A MEDITERRANEAN SOCIETY

S. D. GOITEIN

A Mediterranean Society

THE JEWISH COMMUNITIES OF THE ARAB WORLD
AS PORTRAYED IN THE DOCUMENTS OF THE CAIRO GENIZA

VOLUME V

The Individual:
Portrait of a Mediterranean Personality of the High Middle Ages as Reflected in the Cairo Geniza

UNIVERSITY OF CALIFORNIA PRESS
Berkeley • Los Angeles • London • 1988

University of California Press
Berkeley and Los Angeles, California

University of California Press, Ltd.
London, England

First Paperback Printing 1999

Goitein, S. D., 1900–
A Mediterranean society : the Jewish communities of the Arab world as portrayed in the documents of Cairo Geniza / S. D. Goitein.
p. cm.
Originally published: Berkeley : University of California Press, 1967–c1993.
Includes bibliographical references and indexes.
Contents: v. 1. Economic foundations – v. 2. The community – v. 3. The family – v. 4. Daily life – v. 5. The individual.
ISBN 0-520-05647-7 (cl. : alk. paper)
ISBN 0-520-22162-1 (pbk. : alk. paper)
1. Jews–Islamic Empire–Civilization. 2. Islamic Empire–Civilization. 3. Cairo Genizah. I. Title.
DS135.L4G65 1999
956′.004924–dc21 99-36039
CIP

Printed in the United States of America

08 07 06 05 04 03 02 01 00 99

10 9 8 7 6 5 4 3 2 1

The paper used in this publication meets the minimum requirements of ANSI/NISO Z39.48-1984 (R 1997) (*Permanence of Paper*). ♾

Contents of Volumes I through V

NOTE: The title originally planned for Chapter X, *The Mediterranean Mind,* was relinquished to avoid the erroneous impression that the personality emerging from the Geniza documents is regarded as representative of a hypothetical human type common to the Mediterranean area.

Contents

Foreword

On the morning of February 6, 1985, Shelomo Dov Goitein died of a heart attack at his home in Princeton, New Jersey. Shortly before his death, he had dispatched the 1,455 page typescript of this fifth and final volume of *A Mediterranean Society* to his publisher, the University of California Press. The task of seeing this volume through the press was thus left to his colleagues, students, and friends.

Some two weeks before his death, in a letter dated January 21, 1985, he wrote to his editor:

> Dear Terry,
>
> The University of California Press confirmed that it received the manuscript of Volume V of A Mediterranean Society on December 26, 1984. I am not sure, however, whether it has already reached you, because, I believe, it has to pass first through one or two committees. Anyhow, I am enclosing a correction of ten lines on pages 398–399. Please insert it when you get the manuscript. When a number of other corrections have accumulated (smaller ones, I assume), I shall send them to you.

Corrections were already accumulating in the author's file. Had he lived to see this volume through the press, the text would certainly have benefited from numerous further corrections, changes, and revisions. Together with Goitein, however, we can assume that for the most part these would have been "smaller ones." He might have changed some formulations here and there, rewritten or removed a paragraph. No major revisions were envisaged. He had made his statement about Mediterranean society, and was, even on the day he died, preparing to move on to other things.

The genesis of this project and its evolution from the three volumes originally projected to the five eventually produced (actually six if one counts the planned 400-page volume of indices most of which Goitein had prepared well in advance) are in themselves illustrations of the intellectual vitality and curiosity which permitted Goitein in his sixties, seventies, and eighties to create this great work of historical scholarship.

Goitein was born in April 1900, in the tiny Bavarian village of Burgkunstadt where his father served as a district rabbi and leader of the local Jewish community. At an early age, he moved to Frankfurt to pursue studies at the gymnasium and later at the university level. In a memoir recalling this period, he wrote that "the real formative years of my life were the years 1914 to 1923 which I spent in Frankfurt and partly also in Berlin. It gave me inspiration, knowledge, and friendship. It was a time of great enthusiasm." It was also a time of dreams and striving when the major, enduring commitments of his life were formed: his determination to emigrate to Palestine; his commitment to his own very original blend of spirituality combining general humanistic values with those of his Jewish heritage; and his dedication to the scholarly study of the history and civilization of the Islamic Middle East.

His early training was that of a philologian and not of a historian. At Frankfurt University he concentrated on Arabic and Islamic subjects under the guidance of Josef Horovitz. His curiosity and his studies were, however, by no means restricted to Orientalism. Goitein reminisced that "these were years of mad activity. . . . I attended twenty-four to thirty classes a week because I had resolved to go to Palestine and wished to have as broad an education as possible. In addition, every morning at 6:30 I had an hour of Talmud with the greatest Talmudist in Frankfurt, who happened to be a banker. . . ." This wide-ranging curiosity and diligence were traits which accompanied him throughout his life.

In 1923, upon completing his dissertation on the subject "Prayer in the Qur'an," Goitein fulfilled his long-held ambition to emigrate to Palestine, and began his career there as a high school teacher in Haifa. He remained an educator for the rest of his life. He was a member of the founding faculty of Hebrew University in Jerusalem, which opened its doors in 1925, and became its first instructor in Islamic studies. While the world of scholarship and the university dominated the rest of his career, he retained his original interest in the education of the young, publishing books on the teaching of Hebrew and the Bible and serving as senior education officer under the British Mandate in Palestine, a post he held from 1938 to 1948.

Shortly after joining the faculty of the Hebrew University, Goitein began to do fieldwork among the Yemenite immigrants to Palestine, a research that intensified with the mass migration of the Jews of Yemen following the establishment of the State of Israel. He published works on their Arabic dialect and their way of life. Indeed this early ethnographic work among what he called "the most Jewish and most Arab of all Jews" would profoundly influence

Goitein's study of the life of medieval Jewish communities reflected in the Geniza documents.

Perhaps his most ambitious scholarly undertaking during his early years in Jerusalem was directing the critical edition of Balādhurī's *Ansāb al-ashrāf* on the basis of a single extant manuscript. In preparation for his own volume in the series, Goitein immersed himself in the study of early Arabic literature and society. The volume he produced was a model of its genre, and the experience garnered on this project stood him in good stead later when dealing with the unique fragments of the Cairo Geniza.

Goitein's serious research in Geniza materials occurred rather late in his career. As he himself has testified, it was almost by accident that he discovered their exceptional value for many hitherto poorly documented aspects of Near Eastern history. For the rest of his life Geniza research was to consume most of his scholarly energies. Indeed, it was to facilitate this research that he moved, in 1957, from Jerusalem to the chair of Arabic studies at the University of Pennsylvania. Upon his retirement from Pennsylvania in 1971, Goitein came to Princeton as a long-term member of the School of Historical Studies at the Institute for Advanced Study. Goitein thrived in Princeton. In the calm and supportive atmosphere of the Institute, Goitein completed the last three volumes of *A Mediterranean Society* and produced three other books and numerous articles most of which were based on his Geniza work. He continued to have contact with his former students and to serve as an informal advisor to younger scholars embarking on Geniza research.

After more than thirty years of pioneering Geniza research, Goitein's work, through some remarkable and mysterious symmetry, ended where it began—with the medieval Indian Ocean trade. On the day of his death, the outline of his next major project, a three-volume edition and translation of the Geniza texts relating to the Indian Ocean trade, was neatly arranged on his desk.

A study of the Indian Ocean commerce was his original project. In 1950, while investigating the interplay between Islamic and Jewish law on the basis of Judeo-Arabic court records from the Cairo Geniza, he was able to reconstruct the entire dossier of a series of lawsuits brought against a Tripolitanian merchant who, while traveling to India had lost part of the merchandise entrusted to him by some of his Tunisian and Egyptian colleagues. As he later wrote, this discovery "electrified" him and changed the course of his research and of his life. "The Geniza treasures had been known to the scholarly world since the 1890s, and I had assumed that their main contents were well known. That discovery showed that the study of their socioeconomic aspects had hardly begun." By 1957, he had assembled about two hundred documents dealing with the trade across the Indian Ocean. These were unique. No other documents concerning that commerce during the High Middle Ages are known from any other source. Goitein's move, during the same year, from Jerusalem to the University of Pennsylvania was undertaken primarily in order to complete work on his India book. However, as he wrote in 1978, "after a year of great toil it became evident that this was a questionable undertaking: The India trade, as represented in the Geniza, was only one of many activities of a highly developed urban Mediterranean society. One cannot study the branch without knowing the root. By the summer of 1958 I was off India and on the Mediterranean."

For the remaining twenty-seven years of his life, it was the Mediterranean world of the eleventh through the thirteenth century that was at the center of Goitein's research, writing and reflection. Methodical and disciplined scholar that he was, he formulated and announced the grand design of *A Mediterranean Society* not only well in advance of its completion but even of its composition. The table of contents of the entire oeuvre was confidently published in the first volume when it appeared in 1967, and again reprinted in Volume II, in 1970. Goitein projected a three-volume study consisting of ten major chapters: four to be devoted to economic life (Volume I); three to be devoted to communal life (Volume II); and three to deal with the family, daily life, and the individual. As these last three chapters assumed rather voluminous proportions, Goitein seriously considered some radical abridgments. Mindful of Goitein's unique and intimate familiarity with the Geniza texts and the society that produced them, his friends and colleagues urged him to give full reign to his insights and to his pen. Happily for all, Goitein heeded this counsel and the projected chapters on the family, on daily life, and on the Mediterranean mind each developed into full, separate volumes. In the end, Goitein adhered to his masterplan of 1967; but the three volumes originally projected now grew to five. It is the fifth and concluding volume which is here being presented to the readers.

Goitein spent more time on this volume than on any other in the series of Mediterranean Society. It was the most difficult to conceptualize and to write. It is a pioneering work in the literal sense of the term, dealing not with the externals of the life of a medieval society, but with the internal universe of individual Mediterranean men and women of almost a millennium ago, their feelings, attitudes, and mind-sets. Neither in Islamic nor in Jewish studies was there a precedent for such an effort. It is a history of the "mentalité" and the soul of Mediterranean man during the High Middle Ages, and Goitein, alone among his peers, was capable of bringing to fruition an enterprise of this kind.

Goitein was a man of rigorous and exacting scholarly standards. In *A Mediterranean Society* he succeeded in bringing to life an entire world of the eleventh through the thirteenth century in all its vivid and colorful details. It comes as somewhat of a surprise, therefore, to find Goitein himself so frequently present in its landscape. Goitein's personal involvement with the society he was studying was quite self-conscious and explicit. In the preface to this volume he tells us that in doing history "much depends on the mind and life experience of the historian," and he adds, "the diversity of my own life experience helped me in understanding the Geniza world. . . ." This is probably true for any historian. Goitein, however, did not hesitate to draw, quite frequently and explicitly, upon his own background to explain, clarify, or compare some aspect of eleventh-century Mediterranean life with his observations of recent or contemporary life and history. Nowhere is this intervention more frequent or the personal involvement as great as it is in this concluding volume of *A Mediterranean Society*.

Like a Renaissance painter, Goitein is identifiable in his oeuvre not only by his signature in the corner of the canvas, but by the auto-portrait he sketches in the midst of his "Mediterranean people." To illustrate his point that in Geniza society charity was viewed not only as a bounty to the recipient but as a benefit to the donor as well, he recounts the following incident from his early days in Jerusalem: "During my first years in Jerusalem, when, still unmarried, I had to go for lunch to a certain place (there was almost no other one at that time), I used to meet, at a street-crossing, a wonderful old beggar. He invariably stretched out to me his big open hand, saying with a radiant face, *zekhē 'immii*, 'acquire religious merit through me' . . . , and I, of course, never failed to put something into his hand. He certainly had no doubt that he did a bigger favor to the young man than I did to him" (x, C, 3 n. 26).

His experience with the Yemenite Jews in Palestine is invoked to highlight the importance of astrology and of auspicious moments in the choice of times for important events in the life-cycle: ". . . I experienced this myself. In the early 1950s I was invited as guest of honor to a wedding in a community of immigrants who had recently arrived from Yemen. I took the trouble to get to that place, and everything was ready for the ceremony. But the wedding was postponed, for the person expert in these matters . . . had just found out that the hour was not propitious. That person had already left, so I could not find out how he arrived at his lamentable decision" (x, D n. 35).

Judah ha-Levi, the celebrated thirteenth-century Hebrew poet and philosopher to whose biography Goitein's Geniza research contributed so much new information, is present with Goitein in the English countryside close to the letters and documents that ha-Levi left behind in the Geniza. In a note to his deft and sensitive portrait of Judah ha-Levi's last years, Goitein recounts the following: "Leon Roth, a former professor of philosophy and rector of the Hebrew University, and I often took walks in England between Cambridge and Grantchester, a village nearby, and Judah ha-Levi was frequently discussed. While we were inclined to agree on many topics, Judah ha-Levi was not among them. Philosopher and historian do not always see eye to eye" (x, D n. 167).

There are moments when the intersection between eleventh-century sensibilities and Goitein's biography are more profound and moving. Before migrating from southern Iraq to Egypt in the late tenth century, the members of the famous Tustari family looked into the scriptures for guidance in making their choice. They stumbled upon verses which they interpreted as encouragement to make the move, and they did. In a longish footnote to this episode (x, C, 1 n. 49), Goitein recalls the following about himself:

> I can make a personal contribution to this topic. I did not have to "look" into the Scriptures; I was in them. It happened on September 11, 1923, when Erich Fromm (to become renowned for his psychoanalytical writings) and I officiated as cantors at the Jewish New Year's service in the house of the philosopher Franz Rosenzweig in Frankfurt-am-Main (cf. Franz Rosenzweig, *Briefe* [Berlin, 1935], p. 446, which refers to 1922). When I recited Genesis 21:12, "God hears the voice of the boy wherever he might be," I suddenly paused; for it occurred to me that "the boy" could very well be me; I was to leave the next day for Palestine, then a voyage of eight days (not today's flight of four hours), and the country was very, very much underdeveloped. That the boy in the biblical story was Ishmael seemed to be altogether appropriate for a fledgling Arabist.

The real culmination of this book—indeed of all five volumes of *A Mediterranean Society*—is to be found not in its epilogue, but in the passionate concluding portrait of Abraham Maimonides whom Goitein characterizes as "a perfect man with a tragic fate." These final pages are written with a fervor and devotion unlike anything that precedes them. Goitein is quite frank and unabashed in his admiration and sympathy for this exceptional figure: ". . . beginning in the year 1936–37, when I translated his Arabic responsa into Hebrew, I developed quite a personal affection for him" (p. 482). For almost fifty years, Goitein continued to search the Geniza documents for additional evidence concerning this man who not only "was possessed of a most lovable personality" but who "combined the humility and meekness to be expected in an ascetic with the firmness and determination required in a communal leader. His fervent religiosity and his strictness in the enforcement of the law were paired with common sense and humane consideration for special circumstances, while the lucidity and grace of his exposition revealed a disciple of the Greeks" (p. 482). It seems clear that to Goitein, Abraham Maimonides was a forerunner—possibly even a model—of his own hopeful vision of how tradition and modernity should and can coexist and collaborate. "Abraham united in his single person three spiritual trends that were usually at odds with each other: strict legalistic orthodoxy, ascetic pietism, and Greek science—sober, secular humanism. He represented all the best found in medieval Judaism as it developed within Islamic civilization" (p. 481). He earned his livelihood as a physician in the court of Egypt's sultan and served as the religious and political head of the Egyptian Jewish community from the age of nineteen until his death.

His daring and ambitious project of religious reform in Judaism had little or no effect on subsequent generations. Goitein wistfully regrets "the doleful circumstances that limited the extent and duration of his impact. The nobility of his mind and the excellence of his spiritual gifts were deserving of richer response." Abraham Maimonides combined piety, public service, and professional excellence with an openness to universal values and ideas. A reformer and radical in Judaism, he sought to absorb and Judaize all that was best in the Islamic and Greek cultural traditions to which he was exposed. While he does not say so explicitly, Shelomo Goitein, as man born with the twentieth century, as a historian and longtime resident of the Middle East, and as a human being nurtured a similar hope for his own times. Classics, Islam, scholarship, and public service were all part of his curriculum vitae; in each he left an impact, and in each he was, to one degree or another, disappointed, but never despondent or without hope.

The concluding paragraph of *A Mediterranean Society* attempts a summary of Abraham Maimonides' career. With minor adjustments this could equally well serve as a characterization of the author's life and achievements. "Abraham Maimonides lived near the end of 'humanistic Islam.' He was a son of his time. In addition to his unique personality, his life and teaching convey so harmonious an impression because they were in conformity with the best and most congenial elements in the contemporary surrounding civilization, and at the same time represented the most perfect realization of the religion of his forefathers" (p. 485 f).

Shelomo Goitein described himself as a sociographer. By that he meant that he was a describer, a writer about old societies based on their texts. He was particularly sensitive to the importance of documents, and he knew how to read them in depth. In his work on the Geniza material, he exhibited his unmatched gift for recreating a whole society in all its vividness, exposing its many levels and penetrating to the soul and mentality of the people about whom he wrote. From this point of view, the five volumes of *A Mediterranean Society* are a unique contribution to our vision of premodern Jewish and premodern Near Eastern societies, and stand as a model for the study of both.

Twentieth-century historical scholarship has produced two grand visions of the Mediterranean world, that of Goitein and that of Fernand Braudel. These "two Mediterraneans" complement each other. Braudel's Mediterranean is vast. It stretches from the gates of Hercules to the gates of Peking. It is full of plains, plateaus, and peninsulas, of climates of seasons and of world empires. It moves with the majestic, leisurely rhythm of the long durée. Goitein was more modest, and his Mediterranean is much more modest and circumscribed. It is the Mediterranean coast between Tunisia and Egypt, with a little extension in either direction. It is only a part of the Mediterranean; but its shores are teeming with people, their quarrels, their wedding contracts, their dowries, their house furnishings, their table ware, and also their dreams and visions, their religion, and their most intimate feelings. His universe was not on the measure of the sea. Goitein's, like Braudel's, is a total history, but a total history tailored to the measure of man.

In summarizing his life's trajectory, Goitein wrote:

> I started out as an essentially medieval being, that is, one for whom there exists only one real issue of mind, overriding all others, religion. I have remained, I believe, *a homo religiosus,* but I have become a thoroughly modern man with all that is implied in this change. Finally, there was a constant discrepancy between a particularly happy personal life and a heartbreak or wrath at the sight of so much misery and degradation ex-

perienced during this century. Often I asked myself, how was I able to live with all of this? How often did I cry out with Job, "is my strength the strength of stone, or my flesh made of bronze?" and how often did I feel like the Book of Deuteronomy when it said, "you will be driven mad by the sight that your eyes shall see"? As one who was brought up to regard his life as a service to the community, I felt that question of Job, that curse of Deuteronomy, stronger than any satisfaction that I ever derived from personal happiness.

Personal happiness was tied to his family life, and most particularly to his wife Theresa. The first volume of *A Mediterranean Society* is simply and eloquently dedicated "to Theresa, 'Mine and yours is hers.'" All who had the privilege of entering their home were enriched by the tenderness, the profound and almost total sense of sharing, complicity, and friendship that existed between these two remarkable human beings.

I cannot conclude without pointing to some of Goitein's personal qualities which many of us admired and rejoiced in. He was always ready and eager to venture on new paths. For the first sixty years of his life he was a philologist. At age sixty, the documents and material he was working on propelled him into new areas and he transformed himself into an economic historian. In his seventies, when he was working on documents concerning family life, he acquired the skills of a social historian. He read a great deal in sociology and anthropology, and applied what he learned to the merchants and craftsmen of the Geniza world—and to their wives as well. The resulting volume (*Mediterranean Society,* Vol. III) constitutes one of the finest examples of social history of the Islamic Middle East. In his eighties, Goitein became a historian of what the French call "mentalité." The results of this new turning in his thought are embodied in this fifth volume of *A Mediterranean Society*. In the Fall of 1984 he was a faithful participant in an evening seminar on Islamic and middle Eastern studies jointly sponsored by the Institute for Advanced Study and Princeton University. He had no hesitation about offering for discussion chapters from his work in progress. He graciously accepted comments and criticism from colleagues his junior in both years and learning and frequently revised his text accordingly. Parts of this volume were subject to this kind of discussion and revision. With Goitein one had the feeling that the past was never finished. He looked upon himself as an unfinished product. He had an almost mystical need to keep struggling with himself and to work on improving himself. Next to his radio he kept a list of various musical works. "When I will have the time," he would say, "after I finish the India Book, I'm going to buy all these records and listen to them." If Goitein at age 84 was still improving himself, then anyone who had any contact with him was made to feel that things were not hopeless. One always left his presence feeling good, feeling that he carried one upward.

"I hope," wrote Shelomo Goitein in April 1970, "to return to the dreams of my youth—my role as an educator. Numerous publications of mine tried on the one hand to interpret the classical sources of Judaism and the spirit of our times as I understood it, and on the other hand to further the understanding of the world of Arabic Islam and its relationship to the Jewish people. The Geniza publication should contribute to both ends. Ecclesiastes has said: 'in the morning sow your seed and in the evening do not let rest your hands.' Even in the evening of our lives we should not stop sowing. One day the seed might bring forth fruit."

Many people gave generously of their time and effort in seeing this volume through the press. Three in particular must be singled out. Terry Joseph, whose superb skills as an editor are known to the readers of the preceding four volumes of *A Mediterranean Society,* performed her usual magic on this text as well. Paula Sanders, Goitein's former research assistant and for whom he had a very special regard and fondness, gave selflessly of her time in spite of her demanding schedule as an assistant professor at Harvard until the summer of 1987. Many pitfalls were avoided because of her thorough familiarity with the organization of the Goitein archive and with his method of working. My Princeton colleague Mark Cohen was a pillar of strength and of quiet, sure dedication. His help was invaluable. I am also deeply indebted to him for his help and counsel in preparing this preface. I take this opportunity to acknowledge the gracious cooperation and the material support of Shelomo D. Goitein's children, Elon Goitein, Ayala Gordon, and Ofra Rosner.

Princeton University
December 15, 1987

Abraham L. Udovitch

Preface

The story of the genesis of this book and its purpose are outlined in the Preface to Volume I, especially on pages vii–ix. *A Mediterranean Society* was intended to provide a portrait of the society depicted in the documents and letters of the so-called Cairo Geniza. What the Geniza is and how it can be used as a source for social history are explained in the Introduction to the same volume, pages 1–28.

The approach was to be descriptive, not dogmatic, or, as I defined it elsewhere, "sociographic," not sociological, and at the same time, "interpretative": value judgments were not avoided, but, wherever available, were made from the point of view of the actors on the scene. The people speaking to us in the Geniza papers were most conscious of themselves and others, and very outspoken about both; their words and deeds are living commentaries on the social phenomena encountered in their writings. Naturally, I had also to make use of my general knowledge of Islam and Judaism. I do not believe that the saying "history is made by the historian" contains the whole truth. Much depends on the "history," that is, on the nature of the sources available, and on the mind and life experience of the historian. How the diversity of my own life experience probably helped me in understanding the Geniza world I tried to explain in the Preface to Volume II, pages viii–ix.

To enable readers to take a direct approach to the Geniza and judge for themselves, a "companion volume" was planned, to be called *Mediterranean People* (originally *Readings*). Its first volume was written even before *A Mediterranean Society* was begun. An asterisk after the shelf mark of a manuscript in the Notes of Volumes I–III indicated that the source referred to had been, or was to be, incorporated in *Mediterranean People.* In the course of the years, however, it appeared that the "companion," as planned and partly written by me, was to become more voluminous than the main work. Moreover, numerous sources had been published by me and translated into Hebrew or English or both, and younger scholars in the field had made most substantial contributions. My book *Letters of Medieval Jewish Traders Translated from the Arabic*

(Princeton, 1973) may give the reader an idea of the planned series *Mediterranean People.*

The objective of *Mediterranean People*, which was to bring the reader into direct contact with the sources, has, I hope, been achieved (perhaps even more effectively) by the method of exposition used in this volume, that is, summaries of actual cases or stories, short quotations, in addition to representative selections of complete or essential parts of letters and documents, most of them accompanied by detailed comments. In this volume, in which individuals of the Geniza are studied, the texts in which the sources speak equal or surpass in space my exposition.

Volume V divides into two unequal parts: a larger one, sections A and B, describes the "natural" Mediterranean person, his admirable sociability, polarized by an intricate awareness of individuality; and a shorter one, sections C and D, shows him as formed through religion and study. This dichotomy is not absolute. Communal prayer, Sabbaths and holidays, family events, all accompanied by religious ceremonies, hospitality with its religious halo, were the most common opportunities for social gatherings. The challenges of life had to be met with charity, a duty before God almost more than an expression of mercy or of a sense of obligation toward one's fellowmen. Belonging to a religious community, benefiting from its strength and cohesiveness, defined a person's status within society; this was the decisive element in his social life. The frequent cross-references between the two parts of this volume illustrate the situation.

Cross-references sending the reader to the preceding four volumes are also abundant. Life is a unit; we must dissect it when we examine one of its aspects in detail; cross-references help to hold the *membra disjecta* together. It is left to the discretion of the reader how much to make use of them. Sometimes they are indispensable. The prestige of the medical profession is treated very briefly in this volume (pp. 419–420), but the relevant section extends to more than twenty pages in *Med. Soc.*, II, 240–261. The letters assembled below in the subsection "The personal touch in letters to and from women" (pp. 214–241) are apt to convey a truer and more favorable impression of the position of women in the Geniza society than given when mentioned in different contexts in earlier volumes of this work. In general, the cross-references serve not only to clarify and supplement but also to qualify. Considerateness for the person of the recipient in letters exchanged between males can be studied throughout the book, in particular in the subsection "Challenges," pp. 45–128.

The reader might miss in this book a chapter on the international subculture of magic, witchcraft, and superstitions. I have touched on these topics in various contexts, but did not feel it necessary to treat them in a special chapter. I leave that for younger colleagues to do.

The Index to this volume follows the pattern of Volumes II–IV, that is, it does not include the material in the Notes. The names, subjects, and terms in the Notes are included in the cumulative general Index in preparation for Volume VI which also contains a full index of the Geniza manuscripts used in the five volumes.

The comprehensive collections of photostats, microfilms, and copies I made in the libraries possessing Geniza fragments freed me from the necessity of additional visits. Nevertheless, I cannot part from this book without reiterating my deep-felt appreciation and thanks to the librarians and members of the staffs of the libraries I frequented (named in the Prefaces to Vols. I–IV) for the help extended to me and for all they have done for the furthering of Geniza research. I am grateful to Dr. Harry Woolf, the Director, and to the Faculty of the Institute for Advanced Study for their continued interest in the Geniza project.

My friend Theodore Draper, who encouraged me during all the stages of the writing of this volume, was helpful in many ways. My long-standing companion in Geniza studies, Professor A. L. Udovitch, read considerable parts of the manuscript and made important suggestions.

My former assistant, Paula Sanders (now Ph.D. and assistant professor of history at Harvard University), was an invaluable help during the preparation of this volume. She also created the computerized Index of the Geniza manuscripts used in the five volumes, and the general Index for Volumes I–IV. Amy Singer, my present assistant, proved her competence during the difficult concluding stages. Linda Y. Sheldon typed most of this volume, and by her dedication and resourcefulness alleviated much of my burden.

Teresa Joseph edited this volume, as she did the preceding four. Her name will be connected with *A Mediterranean Society* as long as this book is studied. I am also very grateful to James Kubeck of the University of California Press for his unflagging commitment to the progress of this book.

The Laureate Prize Fellowship awarded to me by the John D. and Catherine T. MacArthur Foundation (as of 1 February 1983) is a source of great encouragement. I am deeply obliged to John E. Corbally, the president of the Foundation, and to J. Roderick

MacArthur, chairman of the MacArthur Prize Fellows Committee, and to all others who were instrumental in bringing about this public recognition of the work on the Cairo Geniza.

The Institute for Advanced Study S. D. Goitein
School of Historical Studies
Princeton, N.J.

Author's Note

Readers are reminded to acquaint themselves with Author's Note and Abbreviations and Symbols in *Med. Soc.*, I, xvii–xxvi. See also Dates and Names; Coins, Weights and Measures, in *ibid.*, pp. 355–361.

Two different styles are used in references to *Med. Soc.*, I–V:

Med. Soc., III, 17 and n. 6 (no comma after 17) sends the reader to the *text* on page 17 which is marked by note 6;

Med. Soc., II, 546 n. 20 sends the reader to *note* 20 on page 546.

In books consisting of more than one volume, the volume number is indicated by a roman numeral and the page numbers by Arabic numerals, e.g., Mann, II, 350, means Jacob Mann, *The Jews in Egypt and in Palestine under the Fatimid Caliphs*, Volume II, page 350, or EI^2, V, 110–115, means *Encyclopaedia of Islam*, second edition, Volume V, pages 110–115.

Some readers may be puzzled that most common words such as *abū* "father of" or *fī* "in" are often printed without macron, the sign for a long sound. The reason for the change is that in closed syllables, like *abu ʾl* or *fi ʾl*, *ū* and *ī* become short.

The Holy Scripture of Islam is spelled Koran in the earlier volumes, as usual in English. In this volume the spelling is Qurʾān.

The often referred to Goitein, *Palestinian Jewry*, stands for *Palestinian Jewry in Early Islamic and Crusader Times* (Heb.) (Jerusalem, 1980). In *Med. Soc.*, III, xx (1978), the abbreviated title was different.

Abbreviations

The abbreviations listed in *Med. Soc.*, I, xix–xxiv; II, xv–xvi; III, xix–xxi; and XIV, xix–xxvi are used in this volume.

Additional abbreviations, not used in Volumes I–IV:

Abraham Maimonides, *High Ways* [*to Perfection*]	Abraham Maimonides, *The High Ways to Perfection*, ed. and trans. Samuel Rosenblatt. Vol. I, New York, 1927; Vol. II, Baltimore, 1938.
Altmann, *Saadya Gaon*	Alexander Altmann, *Saadya Gaon: Book of Doctrines and Beliefs*, ed. Alexander Altmann, 1946. Reprinted in *Three Jewish Philosophers*, ed. Alexander Altmann. New York, 1982.
Ariès, *The Hour of Our Death*	Philippe Ariès, *The Hour of Our Death*, trans. Helen Weaver. New York, 1981.
Baer, *Prayer-Book*	Seligman Isaac Baer, *Avodath Yisrael.* Rödelheim, 1868. Photographic reprint, Schocken Books, 1937. The standard Jewish prayer book with a Hebrew commentary.
Brain, *Friends and Lovers*	Robert Brain, *Friends and Lovers.* New York, 1976.
Brandon, *Judgment of the Dead*	S. G. F. Brandon, *The Judgment of the Dead.* New York, 1967.
Brauer, *Ethnologie der Jemenitischen Juden*	Erich Brauer, *Ethnologie der Jemenitischen Juden.* Heidelberg, 1934.

Carmi, *Hebrew Verse*	*The Penguin Book of Hebrew Verse*, ed. and trans. T. Carmi. New York, 1981.
Cohen, Gerson D., *The Book of Tradition*	Gerson D. Cohen, *A Critical Edition with a Translation and Notes of the Book of Tradition* (*Sefer Ha-Qabbalah*) by Abraham Ibn Daud. Philadelphia, 1967.
Cohen, Gerson D., *Soteriology*	Gerson D. Cohen, "The Soteriology of R. Abraham Maimuni," in *PAAJR*, 35 (1967), 75–98; 36 (1968), 33–56.
Cohen, Mark R., *Self-government*	Mark R. Cohen, *Jewish Self-government in Medieval Egypt*. Princeton, 1980.
Elbogen, *Gottesdienst*	Ismar Elbogen, *Der jüdische Gottesdienst in seiner geschichtlichen Entwicklung* (The Synagogue Service in Its Historical Development). Leipzig, 1913.
Essays in Medieval Jewish and Islamic Philosophy, 1977	*Essays in Medieval Jewish and Islamic Philosophy*. Studies from the Publications of the American Academy for Jewish Research selected by Arthur Hyman. New York, 1977.
Gil, "Megillat Evyatar"	M. Gil, "Megillat Evyatar," in *Chapters on the History of Jerusalem in the Middle Ages*, ed. B. Z. Kedar and Z. Baras. Jerusalem, 1979. Pp. 39–106. Hebrew.
Gil, *Palestine during the First Muslim Period (634–1099)*	Moshe Gil, *Palestine during the First Muslim Period (634–1099)*, Vol. I, *Studies*; Vols. II and III, *Geniza Documents*. Tel Aviv, 1983. Hebrew.

Gil, *The Tustaris*	Moshe Gil, *The Tustaris, Family and Sect.* Ramat Aviv, 1982. Hebrew.
Goitein, *Braslavi Volume*	S. D. Goitein, *Braslavi Jubilee Volume.* Jerusalem, 1970.
Goitein, *Palestinian Jewry*	S. D. Goitein, *Palestinian Jewry in Early Islamic and Crusader Times.* Jerusalem, 1980. Hebrew.
Goitein, *Side Lights on Jewish Education*	S. D. Goitein, "Side Lights on Jewish Education from the Cairo Geniza," in *Gratz College Anniversary Volume*, ed. I. D. Passow and S. T. Lachs. Philadelphia, 1971. Pp. 83–110. Hebrew.
Goitein, *The Yemenites*	S. D. Goitein, *Ha-Tēmānīm: History, Communal Organization, Spiritual Life.* Jerusalem, 1983. Hebrew.
Habermann Memorial Volume	*Yad le-Hēmān: A. M. Habermann Memorial Volume*, ed. Z. Malachi. Lod, 1984. Hebrew.
Ibn Abī d-Dunyā, *The Noble Qualities*	Ibn Abī d-Dunyā, *The Noble Qualities of Character*, Arabic text, ed. with a detailed Introduction and trans. of the verses by James A. Bellamy. Wiesbaden, 1973.
JNES	*Journal of Near Eastern Studies.*
Lamm, *Death and Mourning*	Maurice Lamm, *The Jewish Way in Death and Mourning.* New York, 1969.
Lieberman, *After Life*	Saul Lieberman, "Some Aspects of After Life in Early Rabbinic

	Literature," in *Harry Austryn Wolfson Jubilee Volume*. Jerusalem, 1965. Pp. 495–532.
Malter, *Saadia Gaon*	Henry Malter, *Saadia Gaon, His Life and Works*. Philadelphia, 1921.
Morris, C., *The Discovery of the Individual*	Colin Morris, *The Discovery of the Individual: 1050–1200*. London, 1972.
Nemoy, *Karaite Anthology*	Leon Nemoy, *Karaite Anthology*. New Haven, 1952.
Outremer, 1982	*Outremer: Studies in the History of the Crusading Kingdom of Jerusalem*, Presented to Joshua Prawer, ed. B. Z. Kedar, H. E. Mayer, R. C. Smail. Jerusalem, 1982.
PAAJR	*Proceedings of the American Academy of Jewish Research.*
Richardson, *Old Age among the Ancient Greeks*	Bessie E. Richardson, *Old Age among the Ancient Greeks*. New York, 1933.
Rosenthal, *Complaint and Hope in Medieval Islam*	Franz Rosenthal, *Sweeter than Hope: Complaint and Hope in Medieval Islam*. Leiden, 1983.
Rosenthal, *Knowledge Triumphant*	Franz Rosenthal, *Knowledge Triumphant: The Concept of Knowledge in Medieval Islam*. Leiden, 1970.
Rosenthal, *Study of Muslim Intellectual and Social History*	Franz Rosenthal, *The Study of Muslim Intellectual and Social History: Approaches and Methods*. The Third Annual United Arab Emirates Lecture in Islamic

	Studies. Ann Arbor, Mich., 1980.
Saadia Gaon (Rosenblatt)	Saadia Gaon, *The Book of Beliefs and Opinions*, trans. Samuel Rosenblatt. New Haven, 1948.
Saadya Gaon, *Siddur*	*Siddur R. Saadya Gaon*, ed. I. Davidson, S. Assaf, B. I. Joel. Jerusalem, 1941.
Schechter, *Saadyana*	S. Schechter, *Geniza Fragments of Writings of R. Saadya Gaon and Others.* Cambridge, 1903.
Scheiber, *Geniza Studies*	Alexander Scheiber, *Geniza Studies.* Hildesheim and New York, 1981.
Schirmann, *Hebrew Poetry in Spain and Provence*	H. J. Schirmann, *Hebrew Poetry in Spain and Provence.* Jerusalem, Vol. I, 1954; Vol. II, 1956. Hebrew.
Schirmann, *New Hebrew Poems from the Genizah*	H. J. Schirmann, *New Hebrew Poems from the Genizah.* Jerusalem, 1965. Hebrew.
Schirmann, *Studies*	H. J. Schirmann, *Studies in the History of Hebrew Poetry and Drama.* 2 vols. Jerusalem, 1979. Hebrew.
Stern, *Fatimid Decrees*	S. M. Stern, *Fāṭimid Decrees: Original Documents from the Fāṭimid Chancery.* London, 1964.
Ullmann, *The Individual and Society in the Middle Ages*	W. Ullmann, *The Individual and Society in the Middle Ages.* Baltimore, 1966.
Weiss, "Halfon b. Manasse"	Gershon Weiss, "Legal Documents Written by the Court

	Clerk Halfon Ben Manasse (Dated 1100–1138): A Study in the Diplomatics of the Cairo Geniza." Ph.D. diss. University of Pennsylvania, 1970. 2 vols.
Weiss, "Hillel b. Eli"	Gershon Weiss, "Hillel Ben Eli: Documents Written by Hillel Ben Eli: A Study in the Diplomatics of the Cairo Geniza Documents." M.A. thesis. University of Pennsylvania, 1967.

A MEDITERRANEAN SOCIETY

Map of Medieval Egypt

CHAPTER X

The Individual Portrait of a Mediterranean Personality of the High Middle Ages

NOTE ON THE SOURCES

In this concluding volume an attempt is made to draw a composite picture of the Mediterranean personality of medieval culture which emerges from the letters and documents of the Cairo Geniza. With few exceptions the authors of those writings originated and lived in the Mediterranean area, predominantly its Muslim region. They belonged to a special group: they were Jews. Since—unlike European Jews in the later Middle Ages—the Geniza people were not hemmed in by occupational, geographic, or cultural ghettos, they had many things in common with other, contemporary societies, Muslim and Christian. Consequently this study of the Mediterranean individual, undertaken with regard to a specific community, active within a definite period of time, may have some bearing on the understanding of the spirit of that area which has played so significant a role in human history.

Contrasts between different countries represented in the Geniza, and even between neighboring cities, between the various layers of the society, as well as between individuals belonging to the same milieu, have been pointed out throughout these volumes. It is precisely such variations that attract the attention and interest of the historian. Notwithstanding, an integrated portrait of the Geniza personality is not beyond reach—for the simple reason that it did exist. That society was strong enough to create a clearly recognizable type of human being.

The main sources for this delicate task are letters. Leafing through *Letters of Medieval Jewish Traders Translated from the Arabic*[1] one realizes that a rich repertoire of colorful and polite phrases was at the disposal of their writers. Here we are confronted with a problem: are these profuse expressions of piety, regard for other people, affection, gratitude, admiration, or of aversion and scorn, mere words, thoughtlessly jotted down, and, consequently, of little weight, or can we take them at face value?

Several considerations are in place here. The phrases constantly used in a society are indicative of what it regards as "natural," as universally valid, as accepted standards. Goethe said that all we have to do to become perfect is to live up to the nice phrases we use day in, day out, and to translate them into actions. He took it for granted that the polite verbiage customary in his time represented eternal human values. Only we, who live in a period where everything has become relative, have difficulty in understanding the message contained in formed, traditional speech. By "colorful phrases" I do not mean standard expressions such as "if God wills," but the more diversified wording with which a basic idea was elaborated. Even the constant use of "if God wills" and the like, whenever a future action or event was intended, should not be regarded as being without significance. *We* do not feel the necessity of making such a remark when we say "I shall be coming tomorrow," or when we write an address (as they did: "To Fustat, Square of the Perfumers, if God wills")—and this is the whole difference. The Almighty was regarded as the molder of man's thought and fate, and any neglect of the recognition of this fact was dreaded as dangerous. Many did "forget" God, behaved as if he did not exist, but hardly anyone would deny his threatening presence, if reminded of it by others or by his own misfortunes.

Furthermore, the frequency with which a certain idea is repeated and the variety and adornment with which it is expressed reflect its importance for the writers. One of the most common, extended, and varied openings of a letter is the wish that the social rank of the recipient be strengthened and enhanced and his adversaries humiliated and crushed. When this wish is found at the beginning of a letter by a son to his old mother, a woman in modest circumstances, it makes no sense in the place in which it appears. It is, however, characteristic for the life-style of the society to which the writer belonged.

Finally, the student of a Geniza letter is often in a position to assess the weight of traditional phrases by considering the context of the letter and its whole tenor, often also by comparing it with other missives of the same person, frequently addressed to the same recipient. Many expressions were used by a son assuring his father of his dedication and obedience. When we find such words accompanied by real concern and by actions reported, we understand that they represent the state of mind of a society heeding (or, at least, honoring) the fifth commandment—that most difficult of the Ten Commandments to observe (as the Talmud says). In *Med. Soc.*, III, 17, are reproduced several passages from letters addressed or referring to a younger brother which contain most intense expressions of affection and of almost fatherly care. Another brother, however, is described as worthless; one attended his wedding in order to keep up appearances, but otherwise one did not wish to have anything to do with him. The very tone of the passages related to the younger brother is testimony enough to the sincerity of the writer's feelings. Comparison with what he has to say about the other brother confirms that, while using warm expressions of endearment, he meant what he wrote. It is the historian's task to read between the lines. The richness and formality of the vocabulary possessed by the Geniza correspondent reflects the strength of the society whose tools of communications he used.

Legal documents, by their very nature, are impersonal. Even wills, whose financial dispositions reveal, of course, the testators' concerns, are rarely outspoken. "I do not give preference to one child over another" (directed against the biblical law of primogeniture), "I am an expecting mother and do not know what will happen to me," "I am not satisfied with my burial outfit" are examples of thoughts expressed; in most cases only the decisions made betray the intentions that guided them.

Court records are the most informative of all documents; they are like news reports. But news is usually made by breaking the law, not by observing it; how can one arrive at a balanced judgment on the basis of such material? The frequency of cognate cases coming before the courts, the types of parties involved, and the way in which the participants in a court session, including the judges, react to the pleadings give us an intimation of how widespread the misconduct or exemplary behavior apparent in a case must have been, in which milieu it was rampant, and how society generally related to it. Documents, even more than letters, require interpretation.

Book lists are another source that should not be neglected. Although this work is based on documentary, not literary, sources, the books a person possessed are, naturally, an important indicator of the quality of his professional equipment, as well as of his general interests and his avocations. "You are what you read."

A final reservation must be made. The writings preserved in the Cairo Geniza did not originate evenly in all sections of the Jewish population of the Egyptian capital. The members of the upper class of higher government officials, court purveyors, and physicians in attendance are represented mostly by letters sent or referring to them, and only sparingly by missives addressed by them to their peers. Most such persons lived in Cairo and used Arabic script, so that they had neither the urge nor an easy opportunity to deposit their writings in the Geniza chamber located in Fustat. The Muslim historians of the medical art tell us much about Jewish court physicians. With few exceptions[2] these often interesting personalities are not represented in the Geniza. For instance, we would have liked to know more about Ephraim Ibn al-Zaffān (Jester, a family name), who was not only a medical celebrity but also a renowned bibliophile: after having sold about ten thousand volumes of his library to al-Malik al-Afḍal, the viceroy of Egypt (1096–1121), he still left at his death twenty thousand other manuscripts. More than 150 years after his demise volumes with his ex libris were still available in the bookstalls.[3] The Geniza has preserved a legal document in which a man of this name and period releases the family of a partner of his from all responsibilities emanating from a business venture shared by them with a Muslim. Even if we could be sure that the Ephraim Ibn al-Zaffān of that document was identical with the famous physician—which is likely—there would be nothing noteworthy in that fact. Partnerships constituted the most common form of investment in those days, and the conclusion of one with a Muslim was nothing exceptional. That release had to be given in a Jewish court in order to enable the family to initiate the inheritance procedures in accordance with rabbinic law. The Geniza document could thus not be taken as a proof for the famous physician's special attachment to the community to which he belonged.[4]

The nature of our sources, then, has the consequence that the personalities whose composite portrait is drawn in what follows belonged to the more traditional section of the community, the one that used Hebrew script and was concentrated in Fustat or other places with compact Jewish habitation. The disadvantages of this situation are obvious. The depth of the influence of a surrounding majority is best assessed, however, where that influence is exercised in the main indirectly, where the minority in question remains unassimilated. While preserving its own identity, the minority absorbs the impact of the environment in many facets of its culture. It is this interplay and blending of seemingly disparate elements in a homogeneous culture which forms the object of the study undertaken in this volume.

A. A SOCIAL BEING

1. Gatherings

Introducing the people of this book.—The individual encountered in the Geniza documents was eminently sociable and outgoing. He hated loneliness and thirsted for congenial company. He cared very much what people said about him and entertained definite opinions about others. He was an ardent partisan, prone to take sides. His intense preoccupation with his social ambiance sharpened his eye for human weaknesses and wickedness and taught him to appreciate goodness and nobility. Being warm and compassionate was regarded as the most precious human quality. Women and men, uncomfortable in the company of more than one member of the opposite sex, enjoyed being with relatives and friends of their own gender.

Bartering a wide variety of objects for equally disparate goods (money in those days was also a merchandise "bought" and "sold") seems to have been the passion and pastime of the populace. It required acquaintance with a wide selection of dealers and craftsmen (often united in one profession). The bazaar, besides the house of prayer, was a person's other home. Conversely, the precariousness of life—general economic insecurity, uncontrollable diseases, famines, epidemics, wars and revolts—forced the individual to create for himself a limited circle of dedicated persons on whom he could rely in times normal and adverse. Exerting oneself for one's relatives and friends was the virtue most highly appreciated.

God could be approached only through the channels created by the religious community to which one belonged. Thus religion, which formed the basis of a person's inner life, determined also his status as a social being. Within the community, down to the lowest layers of society, there were conflicting trends and factions about matters of belief, or ritual, or the choice of a leader; participation in the disputes over such issues was vociferous.

The attachment to one's city, native or adopted, rather than to one's country, has been demonstrated in Volume IV with many examples from the Geniza.[1] Of late it has been pointed out that it was almost universal practice in Islam to identify a person by his city of origin or residence and not by any broader geographical unit.[2] As far as this is true, the practice itself had deep historical and socioeconomic roots, also as pointed out in Volume IV, and therefore affected so tangibly the attitudes of the inhabitants. One owed allegiance to one's family, friends, faith, and faction, but the city was one's *waṭan,* the larger unit to which one belonged.

Because of the mobility of the Mediterranean and Islamic peoples in general, the population of a city was composite in every respect: race, creed, occupation, and standard of living. It was a mirror of the world. The very character of a bustling mercantile emporium like Fustat turned its inhabitants into citizens of the world.

A similar polarity between parochialism and openness can be observed in the spiritual world. One belonged to a specific religious group; everyone else was a stranger. Yet the situation was entirely different from that prevailing, say, in central and northern France and western Germany, the countries that most typify Judeo-Christian confrontation in medieval Europe. There Jews were confined to their religious learning and used Hebrew as the means of literary expression. In Islamic countries like Spain or Egypt, Jews wrote even their theological and ethical treatises in Arabic and took full part in the study of the philosophic and scientific works of the ancients which they read, of course, in Arabic translation. The reason for this difference, discussed in previous volumes,[3] was the openness of Mediterranean society during the good years of the High Middle Ages: Jewish houses bordered on those of Christians and Muslims, and there were no occupational ghettos; members of different religions who exercised the same occupation could be more akin to one another than they were to people of their own religion belonging to another class and doing entirely different work. Occasionally one was also reminded that all prayed to the same God, "the Lord of the World," and that one shared with members of the other monotheistic religions more than the clay from which we all were formed. How characteristic is this question submitted by a simpleminded lover of wine: "May a Jew not be permitted to drink wine prepared by a Muslim, seeing that Muslims do not bow to images, and perhaps even by Christians (because they do not believe that the images are God)?" The blessing for a dead person, "May God have mercy upon him," is found in the Geniza referring to a Muslim more than once.[4]

Nor did the "pagan" world remain outside the orbit of a Geniza person. India and China were certainly far away, and Africa was regarded as "another clime." But the products and artifacts of those regions filled the markets and houses. Africans and Indians often served in households or businesses. Daily contacts would not seldom reveal that such foreigners were valuable human beings like anyone else, and the attitude toward them would be conditioned by their worth rather than by their race. Servants were often treated as family, and after their manumission became members of the community.

The ancient Greeks had been dead for aeons. But when one consulted a physician or an astrologer, one was assured to have been treated or helped by the most reliable books of the ancients. Their idolatry had been forgotten; their scientific attainments were avidly studied. Translations from the Greek formed a substantial part of any respectable library not confined to religious matters, and numerous lists containing such works have been preserved in the Geniza.

In daily life a Geniza householder used clothing and food, draperies and utensils, medicines and chemicals brought from the four corners of the earth, items often named after the countries or cities where they were first produced. The walls of his house encompassed the world. He probably had acquaintances who had visited such foreign places or hailed from there, or he invested in business ventures carried on in faraway markets. When he traveled abroad—and not only great merchants traveled but frequently also ordinary people and even beggars—he was not a complete stranger. He had been familiar with the money circulating in the country visited and the goods customarily imported from or exported there. He probably had business friends there, occasionally even relatives. In short, as parochial as the Geniza person was, dedicated to his extended family, religious group, party, and native city, he, being intensely social and outgoing, could also become a thorough cosmopolitan, making contacts in foreign parts and feeling at home there.

It is this touch of an expanded existence which makes reading the majority of the Geniza correspondence so pleasant. It was a civilized world, of people who knew how to behave, who were considerate, paying proper attention to their fellowmen. He knew his station in society but was not unduly deferential to his superiors. To be sure, the very cadence of Arabic speech sounds hyperbolic to our ears. But, in general, as befitting busy people, their statements were concise, clear, and to the point—somehow reflecting the clarity of the Mediterranean sky.

Since our letters and documents deal almost exclusively with practical matters, there was little opportunity for discoursing on the demands of religion, or, rather, since they were taken for granted, there was no point in enlarging upon them. The deep theological problems that had occupied the Islamic world and the Jewish community within it during the eighth through the tenth centuries had been either settled or at least clarified; the battle lines between conflicting views and practices (inside Judaism, for instance, Karaites against Rabbanites) had been drawn; everyone knew where he stood, what to believe, and how to act. The eleventh and twelfth centuries were comparatively sedate. Few new questions were asked, and for those that were, answers were ready. The most tangible of all, that of human suffering, found its ever ready explanation in God's inscrutable ways. One was assured that all that occurred was caused by God and all done by him was to the good. Such teaching certainly had a soothing effect on grieving souls but was fraught with danger. He left too much to God and did too little himself—especially to alleviate human misery or work to perfect himself.

This acquiescence led to disregard for the spiritual needs of the sincerely pious on the one hand and the searching intellectual on the other. At the turn of the century, from twelfth to thirteenth, the crisis became visible. The pietist movement led by the two Abrahams—Abraham, the son of Moses Maimonides, Nagid, or head of the Egyptian Jews, and his elder contemporary Abraham (b. Abu ʾl-Rabīʿ Solomon) the Pious—was actively opposed by the congregations in Fustat and Alexandria and seems to have found only feeble following in subsequent generations. It is certainly not entirely fortuitous that *The Complete Guide for the Pious* by Abraham, the Nagid, has not come down to us in its entirety. Moses Maimonides' *Guide of the Perplexed* certainly provided an intellectual haven for those who seriously were seeking one. Many intellectuals who had become aware of the doubts to which the three monotheistic religions were exposed, especially after the sweeping victories of the heathen Mongols, preferred to join the more convenient ruling religion, while the spiritually dissatisfied, simple Jews began to listen to the sermons of fervent dervishes. The community lost many of its most valuable members.

Naturally, the loss resulted largely from the state of oppression to which minorities were subjected in Mamluk times (as described in detail in E. Strauss-Ashtor's volumes on the subject). No doubt, a complicated spiritual situation contributed much to religious dissatisfaction and doubts and by this to the weakening of the bonds that kept the communal society together. It was precisely the physical and educational symbiosis between Muslims and Jews, experienced during the preceding centuries, which eased the transition to the dominant faith. Another factor was the absence of serious theological obstacles as were those presented by Christianity with its Trinity and images. One was prepared to die on the stake for denying a God who had partners (as the Trinity was misunderstood), but not for refusing to sip a bowl of soup cooked with camel's flesh. And had not Abraham Maimonides himself written that the pious of Islam were truer followers of the Prophets of ancient Israel than many of his Jewish contemporaries? The core of the Jewish community, which was clinging to its inner security untroubled by theological problems or the stirrings of the God-seekers (and, to top it all, was exposed to multifarious, inexplicable, and unending suffering), had little to offer to wavering spirits. The presentiment of decline, expressed by Maimonides in his old age, is echoed in Geniza letters of the thirteenth century.

Yet we should not belittle that inner security of the Geniza person of the Fatimid period, the main object of our inquiry. His was an orderly world, conducive to the formation of a harmonious personality, identifying himself willingly with the strong body of the society to which he belonged. "Fear God and heed his commandments; for this is the whole man." There were many commandments to be heeded, and much study was required to know them all properly. But not everyone was expected to reach excellence in religious knowledge or practice. In religion, as in social life, varying standards were recognized. Just as one found approval when one behaved in accordance with his station, low or high, so were different attainments in the study of the law and its observance tolerated.

The ideal person was the eternal student, who "pondered over the words of the Torah day and night," whatever the profession by which he earned his livelihood. Only a learned man (or one who had the reputation of being one) could be a communal leader. Rabbinic Judaism was a religion for scholarly minds. It was a great blessing for this type of Judaism that it was codified and canonized—between Saadya Gaon (d. 942) and Moses Maimonides (d. 1204)—within the orbit of Islam, which had similar ideals. It seems to me, although the generalization may be hazardous, that the scholarly person as a religious *ideal* was more widely popular in Judaism than in Islam. To be sure, Islam, with its ample economic resources, was far more able to realize this ideal, namely, by making learning a salaried profession. The pittance paid to its officials even by the Jewish community of Fustat did not enable them to devote much time to study. The students were merchants, physicians, even craftsmen, who had earned (or inherited) or were earning enough to find leisure for learning. It was this aspect of study undertaken for its own sake and as a kind of worship which brought it so much esteem within the Jewish community.

The erudition of a Geniza person meant primarily familiarity with sacred Scripture and the law codes, together with their commentaries and all that was connected with them, occasionally including the ability to evaluate and write Hebrew poetry. In Fatimid times, however, one's orthodoxy was not suspect when, in addition, he pursued the secular sciences. For a physician this was, of course, imperative. For others it was a title of honor to be described as both *ḥākhām* (Heb.), "religious scholar," and *ḥakīm* (Ar.), "student of philosophy and the sciences." The India trader Ḥalfōn b. Nethanel, a native of Egypt, was greeted in Spain with these two epithets and, judging from his correspondence and the books he acquired, he was not worthy of the titles. Ḥalfōn was of a family of religious functionaries, but, as far as we know (and we know much about him) he never held public office. He was also praised as "the center of all the leading personalities of his time." He was able to fulfill this role, for he clearly felt himself as at home in Yemen or Syria as in Spain or Morocco. He was the model of a Geniza person also in that his life was by no means easy. He endured grave disappointments in his mercantile undertakings as well as in the communal affairs in which he took so prominent a part. Moods of depression were by no means alien to him as well as to some of his contemporaries. Life meant strife.

A very conspicuous element of the medieval scene is absent from the ambiance of the Geniza person: the glamour of arms and the romance of bloodshed. Weapons were rarely used by the civil population in defense against bandits and burglars. The conduct of war was left to professionals, mostly of foreign origin. Yet the Geniza correspondence is pervaded by an atmosphere of contest and tension. Everything was urgent and often repeated twice or several times. They seem to have thrived on stress. Clashes in family, occupational, and communal life kept the scene constantly in movement. Since most of the longer letters extant were exchanged between friends, they also preserve for us the beautiful picture of a type of friendship which may be compared to *Kampfbrüderschaft,* "comradeship in battle," emphasized by a keen observer as one of the binding forces of medieval society. Geniza society embodies the romance of daily life.

Weekends and holidays.[5]—The flow of daily life and the mingling of various sections of the population which accompanied it have been described in the preceding volumes. Here the special occasions on which people gathered together—and how numerous they were—are briefly reviewed.

Day began with prayer. Judaism, more than Islam, emphasized the meritoriousness of daily attendance at the public service. I have not found any indication as to whether and how far this recommendation was heeded in Geniza times.[6] There can be no doubt, however, that Monday and Thursday, the holy weekdays, on which a lection from the Torah was recited and the service was followed by regular sessions of the rabbinic court, were marked by increased numbers at communal prayer. Judges, clerks, litigants, and witnesses, as well as the ubiquitous "righteous elders," who always intervened helpfully when a case appeared to be hopeless, or people who wished to learn or to gather news, would join the congregation. Tuesday and Friday, the days on which loaves of bread were distributed to the needy and other beneficiaries—in times of stress up to one fourth of the community—were also opportunities for large gatherings.

The Sabbath, "the Day of the Lord," was in Geniza times, however, very much also the day of the people; the cherished opportunity for getting together, for visiting family and friends in the capital, or in the countryside, or even in a faraway city. I wonder whether this special character of the Sabbath, as it emerges from the Geniza papers, is not influenced somehow by the model of the Muslim weekly holiday which was not a day of rest, but, as it is called, a "day of assembly," originally a day of manifesting one's allegiance by attending the public service. During the Jewish (and Muslim and Christian) service, allegiance was indeed expressed by prayers for the spiritual and secular leaders of the community. But the allegiance created and confirmed by the common attendance (everyone was present; there was nothing else to do) had a wider, and, at the same time, more intimate application. The members of the congregation, seated or standing close together, could feel themselves as one body, while the hours left free from service and study were dedicated to the attention one owed to family and friends. The prayers and literary sources emphasized the atmosphere of repose and sanctity to be found on the Sabbath. The element of sociability reflected in the Geniza was perhaps also due to the mundane character of the Jewish community of Egypt.

In addition to the morning service, held early in the day, the congregation, and often both rabbinite congregations, were convened again in the afternoon to listen to and to participate in a public lecture expounding the Scriptures given by a local scholar or an itinerant preacher. After the service or lecture, people did not hurry home but tarried in the synagogue plaza, and no one could pass without being observed.[7] Even without references in letters to meetings on Saturday we can imagine what they were talking about on those occasions. One inquired about the health of a relative, invited friends, and even touched upon business matters (although this was disapproved in the Bible and, of course, in Jewish law).[8] When someone had an errand in the capital, he tried to arrive on Friday in order to talk things over on Saturday; he would remain on Sunday, not because it was another weekend day but because on Saturday, although he could meet people, he could not finalize matters that required writing (forbidden on the holy day). We have had the case of a man, though, who made the long journey from Alexandria and stayed in Fustat only for the Sabbath.[9] Visitors who remained in town for a more prolonged period were invited to pass Saturday in private homes,[10] and, if they happened to be scholars, would be honored by being invited to expound the Scriptures weekly to a wide circle convened in the host's house every week.[11]

Mundane pastimes are mentioned in our sources only when they were disapproved by religious authorities or the pious. A beautiful sermon on the love of God emphasizes that the Sabbath was the ideal time for joy in and nearness to God and therefore one should refrain from wasting time by taking walks for pleasure in promenades and gardens.[12] When the Jewish community in the provincial capital al-Maḥalla was split by strife, its members were scolded for "sitting most of the time in the streets and shops or in the shade of sycamores, thereby spurning the synagogues."[13] As these citations reveal, taking walks was not reprehensible when it did not interfere with the proper fulfillment of one's religious duties. A Maghrebi scholar, writing from Jerusalem, says: "I am shut up in the house, occupied with study, until noon, when I go out walking around for an hour until the afternoon prayer."[14]

Swimming, which was regarded as a profanation of the sacred day, was a different matter: A summons to the court of the Nagid superscribed "It is time to act for the Lord" (Psalm 118:126) invites persons claiming to have seen Jews swimming on Saturday to appear and deposit their testimony. The reverse side, headed by the same verse, contains a list of the culprits, eight altogether, which must have been rather embarrassing for the Nagid: it was headed by the names of two sons and one daughter's son of a beadle and the son of a *parnās,* or social service officer, both officials of the synagogue. The writ was issued at the beginning of the thirteenth century. I am not sure that the prohibition was enforced prior to the arrival of Moses Maimonides in Egypt or that it was meticulously observed afterward.[15]

Besides service and study the main social pastimes on Saturdays (and holidays, of course) were parlor games with dice or the like. In the atmosphere of strict observance created by Maimonides even these became suspect. Here is a question addressed to him:

> *Question:* People get together on Sabbaths and holidays for drinking wine, playing with dice made of ivory bearing signs. The stakes are goblets of wine. He who wins, drinks. They have also other customs, using kinds of seeds; for instance, one takes three and a half grains in his hand and lets the others in turn guess their number. He who hits the right number, drinks and plays the next game. Are these and similar things permitted on the Sabbath and holidays, or not? Many and highly esteemed persons occupy themselves with this. May your excellency instruct us.
>
> *Answer:* Touching dice on Saturday is forbidden, touching seeds is permitted. But this is a gambling game [and prohibited for this reason].[16]

It is unlikely that the ban on such extremely popular entertainments was entirely successful. The man who asked the question was probably from the Muslim West (see the note). But Egypt was not the Maghreb.

Invitations to spend the Sabbath in a provincial town or promises to do so have been found in considerable number. They are of different types, sometimes rather casual: "If my brother (= my friend?) Abu ʾl-Ḥasan is free, have him come on Friday; I shall accompany him back to Fustat on Sunday."[17] "I was forced to spend the New Year in Cairo, but shall pass the 'Sabbath of Atonement' nowhere else than Bilbays [the addressee's place]; this is absolutely definite and real, provided God wills so." From the letter it is evident that the writer intended to return to Cairo immediately after that weekend.[18]

A visit from the city on Sabbath was an event in a provincial town, and, if the visitor was a distinguished person, it boosted his host's prestige. When young Solomon, son of the judge Elijah, served as teacher in a Bible school, also holding other religious offices in Qalyūb, north of Cairo, he reminded his father to make good his promise to visit him on a Sabbath, "after kissing the ground before the exalted fatherly Seat" and expressing yearning for the venerated mother—"may God enhance her honored state."

The judge was also expected to perform the sacramental killing of an animal for the local community. (Even the high priest in the Temple of Jerusalem had to fulfill that function on special occasions.) The judge would leave his razor-sharp knife to his son, who would perform this service for the community in the future.[19] We do not know whether Elijah fulfilled his son's wishes this time, but we have a letter from him saying that he had to settle some matters in Qalyūb in connection with a pious foundation there and would try to come for the Sabbath; if he could not make it, he would arrive on Sunday.[20] A note of nineteen lines repeats five times that the recipient was urgently invited to a circumcision ceremony to be held on Friday—"on condition you stay on for Saturday, for the eyes of all Israel are fixed on you—may God elevate your honored position, and mine!" As customary under similar circumstances, he was promised an escort back to the capital on Sunday. We see that putting up the distinguished guest on Saturday was more important to the writer than his attendance at the family event.[21] A similar attempt at inducing a person of higher standing to extend his visit in a small place over the Sabbath forms the content of a beautifully written letter addressed to an Amīn al-Mulk (Trusted Servant of the Government) with the Hebrew title "Diadem of the Princes." The writer, known as spiritual leader of the Bilbays community during the years 1204–1215, but probably serving there in this capacity long before, had been asked by Amīn al-Dawla to forward certain papers to the secretary of a government dignitary. A Muslim merchant was prepared to serve as intermediary, but it was preferable that the addressee do it in person and use the opportunity to stay in town over the Sabbath. Not even an inadvertent transgression of the Sabbath laws was to be feared in the writer's house.[22]

When one failed to have a guest stay over the weekend, one grieved over his absence. "I had a very bad Saturday, realizing that you went away, and without a fellow traveler to keep you company."[23] "Since we parted my tears have not dried for yearning after you, on weekdays and even on Sabbaths" [when one was not supposed to grieve].[24] The prolonged absence of a dear relative was particularly felt on Sabbaths and holidays, when one was accustomed to being joined by him at the congregational prayer.[25]

If the Sabbath, which, ideally, should be dedicated entirely to devotion, included a generous measure of mundane getting-together, how much more was this the case on holidays, which, by official definition, belonged "one half to the Lord and one half to you," namely for mutual enjoyment.[26] The lengthy feasts of spring and autumn offered plenty of opportunities for timely and protracted vacations and, in particular, for ceremonial gatherings of families and friends (comparable with the American Thanksgiving Day). Other feasts, as well as fasts, were occasions for the display of sociability. People from the provinces streamed into the capital to be edified by well-attended services that were embellished by the vocal art of famous cantors.[27] Various branches of the families or circles of friends vied with one another for the honor of playing the host. A letter to Qalyūb near Cairo, jointly addressed to a father and a father-in-law (probably relatives living in an inherited common house), reminds them: "All our lives we have passed the holidays with you." Now it was time for the grandparents to favor them with a visit and pass the holidays with them, especially because they would be celebrating their son Abu ʾl-Khayr's betrothal on that occasion. The sender (the letter was dictated to Abu ʾl-Khayr) addresses his mother-in-law in particular, imploring her to give her daughter the pleasure of being the hostess. The children greet the mother's brother (probably a favorite uncle), who is, of course, also invited.[28] A father is asked in a letter to spend the holiday in his son's house, as he was accustomed to do, although at that time he had urged the writer to visit with him. "By the truth of what we believe, your coming to us will be a great merit for you with God since I enjoy your presence. The children greet you."[29] How simple people expressed themselves about these matters we read in this note: "My lord [a stepfather is addressed], let my brother Abū Isḥāq spend the holidays with me. . . . If you [the brother] do not come for the holiday I swear that I shall never talk to anyone of you in the future. Peace upon you and peace upon my mother. And do not bring bowls and dishes with you. I have plenty of everything. I am lacking not a thing, except ye [plural]." The brother was, of course, expected to come with his family and, it seems, with the mother of the two brothers as well.[30] To be remote from one's mother on a holiday, says another invitation, was "a grave matter," almost a sin. Waiting on one's teacher and parents was comparable to appearing "before God" on a feast of pilgrimage to the Temple.[31]

How intellectuals flocked together for spiritual and other enjoyment during an extended holiday week is apparent in this passage from a letter addressed to an illustrious scholar in Granada, Spain, by Isaac, the son of the great Abraham Ibn Ezra, himself a poet. After describing his own "company of friends," four mentioned by name, and others, he reports about a prominent friend, a poet, philosopher, and (later) judge, who had just arrived at his place:

> I believe Mār Joseph is traveling to your place to pass there the Passover with Ibn al-Fakhkhār, for the latter has made him desirous of spending the holidays in his house, where he would have a good time. Mār Joseph had planned to go to Seville, but he has changed his mind and is coming to Granada. Take notice of this. I decided not to let this letter go without some foolish poetry of mine. Last night I drafted the nonsense you will see. Mār Joseph has chosen them, and you will pardon me.

The idea behind the letter was, of course, that the poem or poems selected by Joseph from the writer's nightly creations would be read out in the presence of the scholars, poets, and connoisseurs assembled in the hospitable house of the Granada notable during the holidays. We know of many Jewish savants sojourning or visiting there in the late 1120s. Most probably, Ḥalfōn b. Nethanel, the India trader from Egypt, was among them. This would explain how a letter sent to a scholar in Granada, Spain, found its way into the Cairo Geniza. Ḥalfōn, who was in close contact with the poet, as the letters addressed to him by Isaac Ibn Ezra prove, had been given our letter, which is written in a particularly beautiful, clear script, at that reunion (shortly before his return to Egypt, referred to in another letter from the same time).[32]

The great feasts of the spring and the autumn had a specific meaning for the community of Mediterranean traders: some time after Passover-Easter they sailed for the summer season; they came home for the holidays of the autumn. "All the young men are back in Qayrawān [then the capital of Tunisia]" we read in a letter written on the eve of the Day of Atonement, "and celebrate the holidays with their families most happily. Your boy Ṣadaqa has become a big man, an efficient merchant, for whom one can only wish that he follow in your footsteps."[33]

The holidays and fasts, which punctuated the cycle of the year at fixed intervals, were convenient terms for the fulfillment of contractual obligations or the payment of debts. It was the same in medieval Christendom and, perhaps to a slightly lesser degree, in Islam.[34] Not only the three biblical holidays Passover, Pentecost, and the Sukkot feast of tabernacles but also Hanukka, the feast of lights (approximately at Christmas time), served these purposes.[35] One is surprised to read in court records clauses like this: "He will pay these 40 dinars on the Passover feast," since a Jew was not expected even to touch money on a holiday, let alone to take any action with it. The reference is to the so-called *wasṭāniyyāt,* middle days between the sacred opening and concluding days of Passover and Sukkot. How far profane occupations should be permitted on these "middle days" was a moot point, but during the Geniza period people understood that at a time people flocked together anyhow, it was practicable to give them an opportunity to settle urgent affairs. Many documents to this effect are preserved, including one in which a loan was taken (not repaid) during the expensive Passover week. "We have survived the holidays only to encounter skyrocketing prices and sluggish business," complains a Geniza letter, and the Yemenites say: "Gone is the feast and its luster; its debts [the debts incurred for it] have remained."[36]

Before we leave this topic, a curious feature of the Geniza correspondence must be noted: a disproportionally large number of letters were written on the day before or after a holiday (on which writing was prohibited). When a lengthy letter from a Tunisian port, dated "eve of the Day of Atonement," concludes with the excuse that it was written in a great hurry "because the passengers are already boarding the ship," we understand that some last-minute items had to be settled.[37] In many cases, however, no such explanations are given. The famous epistle of Moses Maimonides to the Jewish scholars of Montpellier, France, was written on the day after the Day of Atonement of the year 1195. I assume that during the long-drawn-out litanies sung by the cantors on that day of fasting the Master had time to ponder the profound questions he had to deal with in that important missive.[38] In general, however, I am inclined to ascribe the frequency of letters written immediately before and after a holiday to psychological factors. Six times a year writing was taboo on two successive days. But the holidays were when one was wont to be in the company of one's friends or yearned to enjoy them. Writing replaced or expressed these realities. This explains the curious fact that best wishes for the holiday are expressed in many of those letters although weeks would pass before they would get into the hands of those for whom they were destined.

This custom of conveying congratulations in letters that were expected to arrive long after the occasion for which they were written is perhaps not as strange as it may appear to us. We express good wishes on the occasion of a holiday. For them the holiday itself was a blessing whose beneficial power was to endure for many days to come. Each holiday had its specific blessings, as is considered briefly below in the context of the religious meaning of the yearly cycle.

Holy shrines and pilgrimages.—The sacred times of the year have their parallel in visits to choice sites designed for special devotion. Both unite those who belong together in joint observance, both relieve them of their daily chores, and both are apt to transport the devotee beyond himself to spheres not easily attained otherwise. The very frequency of such events, however, has its pitfalls. Repetition breeds neglect. Just as holidays may become degraded to mere pastimes, so visits to holy sites may deteriorate into outings for the enjoyment of company and nature and less desirable distractions. And, who knows, in remote times when such places began to assume their specific character, if social, or even political agents might have been primary and stronger than intrinsically religious factors, as was the case with Safed, Palestine, sometimes revered as a holy city. In view of this, the secularization of some holy sites should not be regretted too much. The end of their life cycle may have become similar to their beginning.[39]

Various types of holy sites are to be discerned. The great central sanctuaries, such as Jerusalem or Mecca, are in a category by themselves. They were meeting places attracting peoples from widely different countries; one tried to go up there in groups, and, as the story of the company of Karaites from Cairo visiting Jerusalem for a period of mourning (told in *Med. Soc.*, III, 74–75) shows, one could be occupied there with quite mundane affairs. Nevertheless, the universally and officially recognized character of a holy city as "the city of God" made a posture of devotion and ethical decorum imperative. The study of the pilgrimage to such places belongs to the sociology of religions in a more specific way than that of the shrines described in the following.

The sanctuaries of large and influential communities bore a semi-ecumenical character. The Jewish population of "Babylonia" (Iraq and western Iran), which, in early Islamic times, was superior to other sections of the Jewish people in number and religious scholarship, worshiped at the (spurious) tombs of the prophet Ezekiel and of Ezra, the Scribe. As the Geniza shows, these tombs were also visited by Jewish pilgrims from the farthest Muslim West as well as by Egyptian India traders on their way from, and probably also to, India. Ezekiel was the patron of the seafarers, probably not so much because of his beautiful description of a magnificent ship (Ezekiel 27:4–9) but because the India traders from Baghdad, while traveling to the Persian Gulf, were wont to stop at Ezekiel's tomb, praying there for safe return. Unfortunately, the Iraqian India trade is beyond the orbit of the Geniza.[40]

Here we are mainly concerned with the local shrines, intended to satisfy the religious and social needs of the surrounding population. In this respect, too, a clear demarcation line exists between the numerous smaller shrines and those that were venerated throughout a country and beyond, such as the tomb of Aḥmad al-Badawī in Tanta for the Muslims of Egypt (mainly from the fourteenth century) and the synagogue of Dammūh for its Jews (mainly prior to the same time).[41] In the late Middle Ages the cult of saints became a mass phenomenon and, because of the voluminous material on the subject, much has been written about it.[42] I. Goldziher's famous chapter on shrines dedicated to saints (including Aḥmad al-Badawī) is still a classic, not only because of the incredible extent of reading and observation displayed but also in view of the author's humane and deep insight into the psychological and historical roots of this phenomenon. A modest, but not insignificant contribution to its history is provided by the Geniza.[43]

During the eleventh through the thirteenth centuries—the classical Geniza period—the Jewish holy shrines of Egypt are never ascribed to a saint; the synagogues themselves were holy, although in later literary sources, both Jewish and Muslim, the places were connected with biblical figures, and wondrous legends were told about the effects of their presence there. To be sure the veneration of the tombs of saints preceded this period by centuries. The Islamic keepers of the law condemned it as an innovation taken over—with other bad things—from the Jews, and the Karaites scolded the Rabbanites for "praying to the dead" like the Muslims. Both accusations were probably correct. In early Islamic times the practices of the preceding monotheistic religions were partly taken over; later, the example of the majority population was followed by the minorities.[44]

The rather sober-minded Egyptian Jews of the High Middle Ages were, of course, aware of their country having been hallowed by the miracles wrought by Moses; the more sophisticated among them knew also that Jeremiah ended his prophetic career there,[45] and Ezra, the Scribe, was ubiquitous, as his tomb in Babylonia-Iraq (a country that he left according to the Bible) shows. But for a rationalist mind the holiness of a place and the efficacy of prayer there were sufficiently guaranteed by its very nature. In a synagogue where the name of God was invoked day and night in prayer and study, God surely was present. There was no need for intercessors, for "conveyors of prayers," as a moving Hebrew liturgical poem, conceived in another spiritual environment, demanded.[46]

As mentioned earlier in passing, the sanctuary most highly venerated by the Jews of Egypt and, consequently, often mentioned in the Geniza, was the synagogue of Dammūh, a place on the western bank of the Nile south of Fustat. What was the importance of that obscure place, the very spelling of whose name is not yet finally settled?[47] In his painstaking study on the subject, Norman Golb has convincingly shown that this was the only remaining synagogue of ancient Memphis, once the royal capital of Egypt, and in Roman times still a large urban conglomerate, second in importance only to Alexandria, the Greek city.[48] In Byzantine times the decimated population moved to "The Roman Fortress" on the eastern bank of the Nile, which was to be included in the Islamic city of Fustat, just as in the later Middle Ages Fustat was largely deserted and replaced by Cairo. The cities were given up, but not their synagogues (and churches, and, in Fustat's case, mosques). First they were venerated as houses of worship in a capital city, where crowds always assembled for prayer and seekers of knowledge for study, and where law was administered. When the glory of life moved elsewhere, the halo of venerable age remained and even became enhanced. The house of daily worship was converted into a place of seasonal pilgrimage. What happened to Dammūh of Memphis was also the lot of the "great," or main synagogue of Fustat, that of the Palestinians (the Geniza synagogue). In a still later period, when even the halo of old age began to fade, the Fustat synagogue became a tourist attraction. I do not mean the year 1985, but 1655, when a Karaite scholar from the Crimea (southern Russia), after describing the place, added this: "All the walls of the synagogue are covered with the names of persons coming from foreign countries; some write their names with their hands, others have them incised in wood.[49] We, too, inscribed our names." Those visitors were probably devout Jews like the scholar from the Crimea, but they could hardly be described as pilgrims.[50]

Dammūh, according to a Muslim historian the largest place of worship possessed by the Jews of Egypt,[51] was a rallying point for all sections of the community, men and women (especially the latter, who were happy to escape their seclusion once a year), young and old, low and high, learned and plain, who all flocked there for edification, or enjoyment, or both. Sometimes Muslims were invited by friends (as was so common at the tombs of Jewish saints of Morocco in later times) and even Jews who had converted to Islam could not withstand the attractions of the cherished outing.

How life looked at the *ziyāra*, or visit, to the sanctuary, *miqdāsh* (Heb.), of Dammūh, can best be reconstructed by studying a lengthy statute condemning and prohibiting all the alleged abuses in vogue there. I have no doubt that this document was issued at the time of the rigorous enforcement of Islamic law and mores by the caliph al-Ḥākim (996-1021). When the Jewish authorities realized what was happening in their environment, they understood that they had better put their own house in order. Like al-Ḥākim himself they overreacted, and, as happened with the caliph's reforms, the disapproved practices at Dammūh probably surfaced again after some time.[52]

In order to enable the reader to join me in the study of this intriguing document, which is almost a thousand years old, I provide here a full analysis of its contents. As so often happens in the Geniza, about one half of the sheet is torn away and much precious material is lost. It is all the more remarkable how much can be learned from what has been preserved.

The Hebrew preamble states that "the Court," that is, the judge, and the elders had proposed to the members of the community to take action to remove all abuses from the sanctuary of Dammūy,[53] that the community had accepted the proposal, whereby it had become a statute binding for all and forever, like an ordinance imposed by the God-fearing sages of old and approved by God.

In the Arabic text, as far as preserved, the following points are stressed, enumerated here in the sequence they appear in the manuscript. The reader must keep in mind that originally there was at least one item between each two items noted here.

1. All should attend solely for devotion. No merrymaking would be tolerated.

2. Marionette shows ("Chinese shades," the medieval movies) and similar entertainments are not permitted.[54]

3. No beer should be brewed there.[55]

4. No visitor should be accompanied by [a Gentile] or an apostate.[56]

5. No woman should be admitted except when accompanied by [a father, a husband,] a brother, or a grown-up son, unless she is a *very* old woman.

6. The synagogue building should be respected and revered like any other synagogue.[57]

7. Boys, or a grown-up man together with a boy, should not [. . .], in order not to expose themselves to suspicion and make for themselves a bad name.

8. Both men and women should take utmost care not to desecrate the Sabbath in any way.[58]

9. Playing chess and [. . .] is forbidden.[59]

10. Likewise games like "watermelon and clay" and [. . .].

11. Making noise by hitting something with a bang or clasping hands is disapproved.

12. No instrumental music.

13. No dancing.

14. On Sabbath water should be drawn from the well only when needed for drinking.[60]

15. Men should not mix with women, nor come near them [. . .], nor are they permitted to look at them.

16. In the synagogue women should pray in the gallery upstairs and men in the hall downstairs, as is established by ancient custom, *sunna*.[61]

17. Visitors to the place[62] (in times other than those of pilgrimages) should go there only for a serious purpose, not for pleasure or for something that, by deed or word, might endanger them or others or damage the compound. They should provide themselves with keys and not tamper with the locks, nor enter through the gardens or by scaling a wall.[63]

18. The community has empowered [. . .] to represent them in anything concerning that synagogue—may God keep it.

The statute summarized above had no reason to mention one important aspect of the pilgrimage to Dammūh besides prayers and pastimes: the place and time when so many people flocked together provided a convenient opportunity for public announcements, especially those that had serious consequences for the persons concerned, such as bans and excommunications. This was the practice at the yearly assemblies on the Mount of Olives overlooking Jerusalem, and it was not different at Dammūh. We read about a man against whom a ban was pronounced in the synagogues of Fustat and Cairo, and at Dammūh, because he had taken a second wife without the consent of the first. Apparently the ban was effective; the man temporarily expelled from the community appeared in Qūṣ, Upper Egypt, with his first wife, claiming that he had already divorced the second one. But the writer of the letter emphasizes that a ban may be revoked only in the same way in which it had been pronounced. This happened in June 1234, at the time when Abraham Maimonides (who generally was disinclined to approve the pronouncement of bans) was head of the Egyptian Jewry. To remark in passing, both Abraham Maimonides and his father, as well as his father-in-law, Hananel b. Samuel, were much concerned with the upkeep of the sanctuary of Dammūh, and several documents to this effect have been preserved. The temporary religious revival of Egyptian Jewry set into motion by Moses Maimonides' teaching and reforms and by his son's pietism may have resuscitated the veneration for that ancient holy place.[64]

According to later sources the general pilgrimage to the "Synagogue of Moses" took place on and around Pentecost (April-May), the holiday dedicated to the revelation of the Ten Commandments to Moses on Mount Sinai, and a visit, less attended, on the seventh day of Adar (February-March, regarded as the day on which Moses died—and was born). The seventh was celebrated by a fast, followed by a feast on the eighth. This custom might have been influenced by the Fatimid celebration of Muhammad's day of birth and death and its growth into a popular festival during the thirteenth century.[65]

The findings of the Geniza seem to indicate that the great get-together could last for days, occasionally even for more than a week. A letter to the chief justice Hananel b. Samuel speaks of "the days" (not: the holiday) spent in his company at Dammūh (1235).[66] A Nagid (like everyone else) was supposed to be accompanied by his wife. When the widow of a Nagid married her brother-in-law (who also inherited the office of her late husband), it was formally stipulated that, at the time of the pilgrimage, he might stay there with his first wife "not more than two [consecutive] days per week" (so that the prerogatives of the original Mrs. Nagid should be sustained). The fact that it was necessary to emphasize this detail in the comparatively very short marriage agreement shows how important the pilgrimage was for both communal and personal life (1482).[67]

The western bank of the Nile was unsafe. The administrator of Dammūh had to pay a yearly protection fee, *khafāra,* to the sheikh who held sway over the environs and a bonus to the *khafīr,* or watchman.[68] During unrest in the country (we read about times when Gizeh itself, the suburb of Cairo on the southwestern bank, was in the hands of Bedouins and Sudanese), travel to Dammūh was dangerous. A remarkable letter, which deserves full translation, was written in such a situation. It concerned a short visit for devotion—possibly that of the seventh of Adar—not the yearly pilgrimage. The sender sojourned in Dammūh—perhaps for solitary meditation, as the pious of Islam did—but had come purposely to Fustat to warn his companions and relatives (in this sequence) not to go to Dammūh at that time. The addressee was the father of one of these young companions, who was adamant about going by foot. (When necessary they were prepared to walk even for days.) What happened next was this: after long adjurations the young man agreed to join the writer and go by boat; they arrived safely, and being ten—the quorum required for a Jewish public service—they performed the rites usual on such an occasion. The young man insisted on staying overnight with his friend in Dammūh, whereupon the latter sent this strongly worded missive to the father (certainly with the rest of the company which returned to Fustat), assuring him that his son's decision was entirely his own, that he was well. "*Do not hold me guilty without reason.* I shall see to it that he gets back to Miṣr."[69]

Relics of saints or of the founder of the religion himself were the great infatuation of medieval Christianity and, to a lesser degree, also of Islam. The desire for movable objects of adoration—and not only immovables like houses of worship and tombs of saints—was satisfied in Judaism by Torah scrolls which were regarded as particularly "awe-inspiring and holy." One Torah scroll was—and had to be—exactly like the other; every iota of what was written in it was meticulously prescribed. So how did a scroll become holy like a relic and consequently the goal of pilgrimages? By its age. When, by look and according to tradition, it was sufficiently old, it could be ascribed to anyone of the great of the past. An eminently knowledgeable traveler visiting the synagogue of the Palestinians in 1753 could note in his diary that they had there a holy and awe-inspiring scroll written, they say, by Ezra, the Scribe (who brought the final version of the Book of Moses from Babylonia to Jerusalem about 2,200 years prior to that visit).[70]

The Torah scrolls in Dammūh and Taṭay—a minor holy shrine—were highly venerated and in times of the breakdown of public order, as in the 1070s, kept in the capital in the synagogue of the Palestinians.[71] Of particular interest is the history of the Holy Scroll in al-Maḥalla, a provincial capital in the Nile delta with a considerable Jewish community. To this scroll a yearly pilgrimage was made on the New Moon day of Iyyar, about a week after Passover. No legendary attribution to a saint of antiquity could be made here, for the case in which the scroll was preserved bore an inscription stating clearly that it was given to the synagogue of the Palestinians in 1182, to be preserved for the donor and his extended family. A member of the family, perhaps even the donor (or depositor) himself, moved to al-Maḥalla and entrusted it to the (main) synagogue there. Thus we see that old age alone was sufficient for arousing pious emotions. Just as an ancient place of worship became a holy shrine because the name of God had been invoked in it for so many years, thus a copy of the Holy Scriptures, which had pronounced his teachings day in day out, was worthy of being venerated. A letter dated as late as 1847 deals with donations made in al-Maḥalla by pilgrims from Cairo, Alexandria, Palestine, and Syria.[72]

In the scientific-technological civilization in which we live, it is the quest for knowledge, or the striving for the attainment of political, socioeconomic, or other practical aims, which serves us as incentive (or pretext) for the satisfaction of our natural craving for travel and getting together. In a religious age, religion, in its highest and lowest forms, fulfilled a similar function. The pilgrimage to Jerusalem (or Mecca), however, was sui generis. It is described in the context in which it mainly belongs.[73]

Calls and visits, congratulations and condolences.—The gatherings on Sabbaths, holidays, and pilgrimages were hosted, so to say, by God; all participants were equally bound, by law or custom, to attend; they formed a flock whose faces were turned toward the Shepherd. It is evident, however, that the social obligations described by the legal terms forming the title of this subsection—meetings with purely human concerns as their object—were taken as seriously as the religious duties. The rabbinic court of Fustat opined that a wife must be permitted to leave her husband's house to pursue all these activities. In Ṣanʿā, Yemen, it was customary for Jewish women to get together in the afternoon in spacious houses, taking their needlework with them, for what was called "talk and spindle." For the little girls accompanying their mothers and imbibing their news and judgments, these gatherings replaced the Bible school of their less fortunate brothers. In Fustat, where, unlike the capital of Yemen, the Jews did not live by themselves in a separate quarter, such get-togethers were probably less regular. But the many business transactions and lawsuits between women recorded in the Geniza can hardly be explained except by the assumption that women had frequent opportunities to meet, albeit not as regularly and comprehensively as men, who spent their lives in the bazaar and the house of worship, study, and communal activities as much as in their own homes.[74]

Moreover, inquiring after the well-being of one's neighbor, keeping him company, and sharing his joy and sorrow were obligations one owed not only others but also, and perhaps even more so, oneself. One could not live properly without the company of congenial fellow creatures. The Talmudic maxim "Company or death" is echoed repeatedly in the Geniza. "There is no one who talks to me; death is better than this," writes a newlywed to her sister.[75] A communal leader in Ramle, Palestine, who had joined the wrong party, complains: "All the notables of the town keep their distance from me, they cut me and relate to me in a way which any reasonable person would regard as death."[76] The Geniza people possessed a rich vocabulary for expressing loneliness, desolation, separation, and feeling as a stranger, an orphan, or "a lonely bird on the house top" (Psalms 102:8). The desire to retire from the world, not unknown to a Moses Maimonides, was alien to them. Theirs were the practical ethics of Saadya Gaon, who, in the tenth chapter of his *Beliefs and Opinions,* strongly disapproved of living as a recluse.[77]

Most letters open with often extended expressions of yearning and longing for the addressee and the hope of being united with him soon under the best of circumstances and of finding him in perfect health and happiness. In a period when travel was tiresome, costly, and often dangerous, when separation was prolonged and communication slow, such stereotyped assurances of missing the company of a relative or business friend carried more weight than they would in our own times (when we do not use them so prolifically, anyhow). They reflect the attitude of a society that regarded intensive personal contact with one's peers as a way of life. The lists, often long, of relatives and friends to whom greetings are extended and mentioned by name at the end of a letter, underline this fact. If someone was ill, a visit or an inquiry after the patient's state was imperative; strong excuses had to be adduced for failing to do so. In such a case it was customary to state that one refrained from writing out of consideration lest the patient be inconvenienced by feeling impelled to answer, but the writer was constantly inquiring about the recipient's health from everyone coming from his place.[78]

Naturally, practical matters—personal, communal, commercial—were often best settled face to face. Consequently, we frequently read: "I would have preferred to be with you in person instead of sending this letter." In town, one sent a boy with a note, announcing one's coming, inviting the addressee to a meeting, or asking him to visit. Numerous notes of that kind have been preserved. A few examples illustrate their scope. On an irregularly cut slip of paper, 3¼ inches wide and 2½ inches high, Solomon b. Elijah, the schoolmaster and court clerk, informs a colleague that he would come later in the day with two trustworthy witnesses to settle a juridical case (a debt to be paid). The messenger brought the note back. We know this, because on the reverse side—and without crossing the first message out—the careless clerk wrote another message, this time to his tailor, asking him to come to take his measurements and cut up the cloth for a *maqṭaʿ* robe, which the tailor, together with his partner (or employee) "sheikh Abu ʾl-Barakāt," was to sew. It seems that the latter was also expected to be present at this critical meeting.[79]

On an only slightly larger, but evenly cut, piece of paper, Moses Maimonides invites al-Wāthīq (Heb.), the administrator of the holy shrine of Dammūh, whom we have already encountered, to meet him "on Sabbath" (meaning after the service in the synagogue compound) "where, in the presence of the elders, something will be decided which you will like." Maimonides adds that a message sent to him by al-Wāthīq had become illegible because of water damage.[80]

Opportunities for congratulation parties were numerous. In addition to the great family events of betrothals, weddings, and births, good wishes had to be extended when a person entered a new home or acquired other valuable property, when he was honored with a new title or a robe of honor, or was appointed or reinstated to an office at court, government, or the Jewish community, when he was restored to good health after a dangerous illness, or—when he was released from prison. (Then, as now under certain regimes, prison walls confined men of standing.) The safe arrivals of overseas traders and other travelers returning home "with a happy heart and a full purse" after a prolonged absence were recurring occasions for jubilant gatherings. These and other congratulation parties (and excuses for the inability or unworthiness to attend them) have been noted in the preceding volumes. In accordance with the practical and rather jejune character of the Geniza world, wedding celebrations seem to have been less extended, less encumbered with magical and symbolic ceremonies than prevailed in pristine communities such as those of Morocco and Yemen, although these elements were by no means absent. A person attended mainly to fulfill a social obligation (including alms-giving) and to enjoy. Poetic creations in honor of an event, including release from prison (then an experience often shared by prominent persons), were not entirely missing, but not as profuse and of the standard as those common among the sophisticated Jews of Spain.[81]

Two important types of congratulation parties not observed in Geniza times should be noted. Nowhere have I found a reference to good wishes for a birthday, something by no means easy to explain. Everyone knew from the Bible that Joseph's Pharaoh celebrated his birthday by promoting one official and hanging the other, an impressive way of making the day memorable (Genesis 40:20–21). Greeks and Romans kept birthdays of private persons, or, rather, of the god to whom the day was dedicated (*deus natalis,* a custom reminiscent of the Catholic calendar, which sanctifies each day of the year by a saint or the like). In Geniza times, at the birth of a child the exact date according to the Jewish and Muslim calendars was noted, sometimes also the Christian, together with the hours and the horoscope. Thus the day could easily have been remembered and celebrated—had it not been for the belief that numbers were ominous, attracting the evil eye. Even in our own society the question "how old are you" is generally avoided, superstitious apprehensions having become matters of good manners.[82]

The Bar Mitzvah, the rite of passage by which Jewish children become obliged to fulfill the commandments of their religion, in present-day American Jewry an occasion for grand gatherings of family and friends, comparable almost to a wedding, left no trace whatsoever in the Geniza. The situation was probably similar to one that I observed in the traditional Yemenite community about fifty years ago. Since those Yemenites gave their children a strictly religious education starting at the age of four or so, there was no marked passage from childhood to adulthood worthy of an elaborate celebration. When a father noted that his boy was ready and eager to comport himself religiously like an adult, he adorned him with the prayer trappings described in the Bible (Deuteronomy 6:8) even before he reached the obligatory age of thirteen.[83]

Expressions of sympathy and "parties of condolence" are discussed in the subsection on the social aspects of death in A, 3, below.[84]

Hospitality.—Thomas Henry Huxley, visiting the United States in 1876 on the occasion of the centenary, noted among other characteristics of the Americans "extreme hospitality, said to be a savage trait."[85] This allusion to the potlatch of the Indians of the Pacific Northwest, the wasteful entertaining of prominent guests from another tribe, finds its parallel in the Muslim prophet's criticism of the pre-Islamic Arab who bragged, "I have wasted enormous wealth" (on my guests).[86] The proverbial Arab hospitality had various roots but does not occupy us here, for the trait of hospitality conspicuous in the Geniza was of a different type. It was religiously motivated and was extended mainly to needy people and strangers, or to others who had a claim to help, to scholars, whose learning was honored, and, of course, to family and friends, where the motive of reciprocity was also present. "Putting up the wayfarer" was among the religious merits, "whose dividends may be earned in this world, while the capital remained intact for the world to come," meaning that this was intrinsically a deed of piety for which no reward should be expected, although reward was likely.[87]

A beautiful Hebrew letter of introduction, written by a high dignitary in Iraq for a man traveling to Syria and Egypt, contains a veritable sermon on the meritoriousness of hospitality. This virtue was gratefully appreciated (and rewarded) by the saints of the Bible, such as Father Abraham and King David, while inhospitable people like Ammon, Moab, who failed to welcome the Children of Israel "with bread and water," were gravely punished. The letter concludes with the admonition: "Exert yourselves, be not remiss, for all you do will be rewarded" (that is, by God) (II Chronicles 15:7). This sounds as if hospitality was not always taken for granted. But the letter was written in the fall of 1031, at a time when the people of Fustat, renowned for their hospitality, might not yet have recovered fully from the aftermath of the great famine of 1025–1027.[88]

In general, one should remember that hospitality was often required in times that were hard on the host himself and in places where demands on charity were made constantly. This was true, in particular, of Alexandria, which bore the brunt of captives brought by pirates to the Mediterranean port, to be ransomed and put up there, and of refugees, who arrived there from many parts of the Muslim and Christian worlds. In a long letter written in Alexandria in September 1212 we read this short note:

> On the very night I am writing you this letter, there arrived here seven of the rabbis [of France], all great scholars, accompanied by one hundred souls, men, women, and children, all in need of eating bread, as if we had not enough beggars of our own here in town—we have about forty.[89] Most of the community are in trouble because of the sluggish business, and now such a great imposition is thrown upon them; let's see how they will tackle it.

Another group of learned Jews, fleeing inhospitable France, had arrived in Alexandria the year before; so the recipient of the letter knew wherefrom the refugees had come and of what type they were.[90]

In 1234, new royal decrees made the life of Jews in northern France almost impossible. No wonder that in a letter from Alexandria, written in May 1235, we read that a traveler coming from France reported on a large number of French Jews preparing themselves to emigrate to Egypt—whereupon the writer remarks:

"May God guard us from the troubles they will cause." He seemed to have had experience with such arrivals.

Naturally, there were also people who were notorious for their lack of hospitality, or had reason to change their attitude while the guest was still with them, or both. Of Tinnīs, the eastern seaport of Egypt, a Tunisian merchant staying there writes: "In Tinnīs there is no one from whom a foreigner can derive benefits."[91] Shamṭūniyya was a town halfway between Baghdad and the tomb of the prophet Ezekiel, the most holy shrine of the Jews of Iraq and Iran.[92] A physician on his way to that shrine with his young son made a stop in that town and reported that they were well attended to by a *pāqīd,* or representative of merchants, whose household "was not remiss" in the duties of hospitality.[93] (They stayed in a caravanserai.) When an epidemic disease, which had already been rampant when the travelers arrived, affected the family of their host, the latter took no further notice of his guests, which caused them great discomfort. To this the physician, somewhat surprisingly, adds: "You know, the people of Shamṭūniyya, even if they are in good health, pay no attention to travelers."[94]

A noblewoman from Jerusalem who left the town with her family, it seems, after it had been occupied by the Seljuks (around 1072), for Tripoli, Lebanon, writes that her brother-in-law "had not been remiss" (in the duties of hospitality) until her husband, who had meanwhile disappeared in the confusion of the wars, had claimed some inheritance due him. This led to a complete rupture, and the woman and her children were left without the barest means of existence in the foreign country. She writes now to her relatives in Egypt asking for help, but does not say a word of complaint about her brother-in-law, the negligent host.[95]

Hospitality began before the guest arrived in town. Family and friends, and in the case of a scholar or other VIP, representatives of the community went out to meet him at his latest lodging station or any other place agreed upon, to welcome him and to bring him safely through the gates of their town. At the very least, a messenger was sent to perform this duty. Two entirely different reasons gave rise to this procedure. At the entrance to a city, a traveler had to pay customs dues and was exposed to all kinds of searches, in the course of which unexpected and unpleasant things could happen. Passing the gates of a city was so dangerous that when someone got through them unscathed, he was obliged, according to the Talmud (referring to Roman times, of course), to pronounce a benediction of thanksgiving. When the guest was accompanied by local people he could be sure, or, at least hope, to be spared such discomfort.

Another reason for meeting a guest outside the city was the endeavor to show him respect and affection, as was the duty of the population when a new ruler or governor arrived. Naturally, this aspect of hospitality was very cumbersome, and it was regarded as a sign of particular solicitude on the part of the guest when he refrained from announcing the time of his arrival so as not to inconvenience his hosts. If the visitor was a very distinguished personage, for example, a Great Rav, this was impossible, of course. Letters of welcome, certainly containing information about the whereabouts and other details of the prospective meeting, greeted him when he was still far from his destination. In a report about his safe arrival, the proud guest would include a list of the most important of the notables who came out of the town to meet him, adding (of course) that all immediately inquired after the well-being of the recipient of the letter.[96]

The arrangements for lodging in Geniza times held a surprise for me. I had taken it for granted that the first duty of the host was to put up the guest in his own home. This was not the practice. The main concern was to provide the newcomer with privacy, with a place belonging exclusively to him, where he could himself receive visitors, and spend his day and night as he pleased. Did not the righteous and pious expect to be honored even in paradise, "each with an apartment only for himself"?[97]

This is a report about being met outside the provincial town Bilbays by some notables of the place and being provided with desirable lodgings.

We[98] arrived safely in Bilbays, except that I was dying of exhaustion. They had made ready for us a beautiful place for lodging, an excellent house with an upper and lower floor [in this sequence], entirely reserved for us. We were met outside the town by the *dayyān*[99]—[may his] R[ock] k[eep him], his sons—Rk—R. Berākhōt al-Ashmūnī,[100] my lord the Scholar[101]—Rk—al-Makīn[102]—Rk. They inquired very much about your well-being.[103]

A traveler arriving in Qūṣ, a provincial capital in Upper Egypt, after a harrowing Nile voyage, writes this: "Your servant arrived in Qūṣ and experienced on the side of our coreligionists a measure of hospitality which I am unable to describe even in part. They kindly took an apartment for me, a place which can be locked, before I arrived. . . ."[104] A welcome in Alexandria is described thus: "We have been lodged in a fine, pleasant house, get invitations every day, and have it very good here, I and Saᶜīd; we eat. . . ."[105] A *ne᾿emān,* or trustee, a welfare official of the community in Ramle, then the administrative capital of Palestine, describes to his superior how he welcomed a distinguished visitor: "The scholar from Mosul arrived on the eve of the holiday, I mean Passover. I held at that time the office of the trustee. I readied for him a place appropriate for a person of his station, put there all he needed, and provided for him as is proper, before and after the holidays. On the holidays themselves I invited him to stay in my house."[106]

When the Spanish Hebrew poet Judah ha-Levi arrived in Alexandria on his way to the Holy Land, everyone was eager to put him up; a local merchant, who had traveled with him on the same boat, went so far as to use his influence with the governor of the city to exercise pressure on the poet to accept an invitation for dinner. But ha-Levi rented a domicile for himself, and only during Sabbaths and holidays did he stay with Ibn al-ᶜAmmanī, the Jewish local judge and spiritual leader, who was also a physician (and a maker of verses).[107] During the week the poet was visited in his own premises by local notables, and in one letter we read that the visitor brought his dinner with him. He certainly was not the only one who did so (a kind of brown bag dinner party).[108]

When a distinguished stranger was put up in a private home, some special intent was involved. The learned Tunisian merchant Yeshuᶜā b. Ismaᶜīl-Samuel, who had settled in Alexandria,[109] writes this to another learned Tunisian, Nahray b. Nissīm, who resided in Fustat:

> A Spanish man, whom Rav Daniel [b. Azaria] had given the title "member of the [Jerusalem] yeshiva," has arrived from Tripoli [Libya]. He is learned and an excellent preacher. I put him up in my house. On the very first Sabbath [after his arrival] he delivered a sermon, and many pledges were made for him. When he travels to your place you will hear him preaching, if God wills.[110]

Today it is customary to assign an honorarium to a speaker in advance. They were then more cautious, contributing awards in accordance with performance. The numerous pledges in Alexandria were reason enough to invite the preacher for one or several appearances in Fustat. The detail that the writer put him up in his own home is mentioned as an additional recommendation; it was a delight to have constant opportunity to converse with so learned a guest.

"The distinguished member of the Baghdad yeshiva" of whom we have read that he did not announce his coming to Alexandria, so as not to inconvenience the local notables with meeting him outside the city, rented a place for himself (as Judah ha-Levi had done[111]). As soon as his whereabouts had become known, however, "we, all the community," that is, everyone who counted, went to welcome him. After the comportment and qualities of the newcomer had been sufficiently explored, he was asked to deliver a discourse first in the main, the Palestinian, and then, the Iraqian synagogue of Alexandria, and for both occasions the members of both communities were invited. The end of the story is told in *Med. Soc.*, II, 217–218.[112]

How a Jewish scholar from a Christian country was received in Cairo on the eve of the First Crusade may be learned from this letter of thanks by Isaac b. Benveniste of Narbonne, France, addressed to Joshua b. Dōsā, a confidant of the viceroy of Egypt. The letter is written in flowery Hebrew and seems to imply that the visitor was overwhelmed by the hospitality extended to him:

> You ordered a house emptied entirely for me and put me up there like a king with his entourage. You obtained for me exemption from all dues, poll tax and others, as well as a rescript from the king [meaning the viceroy], hanging it on my neck so that no one would dare to say a word against me.[113] And this on top of all your benefactions, filling my pantry with provisions of every kind.[114]

Enjoying privacy did not mean staying away from the local community. Quite the contrary. Nothing worse could be said about foreigners than that "they do not attend the synagogue service and do not visit in the houses of [respectable] people."[115] Such visits were followed by invitations, but, as explained in our section on food and drink, the delicacies offered on such occasions, if mentioned at all, were referred to only in the most general terms. On the other hand, spiritual honors, such as pronouncing at the table the benedictions customarily reserved for the host or leading the local congregation in prayer, are reported with special satisfaction.[116]

Just as the welcome of a distinguished or a particularly dear guest was an elaborate affair, so was his departure. No one should fail to attend the farewell party; when a maker of verses was present, it should be celebrated by a poem containing good wishes for a safe journey.[117] How seriously this social obligation was taken may be gauged from this quaint note (enriched by three postscripts), sent during such a party to a relative and friend, who was tardy.

May it be known to you—you, the illustrious elder Abu ʾl-Faḍl—that you are neither a scholar,[118] nor a relative, nor a friend of mine because of what you have done. If you make this good by coming immediately[119]—all right. Otherwise—the choice is with you. And peace!

[*Postscript*:]

When your father R. Elazar—may God, the exalted, keep him and keep his noble character—heard that I was leaving, he volunteered to come and, had it not been for a very urgent impediment, it would not have occurred that he was late.

[*Postscript. Margin*:]

Would that you walked in his ways and acted as he did! *Behave like everyone else*![120]

[*Postscript. Verso*:]

Had anyone else, and not I, told you [about my departure], you would have come without delay.[121]

Seeing a visitor off and accompanying him as far as feasible were essential parts of hospitality, for which the Patriarch Abraham, the paragon of a host, had set the example ("The men stood up . . . and Abraham went with them to bear them company" [Genesis 18: 16]).[122] In a long letter, the writer, who was not the host, but had spoken to the traveler a few days before his departure, excuses himself for failing to bid him farewell, "as was my duty." He had since fallen ill and was unable to sit, stand, or ride, but hoped to do better, when the traveler returned "safe and successful."[123] By contrast, the Tunisian trader Joseph Lebdi, writing from India after a shipwreck and other misfortunes, mentions with gratitude that Ḥasan b. Bundār, the Jewish representative of merchants in Aden, South Arabia, had come down with his brothers to the harbor and ascended the boat to see him off. To appreciate this, one must remember that the passengers boarded a vessel sometimes days before a favorable wind enabled the crew to set sail.[124]

Bidding farewell did not always conclude the duties of hospitality. One had to take care that the visitor arrived safely at the goal of his journey. After the Fustat community had maintained a poor Palestinian woman and her infant daughter, it provided her with travel expenses down to Alexandria, where the local community was requested to help her out until she reached her final destination. For a scholarly person on his way to Jerusalem the Fustat community was instructed to arrange a collection without delay so as to enable him to join a caravan which was about to leave.[125] A telling parallel "from the private sector" is the story of the Palestinian cantor, Japheth b. Amram al-Jāzifīnī, from whose beautiful hand we have several documents. He had enjoyed the lavish hospitality of Hillel, the elder son of the merchant prince Joseph b. Jacob Ibn ʿAwkal and, as the extended Hebrew poem of praise at the beginning of his letter to his host shows, he was well acquainted with the members of the latter's family. Instead of taking the overland route to Palestine, as was usually done at that time (ca. 1040), he traveled to Alexandria, where he hoped to make money with his vocal art. However, the pledges in the synagogues were disappointing; he incurred debts and pawned some of his indispensable belongings. He now asks Hillel to come to his rescue, assuring him that this would be "the end of the hospitality" granted to him; by fulfilling this request Hillel would really "bid him farewell," that is, get rid of him.[126] An indigent traveler, who had already reached Jerusalem with the help of a benefactor in Fustat, asks the latter to enable him to stay in the Holy City where he hoped for a reunion with him.[127]

The gratitude of the guest was expressed by exuberant praise and, in particular, by invoking God for blessings on him and his family. Jewish religious etiquette provided that the benedictions opening a meal were said by the host, and the grace concluding it was recited by the guest so that he could insert in it appropriate blessings. The host's praise sung in verse was particularly appreciated, for words formed by meter and rhyme could be memorized easily and thus would perpetuate the host's fame. We have several such poems from the pen of the Tunisian India trader Abraham Ben Yijū, praising the Jewish representative of merchants in Aden, Maḍmūn (the son of Ḥasan b. Bundār, mentioned above), which contain concrete details about the personality and activities of his host.[128] This could not be said about most similar creations dispersed throughout the Geniza, which are exasperating by their hyperbolic generalities. It is noteworthy, however, that mostly the host is lauded not so much for the special favors bestowed on the writer but for his solicitude for the well-being of any "wayfarer." Throughout, a Hebrew phrase is used in this connection in order to emphasize the religious merit of the virtue of hospitality.[129]

Another, and the most frequently mentioned way of spreading the fame of a benefactor was to pronounce blessings upon him in public, either in synagogues, when the Holy Ark was opened and the writer was called up to read from the Torah, or in warehouses, serving as bourses where merchants met, or simply at social gatherings.[130] A traveler to Constantinople (today, Istanbul, Turkey), wrote the names and titles of six benefactors of his in that city, plus "the entire holy congregation, may they be blessed," on a tiny piece of paper so that, while praying for them in public, no one should be forgotten.[131]

Young people, as some of us might have experienced, dislike writing letters of thanks. Then, as today, papas had to substitute. "Don't take it amiss," writes one of them, "when the boys are tardy in writing; love is in the hearts, not in letters, God the exalted knows that no time passes when they do not praise you and express their yearnings after you. May God grant that we shall soon be united with you."[132] Asking mama to put up a newly acquired friend and his wife (and later the writer himself) was an easier task than writing letters of thanks:

To the Lady al-Ghazāl [Gazelle], *may God keep her.*

[Your servant] kisses the hands of the lady, his mother, may God always keep her and make many like her, beautifying with her the women and the countries. May God let her rejoice in the (wedding of) her dear son, my master, my brother.

May I ask of you the favor to receive in your house, and to pay special attention to the elder Abu ʾl-Faraj Hibat Allah and the one who is with him [his wife], for I am obliged to him for what he has done for me in al-Maḥalla. He is related to the finest families in Damascus, and *the scholarly member of the academy,*[133] [*may*] *his Rock pre*[*serve him*] has recommended him, too. He himself is a man of virtue and piety. Whatever will be done for him is as if done for me.

In short, he should come back full of thanks for what had been done for him while he was staying with you in a fine place.

I am constantly and sincerely praying for you all the time. I might be leaving Fustat together with *our teacher* Solomon to visit in your blessed house.

The request to ready a fine place for the guests, which probably caused the old lady considerable inconvenience, shows again the emphasis of honoring a visitor by the best lodging available.[134]

Women, according to the Talmud, are less happy with guests than men.[135] This is natural. Since travelers were mostly male, the men in the house enjoyed entertainment, whereas the women had only more work and probably also less food, especially in the not so rare case of unexpected visitors. A frightening occurrence of this genre was the arrival of an almost complete stranger in a house in Jerusalem on a Friday late in the afternoon when people had already assembled for the evening prayer, and when, for religious reasons, it was impossible to prepare additional food—and at a time when provisions were scarce, at that. The women "came out [from their apartment] trembling."[136] It is not surprising, therefore, that the pronounced dedication of the women of the house to the welcome of a guest was particularly appreciated. The young, but learned, cantor Japheth b. David b. Shekhanya writes home to his parents in Fustat that three relatives whose hospitality he enjoyed in Tyre, Lebanon, "were not remiss," neither they "nor those who are with them," meaning their womenfolk.[137] In a letter to his brother, dated 6 December 1214, Hilāl, after describing the horrors of his Nile voyage, which took seven (instead of five or fewer days from Fustat to Alexandria), excuses himself for being momentarily unable to send the present promised to his host personally, but encloses six combs and six spindles, two of each for the elder daughter, and the rest for the wife and mother-in-law, respectively, but the present promised to the little daughter would soon follow separately. . . .[138]

The Geniza has preserved an artistic welcome placard containing in its upper band the words "Blessed shall you be when you come in," and on the bottom the conclusion of Deuteronomy 28:6: "And blessed shall you be when you go out." A band of tulip-like red and black patterns placed on a slant in alternating directions separates the two lines of script.[139]

The meaning of the placard is, of course, not that the host will be as happy with the guest's departure as with his arrival. In Hebrew "coming and going" means traveling, being away from home. When setting out on a journey, as for the pilgrimage to Jerusalem (Psalms 121:8), the traveler is wished a secure going out; when finding shelter on the way, he is greeted with a blessed coming in. The placard means to say: May your auspicious stay in this hospitable house augur well for all your travels.[140]

Pastimes.—The natural pastime for an educated Jewish person was study. Since study had the form of a disputation: questions, often surprising, posed; answers, sometimes contrasting, suggested; and decisions by the leader of the discussion made or deferred; the procedure was a continuous entertainment. The biblical "Your Torah is my pleasure" (Psalms 119:174) must be understood literally.

It seems, however, that in medieval Egypt, despite the praise heaped on it in communal letters for its zeal for study and despite the plentiful oil burned in the synagogues during the night, the common man was less a student than in some other countries, such as Tunisia, Spain, or France. It is the pastimes of the rank and file of the community which are examined in this subsection.

Short "calls" and extended "visits," the multifarious activities on Sabbaths, holidays, and pilgrimages, and entertaining travelers occupied most of the free time at the disposal of the Geniza person. There were, however, some special gatherings which were of considerable impact, in particular drinking bouts sometimes accompanied by the enjoyment of music, mainly for men, and get-togethers for whiling away the hours in a bathhouse, practiced mostly by women.

Warming up under the influence of intoxicating beverages, especially if accompanied by the sound of enrapturing tunes, is most conducive to sociability, to bringing hearts together. Meeting with friends over a cup of wine was a pastime befitting perfectly a community as sociable as the Geniza folks. The proverbial sobriety of East European Jewish immigrants to the United States should not be taken as inherent in the genes of the race. In biblical times one drank to get drunk (Haggai 1:6), and the Yemenites, those most Jewish of all Jews, did not take it amiss when one or some of the honored members of the company got a bit tipsy in the course of the main Sabbath meal.[141] Joyous music, instrumental as well as vocal, was indispensable at a banquet in ancient Israel (Isaiah 24:8–9). Wine, that "cheerer of the hearts of God and men" (Judges 9:13), and music of all kinds, which pervades the entire book of Psalms (Psalms 150!), formed intrinsic elements of the Temple service.

Things changed after the steamrollers of ever new conquering oppressors, of which the Roman Empire was the most enduring, had converted most of the populations of the Near East and the Mediterranean area into a *misera contribuens plebs,* an impoverished proletariat. Wine and music, if enjoyed in large quantities, were luxuries, unattainable by the common people. In the course of the centuries the lower classes reacted. Their speakers—prophets, philosophers, theologians, and lawyers—declared the pleasures of wine and music to be sinful, thus punishing at least with a bad conscience those who enjoyed them, or branding them outright as transgressors of laws laid down by God or reason. This condemnation took many different forms, culminating in the complete prohibition of alcoholic beverages and of listening to instrumental music and female voices.

The main body of the Jewish people upheld its appreciation of the nutritive, medical, and convivial values of wine and stuck fast by its central role in sacramental ceremonies.[142] Excessive consumption, however, especially in company, was abhorred and condemned in strong, almost pathological terms, from the time of the prophets of Israel down to a Moses Maimonides.[143]

These attitudes are reflected in the Geniza. Friends convened around a goblet, or goblets, of good wine making the rounds among them, enlivening the conversation. This was common practice among religious and educated people. Naturally, there were differences. The Geniza has preserved early wine songs—early meaning local and popular ones, not those inspired by the stereotyped and literary Hebrew Spanish poems on the subject, which were imported to Egypt at a later date. One of these popular poems contrasts two types of companies enjoying wine: "wise men" who came together to imbibe strong wine, a mixture of two thirds wine and one third water; and weaklings, who, as recommended by the ancient sages, added two thirds water to one wine, but were not able to digest even this mild mixture. It is evident, however, that both groups were conceived as belonging to the same environment of traditional and knowledgeable persons.[144] Being addressed as "the ornament of conviviality and crown of the revelers," or speaking of "the revival of the kingdom" in invitations to wine was entirely within the bounds of accepted mores.[145] Drinking parties in gardens, a standing topic in Arabic and Hebrew poetry, were common among merchants, as among intellectuals and government people.[146] Important matters, such as sending a son overseas, or promising a bequest, would be arranged at a drinking bout; when confirmed by an oath, such arrangements were irrevocable; otherwise, and when not written down and witnessed, they were void.[147] When peace, *ṣulḥa,* was restored in a family, members came together and drank to one another's health. As in the biblical Joseph story, brotherly love was manifested by drinking together. We learn this from a letter by the young cantor Judah b. Aaron from the renowned al-ʿAmmānī family of Alexandria, written in spring 1217, in which he thanks the Nagid Abraham Maimonides for settling matters between him and his uncle, the chief cantor Zadok (after having previously reported that the old man passed most of his time with wine, leaving him to manage the affairs of the synagogue).[148]

Muslims occasionally joined Jewish drinking parties, which caused some difficulty, because wine, in view of its sacramental character, should be handled only by those within the fold. When such newcomers entered, sophisticated keepers of the law would drop honey into the wine. The use of honey was forbidden in the Temple service (Leviticus 2:11); consequently, its admixture converted the tabooed beverage into a regular soft drink. Maimonides ruled that the Egyptian *nabīdh*, which was diluted with honey, was not to be regarded as wine; the benediction for it was that pronounced over water. Thus, there was nothing offensive to the visitors in this procedure. Quite to the contrary: they could enjoy the drink without compunctions. (Those who had expected to get the real thing from their Jewish friends might have been disappointed.)[149]

In times of stress, such as shortages or during the Muslim month of Ramadan, drinking parties, even in the privacy of a home, were dangerous, and the Jewish authorities tried to discourage them. A mother writing to her son from Aden, South Arabia, recounts a story of three Jewish notables who had come together for a drink during the Muslim feast terminating the month of fast; when visited by a Muslim musician, they received him well. The musician reported them to the qadi, the revelers were immediately set upon, beaten up terribly, and had to pay exorbitant fines. I have not come upon such an occurrence in Egypt. But when the spiritual head of a community in a provincial town reports to his superior in Fustat, "I have pronounced a curse upon any Jew who tastes wine in his house," similar outbreaks of fanaticism were feared to happen even there.[150]

Jewish taverns, so frequently mentioned in ancient Arabic literature, are practically absent from the Geniza. I ascribe this not only to consideration for the Muslim environment but to the belief that consumption of food in public was undignified; one enjoyed drinking and eating with friends, but not in a place accessible to just anyone. And wine tasted best when taken together with meat (and bread, of course).[151]

The sinners with wine in Geniza times were not, as in ancient Israel, the leaders who "were at ease and felt secure," and "were not grieved by the ruin of the nation," but fringe persons, sons of well-to-do homes who became addicts, wasting the paternal wealth on foreign wines and on musicians and mixing with people of dubious reputation; they were also, naturally, low-class hangers-on themselves. One of the longest completely preserved Geniza letters is mainly dedicated to the tribulations of the father of a profligate son. The interesting aspect of this woeful description is the young man's yearning not only for Rūmī wine, and drums and flutes, but also for the boon companions he had left in Alexandria. Whenever he got a position out of town, he gave it up in order to join his company in the port city. When the father expresses the hope that this incorrigible wastrel might perish on a voyage arranged for him, we understand how far things had gone. No wonder that a fiancé had to take upon himself the obligation "to shun bad company, their food and drink."[152] Bad company seems to have also been the issue when a boy from a provincial town was sent to his grandmother in the capital to learn a craft and went astray. His father writes to her:

> Your daughter Sitt al-Fakhr [Lady Pride, the writer's wife] says to you: may God reward you for your affection and what you are doing [for the boy]; however, one who drinks and discards [the commandments of God][153] cannot be loved by his family. You caused me grief by letting this little youngster go astray. God does not permit you to have him leave the city without a craft. Take the trouble with him imposed upon you by Fate until he makes an effort to [learn] a craft.[154]

Here again we encounter the notion that the family is inclined to keep its distance from an addict and his companions.

Boon companions enjoy each other's presence, but are also prone to quarrel when they do not see eye to eye over a matter. A Cairene dignitary, describing a brawl in Alexandria in which the son, nephew, and son-in-law of the head cantor (not the one mentioned above; this letter was written around 1100) and several others took part, notes that all participants were drunk, which attracted, of course, the attention of the police.[155] In a report about another brawl, this time in a provincial town, one party, the grandson of a head cantor and son of a beadle, was so drunk that he remained in that condition even after having been imprisoned and brought before the superintendent of police.[156] All in all, we see, alcohol was not a negligible factor in the life of the Geniza person.

Music fared less well than wine. Music worth speaking of required players of instruments and singing girls who had to be hired, or, as far as the latter are concerned, were often kept as slaves. Thus, music was a luxury. Developed Jewish law, as it presents itself in codes and legal opinions during the High Middle Ages, bans instrumental music completely, in particular, of course, when it was combined with drinking bouts and involved the presence of women. In his famous responsum on the subject, Maimonides showed himself aware of the value of music as being able to lift the select few to the highest spiritual experience, enhancing the service of God, but laws, he explained, can be made only for the masses, and listening to music, as it was practiced, made for depravity.[157] This attitude was by no means specific to Judaism. Islamic law displayed the same rigor. Lawyers were the spokesmen of puritanism and poverty, crying out against the indulgence of the rich and the mighty, as alluded to above. The lawyers held their own field—instrumental music never entered the synagogue or the mosque—but they could not prevail over human nature. The development of instrumental music during the Islamic Middle Ages was stupendous. The example of the upper classes made the forbidden permissible to the population at large.[158]

The Geniza society was a special case, inasmuch as its upper class consisted mainly of observant Jews familiar with the law. Music was confined to special occasions, such as weddings—or funerals[159]—and even then in reduced form, or was practiced and enjoyed by the lower classes, for which reason we have few details about it, except condemnations. When the Jewish judge of al-Mahdiyya received the joyous tidings of the birth of a son to his brother in Egypt, "there was great jubilation in the house," *laᶜb,* "play," that is, music and congratulation parties.[160] Egypt attracted foreigners by the sociability of its inhabitants, its good food, drink, and *laᶜb.*[161] This term, which occurs in the story of the profligate son, told above, several times, seems to have had a wider connotation, such as dance (and dancing girls, just as at funerals hired wailing women are no doubt included).[162]

Fulminating against instrumental music and those who listened to it—in one case also the keeping of slave girls—was a favorite topic of reform-minded visitors or itinerant preachers. This happened in the capital, as reported in an enthusiastic letter written in the first half of the eleventh century, or in a provincial town, where, two hundred years later, the local community complained that the preacher harped on his favorite theme although there was no such thing as instrumental music in the town.[163] Jews as players of flutes, lutes, and other stringed instruments (one, also, as a maker of flutes) or as musicians in general are mentioned in the Geniza. I assume, however, that these musicians played mainly in the houses of well-to-do Muslims, where they could make more money than in the then rather unsophisticated Jewish milieu. This seems to have been the case in some Muslim countries even in our own century. We also find entertainers of other types, such as a buffoon or a monkey trainer. Nowhere do we read about the performances or other doings of these musicians and entertainers. They appear solely as family names.[164]

A woman of the middle class would probably offer a cup of wine to her visitors, but no allusion to female drinking parties or to a drunk woman ever occurs. A *nezīrā,* a woman who had vowed to abstain from alcohol, is noted. Temporary vows of this type were made as a sacrifice to God (like fasting) to enhance the efficacy of prayer for the safe return of a son or another beloved relative. The title nezīrā, however, implies that the vow was made out of piety and was permanent.[165]

Vows, for a variety of reasons, were made also by women to renounce the pleasure of the weekly visit to the public bathhouse. This seems to show the importance these social gatherings had in their lives. The rabbinic decision that a husband was not permitted to deny these visits to his wife, and could not force her to live in a place that did not possess this amenity points in the same direction. The standard price for admission (a silver piece, for which one could have five or more loaves of bread) and the precious textiles and utensils used at those visits (appearing in trousseau lists) are all noteworthy. "There are few pleasures," says E. W. Lane, "in which the women of Egypt delight so much as the visit to the bath, where they have frequently entertainments." New moon day, which was for Jewish women a kind of half-holiday, where they refrained from needlework and the like, seems to have been particularly suited to a mass visit to the bathhouse. These get-togethers, during which refreshments were also consumed, might have compensated the women somehow for what they missed by not participating in the drinking parties with the men.[166]

Egypt has been the classical country of storytelling since Pharaonic times. The most interesting parts of *The Arabian Nights* were written there during the Middle Ages. When a Jewish bookseller lent a copy of *Thousand and One Nights* (this title, in its full form, appears, perhaps for the first time in the Geniza) to one of his customers, it stands to reason that the customer copied some or all of it for entertaining private or public audiences. The Geniza has preserved illustrations from the ancient Indian "mirror of princes" known under its Arabic title *Kalīla wa-Dimna,* for instance, a picture of "a raven holding the tail of a rat" (accompanied by part of the story). Once the fragments of fables, folktales, adventure stories, and similar material, told in Arabic, are brought together from the Geniza collections, the extent and nature of popular entertainment literature current in the community during the High Middle Ages will become better known.[167]

It is noteworthy that shadow plays, marionette theaters comparable as a form of entertainment with modern movies, appear as the first item disapproved by the Jewish authorities in Egypt as early as the beginning of the eleventh century, far earlier than the introduction of this Indian pastime into Islamic countries is generally assumed. It was probably already then, as later, of a bawdy character, bordering on the pornographic, which made it undesirable, especially in a place of pilgrimage.[168]

A gamut of parlor games, from the seemingly innocent play with dice described in a question addressed to Moses Maimonides, translated above, to the kingly chess, is represented in the Geniza, all forbidden, if they had even the slightest resemblance to gambling.[169] Outright gambling is strictly forbidden in Islam and Judaism. It has left almost no trace in the Geniza, but because of the strictness of the anathema things were probably hushed up. Franz Rosenthal, who wrote a comprehensive book on gambling in Islam, also notes that "excessive gambling, though evidently not uncommon, is not frequently attested." The story of the scholarly gambler who embarrassed his host, the Jewish judge of Minyat Ziftā, is partly told in a previous volume.[170] The judge had to ask him to leave the town, after the local head of the Karaite sect had banned the gambler from the Jewish community. "Had he remained one day longer, the government would have seized and lashed him with shoes [a punishment of utmost public humiliation]." The escapades of this devotee are well illustrated in the letter. He played with a seller of beer (who probably was also proprietor of a tavern), lost the cash he had brought with him, 200 dirhems or so, then sold his iron pan (which this traveler, like others, carried with him for the preparation of some quick food), then his head cover, finally his outer garment. With some money owed him in town he was able to recover the garment. Each time he swore to give up gambling, and each time he broke his oath; for this, the writer concludes, he will be accountable to God, adding "and Peace," meaning, may nothing bad befall anyone.[171]

Chess was played for money, and therefore outlawed as a kind of gambling. No wonder that an Arabic couplet written on the reverse side of an important letter addressed to a Nāsī warns that playing chess may lead to the breakup of a friendship.[172] The unfortunately incomplete draft of a legal question submitted to the Great Rav Elazar (of Alexandria) seems to deal with such an occurrence: "The two spread out the chessboard and played in accordance with the rules, play after play, and move after move, when a checkmate came in sight to A, without B noticing it." The remaining script indicates that one party was not agreeable.[173] That the beautiful Hebrew poem in praise of chess, "the play for the thinking," which sees "the dead army resurrected and ready for another fight," is really from the pen of Abraham Ibn Ezra (mid-twelfth century), that is, from the orbit of Islamic civilization, is not quite sure.[174]

Pigeon racing, accompanied by betting, was another common pastime that was disapproved because of its resemblance to gambling. It was, however, passionately pursued, so much so, that we read about communal officials using the roof of a synagogue for letting their pigeons loose. Pigeons were kept and fed in pigeon houses and used also as carriers of messages. This was a Jewish sport, familiar and much condemned even in Talmudic times. The passion was nourished under the influence of the Islamic environment which was no less dedicated to this sport. A story had it that Baghdad was delivered treacherously to the Mongols, the caliph decapitated, and the caliphate terminated because the sons of the caliph and his vizier had fallen out over a pigeon race; their mutual hatred affected the fathers, and revenge took the form of treachery. In a remote Islamic country like Bukhara, pigeon racing had Jewish devotees who became a menace to the community even at the beginning of this century.[175]

Birds in general, as we remember from *The Arabian Nights* and other Arabic tales, provided much entertainment to the good people who kept them. A peculiar case is reported about the Nagid Mevōrākh, so often mentioned in this book. He was able to offer his visitors some special attraction: a parrot presented to him by an India trader, which knew how to recite faultlessly two of the most common Jewish prayers, the "Hear Israel" (Deuteronomy 6:4) and "David's Hymn" (Psalms 145:1, preceded by 20:10). These prayers were repeated three times a day; thus the parrot had plenty of opportunities to hear them. I assume, however, that the India trader took no chances, and used the long hours of sea travel to teach the bird. We have the story from the pen of Isaac b. Samuel the Spaniard, familiar to the readers of these volumes as a member of Mevōrākh's entourage, who found it remarkable enough to include details about it in one of his commentaries on the Bible. Combining pleasure with religion is natural in a religious age.[176]

2. *Challenges*

Hard times.—Beginning with the historical survey in *Med. Soc.*, I, and throughout the unfolding of economic, communal, family, and daily life numerous examples of misfortune and human suffering have been encountered. In this section selected cases and situations, some exceptional, others ubiquitous, are studied in order to explore how those affected by, or learning about, them reacted and communicated about them with their fellowmen.

The course of events in remote countries during the Middle Ages is not strange to us anymore. We, who are privileged to live in this turbulent last quarter of the twentieth century are in a better position than, say, our grandparents had been, to comprehend the state of mind of people for whom abnormal times were the norm.

Geniza letters usually open—after proper blessings for the recipient—with the assurance "written in a state of *salāma wa-ʿāfiya,* which we translate as "well-being and good health." The root *slm* (from which also Hebrew *shalom,* "peace," is derived) actually means unimpaired, complete, not damaged. The second term has a similar connotation: unharmed, free from disease and other troubles. This and similar phrases imply that bad things always lie in wait for us; we must be grateful to God when he keeps them away. Consequently, in the introductory blessings upon the addressee, God is asked to prolong his life and so forth, to avert the bad things, *al-aswāʾ*, from him and turn them upon someone else (preferably his enemies, as many letters have it), for the bad things desire to act. The almost obligatory phrases "May I be your ransom," "May I substitute for you," used when writing to a close relative or another person to whom love is due, mean that we must always be prepared for hard times, but we prefer that they should affect ourselves rather than those near to our heart.[1]

This stereotyped reference to the writer's well-being is made out of consideration for the recipient not to convey actual information. Bad as things may be, *he* should not worry about his friend's state. Take this opening of a letter by Barhūn b. Mūsā Tāhertī, a member of one of the leading Jewish families of Qayrawān (then the capital of the country known today as Tunisia), written shortly after the ruinous pillage and devastation of that city by Bedouin hordes (1057): ". . . I am writing from Tripoli [Libya] in a state of well-being and good health. Praise be to God for this. I intend to travel to al-Mahdiyya,[2] for my family moved there after great tribulations. The tidings I received about our city, its trials and afflictions, are indescribable. May God turn the end to the good. My brother Abū Saʿīd is in Sūsa,[3] which is besieged so he cannot leave it. That town is in turmoil."[4] This frightening news is followed by about eighty lines of business as usual, instructions to Barhūn's junior partner (Nahray b. Nissīm), also a native of Qayrawān, who then sojourned in Egypt.

Consideration for the recipient is noticeable also in these types of opening remarks: "I am writing in a state of well-being—may you never miss it—and comfort—may you never be deprived of it—and praise be to God, the Lord of the worlds."[5] Even more sophisticated is this untranslatable, by no means exceptional introduction: "I am well and at ease—due to your prolonged life," meaning there can be no happiness except when you are with us.[6] Another twist of the same idea, also fairly common, is provided in response to a letter of the addressee: "[I was delighted to learn about your] well-being—may God make it permanent for you, and for me in you"—that is, when you are well, I am well, too.[7]

In view of this profusion of politeness the state of the writer of a letter can be gauged when the traditional formulas are followed at least by a hint of the realities, as in this opening of an important business letter from Tunisia: ". . . I am well and in good health. Things have stabilized," an allusion to the usually troubled state of the country. Excessive expressions of thanks to God for the return to "normalcy" were probably destined to encourage the business friend staying in Fustat to send on the commodities ordered without hesitation.[8] When exaggerated assurances of one's well-being are made, one can be sure that they are followed by something adverse or unpleasant. A letter from Ascalon, Palestine, which was then occupied by the Crusaders, opens thus: "Thanks to God's benevolence I have been living in Ascalon in six thousand states of prosperity." Later we hear that the writer stood security for a particularly high sum of ransom demanded by a Crusader for the sister of a friend and was unable to pay it.[9] A mother is assured that her daughter lives "in a thousand states of comfort" with her new husband, but then it appears that the young couple quarrels because parts of the dowry, some of the copper and the clothing, had not yet been delivered. Clearly the parents had got an inkling of the real situation and kept the things back, wherefore the writer, a cousin of the mother (and probably also her in-law), emphasized that in general, everything was all right.[10] The following description of the writer's well-being is altogether exceptional: "I am completely comfortable in my body and all my affairs. My clothes do not hold me for all my happiness and success." The story was indeed complicated. A Byzantine Jew had married a Muslim woman, certainly a captive whom he had ransomed. When the couple moved to Palestine, they separated, and the wife took residence in Egypt with her daughter, who had meanwhile grown up. The mother fell on bad times, and in this letter the father tries to persuade the girl to return to him and the Jewish fold, pointing out that he (in contrast to her mother) was in excellent health and enjoyed material prosperity and thus was able to provide for her.[11]

Bad tidings, as a rule, were introduced by allusion rather than by direct statement, and detailed information was generally provided only when action on the side of the recipient was requested or expected: "[I am writing . . .] in a state of well-being, but a troubled mind, as willed by the *Creator of the world, may his name be blessed*; may he be praised and thanked *for all he does.*" The excessive thanks to God proves that things were indeed very upsetting, for "one is obliged to bless God for the bad in the same way as for the good."[12] In the course of the letter there is an allusion to losses, for God is asked to replace them soon; transport by sea from Tunisia to Egypt had become irregular so that the writer recommends sending letters by land (which, at the time of the writing, was generally shunned), and, above all, "the entire population is looking out for the Nile, may God bring it soon," that is, the inundation of the fields, without which the country was condemned to famine.[13]

Others were less effusive. "I am in a state as willed by God."[14] God's knowledge, instead of his will, is frequently invoked as testimony to the extent of the writer's sufferings: "I was in a state which only God knows—a miserable life and anguish in the breast." The turn for the better is described in greater detail.[15] Not rarely the writer notes that news about his misfortune will reach the addressee through others. "[I am writing] in a situation which God has ordained; you will learn about it from the letters of our coreligionists. I ask God for relief in any way he deems fit."[16]

The instability of human life which seemed to spare no one, as prosperous as he might appear to be, loomed large in the mentality of the Geniza person. Asking a friend to employ someone who had lost everything because he was unable to return to his hometown, the writer adds: "As long as this *wheel* [of fortune][17] turns, nothing remains in its accustomed state, except for one to whom God grants a respite. May the Creator spare you and me the hostilities of Time and its vicissitudes, and may he not let us taste, or even see again, anything like that we have gone through and may he accept it [what we have gone through] as *an atonement for our sins.*"[18]

Because of the fragmentary state of the letter, I do not try to identify the particularly hard times through which both its writer and recipient had gone, possibly one of those recurrent famines caused by a failing Nile. "Time" harbors inveterate hatred (this is the Arabic word used) against man.[19] Better times are only "a respite" granted to him by God, or, as another letter has it, a miracle wrought by the Almighty. "Praise be to Him who works miracles and proofs[20] with me *every moment and every hour*[21] in his grace, not that I am worthy of it."[22] As a matter of fact, this letter is one of the most emotional and pessimistic ones I have read in the Geniza. The writer, a learned man, flings a most terrible curse against a slanderer, who gives him a bad name, so that even his best friends—including the addressee—begin to doubt him; after expressing the usual phrases of consolation on the death of a son of his friend, he adds: "Finally, anyone who dies in this time is more fortunate than one who lives, only to witness misery and calamities. What the Creator has chosen for the boy is the best, there is nothing else." In another part of the letter, the epoch is described as one of complete anarchy, where no one has remained to guide the community and to decide matters. But this man, who does not ascribe any merit to himself, trusts that "God who has shielded me thus far will protect me for the rest of my life."[23]

Great calamities, as mentioned in the passage about "the hostilities of Time" translated above, have the mitigating side effect that the sufferings of those whom they befall might be accepted by God as an atonement for sins, with the possible consequence that the sufferers might be spared further castigations. This concept was general, and is endlessly repeated whenever consolation was needed. And not only as an encouragement, but also as an admonition: one must "*understand the Times.*" When catastrophe strikes, one must examine oneself and try to mend one's ways. This idea is expressed at unusual length in a letter addressed by the rabbinical courts of Fustat to the community in al-Maḥalla at the very beginning of the twelfth century. Jerusalem had been conquered by the Crusaders in July 1099. Egypt was flooded with refugees. The country of the Nile had itself been visited by a catastrophic epidemic and civil war. The al-Maḥalla community was divided and had quarreled with its spiritual leader; he left, and the absence of competent leadership had had most undesirable effects. In this letter, of which various versions are extant, the community is advised in the strongest terms to take their *dayyān* back. "You must understand the times and know what the world faces. It is inconceivable that in such a time a man of Israel should harbor in his soul *enmity and strife* and partisanship in worldly affairs." He who disregards the lesson to be learned from sufferings will be visited by even harder tribulations.[24]

Because of the general instability, reports about the state of a city or country—and not only about personal or business matters—

were essential. They were called *akhbār,* "news," with the additional meaning of "intelligence," as the government office with this function was named. Because of the secret police—and competition—one had to be careful in the wording of messages.[25] If nothing "exceptional" had happened, and if no action on the side of the recipient was foreseen, such news was held to a minimum. "A number of people have arrived [from Egypt with family names pointing to Syria, Palestine, and the Maghreb], and we have received from them only good tidings, [especially about relations] with the government"—we read in a letter going from Aden, South Arabia, to India, most probably an allusion to relief in customs procedures.[26] Another letter sent in the same direction was even shorter: "As to the news about the countries [meaning, of the Mediterranean, of which the traders out in India were natives], it is gladdening, praise be to God and many, many thanks."[27] No news was not always good news. The representative of merchants in Aden writes to his client in India: "For two years in a row no one has arrived from Egypt because of the epidemics prevailing there. Recently a small boat arrived with four merchants on board who reported that the situation had improved, prices had fallen, and the government was [in control]. May God grant relief to all people."[28]

Traders out in India could not do much in response to news from Egypt and countries farther away. Letters exchanged between merchants of substance in cities, say, like Alexandria and Cairo, who had to consult with one another and take action, usually, however, contain specific "intelligence" about the place of the sender, whether good or bad. Here is the summary of a detailed report comprising both:

A Tunisian from al-Mahdiyya writes to a compatriot staying in Fustat sometime after his arrival in Alexandria. The experience was frightening. The markets were at a standstill; no one dared to sell or to buy; because of a siege the Nile boats could not get through (on the canal connecting Alexandria with the Nile); the city was without a governor. On the other hand, the ships from all over the Mediterranean had arrived with the sole exception of the Sultan's ship *The Bride* and a smaller one from Tripoli. This meant that a good part of the summer had already passed, and before long, in September, the ships would have to set sail for the way back. Only the Byzantine merchants from Constantinople had made up their minds and were prepared to buy, but only pepper; those from Venice and Crete held back. The Sicilian and Spanish traders offered their silk fabrics but were reluctant to open their trunks containing clothing. The situation was particularly unpleasant for the writer inasmuch as the business friends in Fustat, who were insufficiently informed about the happenings in the Mediterranean port, felt themselves neglected by him.

But our Nissīm (this was his name) was not discouraged. He had brought with him good tidings from home. "As to the akhbār of the West, I mean al-Mahdiyya: safety and low prices prevail; there was a huge harvest of grain and a plentiful supply of olives," which meant that oil, the main agricultural export of the country, was inexpensive. Before presenting the main part of his akhbār, the prices and the market for a long list of Oriental spices and other goods, he notes also the current value of the quarter dinars coined in al-Mahdiyya. For long before a Nobel prizewinner made the discovery that money was a commodity like any other object of trade, the contemporaries of the Geniza had been aware of that economic reality. The report concludes with the note that the addressee's wife and baby daughter, who had, of course, remained back in al-Mahdiyya, were perfectly comfortable. Nissīm was immensely happy that the goods carried for his friend had arrived safely; once the city was relieved, he in person would carry 2,000 hides with oil destined for him to Fustat and decide concerning the other goods whether to transport them or convert them into cash in Alexandria. God is repeatedly invoked to grant relief, the city to be "opened," the Nile boats to get through, and the governor to enter. Then, Nissīm asserts, the friends will become aware of what he had done and was doing for them.[29]

"Relief after hardship," *faraj baʿd al-shidda*—this is the great theme running through most of the Geniza reports about adversity. As a matter of fact, any tale of disaster must be concluded by a prayer or an expression of hope for relief and recompense. For everything is wrought by God, "all that God does is good," as we read in the letter of a man exiled and reduced to abject poverty after having occupied an honored post in the caliphal mint.[30] The tone and other aspects of the story, however, reveal to the reader whether misfortune is really borne with endurance and trust, or whether the common phrases obligatory in such circumstances, especially the ubiquitous "may God turn the end to the good," are perfunctory and empty shells.[31] Naturally, feelings, as we all know, are multifaceted; sometimes one can observe changing moods in a single letter. Yet, when writing to a friend we are prone to betray ourselves; ink and paper are often truer messengers of our minds than the breath of our mouths.

For instance, the long letter from beleaguered Alexandria just summarized clearly reveals its writer as confident that the alarming happenings were a passing event, which would soon be resolved, whereupon he himself would be vindicated and recognized as a dedicated and successful manager of the affairs of his friends in Fustat. He invokes, of course, the name of God repeatedly, not so much for help, but as a confirmation of his own optimistic assessment of the situation.[32]

Conversely, the much involved missive of the unhappy father of a profligate son, repeatedly referred to above, shows him as devout and resigned to the will of God, but completely hopeless and desperate—so much so that he did not send the long epistle off, although it was a carefully written masterpiece of calligraphy.[33]

Concerning the exaggerated complaints and profuse assertions of his own rectitude, as well as the affirmations of his trust in God of Abūn b. Ṣadaqa, writing from Jerusalem, I was for some time in doubt whether the certainty of God's expected help was not invoked repeatedly in order to underline the writer's own worthiness. After having identified a number of other letters of this man, however, I guess he really was at peace with his God. And did he not live in the Holy City, of which the Prophet Isaiah had promised that "those who dwell there will be forgiven their sins"?[34]

Finally, the challenge of disaster was met also by what the French call *corriger la fortune,* calling on God, of course, but taking matters into one's own hands. This was good Jewish ethics, as exemplified by the very popular story of the Patriarch Jacob while expecting to meet his elder brother Esau: he prayed for help, but carefully (and successfully) made preparations for all eventualities.[35] Probably everyone tried to act similarly. In many Geniza letters God is asked to grant a substitute for a loss, to recompense the unhappy writer. In some, the successful restitution is reported together with the damage endured.[36] A most impressive and characteristic action in response to a great catastrophe is reported by Maḍmūn b. Japheth, representative of merchants in Aden, South Arabia, at the end of a long business letter sent to India. After having described the enormous losses endured by him when a ship of his went down to the bottom of the Arabian Sea, he continues: "May God the exalted recompense and substitute what has been lost. . . . I asked God for guidance[37] and fitted out a new ship, the *M*[*ubārak*], which will sail to Mangalore. . . . May God ordain its safe arrival. I have done so because I dreaded that [my enemies] and whoever has no good in him will gloat over my misfortune." A prominent man must be successful. Ill fortune impairs his honored position. Maḍmūn took no chances, but tried immediately to roll the wheel of fortune back—upward. He seems to have been rewarded for his resolute response to disaster. The *Mubārak* (Blessed Boat) commuted between Aden and India.[38]

The motto "Relief after hardship" gave its name to an entire genre of classical Arabic literature, whose general theme was approximately "all's well that ends well." When the eminent Qayrawānese scholar R. Nissīm b. Jacob was asked by a relative, who had lost a son, whether he could not write for him a book of consolation consisting of entertaining stories, the like of which the Muslims possessed, R. Nissīm complied with the request, although he noted that he had no experience with that type of literature. But his *Relief after Hardship,* a collection mostly of Talmudic tales rendered into Arabic spoken by Jews, was a tremendous success, as proved by the direct evidence of Geniza letters and the large number of manuscript fragments of the book preserved. The comparatively short book, now available in a painstaking and well-annotated English translation by William M. Brinner, gives an excellent idea of how Jewish preachers addressed their audience in Geniza times.[39]

It seems to me that there is a noticeable difference between the Islamic and the Jewish materials. Islam has absorbed much of the social notions and ideals of pre-Islamic Arabia, where *ṣabr* (patience, perseverance, steadfastness, watching for the proper opportunity) was a highly regarded virtue. "He who takes revenge after forty years is in a hurry."[40] In the Islamic stories relief is often the reward for sheer persistence, for instance, in unrequited love, which finally reaches its goal. In R. Nissīm's book and in Geniza letters it is the worthiness of the sufferer (in the stories often exemplified by a single good deed) which saves him. Moreover, the Jews, a small, dispersed, and often persecuted people, frequently had the opportunity to experience hardship which was followed not by relief but by even worse tribulations. The Talmudic dictum "new disasters let us forget the old ones" appears in the Geniza as "one disaster makes one forget the other."[41] However, as a rule, one refrained from expatiating on one's own misfortunes. One lamented national calamities, such as the death of a renowned spiritual leader like R. Nissīm b. Jacob, "under whose wings we live among the nations,"[42] or the devastation and partial destruction of the city of Qayrawān (1057), which was then a holy city for Jews as it still is for Muslims. Only people in need of help were forced to forego the rules of good manners and to describe their deprivations in detail.

Why, then, do we read so much about hard times in the Geniza? Because "intelligence" and the cooperation made possible by it were apt to turn disaster away or, at least, to mitigate its effects; they were also intended to preserve relations between people when communications were difficult, and the writer had to explain why he acted as he did. International trade could not be conducted without unvarnished and detailed reports about the state of the markets, as well as of the country concerned in general. In times of scarcity, hints about the provisions still available, or unavailable, at the place of writing were a matter of utmost urgency. Information about the breakdown of order and pillages, let alone war, were often as vital for the recipient as for the sender. Naturally, as in the four cases analyzed above, the tone of the missives depended on the seriousness of the circumstances and the mood of the writer.[43]

A number of examples chosen from various spheres of life illustrate the points just made. The report of the Karaite elders of Ascalon, Palestine, about the fate of the Jewish community of Jerusalem at the conquest of the city by the Crusaders in July 1099 is indeed exceptionally detailed. But a close examination of the letter reveals that each fact stated had some implication for future action, such as the ransom of captives, the care for refugees, the salvage of books looted by the conquerors, or the legal state of the women saved. The general mood of the missive is solemn and somber, but not dejected, although the senders themselves (as well as the recipients) had been afflicted by misfortune. It seems that the alertness to the necessity of quick and comprehensive action left no room for despair and lamentation.[44]

A similar or even more heightened spirit of resistance to the impact of disaster is to be seen in the proclamations circulated by Moses Maimonides and the practical measures initiated by him after the Egyptian town of Bilbays was taken by the Frankish king Amalric in November 1168. After the carnage, when many prisoners were carried away to Palestine, Maimonides collected ransom money, participating in person in the financial aspects of the drive, appointed two respected Jewish judges as his representatives in Palestine to arrange with the Franks and the captives themselves for their liberation, and dispatched ever new circulars to congregations still tardy in making their contributions. The conclusion of one of those circulars is an eloquent testimony of the Master's mind (who then was still in his thirties):

Do not blame me, dear brethren, for the strong tone in which I have spoken to you. This letter is to be read out to everyone, young and old, so that your hearts should be shaken. A preacher cannot avoid reprimanding.

May God, the exalted, privilege me and you to see the realization of what was said in his name: *The Lord has anointed me to bring good tidings to the afflicted, has sent me to heal those whose hearts are broken, to proclaim liberty to the captives and freedom to the prisoners* [Isaiah 61:1].[45]

The endeavors of Maimonides—then almost a newcomer to Egypt (but experienced in meeting disaster because of the persecutions of the Almohads to which he had been exposed in Spain and Morocco)—must have been at least partly successful, for Bilbays became one of the most flourishing Jewish communities in the country not long after the castastrophe of 1168.

Two private letters from Alexandria, written in 1219, when the Crusaders invaded Egypt, apparently with some success, show us again, how an event of world-historical dimensions affected the lives of the common people. At the time of the writing of these letters the Crusaders were besieging the port city of Damietta, a key to the conquest of Egypt. The first of the two letters was written on October 21, about two weeks before Damietta was taken by assault. We know that the Crusaders ultimately were not successful. During the year 1219 the Egyptians were afraid that the opposite might come true.

A man writing from Alexandria to his sister in remote Cairo knows that even there people were terrified and beset by hardship. In Alexandria, which, like Damietta, was threatened any moment by an attack from the sea, the situation was far worse: food was scarce, the bread "inedible"; and the impoverished population had to make a high "voluntary contribution" for the war effort. There were other, perhaps even more serious, troubles, as we shall learn from another letter, written about seven months earlier when the invasion had just begun. But the mind of our man was totally occupied with his personal misfortune. He makes mention of the state of the city only to explain why he could not find there either work or support. Actually it was up to him to appear before his sister in person, to implore her for help. But for ten reasons, which he carefully enumerates, he was unable to do so. He had neither clothing nor money needed for the travel. Arriving in the capital he would be arrested immediately for nonpayment of the poll tax and would then cause his sister even more trouble; his children and wife (in this order, of course) lacked food and proper clothing even when he was with them, let alone when away; moreover, his wife did not permit him to travel away from her; anyhow he could not appear publicly setting out to leave Alexandria because he was indebted to people in the city. The tenth and, as he emphasizes, most stringent reason for not making the trip to Cairo was the certainty that his enemies seeing him in such a state of humiliation would rejoice over his misfortune. It is characteristic that this unhappy man concludes the story of his misery thus: "I am powerless. *All that the Merciful does is good.*" Despite the careful enumeration of all his afflictions he forgot one, possibly the worst of all, which he added as a postscript to his long letter: "Because of my worries I got dry pimples and my skin peeled off my bones." Of all concerns, bad health is most apt to move hardhearted relatives.[46]

The earlier letter from Alexandria written during the invasion of Egypt by the Crusaders in 1219, is of an entirely different character. The first preserved sentence reads thus: "The city is in a dire state because of the digging of the ditch. The city is locked up, and forced labor is imposed upon the population." This purely factual statement is immediately followed by a detailed report about the successful treatment of a woman who had been injured in an accident (the people back in Cairo knew about the injury, but not about the outcome), some small errands, and an important family affair (re Abu ʾl-ʿAlāʾ, see below), and, at the end, greetings to at least fifteen persons. Two postscripts are added:

As to sheykh Abu ʾl-ʿAlāʾ—when I arrived, I found the city locked up; no male person could appear in the streets, because he would be taken to the [digging of the] ditch. That's why I was unable to meet him.

As to the *malḥafa* [a blanket serving also as outer garment], the bazaars are locked and no one sells and buys. I am telling you this that you should not think that I am neglectful of your affairs.

Clearly this writer was not eager to convey news about the conduct of the war. Let the kings and generals fight it out. He relates the news for the sole purpose of explaining why certain errands asked from him could not be carried out.[47]

Another[48] letter from a troubled Alexandria, one written in the 1160s, reveals again a different situation and a special state of mind. After prolonged separation from his brother the writer arrived with his wife and only remaining child in Alexandria by sea, but was unable to enter the city with his belongings, for the city was without government and the scene of bloody warfare between Arab and black tribes. Despite the dangers, privations, and uncertainty of the future the letter is entirely engulfed in the joy of the prospective reunion. After a somewhat unusual proem, partly in Hebrew, expressing the wish that, instead of his few lines, the writer could behold the pleasant figure of his brother, the beloved of his soul, and kiss him, and after heaping on him blessings, especially that he should always be God's friend and preferred favorite, he continues:

I have good news: we arrived in Alexandria, I, my wife, and my boy Joseph, the only one who remained, under the best of circumstances inasmuch as we are now near to you—may God grant that we shall be reunited soon. Our arrival happened to be on the early morning of the New Year's Holiday. We remained on the roadstead until Sunday, when we wished to disembark, but were not permitted to do so.[49] Disembarking on Monday, we found the city at a standstill,[50] Lakhmī [Arab] and Ghurābiyya [black] tribesmen[51] fighting each other with about a hundred men between them killed. The governor[52] has gone away, and the city is left forsaken, run-down,[53] and locked up. The finest stores have been plundered.

We did not dare to enter the city via the Dockyard[54] gate, but stayed in the Dockyard until the *eve* of the Day of Atonement. Then we each donned a piece of [festive] clothing and entered the city, passing the fast there, while our belongings remained in the Dockyard. A company of coreligionists, headed by the judge R. Ḥiyyā—[may the] R[ock] k[eep him]—came from Fustat. For the entrance into Alexandria from the Canal [which connects the city with the Nile] they paid a toll of only one dinar.

All this is the reason why I had to stay here and could not come in person instead of my letter. I met Abu ʾl-Maʿānī, who reported to me about you, for which I was grateful to him. He said that you intended. . . .[55]

The end of the page is torn away, but it is not difficult to guess what the writer wished his brother to do: to come to Alexandria, as soon as the situation improved, and, in accordance with the rules of hospitality, accompany the newcomer and his family on their way to the capital. The writer alludes to this in the seemingly stray note about the arrival of R. Ḥiyyā and his company, which included the man who reported about the brother. From time to time prominent Jewish dignitaries from Fustat would pass the high holidays, particularly the Day of Atonement and the subsequent Feast of Tabernacles, in a community outside the capital where they led congregations in prayer and study groups and gave sermons (for which they were compensated by voluntary contributions from the members). The letter demonstrates that R. Ḥiyyā, who was no longer a young man, and his entourage dared to make the trip, and not only that: the toll taken from the company amounted to only one gold piece, which, considering that the gate was held by one of the warring tribes, was not excessive. The brother should not be afraid to follow R. Ḥiyyā's example.[56]

This short letter is quite remarkable. Instead of bewailing his fate and expressing bitter disappointment on experiencing only dangers and discomfort upon his arrival in Alexandria, instead of finding his brother awaiting him there, the writer takes his wishful thinking for reality; the dominant motif of his letter is the happy reunion; the terrifying events reported are only a temporary interruption of his beautiful dream; he is a bringer of good tidings, as he writes at the beginning of the letter.

Catastrophes befalling the community and not followed by comprehensive rescue operations (like those undertaken after the capture of Jerusalem by the Crusaders in 1099) are described realistically and in detail, accompanied only by affirmations of submission to God's judgment. The magnitude of the disaster spoke for itself; there was no need for the writer to express his own feelings. Telling Bible quotations, inserted between the details of the story, are far more eloquent than his pen would have been able to describe, and later the poets, the mouthpieces of the people, would recite their dirges.

The havoc wrought in Jerusalem and Ramle by Bedouin tribes overrunning Palestine in 1024–1025 is referred to in several Geniza letters. I summarize one written in Hebrew, which, although much damaged, is the most comprehensive one on the subject known to me. The writer emphasizes at the beginning that Muslims and Christians suffered the same fate as the Jews. Atrocities like those perpetrated by the Bedouin hordes had never been witnessed in the country under Islam. The first aim of the sons of the desert, "who covered the surface of the earth like locusts," was plunder. Whatever caught their eye was taken, and indescribable tortures were applied to get possession of presumed hidden treasures. Men and women died from their sufferings or committed suicide by throwing themselves into a well. Ramle, which was taken by assault, fared even worse. Many were killed on sight; others were pushed from roofs or into wells, or hanged on trees, even women; virgins and boys, big and small, were seized and violated; the pillage of Ramle, the economic center of the country, was even more devastating than that of Jerusalem; many of those who escaped to the countryside died of exhaustion or under the blows of their persecutors.[57]

This description by an eyewitness, who lived in Jerusalem, is confirmed by the renowned elegy on these events by the Spanish Hebrew poet Joseph Ibn Abitūr, who sojourned at that time in

Palestine or its vicinity.[58] It is entirely different from the gruesome report about the almost complete (but temporary) liquidation of Judaism in Morocco sent in January 1148 by Solomon, son of Abū Zikrī Judah b. Joseph ha-Kohen Sijilmāsī, to his father, who was on his way back from India. Solomon wrote in the capital of Egypt, which is the easternmost country of North Africa, whereas Morocco is its westernmost territory. But, he insists, he writes not from hearsay but recounts what persons who had witnessed the events had told him. As the name Sijilmāsī indicates, the family itself had come from Morocco, or at least had lived there for an extended period, and, as we learn from the passage translated below, close relatives had been affected by the catastrophe. Moreover, the destruction of a populous Jewish center, renowned for its learning and religious observance, was a national disaster of unfathomable magnitude. It also caused an economic upheaval, inasmuch as Morocco formed one of the major western terminals of the India and Mediterranean trades. Clearly, father and son were familiar with the country and were, therefore, interested to know what happened in each town. The number of Jews killed or saved sounds realistic. The remark added at the end of the report that 100,000 persons (Muslims and Jews) were killed at the conquest of Fez and 120,000 at that of Marrākesh is not to be taken literally. It corresponds to what we know from Arabic sources, namely, that the male population was put to the sword (and the women were sold into slavery).

The conquerors were members of a Muslim sect calling themselves *al-muwaḥḥidūn,* "true believers" (Almohads in European languages), who outlawed anyone refusing to accept their tenets. Staging bloodbaths among their orthodox Muslim brethren was therefore permissible, if not meritorious, which is no surprise for contemporaries of similar atrocities. The Almohads, who were of Berber stock, took religion seriously. Jews who accepted Islam—their Islam, of course—were not killed. Their leader was ʿAbd al-Muʾmin, who assumed the title caliph (signifying that he did not recognize any authority in Islam above himself), and he put an end to the rule of another sect, al-Murābiṭūn, "Frontier Warriors" (Almoravids), whose leader Tāshfīn, mentioned in our letter, was a grandson of the founder of the Almoravid dynasty. All the towns mentioned are well known. (In some cases, the European form of the name is added in brackets.) The course of events as described here corresponds in general to what is known from Muslim sources.

After commenting on his father's letter (sent from Mirbāṭ, a port on the southeast corner of the Arabian peninsula, still in existence) and on the consignments sent by him, Solomon reports about the standstill of business in the capital of Egypt (possibly connected with the events in the Muslim West) and tertian fever which endangered his life for nine months, followed by two months of labored breath. To restore his health he gave up his commercial activities and dedicated himself to study. After dealing with some smaller business matters and having arrived at line 37 of his long letter, he continues:

You certainly wish to know the news from the Maghreb, "*the ears of all who hear about it will tingle*" [Jeremiah 19:4]. The travelers have arrived, among them groups of Jews, who were present at the events. They reported that ʿAbd al-Muʾmin the Sūsī [from the Sūs region in western Morocco] attacked the amīr Tāshfīn in Wahrān [Oran], besieged him, annihilated his army, killed him, and crucified his body. Then ʿAbd al-Muʾmin conquered Tilimsān [Tlemçen] and killed everyone in the town, except those who *apostatized*.[59] When the news arrived in Sijilmāsa, the population revolted against their amīr, declared themselves in public as opponents of the *murābiṭūn* [Almoravids], drove them out of town, and sent messengers to ʿAbd al-Muʾmin surrendering it to him. After he entered Sijilmāsa, he assembled the Jews and asked them to *apostatize*. Negotiations went on for seven months, during all of which they fasted and prayed.[60] After this a new amīr arrived and demanded their conversion. They refused, and a hundred and fifty Jews were killed, *sanctifying the name of God*.[61]

The Rock—his deeds are without blemish
and all his ways are justice (Deuteronomy 32:4).
Blessed be the true judge,[62] *whose judgments*
are just and true.
The King's word has power; who may say to
him "what are you doing" (Ecclesiastes 8:4).

The others apostatized; the first of the apostates was Joseph b. ʿImrān, the judge of Sijilmāsa. *Because of this I lament and wail*, etc. (Micah 1:8).

Before ʿAbd al-Muʾmin entered Sijilmāsa, when the population rose against the Almoravids, a number of Jews, about two hundred, took refuge in the city's fortress. Among them were Mār Yaʿqūb [Jacob] and ʿAbbūd, my paternal uncles,[63] Mār Judah b. Farḥūn, and [one word]. They are now in Derʿā, after everything they had was taken from them. What happened to them afterward we do not know.

Of all the countries of the Almoravids there remained in the hands of all dissenters[64] only Derʿā and Miknāsa [Meknes]. As to the *congregations* of the West, *because of [our] sins*, they all perished;[65] there has not remained a single one described as a Jew between Bijāya [Bougie] and the Gate [street] of Gibraltar,[66] they either apostatized or were killed. And on the day I am writing this letter news has arrived that Bijāya has been taken and other matters which. . . . [67]

At ʿAbd al-Muʾmin's conquest of Fez 100,000 persons were killed and at that of Marrākesh[68] 120,000. Take notice of this. This is not hearsay, but a report of people who were present at the events. Take notice.[69]

The letter continues for another sixty lines or so, sprawling over a great variety of topics, among them news about refugees from Morocco, one a Sijilmāsī, a scholar ordained by the chief rabbi of Spain Ibn Migash; the newcomer "had scenes" with the "Rav," the Jewish mufti of Fustat (Ibn al-Qaṣbī, himself a Maghrebi), and could not find an appointment because he was a madman; a notable from Fez, who escaped from that city together with his brother and was able to save a Torah scroll once sent to him by the writer's father and carried it with him as far as Bijāya [Bougie]; and a Kohen from Fez, "who claims to be a relative of ours," a man with restricted income; "he opened a clothing store in the bazaar of the secondhand dealers."

The letter concludes with a beautiful expression of filial piety[70] and greetings, without returning to the topic of the Almohad persecutions. It was customary to recapitulate the main topic(s) at the end. But Solomon was probably weary of his role as bearer of saddening news.[71]

The reader may be surprised that only words of regret, none of blame (let alone curses), were uttered about the apostates, especially the leader of the Sijilmāsa community. In times of general upheavals, when one short-lived dynasty followed the other, it was doubtful whether martyrdom was obligatory. Maimonides discussed these matters in his famous *Epistle on the Sanctification of the Name.* Half a century later, when a similar situation occurred in Yemen, the head of the Jewish community there led his flock into conversion, but saw them return to the faith of their fathers in the course of a few years, after the self-styled caliph who had engineered the persecution had been killed.[72] The situation in Morocco, though, was different. The converts, as far as we know, were forced to remain Muslims, but were terribly mistreated and reduced to the state of a pariah caste, so that their lot had a certain similarity with that of the Marranos, the forced converts to Christianity later in Spain and elsewhere. Yet Jews surfaced in Morocco not long after the time of the conquest. The Maimonides family left Spain for that inhospitable country, and Moses Maimonides himself reports about arguments about Jewish law he had with R. Judah b. Farḥūn mentioned in our letter.[73]

The meteoric victories of the Almohads may have been seen in Egypt as ominous portents for the safety of their own environment. At the time of the writing of our letter, Egypt was ruled by a Shiʿite sect,[74] which originally had its base in North Africa, and from there, mostly relying on Berber tribes, had moved eastward. But Solomon Sijilmāsī was far too occupied with relating to his father all this catastrophic news to have a free mind or time to tell him how the news was received in the capital of Egypt.

The letters discussed thus far, and indeed the great majority of those found in the Geniza, give the impression that they enumerate events rather than describe them. They rarely dwell on a single occurrence or experience. The reason for this should not be sought in the lack of susceptibility to impressions or of the ability to express them in writing. I believe the Geniza person possessed both. Yet letter writing, as repeatedly emphasized, was geared to the recipient. One wrote what *he* needed to know, or what one wished *him* to learn. In the very rare case that the writer poured his heart out, he had to use strong quotations to justify such a deviation.[75]

When something extraordinary happened, however, it was deemed worthwhile for the addressee to visualize it almost as experienced by the writer, and the latter would spare no words in describing it. Even we, so remote in time and place, are able to participate somehow in the events.

I have selected three such incidents to present them to the reader in full: the earthquake that shook Ramle, Palestine, on 5 December 1033 (eight years after its pillage by Bedouins mentioned before),[76] as described by an eyewitness at a time when the population still remained outside the town, fearing a recurrence; a gruesome encounter with Mongols, then the scourge of the civilized world, in 1236; and an attack from the sea on the port city of Aden, South Arabia, in 1135, as related in two letters, one going east to India, and one west to Egypt.

The eyewitness to the earthquake in Ramle was none other than the Gaon Solomon b. Judah, the President of the Jerusalem yeshiva and head of the Jewish community of the Fatimid empire. Despite his age—he must have been close to seventy—and the terrifying events, the thirty-six long lines of his letter, written in his well-known hand, are flawless, a calligraphic masterpiece without any deletions or corrections. His presentation is even more impressive. Not a word of complaint is said about what he personally had experienced and was still going through. Instead, compassionate participation in the sufferings of others and a most graphic and detailed description of what had happened and its results. There is more to it. In disasters caused by men—wars, pillages, oppression, persecutions, and the like—God is, so to say, only the remote mover. But at an earthquake one was confronted with him directly. The head of the yeshiva writes with awe, almost with admiration, about God's doings and says of himself, with a touch of irony: "What could I do except summon the people to fasting and prayer?" The heaping up of Bible quotations had an additional significance; the ceaselessly repeated predictions of the prophets of ancient Israel that sins would be punished by earthquakes had come true. "The Lord is a true God." This implies that just as the foretellings of evil had been fulfilled, thus there was hope for the coming of peace and all the good promised in the Bible. As politeness required, the favorable future is connected mainly with the addressees. No doubt the letter was destined to be read out in the synagogues.

The upper part of the letter is lost, but as the length of the sheet preserved indicates, only a small part is missing.

. . . they went out of their houses into the streets because they saw the walls bending and yet intact, and the beams become separated from the walls and then revert to their former position. Strong buildings collapsed and new houses were leveled. Many died under the ruins, for they could not escape. All went out of their dwellings, without looking back, leaving everything behind. Wherever they turned they beheld God's powerful deeds. The walls collided and collapsed. Those that remained are shaky and split. Nobody stayed in them to this day for their owners feared lest they tumble down over them.

The hand would weary to describe even a part of the happenings. Also the mind is distraught from what the eye saw and the ear heard. What has been said has been fulfilled: "Behold the Lord strips the land and lays it waste, distorts its face and scatters its inhabitants" [Isaiah 24:1]. The prudent will understand. For all were alike, "as with the people so with the priest, as with the slave so with the master" [*ibid.*, 2], when they left their palaces and sought refuge for their lives. Many resigned themselves to the divine judgment, saying, "The Lord is truly God, a living God, an everlasting King and at His wrath the earth quakes" [Jeremiah 10:10]; "Who shakes the earth so that it is frightened";[77] "Who shakes the earth out of its place and its pillars tremble" [Job 9:6]; "He shoves the earth so that it melts and all who dwell in it are miserable";[78] "who can stand before His wrath?" [Nahum 1:6].

This happened on Thursday, Ṭevet 12th, suddenly before sunset, alike in Ramle, in the whole province of Filasṭīn,[79] from walled city to open village, in all fortresses of Egypt from the sea to Fort [. . .], in all cities of the Negev and the mountain [of Judea] to Jerusalem and surrounding places, to Shekhem[80] and her villages, Tiberias and her villages, the Galilean mountains and the whole of the Land of Glory.[81]

Those that traveled on the high roads relate the mighty acts of the living God. They say, "We have seen the mountains shake, like leaping stags, their stones broken into pieces, the hillocks swaying to and fro, and the trees bending down. The water in the cisterns reached the brim in some places." The tongue is inadequate for the tale. Had it not been for God's mercy that it happened before the day was gone, when people could see and warn each other, and not at night when everybody was asleep, only a few would have been saved. But His mercies are many and His kindnesses numerous. Though he decrees [punishment], he does not utterly destroy. He, moreover, in His great goodness, let appear clouds heavy with water, and big drops fell before the earthquake occurred. Two great rainbows appeared, and it seemed as if one of them split up into halves, and fire was visible from the southwest. At that very moment the earthquake took place, the like of which has not been seen since ancient times. On that night the earth shook again. All were in the streets, men, women, and children, imploring God, the Lord of the spirits, to quieten the earth and set it at rest and save both man and animal. On Friday, as well as on the following night, the quakes recurred. All were terrified and fear-stricken. "Earth and its inhabitants were molten" [cf. Psalms 75:4]. They all wept and cried with a loud voice, O merciful One, have mercy and retract from the intended punishment. Do not enter upon judgment. "In anger remember to be merciful" [Habakkuk 3:2] and "pay no heed to former sins" [cf. Psalms 79:8]. All were clothed with trembling [Ezekiel 26:16], / sitting on the ground, / shaking every moment / and swaying to and fro. /[82] For eight days the mind has found no quiet and the soul no rest.

What could the writer of this letter do but to address the people, to declare a fast, summon a solemn assembly, that the people should go out to the field, the cemetery, in fasting, weeping, and lamentation, and recite, "Tear your hearts, and not your garments, and return to the Lord your God, etc." [Joel 2:13]; Come, let us return to God, etc. [Hosea 6:1]. And let us ask for mercy. "Who knows, [perhaps] he will retract and repent. Perhaps he will go back from his fierce anger, so that we perish not" [cf. Jonah 3:9]. It was a great miracle that all the days which the people were thrown in the streets and in the open, no rain fell. Also the governor of the city, with the men in the Caliph's employ, pitched tents for themselves outside the town, and are still there.

May the Lord, the God of the universe, look down mercifully upon his world, have pity on his creatures, save man and animal, and have compassion with babes and sucklings and "those that know not to distinguish between right and left," so that we perish not [cf. Jonah 4:11]. May he deliver you from this and the like, protect you from all harsh decrees, hide you in his tabernacle on the day of evil, and shelter you in the protection of his wings. May he exalt you, and may your good acts, kindnesses, and righteous deeds stand you in good stead. "May He make you dwell securely and at ease, without dread of evil" [cf. Proverbs 1:33]; "May you be at peace, your houses and all that belong to you at peace" [cf. I Samuel 25:6]. Receive ye peace from the Lord of Peace.[83]

The following passage seems to differ from what has just been presented in every respect. The report is confined totally to the person of the writer, telling of his escape from merciless killers; not a single verse of the Bible is cited; and no elation about the miracle is expressed. Yet the very matter-of-factness of the account and its heaping of dry but dramatic details convey clearly the frightful message that any country overrun by those Mongols (whom the writer calls Tatars) faces an inescapable holocaust.

The writer of the letter was a member of the nāsī family of Mosul (a town in northern Iraq), which regarded itself as a branch of the progeny of King David. The addressee, Solomon b. Yishay (Jesse), was the doyen of this (fictitious) nobility.[84] Fortunately, a number of letters (mostly fragmentary) addressed to the doyen by our writer have been preserved, showing him as a prominent and learned member of the community. In one letter he describes—with the same predilection for graphic detail—a visit of his, when he was still a young man (but already father of a little boy), in the house of Moses Maimonides, to whom he had to deliver a message.[85] Our letter was written in Damascus, Syria, in December 1236, at a time when the writer must have been at least around sixty and when weeks had passed since the encounter with the Mongols. The purpose of the letter was to induce the doyen to participate (with two others and the writer) in the renovation of the family mansion in Mosul which had fallen into bad disrepair. He had expected to find Solomon b. Jesse in Mosul and expresses in effusive terms his disappointment over the other's absence.[86] In another letter from Damascus, he reports on 16 May 1237, that according to messages received by him, an earthquake had wrought havoc with the family mansion as well as with a number of other fine Jewish and Muslim houses designated by name. He would have preferred to spare the addressee the bad news, but thought he would wish to know.[87]

The encounter with the Tatars took place around al-ʿImrāniyya, a village east of Mosul, where a cave, renowned as "Cave of David," served as a holy shrine visited by Jews, and probably also by Christians and Muslims, for the Muslim geographer, who describes it, does not mention Jews in particular.[88] David, before becoming king, was forced repeatedly to take refuge in a cave (I Samuel 22:1, 24:3 ff.; Psalms 57:1, 142:1). But how this particular one was transplanted from Palestine to the faraway surroundings of Mosul is difficult to say. Perhaps because a noble family who claimed to be descendants of David had their seat in that town. Our writer, who mostly appears in his correspondence as living in Egypt and traveling to Palestine and Syria, made the long journey to "the tombs of his forefathers" (as one would say in the Geniza) both for business, such as inspecting the deserted family mansion, and for a visit to the local holy shrine. There, however, he was overtaken by the onslaught of the Tatars. These are the first thirty lines of his letter:

In Your Name, O Merciful! Do not ask—my lord and master, the illustrious, noble benefactor, the doyen of the House of David and the Sharīf[89] of the Jewish community, *the great prince, fortress, tower, Prince of the Diaspora of Israel, his h[onor], g[reatness], and h[oliness], our m[aster] and l[ord] Solomon, may God exalt the throne of his princedom and grant him his wishes and desires in eternity*—what *troubles*[90] were endured by your servant since he arrived in these places, after he had been in danger from the Tatars three times.[91]

The last was that they arrived on Friday[92] morning, when we were in al-ʿImrāniyya. They remained *outside the town* killing everyone who was on his way to or from the place, while we stayed in the synagogue waiting for what the enemy would do from hour to hour. Indeed, God had mercy upon us and they went away from us. When night had fallen, we tried to get to the mountain, without having eaten. However, we did not find the way. Thus we passed the night under the hedge of an orchard right until morning, when we tried again to reach the mountain. However, as they came between us and the mountain, we turned back to get to the village but saw on our way fifty riders, and, when we tried another route, we saw on it about a hundred. I and those who were with me said the *confession of sins,* for we were sure to be killed. However, God put it into my heart to cross over to a hedge of blackberries—a thick one, and I took cover under it, I and the boy. The Tatars went by that hedge, twenty-five riders of them; had one of them stretched forth his whip it would have reached us. We remained there till noon, when they rode away from that vicinity, and went up to the mountain, where we remained eight days, eating the leaves of oak trees and old bread.[93]

Finally we went down, finding the country full of corpses. When we arrived, we learned that in that night rumor had spread that we had been killed. But God helped, had mercy, and saved us. However, the fact that I had not the privilege of seeing you and that I arrived and did not find you was almost as though I was killed. May God unite as he has separated.[94]

In the subsequent fifty-five lines no further mention of the Tatars is made.

A comprehensive business letter, sent by Maḍmūn b. Japheth,

representative of merchants in Aden, South Arabia, to his client Ben Yijū in India, contains, in the fourth of the twelve sections preserved, a short report on an event most crucial for the India traders: an attempt by the ruler of Kish, an island in the Persian Gulf, who had usurped control over the trade route between Iraq and India, to be granted possession of "a part of Aden," probably one of its two port facilities. His success would have been a tremendous blow to merchants coming from the Mediterranean countries, for then they would have been plundered by the rulers of both Aden and Kish. Ben Yijū, the recipient of the letter, was a native of Tunisia, who later settled in Egypt. Here is Maḍmūn's report:[95]

This year, at the beginning of seafaring time, the son of al-ʿAmīd, the ruler of Kīs,[96] sent an expedition against Aden. He had demanded part of the town, which was refused, whereupon he sent this expedition. It consisted of two large *burma*s [roundships], three *shaffāra*s [galleys], and ten *jāshujiyya*s [launches], altogether manned with about 700 men.[97] They anchored in the *makalla*ʾ [harbor] of Aden, lying in wait for the incoming ships, but did not enter the town.[98] The people of the town were much afraid of them. But God did not give them victory and success. Many of them were killed, their ships were thrust [with spears], and they died of thirst and hunger.

The first of the [merchants'] ships to arrive were two vessels of the *nākhodā* [shipowner] Rāmisht.[99] They [the enemy] attacked them, but God did not give them victory.[100] As soon as the two ships entered the port,[101] they were manned with a large number of regular troops,[102] whereupon the enemy was driven from the port and began to disperse on the open sea. Thus God did not give them victory. They made off in the most ignominious way, having suffered great losses and humiliation.

A description of the same event is inserted into a letter sent by Khalaf b. Isaac, a first cousin of Maḍmūn b. Japheth, from Aden to a business friend in Egypt:

As to the news from here and all that befell us since you left—to explain all this would take too much space, and even if I filled ten leaves to describe only a part of what befell us, it would not suffice. I shall write concisely, in particular as all our friends, who departed from here, will inform you about what happened and what they had heard and saw. In short, we faced the enemy for two months, the enemy being on the sea and we on the land. There did not remain in the town high or low; everybody took refuge in the castles, while below the castles were only empty houses and fight with the enemy; we faced each other, but they did not dare to land, while the people of the town had no vessels for attacking their ships. Thus each was afraid of the other.

[Slowly] about 2,000 men were assembled. Had there been in the town [before] only 500, the people would not have fled from their houses, but the soldiers arrived only when the enemy had already entered the harbor [*makalla*ʾ]. The people remained far from their houses, until God overcame the enemy and made the sea bad, while they were in Ṣīra in the morning. They joined battle with the people of the town, a number of them were killed near the houses, their heads were cut off, and what they had brought with them to Ṣīra was taken as booty, for they had conquered Ṣīra and stayed there a night and a day, when the disaster befell them and they returned to their ships, while our men were on the land.

Finally, there arrived Rāmisht's two ships. The enemy tried to seize them, but the wind was good, so that they were dispersed on the sea left and right. The two ships entered the port safely, where they were immediately manned with troops. At this juncture, the enemy could not do anything more, either in the harbor or in the town. They retreated behind the mountain [of Ṣīra], until the wind became good for them and they made off. It would take too long to go into details. In any case they left after having been beaten and suffering heavy losses and humiliation. May God, praise to him, preserve us from their evil and never show us their faces again.[103]

The different lengths and characters of the two reports beautifully reflect the different circumstances in which the writers and recipients found themselves. Maḍmūn's letter to India conveyed the news of the attack; for Ben Yijū, who commuted between India and Aden, information about the type and number of vessels used by the pirate-king and the strength of his troops was vital; the fighting role of Rāmisht's merchantmen is emphasized; from other letters we learn that Ben Yijū transported goods on these ships, but Maḍmūn confined himself to the essentials, for his long letter closed the accounts for the year and neither side had time for stories.

Khalaf's situation was different. His Egyptian client had left Aden before the attack. The main business between the two had been settled. The letter, sent at the end of the seafaring season, contained an order: spices and other Oriental goods were sent, for the proceeds of which a large amount of clothing and tableware, mostly ceramics, was ordered, probably for an impending wedding.[104] The merchants returning to Egypt had spread the news about the attack. It is natural, however, that the business friend in Fustat expected to find authentic information about the event in a letter addressed to him. Khalaf did not disappoint him. As we learn from another letter of his, he had more indeed to tell than he did. The two forts protecting Aden were commanded by two cousins, who were at loggerheads with each other, a situation that, at a certain juncture, caused great trouble to the population of the city, left it almost unprotected, and was probably the reason that induced the ruler of Kīsh to launch his expedition. An allusion to the lack of proper defense at the time of the attack is found in the report. More was not needed. As it stands, the report makes a good, coherent story which the writer was obviously eager to tell.

A disaster which struck the government and its entourage, but which affected the population at large only indirectly, was related as an interesting news item, satisfying the curiosity of the people on the receiving end, but with detachment and no comments. Rumor had spread that a fabulous present sent to the Fatimid caliph, certainly from India, had been seized by a Bedouin chieftain. A merchant traveling on the route to the country was asked to inquire. Arriving in Qūṣ, Upper Egypt, after a voyage of only fourteen days on the Nile, and after having reported the arrangements he had made for the continuation of his journey, he writes this: "As to the news, *akhbār,* the Bulyanī has seized the present. It comprised 1,000 sacs [bahār, containing pepper and other Oriental spices], seventy slave girls, each accompanied by a eunuch, and each girl bearing a necklace of jewels; seventy trunks with textiles; an amber chain ornamented with jewels weighing two hundred pounds, and many other things of which I have no knowledge."

"The Bulyanī" was well known to the India traders in Cairo, since on their way to the East they had to traverse the desert between the Nile and the Red Sea, which was the territory of the tribe, of which the man whom they called Bulyanī was the chief. The merchants traveled under his protection, for which they paid, of course; that he could dare to confront the government in Cairo to such an extent was certainly a surprise. We do not know how this affair ended. In a similar case, the rapacity of the Bedouins led to a war in which, however, the regular troops were not successful. The numbers provided in our letter seem to be grossly exaggerated. But we read the like of it in connection with princely presents in many Muslim historians.[105]

The merchants in the capital inquired about the fate of the extravagant convoy sent to the caliph not only out of curiosity but also in order to gauge the extent of lawlessness menacing the country. The future of business and, indeed, of the normal conduct of daily life depended on such advanced knowledge. Above, a detailed report from December 1148 about the catastrophic consequences of the conquest of Morocco by the Almohads is analyzed. As early as December 1141, however, we read in a letter from Fez that a general depression had set in there because of the "usurper," the Almohad chieftain, who was then still far away in the opposite corner of the country.[106] The year 1062 was only the beginning of a long period of devastating anarchy in Egypt. But as a letter from August of that year shows, the merchants in both Cairo and Alexandria were prepared for the worst.[107] At the time the Seljuks were on the way to taking possession of Iraq and the neighboring countries (early 1050s) we read this Hebrew passage in an otherwise Arabic letter from Jerusalem: "*The tidings we get about Babylonia and its environments are hard. May God let us live in safety, quiet, and security and shelter us under the protection of his wings.*" Less than about twenty years later Jerusalem was conquered by the Seljuks and deserted by most of its Jewish (and probably also of a large part of its Muslim) population.[108]

Failures of the government, such as defeats in war, rampages of its soldiers, inability to supervise the food supply (action against the hoarders of grain and the like), let alone oppression of the defenseless, including the minorities, or atrocities in the wake of court intrigues, are never connected with the person of the ruler. The cause of this practice seems to have been not so much precaution, the fear of being denounced for lese majesty, but rather the yearning after an absolute authority. Cursing the king was like cursing God (I Kings 21:10 and 13), making the world a derelict place, a property without an owner.[109]

Incidents of pillaging by rebellious troops or marauding tribes, which emptied the towns and made travel unsafe or impossible, were the afflictions most heavily weighing on the population. They were reported like natural disasters. It is the nature of the warriors to live at the expense of the working masses, just as wild animals feed on quarry. Such cases are noted throughout the centuries, labeled as "the plunder of this or that town," followed by the names of persons affected or saved, or expressions of fear or hesitating hope. Robberies in the course of overland travel and piracy at sea were not confined to times of anarchy or war. Wherever a population has to rely for its protection on foreigners, mercenaries, slave soldiers, "volunteers," or the like, its security is in jeopardy (details in the note).[110]

One of the recurrent causes of mutinies and subsequent pillages was a bad year. Agriculture provided the main revenue of the state, and if a low or altogether failing Nile left the coffers of the government empty, the soldiers went berserk. The Nile was watched not only in Egypt but also in neighboring countries.[111] "This hard year," accompanied by the sigh, "may God bring us out of it unharmed," was the standard phrase under these circumstances.[112] In times of dearth, silence was the order of the day. In a "hard, hard year" even a simple communication, such as "no *wheat* is to be had in the East," expresses the fatal word *wheat* in Hebrew in order to avoid the suspicion that the writer or recipient had any specific knowledge of where the vital substance could be procured. The letter mentions the year 1067. Thus we are here in the midst of the frightful years of anarchy, famine, and plague of 1062–1072, repeatedly referred to in this book.[113] It can be shown that a number of letters in the Geniza were written during this period. Yet the historian will seek there in vain anything comparable to the inferno-like descriptions found in Muslim sources. Those descriptions are substantial and seem to be essentially true. In times of general hunger, minority people had to be doubly on their guard not to give the impression that they possessed anything edible or had an inkling of where to get it. I suspect that in such critical times people kept their correspondence to the absolutely necessary minimum. Food sent to a Jew or another person not in a position of power was simply taken away. In one letter the addressee is advised to send the grain with a Muslim whose high rank would enable him to get the consignment through the toll station.[114]

The Geniza contains an immense amount of data about the availability and cost of wheat and bread.[115] But these were market prices, publicized and known to everyone interested. Besides, the great majority of those data were not from the times of catastrophic famines but from those of periodic shortages or simply when, for one reason or another, it was difficult to lay in provisions. The very fact that, as pointed out in the section on Food (*Med. Soc.*, IV, 226 ff.), the acquisition of grain, then the very mainstay of life, created so much difficulty even for middle-class people and gave rise to a correspondence that can almost be described as nervous, must have had an unhealthy effect on the state of mind of wide sections of the population. The reason for this instability was probably not so much scarcity as the avidity of the people around the government who manipulated the grain market. Steps of the authorities against such practices are noted in the Geniza with regard to bakers, when they tried to emulate the more powerful "hoarders of grain, whom the people curse" (Proverbs 11:26).[116]

Pandemics, such as plague and other contagious diseases affecting large sections of the population, often occurred in times of bloodshed and famine. And, as with famines, one has to distinguish between exceptionally catastrophic "plagues," such as those of the 1060s and of 1202–1203, of which it is rightly said that the like had not happened for many generations,[117] and recurrent visitations which were so frequent that we find some mentioned in the Geniza and which have not yet been identified in Muslim sources. How people reacted and communicated in such times of terror is studied in the subsection "Illness."[118]

A charming note admonishing the recipient to bring his attempts at reconciliation with his adversary to a successful conclusion, since "completing a good work was more meritorious than initiating it,"[119] and since all were equally afflicted by the bad times, contains this prayer: "*May God save me and you from poverty, from pillage and collapse, hunger, war, depletion of the purse, and an oppressive government, from harmful errors*[120] *and hard times* [in Hebrew, then continuing in Arabic] and may He gather Israel in its totality together with King Messiah, *may he reveal himself soon.*"[121] The phrase translated here as "hard times" means, literally, "harsh edicts," the usual expression for this notion. The sufferings of the population are conceived as punishments imposed by God on his sinful world, just as a Roman emperor would discipline a mutinous province by singling it out with particularly severe treatment.[122]

The catalog of tribulations contained in this prayer is rather complete. The absence of plague, mentioned in the Bible so often together with "sword and hunger," shows on the one hand that the writer had not witnessed a major outbreak of a pandemic for a long time or at all.[123] On the other hand, his "depletion of the purse," preceding immediately the most dreaded of all, an oppressive government, refers to the often mentioned, albeit not the most disastrous, calamity: a lagging economy, "a sluggish market," business "at a standstill," "a city in ruins," and people "without work."[124] These exclamations, however, like other details in the letter concerned, are not always to be taken too tragically. Only when additional information provided confirms the complaint, or when the writer shows signs of despair, saying "I am out of work," "I have no livelihood," is the depression real.[125] When a merchant writes, "I receive neither letters of intelligence nor notes about shipments," or when a craftsman emphasizes "I am looking for work, not for alms," or when an intellectual describes his misery of being without office, the writer's personal troubles are connected with the slump referred to by him.[126] In general, economic depressions, if not caused by greater disasters, such as war, anarchy, persecutions, famine, or plague, were braved with courage. Here, where those affected by misfortune could try to improve their lot with their own means, they, hardened by experience, ready to accept adversity, did not mind words about their losses but relied on God and acted. In sum, the first and constant reaction to misfortune was the precaution not to offend the majesty of its first cause, God, "the true and just judge," "all of whose deeds were good." Bitter complaints could only make things worse. Second, man's own dignity had to be preserved: depicting one's plight too elaborately would let the writer appear as luckless, as a man who was not "a favorite of God," even a sinner. Finally, one should not impose on one's friends; even a slight allusion would be sufficient for them to comprehend the magnitude of the disaster that had occurred.

Add to this the magic of words and the power of wishful thinking. When you did not mention the evil, it was not there. When confidence was expressed that there would be "Relief after distress," and that "God will turn the end to the good," the desired turn of events was already in sight. Naturally, tempers were different. A proud man would take matters into his own hands, would not permit his enemies to rejoice in his misfortune; he would try to turn "the wheel [of fortune]" around. Others could hardly conceal their despair. But only "when the knife cut through to the bone," as was said in Arabic, or "when the waters have come up to the [seat of] breath" (Psalms 69:2), would the writer let himself go and describe his deplorable state in all its abject misery.[127] Extreme and undeserved poverty as well as painful and prolonged illness would induce the sufferer "to uncover his face," to reveal his dreadful plight in full.

Cases of general calamities, such as economic depressions, breakdown of authority and wars, or famine, pandemics, and earthquakes, were different. They did not require attention to the susceptibilities of others or care for the preservation of one's own prestige. Exact details were often vital for the recipient, and horror about the events could be expressed freely, mostly, however, veiled in the form of Bible verses. In the case of events afflicting Jews in particular, those quotations had the additional role of showing the people unified not only in space but also in time, if not beyond—the messianic, eternal, almost transcendental meaning of suffering.[128]

Poverty.—The study of poverty in the Middle Ages has made great strides during the last three decades or so. Suffice it to mention the comparatively brief but concentrated *essai de synthèse* by Michel Mollat, the doyen of researchers in this field, and the massive work of Evelyne Patlagean on social as opposed to economic poverty in early Byzantium, both accompanied by detailed bibliographies; Demetrios J. Constantelos's illuminating survey of Byzantine philanthropy and social welfare; and Brian Tierney's attractive exposition on canonical poor law, which draws attention to similar notions in Judaism and Islam.[129]

A number of causes led to this new interest and systematic research in medieval poverty, in the main perhaps the discovery that it was not so much scarcity, the failure of good Mother Earth to provide her children with sufficient sustenance, as the wickedness and incapability of men which were responsible for the deprivations of large sections of the population.[130]

The Geniza documents must be regarded as a major source for the history of poverty in the Middle Ages, as far as the Mediterranean area is concerned. Most of the pertinent topics have been treated in the previous volumes, each in its relevant context, and are again touched upon here and in some of the subsequent sections below. A quarter of Volume II is dedicated to the social services, that is, the works of charity operated by the community, for these were one of the most conspicuous constituents of its very existence. Charity was a religious duty. Consequently, care for the indigent was the natural preserve of a community based on faith. Appendixes A–C in Volume II contain summaries of Geniza documents describing houses and other real estate "given to the Poor" for their permanent support (A); the beneficiaries of public charity and the benefits they received (B); and lists of contributors and of what they provided in cash and kind (C). Add to this Moshe Gil's weighty volume on the Jewish pious foundations based on the documents discussed in Appendix A and some others identified by him later. When equally (or nearly equally) gifted and knowledgeable authors like M. Gil undertake similar studies based on Appendixes B and C, communal charity, as reflected in the Geniza, will become fully apparent in its multifaceted ramifications.[131]

A provisional analysis of the economic data contained in about four hundred engagement and marriage contracts attempted in Volume III resulted in a picture of the approximate composition of the Geniza population, one fourth of which seems to have been either entirely destitute or very poor. In times of high prices and plagues one would say hyperbolically that *the takers* were more numerous than *the givers.*[132] This frightening statistic is matched by a computation of the relative numbers of contributors to public charity and the paupers in receipt of handouts. In the lists from the middle of the twelfth and the beginning of the thirteenth centuries, there was one relief recipient to four contributors. One must keep in mind that not everyone of the poor was prepared to expose himself to the shame of applying publicly for help or was regarded as eligible. It is noteworthy that according to an estimate given to Kenneth L. Brown concerning the Jewish *mellah* of Salé, Morocco, at the beginning of this century, about one quarter of its population depended on charity.[133]

Referring to this computation, Salo W. Baron made the pertinent observation that not everyone above the poverty level was able or willing to donate for communal charity.[134] Weigh against this the fact that pledges of donations were made on special occasions (such as the Day of Atonement), when everyone was expected to attend the public service, and, just as some people were reluctant to register their need for help, thus even persons with limited means (or perhaps especially these) would be afraid of losing face by not participating in pledges at public appeals. Paying was probably another matter. When we find in the Geniza—as in Talmudic times—the problem of tardy fulfillment of vows or of failure altogether, one of the reasons was probably that the response to public appeals was fairly general, whereas its implementation was less so.

The "wretched poor," widows, divorcées, orphans, especially female orphans without fathers or brothers, as well as neglected and abandoned wives, formed a very prominent segment of the indigent population; their lot is described in detail in Volume III. Finally, knowledge of the nature and the vicissitudes of Geniza economics, as presented in Volume I, is a prerequisite for the understanding of the causes of poverty, so paramount in our documents.[135]

In accordance with the general character of this chapter, destitution as seen by the destitute is studied here, notably how he (or she) responded to the challenge presented to him, and how he communicated with others about it. Since we have to rely on letters, the illiterate among the poor—especially the women—would thus remain "voiceless," but this situation is not without remedy. Professional scribes were available everywhere. Mothers dictated their letters to their boys who had learned letter writing in school. The records of court sessions and personal appeals to the authorities or the community assembled in the house of worship, which we read now, were of course written by trained clerks, but they were advised to render the arguments of the complainants verbatim, and this procedure was observed by and large. Moreover, some general considerations about the attitudes toward poverty will add voice to the voiceless. In this section, where private charity is discussed as an element of the life-style of the bulk of the population, in particular, of the well-to-do, the general picture is rounded off.[136]

We learn about want when the person afflicted despairs of his ability to cope with his dire situation and stretches out his hand for help. This fatal step is described in Arabic with the phrase "uncovering one's face" (becoming "barefaced," which is stronger than "losing face"). One should be *mastūr*, literally, "veiled," screened off from the curiosity of outsiders by one's means or work, or at least by enjoying the protection of the family or of an influential patron. The opposite of the mastūr was the *ṣaʿlūk*, which has the double meaning of beggar and bandit, an unfriendly combination not unknown in other societies. In the Geniza world, where self-respect and shame counted more than anything else, it was natural that writers of begging letters emphasized that they had never before "uncovered their faces." The ways in which they described or hinted at their plight and the arguments with which they underpinned their requests for help differed widely, which was to be expected in view of the variety of situations concerned and the dissimilarity of human minds.[137]

In the following a number of such letters are analyzed, beginning with three from early Ayyubid times, from which we have more letters requesting help than those concerning business affairs. The first one, written in or around 1181, is remarkable for its exact biographical details, which the writer had good reason to provide, as our comments show. He was a native of Ceuta (Arabic Sabta, in Spanish Morocco, on the Straits of Gibraltar), and escaped from there—albeit robbed of everything[138]—before the town fell into the hands of the Almohads (1146), who, we remember, massacred or converted by force Jews and others who did not hold their tenets.[139] He lived for many years in Palermo, Sicily, and then in Fustat, Egypt, and suffered heavy misfortunes, though of different character, in both places. As his script and his Arabic and Hebrew styles prove, he was a learned man, maintaining himself as a silversmith at the same time, a common way of life among the Jews of Morocco or Yemen.[140] That his misery did not let him lose his self-respect is proved by this letter, which is also not devoid of a touch of humor.

After an introductory passage,[141] in which the addressee is wished to be blessed "with male children, studying the law and fulfilling its commandments" (this instead of the obligatory greetings to the recipient's sons), and in which the eminent learnedness and scriptorial art of his late father are extolled, the letter opens, as usual, with biblical quotations. Here they emphasize the heavenly rewards for piety and generosity and the blessings derived from male progeny. The last verse quoted says: "*My help comes from the Lord, the Creator of Heaven and Earth*" (Psalms 121:2). Religious etiquette required that one should always profess trust in God before seeking support from men.

The letter itself opens with many good wishes, in particular, as usual in such circumstances, that the recipient may remain all his life a supporter, and never become supported, and always be a giver of loans, never a taker. The latter wish—uncommon—reiterated in strong Bible quotations, suggests that Moses b. Nathan, the recipient (not known to me otherwise) was a banker.[142]

After these proems—for our taste too long, but then probably regarded as the minimum, Ephraim b. Isaac goes on to write this:[143]

Your submissive slave, the lonely, poor foreigner, informs your excellency that I am a Maghrebi, a native of the city of Ceuta, which I left before the *forced conversion* thirty-five years ago today. I lived in [the capital of] Sicily[144] for about fifteen years. There, too,[145] I witnessed a pillage; I was robbed and all I possessed was lost. I came to this country, and needed nobody's support, for I earned my livelihood as a silversmith. I have been here now for seventeen years.

Three years ago I fell ill with ophthalmia, and lost half of my eyesight. As an expedient I took on four boys[146] as a Bible teacher, which brings me four dirhems a week. The Holy one, may He be blessed, knows that one cannot make more with this. Ten of my masters and lords united to help me, the poor stranger, paying the poll tax for me.

Now, my master and lord, I ask you to be so kind and write to my masters and lords, your brothers, *the two olive branches, two, full of oil, two funnels of gold* [who let gold flow] [Zechariah 4:13–15], to be remindful of their slave, and [I request from your pie]ty and generosity some flour for my sustenance *according to the blessing of the Lord which he has given you* [Deuteronomy 16:17]. God knows and witnesses that one never has to ask you twice. And plead for me with our Jewish Maghrebi friends, in particular, Ephraim b. Abu ʾl-Khayr and Joseph the merchant, known as Ben Eli. The Holy one—may he be your helper and supporter—will carry out what is written *God will keep you from all evil, keep your soul, and keep your coming and going, now and forever* [Psalms 121:7–8].

I have written this,[147] Ephraim, the son of Isaac [may he] r[est in] E[den] from the city of Ceuta, the birthplace of your slave, I grew up and received my education in the [capital] city of Sicily.

To his honor (my) m[aster and] t[eacher] Moses, who has come to live in the country of Egypt, as one comes to the Land of Life.[148] May God give him success for my sake and the sake of other Maghrebis. *Shalom.*

At first blush, this letter is a puzzle. The writer was well known to the recipient, of whom he says that he had never to remind him of a request. At the end he says to him jokingly in Hebrew: You have come to this country and made good here; so please be mindful of me and of your other countrymen. The reference to R. Moses' two brothers is also a joke: a favorite technique of quoting a Bible verse was to cite only a part, but to leave it to the reader to complement the remaining section, which contained the intended allusion, in our case: [*who let gold flow*], the meaning being, of course, "your brothers are well-to-do and generous; have them live up to their reputation." Seeing that Ephraim was on such friendly terms with the addressee and his brothers, why did he provide him with so detailed a biography, the like of which is found hardly anywhere else in a letter for help in the Geniza?

The answer is, first, that this letter was intended to be used as an appeal to be circulated among the Maghrebis mentioned or referred to and probably others whom the recipient might choose to approach. Three points are stressed: The writer was a Maghrebi in every respect; he was born in the farthest West, educated in Sicily (which, although ruled at that time by the Normans, belonged culturally to the Muslim-Jewish Maghreb), and lived among and off Maghrebis while in Egypt. Countrymen in foreign parts were like a family; members of a family should help their needy; applying for their help was not shameful. Stressing that the writer belonged to the family of the addressee was a common point in begging letters, but often this was only a hollow phrase. Here the point is made realistically and with conviction.

Second, from his youth to his old age, Ephraim had suffered undeserved misfortune. How could such a person be overlooked when people made their accounts and planned their works of charity? Finally, and this was a most important point: he always supported himself by his work; the Geniza people had no regard for spongers. Unlike others, Ephraim makes no allusion to his being a lifelong student. The letter spoke for itself.

Two other points attract attention. Although he was a very poor man and therefore exempt from the poll tax according to Muslim law, a merciless government exacted from him the tax. Assuming that he had to pay 2 dinars, as was customary at that time, he would have to deliver to the government his earnings of eighteen to twenty weeks. The ten persons paying for him the 70–80 dirhems required were certainly themselves small people, probably former customers of his when he still worked as a silversmith. We see our Ephraim was popular, but the cash that he might have saved for his old age while still earning was siphoned away by the tax collector.

The request for some flour is pathetic. These people lived on a subsistence level, and a very modest one, but seem to have regarded this as nothing extraordinary.[149]

Reading the begging letter of Ephraim b. Isaac's younger contemporary, Joel the schoolmaster,[150] one is tempted to regret that the latter's excellent command of Hebrew, his fine mind, and poetic vein were not applied to a worthier subject. Perhaps he himself felt so, for, after writing about one hundred and twenty short rhymes in prose and a poem of about thirty long verses, he excuses himself, writing on the margin: "I have only been speaking so long out of my great anguish and distress" (I Samuel 1:16). On second thought, both the regret and the surmise expressed must be recognized as misplaced. The letter is addressed to "Abraham the Pious," the founder of a pietist movement, and his brother, Joseph, the "Head of the Pious and Man of good deeds."[151] It is to be conceived as a poetical praise of the two brothers, followed by a passage concerned with the affairs of the writer. Creations of this type formed one of the most common genres of Arabic and Hebrew poetry and should by no means be dismissed lightly as exercises in the art of begging. This poetry had a proper seat in life: being a friend or protégé of a worthy man was one of the most cherished possessions of an intellectual. That Joel himself regarded the poem included in his letter as a piece of art is proved by his suggestion that it might be set to music accompanied by instruments.

Little of the writings of Abraham the Pious is known to us, but our missive shows that Joel had read and understood them. He praises him as the one who had illuminated his eyes and inspired his thoughts. His letter opens—as was usual even in the times of the New Testament in epistles sent to congregations (Galatians 1:3 and elsewhere)—with greetings from God, who bears here, among other attributes, a seemingly strange one: *Perplexer of thoughts,* no doubt a reference to Moses Maimonides' *Guide of the Perplexed,* which must have appeared in the bookstalls of Fustat at the time of the writing of our letter.[152] The two brothers are described as the teachers of the diaspora, leaders of the people, able to explore "the mind of the One who dwells in light" by expounding the Scriptures mystically, and having a purifying effect on the hearts like the Day of Atonement, by both their lucid teachings and way of life: passing their days in fasting and their nights in prayer. (This is a common Sufi expression, but Joel probably learned it from the great penitential poem of Judah ha-Levi where it occurs;

it forms the opening of the vigils in Oriental Jewish communities up to the present day. The Spanish Hebrew poet had visited Egypt two generations earlier, and many of his creations are found in the Geniza.)

Joel knew the two brothers well. He extols Abraham mainly as a theologian and praises Joseph for his share in the sciences. Both were physicians. Abraham's library, which was sold after his death in spring 1223, contained mostly medical books. The customary reference to the recipient's sons is replaced here by the wish that Abraham may be blessed with children who remain alive. The implication is evident.

As to the writer's own affairs he notes that two of his three main troubles would have been sufficient to cause him tormenting nights without sleep: poverty, a big family ("a multitude of little children"), and no savings.[153] Remembering the poll tax melts his heart: for inability to pay it he would be chained and thrown into prison.[154] Moreover, he was in debt to merciless Muslim usurers. But the two brothers who in the past had bestowed clothes upon him[155] and whom he calls "my friends" are trusted to extricate him and let him grow new wings.

Since there is no allusion to hard times for the population at large, the letter was probably written shortly before 1201, when Egypt was visited by a famine and plagues, which caused a rapid decline of the Jewish community of Fustat.[156]

How could such a gifted man fall into such squalid destitution? The answer to this question is to be found in a variety of causes: the general state of affairs where a considerable section of the general population constantly lived at, or below, subsistence level; the limited number and disadvantaged minority status of those who were able to give; in particular, the belief that the inegality between master and slave, man and woman, rich and poor, which can be observed daily in life is God-made and therefore an attempt to change it is futile and almost sinful. Even in messianic times, Maimonides teaches there will be a difference between the strong and the powerless, the rich and the poor. Popular fantasies to the contrary appeared to him as childish. I have touched upon this question in different contexts in this book.[157]

An entirely different atmosphere awaits us in a complete and very long letter which contains neither the name of the writer nor that of the recipient. The latter can be identified by one of his titles and by the blessings for his son, mentioned both by his Hebrew name Elazar and his Arabic *kunya,* or byname. The recipient was none other than Abu ʾl-Barakāt, Judah ha-Kohen b. Elazar, "the

Trusted Servant of the State," about whom and whose family numerous documents, worth a short monograph, have been preserved in the Geniza.[158]

The Trusted Servant of the State, a government official, was one of the most influential and honored members of the community. One would therefore expect that the tone of this letter would be particularly deferential and restrained. The opposite was the case. Here we meet a man who "uncovers his face" completely, or, as one says in Hebrew, has the face of a dog, begging shamelessly for things that cannot be regarded as the basic necessities of life. On top of this he opens his letter with the ominous invocation and warning, "In the name of Him who listens to the needy" (Psalms 69:34). I am aware of the teachings of Jewish ethics that the term "needy" should be understood in its widest sense. To stress this the Talmud says that if a man is accustomed to riding on a horse with a servant running in front of him (which Jews normally never had) he must be provided with them; Hillel the sage, that paragon of Judaism, did so, and once, when no servant could be found, he himself ran in front of the rider for three miles. But this was certainly not the concept of charity in vogue among Geniza people.[159]

Moreover, one might assume that the writer was so at ease because he was very close to the recipient. No trace of such familiarity can be discovered in his letter. True, he calls himself the "Trusted"'s *ṣanīʿa*, "creature," client, a term common in government circles and frequently used in calls for help, but we do not even learn in which capacity he had served his alleged patron. True, also, that his request, written in Arabic, is preceded by an enormous proemium in rhymed Hebrew prose, all sixty-six or so units having the same rhyme. But how different is his performance from that of Joel the schoolmaster discussed above. Joel clearly brings out the things that counted for his addressees and even has an eye for the differences in interests between them; our ṣanīʿa's high-flown Hebrew phrases are nothing but empty shells; we look in vain for any real knowledge of the person or work of the recipient. Now, such generalities are our usual diet in Arabic and Hebrew poetry, and I would not be surprised if it would be found one day that the entire proemium was copied from a letter for another person. But in studying the "uncovering of the face" I have already noted, and will note more, cases of strong social or spiritual ties between the needy person and those he approaches. Where such ties seem at most to be superficial, the matter deserves special attention.

After dedicating ten lines to good wishes for the forthcoming Passover holiday, the writer begins his request in line 77 of his letter:

> It is not concealed from you—*may your glory be heightened and your fame increase*—that these are hard times,[160] especially for one who has no livelihood like me, your slave, who is in great need, without income, without means for expenses for the forthcoming holiday. I have married, being now *under the yoke of a household,* and need at present some adornments for the holiday, as I am accustomed to, such as [new] clothing, money for flour, money for a lamb, and other things required at the holiday.[161]
>
> Only God and the generosity of your excellency, which I have experienced before, can help me, as the Scriptures say: "I will care for all your wants" [Judges 19:20]. I am confident that this saying is in the mind of your exalted excellency with regard to your slave, for I am one of your creatures whom you have created in your generosity and mercy.
>
> Your slave had already intended to send you a request on Purim,[162] but decided to make one for the holidays [in general].
>
> I am confident that my table and my house[163] will be adorned on these holy days only through God and through your charity, dedication,[164] and generosity—may you always remain one who is approached for help.
>
> May my sincere prayer for you and your son, my lord, sheikh Abu ʾl-Maʿāli, said in a state of want, be accepted. *May the well-being of your excellency my lord, that of your noble dear son, and of the rest of the family be increased. Selah.*[165]

The writer of this letter was no fool; he knew that he was impertinent. As the Talmud says, however, brazenness (called chutzpah in American slang) prevails even against Heaven,[166] and it is characteristic of societies with very strict standards that they also comprise some persons who feel they fare better by disregarding them. Moreover, I have little doubt that the writer of our letter is identical with Manasse, the Alexandrian schoolmaster, who, years later, sent to Elazar, the son of the "Trusted," two missives: one, a rather barefaced reminder that he had already informed him that his boy had done well when examined by his grandpa, wherefore he, Manasse, deserved proper consideration at the forthcoming Hanukka holiday; the other, an enormous epistle, a bit too intimate in tone, in view of the hint of Elazar's refusal to see him, requesting that his father stop a judge from diverting schoolboys from his Bible class to that of another teacher.[167] Alexandria was different from the capital in many ways. This might have been one of the reasons why the writer of the letter to the "Trusted," part of which is translated above, appears as a rather queer bird compared with other authors of begging letters in the Geniza.[168]

Another interesting case is the poetic epistle addressed to "the Prince of poets," Judah (b. Samuel) ha-Levi, by Judah b. Samuel the Castilian from Badajoz, a town near the Portuguese border, at a time when these two natives of Spain sojourned in Egypt.[169] Here we see a more refined form of a request for help at work, as fitting Muslim and Jewish societies in Spain which possessed a higher literary culture than those in Egypt.

The man from Badajoz does not conceal that he was in dire circumstances and that Judah ha-Levi was destined from primordial times to be "a father of the needy" (Job 29:16) to him and to others in his situation: the travelers coming from Spain and the Maghreb had spread his fame as being both generous and "the refuge of all the sciences." But he does not express any direct request for help; he asks to be granted an interview, "for it is in the very nature of the souls to strive for the contemplation of the highest objects and to meet eye to eye with the spiritual realities," and so on. In the presence of the poet, the visitor would acquire something of the luminous light emanating from his host, as it is written, "the generous acts generously" (Isaiah 32:8)—a fine point, meaning, that ha-Levi would not be stingy with dispensing spiritual gifts[170]—and "who is like the wise man and who knows the interpretation of a thing? [A man's wisdom makes his face shine.]"[171] Besides illumination, the visitor would gain fame by being granted such an interview. In addition to all the praiseworthy qualities found in ha-Levi already mentioned, he is repeatedly extolled for being modest and unassuming, an allusion, of course, that he would not be so proud as to refuse to see the itinerant beggar-poet.[172]

Since the writer must concede that he has never seen the distinguished visitor from Spain, he asks himself, almost jokingly, how he could know so much about him. He answers using a Talmudic phrase: "If *I* have not seen you, my *star* has seen you," which implies that the meeting requested was preordained. In short, we see here an intellectual lifting the veil from his face only hesitantly, but trying to show both his need and the quality of his education as impressively as possible. Unfortunately, he was more successful with the former than the latter.[173]

The plight of refugees and other strangers was one of the most common causes forcing a person to "unveil his face." At home you are known: you do not need to explain yourself. You are *mastūr,* covered. As soon as you are compelled to leave your house and hometown, you are exposed. "Oh my house, concealer, *sātir,* of my blemishes," says an all-Arabic maxim.[174]

Of the countless tales of misery of this type related in the Geniza,

I present here one, where a general disaster is compounded by unhappy special circumstances and complicated personal relations, a predicament as frequent in those days as it is familiar to us in this century of refugees. An additional reason for choosing this story is that we listen here to a woman dictating it to a boy of hers. We know that this is what happened, because in the letter she speaks while the boy signs as the sender introducing himself as a son of his missing father (probably assuming that the relatives addressed did not know his name or of his existence). Some spelling errors reflect mishearing.[175]

The sender of the letter was a refugee from Jerusalem who had left the city with her family in the 1070s after it had been taken by the Seljuks and was in constant turmoil. Her husband, Abu ʾl-Khayr, was closely connected with Muslim authorities in Palestine and also with Judah b. Saadya, the Nagid, or Head of the Jews of the Fatimid Empire, who had his seat in Cairo. Abu ʾl-Khayr had brought upon himself the wrath of the Nagid, probably because, at the time of intercommunal strife, he was not as steadfastly with him as expected from one so close.[176] During the disorders following the Seljuk incursions, Abu ʾl-Khayr disappeared and his brother "was taken by the Bedouins." Frightening rumors circulated about a son of hers, who had probably accompanied his father. The family had moved to Tripoli, Lebanon, where a relative proved to be helpful, but Abu ʾl-Khayr committed the—understandable—mistake of suing him for a share in an inheritance, whereupon the relatives in Tripoli broke all relations with him and his family. Thus, the unhappy woman, who describes herself as *ṣabiyya*, "youngish" (which has the connotation of inexperienced), was left without any male assistance in a foreign and hostile environment. Here we learn how she tackled the situation:

[My lord and] illustrious master, may God make your welfare and happiness permanent. [I have to convey] to you, my dear boy,[177] something which I shall immediately describe . . . [Abu ʾl-Khayr was] with al-Muntaṣir. Al-Muntaṣir died [and Abu ʾl-Khayr disappeared].[178] Consequently we are lacking clothing and food to a degree I am unable to describe. But [our relative] Joseph was not remiss in providing us with cash, wheat, and other things. Moreover, he returned to me the collaterals, which I had given him, so that I could place them with someone else. God the exalted deserves thanks and has imposed on us to thank Him.[179] You must write him a letter of thanks. . . .

About the books of Abu ʾl-Khayr I learned only in Tripoli. For the crate was locked and I learned about its contents only in Tripoli. . . . I witnessed much bloodshed and experienced everything terrible.[180] I was told that, as soon as al-Muntaṣir died, Abu ʾl-Khayr disappeared. He had books and I [pawned] his books and yours for 5 dinars. Your letters concerning them have arrived. If the Nagid—may God keep him in his honored position[181]—manages to send 5 dinars, he will do so in the way of charity and thus ransom all the books, whereupon I shall send them to you. If he [Abu ʾl-Khayr] is all right, he will ransom them and send them.[182]

I learned that Abu ʾl-Wafāʾ was taken by the Bedouins at the time his brother disappeared.[183] I am a luckless young woman, suffering both by the hunger of the family, and especially the baby girl, who are with me, and by the bad news I heard about my boy.[184] If my lord, the Nagid, has sworn that he would not go to my aid and visits on me the iniquities committed by Abu ʾl-Khayr, have mercy upon me, you, your sister, and your mother, as far as you are able to do so.

[*Verso*:] As far as I am concerned, by our religion, the Rūm and the Jewish captives have it better than me, for, when they are captured, they find someone[185] who gives them food and drink, but I, by our religion, am completely without clothing, and I and my children are starving.

Now, do [plural] not neglect me. Be mindful of the family bonds and the blood. Show your affection for me by writing to me.

The brother of this man[186] was not remiss toward him, when he first arrived here, until he sued them[187] for an inheritance. This led to a complete rupture between them, and no one of them talks to me. . . . Miserable days have come upon me.[188] Must it be so? At the time when I was in Jerusalem,[189] your letters and "shares"[190] came to me plentifully, as is proper between two sisters[191] but now[192] you cut me.

I am writing these lines while the people are on the point of sailing. I have not described in this letter even a fraction of my real state.

Accept for yourself my greeting of peace. And may God extend his peace[193] to my lord the Nagid and my lord the Ḥāvēr. Greetings also to your mother and sister, and to his excellency, your paternal uncle. And regards to everyone under your care.

[*Address* (*written upside down as usual*):]

[*Right side*:]

To my lord and illustrious master [. . .] Abu ʾl-Aʿlā, may God keep him.

[*Left side*:]

[From] his grate[ful] A[bu ʾl] Riḍā. Convey and be rewarded![194]

[*Between the two lines in small script*:]

son of Abu ʾl-Khayr, son of . . .

The "youngish" mother of three (at least) stood the test of utmost privation well; she did not lose her head or her dignity. She describes her misery in detail and explains clearly how it all had come about. She is practical in her suggestions, and does not wail and lament as others did, to arouse compassion. Even when referring to the Nagid, she does not fall to her knees and kiss his feet, as is done in letters written in similar situations addressed to persons of even lesser status. She speaks as one who feels herself as belonging to the same level of society. Marriage was a hard school for Geniza women. Having successfully mastered the perilous transition from parental care to subservience in a strange household, she gathered strength to withstand other and even more painful vicissitudes of life.[195]

An entirely different picture emerges from a cry of distress by one Joseph, known as ʿAfīf b. Ezra, an Egyptian physician, who practiced in Safed, Upper Galilee, Palestine, during the first half of the sixteenth century.[196] It is a pitiful document of utmost self-humiliation, addressed to a relative in Egypt (belonging to the Amshāṭī family, which was already well known in the twelfth century).[197] While returning[198] from Cairo to Safed via Ghaza, the family had been in the Mediterranean port for two months at the time of the writing of the letter, kept there by illness. The son was gravely ill. ʿAfīf says that he had sold everything, including his clothing, for the boy's treatment. The wife was confined to bed, unable to see, hear, or speak.[199] Seven times ʿAfīf cries out "Oh my lord Samuel," imploring him to answer this letter, which was preceded by others that had gone unanswered.[200] Now he promises that this would be the last one, asking the addressee at the same time not to force him to send still another one, for writing such a letter was an ordeal, and finding a carrier for it almost impossible.

ʿAfīf rejects with indignation the charge that he had brought this disaster upon himself by his own fault (probably by disregarding the warning that the family would be unable to make the journey).[201] Practicing as a physician in Safed (which at that time began to assume its role as a major holy city) was done "for Heaven's sake." No doubt his inability to gain a livelihood in Cairo was another reason.[202] The frightening prospect of being forced to give up his journey, thus losing both the material and the idealistic bases of his existence, causes him to lose the composure usually maintained by persons of his status.[203]

The six persons in distress portrayed above differed widely in their situations and states of mind, but had in common that they had not yet arrived at the brink of the abyss. They wrote extensive letters awaiting responses; they looked forward to a future. As such they represented a large group of people in want whose misery reflected the economic, social, and political deficiencies of the world in which they lived, but to which they were trying to adapt themselves. Beneath them there was another, perhaps even larger mass of unhappy people who had nothing to look forward to except a piece of bread for supper or an outer garment for covering themselves especially on a cold winter day. Their cries for help give the reader the impression of outcasts, human beings whom society was unable to absorb.

A man whose use of both Arabic and Hebrew reveals that he had seen better days, writes a letter in irregular script and marred by misspellings which can readily be attributed not to ignorance but to what he himself describes: "By constant fasting and hunger my eyesight has become faint and my heart [we would say: brain] blotted out, so that I do not know what I am writing." In a postscript, he excuses himself in particular for being unable to enumerate all the honorific titles of the addressee, explaining that his personality was so noble that he did not need any laudatory epithets.[204] To be sure, in his introduction he had already described Abū Sahl, son of Moses, entitled "the Beloved [of the Yeshiva]," as a learned man, highly respected in the community, and had extended good wishes to his three sons, singling out the firstborn by name.[205] But for what is he giving thanks? For what does he say: "You have saturated me"? For a flat bread, which he cut into two pieces, one for supper and one for lunch. After each "meal," while saying grace, he included a prayer for the addressee, and now he asks "to be kept alive" by something for another supper. In a third postscript, Abū Sahl is reminded to include him when distributing meat and other victuals at a family sacrifice[206] (on the occasion of a wedding, circumcision, and the like), for he was a complete stranger who did not know anyone in town.

Since Abū Sahl was a cantor, who, as usual, also acted as court clerk, keeping the lists of the beneficiaries of the communal distribution of bread, he was probably the first person contacted by the writer of our letter. Strangers not yet registered got only one loaf of bread, as here.[207] Thus, our letter might reflect the specific plight of a newcomer. But references to persons who had no means to obtain even bread as their evening (and main) meal are abundant.

Naturally, not everywhere are such references to be taken literally. A well-written letter consisting almost in its entirety of good wishes for a holiday and for further success in a life crowned with wide renown ends with these four lines: "By the truth of your generosity[208] I do not have the means for buying bread to eat tonight. But God will help. Everything will be good if God wills. *And Peace. God will give strength [to his people and will bless his people] with peace. And Peace.*"

This is a polite reminder that a holiday was an appropriate

occasion for remembering a destitute relative. Our writer was really very poor, as may be concluded not only from what he says but also from the fact that the letter is written on paper cut from a rather confidential communication addressed to him.[209] The unusual postscript with a blessing upon the community is perhaps a hint that the well-off relatives should not force him to expose himself to public charity.[210]

To say that a person was unable to buy bread even for one evening meal was a phrase denoting extreme poverty. It occurs as such even in legal documents, for instance in a question about a grave family matter addressed to Abraham Maimonides.[211] A working woman (an unraveler of silk) in Tyre, Lebanon, who possessed a house and was able to pay a bill for 12 dinars, albeit in the course of several years, claimed in court to be bankrupt and too poor even to buy bread.[212] A similar formula used in a legal context was concerned with lighting, as in a question submitted to Moses Maimonides: "[Because of utmost destitution the husband] does not light a candle for his wife on weekdays and not even on a Sabbath or a holiday."[213] "He has no money for oil" (namely, for kindling a lamp) has remained a proverbial expression in Arabic for a completely destitute person down to modern times.[214]

The weight of a phrase, however, depends on its context. The complaint in the letter to Moses Maimonides continues: "When she wishes to have light, she goes to her mother or to her brother's family, for all live in the same house." So we see that the phrase was real, not hyperbolic. It should be noted that the young woman referred to did not lose her wits by "the extreme humiliation" to which she was exposed owing to the poverty of her worthless husband. Her story is told elsewhere in this book.[215] The expression "they have nothing for an evening meal" becomes all the more credible when substantiated by aspects of poverty other than the need for food, as when it is said that the family of an orphan girl about to marry took up a collection to provide her with one piece of clothing for the house and one for going out which also served as a cover at night.[216]

The writers of requests for help are often specific about the times they went without food. Joseph the Scholar asserts that he had not eaten "since yesterday noon," implying that he had not had supper, and had no means to buy "even one pound of bread," that is, a loaf.[217] The claim of having gone hungry for two days forms the sole content of a note to judge Elijah b. Zechariah, who was in charge of public charity.[218] Complaints that a woman and her children had nothing to eat for three days and nights in a row are found several times, in each case under special circumstances. One was recounted in the subsection on food in connection with an absentee husband.[219] In a second, a widow with small children, a stranger in Egypt, describes her plight to the elders, it seems, of the Karaite community, asking them to help her to get back to her family in the Holy Land.[220] In a third, under circumstances similar to the second, a stranger in Fustat whose widowed daughter and her little son had already gone hungry for three days asks a benefactor (who had helped him out with his poll tax before) to enable him to travel to Alexandria where he had lived before.[221] Three days of hunger thus seem to have been regarded as the maximum bearable, even by women and children, who, judging from the allowances granted to them, were obviously believed to need less food than men. In February 1982 one could see on the television screen jobless Americans claiming that no food had entered their mouths for three days.

One petitioner writes that he eats one day and goes without bread the next.[222] The cantor Yedūthūn ha-Levi, for whom at least ten entries in communal lists, one dated 1219, show that he received a weekly salary of 7 dirhems, asks another Levi for some support, for he got his fill only on Saturdays and went hungry the rest of the week; 7 dirhems is certainly a pittance for a man with a family. The addressee is adjured "by the truth of his generosity" to make the gift in private, not publicly.[223] The letters of the hungry are replete with biblical quotations, the most popular being

> Let your heart go out to the hungry
> And satisfy the desire of the famished [Isaiah 58:10],

a verse from the lection of the Day of Atonement known to everyone.[224]

The stories of complaints about insufficient clothing are no less pathetic and are reminiscent of biblical scenes. A poor and sick young man arrives in town in the evening, but his outer garment (which covered the body at night) is taken away from him as collateral for a debt of 5 dirhems.[225] Such merciless procedures were nothing new. "If you take your fellowman's garment in pledge, you must return it to him before the sun sets; it is his only clothing, the sole covering for his skin; in what else shall he sleep?" (Exodus 22:25–26). In a note addressed to the Nagid David b. Abraham b. Moses Maimonides, "Joseph, the poor stranger," reports that he was forced to sell his upper garment for 20 dirhems to be able to pay the second installment of the poll tax for the Muslim year (6)50 (which began on March 14, 1252), but when the time arrived for the first installment the following year, they had to pawn even (his wording) the *malḥafa* cloak of the wife. Here the manuscript breaks off, but it is not difficult to imagine what followed.[226]

The complaints about insufficient clothing are accompanied repeatedly by those about the absence of bedding. A man of some learning, who claims to have lost 5,000 (dinars?), describes himself as "*naked and bare,* with nothing upon me and nothing beneath" (no clothing and no sleeping mat), "with three children and a wife; less than this would have been enough in these hard times." He stresses over and over that he would be satisfied if, in addition to his own gift, the addressee would appeal to the council of the elders to arrange a public collection for him.[227]

In the same vein, but using even stronger language, a stranger "from a faraway place, namely Raḥba" (a town in Iraq) complains about the bad reception he was experiencing in Fustat: "No cover and no couch, no work. Three months I am here, and none of our coreligionists has paid attention to me or fed me with a piece of bread. . . . Dogs get their fill here with bread, not I. I have uncovered my face before you, my lord. Had I possessed . . . I would not be standing here in this posture." Needless to say, this writer, like others in a similar situation, had no money for paper; he used the back of a letter written in calligraphic Hebrew that had been dictated by a blind man from Europe who describes himself as fasting every Monday and Thursday (out of piety, not of need) and as not having eaten meat for a year (living at subsistence level). He asks Eli, the parnās, to arrange a collection, with the proceeds of which the sender's "wife and boys" may defray the cost of their travel from Alexandria to Fustat.[228] The rhymed phrase "no cover and no couch,"[229] occurring also in family letters, is another of those stereotypes denoting severe privation.

The trouble of defaulting one's rent was almost as common as the inability of paying one's poll tax, and is also mostly reported in family correspondence. "Street people," however, homeless persons forced to sleep in the streets, found so often today in big cities in warmer climates, seem to be absent from the Geniza. Should we assume that they belonged to a class of the population whose voice does not reach us? The worst I have read thus far about a person without shelter is a letter whose author says: "For one month, thirty days, I have been living in a donkey's stable, alone, starving, and ill; most of the time I do not eat or drink. Meat, fish, or rich food do not come into my mouth. My strength fails because of my sinfulness" (Psalms 31:11). The writer's script, style, Bible quotations, and demeanor, however, show that he "belonged," that he was of the same class as the man whom he addresses. All he asks from him is this: "I do not wish to trouble you, but if you can extricate from that man the 13⅝ dinars [he owes me], this will be very kind of you." He also excuses himself for being unable to attend public prayer service because of his present state and participates in a case of mourning reported by the recipient in the accepted manner: "May God grant you—and me—consolation." How the Wheel of Fortune could reduce this man to so base a degree of homelessness is difficult to understand. Probably his aloneness, the absence of family support, is to be blamed.[230]

As this report and many others analyzed above demonstrate, "Poverty follows the poor," misfortunes often appear in confluence, or, as the writer of a Geniza letter who uses the Talmudic saying just quoted adds: "'Time' has hit me with its arrows," meaning, bad luck has more than one arrow ready for hunting us.[231]

The worst of all adversities, however, was poverty, especially chronic, "crushing" poverty, either into which he was born and from which he was unable to extricate himself, or by which he was "ground" and because of which he was worn out and too weak to recover.[232] Many of the recipients of handouts appearing repeatedly in the communal lists of the Geniza may have belonged to these categories: persons described as disabled or handicapped, blind, paralyzed, chronically sick, old, and, of course, widows and orphans, and strangers perennially out of work. We read much about the care for these unhappy people, as insufficient as it was, but they themselves usually do not speak to us directly. It was an indication of their pitiful state that others had to act and speak on their behalf.[233]

The volume of correspondence and other writings concerned with poverty found in the Geniza seems to be out of all proportion. Should we assume that the Jewish community of those parts and times comprised an inordinately high percentage of destitute? Should it be surmised, for instance, that the Islamic poll tax imposed on Christians and Jews had a devastating impact on the lower strata of these minority groups? Or, shall we ascribe the abundance of material on indigence to the specific character of a comparatively small and tightly knit community like the Jewish, where social services and private charity were more developed than among the large and amorphous mass of the Muslim majority?

I am reluctant to answer either of these questions, given the present stage of research on the Jewish, and, in particular, on the Muslim communities. True, the overwhelming testimony of the

Geniza has proved that the Islamic poll tax was not a light burden, as previously assumed. As actually applied, not as formulated by the jurists, it was a cruel and inhuman vexation that caused endless suffering and humiliation to those who were least capable of filling the coffers of the government. But, taken from a wider sociological purview, the effects of the poll tax, as reflected so richly in the Geniza, seem to prove that considerable sections of the population lived on the brink of hunger, fighting to stave off starvation but incapable of accumulating even modest reserves. When the tax collector arrived with his demands for cash, the little they possessed, for instance, in clothing, was taken away, and they were forced to go begging.

The community represented in the Geniza appears, however, not to have been exceedingly poor in comparison with its environment (nor unduly rich, as an eleventh-century Egyptian poet claimed).[234] Otherwise, pertinent remarks to this effect would have been made on some of the countless occasions when reiterated demands on its liberality were made, as happened indeed in the thirteenth century, when the Fustat Jewish community became impoverished in the wake of the famine and plague of 1202–1203 and the general exodus to Cairo. When it was stated above that at certain times one fourth of the Jewish population of Fustat was either completely destitute or very poor, one has to consider that the Fustat congregations with their well-organized social services attracted the needy from both the Egyptian countryside and abroad, even from remote countries such as Spain, Morocco, Iraq, and, of course, from nearby Palestine.[235] In evaluating the statistics abstracted from the trousseau lists it must be repeated here that in all marriage contracts the husband undertakes to provide his wife with clothing. Those bridal lists do not thus represent the entire wardrobe of the future wife. The almost frightening preoccupation of the Geniza with poverty has a special, tangential, but also very meaningful, reason.

The Geniza, remember, was a place in the synagogue compound where writings that had served their purpose and usually bore the name of God were discarded. The documents consisting of lists of contributors to appeals, of beneficiaries of public charity, and of pious foundations are preserved in the Geniza because the pledges, the distribution of handouts, and the administration of the properties belonging to the community were concentrated in the synagogue compound. The documents that were no longer in use were put aside where they had been used. As for the letters, whereas in the Temple of Jerusalem, prayer was said over a sacrifice or other offering brought by a supplicant, in the synagogue, charity, gifts to the poor, "the people of God," replaced this main aspect of the Temple cult: giving to God—as endlessly stressed in begging letters. Christianity and Islam practice the same combination of charity with prayer. Thus, the synagogue service was the proper place and time for handing in a request for help. The house of worship was also a territory where rich and poor, the respectable person and those who were forced "to unveil their faces," could meet on common ground, unlike a private home, where the unhappy needy had to wait outside at the gate.[236]

In the synagogue, the person solicited would respond either immediately with a gift (probably often handed over through a third person), by making a promise, or by deferring the answer to another occasion. Once the matter had been handled, how to dispose of the letter? Since pockets were uncommon in those days, one could stick a letter into his sleeve or turban, but it was more convenient to get rid of it by putting it away in the Geniza chamber nearby. Longer letters, whose style and quotations were appreciated, were probably taken home, but since they were replete with invocations of the name of God had eventually to be deposited in the Geniza. The proliferation of material connected with poverty in the treasure trove of manuscripts known as the Cairo Geniza was thus due to very special circumstances.

The pictures of the synagogue scenes just evoked had deeper implications, greatly influencing the attitude toward poverty as seen from the side of both the solicitor and the solicited. "More than the master of the house[237] does for the poor, the poor does for him."[238] For "charity delivers from death" is said twice in the Scriptures (Proverbs 10:2; 11:4), and who would not heed such a promise?[239] "God stands at the right hand of the needy" (Psalms 109:31). A great teacher urged that this metaphor should be understood literally: "This poor man stands at your door and the Holy One, may he be blessed, stands at his side."[240] If, because of their frequency, these and similar admonitions failed perhaps often to impress the person approached, they certainly eased the strain on the poor who was seeking relief from his misery. He was not alone. The Law, the Prophets, and the Psalmists, as well as the teachings of the Sages, were preoccupied with him and his fate to an extraordinary degree. True, poverty was the worst of all afflictions, but it did not deprive the poor person of his human dignity. The expressions of servility often found in begging letters should not deceive us. They were customary also in business and family letters. True, also, that a wide diversity of personalities and approaches among the seekers of support was to be observed above. But beyond the submissive style and despite the differences between the meek and the bold, the background for all begging remained the same: the poor applied not only to the person approached but also to an authority higher than both. Such feeling provided a certain release, a spark of freedom, even where the writer was beset by utmost distress.

Moses Maimonides' teachings about poverty and charity, as included in his Code of Law, are described in the epilogue to my section on the social services of the community.[241] He had repeated opportunities to tackle this problem, especially when discussing messianic expectations, a burning issue in those days. Popular preachers, he says, wish to make us believe that the Messiah will bring equality between the poor and the rich. Nothing of the kind; the natural course of things will not change; there will always be the powerful and the weak, the poor and the rich.[242] Maimonides' exposition has a philosophical undertone. But the same idea, albeit based on a different argument, is found in a Midrash probably known to the master: King David asked God to safeguard his world by making the rich and the poor equal, whereupon God answered: who then could do true works of lovingkindness?"[243] The poor help those better off to acquire religious merit. They are useful also in other respects: they help the rich to manifest their munificence, a special kind of "conspicuous consumption."

Illness.—The Geniza person occupied himself (and others) very much with physical well-being. Reports, queries, and good wishes concerning health are abundant and found in every second letter. One took good care of himself and was liberal in dispensing useful advice on such matters to others. Moses Maimonides must have been aware of these tendencies of his contemporaries; he included a chapter on health care in the very first part of the first of his fourteen volumes on Jewish law. That part deals with the knowledge of God; to attain this highest goal of human existence man must have a sound body. Maimonides stated categorically that a person conducting himself in accordance with his guidance would never need a doctor all his life. The gist of his advice was choice of the right nourishment agreeing with the climate, season of the year, and physical make-up of the person concerned, and, above all, utmost constraint in the consumption of food and in sexual activities.[244] The Geniza people were indeed modest in their eating habits and were aware of the dangers of excessive drinking.[245]

Interestingly, Maimonides did not find it necessary to sound a warning against the bottle. To the contrary, he repeatedly recommends wine or water mixed with wine as conducive to good digestion. Another piece of advice of the master, also stressed more than once, namely, to exert oneself physically before breakfast, finds its explanation in the eating habits of his time: the morning meal was taken after a substantial part of the day's work had been done.[246] The extraordinary hygienic importance of the weekly visit to the bathhouse and the rules to be observed there stressed by Maimonides are also reflected in the Geniza, as presently shown.

Recreational activities such as swimming (the Nile was so near) and walks in markets, parks, or gardens appear in our sources as enjoyed mainly by younger people.[247] The frequently mentioned visits to places in the countryside were undertaken, however, not only to strengthen family ties and friendships, or for commercial or communal affairs, but also for rest and recuperation of body and soul. Even a physician in the capital is advised by a colleague in a small town to take a day off with him for the same purpose.[248] How much the pleasures of the countryside were appreciated by city dwellers may be gauged from this (draft of a) Hebrew poem, written by Moses b. Levi ha-Levi, a young teacher and cantor, who tried to settle in Qalyūb, about ten miles north of Cairo, renowned also elsewhere for its gardens:[249]

I am full of joy, folks, with the help of Him
  who dwells in Heaven:
This is a medicine which heals all maladies
  and takes away all sorrows.[250]
The wells hold water sweeter than juices,
  the airs are cool.
Orchards gird the town bringing fruits, glorious
  and refreshing,
Dates, apples, and pomegranates, vineyards and
  almond trees, as well as. . . .[251]
Fresh fruit around the year, summer and winter.
Pure animals[252] roam in the groves, and birds nest
  in the trees.
You do not see dust on the ground. All around there
  are only gardens and water.
The wine they press is seasoned with aromatic
  spices of all sorts.[253]
[*And this*:]
The buckets on their waterwheels sing
  with a lovely voice like that of doves.[254]

By far the most impressive aspect of recreational health care apparent in the Geniza was the weekly visit to the public bathhouse, preferably on Friday, followed by the complete rest of the Sabbath. The rest began even earlier. After the bath one avoided doing business.[255]

The Egyptian capital was famous for the number of its bathhouses, probably an inheritance of a thousand years of Greek, Roman, and Byzantine domination. (They were also a nuisance. In those days, people suffered not from car exhausts but from the excessive amount of smoke emitted into the air by the multitude of bathhouses with their steam rooms).[256] The Muslim antiquarians noted these buildings, their names and locations, for they served as landmarks, after which their environments were named, for instance, in this address: "To Fustat, to the Bath of al-Kaᶜkī [the Pretzel-maker], to the store of sheikh Yaᶜqūb b. Mūsā." Paul Casanova in his *Reconstitution topographique d'al-Foustat* enumerates more than fifty bathhouses, but his list is not complete; it does not note, for instance, that of the Pretzel-maker, just mentioned, or the Bath of the Cock, probably called so, because a sign with a picture of that worthy bird decorated its entrance. When it is said of a person that "he lived in the Bath of the Cock" it means, I assume, in the neighborhood named thus. The excellent Muslim historian al-Maqrīzī mentions fifty-two bathhouses existing in the city of Cairo at the beginning of the fifteenth century, of which, however, nineteen were in ruins and three unused. André Raymond's interesting study on the location of these baths has methodological significance also for the situation in Fustat during the Fatimid and Ayyubid periods.[257]

The frequency of references to the public steam bath in the Talmud reflects, of course, the extraordinary importance it had in Late Antiquity "for both health and pleasure."[258] On Friday one readied oneself for the Day of the Lord by cleaning the body; but one visited the bathhouse as often as one could, as often as it was not full to capacity. Hence the prolonged discussions whether one was permitted to enjoy this pleasure also on Saturday. It was, of course, prohibited, but one was at least allowed to stroll around in the magnificent buildings in order to enjoy the walk and to inhale the steam escaping from the overheated sweat rooms.[259]

In his chapter on health care Maimonides recommended a visit to the public bathhouse once in seven days, but did not mark Friday in particular. This would have been impracticable since Muslims and Jews used the same facilities, and Muslims preferred to bathe on Friday morning before attendance at the weekly great prayer assembly taking place at noon.[260] Naturally, visits on days other than Friday are occasionally noted in the Geniza. "He swooned in the bathhouse last Thursday."[261] "I have already entered the bathhouse this week and eaten chickens," writes a merchant from Alexandria who had fallen ill after his return from Sicily and now informs his business friend in Fustat that he has taken a turn for the better and was already able to visit the bathhouse and to consume light food.[262] The belief in the hygienic power of the sweat bath is demonstrated throughout the centuries by reports that a sick person "has recovered and already entered the bathhouse." The hot bath was one of the most effective means of health care, but one had to be healthy enough to endure its strain.[263]

Besides health care it was the pleasure of company which made the visit to the bathhouse so immensely desirable. A vow to forego this amenity was a severe means of self-castigation, undertaken for various purposes such as intercession for a beloved person on a dangerous journey or otherwise showing concern for him; it could also demonstrate how much one suffered by his behavior.[264] A person was not permitted to enter a bathhouse together with an excommunicated person, for this would prove that he did not avoid his company, as required by law.[265]

It was the women, however, for whom joint visits to the bathhouse were needed for their mental health as much as for their physical well-being. True, the Geniza women attended synagogue services and frequented the bazaars. But they could not gather there for leisurely assemblies, as did the men. Therefore law and practice had to preserve for them this vital right to a bathhouse visit. A husband was not permitted to move with his wife to a place that possessed no bathhouses; he could not prohibit her from visiting one; he was worthless when he was unwilling or unable to provide her with the silver coin required for the entrance. These and similar matters are discussed in *Med. Soc.*, III and IV, where the variegated equipment needed at the visit of the bath, so prominent in the trousseau lists and occurring also in lawsuits, are mentioned in different contexts: the ubiquitous bathrobe, often made of costly material and imported from Europe, the box with compartments for the chemicals needed for the cleaning of the body, the scented oils, the makeup, as well as the bowls for the consumption of hot and cold drinks. Boxes of different sizes, one put into the other, are also often mentioned in this connection.[266] The New Moon day, celebrated by women by refraining from all but unavoidable work, was also earmarked as the day for a general get-together in the bathhouse. Even a woman who had vowed to abstain from these pleasurable visits made an exception of the New Moon day. Unfortunately, our Geniza, dominated by males unattentive to "the other nation," does not reveal to us what was going on in the *ḥammām* on such occasions.[267]

There exists a considerable amount of literature on the medieval steam bath of the Near East, its architecture and the hygienic and social activities observed there.[268] The term "public" used before means that admission, with few exceptions, was open to everyone who paid for it. The place was owned by a private person or one connected with the government, or by a pious foundation. Very rich people, like Abū Saʿd al-Tustarī, the "vizier" of the dowager, the mother of the caliph al-Mustanṣir, could keep one for himself and, naturally, for his family and friends. A lengthy, but enigmatic list of possessions of thirty well-to-do Jews in the Egyptian capital concludes thus: "In the bathhouse of Cairo their money is in the second room. In the bath with the salty water[269] all have their money on the upper floor. Abū Saʿd kept the money of all in the [= his] bath in rooms One, Two, and Three."[270]

The list was written in the 1050s, when only a comparatively few people not connected with the government lived in Cairo, wherefore probably only one public bathhouse was owned by a Jew. Traditionally the bathhouse was divided into three main sections: the entrance hall, where the visitors also rested after the bath, the undressing area, and the bath proper, consisting of various compartments, such as the basin with hot water and the steam room. The coins were certainly buried under the marble tiles of the ground floor and the rotunda beneath the dome. Hiding money in a place where no one would suspect it, namely, where people of all descriptions constantly visited, was certainly regarded as particularly smart.[271]

The description of a bath in Zawīlat al-Mahdiyya, Tunisia, sold by one Jew to another, has some special interest, inasmuch as Tunisia, the ancient province Africa, was particularly exposed to Roman influence. The document itself is absolutely exceptional by virtue of its huge characters. It is a masterpiece of calligraphy. A quaint circumstance saved it, or rather a vital part of it, for us. Someone cut out a piece in such a way that its upper end formed a triangle, on the tip of which a little cord was fastened for hanging the part cut out on a wall. No doubt, this was a charm for a woman in childbed, and since no one in the maternity room was suspected of being able to read, this impressive and beautiful piece of writing must have had a soothing effect on anyone who looked at it. So much so, indeed, that someone took the trouble to carry the charm all the way from Tunisia to Egypt. The beginning and end, and in particular, the left side is lost (as indicated by the open brackets in the translation). In the part not translated here the seller mentions that the bathhouse had been acquired by his brother, as proved by the document of purchase produced in court. After the usual legal phrases he continues:

> I have sold to him [a R. David] for the above mentioned sum this bath [. . .
> In Zawīlat al-Mahdiyya together with its furnace,[272] which is adjacent to it [. . .
> Containing marble columns. Its borders: from the house [of . . .
> To the East, stretching to the gardens known by [So-and-So . . .
> A Muslim. To the South, to the street [. . . and the house known
> By our father previously. The borders of the furnace [. . . The property is
> Complete, undivided [. . . sold to him for the sum mentioned above,
> Which I have received from him, a definite sale, namely [. . .
> The bath, the furnace with all [they contain.]
> Then the middle room, then the room with the basin [all the rooms
> Inclusive of their stucco work [
> Their waters, their toilet]
> Their spacious well [and the pipes (?)
> Which conduct the heat into its basin [.[273]

The furnace is conceived as a separate structure with borders of its own, although connected, of course, with the main building. The term "middle room" again indicates the tripartite division of the bathhouse. The marble columns and the stucco work are expressly noted because they were removable. The fact that this steam bath was situated near a house formerly owned by the seller's father and that his brother had acquired it shows perhaps that it had a semiprivate character, possibly closed to the general public on certain days. For understandable reasons a person tried to live in the vicinity of a bathhouse.[274] He who could afford it, bought one.

In view of the social importance of the bathhouse stressed

above,[275] I have often wondered why I have not found references in the Geniza to friends met there, conversations held, and the like. A religious taboo was involved. In a place where people disrobed and cleansed their body and stood most of the time entirely (or almost entirely) uncovered one could not pronounce the name of God or quote a verse from the Bible; but how could one conduct a conversation or even say hello without mentioning God? Needless to say this problem occupied the ancient sages. "On entering the bathhouse: where all people have their clothes on one may read the Scriptures and pray, and, of course, say greetings; where some people are disrobing there is no Bible and no prayer, but greetings are permitted; where all are naked, greetings, too, are forbidden."[276] Thus it appears after all that the medieval steam bath, as represented in the Geniza, served, at least for males, mainly physical pleasure, and, in particular, what was regarded as good health care.

Bloodletting (nowadays "revived for a wide variety of modern ills") was, like the steam bath, a regular feature of medieval health care. It was preferably performed on a Friday so that one could rest afterward on Saturday. This was already recommended in Talmudic times and is beautifully documented in a detailed letter written by Nathan b. Abraham (later occupying temporarily the post of head of the Jerusalem yeshiva) during a sojourn in Fustat. Having undergone bloodletting on Friday he was unable to attend synagogue service on the Sabbath, but was visited—in the house of a friend—by a huge crowd who stayed all day long; he then intended to set out for the Mediterranean port Tinnīs on Monday.[277] As in Late Antiquity, another aspect of the care after bloodletting was the consumption of wine, enjoyed best in congenial company conducive to reviving the weakened body and the spirits.[278]

Cleanliness as health protection was desired with regard to food products and living quarters, and is listed as one of the virtues of a good housewife.[279] Frequent washing of the hands (more than modern man usually does) was imposed by religion.[280] Anointing the body with sweet-scented oils was considered such a requisite of personal hygiene that as a means of self-castigation it was prohibited on the Day of Atonement, along with food, drink, and washing. In the Geniza we read about these matters in connection with the precious containers of fragrant ointments brought in by brides.[281]

Application of kohl to the eyes was believed by Yemenite men to be a protection against glaring sunlight. Whether this belief and practice were shared by Geniza people who traveled much, or who lived in Fustat and commuted daily to Cairo for work, is not known to me. But one should not forget that the oculist was called *kaḥḥāl,* the one who applies kohl, an indication of the medicinal value of this substance. The tooth powder, *sanūn,* like our toothpastes, seems to have been mainly preventive and widely in use, for in a partnership contract on a pharmacy, dated June 1139, one partner receives for himself the exclusive right to sell this item.[282]

The challenges of weather as reflected in Geniza letters may come as a surprise to the reader. Complaints about oppressive heat and all that goes with it are practically absent, while those about cold and wetness are common. A Sicilian who had come to Egypt in order to study with Moses Maimonides and with Isaac b. Sāsōn of Cairo, Maimonides' peer, writes that despite his long sojourn in the country (where all his children were born and died) he could not bear its hot climate; during the *wakham,* or unhealthy air, prevailing between the Purim and Passover holidays (March–April, now commonly referred to as *khamsīn*), he had fallen seriously ill and wished now to return to his hometown Messina, where his learned father lived.[283] I found no such reports by indigenous Egyptians in the Geniza. One might argue, as a tenth-century observer remarked sarcastically, that the inhabitants of Fustat were used to the bad air of their city and were therefore not harmed by it.[284] But consider the British who are constantly irritated and almost offended by their bad weather. It seems, rather, that the combination of an arid desert climate tempered by the Nile and by the breezes blowing from the Mediterranean (and conducted by the wind catcher into the interior of the houses) made for a certain ease of body and mind. Maimonides and his medical colleagues, including the famous Ibn Jumayᶜ, the Jewish physician in attendance on Saladin, paid much attention to the peculiarities of climate and weather, even of particular cities, such as Alexandria. In private correspondence the topic did not occupy even remotely the place it has (or had) in our own letters.[285]

The frequency of remarks about cold and rain had its cause in their relative rareness, and therefore, in the unpreparedness of the population to meet the challenge by appropriate clothing, housing, and heating (Americans visiting Egypt during wintertime have had similar experiences). The unpaved muddy streets and roads made walking and riding difficult and occasionally impossible.[286]

A few selected items illustrate the widespread sensitivity of the Geniza people to the hardships of the winter season. A merchant from Sunbāṭ, the very heart of the Nile Delta, who claimed to have served the local community by leading it in prayer and otherwise, especially by circumcising the boys of the district, but without any remuneration, tells this story as proof of his selfless dedication. Once, when he learned that a boy who was already three months old was not yet circumcised (it should have been done when he was eight days old), he immediately traveled to the child's place, crossing three canals, *buḥūr,* and that at a time of rain and cold weather; in addition, he donated the things needed for that little ritual operation.[287] Writing from Minyat Ziftā, also in the Nile Delta, a scholar from Fustat admonishes his wife back home not to let their little boy play in the courtyard, where he might be harmed by the cold weather and rain.[288] A man from Alexandria writes to a friend in Fustat that he had set out several times on his way to see him, but had to return because of the rain.[289] Even the mail courier from Alexandria was forced to give up his weekly run to Fustat because of the rain and the storm, *naw*ʾ, and this after he was already one day out.[290] Because of the cold and the frost in Fustat an urgent journey had to be postponed.[291] A real prayer of thanksgiving to God for saving him and his pack animals from the rain on his way from Rosetta (Rashīd) to Alexandria is found in the letter of a merchant after his arrival. Ten consecutive days of rain followed. No one left the house. No business was conducted.[292]

In the subsection on poverty above, the lack of warm covers for the night is noted as a standard complaint in letters of request for help.[293] The same is true with regard to insufficient clothing during a hard winter. A communal official, who says of himself that beggars knocking at doors make more money than he does, reminds the addressee by a discreet allusion to a biblical verse ("the work is much, but it is the season of the rain") that besides money for medication and daily expenses his family was in need of proper clothing.[294] A schoolmaster who also had to beg for medication concludes the story of his misery with the words: "We perish because of our poverty and the cold."[295] A man who mentions himself only by his first name, which means that he was a close acquaintance of the notable whom he addresses, says of himself: "The cold and hunger kill me," but asks only for some "assistance" for the purchase of a *thawb,* a regular robe.[296] Finally, a mother pleading for her imprisoned young son emphasizes that he suffered from cold and mistreatment (in that order).[297] The rainy season in southwest Asia is often mentioned as making travel impossible, or a dangerous hardship, especially if the writers of the letters were Egyptians or persons from a similar climate.[298] I was particularly impressed by this story: When, on a rainy day, the qadi of Ramle, Palestine, ordered a Jewish merchant to proceed to Egypt under the supervision of a guard (which was a costly affair), Muslims and Jews present (in this order) had mercy for him and persuaded the qadi to grant him a stay of fifteen days.[299] Hypersensitivity to cold and wet weather seems still to have been common in our grandparents' day.

Turning now from health care to illness, one finds that the frequency of the latter theme in the Geniza correspondence has its origin partly in practical considerations. As soon as a merchant fell ill and did not show up as usual at the accustomed time and place in the bazaar, rumors or commercial intelligence spread the news in and out of town. One tried to keep one's poor condition secret in order not to disquiet friends or have enemies gloat.[300] Hence the alarmed inquiries about the health of a friend or relative after receiving tidings about him from travelers, or the assumption that he was ill after not having heard from him for longer than usual.[301] Vice versa, one reads assurances that despite the illness about which the correspondent knew, the writer had carried out an errand expected by the correspondents, or that the writer had set out on a planned journey (despite failure of health, which was common on protracted voyages).[302]

Even more common, naturally, are the instances where the authors of business or family letters note with regret that because of poor health the desired actions could not be taken. To give force to the excuse, writers occasionally become quite specific, and the present-day reader is not rarely quite surprised at the duration, seriousness, and spread of a disease.

My letters tarried because I and every other human being in the house were ill. For forty days I have not left the house. My state is now better, and I hope that God will grant me full recovery. In your kind letter you advised me to deliver the bundles of silk to Abū ʿAmr b. al-Baghdādī. Up till now he has not received a thing; I have no one who could transport them. My brother Abū ʿAmr fell ill on the very day he arrived here from Fustat, and I have no one who could do work for me, for sheykh Abu ʾl-Najm and his son [factotums, or partners] are also ill.[303]

The writer of the passage to the nāsī Solomon b. Yishay on an attack by Mongols in 1236, translated above,[304] excuses himself in a letter addressed to the same communal leader for having neglected the service of his master for an unseemly long time:

As for me, I was overtaken by diarrhea, but endured it. However, when it grew and multiplied, the indisposition became a disease and I was treated by a physician, the noble head-physician Doctor[305] Sulayman, the son-in-law of our master, the late R. Menaḥēm [former Jewish chief judge of Cairo]. The medical potions were prepared in the house of R. Menaḥēm every day, from seeds of . . . and others, and my fare was chicken, but the illness recurred. When it finally became easier, I was affected by ophthalmia which was even worse. In the night of Sabbath "Judges"[306] I was overcome by such pain that I screamed throughout the entire night unable to restrain myself. . . . I wished God would afflict my enemies as I was afflicted. Thus my illness became known to everyone. I was unable to bear what I suffered. . . . [May the end be good], if God wills.[307]

Personal misfortune aggravated by stormy times appears, as so often, in this letter of excuse whose writer explains to a business friend with whom he had many common interests why he had not communicated with him for a very long time. When the caliph al-Mustanṣir died in 1094, the powerful viceroy al-Malik al-Afḍal put the caliph's youngest son on the throne, whereupon the eldest, Nizār, fortified himself in Alexandria, claiming the caliphate. A long siege followed, during which the population was forced to bear the cost of the war. These events are echoed in a number of Geniza letters.[308]

I need not tell you, my lord, what happened to me after your departure: six months of grave illness and hopelessness, during four of which I was confined to bed. Everyone had given me up because of the seriousness of the illness and the siege, every day bringing new calamities. I spent for medication—one and a half ounces—1 dirhem daily and for chicken 2 dirhems and had to buy three waybas of wheat.[309] In this way I have passed six months up to this day. On top of this they assessed me at 5 dinars for that forced contribution, may God the exalted punish the one who assessed me thus. Abu ʾl-Faḍl Ibn al-Dhahabī ["Goldsmith"] paid 35 dinars, and they want to get out more from him.[310]

The writer's assertion that he was still sick is borne out by the numerous slips marring a letter otherwise written in good script and correct style. He must have made strong efforts to work for his friend during the two months he was no longer confined to bed, for he has to report about several business and legal affairs settled, and conveys useful commercial intelligence. He does not describe the nature of his illness at all, but emphasizes only its duration, seriousness, and costliness, all apt to explain his long silence.

Literally countless Geniza letters are in the same vein. "For sixty days I was unable to work," and he still writes with difficulty.[311] "With one exception, I could not go out to the bazaar for five months"—and other people in the house were ill as well.[312] A merchant from Fustat was kept back by illness in Constantinople, the capital of Byzantium, for two and a half years.[313]

In family letters, too, the long duration and seriousness of an illness are depicted without details about its character. "She dies before my eyes every day a thousand times," writes Amram b. Isaac of Alexandria about his wife, and a year and six months later: "She is dead upon the earth."[314] Simḥa Kohen of Alexandria complains to his relative, the judge Elijah, that his wife had been bedridden for over a year. Those protracted illnesses probably defied diagnosis.[315]

We should not assume, however, that those people were unable to observe and to report. I render here four descriptions of cases of sickness either of the writer or of a relative, each provided for a definite purpose, evident from the content.

With regard to the first, a patient reporting to his physician, a word must be said about the paper on which the message was written. The slip, about five inches long and two-and-a-half broad, is much torn on the right side. As the configuration of the script shows, most of the damage must already have been present when the note was jotted down. Only a very sick person or a friend (the latter seems to have been the case here) could have permitted himself such disrespect toward the medical profession. The doctor is addressed as Ra'is or chief (namely, of a department in a hospital); this was customary with regard to any physician of some consequence, as far as the Geniza correspondence shows.

A patient reports to his physician

I[n Your name, O] M[erciful]

My lord, the chief physician Abū Riḍā.

May your Excellency take notice that cold and heat have shaken me from Sunday until this hour. I cannot taste anything edible. Yesterday I rolled bread crumbs[316] into two little balls, but after having eaten about a quarter ounce of bread I hiccupped until midnight, and believed the hiccup would never stop.[317] Then my soul desired a bit of fried cheese,[318] but. . . . For three days more [the call of] nature has not come to me.[319] Fever, headache, weakness, and shaking do not leave me all day long. Moreover, I cannot taste anything, not even lemon with sugar. I am also unable to give myself an enema.[320]

So, what do you prescribe for me? I drink very much water.

May your well-being increase and never decrease.

And Peace!"[321]

A husband describes the condition of his sick wife

In a short letter from a provincial town the writer sends thanks for the forwarding of a prescription by one doctor and requests one by another. The latter was perhaps a Muslim or Christian, since the addressee is asked to transcribe the prescription from Arabic into Hebrew letters, although more prominent Jewish physicians might have preferred to write all their prescriptions in Arabic characters. The writer, although the cousin of a prominent judge, does not expect the illustrious physician to come and see his sick wife in person. In a later letter of his to the same addressee he reports that his wife was recovering but that he was advised not to let her stay in the kitchen as long as fire was burning there.[322]

To . . . Nathan ha-Kohen . . . the judge, son of . . . Solomon, the pious, o[f blessed] m[emory],[323]

From his servant Tōviyā ha-Kohen b. Eli, o[f blessed] m[emory]

In Y[our name], O Me[rciful].

Your note, containing the prescription, in which you also inquire about her condition, has arrived. Please kiss the hands of his Excellency, my lord, the illustrious Rayyis Abu ʾl-Bahā, for me. Likewise, favor your servant with the answer to be given by my lord al-Amīn. *May your reward be double.*[324] And please transcribe for me the prescription into Hebrew letters.

She has six attacks[325] during the day and four during the night. Perspiration overcomes her from the sockets of her eyes to her chest. Owing to the high fever she has a feeling that her neck first burns and then becomes cold. At the same time,[326] she suffers pain in her knees. Owing to her grave sufferings her menses have stopped. Finally, because of [her] great anxiety she is affected by mild palpitation of the heart.[327]

The writer (who is known to us through a number of letters preserved) probably knew how to read Arabic, but was not sure that he would be able to decipher the doctor's handwriting (we sometimes have similar problems).

In the preceding two letters relief for a sick person was sought. Consequently, exact and detailed descriptions were necessary. The two missives translated below had different purposes. A father informs the family that his illness was far more prolonged and painful than obviously assumed by them, but emphasizes that he should by no means be given up; he might even appear among them—probably a polite solicitation for an invitation during the forthcoming holidays. The second passage is taken from the long letter of Solomon, son of Abū Zikrī Sijilmāsī Kohen, whose description of the Almohad massacres is translated above.[328] By the detailed information about the state of his health Solomon wished to bring home to his father, who was far away on the India route, that not much initiative could be expected from him in business and other matters. In each case the description of the illness is tailored to the effect intended.

After partial recovery a father describes his state to the family

The letter is written calligraphically, probably because it also contains best wishes for a forthcoming holiday extended to various members of the family and friends. It does not give the impression of having been dictated. The illness concerned seems to have been smallpox.

I need not describe to you my present state after the grave illness experienced by me, so that I despaired of life. My body became completely bloated,[329] then the disease eased a bit; then the blisters[330] covered me even more malignantly than before, and became permanent.[331] I had to lie down, unable to sit up when I wished so. I hated life. Then the Creator chose to grant me health, and a complete turn occurred. Then the pockmarks[332] became apparent on me so that the improvement was not beneficial.

But you [plural] should not think that I am already dead. Do not give me up. So, if the Creator chooses to grant me health, you will see me. Otherwise, nothing can be done.[333]

Detailed wishes for the holiday and an admonition to take good care of an old woman (a grandmother, aunt, or the like) follow. Despite his strong presentiment of death the writer betrays vivid interest in the living. The script seems to be of the eleventh century.

A son informs his father about the state of his health

As for me, after having opened a shop, a great general depression occurred.[334] I was ill for nine months with tertiary fever[335] and fever of the liver. Neither I, nor anyone else believed that I would recover from this. In the wake of the illness difficulties in breathing befell me, which lasted two months. Had I not made up my mind to leave the business, I would have perished.[336] At present, I do nothing, sitting partly in the *qāʿa* [workshop or Bible school] of Joseph and partly in the store of the Son of the Scholar. I study a good part of the night with him every night.[337]

Looking back at these four missives one notices a certain spirit of matter-of-factness in the face of great suffering and even death, a gift for observation, and an endeavor to get and convey exact and definite information. When one writer wishes to have for himself a Hebrew copy of the Arabic prescription, he most probably possessed some knowledge of pharmaceuticals. Such interest of lay persons in medical matters was nothing exceptional in the Geniza society.

The general predilection for graphic detail must also be taken into account. While describing an attack of bandits on a Nile boat anchoring near Dahrūṭ, Upper Egypt, the passenger, Jacob b. Isaiah b. Khalaf, does not content himself with stating that he, his father, and another traveler were wounded by spears, but says: "I was wounded beneath the breast, my father in the forearm, and a Jew from Baghdad in his thigh."[338] A cantor, in a small town, applying to "our lord, *the prince of Israel and their king*" for a raise, provides him with this detail: "I am chronically ill; I am unable to get up from my place even one span of a hand except while screaming with pain; God is my witness; I can pray only while seated."[339] The eccentric Maghrebi India trader, Makhlūf b. Mūsā, writes this to a business friend about his toothache: "*Pangs have seized me like the pangs of a woman in travail, I am too confounded to hear, too frightened to see* [Isaiah 21:3]; because of the illness I cannot go out in the morning or the evening because the cool air makes the pain worse. During the night I pull on a rope crying to God for release from the toothache."[340] As noticed above, people generally tried not to be heard when overcome by pain.[341]

Since the causes of illnesses often remained unknown, it was natural that they were attributed to the First Cause, as the philosophers said, to God. "I do not write about the aggravation of my illness, for this is what God has ordained, and there is no escape from accepting his judgment. May his name be praised."[342] The implication was that illness was a retribution for sin. Popular notions such as the belief that leprosy was caused by opulence and overeating belong here.[343] This disquieting concept is less frequently cited than one would expect (compare Psalms 41:4–5 and others), and then is expressed in standard Hebrew phrases, such as "*because of my many sins.*"[344] One also finds, however, more seriously meant testimonies of this attitude, as when Ṣāliḥ b. Dāʾūd writes this in the midst of a long business letter to Nahray b. Nissīm: "As to the illnesses that have befallen me and their permanence, I ask God to accept my sufferings as an *atonement and to grant me pardon.* While writing these lines, I am unable to . . . the doctor comes to see me every day. I ask God to give you good health and to have mercy on me out of regard for the little ones with whom he has blessed me."[345]

If God is rarely mentioned as the one who "smites and strikes," he is invariably invoked and thanked as the one who "bandages and heals" (Hosea 6:1–2). For God has said: "I am the Lord, your physician" (Exodus 15:26). The miraculous healings reported in the Bible, such as those of Miriam, the sister of Moses (Numeri 12:13–15), or of Hezekiah, the king of Judah (Isaiah 38:1–22), are adduced in letters of good wishes for recovery as encouraging examples of God's healing power.[346]

While a person afflicted by illness might regard his plight as a punishment or atonement, his friends and admirers writing to him would describe it as a visitation by a loving God who tries the pious and saintly who are most near to him. "For him whom the Lord loves he reproves, as a father does to his son in whom he takes delight" (Proverbs 3:12). This and many similar quotations are found in a letter addressed to Abraham b. Yashar, who is none other than the Fatimid "vizier," Abū Saʿd al-Tustari. He was ill and obviously had asked the writer, a Karaite scholar, to compose for him an efficacious prayer. The scholar took King Hezekiah's prayer (Isaiah 38:9–22), enriching each verse with appropriate other Bible quotations. Since Abū Saʿd was murdered while riding on a horse, and did not die of illness, the prayer for recovery must have had the desired result.[347]

This great topic of *sufferings (out) of love,* that is, mutual love, of the loving father probing his child, and the child submitting to the trial with understanding, is often touched upon in Geniza letters as it is in the Talmud. As is perhaps natural, not all types of illness were regarded in the Talmud as sufferings of love, and the same seems to have been the case in the Geniza correspondence. I return to this subject in the disquisition on death.

Because of its ubiquity, and often long duration, illness was one of the most frequent situations in life where we find the individual confronting society. Initially, the indisposed tried to conceal his undesirable state. When the situation endured and became aggravated, however, the patient got to feel how family, friends, and people at large related to him. Constant inquiring about his state, *iftiqād,* was incumbent upon everyone. This is evident from countless Geniza letters where such inquiries are actually made or where writers excuse themselves in various ways for not having done so: they had learned about the sickness only when the addressee had already recovered and visited the bathhouse, or they had had regular reports about his progress from travelers coming from his place and did not wish to inconvenience him with questions; or, to soothe their anxiety, friends would ask for the favor of a special report.[348] When the patient's state had turned for the better, one asks God to make the recovery complete, and, in particular, to guard him from a relapse, for "a relapse is worse than illness," and, indeed, many relapses are reported.[349] One patient writes sarcastically: "I had a relapse only twice."[350]

Concern for the addressee's health had to be expressed not only in words but also in deeds. A man writing a long business letter from Qayrawān, Tunisia, to Egypt, vows to keep fasts and give alms as a "means of intercession for the patient."[351] A mother fasts for her sick son. (Her niece, who tells us about this, remarks that the son's body was covered with harmless scabs and that there was no danger to his life.)[352] A father vowed to abstain from wine and let his hair grow wild like Samson, when his son had an eye disease. (This was a hoax to induce his mother-in-law to visit her daughter.)[353] Public prayers were arranged not only for persons of high social standing (who would be expected to show their gratitude to the communal officials after recovery) but also for a woman of the lower middle class.[354]

The most obvious duty of anyone regarding himself as connected with a sick person was to visit him as often as feasible, shows of concern that were believed also to alleviate the patient's sufferings. (The Talmud says that each visit takes away one sixtieth of the illness; they expected many, many visitors.) A business letter sent from Qayrawān, Tunisia, to Egypt, reports that the Rāv (the highest religious authority in the Tunisian Jewish community), and "the elders," that is, the notables, had visited the writer during his illness often, especially on Sabbaths when such courtesy was particularly welcome. That this detail is emphasized in a letter going overseas shows how important those visits were for the writer's self-respect—and health.[355] A communal official was expected to travel from the countryside to Fustat to pay his respects to the sick Nagid, Sar Shalom ha-Levi. An excuse for failing to do so was—that the writer himself was ill. As a second best, he writes that he prayed for the Nagid, hoping that the prayer might be conducive to his own recovery as well.[356]

The concern for a friend or prominent public figure reached its pinnacle when he recuperated from a serious illness. The letters of congratulations are most effusive, and impress one as sincere. Of one, written (and probably also composed) in rhymed Hebrew prose by the court clerk Mevōrākh b. Nathan, we have two fragments, fifteen plus sixty lines long, respectively. The patient was none other than ʿAzaryāhū b. Ephraim, the head physician, "whose praise is in the mouth of the Muslim doctors"; the day he got up from his sickbed was a day of work stoppage, banquets, and jubilation. "Rejoice, Jerusalem, for God has remembered his people." This verse shows that this physician, like other members of his profession, worked also for the public weal. The letter was written in spring 1172, just after Saladin had taken over Egypt from the Fatimids, when intervention with the new government certainly was needed more than once.[357] As was customary at such banquets, poems in honor of the event were recited. We have one in the Geniza written on the occasion of the recovery of Abraham Maimonides from a grave illness (the Geniza contains several references to his poor health). The poem is jubilant, and praises, of course, also Abraham's illustrious late father, other ancestors, his two sons (who must have been mere boys at that time), and the happy community, for which he had been spared.[358]

One did not wish to be remiss in offering congratulations. A detailed business letter to Nahray is characteristic in this respect. At the end of the letter, the scribe had congratulated him on his recovery from a serious eye disease (often mentioned in the Nahray correspondence; the scribe had learned about its gravity from a traveler). When the sender had read the letter, he asked the scribe to add: "My lord Abū Yaʿqūb also wishes to congratulate you on the healing of your eyes."[359] The pattern of such congratulations is well represented in the opening section of a highly interesting letter of Labrāṭ I, b. Moses I, the Jewish judge of al-Mahdiyya, to Nahray. After having read the bad tidings in Nahray's missives, he had become disquieted and frightened, and passed his sleepless nights in asking God to accept himself as Nahray's ransom and to heal him. He had also passed the news on to "the Light of the World" (the spiritual leader of the Tunisian Jews), who was also very worried about it; his prayer for Nahray, Labrāṭ is confident, would be accepted. Finally, the merchants arriving from Egypt reported that Nahray was well and his eyes restored, whereupon Labrāṭ praised and thanked God. He would be set at rest, however, only by a personal letter from Nahray confirming this happy turn of events.[360]

As we have seen, God was very much present in time of illness. Those assurances of concern were more than conventional phrases. The disability or death of a friend was not only a cause of grief but a material and social loss. The strength of a person was based not only on his own mental and material assets but also on his family and friends, on whom he could rely. And as to the sick person himself, he probably felt insecure with regard to his own merits and worthiness, and even more, God's inscrutable intentions; but one matter was beyond doubt: God's power. He could help and heal—even in the most desperate cases—if he wished so. Whatever the philosophers and theologians of that time might have said about man's ability to influence God's decisions by his deeds, the heart believed that they could be efficacious, that intense and sincere prayer, almsgiving, and fasts could keep catastrophe away.

At the same time, however, even the simplest Geniza person was a member of that hellenized Middle Eastern–Mediterranean society which believed in the power of science. No one had scruples about consulting a physician. One was even eager to know what the books of those renowned ancients had recommended for a sickness diagnosed, and educated laymen occasionally acquired medical treatises. Illness was conceived as a natural phenomenon and, therefore, had to be treated with the means provided by nature. The fact that the Jewish community harbored a disproportionately high percentage of physicians, druggists, and traders in spices and pharmaceuticals might have contributed to the vivid interest and knowledgeability in medications found in the Geniza correspondence.[361] Clearly people often ordered for themselves medications not prescribed for them by a physician but known to them otherwise. Invariably, pious formulas and practical advice or requests mingle in the same letter. Evidently, no conflict was felt between invoking God and relying on nature. When Moses Maimonides put his eloquent chapter on health care, as summarized above, at the beginning of his Code on Jewish Law, he could do so because the Law given by God and the commands of nature were essentially one; both had to be understood and learned by reason. Thus we see that the acute state of illness was apt to present to the Geniza person both the dichotomy and the unity of the world in which he lived. He would not be aware of this, because we do not pay attention to the things surrounding us day in, day out. But his personality was formed by this polarity.

In conclusion, I wish to draw the attention of the reader to two topics which belong here, but which, for reasons presently becoming evident, have not been treated on the preceding pages.

The Geniza correspondence contains considerable material concerning epidemics, plagues, and the like. Plagues in the medieval Middle East have attracted considerable attention of late, but there is no point in discussing the medical and demographic problems mainly connected with this topic here, where we are concerned with how the Geniza person met the challenges of his life.[362] The moot question whether or not the Geniza terminology differentiated between the various types of epidemics may be answered thus: sometimes, when they felt an urge to emphasize the gravity of a disaster, they would heap even four terms together in the same sentence. Epidemics in general seem to be described as "illnesses" related to a town or country (and not a person); the general word for plague was *wabāʾ*, and a particularly bad case, *mawt,* "death."[363] In Hebrew, one also differentiated between "great plague" and "small plague."[364] The word mawt is used in the letter of a community official visiting the provincial town, Minyat Ziftā (mid-twelfth century), in which he reports that ten to twelve persons died every week; it was almost impossible to arrange a proper burial; not ten healthy adult males remained of the congregation, wherefore, no public service was held.[365] A lighter form of epidemic was *wakham,* a kind of sweating sickness, seemingly connected with the climate.[366] In a letter sent from Fustat to Qayrawān, Tunisia, we read this: "A wakham like this I have not seen since I have come to Fustat. I was ill for a full four months with fever and fits of cold, which attacked me day and night. But God, for the sake of his name,[367] not because of my merits, decreed that the illness leave me; I am now restored to complete health. The wakham has ceased, and all our friends [meaning the compatriots from Tunisia] are well."[368] Epidemics of this type also occurred in Alexandria. In a letter sent from there to Fustat, around 1160, the writer reports that everyone in the house was ill because of the great wakham in his place, and wishes that Fustat be spared "those illnesses."[369] Naturally, some persons could be more affected by unhealthy weather than others. In a lovely family letter, addressed to Fustat (early thirteenth century), the writer emphasizes four times that his heart is with "the little one [the recipient's wife] because of the wakham."[370] Sometimes, the writer does not care to define "the illnesses in the town" lest it make business sluggish, or is clearly unable to do so. Thus, a physician who was on the pilgrimage to the tomb of the Prophet Ezekiel in Iraq reports after arriving in the town of Shamṭūniyya that the entire population was affected by an epidemic, that he himself and his boy, too, fell ill, and he describes in detail what happened to the two of them (it seems for the benefit of a relative who was also a physician), but refrains from giving that epidemic a name.[371]

Two of the most distinguished leaders of the Jewish community of Egypt were afflicted by a "great plague." Mevōrākh b. Saadya, the Nagid, died of one in December 1111, together with sixty thousand other persons who perished in that catastrophe in the Muslim year 1111/2. Abraham b. Nathan Av, the Jewish judge of Cairo, barely escaped death.[372] Abraham Maimonides was dangerously ill during the plague of 1216/7. In both cases, contemporary letters use the expression *wabāʾ ʿaẓīm,* already discussed. The passage on Abraham Maimonides provides a striking silhouette of life in a town visited by a plague. The "great plague" referred to cannot be that of 1201/2, for at that time, Abraham was a boy of fifteen, whereas in the lines following here, he is the head of the Egyptian Jews and a physician who regrets being unable to treat his sick daughter. In our letter, however, as in the two others just referred to, the phrase "great plague" is used, and it is likely, although by no means absolutely sure, that the year 1216/7 is meant. The writer of our fragment is the same *nāsī* "from the house of David" whom we have already met repeatedly. He explains to the recipient why he is unable to intercede for him with the Nagid Abraham, or the latter's father-in-law, the chief justice Hananel b. Samuel, or with anyone else.

As to us, our lord, the Rayyis,[373] the Nagid [may his] gl[ory be] in[creased], the chief [Rāv] is seriously ill, may God heal him, and so is his daughter; he is unable to treat her, and confined to his bed; throughout the week he could not get up, neither at night, nor at daytime, which caused him great grief; may God grant him health. Yesterday, I received a note from his father-in-law, our master, Hananel, the chief justice, may his high position endure, saying: "These days are like the Last Judgment; everyone is occupied only with himself."[374] Everyone strives to save himself from the great plague. In Miṣr [Fustat] and Cairo, there is no house belonging to important persons and, in fact, to anyone else, where not one or several persons are ill. People are in great trouble, occupied with themselves and unable to care for others, let alone for strangers in other towns.[375]

In a letter sent early in March 1217 the teacher, cantor, and court clerk Judah b. Aaron Ibn al-ʿAmmānī writes to the Nagid, Abraham Maimonides, how much the community in Alexandria was frightened by his brush with the plague: they held fasts and prayers of intercession, and "did other things" (meaning, probably, public almsgiving or confessions of sins). The letter itself gives an impression of the words used during those assemblies. The letter speaks about "that plague which was in your place" as a matter of the past and not affecting Alexandria. In a text, which is in Arabic, the biblical term *dever* is used, as if it was improper or even dangerous to mention the regular Arabic word.[376] We find the same in another letter from Alexandria, written at the beginning of the most catastrophic period of plagues, famine, and anarchy which Egypt witnessed during the Middle Ages (1065–1072). "We are worried about the *dever* in Fustat, about which we hear." In the same letter and in another missive by the same person, the *nahb al-Maḥalla,* the pillage of that provincial capital, is noted.[377]

The avoidance of the term "plague" in times of great distress (probably in order not to arouse panic, or not to talk of the devil), if such a taboo did, indeed, exist, solves a problem that has occupied me as long as I have been doing Geniza research. Familiar with the graphic descriptions filling the works of Muslim historians describing the period of horror around 1070, I was looking for similar material from private sources. We have, in the Geniza, a good number of letters and documents from this period, and many references to the difficulties of obtaining wheat and other victuals. But there is next to nothing about the plague and famine, and the horrible atrocities connected with them. Perhaps there existed not only a social ban but also a government prohibition against writing about these matters. The silence is too eloquent, too complete, not to invite some tentative explanations.

Since the plague was regarded as an outbreak of God's wrath over the corruption of mankind, or, in any case, as sent by God, the Muslim theologians discussed the problem whether people should flee from it, a doubtful undertaking, as if one could escape God anywhere.[378] Naturally, even pious people did flee. Such a case is reported in a Hebrew letter sent from Jerusalem in later medieval times by a woman calling herself Donna Jamīla, the widow of Judah, addressing two brothers-in-law in Cairo. "The reason for not coming with this caravan [in which the letter was sent] is that the Jews of Damascus who fled from the pest came to me and stay with me, they, their wives and children." She promises to come with the next caravan. The relatives in Cairo certainly knew who was meant by the general term "the Jews of Damascus." Donna Jamīla obviously was not afraid of contagion.[379]

A memorial service in honor of two families who suffered great losses in a plague, which was still raging, may conclude the survey of Geniza material on epidemics. The congregation that paid honor to the mourners is addressed. "May the All Merciful stop the pest, the wrath, and the destroyer[380] from our houses, and your houses, and the houses of his people of Israel. May the maker of breaches wall up this breach,[381] and have mercy with our children and grant consolation to the hearts of these mourners. He who makes peace in his heights [Job 25:2] may bless his people of Israel with peace."[382]

There follow lists of several generations, first of a family of Levis, then one of Kohens (an unusual order), but it should not be assumed that all had perished together in the plague. It was customary to mention ancestors together with the dead for whom the service was held. In addition, a Kohen, already mentioned before, is singled out because of a special prayer for his unmarried daughter, "the chaste rose" (whose name, as usual, is withheld). The usual prayers for the dead (may they rest in peace, be united with the pious in Paradise, and soon be resurrected) follow. The ceremony concludes with a general confession of sins ("You, God, are justified in having brought all this upon us, for you have acted faithfully and we—wickedly" [Nehemiah 9:33]), and thanks to the congregation for their attendance, which was regarded as a deed of charity.[383]

Since the epidemics followed one another in intervals of comparative shortness,[384] the disruption of life, the horrors and panics, and the frightening losses must have contributed to a certain measure of nervousness discernible in the Geniza person. This is apparent also in another phenomenon not treated above: the frequency of reports about the adverse effect of mental excitement on bodily health. Many years ago, when I read Moses Maimonides' words about how he became bedridden for a year after having received the tidings of the death of his beloved younger brother, I believed that only such a sensitive, great man could react like this; the study of the Geniza convinced me that in this, as in other respects, Maimonides was a child of his time and society.[385] I return to this topic in the subsection "Moods" (p. 241, below).

Old Age.—In biblical and later Hebrew and in classical and Christian Greek, as well as in Arabic, the word *old* carried with it the connotation of "experienced," a quality that entitled its bearer to guide the family and others with advice and directions:

> Let days speak
> And many years teach wisdom [Job 32:7].

This leadership in counseling conferred authority and invited respect, and even reverence. The ancient Oriental wisdom,

> The glory of young men is their strength
> and the honor of old men is their gray hair [Proverbs 20:29]

found its legal expression in commandments such as

> Rise up in the presence of gray hair
> and honor the face of an old man [Leviticus 19:32],

and, of course, in the fifth of the Ten Commandments,

> Honor your father and your mother.

Commandments were necessary, for honoring the old is not the natural way of things. As an ancient Aramaic maxim says, "A father loves his sons, but his sons love their own sons [and not him]."[386] It took the ancient Near East and the three monotheistic religions uncounted centuries until the natural, animal attitude toward old age was replaced or mitigated by a more civilized relationship, honoring experience and the authority carried by it. Authority is a tenuous, almost enigmatic social phenomenon. Why, in a traditional society, do fully grown, strong men bow to directives given to them by their toothless elders? Because they themselves will be, after a few decades, in the same situation?[387] As far as I was able to observe in the Yemenite society decades ago, the reverence for the elderly was dictated by religious awe, and much depended on personal circumstances. Animal instincts were always present within the religious civilization. Needless to say, the same was true of the Geniza world.

The term "old man" as an honorific title (Heb. *zāqēn*, Ar. *shaykh*), describing its bearer as occupying a certain social position and mostly also as exercising certain communal functions, is rendered in this book by English "elder." See the subsection "Relationships between grown-up children and their parents" in *Med. Soc.*, III, 240–248, as well as the discussion of the duties and prerogatives of "elders" in the Geniza society in *Med. Soc.*, II, 58–61, especially the term "old young man," meaning a person possessing the social rank of an elder without physically having attained old age. For the ancient use of *zāqēn* in the meaning of distinguished scholar, see p. 265.

A most important factor in the appreciation of old age people is their proportion to the total population. Does the Geniza supply an answer to this question? I believe it does, and most tangibly. We possess the names of literally thousands of persons, appearing either as signatories or otherwise in documents or letters. In the vast majority of cases, I should say, eighty-five percent, the fathers of these persons are eulogized as dead. This means that most of the people appearing in the Geniza as grown-ups attending to their daily affairs had already lost their fathers. To this must be added that court clerks or letter writers often did not know, or care, whether or not a person's father was alive; even in personally signed papers we find occasionally that a person omits the blessing to be said over a dead father, especially when considerable time had lapsed since the death. At marriage, the two spouses, especially the bride, were usually very young. Yet, in many instances, the fathers of the bride or groom, or both, are noted as dead. The extraordinary predominance in the Geniza of the brother assuming the role of protector of his sister in disputes with her husband is to be explained by the fact that the father had died at an early age and the brother substituted for him.[388]

Documents signed by a large number of persons are of particular interest. A power of attorney issued in the Mediterranean port city of Tinnīs is signed by eight persons, all mentioning their fathers as dead. Their handwriting, with the exception of that of the judge, betrays the signatories as ordinary people.[389] In another power of attorney written in Ramle, Palestine, in the fall of 1056, all six signatories add a blessing upon the dead to the names of their fathers.[390] Of twenty-six persons signing a petition to a Nagid from a small town, eighteen mention their fathers as dead, three as living, seven refused to sign, three were out of town, and in five cases that detail is not preserved. Thus, most of the heads of households in that small place had lost their fathers. Their handwriting is shaky, which shows that they were uneducated persons.[391]

In view of the scarcity of demographic details about the life of the common people during the High Middle Ages, a comprehensive study of this phenomenon of the dead fathers seems to be desirable. Each detail must be thoroughly investigated and weighed, and the whole computerized. So much, however, may be said even now: The percentage of old people in the Geniza society was very much reduced, and probably not much different from that prevailing in ancient Greece, so meticulously studied by Bessie Ellen Richardson in her analysis of the epigraphic evidence. Her examination of 2,022 funeral inscriptions showed that forty-nine percent, practically one-half of the population, died between the ages of sixteen and forty, the period during which most fathers sired their sons. Only sixteen percent reached the age of fifty, and only five that of seventy. Since the conditions of climate, nourishment, and clothing were similar around the Mediterranean, and since Greek medical art was available also in the more advanced Muslim countries, it is likely that conditions were similar in the Geniza area.[392]

In medieval Hebrew poetry, old age began at fifty. A famous poem by Judah ha-Levi, written most probably in 1140, opens with these lines:

> Chasing after youth at fifty
> when your days are about to vanish?![393]

His younger contemporary, Abraham Ibn Ezra, is even more outspoken:

> At fifty man remembers life's futility,
> and mourns, for mourning is near.
> He despises the pleasures of this world
> and fears that his hour has come.[394]

A century earlier, Samuel ha-Nagid strikes a similar chord.[395] In the Geniza, age is rarely indicated by number, for numbers, as noted, were ominous. A schoolmaster from Tunisia, who had taught a Bible class in Alexandria together with his son, writes after the latter's death: "I cannot teach alone, for I am sixty" (although in those days classes were often very small).[396] Amram b. Isaac, the relative of the noble India trader Ḥalfōn b. Nethanel, paints an excellent picture of old age in his verbose letters. Quoting Judah ha-Levi (who then was visiting Alexandria), and alluding, of course, to himself, he writes: "Our master—may he live forever—has rightly said: a man who has reached the decade of his seventies—no one listens to his words and no one pays attention to his advice, *let him return to his origin*" (the earth [Genesis 3:19]).[397] When it is said of a "very old" woman that her age was seventy-five, the number is introduced only to emphasize how extremely old she is.[398]

In view of the richness of information about illness in the Geniza, one is surprised to read comparatively little about the infirmities of old age. In requests for help, the writer's senectitude is often mentioned, but he or she rarely goes into detail. There was no need for it. Illness is an individual affliction; the defects of old age are ubiquitous. And can the description of "the evil days," "the unpleasant years," in Ecclesiastes, chapter 12, be bettered by anyone? A characteristic complaint was the lack of *nahḍa,* "get-up-and-go," of resolve, of initiative. A scholar from Baghdad complains to his colleague in Cairo: "I am really pitiable, of little nahḍa. I don't dare to buy books and have no nahḍa for copying some."[399] The lack of nahḍa is lamented also with regard to less noble aims. Women, the workers in the house, complain about weakness and inability to do their chores.[400] Here is a description of old age in the hand of Solomon b. Judah Gaon, the president of the Jerusalem yeshiva and official head of the Jews of the Fatimid empire, written nineteen years before his death. The time was excruciating for him: things in the yeshiva and the community at large did not go according to his wishes. Abraham b. Sahlān, a leader of Egyptian Jewry, Solomon's "peer,"[401] with whom he had probably studied many years before, had just died, and his own son was on his way to Aleppo in northern Syria, a voyage fraught with danger:

> I am a descending sun, soon to set. My soul is very much depressed since my peer passed away, may he rest in Eden. I ask God only to keep me alive through this year so that people should not say: "Both died within one year."
>
> Take notice, my dear, that I am going about like a shadow [cf. Psalms 39:7]. I have no authority, only the title. My strength is gone, my knee is feeble, and my foot staggers. My eyes are dim, and, when I write, it is as if I was learning it, sometimes the lines are straight and sometimes crooked, and so is my style, because my mind is disturbed since the day my beloved [son] traveled to Aleppo to fetch some goods he had left there. I pray to God to bring him back in safety "before I depart and be no more" [Psalms 39:14].[402]

Similar litanies, including the simile of the setting sun, are found in other letters of Solomon b. Judah.[403] But old age, like life in general, has its ups and downs: the rich correspondence of the Gaon shows him as being active in affairs and rich in style during the long years following the passage translated above, although a premonition of death is certainly felt in it.

Who took care of the elderly in those days? As the Geniza seems to show—the elderly themselves, for the most part. Those with means saw to it that their resources were ready for use when they retired, whether in hard coin safely buried in the ground or in promissory notes so that the capital was still working. Rights to real estate were fixed in legally binding contracts.[404] Some went further. A Persian Karaite who wished to dedicate himself to devotion during his declining days entrusted "all his treasures" to three reliable merchants, who took complete control of them without demanding any remuneration, acting "solely for God's sake." No written contract seems to have been made, although the arrangement remained in force "for many years." When the old man suddenly died without having made a will, the three trustees took part in the additional task of distributing the estate among the four sons of the deceased and in administering the shares of two of them who had not yet attained maturity.[405]

That happened in summer 1004. I wonder whether a deathbed declaration appointing five executors made two hundred years later (1201) in Alexandria was not made under similar circumstances, meaning that the newly appointed executives had taken care of the dying man's property during the last years of his life.[406] When a father provided for two minor daughters (probably from a second marriage) by handing over to a trusted merchant the sums he had earmarked for them, on condition that he himself could never take back the money, such action must be regarded as a provision for old age, namely, freeing oneself from obligations that one might not be able to fulfill in later years.[407]

Persons with limited means and lacking the support of a strong family made arrangements similar in certain respects to an insurance contract. In the subsection on the socioeconomic conditions of housing, I gave examples of parts of a house given by old men and women to a person whom they trusted on condition that they themselves would be maintained as long as they lived and would receive a proper funeral when they died. Conditions naturally differed widely according to the circumstances. Thus, in a deed of gift of real estate to a woman, she was only obliged "to serve" the donor, that is, to do for him what a wife would do for her husband (a kind of "homemaker" agreement).[408]

A full-fledged legal document of fifty-four long lines from summer 1122, contains this characteristic story. Elazar, an old man from Tripoli (probably Lebanon), appears in court and declares himself no longer able to work and earn a living. Ṣedāqā, a distant relative, also a native of Tripoli, had admitted Elazar to his house out of family sentiment and consideration for a compatriot and out of his charitable and noble character; and he desired to acquire a religious merit. Now he, Elazar, gives Ṣedāqā all he possesses, about 50 dinars, of which 14 dinars in cash were deposited with the knowledge of the court, earmarked for funeral expenses, while the rest consisted of promissory notes provided by six different persons. Besides this and the clothing on his body, Elazar possessed nothing (except a quarter dinar to be given as a compensation to presumptive heirs [see below]). Ṣedāqā would have free hand over all Elazar's possessions, including the 14 dinars in cash, for the latter trusted him to choose the appropriate type of funeral. A sum of 50 dinars was by no means negligible in those days. This gift gave the old man the satisfaction of enjoying good care by right and not merely as a deed of philanthropy.[409]

Such arrangements were also made on an impersonal but businesslike basis. The judge Nathan b. Samuel he-Ḥaver kept a kind of hospice for old and sick people. A woman gave him her savings of 17 dinars on condition that he maintain her and arrange her funeral.[410] A merchant of means made a legal declaration in Nathan's place a day before his death, detailing his wishes for his funeral attire. The circumstances make it clear that the dying man had stayed with Nathan under a contract in which the latter was obliged to provide him with a dignified funeral.[411] We have found Nathan's colleague Nathan b. Solomon ha-Kohen in a similar role.[412] Both were refugees from Syro-Palestine and probably needed additional income. As judges, they enjoyed trust and were able to solicit funds for those in their places who were unable to pay, especially for medical expenses.[413]

Even between closest relatives such contractual safeguards for the elderly were by no means rare. Here is a typical example. The widow of a grocer gives to her son a quarter of a house which she had received from the estate of her late (certainly second or third) husband, retaining for herself one eighth (which she probably had inherited earlier). Against this, her son would maintain her for the rest of her life. If she preferred to separate from him, he would have to pay her half a dirhem per day. Failing to carry out these conditions, the son would have forfeited the gift.[414] An even more detailed contract between a mother and her daughter and son-in-law conveys to the daughter part of a house on condition that the mother should never be separated from her daughter while the son-in-law would take care of medical expenses and the burial. The mother retained for herself the income from another part of the house for the forthcoming five years.[415]

The maintenance of old parents by their children was a moral obligation, not a legal one. The Talmudic maxim "One compels the son to maintain his father" was a means of protection for the community so that persons who possessed the necessary means should not devolve their filial duties to public charity. Fathers were reluctant to bring their sons to court. "You know what I am suffering from the quarrel with the blessed son Abū Manṣūr, who does not pay attention to what I say, and does not accept advice from me. This is a misfortune which only God can right. If I bring him to court, it is my son whom I bring to court."[416] In a large draft from the year 1232, a man undertakes to provide his father with food and drink and, above all, the money for the poll tax, either reduced, as it was paid then, or in full (emphasized three times). All this was done "for God's sake," that is, voluntarily. The old man had traveled widely on business and was now too exhausted for regular work.[417]

As a rule, a widow lived in the house of her son, actually in the home she created during her married life, for a son usually inherited the house of his father. Even noble families, however, deviated from this rule; elderly widows often stayed with distant relatives or elsewhere.[418] The situation of the father—so long as he did not remain pater familias, or head of the household—was even more complicated. Old men rarely stayed unmarried. Thus, there often arises the question of several nuclear families living in one place, and it seems that often the old couple preferred (or was forced by the circumstances) to live separately. Hence we often find a father sojourning (with a second or third wife) in a town other than the domicile of his sons and complaining about being without news from them or being otherwise neglected by them.

Such complaints are numerous. A mother with a Greek name, writing from al-Mahdiyya, Tunisia, notes that her son has forsaken her for eight years. Another mother wonders how her daughter could have forgotten the education given to her and left her mother without a letter for seven years. Even Moses Maimonides' sister uses bitter words about her son who had disappeared "as if he had fallen into a well," and requests her illustrious brother to find the young man and remind him of his duties. A father goes so far as to disinherit his younger daughter and her husband (compensating them with the proverbial quarter dinar) because they left him without clothing and food during a grave illness.[419]

Remoteness in habitation did not always mean "out of mind." An old man who had retired to Jerusalem, where a young son of his, born to him late in life, died, thanks another son in Cairo for sending him a precious piece of clothing (which had to be sold, however, to cover medical expenses for the dying boy); meanwhile, much time had passed, and the father implores the son to make an effort to travel to the Holy City so that he might enjoy his company before departing life.[420] We find sons inviting their old fathers; one father, married for the third time, had three married sons and one married grandson; they ask him to come and stay with them (with the eldest brother, it seems) "so that you may be happy while being with them for the rest of your days."[421]

The frequency of complaints about neglect should not induce us to believe that the Geniza people were generally lacking in filial piety. When old parents lived with their children, and were cared for by them, there was no need to write letters or to draw up documents. The latter was done only in special cases when their rights had to be safeguarded, as when parents had given a house to one of their children, but stipulated that they (and another child) should have the right to live there if they wished to do so.[422] It must be noted, however, that such unhappy attitudes toward the elderly were by no means confined to the poor classes. I was particularly moved by the letter of a father reproaching a friend with whom his son stayed (probably as his employee) for being remiss in reminding the young man of his filial duties. His mother had died of grief because the son failed to write or inquire after her. The letter was written in Arabic characters by a Jewish religious scholar, which seems to mean that the recipient was a government official or the like, for whom it was easier to skim Arabic script than the rather clumsy Hebrew letters.[423]

I conclude this survey of attitudes toward old age with two documents, one a monstrosity of hard-heartedness and neglect, hopefully rare, but certainly not entirely exceptional, and another one with a warm, human touch, probably representing the generally accepted moral standards.

The first is the story of an old, blind woman, mother of several sons and grandsons, who had certainly once seen better days, since her late daughter left an "estate" and other things. The letter is addressed to the Gaon Maṣlīaḥ (1127–1138) and represents a refreshing mixture of the accomplished style of a court clerk and the woman's *ipsissima verba.* After eight lines of biblical quotations and an introduction in Hebrew, the letter continues:

> I wish to inform your high excellency that I am a blind woman. For a long time, I have been sitting in a corner [forsaken], with no access to this world [no regular income], but as long as my daughter lived, she was always around me and cared for me. Now she has died, and her brothers and their sons have taken what she possessed. My son, Abraham, the firstborn, took the estate, and has not provided me with anything since she died, not even a loaf of bread.
>
> I have now entrusted my spirit to God, the exalted, and to you [singular]. Shout at him and tell him that he should give me what is indispensable.
>
> May the Holy One never let fail your strength and may he guard you from the blows of Fate, such as blindness and indigence, and *shield you under the shelter of his wings.*[424]

The second example was chosen from similar documents because its writer is known to us for a period of at least forty-two years, if not much more, so that his milieu, too, is quite known. He was a scion of the Ibn Nufay^{c} family, which can be traced in Geniza documents through two centuries, mostly connected with Alexandria. The letter was written in Tyre, Lebanon, on October 28, 1090, that is, not long before the advent of the Crusaders. Tyre was at that time the seat of the Jerusalem yeshiva, which was transferred there after the capture of the Holy City by the Seljuks. Our writer served as cantor (who led the community in prayer), as notary, and probably also as a schoolmaster in the small Jewish community of Jubayl, north of Beirut, the ancient Byblos. He traveled to other port cities of Lebanon and Palestine in order to make some money by singing at weddings, circumcisions, and other festive occasions, but in particular, to Tyre, the seat of the yeshiva, where he intended to marry the girl he had betrothed.

The main purpose of his writing was to ask his father's indulgence for accepting a post so far away from him, for a son should always be with his father and serve him (Malachi 3:17). It was not his fault, but dire necessity (or God, as he says) which forced him to be away, and he would return to Fustat as soon as possible. Even more, he would marry an orphan girl without a penny with the sole intention that no other family ties should keep him from returning to Egypt and to his filial duties toward his father. For in order to protect the newly wed, it was common practice to keep her in the place of her parents, brothers, or other close relatives. The biographical data about the writer stretch from his school days, when he filled in the hollow letters in exercise books with colors, his first acquaintance with the scribal arts, to the year 1132 (forty-two years after the writing of our letter), when he occupied the post of chief cantor, and court clerk in Alexandria. The persons greeted or otherwise mentioned in our letter show our young man moving in the circles of religious divines, government officials, and prominent merchants.

A son should always be in attendance upon his father[425]
A Letter from Tyre, 1090

[*Address* (*verso*):]

To my father, whom I love, my lord, the elder Abū [Naṣ]r Salāma b. Saʿīd, known as Ibn Nufayʿ. [May God prolong his life] and make his honored position permanent.

His son—may he be made his ransom.[426]

[*Text* (*recto*):]

I am writing to you, my father—may God prolong your life, make permanent your honored position and his support for you, and smash your enemies—from Tyre. I am well and healthy, thank God, the Lord of the [worlds]. I strongly yearn after you, may God unite us in his mercy if [he wills].[427]

This is to inform you that on the day I am writing these [lines, I intend to] depart for Acre, to make there some earnings, and to return if God [wills to Tyre] for marrying here the one whom I have betrothed and to stay h[ere a few days more]. I have sent you a letter with the son of the elder Abū Naṣr Ju[dah] of Damascus, in which I informed you about what was agreed upon in Jubayl, [namely] that they have fixed emoluments for me which are sufficient for me and my house [i.e., wife] and all tha[t I need].

I deeply regret that we are separated. I must work for our reunion. I must go up[428] and be [together with you]. Please remember me in your pious prayers.[429] God knows that it was not I who desired the separation. God is witness be[tween us; it was he] who withheld sustenance from me and separated us. The life of a young man who is idle and without proper earnings and the company of friends is worthless to me. I t[ried] to go up to you, but was not able to do so, lest you might worry.

And I have joined myself to an orphan girl who does not possess a penny, solely with the intention that she would be ready to travel with me to Miṣr [Fustat].

I entreat you again never to cease p[raying for me, for] all the time I experience the dangers of sea voyages. Always send your l[etters] for me to Tyre, to his excellency, my lord, the President [of the yeshiva] for he will forward them to me to J[ubayl].

[Greetings are extended here to an overseer of the caliphal mint, to a representative of merchants, to a head cantor, and a fourth person, whose name has not been preserved].

Written today, the first of the month of Ramadan 483.[430]

The main theme of old age in the Geniza, as fitting a mercantile society, was: "Old age—a success story." "May your end be blessed even more than your beginnings." This good wish addressed to the elderly illustrates the situation. It is taken from the Book of Job, 42:12, and summarizes its story: a life of vicissitudes and sufferings, of steadfastness and virtue is crowned by the heavenly blessing of a successful old age.[431] The abbreviated form of the wish "May God grant you *a good end*" retained the biblical phrase.[432] One expressed the same idea in Arabic: "Respectful greetings to the illustrious lady, may God make her concluding days beautiful."[433]

A business, inherited or newly created, after many ups and downs, justified the efforts invested: safe provisions had been put aside for the family and for the old man himself; he lived in his own house, blessed with children and grandchildren. Old friends, the witnesses of his youth, who, as children "read" (i.e., studied) the Scriptures and other religious writings together with him under the guidance of a revered master, were still around, creating the pleasant illusion of the permanence of life. Honorific titles that expressed the philanthropy, public service, or learnedness of the old man bestowed on him by the community, the Jewish authorities, or government agencies had been accumulated during a lifetime and were constantly used in public when the thus honored was called up to read holy texts during the synagogue service. The highest gratification of old age was a congenial son or an attentive disciple, as we witness in the correspondence of Nahray b. Nissim or Moses Maimonides.[434]

The aged head of the family retained the management of his business and the domestic affairs. Joseph Ibn ʿAwkal, the dominant figure in the mercantile Geniza correspondence of the first third of the eleventh century, had three sons. One or more of them are regularly greeted in letters addressed to him. But the conduct of the business, as we are able to observe through four decades, was clearly in his own hand. Nahray b. Nissīm, whose correspondence stretches over fifty years (1045–1096), remains active in business as well as private and communal affairs until his death. Maḍmūn b. Ḥasan, representative of merchants in Aden, South Arabia, the pivot of the Jewish India trade during the first half of the twelfth century, had two sons who became his successors. But during his lifetime and to his very end, all correspondence is addressed to, and seemingly also handled by, him in person. Similar observations can be made with regard to less important merchants.[435] A fragmentary letter contains this outcry: "I have been in business for sixty years, and even when I was still a beardless youth, no one demanded from me an oath. Now these people want to impose an oath on me." It was taken for granted that advanced age was more reliable than youth.[436]

The study of old age in ancient Greece analyzed above showed that only five percent of the population, that is, one out of twenty persons, reached the age of seventy.[437] It was assumed that a similar percentage prevailed in the Geniza society. It is likely that most or many of those who reached that exceptional state were also exceptionally well fit. The most conspicuous example of vigorous old age is presented by Hay Gaon, the head of the Pumbeditha yeshiva of Baghdad, who happened to be the prominent leader of the Jewish world in the first third of the eleventh century. Many of his writings have been preserved. He died in 1038 at the age of ninety-nine. (His father and immediate predecessor Sherira Gaon also died in his nineties.) We have a letter written by Hay, a few months before his death, whose script, style, and content betray astounding vitality. His ecumenical standing may be gauged from these lines in an elegy on him, written by the then leader of Spanish Jewry Samuel ha-Nagid:

> And though he departed without leaving a son
> he has [spiritual] children all over the lands of Islam and Christendom.[438]

Hay's contemporary, Dosa, head of the rival Nehardea School of Baghdad, had to wait seventy-one years before his turn came to succeed his father, the eminent Saadya Gaon, in 1013; he managed to occupy the office for four years, during which he was able to assure his followers in faraway Qayrawān, Tunisia, that he enjoyed good health.[439] The Gaon of the Palestinian yeshiva Elijah ha-Kohen b. Solomon succeeded his father about forty years after the latter's death, held the post for twenty-one years, and was privileged to install his son as successor while still serving himself.[440] Arabic literature provides numerous examples of writers and scholars, active in their eighties, and there is no difficulty in finding outstanding examples of longevity in ancient Greece. Sophocles, the tragic poet, died in his nineties (and his most important tragedies were written after fifty), and Plato at eighty-one. Zeno, the head of the stoic school of philosophy and ethics, reached ninety-eight.[441]

In the Bible-oriented society of the Geniza, good old age was the natural reward for (and, therefore, proof of) a virtuous life. "Abraham was old, well advanced in years, and God has blessed him with everything" (Genesis 24:1). Senectitude was not a horror (as it was to so many Greeks) but a crown of dignity, to be worn with pride, albeit often weighing heavily upon its bearer. The Psalm opening the Sabbath service (and, therefore, known to everyone by heart), concludes with this praise of old age:

> The pious flourish like the palm tree
> And grow like a cedar in Lebanon.
> They bring forth fruit in old age.
> They are full of sap and freshness
> [Psalms 92:13,15]

3. Death

Expectations and preparations.—

My God! The soul you put into me is pure.[1]

You created, you formed, you breathed it into me, and preserve it within me.

You will take it away from me and give it back to me at some future time.

As long as the soul is in me, I am grateful to you, my God and God of my fathers, lord of all creations, and master of all souls.

Blessed be you, O Lord, who gives back souls to dead bodies.[2]

This opening benediction of the Jewish morning prayer is a response to the miracle of the nightly separation of body and soul and their reunification after awakening in the morning. The new day begins with a review of the entire life cycle of an individual's soul. The end is not the horror of the Last Judgment but resembles the beginning: the soul as a gift of God, for which man has to show his gratitude in word and deed.

So staunch an assertion of the belief in the continuity of the body-soul coexistence—despite the obscurities, contradictions, and glaring impossibilities contained in it—colored all ideas and images of life after death, in "the twaddles of old women" as in the minutiae of the theologians. It was a long way to go, for which many preparations were required.

An announcement of an actual case of death, an exemplary death, gives us an idea of how the belief formulated in that prayer found its expression in the Geniza milieu. The announcement was sent from Tunisia to a compatriot in Egypt at an extraordinary time: the Arab Hilāl tribes had pillaged and partly destroyed Qayrawān and other Tunisian cities (1057); their population had been robbed and dispersed. The writer wonders whether Armageddon, "the End of Days," prophesied in the Bible, was not already under way, or something even worse. He himself had lost all that had been accumulated by his father and himself. In the midst of all those upheavals, this model picture of a peaceful demise opens his letter:

I beg to inform you, my brother and lord, may God keep you alive, may he grant you life, *and list you in the Book of Life,*[3] that on top of our captivity, dispersion, general collapse, and the destruction of our dwellings, God has signed [confirmed] the register of our sins *by taking away from us the crown of our head and accepted into the Garden of Eden* the noble elder, *the pious, good, and upright perfect saint,* Mr. Barhūn b. R. Moses. I am sorry to tell you that his death—*may he be remembered with blessings*—has hit us all at the time which I have described to you before. He has gone away *to the Garden of Eden because of our wickedness, we who are shamefully stripped of all merits.*

He left a complete, full will, appointing his brother, Joseph—*may God add to his days and years*[4]—the illustrious elder, *the pure, pious, blameless, manly, unique,* as executor of all his affairs and guardian of his son, *may he live forever, flourish and prosper, grow and multiply, and may the Scripture be fulfilled which says: A righteous man who walks in his integrity—blessed are his sons after him* [Proverbs 20:7].

The death occurred on Friday morning, and he rested in his tomb already in the night of the Sabbath [Friday night], as befitting *a perfect saint.* The beauty of his cortege and burial—everyone—except us[5]—would wish such ones for himself. But we could not find any consolation. May God strengthen our hearts and leave us his son, Moses, *may he live forever.*

I informed you of this so that you should know to what extent disaster has struck us.[6]

The deceased, Barhūn (Abraham) b. Moses, was a highly respected member of the Tāhertī family, the most prominent one in the Jewish community of Qayrawān. The writer and recipient of our letter were related to them. Barhūn is described as *a perfect saint,* a very exceptional epithet.[7] Thus his immediate admission to Paradise is taken for granted. This image of postmortem reward for a good life is, however, somewhat blurred by another: peaceful rest in the tomb. As befitting a saint, Barhūn died on the eve of the Sabbath, so that he could immediately enter the Sabbath rest in the life to come.[8] The idea behind this is that the body in the tomb is not entirely devoid of life; they could not accept that he should immediately lose all contact with this world.

Despite the turbulent times, Barhūn was privileged to complete in full the most important preparation for his departure: the settling of all his affairs in this world and entrusting his minor son to his equally esteemed brother, with whom he had cooperated all his life, as their preserved correspondence shows. Moreover, his funeral was splendid. (He must have enjoyed it; have not the sages warned the orators at burials to tell only the truth, for the man carried to his tomb might listen to what they say.)

From beginning to end, this announcement is dominated by the communal aspect of death. The bereavement is regarded as a punishment of the community for its long list of sins; not only that, its wickedness was the very cause of Barhūn's death (seemingly untimely: he left a minor son). Death and its sufferings were regarded as an atonement for sins. The idea of dying a natural death, and not during disturbances, plague, famine, and the like, was expressed by the phrase, *he died because of his sins* (Numbers 27:3). Since Barhūn was "a perfect saint," his demise must have been a vicarious sacrifice for the community.[9]

With this concept of death as punishment and expiation as related to human behavior, competed the contradictory idea of death as a fixed term, predestined (by God), in Arabic *al-ajal* (*al-maḥtūm*), an inconsistency seemingly not felt by the rank and file.[10]

The idea obviously was already present in biblical times, as phrases such as "I shall make full the number of your days" (Exodus 23:26), or "years of life will be added for you" (Proverbs 9:11), echoed in Geniza letters, show.[11] In Late Antiquity, when astrology became all-pervasive, it was taken for granted: "Plague persisted for seven years, but no one whose time had not come died."[12] The term "fixed end," *ajal,* is common in the Qurʾān, and the (originally Greek) entire phraseology connected with it is Islamic.[13] Thus, it seems that Moses Maimonides was right in claiming, in a special responsum dedicated to the subject, that the idea of a predetermined life span, although in vogue among his contemporaries, was essentially foreign to Judaism.[14]

Many years ago, I was told that the Jews of Yemen did not like to be reminded of death. One out of a hundred made a will. In contrast, a Muslim, even if he suffered only from a common cold, would send for the local *faqīh* (divine, schoolmaster, and clerk) and have him write a testament. At that time, I was inclined to believe that this contrast was general in the Middle East and foreshadowed in the Qurʾān, Sura 2:96, where the "Children of Israel" (a term that often included the Christians) are described as being more avid of life than anyone else.[15] But the Prophet of Islam himself died without leaving a will, and Islamic religious doctrine was of divided opinion whether dispositions in the face of death were meritorious or condemnable.

In reality, no fundamental divergence on this point should be ascribed to the two religious communities. Jewish and Islamic laws on wills are essentially identical. Neither knows the Roman or modern idea of a unilateral testament, but both recognize dispositions made during a terminal illness or in similar situations and dealing mainly with the appointment of executors and the distribution of legacies.[16] These laws reflect a society that trusted living persons more than written documents, which had a certain aversion to stocktaking and accounting,[17] and, last but not least, was bound by God-given laws regulating man's inheritance not to be tampered with.

But men did tamper. Wills were made in order to mitigate or evade altogether the rigors of the traditional religious legislation; they expressed the realities and notions of the contemporary society and, of course, the personal circumstances and wishes of the individual concerned.[18]

With regard to wills, Jewish law was more liberal than Islamic (which, for instance, permits the testator[19] to dispose of only one third of his possessions), the reason being, I believe, that the Qurʾān contains a far more detailed legislation on inheritance than the Hebrew Bible. Thus, freedom of disposition was limited by a written law to a far higher degree in Islam than in Judaism.[20]

Anyhow, the testimony of the Geniza overwhelmingly proves that, in those days and places, making dispositions in contemplation of death was general practice. Everyone—man and woman, rich and poor, learned and plain—seems to have been eager to put his house in order before leaving this world. The mass of such dispositions preserved, differing widely in legal character, content, and scope, is indeed astounding. To have died leaving "a complete and perfect will" was praised as an indication of the worthiness and efficiency of a pious and well-to-do merchant; to have died without a will was noted as something special and leading to complications; after recovery, a person would report that he had made a will, in order to emphasize the seriousness of his illness.[21]

The first and main group of relevant Geniza papers consists of wills made during a terminal illness. The document opens with the statement that the witnesses had found the person involved "ill, lying on his bed," but capable of making legally valid declarations "like anyone else walking on his feet in the market." If complete, the record usually concludes with the assurance that the patient had died "from his [that is, this] illness."[22] Where no such remarks are made, the document represents notes taken by a clerk at the time of the declaration, later to be put to paper properly in a juridically acceptable form. Deletions and additions, as well as the absence of the names of witnesses, dates, and signatures, are characteristic of such papers.[23]

It is remarkable that those people were able to make detailed and exact declarations, often containing many names, sums, and descriptions, only a short time before they died. A sugar merchant makes a rather complicated will on Saturday and dies on Sunday, "the day after," as the document states.[24] A physician, who had left the unusually high sums of 500 and 200 dinars for charitable purposes, explains to a visitor a day before his death that the numbers were written in codes in order to protect the gifts from high-handed government officials.[25] Two wills written by the renowned court clerk Ḥalfōn b. Manasse in 1113 and 1126, respectively, one for a man and another for a woman, were made two days before the testator's demise.[26] On a Saturday night, a man in Bilbays, Lower Egypt, willed his wife 40 dinars if she waited to remarry until after her two minor daughters had found husbands, and 30 dinars if she did otherwise. The man died on the subsequent Wednesday; before a year was over the impatient widow was about to marry.[27] Many last wills that lack one of the two dates (of either the will or the demise), or both, might reflect similar situations, that is, wills made only a day or so before the testator passed away.

Another group of dispositions in contemplation of death consists of documents written in situations of impending danger or risk. Two merchants setting out from Alexandria on a voyage to the Muslim West appointed their wives as executors and guardians of their children, one also entrusting his wife and mother of his boy with all his affairs and possessions and making her his heir. This was absolutely exceptional: a wife never inherited her husband's estate. Perhaps being aware of this, the writer noted that he was not sure whether the wording was legally correct and asked to be judged according to his intentions rather than his command of the relevant terms.[28] A dyer undertaking the pilgrimage to Jerusalem appointed his partner as executor and made detailed dispositions for his family in case he did not return from that journey.[29] A learned India trader from the Muslim West, before leaving Qūṣ in Upper Egypt for the perilous crossing of the desert and of the Red Sea, then infested by pirates, sent home detailed instructions with regards to the goods that he had carried with him to Cairo and Qūṣ for Muslim and Jewish business friends. He included also dispositions in favor of each of his three sons and three daughters, "as if he knew he would die." His presentiment was not unfounded. He was murdered while on the high seas.[30]

When a merchant drafts a comprehensive inventory of his assets and liabilities and, in addition, appoints his only daughter as his heir and her mother as her guardian, it stands to reason that this and similar documents were drafted on a special occasion, such as the departure for an overseas venture.[31]

To the same group of documents belong dispositions in which a person advanced in years expresses the apprehension that he might be overcome by sudden death and forced to leave his beloved, especially his wife, without proper provision. In a fragment of such a will, written by Ḥalfōn b. Manasse at his best, the donor, being in good health, undertakes to specify the legacies made by him, especially in favor of his wife, emphasizing that they were irrevocable (which was indeed the law). But only his gift to a synagogue in Alexandria of a Bible codex, Bible commentaries (or translations), and other Hebrew books has been preserved. Other parts of the magnificent document might turn up one day.[32]

The specter of sudden death was apt to induce old people to act, in particular, when accompanied by other apprehensions, and to distribute their possessions during their lifetime. A white-haired man brings his two sons before four witnesses (all with untrained, clumsy signatures) and explains to the boys that all he possessed in cash was 33 gold pieces. In view of such a small estate, he was afraid they would quarrel, wherefore he decided to arrange the distribution while still capable of acting: 8 dinars were reserved for the widow (a second wife, married late in life), due her as her delayed marriage gift, 7 dinars for funeral expenses for himself and an old grandmother ("the shrouds," that is, the burial clothing for the two, had already been put aside; this was common practice); these sums, 15 dinars altogether, were entrusted to the younger son (the other one probably used to travel out of town); the remaining 18 dinars were divided between the two sons in equal shares. There was some "talk," that is, objection, on this point, the elder son probably claiming rights of the firstborn, but finally all accepted the proposed distribution and the money that went with it.[33]

Expectant mothers were in a similar situation. Wills made by some of them while in good health, but apprehensive of the dangers of childbirth, are of considerable interest.[34]

Several deathbed declarations expressly refer to wills made previously. Some merely contain clarifications, others represent changes. The often mentioned parnās, or welfare official, Eli ha-Kohen b. Yaḥyā (documents signed by him: 1057–1098) had dictated his last will to judge Isaac b. Samuel, the Andalusian, in which he had mentioned that one of his partners owed him 48 dinars. The next day the witnesses came in and reported that the partner, who was also ill, had testified that Eli had withdrawn about 6 dinars; whereupon Eli asked them to include in the declaration that he had been under the impression that the sum withdrawn had been profit made, so that the capital invested had remained intact. Further instructions on this matter probably were reported on another sheet not yet found.[35]

An old widow had freed her maidservant during her last illness and given her one half of a house (all she possessed of it) as well as the rest of her belongings "all as an irrevocable gift." Later, but still on her deathbed, she asked the girl to renounce one eighth of the share in the house, which she wished to give to a daughter of her sister. For the time being, we do not know the end of the story. It is likely that the servant was amenable to the request, since the niece probably would have been assigned a far larger share if she applied to a Muslim court.[36]

Finally, and most noteworthy, in many cases regular gifts, or sales, to relatives were in reality transactions in contemplation of death made in order to forestall troubles and lawsuits in the courts of the community or the state.[37]

Most deathbed declarations were partial in nature dealing with but a few issues, or even with only one, that had not been settled through previous arrangements. A man on his deathbed in al-Maḥalla was asked by two witnesses whether a certain person from (or in) Alexandria or anyone else in the world owed him anything. This was answered in the negative in a declaration laid down in a carefully worded document.[38] On a Saturday, a dying man, Sālim al-Ḥalabī (native of Aleppo, Syria), was visited by friends, among them a creditor, who reminded him of a sum of 16 dinars and 4 qīrāṭs still owed him. Sālim assured him that he would get his money, whether "the predestined end" would come presently or not, but wished to discuss the matter after the Sabbath. When the creditor replied that he was unable to return, Sālim reiterated his pledge, and his son, who was present, confirmed that he was ready to pay his father's debt, even if it was twice as high.[39]

Abu ʾl-Khayr, a *mūrid,* or government supplier, declared on his deathbed that he owed Abu ʾl-Karam, the banker, the very large amount of 238 dinars. These were to be paid out of the sale of a huge quantity of sugar stored in the workshop of Abu ʾl-Barakāt al-Lebdī, the sugar maker (repeatedly mentioned in the Geniza papers). Abu ʾl-Barakāt al-Lebdī, together with the banker, should sell the sugar, the balance to be turned over to Abu ʾl-Khayr's son.[40]

Even where several issues appear in a will, it is often evident that it was essentially made for one main purpose. A Kohen described by the titles "esteemed elder" and "our master and teacher" leaves all his clothing, namely, his turbans, shawls, undergarments, and robes, to one son, and a Nubian maidservant to another son with no one else having a claim against either heir. The document, a draft, states that the man died after having made that declaration. Clearly, all other matters had been settled before. Only the clothing worn to the very end (as is expressly stated) and the servant, who had looked after the patient during his last illness, had remained to be dealt with.[41]

A more detailed declaration of a schoolmaster, the son of a scholar, is of the same type. From beginning to end, it emphasizes that nothing, neither gold or silver nor books, had been deposited with his son; his wife had received her delayed marriage gift in full. A small sum had been deposited with a third person to be used for the funeral expenses, the balance of which should be divided in six equal shares[42] among the four children of his son and the two children of his daughter. It is evident that the schoolmaster had made preferential dispositions in favor of his son and was even suspected of having secretly given him money or books. The purpose of the declaration was to protect the son against any claims.[43]

Wills concerned chiefly or exclusively with the continuation of a business or a partnership also belong here. An *ʿaṭṭār,* or perfumer, on his deathbed entrusts his employee, "a reliable young man," with the conduct of his store, fixing for him daily wages amounting to 2⅜ dirhems. Moreover, he declares him to be "trustworthy like two witnesses whose testimony is accepted in court," with no one, the heirs included, having any claims against him. The carefully written document was not completed.[44] A young Mr. Singer, agent in a business venture in pharmaceutical plants, olive oil, and gallnuts, amounting to the considerable sum of 90–91 dinars, asked witnesses—on a Sabbath, because of the urgency of the matter—to enter with him the house of a Mr. Goldsmith, the dying provider of the goods mentioned. Mr. Goldsmith confirmed that the sum mentioned was indeed all due him and declared Mr. Singer as his trusted agent. He died a few days later.[45]

The situation was somewhat different in a deathbed declaration in which again the partner, a proselyte, called Abu ʾl-Khayr (Mr. Good), is appointed as trustworthy administrator (the word executor is not used in the document, as far as preserved), but which contains several other dispositions. The widow's delayed marriage gift (she was his second wife) should be paid with the price of the husband's books. Moreover, Abu ʾl-Khayr should lock up everything found in the house, sell it, and present the widow and her daughter each with a gift of 5 dinars. There are a number of minor details, but clearly the main point was the admission that the substantial sum of 245 (or 145) dinars kept in the testator's bag belonged in equal shares to the partnership with Abu ʾl-Khayr, who would carry on with it dividing profits and losses at the same ratio. The document states also that the dying man's wife was present and heard everything he said. Arrangements with regard to the heirs must have been made before.[46]

There are, however, deathbed declarations that appear to be all-comprising, seemingly intended to state all that was needed for the proper handling of the testator's estate. When a Maghrebi merchant fell ill in Alexandria, he was visited by his business friends who reminded him that he was in a foreign country and consequently should himself settle all his assets and debits. This he did, furnishing with painstaking precision more than twenty details, mainly descriptions of goods and to whom they belonged or were sent. Characteristically, he himself had only 3½ dinars in cash.[47]

A good example of an all-comprising will has come down to us in two copies, but unfortunately in incomplete form. The signed final document is a huge sheet of paper containing forty-nine broad lines; but this was only the lower part of the will; the upper part, which must have been of approximately the same size (if not larger) and which was glued to it, is lost. The copy or draft, written by the same clerk, covers only the lower part. But the loss is not too serious, for in the first thirteen lines preserved, we are still in the first section of the will: the assets and liabilities, amounting to more than 1,200 dinars. Thus the total probably was a multiple of that sum. The entire will can be outlined as follows:

A. Assets and liabilities.
B. Provisions for the testator's wife (of a second marriage).[48]
C. Appointment of his brother as executor and guardian of his children with far-reaching privileges.[49]
D. Charities and a bonus for an employee.
E. Division of all the possessions of himself and his brother to be distributed in equal parts among the latter and the testator's children.[50]
F. A note on the testator's firstborn.[51]
G. A postscript on two minor details.

Despite its unusual length, this was a genuine deathbed declaration, for the document ends with the remark that the testator died "from his illness."[52]

It is evident, however, that such protracted wills could not have been made without careful preparations, probably with the aid of written material. Of another such draft, also containing forty-nine lines, but not completed, only the left half is preserved, but the text extant contains no fewer than twenty-seven items of assets and liabilities with many names, sums, and dispositions ordered. A man gravely ill could hardly keep all these details in his mind and make decisions on them. We must remember, though, that the Geniza people did most of their accounting by heart and preferred to "close their account" every year in order not to be troubled by debts or sums to be collected. On the other hand, every merchant of good standing kept account books; it was probably these that were at hand at the time of deathbed declarations.[53]

The opposite case, where a last will contains only the barest outlines, namely, the appointment of executors and a few legacies, calls even more for the assumption that it was preceded by preparatory arrangements.

In a will made "in expectation of death" in Alexandria on 6 March 1201, the testator appointed five "elders" present, among them a brother-in-law of his, as executors and guardians of his minor son (who must have been between the ages of five and seven at the time), and accepted them as trustworthy, so that no oath could be imposed on them. He likewise declared his wife as trustworthy so that she, too, should not be troubled by any claims or lawsuits. He gave 50 dinars to each of his two daughters and 10 dinars to the daughters of his sister (it is not stated how many she had). Finally, he ordered a Torah scroll to be written on the account of his estate and donated to the community.

There is nothing unusual in this will except the number of executors. Why five and not the usual one or two? The answer is found in another document, written eight years later, in 1209, after one of the five executors had gone abroad. From it we learn that the estate amounted to 2,550 dinars in cash and kind,[54] a sum having the purchasing power of about a quarter of a million good (1970) U.S. dollars. The executors were supposed to do business with this money, dividing the profits in equal shares among themselves and the sole heir, the boy; moreover, they were allowed an indemnity of 1 dinar "for their work and food," for which period is not stated, possibly for each business venture. About two years later, after another executor had died, the two documents were submitted to the Nagid Abraham Maimonides, because the executors testifying in 1209 had meant that the sum mentioned was that of the original estate, whereas the judge writing the testimony had understood it to be the balance remaining in that year. The executors had assigned the boy daily allowances of 4 dirhems (about four times as much as the usual), in addition to wheat, clothing, and the poll tax.[55] The Nagid decided in favor of the executors, opining that the sum mentioned was that of the original estate.[56]

Five executors were needed because trading with such a large capital was a time-consuming affair. In the will, the dying man simply says to the elders: "I appoint you as executors and guardians." As we know, however, from inventories and other sources, the possessions and assets of a rich man used to be extremely diversified.[57] Experienced merchants could not take over an estate of 2,550 dinars without having made at least a cursory examination, clarified dubious items, and discussed the approximate distribution of their respective responsibilities. Seemingly all-comprising deathbed declarations in the Geniza must be understood as only the last of several or many steps undertaken in contemplation of death.

This applies not only to rich people. In a Hebrew will, written in June 1040, a man declares that his wife did not owe him a thing, but that all due her from her marriage contract—the dowry and the delayed marriage gift—had not yet been delivered to her; in addition, he made her a present of four *ēfā* (a biblical word, probably standing for *irdabb*) of wheat.[58] A sister received 2 dinars, and a niece 1, and the Torah codex was donated to the synagogue of the Palestinians in Fustat. The main point of the will was that the testator's son was the only and exclusive heir who could not be sued by anyone. There was no need to appoint an executor since the heir had complete control of the estate left.[59]

For a poor man, this will seems to be rather detailed. But when we consider how difficult and disputable it was to estimate the value of a dowry decades after it had been given, and that no details are provided as to the assets from which the payments due had to be made, we understand that much pourparler among husband, wife, and son must have preceded the writing of this document.

About two hundred years later, in May 1241, a cheese maker, on his deathbed, gives to his virgin daughter, who had come of age, two thirds of a house belonging to him (the other third was the property of the son of another cheese maker), together with 130 "black dirhems," worth perhaps about 2 dinars; a granddaughter received 2 dinars, his wife, "the perfect woman," 2 dinars due her as her late marriage gift, plus 1 dinar as an additional gift. "The balance of the entire estate" went to the son. The transfer of immovables, especially those held in partnership, where the question of the right of preemption had to be settled, was a complicated affair, and a conveyance tax had to be paid to the government. The monetary gift to the daughter might have been intended to cover this. In any case, in order to be effective, even this extremely modest will needed clarifications in advance.[60]

In some of the cases described above, and in several others, we find that persons present at the deathbed declaration ask the testator for further details, remind him of things, or challenge his statements altogether. A woman, instead of freeing her slave (probably her business agent and not eager to become a Jew), willed that he should be sold and his price divided into two equal shares, one to be used for repairs in the holy shrine of Dammūh, and the other to be kept by the court for needy people unable to pay funeral expenses or the poll tax. When those present conveyed to her the suggestion of "the Diadem of the Scholars" (Nathan b. Samuel he-Ḥavēr) that the money was needed for the restoration of a precious Bible codex preserved in the synagogue of the Iraqians, she refused to yield. Books were not a part of her life experience.[61]

Occasionally, the situation got out of hand. Of one such occurrence we have three statements: one, the beginning of a document in monumental chancellery script containing many additions and corrections and, therefore, not completed; another one, overleaf, in a good cursive, summarizing, not without a long deletion, the main points of contention and bringing the declaration to its end; in a third one (preserved not in Cambridge, England, like the original document, but in New York), Ḥalfōn b. Manasse, who must have been present, impatiently jotted down the controversial matters, but without even mentioning names. A man on his deathbed had given his wife of second marriage, in addition to her deferred marriage gift of 50 dinars, an additional gift of 10 dinars, as well as the clothing and other things he had bought her during her marriage (and which were legally his). When asked by the witnesses whether to free her from the obligatory widow's oath (that she had not received or taken anything from her husband's estate), he made this conditional on her consent not to demand from him a replacement of the *belāyōt,* the clothing listed in her marriage contract, but worn out by use. There was some "talk" on this point, but finally she agreed. Then the witnesses asked the dying man whether his wife should not remain in the house and bring up his children. He replied that he left this up to her; if she stayed on, she would be maintained from the same funds as the children; she wisely took notice of this without binding herself.[62] Since an important detail of the will had been disputed, as a matter of precaution, "the symbolic purchase," which in Jewish law rendered any transaction valid, was made from both the dying man and his wife, albeit the former, as the document expressly states, was not required to do so by law.[63]

In general, however, such situations or interferences of persons present at the deathbed are less frequent than one would expect. This, too, shows that the individual wills found in the Geniza, whether partial or all-comprising in character, normally do not reflect all the dispositions made in contemplation of death by the person concerned. They had been preceded by long deliberations, and in many cases, by important transactions. Taken together, however, these wills are well suited to reveal to us the concerns that moved a person while preparing for parting this life.

Man's first thought was God, meeting him on the Day of Judgment or before. In hours of danger a person said the *widduy,* or confession of sins, and if one was properly prepared, death was believed to provide atonement.[64]

Before trying to find favor with God, one must make peace with his fellowmen. This seems to have been the foremost concern of the wills preserved in the Geniza. All debts due, not forgetting the government, must be paid, and often it is indicated how this should be done.[65] Or it is expressly stated: "No one owes me a thing, neither do I owe anyone anything."[66] One is careful to remove uncertainties with regard to former transactions, partnerships, or other relationships in order to spare people trouble with unwarranted claims or outright accusations.[67] Persons from whom the testator had received favors are expressly released from any liabilities so that they should not be suspected of concealing legacies given to them in return.[68] The list of such precautions taken out of consideration for one's fellowman is endless.

The number one creditor of a husband was his wife. The deferred marriage gift, payable at death, is described in some documents as "debt";[69] the dowry had to be returned, and many other obligations resulting from the couple's mutual relations had to be fulfilled. The most urgent matter was a declaration absolving the widow from that hateful oath imposed on her by Jewish law (unless she had been freed of it in advance by her marriage contract, as was often done), as well as protecting her otherwise from the heirs and the courts.

Second in priority was the desire of self-perpetuation, the urge to leave one's children financially safe and secure. This might be a general human propensity, but in a society seeing "the dead providing for the daily needs of the living," as is proved by the immense proliferation of pious foundations, such a relationship between parents and children was particularly pronounced.[70] At the time a will was written, the daughters were in most cases married and had already received their share in the form of a dowry. A daughter would then be assigned a comparatively small legacy as proof that her father had not forgotten her on his deathbed, although she was now "in the house of other people," that is to say, a stranger.[71] When a daughter was the only child, however, her father would make her his sole heir, which was biblical law, but it had to be willed expressly, since the four main schools of Islamic law never permitted her to take more than one half of her father's estate.[72] In many cases, we find males and females being granted equal shares, and a general tendency expressed by the words of one testator, "I do not wish to give preference to one of my children over another," seems to have prevailed.[73] Similarly, the biblical law giving the firstborn son a double share was usually made ineffective by a will to the contrary. There were, however, fathers who saw in their firstborn their main successor and strengthened his position by specific provisions, necessary because Islam did not know the law of primogeniture.[74] It is also characteristic of a society in which the extended family played a far more important role than in our own that so many legacies were made in favor of more distant relatives, such as nieces, nephews, aunts, grandnieces, cousins, and others. A wide variety of attitudes is evident in all these matters.

Man's personality was preserved not only in his children but also in the way in which he was finally laid to rest. Hence the numerous provisions on "shrouds," meaning the dignified clothing in which one wished to be buried, as well as on the funeral procession, the burial, the grave, and, occasionally, the sepulcher to be erected above the grave. This exaggerated preoccupation with interment should by no means be taken as typically Egyptian. It seems to have been motivated by Jewish, Christian, and Islamic beliefs in afterlife and in the resurrection of the dead, but, in particular, by the endeavor to uphold social standing to the very last. Although this tendency was certainly predominant, there were exceptions.[75]

One had to provide for one's soul as well as one's body. In Psalms 17:15, "I shall see your face in righteousness," the word "righteousness," *ṣedeq,* was understood to mean charity, *ṣedāqā,* namely, that one would "see the face of God," that is, meet him in the world to come after having done works of charity here. Do not the Scriptures promise twice: "Charity saves from death" (Proverbs 10:2 and 11:4)?[76] Some last wills are indeed concerned exclusively with charity and burial.[77] In those documents, charity was of different types: gifts to the needy in general, mostly turned over to the communal chest, and legacies in favor of synagogues, holy shrines, religious scholars, or specified persons in need.

The most important aspect of charity, gifts to the pious foundations, that is, the donation of houses or parts of them to the community, rarely appears in last wills for the simple technical reason that these transactions required careful preparation and execution. Consequently, in judging the dispositions on deathbed about charities, we should apply the same yardstick as that proposed for financial matters: we must reckon with the likelihood that other arrangements had previously been made. When our man with the estate of 2,550 dinars provides a Torah scroll with its silver case, which cost at most 50 dinars, as the only "good work" he leaves during an illness from which he died, we are somewhat disappointed.[78] That man, however, as he approached the end of his life, might have given a house worth 200 dinars or more to the community as a pious foundation. I mention this sum because a tithe, or *maʿaser,* ten percent, seems to have been regarded as the proper share to be assigned to charity in a complete will. At least, this was the case in the deathbed declaration of a businesswoman, a divorcée, who, except in her personal affairs, always tried to live up to the accepted standards.[79]

The manumission on one's deathbed of maidservants, who were legally slaves, was widely practiced in Geniza times, although Jewish law seems not to have favored this deed of charity.[80] By being set free, the maid became a full-fledged member of the Jewish community, and could marry a Jew. Numerous documents show that such marriages were indeed concluded, and also that the former proprietors often endowed the freed woman with the necessary means to marry (cf. Deuteronomy 15:14). Most of the information about these matters is to be found in the chapter on slaves and slave girls in *Med. Soc.,* I, 130–147. An appreciation of its social and religious implications must be reserved for a general discussion of the religious character of the society reflected in the Geniza documents.[81]

The same is to be said about legacies for religious purposes. A rich but illiterate businesswoman wills large sums for the illumination of four synagogues "so that they may study throughout the night." In view of the abysmal chasm that divided the book world of the Jewish men from the oral subculture of Jewish women, one wonders how this and similar legacies are to be interpreted.

An ancient, widespread, and enduring literary genre lets dying persons utter wise words, characteristic of themselves and of significance for their posterity. Of this type are blessings on the deathbed of biblical patriarchs, the sayings of sages of the Talmud, or of Greek philosophers when taking leave of their disciples and this world (as reported so diligently by Diogenes Laertius), and the ethical wills common in the late Jewish Middle Ages[82]—all paralleled in Islamic literature. Nothing of the kind should be expected in the deathbed declarations of the Cairo Geniza. I have not found a single ethical will there. The dispositions in contemplation of death are succinct legal statements dealing with matters of a practical nature. No need to reiterate, however, that they reveal to us much about the concerns and moral and religious notions of the men and women speaking to us in these documents.

In conclusion, I wish to give the reader the opportunity to listen to the very words of Geniza persons readying themselves to depart from this world. The first three selections are mainly devoted to matters of charity and religion. The other two show how the complexities of life are reflected in the preparations for death. Each item is a special case; every human situation is a story by itself—then as now.

"Offerings" and the Erection of a Burial Vault (Alexandria, 1090)

Yeshūʿā b. Samuel (or Ismaʿīl), the dying man, was a Tunisian who had settled in Alexandria. In his youth, he had studied in Qayrawān with R. Nissīm b. Jacob, the most eminent rabbinical authority of his time, whose death he lamented in a letter to his fellow student Nahray b. Nissīm.[83] He belonged to that class of learned merchants who shaped much of our image of the Geniza world.

Here we learn what was uppermost on his mind during the illness from which he did not recover. First, a gift to "the Rav," then the highest religious authority in Egypt.[84] "Honoring a divine is like bringing an offering to God in the Temple of Jerusalem." A gift to Dammūh, the synagogue of Moses, the revered sanctuary of the Egyptian Jews, was second in rank. The lion's share of the sums obtained probably went toward the erection of a burial vault (about which we hear very rarely elsewhere). The Tunisian merchant obviously desired to leave a visible monument of himself in the foreign city after several decades of activity there.

This deathbed declaration, like many others, only reiterated what must have been discussed and agreed upon before. The representative of the merchants in Fustat, Abū Yaʿqūb al-Ḥakīm, must have had confirmed that the considerable quantities of goods mentioned in the will were, in fact, held by him; the friend, referred to here only by his first name and title, must have agreed to take upon himself the onerous task of selling a variety of different types of commodities; and the person charged with the erection of the sepulcher must have been informed in advance that the prices obtained would be sufficient for its execution. Out of the many matters that Yeshūʿā certainly had to settle prior to his demise, he mentioned the three wishes discussed above on his deathbed because "it is a religious duty to execute the words of a dying person"; wishes expressed in extremis were sacrosanct and sure, if possible, to be fulfilled.[85]

The sepulcher is called *maghāra* (Heb. *meʿārā*), cave. In stony Palestine, subterranean vaults, carved out of the rocks, received the bodies of the dead or their ossuaries. In sandy Egypt, structures over the tombs replaced the "caves," as can still be seen in the devastated cemetery of Basātīn near modern-day Cairo.

The beginning of the document is missing, but nothing essential is lost, as the opening words show: the court (in Fustat) confirms having received a complete copy of the declaration (made in Alexandria).

We received a copy of his last will, and here it is, letter by letter. The undersigned testify as follows. We were present in the place of R. Yeshūʿā b. R. Samuel [may he] r[est in] E[den]. He was ill, but sound in mind and fully cognizant, knowing what he said and what was said to him. And this is what he said:

Sheikh Abū Yaʿqūb al-Ḥakīm in Fustat holds for me in his warehouse, on his responsibility, thirty hundredweights of sulphur, four hundred *mann* [weight of about two pounds] of lichen,[86] seven and a half hundred-weights of beads, and a wicker basket with hundred scores of beads.[87]

Sheikh Abū ʿImrān Mūsā, the Treasure,[88] shall take upon himself the sale of all this. From the proceeds, 10 dinars shall be given to our master, the Rav [may the] All[merciful] keep [him], and 10 dinars to the synagogue of Dammū.[89]

Of the balance, R. Samuel b. Judah [may he] r[est in] E[den],[90] will take care and add it to the price of the *maqṭaʿ* robes.[91] With this sum, the cave [sepulcher] will be built. He, I mean R. Samuel b. Judah, will take care of this and no one has any right to interfere with actions taken by him.

From this illness *he departed to his eternal abode.*[92]

This happened in the month of Tishri of the year 4851[93] in the city of Alexandria which is situated on the shore of the Great Sea.[94]

The Dispositions of a Pious Woman
(Fustat, November 1006)

This remarkable deathbed declaration exemplifies how the concern for the community of God, charity, family attachment, consideration for one's fellowmen, as well as the person's own burial arrangements, worked in concert. Prior to the fatal illness, other dispositions had been made. Here the main (or the remaining) possessions of the dying woman were divided. One third was given to the two synagogues of Fustat, and a sixth to a girl, probably an orphan, to enable her to marry. Should she die unmarried, this sixth, too, would be donated to two synagogues which would thus get one half of the total. Another third of the property is divided and given in equal shares to a brother of the testator and the daughter of another brother. One twelfth had been sold previously to Sutayt (Little Lady), the daughter of her stepsister Sayyida

(Lady) for 14 dinars, and much pain is taken (and for good reasons) that this sale should not be contested by anyone. Equally, Sayyida and Sutayt are exempted from any claims that might be brought against them, clearly in connection with gifts made to them previously. If one twelfth of the property was worth 14 dinars, its total value would have been 168 dinars, the price of a good house. It is likely, however, that the niece was granted a discount and that the value of the property was higher.[95]

The remaining twelfth was put aside for the interment of the testator's body in Jerusalem. The casual way in which this important detail is mentioned makes it likely that everything related to the transport of the body to the Holy City had been arranged in advance. Yet, as compared with other deathbed declarations, one gets the impression that this woman was less fussy about the disposal of her body than many persons whose emphatic declarations on this score we read.

It is also noteworthy that, unlike other such documents, Talmudic sayings are twice quoted inappropriately. It is unlikely that the trained scribe who authored this document should commit such awkward slips. I believe that these quotations were the dying woman's own words. She had probably picked up those maxims from a learned husband, but was not quite sure about their application. I had similar experiences with Yemenite women quoting the Bible.[96]

The document is much damaged, especially at the beginning, so that we do not even know the dying woman's name. The translation begins at the end of line six of the preserved document.[97]

[A] I own a house in Fustat, in the Fortress of the Candles, in the Lane of the Poor,[98] which belongs to me with all its exits and entrances, the ways leading to and from it, and all rights connected with it from the depths of the earth to the pinnacle of heaven.

[B] Although the site belongs to the King [government],[99] I hereby give eight of the twenty-four parts of the house to the two synagogues in Fustat, four to the synagogue of the Babylonians, and four to that of the Jerusalemites, so that the proceeds of the monthly rent from a third of this house should be used for [. . .][100] in these two synagogues, as our sages—may their merits protect us forever—have said: "It is a religious duty to execute the words of a dying person."[101]

[C] I have previously sold two parts of the house to Sutayt, the daughter of my sister, the widow of Ṣemaḥ b. David, for fourteen good pieces of gold, of full weight, from the mint of the Caliph al-Muʿizz, which I have already received from her and for which I have bought rafters for the repair of the house. Thus, I have sold these two parts of this house to Sutayt for fourteen pieces of gold in a definite, complete, confirmed, and valid transaction, from now to eternity, to her and her heirs after her; they have, therefore, ceased to be my property and have become her property, as is the case with any buyer, and I hereby invalidate any secret deposition in court or any condition connected with that transaction.

[D] I hereby give four parts to this house to Fā'iza, daughter of . . . ha-Levi, as a definite, irrevocable, confirmed, and valid gift, so that she should be able to marry with the aid of them. If—God forbid—the Holy one should ordain her death, this sixth will become the property of the two aforementioned synagogues, and her heirs will have no right to the sixth of this house. However, if she marries, it will belong to her and to her heirs after her. This condition of mine is valid, like that of the children of Gad and Reuben, who mentioned the positive before the negative [part of the condition].[102]

[E] Two parts of this house shall be sold and the proceeds used for my burial, namely to carry my body to Jerusalem, the Holy City, may it be rebuilt soon.[103]

[F] Of the remaining eight parts of this house, four shall belong to my brother Sahlān and four to Rayyisa, the daughter of my brother Ephraim, as our sages—may their merit protect us forever—have said: "The sons of sons are like sons."[104]

[G] I hereby declare my sister and daughter of my father, Sayyida, and Sutayt, her daughter, the widow of Ṣemaḥ b. David, and her children, the orphans of Ṣemaḥ, released, free, and not bound to respond to any demand, complaint, ban, or to give an oath, or even secondary oath, whether general or specified, before either a Jewish or gentile court.

[H] From this illness, she departed to her eternal abode on Thursday, the fourteenth of the month of Kislev, in the year one thousand three hundred and eighteen of the era of the documents, according to which we are accustomed to date in Fustat, which is situated on the Nile river.

[Two, badly damaged lines follow which contain technicalities and the mostly lost signatures.]

A Dying Woman Frees Her Two Slave Girls and Provides Them with Shelter and Sustenance
(Fustat, mid-twelfth century)

The testator Sitt al-Ḥusn (Beauty) b. Saʿāda (or Saadya) was the wife of the judge and prominent public figure Nathan b. Samuel (dated signatures 1128–1153). He bore the title Diadem of the Scholars, and was normally addressed and referred to thus (as in our document).

Sitt al-Ḥusn was divorced by her first husband under dramatic circumstances in June 1117, years before Nathan b. Samuel made his appearance in Egypt. In 1129 she was still unmarried. Her marriage to Nathan was probably concluded later in her life. He was an immigrant, she possessed real estate in Fustat, and as the marriage gift promised her by Nathan shows (item D, below), she was of a fairly well-to-do family, for the husband's contribution somehow reflected the bride's status. She might well have been the driving force behind Nathan's hospice for old and sick people, about which we have read before. And we can visualize her as hostess to the Spanish Hebrew poet Judah ha-Levi, Nathan's friend, when he visited Fustat in winter 1140–1141. She was named after her hunchbacked mother probably because the latter—as hunchbacks often are—was a somewhat unusual person.[105]

Since the deathbed declaration was made on a Saturday, when writing is prohibited by Jewish religious law, no record was drawn up. After the Sabbath, the clerk jotted down what he remembered. The result was a less well organized but probably more lively account of the happenings. The story behind Sitt al-Ḥusn's action may be reconstructed as follows: In her old age, perhaps childless, she had bought two small girls—probably born to women serving in Jewish households (see n. 111)—and educated them in the Jewish faith. Overtaken by the sudden approach of death (otherwise the declaration would not have been made on a Saturday), she freed and bequeathed them the means to live as free women and, perhaps, also to marry.

The judge hurriedly summoned four witnesses to his house, two of whom he had to introduce to his dying wife. Considering that these are notes made by the clerk for his own use (as he says at the end), one understands why some terms and facts are not self-explanatory.[106]

[A] *On Saturday, the fifteenth of Sivan,* I entered with "*the Diadem,*" *R. Nathan, son of R. Samuel, the Ḥāvēr—m*[*ay he rest in*] *E*[*den*], his house, accompanied by *R. Judah ha-Kohen, the Diadem of the Kohanim and their Support, the Delight of the Nāsīs,*[107] *son of the ho*[*nored*], *gr*[*eat*] *and ho*[*ly*] *M. and R. Jacob ha-Kohen, the judge—m*[*ay his end*] *b*[*e blessed*]); furthermore, the elder Abu ʾl-Faraj Ibn al-Ramlī;[108] the Kohen, the ritual slaughterer, who lives near the Bath of the Cock; the Kohen *who blesses the congregation,*[109] the companion of the Raʾīs, the Nagid Abu Manṣūr[110]—*may his Rock preserve him.*

[B] This house belongs to his wife Sitt al-Ḥusn, the daughter of Saʿāda, known as "the daughter of the hunchbacked [woman]." She was of sound mind, knowing what she said and talked about, and she realized that it was Saturday. Then the Kohen, who blesses the congregation, and the elder Abu ʾl-Faraj al-Ramlī were introduced to her, whereupon she asked us to bear witness that as from now on and after her death she had freed her virgin slaves Dhahab and Sitt al-Sumr[111] and given to them the quarter of the house in the Musāsa[112] which belonged to her in partnership with the Raʾīs Abu ʾl-Munajjā Solomon b. Ṣedāqa—m[ay he rest] i[n] E[den].

[C] Furthermore, she willed one-half of the house, which was her home, to the *community*,[113] with the proviso that the slave girls will have the right to stay in the part belonging to the *community*, namely, in the room in which the will was made, for the rest of their lives on condition that they profess the Jewish faith. Both the gift and the permission to live in the house depended on this condition.

The ruin opposite the house, together with the other half of the house, were willed by her to her husband, *our Teacher Nathan, the Diadem of the Scholars*.[114]

[D] It was said that the two Kohanim, mentioned above, had been among the signatories of her *marriage contract*, which stipulated that the deferred installment due to her was fifty dinars, but the contract was not produced at the time the will was made.[115]

[E] She also said that one-eighth of the house behind the mosque,[116] which belonged to her in partnership with the government[117]—may God strengthen it—and the elder Abu ʾl-Aʿlā b. Tammām—*m*[*ay he rest in*] *E*[*den*], should be sold and the money used for all the expenses of her burial, such as the burial garment, the coffin, the cantors, the tomb, the bearers [of the coffin], etc. In case this was not sufficient, a headband, consisting of eleven ornaments, deposited by her with her husband, should be sold and used for the expenses. Her husband, *the Diadem*, said: "Yes, it is in my possession."[118]

[F] If something should remain from the price of one-eighth of the aforementioned house, it shall be given to the slave girls mentioned above; likewise, all clothing suitable for women. That which is not suitable for women shall belong to her husband, the *Diadem*.

[G] As it was Saturday, we did not make the symbolic purchase from him for his approval of what she had said.[119]

I put down in writing what I heard from her, so that in case she dies and I am asked to give witness, I shall not forget.

Reading in this document how the slave girls are constantly mentioned in conjunction with judge Nathan, one gets the feeling that the dying woman divided her property between her children and her husband. She wished to leave a living memory of herself.

Appendix: Manumission of a Slave Girl (Fustat, October 1176)

In Roman and Islamic societies, the freed slave remained in a state of dependence on his former master. According to Jewish law, the separation was total, although in actual life the situation was occasionally somewhat different, since the slave had been to a large extent a member of the family. A bill of manumission is translated here in full to show the legal status of the freed slave in the Geniza society.

The bill is mostly in Aramaic, the official language of the Jewish courts in the centuries preceding the Geniza period. The manumission was made on Friday, so that the freed woman could join the community on the following Sabbath as a full member.[120]

Friday, the third of Marheshwan, in the year one thousand, four hundred and eighty-eight of the era of the documents, in Fusṭāṭ, Egypt, which is situated on the Nile River.

I, Abraham ha-Kohen, son of Aaron ha-Kohen, or any other name, under which I am known, hereby declare, out of my own free will, without any coercion, absentmindedness, or error, but being in full possession of my mental faculties, that I am freeing you, you, Nāshiya, who were my slave beforehand. Hereby, I am freeing you; now you are free; now you belong to yourself; you are permitted to join the community of Israel, to adopt a new name in Israel, and to do what you like as do all free persons. Neither I, Abraham ha-Kohen, nor my heirs after me, nor any legal representative of mine has any rights on you or on your progeny, which you will establish in Israel. This document is for you a bill of manumission from me and a deed of freedom according to the law of Moses and Israel.

[Witnesses:] Yeshūʿa b. Merāyōt, [the] m[emory of the] r[ighteous is] b[lessed].
Saadya b. Judah, [may he] r[est in] E[den].

A Silk-weaver, the Father of Four Sons, Reaffirms His Dispositions (Fustat, December 1188)

This short, but well-planned and equitable will of a poor craftsman attracted my attention when I first came upon it some thirty years ago in the old building of the Bodleian, Oxford (no longer used by students of Geniza manuscripts). The silk-weaver did not keep any cash, not even for his burial expenses. Everything was invested in his workshop. Of his four sons, one, Abu ʾl-Ḥasan, was absent, it seems, permanently living in another town or country. The testator's main concern was to leave a viable family unit. He sold one half of his house to Abu ʾl-Barakāt, his firstborn (named after his grandfather, as usual), certainly for a nominal sum, since he did not assign him anything in this last will. Abu ʾl-Barakāt was also appointed to carry out the provisions for his brothers, with the exception of Bayān, a mere child, with whose care the orphan court had to be entrusted.

After the unavoidable burial expenses, the first payment to be made was the wife's deferred portion of the marriage gift. Although this promise was made at the wedding about a quarter of a century before, it was regarded as a debt, and no one wished to depart this life burdened with a debt.[121]

[A] On Wednesday, the fifteenth of Kislēv, in the year one thousand five hundred of the era of the documents, the following occurred here in Fustat, which is situated on the Nile river, under the jurisdiction of our lord, our Gaon Sar Shalom ha-Levi—may his name endure forever:[122]

We were asked to visit Sheikh Abu ʾl-Faḍl, the silk-weaver, the son of Abu ʾl-Barakāt, who is known by the name Ben al-Maqdisī [the son of the Jerusalemite]. We found him ill, confined to his bed, but his mind was sound, and he knew what he said and what was said to him. We asked him what time it was and about the identity of the persons present, to all of which he answered in clear language and with a sound mind.

[B] Then he said to us: "May it be known to you that the whole half of the entire house // which is mine // [123] in the Tujīb quarter of Fustat,[124] which is known as my home, is the property of my son Abu ʾl-Barakāt, and is not mine, since I have sold it to him. The other half I hereby bequeath to Bayān and Bahā, my sons, in two equal shares, on condition that if—God forbid—my son Bahā should die without child, the share remaining in his property, he not having disposed of it, shall revert to his brother Bayān to the exclusion of his other brothers.

[C] Furthermore, I bequeath to my son Bayān the entire equipment of the silk-weaving workshop, which I own. However, the rest of my property, such as yarn, silk, warps, and all the outfit of the house, indeed all I possess, shall be sold. From the proceeds the expenses for my burial shall be paid and to my wife Sitt al-Riḍā the sum due her according to her marriage contract, namely fifteen Egyptian gold dinars, in addition to three dinars which she owes me.[125]

[D] Of the remainder of the proceeds, five Egyptian gold dinars shall be paid to my son Abu ʾl-Ḥasan, to be held in trust by my son Abu ʾl-Barakāt, and he shall be responsible for them until they come into the possession of my son Abu ʾl-Ḥasan.

The final residue of the proceeds shall be divided in equal parts between my son Bayān and my son Bahā.

[E] The selling of the yarn and the outfit and the rest of what I own shall be in the hands of my son Abu ʾl-Barakāt and Abu ʾl-Ṭāhir, the son of the elder Maḥfūẓ, the beadle of the synagogue of the Palestinians—*may it stand firm and secure.*[126]

[F] All that will accrue to my son Bayān from all I bequeath to him, *of both immobile and mobile property,* shall be in the hands of his brother Abu ʾl-Barakāt, until he attains his majority and proves his maturity. However, all that will accrue to my son Bahā from the proceeds of the property sold shall be entrusted to *the Court of Justice,* to be used for his maintenance.

[G] To my wife belong the following copper vessels: a mortar, a pail, a wash basin, a bucket, an oil jug, and a bowl.[127]

The aforementioned Abu ʾl-Faḍl *departed from this life out of his illness to his eternal abode and left behind him life for the divines and all Israel.*

"Which is mine" was added and is correct.[128]

All is herewith ratified, confirmed and valid.

Solomon, son of Nissīm, *m[ay he rest in] E[den].*

Levi ha-Levi, son of Abraham, *[the] m[emory of the] r[ighteous is] b[lessed].*

The trust in the firstborn is particularly moving in the silk-weaver document. I intended to furnish here an even more stirring example of confidence and reliance: on his deathbed a man with old parents and a wife who had already borne him three children appoints his mother-in-law as sole executor for his estate and as guardian of his children "because of her love for the children, her efficiency, and her piety." Personality, one sees, is a decisive factor even in a very traditional society. I had to refrain from including that document here because of its length.[129]

A Rich Woman Protects Her Family against Her Husband (April 1143)

This deathbed declaration betrays an extraordinary attachment of the testator to her paternal family, and is remarkable for several other specific traits.

The dying woman's husband was a *tājir,* or great merchant, who traveled widely and was expected to be away from home for years. He probably was on a business trip to India. She had a little boy from a former marriage, who lived with her parents. As his guardian and her own executor she appointed a brother of her former husband, who probably had already served in this capacity at the latter's death. The main purport of the will was to legally protect her parents, brother, and boy against her present husband and to provide a sumptuous burial for herself. She wanted to have Muslim wailing women, presumably because the cries and shrieks of Jewish women exercising the same profession were not shrill enough for her taste. The most impressive detail is her wish to be buried alongside "one of her family," meaning her father, mother, or brother. To them she was attached by natural ties; to her husband she was connected by a contract. Although her son was still very young and stayed with his grandmother—and did not yet attend Bible school—she decreed that the daughter of her brother, who lived in the same house, should be his future wife. I have little doubt that later in life, when the family had to decide about the marriages of the two, this wish, expressed in the face of death, carried much weight.

The document is in the handwriting of judge Nathan b. Samuel. He was perhaps a friend of the family or took the case on because of its importance. He noted the utterings of the woman in the order they emanated from her mouth (items B–J), and then reminded her of other points that had to be settled to make the will legally effective (items K–P). Our document is interesting not only because of its content, but also because it reveals in detail the process of a deathbed declaration.[130]

[A] *This testimony was given in our presence, we, the witnesses signing at the end of this will. This happened* on Wednesday, the 26th of Iyyar *of the year 1454 of the Era of the Documents* (= April 13, 1143), in Fustat, *which is under the jurisdiction of our lord Samuel, the great Nagid, may his name endure forever.*[131]

We entered the house of the elder Abu ʾl-Munā, the druggist, the Alexandrian, and found his daughter Sitt al-Ahl, the wife of Abū Naṣr of Aleppo, the merchant, ill and confined to her bed—after having properly taken cognizance of her. She was in possession of her faculties, and made her declaration in clear language and with a sound mind. This is what she said to us:

[B] When my father gave me this large house in the Ḥabs Bunān[132] a year and a half ago, a document about this gift was made out before Muslim authorities. But before this he imposed on me the condition that he, my mother, and my brother, the elder Abu ʾl-Surūr, should never be forced to leave the upper floor, as long as they lived in this world. [*Above the line*:] My father should stay in that apartment as long as he lives.[133] I wish now that this stipulation should be carried out unchanged, for it was made in the presence of my husband, the elder Abū Naṣr.[134]

[C] When that which is ordained for me comes to pass, I wish to be buried in this house in which I am now and not carried out [to the cemetery] except when one of my family dies, I mean, my father, mother, or brother. Then I might be carried out together with the one who will die.

[D] The maidservant Fūq[135] does not belong to him [her husband]; my mother gave me the money with which I bought her. She has a daughter, who belongs to my mother, not to me.

[E] My boy shall stay with my mother as he does now. No one shall separate him from them [the party upstairs].

[F] I receive [from my husband] 2½ dinars per month for expenses, which makes 30 dinars a year, as well as 12 irdabbs wheat.[136] Of this, I relinquish to him 4 irdabbs and half a dinar per month, so that he will have to pay to my son Mūsā (Moses) 2 dinars every month and 8 irdabbs wheat a year.

[G] The rent for the middle floor, where Hiba lives, will be given to my mother until my husband returns. I possess a *document*[137] assigning the rent to me during his absence.

[H] I wish to have a [new] burial attire, since I have none with which I am satisfied. There should be bought for me a robe of fine Dabīqī linen with a hood, a mantle, and a cloak, and *niṣāfī* material for the bier and a braid. All this to cost about 25 dinars. And a coffin costing 9–10 dinars.[138]

[I] Wailing should be done by Muslims.

[J] I wish to have the daughter of my brother Abu ʾl-Surūr for my boy Mūsā.

[K] After having made all these declarations in our presence, she appointed as her executor *our master* Aaron, ha-Kohen, the *honored* [elder], son of our master Joshua, ha-Kohen, *the elder,* [*may he*] [*rest in*] *E*[*den*], concerning all this and concerning her will, and [said: "He is my representative] after my death and my executor also with regard to my father and mother."

When [we heard what she said] we wrote it down on the aforementioned date, *so that our testimony should serve as a document conveying rights.* The word . . . *is erased and should not be considered. All the rest is confirmed.*

[L] She accepted the aforementioned Abū Mūsā Hārūn,[139] the Kohen, as *trustworthy as two witnesses admitted in court* with regard to all his actions in matters of her will.

[M] This includes the [expenditure for] the seven days of mourning for me, to be taken from the expenses due me.[140]

[N] He is the executor for the son of his brother.

[O] *Everything is correct, valid, and confirmed.* She further declared in our presence that she kept nothing [belonging to anyone else, especially her husband] on her premises.

[P] She also said: I release my mother, my father, and my brother Abu ʾl-Surūr from all claims and suits which may be brought against them in my name. No one is entitled to molest them by asking them to give an oath of any kind.

Confirmed.

[*Written between the lines*:]

She said I.

Confirmed.

[*Also written between the lines*:]

My father should stay in that apartment as long as he lives.

Everything is confirmed.
Joseph ha-Levi, son of Thābit [*may he*] *r*[*est in*] *E*[*den*].
Solomon, son of Nathan he-ḥāvēr, [may he] r[est in] E[den].

The document does not state, as usual, that the patient died from the illness regarded as fatal. Shall we assume that, after all, Sitt al-Ahl survived and was reunited with her widely traveled husband?

A communal event.—Death scenes are not reported in the Geniza. Descriptions of a demise are furnished when it happened unexpectedly and under special circumstances. "He ate his supper, lay down on his bed, and was dead next morning; people say his [face] was black like ink." "He went to rest in the evening and did not awake in the morning. It was the first day of the holiday, and he was buried on the same day; he left a fine boy of sixteen, who studies with me." Burial on a holiday was inauspicious, for on a holy day no mourning was permitted. The writer of the letter was a friend of the deceased.[141] The case of a banker who died on the evening of the day on which he declared his bankruptcy has been noted before.[142] When the two sons of Saadya Gaon (d. 942) remembered, eleven years after his demise, that he died "at the end of the middle night watch," we may assume that such details were noted only for persons of high rank who died in harness, where the exact time and number of days of their "ruling" in office was of interest.[143] When it is reported of an esteemed member of the community that he died on a Friday morning and was buried on the same day, it is emphasized in the letter that this was an auspicious sign for him, since the pious were expected to enter the Sabbath rest of the World to Come straight after their demise.[144]

The days or hours immediately preceding death, of such tremendous significance in Talmudic religiosity and even more so in later Christianity,[145] are not represented in the Geniza by expressions of dread, contrition, or confidence in God's mercy, uttered by, or attributed to, dying persons. Even the recitation of the confession of sins in a situation of extreme danger, reported once, gives the impression of the fulfillment of a religious duty rather than that of an inner urge of remorse.[146] It was not the hushed atmosphere of passing away that left us memories in the Geniza (if we except the deathbed declarations confined to practical matters), but the noisy public events that immediately followed demise. To be sure, death was a communal affair even before it occurred: during a fatal illness, prayers were recited in the house of worship, often accompanied by fasting and distributing of alms by relatives and others.[147]

At the moment of death, the news spread like brushfire. We do not read about the blowing of ram horns, as customary in Talmudic times; but the wailing and striking of the face and breast, or of the hands one against the other, by the survivors were sufficient to tell what had happened.[148] "When a death occurs in town," says a great rabbinical authority, "the inhabitants are not permitted to do work," the idea being that everyone was obliged to follow the bier.[149] I am not sure that the people in the small town referred to in the passage translated in the following were cognizant of the sage's dictum. But they certainly were adhering to a widely accepted custom. They decided for themselves also the question whether participation in a funeral was in honor of the deceased or of the survivors.[150] The old man whom they accompanied to his last rest was a solitary person with no family around—as old people often are—but he belonged to the community; everyone had, so to say, a share in him.

> The local people, old and young, left their work until they had laid him to rest. He had a beautiful burial. He went away *in peace, old and in the fullness of his days.* I was pleased that I happened to be present, for people who did not know me spread the rumor that the deceased had not left any estate. Since I was around, I went to the notables of the town and explained to them the situation. They assisted me and were not remiss. May God recompense them . . . and grant consolation to the heart.[151]

A letter from Alexandria, the second largest city of Egypt, presents a similar picture. "On the Sabbath [of the week of mourning], no one, neither low nor high, men nor women, remained in Alexandria." Everyone came to the house of mourning to express sympathy. A few lines ahead it was reported that the *ḥāvēr,* or spiritual leader of the community, had sent the chief cantor to the house to recite "the famous poems which arouse grief in the heart"; the writer of the letter himself eulogized the deceased using the words of Ecclesiastes: "A good name is better than choice ointment" (7:1), but was even surpassed in the praise of the dead by some of the guests. He did not forget to report that he had acquired a particularly large pall, for the cover of the bier, the showpiece at a funeral. The much defective letter concludes with an admonition directed to the family in Fustat to honor and support the widow, who was childless, and therefore legally constrained to marry one of her brothers-in-law. This was usually avoided by undergoing the ceremony described in Deuteronomy 25:7–9, and one was, of course, eager to free the widow from this bondage as quickly and smoothly as possible.[152]

Another letter from Alexandria, written in the second half of the eleventh century, teaches us how the community participated in the funeral of an entirely destitute person, a schoolteacher, an immigrant from Tunisia, who had lost everything in his native country. He died from an acute illness (described in another letter), but his father and partner in the Bible school, a man of sixty, could not take recourse to public charity for the funeral, for his brother was the well-known merchant Mūsā b. Abi ʾl-Ḥayy, who, at that time, had his seat in Fustat; the family was first in line to take care of such an emergency. The minimum required for honoring a poor dead was already fixed in the Mishna. In discussing, among the obligations of a husband toward his wife, the bearing of the cost for her burial, it was stated that even a poor man was required to hire for her funeral two flute players and one wailing woman.[153] Playing flutes at weddings and funerals, the two family events that required, according to the Law, the highest possible publicity, was ancient Palestinian custom.[154] Yet among the countless documents in the Geniza dealing with death, as far as I remember, only this letter from Alexandria makes mention of "play," *laᶜb,* instrumental music, at a funeral. The Jewish community of Alexandria, which was so closely connected with the Holy Land, retained practices customary there (for instance, the system of dating according to the Creation, and not only the Era of the Documents, as practiced in Fustat). Together with condolences, food was brought to the mourner during the week immediately following the burial when he was not supposed to leave the house. One helped the poor man with what he could not do himself.

The main cost of the payments for the coffin and to the funeral personnel (such as washers, pallbearers, grave diggers, cantors singing the prayers) had to be borne by the family. In this case, they amounted to 2½ dinars, known as the minimum also from elsewhere. To this had to be added 1¼ dinars for tidbits offered to the visitors extending their sympathy and for alms distributed to the needy.[155] The writer stresses that these expenses during the week of mourning were made "for him"; the deceased was, so to speak, the host, and, since hospitality and charity were such highly esteemed social virtues, these expenses were inevitable. I furnish here an abridged and partial translation of the letter of the pitiable mourner to his brother.

At the hour of the writing of this letter, I stood up from [the seven days of mourning for my son] Abu ʾl-Ḥayy.[156] I informed you about his demise on the day he died.[157] I went to ʿAllān and said to him: "I am applying to you; regard me as a *captive*[158] and take care of him for me." He replied: "I do not give you a thing except on instructions from your brother." Sheikh Abu ʾl-Najm Hilāl appeared and asked him: "What did he say to you?" He replied: "He asked me to make payments on account of his brother, which I refused." Said Hilāl: "I will pay. First, this is a meritorious deed, for this is a *dead whose burial is incumbent on the community.*[159] Second, nothing is lost with his brother; he is a man who loves to acquire *merit* by helping the poor, let alone his brother." He went and bought the coffin and the underpants.[160] He paid an additional 50 dirhems on the general expenses. Altogether this amounted to 2½ [dinars]. They hired the musicians for him at the time of the funeral . . . and bore the expenses of the week of mourning for him[161] in the amount of 1¼ dinars. [After describing to his brother his dire plight and asking for his support, he adds:] To this very hour people are coming condoling me.[162]

As soon as a death occurred, the community, represented by its appointed officials, took over. Even a rich man's possessions were sealed by the rabbinic court on the very day of his demise,[163] and many other things had to be done. Such haste seems to be somewhat inconsiderate, but it was dictated by the very stringent biblical command to protect the rights of orphans and widows. Under normal circumstances, there was no need to record the actions taken in a document. When the dead person was a foreigner, however, whose family lived in another town or country, each step was of significance and had to be put in writing. The document translated below was such a case and serves to illustrate what may have been happening in a house after a death occurred.

A number of persons betook themselves to the place of the deceased: a judge, to watch over the legality of the procedures; two *parnāsīm,* or social service officers, to serve as trustees with whom money and other valuables could be deposited, if needed; two elders, certainly chosen as experts in clothing, jewelry, furnishings, and goods; a cantor, to supervise the preparations for and the conduct of the funeral; a compatriot of the deceased and a person living in the same house, both probably familiar with his affairs; the beadles of the synagogues of the Palestinians and the Iraqians, to do the physical work required to take stock of the estate; a court clerk, to note the steps taken and list all the valuables and other objects found; a grave digger, to measure the dead man to determine the correct dimensions of the tomb; and, finally, two "washers," to take care of the body. Other persons, probably curious bystanders, were also present.

The absence of any reference to a government office is explained by the date (January 1105). It was the time of the comparatively benign rule of the viceroy al-Malik al-Afḍal (1094–1121), who confirmed the rights of Christians and Jews to deal with the estates of their coreligionists, unlike what happened in other, especially later, times. It is likely, however, that even during this period, the rabbinical court reported the circumstances of each case to the appropriate government authority, albeit probably not, as was required later, on the day of the demise.[164]

Besides the judge, at least six other persons signed. Most of their names, however, are thoroughly crossed out, and only that of Isaac b. Samuel (the Andalusian, *Med. Soc.*, II, 512, sec. 13), who used monumental script, and that of ʿUllā ha-Levi b. Joseph, one of the two parnāsīm (ibid., p. 78), are safely legible.[165]

We, the undersigned, entered, together with those mentioned with us, on Sunday, the thirteenth Teveth 1416 [2 January 1105] the place where Joseph b. Ismāʿīl al-Būnī[166] of Alexandria lived, after having been advised that he had died on Saturday morning. We were informed about this only on the subsequent day, on Sunday, as dated above.[167]

When we learned about his death we were of the opinion that we should not tarry to take legal steps on his behalf. Therefore, we assembled: the Court;[168] the two parnāsīm and trustees of the court; and also the elder Abū ʿAlī Ibn al-Sukkarī,[169] the elder Abu ʾl-Surūr, known as Son of ʿAṭiyya; the cantor Abū Alī b. Shekhanyā;[170] Barakāt b. Khulayf of Alexandria, the flax merchant;[171] R. Ḥalfōn ha-Kohen, who lived in the same house as the deceased; the beadles of the synagogues; the scribe Ibn al-Qaṭāʾif;[172] Simḥā;[173] the washers of the dead, Elijah and Masarra;[174] and other people, whom to note[175] was impossible. Standing, all of us, before the room,[176] we noticed that it was locked from the outside and the inside. We opened it and let the washers carry him out to the courtyard of the place; he was dead and disrobed.[177]

A large part of the next twelve lines describing the rummaging in the room is destroyed, but the remaining words, together with the subsequent six complete lines, clearly reflect what happened. Besides numerous objects, of which a detailed list is furnished on the reverse side,[178] 41 dinars in gold and 8¾ silver dirhems were found. The coins were immediately weighed. Of these, 6 dinars, together with the 8¾ dirhems, were set aside for the funeral expenses and handed over to the two trustees, the cantor, and a fourth person. Four persons were needed; things had to be done quickly, since the dead man was probably buried on the same day. The remaining 35 dinars were deposited with the "Trustee of the Yeshiva" (one of the two mentioned who bore that honorary title). Then the room was locked and sealed, awaiting the arrival of an heir.

Six gold coins amounted to a considerable part of the 41 dinars recovered. As we have seen, a funeral could have been had for less. But the judge and his advisers took into account not only the interests of the heirs but also the rights of the deceased. A sum of 10 dinars appears to have been the average spent on a modest but decent funeral, even, it seems, in the far richer Muslim community of Egypt. Had the foreigner been able to make a will, he would probably have assigned something like that amount for his funeral. The judge and his committee chose the middle way between expenses made for a pauper and those spent by a lower middle class family.[179]

To complement the document illustrating the actions of the communal authorities immediately after the occurrence of a death, another document is presented giving us an inkling of the happenings on the way from the house of mourning to the cemetery until the tomb was closed.

A sum of 10 dinars had been willed, or—more probably—adjudicated by a judge, for the burial expenses of a middle class male individual. Here, the person in charge gives an account of how the money was spent. The superscription is to be explained by the fact that "the shroud," that is, the attire of the dead man, was the most expensive item in the cost of the burial.

Account for the Shroud

[A] A tunic[180]—19 qirāṭs; a robe of Dimyāṭī [linen] and another of green silk—2 + ⅔ + ¼ dinars; a scarf[181]—10½ qirāṭs; underpants—9 dirhems; a turban—30 dirhems; a cloak—1 dinar.

[B] A coffin—1½ dinars; trestles[182]—9½ [dirhems];[183] odorous wood, camphor, and rose water—2½; a saw—½; the tailor—3; the way to the desert—3 (+ ?).

[C] The judges and cantors—24; the washer—7; the bearer of the trestles—1½; the bearers [of the coffin]—10; the grave digger—15; given to his wife for expenses—5; the builders [of the tomb]—12; a watchman[184]—1; the man who filled up [the tomb with earth]—1.

[D] Balance—2½.[185]

Burial attire has been treated in the section on clothing in *Med. Soc.*, IV, here in the preceding subsection "Expectations and preparations," and *passim.*[186] Attention should be drawn perhaps to the green color of the silk robe, for green was the color of Paradise—a Muslim concept. Once, when the Jews of Baghdad, in a fit of Messianic excitement, expected to be flown to Jerusalem on a certain night, they waited on the roofs of their houses clad in green robes.[187]

It must be stressed, however, that belief in the resurrection of bodies with their clothing on had received, so to speak, official sanction from Saadya Gaon (d. 942), the theologian whose precepts were dominant in Eastern Jewry during the two centuries after his death. After stating that no believing Jew shed doubts on physical resurrection, he assures the readers of his *Book of Beliefs and Opinions* that returning the clothes to the revived body was certainly a minor miracle compared with resurrection itself.[188] Saadya Gaon was so positive on this point because it had been accepted in Talmudic times; one of the Talmudic sages had even demonstrated it by a logical conclusion: "The pious will be resurrected in their clothes. Look: God puts a seed of wheat into the earth naked, and it comes out covered with husks. Why should man, who is buried in his clothing, not be revived in the same state?"[189] To prove bodily resurrection by comparing it with the growing of plants out of the earth is common in the Qur᾽an, and Muhammad was credited with the statement that the dead would be resuscitated in the garments worn at their deaths.[190] Thus the rank and file of Jews living in an Islamic environment had no reason for doubt and, as the Geniza shows, acted accordingly. (Funeral homes in the United States today prosper because their customers seem still to be haunted by residues of such concepts.)

Moses Maimonides (1138–1204), a physician trained in philosophy, naturally, looked at these matters differently. In his Commentary on the Mishna, completed when he was a man of thirty, he says this about his contemporaries: "Everyone, the common people and even the educated, ask only *how* the resurrection of the dead will be effected, whether men will appear naked or clothed, and if so, whether they will be clad in the very attire in which they have been buried with all its stripes and patterns and beautiful tailoring, or whether the clothing will serve only as a cover for the body." In his *Treatise on Resurrection,* Maimonides goes so far as to equate those who believe in bodily existence in the world to come with those who imagine God as a body, which is worse than idolatry.[191]

The picture of burial customs, practices, and beliefs presented by the Geniza must be examined in the light of Jewish and Muslim traditions.[192] Fumigating and sprinkling the body with camphor and sweet-smelling fluids, as here, is known from both, although the sources rarely had the opportunity to maintain this. Coffins were common in Talmudic times but not in early Arabic Islam. The profuse use of this costly item (wood had become scarce in the Near East) by the Geniza people probably had its origin in the molestations of non-Muslim corteges by the street mob (about which more later). It seems, however, that the body was not buried in the coffin. Hence we read that people wished to have a new coffin, and even that the one bought or made for them should not be reused for someone else (an interesting taboo).[193] Boards for coffins were available in the bazaar, of course, but sometimes, as in the cases referred to here, a saw was needed for adjustments. It is strange that the portable trestles on which the coffin or bier (or both) was laid during the eulogies and lamentations on the way to and in the cemetery also had to be bought. Did the coffin taboo apply also to them?[194] It is doubtful whether it was possible in an Islamic environment to retain the ancient custom of halting seven times on the way to the cemetery—as if the community wished to keep its departing member back. The ceremonies were probably performed in the cemetery itself. In Alexandria it was customary for the cortege to make a halt in the synagogue. This beautiful gesture of farewell by the community was probably a Palestinian practice and seems to have been unknown in Fustat.[195]

The "way to the desert," southeast of Fustat, where the cemetery was situated, was long, and safety on it had to be bought with money.[196] With the progress of time the cost of protection multiplied. In an account of January 1105, written during the reign of the viceroy al-Malik al-Afḍal, no mention of any government interference was made. Compare that with the next report written in or around 1159, when times in Egypt were rough and the country was ruled by the strongman Ṭalāʾīʿ Ṣāliḥ Ibn Ruzzīk, who was notorious for his avarice.[197]

Funeral expenses for Mubārak b. Abu ʾl-Munā from Damascus

Coffin	40 dirhems
Release [given by the office of inheritance tax][198]	9 dirhems
For the "way" [permit to use the route to the cemetery]	3½ dirhems
Digging and building of the tomb	15 dirhems
The washer	3 dirhems
The cantor	2 dirhems
Poll tax, messenger, and release [by poll tax office][199]	15 dirhems
An underling [or: slave] of the guardsman[200]	5 dirhems
Total	92½ dirhems

The payments made here to offices, officials, and police amounted to 32½ dirhems, over a third of the total cost of the burial. As always, the minorities were particularly exposed to the rapacity of an oppressive government.

Turning now to the funeral personnel, with which the mourner had to cope, no uniformity should be expected. But there was a minimum dictated by the nature of things. The cantor, or leader of the congregation in prayer, appears regularly in documents connected with funerals. The Jewish cantor should not be compared with the *imām,* the leader in Muslim prayer. The Jewish service was a musical performance; the cantor was a singer, known to everyone, including the women listening to his voice from their gallery upstairs. The cantor often served as court clerk and also as ombudsman for the members of the community, male and female.[201] Thus he was the ideal person for the role of a public funeral director, a function designated by the Arabic term "who brings the deceased out [to the cemetery]," probably a translation from Hebrew.[202] The cantor also sang the prayers, of course, wherefore we often find a number of cantors in a cortege.[203] In her detailed will the business woman Wuḥsha says: "The remainder of the 50 dinars [assigned by her for her burial] shall be distributed to the cantors who will walk after my coffin, each according to his rank and renown."[204]

This custom of the men following the coffin was probably general, and since, in later Judaism and in Islam, women and men were kept apart at communal events, the former, as participants in the funeral procession, would walk before the coffin, preceded by the wailing women.[205] Like the cantors, they were by no means of uniform status. Among them we find paupers, but also one who possessed a house of which she left fifteen out of twenty-four shares to the Karaite and Rabbanite communities in equal shares.[206] As we have seen, one differentiated also between Jewish and Muslim wailing women.[207] It was certainly risky for Jewish women to make much noise while passing through Muslim quarters. That it was indeed not only the contents of the lamentations, but the noise accompanying them that was appreciated may be concluded from this sad document: a widow—certainly not a rich one—had inherited from her daughter 10 (or 20) dinars. She dedicated the entire sum to her "for the burial and screaming," *dafn wa-ṣiyāḥ.*[208] As in biblical times (Jeremiah 9:16–20), men, too, were lamented by wailing women. Otherwise, a man on his deathbed would have no need to expressly forbid their employment at his funeral.[209]

Judges (the rabbis of the Geniza period, so-called because they had to deal much with civil cases) seem to have participated in the time-consuming funerals and visits to houses of mourning only in special cases. "Study should not be interrupted even for an hour."[210] When a dayyān appeared at a funeral, he was expected to make a speech in honor of the deceased. What could happen in such a situation is beautifully demonstrated in this exchange of short notes.

A Funeral Speech

As was customary among close friends, neither the short note nor the answer to it translated here are signed. Both persons, however, are familiar to the readers of this book, and their handwriting is well known to the student of the Geniza. The first belongs to the judge Nathan ha-Kohen b. Solomon, from whose hand many documents from the years 1125–1150 have come down to us from Fustat, but he also signed as "first" a document in Tyre in 1102. The answer is in the hand of his younger colleague, Nathan b. Samuel he-ḥāvēr, "the Diadem," as he was affectionately called with an abbreviation of an honorary title of his.

The woman at whose funeral the judge was expected to speak had obviously been renowned for her particular kindness to her daughter-in-law, who, like many young wives in those days, had come from a distant country.[211] For this reason, she was compared with the biblical Naomi, who conferred so much care on her daughter-in-law, Ruth, a foreigner from the Land of Moab. "The Diadem," it seems, was a relative of the deceased woman. As may be remarked in passing, the Geniza has preserved dirges written by him on the death of a noble lady.[212]

This is to inform you, my lord, "The Diadem," m[ay] G[od preserve you], that my mind has become rusty, I am no longer what I used to be and I have no ideas. Tomorrow they will ask me to speak. Kindly write a short alphabetical [eulogy] on the reverse side of this note,[213] giving the essence of the story of Naomi adapted to the case of this lady. Proceed in this composition according to your own taste and send it over immediately.

Answer (on the reverse side):

Your servant kisses your gracious hands and accepts your order with obeisance and reverence. However, this disaster has shaken me[214] and I am in deep sorrow. Give your servant respite until the night, when the commotion will have abated. Then I shall write down what you have ordered and send it to your excellency at daybreak.

May the well-being of your honor increase.[215]

Samuel Krauss, the eminent expert on Talmudica, doubted that eulogies were delivered at the burial of women. Here we see that it was regarded as a matter of course that a dayyān present on such an occasion would "say something," and numerous Hebrew dirges on women have been preserved.[216]

A male lamenter was still heard of at the beginning of the eleventh century. Later the cantors and dayyānīm made this profession redundant. Years ago, at a Yemenite funeral, I had the opportunity to listen to such a professional lamenter. He had hardly begun his eulogy when the entire crowd burst into tears. What he had to say consisted mostly of commonplace quotations that had no specific reference to the deceased. But everyone wanted to weep and waited only for the proper opportunity to relieve his sorrow.[217]

Of the technical personnel with whom the mourning family had to cope, the washers, as their emoluments indicate, seem to have varied in type and quality.[218] Those demanding high fees probably also provided preservatives and spices. They repeatedly appear in the plural, because they were inclined to form partnerships.[219] They functioned as purely commercial undertakings, and should not be confounded with the far later "holy brotherhoods" in which distinguished members of the community acted as washers of the dead. As a very young man, I was admitted to such scenes, probably for the purpose of initiation, but was far too insignificant to be allowed to do the actual work.[220]

The grave diggers, too, sometimes formed unions, even competing ones, called *ḥizb,* the modern word for party. A document written in the first quarter of the eleventh century shows that the elders of the community had to interfere and to regulate their employment which gained the final approval of the community as a whole.[221]

The builders of the tomb represented again a group by themselves. As the "Account for the Shroud" (translated above, p. 160, item C) clearly shows, "building" is a reference not to a sepulcher erected above the tomb but to the very interment. The deceased was laid within a coffin-like structure of bricks, which was covered with a roof of flagstones or bricks. He should have it comfortable there and not be drowned in the sand of the desert. The high price paid to the builders reflects the fact that their task was by no means without danger. In a document from Bilbays, Lower Egypt, from spring 1253 we read about a man "who was killed when a tomb fell on him."[222] When a burial took place late in the evening, as it often did, the tomb was not filled in immediately, since the falling earth could damage the newly made roof of bricks above the corpse. Therefore a watchman had to keep men and animals away, and another person would do the filling the next morning.[223]

In accordance with the biblical concept of dying as "being gathered to one's fathers" (Judges 2:10), one wished to be buried near one's parents or other paternal relatives. We have read this in the will of rich Sitt al-Ahl (p. 153, item C, above). The man, who in his deathbed declaration was content with five outer garments, wished to be buried near his paternal uncle or his first wife (in that order).[224] The octogenarian from Āmul in northern Iran, who undertook the long voyage to Jerusalem to rest near his father, and the remarkable letter inviting a native of Jerusalem to return there not because it was the Holy City but because it was "the city of the tombs of your forefathers" are other examples.[225] We hear comparatively little about these matters, certainly because those who could afford it possessed family burial grounds, so that no special arrangements for this aspect of a funeral were required. This ancient Jewish custom was followed wherever the circumstances permitted it, but was, as far as we are able to judge, less common than one would expect. The often small communities were like a family.

A reader of the Account for the Shroud might have taken offense at the insignificant amount of the item "given to the wife for expenses—5 dirhems," and wondered why this item is noted immediately before the building, that is, closing, of the tomb.[226] The scribe arranged the details of the account in the sequence they happened. What happened was this: We have learned that on the very day a person died his possessions were sealed by the rabbinical court. Since the household money was customarily, although not exclusively, in the hands of the husband or a male relative appointed by him, the widow, if she did not possess means of her own, could remain penniless when death overcame her husband. During the week of mourning no transactions were permitted, and food was brought to the house. The pittance given to the widow in our account was for occasional small expenses. As soon as the inventory of the husband's possessions was made, the widow received the share due her.[227] Mourning in the ritual sense of the word began when the tomb was built, that is, when the corpse ceased to be visible. From that moment on, the mourners no longer belonged to themselves. They had to respond to the condolence ceremonies following immediately at the cemetery and, when they returned home, to be prepared to receive visitors and beggars, and to listen to prayers, sermons, litanies, and lamentations day and night. Thus we understand why the official in charge of the funeral squeezed the 5 dirhems, wrapped in a piece of paper, into the hand of the widow just before the building of the tomb.

The closing of the tomb signaled the inception of "living with the dead," the topic of the next subsection, in which the rites and rationales for the remembrance of the deceased are studied. Here the material aspects of the departure of the deceased, the stocktaking of his possessions, the final testimony of an active life, are considered. Numerous documents to this effect have been preserved, mostly in the form of lists, often partial, or drafts. As an example for discussion, a full report has been chosen, which shows in detail the process of stocktaking and, in particular, the role of the widow during and after the proceedings. This well-prepared and carefully executed visit of the appointed representatives of the community after the week of mourning forms a telling counterpart to the hasty listing of the belongings of a dead foreigner prior to his burial discussed above.[228]

The importance of the person whose possessions had to be inventoried can be gauged by the fact that the three chief judges of Egyptian Jewry found it appropriate to visit his place together. The deceased, Abū Yaʿqūb Joseph of the prominent Ben Nahum family,[229] was probably a grandson of his namesake, who, around the middle of the eleventh century, was active in Fustat in business with Palestine and in matters of the Jerusalem yeshiva.[230] Our Abū Yaʿqūb's wife, so prominently mentioned in our document, was the daughter of a R. Shela whose honorary title was Benefactor of the Community. She bore the beautiful names Joy of the Eye, Fairest of the Fair, known to us from an agreement about the ownership of a house made by her with her sister in 1120, six years after the death of her husband.[231] The deceased was, at least at some time, a goldsmith, since the visitors inquired about jewelry that he might have fashioned for himself, but, as usual in those days, might have accumulated wealth through a number of different economic activities.[232] Before discussing the general import of this document, I prefer to furnish a full translation.

Inventory of the estate of a rich goldsmith[233] (Aug. 11, 1114)

[A] On Tuesday, the seventh of the month of Elul 1425, according to the Era of the Documents, we, the three judges who have our permanent seats in Cairo and in Fustāt, Egypt,[234] visited the home of the deceased elder Abū Yaᶜqūb—may God have mercy upon him, Mr. Joseph, son of Mr. Samuel, known as Ben Nahum, in order to make an inventory of all his possessions, to establish a claim and proof for the orphans—may God comfort them.

This is [what we found]:

		Dinars
[B]	Note signed by the elder Abū Sahl for the amount of	63⅙
	" " " " latter's son, Abū Sulaymān " " "	100
	" " also by Abū Sahl	42
	" " also by Abū Sulaymān (dated Dhu l-Ḥijja [50]7; ended on June 6, 1114)[235]	106¾
	Two notes signed by the elder Abu ʾl-Ḥusayn al-Ḥalabī (of Aleppo), one for the amount of	4⅔
	and the other " " " "	4⅓
	Note signed by the elder Abū Sahl for the amount of 490 less ⅓ dinars, of which 16,000 dirhems were withdrawn, balance remaining approximately	60
	Note signed by the elder Abū Sahl	38⅓
	" " " Abū Sulaymān (to be paid in monthly installments of 1 dinar, dated Ramḍān (50)7 [February 1114])	40
	Note signed also by Abū Sulaymān (dated Shaᶜbān (50)7 [January 1114])	12
	Note signed also by Abū Sulaymān	84½
	Note signed also by Abū Sulaymān (dated Dhu ʾl-Qaᶜda (50)6; ended on 20 May 1113)	100
	Note signed by the elder Abu ʾl-Faraj Ben Qasāsa	29½

[C] A lampstand, a washbasin, a shallow bowl,[236] a sprinkler, five dishes, and a bracelet, all of silver.

[D] New dinars, weighing 400 dinars, less half a dinar.
Another sum of specie, consisting of excellent ancient dinars, weighing 54⅙ dinars.

[E] Bars of fine silver,[237] weighing 85 mithqāls, and worth, according to

the [son-in-law of the deceased, see below] elder Abu ʾl-Ṭāhir, 15 dinars.
Molded pieces of silver with gold luster,[238] weighing 75½ dirhems.
A bar of gold for gilding,[239] and rings of a total weight of 18⅙ dinars.
Silver dust,[240] weighing 5 dirhems.
Rejected dinars, 37 less ⅓.
Two covers of silver and three rings of silver.

[F] On the day of the demise of the elder Abū Yaʿqūb, the widow received from the Court a sum of 1,250 dirhems for the *expenditure for the burial.*[241] When asked about it, she declared that the whole had gone toward the expenses for the deceased.

[G] Three of the notes listed above, namely, two signed by al-Ḥalabī, the elder Abu ʾl-Ḥusayn, totaling 9 dinars, and that signed by the elder Abu ʾl-Faraj for the amount of 29½ dinars, are due and have to be added to the cash in gold.

[H] The elder Abu ʾl-Ṭāhir, the son-in-law of the deceased elder Abū Yaʿqūb, informed us that the elder Abu ʾl-Ḥasan b. Ayyūb owed 61¾ dinars from a *jāʾiz*[242] to the amount of 65, of which 3¼ dinars fees are to be deducted, leaving a balance of 61¾ dinars. This amount is included in a note of Abū Sulaymān, which [was] in the possession of the late elder Abū Yaʿqūb.

[I] This is the total of his possessions on which we, the Court, had put our seal on the day of his demise.

[J] We, the Court, also asked the widow whether the deceased had possessed any other precious vessels, in addition to those listed above in this document. She said: "He had none." We further asked her whether he or she had possessed jewelry listed in her marriage contract or which he might have had fashioned for himself. To this she replied: "With all these things I fitted out the daughter whom I married to the elder Abu ʾl-Ṭāhir. Therefore, there is no need to list anything in addition to the items mentioned before."

We have written and signed this inventory, to establish a claim and a proof, on the above-mentioned date. Ratified and valid.

[K] Among the documents submitted to us were certified notes, some in Arabic and some in Hebrew [characters], as follows:

An Arabic note on the account of Mūsā b. Musallam, the silk-weaver, on 90 dirhems.

A note[243] on account of Mūsā b. Faraj, the Christian, on 10 dinars.

A note on account of Ṣāfī b. Naḥrīr, on 64 dirhems.

A Hebrew note on account of Maṣlīʾaḥ, the Sicilian, showing a balance of 10 dinars.

A Hebrew note on the account of Abu ʾl-Ḥasan, the spindle maker, showing a balance of 16 dinars.

A Hebrew note on account of Abū Isḥāq b. Ṣalḥān, showing a balance of ¼ dinar.

[L] We have written [there follow some remarks about words written between the lines]. The deceased also possessed two slave girls. We have written [etc.].

[M] Signatures of the three judges, of two other persons, probably experts in banking and precious metals, and the clerk.[244]

[N] [There follows an appendix, written (albeit with two slips) in an unusually large good hand, that, it seems, of the first signatory after the judges.[245] Before any shares were distributed to the heirs, the widow received the "deferred installment" due her according to her marriage contract. In this case, the sum due was 75 dinars (the same paid to her sister-in-law Munā at her divorce).][246]

The widow has received five dishes, a sprinkler, a cover, a bracelet, a shallow bowl, a washbasin, a lampstand, and bars of silver, eighteen pieces, and one small piece, the price of the total being 75 dinars.[247]

This document is an excellent illustration of how people, circumstances permitting, readied themselves for the inspection and intervention of the communal authorities. Not a word is said about real estate. The clerk carefully formulated "we entered the home, *manzil*," not "house," so that no misunderstanding could occur concerning the ownership of the place, which, as so often happened, was probably the property of the wife.[248] Furnishings, clothing, and houseware, prominent in other documents, are completely absent. It is likely that they were given in part to the daughter at her marriage and were temporarily reserved for the wife, that is, given to her in the husband's lifetime. Silver vessels and jewelry were another matter. The Fairest of the Fair was certainly asked by her husband more than once in which form she wished to receive the part of the marriage gift due her at his death. She preferred silver; as the wife of a goldsmith, she knew that silver was scarce in those days and possessing it in vessels and bars lent security. Each piece had certainly been selected in common consultation (see n. 247).

But why not jewelry? (Only one silver bracelet, a minor item, is mentioned.) And how could she testify that all the ornaments listed in her marriage contract as well as those created for her[249] by Abū Yaʿqūb had been given by her to the daughter whom she married out to Abu ʾl-Ṭāhir, probably a goldsmith like his father-in-law (item J)? It is difficult to assume that a woman of a well-to-do family, even of advanced age, should divest herself of all her ornaments. The goldsmith's wife could, of course, have possessed jewelry other than that forming part of her dowry or given to her by her husband. But looking through the wills and deathbed declarations of women of ease read above, we notice that strong-willed Sitt al-Ahl makes no mention of ornaments at all: the businesswoman Wuḥsha gives away a few silver rings, the least valuable jewelry, and even these seem to have been unredeemed collaterals; the wife of judge Nathan b. Samuel possessed a headband of eleven pieces, but it was deposited with her husband for the expenses of her burial. She did not wear it. One cannot expect uniformity in these matters; yet the question is what the prevailing custom was, and, considering the enormous role of jewelry in the life of the Geniza woman, this is indeed a problem. Divesting oneself of one's ornaments was a sign of mourning (Exodus 33:4, after the story of the Golden Calf: "The people mourned, and no one put his ornaments on"). But when did mourning begin for a wife and mother?[250]

Another remarkable trait of this document is the fact that it was not a cantor or any other official of the community who was in charge of the burial but the widow herself. Had it not been readied in advance, the very high sum of 1,250 dirhems, worth about 35 dinars at that time, could not have been at the disposal of the judges putting their seal on the possessions immediately after the death occurred. Abū Yaʿqūb had certainly discussed every detail with his wife, and the money was handed over to her in silver coins, so that it could be more easily distributed to all who had claims, including the beggars and visitors who had to be fed during the week of mourning. A son-in-law was around and took active part in the preparation of the inventory. But it was not *always* the males who were entrusted with responsible tasks such as a funeral, a communal event of the highest order. An experienced woman of valor, familiar with all the social connections and obligations of her husband, was the natural choice. Being occupied with her chores would also help to soothe her grief.

The reader should not be surprised that she was not asked to render an account of the high sum spent on the funeral and all that went with it, or of the precious objects kept by her. Here we see again the family protecting its privacy from interference by the community. No doubt, Abū Yaʿqūb, on his deathbed or before, had stipulated that no one, not even a court, was entitled to impose on his widow an oath or even ask her to render an account. Her word had to be accepted as would that of two male witnesses recognized by a court.[251]

The perfectly systematic arrangement of the inventory with its exact data ranging from 1/6 to 490 dinars was clearly the fruit of protracted planning over months, if not years. One major aspect stands out: whatever Abū Yaʿqūb might have possessed, his workshop, with its implements, merchandise, partnerships in business ventures of others, real estate, cattle, or whatnot, had been converted into dinars, either in the form of bankers' notes or in specie, good gold coins, new and old.[252] This way of hoarding by persons approaching death had its source, on the one hand, in the confidence in the rather constant value of the Fatimid dinar, which thus provided security after retirement from work.[253] On the other hand, there was the consideration of what would happen after death, namely the practice of the courts to convert an estate into sums of dinars, which could be divided more easily among the heirs and handled more conveniently in the (so frequent) cases of endless lawsuits, or of minor orphans maintained by the estate.[254] Abū Yaʿqūb certainly believed that he was better equipped for converting his variegated possessions into sums of gold than were the authorities of the community. One transaction was made as late as May/June 1114, two months before his decease. The difficulty for a court to handle an unorganized estate consisting of a multitude of different items may be gauged from inventories referred to throughout this book; for instance, the inventory of the estate of a prosperous coppersmith with its mixture of store and household; or that of (the son of) a seller of potions, a sharābī, adduced about twenty times because it touches on so many different aspects of life; a physician's possessions, where objects required for his practice mix with furnishings and wardrobe; or those of a farmer of the sales tax on silk comprising notes written by Muslim and Jewish notaries on hundreds of dinars, gold coins from different mints, paper bags with silver and copper dirhems, and vessels and ornaments made of gold and silver, whose evaluation would certainly cause many a headache, which the supervisors of our Abū Yaʿqūb's estate were spared.[255]

Death exposed the deceased and his family to the public. On one hand, this had some positive aspects, inasmuch as it was an extraordinary occasion for general expressions of affection and esteem. On the other hand, it was a grave intrusion into privacy.

The more quietly the inevitable event was envisaged and the more carefully it was prepared, the more was privacy protected and the community kept from trouble.

This discussion of death was introduced by a report of the decease of Barhūn b. Moses of Qayrawān, Tunisia, whose end was described to have been as exemplary as his life. No will of his or list of his possessions has come down to us. The inventory of Abū Yaʿqūb's estate, translated above, may serve as a model of so orderly a departure from life. He died in peace with himself and highly esteemed by the community. Otherwise, his family would not have been honored by the joint visit of the three high justices of Egyptian Jewry for a legal action that proved to be, in fact, a routine ceremony. Everything was ready and required only formal endorsement by the authorities. Life ended like a business year, when a person closed accounts trying to leave no loose ends and obligations to others.[256]

Living with the dead.—Keeping alive the memory or, rather, the presence of a beloved was first achieved by the commotion that his or her departure aroused. The reader of the Bible is familiar with such expressions of mourning. Even high-standing persons would weep in public and lament with raised voices; mourners tore their garments and disfigured their face by throwing ashes on it, or by other means. Clothes are symbols, or, one might say, substitutes for the body. Rending or throwing off one's clothing, or deforming one's appearance, represented an outpouring of the feeling that with the death of the beloved a part of one's own self had gone. Inconsolability, the refusal to accept the departure of the dead person as a reality, was also regarded as an expression of the degree of dedication to the deceased. Finally, the inability to return to normal life, the prolonged neglect of one's usual occupations, is described even by a Moses Maimonides as an almost natural response to the loss of an unforgettable beloved.[257]

Vehement expressions of mourning were laudable because they demonstrated reverence for parents or teachers or strong attachment to relatives or friends. There was, however, the ever present danger that excessive grief might induce defiance, at least in words, toward God's decrees (Job 1:20–22; 2:9–10). During World War I, when I was asked to eulogize a fallen friend before a large and very conservative audience, I opened my *oraison funèbre* with Ecclesiastes 10:5: "As if an error had been committed by the Ruler." Only my youth could excuse this blunder. In order to avoid such and similar pitfalls, the sages of the Talmud (like the religious authorities of other communities) tried to regulate the expressions of mourning. Their approach was twofold. On the one hand, old usages, after having been cleared of superstition and standardized, were turned into law; these official mourning rites were intended for heartless people who neglected the duties of filial piety or family affection. For instance, the rending of the clothing after the death of a close relative was made obligatory, but its measures were defined. For a full week after the closing of the tomb, the mourners were advised to stay at home, to sit on the floor, and to refrain from work, so that they could dedicate all their time to the memory of the deceased; many other practices were connected with this. Minor rites of mourning had to be observed for the first month after the death, and, for parents, for a year. On the other hand, these injunctions were also conceived as limits: "Three days—crying; a week—mourning; a month—no pressed clothes and no haircut; are you more merciful than me, the All merciful?"[258] Above all, the mourners were held to recite the "justification of the judgment," a prayer pronouncing the justice of God's decrees, at the funeral. Excessive lamentations impinged upon the belief in God's goodness. The sages went so far as to say: "He who is persistent in his inconsolability will soon mourn for another dead."[259]

Inconsolability, however, seems to have been regarded as the mark of a noble man; at least that is the impression I derived from the letter of a young court physician to his father, translated below, in which this trait is ostentatiously displayed. The beginning of the letter (as often happened) is lost, and with it the address, written on the reverse side, containing the names of the sender and the recipient. But the identity of both can be established by two other letters, one written by the young physician and another addressed to him by his father.[260] Abū Zikrī b. Abu ʾl-Faraj b. al-Rayyis was in the service of Sultan al-Malik al-ʿAzīz (ruled Egypt 1193–1198), the son and successor of Saladin. As our letter reveals, the Sultan showed personal interest in him, which is somewhat surprising because Abū Zikrī, according to all we know about the family, must have been very young at the time, probably less than twenty. (Al-Malik al-ʿAzīz himself, who was born in 1172, was appointed by his father as viceroy of Egypt at the age of fifteen.) Abū Zikrī's quick promotion—he specialized as an ophthalmologist—is easily to be explained by the fact that his father was already in the service of al-ʿAzīz; the personal relationship had its origin perhaps in the practice of taking medications first thing in the morning and preferably in the presence of a physician; at that inconvenient early hour a beginner conducted the service.[261] I stress the youth of the writer of our letter because I believe that its tone has much to do with his age.

Abū Zikrī describes what happened after a letter of his father, announcing the death of a younger brother, had been received and read by him (probably at the house of an acquaintance), whereupon he hurried home.[262]

[A] Of all the clothing I had on me nothing remained on me as cover except the loin cloth and the turban, half of which was on my head and the other half thrown into the mud.[263] Whoever saw me in this state went after me and tried, if he could, to talk to me, but soon found out that I was not one who could be talked to. When I came home, I did not pass a fireplace or an oven without putting the ashes on my head. My senses were lost altogether.

[B] Then the physicians came, and Mufaḍḍal,[264] all the sheiks, and Shams al-Dīn Alkyn and his two brothers with their wives;[265] also Fakhr al-Dīn Taṭṭar[266] with the entire entourage of al-ʿAzīz; then the faqīh [Muslim jurisconsult] Zayn al-Dīn and the ḥājj [Mecca pilgrim] al-Shāṭir. For everyone who had seen me in that state went away and spread the news,[267] whereupon people came whom I knew and those whom I did not know, but no one was able to calm me.

[C] Finally, ʿAzīz al-Dawla al-ʿAzīzī,[268] and with him Murshid, came, after the faqīh Zayn al-Dīn had left me, and said: "We—the Sultan has sent us, after the faqīh had informed him about what he had heard and about your state. He sent us to console you. This is what he wishes to tell you: 'Accept the loss of your brother as I did when my brother al-Malik al-Amjad died. The beloved one is a treasure deposited with us by God; the proprietor takes it back. What can you do?'" They did not cease to adjure me and to swear by the life of the Sultan that, if I did not accept their words and wash the ashes from my face, no one of them would ever greet me, and they would report to al-Malik al-ʿAzīz that I paid no attention to his message.

[D] I washed my face before they left and remained in my room alone, forsaken [lit., thrown away], until the evening. I did not see a Jew who would cheer me up in my misery, or comfort and calm me.[269] Then my ophthalmia came back.[270] I screamed because of the grief in my heart and the pain in my two eyes. I had sent Nahum *al-muʿallim*[271] to the [Jewish] elders and physicians, and adjured them not to bring me anything [to eat] worth even a penny, when they came to see me. They came at night and scolded me for what I had done [the excessive mourning]. I said: "My brother has gone. I have done for him something for which you should reward me." They sat with me the entire night, and each of them comforted me and cheered me up, as much as he could.

[E] I passed the day in fasting, also the night, till noon the next day. The elder Yaʿqūb b. Abu ʾl-ʿAynayn came in, when Nūr al-Dīn b.

Alkyn[272] and Shams al-Dīn were sitting with me, and complained to them about my refusing to take food. They adjured me to break my fast. I gave him a dirhem and he bought lemons and lettuce for me. He went again and brought me *laban* (milk or sour milk), with which to wash my eyes.

[F] I remained in the house for four days and did not leave it until the faqīh Zayn al-Dīn and Murshid came, while Ibn al-Yemenī was with me, and adjured me to go out, because a Mamluk whose eyes were ailing had complained about me to the Sultan, and he had sent them after me. I went with them and treated the Mamluk while my own eyes were bandaged. I returned home and did not go out until after the Sabbath when a second complaint was lodged.[273]

[G] And now,[274] my lord and father—may I be made your ransom—had it not been for your letters containing words of comfort and an allusion to "a widow," I would not have sent you a missive or reply. How much hope did I have for his recovery, vouchsafed in a letter to you; then you wrote that you inquired about him and were informed that an assistant of an eye doctor in Akko had died. This made the matter certain, and I understood that your previous letters were intended to console me, as God does.[275] God has given and God has taken, may long life be granted to you, my lord, may I be your ransom from all evil, and may I never witness an inauspicious day for you.

[H] And console the lady, my mother, on her loss, which grieves me so much. She has reared a child and taken pains with him and, at the end this terrible misfortune! May God strengthen her heart and grant us all consolation; and may he *accept his death as an atonement for all his sins and the sins of his family.*

[I] Your letter mentioned that he was ill three months and died on the tenth of Marheshwan . . . and that he willed, to my regret, to be buried in Haifa, which, for some reason, could not be changed.[276] So let us accept His judgment. I say this reluctantly; but His judgment is accepted by me under all circumstances. Yet you have people [family] around who cheer you up and comfort you, and I have remained like an orphan whose parents are alive.[277] May God bring us together soon.

[J] After my eyes recovered, the tall Levi who lived with me in the house died, whereupon my eyes were again affected with ophthalmia. However, while writing these lines I am recovering and even better than before.[278]

[K] And I say that whoever changes his intention to settle in Jerusalem will not fare well. I had in my mind to remain here only shortly in the service of the Sultan and then to go there, but something happened which made it impossible.

And, also, everyone who leaves Jerusalem will be afflicted, either he himself or through his children; this has become evident in all the misfortunes that have befallen us. May God turn the end to the good and unite us wherever he wills.[279]

[L] Finally, my lord, I adjure you by your belief in the teachings of *our*

Teacher Moses, let yourself not be overcome by distress and grief, and let not the lady weep, for God's sake! My lord knows what *the sages of blessed memory* have said on this: "*Three days—for weeping; seven—for mourning; thirty—no haircut, he who weeps longer than this may, God beware, weep about someone else.*"[280]

[M] Yet, by our religion, the illness that befell my heart and my body when I learned about what happened has not yet ceased, and through it the labored breath, about which you know, increased, and I do not know what will happen. May God strengthen the hearts of all of us. Amen.[281]

Answer quickly to cheer me up. . . . *And Peace.* Written on the 21st of I Adar.[282]

[N] [*Written in the margin*:]

What has come about has come, and God has done what he willed. By the education you have given me, had I strength or a support on which I could rely, I would let the doctor come and see me every day and use his prescriptions. But I have no support—except God the exalted. If I let myself go, my enemies will rejoice in my misery—as if what has befallen me were not enough for them. May God look upon us all with the eye of his bounty and goodness.

[O] And console my dear sister on the loss of her brother, who loved her so much. May God strengthen her heart and ours.[283]

[P] My lord, do not reproach me for what I have written. I believe I flung this letter ten times or more from my hand, overcome by tears.

The markedly excited tone of the letter (written about four months after the death of the brother!) was certainly attributable partly to the neurotic constitution of the writer, known from other missives of his, and partly, as alluded to above, to his youth, but it also represented what was regarded as proper, if not laudable. Practically all facets of traditional behavior while mourning a beloved are visible here, mostly in exaggerated form. The rending of the garments was overdone by throwing them away altogether and running through the streets disrobed, covered only with a loin cloth. Disfiguring the face with ashes was biblical (and probably also Egyptian) custom, but not Jewish law; Abū Zikrī did it profusely (it was winter, and plenty of ashes were available). The custom—almost law—not to eat one's own food on the first day of mourning was surpassed by fasting altogether. And now the week of mourning! The list of dignitaries coming to extend their sympathies—civil, military, religious, professional—some even accompanied by their wives, or appearing repeatedly, was, of course, an indication of how popular Abū Zikrī himself was at the Sultan's court. But there was more to it. Receiving condolences throughout the week, even through the nights, kept the brother's memory alive. Sultan ʿAzīz himself compared the death of Abū Zikrī's brother with that of his own brother al-Amjad.[284] Could there be a greater honor for the deceased? The very last words of the letter, scribbled in the margin and stating that its writer was overcome by tears about ten times while writing it, should demonstrate that after four months the grief over the loss of the brother was as potent as on the day the bitter message arrived.

We miss one thing in this letter: not a word is said about the dead brother, his good qualities and merits, which would make the greatness of his loss even more conspicuous. It must be noted that in the letter, mentioned above, which Abū Zikrī's father wrote to him while on his way to Egypt (and sent to Jerusalem with the Sultan's envoy), he admonished him in the strongest terms to stop quarreling with his brother, not to preach to him, which the youth loathed, and not to bring shame upon the family by letting their squabbles out in the open. Only a few years, at most four, could have lapsed between the father's letter and that of Abū Zikrī's translated above. While the tense tone of the latter could be partly explained as a kind of overcompensation, one might understand why Abū Zikrī had nothing to say in praise of the deceased.[285]

I believe, however, that this was not the cause of the seeming omission which we noticed in Abū Zikrī's outpouring. People write letters of condolence and compose elegies in the style and tradition of their society. There exists a whole literature of elegies and lamentations in medieval Hebrew (and, of course, Arabic), but even in long poems one finds few, if any, hints as to the deceased's individuality. When a Maecenas was eulogized, one knew what was to be said about him; one had only to say it forcefully and in striking phrases not used by everyone. When a brother passed away, one knew, or was supposed to know, what the loss of a brother meant; one had only to express it convincingly. As a counterpart to Abū Zikrī's letter, I examined a cycle of eighteen poems dedicated by the great Samuel ha-Nagid of Granada (d. 1056) to his late elder brother. The poems are moving and very expressive, even factual; they portray the brother from the moment Samuel brought a physician to him, describe how Samuel was overcome by the news of the demise, how he, in person, washed the dead body and clothed it, and, again, in the cemetery, descended into the grave to prepare the proper bedding for him, and so on through the week of mourning, a visit to the tomb, and finally, the first anniversary. But in the total of about one hundred and eighty lines, only three furnish us with some individual traits of the dead brother: he was a munificent and powerful communal leader under whose staff "bear and cow grazed together" (cf. Isaiah 11:7). Despite its specifics, the cycle of elegies by Samuel ha-Nagid was so general in nature that parts of it could easily be adapted to other cases of mourning. That this was so may be concluded from a letter of an Alexandrian notable to the Jewish judge in Cairo written about half a century after Samuel's death, where he quotes three verses from one of the poems of that cycle in a way that suggests they very likely were commonly known among the Jews of Egypt.[286]

The Geniza tells a story about a poet who was visited by his patron at midnight with the request to write a letter of condolence for him in verse. He found the poet already engaged in writing such a letter; moreover, he composed booklets of dirges, each of which was to be recited by "Israel," that is, the local community, on a different day of the days of mourning. There seems to have existed a veritable industry of composing dirges. Judah Ibn al-ʿAmmānī, a cantor, schoolmaster, and court clerk in Alexandria, writes to a senior colleague staying in the capital: "You asked me to send you dirges for the deceased. Wishing to provide a lot, I copied about thirty and dispatched them to you. You answered: 'I have them all with the exception of two or three.'" Whereupon Judah suggested that his colleague advise him of the first lines of the poems to avoid unnecessary duplication. This refers not only to creations of famous poets, such as Samuel ha-Nagid of Granada, just mentioned, but also to funeral poems composed locally for special occasions. In another letter by Judah to the same address we read: "You mention that the dirges have arrived and that you have everything. That is impossible. Had you said 'I have one out of ten,' all right; but that you have all of them is impossible, for some of them were composed [meaning recently] by my uncle Zadok—may his Rock keep him."[287]

Unlike Abū Zikrī b. Abu ʾl-Faraj, the writer of the long letter translated above, a brother, trying to comfort his sister on the loss of their mother, repeatedly dwells on the personality of the deceased. It seems to me, however, that in a society that "put reverence toward parents on the same plane as the service of God, or rated it even higher,"[288] any mother could be praised in the same vein. Readers will judge for themselves.

The woman here consoled on the death of her mother was no longer young, for she had already reared a son who caused her much grief. Moreover, the phrase concluding the letter seems to indicate that she still expected to remarry. She had obviously expressed excessive despair over the death of their mother in a letter to her brother, and he responded with the epistle translated below.

To appreciate our letter, observe the extreme attachment and devotion of a middle-aged woman to her old mother—as is often found in traditional communities. The letter combines phrases normally used in letters of condolence with others betraying special features. Our writer could be so intimate, because his sister was literate. He calls her learned, advises her to read certain books of the Bible, and sends her a "Book of Comfort" written in Arabic to keep her busy in her mourning. The script of the letter is pleasant, but not that of a trained scribe.[289]

As one whom his mother comforts, so I shall comfort you; and you will be comforted through Jerusalem.[290]

From her brother Barakāt—may he be granted that no evil should anymore befall her.

[A] My most noble, prudent and learned sister.[291] I wish to comfort you over our loss of that precious pearl,[292] our lady, our mother—may God place her in the Garden of Eden. With her, all our happiness has gone and our joy has passed away; the crowns have fallen from our heads, for we have always lived by her *merit* and prayed to God on the strength of her good deeds.[293] She was taken from our midst because of our sins—may God have mercy upon her and compensate us for her loss.

[B] Now, dear sister, you know and understand better than anyone that no one is spared this cup of sorrow. She is a saint wherever she is. Our sages have said of a pious person like our mother: "She is like a pearl that is lost; wherever she may be, she remains a pearl; only those who have lost her have become poorer."[294]

[C] I entreat you, Rayyisa, fortify yourself as much as you can. For were you to weep even a thousand years, it would be of no avail. You will only become ill and you yourself will perish. I implore you, dear sister, be composed for God's sake, and he will richly reward you. Read, sister, the book of Ecclesiastes, the words of our lord Solomon;[295] this will improve your faith. In addition, I am sending you the book *Relief after Adversity*; please study it.[296]

[D] I, myself, am writing this note after having soaked my eyes with tears over the loss of our mother and her motherly love. However, what can we do against God's decree, "and who may say to Him: What are you doing" (Ecclesiastes 8:4)? May God strengthen our hearts; your being alive consoles us; a woman who has left behind a daughter like you is not dead.[297]

[E] Again, dear sister, do not do harm to yourself by useless excess. Remember that others lost their mother, father, and children, and still accepted God's judgment with resignation. No one need teach you, for you know well what happened to the prophets and others, and take good care of yourself, so that you do not perish. Attend to the words of the prophet: "Do not weep for the dead, nor bemoan him; weep sore for him that goes away."[298] Read the books of Ecclesiastes and Proverbs and submit to the judgment of your Creator, the True one.

[F] Remember that our lamented mother had always wished and prayed to die in your arms and those of your brothers. Now she has died, with her eyes resting upon you and full of joy that you were there. May God replace the grief for her [with something better].[299] Now, dear sister, know that I revered our mother, although I was far away from her, but despite my being so far away, this separation by death caused me unsurpassable grief. How far more you, poor woman, must have been affected, you, who have never had a happy day in your life, and had revered her so much. Now, you have lost her company and the blessings of her merits—may God keep you company in his mercy and help you with his might and may he not make you lonely separated from your only (son),[300] nor may he cause you shame from him; but may he guide him and me to his holy law.[301] And may he let us die like her: *after a life of piety and good deeds.*

[G] Please excuse me for not coming in person to comfort you. We all need comfort after this loss, and I in particular. May God help and guide you, and may he grant you and me the blessings of her merits; for she is in a state of beatitude.[302] Finally, may he fulfill all the joyous hopes which I entertain for you and support you.[303] *And peace upon you.*

This unassuming and straightforward letter is a good introduction to the thinking of the Geniza people about the enigma of spiritual contact with our beloved after they have been separated from us by death. The loss is absolute; we no longer enjoy the feeling that we are protected by their presence (item A). Yet, a relationship continues, which may be compared with the mutual responsibility of relatives, as far as material possessions are concerned. Relatives (and, to a certain extent, the members of the community) share mutual responsibilities. They are usually helpful to one another during lifetime and inherit from one another after death has occurred. In a period when "the dead provided for the daily needs of the living," inheritance played a more general and tangible role than seems to be so in our own society. Inner life was structured in a similar way. Our letter, which opens with the outcry that with the death of the mother her children have lost the protection enjoyed by her good deeds, can no longer dare to pray to God, that is, to approach him (item A), concludes with the wish that God may grant them the blessings of her "merits" (G), while they themselves would try to emulate her (F). Even more so: her worthy daughter embodies the mother as if she were still alive (D).

I assume that the question of how the postmortem operation of merits was conceived, whether as a kind of inheritance now owned by the heirs or as a continuous emanation of blessings by the deceased, or both, did not occupy their minds much. As children revering their mother, they believed that she still possessed some form of life (B), and that she was destined to dwell in Paradise (A).

The names of the dead, even more than those of the living, should be mentioned accompanied by a blessing, such as "resting in Eden," or "of blessed memory," and many, many others. These expressions must be understood as wishes, or, rather, as prayers: May he rest in Eden, may his good performance here be a blessing for his survivors and, even more so, for him himself. For two books are kept in heaven, one for recompense in this world and one a record of deeds to be scrutinized when admission to the World to Come is considered. Omitting the obligatory blessing over a dead person in the presence of a relative of his was regarded as an offense, just as was the omission of the blessing for a living one.[304]

In documents of the eleventh century it was common to mention one's father with the blessing "may he be granted eternal life," written out in full crosswise above and below the signature.[305] Since eternal life belongs to God alone, this formula was replaced by "may his record be [accepted] for life in the World to Come."[306]

But when would the World to Come come? With the Messiah, or after Resurrection, or prior to both? And which form would it take? The concepts and beliefs about these matters were multifarious.[307] Hence the many different types of wishes and blessings one had for the deceased. Since one wrote mostly in Arabic, Muslim influence on the phrases used is recognizable, although this was mostly a matter of form rather than substance.[308]

Whatever the content or shape of these wishes or prayers, the idea behind them was that just as we expect to benefit from the blessings of the dead, especially parents and other forebears, thus we must also do something for them, especially invoking God's mercy, whenever their name is mentioned and above all on occasions specifically set aside for this purpose. True, man's merits are his strongest advocates, but "there is not a righteous man on earth who does good and never sins" (Ecclesiastes 7:20).[309] Only God's mercy and forgiveness can vouchsafe the deceased their share in the World to Come. Therefore, God must be reminded constantly of *his great name,* one of the most common phrases in the Geniza (the name is: "merciful and gracious," self-proclaimed in the theophany in Exodus 34:6). Immediately after the tomb is closed, a prayer for the deceased is recited, referred to by the term *raḥḥam,* invoking God as the merciful.[310] The prayer is repeated in a more elaborate form again and again in the house of worship, often for generations after the thus remembered person had died.[311]

The dead needed to be protected by the living in other respects as well. No blame should be attached to the deceased and no claim be made against them. To be sure, the heavenly record books noted all deeds of men; but it was safer, as the Hebrew phrase goes, "not to let Satan open his mouth." Therefore, it was common usage, especially in the eleventh and early twelfth centuries, to add to the name of a deceased person (especially the father of a person addressed) the phrase *he-ḥāsīd beʿōdō* (Heb.), "who was pious throughout his life." In any more elaborate contract of release, the absolved party is freed of any responsibility in this world and the World to Come; or in a business letter the customer is assured that he may send the goods ordered in whichever way he prefers (for instance, by land or by sea) with no responsibility for himself "in this world and the next."[312]

One may argue that these are worn-out phrases of the type appearing in the parts of a contract which we are inclined to skip over when we read and sign it. This may be partly true. The difference is that phrases of that sort are not found in our legal papers and there must be a reason for this difference.

Moreover, occasionally not only is a living person released from responsibility in the World to Come, but a deceased himself. "I declare herewith before you that I release the above-mentioned Moses, [*may he*] r[*est in*] E[*den*], from all transactions that have occurred between us, especially from the partnership in those bales of textiles, in which I and that Muslim had shares, as well as from all dealings between us from time immemorial until his death, *may it be an atonement for him, his family and all* [*Israel*]. Likewise, I release herewith his son, Ḥalfōn, the latter's mother, the widow of Moses, and his daughter, and all his other survivors. . . ."[313]

The natural meeting place of the living with the dead was the cemetery. The presence of the survivors at the tombs assured the departed that they had not been forgotten, that their memory was alive, while the visitors must have expected somehow that their most intimate prayers would be heard there and be transmitted to where they might become effective. An elegy put into the mouth of the Nagid Moses, the son and successor of the Nagid Mevōrākh b. Saadya, while visiting the grave of his mother on the thirtieth day after her funeral, tries to express such feelings. He calls his mother "my protectress" (ll. 7 and 33), and exclaims:

> To whom have you abandoned me, my lady:
> Whom have you appointed as my support? (l. 13)

The mother assures him that the separation from him was as bitter to her as death itself, and encourages him:

> Come to see me every day.
> Linger at my grave.
> Your lamentation will awake me.
> Arouse my compassion
> And we shall weep together. (ll. 59–61)

Especially, the anniversary of her death should never be forgotten. He replies:

> If I forget your demise,
> Let my right hand wither.
> By the belief in my religion,
> I shall remember you forever. (ll. 63–66)

The elegy concludes with words of consolation. God will comfort her son and replace what he had lost. There is an allusion to his wife (l. 69), cf. Genesis 24:67, where Isaac is comforted after the death of his mother Sarah after he married and loved Rebekah. The mother herself is confident that her good deeds on earth—all of which were for God's sake—will speak for her, she will have a peaceful and pleasurable rest in the Garden of Eden under the Tree of Life until she will be resurrected and summoned, in the company of noble men and women like herself, to whatever fate God will have destined for her. (The latter, very common, phrase is from Daniel 12:13, the concluding words of the book.)[314]

This long and rather emotional poem of seventy-six lines seems to lack one feature: expectations for a reunion in future life (as Jacob expressed in Genesis 37:35, or King David in 2 Samuel 12:23). I do not remember having met this theme anywhere in the Geniza. One wished the deceased person to be united with some sitting biblical heroes, with the righteous, and in general, a company suited to him, in particular, of course, with his own ancestors and other dead members of the family. A poet or writer of a letter often expresses the platonic regret not to have died instead of the lamented. But to say that he desired to join him when his own hour came was not done: one shied at mentioning the prospect of the death of a living person.

The David Kaufmann Collection, Budapest (DK 167, ed. A. Scheiber in *Habermann Memorial Volume,* pp. 153–158) contains an elaborate poetic dialogue between a mother and her children visiting her tomb a year after her interment. Only a few lines are missing at the beginning, where she is speaking, complaining about the worms tormenting her. The children, sitting around the tomb, bewail her absence and complain that all good fortune and happiness have left their dwellings since her departure. They ask her to pray for them and also to arouse the heart of her husband Nethanel, who since her death had been elevated to the position of Head of the Congregation, to join her in her supplications for her children. The mother expresses words of consolation, while the children thank her for all the good she has done and wish her to be placed in the Garden of Eden together with all noble men and women and to be resurrected at the End of the Days to new life. The mother concludes the dialogue with the words of comfort with which only a mother is able to comfort her children (Isaiah 66:13).

The poetic dialogue between a mother and her daughter while visiting her tomb (by Judah ha-Levi, in Carmi, *Hebrew Verse,* pp. 339–340) is of a different kind. The women wail, and the daughter gently accuses the visitor that she let her have her wedding in the tomb, but finally makes peace with her mother. No doubt, such poems were written for women who knew Hebrew.

The classical Geniza is strangely reticent about cemeteries. From a poem written around 1125 we learn that the cemetery of Fustat, then as in later times, comprised tombstones with inscriptions, mausoleums, and enclosures or structures that served as family burial grounds. A vizier had ordered that all these should be destroyed and that Jewish funerals should take place only at night. But the vizier perished before his decrees were carried out.[315] The way in which documents of the eleventh and twelfth centuries speak about sepulchers seems to suggest that they were not very common but were by no means exceptional.[316] In August 1227, when Abraham Maimonides functioned as Nagid, the proprietorship of the Jewish community of Fustat over its cemetery was unsuccessfully contested by Muslim hotheads, but as far as I know, nothing is said about this in the Geniza.[317]

Cemeteries were the scenes of public supplication in time of calamity. The forebears resting there could not remain unmoved by the sufferings of their progeny and might protect it with the shield of their merits.[318] When a solemn excommunication was to be announced, the Torah scrolls were carried out to the cemetery and the congregation gathered there as a memento mori and warning to the evildoers, and probably also as an invitation to the large community of the dead to witness, and to consent to, the (sometimes dubious) action.[319]

We do not read, however, about seasonal mass visits to cemeteries, so common all over the Middle East, and practiced in Cairo in modern times until the dissolution of the Jewish community of Egypt in the middle of this century. In the night preceding the eve of the Day of Atonement everyone who could make it repaired to the Jewish cemetery south of Cairo; by midnight, at the dim light of a moon nine days old, thousands had assembled to visit the resting places of members of their families as well as the tomb of Rabbi Capusi, a seventeenth-century saint of Maghrebi origin. So popular was the demand for this visit that, about a hundred years ago, the Jewish financier Felix Suarez, after having built a railway connecting Cairo with Ḥulwān (about 25 kilometers south of the capital) built one to the cemetery on condition that the trains operate there throughout that night. Before daybreak, everyone had left. Since that Maghrebi saint originally had a *ziyāra* (pilgrimage) to his tomb on another date, it is not excluded that the mass vigil on the night before the eve of the Day of Atonement goes back to medieval times, whereas the visit to Capusi's tomb was later combined with it.[320]

The scarcity of data on communal visits to cemeteries in the Geniza may reflect realities: the unsafety of the way there and the molestations experienced on it; the prominence of the Karaite community in Cairo; the Karaite disapproval of the cult of saints and of "prayers to the dead"; and, without doubt, the existence of holy shrines, especially of Dammūh, venerated far beyond the borders of Egypt, and others, which furnished opportunities for seasonal religious gatherings.[321]

The proper place for remembering the dead was the synagogue. I have repeatedly had occasion to speak about the mass of "memorial lists" preserved in the Geniza. In the case of mourning these were summaries of prayers for the person who had recently died, for his ancestors and other deceased relatives, and, finally, for the community attending the memorial service. On the Day of Atonement, other holidays, and special occasions (for instance, when a close relative returned from a voyage overseas), the prayer for the deceased ancestors and members of the extended family was more detailed, and special attention was paid to the person who had initiated the service (and probably also made a donation), for his nearest relatives, as well as for the congregation and its leaders.[322]

The combined prayer for the dead and the living is a most eloquent testimony to the awareness of the continuity of life, the individual forming a link in a chain, inheriting, contributing, and passing on. There was no room for Death Triumphant. The predominant mood was the opposite, that expressed by the often quoted prophetic vision: "The Lord has vanquished death forever, and wiped away the tears from all faces" (Isaiah 25:8).[323]

B. AWARENESS OF PERSONALITY

1. The Ideal Person

Character study.—In the preceding pages of this volume the Geniza person is described as an eminently social being, as an embodiment of the world to which he belonged. It seems, however, that the intensity of the contact or clash with the immediate environment had the effect not only of shaping the individual but also of polishing him, of visibly bringing out the core of a person both as observed by others and as felt by himself. It is remarkable how much the writers of our letters not only paid attention to the personalities of others but also occupied themselves with their own psyche. This facilitates somewhat the delicate task of trying to penetrate the interior of their makeup.

A person's character was regarded as a force over which he had little power. "Characters are, as is well known"—they cannot be changed.[1] A father complaining about his leniency toward an unworthy son writes: "My character is not hidden from you."[2] Another father admonishing his elder son not to be too strict with his younger brother warns him: "His character cannot stand this."[3] These and similar words of praise are frequent in business letters: "Taking care of the affairs of others belongs to your character by nature. I am confident that if a complete stranger asked you to look after his business, you would toil for him" (for this reason, no doubt, the writer permits himself to trouble the recipient to run a few of his own errands).[4] The accumulation of synonyms (character-nature) should indicate that man is compelled to act in accordance with his innate disposition. *Khuluq*, imperfectly translated here as character, means, literally, "the form(s) in which one is created." The word, which probably was a plural itself from the beginning, appears here, and often elsewhere, as *akhlāq* ("the plural of the plural," as one says in Arabic), denoting the totality of a person's traits, and, in scientific usage, the study of ethics.[5] Since God is the creator, man's character has to be taken as His work. Addressing a friend, a writer says: "I am grateful [to God] for your [wonderful] qualities," a phrase echoed in various combinations.[6]

For comparing two persons or oneself with others, the notion of character and its synonyms that describe the totality of a personality are used. "His mind is not like that of his brother; he is far nobler," writes a communal leader in Qayrawān, Tunisia, about two of his colleagues.[7] Labrāṭ I of al-Mahdiyya, after having spoken to his younger brother in Egypt with great tenderness, says of another brother who had remained in Tunisia: "Our brother—may God keep him—you know the lowness of his character and nature" (again the duplication of synonyms, here in a pejorative sense).[8] When sheikh Abu ʾl-ʿAlā of Alexandria, Egypt, whom we have met before, was involved in a lawsuit with a woman relative in Fustat, she asked him to visit the capital for this purpose. A traveler to Alexandria, whom she had asked to convey the message to him, reported that sheikh Abu ʾl-ʿAlā insisted that she come to his place instead, and added: "His soul is like the soul of your wife" (the relative concerned).[9] When a person in dire circumstances was advised by his sister to follow the example of his maternal uncle (a nephew was supposed to resemble the brothers of his mother), he retorted: "My uncle wants one thing and I, another. My mold, *qālab,* is the opposite of his." The general assumption was that character was in the genes. "He is excused," writes an India trader sarcastically, complaining about a relative who caused him the enormous loss of 4,000 dinars. "He has proved to be like his father; his father ruined part of what my father left me, and he did the same with my own property."[10]

In many letters persons object to being compared with others. "When I am described as energetic and dedicated, while others are negligent—this is true," writes a merchant.[11] Another writes to a relative: "[I have done as you requested], so that you should not criticize me in your letters; a man like me should not be criticized, for if I could make a thousand dirhems with one dirhem of yours or of anyone else, I would do so."[12] A communal official in a provincial town, explaining that his rival in a nearby place was stirring up much publicity for himself, adds: "But I am not like that."[13] But when blaming a person for what he has done, one would say to him: "Your exterior betrays your spirit," that is, you act in conformity with your character.[14] After having expressed surprise at the (unseemly) behavior of the addressee, one might add, with reference to persons notorious for the same vice (as is done in a letter to judge Elijah b. Zachariah): ". . . unless you have adopted [or simulate] the characters of sheikh Abū Saʿd and Abu ʾl-Thanā."[15]

People sometimes note a change for the worse in their own

character. A husband writes to his father-in-law: "Because of my pains and illness, and the meager support I received, my character became constrained. I was irritated, and began to exchange words with the lady of the house" (his wife; he asks the recipient to talk to her).[16] A father who confesses to his friends that he was unable to describe (that is, to understand) the difficult character of his son, writes to the young man himself: "I have never seen a character or religion like yours and never heard of the like." At the end of the letter, however, he adjures him: "Return to God and bring your [sound] mind back to yourself."[17] Another father uses this strong phrase in addressing his son: "Exchange your character and make it your concern to act reasonably."[18] Naturally, God's help is needed for such a change. "I do not hate her, I hate only her character," complains a husband about his young wife. "I say to her, 'don't do this.' She says, 'Yes, I shall not do it'—and immediately forgets what I have told her, and does it. I hope God will correct her and her blessed character and her blessed movements." In contrast, a woman asking for a divorce complains about "the vexations and character" of her incorrigible husband.[19] Or, in despair, one might write: "He cannot get away from the [bad] nature of the people of the Maghreb [namely, not to answer letters]."[20]

The expectation or exhortation addressed to a person to live up to the proved excellence of his character is a very common topic, especially in personal letters and in recommendations for people seeking help: "Be the person people think you are!" "Be as you are known!" Or, a stereotyped phrase in this connection: "I am asking you to deal with him [for instance, with a bashful refugee from Spain], as is your beautiful habit with regard to any stranger."[21] Or, after having censured a man's action severely, one might praise him for the good "hidden in the folds of his innermost mind."[22]

The preoccupation with the character of an individual in the Geniza correspondence and the profusion of Arabic terms denoting it should not surprise us. It was conditioned by the exigencies of life. The dickering and haggling that accompanied any transaction required a quick perception of the nature of the person with whom one was dealing. In view of the endless troubles caused by the difficulties of communication and transport, by an unstable economy, and by the general insecurity, businessmen had largely to rely on the ability, honesty, and dedication of the person to whom they entrusted their goods and money. The intense competition in social and communal life, requiring constant rubbing of shoulders with (real or imaginary) friends and enemies, forced everyone to check whether he had made the right choices. In short, watching character was not a mere pastime.[23]

It seems to me, however, that more was involved here. In the early nineteen-thirties, when I devoted a considerable part of my time to the study of pre-Islamic, and, in particular, early Islamic, Arab narrative and poetry, I was intrigued to meet in it scores of synonyms denoting "character" in the sense of the totality of a person's distinctive traits, or, at least, of his most dominant attribute. Since saying the same thing in different words was one of the most cherished means of artistry in Arabic poetry and rhetoric, synonyms were found everywhere. But their profuse occurrence with regard to the term "character" set me thinking.[24] It had to do with life in a merciless desert, which sharpened the eye for the observation of human nature. The question "friend or foe" had to be decided only too often. Because of the vast distances, the wandering poet's praise or blame formed part of political and military intelligence. In an atmosphere where only the strong (in reality or by reputation) could prevail, competitiveness, "the striving for the highest," was a necessity for survival. These social notions became embedded in the Arabic language, and, with it, in the minds of its speakers. They were kept alive during the upheavals of the Muslim conquests, and, later, in the competitive economy of the High Middle Ages, in which the people who left us their letters had a share.[25]

The Geniza vocabulary possessed a number of ways for classifying human character. The attributes "difficult," "low," and "noble" mentioned above need no explanation. The common phrase *ḍīq al-khuluq* or *al-ṣadr*, being of a narrow, constrained, nervous character or "chest," describes both a natural disposition and a passing state of mind. It may be translated as worry, namely about one's own affairs (which leaves little time for those of others), but also as sadness about the misfortune or illness and the like of a friend or an esteemed public figure. "I am aware of the constraint of your character and your many affairs," writes Judah b. Joseph of Qayrawān in an amiable letter (on vellum) to the eminent Ismaʿīl b. Barhūn Tāhertī, sojourning in Egypt. "I do not intend to burden your heart with taking care of my affairs in person; I shall be satisfied if you assist my relative ʿAyyāsh with your guidance and advice. I shall regard this as if you had actually dealt with them." As a return service, Judah reports that he had arranged with both the purser and the captain of the boat in which Ismaʿīl's goods were transported, that both his heavy and light baggage would be stowed in the best places available. This assurance was certainly apt to widen and smooth a "narrow chest."[26] "Constraint of the chest" is often mentioned as caused by special circumstances, for instance, in this passage, by the absence of a friend's letter: "By the truth through which we are united in God, smooth my soul with a letter from you. Whenever I tried to write to you, I did not find a joyous mood or a widening of my soul. I gave up writing you letters only because of the constraint of my chest and said to myself: 'I shall not write him unless I am in a joyous mood.'" The opposite of a narrow chest is, of course, its wideness.[27]

Other pairs of descriptions of opposed characteristics were light (moving easily) or heavy or hard, and warm or cold. Barhūn b. Isaac Tāhertī of Qayrawān recommends to his younger partner in Egypt to do business with Abu ʾl-Qāsim ʿAbd al-Raḥmān (a Muslim): "he is light [nimble, obliging]; this is his nature" (August 1048). "Mr. Heavy" could become a derogatory nickname.[28] Abraham Ben Yijū writes about his brother Mevassēr: "He is not a man; he is indolent, possessed of a hard heart" (ca. 1152).[29] Of a person who was reminded by hints to pay his debts and proved to be unresponsive, it is said: "He has a cold brain"; of one who neglected his wife and children: "He is cold in heart and volition"; but "warmth" is one of several terms describing a person who exerts himself for others.[30] "A fresh, supple brain" designates a responsive and pleasant interlocutor.[31]

The principal virtues.—The most common and most comprehensive quality sought in "the right person" was the multifaceted, untranslatable *muruwwa*, literally, "virility," "manliness," derived from *mr*ʾ, man, just as Latin *virtus*, "virtue," took its origin from *vir*, which means the same. The original meaning of bravery, that is, defiance of danger and difficulties, was still underlying its usage in Geniza times, as when a man is exhorted to follow the example of Queen Esther "who jeopardized her life out of her muruwwa, prowess, when she came to the King of Persia without being summoned."[32] A son writing to his father could say of himself: "My prowess emboldens me to write this note to your exalted seat."[33] In general the term is the mark of a man who does the right thing, or, at least, what was expected from him, discounting possible drawbacks for himself. As such, it designates the totality of the mundane, natural virtues, as opposed, or, rather, complementary, to those acquired by the educational influence of religion, described as *dīn*.

Even a fledgling student of Islam knows that the opening chapter of *Muhammedan Studies* by I. Goldziher, "the father of Islamology," is entitled "Muruwwa and Dīn." In that chapter Goldziher analyzes the spiritual situation of the ancient Arabs at the advent of Islam. The Geniza letters show that the awareness of virtues outside of, and alongside with, the spheres of religion was a mark of the medieval civilization of the Near East as revealed in the day-to-day life of a minority group. Compared with the ethical world of Talmudic Judaism or of the Jews in medieval western Europe, this dichotomy is remarkable.

In commercial contracts, the two sides would promise to act in accordance with dīn and muruwwa.[34] When a local official, describing himself as an underdog, requests a prominent scholar in the capital to intervene for him with the Head of the Jewish community, he writes: "He who is possessed of dīn and muruwwa, supports him who has no helper and support." At the end of the long letter he becomes even more explicit: "I know of the dīn of your excellency, that your muruwwa urges you not to be remiss, similar [to Boaz in the Book of Ruth 3:18, of whom it was said] 'the man will not rest until he will have settled this matter today.'" In other words, the commandments of religion were bolstered by the recipients' natural propensity for helping the weak.[35]

In many cases the translation "gentlemanly nature" or the like, in the sense of a person who has power over others but does not misuse it to his own advantage, may be appropriate. A representative of the family of a newly married young woman, who was mistreated by her husband, writes to him: "We trust in your sense of honor, your gentlemanly character, your religiosity, your learnedness, and your noble descent. In any case, we all are agreed upon your gentlemanly character and know that you will not harm her, but will placate her heart by your guidance and fine behavior. May God give you success in this world of yours and the next." Learnedness is mentioned because it was supposed that he who knows the law would also keep it; but the stress is on muruwwa.[36] Of a town on the India route where anarchy prevailed, it is said: "This is a place where no one pays debts except when [motivated] by his own gentleman-like character," that is, does voluntarily what he could not be forced to do.[37]

From this it is only a step to the specific meaning of generosity, then outright alms-giving, which muruwwa assumed, especially in later times. When a Nagid instructs the two congregations of Fustat to arrange a collection for an old man who desired to travel to Jerusalem, he adds: "This is the time for muruwwa," for the display of willingness in giving.[38]

Synonyms of muruwwa derived from *rajul,* "man," are found in the Geniza only occasionally. "The time is difficult, but manliness, *rujla,* and high aspirations become apparent only in times of hardship."[39] "Behave like a man in this matter as much as you can."[40] Of a mean person one said: "He is a small man," *rujayl* (as we do), about a creditor who did not grant a delay in payment (as was customary), wherefore the recipient of the letter was advised to make payment to him immediately.[41]

The virtue muruwwa, as we have seen, possesses widely different images in the Geniza correspondence. A basic unity, however, is perceptible in all these facets: a quality of moral strength that enables a person to do his duty—and a bit more than his duty. Therefore, the term "muruwwa" can appear in the midst of a related expression but stands out markedly. "He who is famed for his goodness, muruwwa, humaneness, and religiosity."[42]

A virtue cognate with muruwwa, but definitely distinct from it, *nakhwa,* or high-mindedness, sense of honor, generosity, is also often invoked in the Geniza. Whereas the former emphasized the moral aspect of generosity, the latter underlined its social role; nakhwa was connected with status. In pre-Islamic times it could denote the haughtiness and (often baseless) boasting of the tribal noblemen, and, as such, was condemned by the Prophet Muhammad in his farewell address to the assembled participants in the pilgrimage to Mecca a year before his death.[43] The verb derived from it could be used in the derogatory sense of treating a person superciliously. But in the Geniza the word always occurs with a laudatory connotation, and the verb derived from it meant being generous and helpful. I need not emphasize that the writers of the Geniza letters spoke the same Arabic as their non-Jewish contemporaries belonging to a similar social ambiance.[44]

The place occupied by nakhwa in the code of virtues of a Geniza notable is beautifully exemplified when one in charge of communal affairs is praised for his *fear of Heaven* (in Hebrew), muruwwa, and nakhwa, that is, his religious, moral, and social distinction.[45] Even more impressive is an extensive letter in which the writer, after having ascribed to his benefactor, in Hebrew rhymed prose, almost every virtue imaginable, addresses himself in the main Arabic part only to one, his nakhwa, his generosity tested through extended personal experience.[46] Being generous with one's time was not less praiseworthy. "This is the time for action [or 'good deeds'] and generosity," writes a "distinguished member of the [Jerusalem] Academy" from a small place, describing the illness of a patient in detail and requesting three friends in the capital to leave all their affairs, to approach a physician, procure the medications prescribed by him, and send them with the man who carried the letter and the money attached.[47] Finally, as already described, nakhwa could express the general idea of self-respect and sense of honor.[48] Once, when a house opposite the women's entrance to the synagogue of the Iraqians in Fustat was rented by the head of the congregation to a Muslim, an indignant member published a protest ending with the cry: "Where is your nakhwa, your self-respect, and sense of honor?!"[49] Of a foreigner who had received many favors from the community, but proved to be a worthless person, it was said: "He showed little nakhwa and muruwwa in respect to his Creator, his religious community, his wife, and his children."[50]

In connection with nakhwa and/or muruwwa, the faculty of resolute dedication, the willpower to do things, is highly appreciated in the Geniza in many different contexts, and various terms are used for it, the most common being *ʿaṣabiyya*, literally, "dedication to one's kin," but in the Geniza describing a person exerting himself for any good cause, public or private. "You decide on a matter and succeed in carrying it out" (Job 23:28).[51] In an environment where many promises were made but not so many kept, this virtue of firmness in word and deed was particularly valuable. Hillel, the son of the merchant prince Joseph Ibn ʿAwkal, is praised for his "high-mindedness, dedication (ʿaṣabiyya), compassion, and gentlemanly character."[52] An India trader who had endangered his own life by saving the assets of his partner, who had died in Dahlak on the Sudanese coast, is commended by the rabbinical court of Fustat for "his dedication and high-mindedness, his burning desire to be helpful to the orphans, his vigor, and intrepidity."[53] The burning desire to help others was also religiously motivated; hence the frequent phrase "exert yourself for [him or] me *for Heaven's* sake," or Arabic was replaced by postbiblical Hebrew *zerīzūth*, eagerness, as in the combination *fear of Heaven and eagerness.*[54] As in ancient Arabic poetry, the ideal person should crave hardship; religious merit could not be acquired except by zest for trouble. "I need not remind you," writes an Alexandrian to his brother in Fustat, neither of them young anymore, "that for the matter requested from you by me, you must be desirous of toil, prepared to take heavy loads upon your back, and prove that you are worthy of your renown; do not fancy that what can be obtained only by drudgery may be gotten with God's help while taking things easy." It is a pity that we do not know what the writer's request was.[55]

A quality uniting muruwwa and nakhwa, but superior to both, and mostly comprising also noble descent and high standing, was *faḍl*, literally, "superiority," but designating mostly a nobility of mind attained by inheritance and self-education. A person possessing this quality would do more than people normally expected. The following quotations, randomly chosen, refer to four leading personalities of the Jewish Mediterranean community active from the end of the tenth century to the middle of the twelfth.

Joseph Ibn ʿAwkal, whose activities in business, communal, and religious law affairs stretched from Iran and Iraq to Morocco and Spain, was not easy to get along with, but he was by all measures a remarkable figure. A competent merchant of Sicilian origin living in Qayrawān, Tunisia, writes to Ibn ʿAwkal in Fustat that he granted him extraordinary conditions because he held him in deep esteem in view of his illustriousness, high nobility of mind, and religiosity.[56]

Abraham b. Isaac (Ibn) al-Furāt (the river Euphrates a symbol of affluence and munificence) was a physician in attendance to a Fatimid vizier who functioned during several decades around the middle of the eleventh century as the main representative of the Jewish community before the Muslim authorities; he was "the eye with which one sees and the support on which one leans." Matters great and small were entrusted to him, and even Muslims sought his protection. The fact that he was a scion of the priestly family of the Gaons of Jerusalem (an office similar to that of the Christian Patriarchs) was apt to enhance his prestige, although, as far as we know, he did not occupy any office within the community. Numerous letters of thanks and praise addressed to him have been preserved. I wish to single out one sentence: "God has favored you with religiosity and nobility, *with a generous heart and fear of heaven*"—one sees again that religious and secular excellence are held in equilibrium.[57]

Around the turn of the eleventh century the Jews of the Fatimid empire were led by the Ra'īs al-Yahūd, or Head of the Jews, Mevōrākh b. Saadya, certainly one of the more prominent personalities of the Geniza period. A leader of the Maghrebis in Alexandria, who had known Mevōrākh intimately during the period when he was in disgrace and exiled to that city, writes to a friend that Mevōrākh's reinstatement was greeted with the highest expectations, "for his religiosity and nobility of mind, in which God has perfected all the noble qualities, surpass everything that had been before."[58]

The idea that faḍl was something special, superior, is forcefully expressed in words of thanks included in a letter by the prominent merchant Joseph b. Abraham b. Bundār of Aden, South Arabia, to Ḥalfōn b. Nethanel of Fustat, who was characterized as "the center of all the leading personalities of his time." Joseph writes: "God gives nobility of mind only to him who was born for it. To you God gave it as something exclusive."[59] An enthusiastic letter of friendship sent to Ḥalfōn from Granada, Spain, in May 1130, ascribes his privilege of meeting Judah ha-Levi, the Spanish Hebrew poet laureate, to his personal excellence: "Knowing your noble mind and lofty character, God has been beneficent to you and sent you the quintessence and embodiment of our country, our glory and leader . . . Judah ha-Levi. Irrespective of how much I regret to be separated from him [the poet had traveled from Granada to Ḥalfōn's place, probably Almeria], I congratulate you heartily on meeting him; may God, the exalted, give you enjoyment one from another."[60]

Moses Maimonides (d. 1204) renders the Hebrew term *ṣaddīqīm*, as he understood it, as *fuḍalāʾ* (derived from faḍl), "the outstanding ones," those who have attained spiritual perfection, the only ones who will be ingathered to eternal life, not, of course, with their bodies, which will disintegrate, but with their intellects, acquired through hard moral and mental work in this world.[61]

Greatness must be coupled with humility. Only God is great,[62] and man must know his own limits. He must demonstrate his humbleness not only while standing in prayer before his Creator but even more so in his demeanor toward his fellowman. The outstanding scholar should not embarrass the less learned, the rich should be careful not to cause shame to the poor, and a man in power should not let those under his control feel his might. One of the surprises I experienced while studying the Geniza correspondence was the ubiquitous and pointed emphasis on meekness and modesty, mostly expressed by the Hebrew term *ʿanāwā* and its derivatives. A poor scholar in Jerusalem, who had received a gift of one dinar from Mevōrākh b. Saadya when the latter was already famed, but not yet Head of the Jews, writes: "Your reputation is high and elevated in all communities of Israel, especially for your humility" (in veiled contrast with a relative of the writer, who put him to shame, but did not support him sufficiently).[63] In an enthusiastic letter, in which a leader of the Jews of Yemen congratulates Mevōrākh on his appointment as Head of the Jews (Yemen belonged at that time to the sphere of influence of the Fatimid empire), he relates the happiness of "all the people in our country" over this turn of events, for "you are famous by your meekness and fear of sin; you humble yourself, although you are great in the eyes of everyone else." At the end of the letter he expresses the hope, or, rather, certitude, that "you, our lord, in your wisdom and humility will guide us and all the other communities on the good and straight path, as it is written 'you will make known to them the way they are to go and the practices they are to follow'" (Exodus 18:20). This verse was said to Moses, of whom the Bible testifies: "The man Moses was meek more than anyone else on earth" (Numbers 12:3).[64]

The letter in which Moses Maimonides is beseeched by a father to accept his son, a student of medicine, as his disciple, is superscribed with the biblical verse: "The meek will inherit the earth" (Psalms 37:11), meaning that Maimonides will not regard himself as too high to accede to the writer's request.[65] This superscription is found elsewhere, as when a minor poet offers his products in Hebrew and Arabic to another whom he regards (or pretends to regard) as superior.[66] In a letter to his father, a young scholar from Ramle, Palestine, describes Abraham b. Nathan, the Jewish chief judge of Cairo, after having visited him repeatedly, thus: "His Creator has made him perfect in every respect: religiosity, humility, and learnedness."[67]

It is noteworthy that the leading minds of the period paid special attention to this quality of humility. One of these was Hezekiah b. David, Head of the Diaspora for more than forty years and, after 1038, also successor of Hay Gaon as Head of one of the two yeshivas of Baghdad. After praising a scholar for his general excellence and learnedness and his faculty of getting along well with his peers, he writes:

> We wish to have you near us and to enrich ourselves by you because of the pleasantness of your character and the mildness of your disposition, your *ʿanāwā*, as the Sage [King Solomon] has said, "It is better to be of a lowly spirit with the humble than to divide spoils with the proud" [Proverbs 16:19], and as Rabbi Joshua b. Levi has said, "He whose mind is meek is worth as one who has brought all the offerings usual in the Temple," as it is written, "A contrite spirit is like sacrifices [in the plural!] offered to God, and his prayer is never rejected [Psalms 51:18–19]."[68]

When Moses Maimonides, as he writes, became disconsolate with the world (probably after the great famine and plague of 1201/2), he found consolation only in the study of philosophy and in his teen-age son Abraham, "for he is humble and meek more than anyone else; add to this his fine demeanor, his sharp intellect, and his beautiful character; with God's help he will be renowned as one of the great."[69] At the death of his father, Abraham was only about eighteen years old; thus it is somewhat surprising that of all good qualities Maimonides singled out his son's modesty. Sons of famous men have a difficult time. They are inclined either to minimize the attainments of their parents, as is done so often today, or to become proud and condescending, as was more common in the past. Maimonides the father appreciated his son correctly. Abraham left us numerous letters in the Geniza, all written while he was Head of the Jews; they all betray an extreme degree of leniency and considerateness. In his magnum opus, named by him *Comprehensive Guide for the Servants of God,* he dedicated a long chapter to the concept of humility, which proves that he thought deeply—probably based on extended personal experience—about its problems, such as those confronting a leader, who is expected to exercise authority, or a scholar, who must defend the truth of an opinion.[70]

The emphasis on humility in the Geniza world calls for comment. A reference to the Talmudic scale of religious values, where humility is one of the higher—according to one opinion the highest—superior even to sanctity, is justified only under the assumption, probably correct, that the social ambiance in the small Jewish communities of Late Antiquity was not much different from that of the Geniza period.[71] People complained of the overbearing leader of a congregation, who behaved autocratically as if he were a Roman governor or a Muslim sultan (the word for this was *mitgāʾē,* lit., "behaving proudly"); a scholar entering the house of study was advised to pray that he should not enjoy putting a fellow student to shame during a learned discussion; and gifts providing embarrassment more than help were only too common. The contentiousness endemic in the Near East was particularly painful in small, closed societies. Hence meekness was rated so highly.

Naturally, humility is appreciated everywhere. Thus an Egyptian poet, a contemporary of the Geniza people, says of a man praised by him: "He is meek—while the stars are beneath his station. This is the most noble trait of the famous."[72]

But I have the impression, possibly erroneous, that this quality plays a less significant role in Islamic religious ethics. The relevant section in Ghazali's classic *The Revivification of the Religious Sciences* falls, in extent and treatment, behind Abraham Maimonides' chapter bearing the same name.[73]

Humility describes a person who knows his own worth but values what is good in others, even if they are far beneath him. Bashfulness, also often occurring in the Geniza correspondence, is the mark of an entirely different type: one who is diffident, insecure of himself, feeling uncomfortable in the presence of others, and therefore entitled to be treated with consideration. The bearers of letters of recommendation are often described as such.[74] A father recommends his son thus: "Poor boy! He is shy and extremely bashful—but how to treat flax, he knows well."[75] One should have regard even for a diffident debtor: "He is a bashful young man; he should be approached with consideration; I hope he will admit the debt and pay."[76] Seven elders of the Jewish community in the provincial town of Minyat Ziftā, in recommending the son of a previous judge for appointment or confirmation, have this praise for him: "Extremely modest, *bashful, humble,* taciturn, forbearing, inexperienced in troublemaking"—all this in contrast with his rival, who is described as the very opposite in every respect.[77]

Shame, *ḥayā'*, was praised by the Prophet Muhammad as the highest of all virtues; at least, 'Ā'isha, his favorite wife, was credited with transmitting this praise in his name. When Ibn Abī d-Dunyā (823–894) wrote his book on the ten most noble character traits, he put shame first as his opening chapter.[78] Of someone who has no shame the Talmud says: "This man's forefathers were not present at Mount Sinai," that is, he is not a genuine Jew, and the same idea is expressed in various other forms.[79] An echo of this seems to be found in the Ḥadīth, the Islamic literature on the oral teachings of the Prophet, where the following remark is ascribed to him: "Every religious community possesses a characteristic trait specific to it; that of Islam is shame."[80] As is well-known, the place of shame in the mentality of the Mediterranean society at large has attracted the attention of contemporary sociologists.[81]

The more surprising is it that shame as a virtue is practically absent from the Geniza vocabulary. Perhaps the very word was avoided. The Geniza has to report so much about people in shameful situations not because of what they had done but because of what had happened to them—for example, disasters of all descriptions, undeserved sufferings, perennial poverty—that it would have been awkward to praise a person for his shame (as is done in ancient Arabic poetry). It seems to me that the idea of humility and modesty (often expressed in the Hebrew term), so prominent in the Geniza, stood in for shame.[82] By humility we profess that we are aware of our shortcomings, which is the essence of shame. For as a virtue shame means that we are ashamed before ourselves, not only before our fellowmen. The eminent scholar and judge Isaac b. Samuel the Spaniard of Fustat wrote in minuscules crosswise above and below his signature: "In you, O Lord, I take refuge that I may never be put to shame; save me by your justice" (Psalms 31:2). "Never" translates Hebrew "not in eternity," and is to be understood in the light of the ancient prayer, included in the Jewish grace after meals: "May we not be put to shame in this world and not be disdained in the World to Come."[83] Even more poignant are the minuscules adorning the signature of a later judge: "May I not be disdained," meaning in the World to Come; I do not care what people say about me, but I wish not to be disapproved by my Creator (or myself).[84] Shame in the higher sense was certainly present in the Geniza society. The notion was expressed in a variety of ways.

Honor and honesty.—The counterpart of shame in the negative sense of the word, constant regard for "what other people say," is honor, *ʿirḍ*, reputation, the good name a person has or wishes to possess. Bichr Farès, who dedicated a book to this notion in Islam, finds that ʿirḍ designates, literally, "a curtain which separates an individual from the rest of mankind."[85] As *A Thousand and One Nights* and the utterings of common people preserved in the Geniza show, the medieval Near Easterner was very vigilant in this respect.[86] Talmudic literature reveals that the Jews of Late Antiquity, despite (or because of) the wretched conditions in which many of them lived, were extremely sensitive with regard to their honor.[87] All this seems to prove that self-respect, the faith of a person in his own value, was highly developed in the individuals of that area of ancient civilizations.

Honor is invoked in the Geniza with regard to all concerns of daily life: family, religion, business in the widest sense of the word, communal affairs, and, of course, relations between people in general.[88] In modern Arabic usage ʿirḍ seems to be predominantly related to a woman's chastity and faithfulness. This was not so in Geniza times. Even in the first instance presently discussed, where a husband gives his wife *a bad name* (the Hebrew term is used), I am not sure that infidelity was intended. It could mean that she neglected her duties as a housewife or the like.[89]

The document translated is an appeal to a Gaon, the highest juridical authority of the Jewish community, probably Maṣlīʾaḥ Gaon, Head of the Jerusalem yeshiva, who had his seat in Cairo during the years 1127–1139.[90] In order to understand why our document does not contain any name, we must remember that the Gaon, like a caliph or sultan, held public audiences, where everyone was permitted to submit an appeal. The petitioner wrote his complaint on a piece of paper (mostly of modest size), which was picked up by an attendant and brought in to the Gaon. The Gaon wrote his decision on the blank space left, or gave instructions otherwise, whereupon the complainant was instructed accordingly.

The large, clumsy letters, the erratic spelling, the colloquial idiom, and the straightforward, extremely informal way in which the Gaon is addressed, probably indicate that the petitioner wrote this little document with her own hand. Perhaps she earned her livelihood by teaching embroidery and other needlework, together with some prayers, to young girls, that is, she might have worked as a *muʿallima*, or teacher, as poor women often did.[91]

I[n Your name, o Merciful]

I hereby inform your Excellency, our Gaon—may his Rock preserve him—that I am a lonely orphan girl whom they have married to a man with no means of support. I have been with him for ten years, and he has always taken what I earned. Finally, when I was in shreds, with nothing to cover me properly, I said to him: "I shall not give you a thing anymore. I'll buy myself clothing with what I earn." He is not worth a thing, not even one dinar.

For a year or more he has given me *a bad name*. I went to the judges and offered to buy myself free with everything due me from him to save my honor. But they did not grant me a divorce. By God, my honor is worth something to me!

I am requesting now that the *Torah scroll* be taken out and that he who acted in this way and tells lies about me be excommunicated, and that I be given a certificate clearing [my honor] for God's sake.

Thus you will save me from a Hell, which no one knows except God.

May your welfare increase and never decrease. Amen, in eternity, Sela.

Unlike the suppliant in *Med. Soc.*, III, 186, who insisted on getting the sum due her at the divorce, this one is prepared to renounce it; she wishes only to get rid of an unworthy husband and to clear her honor, which she emphasizes three times. For this purpose she requests the procedure named "ban in general terms," described *ibid.*, II, 340–341, a ban to be pronounced over anyone who tells lies about her, and for herself she wishes to get a certificate of blamelessness. She is a miserable, poor woman, still "my honor is worth something to me."

Any disturbance in the relations between spouses was a disgrace, especially for the husband. When a merchant who fancied that he had provided generously for his wife during his absence heard rumors to the contrary, he got very excited, described all he had done for her, and invoked God's punishment over those who diminished his "worthiness."[92]

Another touchy area where people could easily feel their sense of honor hurt was religion. The Jewish faith imposes on its believers many ritual injunctions, some of which by ignorance, carelessness, or other reasons were not always meticulously observed. Of one community official we have three documents, stretching over more than twenty years, showing him reprimanding and chastising people in public for their shortcomings. Since in the case of the unhappy woman, just discussed, we do not know whether she got the coveted certificate of clearance, I present here one, publicly clearing a person accused of having committed a transgression:[93]

This is what happened in our presence, we, the undersigned witnesses: in the month of Marḥeshvan 1484 according to the Era of the Documents (Fall 1172); on a Sabbath, there occurred altercations and arguments between Abū Zikrī b. Mevōrākh and Abraham al-Najīb, which to report would be cumbersome. Finally Ibrahīm[!] charged him with offense and instigated against him, and suspected him of having committed *a transgression* defaming his honor. We said to him: "Explain what you say."[94] But he could not adduce a witness or a proof.

We know that Abū Zikrī is renowned for his religiosity, his piety, and meticulous observance. We wish to write this certificate so that it should be for Abū Zikrī a title of right and a proof.
Moses b. Joshua [may he] r[est in] E[den].
Peraḥiā b. Nādīv [may his] e[nd be] g[ood].

The second signatory is the clerk who wrote the document. Since the paper was reused by the same hand to note some Hebrew quotations, Abū Zikrī clearly preferred not to go to court with the cantankerous official to save his honor.

Far more serious is the story of a cantor or teacher, or both, in a small place near Cairo, who was accused of having assembled young men and danced a *zuhdī* dance with them, a dance accompanied by songs of world renunciation and mysticism. In a sex-conscious society any physical contact between a grown-up man and younger companions could arouse suspicion. Here we see that the writer was really shaken in his sense of honor because of such an insinuation. The note is addressed to the writer's superior in Cairo. It is a sign of his excited state of mind that on the reverse side, instead of the usual phrase "deliver and you will be rewarded [by God]," he writes in huge, calligraphic quadrangular letters: "*Cursed be he* who does not bring this to the knowledge of R. Joseph."[95]

Your humble, wretched servant.[96]

A service [a note] submitted to the presence of my lord, [*his*] *h*[*onor and*] *h[oliness, our] m[aster and] t[eacher], our light and pride, the crown of our heads,* R. Joseph [*may his*] *R*[*ock*] *p*[*reserve him*].

I contracted fever and, following it, dizziness. When I was about to recover, I received a note from you that you had heard about me that I assemble young men and dance a zuhdī dance with them. When I learned about this matter, I became alarmed and relapsed. I decided to go to Cairo to clear my honor from that talk about me; but when I arrived at the Nile, I fainted. Such an occurrence is not unknown. But I wish to clear my honor against the one who told this about me. If people have indeed given witness about this, whatever I shall be obliged to do, I shall [not] dodge.[97]

Honor in the sense of a reputation acquired through integrity, reliability, and honesty was the most precious capital of a merchant in a time when so much depended on the person entrusted with the affairs of others. Consequently, complaints about honor impugned are rather common in the Geniza business correspondence. In the very first letter in *Letters of Medieval Jewish Traders,* we find two such grievances on one page.[98] The cases are typical, one being of the usual type, the other more special and refined. Samḥūn the Sicilian writing in Qayrawān, Tunisia, had advised Joseph Ibn ʿAwkal in Cairo to pay two Tunisian merchants staying in Egypt what Samḥūn owed them; he would be repaid with goods bought for him and paid and sent by Samḥūn. Ibn ʿAwkal not only failed to do what he was asked but did not even inform the two merchants about Samḥūn's instructions. The Tunisian merchants' plight became known back in Qayrawān, and Samḥūn felt doubly disgraced: by the inconvenience or damage caused to his customers, and by the shame of Ibn ʿAwkal's not relying on his communication that the goods had been sent. His other complaint was even more pungent. In a previous letter he had written that he would be delighted to do any errand or business for Ibn ʿAwkal in Qayrawān. A formula of this sort concludes any business letter of some length. But Ibn ʿAwkal understood it as meaning that Samḥūn wished to take the place of his regular business representative (mentioned by name) in Tunisia and said so to a merchant from that country. Samḥūn was infuriated; he was not one who would take another person's livelihood away from him. "I and my honor should not be treated in this way." "I and my honor" seems to be a strange way of speaking. But we find it elsewhere: "He disgraced you and disgraced your honor! . . . Save your soul from his tongue."[99]

The honor of communal leaders, in particular their repute for integrity in financial matters, was protected by the authorities. When the Nagid Joshuah, the Maimonid (1310–1355), advised the Fustat congregation about the yearly closing of the accounts of the poll tax, he strongly warned them of "talks" about the dealings of one of five notables who had advanced payments for the community members to the government. "Accounts have been made with him and everything has been settled. No one has the right to make remarks about him, and whoever does make remarks about his honor will be punished in accordance with the law."[100]

Although the idea of honor extended to the area of religion, it was mainly applied to good repute in worldly matters. No wonder, then, that, like *muruwwa,* when combined with *dīn,* it made the person so described a model of desirable conduct. "Had God guided me at the time of my arrival, [my] religion and honor would have remained intact among them," writes Abraham b. Nathan, former Jewish judge in Ramle, Palestine, and later in Cairo, deeply regretting the mistakes committed by him during communal strife in Tyre, Lebanon.[101]

In daily life a person would swear by his honor as he would swear by God, the Torah, the Sabbath, the ruler, or his own father. I still was surprised when I read in a huge and exceptionally calligraphic letter addressed to Samuel ha-Nagid b. Hananya these lines about a gift made to the writer: "The dayyān [judge] sheikh Abū Naṣr saw me in my misery and gave me a dinar, worth—by my honor—one silverpiece." A dinar was worth thirteen full-silver, or forty or so regular, dirhems. Whichever the writer had in mind, his assertion must have been wildly exaggerated. Honor came so easily to his tongue (and pen), because honor, like the other objects of veneration mentioned above, was ever present in one's mind.[102]

As the preceding examples show, honor is usually invoked when it is contested (which is perhaps natural). It is remarkable, however, that a person's trustworthiness in deed, or truthfulness in word, or reliability in general is praised even in legal documents of variegated character to justify why he was chosen for the function entrusted to him. This was done not only at the time of his appointment, as when the prominent trustee of the court ʿUllā b. Joseph, in taking over the affairs of an infant in Damietta, whose father had died in Fustat, was praised for his religiosity and worthiness, as well as for other commendable qualities.[103] Even when a guardian had completed his task and was returning everything entrusted to him to the orphans, the relevant document finds it necessary to state that he was selected by them because they knew of his trustworthiness, equity, and circumspection.[104] When a father left substantial assets to his daughter and only child, he noted that the amount of the principal and profit of a partnership included in the estate had to be accepted according to the word of his partner, because the partner was known for his trustworthiness and religiosity (in this order).[105] In a letter of friendship sent to the India trader Ḥalfōn b. Nethanel while sojourning in Spain, the first two "gifts of God" mentioned as granted to him were religiosity and trustworthiness.[106]

When honesty is singled out as a particularly praiseworthy virtue, one is induced to believe that it might have been a somewhat rare commodity. This is a difficult problem, touched upon in many different contexts in this work: in the sections on business practices, fraud and evasion of customs, court procedures, and on numerous other occasions.[107] From my observations the general trend seems to have been that unless an oppressive government made orderly business next to impossible, or unless people found themselves in extremely dire circumstances, the middle class merchants had discovered that honesty was the safest way to lasting success. "I have been in business and concluded partnerships for sixty years, and never has anyone appointed an attorney against me, or brought me to court, and never have I owed a carob seed to anyone, and that at times when goods to the amount of about 10,000 dinars used to come to me from Syria and Egypt every year," writes a man sadly when, at the end of his life, a suit was brought against him.[108] The habit of the yearly "closing of the account" was certainly conducive to the proper conduct of interurban and overseas trades (about which, naturally, we mostly read in our papers). "My endeavor is, if God wills so, not to remain owing anything to anyone," writes a merchant from the Maghreb in a letter, announcing the dispatch of many items in cash and kind.[109] A son permits himself to give his father this blunt directive: "Do not remain owing anyone a grain in Miṣr [Cairo-Fustat], put everything you buy in the storeroom, and come down." Probity was apparently built into business practice.[110]

I account for the ubiquitous bribes through the fact that the lower officials were paid little or nothing by the government agencies employing them and had to rely on the gratuities pressed into their hands by the persons making use of their services.[111] I had in mind what Thomas Paine, the renowned author of *Common Sense*, while still in England, wrote in his pamphlet denouncing the low salaries of the officers of the Excise who were accused of corruption: "The most effectual method to keep men honest is to enable them to live so." The small considerations paid to sailors (probably for not pilfering the goods carried by the merchants) were referred to with the ominous biblical word "bribe," but the amounts, like the gratuities paid to underlings in addition to customs dues, were listed in the accounts, that is, formed part of normal procedures. In a letter sent by a member of the noble Tāhertī family of Qayrawān, Tunisia, from the flax-growing center Buṣīr, Egypt, to his cousin, staying in Fustat, we find this passage: "Please bribe the official in charge of the scales, for the bales are overweight. However, if people have been warned of such practices, convey the warning to us." This isolated notice should not lead us to believe that cheating of customs was general. It gives rather the impression that special circumstances were involved here. Only a complete examination of the entire material, including the accounts, may clarify the accepted practices at toll stations.[112]

The ease with which absurd allegations and unfounded demands were made appeared natural to me in the world of the bazaar, where no one would assume that the price mentioned first was final. The sum actually paid was the result of negotiations; how much it represented the true value of the object changing hands was quite a different matter. "'Bad, bad,' says the buyer, but after he has gone away, he boasts" (Proverbs 20:14). My surmise that the ways of the bazaar dominated the thought and talk of the people seems to be brought out by the overwhelming majority of court records that do not tell us about decisions made according to law or reason but represent settlements reached after utterly contradictory depositions. In many cases the clerk does not deem it worthwhile to report those happenings, but notes dryly: "Many altercations took place, which to put down in writing would lead too far afield."

The question of honesty in Geniza society invites further exploration. The general standards of behavior were set by the ethical codes of the three religions (which, at that time, probably did not differ very much from one another), by the common law of the merchants (which was recognized as valid by the courts), and by public opinion (about which we are informed by the reactions of the writers of our letters). How far an individual lived up to these standards depended on his personality; hence the immense interest in character, an interest we should emulate. We may proceed almost statistically: there is much praise and much blame in the Geniza records and much can be read between the lines. I do not wish to prejudice future research in this matter, but how one who planned to do so might proceed. Statistics aims at completeness. It is, however, in the nature of the Geniza that many pieces are isolated, dealing with persons and situations not known from other sources. Such items must be noted, of course, but research must be based on letters and documents containing data enabling us to locate them in the proper social ambiance and historical circumstances in which they originated.

A classical test case for the problem of honesty in the Geniza society is the fervent appeal of the prominent merchant Ibn ʿAllān to the rabbinical court of Fustat, made in 1041/2 with the request to transmit it to the Jewish authorities in Qayrawān, Tunisia, the domicile of his former partner, Yaḥyā (or Yiḥye) b. Moses Ibn al-Majjānī. Ibn ʿAllān had had extensive, indeed, very extensive, dealings with Yaḥyā's father, who had recently died, and, although he had many claims against Yaḥyā himself, on that occasion he wished to confine himself to Yaḥyā's handling of his late father's affairs. Suits against Yaḥyā had been brought by Ibn ʿAllān before: "He wronged me and robbed me of my money, not fearing God." He accused him of having submitted misleading accounts and influenced the weigher of the bales in an illicit way, all things "unworthy of a man adhering to the law of the Torah." Outrageous accusations like these were next to unheard of between merchants of high standing.[113]

In accordance with the accepted procedure of closing the accounts every year, Ibn ʿAllān submitted first the details of his dealings with Yaḥyā's father for the year 1037/8, the last one in which the latter was still alive. The goods sent by Ibn ʿAllān, the ships in which they were carried, and the total price obtained for them by Moses Majjānī are specified in the document, as well as the items bought in Tunisia, all of which arrived safely and were sold in Egypt. The total value of the transactions was over a thousand dinars (corresponding in 1982 to about $200,000 or more), and the balance in favor of Ibn ʿAllān was something between 5 and 6 dinars, that is about 0.5 percent. According to all we know about Mediterranean trade in the eleventh century this closing was exceptionally well done, and shows us the two as experienced traders, versed in the fluctuation of the markets and the seaworthiness of the ships. Small sums like 5 or 6 dinars were customarily not sent overseas but carried over to the account of the following year.

In 1038/9 Ibn ʿAllān sent a great variety of items from Syria, Lebanon, Egypt, and Tripolitania to Moses Majjānī, all of which arrived, however, after the latter's demise. His son, Yaḥyā, entrusted their sale in the countries of the western Mediterranean to a relative, and Ibn ʿAllān now demanded their proceeds in full.

A glance at the date explains why Yaḥyā was late in dispatching the goods bought for Ibn ʿAllān. During the years 1038–1042 the Byzantine navy launched a massive attack against (then Muslim)

Sicily, and the sea route between Tunisia and Egypt became practically impassable. Fortunately, we have a letter of Yaḥyā to a friend in which he lamented the calamities befalling him after the death of his father. He had tried an entire summer to arrange the transport of the goods bought for Ibn ʿAllān, but no one was in a mood to undertake an overseas voyage. A merchant in Egypt, other than Ibn ʿAllān, had sent a power of attorney against him to Tunisia, which caused him a damaging loss of face, and three others there were about to do the same. He denied all their demands, but in Tunisia, too, he was harassed with claims of which he did not know a thing; those he did acknowledge exhausted all his resources. But he hoped that the Nagid, or Head of the Jews of Tunisia, who was familiar with his affairs, would extricate him.[114]

The Majjānīs, father and son, as representatives of merchants, operated a warehouse, *dār wakāla*, in which the foreigners stored their goods and through which they conducted their business. Documents to this effect from spring 1040, issued in Fustat, and from summer 1047, written in Zawīlat al-Mahdiyya, Tunisia, prove that Yaḥyā survived the difficult period of the demise of his father and of naval warfare.[115]

A dār wakāla was a semipublic institution, and the Nagid was concerned that it should not go under. Moreover, as Yaḥyā remarked in the letter just summarized, the Nagid implied to him that he should not be unduly worried about Ibn ʿAllān's action, for it was not the first time he had behaved in that way.[116]

The picture emanating from all this is a breakdown of confidence in the honesty of fellow merchants during a period of crisis. Ibn ʿAllān's unheard-of behavior,[117] as mentioned above, was partly ascribed to his character, which means that it should not be taken too seriously; but it was a disgrace that allegations of the type noted could be deposited in a public court session at all. Yaḥyā Majjānī's performance, too, was dubious. The least that could be said of him is that, while taking over from his father, he did not (yet) enjoy the trust due the keeper of a dār wakāla.

Most disturbing are the references to people taking advantage of the tribulations of others, as mentioned in Yaḥyā's letter, and comparatively common in the Geniza correspondence. We, too, read and hear daily about such matters, but the huge, dehumanized world of modern commerce is different from the trickle of trade conducted on a personal level in those days. Yeshūʿā b. Ismaʿīl, the Tunisian, settled in Alexandria, whose deathbed declaration is translated above (p. 145), was once so ill that his friends found it necessary to alert the people back in Tunisia about the seriousness of his condition.[118] After recovery, he reports how various merchants tried to take advantage of him in his state of helplessness. We have a number of letters written by this man; like Ibn ʿAllān, he seems to have suffered from what the Geniza people called "a constrained chest," exaggerated worry for his own interests, and an inclination to be suspicious of others. Remembering the Talmudic maxim, "people are prone to suspect others for vices they possess themselves" (quoted in the Geniza), one believes that it does not count so much whether the allegations noted by Yeshūʿā were real, but that they could be made by him at all. He was a student of the great Rabbēnū Nissīm b. Jacob of Qayrawān and an intimate friend of Nahray b. Nissīm, "the eminent member of the [Jerusalem] Academy," that is, he belonged to the inner circle of learned merchants, who formed the core of Geniza society. One might have expected more from such a person. Perhaps one should rather pity him and his fellow merchants with "a constrained chest," seeing how hard it was in those days to make a dirhem.[119]

A favorite way of responding to, or anticipating financial demands, was to counter them by making others. Ibn ʿAllān alluded to such an attempt made by his former partner, and I now illustrate this pernicious habit with two examples, one from the early eleventh, another from the early twelfth century, and both connected with the highest circles of the Geniza society.

The first item introduces itself as an enclosure, and as such does not bear the name of the sender and addressee. But the content, style, and script show that its sender was Joseph b. Berechiah, of Qayrawān, Tunisia, representative of the Jewish seats of learning in Baghdad and Jerusalem for the Muslim West. It was addressed to Joseph Ibn ʿAwkal of Fustat, so often mentioned in this book, who served as middleman between the yeshivas and the Maghreb. Several such letters, each of significant historical value, have been preserved. A renewed examination of the entire material showed that the story contained in the text translated below is referred to in a letter written slightly later and addressed by the same writer to the same recipient, which makes understanding of both missives easier.[120]

It was a time of gloom, almost despair. Shortly after the termination of a civil war, Bādis, the ruler of Tunisia, had died, and was succeeded by his son, Muʿizz, then a boy of eight (1016). "The entire Maghrib," the letter says, "has perished. The roads are unsafe. The rulers have changed. Justice and government have ceased to exist in our town Qayrawān. Livelihoods have become rotten. The peasants are oppressed. And every man is let loose against his neighbor because of our sins and prodigality."[121] Our text should be read against this background.

I am sending you, my lord and master, this separate note concerning a special matter so that you may be able to deal with it more intensively. I am informing you herewith what I have done for Isaiah al-Fāsī: I saved his life from the hands of the Muslims and extricated him by delicate negotiations and by standing surety for him. In that perilous time, the Muslims took me and imposed on me an oath. It was, however, impossible for me to swear, so that I could not defend myself except by paying 60 some odd dinars.[122] This was done with the knowledge of our coreligionists. Three years ago I wrote to Isaiah, asking him to pay this sum [lit., "the dinars"] to the Head of the yeshiva of Jerusalem through you. I informed him [the Head of the yeshiva] of this. Isaiah did not do what I asked him and was not ashamed to deny what I had done for him; he even claimed that I owed him something.

I took out a court record concerning the silver pieces[123] I paid at that time, which I am sending with this letter of mine. Also a letter to my illustrious lord, the Head of the Jerusalem yeshiva in reply to his letter forwarded to me through you—may God support you—in which I informed him about the truth of the matter. Furthermore, a letter by my brother and lord, sheikh Abū Yaʿqūb,[124] also to the Head of the yeshiva, since I had made the payment through him. Finally, two letters to our friend Abū Ibrahīm Ibn al-Sahl.[125]

All these I am sending to your illustrious excellency—may I never miss you—with the request to deal with them intensively and send them with a trustworthy person to the Jerusalem yeshiva. Write me a letter immediately, if God wills, which will be a relief for me that they have arrived and that you have sent them off. You will earn by this my gratitude and thanks and be rewarded and recompensed [by God]. *May your well-being increase. . . .*

The villain of our story, Isaiah al-Fāsī, that is, from Fez, Morocco, was probably a native of that city, and stayed in Qayrawān only temporarily.[126] He must have given the impression of a respectable, well-off person, otherwise Joseph b. Berechiah, the experienced treasurer of the yeshivas for the North African communities, might not have posted surety for him. Why the Fāsī's life was endangered and how exactly he escaped is not told. Anyhow, he left for the east and commuted between Cairo and Jerusalem. As the wording of the enclosure shows, Ibn ʿAwkal was familiar with his name but not with the circumstances of the case. The strange fact that three years had passed before Joseph b. Berechiah took serious action may be explained by the extraordinary times. In Egypt, Christians and Jews had been outlawed and their houses of worship ruined in the wake of the edicts of the caliph al-Ḥākim, and in Tunisia, on top of the general breakdown of authority, a famine occurred in 1018/9, the approximate time of the writing of the enclosure.

Instead of asking Isaiah al-Fāsī to send the money owed back to Tunisia, Joseph b. Berechiah had instructed him to deliver the sum to the Jerusalem yeshiva. A donation of 60 some odd dinars was high, but a similar sum was sent to Jerusalem a short time later, as mentioned in a letter from 1035.[127] Joseph had informed the Head of the yeshiva of the gift, but the latter had responded that it had not been received.

In the letter written to Ibn ʿAwkal sometime after the enclosure, Joseph b. Berechiah remarks: "The affair of Shaʿya [the Arabic form of the name Isaiah] has not yet been settled and no agreement has been reached. Recently, the Nagid wrote to him and has also asked that a proper clarification of the case should be made in court and in the presence of the elders." In the following, incompletely preserved lines, Joseph mentions letters sent by him "to them in Jerusalem," which shows that the letters attached to the enclosure translated above had been to no avail.[128]

The remarkable aspect of this correspondence is that Joseph b. Berechiah did not get excited and did not lament. He took it for granted that persons from his ambiance acted dishonestly, told lies brazenly, and evaded sacrosanct obligations when circumstances made it difficult to bring them to court.

The same realistic spirit was evident in court procedures. Depositions were not made under oath; one could tell lies unpunished. But when the case required an oath, for instance, when one party acknowledged only a part of a claim—a most common occurrence—an oath was to be administered. Yet the ubiquitous elders knew human nature: since in regular speech every second sentence was confirmed by swearing, people could forget that they were in court, that a false oath was an impingement upon God's majesty, a terrible crime (see the third of the Ten Commandments); the elders intervened and brought about a settlement, and if one could not be reached, "a ban [and curse] in general terms" was pronounced over anyone making a false statement in the matter concerned, with the person relieved of the oath present and saying Amen, a procedure perhaps not less efficient than our lie detector.[129]

In conclusion, I examine a short court record containing grotesque discrepancies in the statements made. At first blush one wonders who of the two contenders might have been the bigger liar. On closer examination, however, it will appear that it is necessary to know more about the persons and their situations before being able to judge how far, if at all, they might have been regarded as dishonest.

The date falls in the time when Egyptian Jews were headed by Mevōrākh b. Saadya, the most efficient leader they ever had. The undersigned judges were the most competent and experienced ones known to me from the Geniza. Thus, what we read in the short text is what could happen in a court of Old Cairo in the best of circumstances. The only person mentioned by the parties by name, Abu ʾl-Munajjā (Trusted by the government), was one of the most prominent Jews of the period. In view of this, the parties themselves certainly were not low-class people. More about them is said below.

Two Contradictory Depositions in Court (August 1098)[130]

Monday, the twenty-eighth of the month of Elul, in the year 1409 according to the era used by us in Fusṭāt, Egypt, which is situated on the Nile River.

M. Tiqwā b. R. Amram appeared in a session of the court and claimed from M. Shelah b. R. ʿAyyāsh 48 dinars, which he had sent to him to Damietta through Abu ʾl-Munajjā b. Abū Sahl Thiqat al-Mulk.[131] He had asked him to take this sum with him to Palestine and Syria and to buy merchandise for him there; now he had come back, but had not delivered to him a thing. Furthermore, Tiqwā claimed expenses for a slave child of tender age, whom he had brought up for him. Finally, he demanded rent for an upper story // and a loggia // [132] for a duration of two years and three months to the amount of 9 qīrāṭs per month.

When asked about this, M. Shelah replied as follows: The 48 dinars are my property and my own; they are the proceeds of Murābiṭī dinars,[133] which the aforementioned M. Tiqwā received from the Aleppans, // the money-changers in Old Cairo, // and sent to me with the aforementioned to Damietta. Not one single penny of them belongs to him.

As to the expenses for the slave girl, I left her with her family on condition that they cover their expenses by making use of her services, while I had only to pay for her clothing.

As far as the upper story and the loggia are concerned, I have not rented any of those, but I had left with him some minor items of my belongings.[134]

These statements were made in our presence, and we have written and signed them, so as to establish a claim and a proof.

Signed by the two permanent judges of Fustat of those days, Isaac b. Samuel (from Spain) and Abraham b. Shemaʿya (from Palestine), with Nissīm, son of the famous Nahray (from Tunisia), as adjunct. The document, like many others, is in the handwriting of the experienced scribe Hillel b. Eli (from Baghdad).[135]

Thus far, Tiqwā (Hope, Heb.) b. Amram, referred to in Arabic as the sheikh Abu ʾl-Munā (Desire) of Ascalon, a seaport in southern Palestine, is known to me from three dated, one datable, and one fragmentary document. Our court record from 1098 is the earliest bearing a date. From a deathbed declaration, written slightly later (but after November 1098) we learn that the renowned trustee of the court, Eli ha-Kohen b. Yaḥyā, who had served the community for forty years (1057–1098), had a partnership with Tiqwā into which he had paid 48 dinars (by chance the same sum as the one noted here).[136] A huge document from June 22, 1100, certifies that Tiqwā had delivered to the representatives of two nephews of Eli b. Yaḥyā 20 dinars which their uncle had willed them.[137] In a short note from Cairo (not Fustat), a letter is presented to the court, which Tiqwā had brought from Faraḥ b. ʿAyyāsh, possibly a brother of our Shelah b. ʿAyyāsh.[138] A much damaged fragment may serve as an illustration of what has been said above about the apprehension people had about taking an oath. Tiqwā was sued for a promissory note worth 5 dinars; he denied the charge and was prepared to take an oath "by the Torah." Elders intervened, and in the same session "a ban in general terms" was administered.[139] Finally, in 1137/8, that is, a full forty years after the court session of 1098, Tiqwā confirmed a legal action of his wife, it seems, a last will, since an executor is named. Thus, at the time of that session he probably was a man in his thirties, if not less. His father was still alive in 1100, but dead in 1105.[140]

The fact that an experienced and highly esteemed person like Eli ha-Kohen entrusted Tiqwā with his money and made him a (partial) executor of his will makes it likely that he was known as tolerably reliable. The respectful way in which Tiqwā is mentioned in the record of 1100, which was witnessed by the same judges and the same clerk who had been present at the session of 1098, shows that his behavior on that occasion did not impair his reputation. What, then, was behind Tiqwā's queer statement, which does not seem to hold water against Shelah's factual rebuttal? The two had been good friends. When Shelah, before embarking on a protracted voyage (it lasted two years and three months), dissolved his household, possibly because his wife had died, Tiqwā agreed to take care of the little slave girl and to store Shelah's belongings. Moreover, he took it upon himself to exchange Shelah's Maghrebi money profitably. For services some recompense was expected, but, as between friends, nothing particular was stipulated. Things worked out differently. Mrs. Tiqwā probably found out that having an infant slave girl in the house was a hindrance rather than a help, and that she could make better use of the place occupied by Shelah's clothing, bedding, and houseware. Tiqwā expected perhaps that Shelah, as was occasionally done, would assign him some fast-selling merchandise brought back by him for dealing with the issue. When he returned from his voyage and nothing happened, Tiqwā became furious and made his preposterous statement. An honest man should not act like this. The ease with which he took upon himself a "ban in general terms," too, was not the behavior of a respected merchant. It seems that the distance between absolute trustworthiness, so highly esteemed, and outright dishonesty, which disqualified a person, was wide; and many felt comfortable in the middle. The cult of eloquence (and disregard for content), so eminently noticeable in Arab civilization, was probably partly responsible for this phenomenon, but this cannot be the entire story. Socioeconomic hardships, again, must also be considered. In any case, the detailed examples supplied in the preceding pages serve to illustrate, but do not claim to have solved, the problem of honor and honesty in Geniza society.[141]

2. *"Your Noble Self." Considerateness*

A Geniza letter is usually concluded by these words: "Special greetings for your noble self," literally, "Single out your exalted self [to accept 'choicest'] greetings." Even a mother would write thus to a young son, see note 32, below. The word translated as noble, *sharīf*, means "put on a high place, elevated above others." This standard phrase expresses in a nutshell both the special attention the writer owed to his fellowmen and the respect he claimed for himself. The cult of individuality was basic to the lifestyle of the society described in this book and applied to women as well as to men.

The personal touch in letters to and from women.—When I was awarded the Levi Della Vida Medal by the Gustave E. von Grunebaum Center for Near Eastern Studies, University of California, Los Angeles, in 1975, I was asked, as is the rule of that award, to select a topic for the conference connected with it. My choice was "Individualism and Conformity in Classical Islam"; my own lecture bore the same title.[1]

That problem had first attracted my attention when I wrote my

Ph.D. dissertation, "Prayer in the Koran." The more I progressed in the study of the subject, the more I became intrigued by the seeming contrast between the intensity of the Prophet's personal prayer (mostly put into the mouths of preceding prophets) and the traditional Judaeo-Christian character of liturgical and hymnical pieces in the Qurʾān. My interest in this phenomenon of individual originality within a strong social ambiance became a fascination during the long years I was occupied with the study of ancient Arabic narrative and poetry.[2] Those ancient narrators created a multitude of terms for character and character traits because they possessed sharp eyes for discerning them. From their anecdotes and short notices there emerge shining silhouettes of captivating personalities, many of whom were outspoken about their own precious selves. At the same time, the speeches, sayings, and, in particular, poems inserted in the narratives betrayed social notions shared by a fairly homogeneous community. What, then, was the relationship between the self and society, between individualism and conformity? A cognate phenomenon, albeit for different reasons, became apparent in fully developed Islam. My acquaintance with the problem was purely empirical, unprovoked by theoretical interest or preconceived ideas.

Geniza society presented a similar situation. One was constantly aware of his own self; one talked much about pleasing and repelling natural dispositions, wished to be recognized as different from other, less desirable types, and extolled the particular virtues of esteemed personalities. At the same time life was dominated by an all-comprehensive religion and a code of social behavior carrying almost equal authority. The tension between the individual and his immediate or wider ambiance is a general human experience, which adopts, however, specific forms in each historical period and in each society. How should we understand the state of the problem in the time and in the communities reflected in the Geniza?

In his lecture "Individualism and Conformity in Medieval Western Europe," read at the Los Angeles Levi Della Vida Conference mentioned above, John F. Benton (known to many for his *Self and Society in Medieval France*) discussed methodological guidelines for the treatment of the subject. The term "individualism" as a historical phenomenon was introduced early in the nineteenth century as denoting the revolt of individuals against the established values of religion and social order. Jacob Burckhardt in his *The Civilization of the Renaissance in Italy* elevated "excessive individualism" to the role of a driving force in bringing about the revival of the peoples of Italy and western Europe during the fifteenth and sixteenth centuries. After Charles Homer Haskins had made *The Renaissance of the 12th Century* (Cambridge, Mass., 1927) a common notion in medieval research, the "Discovery of the Individual" was placed in the same century and even a bit earlier by more recent authors, dealing mainly with literature, art, and legal status. Benton goes on to analyze the various aspects in which "the concern for the individual" could express itself; the reader is advised to make use of his illuminating observations.[3]

The term *individualism* is ambiguous and bears the mark of a doctrine. In the Geniza documents we are meeting with actual personalities, not with claims based on theories. People wished to be special, but, with comparatively few exceptions (to be considered later), did not question the generally accepted standards. Differences of opinion, especially with regard to the minutiae of religious law (*maḥlōqeth*, Heb., *ikhtilāf*, Ar.), were regarded as a blessing rather than a curse both in Islam, "the benign religion," and in rabbinic Judaism. ("These and those are words of the living God.") Deviations, as long as they did not infringe on "the fence around the Torah," were tolerated, considering a man's personality, education, and fate. Consequently, what we have to consider here is not individualism versus conformity but individuality constrained by integration.

The family was the strongest and most traditional social institution of the Mediterranean area. How much the individual was capable of expressing himself within it both in word and deed is all the more significant. Three letters of husbands writing to their wives are translated in full in *Med. Soc.*, III, 218–223. Grief over separation and hope for speedy reunion are their common theme. But how completely different are the three! The third, written by a learned merchant of advanced age, is pervaded by regard for his wife (of a second marriage). In the first paragraph he mentions, but avoids describing, serious ailments suffered by him. "I would not like to disquiet you and increase your apprehensions." In the second, after emphasizing his happiness at receiving her letters, he adds: "Before opening them I became troubled for fear of disquieting news." Her complaints about separation and solitude and "the sickness of the heart that brings about the illness of the body" were indeed hurting him, "for, God knows, I am not one who has to be aroused to compassion and tenderness, since I possess of them more than I am able to describe." After explaining briefly how the technicalities of buying and selling make an early return difficult, he says that he was hardly able to eat, for "when I stretch out my hand to take something, I think about you, your suffering and your loneliness, and the loneliness of each of us." (The very feeling of shared loneliness contains an element of togetherness.) The worst time was Friday night, the height of Jewish family life, when he had to light the candles and to set the table himself—almost sacral tasks reserved for the housewife. The letter ends with a light reproach: a Muslim friend had reported that she had visited his store and wept. That was too much. Successful business needed time. "Maybe, when I come home, you will regret and say 'I wished I had let him stay longer.'" But one should not finish on such a note. Detailed greetings are extended to twelve different persons. The last line returns to the main theme: "While reading this letter after having completed it, only God knows how I feel."[4]

The first of the three letters translated in *Med. Soc.*, III is the complete opposite of the one from the elderly merchant. The writer, a young scholar from a provincial town, is solely occupied with his own dear self. He reports about a successful lecture given by him in the capital and reiterates his yearnings after his "woman of valor," describing himself as a God-fearing husband who loves his wife. His only concern, however, is that she join him in the capital, to which she and her father, the local judge, objected. The writer's concluding sentence belies his polished phrases and reveals his coarse character: "Come! Otherwise I shall leave the country and disappear!"[5]

The second letter translated shows us again an entirely different person. A fledgling cantor on a vocal concert tour in the small congregations of the Egyptian Rīf sheds tears over his separation from his beloved, for "when all gates are closed, the gates of tears are never shut." God sees them and will soon bring him back, true, "without a full purse, but with a happy heart." The letter is studded with humorous allusions to Bible verses. Despite his protestations, sounding sincere, of love and esteem for his wife, clearly his heart goes out for his cherished little boy. "Although you need no admonition from me, act for the sake of your soul by taking utmost care of our dear boy. That will be the best proof of your love."[6]

With these letters should be compared a very long one, translated in Goitein, *Letters*, pages 220–226. It was sent home to Cairo from Aden, South Arabia, after the writer's return from India and countries beyond. The writer was an educated merchant and, it seems, also a public figure, for he opens his letter with a eulogy for a judge (known otherwise, no relative), of whose death he had just learned.[7] He introduces himself as "their father, who is yearning after them," not addressing his wife at all, and, except for a note at the very end, where the children receive some Indian clothing, no mention is made of them in the letter; the writer does not even inquire about their well-being or give advice for their education, as is often done in letters from abroad; he is exclusively occupied with the thought about his spouse, and for good reasons.

He had been away for years. "After I was resurrected from the dead and had lost all that I carried with me, I took a loan . . . and traveled to countries beyond al-Maʿbar" (the southeastern coast of India, probably to Sumatra, Indonesia, the country of camphor and other precious products). During all those years, his heart remained with her, constantly thinking of her, regretting that he was unable to provide her with what he so much desired, "her legal rights on every Sabbath and holiday"—an unusually outspoken reference to the conjugal duties. In this state of yearning, from the moment he left her until he arrived in India, and from India back to Aden, he was constantly drinking, "not out of my free will," but led an exemplary life (no sex), "curing my soul by fasting during the days and praying during the nights" (when did he have time for business and the bottle?). The congregations in Aden and in India often invited him to lead them in prayer. "They regard me as a pious man, and so do I."

Despite his vehement affection he enclosed a conditional bill of divorce, which would set her free whenever she liked. The letters received by him in Aden from her and her father, who had meanwhile died, were ambiguous on this point. "If that is your wish, I cannot blame you. The waiting has been too long . . . but if this is not your decision, do not lose these long years of waiting. Perhaps relief is at hand, and you might regret at a time when regret will be of no avail."[8]

The women addressed in the four letters analyzed above were literate, they knew how to read. Otherwise their husbands could not have addressed them in terms so personal and even intimate. Comparatively few such letters have been found in the Geniza, and for easily understandable reasons: who would discard missives of such a character in a place accessible to everyone? But many must have been written, for economic conditions often forced husbands to be away from their wives, and when one is alone and preoccupied with his own ego, one feels an urge to explain oneself, in particular to the wife, whose understanding matters so much.

To a certain degree the same tendency is apparent also in letters that were transmitted to a wife by a friend and relative (probably charged also with reading it out to her, although this is not sure in each case). The moving passage translated in *Med. Soc.*, III, 228, is the central piece of such a letter. From beginning to end only the writer's wife, who had given birth to a girl during his absence, is addressed. After expressing his happiness and gratitude to God for her safe delivery and her ability to take up again the management of her house, he indignantly rejects her insinuation that his prayer in the synagogue "for what I wish for you" (namely a son) should have been somehow a reproach for her. She should put such unfriendly thoughts out of her mind; even a son could not replace her love, if lost. But he does not fool himself or her: unless her family fulfilled the promises made at the marriage, he could not come home: "We would make peace, and soon quarrel again, for you and I need a minimum of comfort for good life." We are almost witnesses to the conflicting feelings and considerations crossing the writer's sensitive, but realistic, mind.[9]

Messages destined for a woman, but addressed to the person in whose house she was staying, were commonplace. A letter sent to a brother of the writer's wife, but dedicated entirely to her, is now available in a full translation.[10] A Maghrebi proprietor of a bakery, whose good Arabic style and correct use of biblical and other Hebrew quotations betray him as a person with some education, writes to his brother-in-law, a physician, asking him to persuade his wife (with the proud name Sitt al-Sāda, "the Mistress over the Lords") to return to him. The cause of the separation was his insistence, repeated in the letter, that, except for visits to the prayerhouse[11] and the weekly enjoyment in the public bath, she should stay at home, whereas she cherished her participation in an embroidery circle (whether for pastime or earnings is not quite evident). He, as a native of the traditional Maghreb, was perhaps more resolute in restricting the freedom of his wife's movements than was common practice in Cairo.[12] Otherwise, he promises, "she will be the mistress, the queen, and I the slave, I shall be with her better than I was before. I shall serve, obey, honor, respect, and treat her with deference, as is my duty"; she is "my wife, the lifeblood of my heart, my beloved." For love the master baker has a clear definition; as he emphasizes four times, in both Arabic and Hebrew, leading the life of a bachelor in Cairo was impossible for a chaste man. The separation had lasted too long. If she did not return immediately, he would divorce her and (here we must read between the lines: although he knew well that he could not get a fine urban woman like her) he would go out to the countryside, where he would find a choice one, a girl, or (if it must be), a widow. Although addressed to her brother, a more outspoken self-revelation to the person really intended could hardly be imagined.

Wives writing to their husbands would dictate their letters to a younger brother, a schoolboy son, or a daughter. The reason for this was probably not only that most women had not learned how to write but that the commonly accepted code for conjugal behavior required that the wife should make her feelings perceptible indirectly, not by word of mouth.[13] Yet, the few examples preserved show the personality of the author shining through quite distinctly.

Our first selection was authored by the young wife of the prominent Tunisian merchant and philanthropist, Judah b. Moses Ibn Sighmār, who had settled in the capital of Egypt, and married into "an illustrious and fine family." See the passage translated in *Med. Soc.*, III, 57 and note 36. From another missive sent to him we learn that she had borne him a son, *ibid.*, p. 17. Our letter was written in between, when she was expecting.[14] It was a terrible time of civil war and complete breakdown of authority, and subsequent famine. Many slave girls were running away to the Bedouins roaming around Cairo, and she suspected that the business agent (a slave), whom Judah had left with her, had similar plans. The house was broken into, and sacks of wheat laid in for the family had been taken away, a daily occurrence in the city, for people were hungry as she dryly remarks. The chief vizier was now So-and-So, who had banned all the other viziers from the city, and there was no one to rule. Friends and members of the extended family had left, but because of her state she was unable to follow suit; anyhow some of those who had traveled away were robbed clean. She was, of course, frightened, but did not reproach her husband; she only remarks: "I cannot grasp that I should be in one town and you in another." (Later in life she would have more of this experience.)

The main topic of the long letter was her father. "No one has suffered more by your absence than my father." The mother clearly was dead, the father, "in the state you know." "He sits in the store," trying to conduct the family business as usual, but was unable to cope with unjustified demands made upon him. She provides the details and asks Judah to act. Here we see the young woman of valor, who, after the death of her mother, takes over as the mistress of the house and does not lose her head despite the terrifying happenings. Only at the end of the letter do we feel the pinch of her heart: When she dictates the date, it was the Feast of Tabernacles, she exclaims, "What a lonely holiday! A holiday without you!"

From beginning to end the woman speaks in the first person singular, but I do not believe that she wrote the letter herself. As sender of the letter a boy signs (in Arabic characters), and he and his sister convey greetings to the recipient, but not in the way children would address their father. No other people, except the maid, send greetings. Thus it stands to reason that the two were younger siblings living in the house. Of her own father she says only that he constantly prays for Judah's safe return. I assume she sent the letter without the old man's knowledge. The boy had difficulties with spelling and grammar (for instance, in the text of the letter, written in Hebrew characters, he misspelled even his own name), but, as I hope my summary has shown, rendered his elder sister's dictation quite faithfully.[15]

As second choice, I selected the letter translated in full in *Med. Soc.*, III, 193–194, because I regard it as a typical example for the form of a missive sent by a middle-class woman to her husband. It purports to be the letter of a son to his father, just as the unhappy India trader writing to his wife (see pp. 217–218, above), introduces himself solely as the father of his children. No doubt the letter is dictated from beginning to end by the mother, but its form gets her into awkward situations. The boy cannot write "I weaned the baby." But "we" can do, both as the so-called plural of modesty, referring to the mother, or meaning that the entire household was turned topsy-turvy by the event. Only when she arrives at the point that touches her heart most, the expectation that the toddler survive the dangerous period after weaning, she forgets herself and says "I hope."

This woman, the daughter of the highly esteemed ʿArūs b. Joseph from al-Mahdiyya, Tunisia (see the Index), was less refined than the wife of Judah Ibn Sighmār, whom we have just met. It is astounding how many complaints she was able to squeeze into a comparatively short letter, all implying a certain attitude of neglect or lack of foresight on the part of her husband, who had traveled to North Africa. The worst of all was that her own father (in whose house they lived) had also gone away (probably to upper Egypt or farther afield, where we find him in other Geniza letters), so that no man had remained to look after the family. Yet, the good forms of approved conduct are heeded. The complaints never assume the character of outspoken accusations, and care for the well-being of the recipient is properly emphasized.

It is interesting to compare with this a short letter written home, years later, by the same husband, ʿAllān b. Ḥassūn, from the Sudanese port ʿAydhāb before embarking on his passage to India. He addresses his sons, admonishing them to take good care of one another by forming a family partnership, and adds: "Had I known how much I would be longing after you, I would not have undertaken this voyage altogether." Two other letters, sent from Aden, one written when he was a novice in the India trade and another, when he was on the height of his exploits, show ʿAllān as a competent and courageous man.[16]

A girl serving as her mother's clerk has been found by me in the Geniza only once. She was one of three sisters, Spanish, and from the well-known Perdinel family; since apparently no boy was around, her father had taught her Hebrew script and the Arabic phrases needed for letter-writing. The specifically Semitic sounds of Arabic were impossible for the Spanish girl to pronounce, wherefore she mercilessly mixed up *k* and *q*, *t* and *ṭ*, *ʾalif* and *ʿayin*, and was unable to discern between short and long vowels, so absolutely vital in Arabic. But she brought her message through. "My lady, my mother" is in her *x*th month (she forgot which), wherefore the father of the house should come home soon. The entire letter vacillates between anxiety for his health (for he forgot to say in his letter, "I am well," as usual, and the climate of Mocha, where he stayed, was not salubrious), and orders for South Arabian fabrics, gold threads, and other products. Each request or reminder of a promise made is followed by the assurance that his health was more important. Of one sister it is reported that she could not eat or drink for worry over her father's absence. She was perhaps the least popular in the house, wherefore she in particular is lauded for her affection. Mocha (from which our mocha is derived) did not become prominent until the sixteenth century; it is likely, therefore, that our letter was written at that time and thus does not belong to the "classical" Geniza, which is the subject of this book. But the same Arabic phrases were used around 1200: "Your [plural] daughter Najme [Star] kisses your hands and feet," "We were happy with your letter which was like looking at your dear countenance," and so on. A special flair permeates this all-female missive making it stand out somehow, regardless of the grotesque spelling.[17]

Widowed mothers addressing their grown-up sons were the most outspoken female letter writers. Motherhood as such conveyed authority, especially after the main male voice in the house had fallen silent. In the household of a son the old lady became the "big" one, and experienced advice inspired by love was in general heeded and respected. But much depended on the circumstances, and, above all, on the personalities involved.

Here is the summary of a letter sent by a widow from Aden, South Arabia, to a son who had traveled on business to the capital of Egypt; another son had left for a town in Arabia for the same purpose, and several girls were at home. She was clearly in command of the household and also kept a watchful eye on happenings in the town, which, of course, might have had repercussions for the members of the family. Her tone is brisk and domineering, betraying little sensitivity for the recipient.

> You say, you have received no letter from me!? I wrote you nine, and none was answered. The dress you sent me, you had better have kept with yourself. You made me a laughingstock. Next time send me a fine one for the Day of Atonement.
>
> You boys cause me only trouble; the good you have goes to someone else.[18] I had to give part of the house as a surety for 30 dinars for the poll tax of the two of you. For what are you going away? Seeking profit by traveling over land and sea is futile. Staying in town is more rewarding.

Among the news reported was one long story, which served both as business intelligence and as a moral warning. A Jewish merchant, for whom her son did business in Cairo, and other acquaintances of his had gathered for a drinking bout during the Muslim feast concluding the fast of the month of Ramadan. Now, Jews are, of course, permitted to drink wine at any time, let alone during a feast of their neighbors. But, she added, "You know in what situation we live." A Muslim merchant, who was at odds with her son's business friend, smuggled a Muslim musician into the revelry, the police were alerted, the son's friend was beaten almost to death and was fined the enormous sum of 400 dinars, which could mean bankruptcy for him. The mother advises her son to hold back all consignments destined for that merchant until the situation cleared up. But she had something more to say, or to hint, in this matter. The Muslim feast coincided with the Jewish ten days of atonement (between and including the New Year and the Day of Atonement): your friends could have saved themselves all this trouble if they had paid more attention to the sensitivities of Muslims and of their own pious coreligionists. Warnings against drinking are often sounded by mothers writing their sons.

Other news and orders conclude the letter, but, as a postscript, she had to add another motherly piece of advice. She had learned—nothing could remain hidden from her—that her son had given greetings in a letter to a person who was not a friend of his, to say the least. "What for?" she exclaims. "One who does not care for you, don't care for him!" The reverse side of her letter is headed by Psalms 118:6: "God is on my side; I have no fear," rarely seen elsewhere, but occasioned perhaps by the first sentence on that side: "You know in what situation we live."[19]

After some years, when the young men would have founded their own households, this strong mother might have experienced difficult times. A similar, extremely doleful situation is reflected in a letter sent from the town of al-Raqqa on the Euphrates river (now Syria), by a noble but far weaker woman to her younger son Dōsā b. Joshua, in the capital of Egypt. The Dōsās were an old family, active for many generations in Jerusalem; one branch, to which our Dōsā belonged, had settled in al-Lādhiqiyya, Syria, a flourishing seaport.[20] The city changed hands, whereupon the family dispersed; each of the three, the father and his two sons, settled in a different place, a situation, she says bitterly, that could make only their enemies happy. After the father's death, three years prior to this letter, the sons decided that she should live with her married daughter in al-Raqqa. For her this was Hell. "How long can a person live in other people's houses," she cries out, forgetting that she dictated the letter to her own son-in-law with whom she was living (who signs as the sender).[21] "I ask God not to reckon these three years as part of the life-span granted to me." The sons do not answer her letters, and, if they do, they make promises they do not keep. "Why do you kill me before my foreordained end?!" One son had children old enough to accompany him on a journey to Jerusalem to pass there the month of the high holidays. (He should, she adds, extend the trip to visit her, but did not believe he would do it.) She was particularly concerned for the son to whom this letter was addressed and who, it seems, was of a delicate physical constitution. "Even when you are with me and I observe you walking and going uphill and downhill, I am not quiet, let alone after not having heard from you throughout the summer." She speaks to him in the most extreme expressions of yearning.[22] After being privileged to look at him for a moment, she would be satisfied to be extinguished like a candle. Not a word about the in-laws, in whose house she lived (the father of the in-laws was still alive), not even about her (obviously only) daughter; only the obligatory greetings are noted. Although she begins and ends with the remark that she was tired of writing letters to her sons, she notes that she had sent some to each of them twelve days earlier.[23]

We are perhaps inclined to regard this performance of the unhappy mother almost as pathological. We should not forget, however, that women in those days had few real joys in life, attentions by dedicated sons being certainly some of the most desired ones. Still, it seems that this noble lady drove the preoccupation with her disappointment a bit too far. She was oblivious of one of the basic elements of human contacts evident in the Geniza correspondence: sensitivity for the feelings of others.

The unassuming woman whose letter is translated in the following was far more refined and considerate. She was anxious that, after her husband's death, the elder son should take good care of the younger, for both had traveled to another country. She does not preach or admonish; she is confident (or says so, at least), that reason, piety, and character would guide her firstborn to do the right thing; she also knows that nothing would make him happier than giving her happiness, and what could give her more joy than the letter just received from the younger son praising the elder (for his goodness).

I called that woman unassuming, one may even say simple, because of her extremely primitive style. The letter presents an enigma. It is written on a carefully cut piece of vellum or parchment, as was occasionally still done during the first half of the eleventh century, which from top to bottom is completely filled with beautiful oblong script with no space between the lines, so that the whole gives the impression of a carpet-like piece of fabric—in short the work of an experienced scribe. But the text is so crude and faulty, that I can explain it only by the assumption that the woman had ordered the clerk to write exactly what she told him. We find such situations elsewhere.[24]

In the name of the All merciful, the All merciful![25] My son, may God prolong your life, make the days of your well-being permanent, and be for you and with you a helper and protector in all your affairs. I am writing to you being healthy and well in all your[26] affairs.

My son, during the absence of your letters I learned what happened to you two on your journey. I wrote you one or two letters, but did not see a reply until I received your dear letter, in which you, my lord,[27] described a bit of what happened to you. I praised God that the end was good. Praise and thanks to him who will renew his blessings upon you all the time.

My dear Abū Sulaymān [David],[28] I am pleased with you! May your Creator be always as pleased with you as I am!

Now, my dear, by the rights I have upon you, I am entrusting you with Abū Ṭayyib; be as gentle with him as you are with yourself, quiet my heart, as it was quieted when I received a letter from him, thanking [God for your goodness], for his thanks are a justification of you before God.[29]

Now, my dear, you need no advice. Because of your intelligence, piety, and character[30] you would take good care even of a stranger living with you, let alone your brother, and even more so, because by doing so you bring happiness into my heart. May the Creator give you what you wish.

Now, when you send me a letter, give thanks to Nissīm, for he never fails to visit me, inquiring all the time about your letters. Thank also Abū Barham b. al-Zannī, Faraj, and Yiḥye, for no one remembers you as constantly as these three; they ask about you, read your letters, and inquire about your welfare.

Now, tell me what happened between you and the Ṣiraqūṣī, for he has hurt your honor very much by saying in his letter to Mryh: "Abū Sulaymān regards himself as more experienced in courting women than . . . and does ⟨not⟩ need anyone else."[31]

Finally, be with Khalaf only good, better than you have been before, for you are now in the place of your father.

And special greetings for your noble self.[32]

[*On the margin*:]

And peace upon you and God's mercy and his blessings. Peace. And greetings to your brother(?)

[*Address* (*written in perfect majuscules*):]

To Abū Sulaymān b. Nuʿmān, may God prolong his life. From his Mother. Should arrive in Barqa, God willing.[33]

A letter expressing the deep concern of a mother for the spiritual life of her daughter is remarkable in that it reveals sharp contrasts of attitudes within one nuclear family. The grandmother of the child was "a servant of God," a pietist, which implied that she had given her daughters a religious, that is, a literate, education. The writer of our letter was made in the image of her mother. The writer's sister, to whom the letter is addressed, went other ways. Even worse, her own elder daughter seems to have gone astray, for, with the exception of leaving her a maidservant, she disinherited her. The more eager was she that her baby daughter should receive a proper religious education. Her letter to her sister on this matter, written in expectation of death, is the more moving, as her doubts about its effectiveness are only too apparent. Since she was a literate woman, the beautiful and very personal handwriting was probably hers. The letter is translated in full in *Med. Soc.*, III, 353–354.

The story of a poor, but resolute, schoolmistress, who lived separated from and independent of her unworthy husband during most of twenty-five years of marriage (which produced, however, two sons, whom she trained as her assistants), and that of the highly successful businesswoman, Wuḥsha, who was divorced after a short-lived marriage and later gave birth to a son out of wedlock, are impressive examples of female individuality as apparent in the Geniza.[34] The strangely outspoken and bitterly sarcastic letter of a woman from the Ibn Sabra family (translated *ibid.*, pp. 175–176) demonstrates how even utter misery cannot entirely break a basically proud person.

It is noteworthy that the short appeals by women in misery to a congregation assembled in the house of worship or to a religious authority are often not devoid of a personal touch. Concerning the lonely but undaunted orphan girl who, although rebuffed by local judges, fought for her honor in a public audience of a Gaon, we assumed that she wrote her petition with her own hand.[35] But in most cases, where the appeal was executed by a clerk, the voice guiding his pen is also audible. Two complainants, one, a young wife, married to a senile cousin, a good-for-nothing, and one, an orphan girl driven from her home by two elder sisters, go so far as to threaten to apply to a Muslim court if they are not given satisfaction—an action regarded as a grave sin. But whereas the wife speaks in a tone of resignation, "God, whose judgment we accept, has made me miserable by marrying," and so on, the young orphan is not afraid to insist on threatening to apply to a Muslim court, although she was told that this could lead to excommunication.[36] A similar contrast can be recognized between the long and doleful story told quietly by a poor foreigner abandoned by her fugitive husband and the outcry, "I am a captive; free me," of a wife complaining about the vexations endured from a husband whose character made it impossible for her to stay with him.[37]

Appeals for charity (not for justice) such as that of a woman saved together with her little boy from Crusaders' captivity, or one whose only remaining son was murdered by Seljuks, or a blind woman who had to pay a Muslim physician for the treatment of her daughter were the carefully worded products of trained scribes, who, by formulating them (gratis, of course), performed a work of charity.[38] Appeals for justice were different because the claimant was an individual, and court procedure required that the depositions be recorded in the individual's own words (albeit often reformulated by the presiding judge in his presence). Thus the impression that in those short pleas for justice a personal touch is felt is not a guess but the result of accepted procedures that encouraged the individual to speak his mind.

This was even more the case in deathbed declarations, where every phrase could have legal implications. How instructive to compare the depositions made by the woman who wished to be buried in Jerusalem (November 1006) with the detailed will of the wife of an overseas trader, her second husband (April 1143). The former is solely concerned with a variety of works of piety and charity and leaves for her own burial a sum almost too small for the purpose; she uses phrases from religious texts (heard, not read, it seems) in order to explain the decisions made by her.[39] The rich woman wishes to have a sumptuous and impressive funeral with Muslim wailing women and concentrates all her thoughts on the protection of her parents, brother, and little son from a previous marriage against possible encroachments of her new husband. No deeds of charity are envisaged. Her boy was staying with her mother. Arrangements for his future education had possibly been stipulated at her marriage, but, if so, are not reiterated in the will.[40]

The upshot of all this seems to be that the individuality of women is no less pronounced in the Geniza than that of men. It could even be argued that despite the limited radius of her activities, a wife had more opportunity to strengthen her personality than did her husband. He remained in or around his parents' house, he strengthened his social position through the new family connections, and his economic status was enhanced by whatever his future wife brought with her. She came into a strange, often inimical, household, and it could take her a long time before she regained love and esteem in a measure comparable with what she had enjoyed "in her mother's chamber." Hence the abundance of documents on marital strife and the frequency of divorce witnessed in the Geniza. Economic matters loomed large, but incompatibility of characters was not much less to blame. It is significant that although the law permitted only the husband "to send his wife away," in the majority of cases forming the object of litigation it was the wife who initiated the divorce procedures. The common phenomenon of retaking one's separated or divorced wife is another indication of the value attributed to the person with whom one had shared life—only that this recognition matured during her absence (and, occasionally, replacement by another spouse).[41]

The genes of the father and paternal uncle, as well as the male ancestors in general, were regarded as responsible for a person's character. Nobility could be transmitted also by the mother when she came from a distinguished family, and the same was true of depravity. The vituperative "as the mother so the daughter" (Ezekiel 16:44, quoted as a proverb) is echoed in the Geniza.[42] Above all, however, the individual was formed by God; he was one of the wonders of the creation; consequently, whenever someone good, such as a helpful person, came along, God was praised.

Expressions of sensitivity.—The self-respect of the Geniza person, his intense concern with the place he occupied in the hierarchy of his world, was salubriously counterbalanced by the understanding that his fellowmen expected from him a similar regard for their susceptibilities in accordance with their status in society and their specific personality. That attitude is clearly evidenced in the vast mass of correspondence preserved in the Geniza. "My letter should substitute for my presence" writes a husband to his impatient wife, and, reading it, one is inclined to surmise that in writing he revealed perhaps more about himself than he would have dared to say face to face.[43] The common phrase is echoed by the even more frequent expression "Your letter was for me like seeing your noble countenance," often formulated as a request: "Do you not know that a letter received from you stands for your face?!"[44] A missive from a particularly dear or esteemed person received special attention even before it was opened: the recipient would kiss it and put it on his head and eyes, like an embrace given to a living person. An elderly man from Toledo, Spain, who had settled in Jerusalem, writes to his sister in his native city: "Since my departure I have received from you four letters. I keep them with me folded and derive blessings, *baraka,* from them." Baraka is more than simply joy. It is the strength that one derives from the direct contact with a worthy human being.[45]

In short, if we wish to learn how the Geniza person felt and behaved in relations with others we must study his letters. The letters were created in an environment that craved, and was proud of, command of the word, or what we would regard as unbridled verbosity. Much of this is found indeed in the Geniza, but mostly only in letters of request or thanks for support, and even there one can mostly recognize how urgent the request and how generous the help had been.[46] In general, the matter-of-fact spirit of a busy middle class is conspicuous in its correspondence. The wording, as a rule, indicates the situation in which the missive was written, the kind of connection that prevailed between the writer and the recipient, and of course, the personalities of both. The longest business letter known to me from the Geniza (about 3,700 words) needed half a line as introduction and less than this as its conclusion; there were so many urgent matters to be reported, and the relations between the two correspondents were somewhat strained.[47] When Abraham Ben Yijū arrived back from India in Aden on his way home (which did not exist any more; his siblings and their families had taken refuge from Tunisia in Sicily), he goes in his first paragraph straight to the main topic: "I have accumulated riches sufficient for my own family and for yours."[48] Moses Maimonides is addressed by his younger brother David without any formality (no kissing of the hands, no "may I be your ransom," or similar expressions due in a letter to a highly regarded elder brother). David had to deliver an urgent and delicate message: that he was boarding a ship sailing for India against the express instructions of Maimonides.[49]

Yet the Geniza people disposed of a massive arsenal of polite expressions and sentences known and handled by the individual writer in accordance with his literacy and character. Taken together they could form an impressive handbook of good manners.

The first and all pervasive principle of such a manual was the expectation that the writer put himself in the place of the recipient and perceive how he would react to every single point made in the letter. The constant concern for the person, family, affairs, and interests of the addressee should not be kept out of sight for a moment. We conclude our letters with a meager "best wishes" and the like. Not so the Geniza correspondent. For him the well-being of the recipient should be the first and foremost concern. Wishes to this effect begin with the very first word; God, of course, is the subject of the sentence, since everything is done by him, and is the second word because in Arabic and Hebrew the verb normally precedes the noun.

Good wishes opening a letter follow a fairly constant order of blessings, namely, those a person would find desirable for himself: "May God prolong your life; make permanent (or: elevate, heighten) your honored position; crush and destroy your enemies (frequently repeated as a good wish within the letter and without any visible connection with it); preserve and enhance your welfare; may you see your children living, studying the holy Torah, and marrying; (in case there were none, or only girls:) may God give you *male children*, who will be prosperous and even more successful than you." Frequently such wishes are clad in a form showing the writer participating in the recipient's good fortune: "May God grant me your longevity," and similar phrases.[50] In a religiously minded family a son could bless his father with the wish, "May God let you succeed in obeying him and in eliciting his favor," but such expressions are not common.[51] Some prefer to have God select the most suitable choice for the recipient.[52]

The introductory good wishes are followed by the *shawqiyya*, the section expressing the writer's yearning, *shawq*, for the recipient.[53] The reason for this seemingly indispensable element of letter writing is this: relatives and good friends should normally live together in one place. The abnormality that they are separated by physical distance should be mitigated by the intense feeling that in thought they are really wanted. Here is what Jalāl al-Din Rūmī, the Persian mystic, says in his beautiful ode "I and you":

> How wonderful that we are sitting here together in one nook, I and you,
> While in reality we are in Iraq and Khorasan, I and you.[54]

Modern man with his telephone and airplanes does not know what yearning is. In those days, when one had to wait months, or a year, for an answer to a letter sent overseas, and when one was by no means sure that one would see his friend or relative ever again, the words expressing yearning, even if worded traditionally, were not necessarily empty ones. The following from a letter by Khalaf b. Isaac, Aden, South Arabia, to Abraham Ben Yijū, India, is entirely patterned in the usual way: "You mentioned, my master, that you were longing for me. Believe me that I feel twice as strongly and even more than what you have described; may God decree our coming together soon in complete happiness through his mercy, if God wills." This, however, was not enough for the writer. He concludes his letter with these words: "May God, the exalted, unite me with you [me with you!] *in his mercy and compassion*." Not content with this, he signs overleaf as the sender: "His servant, who is longing for him." To be sure, Khalaf and Ben Yijū were personal friends, who also exchanged greetings between their families.[55] Sometimes the expression of yearning strikes a very personal note, as in the passage from a letter sent by a Tāhertī after his return to Qayrawān, Tunisia, from Egypt, where he had visited the three senior Tustarī brothers (one of whom was the father of Abū Saʿd, later "vizier" to the dowager mother of the caliph Mustansir): "I ask God to multiply people like you in the nation, for you are its ornament. By my father, although I am now back with my family, I am extremely unhappy to be separated from you. For being with you makes the soul strong with God." This succinct but forceful declaration is the more remarkable as the writer was a staunch supporter of the Rabbanite Jewish denomination, and the Tustarīs were the most prominent representatives of the Karaite sect.[56]

The theme of yearning is often followed by two cognate motifs: the assurance that although being separated from the recipient, the writer is always with him, inquiring about his well-being of travelers coming from his place or of people receiving letters from him. If he himself did not write as frequently as the duty of friendship required, he acted so in order not to encumber him, so that he should not feel obliged to answer. One wrote when urgent business was at hand.

With this was often combined another assertion. The writer was always with his correspondent because wherever he happened to be in a congenial company "of those who know you and those who do not know you," he would sing the praises of his friend (to be sure, mostly in the usual form of thanks to God). This topic seems to have been de rigueur in Spain, whereas in the East it was reserved for or mainly applied to persons to whom the writer or the community had a particular reason to be grateful, describing him, for instance, as an "instrument of God" in performing good works.[57]

Neglecting these duties of constant communication was regarded as an offense. We read in a letter to a brother:

> What is this, may God be praised, that you never send me news from your side and do not inquire about me with people, Jewish or Muslim, coming to you [the writer had checked!]?! What an enormous rudeness is this from a man like you [who should know how to behave] with regard to me? Now please, make an effort and wash your face for me [atone for your bad behavior by a good deed], and make the utmost effort to help the bearer of this note, a "beggar" [a small merchant], seeing to it that each of his affairs will be dealt with, and not a single one neglected. What is done for him will be rewarded by God, the exalted [no earthly profit is to be expected]. [After some other strong admonitions the note concludes:] You certainly need no advice from me concerning all that has been said above.[58]

As proved by script and style, this missive is late, perhaps from the second half of the thirteenth century, when the fine epistolary manners of the High Middle Ages had given way to a more popular phraseology. The good manners missed in the brother were expressions of the awareness that regard for the well-being and feelings of those with whom we are connected in any way was a first priority in civilized behavior.

In writing, as in conversation, one should never forget whom one addressed. Hence the frequent repetition of the word "my lord," or "O so-and-so," or "my progenitor" (*yā wālidī*, the polite word for father), said to an older person, who had done, or was expected to do, a favor to the writer, or "my brother," to a friend, and even "my boy," to a younger acquaintance with whom one entertained warm relations. Then there was an endless selection of addresses, differing according to the status of the two persons and the tastes of the period or place. A private, let alone an official, letter to a judge would open with the phrase: "The meanest of your servants kisses the ground before your eminent seat"; in the thirteenth century one might add "and covers himself with the dust of your feet."[59] In Spain, where the epistolary style was far more influenced by classical Arabic than in the East, these addresses were often much refined.

When the name or title of the recipient is mentioned, it should be followed by a good wish, the most common being the untranslatable phrase *aʿazz ak Allāh* ("may God strengthen you," "may he enhance your honored position," and the like). The same applied to his relations, house, or goods, and very often also to third persons mentioned, even when the writer was at loggerheads with them (as in the passage immediately following), or said of a governor, even when the missive reported his misdeeds. Such good wishes were heaped when the content of the letter itself was delicate, as in this example:

> I intended—may God prolong your life and make permanent your honored position, happiness and welfare—to come to your house—may God keep it prosperous through your long life—when I learned that my brother [that is, friend] Abū Zikrī Yaḥyā b. Manasse—may God protect him—occasionally visits you; and you—may God always support you—know that there is a matter of discord between me and him, and, consequently, he might utter some remark against me which might embarrass you—may God preserve your honored position—because of me; but my desire is to make your heart prosper with joy and not to sadden it. Therefore I changed my plan and canceled my visit.
>
> What I am asking you now is that you send for me when you are alone [lit., "when your face is not shared by others"], whereupon I shall get up immediately and come.

The matter they had to discuss was indeed serious, "restraining the hands of those who hold sway by force."[60]

Making the recipient happy and "not saddening him" was a main principle of good behavior, as is evident in really countless letters. The Geniza people so often had opportunity to cry for help: refugees of noble families, government officials demoted, well-to-do merchants who lost everything in one or several disasters, underpaid intellectuals, and simply poor people, but in most cases, they succeeded in describing their misery as briefly as possible (and often we regret that they did not become a bit more explicit). After a person trying to settle in Fustat had described his misery by a mere allusion to Exodus 23:9 ("You know the heart of a stranger, for you were strangers in the land of Egypt"), he adds: "It is not good manners to complain more than I have done with this."[61] A gentleman and merchant from Spain, who had arrived in Tyre, Lebanon, after a disaster had befallen him, in which he certainly lost a lot, refers to it in the following short passage. He did not start with this—as we would probably have done—but precedes it with matters concerning and pleasing the recipient. "I experienced troubles on this journey, but the end was to the good. God, praise to him, saved me, and granted me replacement for what was lost. After the great afflictions which others experienced on the sea, what happened to me is insignificant. Only because I know that you—may God crush your enemies[62]—always inquire about my well-being, I informed you, so that you should not worry. God has already [re]paid me more."[63]

The writer does not report his misfortune. He had traveled from Spain via Tripoli, Libya, and Egypt, to al-Lādhiqiyya on the coast of Syria, and then via Aleppo back to Tyre. On this long voyage much could have happened. But since business was good, the losses incurred were discounted. Sufferings endured were not regarded as stuff for entertainment. Even where the horrors and losses of seafaring were terrible, the writers of Geniza letters would write "on sea I incurred incredible sufferings; reporting what I passed through would lead too far," or used similar phrases. As if by silencing it, the entire matter could be regarded as never having occurred. At least, the friend receiving the missive should be spared.

There were situations where the facts did have to be reported or referred to, such as the death of relatives, friends, or a public figure. Then the dire news had to be counterbalanced by strong wishes turning the evil away from the recipient. Common expressions in such circumstances were "may God [let the angel of death] forget your preordained end," "may you live forever," or, when the death had been reported by the recipient in a preceding letter, "I was very much saddened by the news—may God never sadden your heart," and the like. Such wishes sometimes take exaggerated forms, for instance: "May God crown us with your life; may he take away from our days and add them to yours," an elaborate version of the common expression: "May I become your ransom."[64]

The sensitivity for the feelings of others was probably coupled with a half-conscious belief in the magical power of the word. When death was around, one had to chase it away, not from oneself but from the person addressed. Similarly, when one reprimanded a person for any offense, immediately some good wish was required to remove the possible impression that the reprimanded was cursed. This was particularly true for remarks of persons, like parents, whose blessings (and curses) were regarded as specifically effective. In the letter of the domineering mother from Aden, South Arabia, summarized above (pp. 222 ff.), we find this passage: "So-and-so received his mail from Cairo, among it a letter from you; no letter to me was attached to it, and no greetings to me were extended. I was very much upset about this—I wish you good health."[65] Utterings of this type could easily be multiplied.

When one had to report something good about oneself, it was de rigueur to wish the recipient the same and more. A common expression in this context was "I am well and healthy—may God increase your well-being and give you health forever." On many occasions the rule of good manners was applied in a more refined form. An old aunt, in reporting how wonderful her daughter's wedding was, must remember, before everything else, that the recipient, her nephew, was not present; so, she begins her report by saying: "Needless to mention that we cannot be really joyful when you are not present"; after detailing all that had made her so happy, she ends with the good wish "may God grant you the same with your daughter."[66] A father writing from Jerusalem to the capital of Egypt was aware that his trusted friend had only two unmarried girls and no son at all; consequently, in a very long letter he squeezed the message about his own good luck into barely three lines, the major part of which was reserved for good wishes: "I arranged a match for my younger son Abū Naṣr on Passover. It was a beautiful betrothal. May God let you have the same joy with Sitt al-Ahl and the other one [the name, unfortunately, had escaped him] and grant you *a male son, who will survive and prosper; and may He not wipe out the name of your fathers.*"[67] Here too, a magical element might have been involved: the recipient of the good news about the sender's success might become jealous, and jealousy, the "evil eye," is dangerous. Hence the wish, so often found in letters, "may God crush your enemies" is frequently complemented by the invocation "and destroy those who envy you."[68]

Good tidings about boons of God experienced by the writer, such as an escape from danger, could be made more palatable by ascribing them to the religious merits or usual good luck of the recipient. A letter to Joseph Ibn ʿAwkal, the merchant prince, opens thus (to be sure, after four long lines of introduction): "I suffered on this voyage things that are beyond description, and others that to specify would take too long. Praise and thanks to God who turned the end to the good, and this owing to the blessing and beautiful successfulness of my Lord, may God never deprive you of success." Good luck—given, of course, by God—was as contagious as misfortune. "Get near to one perfumed and you will get perfumed yourself." It was propitious to be in close contact with a great person. Telling him this made the contact even closer.[69]

Common relatives or acquaintances should be referred to in terms of their closeness to the addressee, not the writer. A man writing to his brother-in-law referring to his own sister would not describe her as such, but would call her "the mother of your children." A son with an excellent hand and style, writing to his father, thanks God that "you and the one who is with you are well and in good health." In the frequent case when sons extend greetings, the father would write "your servants X and Y kiss your hands" and the like, and only if one knows from another source that X and Y are the sons of the writer would one be aware of their relationship to him. An extreme instance of this polite custom is this line in a letter of the judge (and poet) Nathan b. Samuel of Fustat writing to a friend in Damascus in autumn 1141: "My three cherished ones, *your* sons . . . kiss your eyes." It took me some time until I understood these subtleties of Geniza sensitivity.[70]

A deft way of "not saddening the addressee's heart but making it joyful" was to mention the pleasant aspect of a matter, not its repugnant one. A petition to the Gaon Maṣlīʾaḥ, written for a poor woman with a blind child, had to make mention of the death of a baby daughter of his, which had just occurred; but the mournful event is not expressly referred to; instead, we read: "May God, for the sake of his great name ["the Merciful"] compensate you with a male child, who once will take your place, as it is written: 'Your sons will replace your forefathers; you will appoint them princes throughout the land'" (Psalms 45:17), a wish, by the way, that did not come true.[71] In the frequent case, when a person was urgently requested not to delay action, he was sent to this biblical verse: "Hope deferred makes the heart sick; a desire fulfilled is a tree of life" (Proverbs 13:12), but only its second part was cited.[72] Only in a case of grave neglect, and only between relatives or good friends of equal standing, could one permit himself to cite only the first.[73] A particularly refined example of conveying a grave message that carries an ominous warning is this short note sent to the court physician Abraham b. Isaac Ibn al-Furāt:

May God make my lord, the illustrious sheikh *The Prince of the Community, The Pride of the Priesthood*[74]—may God bless him—a refuge for all those seeking help from him.

The people carrying this note of mine report that one of them is imprisoned and threatened with *execution* tomorrow. They are crying and are in despair because of this. I am asking you now—may God crush your enemies—to strive for religious merit and to deal with the affair of this pitiful man as much as you are able to do. You know what the Scripture says: "Rescuing those taken off to death, *etc.*?" *May the Lord give you the possibility of acquiring all the merits. Salvation*!

The decisive word in this short message is *etc.*, for it is the continuation of the biblical passage: "If you say, 'we knew nothing of this,' surely He who fathoms hearts will be aware; He who watches over your life will know; and He will pay each man for his deeds" (Proverbs 24:11–12). From the fragment of a letter written by a communal official about the same affair to the same address, the threatened person was "the rabbi from Rūm" (Byzantium or Western Europe). He had probably tried to induce a coreligionist who had embraced Islam to return to Judaism, a crime punishable by death. The "etc." in the short note translated above was meant to alert the recipient to the danger he would incur if he failed to intervene for the man facing execution.[75]

A person to be referred to in an unpleasant context should be mentioned by allusion, not expressly by name, and the same was true of the subject matter. A son writing to his father about an uncle unwilling to contribute to a worthy cause says this: "That man whom you know has not changed his character . . . whenever I come to see him, he says: 'I have maintained my mother and my father—until the day of their death because then I was able to do so. Today, not a penny has remained with me, and I am weak and old.' I was not able to get from him a thing."[76] When the writer of a letter had to report something bad done or said to him, he would not speak in the first person or call himself by name, but instead would use *fulān*, Mr. So-and-so. This not only was a magic means of self-protection but also showed consideration for the recipient so that "his heart should not be saddened" by what had happened to his friend, the writer. Conversely, complete anonymity could provide the iciest form of reproach. Here is a note of seven short lines, written in the most beautiful oversized majuscules (to show the writer's perfectionism), but cut out of an old letter in Arabic script (emphasizing his disrespect for the recipient), and mentioning no names or facts: "Everyone knows that a competent, experienced, and discriminating banker, *ṣayrafī*, does not permit himself vain assumptions or mistakes but knows what kind of work, or word, or else he is likely to expect from a person. *May God's name be praised.*[77] Your servant has heard something. This is my answer. *And Peace.*" The message is clear: the mean thing you did, or said about me, is exactly what I expected from a rascal like you.[78]

In the ubiquitous cases when letters were not answered, or when consignments promised had not arrived, good manners required that the emphasis be not on the disappointment of the writer but on the welfare and good intention of the addressee. The standing formula for the first instance was this: "I have sent you a number of letters but have not seen an answer to any one; I hope you were occupied [or: God has occupied you] with good things," that is, your failure to answer was not caused by illness or other unpleasant happenings. In expanded form: "I am disquieted because it cannot be expected from you to be silent for such a long time. I hope God will let me hear good news about you."[79] After having waited in vain for goods or presents the dispatch of which was announced or promised, one would first thank profusely for the good intentions and, at the end, note briefly that nothing had been received.

Regard for the susceptibilities of the recipient had to be shown in particular when a suggestion, advice, or admonition occurred in a letter. These had to be followed by a qualification that it was essentially superfluous but was made or given only because the addressee was best suited to carry it out. A considerable arsenal of appropriate expressions in Arabic and Hebrew was at the disposal of the writer for that purpose. After having bombarded a friend with Bible quotations admonishing him to return to Jerusalem despite the losses he had suffered in the Holy City, the writer concludes: "Finally, there is nothing that can be said in the matter which you—may God keep you—do not know." Even a mother advising her son to deal with his younger brother delicately finds it necessary to say: "You need no advice," and the same is said at the end of the very strong note of one brother to another translated above (p. 232).[80]

Suggestions are normally concluded with the phrase: "Your opinion is the highest one" or "is the one to which God gives success," turns of phrase probably derived from applications to a juridical or administrative authority.[81] Exhortations are followed by Hebrew maxims such as "*one urges only one who feels an urge in himself*"[82] or "*give advice to the wise and he will become wiser*" (Proverbs 9:9), meaning that only wise men appreciate advice given to them.[83]

Propriety required that one should avoid mentioning ugly or ominous matters, wherefore one was occasionally forced to speak in allusions. A Jewish court had ordered a bachelor to part with his slave girl. Instead, he lodged her in his sister's roomy house, "and other things were told me," reports a confidant of the Nagid Samuel b. Hananya, "which to repeat would be improper." When a respectable merchant began to speak in public about esoteric topics, such as the resurrection of the dead, astrological computations, "and other matters that cannot be mentioned in letters," the writer excuses himself for not being more explicit by "the pitfalls of letters" (letters could end up in the hands of unauthorized persons).[84] When one wished to alert the addressee that there was far more to say about a matter than one deemed fit to report, then one would add in Aramaic or Hebrew "*a hint for the wise man* [*is sufficient*]," or "my lord has wisdom like the wisdom of an angel of God" (II Samuel 14:20), or similar expressions.[85] In the opposite case, when one was forced to say more about things for which brevity would have been preferable, one would end by saying: "Had I said less in this matter, it would have been enough" or "less than this would have been sufficient for you."[86]

Respect for age paired with a sense of individuality might have been the cause of the seemingly strange custom that, in letters sent by or to family businesses, the names of the members (fathers and sons, brothers) are noted in the address, but in the text of the letter only one person speaks, and only one is talked to. In a letter to the Ibn ʿAwkals, father and son, only the father, Jacob, is addressed; Joseph, the future merchant prince, is not even greeted; he appears solely in the address.[87] The three senior Tustarī brothers, members of the most important Jewish merchant family in Egypt in the early years of the eleventh century, repeatedly appear as a firm; but the three brothers are mentioned only in the addresses and when blessings are said for them; otherwise the missive is a dialogue of a definitely personal character, even when the senders, too, happened to be brothers. For instance, when two Tāhertī brothers from Qayrawān, Tunisia (two other brothers were in Egypt at that time), wrote to the three Tustarīs, their "speaker" says: "I know that you [singular]—may God support you—are more eager to save a dirhem for me than I, and that you also have the capacity to do so."[88] Even a most personal letter of one of the Berechias of Qayrawān to Joseph Ibn ʿAwkal about the loosening of the bonds of their friendship is written in the name of the family partnership, although the letter does not deal with business. Similarly, a letter addressed to Ibn ʿAwkal and his two elder sons speaks just to the father and contains a highly sensitive and confidential message (as the writer himself emphasizes).[89]

This custom still prevailed around the middle of the eleventh century, as when the brothers Barhūn and Joseph Tāhertī (known to the readers of this volume by the story of Barhūn's death told above [pp. 129–130]) send a joint letter to Nahray b. Nissīm, but only Barhūn is speaking, for instance: "I strive to obtain for you more than for myself" or "I am here for you more than an agent"; and he mentions his brother Joseph in the third person, using of course his honorary byname Abū Saᶜīd.[90] By the beginning of the twelfth century, family partnerships, and with them the practice described, were going out of fashion. The practice itself certainly reflected what happened when extended families met: the fathers or eldest brothers led the conversation.[91]

Finally, just as one paid much attention to his fellowmen by appearing before them in proper clothing suited to one's station in life, thus the external aspects of letter writing—paper, script, use of language, and style—were a serious concern for the Geniza people, especially those of the educated class.[92] The sensitivity of the letter writers in this respect is recognizable not only in what we see in the products of their endeavor but also in what they say. The expressions of craving for indulgence for imperfections are endless: the paper was not as elegant as desirable, but the urgency of the matter did not permit searching for a better one (to me the paper appears to be perfectly satisfactory); sore eyes or other indispositions were interfering;[93] and the most common excuse: the letter had to be done in a hurry since the friend or courier prepared to carry it stood over the writer's head; one did not even hesitate to ascribe to himself sheer ignorance.[94] One letter has this postscript: "You know that I am weak in [?] and style. Do not hold me up to ridicule because of this. No one should read the letter except you."[95] Requests to destroy a letter immediately after it has been read, and reports that this has actually been done, are not rare. But in all cases, I believe, the motive for this was the delicate nature of the contents, not the outer form.[96]

When a writer wished to address an esteemed person but did not rely on his own penmanship, he asked a trusted friend to substitute, preferably one known to the recipient. We had the case of ᶜAllūn b. Ḥassūn, who, while on the Sudanese coast, wrote a personal letter to his sons in his own hand, but, when reporting his adventures on the India route to his revered uncle and father-in-law, made use of the services of a business friend. When the Adenese shipowner Maḥrūz wished to invite his brother-in-law Abū Zikrī Kohen, the distinguished representative of merchants in Fustat, to join him in his own boat on the way back from India, he asked the learned merchant Abraham Ben Yijū to write the invitation, which he did by displaying his scribal art at its best.[97]

This practice, the fruit of respect for the honored and reliance on friendship, pervades the Geniza correspondence throughout its better time. Often, both the sender and the writer are known to us from other sources. We find it applied early in the eleventh century in a letter addressed to Joseph Ibn ʿAwkal, in the later part of the same century in many letters, preserved in the Nahray corpus, and in the twelfth century in writings connected with the India trade, and elsewhere.[98] Not rarely, the writer sends greetings without mentioning his own name, because his handwriting was known to the recipient.[99]

The reverence for an esteemed person went even farther: one did not write to him at all, but paid respects by asking one of his confidants to convey to him his good wishes or whatever the message was. The brother of Ḥalfōn b. Nethanel, and another relative of his, Abū Naṣr b. Abraham, excuse themselves with their linguistic and other shortcomings for not addressing the Spanish Hebrew poet Judah ha-Levi in a letter and ask Ḥalfōn, who played host to the poet during his stay in Egypt, to substitute for them. We have several letters from the hands of both, and both have a complete command of Arabic, as it was written in those days, and the handwriting of Abū Naṣr is superb; but he felt that his use of language and style were not good enough for addressing such an eminence.[100] One is reminded of the vizier Ibn Saʿdān (d. 985), "whose handwriting was the limit of beauty, and whose style could not be more perfect," but who let his letters be written by others in order not to be caught in a mistake.[101] Saʿdān, as he himself explained, acted so "to preserve his honor": Abū Naṣr wished not to inconvenience an illustrious visitor. But, to repeat, self-respect and sensitivity for others are two aspects of one basic feeling: the respect for the value of the individual.

Moods.—Looking back on the two preceding subsections treating the pronounced self-esteem of the Geniza person, which was coupled with due regard for others, one comes away with the pleasant impression of having been in the company of civilized people. True, they were inclined to be somewhat exuberant; but they knew how to behave and control themselves, being steadfast in adversity and sensitive to the feelings of their fellowmen.

Yet life was hard. Making a dirhem required considerable efforts, and unforeseen events, over which one had no control, frequently undid careful preparations. "The race is not won by the swift, nor the battle by the valiant; bread is not gained by the wise, nor wealth by the smart, nor favor by the skilled" (Ecclesiastes

9:11). This sad experience was as familiar to the Geniza people as to those who listened to the "Preacher" in biblical times.[102] "One disaster makes one forget the other" was as proverbial in the Geniza as in the Talmud, when this saying was coined.[103] When troubles accumulated, even healthy and well-educated people were liable to lose their composure and give vent to their changing moods.

Characteristically, the persons affected usually themselves felt that they were transgressing the limits of accepted propriety. A merchant who had been out of work for a year and a half and suffered heavy losses asks another one, into whose family he had recently married, for an unusual favor. "It is not hidden from you that this state of being out of work and suffering losses has constrained my chest and turned my mind upside down. Were I to get something that would at least cover part of my expenses, my chest would be widened and I would again be as I should be." He ends his letter with another apology: "A person whose character has changed and whose chest has become constrained should not be blamed."[104]

Letters written in such a state could frequently open with a kind of warning: "I am well in body, but sick in heart" (for instance: "because of the happenings in this blessed year"), or "disturbed in mind," sometimes with the addition: "in every respect."[105] Reports about unusual behavior are accompanied by pleas for indulgence: "A man who is grieved should not be held responsible," writes a schoolmaster in a small town after having said some unfriendly words to, or about, his brother, the addressee.[106] Another very unhappy man describes his state as "drunk, but not with wine" (Isaiah 51:21, but said in Arabic).[107] Even so prominent a man as the president of the Jerusalem High Council Daniel b. Azarya writing from Damascus to his esteemed friend, the court physician Abraham Ibn al-Furāt, in Cairo says of himself: "I am tired and exhausted, my heart burns without repose and stability, wherever I happen to be."[108] Promises to write again after quieting down are not uncommon, for instance, in a letter of Zakkār b. ʿAmmār, representative of merchants in Palermo, Sicily, describing losses suffered in an attack by pirates.[109] In that situation one would prefer not to act, quoting Isaiah 26:20: "Hide a little while until the wrath has passed."[110]

People occasionally explain why they had not done something that was expected of them by their frame of mind, their mood, or their lack of *nahḍa*, energy, verve, bounce, pep.[111] Complaints about absentmindedness and a divided heart or mind are commonly uttered in different contexts. "I do not remember anything of what happened, I was absentminded, *ghā'ib al-dhihn*" is how the younger brother of the court clerk Mevōrākh b. Nathan excuses himself after having made fun of the son of a VIP; or that, at least, is what Mevōrākh ascribes to him.[112] "My mind was divided. I did not know what I did, *mutaqassim al-khāṭir*," asserts a merchant when he was unable to verify whether certain orders were carried out. "My heart is divided, up and down," writes a sister to her brother, informing him about the illness of her children, doing so only because she feared his reproaches should she fail to do so.[113] All three notions of absentmindedness, divided thoughts, and worried heart are offered by the warmhearted Saʿdān Baghdādī to explain why he was unable to write properly after the death of his mother and the departure of his brother.[114]

A vast topic in the Geniza correspondence: the physical effects of emotions, small and grave, seems to be connected with the general, somewhat exaggerated, concern with health described above.[115] "You would not recognize your sister," writes a woman to her sister after complaining about her maid, who threatened to run to the qadi.[116] A Spanish merchant writes from Fez, Morocco, to his father that because of the arguments he had with the customs office he was ill for three days.[117] More serious is this note in the letter of a government official who had been dismissed and found himself and his family in a state of utmost deprivation: "Because of my distress (*hamm*), I contracted a dry tumor, and my skin is falling off my bones."[118] I spare the reader similar outpourings.

The most common case of physical suffering and inability to act caused by emotions was the grief over the demise of a beloved or highly esteemed person. The eccentric physician Abū Zikrī, whose extremely emotional letter is translated above (pp. 175–177), writes to his father, the judge Elijah b. Zechariah, a beautiful letter of congratulations for a holiday with many greetings to important persons, and in between remarks that he had been ill since coming home. At the end, when he explains that the illness was caused by his sadness over the death of a pious person, we are somewhat in doubt about his diagnosis.[119] The notion that the writer, or another person was unable to take food because of a case of mourning is frequently found.[120] When an old man writes from Jerusalem to a grown-up son in Egypt that he was confined to bed and unable to move since his little boy (from a second marriage) died, we believe him, remembering what Maimonides wrote about how he was affected by the death of his younger brother David.[121]

A perfect picture of the influence of emotions on physical and mental health is found in the long letter written by the noble India trader Ḥalfōn b. Nethanel nine months after his return to Egypt from a long sojourn in Spain. As expected from a man like him, he dedicates the first twenty lines to the praise of his gracious and learned hosts, whom he so greatly missed. Then he goes on to bemoan one after another the disasters that disturbed his mind: civil war, anarchy, the high cost of living in Egypt, the death of the Head of the Jerusalem Academy (which then had its seat in Cairo) and of several luminaries of the Jewish spiritual and social upper crust; hardly had the months of mourning for those passed when Ḥalfōn's misfortune was topped by the demise of his eldest brother, who was the president of the Jewish High Court of Justice. He found himself unable to act, even to supervise the unloading of his goods, and let the perishables rot. During his long stay in Alexandria his body and soul never enjoyed full health, but he was also unable to bring himself to go up to Cairo: how could he visit the place vacated by his brother? Family and friends came down to Alexandria to induce him to return home, but he did not find in himself *nahḍa,* energy, to do so. For this reason, he was also not in a position to send to his friends in Spain (mostly physicians) the pharmaceutical plants promised, for these were to be had only in the capital (the terminal of the India trade), not in the Mediterranean port. Nor for the time being was he in a frame of mind to continue writing the learned discussions that were started during his sojourn in Spain. He concludes with a refined twist; he really did not want to send this letter but he was overcome by yearning for his Spanish friends, and asks them, considering his state of mind, to overlook his shortcomings in style and script (in that order).[122]

When situations became unbearable, one wished oneself dead. When the seasoned merchant Yaḥyā b. Mūsā Ibn al-Majjānī, whose affairs occupied us before, writes, "my mind became distraught and I wanted to leave this world," one is not quite convinced that he meant what he said.[123] But when a very unhappy man reports the death of his own child and adds, "who knows, perhaps death is better than life," we understand.[124] Finally, when a learned and highly esteemed Maghrebi, who passed the later years of his life in Jerusalem, harps again and again on this subject, one believes that he is in earnest. He was unhappy with many things: the general difficulty of life in Jerusalem, the cost of living, the unreliability of people who requited good with evil, and, on top of all this, the passing away of the worthy. Quoting Job 3:21 ("who long for death and it comes not and dig for it more than for hidden treasures"), he writes: "I have often wished to die." Returning to this at the end, he adds: "Even as I write this letter I sigh: Oh that death were near!"[125]

From the wish to die it is only a step to thoughts about suicide. Reading through the Geniza letters I was somewhat surprised by the frequency of this topic, but Muslim and Jewish religious literatures deal with suicide quite extensively and take perhaps a somewhat more lenient, or, should we say, realistic, attitude than we might anticipate.[126] The basic attitude to the problem is well illustrated in the story of the veteran India trader Abū ʿAlī b. Abū ʿAmr (or Omar). He had previously traveled as far as Ceylon (today Sri Lanka). When he was again on his way to the East, he lost everything when the Ghuzz (a Seljuk contingent) ransacked the town of Minya in Upper Egypt. He was tired and writes to his son: "Had my spirit been in my hand, I would have given it up." Our soul belongs to God (see p. 128, above); how could we be permitted to destroy God's property?[127]

A man depressed by several private and public disasters (the first mentioned: his wife's state of health) exclaims: "Could I find death without sin, I would not hesitate."[128] A Maghrebi who had lost everything in shipwreck and, on top of it, was worried about the fate of his family and friends in the turbulent Muslim West says that he would prefer to throw himself into the Nile, were he not "afraid of losing both this world and the World to Come."[129]

In the three examples summarized, the writers accept without hesitation the traditional notions about the nature of the soul, of the World to Come, and of suicide as a sin. This was not always the case, especially in later centuries. Here is an actual treatise on the problem of suicide, found in a letter from Safed, Palestine, written by a man from Cairo, who had traveled there, mainly, it seems, to settle a family affair. Everything went wrong, and whether he receives letters or writes some, "tears are my food day and night" (Psalms 42:4). Nothing was achieved. "Naked I came from my mother's womb, and naked shall I return" (Job 1:20). "For man is not in command of his way, he cannot direct his own steps" (Jeremiah 10:23). Consequently, "had I any doubt about eternal life, I would commit suicide." The term used here for eternal life is not, as usual, a Hebrew expression, but the Muslim term *yaqīn*, "certainty." But is it so certain? The writer clearly wrestles with the problem, and tries to solve it both by traditional belief and rational proof. The final confirmation for him was the word of the Prophet Habakkuk 2:4, "the righteous lives through his faith," namely in the World to Come (for in this world, as we realize, faith does not always save life).[130]

Do we have actual reports in the Geniza about suicides? The evidence is ambiguous. A prominent Jewish merchant who had done business in large sums (100, 400, and 700 dinars are mentioned) with everyone who counted, was found dead in the sea; his hands and feet bound and stones in his clothing. Some said he committed suicide, others, that he was robbed and murdered. The Jewish authorities in the capital were asked to approach the viceroy to instruct the local Muslim judge to conduct an investigation. The only thing to be learned from this story is the fact that people could assume that a high standing person incurring financial difficulties would seek escape in death.[131] An important but late list of contributors notes a person named Ibn al-Mushnaqa, which may be translated "the woman who hanged herself," or "who was strangled." It was common usage in Geniza times for derogatory nicknames to stick as family names.[132]

Besides the deviations from accepted behavior caused by extraordinary circumstances, there were others inherent in the makeup of a person: moodiness, excitability, and depression, not as passing states but as psychological constituents. The Geniza is by no means devoid of human beings of this type.

The letters of such persons are immediately recognizable by their writers' excessive preoccupation with themselves, turning to the addressee only sporadically or where it is unavoidable. Doing so they fail to observe the main principle of civilized correspondence apparent in the Geniza. They speak without restraint about their weaknesses, failures, and misfortunes, and do not try to save face, as most people were so eager to do. By detailing and reiterating their story, they seek—consciously or unintentionally—to arouse interest or compassion. The letter of condolence of the young physician Abū Zikrī translated above, is such a case. Other letters by the same person confirm the impression.[133] The outrageous accusations made in court by the excitable Ibn ʿAllān described above are another example of the actions of a person not being taken fully seriously because of his unbalanced character.[134] The learned, but difficult, ever anxious and oversuspicious Yeshuʿa b. Ismaʿīl of Alexandria also wavered on the border of undesirable comportment.[135]

In the following I wish to present the portrait of an experienced and learned merchant, whose life story can be followed from Spain to India through about forty years and who despite his manifold contacts and undertakings remained the opposite of a person who behaved "as was proper." His full name was Makhlūf (Replacement, for a predeceased brother) b. Mūsā (or Moses) al-Nafūsī

(Ibn) al-Yatīm (Orphan, family name). Nafūsa is a mountainous region on the border between present-day Libya and Tunisia, but Makhlūf had settled in Alexandria, Egypt, where he possessed a valuable house. He also possessed a house in Barqa, eastern Libya.[136] The first dated document related to him was written in spring 1103, when a young man from Tripoli, Libya, came to see him in Cairo, to inquire about living conditions in India. The information given by Makhlūf must have been encouraging, for the novice immediately set out for the East. Thus Makhlūf must have been known as an India trader at that early date.[137] At approximately the same time, we read in a letter from Alexandria: "No one has yet arrived from the West, except the ship from Spain, in which Makhlūf b. Mūsā al-Nafūsī traveled."[138] This note finds its explanation in Makhlūf's letter translated below. He dealt with the affairs of the passengers. Of another Jew we read in a Hebrew letter that in a large ship, in which thirty-six or -seven Jews and about three hundred Muslims traveled, he was "the treasurer and commander" (probably fixing the fares and deciding where the goods of the merchants should be stowed). Like Makhlūf, this "treasurer" was a scholarly person and used the time before the departure of the boat to study with the writer of that Hebrew letter, a rabbi from Christian Europe.[139]

The latest dated reference to Makhlūf I know of is from May 1141, when he boarded a ship sailing from the Sudanese port of ʿAydhāb to Aden, South Arabia, where he indeed arrived.[140] We know of his arrival, because a long-standing lawsuit between him and the India trader Abraham Ben Yijū, to which he referred in other letters, was settled through the good services of Maḍmūn b. Ḥasan, representative of merchants in Aden. (Makhlūf received 300 dinars; Ben Yijū was in India at that time.)[141]

Makhlūf was a prolific letter writer. Maḍmūn mentions that he received more than twenty letters from him on his affairs with Ben Yijū, and describes him as senile and foolish, not knowing what he was doing.[142] At that time Makhlūf must have been in his late sixties, if not older, and one is astounded that he should have undertaken the protracted and arduous voyage to Aden at that age. The letter translated below was written ten years earlier (1131). But all the letters we have from his hand are in the same vein of preoccupation with himself, disregard for or oversensitivity to the recipient, a general feeling of urgency, and fear of being taken advantage of by others or persecuted by misfortune. Writing to a merchant well known to us, he flatly accuses him of conspiring with another equally esteemed business acquaintance to rob him.[143] In another letter, addressed to the distinguished Abū Zikrī Kohen, representative of merchants in Fustat, Makhlūf reports, almost with gusto, about the lawsuits and other troubles he had with four different customers and partners, among them the Ben Yijū mentioned above.[144] In a short note from Alexandria announcing the dispatch of 101 dinars of Sicilian currency he dedicates eleven lines to an apology for not buying his friend a Sicilian turban ordered; the only reason, as he confirms by two oaths with God's great name, was that he thought about the order all the time, but finally forgot it; the only reason, he repeats, was forgetfulness.[145] Castigating a friend for choosing the wrong company, he excuses himself profusely for not seeing him off at the Sidra gate of Alexandria, when leaving for Fustat: the weather was bad for his health, and his toothache, twice referred to and graphically described with the help of a Bible quotation, had become unbearable in the night preceding his friend's departure.[146]

There is no need to search the Geniza for other examples of Makhlūf's correspondence. The letter translated below is sufficient testimony for the psyche of a person who, despite his standing in the merchants' community, lacked self-control to an almost pathological degree. It should be noted that Makhlūf's handwriting is symmetrical, orderly, and pleasant, his style good, and his quotations plentiful and correct. Should we assume that the extraordinary sufferings of a man in his late fifties described below caused permanent damage to his mind?[147]

At the time of the writing of the letter translated here, Makhlūf served as an "overseer of the Sultan's ships."[148] His superior was not the captain of the ship in which he traveled or any other naval authority, but the qadi, or chief Muslim judge of Alexandria.

In the letter Makhlūf describes his manifold misfortunes, which were partly connected with his profession but mostly caused by the profligacy of an unworthy son. When the rapacity of an oppressive minister of finance played havoc among persons of some prominence, our overseer, like many other government officials, was forced to hide and to flee from the country. For a year or more, he suffered terrible privations in the deserts of Libya and Egypt. Meanwhile, his profligate son had sold everything in the house and spent the proceeds on wine and musicians. Makhlūf managed to be transferred from a ship going to Spain to two others sailing to Tunisia, and, in order to forestall further mischief, took his son along on the journey.

Despite the hardships and misfortunes endured on this trip the boy did not improve. When his grandmother and his father obtained a position for him in the office of the director of finance of the Buḥayra district, he remained at his post only for a short time and returned to Alexandria to enjoy music and European wine. Attempts to remove him to Syria and to Yemen were not successful. Moreover, the old man, as an inspector of the Sultan's ships, was unable to secure commissions for merchandise which would have made his journeys profitable or even possible. For it seems that his salary was pocketed by his superior, the qadi. In his despair, the overseer turns to an old friend, obviously a high government official, with the request to employ his son, who meanwhile had reached the age of twenty-two.

It is remarkable that a father should write so many hard words about a son for whom he seeks an appointment. Even more astounding is the remark of the son to his father quoted in the letter: "As long as you are alive, I will be a good-for-nothing; only after you are dead, will I be successful." While the father, as his Bible quotations and his whole way of expression show, was a religious and scholarly person, the son was submerged in the cosmopolitan and pleasure-loving society of Alexandria.

Saving face was one of the foremost principles of personal conduct; as a rule, letters were very much restrained. To enlarge on one's misfortunes was regarded as bad taste, a rule both practiced in the Geniza letters and quoted in them as a maxim. Nothing was more dreaded than becoming the butt of other people's gossip. The writer of our letter, however, in his bottomless grief not only describes his troubles and failures in an unusually frank way but even enjoins the addressee to make them the subject of his conversation everywhere. Still, our writer himself believed that he had gone too far. At the end he craves the indulgence of the recipient by explaining that he had to give vent to his feelings.

The time of our letter can be accurately pinpointed because of the references to "the Monk," the notorious finance minister Abū Najāḥ who, after many misdeeds, was killed in 1129.[149] Makhlūf arrived in Alexandria in the spring following Abū Najāḥ's death, traveled to Tunisia in the summer of the year 1130, and wrote the letter the following summer, that is, 1131.[150] A number of persons mentioned in the letter are known from other Geniza records as having lived at that time.

[*A story of tribulations*]

I am writing to you my lord, the illustrious elder—may God prolong the life of your excellency, and make permanent your honored position, affluence, highness, eminence and power, and humiliate your enemies and all who envy you—in order to inform you that if I tried to describe only a fraction of the troubles, tribulations and humiliations that I have endured in this world, the account would be too long; no letter could contain them and no epistle do them justice.

[*In the deserts of Libya and Egypt*]

[L. 7] In addition to the troubles that I previously had to bear, I was overtaken by the disaster caused by the Monk. I fled to Lukk,[151] which was most unfortunate; had I gone to the country or to Upper Egypt, I would have fared better.[152] A man stronger than I would have weakened on this journey.[153] But such is what God willed.

[L. 11] When leaving [Alexandria], I had 10 dinars with me. For twenty-five days I was on my way and was overtaken by the Feast of Passover [Easter]. During the eight months that I spent in Lukk bad news continued to come from home. At the end of *Elul* (August-September) I went to Barqa for the High Holidays and the Fast.[154] Then, when I learned of the death of the one *whose bones will be ground in Hell* (the Monk), I returned to Lukk, in order to join other travelers going to Alexandria, but found none. Therefore I went to Santarīya,[155] a place never visited by a Jew, as it is a rough country with no water, a desert without vegetation, no wood for fuel and no pasture for the camels, so that their fodder must be carried from afar. I experienced *hardships* on the Sabbaths which I am unable to describe.[156]

[L. 21] From there I traveled to the Oasis,[157] on a stretch of land still more difficult and more terrible than the one described, and then to Upper Egypt and down to Fustat—altogether six months.[158] For the Sabbaths and holidays and for protection[159] I spent seven and a half dinars so that only a little over two dinars were left me. Thus, I passed a year and a half in other people's houses with no rest or comfort, most of the time begging for a *ṣāᶜ* of barley, which I ground with my own hands in strange people's places.[160] From Lukk I sent with Ben Ṭibān two flatcakes of unleavened barley bread, each weighing only fifteen dirhems, to show them on what food I lived.

[*A profligate son squanders his father's possessions*]

[L. 28] My son took advantage of my absence and left his post in the country and went to Alexandria.[161] Some said that he also traveled to Tripoli. He thought I would *never* be seen again. In my house, there was a rabble of mankind[162] with drums and flutes and music, and all I had left was gone. He sold everything he found in the house—*all that had been spared* from his former exploits. Thus he ruined me, besides causing troubles the like of which no one has experienced before.

[*Everything goes wrong in Fustat*]

[L. 34] In Fustat I lived for two months in the Street of the Lentil-cooks (*al-ᶜAddāsīn*),[163] for I feared the qadi would put me in charge of a ship going to Spain. Al-Qayṣarānī owed me a buhār [three hundred pounds] of pepper and one of lacquer. When I went to collect them, I found he had died and his house was sealed.[164] When I looked for al-Māṭishī[165]—he had gone.

[*Sent to Tunisia instead of Spain, Makhlūf endures utmost misery*]

[L. 37] Then I traveled to Alexandria during the week preceding Passover and arrived there on the eve of the *holiday*. I found my house ruined and nothing fit for sale left in it. So I took a hide which I had bought before my departure and two Chinese [or porcelain] dishes and sold them on the market.[166]

[L. 40] As expected, the qadi sent word that he wanted me to embark on a ship sailing for Spain. I explained my situation to him, whereupon he put me in charge of two ships heading for al-Mahdiyya and assured me saying: "An overseer cannot be prosecuted; I take the responsibility for this." I could not disobey him, but complained to him about the good-for-nothing [his son] and said: "In the end, he will sell the doors of my house and ruin it entirely." On hearing this, the qadi bade the boy appear before him and made him take the most solemn oaths that he would travel with me.

[L. 45] Thus we were about to depart, but God had not yet willed that we sail, for my son could not leave because of his many debts and the promissory notes signed by him. I paid everything during the night before my departure. *By God's covenant,* I ended up with not more than thirty-five dirhems, which I left to his brothers.

[L. 49] On our voyage we experienced misfortunes and tribulations. Moreover, I lacked provisions, because I was overtaken by our sudden departure. *God is my witness and judge,* not one loaf of bread went with me on board. A favorable wind started to blow at early dawn Friday so that we found no time to bake or to prepare a thing before sailing.

[L. 52] We came back and I hoped that he would have learned from our hard experiences. However, his gratitude to God manifested itself only in that he relapsed into his old ways. I myself was stripped of everything.[167] For all I had with me was a basket of indigo and a buhār of lacquer and this was taken from me and sequestered.[168] To explain all this would take too much time.

[*A post secured for the son is quit by him*]

[L. 56] After this I and the old lady [the boy's grandmother] asked Abū ʾl-Munā, the director of finances of the Buḥayra district, to take him into his employ. We entreated him, and he, Abū ʾl-Munā, did not disappoint us. He [the young man] had it better with him than with his own grandfather, when the latter was still alive. We were happy and believed that he would renounce the company of the musicians. However, after having been away for the month of *Elul,* he missed the company of the musicians and appeared again in Alexandria. When questioned, he explained that he had come on business, but would return after the high holidays. However, the holidays passed and he relapsed into his old habits, made debts, signed promissory notes, and, when he had to flee from the European wine-sellers and others, went up the Nile to Fustat.[169]

[*A second unsuccessful trip to Fustat*]
[Margin:]

Shortly before the Fūr-day [Purim], I, too, went up in order to get goods on commission, which would be an assistance to me on my impending voyage. I met him in al-Buḥayra. He had received a letter from our lord, *the Gaon*,[170] and returned with me to Fustat. I arrived on the day of *Purim*, and was busy with my lawsuit against Tamīm[171] until Passover. Several merchants intended to entrust me with some buhārs of lacquer. When they learned, however, that I was an overseer of the Sultan's ships, they held back and refrained from doing so. Thus I left Fustat during the middle days of Passover, and *by God's covenant* without taking with me dirhems to the amount of one half of a dinar for the expenses of my journey. Only Abū Zikrī al-Sijilmāsī granted me a loan.[172]

[*Unable to retain his position as overseer of the Sultan's ships, Makhlūf is forced to remain in Alexandria and to pay his son's debts*]

On my arrival in Alexandria, I found that the ships had already been pushed into the sea. I explained my plight to the qadi and informed him that no one had entrusted me with goods, and that I had no merchandise of my own which would support me and my son. I had left my son in Fuwwa,[173] for he could not enter Alexandria for fear of the European merchants. I swore to him [the qadi]: "I do not even have money for provisions, nor do I get a remuneration from you. In short, I cannot undertake the journey." Hearing this, he shouted at me angrily and left me in the clutches of the Europeans, who brought me before the qadi[174] and caused me great trouble. In the midst of these calamities, my son came to Alexandria and I informed him that I was out of work and in straits. I let someone talk to the Europeans, paid them what my son owed them, and took the promissory notes from them.

[*Other misdeeds of the son*]
[Top margin:]

While in Fustat my son was fooled by Ben Baqā in revenge for his having cursed him in Alexandria. Ben Baqā said to him: "I shall give you a loan of twenty dinars, properly witnessed, on which you can make a living, although you are at present broke and without proper clothing." My son accepted and wrote the promissory note, but Ben Baqā did not give him anything and swore that he had returned the document to him. I went to his house and asked his wife and, later, him personally, to give me the note, but he refused.

[*Verso*:]

[L. 2] Finally, I heard of something even graver than this or his former dealings with the Europeans. Ḥayyūn the Lame had given him two *maqṭa*ʿ cloths against a promissory note to the value of ten dinars, signed by four proper witnesses. He took the cloths and pawned them with a wine merchant against four *qisṭs* of wine worth sixty dirhems.[175] When I heard this, *my bones shook, my heart moaned and my hands waxed feeble.*[176] I was at the end of my wits. I took copies of the Bible and on them swore solemn oaths *never* to pay even one dirhem for Ḥayyīm,[177] whether he stayed with me or not.

[*Attempts to send the son to Palestine or Yemen failing, he finally disappears*]

[L. 8] For a month he lived in hiding. Then Ben al-Raṣṣāṣīya,[178] the son of his maternal uncle, wanted to travel to Palestine to his father. His mother, who feared to let him travel alone, sent my son with him to Damietta and wrote to Ben al-Murashshaḥ,[179] asking him to make arrangements for their passage. My thought was that *the Lord might smite him, or his appointed day to die would come*, or perhaps he would improve his ways while being abroad.[180] However, the ships had sailed from Damietta before he reached them and no travel was possible any more. Now the possibility that Ḥayyīm [i.e., Ḥayyūn the Lame] might throw him into prison would give more trouble than his going into hiding; thus he disappeared from Alexandria. I asked Nahrāy[181] to talk for me to Ḥayyīm and to entreat him to take back the two *maqṭaʿ* cloths and to release my son from his promissory note. However, he did not agree, but pocketed 10 dinars which he owed me.[182]

[L. 15] Last year I heard my son say to his mother: I would like to go up to Fustat, to the elder Abu ʾl-Ḥasan, in order to get employment with him, or with Ben Baqā, in the Sugar House. I said to him: Ben Baqā has no use for you, for he has someone whom he is unable and unwilling to dismiss. Work for two months in the country; after the Holidays, Hiba al-Ḥamawī[183] will travel to Yemen and I shall ask him to take you with him. However, my son did not agree to this, and left Alexandria. At present, I have no knowledge of him.

[*Fear that the boy might farm taxes from the government, squander the revenue collected, and have his father's house be taken for the payment of the debts*]

[L. 21] Now it could be that *a brood of sinful men*[184] in the Rīf say to him: "Let us be tax-farmers in partnership. You eat and drink, and your father will be held responsible for your debts." You know my character. However, were it not for the curses upon me after my death, I would give the house with [the loss of] which they threaten me to the poor or to the government, so that no threat would remain. What shall I do with it after years, when I shall pass away? Shall I take it with me? *By God's covenant*, were it now possible to sell properties, it would not remain in my possession. I would take its price and travel abroad, and no one would *ever* see me again.[185]

[*The main purpose of the letter: the addressee is asked to find a position for the son*]

[L. 27] *Without more ado*, I would like to come back to something practical, my lord. Your activities are manifold and your employees numerous. Perhaps you have a post for him where you could use his services. Or else, could you find a position for him with someone else as an assistant or associate overseer? Whatever you regard as appropriate, please do. He will certainly make good with you. Kindly inquire about him. While I was in Fustat during the month of Nisan, I intended to talk to you about this, but I believe I saw you only once. In any case, if you do something for him, and it will prove to be beneficial for you and for him, good, then retain him. However, if he proves to be a good-for-nothing, send him away. The decision rests with you. To have said less about this to a man like you would have been enough. Had it not been for our old friendship [lit., the bread and salt taken by us in common], I would not have troubled you in this matter.

[*The summit of sufferings: the unheard-of behavior of the twenty-two year old son*]

[L. 36] Best personal regards; should you have any business or service for which you believe I could be of use, kindly charge me with it, although I am not good for anything any more except for the worms. My son's deeds and his bad state have wrecked my life and destroyed my body. To see him is for me like seeing the Angel of Death. I brought him up, and now he curses me *boldly*. When I say to him: "Take a warning, look at the sons of the Alexandrian beggars![186] Do you want to become like one of them?" he replies: "As long as you are alive, I will be a good-for-nothing. Only after you are dead will I be successful."

[*A final outcry*]

[L. 41] *By God's covenant* and the Holy Law *given* to *our master Moses on Mount Sinai*, on Sabbaths and holidays, at parties and meetings, have no other subject of conversation except my story and my misfortune. For I am finished, and the Saint [King Solomon] has said: *When sorrow is in a man's heart, he wants to communicate it to others.*[187] I am alive, but dead, a soul without a body and a body without a soul. I have begot Abū Zikrī[188] and brought him up, and now he is twenty-two. I implore you, do for him what will profit you before God. *I speak so that I may find relief.*[189]

[L. 47] My special and most devoted regards to you and regards to your brother. A boy who sells his garment, his turban, his kerchief, and his nightgown and consents to walk around unclothed! Not to speak of other misfortunes *the like of which have never occurred*! Excuse me for slips and errors.

3. Rank and Renown

A saying attributed to the caliph al-Ma'mūn (813–833) is apt to illustrate the changes undergone by Middle Eastern society during the early centuries of Islam: "Social rank is kinship, making its members one family. A prominent Arab is closer to a prominent Persian than he is to a low-class Arab; a prominent Persian is nearer to a prominent Arab than he is to a low-class Persian. The high ones form one class, *ṭabaqa*, the low ones another."[1]

Who are the low ones? According to another dictum ascribed to al-Ma'mūn: "The people of the bazaar [the shopkeepers] are base; the artisans are despised; the merchants are stingy; but the bureaucrats are kings over the people."[2] A younger contemporary of the caliph, the eminent author al-Jāḥiẓ, in an essay especially devoted to the subject, preferred the independent merchant to the government official, who was exposed to the whims of his superiors.[3] In any case, in the developed society of the High Middle Ages it was no longer only race and religion but also class that divided the urban population.

One may ask whether this also applied to the comparatively small and closely knit Jewish world. The Geniza reveals that it did. In the letter of Makhlūf Nafūsī just translated, the proud overseas trader found nothing more deterring to say to his unworthy son than that he would end up as a small shopkeeper in his home town (whom he calls, as was usual, "a beggar").[4] Our book opens with a study of the stratification of Geniza society.[5] Besides birth, wealth, and connections, it was strength and nobility of character (mostly expressed in acts of altruism and charity), piety and integrity, erudition and public service that gained a person his place in society.

The idea of high rank was expressed by the Persian term *jāh*, literally, "place," also rendered with corresponding Arabic and Hebrew words.[6] It is not excluded that Persian social notions had influenced Jews and Arabs even before Islam threw all these peoples closely together. Jāh, as may be expected, was a composite phenomenon, difficult to define; basically it describes a position of power and influence, obtained in very different ways and used for a large variety of causes.

The constant recourse to jāh for success in simple day-to-day business transactions was perhaps learned from the shrewd Persian merchants. In a letter to the prominent Judah b. Moses Ibn Sighmār, which dealt with most important public affairs, such as the ransom of captives and communal leadership, he was also asked to accompany a friend to the Square of the Perfumers; the friend would do the buying of small quantities of a number of Oriental spices, but the jāh of Ibn Sighmār would assure that the spices bought would be of good quality.[7] When I first read this thirty years ago, I was surprised. Soon similar statements were found. The court physician Mevōrākh b. Saadya, one of the greatest leaders Egyptian Jewry ever had, is a familiar name to the readers of this book. In a long letter from al-Mahdiyya, Tunisia, dealing with Hebrew manuscripts which he was interested in acquiring, he is also asked to use his jāh to safeguard the smooth transport of goods belonging to the writer of the letter from Alexandria to al-Mahdiyya. This was before Mevōrākh obtained his post as official leader of the Egyptian Jews. Characteristically, the writer adds: "If I myself were there, this would be of no avail."[8] The angry Tunisian who complained so about his treatment by the eminent Joseph Ibn ʿAwkal says that he did business with him in order to benefit from the connection with Joseph's jāh.[9] When a merchant in Fustat wished to help two young brothers who had arrived from faraway Iraq, he told them that he would not join them as partner in their newly opened business; their link with his jāh would be sufficient help for them.[10] Similarly, a friend of Judah Ibn Sighmār, describing his manifold undertakings, notes concerning one of them that his intention was not to make money but to gain (or uphold) jāh, best translated here perhaps as "connections."[11]

There is no need to reiterate that this emphasis on social rank was not specifically Jewish. When I enlarged on this topic in my address to the Colloque sur la sociologie musulmane, Brussels, September 1961, Sir Hamilton Gibb pointed out in the discussion that the Tunisian historian Ibn Khaldūn had paid much attention to the role of jāh in his chapter on livelihood. Now, Sir Hamilton stated, Ibn Khaldūn's remarks about the concrete living concerns of the middle class received substantial illustration from the stories reported in the Geniza documents.[12]

The general Arabic equivalent for jāh was *ʿizz*, strength, power, respect, the state of a person being treated with deference. In the openings of letters, after the usual good wishes for a long life—and not rarely even before them—were expressions that one's ʿizz and excellence, prominence, and highness be preserved permanently or enhanced. Man's dearest possessions besides life, his children, are mentioned in one breath together with his honored position.[13] Professions besides business, in particular those depending on reputation, such as medical practice and (private) Bible schools, had to fight to uphold their position. That's why we read in the letters of successful physicians and schoolmasters that they could not leave their places even for one day.[14] This passage from a letter to a female relative by the master of a school is instructive: "As you know, I am now in Fustat. They are kind to me and honor me; my jāh is secure; may God make it enduring in his grace!" But in reply to an invitation by the addressee, he writes: "I cannot go outside Fustat for a span; I would spoil my situation."[15]

Family life was another field where "rank" was vital. As a rule, matrimony was created by an agreement between the families concerned, and many factors determined the standing of each. When a wealthy and influential but not well-educated and not so young man asked for the hand of the daughter of a scholar, he requested that the answer, if negative, be kept in utmost secrecy, for "a man exists by his jāh," his reputation.[16] The topic is touched upon in *Med. Soc.* III in various contexts. The decisive values, naturally, were those recognized by Geniza society. Piety and erudition were titles of nobility; a wife earning money by her work was a disgrace and a loss of face for her husband. The ideal was "mixing grapes with grapes," joining peers in marriage.[17]

Persons in public service, either as communal leaders, as higher government officials, or as court physicians (the last being for Christians and Jews the favorite avenue leading to contacts with a caliph, viceroy, or vizier), were regarded as *the* holders of rank, men of power able to achieve goals unattainable to others. Yet, they, too, were dependent. As a community leader, the primus inter pares, the first among equals, needed the approval of his peers; the government would not confirm or uphold his appointment without consulting the acknowledged notables, "the elders"; and although formal elections were unknown, the common people would make themselves heard if they strongly disapproved of a leader's conduct. The position of a person in close contact with the ruler and his entourage was even more precarious. It was difficult to move into such a position and not less toilsome to keep it. Temporary downfall and resurgence were common events. Dangerous intrigues required constant watchfulness. In practically every letter to a man of rank, God's special providence was sought for him.

When the influential court physician Abraham b. Isaac Ibn al-Furāt was called back from Ramle, Palestine, to the Egyptian capital, he was wished "to obtain the fulfillment of all his aspirations with regard to his person [a good match], his jāh, and his wealth."[18] Of Abu ʾl-Munajjā, the builder of the canal that bore his name in the service of the viceroy al-Malik al-Afḍal, a private letter reports: "He occupies today a prominent jāh and place."[19] The capricious court physician Abū Zikrī b. Elijah is congratulated on the news that his jāh had become stabilized, but God's intervention is invoked "to suppress the machinations of the sinful men who plot to shed his blood."[20] Even the Head of the Jerusalem Academy and High Council, whose appointment was mainly a matter of traditional succession, was wished, like any other man of rank, "to find favor and approval in the eyes of God and man" (Proverbs 3:4), meaning, that although his position was for life and confirmed by the government as the highest judicial authority, he was under constant scrutiny by the heavenly judge above him and by the flock entrusted to his guidance.[21] On the other end of the social ladder, a local notable in Alexandria, who was the bearer of only one honorific title of little significance, is wished by a relative "to become secure in his honored position, and a famous name and blessing throughout the land" (Isaiah 19:24).[22]

The most prominent example of a man of rank in Egyptian Jewry falling from favor during the Fatimid period and losing his title of leadership temporarily was none other than Mevōrākh b. Saadya. First, he was forced to flee to the Fayyūm oasis south of Cairo, and then, banned from the capital, he took up residence in Alexandria. He lost his position but not his jāh. Thanks to his personality, erudition, and long-standing service to the community, he was still regarded as the leader, in some congregations even officially during public prayer.[23] In Alexandria he was able to pursue his affairs (medical practice and probably also some commercial undertakings), and, in addition, occupied himself with the supervision of Jewish education. Unfortunately, the circumstances of neither his downfall nor his reinstatement are known. A source close to him attributes the former to the machinations of David, the youngest son of Daniel b. Azarya, the late nāsī and Head of the Jerusalem yeshiva (d. 1063), who replaced Mevōrākh as official leader of Egyptian Jewry during the years 1082 to approximately 1094.[24]

A person could lose his jāh through no fault of his own and without falling victim to intrigues directed against him; for instance, when he owed his rank to his family. When Daniel b. Azarya died prematurely leaving three young sons, a long missive announcing his death, the middle part of which has been preserved, was sent out.[25] I am pretty sure that this calligraphic and highly rhetorical epistle was written by Samuel, his eldest son. For it was customary for a head of a yeshiva to train his eldest son as his secretary to introduce him into the legal, religious, and communal issues with which he would have to deal should he occupy the office of his father later in life. Besides, Samuel's hand is known to us from elsewhere.[26] After describing his pain—also physical—over the loss of his father and his state of disconsolation (quoting Lamentations 2:13), he continues: "You, the illustrious sheikh, have already learned how God the exalted has afflicted the people of Israel and, in particular, myself with the eclipse of the honored position, jāh, possessed by me through the vanishing of the crown, the glory, the power, the splendor . . . the nāsī . . . and Head of the yeshiva. . . . " Samuel was far too young at that time to be considered as a suitable successor to his father.[27]

In conclusion, the ideas about rank entertained by the Geniza people are perhaps best seen in the following passage written by Solomon b. Judah Gaon, Head of the Jerusalem yeshiva, ca. 1025–1051. He, a native of faraway Fez, Morocco, was chosen for this prestigious office in preference to Jacob b. Joseph, a local man, whose father had been President of the High Court, the second highest rank in the yeshiva hierarchy. Jacob, who lived in Fustat, had written two insulting letters to Solomon, one directly, and one through Isaac Ibn al-Furāt, the father of Abraham Ibn al-Furāt, mentioned before. In a letter to Isaac, Solomon expresses astonishment that the letter was forwarded to him at all and continues:[28]

He [Jacob] is a man who has a very high opinion of himself and wants to have the uppermost rank. Naturally, everyone wishes that, but a reasonable person *knows his place*. . . . By the soul of my father—God's mercy upon him!—our master Solomon ha-Kohen Gaon [our Solomon's predecessor] honored him with the title *ḥāvēr* [member of the Academy] only at my request. But he adjured me not to give him a higher rank [as an officer of the High Council]. Had he evaluated himself correctly, he would have been content with the title "member," which is of a general nature; this would have been the attitude of a sincere person, to whom no one would object. However, he who aspires to high office, all eyes are directed toward him and achievements are expected from him of which he might not be capable. I myself wish occasionally I could stay away from things incumbent on me, for I know my place.

[Solomon had returned Jacob's first letter to him and enclosed the other in his missive to Isaac, for "peers"—as he writes—meaning scholars, should not send messages to one another that were apt to poison their relations forever. The fact that he himself occupied now the highest position did not diminish his feelings for others.]

I am not of the type of those who do not think about anyone else, once they have obtained their rank. For I know what I have to expect when I meet my Creator, and wish to be careful with what I say. Jacob[29] believes that he is an excellent speaker. *God knows* that I am able to refute every word he wrote. But this would lead to estrangement, and I wish to preserve our friendship.

Jāh, high position, entailed visibility, reputation, a "name" familiar to many, and this is what everyone who counted was wished. Solomon b. Judah took a higher and more personal view of rank: it had to be justified by qualification, the ability to live up to one's responsibilities, with the proviso that the competent judge of this should be none other than the bearer of the dignity himself. Solomon quotes the Mishna, which teaches that knowing one's place was the mark of a true scholar.[30] In fact, Solomon's attitude in this matter, apparent also in other letters of his, was in keeping with the general mood of the Geniza period, where self-examination and preoccupation with one's own person were so common. With his further contention that his relations with others were not impaired by his attainment of high rank, he also did not stand alone. The unrelenting praise of the virtues of humility and modesty pervading the Geniza correspondence served as a kind of antidote against the arrogant comportment of all too many who had attained high positions.[31]

Striving for superiority, Solomon b. Judah states, is a general human propensity. It certainly is, as we all are aware. But the degree to which the ideas of jāh and ʿizz, position and power, dominated the mind and daily life of the Geniza person appears to us as something unusual. So is another characteristic of his cognate with it: hunting for titles. In order to feel safe in his attainments, the Geniza person needed an official, public, and permanent confirmation, a prestigious title, by which he was addressed during his lifetime and remembered after his death. As the Geniza shows, a title often replaced a person's name; he was referred to only by title, he became identified with his status. Titles, of course, are still with us. The British queen's yearly "list" still makes news (at least in the United States), universities grant honorary degrees, and titles are dispensed to persons of different professions in many countries. Yet it is remarkable how this craving for prominence permeated all layers of Geniza society, creating fine nuances of class distinction and personal aspiration which we cannot claim perhaps to have fully comprehended. We are often inclined to see in this vast potpourri of incongruous appellations only ridiculous expressions of human vanity. But one should never dismiss as nonsense things that other people took so seriously. To bring home the extraordinary role of this social phenomenon in the medieval Middle East it is sufficient to draw attention to the 1982, detailed and solid article on titles in the *Encyclopaedia of Islam* by C. E. Bosworth.[32]

That article deals with the titles borne by caliphs, other rulers, and the higher echelons of bureaucracy, military, and clergy. The special contribution of the Geniza is that it shows, in hundreds of examples, often exactly defined by place, date, and other details, that the practice of dispensing titles had seeped down to a middle class, not, or only tenuously, connected with the court or government service. Whether the Muslim environment was affected by this process to the same degree can be known only after more research has been done in this field with regard to Muslim society.

Although Byzantine and Persian antecedents were not lacking, the proliferation of titles in the caliphal realm seems to have been mainly attributable to inner-Islamic developments: the increasing endowment of the caliphate with a religious halo, to be expressed in high-sounding appellations; the ever-growing bureaucratization of the government, where everyone had to be assigned his proper place and station; and the loss of power by the caliphs, which gave the dispensation of titles the semblance of overlordship and helped to fill their empty coffers with precious gifts, presented to them in anticipation of, or thanks for, favors granted. Soon the pouring forth of titles was lamented as a sign of the decay of the caliphate. By the end of the tenth century (the fourth of Islam) a poet mocks:

> The caliph of ours has few dirhems in his hands,
> So he lavishes honorifics on people.[33]

About a hundred years later, the Seljuk vizier Niẓām al-Mulk complains in his book on statecraft (written in 1091–1092): "In these days, the meanest official gets angry and indignant, if he is given less than seven or ten titles" (a situation that kept the higher officials busy making suggestions and writing recommendations).[34]

In this atmosphere the Jewish community could not fall behind; the impact of the court and government circles is indeed clearly visible in this matter of titles. Yet, the community had carried over from antiquity remnants of corporational organization which accounted for specific developments in this field, as shown presently.

It was natural that the exilarch "from the house of David," the official Head of the Diaspora, who was a dignitary at the court of the Abbasid caliphs, bestowed honorific titles on members of the Jewish community. Since no Geniza documents have been preserved in Baghdad, we learn only rarely about such occurrences. The *nāsīs*, the "princes from the house of David," however, who sojourned, or settled wherever they were welcome—in northern Iraq, Syria, Egypt, and Yemen—lavishly distributed titles, such as "Standard-bearer," "Helper," "Diadem," or "Favorite of the *nesī'ūth* [the office of the nāsī]." Even the great Nagid Mevōrākh b. Saadya did not disdain to note the first of these four titles near the beginning of the fourteen he held. The position of the nāsīs must be appreciated as an expression of the thirst for authority derived from the glory of biblical ancestry, as threadbare as their claim was.[35]

The main dispensers of titles were the two yeshivas of Baghdad, followed reluctantly by the yeshiva of Jerusalem.[36] In Geniza times these academics and high councils, the uppermost authorities in matters of religion, legal practice, and communal affairs, suffered much by the increasing devastation of Iraq and Palestine, and often were even more in need of funds than academic institutions anywhere. Moreover, they themselves had a tradition of titles: they were hierarchic organizations. The rank of a member was defined by the row in which he was seated; promotion was signified by physically moving forward. The place he occupied bore a name. These "names" were later given to scholarly persons living anywhere in the Jewish world, often serving there as communal leaders. The historical development was probably that originally persons so honored had sometimes attended the yeshiva, and some such cases are known. In the course of time, the "names" were also given to learned communal leaders, say in Tunisia or Morocco, who had not visited Baghdad at all.[37]

Another type of title—the list is endless—was given to supporters. The main supports of the yeshivas were the scholarly leaders (often well-to-do merchants), who generally were also responsible for the collection of funds in each country. But there were many benefactors who had no claim to scholarship. Numerous fancy titles were invented to reward their efforts and generosity. But as long as the yeshivas were strong, the dividing line between religious erudition and laity was observed.[38]

Since titles were coveted and dispensed to enhance the renown of benefactors or leading scholars, they were awarded with as much publicity as possible. (Cf. the modern "commencements.") In Baghdad this was done during the two months of common study in spring and autumn described in *Med. Soc.*, II, 197–198, where a German Jewish traveler who witnessed the occasion once found two thousand participants listening to the Gaon, or Head of the yeshiva (who was assisted by a number of *meturgemāns*, or broadcasters). Sherira Gaon (d. 1006) wrote to an honorary *allūf*, who had complained about the little publicity given to him, that his "name" was read out in the presence of "many thousands," among whom, he tactfully added, were many who were familiar with the complainant's name anyhow.[39] In Jerusalem the titles were awarded at the yearly reunion on the Mount of Olives on the autumnal Feast of Tabernacles, that is, a prayer was said for the recipients, mentioning them by their new designation. In a small town like Jerusalem, surrounded by a largely devastated country, no big crowds could be expected. Yet the Holy City, more centrally situated than Baghdad and close to the Mediterranean, was a goal of pilgrimage, wherefore the recipients of honorary titles could more easily be present in person. This, of course, enhanced the publicity effect of the ceremony.

In the following I translate a passage from a letter by Daniel b. Azarya, Head of the Jerusalem yeshiva (d. 1063), addressed to Abraham (b. Isaac) Ibn al-Furāt, an exceptionally dedicated benefactor of the community at large and of Daniel in particular. Ibn al-Furāt, a busy court physician, was unable to attend the award of a new "name" given to him to be added to two he already possessed. Therefore, the Gaon had to explain to him the significance of the new one. To be attractive, a title had to be very special, either new, or, if borne before at all, given earlier only to a very distinguished person. This was indeed the case with the title "Splendor of the Elders." Abū ʿAlī I (the elder) Ibn Faḍlān, a banker of a famous family of Baghdad, had been honored with it over half a century before. Titles conferred within the community were always in Hebrew. Hōd, Hebrew for splendor, as Daniel himself notes, was a translation of Arabic Bahāʾ. The title Bahāʾ al-dawla, "Splendor of the government," was borne by a Būyid ruler and several viziers contemporary with the audacious banker Ibn Faḍlān, who had the temerity to deny a loan to a powerful emir.[40] "The Elders" were the government of the Jewish community. Consequently, the new title conferred meant that Abraham Ibn al-Furāt was actually the leader of the Jewish community of Egypt. This was by no means an expression of adulation. The passage on the award of the title is written mainly in Hebrew but is followed by a report in Arabic about the instructions given by the Gaon to the member of the academy Eli b. Amram, the official Head of the Fustat congregations. He ordered him to consult and obey Ibn al-Furāt in all matters concerning the mundane affairs of the community and to pray for him in public calling him by his new "name," adding "may God crush his enemies" (the recipient was aware of the meaning of Daniel's allusion). Ibn al-Furāt had no official standing in the community whatsoever. But soon everyone would know what the new title meant.[41]

I crave the indulgence of the reader for the long introduction. But without some acquaintance with the historical circumstances, the title conferred on Ibn al-Furāt extolled in Daniel's letter would have remained entirely meaningless. The beginning and the end of the letter were torn away. The passage preserved begins in the midst of a sentence.[42]

[I am describing now] the proclamation of the new name, which was added to your exalted titles. This was the text:[43] "Our mighty, noble, and leading man, his honor, greatness, and holiness[44] of *my* master and *our* lord[45] Abraham ha-Kohen, the Chief of the Community, the Splendor of the Elders, the Glory of the Kohens." I added to this blessings for you and prayers for your noble ancestors, may they be remembered with blessings on the day of resurrection.

The new name is Splendor of the Elders. With this name sheikh Abū ʿAlī Ibn Faḍlān was honored in Baghdād many years ago, and from that time up till now no[46] one has received that title. Since you, the illustrious sheikh, are the splendor [Ar. *bahāʾ* is used] of Israel, I entitled you with it and ordered that it should be mentioned in public prayer in addition to the two excellent titles you held before. May God make the new name a good augury for you and for the enhancement of your esteem, the increase of your renown, for the permanence of your exalted position, and for many happy years to come.

In the continuation, written in Arabic, Daniel emphasizes that the grand title awarded to Ibn al-Furāt was not a sufficient recognition of his merits but he trusted in his pleasant nature to accept it in good spirit. The excuse was appropriate. In the three titles given by the yeshiva[47] to Ibn al-Furāt there was not the slightest hint of the possession of Jewish learning, the most coveted honor for a Jewish leader. In a letter to Ibn al-Furāt by Eli b. Amram, the Head of the Fustat community, he is praised for his profound knowledge in Bible and Talmud. Had this been true, Daniel would not have failed to acknowledge it by an appropriate title. Despite the debts he himself and the community owed Ibn al-Furāt, Daniel could permit himself to avoid the sin of flattery because he was well aware that Ibn al-Furāt knew his own place: he did not belong to the inner-Jewish hierarchy; he was, as the Geniza correspondence proves, the shield of the community against government authorities and any other oppressors, high or low.

The yeshivas waned, but the appetite for titles waxed. How could it be satisfied? Yeshivas in the classical sense did continue to exist in Egypt and Syria throughout the twelfth century and in Baghdad even longer. In a list of forty or so titularies, carefully compiled early in the 1140s, about thirty were in one way or another—as actual or honorary members, or as benefactors—connected with a yeshiva. Yet each of these bore one or more titles; the yeshiva connection seemed to have become commonplace and easy to acquire.[48] The official heads of the Jewish community of Egypt, who more and more replaced the heads of the yeshivas in the religious field, often bore numerous "names" but seem not to have made the dispensing of titles part of their regular activities. Being mostly court physicians they were too busy; moreover, they were givers, not takers; they had no need to engage in the lucrative but time-consuming occupation of inventing and distributing appropriate titles. So, who else did the job?[49]

The answer is provided by the titles themselves. They reflect the congregational, one may say, the democratic character of the Jewish community. Membership in a congregation was entirely voluntary. But the demands on the congregation were many: the upkeep and illumination of the houses of worship; the payments, albeit modest, of community officials; the regular and special handouts of bread, meals, clothing, and cash to the needy; the general care for widows and orphans, the sick, and the old; the education of the children of the poor; and extraordinary drives for ransoming captives or intervening with government authorities. Success in all these fields depended on the capacity and willingness of the members; those who contributed their share or more were rewarded with an appropriate "name." Titles composed with the term *qahal*, congregation, were almost as frequent as those given by a yeshiva; the title is often in the plural, *qehillot*, for works of charity were frequently carried out by the two congregations of Fustat, the Iraqians and the Palestinians, together, and occasionally the congregations from the countryside cooperated as well. Benefactors of both Rabbanites and Karaites were honored with titles composed with the phrase "[the House of] Israel," or with simply "the two groups."[50] "Head of the congregation[s]" during most of the Geniza period was, unlike antiquity, not the name of an office but an honorific title.[51]

Who awarded these and similar honors expressing the gratitude of the community? It had to be done as were all decisions on public affairs: the elders of a congregation or local community arrived at an agreement (usually by consent, not by vote) on the person and the title he deserved; they inquired whether there was any opposition to the award among those regularly attending service. If none was to be expected, they instructed the cantor to invoke God's blessing over the thus honored, calling him by his new "name," with the understanding that the same would be done in the future, even after his death, in any prayer said for him.[52]

The name of a respectable person of some standing was normally preceded by phrases like "the illustrious sheikh" in Arabic, or "the esteemed elder," *zāqēn*, in Hebrew. These were not titles, but forms of address, which the writer would choose according to the circumstances. It stands to reason that we have here Hebrew adaptations of Arabic usage, for the genuine, Talmudic honorary zāqēn designated a distinguished scholar.[53]

Besides the "Holy Congregation" there were other groups with religious connotations which provided material for titles. When a judge (who functioned also as a rabbi) was labeled "distinguished," "expert," or "recognized," epithets that designated a rank in Talmudic literature, the same was probably true in the Geniza period, where we find judges thus "named" presiding over the court.[54] Other laudatory by-names, such as the "Efficient," the "Stalwart," or the "Diadem of the Judges" and the like were, however, honorific titles.[55] A similar differentiation prevailed with regard to the cantors.[56] They were the most popular class of community officials. Everyone heard them when attending a service, and since they very often doubled as court clerks or court messengers (for instance, visiting private homes to restore peace between husband and wife), they were in personal contact with many. Hence the proliferation of titles for them, and just as high-sounding. Even a chorister could be honored with the title "Splendor," but this was exceptional.[57]

Persons named Kohen or Levi had no official functions in the community but possessed certain religious prerogatives, for instance, during the service the Kohens pronounced the priestly blessings (Numbers 6:23–26), now pronounced in many churches by the officiating minister (and following this practice, in most U.S. synagogues by the rabbi, even if he is not a Kohen). In the twelfth century, titles composed with tribal names, such as "Splendor," "Glory," "Leader" of the Kohens, or "Pride of the Sons of Levi" became extremely common, probably because not much else that was praiseworthy could be said of the person concerned, except generosity, which was usually lauded by an additional title. For example, Ibn Jamāhir the Levi was certainly a prominent India trader, active and influential in communal affairs, and his second title "Crown of the Generous" must have been earned somehow, but the stories told about him in *Med. Soc.*, I, 133 and 146, cast doubts on his moral qualities. Yet the importance attributed to membership in tribal units, once so prominent in the rites of the Temple of Jerusalem, was connected with messianic expectations and should not be dismissed entirely as empty phrases.[58]

A plethora of titles, others than those granted by a yeshiva, was related to religious study and instruction. This was only natural. First, there were the select few who attained a high degree of scholarship while studying with renowned masters far away from the seats of yeshivas and, for one reason or another, were not eager to get a "name" from a Gaon. Such persons were distinguished by the title *talmīd*, "disciple," which described them as eternal students.

The father of judge Abraham, "the Son of the Scholar," talmīd, so often mentioned in these volumes, probably acquired his erudition and renown in Qayrawān, Tunisia, a flourishing center of Jewish learning in the first half of the eleventh century.[59] There were local midrāshim attended by people wishing to acquire a modicum of Jewish learning for its own sake, which might also be helpful when they chose to serve as one of the lower community officials. As far as the Geniza goes, these midrāshim did not award degrees. A personal title, as required by the circumstances, would have the desired effect.[60] Finally, studying "all the days of your life" was a religious duty, and some at least—we have no statistics—took this command seriously. Evening courses were available during the week, and public disputation lectures were welcome events on Saturdays and holidays. Devoted participants excelling in the discussions were rewarded with a title, some, we may surmise, even without craving for such an honor. These matters have been treated in the subsections "Adult Education" and "Higher Studies: Organization," *Med. Soc.*, II, 192–205, and are taken up again, from the religious point of view, in sections C and D, below. Here a few cases apt to illustrate the meaning of such titles are discussed.

The most prestigious title for attainments in religious learning was talmīd. A beautifully written ancient missive, probably from the tenth century, describes the affair of a "bogus-nāsī," as Jacob Mann characterized a spurious scion of the family of the Head of the Diaspora, who succeeded in usurping complete mastery over the Jews of Egypt, Palestine, and Syria for two whole years. To explain the astounding fact that a person like that could exercise the highest authority in religious and legal matters, and collect contributions everywhere, the writer emphasizes twice, that the most learned men, members of the yeshivas as well as talmīds, bowed to his decisions.[61] By the end of the twelfth century, when the title ḥāvēr, "member of the yeshiva," had lost much of its luster, talmīd became the common title for a religious scholar, occasionally accompanied by an additional name of distinction. For instance, Maimonides' nephew, who studied with him, was called al-talmīd *al-zakī*, the sharp-witted, the bright, and the same title was given to others.[62] The Hebrew equivalent *ha-talmīd ha-mēvīn*, the discerning, the thinker, goes back to Talmudic usage.[63] Of particular interest is a family tree, where in the first two generations three persons had the title ḥāvēr and one was a judge, dayyān; in the third there were two talmīds; in the fourth, one; in the fifth none. In another branch of the same family, which contained eight generations, there was none bearing a title in generations four to eight. That a person should pride himself publicly on the learnedness of forefathers who lived six or more generations back shows in what high esteem religious scholarship was held even long after it had died out in the family.[64]

Local midrāshim were headed by persons of different types and ranks, sometimes even a learned cantor, and were attended for different purposes.[65] In the list of titles from the early 1140s, repeatedly referred to, a physician is called "Chief speaker" and "Master of the Midrāsh." The physician attended the institution, probably in the evenings, to enlarge his religious knowledge, and took the floor with conspicuous frequency. The title Chief speaker was borne by an illustrious sage about a thousand years before, more than six hundred of whose dicta are quoted in the Mishna. In the twelfth and thirteenth centuries it designated a studious layman pursuing serious study.[66]

Quite another type of attendant at a midrāsh appears in the letter of the father-in-law of Maimonides' son, Hananel b. Samuel, "the Great Judge," who, among many other activities, presided over the midrāsh in Fustat. Addressing the father of a young man who was sent from Alexandria to Fustat for study in the midrāsh of the capital, Hananel congratulates the addressee on "his noble offspring, the illustrious talmīd Joseph," praises him that all his intentions are religious, like those of his forefathers, and reports about him later in the letter: "From the time he arrived in Fustat he has not ceased to attend the midrāsh. In addition, he studies [lit., "occupies himself"] with his cousin R. Peraḥya, the esteemed scholar, who lauds him much for the intensity of his aspirations and the quality of his mind." The youthful (and newly married) Joseph is politely called illustrious talmīd because he was on the way to becoming one.[67]

Some titles extol the intelligence, the discernment of the persons bearing them. Whether this honor was acquired through diligent participation in the communal study of sacred texts, or by serving as an assistant lay judge, or by otherwise giving good counsel in public meetings cannot be said, and possibly was different in each case. Abu ʾl-Maʿālī Samuel b. Judah Ben Asad, "The Master of the Discerning," appears in numerous court records dated 1133 through 1167, but, as far as I can see, his high-sounding title is first used in 1159; by 1166/7 he is being referred to simply as "The Master." His dedication to the cause of orphans and others, where a high degree of both reliability and circumspection was required, probably earned him the honor.[68]

In later times, such noble titles did not always command respect, as this rude note from the early thirteenth century indicates.

"Hope deferred makes the heart sick" [Proverbs 13:12].[69] "It is better not to vow than to vow and not fulfill" [Ecclesiastes 5:4].

Your excellency, my lord, the illustrious sheikh Abu ᵓl-Ḥasan, The Prince of Wisdom—may the Keeper of the souls of the pious keep you—promised me a small quantity of sugar which I could cook in my workshop. When my messenger arrived, you said to him: "I shall send it," but you did not. God beware that you should not keep your promise, for the sages have said: "Saying 'yes yes' is an oath" [and not keeping an oath is a serious sin].[70]

"The Prince of Wisdom" was perhaps somewhat demanding in matters of religious observance, wherefore he was reminded of the beam in his own eye by three sacred texts.

In a letter to an important merchant he is called Glory of the Elders, Crown of the Understanding; these two appellations rhyme, though, and are followed by two other rhymes with good wishes, they should probably be regarded as forms of address, not as formal titles. It should be noted that in the long line of titles borne by the leaders of the community in later times some of them were indeed rhymed.[71] Needless to say, honorific epithets in Arabic, such as The Sagacious, Smart, Smartest of the Smart, are nicknames that in due course occasionally became family names.[72]

By the end of the twelfth century the proliferation of official titles, that is, those noted in legal documents, got out of hand. One example suffices. The cantankerous communal official Abraham al-Najīb, whom we have met before, and who appears frequently in the Geniza as collector of rents and performing other minor services, leased a field adjacent to the holy shrine of Dammūh at a token payment of 6 dirhems per year. He promised that he "and his son after his death" would develop the land and return it to the community after thirty years, a type of contract common in the land of the Nile. The scribe of the short document found himself obliged to ornament al-Najīb's name with these seven appellations: "The Esteemed Elder, the Crown of the Levites, the Delightful Notable, the Favorite of the Remote and the Near Gaons,[73] the Joy of the Elders, the Man of Good Advice." As reported above, the eminent vizier Niẓām al-Mulk complained in his book on statecraft that even the meanest government official was dissatisfied if he did not get at least seven titles. This happened in Baghdad, then the capital of the Seljuk empire, near the end of the eleventh century. The filtering down of pompous titles to the lower ranks and their subsequent depreciation occurred in Egypt somewhat later and reached its nadir by the end of the twelfth century, when Egypt, under the Ayyubids, had become a Seljuk successor-state.[74]

In conclusion, this matter of titles awarded within the Jewish community illuminates a serious social phenomenon. During the most solemn service of the year, held on the Day of Atonement, God's blessings were invoked for the ruler of the country, the Fatimid caliph, the Head of the Jewish community, the learned divines, the spiritual leaders of the local congregations, and for "the bearers of titles," as if, before getting special attention up there in Heaven, one must first achieve something similar here on earth. In a general way one received a "name," a noble appellation, when the name of a respectable person was preceded or followed by the epithet "the esteemed elder," later on also "the esteemed *sār*" (chief or notable), and in ever increasing degrees by special titles. This striving for renown had the beneficial effect of inspiring a person to exert himself to obtain a certain measure of excellence in one or more fields, such as charity, study, religious observance, or activity for the common weal. It had the disadvantage of accentuating the hierarchic structure of society and nurturing a certain contempt and even disregard for the underprivileged.[75]

The Hebrew titles awarded by the Jewish community and its authorities showed only one side of the story. During the High Middle Ages Christians and Jews participated more intensely in the life of the general, now preponderately Muslim, population than in any other medieval period. Distinction was now sought in Arabic titles carrying prestige in the public at large. They were given mostly to persons connected in one way or another with the government or the army: government officials, clerks, and agents of higher standing, physicians who had treated members of the court, a vizier or a general, as well as prominent merchants and bankers. The obvious assumption that Christians and Jews were honored only with titles of low rank is refuted by the abundant testimony of the Geniza, and, as far as physicians and other men of science are concerned, also by Muslim biographical literature.[76]

In *Med. Soc.*, II, 356–357, it was asked how a Jewish administrative officer could be honored (in 1098) with the title *Thiqat al-Mulk* (Trusted by the Government) borne at the same time by the chief qadi of the Fatimid empire. The answer advanced was that titles probably did not carry with them the same weight in each section of the bureaucracy. Usages in this respect probably differed from one place to another and changed with the times and governments. On the other hand, titles were tenacious of life. In a document dated 1038 "a physician of the exalted majesty" from a family of doctors who had served the Fatimid caliphs in both Tunisia and Egypt, bears the title *al-Sadīd*, translated by me as "the Sound."

Two hundred years later, in and around 1237, we still find a physician bearing that title, and many others in between.[77] The title was expanded to (or perhaps is abridged from) *Sadīd al-Dawla,* "[Recognized as] Sound, by the ruling dynasty," awarded to the Jewish physician Abū Saᶜd, and to *Sadīd al-Dīn* "[Recognized as] Sound, by the [Islamic] religious community," a Christian physician, and to a qadi, who acquired fame as a medical man.[78] Even Moses Maimonides, who disdained titles, was addressed as *al-shaykh al-sadīd.*[79] Perhaps this and similar titles were not merely honorific but were given by teachers or superiors as a kind of certificate of a certain degree of competence. It should be noted that a Jewish *kātib,* or government official, and a Muslim judge, doing business on the trade route to India, bore the same title.[80]

Al-Asᶜad, "the Auspicious," even in the form *Asᶜad al-dīn* "[Regarded as] Auspicious, by the [Islamic] religious community," was the byname (used also as the proper name) of a Jewish physician from the Sabra family in al-Maḥalla, Lower Egypt. He was renowned both as a practitioner and as a medical author, for instance of a treatise comparing the climates of Damascus and Cairo. (He had practiced in both these cities). Ibn Abī Uṣaybiᶜa, the Muslim author of a huge biographical dictionary, recounts how this al-Asᶜad was a friend of an uncle of his and cured a female member of the household, after all other attempts had failed. Such an intimate detail helps perhaps to explain the strange title Asᶜad al-dīn, connecting a Jew with the Islamic community. Al-Asᶜad of al-Maḥalla appears in the Geniza in a number of different contexts.[81] A contemporary of his with the same title was a banker acting as administrator of the Jewish pious foundations, in which capacity he had contacts with a Muslim emir.[82] A Jewish *kātib al-ᶜArab,* chief clerk of a Bedouin levy, was also an Asᶜad, and so was a representative of merchants, it seems, in Aden, South Arabia, and the director of the customs house in ᶜAydhāb, the important Sudanese terminal of the India trade. The same variety of occupations is noticeable among the bearers of similar titles expressing a certain quality of excellence.[83]

Arabic titles composed with *dawla,* "ruling dynasty," or *mulk,* "government," besides those already mentioned as awarded to Jews, are common in the Geniza.[84] We even have a dignitary bearing two such titles: Amīn al-dawla Thiqat al-Mulk, "Trusted by the Dynasty, Relied upon by the Government." He certainly was connected with one or several courts, for he is wished "to find plenty of favor in the eyes of kings and ministers."[85] In Iraq any Jew of some prominence was supposed to have a title of this type. There was a wide variety of them, including some curiosities, for instance *ghars al-dawla,* "Plant of the Ruling House," borne by a man praised for his scholarship.[86]

All in all, it seems that the proliferation of honorific titles common to Muslims and members of the minority communities points to a certain degree of acceptance of the latter by the former, at least in circles of the more secularly minded professionals. We have seen that so eminent a Muslim author as Ibn Abī Uṣaybiʿa could unhesitatingly report that friendship had existed between his own uncle and the Jewish physician Asʿad al-dīn, although Islam disapproves of such relations with non-Muslims. This positive aspect of official titles borne by Jews, however, was counteracted by sinister developments. Almost all dated or datable documents revealing the popularity of Islamic titles among Jews originated during the last third of the twelfth and, in particular, the thirteenth century, and later, a period of palpable decline of the Jewish population in Egypt. Acceptance led to assimilation, and finally to absorption. The majority of the Jewish elite, by avidly seeking distinction, ended up in extinction. They were later partly replaced by immigrants from faraway countries with different social concepts.

4. *Friendship and Enmity*

On the nature and history of friendship.—"A thousand friends, and not a single enemy!"[1] That was the ideal. Reality was different. Even the best of men has enemies. "Rain [a blessing for the earth, an embodiment of goodness] is hated by two, but loved by only one."[2] Why should it be so? An answer is advanced in another piece of Near Eastern wisdom: "Love dependent on something does not endure; love not dependent on something lasts forever. Which is love of the first kind? That of Amnon and Tamar. And that of the second? The love of David and Jonathan."[3] When Amnon, the son of King David, was infatuated with his half-sister Tamar, nothing seemed to exist for him in the world except his desire. With passion spent, love turned to hate (II Samuel 13:1–22). How different with Jonathan, the warlike son of King Saul, and the youthful hero David! "The soul of Jonathan became bound to the soul of David" (I Samuel 18:1–3). Love between souls—invisible and timeless—is inexplicable and enduring. The bond between the two was something beyond them: the glorious defense of a people menaced in its very existence. Since the love of the multitude is mostly dependent on things tangible, which, moreover, are often desired also by others, true love is rare and hatred common.[4]

Quotations like those and similar ones, from "what the people say" and "what is written in the Scriptures," "what the Sages taught" and "the Ancients [the Greeks] opined," would have been brought up when the Geniza people discussed the nature of friendship, a topic that occupied their minds very much, as their letters show. To be sure, they were practical people: a friend was a man who exerted himself for you and expected to be repaid in the same way. The vicissitudes of friendship, so often lamented, would not be described by them as inexplicable. They had a better word: God. He binds the hearts together and he loosens their bonds, if he pleases so, for "who may say to him what are you doing" (Job 9:12). This attitude, expressed in the first letter translated below, is not entirely one of resignation: as in other matters, it is hoped that God will turn the end to the good. The highest, the true type of friendship, was common exertion under the banner of faith, friendship for God's sake, getting strength through contest with a worthy man who exemplified the religious ideals of the period. Friendship in God, by its very nature, is imperishable. The passages from the second letter translated below illustrate this aspect, often touched upon elsewhere, although mostly in shorter form.

Men of excellence are rare. Therefore it is natural that many are attracted to them. Friendship in the Geniza was a relationship not only between two but also among a circle of people, hopefully centered around an outstanding personality, such as Nahray b. Nissīm, whose relationships with others we are able to trace through half a century (1045–1096). The Geniza has preserved hundreds of letters addressed to him, and many exchanged among the members of his circle. In this mass of correspondence he appears in his later years as primus inter pares, and, since he functioned then as Rav, or religious authority, and as communal leader, he took on the stature of a master gathering around him disciples. Another type of central personality was Ḥalfōn b. Nethanel ha-Levi, the India trader who commuted to Spain, Egypt, and Aden, South Arabia (occasionally also to India, first half of the twelfth century). He was not a towering figure, but, owing to his noble descent, his family, connections with the leading circles all over the places mentioned, and his thirst for knowledge, he acted as a bond among the best minds of the community. His personal friendship with the Spanish Hebrew poet Judah ha-Levi is a chapter by itself.

Partnerships were formally concluded, mostly for a year, for a business venture, or for some other short period, then formally dissolved, but often renewed between the same persons countless times. Friendships grew slowly and were not formalized. Pacts of "friendship in God" seem to have been known in the Jewish communities in Christian countries from the thirteenth century, but in Egypt and the adjacent countries much later. Nevertheless, friendship was more than an intimate and often transitory relationship between two persons. A person was known as the *ṣāḥib*, or friend, of someone else, meant as a mark of distinction or simply as a means of identification. It is surprising that we never read about a formal contract with a *rafīq*, a travel companion, although one bore heavy responsibilities for him. I assume that the very fact of two sharing a cabin in a boat, or a room in a caravanserai, or a rented apartment in a foreign city was proof enough for the authorities to assume that a close relationship existed between them. We read much in the Geniza letters about the choice of a travel companion, expressions of satisfaction or disappointment.

The multifaceted image of friendship in the Geniza reflects the heritage of ancient concepts, institutions, and thought connected with the subject. A short survey of this heritage may contribute to a better understanding and appreciation of that image. The Geniza people themselves were not unaware of the past. The Bible and Arabic popular narrative furnished much relevant information. The intellectuals, who combined secular with religious education, as their letters reveal, were familiar with Arabic literature.

Friendship as a social institution and spiritual bond, and not merely as a more or less passing human relationship, was known to the ancient Near East. From the Bible we might remember that King David had an official companion styled "friend of the king," and so did his son King Solomon.[5] Their eldest sons, the crown princes, too, had their official friends whom they consulted in difficult hours.[6] The friendship between David and Jonathan, the son of King Saul, is to be understood against this background. Jonathan, the crown prince, chose David as his permanent companion, because, as the Bible says, he loved him as his own self, an expression echoed in the writings of the Greeks, and later the Arabs, as well as in the Geniza.[7] Jonathan, the Bible tells us, stripped himself of his robe, armor, belt, and sword, and put them all on David. Jonathan's attire represented his personality. By donning it, David became Jonathan, the two fused into one. This formal act of the conclusion of a friendship had a name. It was designated by the term "covenant," *berīth*, the same word the Bible uses for the bond between husband and wife.[8]

Besides this formally concluded friendship between two individuals the Bible tells of groups bound together by ecstasy and of prophetic rapture induced by music. We read about them in the stories of Samuel and Saul. The procedure of initiation into the group was the opposite of what we have just met within personal friendship. The novice was expected to be carried away by the enthusiasm of the group, to be seized by the spirit, until he forgot himself and threw off all his clothing, piece by piece, and stood naked among the prophesiers day and night; in other words, he divested himself of his individuality, he became one with the group and was possessed by the spirit.[9]

Within the group there was room for formal *personal* friendship, namely, between master and disciple, between the leader of the group and his prospective successor. The First Book of Kings tells us that the future prophet Elisha originally was a farmer, ploughing his fields and supervising the work of his farmhands himself when the prophet Elijah, as was his habit, appeared suddenly and cast his mantle upon him, meaning, as in the case of David and Jonathan, that the two had become one.[10] A similar act was performed in the biblical wedding: the bridegroom spread his robe, or rather the skirt of his robe, over his future life companion symbolizing what is written in the Book of Genesis: "They become one flesh."[11]

In the heroic age of the Arabs, in pre-Islamic Arabia, friendship was of little import. Pre-Islamic poetry contains some noble verses on friendship,[12] but we would look in vain for a pair like Achilles and Patroclus, around whose brotherly love the whole story of the Trojan War turned.

We learn about the social institution of the boon companions, *nadīm*, mostly two, who shared the revelries of a poet or hero and served as his lookouts and guards on his amorous nightly adventures. These two boon companions are mentioned, however, most prominently in stories about the Arab kings of Ḥīra, who were under Persian domination. Thus, it is likely that the nadīm, together with the wine and the singing girls, came to the Arabs from Persia, where, as we shall presently see, the ancient Near Eastern institution of the friends of the kings had remained fully alive.

The minor role of friendship in pre-Islamic Arabia is to be explained by the preeminence of the bonds of blood and kinship. Or, as the Arab poet has explained it:

> Take for your friend whom you will in the days of peace.
> But know that when fighting comes, your kinsman alone is near.[13]

Formal friendship, *ṣuḥba*, came into the Arab world with religion, with the Islam of Muhammad. Conversion was conceived as a personal bond between the new believer and the founder of the religion. It was symbolized by a handclasp, the joining of hands by which the ancient Arabs used to confirm a contract or a covenant. Muhammad's adherents were called his friends or companions, *aṣḥāb*, or, in relationship to each other, brothers, *ikhwān*.[14]

From that time on, spiritual bonds of the widest variety became the base of sustained personal relationships transcending family attachments, the strongest being those connected with Islamic mysticism known as Sufism. According to the developed theory of Sufism, only a specific and lasting relationship with one single master can initiate a novice properly into the Path of Truth. It cannot be learned from books or by changing from one master to another. The two symbolic acts of initiation practiced by the ancient prophets of Israel, namely, the clothing of the novice with the mantle of the master and, conversely, the throwing away of all clothing in the ecstasy induced by music were exceedingly prominent features of Sufi life, but there seems to have been no historical connection between these *ancient* Near Eastern and *medieval* Near Eastern practices.

The matter was different with regard to another type of formal friendship, the friends of the kings. The Persian dynasty of the Sassanids continued this ancient institution, much as the Hellenistic rulers and Roman emperors had done before. The Muslim ideas about kingship were largely molded by the Sassanid heritage, wherefore the problem of the friends of the kings is copiously ventilated in Islamic literature. In a remarkable memorandum submitted to Manṣūr, the second Abbasid caliph (754–775), called "Book of Companionship," a Persian nobleman, Ibn al-Muqaffaᶜ, surveys the types of persons who should become a caliph's intimates. I have discussed this memorandum in my *Studies in Islamic History and Institutions* under the title "A Turning-point in the History of the Muslim State"—"turning-point," because it was not the aristocrats recommended by Ibn al-Muqaffaᶜ but the technocrats, so much more needed by the Muslim state of those days, who finally became the caliphs' confidants.[15]

A third source for thought on friendship in Islam was Greek philosophy and rhetoric which reached the Arabs in many different ways. The most detailed exposition of the topic is found in Miskawayh's book "Training of the Character," the classical and most influential treatise on Islamic ethics. Man is by nature a social being. Consequently, his intrinsic and highest destination, spiritual perfection, can be reached only through association with a congenial friend.[16]

Notions alive in the upper classes filter down in the course of time, undergo adequate transformation, and reach the broader masses of the population. As the writings of the Cairo Geniza show, it was not different with ideas about friendship. Terms coined for the description of this relationship by religion, statecraft, or philosophy became part and parcel of the daily speech of the common people. Ṣuḥba, or formal friendship, itself became an all-important institution; it was actually the organizational backbone of international trade.

Because of the enormous risks involved, people normally participated in many different business ventures simultaneously. Above and beyond these, however, any respectable trader had a ṣāḥib, or friend, on the other side of the sea who acted for him not merely as legal and business representative but as his confidant in every respect. The list of services to be rendered by a ṣāḥib was interminable. Often the ṣuḥba was based on a relationship of master and disciple, that is, a fledgling overseas trader left his hometown, worked for some years under the guidance of an established merchant overseas, and, in gratitude for this education, as it was called, became his ṣāḥib after his return to his native city. In the India trade every consignment sent to a ṣāḥib was accompanied by presents, as appropriate between friends. Since this custom was not practiced in the Mediterranean trade, it probably was learned by the Near Easterners from the Indians.[17]

A particular type of commercial friendship was the institution of the travel companion, *rafīq*, mentioned in numerous documents and letters. People endeavored to travel in groups, large or small, but each individual traveler was specifically connected with another by far-reaching bonds of mutual responsibility. Each was supposed to know the sums of money and description of goods carried by the other, to look after him in the frequent cases of illness or other mishaps, and to take care of his possessions after his death.[18] A Yemenite Jew, writing from Jerusalem at the beginning of the thirteenth century, reports that the government had confiscated all the belongings of his dead travel companion and that because of this he was in great fear for himself.[19] I have not found in the Geniza a contract on travel companionship and do not expect to find one, for it was a relationship of personal confidence comparable with the ṣuḥba, not a legal obligation—despite the disastrous legal consequences it could sometimes have for a surviving rafīq.

Before passing now to the Geniza testimony on friendship, I wish to draw the attention of the reader to Robert Brain's *Friends and Lovers*.[20] I appreciate the book because of the strong involvement of the author, an anthropologist, in his subject and his clear vision of friendship as an indispensable human condition. Surveying biblical, classical, medieval, and, in particular, contemporary concepts, he brings everything into focus by using his findings among primitive societies in Africa, Asia, and the Pacific. (He himself was born on the island of Tasmania, Australia.) He attempts a cross-cultural, comparative study of the elusive topics of friendship and love, no less, in fact, than to define the nature of friendship beyond the differences of cultures, times, and places. "Friendship is a social and psychological need (cemented by formal behavior and ceremony). . . . The prime bond of friendship is a moral, even spiritual one." The author spent two years among the Bangwa, a people in the Cameroon, central Africa, once notorious for its bellicose character. It soon became clear to him that friendship among them was endowed with deeper intensity of meaning than in our own society. The relationship between Jonathan and David would be normal and comprehensible to them. "Moreover, they would not be in the least tempted to presuppose or imagine any homosexual overtones [in that friendship], since, as far as I could make out, and I certainly made enquiries, these practices were unknown between adult men." Like David, the friend of a dead Bangwa shows vehement expressions of mourning, sings in public the praise of the demised, and laments his separation from him. Throughout the book, the author does not pass any judgment on homosexuality; he only emphasizes: "We must not equate friendship with sex."[21]

Brain compares friendship in British private schools, as described so eloquently by Disraeli in *Coningsby*, to what happens in Thailand villages. "In a Thailand village, emotional friendships are recognized, openly encouraged, and even institutionalized. Villagers live in an atmosphere of open mistrust and suspicion . . . which is relieved by a bond between men known as 'friendship to the death.'"[22]

The Geniza world was certainly remote in every respect from that of the Thailand villagers. While reading the pages that follow, one should keep in mind the traits of friendship developed in an ambiance of dread of enmity as described by Brain.

The quotation about the nature of friendship that starts this subsection should be complemented by one from "the Ancients," meaning the Greeks, as available in Arabic translations or simply ascribed to them. After describing his misfortunes and losses at sea when his boat ran aground and could not be moved, an experienced trader had this to say to a younger friend, possibly a nephew: "You know what the Ancients have said: 'Four things reveal the true friend: showing a cheerful face whenever meeting the friend; always looking for him [or: visiting him frequently];[23] taking care of his affairs; sharing his worries.' I am asking you now that you add to the expressions of your affection, well known to me, that you neglect ['leave'] your noble self and take care of my affairs." An endless list of things to be done follows. The ancients were invoked because the demands of the writer were indeed extraordinary.[24]

The word used for friend here, *ṣadīq*, was the one common in Arabic literature, when Greek philosophy dealing with the topic is referred to. The most famous Arabic treatise on ethics says this: "Friendship, *ṣadāqa*, is a type of love, *maḥabba*, more exactly of affection, *mawadda*."[25] These terms are constantly used in the Geniza. One signs (always on the address) *muḥibbuhu*, "the one who loves you," or *ṣafī waddihi*, "the one who is sincere in his affection," but, unlike our "sincerely," such expressions are exchanged only between close acquaintances. When an old friend of judge Elijah b. Zechariah excuses himself with the nearness of holidays for traveling from Bilbays, Lower Egypt, to Alexandria directly, without making the detour to Fustat (to pay his respects to him), he adds: "You know the true nature of love, *maḥabba* [meaning friendship]; God, the searcher of the hearts is my witness that there are no pretexts in what I say."[26] In Hebrew the general word for friendship was *ahavā*, love, the same as used for the love for one's wife or God, and the relevant biblical proverbs are quoted, for instance: "There is a friend who sticks closer than a brother" (Proverbs 18:24).[27] In both Hebrew and Arabic the relationship is described as a covenant; when one travels to a friend's place to see him, one speaks of "the renewal of the covenant."[28]

There are other words describing a person as a friend, for instance, "brother" in both languages (which carries less weight than one might expect). It seems, however, that the almost technical term for an enduring companionship involving mutual obligations was the often mentioned *ṣuḥba*, used also for the lifelong dedication of husband and wife. "You would have been obliged to do this even if there had not existed between us a partnership, affection, and ṣuḥba," the latter clearly representing the culmination.[29]

Needless to say, friendship came into being in many different ways. It could have been a relationship inherited from one's fathers. In business letters the son of the writer is referred to as sending respectful greetings to the recipient and also to his sons, in order to prepare the younger generation for future cooperation.[30] In a letter from March 1029, Abraham b. Da'ūd is reminded by Nissīm b. Isḥāq, "who loves him": "Keep fast to your friend who was the friend of your father" (cf. Proverbs 27:10).[31] True friendship should be like a family relationship. When the connection was really close, the writer of business letters would ask to be honored not only with commercial orders but also with buying presents for the recipient's children and even wife: "I regretted that you did not charge me with buying things for your boys and the inhabitant of your house [wife], for I am most happy to carry out such orders for you."[32] The complete confidence in the ṣāḥib is best expressed in this phrase: "I am not absent where you are present."[33]

As in our own days, common study, especially with a revered master, was another atmosphere that bred friendship. The intimacy of the gentle Nahray b. Nissīm with the excitable Yeshūʿā b. Ismaʿīl is a good example.[34]

In many Geniza letters a person traveling to another city or a foreign country is introduced to the recipient with the request to assist him in handling his affairs. If first contacts were successful, enduring friendships could develop between persons living in different places. We are able to observe such a development in the relations of the India trader Ḥalfōn b. Nethanel ha-Levi, whose family name was Dimyāṭī, that is, from Damietta, but whose permanent seat was Cairo-Fustat, and Abū Naṣr, who was to become his representative in Alexandria. In spring 1134, Abū Zikrī Kohen, representative of merchants in Fustat, concludes a long letter to Ḥalfōn, then staying in Aden, South Arabia, with these words: "I need not admonish you to assist Abū Naṣr b. Abraham in all his affairs." This shows that a trip to Aden was a new venture for Abū Naṣr and that he himself had been introduced to Ḥalfōn in a previous letter.[35] Three years later, in spring 1137, Abū Naṣr writes to Ḥalfōn, inquiring about arrivals from the India route and describing his own difficulties and the general economic depression in Alexandria in a way betraying a certain familiarity between the two. A brother of Abū Naṣr adds greetings.[36] Finally, from autumn 1140, we have (so far) seven letters from Abū Naṣr addressed to Ḥalfōn, which shows that Abū Naṣr had become his confidant, representing him in the Mediterranean port city. He also substituted for Ḥalfōn in taking care of the Spanish Hebrew poet Judah ha-Levi at and after the latter's arrival in Alexandria, which proves how highly Ḥalfōn esteemed and relied on him. Commercial, public, and private affairs dealt with in these letters display a wide variety of interests shared by the two friends. The greetings exchanged reveal that the extended families on both sides plus a number of friends were already included in a growing circle of human contacts. After describing the troubles endured by Judah ha-Levi in Alexandria and his own actions in this matter, Abū Naṣr adds: "The prayer for relief is shared by both of us, for I am united with you in happiness and distress"—as friends indeed should be.[37]

How strongly friendships based on reciprocal involvement in business and public affairs could be charged with sentiment is brought home by this letter of Joseph b. Berechiah, Qayrawān, to Joseph Ibn ʿAwkal, Fustat.

Both the sender and the receiver of this letter were most prominent in and beyond their respective community. Ibn ʿAwkal, who had his seat in Cairo, would forward to the Jewish academies of Baghdad the donations and legal questions dispatched to them from North Africa and sent to the West the learned answers and other letters that came from Baghdad. He must have tired of this burdensome task, though, for Joseph b. Berechiah's predecessor as representative of the academies, Jacob b. Nissīm, who died in the winter of 1006/7, already makes complaints similar to those following below.[38] In this letter, Joseph Berechiah regards his friendship with Ibn ʿAwkal terminated, but still writes to him to uphold the rights of a poor freedman, which was a religious duty.

(The damaged manuscript has a big hole extending over eight lines in the middle of the page, and the last three lines are almost entirely lost.)

My noble and highly respected elder, may God prolong your life, guard you, and always grant you success.

I am writing to you, my elder—may God protect you from what one fears and let you attain what makes one happy—at the end of the month of Av (July/August). I am sound in body but sore in mind because of the absence of your letters and because you neglect me and turn your mind from my affairs. All the caravans and ships have arrived, but I have not seen any letter or commission for me. Even more so: in the letters received from you by my friend Abū ʿImrān Ibn al-Majjānī[39]—may God keep him—no mention is made of me.

Now, my lord, I know well that it is a gift of God to be favored with affection and to be close to the hearts of friends, as he has said: "The Lord made all that Joseph did to prosper in his hands, and Joseph found grace in his sights" [Genesis 39:3–4]. If this heavenly favor is withheld from a man, he is forgotten by his friends, and consideration for him becomes slender. When things come to this, a believing man should not make accusations of being neglected and slighted, but thank God, as we must, for both good luck and misfortune.[40] In this sense, his saint[41] has said: "I lift up the cup of salvation and call upon the name of the Lord, and although I found trouble and sorrow, I call upon the name of the Lord" [Psalms 116:13 and 3–4].[42]

However, the hardest thing for me, my lord, was this. You mentioned in one of your former letters to Abū ʿImrān that you had received quires[43] and letters from our lords[44] and that you would forward them with a trustworthy person. Later on, however, you neglected this matter and we did not hear anything further about it. Through a special favor of God, I received a letter from my lord Hay, which was forwarded to me by the Tustarīs[45] through Abū Ibrahīm Ismaʿīl b. Barhūn, after having been copied as a matter of precaution. . . . This letter was a real consolation and remedy for my soul. But I was shocked to read in it that he had not received a letter from me for five years. I do not know [how this could happen]—perhaps because of the adversity of the Time.[46] In any case, God is to be praised for everything. I have made it incumbent upon myself not to trouble you by asking you to write to me or to do any business for me, as I feel that this might be a burden for you. Thus let us wait patiently for a turn of fortune, when our friends will again be the same as they used to be, if God will.

I am writing you this letter on behalf of its bearer, the "boy" Faraj, the freedman of my late paternal uncle. [Details about Faraj's request.] The poor of God are entrusted to your care. Therefore, let him not lack any assistance needed; you will be rewarded [from Heaven].

If you see fit to answer this letter, it will be kind of you . . . in case this is burdensome to you, you are excused. . . .[47]

An entirely different picture of friendship emerges from another letter sent, perhaps a generation later, from Tunisia to Egypt. The writer and recipient had been close acquaintances before the latter had emigrated. Worldly Egypt, as it appears to us through the Geniza around 1040, had its dangers for the pious and observant Tunisians. But the recipient came from a strong family, and he and his son kept the banner of faith flying high. This made the writer particularly happy and induced him to open his letter with enthusiastic praise (supported by learned quotations) of a father succeeding in educating his son in his spirit. Then he continues:

You strengthened the ropes of the faith and made firm the poles of religion[48] through your study of the Torah and your love for the teachings of our Sages, the successors of the prophets. You are walking in their steps, as [King Solomon] has intimated in his Song: "If you do not know, O fairest among women, follow in the tracks of the flock etc." [Song of Songs 1:8].[49] The this-worldly people have not won you over to the vanities of this world and to the attractions of their novelties. You have held fast the banner of our faith, you and your family, and have kept [God's commandments] when "Israel went astray from him" (Ezekiel 44:15).[50]

You have become a light in the darkness. You will be happy and prosperous [Psalms 128:2]; happy in this world and prosperous in the world to come.[51]

I need no [excuses], since you know for certain the sincerity of my love and the genuineness of my affection. The proof of this is your awareness of what is written: "[As water reflects the face,] thus the heart of a man reflects that of another" [Proverbs 27:19].[52] This is love for God's sake, which is guaranteed to endure. It was I who opened our correspondence and readied it for continuation, I persevered in my endeavor to [strengthen] the brotherhood with you. God will assure our bonds, since they are for him [lit., "for his face"].

As happens so often in a Geniza letter, its real purpose is revealed near the end. The recipient had ordered a Torah scroll and a volume from the Talmud to be written for him in Tunisia. The order had arrived a bit late in the summer. As the writer of the letter explained, the work would have been done in a hurry, and the scroll, if sent near the end of the seafaring season, when storms were to be expected, might suffer water damage (as had his own letter indeed very much). He had not neglected the matter, but would have it done leisurely during the winter, when the skin used for the parchment could be tanned for its holy purpose, as prescribed by the law. No doubt, a certain element of excuse can be noted in the profuse affirmations of friendship. But the entire letter is pervaded by a sincere feeling of happiness induced by the conviction that the faraway friend still adhered to the old ways, which they had shared when they were together in their native city. Common ideals and practices are the safest bonds of true friendship, provided, of course, that it has come into being at all by the inexplicable miracle of mutual affection and esteem. The letter concludes with the words: "And I shall convey your greetings to Rabbēnū, may God keep him," no doubt Rabbēnū Nissīm b. Jacob of Qayrawān. The friendship was spawned when the two sat at the feet of one of the greatest rabbinical teachers of all times.[53]

Friendship among intellectuals.—The writer of the epistle from Tunisia treated on the preceding pages quotes the Bible and post-biblical Hebrew literature profusely, but his rich Arabic vocabulary shows him to be a man of secular education, an intellectual in the wider sense of the word. The letters of intellectuals extolling friendship emphasize the spiritual benefits derived from personal contacts, especially from enjoying conversation in the presence of an esteemed friend. The classical book in Arabic literature on amiable discourse and diversified exchange of ideas is named

"Providing [spiritual] Pleasure and Companionship."[54] These and a plethora of other expressions describing the inspiration derived from being in the lively presence of intelligent companions are echoed in the Geniza correspondence. The emphatic language used in connection with this theme betrays its intrinsic role in daily life. What else could observant intellectuals enjoy in life besides work, study, and prayer? For a variety of reasons, music, although much loved, was disapproved by Islam and Jewish religion. Listening to narrators of stories like those known to us from *The Arabian Nights*—flourishing in Egypt—or viewing the (often lascivious) showings of the shadow theater were the pleasures of the common people. No wonder, then, that the company of congenial and esteemed friends was passionately sought after. As Robert Brain repeatedly emphasizes, friendship is a product of culture. This was true even of primitive societies, where friendship was a wonderful means for whiling away the hours.[55]

A confidential letter from the spiritual leader of a provincial community in Lower Egypt to a learned friend in Cairo opens with these words: "The reason for writing this letter is my intense yearning after your illustrious presence. I remember those instructive conversations,[56] those sayings full of guidance, those well-founded remarks. All this filled me with profuse love—love that is, no doubt, of a religious nature, since it was caused by motives connected not with physical pleasures but with pleasures of the soul alone."[57]

Concluding a letter of praise addressed to the prominent court physician Abraham Ibn al-Furāt and written entirely in eloquent Hebrew rhymed prose, a nāsī adds words in regular Arabic prose. The first item was "the beauty of his conversation, in which he outshines others."[58] When Ibn al-Furāt was promoted and moved from Palestine to Cairo, the nāsī and Head of the yeshiva of Jerusalem, Daniel b. Azariah, writing from Damascus exclaims: "How can life be without you?!" Daniel mentions him constantly in private and public, but nothing can replace his presence, "his blessed blaze and auspicious resplendence," his face.[59] The same topic is taken up by him shortly afterward, writing from Jerusalem after having obtained complete authority there: "All I am grieved about is your absence. I have no place anymore in this country when you are not here. You have heard more than once my oath that I could not feel well here in Shām (Palestine-Syria) without you," [that is, no one else is there who can compare with you as company].[60]

A few years later, Evyatar, the son and secretary of Daniel's successor Elijah Gaon, harps on the same theme in even stronger terms. The exuberance might be explained by his younger age, nor can the addressee, the parnās Eli ha-Kohen b. Yaḥya of Fustat, have been very old for he lived for at least thirty years after this letter was written. Evyatar reveres his friend like a father, he sees him in his dreams at night and cannot do anything better than talk about him and sing his praise during the day. He wishes to live in Fustat at the side of Eli, but cannot leave Jerusalem, "the House of God," and his own old father, whom he serves. He would like to invite Eli to take up residence in the Holy City, near himself, but would not dare to rob him of the congenial company of his illustrious friends in the capital of Egypt. So he has only one prayer to God: to let them meet again in person at least once before parting this world.[61]

A letter dedicated entirely to the topic of friendship between educated young men concludes this series of stereotypes used:

> I do not enjoy life without you. By God! Have compassion with my loneliness, weakness, and constrained heart, and, by God, satiate me with looks at you before I die.
>
> So, do not absent yourself longer than you have done. For things between you and me have not been like this before. Of all the young men who have been with you, not one of them has mentioned a word you might have said about me, which saddened my heart.
>
> So, as soon as you have read this letter, send me one, telling me how you are. *And Peace.*[62]

All the motifs in this short note may be found elsewhere. But one cannot escape the impression that here they were meant seriously. One needed a friend for friendship's sake.

Perseverance in unrequited friendship (as in the letter just translated) was a mark of pride. We have a heartwarming letter of a cantor in a provincial town, named Berākhōt (Blessings) who had been a member of a circle of friends in Alexandria.[63] Letters had been exchanged for some time, but finally the friends, or, at least, the addressee, the physician Yedūthūn, got tired. On various occasions, physicians loving and even writing (Arabic) poetry have been mentioned in this book. Yedūthūn had certainly adopted that name because it was borne by one of the choirmasters in the Temple of Jerusalem (Psalms 39:1, heading).[64] Knowledgeable cantors, like the writer of our letter, were expected to be able to compose liturgical poetry (in Hebrew, of course) and songs for weddings and other family events. This explains the special relationship between the two. But, alas, Berākhōt had written ten letters—the bearers of the last three are noted—and without seeing an answer. Undaunted, he wrote our letter, which shows him making ceaseless efforts to elicit the latest news from travelers. He was successful and well informed about happenings in Alexandria, revealing his concern for the well-being of his companions. But how to quench his yearnings after his Yedūthūn and his brother? "In the name of *our love* [an oath]; when overcome by yearning for you I take the letters that I have received from you [plural] in the olden times, read them, kiss them, and put them on my head,[65] and say 'may God let us come together before our predestined end.'" He asks for only a few words to assure him that "the old covenant" was still in force. At the end of the letter, he adds that, as before, when he heard a "word" [a piece of poetry or prose] of unusual quality, or a fine poem, he would note it. Of late he had heard such lines of poetry and enclosed them, asking Yedūthūn to show them also to another friend mentioned by name.

Poems exchanged between friends, usually written in the same meter and rhyme, gave intellectuals a convenient medium for expressing their mutual feelings. In this Jews followed the Arabic model, but, as a rule, used Hebrew in their creations. Many exchange poems are found in the divans of medieval Hebrew poets. From the Geniza we learn how average intellectuals (who had studied such divans) proceeded in this matter. A complete letter embellished by a poem is presented below. The recipient Abū Zikrī Yiḥye b. Mevōrākh is repeatedly addressed as a young man and is wished to get married, to see Jerusalem rebuilt, and to become a happy father (in this sequence); moreover, he is described as a *talmīd*, a scholar. A friend greeted is also praised as a scholar and "dearest treasure." Since greetings are extended also to Yiḥye's father, and even to his mother, the writer, who calls himself Isaac b. Nissīm Parsī (Persian), might have stayed with them while visiting their city. It should not be understood from his family name that he himself came from Persia, for his Arabic is that of a native speaker. The letter is full of intimacy coupled with respect.[66]

Like many other Geniza missives the letter is headed by Bible quotations, alluding here to the recipient as a modest person seeking knowledge (Psalms 37:11 and 119:165, often quoted, and therefore not particularly characteristic). The letter itself opens with a poem of eighteen verses, all in the same rhyme and meter. Parsī thanks Yiḥye for his masterly poem but despairs of being able to repay him with a piece of similar quality—for at his departure the friend had taken with him the writer's heart and mind. When Yiḥye's poem arrived, Parsī was afraid that he would have difficulties in keeping up with its refined allusions, for Yiḥye's poem possessed the qualities of the creations of the unique Spanish Hebrew poet Solomon Ibn Gabirol.

> Poetry is your slave for ever,
> and you reduce the poems of others to slavery for yourself.

The first half-line (adapted itself from a famous poem by Ibn Gabirol, written when he was a youth of sixteen) means that its author possessed complete mastery over the intricate art of verse making, the second, that he was skilled in using the creation of others for his own purposes. Numerous examples of such procedures are found in the Geniza.[67] After assuring Yiḥye that he had not found another friend as intelligent and of pure heart like him, he concludes with these verses:

> May God plant you in his garden as a good seedling,
> and show you and me his chosen [the Messiah].
> May you enjoy the knowledge of God and his majesty,
> and relish in the understanding of the mystery of his creation.
> Then this song of mine will mean happiness for you,
> my prince, the beloved of my soul, my friend.[68]

The poem is followed by an extensive Hebrew letter (five long lines, and about thirty-five short lines written in the margin and on top), often passing into rhymed prose. Parsī thanks Yiḥye for several letters which reminded him of the writer's beautiful face and equally beautiful way of life; he encourages him to follow up with similar creations of his pen. The reverse side is entirely filled with an even longer letter in Arabic of approximately the same content, written in slightly more congested script (for which change he excuses himself). There was a good reason for the duplication, found elsewhere in the Geniza. Letters of praise were read out in the circles of family and friends, where not everyone could be expected to possess the high degree of proficiency in Hebrew required for their full understanding.

How the Jewish intellectuals of Spain contemporary to their poet laureate Judah ha-Levi (d. 1141) flocked together for mutual enjoyment of the fruits of their pens is briefly described above.[69] As J. Schirmann has shown, ha-Levi's divan is the broadest and most vivid mirror of that world.[70] The special atmosphere of those circles of intellectual friendship is also well reflected in letters addressed to the India trader Ḥalfōn b. Nethanel during his visits to that country. Ḥalfōn took the letters with him to Egypt, where twenty or so of them ended up in the Geniza. In the following, one of these, written by Joseph b. Samuel Ibn al-Ukhtūsh, a cousin of Ḥalfōn and friend of Judah ha-Levi, is translated in full.[71]

The letter was sent from Granada in May-June 1130, a special year,[72] probably to Almeria, Spain, where Ḥalfōn had arrived not long before from Egypt. For our taste the letter suffers by an excess of verbiage, but, compared with contemporary products, it keeps a sound mean between what was required by politeness and the expressions of true affection and esteem for Ḥalfōn's personality—the essence of friendship.[73]

May God make permanent for my lord and master, the illustrious *rayyis*,[74] his high rank, prestige, happiness and welfare, may he add continuously to his high standing and prolong his life and splendor for his brethren and friends. May you always enjoy the possession of esteem, eminent importance, sublime rank, praiseworthy ways of conduct, and rich gifts of the spirit.

I am writing early in the month of *Sivan of the year [of the Creation 48] 90* from the city of Granada, may God protect it.

After thanking God, the exalted and majestic, for his plentiful benefactions, there is no duty pressing on me and dear to me more than the pleasure of talking about you and occupying myself with you, boasting of your acquaintance and making remarks in social gatherings about your excellence and nobility, and pointing out the spiritual gifts bestowed upon you by God, namely an overflow of religiosity, a strong faith, praiseworthy chastity, godliness, and humility, learnedness, self-restraint, great philanthropy, and many other rich gifts. He—may his name be praised—is to be entreated and his countenance to be supplicated that he may preserve your qualities and protect your perfection from the vicissitudes of fate and, in his mercy, may let us always hear from you what gives us joy, not grief or anxiety.

Last year we received the distressing news of the two disasters that rapped the ears and let the tears flow: the death of our lord, the head of the academy, and that of our lord, *the Crown of the Judges*, your brother—*may they rest in Eden*. Would I try to describe how much our community was afflicted by this, ink and pens would come to an end, but not my words. Your brave and noble soul knows well that I share with my lord everything, be it bitter or sweet, and, despite the great distance, I should have come to you to express my sympathy and consolation. But there are circumstances that render the fulfillment of obligations impossible. May God bestow upon the two the favor befitting them, prolong your life after them, cool their graves, and may he be your company after they have left you.

You know that despite your being away from us, our love of you renews continually. So, do us a favor and send us a message telling us how you have been, stage after stage, from the day of your departure to the day of your arrival, and all that has occurred to you, in general and in detail; and how you have found the upper layer of society, *small and great* [or: young and old] may God elevate you all. Your communication will be an honor to us and a great favor.[75]

Knowing your noble mind and lofty character, God has been beneficent to you and sent you the quintessence and embodiment of our country,[76] our refuge and leader, the illustrious *scholar,* and unique and perfect *devotee,* r[abbi] Judah, the son of al-Levi m[ay his] R[ock keep him]; how much do I regret to be separated from him and how heartily do I congratulate you on meeting him—may God the exalted give you enjoyment one from the other. Let me hear as much as is convenient about your meeting. I need not repeat my request for a note from you, which will be a great favor to me, God willing.

My most special, copious, and lavish greetings to you, my illustrious lord, accompanied with overflowing yearnings after a meeting with you, only to be satisfied by the sight of your gracious countenance. Greetings also to the prominent notables accompanying you; may God enhance their position and bestow on them a good name.[77]

In particular, I ask you to convey my most intensive and well-scented greetings to my illustrious lord, *the Pride of the Merchants,* Abu ʾl-Barakāt b. Ḥārith, my dear, special friend—may God elevate and protect him. Please convey to him my excuse for not writing to him separately, but including him in this letter.[78]

Accept also greetings from my brother Mūsā and your paternal aunt[79] and all our brethren in the country, potter, philosopher, bragger, and cantors,[80] and the community at large in accordance with their esteem of your rank and their admiration for your lofty *mind.* May *the welfare of my lord, master, and friend wax and increase. Amen. Selah.*

[*Address:*]

To the illustrious, *generous, and pious scholar,* the accomplished *rayyis, the chief over the leaders of the house of Levi, our master* Ḥalfōn, *son of his honor,* Nethanel, *may the All(merciful) pre(serve him).*

His favorite, who is proud of him and yearns after his illustrious presence, *Joseph ha-Levi, son of Samuel* Ibn al-Ukhtūsh, *m[ay he rest in] E[den]. Peace.*

Formal pacts of friendship between religious persons working on their spiritual perfection seem not to have been in use during the High Middle Ages, at least, none has been found by me in the Geniza from that period. They seem to have come into fashion in the thirteenth century in Christian countries. In a famous ethical will by Judah b. Asher b. Yehiel, who emigrated from Germany to Spain in 1305, he has this to tell about his grandfather Yehiel. At the age of ten he concluded a pact with a friend, in which both undertook to share all rewards, spiritual and secular. The two, renowned for their saintliness and generosity, kept this agreement all their life. When Yehiel died in 1264 and his coffin, as usual, before being lowered into his grave, was opened, his friend reminded him of the covenant, whereupon a look of joy lit the dead man's face, as testified by all those present.[81] Professor Meir Benayahu drew my attention to a highly interesting pact of friendship concluded in Cordova, Spain, in 1317, where the two partners undertake to settle in the Holy Land and there to share all their possessions; if necessary, one would work for the maintenance of the two families, while the other would be free for religious study, and vice versa. The pact was concluded for a duration of seven years.[82]

In the subsequent centuries, and especially the sixteenth, the formal creation of brotherhoods undertaking to follow the right path became popular in the East and in particular in Palestine. This was caused on the one hand by the arrival of tens of thousands of refugees from Christian countries, such as Spain, Portugal, Italy, and Germany, and on the other the unprecedented expansion of the esoteric teachings of Kabbalah mysticism. The rules of these brotherhoods reveal a profound sense of religious rigor and a refreshing subtlety of ethical conduct. The flight from self-righteousness and from mutual admiration is a noteworthy trait.[83] The movement left a small sediment in the Geniza, a pact of pious friendship, concluded in Cairo on 2 January 1564, to my mind, between two religiously minded teenagers.[84]

W[ith] G[od's] H[elp], We, the undersigned, declare to have contracted a strong and enduring pact of love, brotherhood, and peace,[85] as if we were brothers from father and mother with respect to anything for which we need mutual help.[86]

Any book we may possess, purchase, or copy, we shall lend to each other for a duration of twenty days, either for the purpose of study or for copying it and we shall never conceal any book from each other.

Also, we shall pray together in the synagogue of the great and pious rabbi Samuel Ben Sīd—m[ay] h[is soul] b[e preserved] i[n the bundle of] l[ife]—as long as we live on this earth.[87]

Also, we shall help each other materially by gift or loan,[88] as far as we are able to do so, on occasions of joy or, God forbid, others.[89] So that there should be between us all our lives nothing but consent, friendship, and brotherhood of real brothers, as if we had been one body[90] or brothers from father and mother, from conception and birth.

We have concluded and confirmed this strong and enduring pact for ourselves and our posterity.

[There follow six lines of legal verbiage usual at the end of any contract.]

We have also undertaken that if, G[od] f[orbid], sin causes that one of us should be angry with the other, no twenty-four hours should pass before we restore consent and friendship stronger and closer than before.

All that is written above we have confirmed and accepted for us and our posterity with a grave oath, containing the name of God, and with handclasp, as a public writ, communicated to the great teachers, R. Joseph Caro, R. Moses di Trani, R. Israel de Curiel, R. Meir of Padua, and R. Isaac Ibn Sīd.[91]

Each of us has taken upon himself to fulfill these obligations towards his friend wholeheartedly out of his free resolve and will.

This happened on Sunday, the seventeenth of the month of Teveth of the year 5324. Everything is confirmed and certified.

I, the lowly Elazar Maymōn

I, the lowliest in the company

Yōm Tōv ["Holiday"], son of Sīd [= Sayyid, "Lord"], may his end be good.[92]

I regard this document as having been concocted by teenagers. It is childish to open a pact of perennial friendship with a paragraph on the lending of books. I suspect that the pious youngsters had quarreled about this matter (a very grievous one, as we all know from experience), and, in order to do away with such sinful squabbles once and for all, decided to conclude a contract of friendship of a type in use in their environment. The idea of submitting this insignificant document to five of the greatest rabbis (some of whom were of very advanced age at that date) is also a sign of immaturity. The fact that so much correct legal verbiage is reproduced should not surprise the reader. No doubt they had already acquired this knowledge in school. As in some other communities (Yemen, Baghdad), on Thursday afternoon, when teachers went to the bazaar to buy provisions for the Sabbath, they kept the elder boys busy by having them copy letters and documents (which also prepared them for life with something more practical than memorizing the Bible). In general we must remember that in those days boys and girls assumed adult responsibilities far earlier than is common in our civilization.[93]

The stipulation that the two friends should attend service in the same synagogue "as long as we live on this earth" meant that they should meet at least twice everyday. Trying to be constantly together (as members of a nuclear family should) belongs to the essence of friendship, already taught by the ancients and confirmed by the rules of the contemporary brotherhoods.[94] The paragraph denouncing anger as a big sin (which trails the concluding legal verbiage as an afterthought) is also in the spirit of those rules, which teach that one should not be angry even with persons transgressing the law, and not speak evil of an animal, let alone of a human being.[95]

This unpretentious document reflecting the intense pietism of the Late Middle Ages[96] contrasts with friendship between intellectuals as it appears in writings from the classical Geniza period, which is the subject of this book. Even then friendship "for God's sake" with a religiously minded person was regarded as the highest.[97] In general, the more secular atmosphere of the High Middle Ages provided a broader basis for friendship, comprising cultural elements other than religion.

Breaking off.—One of the curious finds of the Geniza is a notebook of advice composed in reply to questions about a wide variety of matters: seeking office, choosing a profession, taking a wife, going on travels, dealing with friends and enemies, and other decisions a man must make in life. The booklet is in the beautiful hand of the experienced and highly esteemed court clerk Hillel b. Eli, about whom we actually have a report that he gave efficient advice on a delicate matter: the case of a prominent woman expecting a child conceived out of wedlock. A horoscope in his hand, written when he had already retired from office, is also preserved. The booklet of divination, however, stresses expressly that its author does not need any horoscope to arrive at his judgment.[98]

The style of supplying answers about friendship, and about other topics dispersed throughout the booklet, gives the (probably wrong) impression that they were entered at the time they were actually pronounced.

You asked me which of the two of you loves his friend, *ṣāḥib*, more. I see [or: notice, *nāẓir*] that you love him more. May the Creator make the two of you love each other for ever, and may he not let anyone take pleasure in your [plural] failure.[99]

Know that love is from God. He has granted you the love of your friend. Everything comes from God. Therefore praise and thank him that he has made you beloved by him and by everyone.[100]

You asked me which of the two of you loves his friend more. I see that the love of the two of you is even. May the Creator make your love permanent and never separate you.[101]

The questions asked here reflect an ambiance of anxiety and mistrust. How a distinguished merchant dealing with objects worth thousands of dinars could waver in his friendship is demonstrated by these conflicting statements found in a single, albeit very long, letter by a Tunisian settled in Sicily addressing Judah b. Moses Ibn Sighmār, an equally prominent Tunisian living in Egypt. "I see, my lord, that you are desirous of separating from me. I do not wish to exercise any pressure on you, for our feelings for each other are at present not as they used to be. When friendship, *ṣuḥba*, lasts long, it becomes boring. You wish separation?! I wish it even more!" Near the end of the letter, after having told much about himself and detailing a number of actions to be taken on his behalf, he reassures his correspondent. "I know that nothing can happen to us as long as our hearts communicate with each other. By God, I am clinging to the covenant, *ʿahd*, which has existed between us, and I know also that there is no doubt in your love." And he signs (on the address, as usual): "Your loving. . . ."[102]

Such temporary (or perhaps not so temporary) estrangements were kept secret, which could lead to misunderstandings and blunders on the part of others connected with the two friends. We have the much corrected and damaged draft of a long letter dealing with the funeral of the venerated R. Nissīm b. Jacob and with other matters, which had caused friction between the addressee and one Abū Zikrī Ibn Qayyōmā, of al-Mahdiyya, Tunisia, well-known from other letters.[103] The writer of the draft was caught in between and excuses himself. "You, my lord, are my brother,[104] but I have never noticed on the side of Ibn Qayyōmā with regard to you anything but friendship, *ṣadāqa*, praise, and love. None of us imagined that separation had occurred between the two of you or that one was keeping away from the other."[105]

Causes for estrangement, naturally, were numerous, the most common being the discontinuance of correspondence and the failure to carry out services promised. But the Geniza people were not fussy in this regard. In countless letters we find the remark that the writer's missives were not answered and the requests contained in them not fulfilled, but hope is expressed that the nonperformance was attributable to happy circumstances (and not to illness or other undesirable causes). When the silence was prolonged, however, and important affairs—not only of a personal nature—were neglected, and, to top it all, letters from the addressee had been received by other friends containing no greetings or message for the writer, it was time to renounce the friendship. All these elements are found in the noble letter of Joseph b. Berechiah to Ibn ʿAwkal, translated above, and similar complaints are abundant.[106] The most painful offense was the information that when friends met in the addressee's home, the writer's name was not even mentioned. If he was indeed forgotten, it was time to draw the consequences.[107]

Time as the culprit that severed the bonds of love and friendship is a prime topic in classical Arabic and medieval Hebrew poetry, which has left its traces in the Geniza correspondence.[108] In both literatures, Time is used in the general sense of Fate, Fortune, but has not lost its original meaning of the lapse of years affecting friends or members of a family separated physically by the contingencies of life. Because of the mobility of the population, separations were very common, and the difficulties of communication loosened or contributed to the loosening of the bonds of love. Love of kin or friends was, however, so dear a possession that its loss could be conceived only as the machination of some dark power.

Judge Nathan b. Samuel he-ḥavēr (*Med. Soc.*, II, 513, sec. 18) served as secretary of the Damascus branch of the Jerusalem yeshiva, but accompanied Maṣlīaḥ Gaon, when he opened a Cairene branch in 1127. In a letter from Fustat, dated October/November 1141, Nathan complained bitterly about the addressee, Petaḥyāhū ha-Kohen, a close companion of his youth, and two other friends in Damascus, from whom he had not received letters for years. True, in 1141 the Crusaders' kingdom separated Damascus from Egypt. But we know that Jews and Muslims were permitted to travel through the Christian territory, and our letter reports the arrival of a dignitary from Damascus carrying an eloquent epistle to the Egyptian Nagid written by Nathan's friend Petaḥyāhū. Nathan does not complain about the Crusaders. He accuses Time: "I complain about Time, the perfidious, the faithless, which disregards the claims of brotherhood and impedes its growing; it weakens and emaciates the love of friends. This is its character from its very beginning, incessantly urging separation, the treacherous robber! . . . It changed your relationship with me, you, my friend and beloved, whom I have reared on my knees, until I made you my equal."[109]

Knowing the infamy of Time, friends were on their guard against it. After many disappointments it was neglect of his affairs for five years which induced Joseph b. Berechiah to discontinue his relations with Ibn ʿAwkal.[110] We read about "over twenty letters"[111] unanswered in the course of six years. When the culprit finally renewed the correspondence, the considerate friend remarked only that he was pleased to learn that the writer was well and promised to keep writing if it was reciprocated.[112] Inquiries about the cessation of correspondence are very common: One requests an explanation, quoting "you shall not hate your brother in your heart" (Leviticus 19:17).[113] A letter especially dedicated to this problem emphasizes that "brothers" are sometimes angry with each other, but the one who feels hurt must speak out, lest the other suspect him of some different motive.[114] To avoid misunderstandings, a merchant, after detailing some disagreements he had with the recipient's family, adds:

> Transmit my regards to my lord, the illustrious "brother," the elder al-Āfḍal, and to all his boys, *from beginning to end* [he obviously had many]. They are to me like my brothers and my children. I shall not forget them because of this, and shall not bear enmity because of what had been thrown [or: you have thrown] between me and them. "Well meant are the wounds inflicted by a friend" [Proverbs 27:6]. "And love covers all offenses" [*ibid.* 10:12].[115]

"Forbearance with a beloved, and not losing him," is a maxim summarizing true friendship in the Geniza (and is still alive in spoken Arabic today).[116] It is quoted in an amiable and curious holograph by the Nagid Joshua b. Abraham (1310–1355), the great-great-grandson of Moses Maimonides, written on September 30, 1334. I call it curious, because in the holograph Joshua pleads with a physician who was angry with his son, a student of medicine in the capital, who had made debts; Joshua's missive is followed by fifteen lines written by the student admonishing his father to send the Nagid a quantity of sugar molasses,[117] as he had promised (and to send to himself another one in a separate basket). He assured his father that the Nagid was praying for his welfare, that is, was not cross with him. Joshua lauds the student as a fine young man, a cantor with a pleasant voice (he obviously earned his scanty livelihood with this), popular in the community, and walking in the ways of pious Jews. Life in Cairo was expensive; even people with means found it difficult to make ends meet, let alone a poor student. His father, the physician Muhadhdhab, was renowned for his munificence; how could he neglect his own son to such a degree? Joshua concludes: "I am writing you all this because of our love and long-standing companionship. I have become well aware of late that you have given up this relationship. But I have not, and will not. 'Forbearance with a beloved and not losing him!' No one doubts that you are my *ṣuḥba* and love, but God turns the hearts around. I wish you good health and well-being. *And plenty of peace.* Written on the last day of Marheshvan 1646 of the Era of the Documents."[118]

There were, of course, false friends whose unmasking was a

painful experience. A young man who had entered government service recently is advised by his father concerning some officials whose *ṣuḥba* should be sought, and others "who face to face are mirrors [show bright, friendly faces] and behind the back—scissors [cut you to pieces]."[119] The circumstances under which such betrayals were discovered are usually not known to us, because those affected by them preferred to speak in allusions, as did the proud banker whose icy note is translated above.[120] The following is an impressive example of a solemn renunciation of friendship. The short letter is written in unusually large and beautiful Arabic characters, as were used in official documents emanating from a government chancellery. Even the Bible quotations are provided in Arabic translation. The writer, probably himself a government official, no doubt wished to emphasize by this the solemn character of this letter, in which he formally terminated his friendship with the recipient. He mentions that he had considered breaking off their relationship for some time, and now improper acts on the part of the addressee and his son had precipitated the decision. He was almost happy that things had come to the breaking point. But the address does not contain a name—a sign of extreme intimacy—and calls the recipient "intimate friend, friend of my spirit [my soul]," the idea being that an old friend can never be given up entirely.[121]

In the name of God, the all merciful and compassionate. Help is sought from God, the possessor of heaven and earth [Genesis 14:22], in whose hand is the soul of every living being [Job 12:10]. Part of what I had written God has brought forth in you, but something has remained, as God has said: "I shall make the sin of the Amori full."[122] I have acted in a way only God the exalted knows, but you—had it not been for my trust in God, the almighty, I could put you in a situation which you would hate. But let God judge between me and you and my progeny and yours.

I had already intended to separate a long time ago, before I moved to Alexandria, then came to me this bounty.[123] God must be thanked for everything. Indeed, I am just a happy man in the midst of what God the almighty has wrought.

And his prayers may come over Moses.[124]

And praise to God alone.

[*Verso*:]

These lines shall be brought to the intimate friend, the friend of the [i.e., my] spirit."[125]

Our letter demonstrates sensitivity for one's fellowmen, which shows Geniza society at its best. The writer does not heap accusations on the addressee but leaves it to him to become aware of what he has done to an old friend. Another matter is involved. Remaining on paper, black on white, the evil would be perpetuated. Alluded to, but not expressly mentioned, it could become forgotten and wiped out one day.[126] This good practice was not adhered to by everyone, as the following pages prove.

Envy and enmity.—"You know, my lord, that a person has only one who loves him, but ten who hate and harm him."[127] This Geniza description of a human experience is similar in content to the Arabic and Judeo-Arabic proverbs cited above, note 1, but sounds far more pessimistic. Does it reflect the realities of life in the society and period concerned? The answer to this question is somewhat complex.

The wish "may God crush your enemies and destroy those who envy you" was a phrase almost obligatory in any longer letter, and was often repeated in the text itself.[128] People liked to diversify these good wishes. A man from Qūṣ in Upper Egypt with a strong, scholarly hand writes this: "May God the exalted always treat you in accordance with his bountiful ways, crush the eyes [plural, not dual] of those who envy you, and smash the noses of your opponents, may he fulfill with you his trusted word: 'No one will stand up against you all the days of your life'" (Joshua 1:5).[129]

It seems strange that an important business letter of fifty-five lines going from Aden to India should be superscribed with one single wish: "Your hand shall prevail over your foes and all your enemies shall be cut down" (Micah 5:8), even though neither this letter, nor any other in the rich correspondence exchanged between the sender and the recipient, contains details about persons or groups particularly hostile to the latter. Not less odd is a note of four short lines where the addressee's name is followed by the sole wish "may God crush your enemies." An explanation of these usages must be sought in the realities of the wider world in which the writers of these missives lived.[130]

Muslim high society: the court, government, judiciary, and academe, so vividly depicted by Muslim historians and biographers, was an ambiance of constant strife and intrigue. We read endless reports about the rise and downfall of viziers and other courtiers as well as of members of the higher bureaucracy, the appointment and dismissal of judges and professors, and the coteries and machinations that were behind all these turns of the wheel of fortune.

The character of higher Muslim society rubbed off on the communal and private lives of the Jewish minority. Strife within the

Jewish leadership during the High Middle Ages had been known from literary sources. When the Geniza was discovered and assiduously studied, a flood of information about this topic swamped Jewish historiography. Reading Jacob Mann's classic *The Jews in Egypt and in Palestine under the Fatimid Caliphs*, and his chapter on Babylonia-Iraq in his *Texts and Studies in Jewish History and Literature*, I, 63–202, one gets the impression that communal rivalries were the daily diet of everyone in those parts and days. Mann himself, after having toiled much with the turbulent period of the Gaon Solomon b. Judah of Jerusalem (d. 1051), grew somewhat impatient with these "internal bickerings," and wished that Solomon had employed his beautiful command of Hebrew for some better purpose.[131] In Babylonia-Iraq, where the Jewish population, at least during the tenth century, was far larger than in Egypt and Palestine, where its institutions were more important and the issues involved greater, the clashes within the leadership added up to an almost uninterrupted series of crises. There, where, in a time of almost perennial warfare, the Jewish leaders were closely connected with military commanders, their language, too, became coarser. As far as I can see, a Solomon b. Judah never used words and phrases as offending as those dispensed freely by the great Saadya Gaon of Baghdad (d. 942) a century earlier. No wonder that a penitential supplication in Saadya's Prayerbook (not accepted in the general synagogue service) contains these lines: "O Merciful, plant perfect peace in the two yeshivas [of Baghdad], in the Land of Israel, and among those living in the Diaspora, between the students of the Torah, and in every congregation, and keep away unwarranted hatred from your people Israel."[132]

It may even be argued that the advent in Jerusalem of Daniel b. Azarya, a scion of the Babylonian family of the Head of the Diaspora, introduced a harsher tone into Jewish public life in Palestine, which reverberated in the subsequent generation. These are the words of a circular written after Daniel had triumphed over his many opponents, who had sided with the local candidate for the Gaonate of the Palestinian yeshiva: "We [=I] thank the God of our father David, who lifted our heads above our enemies [Psalms 3:4], crushed the loins of our adversaries [Deuteronomy 33:11], ground those who hate us [Psalms 89:24], and smote our foes (*ibid.*). He made a covenant with David."[133]

When the communal leaders were at loggerheads, the man in the street did not remain untouched. In the synagogues (as in the mosques and churches), prayers were said for the men in power, not in general terms, as is the custom today, but specifying names and other unambiguous details.[134] Daniel b. Azarya went a step further. No doubt the circular just cited was destined to be read out during a synagogue service; this we may conclude from another order of his, expressly mentioned by him in a letter to his greatest admirer and supporter in the capital of Egypt, Abraham Ibn al-Furāt. He says that he had advised the spiritual leader of the Fustat congregation not only to bless Ibn al-Furāt during the prayers—this was commonly done for a meritorious benefactor of the community—but always to add "and may He crush his enemies."[135]

In light of the preceding remarks about the infighting of the Muslim ruling class and the dissensions within the Jewish leadership, the wishes for the destruction of one's correspondent's enemies, so easily thrown around in the Geniza letters, should be taken with a grain of salt. The phrases were borrowed by the middle class from the life-style of a higher social level; they should be taken as positive statements: your enemies are mine; I am your friend through thick and thin. When a person writes, in lamenting his own sufferings, "may God afflict my enemies as he has afflicted me," he really does not have particular enemies in mind but intends only to emphasize the gravity of the illness.[136] The more polite Geniza correspondents give this phrase a different turn: "My situation is more befitting *your* enemies and those who hate *you*."[137]

Nonetheless, envy (or, rather, fear of the evil eye of the envier), hatred, founded or unfounded, craving for retaliation and revenge, and gloating over the misfortune of others, are by no means absent from the Geniza. Aggressiveness and violence seem to have been confined to the lower classes. Forgiving offense, even if committed in public, is reported, but this virtue was obviously not very popular. In these matters, much depended on the nervous system of the persons concerned.

Envy and competition were vital factors in pre-Islamic Arabia. Franz Rosenthal, in his stimulating 1980 Ann Arbor lecture, pointed out that the Arabic language created special forms for the elative ("greater than . . . ") and superlative ("the greatest") which Hebrew, for instance, does not possess. Arabic, too, has special verbal forms expressing the notions of reciprocity and competition, almost absent from other Semitic languages.[138] The damage caused by envy was very much dreaded; the last but one chapter of the Qurʾān contains a special prayer for protection from this evil.[139] Satan envied the newly created Adam, when the angels prostrated themselves before him in adoration. Since then, Satan "the stoned" is the embodiment of envy.[140]

Jews in the diaspora had very little to be envied for. A successful

Jew, like the "vizier" Abū Saʿd al-Tustarī, was envied (and murdered) by Muslims; the Jews were proud of that family.[141] When enviers are constantly cursed in the Geniza along with enemies, the influence of the environment is at play. This is felt in the very phrasing, "May God bring us together soon under the best of circumstances and by stoning every envier" (a reminder of the "stoned" envier in the Qurʾān). This wish is found in a letter of an Adenese merchant addressing Ḥalfōn b. Nethanel, who really seems to have been bothered by his enviers, for in another letter from the same town he is assured that only persons excelling in virtue and gifts of the spirit are envied. This, too, was a common topic in Arabic literature:

> I am envied. May God increase the envy!
> A man is envied for his virtues.[142]

No one remains neutral in this world. "He who loves you does not hate you; he who hates you does not love you; enmity is inveterate," wails a man after describing the machinations of his enemies, "who took my money and spilled my blood more than once."[143] A main cause of enmity, although this is not unequivocally clear from our letters, was to have one's livelihood undermined. "He robbed the bread from my mouth and the sleep from my eyes, *may God judge between me and him*" (cf. Genesis 16:5).[144] Although anger at damage caused by fellow merchants is not absent, it is, in particular, the members of the "free" professions of physicians, independent teachers, and community officials who are outraged most by unsavory competition.[145] The excitable young doctor Abū Zikrī, son of judge Elijah, who writes about the gloating of his enemies in the letter translated above, had written home that he had made peace with his competitors in the capital. His younger brother responds with these words: "Our father is well and thanks God that you have made peace with these people in Fustat and that you are keeping your position despite *those sinful men who are shedding blood, may God subdue them, undo their machinations, and requite them for what they have done.*"[146]

In a moving letter, a cantor and ritual slaughterer in Crusader Acre, Palestine, bitterly complains about the leader of an Alexandrian group of catchers of purple snails, who undermine his position in the community and rob him of his livelihood. The only reason for the pernicious enmity was the cantor's censure of the Alexandrians for their frequenting of taverns of bad repute.[147]

A typical case of harassment inflicted on a communal official by a local tyrant is reflected in this letter of a *ḥāvēr*, or member of the Jerusalem yeshiva, appointed as spiritual leader of a community in a provincial town. The president of the community was related to an influential person from a scholarly family, but was not learned himself. The arrival of the ḥāvēr was apt to diminish his standing, so he did everything to humiliate and isolate him and to weaken his economic position. The short passage translated in *Med. Soc.*, II, 291 and n. 6, shows how he offended him. The complaint of the ḥāvēr is subdued, since the letter is a cry for help addressed to the father-in-law of the writer's enemy:

> Since I have come here, he behaves as if he were the master and I his slave. Would it had been so [that he had treated me with the consideration a master owes his slave], and that he had not organized cliques against me and cut off my livelihood. He let them give an oath that they should not pay me a penny and never share my company. And other things like that. He did not pay attention that I walked to his house, greeted and praised him by his name and the name of his father and blessed him [publicly during the synagogue service]. This is what I have done for him, and this is part of what he has done to me. He cut off my livelihood and annulled the collection [to be made for the communal official] year after year; for five consecutive years. I have received nothing because of him and his clique.[148]

In a similar case, where, however, no regard was to be had for family sensitivities, the harmed official gave vent to his feelings without restraint, although he was writing to a Nagid and the two chief justices of Fustat. He had heard that his adversary had written a letter to these highest Jewish authorities in the country, and, although he had no direct information about its content, he could imagine it in view of the hatred between himself and one Zikrī b. Musallam Ibn al-Naᶜja, because the latter envied him to a degree that he transgressed the commandment "you shall not covet" (Exodus 21:17). In fact—as he adds sarcastically—the verse does not apply to that man, for "he does not belong to the children of Israel, but is a remnant of the Amoris" [who were exterminated because of their sinfulness (II Samuel 21:2)]. The only thing that Zikrī knows from the Scriptures is "your sons will replace your forefathers" [a hint to the opponent's claims of noble descent (Psalms 45:17)]. In reality, the verse "You have risen in your fathers' stead, a brood of sinful men" (Numbers 32:14) applies to him. "He has done to me what even Haman, the wicked, has not done to the Jewish people" ["to destroy, slay, and annihilate all the Jews" (Esther 3:13)]. Here, the lower part of the letter is torn away.

In the few lines legible on the reverse side the writer notes that most people in the town knew well what had happened between him and Ibn al-Naʿja, the physician—as he calls him here. An oral report would be given to the Nagid by a person named, and the matter would be related to the justices in a detailed letter.[149]

What could be worse than what Haman the wicked had planned to do to the Jewish people? The answer is found in the only biblical verse written above the letter, alluding, as usual, to the main purpose of its content:

> The wicked are lost from birth
> Those who speak lies go astray from the womb [Psalms 58:4].

The physician had spread false accusations against our writer. No enmity appears to have been more implacable than that caused by slander and denunciation, especially when the thus offended was suspected of misdeeds, which were in truth actions for the benefit of others—sometimes of the slanderer himself. A carefully worded (but much damaged) document, referred to above, praises an India trader who had endangered his own life and property by saving the assets of a traveling companion, who had died in Dahlak, on the Red Sea, a place notorious for its rapacious rulers. The document issued in Fustat around 1130 details all the actions undertaken by the courageous trader until the assets, whether listed in the dead man's papers or not, had safely reached the orphans. That experienced merchant took no chances. He knew that even the most meritorious deeds could become food for evil tongues to spread gossip.[150]

Another man in a similar situation was less fortunate. We do not have all the details because only the second leaf of the letter has been found thus far, probably to be followed by a third one. It was an affair of a power of attorney and a deposit in which the writer believed he had acted in the best interests of his opponent, whereas the latter had accused him in public of the opposite. The interesting aspect of this letter is the endeavor of its sender to understand the outrageous behavior of a person who clearly had been an old acquaintance of his family:

> "*He who casts suspicions on others charges them with his own defects.*"[151] I remember what my father, my lord—*may he rest in glory* [Isaiah 11:10]—has said about him: "Because he mixes with bad company he tarnishes the honor of good people." *By the uniqueness of God,* I have never done them any wrong. Then this man comes and *repays evil for good* [Psalms 38:21]).

May *the Creator of the World* reward me *in his mercy* for all I have done for them in the matter of that *deposit*, harming myself and my children. May God requite them for what they have inflicted on my heart and my body and deliver them into the hands of people suspecting them and *putting them to shame*, as they have done with me in the presence of the most respected members of the community, shedding my blood. *May God pay him according to his actions* [cf. Job 34:11].[152]

The man was so bitter because his opponent had threatened again and again that he would bring this and other matters to the attention of the government, an action fraught with danger for all concerned.[153] Jeopardy there certainly was when Abūn b. Ṣadaqa, the excitable Maghrebi living in Jerusalem, of whom we have a number of remarkable letters in the Geniza, concealed a small sum of money left by a countryman. He did so to save it for the heirs, because the government confiscated the property of foreigners when no heirs were present in town. Soon rumors were spread that Abūn had "robbed the government" (not the heirs!) of 100, 500, 1,000 dinars, when the entire sum concerned was not more than 15–16 dinars. The rumors had even reached Fustat, where the recipient, Ḥayyīm b. ʿAmmār al-Madīnī (i.e., of Palermo, Sicily), a friend of Abūn, had heard of them and was puzzled. Abūn got furious. "No one has ever trod on another man's blood as that one who caused all this did on mine. May God let me see on his body *leprosy and other plagues*, may he not let him leave this world until he will see himself as a leper. I am confident that this will happen, if God wills, for our sages, Peace upon them, have said: *He who casts suspicions on rightful men will be* afflicted on his body."[154] Immediately after having flung this terrible curse on the slanderer, he turns the evil away—by writing a blessing for himself: "R. Yose, Peace upon him, had said; 'May I be of those who are suspected of something they have not done.'"[155] But he cannot conclude the passage without adding "Woe to the wicked forever."[156]

We must condone Abūn's outbursts, for, as is evident from other parts of this letter (pp. 244–245), he was deeply upset by other matters at that time and almost despaired of life. Moreover, he says: "What would have happened, if those rumors had reached the ears of the director of finances or the head of the department of estates?"[157] Less tolerable are those "claims to retaliation" addressed to God, if they are mixed with malicious rejoicing in the misfortune of a poor man, especially when they appear in a letter of mixed content, containing also the most effusive expressions of friendship (p. 285 and n. 61). In between two paragraphs on the current affairs of the yeshiva, as the secretary of which Evyatar, the future Gaon, served, he writes this:

> As to the man of Acre, the words of our ancients have been fulfilled with him: "*He who takes misfortune easily, will be visited by greater sufferings*" . . . I am really grateful to my Lord who helped me in what I desire, and hope that he will complete what our ancients have said: "*Against whomever the sages direct their eyes there will be death or poverty.*" Poverty is already in place; there remains the wrath [bringing death]. No doubt, God retaliates on him, for I have utmost claims to retaliation.[158]

Such rudeness of sentiment and language is not common in the Geniza. I am inclined to see here an echo to the advent of the Iraqians. Evyatar's father had to yield to Daniel b. Azariah; he himself was pushed aside for years by Daniel's son David. The length of the contest, which stretched over more than four decades, blunted human sentiments and created an atmosphere of offensive language as had been in use in Iraq.[159]

There can be no doubt, however, that gloating over an enemy's misfortune and, even more, the dread of becoming exposed to such humiliation were uncommonly dominant in the psyche of the Geniza person. He, who was so sensitive to esteem and renown, felt any infraction to his prestige as intolerable, while the troubles befalling an enemy were a kind of self-justification. One might say that this is a general human propensity. Whether this assumption is correct or not, the correspondence of the Geniza people, low and high, is too replete with relevant utterings to be disregarded.

The unhappy father from Alexandria, whose son had run away to the army (his story, told in several letters, is summarized in *Med. Soc.*, II, 379 and n. 27; IV, 241 and n. 119), tries to bring him back by reminding him of the tears of his mother, but especially by this: "Had you known how many enemies you have left behind you, you would not have traveled away; your enemies are gloating over you."[160] In another letter from Alexandria a son tarrying too long on the India route is admonished by his brother to hurry back: "You must be considerate with regard to your brothers-in-law; they have many enemies, as you know, who are gloating over your absence [taking it as desertion of his wife]." The hurt pride of the brothers-in-law, not the anguish of the lonely wife, is expected to impress the *muruwwa*, or manliness, of the addressee, which is invoked in the letter.[161] A well-educated official who lost his position in the caliphal mint and lived with his family in Alexandria deprived of everything, explains to his sister that he could not return to the capital for ten reasons, the tenth and most compelling one being that he would be unable to bear the rejoicing of his enemies.[162]

The intellectuals seem to have been no different in this matter. When Ḥalfōn b. Nethanel's elder brother Eli, "The Diadem of the Discerning," who presided over the High Court of the Jerusalem yeshiva, then seated in Fustat, passed away, some other calamities occurred in the family. "As if it had not been enough," writes his brother-in-law to him, "that the enemies gloated over the disaster afflicting all of us, when the pearl, my lord the Diadem, was taken from us."[163] When the court physician and later judge Elijah b. Zechariah admonishes his sons to mend their ways and to set aside their squabbles, he quotes in full one of the most sublime passages of the Bible (Jeremiah 9:22–23), but enforces this by adding: "Protect yourselves and your parents from the gloating of people who are not worth being talked to."[164]

Moses Maimonides, as his writings prove, was a keen observer of his contemporaries. Wishing to explain to them that in the World to Come there will be no bodily existence and, consequently, no physical pleasures, such as food, drink, and sex, he adds (inter alia): "In this world, too, there are pleasures other than those connected with the body. Do we not find most men making extraordinary efforts and sacrifices to get high rank and esteem; many people preferring revenge on an enemy to many physical enjoyments; and others avoiding the choicest bodily pleasures because they are afraid of the shame ensuing from them?"[165]

In short, attention to "what other people say" was one of the main concerns of the Geniza person. This state of mind, molded under the impact of the environment, was enhanced by the smallness of the community, where everyone knew everyone, and where one was constantly observed. Sixteen hundred years or so of oppression and humiliation had also the effect that feelings of enmity and vengeance were a matter of thought and word rather than of deed. The actuality of life was better than it looked. Most of the "daily news" provided by the Geniza concerning life during the High Middle Ages is a story of cooperation, friendship, and mutual aid.

Aggressiveness and violence were not entirely absent, but as far as I can see, were confined to the lower classes and, in general, petty circumstances. This little statement of witness is typical:

On Monday, the sixth of the month of Marheshwan [October 1231], came Shamūn Ibn al-Muzanjir [dyer of verdigris-green], sat down in the store of R. Simḥā, and began to sew. Suddenly his brother ʿImrān appeared and said to R. Simḥā: "Arbitrate between me and that one; he should pay me something." Said Shamūn: "I do not owe you a thing." ʿImrān stood up, seized the end of Shamūn's turban and his beard, and choked him with them. But Shamūn did not lift his hand against his brother ʿImrān, for this happened in the presence of Jews, Muslims, and Christians, which is a *desecration of the Holy Name.* And Peace.

Witnessed by Solomon b. Rabbi Elijah, [May his] e[nd be] g[ood].[166]

A woman reports to another about a family brawl, which exploded when a man brought his wife, probably one not approved by the family, into his brother's house; the two brothers came to blows, even the mother (who probably tried to separate the combatants) was hit. The two were brought before the dayyān and were reprimanded and put to shame by him in the presence of the community "in an indescribable manner." Finally, the intruder, together with his brother, went away to the army (probably as purveyors, not as soldiers), leaving his wife with his mother. For her protection, she was, however, taken into the house of the judge.[167]

Such protection was by no means unnecessary, since an undesirable newcomer could be lashed with a shoe by a sister-in-law.[168] Shoes were also used in an attack on a cantor, his wife, and children, an intended act of humiliation.[169] Brawls and fistfights in the synagogue or its court are reported from Ramle, Palestine, Maḥalla, Lower Egypt, and the Iraqians' synagogue in Fustat.[170] In a complaint to a Nagid, a widow alleged that a stepson hit her with the intention of doing her physical harm when she entered a house to which she had a claim.[171] And in turbulent Alexandria, in a time of famine, the administrator of the social services was threatened with death if he did not release quantities of wheat for the poor, which the Nagid had ordered him to retain in the likelihood of a worsening situation.[172] We never read a complaint that someone needed medical treatment after a brawl, however, and, of course, during the entire period, as far as we know, a Jew never committed a murder.[173]

Heavenly intervention was usually invoked to rectify wrong by retaliation in kind. Occasionally the opposite occurs: God is asked to condone the offender as the offended himself had forgiven him. The fragment of a noble letter translated below concerns the sheikh al-Najīb, repeatedly met before, who regarded himself as called upon to correct the mores of his contemporaries. Al-Najīb, as the letter shows, led a study group in the synagogue, not, of course, during the service. He suspected the writer of the letter of having been critical of his teaching and when he came in immediately attacked him:

> Who put such an impossible suspicion into your mind? God forbid that you should *cast suspicion on rightful people.* Brother, if it is embarrassing to you that I am present in the synagogue [while you are teaching], I shall not come in at all. On that Saturday I did not notice that you were teaching a group, until you began to talk, putting me to shame in public—*may God forgive you.* Even a slave should not be chided in this way.[174] Then you, sheikh al-Najīb, did what you did. May God put me among those of whom it is said "*those who have been insulted, but do not insult, have been put to shame, but do not retort,*" and make you a man *standing in the breach,* when Israel is in trouble, using his honored position only for good deeds, and being kind to his friends.[175]

The full text of that remarkable quotation is this: "Of those who have been insulted . . . who act out of the love of God, and accept his afflictions with joy, it is said: 'Those who love him are like the sun when it rises in might'" (Judges 31:5).[176] But the lovers of God are few.

5. Sex

The twentieth century is an excellent teacher on the sociology of human sex. Many things are no longer uncommon in families where they had been unheard-of a century ago. This upheaval was hardly the result of biological changes, although better food and improved medical care may have made the individual bolder and more enterprising. The main cause must be sought in the moral and spiritual transformation experienced by society at large. Individuals and groups are acting under the impact of the new morality. Not having at least experimented with the novelties is regarded almost as backwardness.

This tremendous century of ours, which may well become a watershed in human history, is, of course, very exceptional in its attitude toward sex. The response of individuals and groups to the wider ambiance in such personal matters as sexual behavior should alert the historian to the likelihood that a somewhat similar situation may also have prevailed in more traditional societies. This is particularly true for the task before us: trying to define the place of sex in the Jewish community that formed a sector of the vibrant Muslim society of the High Middle Ages.

The Muslim injunction of *satr al-ʿawra*, the covering of the private parts of the body—which for women meant almost the entire body—was not merely a matter of religious ritual; it reflected a strong social attitude of the common people who took religion seriously. The more the opulent and the mighty felt themselves secure in their wealth and power, the more they loosened their tongues and secluded their wives. The littérateurs, who frequented the courts of the princes and the palaces of the rich, have provided us with abundant and unrestrained reports about sex as it was discussed and practiced in those circles. Some of the sophisticated leaders of religious law and thought, who feared God but were confident of their own merits and trusted in God's mercy, were similarly inclined to allow themselves certain freedoms with regard to sex and other matters and did not mince words on such topics. At the other end of the social spectrum, the people who were not *mastūr*—literally, "not covered," not protected by their means, family, or social standing, in short, not respectable—had had little power to seclude their wives, and no cause to restrain their tongues. Their voice is heard in the chronologically later parts of *The Arabian Nights* and in similar literature.

The sexual mores of the bulk of the urban population, the great masses of skilled craftsmen and artisans, respectable shopkeepers, middle class merchants, and lower bureaucracy are less well known. Abdelwahab Bouhdiba in his grand dissertation on Islam and sex repeatedly speaks of "all layers of Muslim society," but he does not seem to have paid special attention to the problem of differentiation raised here.[1] Historians had little opportunity to speak of the middle class. Books of entertainment, if systematically analyzed according to the social groups that they address, promise important results, but more work is still to be done in this respect. Much is to be expected also from a careful perusal of Islamic religious literature, since a large number of its creators came from families engaged in crafts or commerce or were themselves involved in such occupations. May I draw attention to an extensive paper by Hayyim J. Cohen (which is a condensation of a Ph.D. dissertation written under my supervision) on the socioeconomic backgrounds and mundane occupations of Muslim religious scholars during the first five centuries of Islam. Of the 14,000 biographies examined, about 4,200 yielded information proving that classical Islamic religious literature was to a considerable extent the creation of a mercantile middle class.[2] But writers of books naturally have a purpose: they intend to make a point, to state, prove, or preach something; they address a public. We should like to hear the unmediated voice of the common man when he speaks in private, occupied with his own daily concerns, not *voicing* opinions but revealing them inadvertently.

In this respect the Cairo Geniza is able to make a contribution, albeit a modest and limited one. The general difficulties in the use of the Cairo Geniza for the study of medieval social history are compounded by the fact that respectable persons of the lower and middle class were extremely reticent with regard to anything that smacked of sex, to the extent that in the heart of the classical Geniza period, the eleventh century, one would not dare to put on paper even a word with so harmless a sexual connotation as "my wife." One did not write "my wife," *zawjatī*, but "the one who is with me," *man ʿindī*, or similar circumlocutions, which sometimes were very awkward. The Geniza has preserved more than two hundred and fifty letters addressed to Nahray b. Nissīm, a merchant banker from Qayrawān, Tunisia, who had settled in Egypt, by means of which we are able to follow his fortunes for a full fifty years from 1045 through 1095. Many of the letters were written by close relatives and friends, and often contain references to matters other than business. But nowhere are greetings extended to his wife, and, needless to say, Nahray himself never mentions her in his own letters of which we have about twenty-five. We know the names of his son and his daughter, we hear much about his mother and something about his sister, but we do not know the name of the wife whom he survived. The name of one who outlived him is known only from a legal document written after his death.[3]

The Geniza contains innumerable details about a woman's wardrobe and ornaments but practically nothing about her physical appearance. When a young schoolmaster, who lived far away from home, apprised his mother of his marriage, he assured her that her prayers had been heard and that his young wife possessed all the wonderful qualities of character that he had always admired in his mother. This is said in Arabic, like the rest of the letter. But the additional praise of the girl, namely, that she was very beautiful, is expressed in Hebrew, as we would use Latin when we are in doubt about the propriety of what we are saying.[4]

The limitations of the materials to be presented are self-evident. The first is the provenance of our texts. As far as commerce is concerned, the Geniza is a first-rate source for both the Mediterranean and the India trades. For such matters as sex and family life, however, our information comes mainly from Egypt itself and, in particular, from its ancient Islamic capital, Fustat. But has not Fustat been censured by visitors and by newcomers from other

Muslim countries, including Moses Maimonides, for the looseness of its sexual mores? Al-Muqaddasī, a native of the holy and virtuous city of Jerusalem, says simply: "In Fustat every wife has two husbands."[5] A somewhat malicious religious legend was invented to explain the dominant position allegedly enjoyed by Egyptian women. When Pharaoh and his host were drowned in the Red Sea, the widows, instead of remaining unmarried, freed their slaves and hirelings and took them as husbands. But they imposed on them the condition that throughout all generations the husbands should be submissive to their wives. "Look at the Copts," meaning the really native Egyptians, concludes the narrator of that story. "When you make a deal with a Copt and you believe you are through with him, what does he say to you: 'Wait, I must go home first and ask my wife.'"[6]

Be that as it may, as far as the Geniza people are concerned, the great majority of them were newcomers to Egypt or sons of immigrants. They represent a fair cross-section of the Arabic-speaking population of the Mediterranean and southwest Asian areas, from Iran and Iraq in the East to Morocco and Spain in the West. Nahray b. Nissīm was a Tunisian, and most of his friends and acquaintances were also Westerners. Thus, the sexual mores to be studied by us should not be regarded as specifically Egyptian.

A far more serious limitation is the fact that the writers of the Geniza letters were Jews, members of a minority group. To be sure, the role of Christians and Jews under Islam should never be likened to the conventional picture of the Jew in medieval Europe. In Islamic countries, both Christians and Jews were indigenous to the area and found in almost all walks of life. During the High Middle Ages there were neither occupational nor geographical ghettos, the linguistic assimilation to the Muslim majority had become almost complete, and participation in its cultural life was far-reaching.

With regard to family life and sexual mores, however, matters so intimately connected with religion and social standing, the situation was different. The seclusion of women was far tighter in Islam than in Christianity and Judaism. Christian and Jewish women were required to cover their hair and to dress modestly, but they were not obliged to veil their faces and they could talk to a man of another family without incurring opprobrium. This contrast is beautifully illustrated in a legal question submitted to Moses Maimonides. A Jewish and a Christian family lived in one house. Such arrangements were common. One day the Christian embraced Islam; this change, as the letter emphasizes, caused no end of inconvenience to the female members of the Jewish household.[7] In the Geniza letters it is taken for granted that a male unrelated to the family could come into a home and discuss matters with the woman of the house in the absence of her husband. Since women were very much involved in economic matters, there was ample opportunity for such encounters.[8]

Islam was uneasy with regard to the admission of women to public services in the mosque. In contrast, the churches and synagogues of Fustat had women's galleries, frequented by women, married or not. The entrance to the gallery was through a so-called secret or women's door, a *bāb al-sirr* or *bāb al-nisā*, located on a street different from that into which the main gate opened. It should be noted that the same special entrance for women was found in any large private home. But in the synagogue *court,* men and women mixed freely. In a letter a woman could write to a man: "When we met last Saturday in the synagogue we discussed such-and-such a matter." Thus, the basic attitude toward the seclusion of women was not the same in the minority and majority populations.[9]

Concubinage with one's slave girl was another and even more serious contrast between Islam and the older religions. Cohabitation with a woman whom one could buy and sell on the market was as legal and natural in Islam as marriage to a free woman. In Christianity and Judaism this practice was anathema. It is true that in the Hebrew Bible concubinage with one's slave girl was legal as it was in Islam. Only in postbiblical times, when concubinage with foreign women menaced the very character of Jewish religion, did opposition to it become extreme. This attitude persisted in Christianity.[10]

According to the Bible, sexual relations between males were to be punished by death.[11] It has been argued that the severity of this punishment rested on the assumption that Israel, a small nation constantly at war with stronger neighbors, could not permit a part of its male population to become effeminate or uninterested in producing children. Another, or additional, reason was probably ritual, the prohibition of things that were regarded as unnatural, as is found in the Bible elsewhere. Be that as it may, even in late Roman times, when the Near East and the Mediterranean world had been impregnated with Greek and Iranian ideas about pederasty, it was still asserted that such practices were not found among Jews.[12]

The cult of attractive male youths was originally a privilege of the men in power. But, as often happens with social mores, the example of the ruling classes filtered down and became a style of life for the entire community. A poor schoolmaster teaching the Qur'ān, who did not have the means to marry a wife or to satisfy his desires in a more transitory fashion, would pick up a boy, or several boys from his class. The North African writer Rachid Boujedra, in his autobiographical novel *La Répudiation*, describes himself as a victim of such an occurrence, but does so in a rather casual manner. Such happenings, he writes, were common; parents generally knew about them but preferred to close their eyes and mouths in order not to injure the bearer of the Holy Scripture.[13] Thus we see that what in one civilization was regarded as a horrid crime was looked upon in another as a tolerable pattern of behavior. The three monotheistic religions are unanimous, however, in their condemnation of pederasty.

Up to this point it might appear that there was a marked difference between the minority population and the majority regarding the seclusion of women, concubinage with slave girls, and pederasty. The findings of the Geniza seem to indicate that this assumption is true only in part. The social notions of the majority population had its effect.

According to the socioeconomic conditions of the time for the majority of the population, sexual satisfaction had to be obtained through marriage. Marriage was instituted by God, not only for procreation but for the partners to find full sexual satisfaction without being forced to seek it illicitly. The attitude toward marriage reflects ancient Near Eastern wisdom, as it is expressed, for instance, in an often quoted passage from the Book of Proverbs (5:15–21), which, in abbreviated form, runs like this: "Drink water from your own cistern, rejoice in the wife of your youth. Why should you become infatuated with a stranger?" A Geniza sermon in praise of marriage describes the wife as a protecting wall surrounding her husband.[14] A man imploring his wife to return to him, after she had fled to her relatives, assures her that, in the future, *she* would be the queen and he the slave, for "living without a wife in Cairo is very difficult for blameless and chaste persons." A fully grown man without a wife was regarded as living in sin, and it was not easy for him to find an apartment just for himself. Widowers, unlike widows, rarely remained unmarried.[15]

Love and sex within marriage are discussed in *Med. Soc.*, III, 165–170, and also 47–54. The most important aspect emerging from the Geniza in this respect is the fact, established by both legal documents and letters, that the night of the Sabbath (Friday night) was set aside for the fulfillment of the conjugal obligations a husband owed his wife. In the Talmud this was only a recommendation and then only for scholars. By Geniza times it had become a general observance that could be claimed in court (as a minimum, of course). This applied to the majority of the Jews, the Rabbanites, who followed the teachings of the rabbis of the Talmud. The Karaite Jews, who recognized only the Bible as their guidance, took an opposite stance: sexual intercourse was regarded by them as a desecration of the holy day. In the numerous cases of mixed marriages, mostly a Karaite woman marrying a Rabbanite man, the sensibilities of the wife had to be honored.

And not only in that respect. "Living together without mutual consent is like prostitution."[16] Divorce was often sought by, and granted to, wives. The fact that about 45 percent of all women whose cases are known to us from the Geniza were married more than once should teach us that marriage did not always mean life imprisonment for the female.

Polygyny was permitted by law but discouraged by statute and legal practice.[17] In a comprehensive Hebrew study (certainly to be followed soon by an English version) Mordechai A. Friedman shows that polygyny was somewhat more common in Geniza times than might be concluded from the writings of myself and others. It should not be denied that for the first wife polygyny—even the mere threat of its occurrence—was considered an unmitigated evil. There were, however, exceptions, as when the elder wife accepted the younger one as help, or loved children borne by her, while she herself was barren, or when the two simply enjoyed the company of each other. In *Med. Soc.*, III, 149, I reported a case in which these three circumstances were combined. I observed it in the 1950s, when I studied immigrants to Israel from a Jewish weavers' village in an agricultural environment of Yemen. I add here another example concerning an urban family.

Once, while I was attending a service in a Yemenite synagogue in Jerusalem, a hefty, broad-shouldered young man came in who attracted my attention because most urban Yemenites are slight of build. I asked my neighbor: "Who is this uncommon type?" He answered: "His story is even more unusual." On the way home he reported this: An octogenarian, who had sired seven daughters and married off all of them, was urged by his wife to marry a younger woman, who might be more lucky and give him a male heir. After much reluctance the old man agreed; his wife selected a suitable candidate and arranged a fine wedding for her. The young man in the synagogue and two other healthy boys were the result. One sees that in a polygamous society a second wife is occasionally brought into the house by the first.[18]

Proved adultery of a married woman is known to me only from Alexandria, the city of loose mores, and only in special cases, namely, where petty merchants tried their luck in faraway India and got stuck there for years. Scandals ensued ("she should be burned!"), but, as far as we know, nothing happened to the women concerned except that they produced healthy babies. One of them sent greetings to a brother—out in India—as one letter sarcastically remarks.[19] Elsewhere we read only about allegations (occasionally not entirely unfounded). A luckless woman, who had run away from her husband, reports that her father-in-law had suspected her of having an affair with a brother-in-law, but she mentions it only as an absurdity exemplifying the degree of hatred with which she had been received in the family.[20] More dubious is a story reported by a cantor who served as spiritual leader for a small congregation in a provincial town and was writing his superiors in the capital asking for advice. A young couple lived in the house of the husband's mother, who had remarried. After her death the stepfather began to visit the apartment of the young woman with a frequency that aroused the suspicion of the community; some people were prepared to bring the matter to the attention of the police. Summoned by the cantor, the man promised to discontinue these visits and to pay a fine of 2 dinars in case he relapsed. The amount of the fine shows that we are here on a very low level of society.[21] A similar promise was broken repeatedly by a Karaite who visited a married woman of his community using frivolous language and making indecent overtures. Brought before the assembly of the elders, the woman argued that she discouraged those visits, had complained about them to her husband and the authorities of the community, and, whenever the man came in when she was alone, had asked an aunt to come down. In the presence of the accused, however, she changed her testimony, stating only that she disapproved of the visits. Finally a group of Karaite women testified that she was a person without blemish. At the next prayer service a solemn ban was pronounced on anyone who had positive knowledge about the affair and did not deposit it in court. The carefully written record of four pages is fittingly headed by the superscription: "In the name of Him Who knows the secrets" (cf. Psalms 44:22).[22]

The grotesque story of a Jewish girl and a Christian doctor, who had an affair and were spied on by two Muslim hatmakers, with the matter ending up in Jewish and Muslim courts, is too illuminating to be withheld from the reader.[23]

This is a leaf from an old court record, much effaced and stained and with its lower part, that is, end of page one and beginning of page two, torn away. The main story comes out quite clearly from the part preserved, but its continuation on page two, where a second woman and a defendant called Saʿdān make their appearance, is too fragmentary for reconstruction.

There also appeared in court R. Amram b. Saʿīd b. Mūsā, who reported that he was working in the store of Abu ʾl-Faraj Ibn Maʿmar al-Sharābī, and that a physician named Abū Ghālib used to write out prescriptions in the office of the aforementioned Abu ʾl-Faraj. Then the aforementioned R. Amram b. Saʿīd stated that he frequently observed a woman sitting together with this medical practitioner Abū Ghālib, and that he believed she was a Muslim because he saw her so often. Afterward, however, he learned that she was Jewish; he inquired about her and was told that she was the daughter of Ibn al-Māshiṭa (the Son of the Bride-comber). Some Muslims became excited about this and watched her and suspected her of having an affair with the aforementioned Christian medical practitioner. This went on for about forty days, more or less.

Finally, the woman came to the physician one day and said: "I want you to ride with me to a patient." She remained with him until he had finished his work; then he rode with her, and the two went off together. However, two Muslim men, hat makers, of that group which suspected them, one of whom is known as Sayyid Nāṣir and the other as Abu ʾl-Dīk . . . [. . .] to a place known as. . . .

[Overleaf]

. . . the superintendent of that compound. However, when one of the two women saw the police, *rājil*, coming, she became frightened and turned to me saying: "Oh cousin, don't let us down, we are Jews." This Saʿdān was present and stated that all this was claimed against him in court, but that no claim against him had been established.

[In Arabic script]

I witnessed this and signed, ʿAllān b. Nahum [with his signature and date]

I witnessed this and signed, Ibrahīm b. Yūsuf b. Nathan [with his signature and date]

I witnessed this and signed, ʿAllān b. Ibrah[īm] [with his signature and date].

Comments

As we learn from a long document from the year 1065/6, the store of Ibn Maʿmar al-Sharābī (seller of medical potions, soft drinks, and wines), the scene of the action in the court record, must have been rather roomy, for it served also as a kind of warehouse, where goods and money sent from abroad could be deposited by a court.[24] Thus, the doctor and his girl could enjoy a certain degree of privacy. The calligraphic script points to the middle (or even early) eleventh century. A document from around 1039 describes indeed the mores of Egyptian Jewry as needing some reform.[25] R. Amram, the witness, took her for a Muslim, because it did not occur to him that a Jewish woman could behave in such a way, especially in a much frequented Jewish place. The father of the girl probably acquired his name from his mother, the bride-comber, in catering weddings.[26] The girl was therefore of a modest family, but one well-known around town—another aggravating circumstance.

The doctor is first called *ṭabīb*, physician, but later defined (twice) as *mutaṭabbib*, medical practitioner. In that early period, the differentiation between the two terms was perhaps still felt. Later the two terms were used interchangeably.[27] As his high standing required, the doctor probably moved around the city on a mule. This time, the girl, too, arrived mounted, probably on a donkey, disclosing her desire to go away with him to a more remote place and for a prolonged period. The two Muslim hat makers[28] were members of a group feeling themselves called upon "to order people to do what is proper and to restrain them from what is improper" (Qurʾān 3:104, and *passim*), that is, to expose other persons' misdeeds. It is appropriate, however, to pay attention to the times. If it was felt in the Jewish community that some stricter discipline was needed, probably a similar sentiment prevailed in Muslim circles, especially in those of the common people who were religious.[29]

Thus far I have not found a single reference to Lesbian practices in the Geniza, and do not expect to find one.[30] They did exist, however, in the society described in this book, for R. Nissīm b. Jacob of Qayrawān, Tunisia (d. 1062), dedicated an extensive responsum to the subject, and Moses Maimonides had to deal with it in his Code, which was concluded in Egypt during the last quarter of the twelfth century. Although disapproving of them, Maimonides states that no formal punishment was foreseen by the law for these practices, but women known for such indulgence should not be admitted to one's house, nor should the female members of one's own household be permitted to visit persons of such repute. From the very wording of Maimonides' ruling one understands that such matters did not remain a secret. Who knows, in some circles there might even have been some boasting about them.[31]

Before moving on to the male side some general observations

on the wider ambiance to which the Geniza people were exposed are in order. Poetry played a central role in medieval Arabic culture and one of its dominant themes was that of physical love. This motif, however, had been refined and romanticized long before the advent of Islam. With Islam further spiritualization occurred: enslavement to one's beloved was an exercise in becoming inured to the service of God and even to mystical union with him.[32]

How did all this affect the Jewish community, which had no such tradition, where the sages led endless discussions about "the laws of purity," "forbidden relations," and cognate themes, but where sex as such, let alone romantic love, were not objects for educated conversation or deeper thought? In Spain, from the eleventh century on, an unusual response to the values of Arab culture had taken place: a sublime religious poetry colored by the Arab model came into being, which, however, carefully avoided the blurring of the border between the Creator and the created. Their secular poetry, artfully using the imagery of the Hebrew Bible (as was done in Christian medieval poetry) certainly gave much satisfaction to a changed society.

That change did not occur in the more conservative communities of the East. Thoughts about sex and love were, so to speak, kept away from the people, who had to be protected from them. They were a nuisance, unavoidable, a blessing only in wedlock and there, too, only with the moderation imposed by religion. One could not be an educated person in an Arab ambiance, however, without knowing poetry, and poetry was a vehicle of love. A government official, a physician, a merchant of high standing could not escape from the style of life of an environment with which they had daily contacts. For these people Saadya Gaon (d. 942), the most authoritative interpreter of Judaism in the tenth and eleventh centuries, wrote the tenth chapter of his *Beliefs and Opinions*, in which he examined thirteen leading values of the world in which his educated readers lived. I am summarizing here his chapter on romantic love, because without having an inkling of the ideas prevailing in the circles of those influential Jews who did not leave us their writings in the Geniza, the Geniza world itself cannot be fully understood.

Saadya Gaon on romantic love[33]

Romantic love, *ʿishq* [which had as its essential object physical love of women (other than one's wife) and infatuation with a handsome youth], should really not be mentioned in a book at all. [But just as he had dealt with unbelievers in his book with the intention of protecting the soul from their errors, he does the same with this evil.]

People opine that love is the most noble thing with which a person can occupy himself. It refines the spirit and softens the temperaments until the soul becomes sensitive to an extreme. It begins with looks, continues with desire, and ends up with being conquered. They go even higher, ascribing it to the influence of the stars: when the nativities of the stars under which the two are born are in favorable conjunction, love and intimacy result. They move another step higher and ascribe love to the Creator's own doing: he creates the spirit in the form of spheres, cutting them into two halves, and putting one half into one human being and the second into another, wherefore each part seeks the other. They end up by making love a religious duty, meaning that the self-humiliation before the beloved teaches the lover to humiliate himself before God.

Besides a love poetry of enormous dimensions, the Arabs possessed a good deal of theoretical writings about love. Despite its crudeness and offensive simplicity, Saadya's survey provides a fairly correct idea of the main points usually made. He refutes them in the reverse order. As to the idea that illicit love might be a way to God, it is unthinkable that God should expose men to things that he himself has prohibited. As to that cutting of the "spheres" into two halves, Saadya had already proved in a preceding section of his book that the spirit of an individual is formed together with his body, wherefore no preexistence of souls can be assumed.[34] The predestination of love by the conjunction of the stars would require that when A loves B, B must love A, which is disproved by daily experience. Finally, the eyes and the hearts (read: desire) are dubious guides. "Do not go astray by following your eyes and your heart" (Numbers 15:39); better: "My son, give me your heart and let your eyes observe my ways" (Proverbs 23:26).

There follows a long section describing the dangers and sufferings brought about by romantic passion, all motifs common in Arabic poetry but illustrated here by a profusion of Bible quotations. The end is usually bitter disappointment, especially when consummation is achieved. The biblical story of Amnon and Tamar (see p. 272, above) is the warning example.

The chapter concludes: "This thing is good for husband and wife. He should enjoy her company and she his.[35] The two together 'build the world.' His passion should be spent on her with reason, in observing the religious injunctions, and in a measure preserving their mutual fondness. Anything beyond this must be avoided with all might."

Although this diatribe is directed mainly, if not exclusively, against the "looking at the beardless youth" (to use a Muslim expression), no overt reference to homosexuality is made. Despite the numerous Bible quotations, the death penalty on pederasty is not mentioned. They detested those practices so much that they tried to kill them by silence. No doubt, denunciations and complaints in these matters must have reached the courts, as they have concerning suspicions on female chastity, but none has come to my knowledge. In reality, the Geniza is not without sidelights on the subject, some quite unexpected ones.

The diffusion of a practice is best attested by the endeavors of authorities to suppress it. The Geniza has preserved the statutes of Dammūh, a Jewish holy shrine southwest of Fustat, known also from Muslim sources. The visit to it in springtime had the character of an outing as much as that of a pilgrimage. Among the many things prohibited during the visit, the attendance by unaccompanied boys, or by a man accompanied by a boy who was not a close relative, is specifically noted.[36]

Even more telling is the story of an actual pilgrimage, this time to Jerusalem. Script, spelling, and style identify the writer as a man of very little education. He starts out by assuring the recipient that there had never been more beautiful holidays than those experienced on that pilgrimage. On their way to the Holy City, the pilgrims, who traveled in groups, passed the Day of Atonement, a day of fasting and prayer, in Ramle, at that time the administrative capital of Palestine. During the service, a man from Tyre, Lebanon, and one from Tiberias, Palestine, became enamored of each other, and the one from Tiberias made overtures to the one from Tyre in full presence of the assembled. A fistfight between the pilgrims from Tyre and those from Tiberias ensued, whereupon a local notable called in the police, who remained in the synagogue until the end of the service. The writer does not censure the lovers or the fistfight.[37]

The Geniza has provided us with a Hebrew *maqāma*, a rhymed short story which recalls the episode of the Qur'ān teacher in the novel of Rachid Boujedra mentioned earlier. This particular *maqāma* is so extremely sarcastic that I assume it to be an imitation of an Arabic original, and I shall be grateful to my learned colleagues for helping me to find it. A cantor became enamored of a boy.[38] In order to win his favors, he sold all the learned books he possessed and gave the money to the boy, but the latter did not return his favors. Then, one by one, the love-mad cantor sold the weekly lections of the Five Books of Moses—there are fifty-two of them (reminiscent of the sixty *ḥizb*, or parts, of the Qur'ān). Finally, he even disposed of his prayer mantle, but the boy did not budge. In the face of this calamity, the cantor filed suit against him before the rabbinical court and the elders of the community: "I have made a deal with this boy, I have done my part, I have given him all I have; but he has not fulfilled his obligation; please let me have the well-deserved satisfaction." The comedy ends with the discovery that the cantor was not really a Jew but a sham convert who had come from far off in the West, where he had been notorious for similar escapades. I am not convinced that the unexpected twist at the end was a part of the original story.[39]

It seems that a section of the Jewish intelligentsia, especially in Spain, had accepted the cult of the ephebes, or beautiful boys, as an essential ingredient of the high civilization to which they then belonged. There exist medieval Hebrew poems, some found also in the Geniza, which are dedicated to this topic.[40] It has always been contended that those poems were literary exercises composed to prove that the Hebrew language was able to express everything. This assumption no doubt is partly true, but J. Schirmann has shown that it is not the whole truth. One must keep in mind that in the Muslim Near East the *amrad*, "beardless youth," who often served as a cupbearer in drinking rallies, was by no means always an object of sexual attention. Youthful beauty was regarded as a symbol of the eternally young and beautiful, of God. The end of the quotation from Saadya Gaon's chapter on romantic love (translated above, p. 318) proves that the Jewish thinker was well acquainted with such and similar ideas of Muslim mystics.[41]

Even the Holy Language (as Hebrew was called by Jews and some others) was used to glorify male homosexuality. I wish to illustrate this by two strophes of a tenth-century Hebrew poem—also from the Geniza—written in southern Italy, a region exposed at that time to both Islamic and Byzantine influences:

> Behold, ships, behold, ships coming into the port.
> Go and see what merchandise they bring.
> Beautiful girls.
> Go and see what they were sold for.
> For a barrel of straw.
> Ah, captain, you have been paid too much.
>
> Behold, ships, behold ships, coming into the port.
> Go and see what merchandise they bring.
> Handsome boys, finer than gold.
> Go and see what they were sold for.
> For a barrel of gold and gems.
> Ah, captain, you have been paid too little.[42]

Even if this was only an exercise in translation, one wonders for which type of audience such verses were intended.

The natural outlet for extramarital relations was concubinage with a slave girl, which, in Islam was perfectly legal. The Christian and Jewish minorities had some difficulty in keeping this disturbance of family life away from their communities. For to choose a female according to one's own taste and to have complete disposition of her could be preferable to a wife selected for the future husband by others, a wife, who, on top of this, was constantly watched and protected by her family. Yet, there were circumstances that called for restraint. First of all, the cost. A simple maidservant could be had for about 20 gold pieces (a sum almost sufficient for the sustenance of a modest family for a year). An attractive slave girl could cost four or more times as much, and if she was a trained musician, even far more.[43] Since three quarters of the Jewish male population were unable to produce 20 dinars in cash as the first installment of the obligatory marriage gift, only a small minority could have been in a position to acquire a satisfactory concubine.[44]

Moreover, if the girl was, or claimed to be, a Muslim, her non-Muslim master could be fined or suffer more severe punishment. Finally, whenever the Jewish (and probably also the Christian) authorities were strong enough, they forced the possessor of a concubine to sell her, a painful experience, both sentimentally and materially, especially when, as an act of atonement, the price was to be distributed among the poor.[45]

We do not know, of course, what was going on in the opulent Jewish high class that had its domiciles in the new capital Cairo and did not leave us any writings in the Geniza of Fustat. They had to be treated with utmost consideration by the Jewish authorities, especially with regard to their private lives. Here is a short passage from a very long letter from Daniel b. Azarya, the nāsī and Gaon of Jerusalem, to his friend and main supporter in Egypt, Abraham Ibn al-Furāt: "I wish for you—*may our King* [*God*] *strengthen you*—that you take care of yourself with regard to that matter which we have repeatedly discussed. Do not neglect it, but act in it in a way for which you hopefully will be able to praise yourself, while leaving it might be regarded as a bad omen. *May God give you success in doing his will.*" This sounds as if the Gaon had advised his illustrious friend to get rid of some illicit relationship.[46]

We have already read about Daniel b. Azarya's holy war against slave girls serving as concubines, instrumental music, and other matters disapproved by religion, when he first visited Egypt in or around 1039.[47] Isolated complaints about concubinage reached the courts down through the centuries. Of particular interest is the case of an Indian slave girl who had borne a son to her master but who was allegedly abandoned by him, together with the baby, in an African seaport on his way home. When, at arrival in another port, the matter came to the knowledge of his Jewish traveling companions, they strongly disapproved of his action and drew up the record that we still have. Clearly, not only the wife but the concubine, too, had certain rights that had to be honored.[48] In general, for the reasons specified above, slave girl concubinage was a phenomenon of limited dimensions and importance in Geniza society.

References to prostitution are extremely rare. We have some sporadic and not unequivocal notes concerning the seaports of Acre, Palestine, Alexandria, Egypt, and Aden, South Arabia, perhaps also Cairo; for Fustat I know only of one case, where, however, the word "prostitute" seems to be used in a general pejorative sense. A member of the highly respected Ibn Sighmār family was suspected of having an affair with a Muslim woman; he had already paid a fine of 120 gold pieces, an enormous sum, and had already been imprisoned for a month and a half at the writing of the letter reporting the scandal to someone in Qūṣ, Upper Egypt; twelve court records had been written in this matter. Clearly the female concerned was not a regular prostitute, but one of those independent women familiar from the amorous stories of *The Arabian Nights.* We are here in the 1030s, a period notorious for the loosening of communal discipline.[49]

The world of the learned and religious merchants, which provides the bulk of the Geniza correspondence, presents a different problem. Those merchants were engaged in the Mediterranean, partly also in the India, trade, and were regularly absent from home for months, a year, or more. I do not recall in this vast corpus of writings a single reference or allusion to concubinage with a slave girl or to a visit to a place of ill repute, let alone to the infidelity of a married woman. I have often asked myself what these people did about sex, especially during those long periods of separation from their wives. Was friendship with persons of the same sex the answer? No. It was true that formal friendship was a strong socioeconomic power in the middle class society of those days. In those circles of learned religious merchants it was not a relationship for the satisfaction of bodily desires.

Practicing abstinence while away from home should not appear so strange considering the socioeconomic and spiritual conditions in which those men found themselves. Life was hard; it was difficult to make a dirhem; travel was fraught with hardship and danger.

The eating habits were unimaginably frugal, and where there is no Ceres there is no Venus. Furthermore, the rhythm of life was punctuated by the obligatory daily prayers, and for those educated merchants, by regular readings from the Holy Scriptures and the sacred Law. In other words, the little time left free from business was constantly occupied by religious activities normally pursued in company. Finally, communal life and strife were very intensive and consumed much of the attention and energy of the middle class people, both at home and while traveling.

Maimonides includes the sex laws (not those of marriage) in his Book of Holiness, one of the fourteen volumes of his Code. This was in conformity with the Talmudic interpretation of Leviticus 19:1: "You shall be holy, for I, the Lord, your God, am holy," which was understood as referring to sexual behavior.[50] Encouraging sexual relations on the Sabbath, the holy day of the week—in contrast with the Karaites, as explained at the opening of this subsection—manifests an attitude that accepts the human being as a harmonious aggregate of natural and supernatural inclinations.[51]

C. THE TRUE BELIEVER

1. *Trust in the Merciful*

Our universe is the physical world, which we try to dominate so as to make our life as pleasurable, meaningful, and extended as feasible. The people who left us their writings in the Geniza (and probably also their Muslim and Christian contemporaries) pursued similar goals: they wanted a decent livelihood, a happy family, and a secure and friendly ambiance. But the reality they had to face was different: it was God, who directed a fickle and often indomitable nature, a heterogeneous and frequently hostile human environment; and man, who knew much about his Creator but little about himself, and was often prone to go astray. Accommodation with God was the problem. His kingdom represented the physical, moral, and political world order.

This does not mean that those people were always aware of God's presence, although they certainly bore his name constantly on their lips in accordance with the habits of speech common in those parts and times.[1] But, just as we often live in a thoughtless fashion wasting our resources and forsaking our principles, so, in Geniza times, many were "forgetful of God" (Psalms 50:22, Job 8:13), either temporarily or in a sinful way of life. There were, however, many agents that reminded them of God's power: critical situations, unbearable sufferings, the ambiance (family, friends, communal and other authorities) and, not least, the inner voice: "The burglar, while breaking into a house, calls on God to assist him."[2]

God was not conceived as a stern father figure. The invocation "Our Father in Heaven," familiar from Talmud and Midrash (and, of course, to every Christian from the paternoster) is extremely rare in the Geniza, and, where it occurs, has the flare of a quotation.[3] God's main characteristic was his mercifulness. In the Talmud, the name of God is Raḥmāna, the Merciful, an appellation based on biblical precedence. God introduces himself as such to Moses after the disaster of the Golden Calf in the theophany in which, according to Exodus 34:5–7, his thirteen attributes are all expressions of compassion and forgiveness.[4] God's "power" and "great name" manifest themselves in overcoming his wrath and showing mercy, as Moses reminds him on another occasion: "I pray you, let the power of the Lord be great, as you have said: the Lord is slow in anger and abounding in love, forgiving sin and transgression . . . pardon the sin of this people . . ." (Numbers 14:17–19). These thirteen attributes of mercy are endlessly repeated in the Jewish penitential liturgy, because the efficacy of their recitation was promised by the sages of the Talmud;[5] the Christian knows his *kyrie eleison* ("Lord, have mercy"), and the Muslim begins every prayer, document, or other undertaking with the *basmalah*, "In the Name of God, the Merciful, the Compassionate."[6] God's emotions are compared with that of a mother: "Can a woman forget her babe, or not be compassionate to the child of her womb. Though she might forget, I shall never forget you" (Isaiah 49:15). The verse "as a mother comforts her son, so I will comfort you" (*ibid.* 66:13) is rarely absent from a Geniza letter expressing sympathy.

Now, since "God is good to all and his mercy is upon all his creations" (Psalms 145:9),[7] the eternal question, Why is life so cruel, why do innocent people suffer so much, presents itself to each generation anew. Some of the Jewish theologians of the Geniza period, like their colleagues of other monotheistic faiths, tried to tackle various aspects of this problem, such as God as "first cause," his prescience, his justice. The rank and file of the Geniza people, including the learned merchants, who frequently had to report about disasters befalling others or themselves, rarely pondered these problems. For them the law provided, if not an answer, at least a way of conduct in such situations: "One is held to bless God for bad things in the same way as for good ones" (Mishna, Berakhot 9:5); "in the same way," that is, wholeheartedly, as it is written: "You must love your God with all your heart, and all your soul, and all your might" (Deuteronomy 6:5). While hearing or reporting good news, one says: "Blessed be the Good One who dispenses goodness" (based on Psalms 119:68); bad news, "one thanks God," according to Saadya Gaon's formula, by saying: "Blessed be the True Judge." These two benedictions pervade the Geniza correspondence, and, since Saadya's prayer book was accepted during most of that period, "I thanked God" meant I pronounced the blessing upon the True Judge, while experiencing, or learning about, misfortune.[8]

The basis for this salutary discipline imposed on human behavior in adversity was the teaching that "all that the Merciful does, he does for the good,"[9] even if it appears to be the opposite, for, as a Geniza letter explains: "God does with his servant what is good for him, although he may not be aware of it."[10] Another, even more frequent corroboration of God's goodness is the inconstancy of human life: "It is inevitable that some relief, some sign of the Creator's mercy, comes; nothing remains constant, neither hardship nor anything else."[11] Hence the conclusion of any report about misfortune and even extreme sufferings: "God will turn the end to the good."[12] The superscription of countless letters "In your name, O Merciful" (appearing in many different forms) should be understood not as an imitation of the Muslim basmalah but as an abbreviation of the ancient "In your name 'Merciful' we trust," meaning we are confident that you will live up to your name (still found in this form in a Geniza letter from Yemen).[13]

Even a reader who possesses only the slightest acquaintance with the Hebrew Bible is aware of the fact that the concept of God as the embodiment of compassion and forgiveness is only one of the images in which he was conceived in ancient Israel. The more remarkable is it that in postbiblical times this idea became so central that "the Merciful" was adopted as the very name of God. Before trying to find an explanation for this change, a look at other prominent attributes of God prevailing in the Bible and still of significance, although qualified, in the Geniza period, is imperative.

For the ancient Israelites, who had to fight so many wars, God was above all "a man of war" (Exodus 15:3); his most holy name was "The Lord of Hosts," who led the armies into battle (Psalms 24:8–10); even Isaiah calls him thus in the theophany granted to him, although it was envisioned as taking place in the heavenly sanctuary (Isaiah 6:3).[14] At the time of the Geniza, it was many hundreds of years since the Jews, like most other peoples of the Near East, had borne arms. A warlike God was no longer a reality.

There was, however, another closely connected concept that was very much alive: "the great, mighty, awe-inspiring God" (Deuteronomy 10:17), an epithet to be repeated three times a day in the first benediction of the obligatory (both communal and private) prayer. Any extraordinary experience, such as glimpsing the Great Sea, high mountains, or a terrible rainstorm, had to be acknowledged with a blessing of the God "whose power and might filled the world."[15] A frightening natural event was seen as a manifestation of God's wrath. The description of the devastating earthquake of Ramle, Palestine, in 1033 by the Gaon Solomon b. Judah (pp. 63 ff., above) clearly shows that, despite the horrors experienced, the writer felt privileged to have been worthy of witnessing "the mighty acts of the living God."

The awe-inspiring presence of the Creator fulfilled a disciplinary role. "As a man castigates his son, thus I castigate you" (Deuteronomy 8:5). It is true that the attribute of God as fatherly disciplinarian is hardly mentioned in the Geniza, but the problem of suffering as a test and, even more, as punishment is very much in evidence.

One has the feeling, however, that those ubiquitous phrases "because of our sins," pronounced, for instance, in a report on the horrid bloodbath by the fanatic Almohads, and "the sin has caused this," stated in connection with personal losses, are to be understood as traditional acknowledgments and justifications of God's decrees. No compunction or need for personal atonement seems to have been expected. Even when the Gaon Solomon b. Judah, on the occasion of the Ramle earthquake, declared a public fast accompanied by a communal confession, he added: "What else could I do?" meaning: besides this routine response.[16]

When people express the hope, also common, that the misfortune suffered might contribute to the expiation of their sins (in this world and the World to Come), they seem to be more in earnest. This should not be understood as a confession of specific sins committed. "No one on earth is righteous, who does only what is good and does not sin" (Ecclesiastes 7:20). There is no particular shame in the assumption of having committed a sin. Hoping for God's forgiveness is a sign of piety and includes the expectation of being spared further troubles.

For thinking people, accepting and submitting to God's judgment was not an easy matter. The pious Persian Isaac Nīsabūrī of Alexandria, after suffering extraordinary losses by shipwreck (320 dinars!), and reporting even more terrifying news about the fate of the passengers, says approximately this: "God filled my heart and the hearts of other merchants with hope so that we would buy much to send overseas, and our losses would be excessive; but his judgment is accepted, and the end will be to the good." God appears here in a role not much different from that of the biblical Satan. But God, who was felt near, almost like a member of the household, was preferable to any dark force that by its very nature was inimical.[17] Nīsabūrī's often mentioned contemporary and compatriot Yeshūʿā b. Ismaʿīl (Samuel) reports to Nahray b. Nissīm about two disasters happening to him. The first is justified by the common: "What has caused this? the sin"; the second is introduced thus: "God has ordained what he willed and *what he knew in advance*; everything was lost; not a thing was saved. I can only say: 'blessed be he in whose decrees there is no injustice.'"[18] A third personality, who sojourned in Alexandria approximately at the time of the writing of these two letters, complains about his fate, in a way even stranger than they: "I am in immediate danger and my future is in jeopardy. I have not acquired a portion in the World to Come, or a good reputation here, or material gains." "*Had God guided me*, when I first arrived among them, my religion and my honor would have remained untainted." The writer of this letter was Abraham, the son of the late Nathan, President of the High Court of Jerusalem, and himself, at the end of his life, Jewish chief judge in Cairo.[19]

What these three men (who might have met in Alexandria near the end of the eleventh century) had to say about God's inscrutable ways—knowing in advance that an undertaking would fail, putting wrong advice into a man's mind, or withholding his guidance from him altogether—was probably the utmost that persons of rabbinic, but not philosophical, erudition would dare to put on paper about the subject. They would hardly have accepted the expedient constructed by the philosopher Gersonides (Levi b. Gerson, d. 1344) that God ordains and knows only the general nature of things, the choices before man, leaving it to his free will to make a personal decision. Those men of the eleventh century were perplexed but not desperate. The commandment to praise God for misfortune in the same way as for good things, strictly and continuously observed in the Geniza correspondence (they had much opportunity to do so), instructed man how to behave in adversity and turned his mind to hope for the better.

Pronouncing the traditional benediction for a bounty received was not enough; a person had to emphasize that this was not a reward deserved but an overflow of God's grace. In this respect, too, they were very consistent. When a notable from Sfax, southern Tunisia, which was at war with the ruler of al-Mahdiyya, was captured by the Sultan's mariners, chained, five times handed over to the executioner, and finally released, he naturally became effusive: "God blessed me with his pardon [in Arabic], not because I had any merits or good deeds [in Aramaic]."[20] And when one of the foreign merchants visiting Aden, South Arabia, was spared, together with the other foreigners, the forced conversion to Islam, to which the local Jews had been (temporarily) exposed, wrote: "God the exalted wrought a miracle with us and saved us *not because of our might and power* [meaning merit (Deuteronomy 18:17–18)], but by his grace and bounty."[21] But one wrote such declarations also after an eventful, but by no means particularly dangerous, voyage, an illness, or other troubles.[22] In order to remind the believer never to ascribe to himself any merit, a special benediction (repeatedly cited in the Geniza) was instituted: "Blessed be he who bestows bounties on sinners, who favored me with his bounties," to be said after return from travel, recovery from illness, or release from prison.[23]

Trust in the Merciful should be expressed by the constant awareness of his watchful presence. The simple statement, "I am well and prosperous," in a letter from Damascus is followed by the qualification, "but God alone decrees."[24] David Maimonides' cocksure assertion, "I am confident that this letter will reach you when I, God willing, shall have already made most of the way," is mitigated by the addition "*but the counsel of God alone will stand*" (Proverbs 19:21). It did. David perished during his passage to India.[25] Writing in the night after the Day of Atonement, a man from al-Mahdiyya, Tunisia, informs his correspondent: "God willing, I am planning to leave between the two holidays [i.e., about a week later], provided God grants me life so long." For prolonged travel one had to be in good health. Still, the writer was not sure it would last a week unless decreed thus by Heaven.[26] When a court clerk sat down with his wife to note what he had to bring home from the market for a forthcoming holiday, he superscribed his list thus: "Expenditure for the Pentecost—if I live so long with the help of the Almighty." The chickens included in the list certainly did not remain alive in the house for more than a few hours.[27]

In short, the Geniza person must have had a strong feeling that the Merciful was looking over his shoulder, and formulated his writings accordingly. This was particularly de rigueur in applications for help and in letters of thanks. One should always apply first "to the gate of God" before asking for human assistance, and praise him for inspiring the benefactor to act as he did. These ideas are expressed in endlessly different ways, sometimes quite awkward ones, for instance: "There is only one on whom I rely, God the exalted and you, may God keep you and protect me."[28] Or when a son acknowledges the receipt of a shipment sent by his father: "I received from God and from you a robe and a turban," to which, however, he proudly adds: "And paid the dinar for the poll tax with the money earned by my own work."[29]

We should not assume, however, that the Geniza people were entirely prisoners of their pious formulas. When they had an intense feeling of their powerlessness in the face of God, they showed it. "No one has control of his own self," complains a son to his mother, after a well-planned journey proved to be useless.[30] Another who suffered greater misfortunes, writes this: "No one can evade the decrees of the Lord of the Worlds, as the Saint [Jeremiah 10:23] has said 'I know, O God, that man's road is not his to choose;' there is no escape from his judgment, and there is no one to whom one may complain except him."[31] In cases of death or communal disasters such thoughts were commonplace.

A way to give vent to one's feelings of powerlessness was to accuse insidious Time or Fate, or one's own weak star or an unlucky constellation (Heb. *mazzāl*). The Wheel of Fortune was an idea not unknown in the Talmud,[32] and the belief in the dependence of human life on the movements of the celestial bodies was, of course, widely accepted in Late Antiquity. True, the most prominent Jewish sages of the third century, R. Johanan in Palestine and Samuel in Babylonia (himself an astronomer), ruled that Israel was not under the rule of the stars. Has not the prophet Jeremiah (10:2) taught: "Do not learn the ways of the gentiles, nor be dismayed by the portents of the sky, because the nations are dismayed by them."[33] An eleventh-century Hebrew poet living in Italy dedicated an impressive penitential poem to the contrast between the trust in God and the fear of the portents of the sky; and Moses Maimonides, well versed in astronomy, strongly condemned astrology as a pseudoscience.[34]

Yet, at the peak of the classical Geniza period, the respect for the sciences of the ancients, including astrology, was predominant, so that the phrases borrowed from it had become household words. The images of perfidious Time and treacherous Fate, which permeated Arabic poetry and daily speech, were likewise commonplace in the Geniza correspondence. Each and every turn in the Hebrew passage written by the learned Nathan b. Samuel (translated above, p. 294 and n. 109) may be paralleled by a quotation from Arabic poetry. While composing these pompous lines, it certainly did not occur to Nathan that the role allotted by him to Time infringed somewhat on the concept of God's omnipotence; nor is such an inconsistency felt when God and Time are mentioned together, as in this letter for help.

"God had granted him well-being, distinction, and high rank. Then he was overwhelmed by the calamities of Time, its disasters and arrows."[35] Time is brought in when something unexpected, sudden, or particularly cruel happened: "I fought Time until I was overcome by it; my wife and children died of hunger [not, it is hoped, to be taken too literally], when I had to go into hiding because of the poll tax."[36] When a friend causes losses, one exculpates him by saying: "My ill luck and Star are guilty; no blame befalls you."[37] In a short but eloquent Hebrew letter, the writer says that he is attacked by Time, which roars like a lion and by the weight of which he is oppressed.[38] Time ensnares man in its net and, in general, betrays him.[39]

Despite such picturesque language, Time and the celestial configurations should not be understood as independent demonic powers. A most common wish following the name of the addressee was "may God make your Star strong [Aram.]" or, "high [Heb.]."[40] These ancient phrases with astrological connotation had the advantage that the name of God did not have to be mentioned too often on both joyous and sad occasions. Marriage contracts were invariably superscribed with wishes for a good omen, an excellent augury, a propitious hour, or a friendly mazzāl, and not with the name of God. In documents, which often were subject to litigations, the name of God was avoided, but one did not hesitate to use expressions of astrological or magical origin, since these powers, like all others, were directed by their Creator. With reference to the superscriptions of marriage contracts one would wish at a wedding: "May God make it the most auspicious hour," and the common Arabic byname Abū Saʿd, "the Man with the Auspicious Star," was converted into a new, even more widespread Hebrew name: Saadya (not found in the Bible or the Talmud), composed of the words *saʿd*, good luck, and *Ya*, God.[41]

In popular belief, it must be conceded, these phrases about the stars and fate certainly fulfilled an important function: when misfortune struck, they freed the thus afflicted from the pangs of conscience that his sins might have brought about heavenly punishment. Rāvā, an eminent Babylonian sage of the fourth century, makes the astounding statement: "[The length of] life, [success with] children, and livelihood depend not on one's merit but on one's Star," no doubt one of those popular sayings, which he loved to quote.[42] This maxim, which is in flagrant contradiction to biblical and postbiblical teachings, was not recognized as valid, but many a Geniza person would have accepted it without much ado. Even Ezekiel, the younger brother of the India trader Ḥalfōn b. Nethanel, writes: "No one can reach beyond the limits set to his livelihood."[43] Total loss (confiscation by government of his shipwrecked goods in a foreign country) is ascribed by the writer to his weak star.[44] The notion of the preordained span of life has been discussed above.[45]

The state of powerlessness, in which the Geniza person often found himself, nourished a feeling of insecurity, which was counterbalanced by trust in the Merciful (for those who trusted). In hours of difficult decisions one would write not "I asked myself" but "I consulted my Creator." The phrase is Talmudic and quoted in the Geniza.[46] But asking God for guidance or, as one says in Arabic, *istikhāra*, literally, "asking him for the best choice," is a common Islamic idea. The term occurs throughout the Geniza correspondence, especially of the eleventh century.[47] Communications about a commercial transaction, the formulation of a partnership, or the dispatch of a valuable shipment are introduced by this term. One gets the impression, however, that it was used in the Geniza selectively, especially in cases of new or hazardous ventures, or when the recipient of the letter would not have expected such a decision.[48] An istikhāra is almost obligatory before undertaking a major voyage. When a branch of the Tustarī family hesitated to emigrate from southern Iran to Egypt, they "looked into the Scriptures" and found that God's choice was revealed to them by Genesis 46:3: "Do not be afraid of going down to Egypt, for I shall make you there into a great people."[49] However guidance was found, whether by use of the Bible, by semimagical procedures of divination, or simply by earnest prayer until certainty was obtained, the idea behind it all was that man cannot be sure about what is good for him, but the Merciful knows and is ready to guide.[50]

The idea of the God of mercy, so richly developed in the life-affirming religion of an oppressed people like the Jews, had widespread appeal in Late Antiquity, when much of the ancient world's population had been reduced to a *misera contribuens plebs*, which had not much to hope for, except mercy. The idea retained its central place in Islam, despite becoming a religion of highly successful conquerors, perhaps because the insecurity of life was felt intensely also (or particularly) by the classes in power.[51] The Geniza society, firmly implanted in the Jewish tradition, was enriched by the religiosity found within the Muslim environment, but was also affected by its social notions as well as by a rationalistic atmosphere in which the sciences of the ancients were honored. I think that the Geniza person left more to the grace of God than was accepted in classical Judaism, where much emphasis was placed on the "works" (the fulfillment of the commandments) and their merits. One is reminded also of the image of the Muslim ruler, for "the kingdom of earth is similar to the Kingdom of Heaven [and vice versa]."[52] The remunerations received by subjects and officials for services rendered to the sovereign are frequently depicted by the earlier Muslim biographers and historians as gifts by him and acts of bounty. Similarly, the good things one enjoys in life appear in the Geniza as manifestations of God's largesse rather than rewards for worthiness and merit. The fatalism of pre-Islamic Arabs, partly inherited by Islam and corroborated by the scientific teachings on the dependence of human destiny on the stars, enhanced the feelings of powerlessness and insecurity.

These negative tendencies, however, were counterbalanced, and the confidence in the Merciful was underpinned, by a remarkably widespread awareness of the presence of God, fostered by membership in the holy community, to which a person belonged.

2. *Close to God*

"Where are you and where is God?!" meaning, look how far away you are from God, you, his servant, who should always be in attendance, heeding his commandments. This outcry concludes a note by a Jewish judge, which was in essence a summons to court but in form and tone a fatherly admonition. The young man addressed actually ran away not from God but from his wife. Nevertheless, neglecting one's duties toward his fellow creatures, especially those committed to his care, meant being forgetful of one's Creator.[1]

Similarly, the admonition "do in this matter what will bring you near God" ("if God will" [sometimes added]) is frequently used, for instance, when the addressee is asked to exert himself for the benefit of an innocent or needy person.[2] Nearness to God meant basically being chosen to be one of his close attendants, as the Jewish holiday prayer has it. "You, our king, let us come near to serve you." For the select few this would encompass the numinous sense of enjoying God's presence, as expressed in the concluding verses of Psalm 73:

> I am always with you,
> You hold my right hand.

You are guiding me with your counsel.
Whom else do I have in heaven?
And having you, I want no one on earth.
Those who keep far from you perish.
As for me, nearness to God is [the] good.[3]

In general, a person's religiosity was the measure of his reliability and probity in his relations with his fellowmen. This idea was expressed in a wide variety of ways. "Your brother, the elder Abu ʾl-Ḥasan is in excellent standing with God and men, which is a gift of God's bounty," reports a father to his son. A gift, for opinions about other people are not always well-founded, and love of peace for God's sake is often misjudged.[4] "*Being good before God and trusted by men*" was a praise said of a Nagid of the land of Yemen, who had saved the property of a dead India trader for his orphans.[5] The wish "may you find favor and good acceptance in the eyes of God and man" (Proverbs 3:4) is ubiquitous and is mostly said in connection with mundane matters. While forming a partnership the two parties promise to take upon themselves "*faithfulness before Heaven,*"[6] to follow the truth in deed and word, to act with integrity "in accordance with what God has ordered us." This contract between two merchants was written in Fez, Morocco, in January 1138.[7] A partnership agreement between two glassmakers made in Fustat, Egypt, in December 1134, is even more profuse: "Each of the two took upon himself . . . to tell the truth, to be faithful and to act in a praiseworthy way, which will clear him before God, praised be he."[8] Other contracts are more concise, but to be "cleared before God" is a most common condition, mentioned in contracts as well as in letters.[9] In settlements of disputes one would specify that they were granted "wholeheartedly, in this world and for the World to Come, according to the laws of men and the laws of Heaven."[10]

"Religiosity," usually expressed by Persian-Arabic *dīn,*[11] occasionally also by Hebrew *fear of Heaven,* is adduced in Geniza correspondence when moral behavior and business ethics are at stake. When an Alexandrian merchant, before going overseas, instructs his wife concerning a large number of goods some of which are entrusted to various persons, he notes concerning one partner: "Because of his trustworthiness and dīn any claim made by him must be honored."[12] "I believe in your religiosity and nobility," writes an Andalusian from Jerusalem, asking al-Faḍl al-Tustarī politely, but firmly, to make accounts (and to pay his debt).[13]

Religion is invoked mostly when the writer has occasion to be critical of the person concerned. "Such behavior evinces little intelligence and religiosity," writes a merchant, when he had been falsely suspected by a business friend in a matter where the true facts were easily available; unfounded accusations were regarded as a grave sin.[14] The term is used in particular in serious cases. When a man made unfounded claims on an inheritance, it was said of him: "The vileness of his dīn became apparent to everyone."[15] Of the two Jews who had been associated with "the Monk," the rapacious finance minister, who was murdered in 1129, it was deposed in court that "they possessed little dīn."[16] In this sense one would say also in Arabic as in Hebrew: "He does not fear God."[17]

The "religion" referred to in such contexts was not necessarily the Jewish faith in particular. It was a concept of reverence for the heavenly numen representing the ideas of justice and decency. This is evident from such passages as the following. A man, trying to dissuade his sister from marrying her daughter to a certain person from Syria ("as if there were no fine boys in Egypt"), characterizes the foreigner thus: "He is depraved, he is neither a Jew, nor a Christian, nor a Muslim," which takes it for granted that certain basic ideas about morality were common to humanity, or at least to the three monotheistic religions.[18] Even more revealing is this sentence in a letter of a man from Alexandria known to us from another missive of his (summarized in *Med. Soc.*, III, 34 and n. 2) as outspoken and sarcastic: "How do you act with regard to your Lord?! You fast and pray to him; then you make a vow and break it. You do not have the faith of the Jews, nor even that of the Majūs." Majūs was the Aramaic-Arabic name for the adherents of Zoroastrianism, the pre-Islamic religion of Iran. The Zoroastrians had neither "a prophet" recognized by official Islam, like Moses or Jesus, nor "a book," like the Torah or the New Testament, but were accepted by Islamic law as "a protected minority" like the Jews and Christians. Thus they were regarded as a kind of third-class religion. The man addressed in this letter had vowed to maintain his old mother, but did not keep his promise; by the time of the writing the mother had already died. Fasting and praying are mentioned because the writer wished to emphasize that even a most rigorous observance of religious rites cannot atone for the neglect of moral obligations.[19]

It has not escaped the readers of this book that the correspondence of the Geniza people is characterized by the constant awareness of, and even direct appeals to, God. Each and every step in life and every occurrence affecting a person, or his closer or wider environment, are reacted upon or preceded, as the case may be, by remembering God or invoking him directly. Here the question arises: what do all these words mean? Are we here in a situation similar to that decried by the prophet Jeremiah when he complained to his God (12:2): "You are present in their mouth, but far from their heart" (lit., "kidneys")? Or, to remain within the Islamic ambiance, should we concur with a critical observer, who wrote in connection with the pious inscriptions in the Alhambra palace of Granada, Spain: "The routinization in Islamic society of appeals to God seems to have reduced this divine presence to the rather dreary status of a repetitive design on wallpaper"?[20]

The general problem of the use of language in the Geniza writings has been touched upon above in my introductory remarks on the sources (pp. 1–5). Here some additional considerations concerning the sphere of religion must be made.

The Jews, mindful of the third of the Ten Commandments not "to take the Lord's name in vain,"[21] were inclined to mention God's name sparingly, or, at least, to circumscribe it. But when the Geniza people wrote Arabic they used the term "Allāh" almost as profusely and boldly as did their neighbors.[22] A variety of appellations for God appear in the Geniza correspondence, used partly indiscriminately and partly with a special meaning related to the context. A short family letter of fifteen lines contains these phrases: "May the Creator prolong your life, while preserving your honored position forever" (l. 1). "May the Abode,[23] praised be he, turn the end to the good" (l. 3). "May He who grants success to those striving for the good give him and her success" (referring to a young couple, who were about to marry [ll. 4–5]). "May *the Keeper of Israel keep him*" (a scholar [l. 7]). Later on, though, a strong admonition addressed to three young relatives to be steadfast in the study of the Torah and to prompt one another to strict observance is followed by a wish using the special name of the God of Israel: "*May the Lord of Hosts in his great mercy let you dwell in safety . . .* " (ll. 11–12).[24]

As this example shows, the use of different appellations of God was not entirely attributable to the predilection for variety characteristic of the Geniza writers; it could allude to the specific meanings connected with each.[25] In Arabic too, when the term *rabbī*, "my Lord," was used instead of the more common Allāh, the context frequently reveals that a matter of deep concern or warm confidence in God was involved.

As a rule, whenever the name of a person is mentioned it was accompanied by a blessing (or, rarely, the opposite); in many instances, the phrases were routine; but very frequently the expressions chosen have strong emotional overtones, affection, admiration, gratitude—only God is able to adequately remunerate the blessed person. The same holds true for the superscriptions and concluding blessings in missives. Unlike the Muslims with their Basmalah the Geniza writer had at his disposal a wide variety of openings of letters in both Hebrew and Arabic. Any long letter is headed by Bible quotations containing, or referring to, the names of God and alluding in one way or another to what follows. When the nervous Yeshūʿā b. Ismaʿīl superscribes a letter with "In the name of the mighty God," we need to read only four lines to understand why this unusual heading is chosen: "This year was as willed by God," that is, exceptionally bad. God showed his might rather than compassion.[26] At the beginning and the end of bills of lading, God's mercy is usually invoked to grant safe arrival to the shipment. When, in addition to the routine phrases, God is addressed as, "O most merciful of all those who have mercy," the writers must have had reason to give their appeal a most urgent turn. One such bill concludes thus: "O You who do not sleep and are not careless, keep an eye on those who do sleep and are careless," reminding God of his promise in Psalms 121:4, has an almost naïve directness of appeal.[27]

Following an ancient statute, documents, as a rule, were not superscribed with the name of God. But in the text, the scribe could not get himself to say "whatever profit we make" or "whatever we earn," but would write "whatever God will grant," "will apportion," or "whatever sustenance he will provide."[28] These were routine phrases, the likes of which are found in partnership and commenda contracts written in Christian countries of the western Mediterranean from the eleventh through the fifteenth centuries. (Might they have followed their Muslim business friends in this practice?)[29] But when very humble people (a father admitting his son as partner with payments of 6 dinars by each) express the same idea with the words "whatever mercy Heaven may have with us," we believe that they did indeed need special consideration from above.[30]

The direct appeal to God, so prevalent in the Geniza, is emphasized by the total absence of intermediaries. No angel is invoked in cases of deadly danger, as when hiding from merciless raiders, stranded on a shipwrecked boat, or living through a catastrophic earthquake. True, the Palestinian Talmud says: "When you are in distress, don't cry to Michael, don't cry to Gabriel; cry to me, and I shall answer you."[31] But the host of angels is very conspicuous in the Talmudic scenery, whereas in the Geniza even the names of the archangels appear only exceptionally as personal names, and that of Gabriel seems to be completely absent.[32] An unusual form of curses on anyone pilfering a Torah scroll donated by a person on his deathbed contains the names of ten angels (as if the curse by the Lord of Hosts was not enough), among them one occurring only in very late sources.[33] Even in a general way, protection by angels is not asked for. What superscription over a letter addressed to a person on a journey, or one planning to travel, could have been more fitting than Psalms 91:11, "He will order his angels to guard you wherever you go"? Offhand, among the hundreds of headings read, I do not remember one such occurrence.[34]

The absence of angels is matched by the total disappearance of Satan, the tempter and accuser. With reference to medieval England George Gordon Coulton writes: "In most minds, Satan bulked almost as large as God; in some, even larger."[35] At a symposium on John Milton, a searching literary study on "The Idea of Satan as the Hero of *Paradise Lost*" was presented a few years ago.[36] Muslims open every religious activity such as the recitation of the Qurʾān, or the study of the Traditions of the Prophet, with the invocation: "I take my refuge with God from the cursed Satan," as prescribed in the Qurʾān itself (7:200; 16:98; 41:36). Marriage, as an Islamic marriage contract from a noble family states, was instituted by God as "a protection against Satan and his host."[37] The Talmudic literature has much to say about Satan and sketches a lively portrait of him.[38] In Jewish liturgy, as far as I can see, by Geniza times Satan was relegated mostly to personal prayer. A guest, when saying grace after a meal, blessed the host with numerous good wishes, among them, "may Satan have no power over your possessions."[39] The entreaty for protection against many evils, including "the corrupting Satan," said by Judah ha-Nāsī, the codifier of the Mishna, after the obligatory prayer, also found its way into the prayer book.[40] But no echoes to these wishes and supplications have been observed by me in the letters of the Geniza people. They preferred to ascribe unpropitious thoughts and deeds to the influence of the stars or as wrought by God himself.[41]

Miracle-working rabbis or saints, common in Talmudic times, and even more conspicuous in the Jewish communities of the Muslim West in the Late Middle Ages, do not make their appearance in the "classical" Geniza correspondence. Supernatural men seem not to have belonged to the spiritual climate of that society. Belief in the efficacy of supplication by worthy people, however, was very strong. This topic of intercessional prayer is present in a multitude of letters and deserves some special study. When a man during travel, serious illness, or in another dangerous situation asks a religious dignitary, his parents, or other relatives, a pious old woman, or friends to pray for him, he is in earnest. Requesting a friend to implore God for him, might express also the writer's esteem for the person thus addressed as a worthy advocate. Conversely, the extremely frequent assurance that the writer prays for the recipient of his letter (often supplicating regularly after the completion of the obligatory prayer) may reveal gratitude or deep concern for his welfare, especially when the latter was a person connected with the government or otherwise in constant jeopardy.

The basic idea behind the request for intercessional prayer seems to have been the concept of nearness to God. The person asking for it is conscious of his own unworthiness, or, at least, reveals this expression of humility. The person asked for intercession stands, so to speak, nearer to God; his prayer has not far to travel before reaching the heavenly throne. The image of court procedures might also have been influential. Intercessional prayer for you by a man of established reputation could serve as an attestation to your good standing and meritoriousness. Finally, in daily life it was common practice that whenever someone approached a higher authority with a request, he tried to have a VIP support the application with words of recommendation. There were also situations of a more delicate nature. After altercations with family or friends the person traveling away from them would ask them to pray for him; their consent would show that they had pardoned him and "cleared him" before God.

Nearness to God was sought not only through the intermediary of worthy men and women, but also by the numinous character, the holiness, of a place and time. These topics are treated elsewhere in this book.[42] Here, the practice of intercession is illustrated by a letter dedicated completely to this subject and by passages from another letter exemplifying the urgency of the request for such a favor, as well as an additional aspect of it: an entreaty to be exculpated from any misunderstandings that might have occurred between the interceders and the person asking for intercession.

Prayer in the Holy City, especially on the Mount of Olives, in full sight of the Temple area, was regarded as particularly efficacious. If said on a holiday, with all the pilgrims assembled, it was trusted to be even more powerful. When, on top of this, it was led by a man of piety and scholarship, it was believed to be sure of acceptance.

This is the background of the short Hebrew letter translated below. Its writer had made a donation, in recognition of which a public prayer was to be recited in his name for the Jewish community in general and for some specified prominent persons in Jerusalem, Ramle, then the administrative capital of Palestine, and for Fustat, Egypt, in particular. But he had become seriously ill and was unable to attend. Therefore he asked the Gaon Solomon b. Judah, who presided over the ceremonies on the Mount of Olives, to act in his stead and to pray also for his health, taking care not to omit his name from the public prayer.

Solomon took office around 1025. Here the writer wishes safe return to his son Yiḥye who studied in Baghdad with Hay Gaon, Solomon's Iraqian counterpart. Hay Gaon died in 1038 in his late nineties. Thus it is reasonable to assume that our letter was written around 1030.

The beginning and end of the letter are not preserved, but only a few words have been lost. The first six lines, which contained the name of the addressee and the introductory phrases, are too damaged for continuous translation.[43]

My first[44] [request] of you, my most honored, is this: do not spare your entreaties[45] for me; may the Lord, your God, hear from above his temple and the gates of his house and take away from me the illness and grant me health, so that I might view the countenance[46] while I am alive. For I know that your prayer is accepted and granted for everyone, let alone for your intimate friend.

Moreover, tomorrow, on the Feast of Unleavened Bread [Passover], you will pray and bless in my name our brethren, Israel, who live in the country of Israel, Egypt, Damascus, Aleppo, and all other places east and west, and also certain elders of Jerusalem and Ramle, who honor me, and elders in Miṣrayim [Fustat]. Do this while mentioning me in the prayer, for the blessings are in my name. I trust in your piety and righteousness[47] that you will do so.

May God show you soon[48] the countenance of your beloved son, our master Yiḥye, alive and well and let you have satisfaction and joy[49] from all your sons. May he bless your latter days and grant you—and grant me with you—to see his temple rebuilt, his sanctuary restored, his messiah come, the diasporas ingathered, and salvation sped. May he have mercy with the remnant that is left [Isaiah 37:4] and guide their hearts back to his fear and teachings, and forgive and pardon them in your lifetime, soon and in the near future.

May your well-being never cease to be proclaimed by heaven and by every mouth from this time forth and forevermore. And greetings to your flock and to the elders who go with you [to pray on the Mount of Olives].[50]

By enumerating all the good things expected in the future, including his own recovery, the sender wishes to enjoy them in anticipation, in company with his venerable friend. But public prayer for prominent persons was mainly a social affair: despite his poor state the sick man did not neglect this duty.

The second letter discussed here was written on 27 October 1103 by a novice in the India trade and sent by him from Dahlak on the southwest coast of the Red Sea to his brother-in-law in Tripoli, Libya. The writer had originally intended to travel only as far as Egypt, but learning in Cairo about conditions in India he decided to go there, adding sarcastically: "The eyes of the fool are on the end of the earth" (Proverbs 17:24).[51] After describing the horrors of travel on the Red Sea on "a ship with not a single nail of iron in it, but kept together by ropes," and decrying its inhospitable ports (in humorous rhymed prose), he continues (11. 24 ff.):

> I adjure you by the truth of these lines and by the *love* [Heb., meaning friendship] between us and by the bread we have eaten and the cup we have drunk together, that you do not omit me from your prayer, neither you, your mother, or maternal uncle Jacob. I know that you [singular] pray for all kinds of people. How much more appropriate and urgent to do so for your friend [Ar; *ḥabīb*]; and God in his mercy will save me.[52] I, my lord, am about to cross the great ocean, not a sea like that of Tripoli, and am not sure that we may ever meet again. I ask God and ask you [singular] that you pray for me and exculpate[53] me . . . [especially] your uncle Jacob. . . . May God forgive and exculpate you [singular] in this world and the World to Come from all that happened between me and you and your uncle Jacob.[54] Have your mother convey greetings to my sisters and order them to pray for me.[55] My lord, had I the power to halt the ship from setting sail by paying them 200 dinars, I would do so. But God alone is sufficient for me [as helper].[56]

The letter concludes with greetings, including one to "an intimate friend,"[57] who, too, is adjured to pray for him, and some practical matters, for which the brother-in-law is advised "to consult my sister" (that is, the addressee's wife).[58]

The background of this letter can be easily reconstructed. The writer's sister had quarreled with her mother-in-law. He, as her natural protector in the absence of parents, had intervened and had had a row with those in-laws: her mother-in-law, the latter's brother (and protector), and, it seems, to a lesser degree, her husband. To cool off (or for other reasons) he made the short trip to Egypt, which developed into a voyage to India. Now facing death (which he feared so much), he had to clear himself before God of all iniquities he might have committed, especially his altercations with his sister's in-laws. To get God's forgiveness, one must first "emulate his ways" and forgive one's own adversaries. This he did (see n. 54) or, more exactly, asked God to pardon them, and implores them now to do the same.[59]

One wonders why these detours via God were necessary. Could he not simply write: "I have forgiven you what you have said and done to me, and am asking you now to do the same"? The reason was that God was there; one could not evade him. In an hour of great danger one was afraid of being punished by him for one's sins.[60] Any iniquity one was aware of had to be cleared away, and for this one needed the support of the merciful judge in heaven.

How did this ubiquitous fear of, and trust in, God's presence come about? The obvious explanation is that his presence was taken for granted because everyone, to whatever religion he belonged, seemed to accept it as a fact. The very language one used in everyday speech was permeated by his names.[61] An almost unnoticed, but ceaseless, indoctrination and an all-comprising ritual were apt to keep the awareness of God constantly alive in everyone's mind. And the establishment of a personal relation with that awesome power was certainly a need felt by many, each in accordance with his mental faculties and education. The difference between the various religions was the kind of discipline they imposed on their members, the ways in which they tried to make and preserve nearness to God as a reality for their believers.

The type of religion to which the rank and file of the Geniza people were exposed was a belief in the meritoriousness of deeds, of the fulfillment of duties taught by God in his Torah (Pentateuch), not only "Ten," but 613 commandments—248 positive precepts and 365 prohibitions.[62] To do justice to so many duties, one had first to know them; one had to learn. Thus Jewish religion fostered study as worship and required continuous alertness to do certain things and to leave others. By this method the believers were constantly reminded of the heavenly Teacher's presence and were rewarded for their awareness, as an ancient sage had said: "God, wishing to provide Israel with the opportunity for gaining merits, multiplied for them teachings and duties."[63] This was also the professed ideal of the Geniza people. Throughout the centuries fathers were wished that their sons and grandsons should become students of the Torah and assiduous keepers of its commandments.[64]

For the realization of this ideal, life was organized in a way that brought the believer constantly in contact with the object of his veneration. How this was done is admirably expounded in Saadya Gaon's *Siddur*, the authoritative guide on Jewish worship during most of the classical Geniza period. From the moment the believer opened his eyes in the morning to the time he was about to close them for nightly rest he was advised to recite prayers and benedictions at prescribed hours and occasions. A page from the *Siddur* concerning a man's rising in the morning illustrates this practice.[65]

At awakening a person says: "Blessed be you, my Lord, our God, King of the world, for taking away sleep from my eyes. . . . May it please you, my Lord, to train me to do good deeds, not bad ones; let good impulses, not bad ones, rule over me; make me strong for [observing] your commandments and grant me my portion in your Torah; and make me be accepted with favor and compassion by you and all who see me. Blessed be you, my Lord, who grants favors?"[66]

When a person washes his hands, he says: "Blessed be you, my Lord, our God, King of the world, who hallowed us with his commandments and prescribed the washing of hands." As Saadya explains in his comments, this benediction is not said when one cleans one's hands of dirt. It was a ceremonial, a symbolic act, the entrance into the state of purity, in which alone one was allowed to approach God, as when the priests, before entering the Temple, were ordered to wash their hands (and feet).

Then follow ten other benedictions accompanying each and every movement of getting up: stretching the arms, rubbing the eyes, straightening the upper body, dressing, sitting down, standing on the floor, walking, putting on shoes, fastening the belt, and wrapping oneself up in the outer garment. All these are full benedictions; for instance, while rubbing the sleepy eyes, one would say: "Blessed be you, my lord, our God, King of the World, who opens the eyes of the blind" (Psalms 146:8).

Strict compliance with these instructions when starting a day would no doubt be apt to dispel all thoughts from the mind except the remembrance of God. Saadya himself, however, states that most people prefer to say all these benedictions together, and this has remained the standing practice despite Maimonides ruling otherwise.[67]

I summarize that page from Saadya's *Siddur* to illustrate the general trend of rabbinic institutions: they aimed at occupying the mind as completely as possible with the presence of God. Prayer was the most immediate approach, but only one of the many possible avenues, as shown in the following. One should pronounce (at least) one hundred benedictions every day; considering the length of the three daily Jewish prayers (incomparably more time consuming than the five Muslim prayers) and the countless other occasions on which a benediction had to be said, it was not difficult to reach that number. There was, of course, the problem of how to square this ideal with the demands of daily life. The sages wondered whether laborers should be permitted to do their work while reciting at least a part of the service. They reasonably decided in the positive, and also ruled which parts were suited for that purpose.[68]

In one sector of life, and a very important one, rabbinic legislation seems to have been remarkably successful: in converting the weekly day of rest, the Sabbath, into a day really "belonging to the Lord," as demanded in the fourth of the Ten Commandments (Exodus 20:10). By stretching the biblical prohibition "do not do any work on it" to the utmost limits of imagination, they prohibited any activity, thought, or talk connected with one's occupation, or any physical exertion such as walking or otherwise moving more than about three quarters of a mile beyond the limits of a city, or carrying even the lightest weight outside one's house, or activities such as riding or swimming. Thus, there was plenty of time to attend prolonged services, in which the entire congregation had an opportunity to participate in one way or another, or to listen to edifying sermons or learned disputations outside the services. The rest of the day was devoted to festive meals, interspersed with prayers and religious songs, also educational conversation, when a suitable guest was present, as well as functions for which one had no time during a busy week: visiting the ill, congratulating the families of newlyweds, or expressing sympathy to mourners—all not only social but religious duties. No wonder, then, that the Sabbath was regarded as a day when one was free of the tribulations and worries of this world, a foretaste of the World to Come.[69]

The spirit of the Sabbath is adequately expressed in the centerpiece of the Minḥā, "afternoon prayer," of Saturday, as formulated in Saadya's *Siddur* and some Geniza copies:[70]

> You are one and your name is one [Zechariah 14:9, referring to messianic times]; and where on earth is there a unique nation like your people of Israel [I Chronicles 17:21; Deuteronomy 26:17–18]. You have given your people a crown of salvation: rest and holiness. Abraham is joyous, Isaac jubilant, Jacob and his sons rest on this day, [and to your servant Moses you have said on Mount Sinai: "my countenance will appear and you will be given rest" (Exodus 33:14)], rest, as a gift of love, rest in truthfulness and trust.
>
> Be satisfied with our rest, hallow us through your commandments, grant us our portion in your Torah . . . and purify our heart for serving you in truthfulness. Blessed be you, our Lord, who hallows the Sabbath.

To understand the purport of this prayer one must remember that, from the time of the Greeks and the Romans and throughout the centuries of Islam, nothing distinguished the Jews from their environment more than the Sabbath, when an entire people disappeared from the scenes of daily life and dedicated themselves to religious function. The Muslims called the Jews *ahl al-sabt*, "the people of the Sabbath," and often granted them facilities for making its observance possible to them. Such consideration was particularly necessary on caravan travel, when the Jewish traveler had to stay put on Saturdays, and try to join his company later. Such occurrences were so common that an Arab poet could say of the stars during a long night: "Its stars, you might think, were Jews whose journey the Sabbath stayed."[71]

The intensity of the feeling of being different was never so pronounced as on the holy day of the week. According to Exodus 20:8–11, the Sabbath was instituted to commemorate the creation of the world. Only Israel accepted the celebration of the holy day in its totality, with all the inconveniences imposed by it; hence the elated feeling of being special pervading this prayer, and the bold comparison with Moses on Mount Sinai: a true Sabbath rest is like beholding an appearance of God. I put the passage on Moses in brackets, because in later times, and by Maimonides, too, it was omitted from the service; but there can be no doubt that it belonged to the original text; it was indeed its pivotal part.[72]

The Geniza society seems to have been successful in enforcing the observance of the Sabbath. Only a few accusations have reached the courts, and they concerned not flagrant transgressions, but minor or dubious cases. Swimming, for instance (see p. 12, above), is not one of "the thirty-nine major activities prohibited on Sabbath," nor a direct "derivation" of one of them, but a matter of precaution, lest the occupation with that sport lead to more serious violations of the law. Yet the relevant document speaks twice of "the desecration of the Sabbath," a grave sin. In popular opinions, swimming in the Nile did not fit into the atmosphere of the Sabbath, as it was conceived by an observant community.

Some went even further. What could be more innocent than promenading in the beautiful parks and gardens in and around the capital of Egypt? First, there was a legal concern. Strolling around, one might stray farther away from the limits of the city than permitted—a major transgression (see p. 12, above). Second, and mainly, on Sabbath one should seek nearness to God, not the beauty of nature. In the following I translate the summary of a relevant sermon of the type heard in Geniza times on Saturday afternoons.

"A garden locked is my sister, my bride, a fountain locked, a sealed-up spring" [Song of Songs 4:12].

From this verse has been deduced that Israel is called "the bride."[73] Sabbaths and holidays are also addressed as bride, for the sages, out of veneration for them, would greet their arrival with the words: "Come, O bride."[74] The allusion is that, as everyone knows, the bride is constantly close to the groom in the joy of the wedding, always turning to him and thinking of him, so that she rejects everyone else and relies only on him.

It is also well known that the Sabbath and the holidays are the time of love,[75] joy, and nearness to God, may he be praised. Consequently, Israel, who are compared with the bride, must refrain from arranging pleasurable walks in promenades and gardens,[76] even those nearby which are inside the town limits; for them they must be nonexistent, because of the risk of getting to places outside the limits. On Sabbaths and holidays they should be concerned solely with getting close to God through serving him. They should regard every open garden as locked, and every flowing fountain as sealed up.

I heard this exposition in the name of the late R. P[h]in[e]has, when the young men of [. . .] were readying themselves on the holidays to leave the city for the gardens and vineyards.[77]

Comments

We should keep in mind that this is only a summary, which was written by one who was not present at the sermon, but had learned about it from another person.[78] As far as it is possible to follow the tortuous paths of associative (not logical) thinking at all, the main points are evident.

As usual, the preacher opens with a biblical text, which forms the keynote of his exposition. Then he reminds his audience of the traditional rabbinic interpretations: Israel is the bride of God, and the Sabbath, too, is addressed as bride. But soon he gives the verse quoted an entirely new turn. The garden is a real garden; the fountain is real, but they should be regarded as being locked up on Sabbaths and holidays; the young men of Israel should not be diverted from the service of God by the charms of Nature.[79]

The preacher must have been popular, since he is mentioned only by his first name, Pinhas (which is very rare in the Geniza). He might have belonged to the circle of pietists of Abraham (b. Solomon), the Pious.

Going out for a walk in company was much cherished by the

Geniza people and could serve on a Sabbath as an opportunity for an exchange of ideas on spiritual matters fitting the character of the day. The text translated below describes such an outing to a place named after the newly constructed observatory of Cairo, an open space overlooking the Pool of the Abyssinians southeast of Fustat. The observatory was erected on the command of al-Malik al-Afḍal (viceroy of Egypt, 1094–1121) near the end of his life, it seems, but soon after his death was transferred to the high roof of the Gate of Victory of Cairo. Only al-Afḍal's observatory can be meant here, for Cairo was too far for a walk and beyond the limits permissible to a Jew on the Sabbath.

The leader of the company opened the discussion in the Socratic way, by asking the writer a question, namely, about the esoteric meaning of the term "the Mountain of the Lord." It was the Saturday after Pentecost (Shavuoth), when Moses' theophany on Mount Sinai was commemorated, and when Psalms 24:3, which contains the words "Mountain of the Lord," was recited. The writer's reply shows that similar matters had been discussed with him before. The remarks of the mentor begin, as usual, with a question on a biblical text; the explanation of the text contains implicitly the master's opinion about the topic of the conversation.[80]

On Saturday, the eighth of the month of Sivan[81] we went for an outing at the observatory.[82] The esteemed Sheikh Rabbi Elazar, son of the late Rabbi Solomon, was with us and asked me about the meaning of "the Mountain of the Lord." I answered: "We must ask and implore *our forefathers*, may they rest in peace, to get us to where they got themselves, namely, to get to the real "Mountain of the Lord," and to ask the Exalted one to uncover for us the *depth of the mystery*.[83]

[*Remarks of the mentor*:]

"Question: the noble Torah, revealed through the lord, the Messenger [Moses], says, 'Assemble for me seventy of the elders of Israel' [Numbers 11:16], but afterward they could not get near [Mount Sinai] and when they got near, they were consumed by fire, or otherwise perished. But concerning the one who really got up the Mountain, the lord, the Messenger, the lord David has said in the Book of Psalms: "Who may ascend the Mountain of the Lord and who may stand in his holy site? He whose hands are clean and whose heart is pure, etc." [24:3–4]. All this is said about him [Moses], may he rest in peace. Furthermore, "Mountain of the Lord" means the state of uncovering the mysteries, the state of being *present* at Mount Sinai, the state of witnessing the light of revelation, and *the Lord's majesty, may the name of the majesty of his kingdom endure forever.* When you study well the meaning of that psalm and its commentary, you will realize that it refers in its entirety to the Lord Moses, may he rest in peace.

The teaching that the old mentor tried to drive home was simple: one is worthy to penetrate the arcana of mystical knowledge only after having proved oneself by exemplary moral conduct. An old Midrash (homiletic commentary) on the Psalms undertakes to show in the light of Moses' life story that he deserved "to go up to the Mountain of the Lord,"[84] unlike the "elders," who tried to do the same, but did not possess the necessary qualifications and perished.[85]

Style and spelling are absolutely uncommon. Arabic words are used even for Torah (*sharīʿa*). Most of the time Moses is called "the lord, the Messenger," like Muhammad in Islam: terms from Islamic mysticism, such as "the light of revelation," and "true," real, in the esoteric sense, are used. The few Hebrew words occurring give the impression that they were heard rather than learned by reading. Even the simple word mountain, *hr*, is always spelled *hʾr*. Perhaps the writer was a young man, who had been alienated from Judaism and found his way back through contact with Islamic mysticism.[86]

The data assembled in this subsection seem to indicate that a naïve belief in the personal closeness of the individual to God permeated the Geniza world during the High Middle Ages, as well, we may safely assume, as other Mediterranean and Near Eastern societies. In conclusion, I wish to draw attention to a small relevant detail that impressed me when I first read it. A noble refugee from Jerusalem, who was stranded in Tripoli, Lebanon, after her husband had disappeared during a war, writes to relatives in Egypt on matters that also concerned the Nagid Judah b. Saadya and his brother and successor Mevōrākh. At the end of the letter she wished to send regards to the two brothers (whom she knew personally). But how to do it? Letters were usually exchanged between males, who often added regards from their own womenfolk to those of the addressee. For it was improper for a man to send regards to a woman or vice versa.[87] The solution: "May God extend his greetings of peace to my lord the Ḥāvēr." That intelligent woman was in a quandary as to how to address the two notables. She had no qualms about imposing upon God to convey her message.[88]

3. Member of God's Community

The individual's experience of God's closeness had its main root in the conviction that he or she belonged to God's people, to the community with the right faith. "For what great nation is there that has a god so near to it as is the Lord, our God, whenever we call upon him? Or what great nation has laws and precepts as right as all these teachings that I set before you today?" (So says Moses in Deuteronomy 4:7–8). This attitude was not confined to Judaism, but was shared, with enhanced emphasis, by Christianity and Islam, which had been exposed to the same traditions and a similar spiritual atmosphere. As for Judaism, by Geniza time the question had to be asked how was it possible to sustain the claim of superiority in the face of the harsh judgment that history had dealt out to the Jewish people: disinherited from most of its ancestral soil, dispersed all over the world in small and mostly powerless communities, and exposed to humiliation and harassment? How could a Jew in Geniza times preserve his trust in God and, with it, his self-respect?

The fact that he did remarkably well will not surprise the reader of this volume. A religious discipline, developed during long generations with similar experiences, guided the mind: how to remain continuously aware of God's presence, and how to behave in misfortune, and, indeed, in any and every situation. Life was minutely regulated by law and custom. Religion was built into the structures of the day, the week, and the year in a way that let its teachings appear as natural as the course of nature itself. Belonging to a specific community was not a problem; it was a fact: a person was a Jew because he was born one; that one neighbor was a Muslim and another a Christian corresponded to the order of things: both inherited their faith from their parents.

Being a Jew was a matter of distinction. He possessed the uncontested privilege of a unique descent. He could rely, as it was so often said in both liturgy and letters, on "the merits of his ancestors." Remember that claiming any merit for oneself was regarded as unseemly.[1] Doing the same with regard to one's forefathers was an expression of filial piety. The main Jewish prayer, repeated three times a day, opens with thanks to God for his guidance of Abraham, the father of both the faith and the nation. With such an introduction, the favors sought from God later in that prayer were justified.

A high claim to pride for any Geniza person was his ability to read and recite in public the Torah and the Prophets in their original language—a task to which he had dedicated most of his years in school. The emotion accompanying this performance found its expression in the benedictions said by him before and after the recital, respectively: "Blessed be you . . . who chose us of all nations and gave us his Torah" and "who, by giving us true learning [lit., 'a true Torah'], planted eternal life within us."[2] These are high-sounding words, but they are simple Hebrew, and simple are the ideas behind them. A continuation of some form of life after death was assumed by each of the three monotheistic religions. For a Jew, studying the Torah and fulfilling its commandments was a path that could lead to eternal life. A public declaration to this effect, pronounced in the solemn hour of the recital of the Torah, could give the reader and those present the feeling that they were already on their way.

The extraordinary significance of the Sabbath in the consciousness of a Jew who observed it has been discussed in the preceding subsection. An additional consideration is necessary. According to the biblical story (Genesis 2:1–3), the Sabbath was hallowed, that is, instituted as holy, at the time of the creation itself, a concept reflected in the synagogal liturgy.[3] Originally it was not destined for any particular religion, not even for mankind alone, as the commandment to give rest to one's cattle proves (an injunction, by the way, from which severe practical difficulties ensued, as the Geniza shows).[4] The universal claim of the Sabbath is well expressed in the audacious saying of a third-century sage: "He who pronounces Genesis 2:1–3 in the Friday evening service initiating the Sabbath is considered as if he were a partner of God in the work of creation."[5] For rest, freedom from the slavery of labor was part of creation itself.[6] Judaism remained the religion of a people, and the Sabbath its distinctive mark (e.g., Exodus 31:17). But the universal character of the day, underlined by the texts and prayers recited, was apt to give the individual believer a feeling of participation in a spectacle of eternal dimensions.

The holidays were different. They were in various respects of an intrinsically national character, with the understanding, of course, that, as in antiquity, nationality and religion were inseparable. The most sacred holiday, the Day of Atonement, dedicated to fasting (25 hours), confession of sins, glorification of the King in Heaven, and supplication for forgiveness, was paralleled, although not duplicated, by similar sacred days in other religions. It was by no means a day of dejected contrition and mourning, but rather one of joyous trust that the day would fulfill its promise: "On this day He will pardon you to cleanse you; from all your sins you shall be clean before the Lord" (Leviticus 16:30).[7] This is said in connection with the elaborate ritual of atonement performed by the High Priest in the Temple (of Jerusalem). The ritual of that day, combined with repentance and atonement, was to have the miraculous effect of making the penitent a new being (expressed also by the custom, habitual in Geniza times, of donning new clothes on that day).[8] Now that the Temple was no longer, the reading of the description of the ritual in the Bible, in the Mishna, and in liturgical compositions, which visualized the restoration of the Temple, formed the central part of the service. The prophetical teachings about justice, freedom for the oppressed, and help to the needy (Isaiah 58), as well as compassion even for the sinner (the Book of Jonah) were also recited on that day and partly realized by the pledges of the members for yearly or special contributions (about which more below).

The New Year, which preceded the Day of Atonement by seven days, celebrated the "birthday" of the world, the founding and future restoration of the Kingdom of God, the reign of justice and equity. Its most conspicuous ritual was the blowing of the shofar trumpet, by which, in ancient times, a king was greeted as he ascended the throne. "All nations will be united to do the good that pleases you"—as the central prayer of the day has it. Yet, the King is "the God of Israel who dwells in Zion" (Joel 4:17). The shofar is a reminder of the grand trumpet of the Messiah, "which will summon the dispersed . . . to assemble and bow to the Lord on the holy mountain in Jerusalem" (Isaiah 27:13).

In short, the two days of New Year and the Day of Atonement, which were parts of "the Ten Days of Repentance" opening the year, were destined to call on the world and the individual to examine their deeds, to confess, and to mend their ways. As such, they possessed general human appeal of the highest order. At the same time they constantly reminded the believer of the special role and fate of the community to which he belonged.

The same is true of the three ancient holidays of pilgrimage to Jerusalem, "to appear before the Lord": Passover-Easter, commemorating the Exodus from Egypt; Shavuoth-Pentecost, celebrating the Revelation on Mount Sinai; and Sukkot-Tabernacles, originally the important harvest feast of eight days in ancient Israel, but, according to Leviticus 23:42–43, instituted in remembrance of the tent life of the Children of Israel after the Exodus. The "national" background is even more conspicuous in the minor holidays of Hanukkah (The Maccabees) and Purim (Queen Esther), and the fasts, all of which (with the exception of the Day of Atonement) bemoan national disasters, of which the destruction of the Temple of Jerusalem (9th of Āv, in July-August) was the most memorable.

Thus, every special day in the year—and, as we have seen, there were many—connected the individual with the past—and the future—of his community. This situation is richly documented in the

Geniza correspondence.[9] The standard wish for the High Holidays is summarized thus: "May these forthcoming days"—that is, all that is expected in them: repentance, prayer, strict observance, and pledges for charity—"be accepted [by God] from you and from me, and *may you be inscribed in the Book of Life and the Book of Pardon and Forgiving together with me and all Israel.*"[10] A full-fledged congratulation, referring also to the Feast of Tabernacles (following close after the Day of Atonement), reads: "I congratulate you, my lord . . . on this awe-inspiring *Fast* and those illustrious *days of Feast, may the God of Israel inscribe you in the Book of Remembrance, in the Book of Redemption and Mercy, in the Book of Livelihood and Prosperity, and give you many years in joy and happiness, so that you may behold the beauty of the Lord and visit in his sanctuary [Psalms 27:4], you and your beloved [son] and all those connected with you. Amen.*" In other words, the addressee is wished to live long enough to witness the restoration of the Temple and the revival of pilgrimages to Jerusalem.[11] The New Year is rarely singled out, since the "Ten Days of Repentance" were regarded as one unit; when it is referred to with the wish that the addressee and his son "may be privileged to hear the sound of the shofar," the trumpet of the Messiah is intended.[12] Similarly, if he is wished to be inscribed together with his sons "with those inscribed for life in Jerusalem" (Isaiah 4:3), millennial expectations are implied.[13]

The same applies to the days of feast and fast. On Passover, noted for the family sacrifice of a lamb at the pilgrimage (to become a great symbol in Christianity, cf. Exodus 12:2–14, and Isaiah 53:7), one is wished to be privileged to participate in the various offerings made in the Temple on that holiday and to eat from them, as well as to witness the pilgrims arriving in Jerusalem three times a year.[14] On Shavuoth, when the revelation on Mount Sinai was remembered, the wishes were even bolder: "May you be privileged to see the Presence [of God, Heb. *shekhīnā*, from which Ar. *sakīna*] with your own eyes, as it is written: 'They will see with their own eyes when God will return to Zion'" (Isaiah 52:8).[15] Even more outspoken is a large, but fragmentary, letter: "May you be privileged to behold the Messiah, the son of David, together with [. . .] and see the Presence of the Lord with your own eyes, as it is written [. . .]."[16] On the autumn holiday of the Tabernacles, water plays with sacral dances were enacted in the Temple to inaugurate the rainy season. Consequently, one was wished to witness those festive occasions whenever they were renewed, as it is written: "You will draw water with joy from the springs of redemption" (Isaiah 12:3).[17]

The minor holidays of Hanukkah and Purim seem to have been rated higher by the Geniza people than by European Jews. They are described as *mōᶜēd*, Ar. *ᶜīd*, "holiday," which is imprecise, since that term refers to a day on which work was prohibited entirely or partly (which did not apply to those days). One sent extended regards wishing the addressees wonders, miracles, and redemption in their lifetime comparable with those commemorated on those holidays, and, as far as Hanukkah was concerned, that they attend the future reconsecration of the Temple. Teachers expected to receive a consideration on Hanukkah and children "a Purim dinar."[18] During the months in which a fast occurred one was wished that they should be converted into days of joy. The main fast of mourning, the Ninth of Āv, was also an occasion for discreet personal gifts to cantors and scholars.[19]

Before taking food or drink of any kind one would say the appropriate benediction, and grace (shorter or longer, depending on the type of food consumed) after. They ate while seated and not as frequently as we do. (Drinking while standing, as at our cocktail parties, was regarded as damaging to the health.) These expressions of gratitude to God for preserving our life (and that of others, including animals) were usually said aloud, followed by an Amen by those present, so that the children learned them by listening. For them, opening the mouth for food without opening it first for a benediction would soon become awkward and unusual. Many other pleasures in life required a blessing, for instance, smelling delicate scents. In a community counting many members who were dealers in spices, aromatic plants, and perfumes, susceptibility to pleasant smells is not surprising. Saadya Gaon in his *Siddur* lists five different benedictions in this respect. "You cannot say the same blessing for musk, which is taken from an animal, as for odoriferous wood."[20]

Some of the main foodstuffs—meat, wine, cheese (for the rigorous, also bread)—were subject to dietary laws of biblical and, mostly, postbiblical origin. For the believer this signified that he belonged to a very special, a holy community, although in the countries of Islam, where similar restrictions prevailed, such laws and practices were less strange than in environments that were not familiar with them. To ease the observance of these comprehensive and complicated injunctions, or even to make it possible, Jews had to flock together, that is, to live in communities large enough to provide the necessary services and facilities. Thus the dietary laws were another tie that kept the individual closely attached to his community.[21]

Finally, the Jewish community (like the Christian denominations) under Islam formed a legal corporation, which was responsible for its members and had a considerable amount of jurisdiction, religious and civil, over them. Matters differed from one state to another, and from one ruler to his successor. The weaker the minorities became in number and influence, the more the Muslim governments were inclined to meddle in their affairs. In the classical Geniza period, especially in Fatimid times, communal discipline was still high. Bringing one's civil cases before the rabbinic courts, and not only those in matters of family and inheritance, was regarded as a religious duty. This situation was an additional incentive for the individual to study, to make himself acquainted with Jewish law, and also to participate in the public life of the community. The selection of leaders, who would also act as lay members of the rabbinic courts, had significance for everyone. Communal jurisdiction and its impact on the daily life of the individual have been discussed in detail in *Med. Soc.*, II, 311–407.

The semi-autonomous status of religious minorities had profound consequences for their members. Charity in those days was mainly conceived of as a religious duty. In view of this, each community had to look after its own people. When Jews were taken captive in a war between Muslims and Christian invaders, it was not up to the Muslim state but up to the Jewish community to ransom them, an extremely costly affair.[22] Care for the poor and the sick, orphans and widows, the old, and indigent foreigners was in the main left to their coreligionists. Thus, the tiny Jewish community, membership in which was entirely voluntary, had to undertake tasks that are incumbent today on municipal, state, and federal authorities. How the Geniza society acquitted itself of these duties is described in various parts of this book, surveyed at the opening of the section on poverty above.[23] Special attention is drawn to "Appraisal of the Jewish Social Services" in *Med. Soc.*, II, 138–143, and the conclusions drawn about private charity in this volume (pp. 91–94).

Religious communities, which, like the ancient Jews and the early Christians, were constantly in jeopardy, developed a special ethical code of charity. Mercy was God's main attribute, and man should emulate him. Moreover, the members of the community were often in a situation where they had either to ask for help or to give some. Both are onerous, the former, because the needy are proud and easily sensitive to shame, and the latter, because it is not easy to part with limited means acquired by hard toil. Here religion provided succor to both. The very fact that both "giver" and "taker" stood before God in the same prayer hall (which was usually limited in size) ensured that the two knew each other by sight, even when they usually did not talk to each other.[24] This brought about the feeling that the congregants belonged together, and created a certain consciousness of equality, of shared powerlessness in face of the might of Heaven. Destitution, either inherited or brought about by circumstances over which one had no power, was decreed by God; we must thank him for all he has in store for us, and no shame could be attached to the effects of his deeds.

On the other side, the expenses or efforts expected from the "giver" represented only what he returned to God in gratitude for all the good he had received from him. Munificence was a manifestation not only of social status but of acceptance by the heavenly judge, an acquisition of merits. When the Temple functioned, one expressed one's gratitude by offering sacrifices. Now, alms and exertion for worthy causes replaced those lost opportunities. The offerings in the Temple were of different degrees, the highest being the burnt offering, where the entire carcass "went up" in flames on the altar, and no human being participated in its consumption. This symbolized the ideal image of charity, when all that was donated went to the recipient and no recompensation of any kind was, or could be, expected. Support for a meritorious, but destitute, scholar was the favorite example, endlessly repeated in the Geniza. (Unfortunately, there was much opportunity to do so.) Such selflessness was promised the highest reward: eternal life. "Charity delivers from death" (Proverbs 10:2, 11:4) could not be meant literally, but was a clear reference to life in the World to Come.[25]

About all this we read in the appeals for help, many of which are partly or fully translated or summarized in the preceding sections. The persons approached did not write letters; they acted (or not). Their deeds of support are usually reflected in letters of gratitude—realistic and sincere, or routine and hollow, as found mostly in letters with new requests. Praise for the religious virtue of charity pervades the Geniza correspondence.[26]

The religious motivation for good deeds also had legal aspects. The economic law of "no free lunch," that is, everything granted as a gift is recompensed in one way or another, was well known to the Muslim authorities. Therefore, anyone lending a needy person sustained and conspicuous help was suspected of having received benefits from him. Of any such benefits the government and, after some years, even the person concerned or his heirs might demand a share. Therefore, when leaving the house of his patron, or on his deathbed, the person supported would make a legally valid deposition to the effect that all help had been given to him gratuitously and for Heaven's sake only and that he had no claim whatsoever against his benefactor. A number of such declarations have been preserved in the Geniza, as for instance, the moving deathbed declaration of a pauper who was maintained by the congregation and lodged in the synagogue compound. She releases the spiritual leader, "the great Rav" R. Isaac (b. Samuel the Sepharadi), and his children and wife from any obligation toward her; she also releases the female caretaker of the synagogue (who obviously had looked after her), as well as the latter's husband.[27] In the following are presented two telling examples, one from the first half of the eleventh century, the other from the second half of the twelfth.

Release for a Benefactor and his Family (1025/1026)

The item translated here is entirely in Hebrew. It is one of the most competently styled and beautifully written Hebrew documents in the Geniza. It has been pieced together by me from three fragments, the first in the British Museum (now, Library), the second in the (former) series of glasses in the Taylor-Schechter Collection, Cambridge, England, and the third in the (former) series of volumes of the same collection. The fragments fit one into another exactly, so that parts of a word, and even of a letter, are sometimes found on two different fragments. The document contains about 700 words, mostly of legal verbiage, as usual in releases, which are reproduced here only in outline.

The fact that each of the eight members of the family of the benefactor is mentioned here by name shows again how in those days the entire family was held responsible for the actions of its individual members, as apparent even in the declaration of the destitute woman summarized above.

This testimony was given in our presence, we, the undersigned witnesses, on [. . . . . .][28] of the year 1337 of the Era of the Documents, according to which we count [1025–1026] here, in Fustat of Egypt, which is situated on the Nile river.

Turayk,[29] daughter of Abraham [son of Mo]ses, known as Ibn Qurdūsī[30] declared in our presence: Take notice, my masters, that, for more than ten years, I have been living in the house of R. Muḥsin b. Ḥusayn, the representative of the merchants, known as Shimʿān's sister's son,[31] may he be mentioned with blessings. I have lived entirely at his expense, for I possessed nothing, nor was I [able to] earn a livelihood. He acted on my behalf solely for Heaven's sake. May God, be he praised, recompense him for all the good he has done for me.

And now be my witness, make the symbolic purchase from me, write down my declaration, specifying the rights conveyed, sign and give it to them, namely to Muḥsin b. Ḥusayn, known as Shimʿān's sister's son, to his three sons Ṣadaqa (Alms, namely, given by God), Abū Naṣr (Victorious), and Asad (Lion), and to his three daughters, Sarwa (Cypress), Fāʾiza (Triumphant), and Nabīla (Noble), and to his wife Fahda (Cheetah),[32] daughter of Judah, known as Ibn al-Athāribī,[33] the clothier, as a title of rights and a proof.

I declare herewith before you, out of my free will,[34] without coercion or error, being neither incapacitated by illness nor misled, that I have no claim against[35] them or their heirs or representatives on silver or gold, dirhems or dinars, money or property, or any other object large or small, of little or of great value. Therefore I release, clear, and free them from any claims from me and my heirs, and write them this release to be a correct, permanent, valid, and certified instrument in their hand and that of their heirs before any court in the world. I have no claim or complaint against them resulting from an inheritance, a debt, a partnership. . . .[36]

(There follow another three hundred words explaining that any document or witness contrary to this declaration was null and void and that no secret deposition invalidating it had been made. The full names of the "Little Turk" and her benefactor[37] are repeated three times. The text of the document is complete, but there are no signatures. Whether the signatures were cut away, or whether, for one reason or another, this release remained unsigned, cannot be decided.)[38]

Release Given to a Protector
(after 1150)

This case is similar to, but in important details different from, the preceding one. A notable had harbored a widow and her children in his house to protect them from a Muslim creditor of her late husband. He had also settled the affairs of the dead man with his creditor. But nowhere is it stated that the widow was poor or unable to work. The fact that the notable had settled the dead man's affairs made it necessary to clarify that this was a work of piety and in no way a commercial transaction from which profit might have been derived. For this reason, and also because the widow clearly stayed in her protector's house for only a comparatively short time, here, unlike the previous document, the release does not make mention of the family of the benefactor.

The hero of the story, the great merchant (Ar. *tājir*) Abu ʾl-Maʿālī Samuel b. Judah Ibn Asad, appears in numerous documents from January 1133[39] through November 1165.[40] Since our release is in the hand of Mevōrākh b. Nathan (dated documents, 1150–1181)[41] while his father was still alive, it was probably written in the early 1150s. Samuel Ibn Asad lived some time in al-Maḥalla,[42] and was found also in Minyat Ashnā,[43] and our story, too, conveys the impression that it happened in a provincial town. The release was given by the widow and her elder son after arrival in the capital.

The manuscript represents a unique case: it was acquired by its present proprietor, Daniel M. Friedenberg of New York, only a comparatively short time ago.[44] The beginning is missing, but not much has been lost.

(The declaration opens with the happenings immediately after the death of the debtor.)

. . . who had a claim against him. They surrounded the house, took all of us, me and my children, and menaced me, demanding all that my above-mentioned husband R. Isaac owed them. There was no possibility for me to get free and to escape from their hands.[45] But *our honored and highly regarded* elder Abu ʾl-Maʿālī the merchant, *known as* Ibn Asad, namely, *[his] h[onor], g[reatness, and] h[oliness], our master and teacher Samuel, the honored notable, the wi[se] and pr[udent],*[46] *the Master of the Discerning,*[47] *may his Rock ke[ep him]*, son of . . . Judah, *the esteemed notable, [may he] r[est in] E[den]*, in his kindness delivered me and my children from their hands, settled our affairs and those of the deceased with his creditors, and took care of his affairs and his burial. He brought me and my little ones into his house,[48] and we remained under his care until we left that town.

We both, I, Sumr,[49] daughter of Moses, and I, Abu ʾl-Ḥasan, her son, declare herewith in your presence . . . that we have no claim whatsoever against the said elder Abu ʾl-Maʿālī resulting from a debt, a deposit, or any other transaction or any other matter of any kind. Had it not been for the mercy of God and the goodness of the elder and his protection, we would have perished in the hands of that Muslim.

God, the exa[lted], will call us to account and reprimand us[50] should we ever trouble the elder with claims or sue him before either a Jewish or a Muslim court with regard to anything belonging to both of us or the heritage of my father: I, Abu ʾl-Ḥasan.[51]

We also stand security to the elder Abu ʾl-Maʿālī for the minor boy Abū Isḥāq, whenever, after coming of age, he might sue him for the inheritance of his father. We undertake to protect the elder from him and to restitute all expenses and damages that he might incur because of this.

We made the symbolic purchase from Sitt al-Sumr and her son Abu ʾl-Ḥasan, from each separately, with regard to everything stated above. . . . We wrote down that which happened in our presence, signed, and gave the declaration to the said elder Abu ʾl-Maʿālī so that it may be in his hand as a title of rights.

[*Signatures*:]

Mevōrākh, son of Nathan, he-Ḥāvēr, [may his] e[nd be] g[ood].[52] Ezekiel, son of Nathan, [may his] s[oul] a[bide] in b[liss] and [his] p[rogeny shall] in[herit the] l[and].[53]

[*Validation by court*:]

We were constituted as a court of three, when Mevōrākh b. Nathan he-Ḥāvēr . . . and Ezekiel b. Nathan . . . came and testified before us that the signatures above were theirs; whereupon we properly confirmed and validated them [the signatures].

Ḥiyyā, son of R. Isaac, [may he] r[est in] E[den].[54]

Ephraim, son of R. Meshullām, [may he] r[est in] E[den].[55]

Hillel, son of rabbi Zadok, the president of the court, b[lessed be the] m[emory of the] h[oly].[56]

Charity occupies an uncommonly large portion of the Geniza documents. Whether this was owing to the extent of poverty in the Jewish community, or to the readiness of its members to help, or both, is difficult to say. At present we know too little about the distribution of wealth in the Muslim environment and the social services provided by it. The Talmud praises the Jewish people for being marked by compassion, shame (fear of appearing remiss in the fulfilling of one's duty), and doing good works.[57] Inducing others to make contributions was regarded even higher than contributing oneself.[58] This theme is repeated in the Geniza again and again, probably because many were not in a position (or in the habit) of giving much at a time. In a single letter a person is asked five times "to make the rounds" to collect some donations for two families in straits. In the last line, it is politely suggested that he take another man (mentioned by name) with him while making the rounds. The request was modest: 5–6 dirhems—perhaps a *façon de parler*.[59] As a rule, help in distress could be expected only from coreligionists. Things being so, the attachment to one's religion was a matter not only of birth and faith but of practical considerations as well.[60]

4. *Schism and Counterreformation*

At the opening of the preceding subsection it was presumed that the perception by the individual of his propinquity to God was based on the conviction that he was a member of a community on the right path. But what happened when the community itself was divided into conflicting creeds? This situation was indeed faced by many Muslims and Christians of the Middle East a thousand or more years ago, and even the small Jewish community experienced schisms of different size and duration. A Karaite author writing in the late eleventh century remarks that of the fourteen "religions" (lit., "laws") inside Judaism only four had survived in his time: the Rabbanites and the Karaites, and two others (which left no trace in the documentary Geniza).[1]

The appearance and disappearance of schisms in Judaism in early Islamic times is a fascinating story, which cannot be pursued here, because it preceded the period with which we are concerned in this book. It seems that during the fifth through the eighth centuries, the "dark" Middle Ages—dark for us, because we know so little about them—the exilarchate and the Babylonian seats of learning, the central Jewish institutions, had lost much of their authority, making way for the emergence of independent splinter groups. Some groups continued trends already present in Palestine before and after the destruction of the Second Temple in the year 70. Of this type were those following the refusal of the Sadducees to recognize any religious authority except that of the Holy Scriptures, or the messianic activists, who, like the zealots or Bar Kokhba and his followers, rose against a power whose magnitude they entirely misjudged and were therefore doomed to failure. Other early Jewish sects were inspired by their Iranian and later Islamic spiritual surroundings. None of those splinter groups was able to survive long enough to make an enduring impact on the main body of Judaism.

Things changed with the rise, or, rather, revival, of the Middle Eastern bourgeoisie after the destruction wrought by the suicidal Byzantine-Sassanid wars and the Muslim conquests.[2] The Muslim armies consisted mostly of Bedouins, who robbed the conquered peoples and reduced many of their members to slavery. Enslavement was soon followed by acceptance of Islam, which converted the slave into a client of his master or of his master's tribe.[3] Fortunately, however, the leaders of the Muslims were citizens of the merchant republic of Mecca, who understood, as the Arabic saying has it, that one cannot kill the cow and also milk it, and found it both practical and convenient to engage the services of the sedentary subject population. Consequently, a semblance of an orderly administration slowly began to emerge, and the non-Muslims could breathe again (although not quite freely).

The Jews recovered more haltingly than their former oppressors, the Iranians and Christians, which is natural. By the time a substantial Jewish middle class becomes discernible to us, Islam had already developed considerably, and numerous Jews had adopted the Arabic language (mostly retaining also their Aramaic vernacular for centuries). The exigencies of life demanded a measure of contact with the Muslim merchant world, the ruling class, and the Arabic-speaking intelligentsia. This contact, together with the attainment of a modicum of prosperity, had considerable consequences. The *responsa*, or authoritative answers on legal and other matters emanating from the Babylonian houses of learning in ever growing numbers, prove the restoration of Jewish prestige. For practical reasons the Muslim government recognized the authority of their leaders as well as that of the exilarch, or Head of the Diaspora, who was believed to be a scion of the family of the biblical King David. This further strengthened the position of the Jewish establishment. By the publication of treatises and compendiums written in a mixture of Hebrew and Aramaic (similar to the Talmud), the yeshivas regulated and streamlined religious life. At the same time the availability of leisure and contacts with a different, but cognate, culture provided time and occasions for thinking and asking questions.

Some of the questions raised, as in the case of the earlier ephemeral schisms, were not new. In view of the systematizing and stricter enforcement of the so-called Oral Law, doubts emerged again over whether the countless injunctions taught by the Sages, but not expressly mentioned in the Bible, were indeed willed by the heavenly legislator. Did not the Torah repeatedly warn: "Do not add to it" (Deuteronomy 4:2, 13:1), verses often quoted by Karaite authors. Doubts soon turned into certainty, and "Back to the Bible" became a battle cry. Those who acted in this spirit called themselves Benē Miqrā, "Sons of the Bible," and were shortly called Qārāʾīm, "Readers" (of the Bible), usually rendered in English as Karaites.[4]

The beginnings of this movement are shrouded in mystery. Socioeconomic and even personal elements might have been involved in the original break. But there can be no doubt that a genuine religious urge, a search for the truth, was behind it all. Reading the tracts addressed by the Karaite scholars to their Rabbanite brethren, one discovers a missionary spirit of impressive sincerity. Those eloquent preachers were clearly convinced that they were on the right path to God and that it was their duty to save others from their errors. In Islam, too, this was a period of feverish missionary activities, and Leon Nemoy is probably right in assuming that the Karaite writers might have learned from Shiʿite (Ismāʿīlī) propagandists.[5]

The essentially religious motivation of the Karaite movement is evidenced also in the activist ascetic spirit of some of its most prominent speakers, and is discernible in the reports about Karaite life. One of their early exponents, Daniel al-Qūmisī (from Qūmis near the southeastern tip of the Caspian Sea in northeast Iran, who settled in Jerusalem around 900), invites "the merchants of the Diaspora" not to wait for the Messiah and the ingathering of the exiled but to move to Jerusalem. There, vigils were held on the mountains supplicating God to condone the sins of Israel, which caused its dispersion. If the merchants addressed were kept back by the exigencies of their business, they should send at least five men from each city together with their sustenance "to keep the [prayer] watch on the walls of the Holy City" (cf. Isaiah 62:6).[6]

These were not empty words. A young man of eighteen, who traveled (again from northeastern Iran) to Jerusalem to study the Bible with the renowned masters there, financed his long journey by carrying with him the money donated by his compatriots for "the men of God, the teachers of the Bible." (Later he joined the Rabbanites, telling us his story in poems of anti-Karaitic polemics).[7] Sahl b. Maṣlīʾah, a Karaite author active in Jerusalem in the second half of the tenth century, reports this:

> The Karaites have assembled in Jerusalem righteous and pious men and have set up alternating watches for continuous prayers of supplication. They seclude themselves from the desires of this world, having renounced eating meat and drinking wine. They read the Torah and interpret it, acting as both teachers and students. They have abandoned their businesses and forgotten their families; they have forsaken their native land, left their palaces, and live in huts made of reed. They left the cities to go up to the mountains, they doffed their fine garments and don sack cloth.[8]

Of particular interest is a passage in another work by Sahl, because it shows that women, too, were gathering in Jerusalem (probably accompanying their husbands) to mourn and bewail the fate of Zion. "Take notice, brethren, that Jerusalem in these days is the refuge of every fugitive, the aim of every mourner,[9] a resting place for the needy. Here live the servants of God, who gather from every town and 'clan': and here are also women who wail and lament in Hebrew, Persian, and Arabic 'and teach their daughters lamentations and one another dirges' [cf. Jeremiah 9:19]." Some of these women were learned and recited their penitentiary dirges in "the holy language" (as the writer has it). Even more remarkable is the fact that Persian is mentioned before Arabic, which seems to show that more "mourners" came from Iran than from Arabic countries.[10]

The repeated appeals to the "merchants of the Diaspora" show that in the early period of the sect's history there were among the Karaites people with means able and willing to maintain their brethren in the Holy Land. The Geniza correspondence of the eleventh century reveals a similar situation, with the difference that the rich and influential Karaite merchants of Cairo extended their help also to non-Karaite Jews, to Rabbanites living in Jerusalem.

Rabbanites had been found there long before the advent of the Karaites. The novelty of the Karaites' approach toward Zion was their activism, which expressed itself in different ways. They, like the majority of the Jews, believed that the coming of the Messiah and the ingathering of the dispersed could be achieved only by a miracle, by God's will. But, they taught, one must do something about it. God's presence was still in Zion. Has he not said, "Come back to me and I shall come back to you" (Zechariah 1:3 and Malachi 3:7)? Israel is like a wife sent away from her husband's house because of her misdeeds. If she is really yearning to return to him, does she not come to his gate, tapping and rapping, until he opens?[11] That means that whoever is able to do so must be physically present in the Holy Land, not to carry on his accustomed life there but to conduct himself in contrition and utmost self-denial, as proper for a penitent, praying day and night, "reminding God" (Isaiah 62:6). The study of the Torah required the formation of groups, since it was done in the form of a disputation, "where everyone acted as both a teacher and a student."[12] The repeated mention of "going up to the mountains" seems to show that solitude was also recommended as a means of self-castigation. It is probable that the example of the Christian hermits who populated the barren hills of Judea and had formed a model for the Muslim pietists was somehow influential here too.[13] Saadya Gaon, in his condemnation of a life of withdrawal from the world, speaks twice about secluding oneself, or roving, on the mountains.[14]

In addition to the obligation to emigrate to the Holy Land, or at least to stay there for a prolonged period, leading a life of asceticism and mourning, another trait in the Karaite sect's attitude toward Zion seems to have existed: to make Jerusalem its spiritual center. In this they have succeeded almost completely. A galaxy of Karaite scholars lived in Jerusalem during the tenth and eleventh centuries until the advent of the Crusaders put an end to everything.[15] Among the eleven authors discussed by Mann, *Texts*, II, 8–48, were several of the classics of Karaite literature, for instance,

Japheth b. Eli, whose multivolume Bible commentaries, written about 960 to 990, reveal a spirit of observation of human nature not readily encountered in medieval commentators.[16] To the Karaite scholars active in Jerusalem in the eleventh century, described by Mann, should be added David b. Abraham al-Fāsī, author of the massive, and still valuable, *Dictionary of Biblical Hebrew.*[17] Against all this, the Rabbanites living in Palestine (and Egypt) had next to nothing to offer. I can explain the difference only by assuming that the Karaites made a deliberate effort to provide their scholars active in Palestine with at least the minimum of a decent livelihood, whereas the Rabbanites did not care, or were unable to do so. Saadya Gaon taught expressly that the return to God was a spiritual matter; "the ingathering of the exiled" was to be decreed and realized by him. Behind the apparent disinterest of the Rabbanites in the Jerusalem yeshiva was also the claim of superiority by the Baghdad houses of learning.[18]

During the tenth century, Karaite scholarship continued also to flourish in the environment in which it had originated: Iraq and the neighboring countries. Its leading spirit was Qirqisānī, whose *Book of Lights and Watchtowers* (a *summa* of Karaite belief and law) and *Book of Gardens and Parks* (a scrutiny of the nonlegal parts of the Bible) reveal him as an original thinker of great erudition, who did not disdain to discuss matters with Rabbanites, Christians, and Muslims. He is a worthy representative of the "Renaissance" civilization of the Near East around the tenth century, when Arabic had become the language of educated discourse, and when Muslim, Christian, and Jewish men of letters could converse with one another in a civilized manner.[19] It seems that none of his writings was translated into Hebrew. For this reason the later development of the sect in Byzantium and subsequently the Crimea, Poland, and Lithuania, was mainly influenced by the creations of the Jerusalem center of Karaism.

Qirqisānī was also the most outspoken exponent of the right and duty of the individual scholar to arrive at independent judgment based on reasoning, a principle already ascribed to the founder of the sect ʿĀnān (late eighth century). In the first centuries of the Islamic era, the educated individual was forced to take a stand in the face of his encounter with Islam, the new ruling religion, and with various denominations of Christianity, with Judaism, Zoroastrianism, dualism, as well as with disbelief in the accepted religions,[20] and last but not least, with the growing influence of Greek philosophy. Accepted truths became open to discussion. The Sages of the Talmud had based their teachings on the claim of an unbroken chain of *tradition* coming down to them "from Moses on Mount Sinai," and on what they had inherited from their "fathers," meaning teachers. Against this the Karaites held to the words of the Prophet, "Be not like your fathers" (Zechariah 1:4), and of the Psalmist, "They should not be like their fathers" (Psalms 78:8). If the words of the fathers contradict the Torah, they must be rejected, and the truth must be established by renewed investigation of the Scriptures using the method of analogy.[21] The slogan of independent search by rational thinking was almost as strong in Karaite beliefs as the battle cry of the return to the Bible. Unfortunately, when the reasoning itself was faulty, the reliance on the Scriptures became vitiated.[22] There can be little doubt, however, that the Karaite call for a new look at the Bible as well as for independent reasoning—although both perhaps not entirely new—had a healthy impact on the Jewish community at large.

Finally, the Karaite persuasion excelled in its emphasis on the obligatory study of Hebrew; study, not use. Most writings of the Karaites in the period with which we are concerned here were in Arabic, a language in which the art of disputation had attained a high degree of perfection. To be sure, the Karaites were not united in this as in many other respects. Whereas Benjamin Nehāwendī, an early Karaite author, opined that "we [Jews, Karaites?] should speak among ourselves no language other than Hebrew," Qirqisānī taught that language and script as such were not holy but only symbols expressing thoughts; one could even pray and give an oath in any language in which one was conversant.[23] Qirqisānī took pains to prove, though, that Hebrew was the language in which God had revealed himself, and therefore one could not claim to understand the Bible without being thoroughly familiar with the vocabulary, grammar, and ways of expression in which it was written.[24] The standard Code of Law of the Karaites, authored by Elijah Bashyatchi (Adrianople, Turkey, d. 1490) and still in force among them, counts as the sixth of the ten principles of Faith, "the duty to know the language of the Torah and its meaning."[25] Language study became one of the foremost concerns of the Karaite scholars, soon to be overtaken, however, by the rich development of this science in the Rabbanite camp. It was the example of the Arabic environment that affected both. The Arabs regarded themselves as the most language-minded people on earth, and they, together with their clients converted to Islam, soon developed a refined system of linguistic terminology. Based on this and their knowledge of Hebrew and Aramaic, the Rabbanite grammarians went several steps further in their linguistic scholarship. The Karaites, as far as I know, did not actively further these later developments.

The Karaite schism acted initially as a stimulus and reawakening of the Jewish community at large, as well as of its individual believers. This was particularly true for places where the sect was numerically and spiritually well represented, as in Palestine and Iraq.[26] The Karaite emphasis on the study of the Bible and Hebrew—reminiscent of the later European Reformation and Renaissance humanism—their belief in the power of independent reasoning, and their call to live in the Holy Land, or at least to visit there, and to lead an austere life, all invited examination and, at least partial, emulation.

Their attempt at a complete upheaval, that is, the disqualification of the Talmud, which had become the authoritative source of Jewish faith and practice, and formed also the very raison d'être for the existence of the yeshivas, the Jewish central institutions, was doomed to failure. In Judaism, as in Islam, the validity of the current tenets and laws was proved by their acceptance by the majority of the community.

Moreover, the Karaite scholars themselves were inured Talmudists. The religion with which they were familiar was a system of elaborate rituals and injunctions reminding the believer constantly of his duties, and one "where the scholars were kings,"[27] corroborating or initiating laws and tenets through authoritative interpretation of the scriptures. Rejecting the Talmud the Karaites proceeded to create another one.[28] But this was a futile undertaking. Rabbinical Judaism could rely on an age-old tradition, which by the time we deal with it here had grown organically for more than a thousand years. The Karaite movement was ill-timed and badly conceived. In an extremely tradition-bound period they tried radical innovations, and the innovations proposed by them were not attractive, and, in truth, not justified by the biblical texts from which they were derived. Moreover, the extreme freedom of reasoning given to the individual led to absurd disagreements on the practices to be followed, which impaired the reputation of the sect. The following desperate cry for help sent by the Karaite congregation of Alexandria to the leader of the community (then probably in Cairo) illustrates the situation: "Your servant kisses the soil before our lord, may God enhance your prominence. O our lord, do not ask us about our situation, we, your servants, the Karaites in Alexandria; our helplessness, discord, and disputes over all matters. And this *because of our many sins*. This damages all our affairs and leads to disregard of the religious law, disintegration of its authority, and breaking up of the community. . . ."[29]

A few of these novelties must be considered here because they had a tangible impact on the life of the Geniza people. As in the history of the Church, questions of the calendar were most conspicuous causes of division. The Jewish community had lived for centuries according to an astronomically regulated calendar (still in force). The Karaites reverted to the "natural" fixing of the first day of a month by actual observation of the appearance of the new moon, for a number of reasons a very impracticable procedure.[30] This and other reversions to obsolete and complicated practices in fixing the calendar caused discrepancies between Karaites and Rabbanites, and also within the Karaite community itself. Imagine an observant Karaite keeping his store open on the Rabbanite Day of Atonement, when any activity other than prayer was unthinkable; or a Rabbanite baker offering regular bread for sale on a Karaite Passover, the feast of unleavened matzos. Those occurrences could lead to disorders, attracting the attention of the authorities.[31]

Another blatant discrepancy was the austere, almost ascetic, character of the Sabbath prevailing among Karaites: no light in the house, no heating, no warm food, even if kept warm by means other than fire, no sex, and a series of other prohibitions. These restrictions also impeded spiritual contacts: on a Sabbath, Karaites would not enter the well-illuminated synagogues of the Rabbanites, for light in a Jewish place on that holy day was an abomination for them.[32]

A particularly unfortunate outcome of Karaite dabbling in the law was the enlargement of the scope of incestuous, and consequently forbidden, marriages. By teaching that marriage created consanguinity[33] and in addition prohibiting certain unions with blood relatives other than those mentioned in the Bible, the early Karaites made the choice of a mate extremely difficult, especially in a community of limited size like their own. The proliferation of Karaite-Rabbanite mixed marriages in circles high and low was a consequence of such legislation.

Asked by an esteemed scholar—it seems a newcomer to Egypt who was not familiar with Karaites—how to relate to them, Moses Maimonides had this to say:

These Karaites, who live here in Alexandria, Cairo, Damascus, and other places in the lands of Islam, should be approached with respect and treated with sincerity and friendliness, as long as they do not deride our

Sages and the usages practiced by us according to their instructions. We may visit the houses of the Karaites and drink their wine,[34] and, needless to say, support their poor, and bury their dead, and so on, as we are advised to do even with pagans.[35]

Maimonides' balanced opinion is reflected in numerous private letters and documents of the Geniza. The reports about clashes between the two groups, also preserved in the Geniza, should not be taken as representing the day-to-day relationships between the two groups. Rabbanites and Karaites regarded each other as belonging to one *umma*, "a nation constituted by religion," and were recognized in legal documents as "our coreligionists."[36] The Muslim authorities, too, counted both as one community. The Tustarīs, the most prominent Karaite family in Egypt during the first half of the eleventh century, are mentioned in Muslim sources simply as Jews. Abū Saᶜd, the "vizier," and his brother Abū Naṣr, who reached the highest pinnacles of power ever attained by Jews under the Fatimids, were much involved in Rabbanite affairs, supported the yeshivas in Jerusalem and Baghdad, and helped Rabbanite individuals in different locations.[37] Similar broadmindedness is reported from other Karaites connected with the government.[38] A leading Karaite figure contemporary with the Tustarīs, David b. Isaac ha-Levi, deservedly bore the title "Pride of the Two Denominations"; he was asked by the caliph to settle a conflict between Karaites and Rabbanites in Palestine, and, although he was not successful in that particular case, he was so in many others.[39] Karaites in government service were expected to be helpful in inner-Rabbanite affairs, as when a tax-farmer in Minya, asking for protection from unfair competition by Jewish newcomers, suggests that the addressee contact the Karaite *ṣāḥib dīwān*, "finance administrator," of that town.[40]

Joint appeals by Karaites and Rabbanites were natural, since the victims for whom the collections were made were often members of the two denominations. The Muslim pirates who took captives from Byzantine ships and sold them as slaves in Alexandria, Egypt, did not differentiate between the two.[41] Neither did the Muslim moneylenders, to whom the Jews of Jerusalem were heavily indebted.[42] Still, it is noteworthy that, as revealed by the Geniza, in the same decade when serious disturbances caused by religious dissent occurred among the Jews of Palestine, the Jews of Fustat were able to cooperate closely. A letter of help from Alexandria is addressed to "the holy congregations of Fustat of the two denominations, the men of the Talmud and those of the Bible." In the first place "the scribes of the government" (higher officials) are extolled and wished promotion, probably referring to Karaites, although (or because) the writer was a Rabbanite.[43] About twenty-five years later, a letter from Jerusalem refers to the receipt there of about 80 dinars, an installment of a sum destined for the dispensations. One sees that a "united Jewish appeal" was nothing exceptional.[44]

We read little about partnerships and other close business connections between members of the two persuasions; perhaps it was not necessary to indicate their affiliations. It should perhaps be noted that a younger brother of the President of the High Court of the Jerusalem yeshiva residing in Cairo ran a drugstore in the Gizeh suburb in partnership with a Karaite (1126).[45]

Even at a time of serious tension, Solomon b. Judah, the Gaon of Jerusalem, stressed that the Karaites were eager to intermarry with families of his own flock.[46] Numerous documents to this effect have been preserved and many are discussed in this book, especially in *Med Soc.*, III.[47] A wide variety of situations is apparent in them. The contracting parties usually remain in their separate persuasions but take it upon themselves to respect the religious susceptibilities of their spouses. There are, however, cases, on both Rabbanite and Karaite sides, where one spouse embraces the faith of the other. An interesting document specifying the conditions under which a Rabbanite girl marries a Karaite notable contains only socioeconomic, that is, no religious, stipulations.[48]

Serious clashes occurred in the second quarter of the eleventh century, when the peace-loving Solomon b. Judah "ruled" as Gaon.[49] In 1024, shortly before he assumed office, the government intervened on behalf of the Karaites. Their opponents had tried to force the Karaite artisans and businessmen to close their stores on Rabbanite holidays and seem also to have invaded Karaite places of worship. The edict of 1024 outlawed the use of force in matters of religious disagreement, especially with regard to the two acts of violence mentioned above. Another caliphal order was given in favor of the Rabbanites. When I published it, I assumed that it was promulgated approximately at the same time as the 1024 edict, because it is similar in diction to the first and, like it, forbids all interference with "buying and selling." The second government action, however, referred to another important detail: the banishment of the leaders of the Rabbanite troublemakers. This emergency occurred when Solomon b. Judah was in office and is repeatedly and emphatically referred to in his letters.[50]

The middle of the eleventh century was a period of famine in

Egypt and of anarchy in Palestine. Such times were apt to poison life for everyone. The caliph's decree protecting the Karaites seems to have been carried out with particular harshness. The tone in some of Solomon's letters is very bitter indeed. He tried to calm down the spirits, but in vain.

The troublemakers were Joseph and Elijah, the sons of Solomon's predecessor (which is understandable), and Solomon's own son, Abraham.[51] The three are mentioned together in a letter from Jerusalem, written on the eighth of Kislev, about seven weeks after a ban against the Karaites had been pronounced on the Mount of Olives in violation of the caliphal decree. Unfortunately, only the right half of this interesting letter is preserved. Abraham, probably because he was the Gaon's son, was spared imprisonment. Elijah had fled to Nablus. Joseph was apprehended. Finally, Elijah was found, too, and the two were sent to Damascus, where, as the writer learned later, Joseph fell ill with fever. To free the imprisoned scholars, Solomon left Jerusalem for Damascus, but—as we learn from a letter from him—because of the bad weather and his old age, he was unable to pursue this journey. The Karaites, emboldened by their success, went up on the Mount of Olives and smashed the pulpit on which the ban against them had been pronounced. "No Rabbanite shall come to Jerusalem any more!"[52]

Another rally also ended with the victory of the Rabbanite extremists. In order to arouse public opinion against the Karaites a rumor was spread that on Purim, on which the boys would burn effigies of Haman (the bête noire of the Book of Esther), the Karaites burned the effigies of three Rabbanite leaders (perhaps the three just mentioned?). Although this story was strongly disowned by respected elders, the crowd assembled at the Market of the Jews on a fast day (probably proclaimed especially for this purpose) demanded the excommunication of the Karaites. It was done despite the passionate warnings of the Gaon.[53]

This, like the (always temporary) excommunications pronounced on the Mount of Olives, certainly fell soon into desuetude by not being repeated the following year or whatever term was set for it. It represented too severe a rupture in the life of the Jewish community, but such occurrences show the deep-seated rancor of the Palestinian Rabbanites against their Karaite compatriots who could rely on their rich influential brethren in Egypt.[54]

This volatile state of affairs could spill over into personal relationships. In consequence of Rabbanite denunciations, a Karaite artisan, leader of the small Karaite community of Damascus (perhaps mostly artisans themselves), was forced to work in a government workshop. The hard conditions (probably "from sunrise to sunset") impeded him from participation in the religious and social life of his group. Their members had asked a high-standing personality in Cairo to induce the eminent Abū Naṣr al-Tustarī to obtain for him a caliphal order freeing him from that duty; two years had passed, but nothing happened. He himself now asks his correspondent to approach Abū Naṣr anew. Otherwise he would be forced to forsake his congregation and leave Damascus for Ramle. Only the petitioner's own words can bring home the intensity of his grievances:[55]

> The artisans of this profession are Jews, and I am the only Karaite among them. To take revenge from my coreligionists by doing me harm [*ṭalaban tashaffin min aṣḥābī bī*], they denounced me to the officer recruiting workers [*mutawallī ʾl-istiʿmāl*] with the effect that I was forced to work there, which I have been doing now for two years. I had to suffer from them more than from gentiles, and was separated from the company of our coreligionists, from attending their joys and griefs [weddings and funerals], from the management of their affairs, and from participating in their meetings . . . I was indeed completely separated from them [ll. 3–8].

Two visitors from Cairo witnessed the writer's plight and one of them was shocked to see what he had to endure (ll. 9–11).

> I intended to move to Ramle, afraid of what had happened to me, "and the Egyptians let the Israelites drudge in hard work" [Exodus 1:13].[56] However, our community met and asked me not to leave and wrote letters to his excellency my Lord, the Sheikh Abū Naṣr al-Tustarī—may God prolong his life and make his prosperity permanent—informing him what had happened to me and asking him to obtain [*yastanjiz*] an order [*sijill*] from his Pure Majesty to the effect that I should be exempted from all forced work. These letters were properly signed and sent off over two years ago, but no answer was received. Finally, I showed that I was in earnest in my decision to move, but they insisted that I should remain, and wrote letters both in Arabic and in Hebrew[57] to his excellency my Lord Abū Naṣr—may God make his glory permanent—asking him what has been explained above [ll. 12–*verso* 5].

In the remaining, much damaged, part (*verso* ll. 6–18), the recipient is asked to deliver the letters to Abū Naṣr in person, to describe to him what he had witnessed in Damascus, and to impress on him that a favorable caliphal decree, which would enable the writer to remain in Damascus, would strengthen the Karaite congregation there.

The introductory paragraph of the letter speaks of revenge. This could be a reference to a local affair, of which we have no knowledge. It is more likely, however, that the writer alludes to the sufferings of the Rabbanites, when their leading scholars were banished and two of them were brought in chains to Damascus, where they were not treated very kindly. The iniquities of a community are often visited on an individual.

The Karaite artisan from Damascus exemplifies the fact that not all Karaites were rich and influential Merchants of the Diaspora or persons connected with the government. The documentary Geniza shows that utmost frugality, bordering on asceticism, was not only a religious ideal but for many Karaites a reality. Fines for the benefit of the Karaite poor, and not only for those living in Jerusalem, have been met with before. A Karaite with a good handwriting and a decent style reminds his congregation that he had appealed to them repeatedly for a handout "of 10 dirhems or less" but had not received an answer. He could not go begging at a shop or the gates of houses. If pledges could not be made for him on a Sabbath, it might be done at a circumcision festivity (seemingly a frequent occurrence).[58] A Karaite from Damascus deserted his wife and four children, adopted the Rabbanite persuasion, and then, like many other paupers, traveled to Fustat, where the Rabbanite community was renowned for the charity and generosity of its members.[59] In a highly interesting and carefully written, but much damaged letter, a Karaite cantor, who had converted to the Rabbanite persuasion, asks Moses Maimonides to pay for him the poll tax "as you do for two hundred others." Actually, the letter is meant for the community: "Do not [pl.] force me to apply to the Karaites; they will not give me a grain after I have separated from them."[60]

With few exceptions, such as cases of mixed marriage concluded before a Rabbanite court, the Karaites had no reason to deposit their family papers in the Geniza. Despite the limited material found there on the subject, the stratification of the Karaite society appears to have been not much different from the Rabbanite. There is one noticeable exception: during the first half of the eleventh century the percentage of wealthy Karaite brides is larger, out of all proportion, than that in Rabbanite families.[61]

In Palestine and Egypt there seems to have been little spiritual contact between Rabbanites and Karaites during the eleventh century. The repeated assertions of Karaite writers that their opponents avoided with all their might engaging with them in disputations seem somehow confirmed by the silence of the documentary Geniza.[62] The reason for this can be easily understood. Since the

Talmud, the very essence of Rabbinic Judaism ("Rabbinic" means accepting the teachings of the Talmud by the rabbis) was rejected by the Karaites in total, there was not much common ground for theological reasoning. In general, attention should be paid to Salo Baron's sober warning against an overestimation of the Rabbanite response to Karaite polemics or missionary adventures.[63]

The situation was different in the "neutral" fields of the study of the Hebrew language and the final establishment of the text of the Bible (Masorah). David b. Abraham al-Fāsī, the Karaite author of a very valuable Hebrew-Arabic dictionary of the Bible,[64] made use of the linguistic work of the eminent Judah Ibn Qoraysh, with which he could have made himself familiar in his native town of Fez, Morocco.[65] His own work, written, or at least completed, in Palestine, was copied by Abraham b. Shabbetay, a member of the Jerusalem yeshiva, in Tyre, Lebanon, in 1091, at which time the yeshiva had its seat in that town.[66] The linguistic work of Abu ʾl-Faraj Hārūn, "the grammarian of Jerusalem," another distinguished Karaite author, was brought by a Spanish Jerusalem pilgrim to his Rabbanite colleagues in Spain.[67] The still ongoing disagreement between the experts, whether the two most eminent Masoretes, Aaron and his father Moses Ben-Asher, were Karaites or Rabbanites (the latter seems to be favored of late), shows how fluid the borders were in fields not immediately exposed to theological dissensions.[68]

The Karaite response to the fall of Jerusalem in July 1099.—I conclude this survey of the schism in the Jewish community as reflected in the Cairo Geniza with a letter of deep historical significance showing us the leaders of one Karaite community addressing another.

The Karaites paid dearly for their love of Zion. When the yeshiva and with it the majority of Rabbanites had left Jerusalem for Tyre and other places in the early 1070s, a substantial number of Karaites had remained and suffered immense losses of life and in many other aspects, of which the looting of their invaluable libraries by the Crusaders was not the smallest privation. One letter tells how the Karaites of Ascalon, Palestine, which at that time was still in Fatimid hands, and those of Egypt acted in the face of such a disaster. It is a leaf of honor in the history of the sect.

The letter was written shortly after Passover, approximately in April 1100, about nine months after Jerusalem had been taken by the Crusaders. From the Rabbanite side we have a response to this event probably not later than two weeks after it happened. A Geniza text, recently discovered, tells us that as soon as the sad tidings had reached Cairo, some notables assembled in the house of Mevōrākh b. Saadya, the Nagid, whom they found sitting on the floor, his garments rent (as is Jewish law, when mourning close relatives or martyrs). On the spot, 123 dinars were collected and sent to Ascalon to ransom the Torah scrolls and the captives (in this sequence) from the Crusaders.[69] This, of course, was only a first installment, the beginning of a process that lasted years. Other Geniza texts prove that Rabbanites of noble families had fallen into the hands of the invaders. It seems to me, however, that these were not persons captured in Jerusalem. This new text is the only Jewish source that mentions the burning of a synagogue (which had been reported by a Muslim historian). The Karaites did not have a special synagogue building; they had prayer halls, since Islamic law prohibited non-Muslims from erecting new houses of worship.[70]

The major part of the Karaite letter was published by me with a translation in 1952.[71] The missing section, with the exception of a part of the introductory Hebrew phrases, was more recently identified and edited by me. The Arabic text and the signatures, that is, all the essentials, are now available in full. The newly identified section is translated here into English for the first time.[72]

The letter is signed by six notables, all from Ascalon, as is evident from the content. It was not sent from that town, however, but from Egypt, most likely from Alexandria.[73] The senders themselves were refugees. The Crusaders not only occupied Jerusalem but menaced the entire coastal region. An Egyptian army, sent to dislodge them after the conquest of Jerusalem, was unsuccessful. Ascalon itself was saved only by temporary discord among the Crusaders. The fall of the city seemed to be a matter of months. In view of this, the captives ransomed were sent to Egypt by caravan (not by sea, which was almost entirely under the control of the Christian fleets). Almost all of those who had tried to reach Egypt individually had perished. Only about twenty had remained in Ascalon. Now the task at hand was to bring them, too, to "the Land of Life," to provide all the persons ransomed with the minimal necessities of life, and to continue the unending endeavors to save souls and books. The community addressed, no doubt the Karaite congregation of Cairo-Fustat, had already made a considerable contribution, but more was needed, and advice is given on how to organize the appeal, somewhat reminiscent of contemporary practices.

Finally, attention must be drawn to the repeated references in this letter to the troubles caused by the exigencies of war and, in particular, to a plague and other contagious diseases affecting both

Egypt and Palestine (known also from Crusader sources). The impact of this long-drawn calamity is fully evident from another Geniza letter referring to the fall of Jerusalem, one written by a pilgrim from the Maghreb, who was prevented from reaching his sacred goal by the troubles incurred in Egypt. "You know, my lord" he writes, "what has happened to us in the course of the last five years: the plague, the illnesses, and ailments[74] have continued unabated for four successive years. As a result of this, the wealthy have become impoverished and a great number of people have died *of the plague*, so that entire families have been wiped out." Who knows, perhaps the victory of the Crusaders was made possible, or at least easier, because the Fatimid army was in disarray. It was expected to arrive even before the Crusaders reached Jerusalem, but failed to do so.[75]

As a whole, the letter is self-explanatory.[76]

[A. *Introductory blessings*]

[Of the certainly long Hebrew proem, only five lines have been preserved, ending with the expression of messianic hopes:]

"At that time I will bring you home, and when gathering you in, I will make you renowned and famed among the peoples of the earth, when I restore your fortunes before your very eyes" [Zephaniah 3:20].

[B. *Praise for the quick and efficient help*]

We received the letter of your excellencies, our lords, the illustrious sheikhs—may God prolong your lives and make permanent your strong, high, and exalted position, and crush your enviers and enemies. The letter contained instructions concerning the *suftaja* [letter of credit] attached to it, which was destined for our brethren, the Jerusalemites. We have received the sum from the person charged with the payment, which our community much appreciated and highly valued. We regarded it as large, not as compared with your usual generosity but in consideration of your present troubles. We were particularly impressed by this donation because you acted immediately, without delay.

[C. *How the funds sent before were used*]

We thanked God, the exalted, for giving us the opportunity to induce you to fulfill this pious deed and for granting you to take a share in it with us.

We spent the money on ransom for some of the *captives*[77] after duly considering the instructions contained in your letter, namely, to send what was available to those who had [already been ransomed].[78] We have not failed to reply to what you have written us, may God keep you. We answered indeed, but were looking for a man who would carry our reply to you. Then it so happened that those illnesses came upon us: plague, pestilence, and epidemics,[79] which occupied us, either ourselves or one of our relatives being stricken by disease. Finally, a person traveled from here,[80] and we trust that he explained to you the situation with respect to the sums you had sent: that they reached us safely and were spent in the manner indicated by you.

[D. *The plight of the ransomed and of those still in captivity*]

News still reaches us continuously that of those who were redeemed from the Franks and remained in Ascalon some are in danger of dying from want of food, clothing, and from exhaustion. Others remained in captivity, of whom some were killed with all manner of torture out of sheer lust to murder before the eyes of others who were spared. We did not hear of a single man of Israel in such danger without exerting ourselves to do all that was in our power to save him.

[E. *Captives redeemed by an Alexandrian notable*]

God the exalted has granted opportunities for relief and deliverance to individual *refugees*, of which the first and most perfect instance—after *the compassion of Heaven*—was the presence in Ascalon of the honorable elder Abu ʾl-Faḍl Sahl, son of Yūshaʿ, son of Shaʿyā—may God preserve him—who has dealings with the government—may God bestow upon it glorious victories—whose influence is great in Alexandria, where his word is very much heeded.[81] He arranged matters wisely to overcome this emergency; but it would require a lengthy discourse to explain how he did it. He could not ransom some people and leave others.

[F. *On some captives still held by the Franks*]

In the end, all those who could be bought from them [the Franks] were liberated, and only a few whom they kept remained in their hands, including a boy of about eight years of age,[82] and a man known as Abū Saʿd, the son of the Tustarī's wife.[83] It is reported that the Franks urged the latter to embrace the Christian faith of his own free will and promised to treat him well, but he said to them, how could a Kohen become a Christian and be left in peace by those [the Jews] who had already disbursed a large sum on his behalf. Until this day, these captives remain in their [Franks] hand, as well as those who were taken to Antioch, but they are few; and not counting those *who abjured their faith* because they lost patience, as it was not possible to ransom them, and because they despaired of being permitted to go free.

[G. *No women violated*]

We were not informed, praise be to God, the exalted, that *the accursed ones* who are called Ashkenaz violated or raped women, as others do.[84]

[H. *Details about the escape*]

Now, among those who have reached safety are some who escaped on the second and third days following the battle and left with the governor who was granted safe conduct, and others who, after having been caught by the Franks, remained in their hands for some time and escaped in the end; these are but few. The majority consists of those who were bought free.

[I. *Flight of individuals to Egypt*]

To our sorrow, some of them ended their lives in all kinds of suffering and affliction. The privations that they had to endure caused some of them to leave for this country [Egypt] without provisions or protection against the cold, and they died on the way. Others perished at sea; and still others, after having arrived here safely, became exposed to a "change of air"; they came at the height of the plague, and a number of them died. We had, at that time, reported the arrival of each group.

[J. *The transport of the ransomed to Egypt*]

But when the aforementioned honored elder arrived, he brought a group of them, that is, most of those who had reached Ascalon; he passed the Sabbath and celebrated Passover with them on the way in the manner required by such circumstances.[85] He contracted a private loan for the sum needed to pay the camel drivers and for their maintenance on the way, as well as for the caravan guards and other expenses, after having already spent other sums of money, which he did not charge to the community.

[K. *The books ransomed*]

All this is in addition to the money that was borrowed and spent in order to buy back two hundred and thirty Bible codices, a hundred other volumes, and eight *Torah Scrolls.* All these are *communal property*[86] and are now in Ascalon.

[L. *Reduced prices for the captives*]

The community, after having disbursed on different occasions about 500 dinars for the actual ransom of the individuals, for maintenance of some of them and for the ransom, as mentioned above, of the communal property, remained indebted for the sum of 200 and some odd dinars. This is in addition to what has been spent on behalf of those who have been arriving from the beginning until now, on medical potions and treatment, maintenance and, insofar as possible, clothing. If it could be calculated how much this has cost over such a long period, the sum would indeed be huge.

Had the accepted practice been followed, that is, of selling three Jewish captives for a hundred (dinars), the whole available sum would have been spent for the ransom of only a few.[87] However, the grace of the Lord, may his name be glorified, has been bestowed upon these wretched people,[88] who may, indeed cry out as it is written: "You let them devour us like sheep, and scattered us among the nations. You have sold your people for a trifle, demanding no high price for them."[89] Indeed, all the money we have spent to meet this emergency, from the beginning until now, is but insignificant and negligible with respect to its magnitude and the intensity of the sorrow it has entailed.

[M. *Need for further donations despite the dire state of the community*]

Some may rightly adduce as an excuse the impoverishment of this class of the wealthy and well-to-do, as well as the troubles endured by your community during this winter, which harmed it and weakened its strength, [damaged] its fortunes and reduced its numbers, so that everything became disturbed. Finally, he who escaped from this was assaulted by painful illnesses which devoured his possessions so that he had to take loans for his current expenses.[90] We cannot refrain from reporting what we know, however, and what we have done up till now. For we know that you, like ourselves, grieve and mourn for those who have gone and are concerned to preserve those who are alive, especially since your determination to distinguish yourselves in this matter has become apparent, and the loftiness of your aspiration and generosity is now famous. You were the first and most consistent in seizing this opportunity to get precedence over all other *communities* and have attained great honor. You are now in the position of that tribe that was praised because it rushed to perform noble deeds and was in a hurry to accomplish all that is praiseworthy, as it is said: "He was in the van of his people to fulfill the Lord's design and his decisions for Israel" [Deuteronomy 33:21].

We have already indicated that we remain in debt of more than 200 dinars, apart from the sums that are still required for the maintenance of the captives who remained in Ascalon—a little more than twenty persons—their transport and other needs until they will arrive here.

[N. *A special case*]

Among those who are in Ascalon is the honored elder Abi [!] ʾl-Khayr Mubārak, the son of the teacher Hiba b. Nīsān—may God always protect him. It is well known how noble, wise, God-fearing, and endowed with high virtues he is; he is bound by an old vow not to benefit by anything from charity together with the whole of the community, but only from what is explicitly destined for him by name. [He should be enabled] to come here, after you, our lords, have graciously provided what is needed for the payment of the debt incurred for the ransom of our and your brethren.

[O. *Suggestions for a successful appeal*]

Gird now your loins together with us in this matter, and it will be accounted for you *as a mark of merit* in the future, as it has been in the past . . . for we have no one in these parts to whom we could write as we are writing to you. It is proper that we should turn to you and take the liberty of causing you some inconvenience.

The main sections of this letter should be read out to your community, after you have announced that everyone was obliged to attend. The benefit will thus be complete and general, both to those who pay and to those who receive payment. For it is unlikely that there should not be among the people persons who had made a vow; there may be others who owe a sum to *the communal chest*, the use of which has not been defined; such should, then, be invited to earmark their contribution; others might volunteer a gift without strings. Or there may be those who intend to make a contribution to one cause rather than to another. In this manner, you will achieve your purpose, extricate strength from the weak, and deal with us in your accustomed generosity and excellent manner . . . and you will deserve, through this charitable act, to acquire both worlds. . . .

[P. *How to transfer the funds collected*]

We dispatched a messenger to you, who will tell you the details of this emergency, thus exempting us from discoursing on it at greater length. We beg of you—may God prolong your life—to take care of him until he returns, as well as of the sums which God may grant from your side. If you could make out a letter of credit for what will be collected, this would make things easier for him, since he is but a messenger, and speed up his return.[91] If this cannot be done, arrange that an exact statement of how much has been collected be made, and have your letter sent through him [the messenger] and mention the sum in it.

[Q. *Conclusion*]

[Nine lines of blessings in Hebrew and biblical quotations expressing hopes for retaliation and restitution (Isaiah 14:2, Jeremiah 50:33–34*a*, Isaiah 61:9).]

[R. *Postscript and details about the messenger*][92]

The bearer of this letter, *our esteemed m*[*aster*] *and t*[*eacher*] Ṣedāqā, son of the learned and pious Saadya, known as sheikh Abū ʿAmr, the Miller, [may] G[od have] m[ercy upon him], is a respectable and reliable person, helpful and devout, eager to earn praise for the pursuit of good deeds, a man of true liberality. He is not blessed with riches, and has little in hand. However, his noble soul demands from him more than his circumstances permit. He busies himself with the affairs of the [. . .], makes rounds for the needy, and seeks to gain all kinds of religious merits. Now he has ventured to leave his own affairs and to undertake this mission.

We reiterate our request that you take good care of him, carry through his mission as quickly as possible, and support him in every way. The good you do with him will be widely known, the little you donate will be appreciated, let alone the much. Whatever you decide—may God make your welfare permanent—with regard to what we have written concerning this man and expediting his mission, will be right, if God will.

[S. *Six signatures*][93]

[1] Samuel b. Ḥalfōn, *the physician,*[94] sends your excellencies the most special greetings.

[2] Musallam[95] b. Barakāt ("Blessings") b. Isḥāq (Isaac) sends your excellencies the most special and respectful greetings.

[3] *May the entire holy and chosen congregation—may their Rock keep, and their Savior help them, above all, their learned and saintly men—accept my greetings of peace, I, Shelah, the Kohen, b. Zadok b. Maṣliaḥ b. Z . . . m[ay their] s[ouls be]*

p[reserved in the] b[undle of] l[ife]. Take notice that my soul is yearning after you. May our God in his grace bring us together soon. [A]m[en]. [In Hebrew. Shelah, as Kohen, pronounced the priestly blessing over the entire congregation.]

[4] Hananiah b. Manṣūr [Victorious] b. Ezra sends etc. and asks you to pay attention to the content of this letter. And Peace!

[5] The writer of this letter, *the suffering, mourning, and grieved* Isaiah, the Kohen, son of Maṣlī'aḥ, the Pre[ceptor], singles out all your lords for the choicest greetings and asks you to be indulgent with him;[96] for it has not been hidden from you what he has endured and suffered from the moment he parted with you up till this very moment. And [may your] w[elfare] w[ax]. A[men].[97] [Not every Kohen cared or was permitted to pronounce the priestly blessing over the congregation. See signatory 3, above.]

[6] David b. Solomon b. David b. Isaac b. Eli the [Preceptor][98] extends to your illustrious excellencies the most respectful greetings and asks you to take care of the messenger and to attend to him quickly. May I never be robbed of your generosity.

Counterreformation.—Schisms are failed reforms. For reasons explained above, the radical reformation of the Jewish religion attempted by the Karaites led to a schism. The counterreformation connected with the name of Saadya Gaon, the head of the Sura yeshiva of Baghdad, invigorated Judaism and directed its development for centuries.

Muslim scholars leaving more than a hundred writings are listed in the *Fihrist* (The List), a kind of bibliography of Islamic literature, composed by Ibn al-Nadīm.[99] Most of the works of such early writers, standing at the cradle of a new literature, got lost in the course of time, because they were replaced by more sophisticated and more complete creations. Thanks to the endeavors of an Ibn al-Nadīm and other medieval authors writing on the history of Islamic literature we at least know the names and nature of the works of the ancient Muslim authors, and often also something of their life story.

Saadya was as prolific a Jewish author as were numerous Muslim learned men of his age. No such helpful information as a *Fihrist* was at the disposal of modern scholarship with regard to post-Talmudic literature. To be sure, Saadya's preeminence was known. His philosophical chef d'oeuvre and a few other of his writings were available in print. His bibliography and biography, however, had to be pieced together by references and quotations dispersed throughout medieval Jewish literature, a herculean task, accomplished by the giants of the *Wissenschaft des Judentums* (Jewish historical research) of the nineteenth century. Then, toward the end of that century, the Cairo Geniza laid bare its arcana. Countless fragments, large and small, of Saadya's writings, or references to them, became known and were assiduously collected and discussed. By 1921, Henry Malter, a scholar of impressive learning, common sense, and good taste, was able to produce a comprehensive and thorough book, entitled *Saadia Gaon; His Life and Works.* Even during the very printing of that book, substantial new finds were made in the Geniza, and since then the process has gone on. Important works by Saadya, such as his *Siddur,* so often referred to above, or his *Egron,* discussed immediately below, were printed in specialized editions. Specialized studies on him as a philosopher and teacher of ethics and piety, as a translator and commentator of the Bible, as an authority on Jewish law, as a liturgical poet and linguist have made their appearance. Five memorial volumes honored the millennium of his death (Baghdad, 942), three in the United States, one in England, and a particularly voluminous one in Israel. Had it not been the time of World War II, continental Europe would certainly have contributed additional such volumes.[100]

A true reformer is a creative mind, one who holds fast to the accepted values and notions of an ancient heritage, but tries to remodel it by enriching the existing structure with much needed additional layers, thus providing the whole with a new look. Saadya was certainly a man of this stature. That he was a trailblazer is gratefully acknowledged by many of his successors, and may be learned also from the book lists preserved in the Geniza.[101] He himself was aware of his role, when he wrote, referring to his lifework: "God does not leave his people at any time without a scholar whom he gives learning and inspiration so that he may so instruct and teach them that thereby their condition will be improved."[102]

Saadya was born in 882 in the Fayyūm, the oasis-like district south of Cairo, and is therefore often referred to as al-Fayyūmī for short. He himself used FYWMY (Fayyūmī) as an acrostic in several of his poetic creations. His first dated book, the *Egron,* "Compendium," a study on Hebrew, written in the Hebrew language for general use and in particular for poets, already displays the multifaceted spiritual world of its author. In the Introduction the book is dated 902, when its author was twenty years old; in a later, Arabic, version, Saadya notes indeed that he wrote the first edition at the age of twenty.[103]

The *Egron* opens with the then accepted notions about the Holy Language. It was God's own speech, with which the world was created ("God *said*: Let there be light," e.g., Genesis 1:3); in which the angels praise him (Isaiah 6:3); in which Adam and Eve and all their progeny conversed for over a thousand years ("the whole earth had *one language*," Genesis 11:1), until human hubris robbed them of this precious gift (*ibid.*, 2:9). Only the Hebrews kept it even during their servitude in Egypt and all their other tribulations; they are the bearers of the Torah, the words of the Prophets, and all the other Holy Scriptures. But when they sinned, they were dispersed among the nations and began to learn, even as children (as Saadya certainly did), to read and to speak the foreign vernaculars (Nehemiah 13:24). Only when in this, as in other matters, they correct their ways will salvation come and mankind again be united in "the pure speech" (Zephaniah 3:9).[104]

Actually, Hebrew had not "ceased from the mouth" of the Children of Israel. All prayers and benedictions (there were many and long ones) were said in that language. Moreover, it became daily enriched by the unending creations of liturgical poets.[105] But in his youthful enthusiasm Saadya demanded more: "Let the Holy Language never be absent from our mouth, we, our children, our wives, even our slaves.[106] Let the people of our God talk in it, when they go out and at home, when they are at work and in their bedrooms, and even with their babes."[107]

Saadya's immediate concern, however, was to analyze the Hebrew language, so that it could be properly used, and to collect its treasures, so that they were always at the disposal of the liturgical poets, of whom he was one. I even suspect that he first assembled those collections for himself, but then decided to make them available also to others. His ideas about the structure of Hebrew were expressed later in a book—written in Arabic—entitled *The Correct Use of the Language of the Hebrews*. The often-quoted book was lost, but considerable Geniza fragments of it, preserved in Leningrad, Oxford, and Cambridge, enabled Solomon L. Skoss to reconstruct its contents. The linguistic thinking of Saadya, "the earliest Hebrew Grammarian," is very impressive; it was qualified and enriched by subsequent research, but taught the future generations that the use of the Holy Language, as of any other language, required discipline.[108]

The lexicographical collections in the *Egron* comprised both the Hebrew of the Bible and that of the Mishna and the Babylonian and Palestinian Talmuds. This was a declaration of faith. Saadya was completely aware of the fact that "the language of the Scriptures" and that "of the Sages" were different, but he recognized them as two branches of one language. This scientifically correct finding was, of course, a welcome help in the dispute of the Rabbanites with the Karaites, as became even more evident in a much later publication. There he successfully explained words occurring in the Bible only once, or otherwise difficult, by comparing them with quotations from Talmudic literature, pointing out that the Sages, as the disciples of the Prophets, were naturally familiar with the language then in vogue.[109]

The interest in rare and "difficult" words had an additional purpose. The synagogal artistic liturgy, the Piyyūṭ, which flourished around the middle of the first millennium as profusely in Palestine as did pre-Islamic poetry at the same time in Arabia, reached for exquisite expressions, rare or nonexistent grammatical forms, and allusions to faraway topics dispersed all over the vast Talmudic literature. Just like ancient Arabic poetry, a piyyūṭ could not be understood without a commentary. The sublime should be above the grasp of the ordinary mind.[110]

At his beginnings, Saadya was an enthusiastic disciple of this School, almost surpassing his masters. Slowly a change occurred, conditioned, it seems, both by the changing circumstances of his life, and, even more perhaps, by a change of heart, but in any case exerting deep influence on the following generations. The Jews of Egypt were closely connected with those of Palestine, the country where the piyyūṭ was cultivated. I believe even that Saadya studied there in his youth.[111] Anyhow, in his thirties or so he spent several years there. His last two decades he lived in Babylonia-Iraq, where the piyyūṭ seems to have been less popular. In his *Siddur* (Order, of the prayers and usages to be observed during the year), he notes repeatedly that he had composed many liturgical poems for this or that occasion but they were "too long," wherefore he provided only one or a few shorter ones. Most of those we read in the *Siddur* present practically no difficulties in either language or content. This is particularly true of his greater creations, such as the *Tokhēḥā* (Self-admonition, for the Day of Atonement) or his famous two *Baqqashōth* (Personal Prayers) which he says he included "for those who seek the propinquity of God." These personal prayers were highly esteemed by later generations. The very critical Abraham Ibn Ezra (d. 1167) wrote about them: "No one has composed anything comparable; they are in biblical, grammatically proper style, without riddles or farfetched hermeneutics."[112] Because of their holiness Maimonides was asked whether it was not obligatory to recite them while standing.[113] A modern admirer coined the paradox: "Saadya [at the time he lived in Baghdad] was the father of Spanish Hebrew poetry." For various reasons, this bon mot cannot be sustained. It is true, however, that Saadya, during his exuberant life, carried liturgical poetry from and through extreme artistry and learnedness to noble simplicity and rationally oriented piety.[114] Even in his fifties, though, he reverted occasionally to a somewhat artificial form of Hebrew style, probably whenever he felt that that type of expression was the one best fitted for the occasion.[115]

An event that almost created a schism within rabbinic Judaism and had a decisive impact on Saadya's life was a rift between the yeshiva of Jerusalem and those of Baghdad with regard to the calendar. Today the western and eastern Christian churches still have different ecclesiastical calendars with the result that they celebrate their holidays on different dates. A similar difference prevailed between Karaites and Rabbanites. The Rabbanite community, under the leadership of the more prominent Babylonian schools, had adopted an astronomically calculated permanent calendar, which, at the time of the outbreak of the controversy, had been in force for centuries. Under circumstances not fully known, Ben-Meir, then the head of the Jerusalem yeshiva, proclaimed in 921 a calculation differing from the accepted calendar by two days. Saadya, who at that time commuted between Baghdad, Aleppo in northern Syria, and Jerusalem, tried to convince Ben-Meir of the fallacy of his computation. When the latter remained adamant, Saadya put his scholarship and pen at the disposal of the Exilarch of Baghdad and refuted Ben-Meir in public, as we learn from letters, circulars, and pamphlets, partly published in the name of the Exilarch. Ben-Meir realized that even people close to him stuck to the traditional calendar and had to give in, or, at least, we know nothing to the contrary. If I am not mistaken, all our information about this widespread and dangerous dispute comes from a dozen or more Geniza documents, some of which were pieced together from several fragments published at different times in different places. Anyone who wishes to taste the vagaries of Geniza research and, at the same time, its historical significance, is advised to read about the Ben-Meir controversy. A prominent medieval scholar could regard Saadya as the founder of the science of the Jewish calendar because he still could read the complete writings, of which we have only the remnants.[116]

It is not difficult to guess why Saadya had become so knowledgeable in matters of astronomy connected with calendar computation. In 882, the very year in which he was born, the Jews from Babylonia (Iraq-Iran) living in Fustat bought the Jacobite St. Michael's church and installed there a house of worship for themselves, so numerous had they become.[117] But Babylonia was also the cradle of Karaism; the most prominent Karaite contemporaries of Saadya, such as Nehawendī, Qūmisī, Qirqisānī, were named after places in Iran or Iraq. Soon Karaites occupied leading positions in the capital of Egypt. Under these circumstances Saadya's vigilance in defense of rabbinic Judaism against Karaism can easily be understood. It accompanied him throughout his life, not so much in special polemical writings (known only through references and fragments found in the Geniza), one of which was devoted mainly to questions of the calendar, but in all his literary creations, whether he expounded the Bible, the philosophy of Judaism, or Hebrew linguistics. Moreover, as S. Gandz repeatedly emphasizes in his instructive paper "Saadia Gaon as a Mathematician," he seems to have had a propensity for arithmetic and calculations "for he frequently goes out of his way in order to introduce all kinds of computations into his legal and theological disquisitions."[118]

Be that as it may, Saadya's role in the Ben-Meir affair proved his excellence as both a scholar and a public figure. He moved to Baghdad, where he received the title *allūf*, "distinguished member" of the yeshiva. In May 928 he was appointed head of the Sura yeshiva, which was in dire need of a competent leader. Like other Gaons before and after him, Saadya clarified and developed Jewish law by *responsa*, "answers," to actual or theoretical questions submitted to him. His main contribution, however, was systematization in both content and arrangement, as well as the use of Arabic juristic parlance. This was achieved by short treatises on selected fields of law, a kind of lecture to students, fitted with proper introductions. Saadya also wrote a systematic Introduction to the Talmud and a work on the Mishnaic Thirteen Rules for the legalistic interpretation of the Torah.[119]

The use of the Arabic language was justified in order to bring out the precise meaning of the terms in the mixed Aramaic-Hebrew idiom of the Talmud, with which, as Saadya often had opportunity to complain, his younger contemporaries were no longer sufficiently familiar. It was also necessary to streamline the proceedings of the Jewish courts with those of the Muslim authorities, which possessed, of course, overriding authority. If Saadya's Arabic treatise entitled *Law of Inheritance* was actually one of his earliest writings in the field of law, he might have been induced to choose that language because he noted that many cases about inheritance came before both Jewish and Muslim courts.[120]

I am inclined to see in these lecture-like monographs a fundamental reform of teaching, apparently introduced by Saadya while head of the Sura yeshiva. The traditional method of study was—and remained for a long time—reading a section of the Talmud and discussing it; the basis of instruction was an ancient text. The new approach was that the teaching process centered on a topic, the collection of the relevant material, and arranging it in the order required by its nature. It seems that Saadya not only adhered to this principle in his own writings but developed it as a method to be followed in the yeshiva. I have come to this conclusion, because the most eminent among Saadya's successors as head of Sura was the Gaon Samuel b. Ḥofnī (d. 1013), who wrote at least forty-three such monographs that we know of. They comprise the entire gamut of civil law, from the "Transfer of Debts and Letters of Credit" (which belong to the "Law of the merchants" not recognized by the Sages of the Talmud) to the "Digging of Canals, Irrigation Ditches, and Wells," an important topic for a country where the agriculture is based mostly on irrigation.[121]

My surmise about Saadya's intention to realize his educational reforms first in the yeshiva which he headed seems to apply even more to the way in which he expounded the Bible. Eleven years after his death, his two sons She'ērīth and Dōsā were asked to compile a list of their father's writings. A partial copy of their answer, preserved in the Geniza, notes that he translated the entire Pentateuch without a commentary, then wrote commentaries to the first part of Genesis and to Exodus and Leviticus, finally a book called *The Flowers of the Gardens*, elucidating certain points in the Pentateuch from beginning to end. In a later part of the list is mentioned a book of answers to specific questions on the Pentateuch. Among the details concerning the other books of the Bible, Saadya's sons make mention in particular of his extended Introduction to the Book of Psalms.[122]

The strange but indisputable fact that Saadya began his extended commentary on the Pentateuch with the first half of Genesis, then took on Exodus and Leviticus, and finally stopped at the beginning of Numbers is best explained by assuming that he assigned the parts not undertaken by himself to other scholars. This assumption seems to be confirmed by a note copied from a work by R. Joseph Rosh ha-Seder b. Jacob, a Babylonian scholar living in Egypt, from whose hand we have more information about books than from anyone else: "I studied the commentary of the Torah written by three: the first part of Genesis, Exodus, and Leviticus by Rabbenū Saadya; the second part of Genesis, Numbers and the first part of Deuteronomy by R. Samuel b. Ḥofnī; and the last part by R. Aaron b. Sarjādo."[123]

Aaron (b. Joseph ha-Kohen) b. Sarjādo, a scholar who belonged to the Jewish high bourgeoisie of Baghdad, is well known for taking sides with the Exilarch David b. Zakkay in his conflict with Saadya. But this is not to say that sometime before he had not been Saadya's admirer and close colleague, who had an opportunity to become familiar with the master's methods.[124] We do not know to whom the parts later taken up by Samuel b. Ḥofnī had been originally assigned. There are, however, other questions. A Yemenite scholar of the fourteenth century quotes Saadya Gaon forty-seven times—often very extensively—in his biblical studies; those from Genesis are exclusively from the second and not from the first part of the book.[125] In one of his last publications N. Allony notes references in Geniza sources to parts of the second sections of Genesis, to Numbers, and to Deuteronomy, ascribed to Saadya.[126]

An elucidation of these problems is apt to shed light on Saadya's multifaceted activities as Bible commentator. The letter of his sons, analyzed above, and other Geniza references, including those quoted in Allony's article, speak about *nukat*, "difficult points," "short explicative notes," a term common in Islamic literature,[127] about *masāʾil*, "questions answered," and about *tafsīr bilmaʿānī*, "translation with discussions of problems," a full-fledged commentary. Saadya's philosophical, polemical, and linguistic writings comment on the Bible on every page. All of this had one aim: to guide the student to what Saadya believed was the correct understanding of the Bible, leading *to* and not *away* from it. The enormous Hebrew-Aramaic literature of commentaries, homiletics, and the Midrash preceding Saadya took the sacred texts rather as a point of *departure*. He, too, was a preacher; his sons mention a book of sermons written by him. But in his Bible studies he tried to come to grips with the text, its literal meaning and wider implications and connections. For this purpose he wrote his commentaries and cognate creations all in Arabic, the language of the educated people. His youthful ideal of spoken Hebrew had to give way to the duty of achieving clarity and full comprehension by a wider public.[128]

Since Saadya's expository material was available for almost the entire Bible,[129] the Arabic translation of the Pentateuch and many other parts of the Bible accepted in the Jewish communities of the Arabic-speaking countries were regarded as *Tafsīr Saadya*, and rightly so.[130]

There was one biblical book on which Saadya seemingly wrote no commentary. Ecclesiastes, the Preacher and angry censor of this world, must have puzzled him for a long time, as it did many other believers before and after. There was, of course, no doubt about his identity with King Solomon, and, consequently, his flawless orthodoxy. Passages expressing doubts in a future life (3:21) could be explained away by references to others in the book, which seem to take it for granted, for instance 11:9 and 12:7, or, as in the case of 9:4–6, could be ascribed to the evil and foolish people mentioned in the preceding verse 9:3 (Malter, pp. 239–243). But what was the purpose of the wisest of all men in writing this book? Here, attention should be drawn to an ingenious study by G. Vajda, in which he convincingly shows that the tenth and concluding treatise of Saadya's philosophical chef d'oeuvre was indeed a kind of *maʿānī Koheleth*, a discussion of the book of Ecclesiastes. In that treatise, in which Saadya, being in the last decade of his life, tried to convey to the reader his mature advice for proper conduct, he finds the quintessence of all he had to say in that book of the aging king—a form of self-identification after much soul searching.[131]

Having discussed seven major theories about the nature of the soul and having established (in the wake of Plato) its being possessed of the faculties of concupiscence, wrath, and reason (lit., "discernment"), Saadya demonstrates that human bliss is vouchsafed when the balance is preserved between the extremes to which the soul's faculties are inclined. When Koheleth complains about the futility of wisdom (1:17), of pleasure (2:1–2), and of the accumulation of wealth (2:4 ff.), he means to say that each of them must fail, if pursued exclusively and to the extreme. After having illustrated the rule of the golden mean by thirteen examples, among them such touchy topics as asceticism and renunciation of the world, or complete dedication either to the seeking of wisdom or dedication to worship ("fasting during the day and standing in worship all the night"), he concludes his argument about the two aspects of any human endeavor with the quotation of Ecclesiastes 7:18: "It is good that you take hold of one without letting go the other," adding "and this is also my aspiration."[132]

In passing from Saadya's Bible commentaries to his philosophical work, I have dwelt on the concluding treatise of his chef d'oeuvre, to which Ecclesiastes forms a kind of frame. This was done to evince the unity of his spiritual world despite its wide scope and diversity.[133] Saadya's discourse about the seven theories of the nature of the soul shows familiarity with Greek, even pre-Socratic, philosophy. Since it has been difficult to pin down the sources from which Saadya might have derived his knowledge, it has been conjectured that it might have come to him through association with the learned interconfessional circles then flourishing in Baghdad.

Whether works of Arabic literature of the ninth and tenth centuries were derived to a considerable extent from attendance at learned assemblies and only partly from complete books is a problem of Arabic literature in general.[134]

The *Book of Beliefs and Opinions* opens with the problem of how the physical world came into being. For only after it has been demonstrated that the biblical account, creation out of nothing, is the only one acceptable can the main theological problems, such as God, revelation, predestination and free will, resurrection and the World to Come, be approached. Saadya discusses and refutes twelve theories about the origin of the world, not only from Greek thought but also from (Zoroastrian) Dualism, Manichaeism, "Materialism," Hinduism, and others. Here, too, the scholars are of divided opinion concerning the sources he used.[135] But one thing stands out clearly: the world of the Jewish intellectual living in the center of the Islamic world at the beginning of the tenth century was exposed to challenging and conflicting influences. Here Saadya, as he pronounced in his Prolegomena, stepped into the breach.

It was a time when the human mind, after having completely surrendered to "the yoke of the Kingdom of Heaven," wished to reassert its independence. Saadya's Prolegomena is dedicated to epistemology, the ways by which knowledge is acquired. Apart from sensation, intuition, and logical inference, the generally accepted methods, Israel was blessed with revelation and tradition with the aim to facilitate and accelerate the process of achieving perfection. But throughout the book Saadya proceeds along the lines of methodical reasoning, bringing in the Bible—and to a far lesser degree postbiblical quotations—as a kind of illustration and confirmation.[136] Assigning the first place to reason even in disputations within the community had become a necessity: not only had postbiblical religious literature ceased to be common ground for all Jews (witness Karaism). Even the Bible (and implicitly God) had become the targets of biting criticism, if not satire, by a man writing perfect, piyyūṭic Hebrew, accessible only to a scholar; and he was not the only one indulging in such blasphemy, using Hebrew as a medium of dissemination.[137]

I refer to Ḥiwwī al-Balkhī, from Balkh in Afghanistan of all places, whose book of two hundred problems questioning the authority of the Bible had become widely known since the days of Saadya, who wrote a refutation of it in verse. It was mentioned by Bible commentators throughout the Middle Ages, is noted in a Geniza book list, and Israel Davidson, who had the good luck to find a big chunk of Saadya's refutation in the Geniza, published it in a book in 1915.[138] We had to wait until December 1981, though, when Ezra Fleischer, having identified a coherent fragment of Ḥiwwī's creation itself (in the Geniza, of course) put the whole story into the proper historical context. Saadya treated the difficult topic in verse because Ḥiwwī had done so before. This was a Near Eastern tradition, widely followed in Arabic poetry; but it had already been adopted by Saint Ephraem, the great doctor of the Syriac church (d. 373), when refuting the mighty heretic Bardesanes (who had died about a century and a half before him). Ḥiwwī had himself preceded Saadya by half a century, but his verses must still have been in vogue in the latter's time so that Saadya felt called upon to refute him from beginning to end.[139]

Ḥiwwī's "questions" comprise roughly three categories: (*a*) The Bible distorts the image of God, or God is not what we believed he is. He is not omniscient. (Why does he ask Adam "where are you?") He is not omnipotent. (Why is he afraid of the Tower of Babylon?) He is neither just nor merciful. (Why was Jacob afflicted by misfortune, the premature death of his beloved Rachel, and the troubles with his son Joseph, or why had the Israelites to endure slavery in Egypt for hundreds of years without any reported guilt of theirs?) (*b*) The miracles mentioned are fake. (Moses practiced what he had learned from the Egyptian sorcerers. He knew that the tide would return in the morning when Pharaoh and his hosts would attack.) (*c*) Contradictions. (Why was circumcision imposed when even small scratches were forbidden as a desecration of the human body [Deuteronomy 10:14]?) As expected, Saadya's refutations are of different weight and significance. But in all matters that were essential for the Jewish faith, as Saadya understood it, he took a firm stand, as one who was out not to convince others but to be satisfied to have attained the truth for himself. The establishment of the unchallenged authority of the Holy Scripture was a precondition for any Jewish (or Christian or Muslim) theology.

Saadya's *Book of Beliefs and Opinions* makes fascinating reading, dense and tense. One endeavor runs through the whole: proving the irrational by rational argumentation. Everything of consequence was and will be achieved by miracle: the creation out of nothing, revelation, the coming of the Messiah, life after death. This seemingly farfetched theory had a very practical purpose: it kept the candle of hope glowing. The world, as we know it, is rotten. Its end cannot be far away, either because the term fixed by God for the length of its existence is near, or because its corruptness deserves a premature termination by an Armageddon from which only the righteous will be saved. Life after the final resurrection of the dead is ethereal, spiritual; it cannot be imagined by our body-bound mind. Only the pious, both Jew and Gentile, will participate in that miraculous world.[140]

The answers provided by Saadya to the questions, big and small, asked by individual Jews and the community at large during the tenth through the twelfth centuries, seem to have been satisfactory. Saadya did not remain alone. Samuel b. Ḥofnī, his most prominent successor as head of the Sura school, developed the systematic teaching of Jewish law, using the medium of Arabic and followed Saadya in his rationalistic way of expounding the Bible and the Talmud. Sherira, head of the other yeshiva, brought to fruition what Saadya had attempted in various writings (of which only snippets had been preserved): the creation of a historical account proving the uninterrupted continuation of the chain of tradition down to his own time. Sherira's *Iggereth,* his famous "Letter" sent to Jacob b. Nissīm b. Shāhīn of Qayrawān in 987, fulfilled their requirement. It is our main source for the history of the Gaonic schools.[141] Sherira's son and successor Hay, who reached the age of almost a hundred years like his father, was the most gaonic of all Gaons: from his hand are perhaps as many responsa known and preserved as from all his predecessors in both yeshivas. This proves, that the revival of traditional Judaism initiated by the many-sided Saadya was still paramount within the community at the beginning of the eleventh century. The Geniza, which permits us glimpses into the personal life of its members, confirms this impression.[142]

Spain was a different story. The dismemberment of the Umayyad caliphate, followed by the rise of numerous small principalities, enabled Jews to move up the social ladder. This entailed a larger measure of assimilation to the culture of the environment than was customary in the East. The creation of a large body of secular Hebrew poetry with all the social implications connected with it was the most conspicuous aspect of this process. At the same time, traditional Jewish scholarship cultivating strict observance and further development of the law was in full bloom. The central personality in this development was the Nagid Samuel (b. Joseph ha-Levi) Ibn Nagrela (d. 1055/6), whose role in the West can be compared with that of Saadya in the East. Known as one of the most prolific and original writers of Hebrew verse, he served as vizier in the Berber principality of Granada, Spain. In this capacity he had to accompany or to lead armies into the field, leaving poetic descriptions of his military exploits. Captured in a battle in 1049, he faced death; miraculously saved, he vowed to compose a corpus of decisions in Jewish law. "In this book you will find the words of the Ancients and those of the most recent; you will not have the trouble of searching; God has taught me what to take and what to leave." In his youth he had studied the Talmud and gaonic responsa with the greatest authorities in Spain and had continued taking notes all his life. His corpus enjoyed high reputation; it is quoted by about forty authorities.[143]

The example given by Samuel ha-Nagid (as he is commonly referred to) was followed by the Spanish Hebrew poets of the eleventh and twelfth centuries. Along with writing poems on wine, women, and other pleasures of this world, they complied with a strictly religious conduct. Jewish Spain produced works in all the fields in which Saadya had been active: Hebrew linguistics, religious poetry, and liturgy of the highest quality, books on ethics and theology, Bible commentaries, and, of course, studies on religious law. As the Geniza reveals, these creations reached the Muslim East and were studied there but did not elicit local response. No author of distinction made his appearance there (with the exception of some immigrants from Spain). The local population was probably too small and too harrassed economically to produce and support talent.

The arrival of Moses Maimonides of Cordova, Spain, in Egypt, shortly before he reached his thirtieth year in 1168, was certainly the most significant event in the East-West-East relations within the Jewish community of the Mediterranean world. His lifework (with that of his son Abraham) should perhaps be characterized as restoration rather than reform. It designated the end of a period of efflorescence of Oriental Jewry under Islam, just as Saadya's appearance had marked its beginning.

5. Messianic Expectations and the World to Come

Between the death of Saadya Gaon of Baghdad in 942 and that of the Spanish Hebrew poet Judah ha-Levi shortly after his arrival in Palestine in 1141, a considerable change seems to have occurred in the Rabbanite-Jewish attitude toward messianism. The matter assumed an aura of urgency, as if redemption were around the corner, as if one had to do something to hasten its realization, or, conceived personally, to be present when the wondrous event would take place. Saadya had been lukewarm at best with regard to any activist approach (he even removed the phrase "Let new light come forth from Zion" from the morning prayer),[1] but now

"Jerusalem" (in the triple sense of Temple, City, and Holy Land), the scene of Israel's expected revival, was growing more and more central in popular religious sentiment and thought. "Meeting in Jerusalem" had become another way of saying "The Coming of the Messiah." Living, or, at least, visiting there, "seeing it," became a religious merit of the first order, for which often incredible sacrifices were made. Failing that, one desired to be buried there.

The prophetic promise "Come back to me, and I shall come back to you" (Malachi 3:7), already understood literally by the Karaite author al-Qūmisī, is quoted in this sense by a prominent Rabbanite, writing elatedly from Jerusalem, after having braved a snowstorm on the way. He took the second part of the verse as a sign of God's forgiveness and acceptance of his own pilgrimage.[2] The thirst for Zion found its sublime expression in the poetry of Judah ha-Levi. Addressing Zion he says: "The air of your country is life for the souls," meaning that, despite its desolate state, a land where every corner tells a story of a meeting with a divine appearance was the proper place for a soul seeking the nearness of God.[3]

At the end of this subsection are examined the forces that brought about the change of attitudes toward messianism. Here is explored how the new mood was reflected in the day-to-day Geniza correspondence of the eleventh through the thirteenth centuries.

The opening of an important business letter, sent on 5 March 1026 from al-Ahwāz in southwestern Iran to the capital of Egypt, contains this passage: "God knows the strength of my longing for you—may he always support you. I ask Him to bring us together when His holy city will be built."

The letter was addressed to the three senior Tustarī brothers, prominent Karaites, resident in the capital of Egypt. I assume that the senders were Karaites as well.[4]

Slightly later a Spanish Jew, Yehudā b. Ismaʿīl (= Samuel), opens a business missive with the wish: "May God unite us soon in his holy city; he can be relied upon for this and he has the power to achieve it." The letter was sent from Sicily.[5]

Of particular interest is a letter from Sūsa, Tunisia, where, after the destruction of Qayrawān by Bedouin hordes in 1057, the refugees, including the great Rabbenu Nissīm b. Jacob, had found temporary shelter. The writer Labrāṭ b. Moses Ibn Sighmār (later dayyān in al-Mahdiyya, which replaced Qayrawān as the capital) describes the situation of the refugees as hopeless: "death is preferable to life" (Jeremiah 8:3), we "long for death, and it does not come" (Job 3:21), but goes on to write eighty long lines on a variety of business and family matters. The addressee, his younger brother

Judah, whom Labrāṭ had brought up (probably because of the early death of their father) and for whom he harbored tender feelings (as did Moses Maimonides for his brother David), was later to become a great merchant and renowned philanthropist in Egypt.[6] On lines 30–38 Labrāṭ congratulates Judah on his marriage, excuses himself that because of the state of his mind he was unable to write to Judah's father- and brother-in-law, clearly personally known to him, and admonishes Judah to accept his mother-in-law as a substitute for his own mother (whose death is reported in the same letter) and his father-in-law as a replacement for himself, who had been to him like a father. He concludes: "I am writing this letter, overwhelmed by tears, for this is a separation for life, and here I have no one on whom I can rely and with whom I can share my sorrow and my joy. I ask God to unite us soon in his holy city, if God will."[7]

It was customary in merchants' families that one member, usually a father or elder brother, stayed put and the others traveled. Labrāṭ and Judah (like Moses and David Maimonides later) had divided the family business between themselves in such a way. Judah had already gone on a business trip from Qayrawān to Egypt in summer 1048, about ten years before the writing of that letter.[8] Now that through his marriage he had become a member of another firm, so to speak, there was little likelihood that the two brothers would see each other again. Only a miracle, such as the ingathering of the exiled to the Holy City, could achieve this.

In the first two examples given above, the messianic reference might have had a similar meaning. Deserts in one case and the Mediterranean Sea in the other separated the senders of the letters from the recipients. Even though merchants were very mobile in those days, for one reason or another, such as old age, the correspondents might not have expected to meet again.

At first blush it appears somewhat awkward, when a man in Yemen, who remarks in another letter that he visited Aden only once a month, writes to Ḥalfōn b. Nethanel, a renowned India traveler, who sojourned in the South Arabian port: "May God grant me the privilege to meet you in the courtyards of the Temple in Jerusalem." The long letter shows that Ḥalfōn and the writer knew each other personally and had many interests in common: communal, business, religious, and scientific. The Yemenite, however, had deep veneration for the Holy Land and apparently wished to be buried there, for "its soil atones for its people" (Deuteronomy 32:43). The letter to Ḥalfōn was written in the 1130s when Ḥalfōn frequented Aden.[9]

A more substantial hope for the restoration of Jerusalem is expressed in this passage of a letter sent from Old Cairo to Alexandria by the schoolteacher, cantor, court clerk, and bookseller Solomon, son of the judge Elijah b. Zechariah, a prominent member of Abraham Maimonides' court: "May God bring us all together. May he not let me die in this place, but unite us in our city where we will be safe, joyful, and happy with one another. May he do so for the sake of his venerable, awesome name, as it is written: 'Even when your exiled are at the ends of the sky, from there the Lord your God will gather you and from there he will fetch you'" (Deuteronomy 30:4).

During his childhood, Solomon had lived in Jerusalem. His eldest brother Abū Zikrī was physician in attendance to the Ayyubid Sultan Muzaffar, who, in 1219, dreading a Crusaders' attack, laid waste to Jerusalem. At the writing of this letter, Jerusalem was practically uninhabited except for the Temple area and the Holy Sepulcher. Why should it not be filled soon with the ingathered of Israel?[10]

Solomon's messianic outburst was occasioned by a remark made in the preceding line, that a relative was coming to stay with him over Passover. Any mention of a holiday required a good wish, usually paired with the expression of messianic hopes. The standard wish was: "May God grant you many years in happiness and joy, and may he grant you to behold the beauty of the Lord and to visit His Temple" (Psalms 27:4).[11] Since in ancient times a Jewish man was required "to appear before God" on a holiday, the addressee was wished to be granted the same privilege during his lifetime. This wish was expressed in many different forms, often in rhymed Hebrew prose. A commonplace judicial report sent from a small town to the future Nagid Mevōrākh b. Saadya at a time when he still served as a kind of president of the supreme court for his elder brother, the Nagid Judah (in the 1060s), ends with good wishes for holidays: "And may he bring us and you and all Israel together to his sanctuary [meaning Jerusalem], when his congregation will be assembled and his Temple renovated."[12]

Each of the holidays had, in addition to the general wish, a specific one, mostly connected with the Temple service: on Passover, the wish to partake in the sacrifice of the Passover lamb and other offerings due on that holiday, and on Sukkot, the Feast of Tabernacles, to witness the "rejoicing at the water libation."[13] The wish for Shavuot is a combination of Numbers 14:14, referring to the revelation on Mount Sinai, and Isaiah 52:10, God's return to Zion, as for instance in this fragment written in large letters: "May you be granted to see the Messiah, son of David, and to behold the Presence of God face to face, as it is written. . . ."[14]

Hanukka and Purim, which in their liturgy are described as days of miracles, were rated in the miracle-ridden world of the Geniza far higher than in Ashkenazi Judaism of yesteryear. Both were described as holidays: *ᶜīd* in Arabic, *mōᶜēd* in Hebrew, and as "noble days," the same expression as used for the most holy days of the month of Tishri.[15] One sent special letters of congratulation. The standard wish was: "He who wrought miracles for our fathers in these days may do the like for me and you and all Israel."[16] Occasionally it was modified and enlarged to fill an entire letter, comprising ideas about exile, and redemption, or wishing the fulfillment of Isaiah's prophecy on the new heaven and new earth (66:22).[17] On Hanukka one traveled to stay with relatives or friends, as one did for Passover or the Day of Atonement, and one would celebrate Purim in Jawjar, a town whose synagogue, named after Elijah, the harbinger of redemption, was a goal of pilgrimage.[18]

It is almost needless to say that letters and poems of congratulation occasioned by happy family events, such as weddings or circumcision feasts, conclude with the good wish that the person addressed, or all those assembled, "may witness the erection of the House of God, the ingathering of the people, and the advent of the Savior."[19]

When a Gaon or Nagid, that is, the head of the Jewish community at large, was addressed or referred to, he was wished that his leadership should endure until salvation, or the Redeemer, or the Teacher of Righteousness came. His authority was temporary and derived from the real one whose appearance was expected.[20] Salvation, *yeshūᶜā*, was the technical term for messianic times, a usage foreshadowed throughout the books of Isaiah and the Psalms and confirmed in the second benediction of the *ᶜamīda*, the daily prayer. In its Palestinian version, the one in use in the Geniza synagogue, the benediction had this form: "May He let Salvation sprout as quickly as the blinking of an eye," that is, with miraculous suddenness.

How seriously this attitude was taken might be measured by the way in which the Gaons, responding in kind, signed their letters. Extended phrases were impracticable. The Gaon and nāsī (member of the family of the Exilarch and consequently regarded as a scion of the House of David) Daniel b. Azaryah, Head of the Jerusalem yeshiva 1052–1063, signed with one word: *yeshūᶜā*, "Salvation." He, in turn, was wished that one of his sons should become "the Redeemer." Hay Gaon of Baghdad (d. 1038) and his younger contemporary Solomon, Gaon of Jerusalem (d. 1051), signed: *yeshaʿ rāv*, "Complete Salvation," Solomon's predecessor and later also his own son Abraham: *yeshaʿ yūḥash*, "may Salvation be hastened." Lesser dignitaries imitated this practice, using as signature a phrase like "May Salvation be renewed," an allusion to Jeremiah 31:30, or with direct reference to that verse: "A new covenant!"[21]

When a large community addressed another, as when that of Palermo, Sicily, recommended a meritorious Spanish notable to the communities of Qayrawān and al-Mahdiyya, Tunisia, or when that of Tyre, Lebanon, submitted a lawsuit to that of Aleppo, Syria, the good wishes that the addressees may soon be blessed with the appearance of the Redeemer are formulated in a most elaborate and distinguished style. The senders, one feels, expected him to be just around the corner.[22] As we have read in the letter of Solomon b. Elijah written in the 1220s, private persons expressed the desire not to depart this life before the exile was terminated.[23] Two hundred years earlier, in May 1028, a *parnas* from a distinguished family, while signing a court record, adds in minuscules written crosswise above and beneath his name: "May God keep him [meaning: me] alive until the Redeemer comes."[24] The first of three signatories on an old fragment, probably from the tenth century, writes crosswise above and beneath his name: "Salvation during his [meaning: my] lifetime."[25] An inscription containing the ancient prayer "Remember me, O Lord, when you show favor to your people and take note of me, when you bring Salvation" (Psalms 106:4) shows that the writer was anxious not to be left out of an event that could occur any moment.[26]

Finally, attention must be paid to the numerous messianic names present on the Geniza scene. Names in those days were words that carried a meaning and a message: they characterized the society in which they were used.[27] Messianic names such as Sar Shalom (Prince of peace [Isaiah 9:15]), Ṣemaḥ (Sprout [Zechariah 6:12], meaning Sprout, progeny of David [Jeremiah 23:5]), or Mevasser (Harbinger of good tidings [Isaiah 52:7]), unknown during the Talmudic period, were borne by certain Iraqian Gaons even in pre-Geniza times. Thus it is natural that their example was followed by the common people.[28] There were other messianic names such as Meshullam (Isaiah 42:19, of doubtful meaning), which is common, or simply Mashīʾaḥ (Messiah), which is rare.[29] There might have been family traditions in this matter, as when a man is called Mashīʾaḥ b. Ṣemaḥ,[30] or Meshullam b. Mevasser,[31] or Meshullam b. Furqān, the latter being the Arabic equivalent of Hebrew *yeshūʿā* (Salvation).[32]

Yeshūʿā, which is the technical term for the coming of the Messiah, is one of the names most frequently occurring in the Geniza. Although feminine in form, it was given exclusively to boys. M. Steinschneider, in his pioneering study on Jewish onomastics in Arab countries, thought that abstract nouns used as male names such as *yeshūʿā* were found among Karaites and Samaritans, but not at all, or very rarely, among Rabbanites. Geniza research has changed this conclusion. Without making any special investigation, I have noted about ninety persons bearing that name, and, as far as I was able to ascertain, all were Rabbanites. One awaited salvation and wished the son to witness it, perhaps even taking an active role in it.[33]

Millennial considerations could affect the decisions of a practical business man. Shortly before the Muslim year 500 (1111, the beginning of the Crusader period) a merchant, making dispositions in contemplation of death, appoints his only daughter as his sole heir and his wife as her guardian and executor. He draws up a long list of his possessions, assets, and liabilities, but at the very beginning of the document he states: "The girl shall not marry before the year 500 of the Arabs is out, which is the End of the Period." From the writings of the Muslim theologian al-Ghazālī it is known that the turn of the century was expected to bring about "a renovation of the religion" (to which the theologian himself, who died in 1111, hoped to have contributed). From the very succinct way in which the merchant referred to the End of the Period it is evident that everyone understood what that year meant, as far as Jewish expectations were concerned.[34]

The preceding survey demonstrates that belief in the sudden and miraculous appearance of the Messiah was a fact of life. The great event had to be miraculous, not natural, because thus was it foretold by the prophets and expounded in minute detail by the theologians, especially Saadya Gaon, whose writings dominated most of the Geniza period.[35] There was, however, one significant difference: popular messianism was optimistic; it looked forward to an age when Israel would be united, safe, and happy, being dedicated to the service of God, as laid down in the Holy Scriptures; the "Pangs of the Messiah," the catastrophes foreboding his appearance, as described in the traditional theory, are not echoed in the day-to-day Geniza correspondence. The period did not lack Armageddon-like events, such as the destruction of Qayrawān in 1057, mentioned above, or the conquest of Jerusalem by the Crusaders in 1099, terrible famines, plagues, and complete breakdowns of authority: synagogues were destroyed and Torah scrolls desecrated, but I have read nowhere that such occurrences were regarded as Signs of the End of the Days. One mourned the dead, organized help for the refugees and the hungry, and redeemed the books that had fallen into the hands of Bedouins or Crusaders. But the mood was not apocalyptic. The pressure of the Galut (exile) was always present. Yet on holidays, or, as one says in Hebrew, "good days," one yearned for the day that would be "completely good." In cataclysmic times one was not eager to be reminded that even more terrible experiences might be ahead.

This attitude explains perhaps the strange response found in the Geniza to a dire crisis of Islamic messianism, which also affected the Jews of Egypt and Palestine in a very tangible way: the reign of the Fatimid caliph al-Ḥākim (996–1021). Al-Ḥākim was regarded by some Ismāʿīlite (Shiʿite) theologians as the Mahdī, the Savior, "who would fill the earth with justice as it is now full of corruption." Some theologians even declared him to be the Presence of God on earth, and he, at least for some time, did not object. A recent study by J. van Ess has clarified many aspects of this dark period.[36] The caliph was inspired by high ideals, but his mind, as proved by his bizarre edicts, was utterly unbalanced. Acts of messianic self-humiliation (riding on a donkey clad in wool [Zechariah 9:9]) and attempts at enforcing stern justice and chastity alternated with vexatious prohibitions imposed on his subjects[37] and endless executions (the messiah "who smites the land with the breath of his mouth" [Isaiah 9:4], as one Ismāʿīlī theologian put it). All this was done in expectation of the critical Muslim year 400 (lunar years reckoned either from the beginning of the era in 622 or from Muhammad's death in 632). As for Christians and Jews, the Prophet had promised them protection, but now that four hundred years had passed and neither had Christ reappeared nor the Jewish messiah come, their time was up. They had the choice among conversion to Islam, expulsion, or death. Al-Ḥākim, the son of a Christian woman, directed his persecutions especially against Christians. In September 1009 (the beginning of the Muslim year 400) the Holy Sepulcher in Jerusalem and many other Christian buildings were destroyed. Then, as late as January 1013, the caliph intervened personally and saved the lives of twenty-three Jewish notables falsely accused of impugning Islam. This did not hinder him from ordering soon afterward the destruction of the synagogues and applying to the Jews the pernicious edicts inflicted on the Christians. Not a long time passed, however, when the fickle caliph permitted the new converts to return to their original religion and to rebuild their houses of worship.

What echo did these tremendous events find in the Geniza? We read much about the endeavors of the Jewish authorities to replace the destroyed synagogues, but practically nothing is said about the persecutions. Instead, the Geniza has preserved several copies (or fragments of them) of an Egyptian Megilla, "festive scroll," in which the deliverance of the twenty-three notables is celebrated as a miracle, the caliph al-Ḥākim, "who loves justice and hates iniquity" is extolled as a Messiah-like ruler, see Psalms 45:8. A yearly fast and feast were instituted by the Jews in which that Megilla was read. The persecutions were forgotten, the miracle remembered. The wishful optimism of the messianic mood, as described above, prevailed.[38]

The unforgettable Paul Kraus has shown that the Ismāʿīlī theologian Kirmānī not only quoted the messianic passages from Isaiah and Zechariah mentioned above (and others) in Arabic but also reproduced them in the Hebrew original, both in Hebrew script and Arabic transliteration, probably for missionary activity among the Jews.[39] I should not be surprised at all if some day we will discover that Kirmānī, who hailed from northeastern Iran, was himself a Jewish convert to Islam or the son of one. His excessive use of *gemaṭria*,[40] although not unknown in Islam before him, makes him suspect. In any event, the Geniza indicates that Jews in Egypt did read Shiʿite books. I found an extensive fragment of admonitions of a father to his son, in Hebrew characters, which is an abridged version of the caliph ʿAlī's ethical will to his son Ḥusayn, taken from a Shiʿite treatise of the fourth Muslim century. The piece consists of gnomes of pietist ethics, and contains nothing of an esoteric character.[41]

How "an extraordinary document," namely the letter of a *dāʿī*, or chief Ismāʿīlī missionary, to a chief qadi, got into the Geniza, as described by Samuel M. Stern, is indeed puzzling. Should we assume that a Jew was the messenger and disposed of it there? Of keen interest is S. M. Stern's study "Fatimid Propaganda among Jews," in which he shows the methods, both theological and mundane, used, and that indeed a number of Jews of high status, both in the Maghreb and in Egypt, succumbed to worldly allurements. Allegorical interpretations of the Bible and of Jewish laws of the Sabbath and holidays silenced the conscience of the converts.[42]

When al-Ḥākim was murdered, Christians and Jews could ponder that Muslim messianic expectations did not fare better than their own. It did not discourage anyone who was inclined to believe from clinging to the certitude of an impending advent. This is beautifully exemplified by the story of messianic stirrings in

Baghdad in the years 1120/1. The historical circumstances of that event, especially in comparison with nearly contemporary messianic movements, have been extensively discussed in connection with the edition of the text. Here attention is drawn to the way in which the debacle of failure is overcome by deft expressions of faith in the basic validity of messianic expectations.[43]

In a nutshell, the story, told in Arabic,[44] was this: a woman from a physician's family, renowned for her piety both before and after her marriage, had a vision five days before Rosh ha-Shana 1120: the prophet Elijah ordered her to appear in public[45] to announce in his name that *yeshūʿā*, salvation, was near. In response, the Jews assembled (what they did is lost; see below), and the Seljuk Sultan, the actual ruler of Baghdad, became paralyzed with fright: "The Jews say 'our kingdom has come; we shall not leave any other kingdom in existence'" (an allusion to Daniel 2:44). The caliph, who was in charge of the affairs of the non-Muslims, was not less consternated and ordered "the Jews" (meaning, their notables) imprisoned in the Mint (where many of them were active). Then he sent a letter to the chief qadi as follows: "The time of the Jews is up.[46] Either a new prophet [= their Messiah] appears among them or they accept Islam. Otherwise they are doomed. Do not stand in my way and in the way of all the Muslims." But the chief qadi, the keeper of the law, remained adamant: "No one doing harm to that people has ever remained unpunished. Their time is not up. It is steady with God" (Isaiah 66:22). The caliph called Abū Sahl Ibn Kammūna (a man from a Jewish family whose members had been in government service for two hundred years) and asked him to tell him the story of the apparition and who saw it.[47] After learning that a woman had originated the commotion, the caliph laughed and made fun of the Jews. "They must be fools to rely on the intelligence of a woman. Tomorrow I shall burn the woman and declare the Jews' lives forfeited." That happened late in the evening, just before the viziers took their leave. Hardly an hour had passed before the caliph himself was honored with an apparition of the prophet Elijah holding a pillar of fire in his hand. The caliph became frightened. As a result, Ibn Kammūna and later also the other Jews were freed.

We learn what actually happened from a Muslim historian. The Jews, in their messianic excitement, tore off the yellow badges which they and other non-Muslims were obliged to wear on their clothing and, as is evident from the Jewish version of the story, apparently also stopped delivering certain contributions, and even the poll tax. In the end, they had to pay a very heavy fine, 4,000 gold pieces to the caliph and 20,000 to the Sultan. The "Jālūt," that is, the Rosh Galūt, or Exilarch, collected the money.[48]

The story makes no mention of these impositions. There is a faint allusion to the poll tax, euphemistically described as a means of protection (as it is actually defined in Muslim law). Otherwise, the report is essentially a tale of miraculous redemption, accompanied by appearances of the prophet Elijah and replete with hidden workings of the living word of God. The Seljuk Sultan is disquieted by Daniel 2:44, the chief qadi takes Isaiah 66:22 literally, and the caliph reckons with the possibility of an impending advent of a new Jewish prophet. The popular messianism of the Geniza writings was neither apocalyptic, nor universalistic, and certainly not antinomian. It was a burning desire for redemption from a state of humiliation and a yearning to be with God where he was nearest, in his sanctuary in Jerusalem. (Jews lived in a Muslim environment, where the Muslims' thirst for seeing God was quenched by a pilgrimage to the holy sites of Mecca.) There was a third motive involved: because of the immense mobility of the Geniza society, members of an extended family, who ideally should live in one place, even one house, were often dispersed in different towns and countries; and formal friendship, too, counting almost as much as family ties, if not more, was constantly disturbed by separation. The miraculous ingathering of Israel would also bring about the complete unification of families and friends.[49]

I wish to conclude this subject with the translation of a Hebrew placard of a Spanish Jerusalem pilgrim. The paper on which this "script of pilgrimage" is written is of a particular type. It is about five and a half inches high and seven inches wide, very thin, but exceptionally strong. Even in its present, dilapidated state, it remains in upright position when propped against a support. It has a border, about one inch wide, drawn in the same ink as the writing. I assume the pilgrim put this placard up at night as a protection against any evil.

If I forget thee, O Jerusalem, let my right hand wither [Psalms 137:5]. [I am] Abraham, b. R. Judah—m[ay he rest in] E[den], the Spaniard, from the town of Jayyān [today Jaén] called al-Ṣarrāf [the Banker]. May God, for the sake of his name, let me arrive in Jerusalem, the Holy City—may it be rebuilt and established during the lifetime of all Israel—and let me become one of its inhabitants. May this be His will. Amen, in eternity, Selah.

Written. . . . [Here, probably the date of the pilgrim's departure from his hometown was given.][50]

Literature on Jewish Messianism and the place of Jerusalem and the Holy Land in the concepts of the three monotheistic religions is endless.[51] Christian millennial expectations and Islamic Mahdism, as well as the sanctity of Jerusalem in both these religions, have relevance here.[52] Has not the early Karaite writer al-Qūmisī summoned his coreligionists to follow the example of people "from all nations," who come to Jerusalem from the four corners of the earth?[53] Despite the multifarious aspects of Messianism emerging from the Bible, Talmud and Midrash, let alone the writings of the Karaite and Rabbanite theologians of the Middle Ages, the Geniza correspondence of the eleventh through the thirteenth centuries seems to show that the average Jew knew what he was supposed to believe and to hope for.

First, the glowing visions of the Messiah and the messianic age found in the Bible were not realized through the return of the exiled from Babylonia to Jerusalem and the erection of the Second Temple. All the good tidings contained in the prophetic lections read on Saturdays and holidays were a matter of the future.

These were the main changes expected: the end of the wicked empires; the ingathering of Israel in the Holy City and the Holy Land; the erection of the Temple and the renewal of the service in it (hence the special reverence shown to Kohens in Geniza times);[54] an age of peace and plenty, allowing the ingathered to study "the Torah" (and other worthy knowledge) without interference. The notion of the coincidence of the resurrection of the dead with the coming of the Messiah, so heavily emphasized by Saadya Gaon (see pp. 406–407 ff.), is not evident in the Geniza correspondence. Perhaps they avoided speaking of resurrection because they did not like to be reminded of death.

The coming of that golden age would be heralded by the messenger of God (Malachi 3:1 and 23), the prophet Elijah, who, as in his lifetime, would brave tyrants but would also be kind to the weak; the story of the messianic stirrings in Baghdad 1120/1 just told is an example of both.

> How comely on the mountains
> Are the footsteps of a herald
> Proclaiming peace
> Heralding happiness
> Proclaiming salvation
> Saying to Zion:
> Your God is King [Isaiah 52:7].

All this could be achieved solely by miracles wrought by God. Thus was it foretold by the biblical prophets of truth, and thus was it conditioned by the state of a people dispersed in small groups all over the world. When the sober rationalist Saadya Gaon insists again and again on the comprehensive orthodox belief in miracles, he knew what he was talking about: one can be a believer only if one is prepared to accept the most unacceptable. *Credo quia absurdum.*

We must now try to explain why messianic expectations were seemingly intensified from the tenth century onward. People yearn for radical changes not so much when their situation is hopeless but when they have reached, after tremendous effort, a certain, but by no means fully satisfying, state of well-being and are looking for more. Events in the environment can serve as an occasion or incentive for such expectations. All these conditions were present for the minorities under Islam from the second part of the tenth century.

The great empires were tottering. The Abbasid caliphate, which had been exposed to rapid decline since the middle of the ninth century, fell prey to the Daylamites, an Iranian mountain people, around the middle of the tenth. Some of their chieftains made energetic rulers, but they fought one another incessantly, with the result that Iraq-Iran, once the most flourishing part of the Islamic world, was laid waste. The Jewish inhabitants suffered perhaps even more than the rest of the population. The endless requests of the yeshivas of Baghdad for rescue, sent to all corners of the Jewish world, and the emigration to western countries, so widely reflected in the Geniza, illustrate the situation.

Then came the Fatimid onslaught. A militant sect, Ismāʿīlī Shiʿism, took possession of Egypt, Palestine, and the Muslim holy cities of North Arabia. But the Ismāʿīlīs themselves were at loggerheads with one another; the Qarmatians, an Ismāʿīlī terrorist group, invaded Palestine and even Egypt, and the Bedouins, always taking advantage of a state of anarchy among the sedentary population, joined the fray. "Atrocities, the like of which had never been seen in the lands of Islam, were committed by them." Jerusalem had changed hands under Islam before, and more than once. The scope, vehemence, and religious significance of the changes during "the sixty years' war of 969–1029" were exceptional.[55]

After about forty years of respite and relative prosperity, a thirty years' war between the Fatimids and the Turkish Seljuk invaders devastated Palestine again. Before the century was out Jerusalem fell to the Crusaders. The reconquest of the city by the Muslims in 1187 did not end the menace of the European Christians. The demolition of most of Jerusalem in 1219, its being taken over by Emperor Frederic II in 1229 (also echoed in the Geniza), and the catastrophic invasions that soon followed seemed to prove that the Holy City could never find rest except by a God-sent "Prince of Peace" (Isaiah 9:5).

The Islamic "centennial" expectations, which surfaced in the (Muslim) years 400 and 500 after Muhammad (ca. eleventh and twelfth centuries), affected Jews (and Christians) directly and were naturally apt to resuscitate age-old messianic hopes. The role of Fatimid religious propaganda and Karaite "Zionist" activism should not be disregarded. The ever-growing place of the sanctity of Jerusalem and its Temple in Christian and Muslim religiosity was held up as an example to be imitated by the true Sons of Zion. In Talmudic times the tendency to replace the Temple service with repentance, prayer, and charity grew with the years. By the eleventh century the pendulum had swung back.

It seems to me, however, that some wider issue was involved: the Jewish community had become impatient and unwilling to suffer any longer the state of humiliation and inscurity to which a minority population under Islam was exposed. Precisely because the community had attained a modicum of prosperity by the tenth century (as the Geniza proves), and participated extensively in the culture of the Arabic environment, the role of a second- or third-class being became intolerable. The cries of despair, of being given up by God, pervade the Hebrew poetry of the eleventh and twelfth centuries. The lighter aspects of the situation are exhibited in the reiterated expressions of hope for the coming of the Messiah, found in the day-to-day correspondence preserved in the Geniza.

Hay Gaon (d. 1038 in Baghdad), the most influential of all Gaons, describes God as an unnatural father to Israel, his son:

> He has been like an enemy to his children.
> When they died, he did not bury them,
> Seeing their corpses strewn on the ground,
> He did not order to collect their bones,
> Nor did he care to cover them with earth.

In another penitentiary poem (*selīḥā*, not an elegy) Hay says that the children of Abraham, Isaac, and Jacob were kept alive for the sole purpose of not being spared a single torment invented on earth, and concludes: If God has no compassion for his children, he should at least have mercy on the widowed city, Jerusalem.[56]

The Spanish Hebrew poets, each in his own way, expressed similar feelings. Here are the opening and some additional verses from a *ge'ulla* (prayer for redemption) by Judah ha-Levi on the same topic:

The dove you have carried On eagle's wings [Exodus 19:4]
Who nestled in your bosom In innermost chambers
Why have you tossed her away Flipping around in forests
While all around her are Hunters with nets?

Strangers allure her To other gods
While she weeps in secret To the Beloved of her youth.

Why have you given me over to death
While I know that only you are my salvation?

There is no sign, no miracle, No vision, no appearance,
And when I ask to learn The time of the End,
They answer me dubiously: You ask for too much.

Will the Lord reject me forever?
Is there no End to my waiting?[57]

Solomon Ibn Gabirol concludes each of the four stanzas of his forceful ge'ulla with the outcry: "Why do you forget us without end?!" (Lamentations 5:20).[58]

Abraham Ibn Ezra went a step further. In a ge'ulla of his, the despair of the people of Israel is spelled out in these words:

If you wish to redeem me, redeem!
If not—let me know![59]

These poetical expressions of impatience at the sufferings of Israel and the Messiah being long in coming had, on the face of it, a good side: they gave vent to feelings that everyone entertained but did not dare to voice. On the other side, both the unending complaints and the exuberant expressions of hope demonstrated the dangers inherent in messianism. By leaving everything to God and the future, one did perhaps too little for the preservation and development of the present, a proper organization of the community, education, and the social services. It seems, however, that as long as the situation had not become entirely intolerable, as in Mamluk times, the balance between poetical lamentations and everyday parlance of hope performed a good service.

The World to Come

Criticizing the ideas about the World to Come entertained by the common people, Moses Maimonides says this: "They fancy that at the coming of the Messiah the dead will be resurrected and enter the Garden of Eden, where they will eat and drink and remain in good shape as long as heaven and earth exist."[60]

Described as such, these are fantasies of simpleminded people. The combination of a resurrection of dead with the advent of the Messiah is described by Saadya Gaon as the opinion of the majority of the Jewish community, however, and is upheld by him as orthodox in the strongest terms. Maimonides had to do the same in order to save the belief in a bodily resurrection, expressed in Jewish prayer three times a day in unequivocal terms.[61] The reader of the New Testament is reminded of the Revelation to John, the Apocalypse, where the Advent, or Second Coming of Christ, also takes place with a resurrection of dead. All this goes back to Old Testament allegories describing the restoration of Israel as a reawakening of the dead, in particular Ezekiel's grand vision of the dry bones, which will be revived and form a large crowd safely brought back to the Holy Land (37:1–14). Saadya refutes the allegorical understanding of the biblical passages concerned, but since they all refer to Israel, that resurrection at the time of the Messiah will be partial and confined to the pious of Israel alone.[62]

At the End of the Days (Isaiah 2:2), a second resurrection of all mankind, but as eternal life only for the pious, will occur. One is again reminded of the Revelation to John.[63] The second resurrection will be entirely different from the first. The first will be corporeal, the resurrected will be common human beings, identical in shape and even clothing with what they had been during their original existence.[64] After the second and final revival "there will be no food, drink, sex, business, competition, hatred, or envy, but the pious will sit [that is: study] with their wreaths on their heads, enjoying the brilliant light of the Presence [of God], as it is written: 'Beholding God is their food and drink'" (Exodus 24:11).[65]

This poetic vision from the Talmud (formulated by Rav, the founder of one of the two Babylonian yeshivas during the first half of the third century) is accepted by Saadya, albeit in a somewhat pedantic fashion: since God is described on the one hand as a devouring fire (l. 9, Deuteronomy 4:24), whereas on the other hand it is said of him "with you is the source of life, with your light we see light" (Psalms 36:10), God's light is conceived as the nourishment that keeps the pious alive (as it was for Moses when he tarried for forty days on Mount Sinai without food and drink) and as a consuming fire for the wicked.[66] Saadya repeatedly warns his readers that these matters cannot be visualized or fully expressed in words, since both God and the souls of men are incorporeal and not accessible to our senses. God's presence (or glory, as Isaiah 6:3 says) fills, or permeates, the whole world, including ourselves, as our souls are constantly aware of him: the soul is lovesick, longing and yearning to meet him, a desire probably to be fulfilled only after it will be liberated from its earthly shell, in the World to Come.[67]

The Muslim, Jewish, and Christian theologians of the High Middle Ages, who had studied Greek philosophy systematically and identified themselves with its teachings, experienced serious difficulties, since in the three religions corporeal resurrection was a basic article of faith.[68] In his essay "The Problem of Immortality in Avicenna, Maimonides and St. Thomas Aquinas," Harold Blumberg compares how great thinkers of the three faiths tried to solve the problem.[69] Avicenna (Ibn Sīnā, 980–1037), Blumberg asserts, simply avoids the ticklish topic of physical resurrection.[70] Maimonides, like Saadya, accepts a physical resurrection at the time of the Messiah, thus providing joyous hopes for the common people. In the World to Come, and this is the novelty of Maimonides' teaching, nothing remains of the individual souls; only "the acquired intellect," the true notions about the nature of God, acquired during one's lifetime, will survive.[71] Aquinas concedes eternal life also for the individual souls. All three agree that the future lot of the soul depends on the moral conduct and intellectual attainments in this world, which are best achieved by following the golden mean.[72]

Maimonides placed the results of his thinking about the World to Come into his Code of Law, upholding it by Scripture and tradition as the true belief of orthodox Judaism. The relevant exposition is found near the end of the laws of Repentance. The Hebrew word for repentance is *teshūvā*, "return" to God, that is, following the right way after having erred away from it. Since we all are sinners, only teshūvā can pave the way to the World to Come. I translate or summarize selected passages from the chapter treating the subject:[73]

(1) "'The Good in store for the righteous' [Psalms 31:20]—this

is Life in the World to Come; Life, never ended by death; Good, never marred by bad, as the Torah has said: '. . . so that you should have it good and live long' [Deuteronomy 22:7], which is traditionally interpreted as meaning: 'Good, in a world which is completely good; long, in a world which has no end.'"[74]

(2) No bodies or bodily desires exist in that world, as proved by Talmudic quotations to this effect, as on p. 406 and n. 65, above.

(3) The soul created with and living through the body dies with it; the eternal soul is the knowledge of God acquired during life here.[75]

(4–6) There is no possibility to imagine the beatitude enjoyed by our spiritual soul in the World to Come, since all our perceptions here are made through our bodily soul. Hence King David's expressions of longing for that bliss, as he says: "Had I not been confident to see the good that is with God in the Land of Life . . ." (Psalms 27:13).[76]

(7) All the prophecies in the Bible about the redemption of Israel and the glory bestowed upon it refer only to the coming of the Messiah, as the Sages have said: "All the prophets have presaged solely for the days of the Messiah, but the World to Come 'no eye has seen, except God alone'" (Isaiah 64:3).[77]

(8) "The World to Come has not been called thus by the Sages because it will come into being only after this world has perished. It exists already, as it is written, 'the good that is in store' [Psalms 31:20]; it is already in store, namely, for each individual after he has completed his life in this world."

A recent study, "Maimonides' Fiction of Resurrection" by Robert S. Kirschner, contains an abridged translation of Maimonides' *Treatise on the Resurrection of the Dead* (see n. 68) and "proposes that [in the treatise] Maimonides creates a kind of legal fiction by which he virtually eviscerates the doctrine he claims to profess." To this should be added, however, that in the ambiance of atomistic thinking characteristic of medieval Islam (in which Maimonides lived), apparently contradictory doctrines could be harmonized without losing their standing. Maimonides accepted physical resurrection unconditionally because the belief in it was prescribed by the Law laid down by the ancient Sages. The codifier did his duty.[78]

In a stimulating essay, Ezra Fleischer censures the Hebrew poets of Spain for including in their liturgical creations, destined for synagogal service, foreign elements that had no place in Jewish tradition. With the same right one could wonder how the Aristotelian "acquired intellect" could become a basic tenet in a Jewish code. The answer seems to be that as long as a religion is vibrant with life, it can (and must) assimilate the innovations of its time congenial with its own spirit. A poet like Solomon Ibn Gabirol in his "kingly crown" could unroll a picture of the physical world conceived by the science of his time as a true comment on the wonders of the Creation extolled in the Bible. Maimonides' definition of the spiritual soul was a proper translation of the Talmudic concept of the uncorporeal soul into the abstract language of thought acceptable to his philosophically trained contemporaries.[79]

Booklists, legal documents, and letters preserved in the Geniza prove that the creations of a Maimonides, like those of Saadya before him, were read, bought, and copied. The knowledge of Greek philosophy, however, despite intensive occupation with it by the select few, never became a prerequisite for an educated person in Arabic Islam, as was the case, for instance, with poetry.[80] In the day-to-day correspondence, Maimonides' philosophical ideas are not quoted, and even the Talmudic sayings about the World to Come are rarely referred to verbatim. Yet, the teachings of the Talmud and of Saadya, and even of the philosophically minded Maimonides, did seep down. The ideas about the World to Come in vogue among the rank and file have been repeatedly touched upon in the section on death (X, A, 3), above, especially in the subsection "Living with the Dead." Here a retrospective overview is in order.

It was definitely taken for granted that death was not the end of life. Moreover, certain basic ideas about the nature of life's continuation were also common. Of a revered person, male or female, it was assumed that he or she might enter Paradise immediately after death, if God willed so. Hence, being buried on a Friday was a privilege: the soul of the deceased could thus enter immediately the rest of the Sabbath in the joyous ambiance of Paradise.[81] There, he or she would not be alone, but would enjoy the company of the founders of the faith, so familiar from the Bible and prayer, separated, to be sure, according to gender in that world as customary in this: the men would be with Abraham, Isaac, Jacob, Moses, and Aaron, and so on; and the women with Sarah, Rebekka, Rachel, and Leah, and in general, with one of "the seven groups" of perfect saints.[82]

The most common blessing attached to the name of a deceased was "resting in Paradise," followed by "his soul is at rest."[83] This must be understood as a religious antidote against animistic fears for a soul unable to find rest and fluttering around the burial place of the body, which also suffered, namely, from the worms, "as living flesh is hurt by the pricks of a needle."[84] As the Talmudic (and biblical) quotation shows, those concepts must have been popular among Jews. According to an ancient Muslim tradition, ʿĀʾisha, the favorite wife of Muhammad, learned from a Jewish woman in al-Madina about this notion of "the tribulation of the tomb" and how to avoid it by leading a proper life here. Subsequently, the Muslims developed this theme, especially about the first hours in the grave, partly echoed in Jewish sources (but not in the documentary Geniza).[85]

Another, extremely common blessing was "his record [or: 'the record of the righteous'] is [or: 'will be'] a blessing" (Proverbs 10:7). The literal meaning of the word translated here as "record" is "the memory." But this is not intended in the blessing for the dead as accepted in later Hebrew usage. What it meant to express was that the record of the good deeds and achievements of the deceased was so good that, one hoped, it would serve him as a blessing in the World to Come. This was understood quite literally: two books of record were kept in heaven, one for this life, and one, "the book of record for life in the World to Come."[86] These and the blessing commonly used in the eleventh century, "may he be granted eternal life," manifest the belief that only a worthy life here has the prospect of being continued in the hereafter.[87] The alternative was the punishment *kārēt*, "to be cut off from his family and people," to disappear. This seems to have been the prevailing mood in Geniza times. We read next to nothing in our correspondence about Gehinnom and tortures there. Hell, so populous a place in Islamic and Christian imagination, is practically never mentioned. Life on earth was hell enough. One did not need the menace of another hell after death to be held to lead a decent life here.

The copyist of a book completed in 1092/3 put this colophon, or inscription, at its end: "May God grant him to participate in the jubilations at the coming of the Redeemer; to be in the company of the Rocks of the earth [the ancestors of the nation]; and to get a share in both worlds, as is written 'through Me your days will increase [here], and years will be added to your life [in the World to Come]'" (Proverbs 9:11).[88]

As this colophon demonstrates, and as has become evident throughout this section, there were three types of expectations. The first and by far the most often noted was the wish to witness the coming of the Savior in person. The messianic age was conceived by the Geniza people as an intrinsically this-worldly event.[89] The partial resurrection of the dead, namely, only of the pious of Israel, an artificial concept, although accepted by Saadya and Maimonides, seems not to have been brought home to the community at large.[90] The common wish for the dead to be granted a temporary resting place in Paradise in company with the pious of old was rarely developed in detail, but certainly was a widely diffused idea. The resurrection of the dead is far less frequently mentioned. The wish expressed by the two sons of Saadya Gaon eleven years after their father's death, "may God speed up his rising from the dead," is not in common use in the Geniza correspondence.[91] We see that the community heeded the advice given by the Talmud and the theologians not to speculate about matters that the human mind is unable to conceive. This passage from a letter written in Jerusalem around 1063 illustrates the situation. It is addressed to Nahray b. Nissīm, and refers to the latter's cousin Israel b. Nathan, who, after disastrous years in Byzantium, settled in Jerusalem, where his mind became occupied with visions, prophesying, and astrology.

> In the matters known to my lord, R. Israel has increased his activities very much. Before they had been known only to a few, now they have become *public* and much talked about, especially by most of the foreigners. Finally, matters have reached a point where he speaks about topics that should not be mentioned in a letter because of the 'pitfalls of letters,'[92] such as the resurrection of the dead and the signs of the stars, and similar matters, about which he gives witness under oath whenever he sits down [to talk with people].[93]

The resurrection of the dead, albeit a basic tenet in the three monotheistic religions, was not well suited as a topic in educated conversation.

The transcendental hopes held out for the pious: Messiah, Paradise, resurrection, centered on one main theme: return to God, renewal of the Covenant, conceived as both communal and personal.[94] Life in the Diaspora was not only painful and humiliating, but was sensed also as a kind of repudiation by God. One felt forgotten.[95] Hence the immense yearning for rebuilding the Temple in Jerusalem and resumption in it of the priestly service. Pilgrims streaming there three times a year would be the most conspicuous manifestation that the time of wrath was over. The standard wish for a holiday was "to be granted to behold the beauty of the lord and to visit in his Temple" (Psalms 27:4).[96]

The meeting with God in the unknown lands of afterlife was another matter. Everyone believed that he would be called to account in one way or another. When a divorced woman from a merchant family, who was very bitter about her lot, refused to marry another man, "so that *he* [her former husband] should be punished for my sins in the World to Come," we understand that requital in afterlife for our sins here was taken for granted, but the ideas about its realization must have differed widely.[97] It is natural that the old and pious Gaon Solomon b. Judah, confronted with an ethically problematic situation, always took into account what was awaiting him after death. "I know what I have to meet when I shall be with my Creator; therefore I must be careful with what I say." Or: "I do not know what will happen to me, nor when I shall be summoned for judgment."[98] When a young man was about to desert his wife, he was warned by a fatherly judge: "Where are you and where is God?!" meaning, do you not know that God's punishment will reach you, here or somewhere else?[99] Taking into account life after death was not reserved for special occasions. As the Geniza shows, a commercial responsibility would be undertaken for both this world and the World to Come, and not only in legal documents but in letters as well.

Reward for good deeds, especially study, honesty, and charity, and compensation for undeserved suffering were the main expectations. One wished oneself to be granted one's share in the World to Come and prayed for departed relatives or other dead persons to find rest, a seat in Paradise, and, in the first place, God's mercy. One was reluctant to be specific with regard to oneself or to another living person with good wishes for the World to Come; one had to be dead before such good wishes could be fulfilled. There can be little doubt, however, that thinking persons who, through daily prayers and benedictions, as well as the fulfillment of the ever-present rituals and moral injunctions, had enjoyed enduring contact with God were longing for the meeting with him once the inevitable event took place.[100] For the expression of such feelings we must once again consult the poets.[101]

For the purpose I have chosen a poem by the Spanish Hebrew poet Judah ha-Levi, which is found repeatedly in the Geniza but had been known for centuries and, in various places, was (and is) included in the synagogue service.[102]

In content, rhyme, and meter the poem is built on Psalms 116:7.

Get Ready

"Return, my soul, to your repose,
For God has been good to you."

Splendid one, taken from your Creator's splendor,
Arise! This is not the time for rest.

The way is long, prepare your provender.
The hour has come to do God's work.

I am a stranger here like all my fathers,
And the rest of my years is like a passing shadow.
When, if not now—
Can you save your life from perdition?

But when you seek the One who formed you,
And cleanse yourself, holy, from filth,
[Then]:—Come near! Don't be afraid!
Your deeds will bring you near.

Proud one, look at your world!
Do not be deceived by your false dreams!
Your day is short, your destination distant.
What will you say when you meet your God?

You thirst to behold the beauty of the Lord
And to serve in his Presence for time everlasting.
So return, return, O Shulamit,
To the house of your Father, as when you were young.

Comments

"Return," namely to your origin, for the souls of the pious are kept under God's "throne of splendor," or, as ha-Levi says in the opening verse of another famous poem of his, emanate from the Holy Spirit.[103] These poetic and semimythical notions, anticipated in the Bible and expressed in the Talmud, were adopted by the medieval religious thinkers, of whom ha-Levi was one. The spiritual soul, to be differentiated from the soul of the body, which dies with him, is of the same ethereal imperceptible substance as "the glory of God which fills the world" (Isaiah 6:3). Although such concepts border on the idea of a God immanent in this world, the Jewish theologians held fast to their experience of a personal God.[104] So did ha-Levi, and this builds up the tension in our poem and explains its charm. Beginning with presenting the soul as a heavenly substance, it ends with the image of a spoiled child well received after her return to her father's house.

"Not this," the easy life you are enjoying in Spain, the poet says to his soul, is the rest promised to you.[105] "The way" to the perfection which might lead to eternal life "is long: prepare supplies": repentance, good deeds, and humility.[106] Now is the time to leave your worldly affairs and to do God's business.[107]

The next three stanzas develop the theme of the first. Not many years are left. "When, if not now," exclaims the poet, "may you save your life from perdition," that is, from the loss of your eternal existence.[108] The third stanza strikes up a more hopeful tone. Extricate yourself from the filth of this world, then your good deeds may bring you near to God.[109] The fourth stanza takes up a theme common in ha-Levi's poetry: human pride and self-confidence. Ha-Levi was a successful and well-to-do physician, a poet and scholar of renown both in his native Spain and throughout the Jewish world, but his letters and writings reveal him as a man of pious humility.[110] "May you see your world as long as you live," means in the Talmud "enjoy it"; ha-Levi uses the phrase in the opposite sense: "examine your world and you will discover that it is a deceptive dream."[111] The stanza concludes with an exhortation similar to that opening the poem: "Your day is short and much is still to be done. Prepare your plea!"[112]

The poem concludes with elated expectations. The allusion to the (then) traditional good wish for a holiday "to behold the beauty of the Lord" (Psalms 27:4), refers here not to the Temple of Jerusalem but to God's spiritual abode.[113] The final two verses center on the name Shulamit, the beloved in the Song of Songs (7:1), taken in the sense of "a newlywed who proves herself as perfect in the house of her father-in-law and is eager to hurry to her own father's house to report her success." This Talmudic expression (found in a purely legal exposition) derives Shulamit from *shālēm*, "perfect," and illustrates a very common social phenomenon: after the wedding the bride was taken to the home of the husband's family, where she often had to endure distressing hardship from her mother-, sisters-, and father-in-law. When the new family accepted her as an accomplished housewife and companion, she dared to visit her own family, because she had only good things to tell there about her experience in the foreign world to which she had been exposed. The mere name Shulamit elicited the idea that the striving for near perfection in this world was not entirely in vain, while the concluding words "as when you were young" evokes the Psalmist's mighty appeal to the soul (103:1–5), which ends with the wish "may your youth be renewed."[114]

Judah ha-Levi's poem can be understood without elucidation. It is written in simple language; anyone with a modest knowledge of Hebrew can master it. Nor are the ideas expressed in it very special. They are the quintessence of true beliefs about life and death, as discussed in this book on the basis of the Geniza evidence. The allusions to Bible and Talmud occurring in every line do not require great scholarship. Most are quotations from biblical books and Talmudic treatises frequently read or regularly studied. But these allusions give weight to the poem and legitimize it as a genuinely Jewish profession of faith. The special attraction of the poem is the ease of combination of many different elements and the sincerity of conviction.

Any reader of the Qur'ān, or visitor to a Muslim cemetery, who is familiar with ha-Levi's poem, is reminded of the end of Sura 89, which is carved on countless Muslim tombstones: "O you, O soul, be at rest, return unto your Lord, pleased [with your reward] and pleasing [God]; enter among my servants; and enter my Paradise." The connection with Psalms 116:7 is unmistakable. The intermediary was probably a Christian (Syriac) liturgical creation. But this is beside the point. What I wish to emphasize is the essentially optimistic character of the Jewish outlook on the World to Come, which, in its Islamic environment, could be better preserved than elsewhere, as long, of course, as living conditions were bearable. The High Middle Ages, the period of the classical Geniza and the efflorescence of Spanish Jewry, was a time of transition.

D. THE PRESTIGE OF SCHOLARSHIP

A Survey

The Talmudic scholar and student of the Law.—Franz Rosenthal's classic *Knowledge Triumphant: The Concept of Knowledge in Medieval Islam* opens up new vistas on the understanding of medieval Islamic civilization:

> All human knowledge that has any real value and truly deserves to be called "knowledge" is religious knowledge. Moreover, it is not just vaguely some general religious information, but it is specifically identical with the contents of the divine message transmitted by the Prophet (p. 30).
>
> Knowledge remains the goal of all worthwhile aspirations of mankind, the true synonym of religion. These were the ideas that determined the development of Muslim "knowledge" and with it, of all Muslim intellectual life, and, in fact, all Muslim religious and political life. From the Qur'ānic attitude toward knowledge it would be possible almost to predict the course that Muslim theology, mysticism, jurisprudence and the like were to take, as well as the fate that had to befall the liberating influences set in motion by the reception of the Classical heritage in the ninth century. The triumphs and defeats of Muslim civilization are foreshadowed in Muḥammad's understanding of "knowledge" (p. 32).

In Judaism, Torah study was just as pivotal, and the scholar successfully devoting his life to it was an object of veneration. This holds true not only for Jews living under Islam, but (perhaps to an even higher degree) for those dispersed in the countries of the Christian West, for this tradition had its roots in the ancient Near East and in the history of the Jewish people at large. Originally designating any kind of teachings ("listen, my son, to the Torah of your mother" [Proverbs 1:8]), in classical Judaism the term came to mean the Torah of Moses, the Pentateuch, and all the laws and other teachings deduced from it in the course of many generations. Embedded in their Islamic environment the Jews participated, in different degrees, in the branches of study developed there, and some of the prestige enjoyed by the Torah scholar rubbed off on the bearers of other knowledge, especially the physician and the student of theology, philosophy, and the exact sciences. In his translation of the saying "The world stands on three things: Torah, Service [of God], and Charity" in the opening of the *Ethics of Fathers*, Moses Maimonides renders Torah with *ʿilm*, the central Arabic term for knowledge.[1]

In the preceding section (p. 348), reference is made to his benediction at the public recital of the Torah: "Blessed be you, our God . . . who, by giving us true learning [lit., 'a true Torah'], planted eternal life within us." A similar benediction opens the daily Jewish morning prayer and is followed by the reading of this passage (appearing in Talmudic sources in different versions): "These are the things of which a person eats the fruits [meaning: gains interest] in this world, while the principal remains for him in the World to Come: Honoring father and mother, deeds of charity, regular attendance at the public morning and evening services . . .[2] devotional prayer, and bringing about peace between one person and another; but the study of the Torah is worth all these together."[3]

The high rating of study as superior to all-around ethical behavior and concentration of the mind during prayer is explained by the principles that "study engenders action"[4] and that "he who acts because he is enjoined to do so is preferable to one who acts without being obligated."[5] Everything should be done as God has taught.

This sounds complicated, but it was not. As the Geniza proves, it was rather the common attitude. Throughout, fathers are wished to have sons "studying the Torah and fulfilling its commandments" (or the like), and always in that order.[6] Studying the Torah meant many different things. For the common people it meant being able to read and to recite in the proper way the five books of Moses and other parts of the Bible included in the prayer services and, of course, the prayers themselves. More ambitious persons could participate in evening courses or take private lessons.[7] But even for the average people study was lifelong, as repeatedly prescribed (e.g., Deuteronomy 4:9–10), for the real House of Study was not the Bible school, attended, with varying success, by children, but the synagogue. During the service the ritual laws were explained in succinct statements, as found in the *Siddur* of Saadya Gaon and still heard in Oriental synagogues, usually before, or (more commonly) after the reading of the Torah. Moral and religious education was provided by the *derāsh(a)*, a sermon, or rather, lecture, followed, or interrupted, by a disputation, usually connected (often very loosely) with the Bible reading of the Sabbath or holiday concerned. These sermons were often given not during the morning service (before which one did not eat) but later in the day. Here the listeners, when they did not study the sources themselves, could pick up quotations even from rarely read books, as we find occasionally in Geniza letters. The two sermons summarized above (pp. 345–347), one concerned with the observance of the Sabbath, and the other possessed of mystical and ethical trends, serve as examples. The *derāsh(a)*, literally, "seeking," namely, the alleged real (exoteric or esoteric) meaning of biblical passages, was an entertaining form of Bible study. An enormous literature of *derāsh(a)s*, described by the general name Midrāsh, has been preserved, both in the form of books, read throughout the centuries as sources of edification, as well as in Geniza fragments, often of considerable size.[8]

Last, but not least, the extended prayers themselves, all said in Hebrew, either recited by the congregation in unison or read or sung by cantors, who added ever new liturgical creations to their repertoire, represented a lifelong opportunity for learning.[9]

All this created an atmosphere and an attitude, but was no substitution for the systematic acquisition of knowledge. According to Saadya, the prayer said immediately after awakening in the morning, "grant me my portion in your Torah," shows that knowledge, like health, rank, or riches, was regarded as a gift of God, apportioned to each individual in accordance with his natural disposition, social status, and special circumstances.[10] A general—one might say minimal—level of education, as described in the preceding lines, was expected from any respectable member of the community.[11] Excellence in erudition was difficult to acquire, however, in a community lacking the economic means for continuous maintenance of higher institutions of learning. Fustat possessed a Jewish College (also called Midrāsh) for advanced students; Alexandria, it seems, had a less stable school of the same type; and the same was true of Ramle, the administrative capital of Palestine, but we read nothing about their organization or financing.[12] In a letter to Nahray b. Nissīm, written around 1090, when he was asked to convey greetings to all members of the Midrāsh, he was certainly one of them, if not their President, since, at the time of the writing of the letters, he was the rav, the highest expert in Jewish law, in Egypt.[13] When chief judge Hananel b. Samuel says of the son of a rich and influential man in Alexandria that he did not leave the Midrāsh in Fustat for a moment and, in addition, pursued private study with another scholar, it may be concluded that the college had its own premises and faculty.[14] Similarly, when in a letter to judge Hananel he is reminded that three books were deposited with him, one on medicine and one on Arabic poetry (in his house), and a third one, a book on Jewish law, in the Midrāsh, one gets the impression that the judge had an office there and probably was its head.[15] Solomon, the son of judge Elijah, addresses a letter to "the Midrāsh of our Master, the illustrious judge Isaac" in Alexandria, which again seems to show that the Midrāsh was not an independent institution but was under the tutelage of the local judge and spiritual leader.[16] Even the busy judge of the desert town on the Euphrates, who presided over three congregations and had to make strong efforts to keep his unruly flock under control, regarded teaching as his main task. He boasted that even scholars from Christian Europe came to his remote place to study Talmud with him.[17]

Egypt must have been a special case. Although "wandering scholars" were a general phenomenon in both the Islamic and the Christian Middle Ages, practically all of Egypt's leading scholars during the classical Geniza period, from Shemarya b. Elhanan at the end of the tenth century to Moses Maimonides at the end of the twelfth, originated from outside.[18] Perhaps the very fact that the Jewish population itself was largely composed of immigrants or their offspring (first from Iran, Iraq, and Syria, and later from the West) was an impediment to continuity. As long as the Jerusalem yeshiva functioned, well-to-do fathers in Egypt could send their sons there for higher studies. Saadya Gaon from the Fayyūm district south of Cairo most probably acquired his vast knowledge of Hebrew sources, already displayed at the age of twenty, in that center of learning.[19] Finally, the Jewish population of Egypt was of limited size, and leading families, like the Tustarīs, were Karaites, who would support eminent scholars personally, but certainly not contribute to the upkeep of rabbinic institutions.

The main topic studied in Midrāshim was the Talmud with accessories, such as the monographs of Saadya, Samuel b. Ḥofnī, and Hay, and other attempts at codification, commentaries, as well as the responsa of the Gaons. Theology and philosophy, so prominent in the writings of a Saadya, and even logic, often taught in Muslim madrasas, were absent from the syllabus, as far as we know. This course of study may be compared to that of a Law school after a Bachelor of Arts degree in the humanities, the latter mainly provided by the Bible and its midrāshic expositions. As long as the yeshivas of the classical type existed, the members were postdoctorals of all ages and from all stations of active life. There, too, the Talmud and its associated disciplines were the main subject of study. A *talmīd*, "scholar," par excellence, was a man proficient in the Talmud.[20]

In principle, the teaching of higher learning was supposed to be dispensed gratuitously. Attainments in scholarship could not provide a comfortable income. Most of the leading scholars of the Geniza period earned their livelihood either as physicians, like Mevōrākh b. Saadya and Maimonides, or as merchants, like Nahray b. Nissīm and chief judge Hananel b. Samuel.[21] Why, then, was religious scholarship so revered in the rather materialistically minded Geniza society? It seems that precisely because the long hours dedicated to study and taken away from gaining one's livelihood represented a kind of renunciation of this world; it gave the scholar an aura of a holy man, "whose prayers are accepted by God and granted."[22] For it was he who did for the community at large that "portion of God's Torah" for which to strive was the obligation of everyone. Because of this vicarious sacrifice, gifts to him were "like offerings burnt on the altar" (in the Temple of Jerusalem).[23] Finally, these scholars were also the highest authorities in all matters of daily conduct, from the observance of the ritual to family matters and civil law.

The physician and student of the sciences.—Another prestigious occupation was that of the physician.[24] His knowledge, like that of the Talmudic scholar, was esoteric, accessible to others only imperfectly. He was a student of the "writings of the ancients," this time the Greeks. In a bookish civilization, acquaintance with ancient sources, the reliability of which had been tested throughout the ages, was highly respected. When a physician wished to assure his patient that he got the best treatment available, he would tell him that it was recommended "by the most ancient authorities."[25] The names Hippocrates, Galen, and Dioscurides were familiar even to laymen. The study of medicine was conceived as comprising most of the sciences then cultivated, not only those immediately connected with his profession, such as pharmaceutics, nutrition, and climatology, but also general sciences, such as logic and mathematics. The accomplished physician should have a mind trained in philosophy. The term *ḥakīm*, "doctor," designated not only a physician but also a man of comprehensive secular education. In addition, it was taken for granted that he believed in God, the Prophets, and the World to Come (a formulation applicable to each of the three monotheistic religions), and he satisfied the highest standards of morality and comportment (including perfuming oneself when visiting a patient). All these ideas were already contained in "The Education of a Physician," written in the ninth century, probably by a Jew.[26] The Jewish physicians known to us from the Geniza, as far as they were observant and participated in the life of the community, were also often well versed in Jewish scholarship.[27] Renowned and successful physicians were often employed by rulers and members of the ruling class, which provided them with access to the highest ranks of society. Such contacts made them even more knowledgeable (albeit in different ways) and inspired additional prestige.

The astronomer and astrologer.—The master of another science, astronomy (paired with astrology), often an even closer companion of the rulers than the physician, enjoyed high esteem in Islamic medieval society. The indefatigable efforts of Bernard R. Goldstein of the University of Pittsburgh and David Pingree of Brown University have unearthed horoscopes and astrological almanacs of considerable interest from the Geniza, mostly from the twelfth century, when "the passion for astrology," to use an expression by Lynn White, Jr., also reached its zenith in Europe.[28]

These almanacs, which refer only to non-Jewish calendars and holidays, were certainly not created by a Jewish scholar; however, the fact that they were transcribed into Hebrew characters and, as I believe (see n. 28), by none other than the illustrious "scribe of the yeshiva" Nathan b. Samuel he-Ḥāvēr proves that the belief in the influence of the movements of the heavenly bodies on life on earth and trust in the capacity of scientists to foretell their effects were accepted at that time (ca. 1160) even among the divines composing the rabbinic court of the Egyptian capital. Astrologers, male and female, appear, alone or together with members of their families, in lists of communal handouts of clothing and bread. Their very poverty proves that these were mere fortune-tellers (although some had a *dukkān*, or office, in the bazaar).[29]

In legal documents persons are described without scruple as astrologers.[30] In letters one would report matters like this: "The astrologers are of the unanimous opinion that, according to my nativity, *mawlid*, no adverse constellation, *qaṭᶜ*, against me has remained, and that from the eighteenth of this month good fortune will come to me."[31] Even more characteristic is this note (sixteen lines) scribbled on the blank space of a marriage contract from the year 1084: "These are the Bible verses to be read before giving an astrological judgment." The verses that follow, such as Jeremiah 13:18 and 10:11, Ezekiel 21:31, and, especially, Daniel 2:21, and others, speak about the falling down of crowns, of changing times, and of the fall and rise of kingdoms. Thus, this astrologer was interested in horoscopes not for individuals but for mankind in general (as found in the material published by Goldstein and Pingree), no doubt in expectation of messianic upheavals.[32]

How can this "passion for astrology" be explained? Needless to say, we have here again the belief in the reliability of ancient books characteristic of this era of history. For many hundreds of years astrology had been practiced; so its usefulness could not be denied, in particular, since persons of highly technical knowledge were its standard-bearers. The prestige of inherited learning guaranteed the survival of astrology. Another question was, of course, how could this belief be tolerated, since God himself was the Creator of everything, even of a man's secret thoughts. The power of the belief in astrology is evident in the fact that the answer to this question was given in medieval Judaism neither unanimously nor unequivocally. Following Jeremiah 10:2, two leading Talmudic scholars of the third century, R. Johanan in Palestine and Samuel in Babylonia, declared that Israel was not under the rule of the stars.[33] This was formally recognized as the accepted opinion, but was less outspoken than Jeremiah, who had declared that "these beliefs of the nations are futile" (*ibid.*, v. 3). A leading Talmudic scholar of the fourth century went so far as to declare that the length of life, good luck with children, and earnings depended not on one's merit but on one's stars.[34] The good wishes for a propitious hour and a friendly star over marriage contracts were not mere phrases; they had their place in real life.[35] The obvious contradiction between the power of the stars and that of God was neutralized by the belief that the stars act according to the will of God, as we read again and again in Solomon Ibn Gabirol's poetic creation

"The Kingly Crown," which accepts the assertions of astrology in sum. Only Maimonides condemned this science as a fake. In any case, despite the general acceptance of astrology by the Geniza people, not a single Jewish scholar creatively active in this field appears in their writings. But it certainly did not diminish their awe before the attainments of the eminent members of the Cairo observatory.[36]

The master of language.—No branch of knowledge has left more traces in the day-to-day correspondence of the Geniza people than the mastery of language, culminating in poetry and cognate ways of ornate and formal speech. Any letter containing a request, thanks, or good wishes, or written on any other special occasion, or even on current affairs, was likely to begin with biblical quotations, followed by Hebrew verses or rhymed prose conveying greetings, then other verses or rhymed prose praising the recipient's excellence (usually after his name was mentioned). The text itself would often be adorned with special phrases in Hebrew or Arabic, frequently rhymed. At the end of a carefully written long letter the writer would crave indulgence for shortcomings in style (sometimes also script and paper, even if they appear perfect to us. Those who make excuses usually are good stylists.[37]

The interesting fact is that simple people, aware of the litterateur ambiance in which they lived, excused themselves, not out of false modesty but because they knew their limitations. "You know that I am weak in [. . .] and expression; my writing is not worthy of your trouble; let no one read this letter except yourself."[38] Japheth b. Manasse ha-Levi Ibn al-Qaṭā'if, writing to his brother, the court clerk Ḥalfōn, extols the latter's "unique style, [deep] understanding, beauty of expression, and rich ornateness," but adds: "I can hardly understand what you write, let alone requite it."[39]

In public correspondence, especially that exchanged between communities in different cities, utmost care was taken in both script and diction; poetical proems in praise of the addressed were almost obligatory.[40] In spring 1027, when the Alexandrian community was in trouble because of the funds needed for the ransom and maintenance of captives, its dayyān Joseph ha-Kohen had the patience to precede his urgent letter to the Fustat community with four verses on the address and twenty-eight in the opening of the text, followed by seven plus nine lines of "verbiage" (as Jacob Mann called it).[41] His son and successor Yeshūʿā, in a similar situation, produced an even more extensive poetic exordium and did not fail to mention that the entire community of Alexandria admired "the beauty of the verses" in the letter sent from Fustat about the same affair of the ransom and maintenance of captives.[42]

In general, where applicable, a prominent person was praised not only for his religious observance and civic virtues but also for the excellence of his diction and his command of the (Hebrew) language. A long poem recited at the banquet in honor of the circumcision of Nethanel, the son of the Nagid Mevōrākh, extolls the father's beauty of speech:

> Your palate is sweet like honey [cf. Song of Songs 5:16] . . .
> You seize every ornate and distinguished phrase [as easily as others] seize abandoned eggs [cf. Isaiah 10:14].[43]

Mevōrākh's "sweet" (Ar. *ʿadhb* for Heb. *māthōq*) and heart-winning speech is known from the assembly convened immediately after the news of the fall of Jerusalem in July 1099 had reached Cairo.[44] When Jacob, the spiritual leader of the flourishing community of Aleppo, Syria, member of the Jerusalem Academy (and son of Joseph, who had been President of the High Court), was praised by another prominent Talmudic scholar for his delightful talk, "graceful language, and beauty of composition," we understand that cultivated speech was essential to that scholar. A relative writing a short letter to him in Arabic about a family matter and some liturgical creations finds it necessary to introduce it with nine lines of Hebrew rhymes in a highly payyetanic style.[45] Before assuming the office in Aleppo, Jacob had lived in Palestine and Egypt, where he must have been in close contact with two eminent Talmudic scholars who were also most fertile liturgical poets: the Palestinian Samuel, by-named "the Third," that is, candidate for the presidency of the Court of the Jerusalem Academy, and the refugee from Spain, Joseph Ibn Abitur, who had been a candidate for the spiritual leadership of the Jews of that country, but had refused the dignity.[46] How seriously a divine in Egypt took even secular poetry may be gathered from a question submitted to a presiding judge concerning a poem by Solomon Ibn Gabirol and dedicated to Samuel ha-Nagid. The question has the usual form of a request for a legal decision: "What is the opinion of the illustrious . . . presiding judge with regard to a qaṣīda [poem (by Solomon Ibn Gabirol)] of blessed memory [identifies the poem by its opening and ends as usual in such a request] and may you receive double reward from Heaven." The questioner was unhappy with a metrical deviation in one foot (owing, as we see, to an erroneous text in his possession) and with two Hebrew words unknown to him, "onyxed and jaspered," probably improvised by the poet to mean "ornamented with precious stones." The letter itself is mostly in Arabic.[47]

The poet.—The infatuation with formed and ornate speech was an ancient heritage which the Jews had shared with their Christian neighbors, who spoke Greek or Aramaic (Syriac), centuries before the advent of Islam. The conspicuous expression of this tendency was Hebrew liturgical poetry (designated as Piyyūṭ), of which the Geniza has preserved unexpected treasures of immense scope. Successful pursuit of this art required scholarship, a ready knowledge of the themes and words of the Bible and midrāshic literature, the Hebrew classics. This is somehow comparable with the hellenized Near Easterners who studied the Greek classics, from Homer to Menander, in order to get a firm grounding in cultivated speech together with a humanistic education.

Under the impact of the Arabs, who rightly claimed natural gifts and preeminence in poetry and rhetoric, two new elements entered Hebrew literature.[48] First, the theory and systematization of the Hebrew language, in short, its grammar in the widest sense of the word, became a central concern of Jewish scholarship. "Grammar" had been an intrinsic part of Greek education, but, as in the fields of the sciences, theology, and philosophy, linguistic thinking and training had to wait for the High Middle Ages before they became acceptable to a religious community that had been anxiously watching from its ramparts to ward off foreign influences. One talked much about the vital importance of the Holy Language and the meritoriousness of using it, but did little to implement that ideal. Islam, which made linguistics a handmaid serving the understanding of its Holy Scripture, showed the way. The lifelong dedication of a Saadya Gaon and his Karaite predecessors and contemporaries to the study and teaching of Hebrew and the cooperation of Karaites and Rabbanites in this matter reveal how much Jewish society had changed in its Islamic environment.[49] The excellent achievements of the Jewish linguists of the tenth through the twelfth centuries did not fail to influence education. *Naḥw*, "grammar," correct language, including metrics and versifying in general, became part and parcel of a liberal upbringing.

The imitation of the formal elements of language and prosody was one thing; the acceptance of the purely secular motifs of Arabic poetry, such as love and friendship, praise and satire, enjoyment of life or despising it, was quite another. Eastern Jewry had known only religious poetry. For the verses written for weddings, circumcision banquets, weeks of mourning, or for the celebration of scholarly and public events were in form and content essentially religious. Even wine songs occasionally had a religious tint.[50]

Jewish intellectuals, especially physicians (who loved also to satirize one another in Arabic verse), did not neglect Arabic poetry. A leaf in the Geniza contains a list in Arabic script of at least forty-two divans (the authors of many which are unknown to me). If, as is likely, the list represents the (partial) inventory of a library, its proprietor must have had a considerable knowledge of the subject.[51] A small fragment in beautiful Hebrew script contains remnants from creations by the prince of Arabic poets, al-Mutanabbī (d. 955), including the beginning of his famous poem (so often quoted today): *al-sayfu aṣdaqu anbāʾan min al-kutubi*, "the sword is a truer messenger than letters."[52] The record of a public sale of the Arabic section of the library of a Jewish physician, held in November 1190, lists as first item sold six volumes of the *Kitāb al-Aghānī* (The Book of Songs) collected by Abu ʾl-Faraj al-Iṣfahānī (d. 967) over fifty years.[53] I was particularly moved by a detailed list of a dead coppersmith's belongings, which contained among many other items four books, the *Siddur* of Saadya Gaon (see *Med. Soc.*, IV, 416 n. 327, and here, *passim*), another Siddur, a section of the Book of Psalms, and, in Arabic script, a volume of poetry.[54] However, no poet of the East included the lighter themes of Arabic secular poetry in the cadre of his Hebrew creation.

Things changed when the last century of Umayyad rule in Spain and the small principalities replacing it offered the Jews opportunities to penetrate Islamic higher society. They seem to have observed there that Islamic orthodoxy lived in peace with Arab frivolity. Hebrew poetry began to fulfill a role in Jewish society somewhat comparable with that of the Arab in an Islamic ambiance. Any author who used the new strophic forms of poems and the Arabic metric rules felt induced to take over also the mundane topics expressed by them.[55]

Then the "Spanish miracle" occurred. All the outstanding Jewish poets, such as Samuel ha-Nagid, Solomon Ibn Gabirol, Moses (b. Jacob) Ibn Ezra, Judah ha-Levi, Abraham (b. Meir) Ibn Ezra, all Spanish, happened also to be paradigms of piety and outstanding scholars, each in his field or fields.[56] Consequently, everything emanating from their pens was acceptable. Copies of their creations, including secular ones, made during their lifetimes, have reached the Geniza. Innumerable others, copied later, followed suit.[57]

The superiority of Spanish Hebrew religious poetry was soon recognized in the East. A man who wished to become a cantor made for himself excerpts from the divans of Solomon Ibn Gabirol and Judah ha-Levi. Once, on a Day of Atonement, when he sang one of the Spanish penitential liturgies, the congregation became so excited that they asked him to enlarge it by compositions of his own, imitating it. He accepted the challenge and, while a member of the audience recited one stanza of the Spanish poem, he, the cantor, "was inspired by God" and improvised a corresponding one in the same style. He adds: "I sang my stanzas in a melody learned from you."[58]

Judah ha-Levi's theological chef d'oeuvre, the *Kuzari*, was certainly known to the Jewish intellectuals in Egypt even before he arrived in that country on his way to Palestine. He had corresponded about it with the Egyptian humanist-merchant Ḥalfōn b. Nethanel when the latter visited Spain. But ha-Levi's popularity was achieved by his superb liturgical creations, in which the depth of religious sentiment was fully brought out by the perfection of their forms. The extraordinary veneration with which he was received in the land of the Nile owed to the general esteem for knowledge, namely, for the poet's knowledge of what was due to God and man and his mastery of the linguistic tools needed to give expression to his insights.[59]

Seven Portraits

In the following the position of scholarship and scholars in the Geniza society is illustrated by a series of portraits emerging from documents mainly of the eleventh and twelfth centuries.

An all-around education.—The writer of the following calligraphic note belonged to the jeunesse dorée of the Egyptian capital. This can be deduced from the nickname of one of his friends, who is called Devil and Bird of the Jinnies, and even more so from the strange fact that his father, a physician in a government hospital and a renowned Hebrew scholar, gave him the very large sum of 25 dinars on condition that he stay indoors to study. Although the civilization of that time was bookish in general and the subjects to be learned by the unfortunate young man could mostly be studied from textbooks, there were Jewish and general houses of learning in Fustat and Cairo from which he certainly could have profited. The old physician must have known his son all too well and intended above all to keep him off the street and away from the influence of his friends. The young man retorted by secretly sending notes to his companions—like the two that follow, one in translation and the other in outline. He also arranged to meet them at his house during his father's absence. He clearly was afraid that his silence might be understood by them to mean that he had given up their friendship.

Our unhappy student bore the same name as the Gaon and head of the Jewish community in the Fatimid empire, Nethanel b. Moses ha-Levi, "the Sixth," who held office in the 1160s, and was no doubt the same person. He became a physician in attendance to Fatimid caliphs and survived them with a comfortable pension. In addition, Nethanel served as the official head of the Jewish community during the waning years of Fatimid rule. Thus, his father's endeavors had not been in vain.[60]

In Y[our name, O] Mer[ciful]

I have taken note of your message—may God grant you permanent well-being—and read it and understood its content. You speak there of certain things,[61] but, dear brother, believe me, I can in no circumstances leave the house for various reasons, the most important being that I am staying at home to study medicine, language, Talmud, and the science of theology. For studying at home I received 25 dinars, on condition that I do not leave the house—even to visit the public bathhouse.

Dear brother, you cannot imagine what I suffer by being separated from you and from our friend the Devil,[62] the Bird of Jinnies. "For now my calamity is heavier than the sand of the seas; therefore, my words are rash" [Job 6:3]. I can't believe that this time will ever pass. Whenever the day draws to its end, I say: "As a slave, who longs eagerly for the [evening's] shadow, and as a hireling, who looks for his wages" [Job 7:2]. I have been sitting in the house for such a long time that no one's eye[63] has fallen upon me, as Job—m[ay peace be] u[pon him]—said: "The eye of him that sees me, will not recognize me" [Job 7:8]. It is due to my lack of experience and bad planning that I have fallen into this trap. If you think otherwise, dear brothers, "teach me, and I will hold my peace, and cause me to understand, wherein I have erred" [Job 6:24].

I believe that my confinement was ordained by God; it was not my fault; for it is just as Job said: "He shuts up a man, and no one can open" [Job 12:14].

Please[64] excuse the shortness of my answer. I am in severe straits, for my value has decreased and the load of my sins has increased, while I was unaware of this, not knowing. Now, my brother, by God who knows your secrets, do not cease to send me your letters. You did not make mention of my "brother" Abū Naṣr in your note—may God keep him—nor did he send me any answer. I do not know what is the reason for this.

In reply to your remark that you have no access to me owing to my father, please come early in the morning, immediately when you come out of the synagogue service, once or twice every week, for my father is in the hospital from early in the morning until just before noon. Then we can have a talk together. *And Peace.*

Your slave, servant, protégé, and boy,

Nethanel ha-Levi, son of R. Moses, the Sixth in the S[ociety of the scholars]—ma[y the Merciful] pr[eserve him].

[*Written crosswise beneath and above the name*:]

"I[n you, O] G[od, I] t[rust], [may I] n[ever be put to] sh[ame]" [Psalms 31:2].[65]

[*Added*:]

Into [the hand of] "the brother."

The second letter[66] is addressed to a religious and learned "brother from father and mother" (i.e., an intimate friend) and to another companion. It refers also to a missive by "my illustrious lord and master 'Father of a son'" with the nickname written in code.[67] The superscription reads: "*In the name of Him who humiliates and exalts, and liberates prisoners*." The friends obviously had scolded Nethanel for accepting the humiliating house arrest and for not standing up to his father. As in the preceding message, Nethanel emphasizes that he had done so only against an exceptionally high compensation and had struck thus a good deal.[68]

The main part of the missive is dedicated to the literary interests of the two. The friend had asked for a book (see below), whereupon Nethanel replies that he could have it if he would copy it himself, or had someone who could dictate it to him.[69] The friend had failed to comply with a request by Nethanel to send him *karārīs* (Ar.) *al-derāsh*, quires containing a discourse on biblical or Talmudic themes, a failure for which he is slightly reproved.[70] In each of the two letters, three different friends are mentioned, which, together with Nethanel, makes seven, a reasonable number for a close circle of friends. Naturally, Nethanel, who says of the recipient of the second letter that his image was engraved in his heart (so that he saw him constantly despite his absence), might have had additional friends.

Together, the two missives give a good idea of what a member of Jewish higher society in Cairo (around 1140) regarded as indispensable elements of higher education for his son.

Medicine, naturally, provided an honorable way of earning a livelihood. Beyond this it opened the door for gaining access to powerful Muslims and even to the court, as was the case with our Nethanel according to the report of a reliable Muslim historian.[71]

No one without such support could become a leader in a minority community. Since Nethanel was so successful that he became physician in attendance to caliphs, it is not farfetched to assume that he took a serious interest in his profession, aside from the practical advantages it yielded.

A thorough knowledge of classical Arabic was required for the study of medicine and cognate subjects, and, of course, of the sciences and theology. Moreover, its knowledge was indispensable in cultivated speech, spiced with quotations, and, as far as possible, the ability to write verse. Nethanel was not a beginner. His Arabic handwriting (found in the second letter) is as fluent and beautiful as his Hebrew. In the future, he would address the Jewish community in Middle Arabic interlaced with Hebrew phrases and passages from the Bible, Talmud, and Midrāsh. But over two hundred years and more had passed since Saadya Gaon and his contemporaries had emphasized that classical, that is, biblical Hebrew demanded the same degree of attention to its exact pronunciation and grammar as classical Arabic; by 1140 the cultivation of Hebrew was at its height; one could master it only by serious study.

The Talmud and the literature growing around it, which formed the main content of Jewish higher education, was basically a study of Law. Nethanel's father, Moses, headed a *yeshiva shel gōlā*, a local group of men dedicated to this study. His erudition was renowned as far away as Spain in the west and Iraq in the east. That is what the Spanish Hebrew poet Judah ha-Levi, who visited Egypt in 1140/1, said of him in a laudatory poem.[72] Later, our Nethanel became Gaon, or president of that yeshiva, while also occupying the office of head of the Jewish community appointed by the government. From an interesting document from May 1169 it is evident that Nethanel had given up the communal leadership but retained his position of Gaon of the yeshiva, and as such decided legal matters. Saladin (the later Ayyubid Sultan) became vizier in Egypt on 26 March 1169; so it was natural that Nethanel, who was so closely connected with the Fatimid rulers, had to give way. But the Gaonate was a matter of scholarship (and descent). He is still referred to in the document with the words "by order of our Gaon Nethanel."[73]

Bible study is not expressly mentioned in the correspondence. There was no need for it. Bible reading was done throughout the year. When Nethanel quotes from the first twelve chapters of Job five times in a short letter, it stands to reason that he had just completed that part of the book.[74] The *derāsh*, or discourse, which he had asked for from his friend, could have been dedicated entirely to the Bible, but even if it was a Talmudic inquiry, it would have been based on the Bible from beginning to end.

"The science of theology," *ʿilm kalām* (not *al-kalām*), could refer to such Jewish books as Saadya Gaon's chef d'oeuvre, to Baḥyā's *Duties of the Hearts*, or even Judah ha-Levi's *Kuzari*, but probably also to Muslim studies on the subject, since in this field Islamic influence was particularly marked. Moreover, for practical reasons, the Talmudic scholars who served as experts of law and as judges occasionally had an opportunity to meet with their Muslim colleagues on legal matters, and on such occasions it was natural to discuss also theological problems of interest to both religions. Speculative theology could offer a special opportunity for a lengthy discussion between intellectuals of the two religions. We have a report on such a meeting in which Moses Maimonides participated.[75]

The *Iktisāb al-faḍāʾil min kitāb al-masāʾil* (The Acquisition of Noble Qualities through the Book of Questions), probably a commentary, possessed by Nethanel, cannot be defined. Books called *Questions* existed in practically every branch of knowledge in Arabic literature. Since "noble qualities" are mentioned, one might think of the *Questions on the Works of the Souls and the Members* by the ancient Sufi al-Ḥārith al-Muḥāsibī, which deals with the contrast of inner religiosity (souls) and mere observance (members) in a way taken up later by Baḥyā. But this is no more than an educated guess.[76]

The comprehensive education from which Nethanel benefited in his youth left its mark upon him in later life. The titles given to him when he took office and later, while holding it, reflect the prestige he enjoyed. In a document from February/March 1160, designating him as Head of the Jewish community, these three honorific epithets *precede* his name: "one who is unique in our generation," "our prince," "the elect of God among us." These phrases, all in Hebrew, clearly refer to his spiritual leadership as Gaon of the yeshiva. His name is *followed* by another epithet: "the chariot of Israel and its horsemen," the cry uttered by the prophet Elisha, referring to his master Elijah who was carried off to heaven before his eyes (II Kings 2:12). This is not an expression of admiration for scholarship; it means that, at a time precarious for the community, Nethanel, owing to his connection with the court, was able to avert the danger.[77]

The same epithet is found in several documents, even one issued (on 14 February 1160) in a small town, where it is followed by a still more expressive title "the Head [the beginning] of the Redemption," which seems to indicate that the danger averted must have been quite serious.[78] The Elisha exclamation is also used in a letter by the court clerk, later judge, Mevōrākh b. Nathan, addressed to Nethanel shortly after his installation. There the wish is added: "May God turn the heart of *all* Israel toward you" (cf. II Samuel 3:12), which shows that Nethanel's appointment—as natural in a medieval religious democracy—was not uncontested.[79]

Mostly, however, Nethanel is praised for his scholarship. His most common epithet was "a lion of knowledge," found in a document as early as February 1160, also in Mevōrākh's letter, which was almost contemporary with it, and in the latest court record we have from him (dated 15 November 1165), which was written by the court clerk, later judge, Samuel b. Saadya.[80] In the very first document in which we read about Nethanel's activities as judge, he is described, among other things, as "the one who lights up our way."[81] The extraordinary role of titles in the Geniza (and contemporary Muslim) society has been discussed in detail above (pp. 260 ff.). A congregation expressed its appreciation and gratitude by agreeing upon the honorific epithets suggested by the elders and scholars.[82] The majority of titles connected with Nethanel contain an element of this relationship between the community and its leader such as "the elect of God among *us*," "who lights up *our* way," "who is unique in *our* generations," "*our* Gaon," "the crown of *our* head." As the court records related to him show, Nethanel, who was officially "supreme judge [for the Jews] in all towns of Egypt,"[83] attended to legal cases in person and had reports about cases coming before courts outside Cairo sent to him. Benjamin of Tudela, the famous Spanish traveler, mentions only one person in Cairo, our Nethanel, of whom he has this to say: "Among the Jews is Nethanel, the Prince of Princes, the Head of the yeshiva, the Head of all the congregations in Egypt. He appoints rabbis and cantors, and is in attendance to the Great King who has his seat in the palace in Cairo, the royal city."[84]

It was a long way from the unhappy student under house arrest to the Gaon of the yeshiva, the Head of Egyptian Jewry, and the physician in attendance to a caliph. All-around prominence in the community could be attained only by all-around scholarship.

Scholarship as a profession.—A professional scholar was a person who derived his main livelihood from his attainments in Jewish learning, usually in the service of the community. A variety of occupations, usually providing limited income, were open to such persons, see *Med. Soc.*, II, 211–240. Scholars who occupied a leading position in the community, like Nethanel ha-Levi Gaon, whose life story was just analyzed, relied for their subsistence primarily on a mundane occupation. There were, however, especially in the earlier parts of the classical Geniza period, scholars who were in a position to dedicate all their time to their communal duties, above all, the heads and other higher officials of the yeshivas, as well as judges of larger congregations, able and willing to maintain them. Such a person reveals himself to us in the letter translated below, which also gives us a detailed picture of the milieu in which he functioned.

The two letters of Nethanel ha-Levi presented above disclose the propensities and anxieties of a young man; the apparently endless scope and diversity of knowledge which he was expected to master; the apprehension that he might lose the friendship of his companions, his dearest possession; and his doubts concerning the correctness of his decision to accept his father's offer. On the other hand, his desire to get hold of a *derāsh*, or discourse, of which he had heard, and his readiness to lend a book (one not commonly known) from his library on condition that it be treated with care reflects the fledgling scholar.

The letter of Elijah ha-Kohen b. Abraham, translated below, reveals a professional scholar at the height of his success: he was in command of three congregations whose leaders cooperated with him in harmony; he enjoyed the full support of the local ruler; he had "revived the Torah" in his place; his house of learning was frequented even by scholars from faraway Christian countries; and above all, he was confirmed in his position, for which he had been chosen by the local Jewish community, by the Head of the Diasporas and the heads of the yeshivas of Baghdad, especially the renowned Rav Hay Gaon; moreover, this confirmation was valid not only for the town where he was active at that time but also for any other place to which he would like to go.

Unfortunately, the provenance of our letter is not indicated. A note in the margin says that it took eight days on a boat on the Euphrates to get from there to Baghdad. I made great efforts to obtain exact geographical information. Thanks to the praiseworthy cooperation of colleagues, I was able to learn that it could only be the town of ʿĀna. ʿĀna is situated in the corner where the Euphrates makes a turn from a west-easterly to a southerly direction so that the town is protected on two sides by the river. This advantageous strategic position was enhanced by a strong castle. ʿĀna is famous in Islamic history as the place to which the Abbasid caliph was exiled when a mutinous general in Baghdad recognized the

Fatimids of Cairo as the legitimate heads of the Muslim community. This happened about thirty years after the writing of our letter.[85]

As is evident from a later source, the Jewish community of ʿĀna had some contacts with that of Aleppo, northern Syria, despite the long distance between the two towns, for ʿĀna was situated on a highway between Baghdad and Aleppo. Around 1600 there were still two synagogues in ʿĀna, the office of the rabbi was described as "head of the community, judge, and disseminator of the Torah," and he was in receipt of a fixed salary. At times, however, no such spiritual leader could be found (or maintained), and that seems to have been so before our Elijah ha-Kohen arrived. His letter was written after he had held his office for quite a number of years, to the satisfaction of everybody, and especially himself.[86]

Despite the warm personal tone of the letter it must be regarded as having a semi-official character. The detailed greetings sent by groups and persons in ʿĀna (sec. B) to numerous persons and groups in Aleppo (sec. F) seem to emphasize that the community of ʿĀna was enjoying orderly government, justice, and a revival of religious studies, so that it would behoove the sister city to renew the economic and spiritual ties between the two. The rough character of the mass of local Jews was well known, but now they were under the guidance of a benevolent, but resolute, leader.[87]

I have the impression that there was even more to it. Jacob b. Joseph, the recipient of our letter, about whom we possess detailed information (see n. 91), aspired to more than being the spiritual leader of the Aleppo community. As we know from a letter by his elderly friend, the Gaon Solomon b. Judah, he wished to become a member of the Council of Seven of the Jerusalem yeshiva, while Solomon remarks that it was even difficult to get the title *ḥāvēr*, or member of the Academy for him. Jacob's father had been President of the High Court, however, wherefore he thought that he had higher claims. Thus, Elijah ha-Kohen could expect that in the not too distant future the Aleppans would have to look for a new leader. Elijah's successes in ʿĀna would certainly recommend him to them. As Solomon remarks in the letter just referred to: "Everyone strives constantly for a higher rank."[88]

Our letter is written in a bold but careful hand with large, almost quadrangular characters which makes it likely that Elijah ha-Kohen was a native of Palestine. As far as is known, we unfortunately do not have anything else from his pen, for he was undoubtedly an interesting person. It is possible, however, that fragments in his characteristic handwriting may still be found in the Geniza. It would be particularly lucky if these were missives from his earlier years.[89]

Judge Elijah ha-Kohen b. Abraham presided over three congregations: one following the rite of Palestine, the second that of Babylonia-Iraq, and the third that belonging to the dissident sect of the Karaites.[90] Representatives of all three groups sat with him on the bench. Previously, he had held a position in Palestine. He had been for some time at his new post and was eager to receive official renewals by the Jewish authorities of Baghdad, namely, the Head of the Diaspora and the heads of the yeshivas, or high councils. Our letter jubilantly announces that these renewals had arrived.

Our judge must have been an authority on Jewish law of considerable renown, since even scholars from Christian countries had come to study with him. To be sure, "wandering scholars" were a general medieval phenomenon, see *Med. Soc.*, I, 51–54.

Power rested ultimately with the government. The efficacy of any judge, and especially one of a minority group, depended on his good relations with the government and its executive officers. Our judge proudly reports that he was held in great esteem by the local ruler and was openly supported by him.

The community presided over by the judge must have differed considerably from that led by him in Palestine (which also might have consisted of three different groups, see *Med. Soc.*, II, 6–7). The middle Euphrates flows through the desert and the Jews in the writer's town had apparently acquired something of the rough character of desert dwellers, who were inclined to settle matters by force rather than by law.

The recipient was a member of the Jewish high council of Jerusalem, and his father had held its second highest office, that of the president of the high court. He himself was a judge, first in Fustat (at least until 1018) and then in Aleppo (dated document: 1028). Since our letter shows him as a newcomer to Aleppo, it must have been written in the 1020s.[91]

It is in conformity with the spirit of the surrounding Arab civilization that the writer praises his colleague repeatedly, not only for his activities of judge and teacher but also for his eloquence and beautiful language. The writer's style was to the point and not unduly high-flown, compared, of course, with what was regarded as the minimum for urbane expression in his time.

The letter is in Hebrew, as was customary among scholars (not in Arabic).[92]

"You love justice and detest iniquity, therefore God, your God, has anointed you with the oil of joy, preferring you to your companions" (Psalms 45:8).[93]

[A. *Praise and good wishes for the recipient*]

To the seasoned scholar, the charming teacher, and lucid speaker, pure of heart and blameless in conduct, who gathers for himself merits to be rewarded in this world and the World to Come; may his Creator increase his worldly possessions and surround him with his guardian angels; may law and ordinances be learned from his mouth when he sits down to teach and stands up to judge;[94] may the mighty God protect him from error and lead him on a smooth path in honor and beauty,[95] him, our master and teacher *rav* Jacob, the member of the Great Sanhedrin (Council), may our Creator increase his distinction and grant him fame and glory.

[B. *Greetings from a variety of persons in the writer's place*]

Greetings to my highly honored and deeply beloved friend[96] from me, the Court (presiding judge), from my son, ma(ster) Amram, and my colleagues on the bench, the elders of the three congregations, who have been busy with me for years to retrieve possessions appropriated by oppressors, with the help of God, praised be he, and the awe of the Torah, which he has given us, and the dread of the government, which appreciates me greatly and openly shows me its favor. Also from the scholars of the land of Edom, R(abbi) Karmī, R(abbi) Judah, and others who have come here from Aleppo for my lectures to study Mishnah and Talmud with me in their quest for scholarship.[97]

[C. *Thanks for previous hospitality*]

I inform you that I long to see your splendorous face, to listen to your delightful talk, and to enjoy your conversation. I worried when I heard that you had traveled from Aleppo, leaving the company of good and learned people. I had also assumed that you would be coming here, as I learned from travelers, and hoped that our God would present me with the opportunity to return you a little of the hospitality with which you received me in Miṣrayim (Fustat) and in particular my son during his illness, you and the people (lit., men) of your house.[98] Also, when he visited Aleppo last year, you were very kind to him, assisted him in his affairs, hosted him, and pampered him with delicacies.[99] May the King of Glory repay you for all you have done, and grant us the ability to reciprocate at least a little, commensurate with the respect in which we hold you. May he keep and preserve you, prolong your life, make your light luminous and keep away from you all that you dread, but let you enjoy prosperity as it is written: "The Lord will let you enjoy prosperity" (Deuteronomy 28:11).

[D. *Congratulations on the recipient's marriage into an Aleppan family*]

When the festive tidings reached us that you built your house on sound foundations in the midst of our pious and noble masters of the community of Aleppo,[100] we were extremely happy for you and for them that such a wise and prudent man should be in their midst. May God make them happy with you and you with them and bless all your undertakings.

I had written before to your honor, but had not seen any answers. It is well known that you are very busy teaching the two laws[101] and exercising your profession. Moreover, you were occupied with the financial arrangements connected with your wedding. May he who ordains marriages give you from your wife sons who occupy themselves with the Torah. We explained the absence of your answer by your multiple occupations. Or perhaps you have sent us letters and they fell into the hands of people who do not wish me well and hid them.

[E. *Confirmation of the writer in his office by the Head of the Diasporas and the heads of the yeshivas of Baghdad*]

In those letters I had also informed you that our master R. Benjamin ha-Kohen and others, who had known us from this town and the Land of Israel, traveled (to Baghdad) and told our masters, the heads of the yeshivas, in terms that I am unable to detail, about my appointment here and that I revived the Torah of Moses, may peace be upon him, and turned many from sin. In response, they, those most honored and God-fearing men, wrote me wonderful letters which I am reluctant to describe confirming me in my jurisdiction here and in any other city to which I might transfer.

When the travelers returned, letters of renewal of my installation were sent to me with R. Ezekiel the Babylonian from our lord Hezekiah,[102] the Head of the Diasporas of all Israel, and from Hay, the head of the yeshiva, may their Rock (God) keep and reward them, and also in the name of the former heads of the yeshivas. Had it not been for pressure of time, I would have made copies of the letters of renewal and sent them to your honor since I know how much you love me, so that you may partake in my happiness.

[F. *Greetings to a variety of persons and groups in Aleppo*]

I ask you to honor me continuously with your letters, which are ornated with graceful language, rich wisdom, and beauty of composition, so that I may enjoy the knowledge that you, your son, the pleasant, decent, and bashful youth, and all your friends and acquaintances are well. And give my regards to our honored elders, our master Saᶜdēl,[103] the head of the congregations, who is always very good to me, sending well-worded letters recommending me to rulers and officials; . . . to our master R. Ḥayyān,[104] the honorable elder, to R. Japheth and R. Mevōrākh, the pious sons of R. Sahl,[105] R. Yeshūᶜah b. R. Jonah, the teachers, cantors, parnāsīm (social welfare officers), collectors of alms, and all those working for the common weal; also, all the elders, the representatives of the merchants and, in particular, R. Caleb;[106] and the whole community of Aleppo, old and young, each individually by his good name.

May your well-being increase and flourish. And may the end be good.[107]

Elijah, ha-Kohen, Court, son of R. Abraham (may his) s(oul) r(est in) c(omfort) (in the) b(urial place of God's) s(cribe) [Moses] (Deuteronomy 33:21).[108]

Installed by the Princely Gate[109] and the Gates of the Yeshivas of the Diaspora.[110]

[*Postscript*]

[G. *The writer's difficulties and successes in dealing with an unruly community. His good standing with the government*]

Blessed are you who have fixed your domicile among God-fearing, law-abiding, and charitable people. You are lucky with them and they with you. But here I must try to keep the balance between the two denominations, the Rabbanites and Karaites, for these, too, are under my jurisdiction together with the Rabbanites.[111] I try to tutor[112] both, sometimes by pressure, sometimes by mild reproach, and occasionally by force and coercion. Last week I recovered a house from particularly mischievous extortionists, after they had appropriated it for thirteen years, and won it back for an orphan girl. One of these extortionists began to use bad language against me. The matter was reported to the ruler of the country—not by me, but by others and some of their opponents in court. The ruler sent a policeman after me to come to see him; it is the custom that I present myself to him together with the Muslim chief judge, their other judges, and the notables of the city every Monday and Thursday[113] and, in addition, whenever there is any need or any plea for our people, I am never prevented by the doorkeepers from seeing him. Thus, when I appeared in the palace, the king said to me: "What is this that I have heard that one of the . . . cursed himself[114] and you did not inform me." He immediately sent policemen to apprehend him and wrote down a public announcement to be read in the bazaars and the streets that anyone who would hide him would forfeit all his possessions and he himself would be executed. The king ordered his house and store to be sealed.[115] When his relatives realized that evil was determined against him by the sovereign, they came to me and entreated me, lest he perish. I understood and was afraid that he would be [. . .] and flogged, therefore I made a public announcement, as is their usage, and entreated the ruler not to harm him. But he said to me: "Leave me alone. When I chastise him, all the Jews will hear and be afraid and will no longer behave insolently toward you." Later on he [agreed] to leave him. . . .

Most of our people here are of a type from whom it is impossible to recover illegally appropriated property except by recourse to coercion by the government. May the Holy one, praise to him, illuminate my eyes by his Torah and give me success, for even the prophets were unable to restrain this nation. Had it not been for their awe of the government, I would never have been able to recover illegally appropriated property. I wrote you all this, my dear friend, that you should know the troubles I have with them. May the end be good.

[*A Postscript by the Writer's Son*]

And I, Amram ha-Kohen, son of rabbi Elijah, make many bows before my lord, the member of the council, (may his) R(ock) k(eep him).

[A marginal note by the judge, dealing with a power of attorney and a settlement made in Fustat, is too defective to translate. It does contain the interesting information that a trip on the Euphrates from the writer's place to Baghdad would take only eight days. To be sure, Baghdad is situated on the Tigris, but several canals connected the two rivers.]

[*Address*:]

To his honor, our leader and crown, his ho(nor and) gr(eatness), our teacher R. Jacob, member of the great Sanhedrin (Academy), son of our teacher Joseph, (the) m(emory of the) r(ighteous may be) b(lessed).[116] May our Rock increase his learning and rank, and bless the work of his hands.

From me, Elijah ha-Kohen, the Court, son of Abraham, (may he) r(est) in E(den), who loves him with all his soul and is loved by him. Covenant of Peace.[117]

[In Arabic characters, it seems written by Elijah himself:][118]

To my Elder and Head, Abū Yūsuf Yaʿqūb, the scholar, may God prolong his life and make his honored position permanent.

To Aleppo, to the Imām[119] and Head of the Jews.

[In another Arabic script. Note of the forwarding postal agency:][120]

(To . . .) Hilāl b. Ḍaḥḥāk.

Scholarship as an avocation.—A scholarly Jerusalem pilgrim from Egypt, fleeing from the Seljuks, finds a home in Salonika, Greece, Byzantium (ca. 1090). The writer of this letter, a scholar from Cairo, had left his native town in order "to have his bones buried in the Holy City." But during the last third of the eleventh century Jerusalem was not a place where a man could end his life peacefully. Our scholar turned north to Damascus and other Muslim cities and, finding no rest there either, finally entered Byzantine territory. Asia Minor, however, into which the writer of our letter had crossed from the East, was flooded by the Turks, who had crushed the Byzantine imperial army in the battle of Manzikert, 1071, and he was forced to flee westward. He wandered from one town to another for twenty-six years, never staying in one place longer than thirty months. Finally, he settled in Salonika in northern Greece, then a town of Jewish learning, where he soon felt himself at home.

The letter is addressed to his only son in Cairo. He also had five daughters, two from his first wife, repudiated and remaining, of course, in Egypt, and three from his second wife, who accompanied him on his travels. One of her daughters also stayed in Cairo, one died on his travels, and one, born late, who was beautiful and much sought after, preferred to stay unmarried until she would "return" one day with her mother to Egypt—although she had never seen that country.

The chasm between masculine and feminine cultures in medieval civilizations is patent in this letter. The old man from Cairo conversed with his learned cronies in Salonika in Hebrew, just as the Christian wandering scholars of Western Europe used Latin everywhere for the same purpose, and the Muslims used Arabic. The brotherhood of scholarship knew no territorial boundaries. Women had no such international contacts; they simply longed to be with their families and to speak the vernaculars that they knew from childhood.

Only the second sheet of the letter, clearly indicated as such by a *b*, representing the number 2, written on the top, has been preserved. Since it runs to eighty lines and seems to express all that the old man had on his mind, one wonders what the first sheet contained. Probably thanks to God for all his benefactions during his prolonged travels; possibly also religious admonitions, since the son, despite brilliant promise, had not continued his scholarly career. The sheet is a piece of vellum, almost evenly cut, but, as usual with this material, much damaged by holes and the obliteration of words and lines. The difficulties in the Arabic text of the original caused by these damages are discussed in its edition (see n. 121). The text on the second leaf begins in the middle of a sentence.[121]

[A. *Feeling happy in Salonika*]

. . . with an attractive young girl.[122] The Jews here do not treat me as a stranger. I have no means for the voyage to you [plural]. We are three persons and I am afraid we might be a burden on you [plural], in particular, since the good news you broached to me was only that you will not need me—may the *Ho*[*ly one*], *b*[*lessed be*] *he*, let you never be in need of anyone except him.

Despite my blindness and physical weakness, which has befallen me in these foreign parts, I am not lost. On the contrary, I am in a thousand states of prosperity. Praise be to God who provides me with sustenance in his kindness. I am beloved here and honored by all who fear God and trust in him, and are intelligent, and educated. Nothing, though, has remained with me except my tongue and my brain. I am able to listen in my room to the sounds of the synagogue service, when it is conducted by a cantor on Friday night, and on the day and night of Saturday.[123] And although the community in Salonika contains fine scholarly people, no one yet has been able to catch me at an error in the discussion *of civil or criminal law*, or any other of the sciences.

[B. *About the family in Egypt*]

In short, I have no grief except the separation from you. You entreat me in your letter in the name of God, saying: "The moment you have read this letter do not tarry any longer, but come." Please, do not write such a thing again, for I yearn for you a thousand times more than you do for me, but I have no strength.

I cannot tell you, my boy, how happy I was with the letter of your brother-in-law Abu ʾl-Ḥasan, for I learned from it that he comes from a fine family. Be friendly with him, and also with your other brother-in-law—although I have not yet received a letter from him—and with your sisters, your mother and with my daughter, may God keep her,[124] and the family of your father-in-law. Greet them all and their children from me. *May they all be blessed by the Ho*[*ly one*], *b*[*lessed be*] *he, and gain a good name and progeny.*

My boy Ismaʿīl,[125] I was informed in the year 48[126] about the inundation of the Nile. I was terrified and had no rest either by day or by night. For *God's* sake, make an effort and write me about your well-being, also who your other brother-in-law is and how each of you gains his livelihood. Give my best regards to your father-in-law and let me know which rank he has among the "members."[127]

Send your letter to ʿImrān b. Nahum[128] in Alexandria, and he will forward it to me. The address:

To Salonika, the Upper Synagogue, the House of Shabbetay, the son of M. Moses, bynamed,[129] the Head [of the congregation].

My boy, I beseech you in the name of God, do not neglect the pursuit of knowledge. I am also astonished about you that you found only once someone who wrote a letter for you.[130] You forgot also the [honorific title] with which I was addressed in Damascus. Furthermore, my boy, I say that [. . .] divert you from seeking knowledge and you have forgotten [. . .] and how the Head of the Academy used to address me [. . . .][131]

[C. *The writer's twenty-six years of wandering*]

My boy, God is my witness that, in the beginning, I could not come back to you because I had not the necessary means for you. All of you know that whenever I had accumulated some sums I did not leave one penny with me, but spent everything on you [plural], because I loved you and had mercy on you. Second, I wished to bury my bones in the Holy City, for out of this desire *I had left the inheritance of the house of my fathers and separated from them.*[132] But that was at a time of which God disapproved. Therefore, it is now twenty-six years since I left you and did not find rest in any place for more than thirty months, and I had never enough money for traveling back to you.

I learned also that [. . .] the maternal uncle of Joseph perished in a fire, he and all those that were with him; when I left you, you had a partnership with him.

At that time, my means dwindled[133] because of the many expenses and

I saw no hope for me any more in the lands of Islam. The fourth girl[134] died. The Turks swept over the eastern parts of the land of the Romans and I fled before them hurriedly to the western part. My eyesight began to fail and constantly worsened in the course of five years. After this I did not think that there remained with me [. . .][135] for this girl that is with me, although many young men have asked for her hand, did not accept any one of them.

[D. *Refusal to return to Egypt*]

Now your letter and that of your brother-in-law Abu ʾl-Ḥasan have arrived and you ask me not to tarry a moment after having seen your letters. But I have not strength enough to walk from my room to the door of the house without being supported and am generally in a poor state, being hard of hearing and of utmost frailty. If you would see me you would run away a month's walking distance. And consider the enormous perils of the voyage, its expenses, my fright because of my high age and my solicitude for the one who is with me, although she wishes to travel. Do not oppose me in this matter. I am also afraid of becoming a burden to you, I and my family. For you know it is not my nature to save money, but when I have some to consume it.

By God, my boy, do not suspect anything concerning me *and do not think evil of the ways of the Creator.*[136] Do not pay attention to the talk of a group that has traveled from here to your place and of which even the most important men among them have been afflicted by doctrines that I am ashamed to mention orally, let alone in writing. My son, rely on your own judgment and on what you have learned. When you were a boy of thirteen years you dazzled the people by your brilliant mind. Do you not know that these are heavenly things in which no one has a share?! Take a lesson from what happened to your sisters and to you in Cairo. Did I forsake you or even your possessions?[137] Greetings of p[eace].[138]

Comments

1. The writer mentions that he was frightened by the rumors about an inundation of the Nile in 1087/8 (see n. 126) and asks his son about those bad tidings. Thus this letter was written in 1088/9 or 1089/90. It was so frightening for the writer because he remembered what happened in the country while he was still there. See next paragraph.

2. Since he had left Egypt twenty-six years before, this must have been around 1064, a terrible time of famine and complete breakdown of public authority, see above, n. 137.

3. At the time of his emigration he cannot have been far more than about fifty, considering that twenty-six years of hardship still left him "in a thousand states of prosperity" (sec. A). For a sturdy person fifty or so is not an age to "bury his bones in Jerusalem."

Thus he probably left Egypt because the situation there appeared hopeless to him.

4. Clearly there were other, more personal, reasons. He was divorced from his first wife (still alive at the writing of the letter), the mother of his only son and some daughters. He had children from a new wife. Moreover, throughout the letter it is evident that the family knew that he was not without means and expected, in one way or another, to benefit from them. He could not deny that he was successful in making money (probably also on his travels), but, as he humorously remarks, it was not his nature to save money (for others), but as soon as he had some, he consumed it (himself; see secs. A and D).

5. In short, our writer was a merchant who left a country that was in ruins and a family that was a burden. Moreover, like many Geniza overseas traders, he had in himself the streak of an adventurer. Living in at least ten different places in the course of twenty-six years was certainly not a pleasure, but he seems not to have regretted that experience.

6. On top of all this, he had an avocation which he took very seriously: Talmudic law. I assume that he came from a scholarly family and had studied from boyhood, wherefore "the Torah became his delight" (Psalms 119:77; we love what we are accustomed to). His assertion that none of the fine scholars of Salonika could "catch me at an error in the discussion of civil or criminal law" (sec. A) was perhaps exaggerated, but seems to show that our writer had served as associate judge on the rabbinic court of Fustat for years. When he mentions that the Head of the Jerusalem yeshiva addressed him with honorific titles we might assume that the learned merchant contributed to the upkeep of that institution, but the titles for benefactors who were also scholars were special. The family into which he had married his son was clearly of the same type (see n. 127). But the son did not follow in the footsteps of his father and paid little attention to such niceties; for the old man they were most important. He had certainly told the scholars in Salonika about his honorary titles and was probably addressed with one of them. Now a letter from his son arrives failing to address his father with any title, and written in the hand of a simple shopkeeper to boot (see nn. 130 and 131); a most embarrassing situation. Our learned friend and his Salonikan companions probably remembered (but certainly did not quote) a question asked in the Talmud: "Why do the sons of scholars only rarely become scholars themselves?"[139]

7. The head of the congregation of the Upper Synagogue in Salonika put up our writer in his house (or in an adjacent building) and probably also took care of his support, as far as was needed (sec. A). This was not mere charity for an old, blind foreigner.[140] The writer of our letter had been in Egypt in the company of the learned merchants from Qayrawān, Tunisia, a Nahray b. Nissīm, a Judah b. Moses Ibn Sighmār, an Abraham b. (Isaac) the Scholar, and others who had studied with the great masters of that city. He also had lived for a considerable time in Jerusalem, where the Gaon Elijah b. Solomon ha-Kohen and his son Evyathar represented the traditional wisdom of the Holy Land; we have read about his sojourn in Damascus, and on his long way to Salonika he certainly did not miss such important Jewish centers as Aleppo and Constantinople. In civil law, regarded by our writer as his main strength, he might have been able not only to enlarge his theoretical knowledge everywhere but also to observe its practical application in different places, so important in this field. In short, he was a useful amateur "scholar in residence." The dividing line between the professional and avocational student of the Talmudic law was not absolute.

Interconfessional learned contacts.—Among the subjects to be studied by Nethanel ha-Levi b. Moses during the house arrest imposed on him by his father was *kalām*, or speculative theology.[141] This science, so thoroughly researched by Saadya Gaon and his Karaite contemporaries in the first half of the tenth century, was only slowly recognized in Egypt as a basic element in the education of a Jewish intellectual. By the middle of the twelfth century, as Nethanel's letter proves, it was well established, especially for those educated Jews who, by their very professions, had contacts with learned Muslims. We shall read about such contacts in the following. In both examples, Moses Maimonides was involved.

It has long been known that Maimonides was in close contact with Ibn Sanā' al-Mulk (1155–1211), who followed his father al-Rashīd as Muslim judge in Cairo, and was famous in Arabic literary history as a poet, and, in particular, as an expounder of the theory of later, nonclassical, poetry.[142] A poem of his in hyperbolic praise of the medical art of Moses Maimonides is well known and has often been translated. It opens with these verses:

> Galen's medicine, I notice, serves only the body
> That of Abū ʿImrān serves both mind and body.[143]

Franz Rosenthal has published a passage from Ibn Sanāʾ al-Mulk's *Fuṣūṣ al-Fuṣūl* (Gems of Excerpts), in the main a collection of letters addressed to Ibn Sanāʾ al-Mulk's family by the famous qadi al-Baysānī, Saladin's trusted chancellor, a man of manifold interests. Maimonides appears in Ibn Sanāʾ al-Mulk's company and that of another Muslim savant during a long discussion. The topic was the *ʿilm al-kalām*, "speculative theology," which was treated by Maimonides with searching criticism in his *Guide of the Perplexed* (Part One, chapters 71–76).[144]

In a letter sent by al-Baysānī to Ibn Sanāʾ al-Mulk's father, he praises his son for brilliant remarks made in a circle of savants "loving discussion, in particular, on the science of *kalām*." With reference to this Ibn Sanāʾ al-Mulk writes the following: "The *ʿilm al-kalām* referred to [by al-Baysānī] is a section in an epistle in which I commented on a disputation that had taken place between me, the late Sharīf Abu ʾl-Qāsim al-Ḥalabī, and the *raʾīs* [chief physician] Abū ʿImrān Mūsā, the Jew. This was a long session; there is no room for quoting it in this book."[145]

The word used for disputation, *munāẓara*, is the term for a full-fledged debate. Rosenthal includes the biographical details for the Muslim savant, who was already dead at the writing of this passage. He was a Sharīf, a member of the ʿAlid nobility of Aleppo, northern Syria, then staying in Egypt. Thus, three intellectuals of widely different social, geographical, and spiritual origins (at his death in 1186/7, the ʿAlid was eulogized by Ibn Sanāʾ al-Mulk for his opposition to atheism and philosophy) are united here in a thorough investigation of the basic truths of the monotheistic religions. A look through Maimonides' discussion of the subject in his *Guide*, which was written at approximately the same time, proves that he was well prepared for this disputation. Whether Nethanel ha-Levi had had an opportunity to make use of his knowledge of kalām, acquired in his youth, we do not know. It is very likely that he had, for, as the passage quoted states, kalām was at that time a favorite topic when intellectuals came together.

A Geniza document from the year 1182, near the time when the disputation just described took place, shows Moses Maimonides again in close touch with the qadi and poet Ibn Sanāʾ al-Mulk, but under such totally unexpected and, therefore, particularly intriguing circumstances that only an annotated translation can do it full justice.[146]

The document concerned is the copy of a deathbed declaration, entered into the record book of the rabbinic court of Fustat. A part of this record book is preserved in the Bodleian Library,

Oxford. The document is written in Arabic. As usual, words written in Hebrew or Aramaic are italicized here.

Bodl. MS Heb. f. 56 (Cat. 2821), f. 45, *recto.*[147]

On Wednesday, the eighteenth *of the month of Nisan 1493*[148] we were present with the sheikh Abu ʾl-Faraj, *the esteemed notable, the wise and prudent,*[149] son of [his] h[onor], [the] g[reat] and h[oly] m[aster] and t[eacher] Moses, the esteemed elder, known as Ibn al-Kallām, [may he] r[est in] E[den], and found him ill but his mind present.

He said to us: Please take notice that I owe

To our lord, our master and teacher Moses [may his] R[ock] k[eep him], 2½ Egyptian dinars;

Also to him another sum, on the claim of which he is trustworthy.

To the sheikh al-Muwaffaq, [may his] R[ock] k[eep him], 4⅙ dinars for the poll tax, which he paid for me;

Also to him the price of wheat, for the claim of which *he is completely trustworthy,* up to 10 dinars;

To the illustrious Qadi Ibn Sanāʾ al-Mulk, 1 dinar and 12 dirhems;

To the illustrious faqīh Ibn Ṣawla, 4 dinars;

To Abu ʾl-Khayr of Haifa, 5 dirhems;

I am giving to my wife called . . . [150] the daughter of my maternal uncle, the Sheikh Abū Saʿd // [may he] r[est in] E[den] // the entire third of the entire house in the al-Mamṣūṣa quarter in Fustat-Miṣr and grant her complete proprietorship over it on condition that she does not marry again after my death. However, if she marries // after my death //, she will receive only 10 dinars of Egyptian currency promised her as the delayed installment of [my gift noted in] her marriage contract.

He passed away from this illness to his eternal abode.

["After my death" is written above the line.]

We have written and signed that which has occurred in our presence so that it may serve as a title of right and a proof.

Samuel ha-Levi b. R. Saadya, [may he] r[est in] E[den]

Elazar b. R. Michael, [may he] r[est in] E[den].

Who was the dying man? In what position did he find himself that he was forced to incur debts? Who were the persons included in his circle of friends? And what is the significance of the assistance given to him by them?

Fortunately, Abu ʾl-Faraj Ibn al-Kallām is known to us from other Geniza sources. In summer 1156, twenty-six years before his deathbed declaration, he was already described as "the esteemed notable," as here, and appeared as "a trustee of the court," to whom 238 dinars belonging to a rich orphan girl were entrusted.[151] He is also listed as a contributor to a public appeal in the 1140s.[152] Only a very well-to-do person could be entrusted by a court with so large a sum. That our Abu ʾl-Faraj was indeed rich is evident from the poll tax paid for him according to our document: it was the top contribution imposed on a non-Muslim.[153]

If so, why was it paid for him by someone else? This question finds its answer in another strange detail in this declaration. Wheat, the main provision laid in for a household, was bought for him. The combination of payment of the poll tax (which suffered no delay) and the purchase of wheat is found in many a Geniza letter: while away on a business trip during the summer, when the wheat was harvested, a relative or friend was asked to take care of the wheat and the poll tax. Thus, it is evident that our man was overcome by suddenly approaching death on his way back from a voyage. Since we have met him as a contributor to a public appeal in the early 1140s, at the time of this declaration he must have been a man of advanced age. That death was unexpected may also be gathered from the fact that he willed one third of this house to his wife on his deathbed. Gifts of real estate were usually complicated matters and were not left to last-minute arrangements.

But why was Abu ʾl-Faraj, who paid the highest poll tax up to his very end, so short of cash that he had to borrow comparatively moderate sums from five different persons? This strange phenomenon has parallels in other Geniza documents, and had its origin in the guiding business principle of that society: letting one's capital work all the time. "Do not let a single dirhem idle with you." From a voyage one brought home goods, not cash; at home one's money was invested in wares or in partnerships and commendas.[154] It is possible, however, and even likely that in our case, some particular circumstance, a misfortune such as shipwreck or a robbery, followed by Abu ʾl-Faraj's fatal illness, had occurred.

The strangest aspect of our document is, of course, the choice of the persons from whom these loans had been taken. "Our lord Moses," as the date of the document proves, can be no other than Moses Maimonides, who was at that time *ha-rāv ha-gādōl*, the highest religious authority (corresponding to a Muslim Grand Mufti) of the Jews in Egypt and beyond.[155] The sums borrowed were just characterized as moderate; they were not commercial loans, but neither were they negligible. A family could live modestly on a month's income of two dinars. Dinars were made of gold, not paper. Thus the 2½ dinars given by Maimonides (who also contributed another sum) could have been of enormous help under certain circumstances.

The largest sums were contributed by a person mentioned only by his title The Successful, *al-Muwaffaq*, an honorific epithet given to physicians. There is little doubt that this was Ibn Jumayᶜ, a Jewish physician in attendance to Sultan Saladin and one of the greatest medical authorities and teachers of the time. Since he took care of Abu ʾl-Faraj's affairs during his absence, he could very well have been related to him.[156]

The most surprising detail in this document is the fact that we find here the illustrious qadi Ibn Sanāʾ al-Mulk lending Abu ʾl-Faraj 1 dinar and 12 dirhems. Sums of this size are given only to very good acquaintances.

The fourth creditor (of the rather substantial sum of 4 dinars) was a Muslim religious scholar, described briefly as "the illustrious faqīh Ibn Ṣawla," a person obviously known to those present. The man from Haifa (many persons called Ḥayfī appear in the Geniza, mostly in the eleventh century), who bears no title and is noted with 5 dirhems only, was probably a grocer or someone who had sent provisions to Abu ʾl-Faraj's house.

All in all we find here two most prominent Jews and two illustrious Muslims belonging to a circle of close acquaintances who certainly were united by common spiritual interests. Abu ʾl-Faraj was admitted to this group, as elsewhere in the Geniza we meet merchants seeking the company of intellectuals.[157] I have little doubt that he had done many favors and services for his distinguished acquaintances, and thus he found no difficulty in getting some help from them when he needed it. Abu ʾl-Faraj's grandfather was a physician,[158] but I do not believe that he followed in his footsteps. As reported above, he was a trustee of the court who handled large sums belonging to others, for which he had to stand security with real estate belonging to him—not an avocation for a busy doctor.

As is evident from the biographical writings of Ibn al-Qifṭī (d. 1248) and Ibn Abī Uṣaybiᶜa (d. 1270),[159] and other sources, the early Ayyubid period saw an intellectual revival which also opened the way for contacts between the members of different religions. The document discussed above illustrates this situation. We should keep in mind, however, that such contacts, even under the most auspicious circumstances, were of very limited scope and ephemeral character: jurists, like Maimonides and Ibn Sanāʾ al-Mulk (or his father al-Rashīd), who had practical contacts through legal matters,[160] would occasionally also discuss theological problems that occupied their minds; physicians like Abraham Maimonides and Ibn Abī Uṣaybiᶜa, who at times worked in the same hospital, clearly also formed some personal relationship. But the general trend was toward segregation, discrimination, and, finally, persecution. Yet, our deathbed declaration from the year 1182 is a precious historical document.[161] Precisely because it does not refer to a special occasion when a particular topic was discussed, but presents us with the existence of a circle of intellectuals who were accustomed to meet and were concerned with the personal affairs of their acquaintances, it provides an unexpected glimpse into interfaith relations toward the end of the High Middle Ages.[162]

Judah ha-Levi: Poet laureate, religious thinker, communal leader, physician.—In a letter written in Granada, Spain, in the spring of 1130, the poet Judah ha-Levi is described by a younger friend thus: "The quintessence and embodiment of our country, our refuge and leader, an illustrious *scholar* of unique and perfect *piety*."[163]

No one could have found more appropriate words for expressing what ha-Levi meant to his compatriots and contemporaries. Many in Spain wrote verses. Eminent poets, like Moses (b. Jacob) Ibn Ezra, ha-Levi's mentor, then an octogenarian, and Abraham (b. Meir) Ibn Ezra, as well as a galaxy of others, whose considerable merits we are still able to appreciate, were around. But in the combination of his perfection in form and the elementary power of religious conviction ha-Levi seems to have been unique. The letter from Granada does not speak of poetry in particular; poetry was only one aspect of that precious possession that contemporary opinion respected so much: knowledge, namely knowledge paired with piety, both expressed here in Hebrew terms. When ha-Levi's piety is described as unique and perfect (very rarely said about a living person at that time), the knowledge that was the basis of it must also have been sound and outstanding.

We are in a position to check the exuberance of the Granada letter. Many hundreds of ha-Levi's religious (and, of course, secular) poems are available in multivolume scholarly editions and in selections made for different purposes.[164] His philosophical-theological chef d'oeuvre, known as the *Kuzari* (Ar. *al-Khazarī*, called so by ha-Levi himself in the letter translated below, at a time when the work was still in progress) can be read in full or in selective translations in a number of languages.[165] The book is in the form of a dialogue between a king of the Khazars (a Turkish people, whose nobility had embraced Judaism at some time in the early Middle Ages), first with a philosopher, then a Christian, and a Muslim (for only a few pages), and finally with a *ḥāvēr*, or Jewish scholar. The Khazar king does not confine himself to questions but makes many critical and learned remarks. This form of dialogue gives the author the opportunity to touch upon a wide variety of subjects, so that the exposition becomes very lively, perhaps also a reason for the popularity of the *Kuzari*.[166]

The final title given to the book by the author, *The Book of Refutation and Proof concerning the Despised Faith*, reveals its purpose without beating about the bush. Yes, the bearer of Israel's religion is despised like anyone else unable to stand up against his tormentors and disfigured by suffering. But these trials have a meaning. Israel was endowed with a unique religious sense, to be developed in a country particularly selected for that purpose: Palestine. "You alone have I singled out of all the families of the earth. That is why I will call you to account for all your sins" (Amos 3:2, *Kuzari* II:44). Israel is like the seed that falls into the ground and disappears fructifying in the process its daughter religions. But once the people of prophets is restored to the land of prophecy—namely, in the time of the Messiah—it will reappear in its purified, original form and grow, together with the reformed other religions, into a mighty tree of faith (IV:23). The same spirit pervades ha-Levi's poetry. One understands why his Jewish contemporaries were so receptive to his creations.

Ha-Levi has been taken to task for his "mystical and geographical nationalism," which, it was argued, contradicts both the spirit and the letter of Jewish law.[167] It is doubtful whether this argument holds water. On the one hand, ha-Levi lived in an environment where each of the various Christian and Muslim denominations claimed to be the exclusive bearer of the truth. On the other hand, Christians and Muslims referred to Abraham, Moses, and the prophets as ancestors of their own faiths. Why should the Hebrew Scriptures, the obvious source for all these beliefs, not be taken literally? What could be more outspoken than these prophetic utterings: "For as long as the new heaven and the new earth which I will make shall endure before me, so shall your seed and your name endure" (Isaiah 66:22; Jeremiah 31:35–37). In a short, powerful poem ha-Levi chose these verses as his motto, conceiving them not as a promise of God but as a duty for the believer to take the eternal existence of Israel as granted.[168]

The geographical aspect of ha-Levi's beliefs was not essentially "nationalistic." As he has so movingly expressed in many of his poems of Zion, the love for the Holy Land was the longing for God's presence, for the places sanctified by his revelations. The Muslim *ḥajj* to Mecca and the Christian pilgrimages and Crusades to Jerusalem had similar roots, which, naturally, were of double strength in the hearts of the uprooted, "the children driven away from the house of their Father."

One might argue that the themes of Israel's uniqueness, of the holiness of Palestine, and the coming of the Messiah are overdone both in the *Kuzari* and in ha-Levi's poetry. They are, but for good reasons. It was a time of extreme urgency. Constant and gruesome warfare was going on in Spain. As Judah ha-Levi emphasizes in his poems, whenever Christians and Muslims fought each other, the Jews were affected most by the disturbance of peace. The feelings of impotence in the absence of any signs of relief were dangerous forebodings of despair and loss of faith. Here the poet, even more than the thinker, stood in the breach. Using the motifs of love poetry with its anguish of vacillation between trust and doubt, he gave free vent to the endless complaints of Israel, only to counteract them with even more forceful affirmations of God's "eternal love" and unshaken concern for his people. All in all, the voice of encouragement ringing out from ha-Levi's poems was stronger than the whimpers of despair.[169]

A larger issue was involved. The question was whether God was the God of Abraham or of Aristotle, whether he should be sought by speculative thinking or by intuitive experience, by an inner sense, by "taste." ("'Taste' and see that God is good" [Psalms 34:9, *Kuzari* IV:17].) It was a period when the Aristotelian tradition was becoming a leading force in the thinking of western Islam, and ha-Levi clearly made an effort to come to terms with it. The task was not as hopeless as it might appear. As a physician, ha-Levi had accepted Greek medical science lock, stock, and barrel.[170] The Ptolemaic concept of the universe was taken for granted, and since God is visible in his works, Greek teachings about the physical world served the poet as material for some of his poetic creations. A magnificent hymn of his is based on the five times repeated refrain "He is the God of gods and the Lord of lords" (Deuteronomy 10:17), seemingly a strange epithet for a god of monotheists. In ha-Levi's time this was perfectly understood by everyone; the gods and lords were those wonderful powers keeping the world together at God's command: the seven heavenly bodies, "the planets," which then included Sun and Moon and were believed to revolve around the firmament; the twelve figures of the zodiac; the four elements; the earth with its flora and fauna; the human soul and intellect; and, towering above all this, the heavenly choir of the biblical cherubs and seraphim, to which the threefold Sanctus, daily sung by the faithful, responded.[171]

Naturally, no Jewish, Christian, or Muslim religious thinker could accept the "philosophers'" notion of an uncreated, eternal world, let alone their denial of a divinity in the biblical sense. It seems that with the years ha-Levi became disappointed with his endeavors to absorb Greek philosophy. A famous poem of his, replying to a friend who disapproved of his apparently irrational decision to emigrate to the Holy Land, concludes with these verses:

Let not Greek wisdom seduce you:
 it has no fruit, only blossoms . . .
The words of its wise men are confused,
 built on vain foundations and plastered over.
You will come back from them with a
 heart stripped empty and with a mouth full of dross and idle talk.
Why, then, should I seek me crooked paths
 and forsake the straight road.[172]

Finally, and most important, Judah ha-Levi's religious poems were by no means intrinsically liturgical. Many of them have the form of interlocutions between the poet and his God or of a man addressing his soul. This eminently personal character of ha-Levi's creations gave them their charming intimacy as well as the force of an appeal to the individual's sense of responsibility. In truth, there was no difference between personal and liturgical prayer. Ha-Levi is always an advocate for his community, even when speaking as if he stood alone before his father and judge.

In order to bring home this point, I provide an almost literal translation of the first and last stanza of a proem or introduction to the Kaddish[173] (called *reshūth*, "permission" requested by the cantor from the congregation to recite it). Thus, by its very destination, this proem is eminently liturgical. What it really is, the reader will be able to judge for himself.

Introduction to the Kaddish

1.	Oh God, your name	I shall proclaim
	and your true nature	not conceal.
	I lent my ear	and did believe
	I do not ask	and do not probe.
	A vessel of clay	how could it say
	to its molder:	"What are you doing?!"
	I have sought him	and have met
	a tower of strength,	a rock of refuge,
	One who is clear	like shining light,
	unveiled	and unconcealed.
5.	Be alert	and be prepared
	to contemplate	the mystery of yourself.
	Examine	what you are,
	and from where	you were taken,
	Who made you	and gave you reason
	and whose power	is moving you.
	Then have a look	at God's creations
	and become aware	of your own glory.

Study his works / do not lay
but on himself / your hand,
Lest you ponder / on the Beginning
on things yonder / and on the End.[174]

Comments

The Kaddish prayer extols the name of God, that is, his true nature, as far as it can be expressed in words. The opening stanza of ha-Levi's poems states in unequivocal terms that God is accessible, inspiring the heart with trust and the intellect with a clear vision of himself. The next three stanzas develop this theme, and show God revealing himself in the miracles of nature, in the words of the prophets, and in his double capacity as benefactor and judge guiding the individual.

The concluding stanza is based on a famous medieval saying (going back to the Delphic oracle's dictum "know yourself"): "He who knows himself knows his God," an idea on which, according to the philosopher Ibn Sīnā (Avicenna, 980–1037), philosophers and saints are in agreement. In a penetrating study, Alexander Altmann follows the history of this idea through classical, Islamic, and, in particular, medieval Jewish literatures, where he also draws attention to a poem by Judah ha-Levi: "If your soul is precious in your eyes, learn what she is, then seek your Creator."[175]

Having arrived at the climax of his poem ha-Levi becomes exuberant: since we can know God only through his works, man, who is "the glory" of his creation (Psalms 8:6) must only be aware of the mystery of his own existence to get a "taste" of God. But speculations as to when the End (the Messiah) will come, or how the world came into being (beside what is said expressly in the Scriptures) are of no avail.

The introspection demanded here is well illustrated in the poem translated above (p. 451). We are capable of knowing God, because we are a part of him, taken, as it were, from his splendor, and all we have to do is to keep this splendor shining. We should be grateful for all the good we have received here, but never be proud of our attainments. Constant self-examination should keep us clean; we should not feel as sinners but rather as children always able to come home to a benevolent father.

In the letter from Granada referred to at the opening of this subsection, Judah ha-Levi is praised—among other epithets discussed here before—as our refuge and leader, *malādh-nā wa-zaʿīm-nā*. These are two very strong expressions in Arabic. We might assume that he, who as a successful physician had personal access to leading Muslims, perhaps even to a ruler, might have occasionally intervened for an individual or a community in distress. Moreover, renowned for his poetry, scholarship, and piety all over Jewish Spain and beyond, he might have been capable of initiating common actions, for instance, raising funds when needed, even in places faraway from his own domicile. These assumptions have been confirmed, and many other details of the biography of the poet have become known through discoveries in the Cairo Geniza made in the course of the last thirty years or so.

All these materials have come directly or indirectly from one source, the archives of a Cairene businessman, public figure, and scholar. He was called Abū Saᶜīd Ḥalfōn b. Nethanel ha-Levi al-Dimyāṭī, or Ibn al-Dimyāṭī, that is, a man whose family name was derived from the Mediterranean port Damietta; but he did not live there, as had been assumed by the biographers of ha-Levi. Ḥalfōn was a traveler; we find him in India, South Arabia, and East Africa; in Egypt, of course, and in Damascus; and frequently in Spain and Morocco. He was of a noble family, and two brothers of his, bearing, respectively, the honorific titles The Crown of the Judges and The Diadem of the Enlightened, succeeded each other as judges, probably chief judges, of the High Court of the Jerusalem yeshiva, which then had its seat in Cairo. Owing to his social position, his extended travels, his scholarship and generosity, perhaps also owing to his fine personality and the exceptional fact that he was a bachelor, he acted, as a Spanish friend wrote, "as a unifier of the dispersed notables of his time, as leader of his own community [the Egyptian] as well as ours [the Spanish]."[176] The letters addressed to him and those emanating from his pen show that he was on familiar terms with everybody of consequence in Jewish Spain. In addition, his father's sister was married to Samuel Ibn al-Ukhtūsh,[177] a prominent member of one of the leading families of the country.

It is therefore not surprising that Ḥalfōn b. Nethanel, on his repeated visits to Spain, should have made the acquaintance of Judah ha-Levi, which developed into a lasting friendship. Ha-Levi composed a number of poems in his honor both in Spain and later in Egypt, and also dedicated to him a treatise on unusual Hebrew meters and phrases.[178] There was, however, even more to this friendship: Isaac b. Abraham, Judah ha-Levi's son-in-law, was Nethanel's relative.[179] Thus we see that in this case, too, the bonds of friendship were strengthened by family ties.

So far the following Geniza papers of documentary character[180] referring to the poet have been uncovered (pp. 462 ff., below):

1–5. Five holographs of Judah ha-Levi, all written in Spain.

6. A letter by Ḥalfōn b. Nethanel, sent by him in 1129 from Alexandria to Isaac b. Abraham, the poet's son-in-law, in Spain.

7–8. Two letters addressed to Ḥalfōn by his cousin Ibn al-Ukhtūsh, the first dated Granada 1130, the second undated, but certainly also sent from Spain.

9. A letter by Isaac b. Barukh, a prominent merchant of Almeria, Spain, to Ḥalfōn while in Morocco, concerning a payment of 150 gold pieces to be made to ha-Levi through Judah b. Ghiyāth, also a poet.

The remaining twelve items refer to Judah ha-Levi's stay in Egypt on his way to the Holy Land.

10. A letter by ʿAmram b. Isaac, Ḥalfōn's brother-in-law and business representative in Alexandria, announcing to him the arrival of the poet in that town on board the Sultan's new ship on 24 Elul (8 September 1140).

11–12. Two other letters by the same with various references to ha-Levi after his death, for instance, that he had delivered prior to his departure a precious turban to ʿAmram for financing the travel of a relative (or acquaintance) from Alexandria to Palestine.

13. A letter by Abū Naṣr b. Abraham, Ḥalfōn's business friend in Alexandria, dated 12 Elul (August 1140) and expressing concern that the Sultan's ship had not yet arrived as expected.

14. A letter by the same, dated 10th of Marheshwan (13 October 1140), describing in detail the difficulties incurred by the poet in Alexandria owing to the furious endeavors of the town's notables to have the distinguished visitor as their guest, and urging Ḥalfōn to come immediately to Alexandria.

15. A letter by Abū ʿAlī Ezekiel, Ḥalfōn's brother, sent to him in Alexandria from Qalyūb near Cairo, dated 5th of Kislev (17 November 1140), in which he excuses himself for not going there to pay his respects to the poet in person. He believed himself too insignificant to take up the time of so illustrious a visitor.

16. A personal letter from Abu-l-ʿAlā in Alexandria to ha-Levi himself, who meanwhile had gone to Cairo. In this letter Abu-l-ʿAlā describes how the dayyān, or chief judge of the Jewish community in that town, had collected the poems composed by ha-Levi during his stay in Alexandria, and comments on the criticism that that collection had aroused. Written shortly before Passover, approximately February 1141. Incidentally, on his way to Cairo, ha-Levi visited Ḥalfōn's brother Ezekiel and dedicated to him a short poem, *Diwan* (ed. H. Brody, Vol. I [Berlin, 1894], p. 40, no. 30). Ezekiel's

letter indicates that ha-Levi was not expected to come to Cairo at all. See below.

17. Letter to Judah ha-Levi in Cairo from his namesake and compatriot Judah b. Samuel of Badajoz, Spain, asking for an interview as well as for material support.

18–19. Two letters, written by Abū Naṣr b. Abraham (see item 13, above) on one day, 3 Siwan (11 May 1141), one to Ḥalfōn and one to another Cairene merchant, describing almost in the same terms the dangers incurred by the poet in trying to persuade a Jewish convert to Islam to accompany him to Christian Palestine, where he could return to the Jewish faith. Both letters conclude with the remark that ha-Levi had already boarded the ship and was awaiting only a propitious west wind.

20. A short note by Abū Naṣr, which was attached to an epistle of Judah ha-Levi to the Nagid Samuel b. Hananya, written by the poet while he was already on board the ship that was to bring him to Palestine. At the time of the writing of the note, the ship had already lifted sails. Ḥalfōn b. Nethanel is requested to deliver ha-Levi's letter to the Nagid.[181]

21. Another letter by the same, dated 11 Kislev (12 November 1141), referring to ha-Levi's death and to certain arrangements made by him before leaving Alexandria.

22. To these twenty-one items, identified by me, another is to be added, published by Mann, I, 224, note 1, who, however, had doubts whether it referred to ha-Levi, because at that time it was assumed that the poet's visit to Egypt occurred slightly later. The passage in question is contained in a letter dated Marheshwan (October) 1141 by Nathan b. Samuel, to whom ha-Levi had addressed several poems—and reads as follows: "You know of course, what happened to our Master Judah ha-Levi—may his holy memory be blessed—the saint, the pious, who was indeed predicted by the prophets of truth. . . ." We know now from the new material that ha-Levi actually died in summer 1141, so there is no doubt that he is meant here.

23. Finally, attention is drawn to the fragmentary MS TS 12.287, which is almost in the shape of a triangle and on whose first line appear only the words Judah ha-Levi. As in the same manuscript a Jacob (Qurṭubī), of Cordova, Spain, is mentioned, it is possible that once the missing half is found it may prove to contain some information about our poet.

Turning now to the discussion of these finds, we appropriately begin with the holographs of ha-Levi, which, as we have seen, also precede in time most or all of the other documents. None of these letters is signed. That was the custom at that time among intimate friends, especially with shorter letters, which were delivered by a personal messenger and often written in haste, with the messenger waiting. The identity of the writer of item 4 is established beyond doubt by its contents, that of the other four by details and by the similarity of their script with that of item 4.[182]

The latter is of the highest importance for the poet's biography. For in it he explains to his friend Ḥalfōn how he was induced to write his classic, the *Kuzari*: A Karaite philosopher from Christian Spain had asked him certain questions, and in reply he had written that book. He belittles its value and calls it a trifle (*sakhāfa*), a designation that he would hardly have used had the book already had the bulky scope of its finished form at that time. The "occasion" that gave the impetus to the writing of the *Kuzari* is still discernible in the book as we have it, first in the long and dignified dissertation on the Karaite heresy contained in it, and second in its overall thrust: proof for the truth of the Jewish faith, according to Judah ha-Levi, is to be found not in any argument but in its uninterrupted living tradition and testimony, an aspect blurred over by the Karaites.

The poet continues to say that he had dissociated himself (*jaḥadtuhu*) from the book, but that he would show it to his friend. We may rightly assume that it was the encouragement of his friends which is to be credited with the fact that the master overcame his doubts and completed the *Kuzari*.

In the concluding part of the *Kuzari* the author expresses his desire to emigrate to the Holy Land and to devote himself there to the service of God. Similarly, in our letter, ha-Levi reiterates before his friend Ḥalfōn that he has no other wish than that already expressed to him orally, namely, to move eastward. From this, it may be inferred that Ḥalfōn had, like others, tried to dissuade him from undertaking the dangerous journey, especially as the time was one of grave political unrest.

There is another interesting point in this hastily written letter. Its writer apologizes for its appearance (it does make for extremely difficult reading) by explaining that he wrote it on a Friday morning, when, as Ḥalfōn knew and had himself observed, there was always a huge crowd around. This, no doubt, refers to ha-Levi's medical practice: during the week, he was busy serving members of the Muslim ruling class,[183] and on Friday, the Muslim day of public worship, he was free to minister to other patients.[184]

The first three letters are interconnected.[185] They were written in Toledo, which, since 1085, had been in Christian hands. Item 1 repeatedly makes reference to a wicked queen, which can only mean Doña Urraca, the cruel ruler of that town, who died on 8 March 1126. A Jewish girl was held prisoner by her, and Judah ha-Levi tried to collect the usual ransom of 33⅓ gold dinars to gain her release. In Toledo itself, 10 dinars had been brought together: "Ghuzz Turks," perhaps Seljuk merchants, had donated 4 or so; Ḥalfōn had promised 1; it was expected that Malaga would contribute 6 and Lucena, the main Jewish center of Spain at that time, 10; Granada also was taken into consideration.

It seems a little strange that Judah ha-Levi kept his Egyptian friend busy with such an affair. Bear in mind, though, that ha-Levi was then in Christian Spain, whereas Ḥalfōn went on business trips to Malaga, Almeria, and Lucena, which were under Muslim rule. In addition, Ḥalfōn was closely related to one of the leading Spanish-Jewish families. Indeed, in item 2, ha-Levi asks his friend to use his influence with his aunt, her husband Ibn al-Ukhtūsh, and another notable to urge a donor, who had not kept his promise, to pay his share. Finally, as a communal leader, Judah ha-Levi had to satisfy many needs and he did so by devolving some on his close friend and admirer. In the same letter, we read about two such requests from Ḥalfōn, one to help a sick, blind foreigner, who had lost all his former riches, and another, to induce "the Light of Israel" that is, Joseph Ibn Migash, the spiritual Head of Spanish Jewry, who had his seat in Lucena, to send a reply to the community of Toledo on questions addressed to him.[186]

In a short note, item 3, Judah ha-Levi returns the gold piece donated by Ḥalfōn, for it was not good, and sends, in addition, 500 sheets of paper. In my collection of Geniza documents on the India trade there are many instances of paper sent as presents, but the quantities involved were always limited, between 12 and 36 sheets, although the donors and receivers were substantial businessmen. Thus, a consignment of 500 sheets must have been on a commercial basis, which is also implied by the text. Doctors sometimes dealt in books, especially in medical books, and paper was needed in considerable quantity for copying the manuscripts.[187]

About Judah ha-Levi's economic position in Spain we learn from the letter to Ḥalfōn of Isaac b. Barukh, item 9.[188] Here, a payment of 150 gold pieces to the poet is mentioned, certainly in connection with a transaction made for him by Ḥalfōn. In those days people would spread the risk by taking part in a single transaction with only a small part of their capital; 150 gold pieces was a considerable sum. The financing of ha-Levi's travel to, and sojourn in, Palestine (e.g., staying in Alexandria in a roomy place where he could receive guests for months), his generosity toward a relative or friend while in Alexandria (see items 11, 12, above), the expectation that he would dispense gifts to a foreigner while retired and on travel (17), all seem to indicate that he was rather affluent. No wonder; he was a doctor "in the service of kings," and "kings" paid well to preserve their lives. A Geniza paper from exactly the same time, around 1140, tells us about the ruler of Qabes in Tunisia who fell seriously ill and sent his qadi to Tripoli to fetch a Jewish doctor called Abu ʾl-Jūd Tobias. Tobias was paid a hundred gold pieces "before stepping over the threshold of his house" and a pledge was given to him for a payment of a thousand after successful treatment.[189] Judah ha-Levi himself alludes in his poems to his favorable economic situation.[190]

As the Geniza documents come from Cairo, most of the references made in them to our poet are concerned with his stay in Egypt. Before discussing them, three shorter notes mentioning him when he was still in Spain have to be considered. In his letter of 1129 to ha-Levi's son-in-law Isaac, Ḥalfōn expresses his admiration over the fact that Isaac's illustrious father Abraham and his father-in-law Judah were able to pursue their scholarly endeavors in many fields, despite their numerous preoccupations and tribulations and "the yoke of the rulers and the hardships of the exile."[191] This state of affairs is echoed in many a poem of the master.

A less gloomy atmosphere prevails in the letters of Joseph b. Samuel Ibn al-Ukhtūsh, Ḥalfōn's cousin. In one,[192] he sends Ḥalfōn, at his request, a *muwashshaḥ* poem by Judah ha-Levi; perhaps this was the piece promised by the poet in item 4. The letter sent from Granada in the spring of 1130 has been translated and discussed above.[193]

In addition to Geniza letters from Spain containing direct references to Judah ha-Levi, there are others addressed to Ḥalfōn b. Nethanel which mention persons from the poet's circle of friends or which otherwise illustrate the social and spiritual atmosphere of Jewish Spain at that time.[194]

This holds true to an even higher degree with regard to Judah ha-Levi's stay in Egypt. The Geniza yields plenty of information about practically every person or subject matter mentioned or referred to in the numerous poems and poetic letters composed by him during that period. Ha-Levi's biographers have been puzzled by the wealth of material stemming from this time and in particular by its character, for it contains many cheerful and worldly verses which seemed to be in contrast with the mood of a pilgrim to the

Holy Land. Far-reaching conclusions have been drawn from this fact with regard to the duration and character of the poet's stay in the land of the Nile. From the family name of his host Ḥalfōn, Dimyāṭī, and a misinterpreted allusion in a poem dedicated to him, it was concluded that ha-Levi passed two years in the Mediterranean port of Damietta, and, in general, that the fleshpots of Egypt had not failed to impress him. With the new material available, we are in a position to define exactly the dates of his arrival and departure, the month of his death, and the nature of his stay in that country.

Judah ha-Levi arrived in Alexandria on board "the Sultan's new ship"[195] on the morning of Sunday, 8 September 1140. The accompanying ship, that of the Qā'id, or Commander, had arrived on time, but the ship in which our poet traveled was twelve days overdue. After the trials of so long and dangerous a journey, rest was imperative. In addition, the time for seafaring had drawn to an end. One definitely did not travel in wintertime from Alexandria to Acre or Tyre on the Syro-Palestinian coast.[196] Ha-Levi had to remain in Egypt simply to await transport for Palestine. This is best borne out by the fact that he did not move on to Cairo, where Ḥalfōn and others of his friends lived, but stayed in Alexandria three full months. Only around Hanukka, December 1140, was he fetched to the capital by Ḥalfōn personally, and he stayed there until after Passover, March 1141. He was back in Alexandria in time to board a ship for Palestine on Thursday, the 8th of May but, owing to unfavorable winds, the ship was still in the port on Sunday, the 11th. It is interesting that before boarding his ship, the poet left a strongly worded message for Judah Ibn Ezra, who was expected to follow him, saying that he should not go up to Cairo but proceed from Alexandria to Palestine directly.

We have extensive reports about ha-Levi's two stays in Alexandria. Repeated reference is made to two travelers from Spain who accompanied him; one was his "relative" Isaac, the son of the famous Abraham Ibn Ezra, and I am inclined to believe that he is the same "Isaac the son of the illustrious scholar Abraham" already known to us as the poet's son-in-law.[197] Isaac Ibn Ezra remained in Cairo, while ha-Levi's second companion, Abu ʾl-Rabīʿ Solomon b. Joseph Ibn Gabbay, who also accompanied him to Cairo, came back with him to Alexandria; but there their ways parted: Ibn Gabbay went westward and Judah ha-Levi to the east. To this event, the separation from the last of his Spanish friends, ha-Levi devoted a special poem, ending with the words: And this is the end of all my friends from Spain. Before, he had dedicated another poem to this

Abu ʾl-Rabīʿ Ibn Gabbay, describing jokingly how his faithful companion provided him with food and other commodities when he himself had forgotten to do so.[198]

The poet's troubles in Alexandria started even before he disembarked. As a foreigner, he obviously had to wait until certain formalities concerning the tax obligatory on Christians and Jews were settled. Ha-Levi and his companions certainly carried with them the receipts for the tax paid in Spain, just as the members of the minorities did in general; however, exactly in those days, an illegal additional tax was imposed on Christians and Jews in Alexandria. Obviously, it was a moot point whether the foreigners had to pay it. It seems that friends stood security for them; therefore, we find Abu ʾl-ʿAlāʾ, a community leader in Alexandria, corresponding with Judah ha-Levi and his companion Ibn Gabbay about the tax when they were already in Cairo.[199]

The worst tribulation endured by the poet, however, was from his friends. The notables of Alexandria vied with one another to play host to the distinguished visitor, and one, with the family name Ibn Maṭrūḥ,[200] even used his influence on the superintendent of police[201] to get him for a Friday night. Ḥalfōn's business friend Abū Naṣr, from whom we know this and other details, writes that he himself did not ask the poet to his house in order not to embarrass him, but took his own dinner along every evening to Judah ha-Levi's place, so as to share his distinguished company. We can safely assume that many others did the same.

As may be concluded from a number of ha-Levi's poems, and as we learn expressly from two letters, he spent most of the holidays and the Sabbaths in the house of the dayyān of the Jewish community in Alexandria, Aaron Ibn al-ʿAmmānī, who was himself a scholar and a poet, in addition to earning his livelihood as a prosperous physician. Ibn al-ʿAmmānī, whose family had come to Egypt from ʿAmmān in Transjordan a few generations before, represented the Palestinian tradition of scholarship and poetry, and he and his five sons did all they could to make ha-Levi's involuntary stay in Alexandria as joyful as possible. Ha-Levi reciprocated by dedicating to the dayyān and his entourage numerous verses, many of which certainly were improvised and meant only as an act of courtesy.

After the poet had left for Cairo, the flattered judge collected and published these poems, which, as we learn from the letter to ha-Levi already referred to, gave rise to misgivings in two directions. Those who had not been honored by a poem felt slighted, while, in general, the light and sometimes even joking vein in many of these poems was held by some as improper for a *ṭālib ḥajj*, a man on a holy pilgrimage.[202]

The letter to ha-Levi implies that the poet would disapprove of the dayyān's action. We, however, have to be grateful to Ibn al-ʿAmmānī, because his collection, which is now in our hands, gives us a good idea how in those times each and every facet of social life, including such trifles as a present of chickens, or the admiration of a fountain and water basin in a house garden, was echoed in verses. No doubt, the dayyān's example was followed by other Egyptian notables who were eulogized by ha-Levi. This, and nothing else, is to my mind the reason we have so many poems of the social type from ha-Levi's comparatively short stay in Egypt.

On his return to Alexandria and shortly before embarking for Palestine, ha-Levi had a very unpleasant experience. In that town, there lived a convert to Islam named Ibn al-Baṣrī, whose brother in Spain had handed over to Judah ha-Levi's companion a bill of exchange (*suftaja*) in the amount of 30 gold pieces for the convert. Whether at the request of Ibn al-Baṣrī's brother, or out of his own initiative, our poet tried to persuade the convert to travel with him to Palestine, which then was in Christian hands and where he could therefore return to Judaism without incurring danger. Ibn al-Baṣrī, however, denounced ha-Levi who had to appear successively before the head of the secret police, the governor, and the qadi of the town. Had he not been well known and highly respected from his first visit in the town—Abū Naṣr remarked—his life would have been in jeopardy. As it was, the anger of the mob turned against Ibn al-Baṣrī for giving so much trouble to a distinguished and pious scholar from abroad, and he was almost killed.

Abū Naṣr concludes his report[203] about ha-Levi's stay in Alexandria with the remark that all the ships going to Spain, Tunisia, Tripoli, Sicily, and Byzantium, that is, those that were driven by the east wind, had left; only the ship on which Judah ha-Levi had already been for four days had not yet moved, but it would leave as soon as the wind came from the west. As is well known, Judah ha-Levi composed two poems on the west wind, one, a request in which he asks it to fight the east wind which was incessantly stirring up the sea; this, we may assume was said during the long days in which he had to wait to go under sail. But there is a second one in which he expresses his thanks to the west wind, "for bringing me near to the yoke of the love of God and taking from my neck the yoke of the Arab."[204] It is most likely that these verses were composed after the west wind finally had made its appearance so that the ship could reach the coast of Palestine.[205] If this assumption is true, this beautiful little poem would be the last we have from ha-Levi's pen. For two months later he was dead, as we learn again from the Geniza.[206]

A full publication and discussion of all the Geniza letters referring to Judah ha-Levi would fill a book (which should comprise also a survey of the poetry and other writings of his found in the Geniza). This cannot be done here. The holographs from the hand of the poet, however, should not be withheld from the readers of this volume.

Five Holographs by Judah ha-Levi[207]
Letters 1–3
A Collection in the Cities of Spain
For the ransom of a captive woman

The postscript to item 2 shows that Judah ha-Levi wrote from Toledo. Consequently, "the wicked woman," in whose prison the captive languished, could hardly have been any one other than Doña Urraca, who ruled over that city from 1109 through 1126. Urraca, described as ruling "cruelly and femininely," waged war against her husband Alfonso I of Aragon, her son Alfonso II of Castile, and her sister Teresa, the ruler of Portugal. Thus we are not astonished that she showed no mercy for the captive girl. Urraca died on 8 March 1126, and, considering that one of the letters refers to the Jewish autumn holidays, the latest possible date for these letters was late summer 1125.[208]

The standard ransom for a person of any religion or sex all over the Mediterranean was 33⅓ dinars. Ha-Levi speaks of 32 dinars, presumably because he himself, before starting the pious work of collecting the ransom, had contributed 1⅓ dinars. Ransoming was a highly regarded religious duty, wherefore the terms referring to the captive are in Hebrew.

It is surprising that the collection of a ransom for a single captive should have necessitated an action comprising several of the major Jewish communities in Christian and Muslim Spain. Compared with Egypt, where large sums were frequently raised for similar purposes, Spanish Jewry here seems either poorer or less liberal. But no such conclusions should be drawn from these letters. Rampant piracy and continuous warfare accounted for the constant need to provide funds for ransoms, especially in the port cities. This probably explains why Almeria and Denia, which harbored important Jewish communities during this period, are not included in ha-Levi's list. Almeria, as we know from several Geniza documents, was indeed busy with other captives.[209]

1. *Report about the progress of the collection* (TS 8 J 18, f. 5)[210]

My lord and master, may God make your honored position permanent.

I received this letter from our *master and teacher* Judah b. Ghiyāth,[211] lord of mine and admirer of yours, may God elevate you both, and decided to rush it to you so that you may enjoy it—may God let me enjoy your company.

In my previous letter I thanked you for your efforts in the matter of the captive woman. [The girl probably was traveling in a caravan in Muslim territory when it was overtaken by raiders from Christian Toledo.] Kindly alert her father to come to us, for her affair is nearing a satisfactory solution: We here in the town pay 10 mithqāls; the Turks, the Ghuzz[212] have sent 4 or so; and then the mithqāl donated by you. From Malaga we expect 6, and when he [her father] will bring 10 from Lucena,[213] the matter will be settled and we may get his daughter out before the holidays. For that *wicked woman* has changed her mind and does not permit us any longer to take the girl out of the prison on Sabbaths and holidays.[214] If he [her father] prefers to send us what has been collected thus far and to go to Granada in order to secure what might still be missing from the 32, let him do so. But I believe the best thing is to obtain her release as quickly as possible. God may guide us to whatever may be the best. The final term agreed with the *wicked woman* is the end of Tishri,[215] and she does not grant us even one hour more.

Kindly let me know how you are in body and soul, may God shelter them in his grace. And Peace!

[*Verso.* Address:]

To the illustrious *scholar*, the noble leader, *our m[aster and] te[acher]* Ḥalfōn ha-Levi, *may the All [merciful] pre[serve him], son of his honor, our m[aster and] t[eacher]* Nethanel ha-Levi *m[ay he rest in] E[den]*.

2. *Bid for speeding up the collection and other requests* (TS 10 J 15 f.1)

My lord and master, [may God] unite [us] soon under desirable circumstances.

You have strained my yearnings. Please [mend] soon what you have impaired.

May I ask you a favor? Kindly approach your uncle[216] and your paternal aunt and also the Head of the Police Abū Ibrāhīm Ibn Barōn,[217] who values you very much and who is my support—may God make his honored position permanent—that they should talk to Ibn al-Šayyānī[218] with regard to the balance of the *pledge* made for the *imprisoned woman.*[219] For we are in trouble with regard to the small balance remaining as we had been with regard to the large sum.

The bearer of this letter of mine—may God restore his health—asks you to kindly recommend him to someone who could be of help to him. For he was a man of means and has become the opposite; on top of this, he has lost his health and eyesight and is far away from his family and native country. And God may let you be the originator[220] of every charity and good work.

And Peace upon my lord and God's mercy.

[*Verso. Address: same as in preceding letter.*]
[*Postscript, written upside down:*]

Convey my highest regards to the illustrious *Master* [*Rāv*], *the Light of Israel,*[221] *may the All merciful preserve him,* and substitute for me in asking him to reply to the people of Toledo. They rely on me in this matter, and I cannot say that my requests find no friendly response with the *Master, may his Rock protect him.*

And peace upon my lord.

3. *Note on a bad dinar and other matters* (ENA, Laminated no. 40 [now New Series])

This short note is partly effaced and damaged by holes in many places. But it is not without interest.

My lord and master and one to whom I am much indebted[. . .].

I asked God for guidance[222] and, relying on the nobility of your character, I am returning to you the dinar,[223] for it is not good.

You will receive also 500 sheets of paper which were in my possession, and in the possession of the son of m[aster] Obadiah, who is ill at present, and which belong to the son of Obadiah. Take notice of this.[224]

There is nothing new with me except that I shall be on my way to you next week, if God, the exalted, so decrees. And complete peace upon my lord and great master, and God's mercy!

And excuse, please.[225]

[*In the margin*]

The vizier Abū Muḥammad b. Abū Rajā' conveys to you his finest, best scented, and most fragrant greetings. And so does the vizier Abū Isḥāq b. Wāzīᶜ.[226] And peace!

[*Overleaf. Address as above with slight alterations.*]

4. "*Going East*" (ENA, Laminated no. 41 [now New Series, no. 1]; Goitein, *Tarbiz,* 25 [1956], 408–412)

Travel to the Muslim East was so common among the savants of the Muslim West (for study and also for the pilgrimage to

Mecca) that books were compiled dealing exclusively with the biographies of such travelers. Judah ha-Levi had a special reason for going East: he yearned to spend the end of his days in the Holy Land and to be buried there.

The letter is hastily written in an extremely difficult, characteristic, Spanish hand. The left ends of the first six lines are torn away. The translation owes much to the critical remarks of D. H. Baneth in *Tarbiz*, 26 (1957), 297–303. It is discussed above (p. 456).

My lord and master, and God's greatest gift to me—may God make permanent your honored position and unite us in the most pleasant circumstances, in his grace. Your dear, cordial letters have arrived. They did not[227] diminish my longing for you, but excited and increased it[. . .]. We can do nothing but trust in God's bounty, to unite us and fulfill our hopes—if God so decrees. Nor are my secret hopes different from those that I expressed openly in your high presence. I have no other wish than to go East as soon as I can, if I am so enabled by [divine] decision.

My work is as you know. Your dear letter was handed over to me on Friday morning when I was surrounded by a large crowd, as usual, the like of which you have witnessed; but I am answering on the spot. I have already answered two previous letters of yours, acceding in them to your wishes.

As for the Khazarī book, it was the usual kindness of the illustrious philosopher (*ḥakīm*) and accomplished scholar (*ḥākhām*) Joseph b. Barzel to praise me for a trivial thing.[228] I personally would have refrained from submitting it to you. The reason for writing it was a challenge by one of our heretics, living in the land of the Romans, who questioned me concerning certain problems, in reply to which I sent him that book. Later on, I repudiated it. You will see it when we meet.

I am seeking an opportunity to finish what you have asked me to compose,[229] if I can find time for it.

Please excuse the form of the letter; I am writing it surrounded by people, as I understand that the one who undertook to transmit my answer is in a hurry.

> Desire carries me on its wings to you and I say:
> "Love, and not my feet, is the guarantee [of my coming]."[230]

And peace to my lord and master, commensurate with the greatness of my longing and yearning, and the mercy of God.

[*Address*:]

To the illustrious *scholar* and noble leader, *our m*[*aster*] *and t*[*eacher*] Ḥalfōn ha-Levi, *m*[*ay the All merciful*] *k*[*eep him*], *son of the honored m*[*aster*] *and t*[*eacher*] Nethanel, *m*[*ay he rest in*] *E*[*den*].

From him who is always ready to serve you and who longs for you.[231]

5. *An Early Letter of Judah ha-Levi to Ḥalfōn b. Nethanel* (TS 13 J 17, f. 22)[232]

This is perhaps the very first letter written by the Spanish physician and Hebrew poet to the learned India trader. He had treated him and now inquires whether he has fully recovered. Unlike the four notes translated above, this letter is styled and written carefully and elaborately and gives the impression of reflecting a first encounter with a personage never met before. Greetings are extended to two Maghrebi merchants found later in the company of Ḥalfōn on their way back from India in the port of ʿAydhāb on the East African coast.[233] These local people must have taken care of the traveler during his illness, wherefore Judah ha-Levi had had an opportunity to meet them.

To the illustrious sheikh, the scholar,[234] the perfect gentleman, Abū Saʿīd al-Ẓumyāṭī,[235] may God prolong the life of my master and lord[. . .].

I have arrived in safety, thank God, but regret to be deprived of your sweet company and delightful conversation, as everyone would be who has witnessed your brightness, as I have done, and experienced the perfection of your essence and of your spiritual equipments, as I have experienced.[236] In view of this, what I owe you and the obligation to honor and thank you, as far as possible, are above ability. May God in his goodness help me to do my duty.

All this has increased my worry about you and my longing for news from you; may God let me hear from you happy tidings and reports, as one would hope for. I should be grateful if you would kindly inform me about your state of health and the results of the treatment since I left. I ask God that he grant you and me[237] complete recovery and return to your former health; also that he enable you soon to take up again the things you hope for and enjoy.

Please inform me also when your blessed departure takes place, may God give success to your undertakings and make his benefactions to your friends permanent through his power and goodness.[238]

You kindly asked me about my own well-being. Nothing new is to be reported of me except that my mind is occupied with the actions during my treatment of you. May God seal the matter well for all of us.

I am extending to the high excellency of my lord greetings commensurate with my love, corresponding to my yearnings, and expressing my admiration and partisanship for you.

Likewise for the illustrious two merchants Abū Yaʿqūb b. Ezrah[239] and Abū Isḥāq b. Muʿṭī, my master, may God strengthen their honored position.

Finally, greetings, repeated, reiterated, and renewed to my master and lord. And may the mercy of God and his blessings be upon him.

Politeness requires something else [i.e., better].[240]

Despite their brevity, items 1–3 and 5 are welcome contributions to Judah ha-Levi's life story. The case of the captive woman illustrates his role as "our refuge and leader." No doubt, he himself went to the Queen, or submitted to her his requests and suggestions through some courtiers. The "we" in the negotiations with "the wicked woman" (item 1) is the plural of modesty and anonymity, almost de rigueur in medieval Arabic. Greetings extended to Ḥalfōn by two Muslim dignitaries in item 3 also show ha-Levi as mixing with the Muslim upper class. In item 2 he appears as representing the Toledo community before the spiritual Head of Spanish Jewry, with whom he had been in contact for years. The casual way in which Ḥalfōn is requested to remind the Rav of replying to the questions submitted to him reveals familiarity.[241] Then, again, the very formal style in which Ḥalfōn is addressed in no. 5 shows a physician who had made contact with his patient only a short time before. Ha-Levi repeatedly alludes in his poems to his double role as physician searching after patients in the mansions of the mighty and acting as a leader of the Jewish community, for instance, in these terse lines:

> You flee from the service of God
> but long for the service of men
> You seek the face of the many, but forsake
> the face of the One sought for all requests.[242]

In conclusion, from his correspondence, poetry, and the *Kuzari*, ha-Levi appears to us as a man who has made peace with himself, and with God and men. The question whether his poetic complaints about "the transgressions of the youth," "the slavery to desire and lust" reflect biographical facts, or are "confessions of sins," obligatory on any one, might be better understood from a fuller scrutiny of the relevant texts.[243] All in all, his faith was his life: he found rest in the houses of study and prayer, enjoyed his Sabbaths, festive holidays, and glorious Passovers; he loved his family; cultivated an endless circle of worthy friends; and, last but not least, was successful within his medical profession and, consequently, enjoyed a satisfactory economic situation. He emigrated to the Holy Land, not as a refugee but in fulfillment of a lifelong desire; it was for him the place not only of the most sacred memories but of the dearest expectations: the scene of resurrection, "as they say," of "beholding the beauty of the Lord," of coming home. The months in Egypt represented a kind of euphoria. Judah ha-Levi's death within a month or two after his arrival in Palestine was perhaps not premature. It was the fitting conclusion of the life of a true servant and ardent lover of his God.[244]

Pious women.—In view of the limited size of the Jewish population in medieval Spain the number of male Hebrew poets (and their creations preserved) was very considerable. But where were the female poets? Until recently we did not hear of any. The reason for this silence is easily explained. Hebrew poetry required a thorough knowledge of the text of the Bible, as well as of elements of Talmudic and Midrashic lore. Even educated women could not compete in this with their male contemporaries, who had spent their entire childhood and early youth memorizing sacred texts and who were exposed to Hebrew throughout their lives while attending the synagogue service and the study groups attached to it. The men who had poetic inclinations had frequent opportunity to develop their gifts by participating in the get-togethers of litterateurs meeting to exchange the fruits of their pens. In the exceptional case of a woman who wrote Hebrew verse, she lacked an audience, for a woman was not expected to address a group of men. Most women were illiterate, except for being able to recite a few Hebrew prayers. Finally, any Hebrew poet was expected to dedicate a major (or the major) part of his work to liturgical or otherwise religious poetry. In this respect, too, women were disadvantaged because the traditional speaker in a liturgical text was a male.[245]

In April 1984, an interesting discovery was publicized in the *Newsletter* of the Taylor-Schechter Geniza Research Unit of the Cambridge University Library: a short, charming poem addressed by the wife of Dunash Ibn Labrāṭ to her husband (ca. 950). Dunash, generally regarded as the initiator of Spanish Hebrew poetry using the meters and motifs of Arabic poetry, had to leave Spain, probably at the bidding of the then leader of the Spanish Jewish community Ḥisday Ibn Shaprūṭ.[246] I translate from the reduced photograph of the manuscript published in the *Newsletter* (p. 3).[247]

> Will the beloved remember his graceful gazelle
> as on the day they parted, while she held her boy on her arm?
> He put the ring from his right hand on her left
> while she put the bracelet on his arm,
> When he took her cloak as a keepsake
> and also took her chain as a token.
> Will there remain in the entire land of Spain
> its lord Dunash, even if he takes one half of
> the kingdom [Esther 5:3] with him?[248]

Comments

This short piece provides a moving picture of the farewell scene. Naturally, the young wife holds her only child in her arms. The husband takes from his right hand the signet ring with which he seals (cf. Jeremiah 22:24), a symbol of his personality. Bracelets in those days were worn in pairs; but here, where a single one is referred to, must be meant the silver bracelet around the upper arm, worn as a sign of dignity and strength.[249] For a variety of reasons, men occasionally wore the outer garments of their wives.[250] A chain hanging from the neck down over the chest was a sign of office for men (already so in Pharaoh's time, Genesis 41:42) and a precious ornament for women (Ezekiel 16:11).[251] On Judah ha-Levi's visit in Egypt he was surprised to find the men in the entourage of the Nagid Samuel b. Hananya wearing chains on the neck as well as armbands.[252]

The factual and well-rounded little piece appeals to us, and must have been appreciated also by the contemporaries of its author (although their literary taste was so different from ours), for another copy of it is preserved in the Mosseri Collection.[253] I have the feeling that the author of this piece was trained in religious poetry, characteristic for its straightforwardness. But no far-reaching conclusions should be drawn from a single find. It is not even sure that the wife wrote it, although the response to her poem is superscribed: "The answer from him to her." I personally believe that she was the author, although the poem gives the impression of a perfection in composition and style not expected at that early period (especially as compared with the stiff and unimaginative creations of her husband). But, "when sorrow is in a person's heart, he finds words to express it." She was not only desperate that he was leaving, but angry that out of consideration for her and their child he did not find another solution for the dispute that caused his exile. "That he takes my things with him does not make him present here. Keepsakes cannot substitute for a living person." Moreover, a ring could be had for half a dinar, while bracelets, chains and cloaks each could cost tens of dinars.[254]

Another Jewish woman from Spain, a poet writing verse in Arabic, has been the subject of learned discussion. Her name was Qasmūna, daughter of Ismāʿīl Ibn Baghdāla; she had been taught poetry by her father, and three short pieces from her hand, showing considerable mastery of the Arabic language, are quoted in a short treatise on female poets using that language.[255] In correcting another author's mistakes in the interpretation of her verses, James A. Bellamy of the University of Michigan, Ann Arbor, convincingly showed that Ibn Baghdāla was an error of the copyist for Naghrēla, and that Ismāʿīl was at that time the regular Arabic equivalent of Hebrew Samuel. This means that Qasmūna's father was none other than Samuel ha-Nagid, vizier of King Bādīs of Granada, Spain, a prolific poet, an eminent Talmudic scholar, and head of Spanish Jewry.[256]

Samuel ha-Nagid left about 1,750 pieces of Hebrew poetry, mostly short, but some long, and not a few very long; thus one might find it natural that he taught his daughter Hebrew poetry.[257] But this is by no means certain. Qasmūna, daughter of a high-ranking courtier, found an audience in the women of the court, among whom there were certainly some literate, if not learned, ones. This probably explains why the verses of a Jewish poet, a woman, at that, found their way into the book of a Muslim author. Moreover, Qasmūna must have died comparatively young, for in her father's elegy on her death during an epidemic of smallpox, he says that she parted this world before having experienced anything bad during her life. (*She* seems to have been of another opinion; in her verses she complains about her loneliness; she was like an orchard whose fruit had ripened, but no hand was stretched out to pluck it; her father—who received the tidings of her death while on one of his many war expeditions—obviously was too busy to select a worthy son-in-law.)[258]

In short, at a time and in a country of exuberant productivity in Hebrew religious poetry no sure sign of female participation can be discovered. I have no doubt that Jewish women fluent in Hebrew (and Arabic) script occasionally wrote a poem of the type written by (or attributed to) the wife of Dunash Ibn Labrāṭ.[259] Some might have written a Hebrew prayer, although we have not heard of one. But all this cannot be described as a contribution of women to Jewish religious creativity. The role of the Jewish wife in the life of the family cannot be over-estimated. "Everything depends on the wife" (for making her husband pious or sinful), says the Talmud. But her efficacy was confined to the limits assigned to her by Jewish law and social traditions.

Throughout the centuries we read about women described as Nazirites, abstaining from wine and other alcoholic beverages, or as pious, devout or saintly, see *Med. Soc.*, III, 252–254, where also a letter of an educated woman of that type is translated in full. In the following the letter of a pious woman belonging to a humble class, finding herself in a very special situation, is translated. She is fighting not only for her faith and her children but also for the soul of her husband. This was the time when the influence of

Sufism, Islamic mysticism, was at its highest, not only among the Muslim masses but also among the decimated remnants of the minority religions. Biographies of Sufi masters state occasionally that their mystical sessions were attended by non-Muslims, often with the result that the visitors were converted to Islam. This is reported, for instance, with regard to the classical Sufi author al-Qushayrī (d. 1074);[260] the eminent later representative of Sufism al-Shaʿrānī (d. 1565) boasts that many Jews were induced by him to embrace Islam.[261]

Thus far, the participation of Jews in the mystical sessions of Sufi masters had been attested to only by Muslim sources. It is now corroborated by the missive translated in what follows. The Sufi master mentioned in the letter, al-Kurānī,[262] is no doubt Yūsuf al-ʿAjamī al-Kurānī, who died in Cairo in January 1367.[263] Consequently, the Nagid David, to whom the letter is addressed, can only be David II Maimonides, who followed his father Joshuʿa b. Abraham II b. David I b. Abraham I b. Moses Maimonides in 1355 as head of the Jewish community of Egypt.[264] The letter was therefore written during the years 1355–1367.

According to his biographers,[265] Jamāl ad-Dīn Yūsuf b. ʿAlī al-Kūrānī at-Tamlījī al-Kurdī specialized in *taslīk*, the education of fellow mystics which is why Ibn Taghribirdī calls him Imām al-musallikīn, the Master of the Trainers. He had a large following and supervised various *zāwiyas* (convents of dervishes); his own zāwiya was on the Qarāfa al-ṣughrā, the Muslim cemetery east of Cairo, between the town and the Muqaṭṭam mountain, the time-honored refuge of monks and mystics, referred to repeatedly in our letter as "The Mountain." Al-Kūrānī renewed the ṭarīqa (mystic way) of al-Junayd (d. 910), an early Sufi, who was of Persian origin and taught his followers to adhere to the principle of strict poverty. They were therefore called, as in our letter, *fuqarā*, the poor ones, one of the synonyms designating Muslim mystics in general. When the Sultan offered him a pension for himself and his followers, he refused to accept it as inconsistent with his teachings. Al-Shaʿrānī reports many strange stories about him, some of which may be given here in illustration of the general atmosphere in which these Sufi masters lived. When he went out of his cell, his eyes were like burning coals and everyone upon whom his gaze fell was immediately transformed into a superior creature. Once, when he emerged from a seclusion of forty days, his gaze fell on a dog, who instantly became a sort of dog saint, to whom all other dogs flocked as followers; even men visited this creature in order to have their wishes fulfilled through the blessing by its holiness. After its death it was buried by some God-inspired people and its tomb was visited by fellow dogs, just as people did the tombs of human saints.[266] Al-Kūrānī never allowed the convent to be opened to visitors, except when they brought presents for the fakirs. Asked about this seemingly materialistic attitude, he explained it thus: the dearest thing the fakirs have is their time, whereas money is the dearest thing to worldly people; we can spend our time for them, only if they spend their money for us. Once some of the Sultan's attendants, who had fallen into disgrace, fled to his zāwiya; the Sultan came in person to the saint asking him to attend to his own affairs and not to meddle in matters of the state. In order to prove that the refugees had become converted, al-Kūrānī asked one of them to change a stone column into gold by his mere word. This was effected in the presence of the Sultan, who became convinced that the influence of such a saint could only be beneficial. Al-Kūrānī also wrote a book on the initiation of new followers.

It was under the guidance of this sort of person that Baṣīr, the bell maker,[267] a Jew from Cairo, became infatuated by the Sufic way of life on the mountain in the desert near the town, amid a crowd of mendicants (see pp. 474 ff., below, l. 9). He forsook his wife and three small children, and intended even to sell his house, which was, of course, in the Jewish quarter, and to take up permanent residence in the Sufi convent (*verso*, ll. 3–5). The Sufis lived in their convents with their families[268] and it obviously was also Baṣīr's intention to do the same. At this juncture, Baṣīr's wife sent an urgent appeal to the Nagid David, the head of the Jewish community, "to go after" her husband (l. 15) and to bring him back to the fulfillment of his duties as a Jew and a parent. The reasons for urging his return are not without interest. To devote oneself to *taṭawwuʿ* (margin, l. 4),[269] supererogatory divine worship, was, of course, highly meritorious also from the Jewish point of view, but, she argued, the Muslim mendicants had only the *ẓāhir*, the outward appearance of piety, not the *bāṭin*, the inner, the true, essence of religion. In any case, supererogatory works were useless, so long as a Jew did not fulfill his basic duties of attending the three daily services and of studying the Divine Law (ll. 7–8, *verso*, ll. 1–2). The proper place for voluntary devotion was the synagogue (margin, l. 5); furthermore, if the family was to move to the mountain, the children would be unable to visit the Jewish school, to study the Torah (*v.*, ll. 5–6), and finally, there would be the danger that Baṣīr, together with his three children, would be converted to Islam (ll. 11–12).

It may seem strange that Baṣīr's wife, in her petition to the head of the Jewish community, dwells mainly on the religious aspect of the matter, while she puts her complaints about her solitude and her care for her hungry children in second place (ll. 13–14, margin, l. 3, *v.*, margin, ll. 1–2). In integrated Jewish society, however, as may be observed even today, it is precisely the mother of the house who, though participating only indirectly in the religious life, watches most eagerly over its proper functioning; it is she who sees to it that the boys study under good teachers, and it is she who sends the sometimes lax husband to synagogue early in the morning or in the late afternoon after he comes home tired from work. Moreover, Baṣīr's wife evidently had discussed these religious questions, which were the source of all her trouble, with her husband, whom she clearly matched, if not surpassed, in judgment.

It can hardly be assumed that she wrote the letter herself for she would scarcely have had an opportunity to develop the fluent handwriting of the letter; it is problematic that she knew how to write at all. But there are far too many mistakes in it to assume that a learned person, such as the scribe of a rabbinic court, had written it for her. Thus, we have to surmise that a clerk in a business house or some other person of moderate education wrote it for her, reproducing her own words, for the letter bears a very personal character. Although abounding in the usual deferential phrases,[270] it is rather outspoken. The petitioners no doubt had direct access to the Nagid, for she reminds him that he had promised her some medicine for her boy, who suffered from an earache (*v.*, margin, ll. 3–7); we learn here, by the way, that R. David b. Joshua, just as most of his forefathers, was also a doctor. Clearly she realized that the Nagid was averse to becoming involved in a dispute with the militant Sufis, and hence she reminded him that since he was in charge of a whole region (*yudabbir aqlīm*, *v.*, l. 10), he could not fail to succeed in this matter, if he really tried. She uses many Hebrew words and phrases, just as an illiterate Yemenite woman would do, when talking about religious matters, and she repeats herself frequently, as a person in grief is wont to do. The letter is a last attempt to save a desperate situation; all in all, it is a very human document, not without historical value.

A wife's petition (TS 8 J 26, f. 19)

[1] *In your name, You Merciful.*

[2] *To the high Seat of our lord, the Nagid, may his splendor be exalted and his honor be great.*

[3] The maidservant [4–5], the wife of Baṣīr, the bell maker [3], kisses the ground and submits that she has on her neck [6] three children because

her husband has become completely infatuated with [life on] the mountain with [7] al-Kūrānī, *in vain and to no purpose, a place where there is no Torah,* [*8*] *no prayer and no mention of God's name in truth.* [9] He goes up the mountain and mingles with the mendicants, [10] although these have only the semblance, but not the essence, of religion.

The maidservant [11] is afraid there may be there some *bad man who may induce her husband to forsake [12] the Jewish faith, taking with him the three children.*

[13] The maidservant almost perishes because of her solitude and her search [14] for food for the little ones. It is her wish [15] that our Master go after her husband and take the matter up with him according to his unfailing [16] wisdom. What the maidservant entreats him to do is not [17] beyond his power, nor the high degree of his influence.

[*Recto*, margin] [1] The only thing that the maidservant wants is [2] that her husband cease to go up the mountain [3] and that he may show mercy toward the little ones. [4] If he wishes to devote himself to God, [5] he may do so in the synagogue, [verso, l. 1] *regularly attending morning, afternoon, and evening prayers,* [2] and listening to *the words of the Torah,* but he should not occupy himself with worthless [3] things.

Furthermore, he presses the maidservant [4] to sell their house, to leave the Jewish community, [5] and to stay on the mountain, [which would mean that] the little ones would cease [6] to study the Torah. [It would be helpful] if our Lord [7] gave orders to the maidservant in that matter and instructed her [8] concerning it,[271] for his wisdom is unfailing. And Peace.

[9] Our lord—may God prolong his life—is in charge of a vast region; [10] thus his high aspiration could not fail to hinder [11] the above mentioned from going up the mountain and to induce him to attend (verso margin 1) the synagogue and to occupy himself [2] with the upkeep of the family.

[3] P.S. Our lord has promised the little one [4] a medicine for the ear,[272] for he suffers [5] from it. There is no harm in trying it out, [6] seeing that even the barber is playing with it [7] without experience and mercy.

Immediately after these words is some very faded scribbling in Arabic writing, done by another hand and in different ink. It seems to read *laylat-hā* with an abridged signature attached to it, meaning this very night—obviously an instruction given by the Nagid to send the desired medicine at once. Thus the poor woman would have obtained at least one of the objects of her letter.[273]

A perfect man with a tragic fate: Abraham Maimonides.—Abraham Maimonides (1186–1237) stood for everything regarded as praiseworthy in the society described in this book. His mastery of the sources of Judaism—Bible, Talmud, Midrash, medieval authors, and, of course, the voluminous writings of his own father, Moses Maimonides—was prodigious. He quotes the remotest texts with a facility that suggests he knew most of them almost by heart. Although moral duties and esoteric practices on the long road to God were his main concern, he scrutinized the technicalities of the liturgy and the trifles of the ritual with the same dedication. In short, he was a paradigm of learned orthodoxy.[274]

At the same time Abraham Maimonides devoted himself to the sciences of the ancients with a fervor bordering on faith. He went as far as to accuse the hyperorthodox of their disregard for the laws of nature and of the sciences that studied them. By their ignorance they became a laughingstock for the gentiles. Those narrow-minded scholars, who regarded themselves as the elite of the Jewish religious community, did indeed "desecrate the name of God"—a very grave censure. Conversely, a person who restricts his intake of food and drink on a Sabbath, and occupies himself instead with scientific reflections about the cosmos, from the earth to the uppermost celestial sphere really "rejoices in God" (Isaiah 58:14): he becomes aware of the greatness of the Creator through the wonders of his creations. In short, the sciences, if properly handled, do not harm religion but help the select few on the way to obtain "true holiness."[275]

Most important of all: Abraham realized in life what he preached in his writings. He was a great teacher of religious ethics. As proved by the letters emanating from him or addressed to him—both those incorporated in his book of *Responsa* and those found in the Geniza—his gentle nature, his penetrating reasoning, and his strong willpower made him an ideal model of a moral leader and guide. One of his admirers went as far as to address him as "the Presence of God dwelling among us."[276] His father Moses Maimonides praised Abraham's extreme humility, fine demeanor, sharp intellect, and beautiful character, and, when he was hardly more than seventeen years old, expected that "he would be renowned as one of the great."[277] Impressions of his personality on the rank and file of the community are quoted below.[278]

We are particularly well informed about Abraham Maimonides' religious ethics, because that particular section of his chef d'oeuvre, the *Kifāya* (Complete [Guide] for the Servants of God) has been preserved in its entirety. The two volumes of Samuel Rosenblatt's edition and translation comprise this section, which forms the second part, or chapters 11–23, of the fourth volume of the *Kifāya*. The three preceding volumes were dedicated to the obligations incumbent on all believers and deal with many ethical themes. But since only disjointed parts of, or quotations from, these volumes have been preserved, no coherent picture of Abraham's specific teachings on the moral behavior required from everyone, particularly, of course, from the initiated, can be formed. This is a deplorable loss. Seeing that many far-reaching reforms are suggested with regard to institutional prayer in the general part of the *Kifāya*,[279] one might also expect to find there some new approach in matters of ethics.

It lies in the very nature of things that in discussing the special demands to be made from those who endeavor "to walk on the high ways to perfection," Abraham Maimonides touches on many topics which are discussed in a very similar manner by other pious thinkers, both Muslim and Jewish. Samuel Rosenblatt made considerable efforts to identify those parallels or presumptive borrowings, and today more of them may be found.[280] The question is whether this entire intellectual and spiritual endeavor forms an integrated, organic unit behind which stands a strong, single-minded personality. Such was indeed the case.

Abraham Maimonides' surviving volumes convey a sense of urgency, as if one is on a journey, directed by a leader who is in a hurry. In a letter from the year 1231/2, when Abraham Maimonides was forty-five years old, he wrote that—in contrast with several other literary projects—he had completed his chef d'oeuvre, had already revised and copied most of it, and some parts had already been sent to faraway countries.[281] Clearly, he tried to complete this voluminous *Guide* during the best years of his life, for himself and his disciples. It is evident that Abraham longed to found a Jewish *ṭarīqa*, a special "way," a community of novices dedicated to the ascetic life, as conceived in the *Kifāya*, and with himself, of course, as master. How far the plan was historically feasible is discussed at the end of this subsection.

Before unfolding the day-to-day life of Abraham Maimonides, as it has now become known through a large number of Geniza finds, I quote a biographical note about him by a Muslim physician, who worked with him for sometime in the same hospital. It also contains a short description of his physical appearance, the only one we have of any important Jewish person from the period mentioned in this book.[282]

Ibrahīm, the son of the Ra'īs[283] Mūsā

This is Abu 'l-Munā[284] Ibrahīm, son of the Ra'īs Mūsā b. Maymūn. His birthplace was Fustat, Egypt. He was a famous physician, learned in the art of medicine, and excellent in its practices. He was in the service of [the

Sultan] al-Malik al-Kāmil, Muḥammad b. Abū Bakr b. Ayyūb [reigned 1218–1238], and also commuted between the Palace and the Hospital in Cairo, treating the sick there. I met him in the year 631 or 632 [October 1231–September 1233], while working in the hospital there, and found him to be a tall old sheikh of lean body, pleasant manners, refined speech, and distinguished in medicine.

Ibrahīm, the son of the Ra'īs Mūsā died in the year six hundred and thirty- . . .[285]

In this short biographical note Abraham is described three times as the son of his father, although, like him, he was a *ra'īs*, chief physician and Head of the Jews, and was nearing the end of his life. Being the son of a famous father may involve difficulties, even in a society where the reverence of parents was almost on a par with the reverence of God. Abraham solved the problem in an ingenious way.

On the one hand, one cannot imagine a spiritual heir more dedicated to his predecessor than he was. He devoted three separate treatises and a great number of shorter responsa and letters to the defense of his father's philosophical and Halakic writings. His first literary attempt was a book on the principles of his father's Code of Law, the *Mishneh Torah*. In all his extant writings he copiously quoted the elder Maimonides whenever an opportunity offered itself. Even more significant is the fact that he emphasized again and again that he lived according to the principles of conduct adopted by his father.[286] On the other hand, we see Abraham working out a complete system of his own religious thought and practice—a procedure that certainly would not have been necessary, had the son found full satisfaction in the religious practice and literary creations of his father. It seems that the import of Abraham's magnum opus has not yet been fully appreciated. In view of this, before we submit and evaluate the new material from the Cairo Geniza, a few words about that book may not be out of place.

The title of the book, *Kifāyat al-ʿābidīn*, may be translated approximately as "Complete [Guide] for the Servants of God." A Muslim contemporary and compatriot of Abraham Maimonides, ʿAbd al-ʿAẓīm al-Mundhirī, who was born in Egypt in November 1185, six months before Abraham, and who died in 1258, surviving him by twenty years, wrote a book with an almost identical title: *Kifāyat al-mutaʿabbid wa-tuḥfat al-mutazahhid* (Complete [Guide] for the Pietist and a Present for the Ascetic). But this was a small book on Islamic supererogatory prayer and has nothing in common with Abraham's encyclopedic work except some similarity in the title.[287]

Abraham Maimonides deeply admired the Muslim mystics, the Sufis, and went as far as to state that some of them were worthier disciples of the prophets of Israel than many of the Jews of his time.[288] It is obvious that he was much influenced by Sufi doctrines, and those who have written about him have adduced parallels from the classics of Sufism in order to illustrate this fact. Sufism, however, was an extremely ramified movement, and, as I have already pointed out in my review of the second volume of the *High Ways to Perfection*, the task at hand is to find out which particular school of Islamic mysticism served as a model for Abraham Maimonides.[289] An answer to this question is possible because of the specific terminology and also some specific teachings contained in the *Kifāya*. The inquiry is imperative, for the book has been preserved only in part, and we are not able to reconstruct Abraham's thought without finding out first which Sufi school attracted him the most.

Abraham refers to his chef d'oeuvre as *ḥibbūrī*, "my book," although he wrote quite a number of other books.[290] At the same time he always called the *Mishneh Torah* of his father *al-ḥibbūr*, "the book."[291] The scope of the *Kifāya* was very wide. Its original size can be gauged from the parts still extant. The text published by Samuel Rosenblatt represents the second section of the fourth part and formed volume nine of the manuscript. Rosenblatt's edition comprises 248 pages of Arabic text. Since the second section of the fourth part was followed by a third, which, as we shall presently see, must have been rather extensive, the whole manuscript consisted originally of at least ten volumes. On the assumption that the various volumes were approximately equal in size, we arrive at a total of about 2,500 pages of 21 lines each, a text nearly three times as long as *The Guide of the Perplexed* of the elder Maimonides.

This difference in size finds its explanation in the fact that the *Kifāya* combines the subject matter of both the *Mishneh Torah* and the *Guide of the Perplexed.* Since the first three parts of Abraham's *ḥibbūr* dealt with the religious injunctions incumbent on all members of the community, and only the fourth and last part was devoted to the "special way" or "the high paths" (in the plural) of the pietists, why, then, did the son find it necessary to recapitulate the religious duties, after the father had expounded them so completely and so lucidly in his code of law? Fortunately there is no need to guess the answer to this question. The second section of the second part of the book, containing fourteen chapters (as against thirteen chapters that form the second section of the fourth part referred to before), is preserved in a manuscript in the Bodleian Library, and parts of it have been published by various scholars. Moreover, there are copious references to the lost sections in other writings of our author. From all this it becomes evident that the younger Maimonides had to recapitulate the institutions of the Jewish religion first and foremost for the simple reason that he intended to reform them. The section preserved in the Bodleian deals mainly with prayer, and in this field far-reaching changes were suggested by him. Prayer should be accompanied by a great number of prostrations. The biblical gesture of raising the hands in supplication should be observed, wherever a benediction contained a request. The congregation should sit and stand in prayer not along the four walls, as was, and still is, done in Oriental synagogues, but in rows facing the Holy Ark. While seated, members of the congregation should sit upright and not recline comfortably, as was, and still is, usual. The feet should be washed before every prayer, as was done at the sacrifices in the Temple of Jerusalem. And so forth.[292]

Second, it was necessary to restate the laws of Jewish religion and ethics because they were now reinterpreted, deepened, and broadened in the new spirit of pietism. The very names of the various sections of the book point in this direction. Thus, the third part, which deals with the duties toward our fellowmen, *miṣvōth she-bēn ādām laḥavērō*, is called "Rules of Behavior for Companions" ("companion" having the connotation of "fellow traveler on the way to God"), *ādāb al-ṣuḥba. Ādāb al-ṣuḥba* is the title of a treatise by the famous Muslim mystic of the tenth century, al-Sulamī.[293] We have to keep in mind that Abraham Maimonides, although he so often stresses the contrast between the masses and the elect few, conceives of the Torah as given to guide all Israel to the "high paths" for perfection.[294] Accordingly, the words of the Bible have to be interpreted with a view to this aim, and where they seem to contradict it—for example, when they emphasize material prosperity as a sign of God's grace—they have to be reinterpreted. Now one can understand why Abraham saw fit to recapitulate the content of Jewish religion and ethics in the first three parts of his magnum opus before he embarked on the discussion of the specific aspects of pietism in the fourth.

The extraordinary size of the *Kifāya* is also the result of its literary character. According to Abraham Maimonides, pietism, *ḥasīdūt*, is not only a way of life, it is a branch of knowledge, a science (a concept in vogue also in Sufi circles). The definition of its "place within religion" (*maḥalluhā fi ʾl-sharīʿa*, which means: its derivation from the established sources of Judaism) was the master's main concern. Consequently, the *Kifāya*, like the *Guide of the Perplexed,* is largely a book of exegesis. Moreover, Abraham Maimonides was a passionate *darshān,* an exegete and preacher by natural inclination. His explications of the Bible and the Talmud are so graceful, so lucid, so persuasive that one is almost convinced that his *derāsh* is *peshāṭ,* that his moralistic and pietist interpretation represents the literal, the real meaning of the text. Be that as it may, the expository character of the *Kifāya* is partly responsible for its comprehensive size.

Any attempt at an evaluation of Abraham Maimonides' lifework must take into account that most of his chef d'oeuvre has not come down to us. Modern treatments of our author do not seem to have exercised this necessary precaution. The first part of the *Kifāya,* which contained his theology, is entirely lost. This is perhaps not too serious a drawback, since here he probably more or less followed his father, although one cannot be certain. The lack of the tenth and concluding volume, which dealt with the *wuṣūl,* the arrival at the end of the way, the attainment of the goal of the mystic—in other words, Abraham Maimonides' esoteric philosophy—is an irreparable loss. According to all we know from Sufi parallels, this section (the third and last of the fourth part) must have been very extensive. I still hope that fragments of this section may one day turn up among the many thousands of Arabic Geniza papers of literary character which have not yet been systematically scrutinized.[295]

I am encouraged in this hope by a little find: a draft of a short treatise written in Abraham Maimonides' characteristic and almost illegible hand, which once may well have belonged to one of the lost sections. It bears a separate title page; this is not unusual since our master used to publish parts of his huge book in separate sections. He says so expressly in his letter of 1231/2 in which he speaks about his writings,[296] and one section, that about prayer, which we mentioned above, is repeatedly referred to in his responsa as "The Book on Prayer."[297]

The title page of the treatise clearly gives Abraham ben Moses as its author, but the catalog of the Hebrew manuscripts in the Bodleian Library, where it is preserved, did not list the work under Abraham Maimonides. This fact, together with the very difficult handwriting, may have prevented the numerous scholars devoting attention to him from using this manuscript, despite its considerable value.[298] It is a treatise in defense of the *ḥasīdīm,* the pietists and ascetics. Three groups are opposed to them. First, the judges, dayyānīm—we would say rabbis—and the experts in rabbinic law. They are not competent, he says, to pass judgment on the pietists, for *ḥasīdūt*, "piety," is a science by itself, and just as an expert on civil law would not dream of making decisions with regard to *qodāshīm*, the rites connected with the Temple of Jerusalem, so these experts should refrain from dealing with matters of *ḥasīdūt*, of which they are ignorant. Besides, the Talmud clearly indicates that the *ḥasīdīm* rank higher than the students of religious law. Second, there are people who strive with all their might for communal leadership and public office. A person of this description by his very nature hates the ascetics and is therefore not qualified to judge them, even if he should have theoretical knowledge of *ḥasīdūt*. I believe, the author had a particular person in mind as he wrote this. Finally, there is the mass of common people, who abhor the pietists because their whole way of life is so different from their own and whose testimony about the sayings or deeds of the pietists is therefore suspect and should be subjected to most careful scrutiny.

What, then, were the accusations hurled against the *ḥasīdīm*? A *ḥāsīd* may use strange expressions that seem blasphemous to those hearing them. If that accusation was substantiated, the person who uttered them should be made to exercise greater care about what he says concerning his religious experience. Another charge, echoed in the *Kifāya*,[299] was laxity in the observance of the details of the ritual. In our treatise, Abraham Maimonides deals with this aspect only in passing. His main concern here was a third accusation: heretical beliefs and doctrines. If that charge was found to be true, the guilty party was a *mēsīt umaddīaḥ*, a false prophet, who is, according to the Torah, liable to be punished with death.

On analysis, the treatise, taken together with some passages in the *Kifāya*, gives the impression that the pietist movement among the Jews of the Muslim East was not confined to the circle of Abraham Maimonides and of his elder companion and perhaps guide, Abraham Ibn Abu ʾl-Rabīʿ—that is, Solomon *he-ḥāsīd*.[300] In any case, the movement embodied in Abraham Maimonides was very remarkable and deserves a special place in the history of religion at large. For Abraham united in his single person three spiritual trends that were usually at odds with each other: strict legalistic orthodoxy, ascetic pietism, and Greek science—sober, secular humanism. He represented all the best found in medieval Judaism, as it developed within Islamic civilization.

On top of all this, Abraham served as Raʾīs al-Yahūd, spiritual and secular head of the Jews of Egypt, throughout his adult life from the spring of 1205, when he was only nineteen, to his death in December 1237.[301] In this capacity, he had to deal with countless religious and legal questions, with time-absorbing communal and other public affairs, and with the continuous care of the poor, the sick, orphans, and widows, foreigners, and other persons in need of help. These extended and variegated activities all left their traces in the Cairo Geniza. During the years of my research into that ancient hoard of manuscripts, I tried to collect as far as feasible all the evidence related to him. I did so first because of the great importance of the man. Second, beginning in the year 1936–37, when I translated his Arabic responsa into Hebrew, I developed quite a personal affection for him. For those responsa, as well as his letters found later in the Geniza, show that he lived up to the standards that he had set in his writings. Abraham Maimonides was possessed of a most lovable personality. He combined the humility and meekness to be expected in an ascetic with the firmness and determination required in a communal leader. His fervent religiosity and his strictness in the enforcement of the law were paired with common sense and humane consideration for special circumstances, while the lucidity and grace of his exposition revealed a disciple of the Greeks.

The material thus assembled is extensive, about seventy-five autographs. Most of them are short, but some are of considerable length and interest, such as the treatise in defense of the pietists analyzed above. Quite a number of letters addressed to him as Nagid have been preserved, and he is referred to in many documents and letters. My survey of this material places special emphasis on Abraham Maimonides as leader of a pietist movement.

To begin with, there is a strange document, a genealogical list of his ancestors on his mother's side.[302] A similar list had already been published by Jacob Mann,[303] but that does not contain the particular feature that makes our document so interesting. In it most members of the family through nine generations bear honorific titles in which the word *ḥāsīd* (pietist) occurs. Yeshaʿayāhū Rōsh ha-Seder, Isaiah, The Head of the School, who opens the list as in Jacob Mann's text, is called *p'ēr ha-ḥasīdīm we-anshē ha-maʿase*, The Pride of the Pious and Saintly Men. The title *p'ēr ha-ḥasīdīm* is attached to the names of three other members of that family; a fifth is called *segullat ha-ḥasīdīm,* The Elect One Among the Pious; six others are labeled simply *he-ḥāsīd.* Since nine generations comprise about three hundred years, it is very unlikely, although not entirely impossible, that all these titles were actually borne by the persons concerned. In practice, the titles meant that when they were called up to the reading of the Torah these were the epithets used. I have found nothing comparable in any of the many published and unpublished memorial lists from the Geniza studied. Therefore it is reasonable to assume that the family of Abraham Maimonides' mother adopted at some time the ḥasidic way of life and then attributed these pious epithets to their ancestors. A letter to Abraham Maimonides himself at the end of his life addresses him, among many other well-known official epithets, with the very appropriate title *rōsh kol ha-ḥasīdīm* (the Head of All the Pietists), and I have no doubt that at that time this title was mentioned in every public announcement in which his name occurred.[304]

It is a pity that we know nothing about the pietist activities of the family of Abraham's mother, that is, Moses Maimonides' wife. Nor, so far as I know, does Abraham quote any of his five uncles or any other member of his mother's family in his extant writings. The very existence of such a tradition is highly significant, however, and it is possible that we shall learn more about it at some later date.

A number of Geniza texts deal expressly with his disciples. Of particular interest is a letter from Alexandria in which Abraham Maimonides' followers complain to him of persecutions by their coreligionists, who prevented them from practicing their pietist prayer rites. Even more deplorable was the fact that the anti-ḥasidic propaganda was instigated by a *nāsī*, or member of the Davidic family of the Exilarch, who acted out of a personal grudge against the Nagid. The letter itself is a fine testimony to the spirit of its writer, for it does not curse or even blame the persecutors, but describes their behavior as a sign that Israel was not yet ripe for redemption—a state of affairs that could be changed only by repentance and prayer.[305]

Another Geniza fragment reveals the remarkable fact that Abraham Maimonides' circle of pietists attracted novices from distant countries and that among them was also one who wore the cloak of the ascetic but gave himself up to worldly pleasures. The writer of the fragment dissociates himself from the addressee in the strongest terms and admonishes him to rejoin the master's team in study and practice: namely, to fast during the day and to stand up in prayer at night.[306] He advises the errant novice to take up a profession, a principle of conduct for which the master himself gave a shining example. The writer also refers to a letter to him from Abraham who had invited him to come to rejoin the group and in which he had described briefly the addressee's state.[307]

A model pietist is introduced to us in a fully preserved letter of recommendation, in which the bearer is described as a disciple of the Nagid and as one "who had pushed the world of existence out of his heart and was seeking God alone." The young man had some experience in the art of silk weaving but lacked the equipment and the necessary means for exercising his craft. Thus far, the Nagid and the writer himself had assisted the bearer of the letter. Now it was up to the addressee to show his munificence, but, as the writer emphasizes: *be-derekh kāvōd,* "in a dignified way."[308]

A dayyān, or judge, in a provincial town, before addressing the Nagid on a legal matter, expresses his grief at being deprived of his company, company which led men to the blessings of the World to Come, and at being concerned with the opposite sort of occupation. In taking up public office he did not know what he was doing, but he hoped to be able to resign and to join again the master's yeshiva, this time permanently.[309]

The Geniza has preserved two letters of recommendation for disciples of his, written by Abraham Maimonides in his own hand. Although they do not refer to the young scholars as members of his pietist circle, they are not without interest in our context. The first letter, dated October 1235, is addressed to a dayyān in a provincial town. The latter was piqued because the young man had held his wedding according to a custom not approved by the dayyān; he imagined that Abraham had not attended the wedding because of this irregularity. The Nagid retorts that such insistence on customs not warranted by religion was unhealthy and that the dayyān himself should give up his idiosyncrasies in this matter. He, Abraham, had been unable to attend the wedding, because on that particular night it was his turn at the government hospital, and for certain reasons he did not want to defer it. The dayyān was obliged to help the newcomer in his town, first, because the latter had had trouble with the police (he had left the capital city without the required permit), and second because he had married an orphan, who deserved special consideration according to Jewish law. If it was true, though, that "the beloved son," as Abraham calls his disciple, had tried to encroach on the dayyān's right to lead the community in prayer and on his other privileges, he would have to face retribution.[310]

The same consideration for the two parties concerned is displayed in another letter by Abraham to a local dayyān asking him and his sons to grant the bearer's request to marry the dayyān's daughter. The young man was persistent in his love—love, of course, not for the young woman, whom he probably did not even know, but for a family of *ḥakhāmīm wa-ḥasīdīm,* scholars and pious men—and he was prepared to make all the financial sacrifices required. Abraham understands, however, that the family might have reasons for refusing this request. In this case he asks them not to put the suitor off but to give him a clear-cut and definite reply.[311]

The five examples summarized aptly show how troublesome and time-consuming Abraham Maimonides' care for his disciples must have been, but that was nothing compared with his duties as Ra'īs al-Yahūd, the spiritual and secular head of the Jews in the Ayyubid kingdom. The printed responsa vividly illustrate the long-drawn-out lawsuits and intricate ritualistic controversies that were submitted to him. In addition, he was asked many questions to which the writers would have found ready answers in Maimonides' code. Why then, did they apply for information to the Nagid rather than consulting the Code? The reason for this course of action was usually not ignorance but the technique of legal procedure prevailing at that time among Jews and Muslims alike. The local judge was but a *nā'ib*, a deputy, of the chief justice in the capital. Whenever there was even the slightest doubt about a case, the deputy wrote to the chief, in order to be backed up in his judgment by a rescript from his superior. The Geniza contains many examples of this procedure, even on the Muslim side.

The Geniza shows us how Abraham Maimonides' collection of responsa, as we now hold it in our hands, came into being. Those who submitted a question left below it sufficient space for a reply. The Nagid wrote his decision in his own hand in the free space. The decision was copied by a scribe and sent back to the person concerned. The original questions, together with the Nagid's autographic rulings, were preserved in the synagogue archives and finally used for preparing a complete copy of his responsa. The claim of the medieval scribe of the manuscript of Abraham Maimonides' *Teshūvōt* (now in Copenhagen, Denmark), that he had copied from the originals, is fully borne out by the procedure described. It is proven definitively by the fact that a decision given by Abraham and preserved in the Geniza coincides word for word with the text of that manuscript. This was not known at the time of the publication of the manuscript, because Abraham's difficult handwriting had precluded identification of the relevant Geniza text. In the catalog of the Bodleian Library, the piece is described as follows: "Two forms of affidavit in Arabic; the first much injured."[312] It is, in fact, a question submitted to the master, with his reply. It is reasonably certain that the text was already in this unsatisfactory state at the time it was copied by the medieval scribe, for he copied only the answer, and contented himself with summarizing the question, a procedure he did not normally follow.

In order to facilitate the Nagid's heavy task, the local judges and scholars would assemble a number of problems arising from their legal and religious practice before addressing their superior, and he would answer them all at once. Some collected responsa of that type are contained in the printed edition of Abraham Maimuni's decisions, and one, still unpublished, comprising seven responsa has been found in the Geniza. At the end of the query—only the end is preserved—Abraham is asked to write his reply in nontechnical language, intelligible to persons untrained in Talmudic studies. This indicates again that the local scholar wanted to show the answers to the parties and persons concerned, and there is little doubt that the Nagid's letter, as we know from many other instances, was read out in toto in the synagogue. Its content is a typical example of the variety of topics handled by the master day in and day out. The first two responsa dealt with cases of civil law, the third with a similar case, also involving the rights of a firstborn, the fourth with the position of slaves and Karaites with regard to ritual matters, the fifth with a detail concerning the circumcision ceremony, the sixth with the ritual bath obligatory for married women, and the seventh with the question of the extent to which an unscholarly person was allowed to serve as a ritual slaughterer. An average of five lines, couched in simple, straightforward language, sufficed the master to supply the desired information concerning each item.[313] Another unpublished responsum, the answer to a long query concerning the inheritance of a freedwoman who died without heirs, consists of a marginal note of three and a half lines.[314] Such brevity, so uncommon among Ashkenazi scholars, was the only way to survive.

In this connection attention is drawn to the facsimile of two queries written on one page, published by Simḥa Assaf in his *Texts and Studies in Jewish History* (Jerusalem, 1946), page 169. The writer, knowing Abraham Maimonides' habits, left room for an answer of about six lines before he began with his second query. Abraham actually needed only four.

The unsavory subject matter of that question recurs in three other queries addressed to our master, the answers to which have not been preserved or were never given. They all deal with Jewish men who lived with slave girls, mostly of European extraction, either while unmarried or to the neglect of their wives or fiancées. This was a well-known social evil rampant among the Jews of Spain of the thirteenth century. Our Geniza evidence seems to indicate that it was not unknown at that time in Egypt, either. According to Muslim law the female slave is at the disposal of her master. In Jewish and Christian laws the use of a slave as a concubine was a grave sin, and it is out of the question that the writers of those queries were ignorant of this fact. But again, they wanted to have a rescript from the Nagid before proceeding against the transgressors. Abraham's responsum also states that a Jewish man is not allowed to pass a night under the same roof with a maidservant if there is no female relative in the house. All these questions and Abraham Maimonides' dealings with them are discussed in detail in Mordechai A. Friedman's forthcoming book on polygyny.[315]

The Geniza has preserved other questions addressed to Abraham to which no answers have come down to us. Two concern milking sheep on the Sabbath day. Cheese was the main protein food of the poorer population in those times, and strict observation of the relevant laws was required in this matter. Therefore, sheep breeding and the manufacture of cheese were favored Jewish occupations.[316] Two other questions to which the answers have not been preserved referred to Jews traveling to India and the Far East. One mentions a trader who had been away for fifteen years and who died in Fanjūr on Sumatra, Indonesia, the farthest point East reached by a Jew according to the Geniza documents.[317]

An interesting question with regard to the synagogue liturgy was never completed, as the manuscript indicates, and therefore cannot have reached the master.[318]

In addition to giving decisions in writing, Abraham Maimonides acted as judge in the capital. There was of course a rabbinic court in Old Cairo at that time. Through the Geniza we know the names of its members and many of their activities. But the Geniza proves also that the Nagid dealt with much of the regular business of the court. A note in his handwriting, from December 1210, states that the parties had reached a settlement and one would pay to the other 20 dirhems every month.[319] Another fragment shows him signing a *qiyyūm bēth dīn*, validation of the signatures of a legal document.[320] In a third, Abraham instructs a scribe how to make out a declaration that the court of Old Cairo had acceded to a ban pronounced against a certain person by a court in another country.[321]

The scribes of the eleventh and twelfth centuries were scholarly persons with excellent command of legal parlance who always displayed beautiful handwriting. The general decline of the Jews in Egypt in the thirteenth century is evident also in the poor script and sloppy formulation of their legal documents (with the exception of some written by expert judges). Our master must have been plagued by the inefficiency of his clerks, for in June 1218 we see him again correcting a document dealing with a simple matter, the case of a widow acting as a guardian for her children, and adding to it four lines in his own hand.[322]

The incompetence of community officials even of good social standing is evident from the draft of a *ketubba*, marriage contract, from Bilbays, a town on the highway between Cairo and Palestine. It was written in 1221 and submitted to the Nagid with the request to correct any mistakes that it might contain. A ketubba in those days was not a mere formulary, as it is today, but a binding contract, and drafting it sometimes required a legal expert. The ketubba in question contained no unusual conditions, though, and it is hard to imagine why the Nagid should have been troubled with such a trifle. Still, the official who wrote the ketubba must have had some status, because in the accompanying letter he asks whether the wedding could be held in Old Cairo in the Nagid's residence with the Nagid officiating, while he, the writer, would recite the wedding benedictions and hand over his masterpiece, the ketubba, to the bride. We see here, by the way, that in addition to all his other occupations Abraham Maimonides occasionally fulfilled the regular functions of a rabbi.[323]

While the threefold task of jurisconsult, judge, and rabbi might have been frequently troublesome, it was the administrative aspect of the office of Nagid which was the most time consuming and exasperating. The Nagid had to appoint, or to confirm the appointment of, all the Jewish community officials and to define and to redefine again and again their duties and privileges. In case of insubordination he had to rebuke and, if necessary, to punish the recalcitrants. He was responsible before the government for all affairs of Jewish marriages and divorces. And, above all, he was in charge of the Jewish social service. In better times, as the documents of the tenth through the twelfth centuries show, the latter was the domain of the *parnāsīm*, social officers, some of whom were honorary functionaries and some of whom were paid. With the decline of Egyptian Jewry, the old Jewish democratic *kehilla*, community or congregation, gave way to the Muslim autocratic order of things, where the qadi, or judge, united in his hands much of the civil authority, including the social services, insofar as they existed.[324]

The Geniza material about Abraham Maimonides' administrative activities is very rich and reveals the appalling fact that he attended to all these variegated duties in person. He had under him dayyānīm, specializing more or less in the duties of judge, overseer of the poor, and teacher. Even though the institution of the parnāsīm was not yet entirely extinct, the amount of work done by him personally, as we can judge from the papers written by him and still preserved, was staggering. This copious material needs to be treated in a separate paper. I would like, however, to illustrate each of the three main branches of the Nagid's administrative duties with one example.

Here is a letter written in Abraham's own hand to a *muqaddam* of the Jewish communities in two small towns situated on the eastern and western banks of the Nile, respectively. The muqaddam was the spiritual and communal leader, whose exact functions varied from place to place and from person to person and had to be fixed or approved by the Nagid. The letter is self-explanatory. After referring to previous correspondence in the matter, the Nagid continues:

After the sending of that letter the aforementioned Sheikh al-Muhadhdhab, [may his] R[ock] p[reserve him], came and registered a complaint with me contending that you and he had reached an agreement concerning his rights and responsibilities, and that you demanded his due from him but did not undertake what was coming to him.

To make a long story short, the upshot of his words was the following: You are the muqaddam of Minyat Ghamr and Minyat Zifta. The man has no desire to encroach on your position of muqaddam. He does not arrange marriages or divorces and does not act as judge or administer inheritances. This is because of his feeling of what is just and proper. But as for leading communal prayers and ritual slaughtering and the like, which he used to undertake in the days of the *Ḥāvēr*, our Master Moses ha-Kohen, m[ay his Rock] p[reserve him], you should certainly have him as substitute in one of the towns since it is not possible for you to be in two places at once on a holiday or Sabbath; on the other hand, if you appoint someone else and reject him—there is no justification for this! He has more right than another since he is your relative, your cousin, and "for the sake of peace one does not change over from one house in which the *ʿērūv* is placed to another."

These feelings of jealousy are not worthy of you. If you led the congregation in prayer on the first day of a holiday and he on the second day, as your substitute, it would surely not involve any weakening of your honored position. Or, if you led the prayers in one town and he in another as your substitute, what harm would it do? None at all! Whoever hears that you are behaving grudgingly in this will attribute to you something which is [not] befitting of you. A statement signed by you regarding these matters would be useful. Do not think, God forbid, that he goes around gossiping about you. Finally, be on good terms for the purpose of the welfare of Israel and peace. If I had said less in this matter it would have been enough.

May your prosperity increase![325]

The letter shows the impatience of Abraham Maimonides with the petty jealousies of those narrow-minded so-called communal leaders. One of them, submitting a complaint in a similar matter, excuses himself indeed for troubling the master, "whose pure soul, benevolent constitution, and noble mind are repelled by hearing such affairs."[326]

On family laws, a single case, when Abraham issued an order that a man was not allowed to remarry before he had indemnified his former wife in full, is represented in the Geniza by three items and, in one, reference is made to a personal letter sent by him in this matter. The secretary who wrote the main document is superior to the two mentioned before, but he still falls short of the standards of the earlier centuries.[327]

The Nagid's perpetual preoccupation with social service is best illustrated by more than fifty orders of payment written in his own hand in the course of about two months (spring 1218). They concern dues to the government, salaries to officials and teachers, subventions to a traveler from Spain, a *nazīr*, or ascetic, from Persia, and many other needy persons, payment to a mason for work on a house dedicated to the poor of Jerusalem, and sundry additional items.[328]

One of the official duties of the Nagid was the preservation of peace within the community. This involved dealings not only with the community officials and their supporters and opponents but also with the contending members and factions of the more prominent families. Thus Abraham Maimonides succeeded in restoring peace in the great ʿAmmānī family of Alexandria: specifically, between the grandsons and great-grandsons of Aaron ʿAmmānī, the Jewish judge of Alexandria, who became famous through the poems dedicated to him by the poet Judah ha-Levi. In a detailed letter of thanks about this affair, written in March 1217, a member of this family has the following to say: "Everything has been settled through you, my lord, and all we have attained is from God and through your merit, my lord, for everything crooked and difficult becomes straightened out in your days, may God crown us all with your life."[329]

As the most prominent personality in Egyptian Jewry, Abraham Maimonides had also to spend much time with a social duty incumbent on all notables: writing letters of recommendation or otherwise acting in favor of persons approaching him. A Davidic nāsī who wishes to be honored while visiting a provincial town turns to the Nagid, and the latter instructs the local dayyān in person and, in addition, writes a letter in his own hand to the community.[330] A physician and colleague asks him rather impertinently to help him in a matter of inheritance.[331] A gentleman from Alexandria intends to travel to Damascus, so a friend of his asks Abraham to write for him a letter of recommendation to the head of the Palestinian yeshiva, which at that time had its seat in the capital of Syria.[332] And there are letters of thanks making mention of recommendations granted.[333]

The office of the Nagid was political by nature, and, as always in politics, there was rivalry and opposition. Very soon after his arrival in Egypt, Moses Maimonides found himself in opposition to the family of Nethanel ha-Levi "the Sixth," which provided Egypt with two heads of the Jews in the time of the Fatimids and one in that of the Ayyubids. In the fall of 1171—exactly when Saladin abolished the Fatimid caliphate—Moses Maimonides replaced Sar Shalom, a scion of this ha-Levi family, as official head of the Jews, but in, or slightly before, 1177, Sar Shalom regained his position and held it until at least 1195. At the end of his life, Moses was again appointed Raʾīs al-Yahūd and was followed in this office by his son Abraham. His opponents were not idle, however, and as early as Nisan 1205, a year after his father's death, a *taqqāna*, or statute, was made that the *reshūt* (authority) of the Raʾīs should no longer be mentioned during the synagogue service.[334]

The statute was to be valid for thirty years, but it must have been abrogated after a comparatively short period, for as from Āv 1213 we find documents all over Egypt bearing Abraham Maimonides' authorization.[335]

In their attempt to undermine Abraham's position, the opposition, centering on the Nethanel family, used an even more poisonous and dangerous weapon. They denounced Abraham's pietist reforms to the Sultan as a *bidʿa*, an unwarranted innovation, which was anathema according to Muslim concepts. The Ayyubid were very orthodox rulers, especially the extremely conservative al-Malik al-ʿĀdil (reigned 1200–1218) to whom this complaint was submitted. Abraham realized the full impact of that accusation and retorted with a memorandum saying that the new religious practices were confined to his private synagogue and that no one was coerced to follow them. How seriously he took this threat may be seen from the fact that he had about two hundred persons sign the memorandum. Our report about these events, which comes from one of his opponents, states bluntly that the memorandum was a lie, for everyone knew that the Nagid had made changes in the synagogue service everywhere.[336]

Thus we see that political rivalry combined with opposition to the pietist reforms of the son and the philosophical teachings of the father to make Abraham Maimonides' life none too easy. There was also discontent with the new style of rabbinic study, inaugurated by Moses Maimonides' Code of law, the *Mishneh Torah*, and perpetuated by the use made of that great code. It is interesting that it was a Yemenite rabbi sojourning in Egypt who used very strong language against Abraham because in his halakhic expositions Abraham allegedly failed to refer to the Talmudic sources, confining himself, we may assume, to the text of his father's code, wherever there was no reason to go beyond it.[337]

Finally we should not forget that Abraham's profession and main occupation was that of a physician to the court, including work in the government hospital. As such, Abraham had to ride every day from Fustat, or Old Cairo, where he lived,[338] to New Cairo, the seat of the government, a distance of about two miles. How time-consuming and exhausting this occupation was and how much it interfered with his literary activities, he himself described in the letter of 1231/2, referred to above.

When we look back on this long, long list of impediments to Abraham Maimonides' noble endeavors to reform Jewish religious thought and life, we feel what he himself has written about the detrimental effect of communal leadership on piety. Quoting the Proverbs of Solomon, he says: "Can a man take fire in his bosom and his clothes not be burnt? Or can one walk upon hot coals and his feet not be scorched?"[339]

I beg the indulgence of the reader for having exposed him to so many details of Abraham Maimonides' life. It was my belief that only the amassing of facts, of actual occurrences, could bring home the doleful circumstances that limited the extent and duration of his impact. The nobility of his mind and the excellence of his spiritual gifts were deserving of richer response. His medical work "in the service of the King" (as he calls it in his letter of 1231/2) and his hours of study and devotion with his disciples and companions were indispensable.[340] But why did he not give up the headship of the community, which clearly devoured a major part of his time, beginning at the age of nineteen and ending only at his death?

His father, after occupying the headship of the Jews for five or so years, left it to its former incumbent, Sar Shalom ha-Levi, retaining for himself the office of "the Great Rav," the Jewish Grand Mufti, or highest authority on law. During the twenty or so years of being free from that yoke Moses Maimonides wrote (or completed) his two major works, his *Code of Law* and the *Guide of the*

Perplexed, and several other books. Why did Abraham not follow the example of his father?[341]

He answered this question for us in his *Kifāya*: "Leadership cannot help having an injurious effect on *zuhd*, asceticism, as is well known. He that strives for asceticism must, then, avoid leadership and refrain from it, as much as possible, and give it up, if he has already got stuck in that mire [as Abraham had at the age of nineteen], *unless this leads to a neglect of the religious law.*"[342]

In short, Abraham was convinced that without the position of power given to him by two successive Sultans, al-Malik al-ᶜĀdil and al-Kāmil, Jewish religious law would not be properly observed. This applied perhaps mainly to his father's reforms, such as the statute that marriages and divorces, to become legal, had to be supervised by a cleric appointed by the Raʾīs, or to the so-called laws of the purity of the family, such as the monthly visit to a ritual bath by a married woman and all that was connected with it. Documents preserved from Abraham's time show that those ordinances were not generally observed in Egypt, and transgressions had to be punished with heavy fines.

Abraham might have been right that there was no substitute for him in Egypt.[343] But spending his time on small matters like some of those described must have been a tragic error. Perhaps, despite his meekness and humility, there was in some dark corner of his mind a powerful conviction of his own superiority and irreplaceability. To be sure, Abraham could not know that his life would be cut short at the age of fifty-one, during an epidemic, it seems. After all, his father, who died at the age of sixty-six, wrote his main works during the two last decades of his life.

Abraham succeeded in completing the *Kifāya*, but he did not have sufficient time to propagate it, which he himself so much desired, and to create an institutionalized community of disciples who would preserve the book by studying it. The result was that most of the *Kifāya* was lost, including the last part, describing the *wuṣūl*, the "arrival" at the end of the long way to God. Thus we do not know how far he went in his esoteric teachings. A fifteenth-century Yemenite rabbi writing on "philosophic mysticism" repeatedly quotes these famous verses of the Sufi martyr al-Ḥallāj:

> I saw my Lord with the eye of my heart.
> He said: "Who are you?" I answered: "I am You."
> In my subsistence is my annihilation,
> in my annihilation I remain You.[344]

For these and similar utterings al-Ḥallāj was crucified in Baghdad in the year 922. By the time of Abraham Maimonides, his younger contemporary Jalāl al-Dīn Rūmī (d. 1273), the Persian mystic and founder of the order of the dancing dervishes, could write the following and many similar verses without impairing his status as an orthodox Muslim.[345]

> O ye who are seeking God, seeking God.
> Why do you seek what you have not lost?
> There is no need for seeking, ye are God, ye are God.

Abraham Maimonides, master in the art of exegesis, would have had no difficulty in Judaizing similar ideas, albeit probably not in such extreme forms. Was not man created in "God's image" (Genesis 1:26–27)? Does not his faculty of discerning between good and evil make him like "God" (*ibid.* 3:5)? Is not the philosophical maxim "He who knows himself knows his Lord" in the same vein? Since the concluding part of the *Kifāya* is lost, we cannot know how the "arrival" at the end of the high way to perfection was conceived by its author. Should we take this loss as a sign that the community refused to follow him on this way?

Abraham Maimonides succeeded in assembling around him a dedicated group of disciples. But this circle did not develop into a tightly organized, permanent community of ascetics, a process in which Islam was so extraordinarily successful. We have read about Abraham's many preoccupations and the brevity of his life. There were other tragic circumstances. The majority of the Jews of Egypt—disregarded by his educational efforts (see below)—was unwilling and unable to follow him. Nothing is more suspect and feared by common religious people than "reforms," particularly in the conduct of traditional prayers. Would "the angels forwarding the prayers [to God]" recognize Jews imitating the ancient Israelites with their prosternations and outstretched hands and other rituals, long ago given up by the community? Moreover, these little bourgeois, who worked hard to make a dinār, wished to enjoy the fruits of their labors; they had little taste for abstinence.

Finally, and perhaps most important, in the Late Middle Ages the Jewish communities of Egypt and southwestern Asia became so decimated by persecution, epidemics, and apostasy that they did not possess manpower enough to form an elite of the type envisaged by Abraham Maimonides. (The three introductory books of the *Kifāya*, remember, which deal with the obligations incumbent on everyone, were written not for the common people but for the select few to remind them that their high status did not free them from the duties shared with everyone.) Abraham's youngest son, Obadiah, who was a mere boy of thirteen when his father died, wrote "a small manual for the spiritual wayfarer," and there were other writings with a mystical bent, which were probably the work of a Maimonid. But all this did not amount to much. The *Kifāya* did not enter the mainstream of Jewish religious thought.[346]

There remains, of course, the more general question: were the diverse elements of culture so beautifully united in the person and lifework of Abraham Maimonides incompatible by their very nature? Was not their unity doomed to disintegrate with the changes of times and mores? Is not the inward concentration on God's presence and all that is connected with it a bit in conflict with the endless technicalities of religious law and ritual? Does not Abraham Maimonides' criticism of the "judges" and his emphatic assertion that the "pious" are of a higher religious rank than the rabbis underline such a contrast (pp. 480–481)? And does not his passionate defense of the sciences of the Greeks reveal that their value was by no means generally recognized by the Jewish society of his time?

Needless to say, the wider world of the Islamic environment faced the same problems. The question whether the contact with the Greek heritage has really transformed Islamic mentality has been discussed by European scholars throughout this century and has mostly been answered in the negative. A most detailed and well-balanced synopsis of this ongoing discussion has been written by Joel L. Kraemer in "Humanism in the Renaissance of Islam."[347] My own position in this controversy is expressed in the first part of my *Studies*, especially in the chapter "The Intermediate Civilization: The Greek Heritage in Islam."[348] For a variety of causes, familiarity with Greek sciences and humanism being only one of them, the centuries between, say, 850 and 1250 could be described as "humanistic Islam" with all the facets of meaning—mutatis mutandis—included in the term "humanism." In the Late Middle Ages legalistic rigorism, the main power in developed Islam (as in Judaism), eliminated the Greek heritage (except logic, the weapon of the lawyers), and pietism and the mystic "seeking of God" came into disrepute because of misuses associated with them.

Abraham Maimonides lived near the end of "humanistic Islam." He was a son of his time. In addition to his unique personality, his life and teaching convey so harmonious an impression because they were in conformity with the best and most congenial elements in the contemporary surrounding civilization, and at the same time, represented the most perfect realization of the religion of his forefathers.

EPILOGUE

How do these five volumes of *A Mediterranean Society* fit into contemporary "sociographic" history writing? I do not remember having chosen any particular book or school as my model, nor can I say that my procedure was eclectic. I was guided by the command given to me by sources of a very special character. I could not have undertaken so comprehensive a work, naturally, had I not had behind me long formative years of historical training.

My first lasting impression was the study of Jacob Burckhardt's *The Civilization of the Renaissance in Italy*, which I read less than twenty years after the author's death (d. 1897). The concept of the interconnection of the divergent aspects of life in a particular country and epoch (political institutions, religion and other accepted beliefs, literature, art, formation of the individual, and so on) remained with me, if not as a fact, at least as a question, to be asked during the comprehensive study of any society.

Oswald Spengler's *The End of the Western World* (1918) (the usual translation *The Decline of the West* is too weak), although not convincing, was thought provoking and focused attention on many then neglected phenomena, for instance, the possible rising force of Catholicism (giving as examples Poland and Latin America!) as well as of Islam, written at a time when the fortunes of Islam were at their lowest ebb. I might mention in passing that Arnold Toynbee's *A Study of History* (1934 ff.) had no formative influence on me, perhaps because I started by reading about what he called the Syriac culture. He credited it with three achievements: the invention of the alphabet, the development of seafaring, and monotheism. Unfortunately, that civilization never existed. The peoples of Greater Syria never formed an enduring unit, culturally, politically, or otherwise. Despite Toynbee's immense learning, I was in doubt concerning the validity of his generalizations.

In the Henri Pirenne controversy about *Mohammed and Charlemagne* I never took a position; the source material seemed to me hopelessly thin. My guides in medieval socioeconomic history were Robert S. Lopez of Yale and, on the Islamic side, Claude Cahen and some of his younger colleagues.

At the university, I studied classical history along with my main topics, Semitic languages and Islamic studies. I never intended to work in the field of Greek and Roman history, but chose that subject because methodologically it seemed to me to be the most developed historical discipline. I sat at the feet of Matthias Gelzer in Frankfurt and Eduard Meyer in Berlin, two scholars still highly regarded. My reading of Latin inscriptions with Herman Dessau, the collaborator of Theodor Mommsen on the *Corpus Inscriptionum*, stood me in good stead when I had to treat ancient texts later in life.

My model in Islamic history was Carl Heinrich Becker (d. 1933), whose lectures I attended in Berlin. He taught Islam as a civilization (and not merely as a religion), at that time a revolutionary attitude (for which a professor at Cairo University lost his post).

The art of history writing—critical analysis of the sources, combined with graceful and "committed" telling of the story—was embodied for me in the immense work of Julius Wellhausen (d. 1918), leader in both biblical and Islamic studies. His books *Israelite and Jewish History* (1894, numerous expanded editions) and *The Arab Kingdom and Its Downfall* (1902) are classics despite the qualifications they needed even at the time of their appearance.

C. H. Becker used Arabic papyri and other documentary material copiously for the study of Islamic economic and administrative history, a field beyond the purview of Wellhausen. In the wake of the general development of sociology and economic history (Herbert Spencer, Emile Durkheim, Max Weber), and soon also the astounding archaeological discoveries made in the Near East, a new phase of history writing ensued. For my generation it was best represented by the towering figure of Michael I. Rostovtzeff (also spelled Rostovtsev, 1870–1952). His *Social and Economic History of the Roman Empire* (1926), appearing at the same time as his *History of the Ancient World,* Vol. I, *The Orient and Greece*, was a landmark. His universal approach was crowned by his involvement in the historical research of the art discernible in the murals of the newly excavated third-century synagogue in Dura-Europos on the Euphrates (*Dura-Europos and Its Art* [1938]). I liked in particular his *Caravan Cities* (1932), an exhaustive characterization of cities according to their function. Clifford Geertz's "Suq: The Bazaar Economy in Sefrou" in *Meaning and Order in Moroccan Society* (1979) shows how much this art has been refined over the years.

Fernand Braudel's classic *La Méditerranée et le monde méditerranéen à l'époque de Philippe II* (1966) was known to me, but I thought that I could not spare the time for the second half of the sixteenth century while I was so occupied with the eleventh. As soon as the book was available in twin paperbacks (in English) and could be studied away from my desk, I began to read it, and soon regretted not having done so earlier. It reminded me of a book that had impressed me immediately after its appearance in 1923, Emil Ludwig's *Am Mittelmeer* (translated as *On the Shores of the Mediterranean*). Ludwig was internationally renowned as an author of biographies. He treated the Mediterranean region as a personality. It is, of course, a far cry from the fleeting impressions of a popular writer to Braudel's massive "total history."

Most of my scientific research was based on *unedited texts.* The major part of my thirties was dedicated to the preparation of a multivolume edition of the *Ansāb al-Ashrāf* of al-Balādhurī, a comprehensive work on early Islamic history, which was to be carried out by an international group of scholars. My protracted occupation with that work gave me many insights and much enjoyment. Those ancient Arabs had a sharp eye for the observation of human character and also had the linguistic ability to do justice to their impressions in words (see pp. 191–205, above). Work on the *Ansāb* contributed much to my familiarity with classical Arabic language and literature.

For me "unedited texts" were also the Jewish immigrants to Palestine from Yemen, in the 1930s mainly the urban ones from Higher Yemen, and in the 1950s the villagers from Lower Yemen in the south. In between I also edited Yemenite manuscript texts, especially the report written in beautiful Ṣanʿānī Arabic by a learned Jewish coppersmith about Joseph Halévy's famous travels in Yemen in 1870, on which he served as guide.

My original purpose in all this was linguistic; I wished to study original Arabic dialects uncontaminated as far as feasible by strong foreign influences. But soon I learned that one cannot learn the language of a people without knowing its life. I do not think that I knew the term "oral history" in 1930, but what I did was just that: I tried to let my interlocutors talk about whatever came to their minds, and to make my own presence felt as little as possible. (For how this was done see "The Life Story of a Scholar" in the *Bibliography of the Writings of Prof. Shelomo Dov Goitein* by Robert Attal [Jerusalem, 1975], p. xxiii.)

A decisive influence in this field was my friend and collaborator through the years, Erich Brauer, a product of the then famous Berlin School of Ethnology. A scholar of penetrating intelligence and warm human understanding, he did not overlook any aspect of the life of the community studied, whether it was physical anthropology, the plays of children, or religious attitudes, and each was described with equal dedication to detail. Generalizations were avoided. His *Ethnologie der Jemenitischen Juden* (Heidelberg, 1934) is a gem. I began to read assiduously on the methods of anthropology, and during my frequent visits to England, consulted such scholars as E. Evans-Pritchard, Meyer Fortes, and others about my work with Yemenites. The common sense in Evans-Pritchard's BBC lectures "Social Anthropology" (1951) captivated me. In the course of my occupation with newcomers from outlying districts it became advisable to condense the fieldwork experience accumulated by me in a "questionnaire for the study of the Jews of Yemen, especially those from villages and small towns." The questionnaire is now available in my (Hebrew) *The Yemenites: History, Communal Organization, Spiritual Life* (1983), pages 345–355. The users were advised to make themselves familiar with the approximately 800 questions, but not to read them out to their informants.

After some hesitation I began to occupy myself with the Cairo Geniza. Despite some meritorious publications of Judeo-Arabic documents, for instance by the late E. Strauss-Ashtor while he was still in Vienna, it had become evident to me that the vast majority of private and business letters and documents, most of them written in Arabic during the tenth through the thirteenth centuries, had never been touched by scientific investigation. It was reasonable to expect that those untouched sources (again "unedited texts") might provide valuable information about Jewish, Islamic, and also general socioeconomic history, but the Geniza material about Jewish communal history, religion, and literature had been thoroughly researched during the sixty years prior to my entry into the field. Masters of encyclopedic knowledge in Jewish matters turned their attention to the Geniza. It took me years to study their work. I am still not sure that I have done enough (see *Med. Soc.*, I, 23–26). For, to use a phrase of Sir Eric Turner, the late Greek papyrologist, "I was eager to relate what I found to be new to the existing stock of knowledge." It was my belief that the preeminence of one of these masters, Jacob Mann, was not properly recognized during his lifetime. I tried to rectify this shortcoming in my Preface to the 1970 reprint of his *Jews in Egypt and in Palestine under the Fatimid Caliphs* (pp. xiii–xxiv). Jacob Mann created the framework for Jewish history in the Middle East during the High Middle Ages; any future research in this field must have recourse to him.

The writers of the Geniza papers were inveterate townspeople. Thus it became necessary to study the problems of urbanism, especially as far as the Middle East and the Islamic city were concerned, a field in which the French excelled. My attempts to master this topic are described in *Med. Soc.*, IV, 2–6, 347–348. To the publications noted there must be added a newly completed one: the two volumes by Heinz Gaube and Eugen Wirth, entitled *Aleppo: Historical and Geographical Contributions to the Urban and Architectural Designs, Social Organization, and Economic Dynamics of a Near Eastern Metropolis of Long-distance Trade*, Wiesbaden, 1984 (German). The authors of this monumental work see its novelty in (*a*) the completeness of their literary and archaeological data for the earlier periods, and (*b*) new data and concepts concerning the eighteenth and nineteenth centuries (see the summary in English in I, 468–469). Eugen Wirth's chapter "Aleppo, a Characteristic Example of an Oriental and Islamic Metropolis" (I, 59–72) is an instructive attempt at typological generalization, intended also for the Middle Ages.

I am not sure that I have accounted for all the elements that formed my historical thinking and writing. What about the biblical narrative, to which I have dedicated considerable efforts, see my *Bible Studies* (1963) (Heb.). Had not Leopold von Ranke, the father of German historiography, noted about the report on King David's later years (in II Samuel) that it is one of the most perfect examples of history writing (proximity to the events, objectivity paired with emotional involvement)?

Finally, after having completed this volume, I read again (this time with a pencil in hand), the opening essay in Clifford Geertz's *The Interpretation of Cultures* (1973). I wished to check whether my historical "interpretative sociography" was somehow in tune, in intention at least, if not entirely in execution, with Geertz's "interpretive anthropology." His methodical approach: complete as possible and meaningful observation of each individual case, was just to my liking, including, in the often fragmentary Geniza pieces, some reading between the lines. The belief that "understanding a people's culture exposes their normalness without reducing their peculiarity" was fully shared by me. "Bringing home to the reader the otherness of a civilization studied and at the same time letting its members appear as fellowmen comprehensible to us" was certainly my endeavor from beginning to end. I also experienced that "cultural descriptions must have a minimal degree of coherence," as Geertz writes, but "coherence cannot be the major test of its validity." "Sometimes," I had opportunity to observe, "matters do not fall into focus, either because our information is insufficient, or, perhaps, because life itself was not in focus" (*Med. Soc.*, III, viii). Finally, I fully accept that "it is not necessary to know everything in order to understand something. . . . Cultural analysis is intrinsically incomplete." We must face the fact that we are not always able to get to the bottom of things, but we must never give up hope that new questions might provide new answers.

Having presented my credentials as "interpretative historical sociographer"—whatever they are worth—in other words, having described the mental tools I have put into the research of the documentary Geniza, I must now try to outline what I believe I have derived from that effort, for others and myself.

"The breath entered them; they came to life and stood upon their feet, a very large host" (Ezekiel 37:10). "The dry bones," the dispersed Geniza fragments, had to be brought together, "bone matching bone," to form skeletons; "sinews, flesh, and skin" grew over these, philological and historical comments making them viable; finally, a breath or "wind," the contact with the other resurrected, let them come to life as members of "a vast multitude," a flourishing society.

The uncovering of new, or formerly insufficiently known, facts is in itself an enrichment of human experience, and, as such, a service to truth. On the Jewish side, the Geniza reveals that the majority of the Jewish people, who were concentrated in the Islamic lands of the Mediterranean during the High Middle Ages, enjoyed comparatively normal conditions of existence. Consequently, its members appeal to us as a fairly regular type of humanity. We understand better now the socioeconomic ambiance that made possible the diversity and quality of their spiritual creations, still regarded as classic expressions of Judaism.

Wherever applicable, the Geniza society is treated in this book as part and parcel of its Islamic environment. For instance, the Geniza reveals to us the existence of a well-organized commercial mail service connecting cities far away from one another. (See *Med. Soc.*, I, 281–295, also *EI*², II, 969–970, s.v. "Fuyūdj.") The users of this service, whose letters we have, were Jews, but the postal agencies, as these letters show, were normally run by Muslims. A princely mail system had been widely used from antiquity on; but the fact that Muslim civilization had preceded Venice in establishing a mail service for the general population was, to the best of my knowledge, not known, at least not with the mass of detail available in the Geniza. The same is true of many other data on daily life in the widest sense of the word. A distinguished reviewer wrote with regard to Volume I of this book: "Now that we have access to such data, Islam studies will never be the same again." I hope that Volume V, which explores the personal life of the Geniza people, will also be taken as a contribution to a better understanding of the inward world of the High Middle Ages in general.

The Geniza society with its competitiveness and materialistic attitudes has some traits in common with a secularized world. Precisely for this reason its all-embracing religiosity calls for comment. In the Preface to Volume IV (p. xii), I tried to formulate the situation thus: "With the exception of the few really pious and God-possessed, religion formed the frame, rather than the content of the daily existence." Yet that "frame" was fairly substantial. It regulated the day, the week, and the year of each member of the community, and, far more, his physical world picture: God the Creator still was guiding the nature around man, his health and success (or failure) in life, even his thoughts, good and bad. Such beliefs left too much to God and could have the reverse effect of reducing a person's feeling of responsibility. In general, however, the religiosity of the people speaking to us from the Geniza papers is very impressive. Theirs was a great, orderly world, extending beyond death, a world ideally ruled by God, the inscrutable, but believed to be the embodiment of justice and mercy.

The respect for knowledge and learned persons endowed the Geniza society with a touch of spirituality, which enriched its generally materialistic outlook. As for the field of religion, one suspects that they did not do enough. Their upkeep of houses of learning was spotty. The relatively limited size of the community might have restricted its possibilities. Yet when one reads in the communal records of two months of the year 1156 the sums spent on the trousseaux of middle-class brides (Vol. IV, App. D), when, soon afterward, the Spanish traveler Benjamin of Tudela describes the Jews of Fustat as "very rich," and when, a few decades later, Abraham Maimonides is very critical of his contemporary coreligionists, one doubts the effectiveness of their traditional beliefs in the value of (religious) scholarship. Nevertheless, we must be grateful to the Geniza for exposing to us the realities of a medieval religious community, its bright and shadowy hues.

Finally, to return to the content of this volume in particular, the often moving stories of personal experiences, as told in the Geniza, bring us into contact with human destiny at large. Every happening of the past is a nonrecurrent single episode; yet it has relevance to the general experience of mankind. This relevance is manifested in the tales of the narrators. It is the privilege of the historian to conceive the accidental past as ever-present life.

Notes

Notes

CHAPTER X: *The Individual*: Portrait of a Mediterranean Personality of the High Middle Ages

NOTE ON THE SOURCES

[1]Quoted in this book as Goitein, *Letters* (see *Med. Soc.*, III, xx).

[2]Especially physicians serving as leaders of the Jewish community (see *Med. Soc.*, II, 243–245).

[3]Ibn Abī Uṣaybiʿa, II, 105. Cf. Max Meyerhof, "Mediaeval Jewish Physicians in the Near East, from Arabic Sources," *Isis*, 28 (1938), 442–443.

[4]Ephraim b. Ḥalfōn Ibn al-Zaffān: TS 16.11. For partnerships with Muslims see *Med. Soc.*, II, 294–295. The physician could have been identical with, not a grandson of, the Ephraim of TS 16.11. *Med. Soc.*, III, 460, n. 74, is to be corrected accordingly.

A. A SOCIAL BEING

1. Gatherings

[1]*Med. Soc.*, IV, 40–47.

[2]Bernard Lewis in his review of R. Stephen Humphreys, *From Saladin to the Mongols* in *Speculum*, 56 (April 1981), 395.

[3]In particular, *Med. Soc.*, II, 289–299.

[4]Wine: TS 8 J 21, f. 21, ll. 3–6, a question addressed to Abraham Maimūnī. Blessing over a dead gentile: *Med. Soc.*, II, 278.

[5]The relevant chapter in Strauss, *Mamluks*, II, 372–381, is highly recommended. Although the author, naturally, makes much use of sources from Mamluk and even early Ottoman times, most of the details provided certainly apply also to the period dealt with in this book. For life in the synagogue in general, and especially on Sabbaths and holidays, see *Med. Soc.*, II, 155–170.

[6]Officials would, of course, attend the daily service, dedicating some of their time to study. "The schoolmaster comes with me to the synagogue every day, studying *pitrōnīm* [Mishna and the translations of unfamiliar terms into Arabic] and the Bible": DK 121, ed. A. Scheiber, *Sefunot*, 5 (1961), 466. Since the teacher prayed with his pupils, it was not expected that he go to the synagogue.

[7]About the public lectures, which had somewhat the character of a disputation, see *Med. Soc.*, II, 158–159, 215–219. "Being observed": TS NS J 376, a complete memo without the names of the sender and recipient (as was common in notes exchanged between friends), in which the writer apologized for not meeting "his lord" because the people at the synagogue would gather around them. Probably written by Solomon, son of the judge Elijah.

[8](Female) relative: *Med. Soc.*, II, 144–145. Friend: *ibid.*, IV, 255 and nn. 8–9. Business: TS 10 J 9, f. 21, ll. 7–8, *Nahray* 86 (letter from Alexandria), "I met Ibn

Sha'ya on Saturday; after we parted, he informed me that the matter of that shipment was settled."

[9]TS 10 J 17, f. 10: a physician arriving from al-Fayyūm on Friday and returning on Monday, see *Med. Soc.*, IV, 238 and nn. 87–90. ULC Or 1080 J 28, ll. 11–14: a letter by Solomon, son of the judge Elijah, to the husband of a paternal cousin in Alexandria, reporting that a relative was visiting in the town and staying with them from Friday till Monday, when the judge gave him letters of recommendation. A visitor from Alexandria, staying over Saturday only: ULC Or 1080 J 29 (see *Med. Soc.*, IV, 448, n. 17).

[10]TS 8 J 14. f. 12. Postscript: *wa 'anā asbut fī kull sabt 'ind al-shaykh al-Ma'ālī*, "I pass every Saturday in the house of M." The Spanish Hebrew poet Judah ha-Levi, sojourning in Alexandria on his way to Palestine, rented an apartment for himself but spent Saturdays in the house of the judge Ibn al-'Ammānī, who was a physician and writer of verse (see *Med. Soc.*, II, 259, and Goitein, *Tarbiz*, 28 (1959), 351).

[11]See *Med. Soc.*, II, 194–195 n. 11.

[12]TS 13 J 19, f. 7, ll. 10–12: *al-ishtighāl bilfuraj fi'l-basātīn wal-sawāqī*. See pp. 345, ff., and nn. 73–79, below. The sermon is superscribed with verses from the Song of Songs, understood to be praise of Israel as the bride of God. One should take such talk seriously. The eminent educator Helene Barth told me once that she asked an old Yemenite why he and his companions got up on Saturday as early as 3 A.M. to sing psalms and hymns: Should one not have a little more sleep on the day of rest? Answer: "The Sabbath is something so wonderful that one should not waste it with sleep."

[13]TS 20.125, ll. 14–15. Trans. in Cohen, Mark R., *Self-government*, p. 330.

[14]Gottheil-Worrell XXVII*v*, ll. 7–8, p. 126.

[15]ENA 4100, f. 21B. For beadle and *parnās* see *Med. Soc.*, II, Index s.vv.

[16]Maimonides, *Responsa*, II, 327–328, no. 179. "Highly esteemed": Ar. *marmūqūn*, lit., "looked at with furtive admiration," a Maghrebi expression (see Dozy, *Supplément*, I, 558*b*). The man who asked the question came, perhaps like Maimonides himself, from the more observant Muslim West.

[17]ENA 2808, f. 16, ll. 22–23: letter dealing (among other things) with the donkeys bearing young (see *Med. Soc.*, IV, 263 and n. 9).

[18]TS 12.654*v*, ll. 8–10. The *nāsī* Solomon b. Yīshay (Jesse), who temporarily had his seat in Bilbays (see *Med. Soc.*, II, 19, n. 49) is addressed by a relative. The Sabbath between New Year and the Day of Atonement is usually not called, as here, "Sabbath of Atonement," *al-teshūvā*, but "Return," *shūvā*, the first word of Hosea 14:1, the prophetic lection read on that day.

[19]TS 13 J 22, f. 13, ll. 4–10. Despite the propinquity of the capital, Solomon could not get there on a Sabbath or holiday, because he also functioned as a cantor (as he complained in another letter).

[20]TS 13 J 22, f. 15, ll. 9–17. Here, in the address written in Arabic characters, Solomon is called Barakāt (Blessings), an abbreviation of his byname Abu 'l-Barakāt.

[21]TS 8 J 17, f. 5. As usual in short notes, the names of the sender and recipient are not mentioned.

[22]TS 13 J 13, f. 4. Judah ha-Kohen b. Tōviyāhū he-ḥāvēr writes to Amīn al-Dawla, "Yehōsēph [= Joseph], the illustrious judge, etc., son of the late Nathan, the illustrious ḥāvēr and excellent judge." This Yehōsēph is repeatedly referred to in the letters of his elder brother Mevōrākh b. Nathan (so often mentioned in this book) as a young man of means, helpful, but careless and involved in pranks and squabbles (TS 13 J 20, f. 6, ll. 25 ff.; ENA NS 19, f. 31, ll. 8, 13, 16, 18, 19, 24). In his later years Yehōsēph may have become a judge, but I have not found him anywhere acting in this capacity. The title was probably an honorary one meaning that the government official Amīn al-Dawla was learned in Jewish law like a judge. The altogether unusual reference to the recipient's fussiness in observance of the Sabbath laws is probably also not to be taken too seriously. His Hebrew title Diadem of the Princes (*nēzer ha-sārīm*) proves that his excellence was secular, not religious. The person referred to in our letter as "The Diadem" (TS 13 J 13, f. 4, ll. 17, 18)

was Yehōsēph's elder brother Mevōrākh, who, like his late father Nathan, was probably called The Diadem of the Scholars (*ha-ḥavērīm*).

[23]TS 13 J 19, f. 4, ll. 4–5. He wishes to emphasize that both he and his friend were without company.

[24]TS 10 J 12, f. 8, ll. 6–7.

[25]See the emotional passage translated in *Med. Soc.*, II, 16.

[26]BT Pesaḥim 68*b*. Another opinion had it that one belongs either entirely to God or to oneself. The first ruling is in the spirit of biblical legislation, which emphasizes the enjoyment of the holiday in the circle of the family including servants, strangers, and the needy (Deuteronomy 16:14–15).

[27]Flocking to the capital for the holidays: *ʿind dukhūl ahl Malīj*, TS 12.58, l. 25, see l. 12. (The recipient is asked to convey greetings to the cantor of Malīj, who, of course, could not himself come to the capital on a holiday because he had to officiate in his town.) ENA 2738, f. 23: *maʿa man yadkhul yuʿayyid fī ʿaṣeret* (Heb. Pentecost). TS 13 J 19, f. 14*v*, ll. 9–10: no one is like the *ḥazzān sheʾērith* (Pride of the Cantors) in this art, *fann*.

[28]TS 13 J 20, f. 20. Betrothal: *tujmilūnā fī faraḥ bneʿmal li-Abu ʾl-Khayr Faraḥ* (happy event) could also mean wedding, but weddings were not celebrated on holidays, although even the scholar Eli b. Ezekiel ha-Kohen arranged a betrothal (text, *amlakt . . . milāk ḥasan*) in Jerusalem on Passover (*Med. Soc.*, III, 91, where the words "on Passover" were omitted). According to a communication by Mordechai A. Friedman, "on Passover" might be taken as "around Passover." Pleasure: *tijī ʿind bintik tanshalī = tansalī*, the seventh form of *slw*; *sh* and *s* are interchanged.

[29]Westminster College, Frag. Cairens. 109, ll. 14–15: *yikūn lak khayr an* (= *khayran*) *ʿaẓīm min allāh bi-faraḥī bak*. It is the father's religious duty to make the members of his household happy on a holiday (see Deuteronomy 16:15, cf. n. 26, above; emphasized in BT Pesaḥim 109).

[30]TS Arabic Box 7, f. 9.

[31]TS AS 145, f. 22*v*, ll. 1–3. "Grave matter": *amr ʿaẓīm*. The form of the address is remarkably uncommon: "To my mother." Usually a letter is addressed to the male person (often a son) in charge of the household. The duty of waiting upon one's (main) teacher on a holiday: BT Sukkot 27*b* and parallels. The disappointment of a mother and a sister when a son and his family failed to come for the holidays: *Med. Soc.*, III, 115.

[32]TS 12.280, ll. 10–18. The identity of the writer is established by his hand which is identical with TS 13 J 18, f. 19, *India Book* 108, signed by him, and Gottheil-Worrell XXI, pp. 94–95, both addressed to Ḥalfōn b. Nethanel. The three letters touch on similar matters and persons. The addressee of TS 12.280 is Isaac b. Obadiah, referred to in TS 10 J 15, f. 2, ll. 3–4, *India Book* 110, as *al-ḥāvēr al-jalīl*. About Joseph (Ibn Ṣaddīq) see Schirmann, *Hebrew Poetry in Spain and Provence*, I, 544–553, and *idem*, *New Hebrew Poems from the Genizah*, pp. 257–266. In l. 8 he is bynamed *al-ḥashīkh*, "the lean," an Aramaic word known through the proverb "until the fat one becomes lean, the lean one dies," but which I have not seen used elsewhere. Isaac Ibn Ezra was a whimsical man who cherished bizarre expressions. "Foolish poetry," *kalām sakhīf*.

[33]TS 13 J 23, f. 14, ll. 27–28. Judah b. Joseph writes to ʿAyyāsh b. Nissīm b. Baruch. See n. 37, below.

[34]Many contracts in Lopez-Raymond, *Medieval Trade* are geared to Christian holidays. As the Geniza shows, even Jews leased houses on the first of Muḥarram, the beginning of the Muslim year, and closed accounts at its end, but there were no fixed customs in these matters, at least in Fatimid times. The financial calendar of Muslim governments, based on the solar (agricultural) year, has left no traces in the Geniza.

[35]Hanukka: *Med. Soc.*, I, 254, n. 149 (1066). TS 20.83 deals with the same matters. Dropsie 386, l. 62 (delay of payment granted until Sukkot); verso, l. 18 (additional period of grace until Hanukka) (Sfax, 1063). For the popularity of Hanukka in Geniza times see p. 352, below.

[36]The problem is discussed in *Med. Soc.*, IV, 336 and n. 201, in connection with a document issued during "the middle days" on order of Moses Maimonides. A loan of 50 dirhems received in Minyat Ghamr during the Passover week, 1226: TS 13 J 4, f. l. Complaint about costly holidays: Dropsie 394, ll. 19–20. Yemenites: Goitein, *Jemenica*, p. 89, no. 503, with a quotation from the Talmud and Jewish-German to the same effect.

[37]TS 13 J 23, f. 14. See n. 33, above. TS Misc. Box 28, f. 225, *Nahray* 161: A long letter from Jerusalem, addressed to Nahray b. Nissīm, written on the eve of the Day of Atonement, contains good wishes, but otherwise is business as usual. Another, even longer letter from Jerusalem, written on the eve of Passover by a different person: TS 12.279, *Nahray* 154.

[38]Alexander Marx, "The Correspondence between the Rabbis of Southern France and Maimonides about Astrology," *HUCA*, 3 (1926), 357, sec. 29. Maimonides, too, notes, "Written in a great hurry," probably because he had to make an urgent visit to the Sultan's palace, after having been absent for a day. Further literature on this letter in S. M. Stern, "Maimonides' Correspondence with the Scholars of Provence" (Heb.) *Zion*, 16 (1951), 21 n. 6 (for 1194 read 1195).

[39]Safed in Upper Galilee, Palestine, is today mainly a town of artists and vacationers (although some Jews dedicating themselves to study and prayer are still there). Safed became and was called a holy city in the sixteenth century when it was the rallying place for saints and sages. Such confluence, however, was made possible in Mamluk times, when Safed became the capital of a province and attracted Jews with means to settle there. To be sure, the territory of Upper Galilee had been regarded as holy many centuries earlier because it harbored the tombs of renowned sages of the Talmud. Visits to these tombs became a mass phenomenon only after the classical Geniza period.

[40]A Maghrebi visiting "our lord Ezekiel and all the saints" and meeting a man from Sijilmāsa, Morocco, on that occasion: *Med. Soc.*, I, 56. A trader from Alexandria, Egypt, writing on his way back from India that he intended to make the pilgrimage to the tomb of Ezekiel and then to undertake another sea voyage: TS 8 J 15, f. 28, *India Book* 185. For a short description of the tomb compound see *EJ*, VI, 1096/7. The place is called al-Kifl (pronounced *tshifl*), because the Qurʾānic prophet Dhuttʾl-Kifl (Sura 21:85) was identified by the Muslim commentators with Ezekiel. An India trader, who, I assume, was an Iraqi, writing to his partner in Egypt, notes their donations made in India "for our lord Ezekiel, our lord Ezra, and Rabbi Meir" (the latter is located in Ḥilla in southernmost Iraq): TS 13 J 18, f. 2, *India Book* 179.

[41]For Aḥmad al-Badawī see *EI*², I, 280–281. The lengthy article concentrates on the personality of the founder, but provides too little information about the festivities at his tomb. For this purpose the interested reader must use the bibliographical data noted in the article and at its end.

[42]This is true in particular of Morocco (where Aḥmad al-Badawī was born) (see I. Ben-Ami, "Folk Veneration of Saints among the Moroccan Jews," in *Studies in Judaism and Islam 1981*, pp. 283–344, esp. the bibliographical notes 1–3 and 14). The author succeeded in collecting data related to 571 Moroccan Jewish saints (including 21 women); the entire Jewish population of that country amounted to only about 300,000 souls. Since one cannot live without saints, Moroccan immigrants to the state of Israel have already created new shrines there for some of their most venerated holy men. Unlike Egypt, which tends to centralization in everything, in Syria holy shrines are clustered around each of the main urban conglomerations (see, e.g., Janine Sourdel-Thomine, "Les anciens lieux de pèlerinage Damascains," *BEOIF Damas*, 14 (1952–1954), 65–85 (where further literature); Jean Gaulmier, "Pèlerinage populaires à Ḥama," *ibid.*, 1 (1931), 137–152. For Palestine see n. 44, below.

[43]I. Goldziher, *Muhammedanische Studien* (Halle, 1889–1890), II, 305–356 (mainly sections V–VIII of his study on the veneration of saints). Goldziher observed

Islamic folklife while visiting the Near East, and especially Egypt, in 1873/4 and later.

[44]For the attitudes of Islamic scholars and mystics to the tombs of saints, especially in Palestine, see Goitein, *Studies*, pp. 146–147. For the Karaite accusation that the veneration by Rabbanites of the tombs of Talmudic sages (see n. 39, end, above) was a foreign import, see, e.g., in Nemoy, *Karaite Anthology*, pp. 115–116.

[45]Jeremiah 46:13–28, a prophecy promulgated in Egypt, is read on one of the Sabbath services. The sermons given on such a day certainly enlarged on Jeremiah's sojourn in the country of the Nile.

[46]The attitudes toward the sanctity of the synagogue are discussed in *Med. Soc.*, II, 155–157.

[47]I have accepted the "historically correct" spelling suggested by Golb (see the next note), but E. Ashtor ("The Number of Jews in Mediaeval Egypt," *JJS*, 18 [1967], 18 n. 49) adduces a noteworthy argument for the retaining of the "traditional" spelling Dumūh.

[48]N. Golb, "The Topography of the Jews of Medieval Egypt," *JNES*, 24 (1965), esp. 255–259; *ibid.*, 33 (1974), 124–125.

[49]The inscriptions engraved in wood were made not by modern visitors but by donors during the eleventh through the thirteenth centuries (see *Med. Soc.*, II, 147–148, and next note).

[50]Quoted by Benjamin Richler, "New Inscriptions from the Synagogue of the Palestinians in Fustat" (Heb.) *ʿAlē Sefer* (Bar-Ilan University, Ramat Gan), 5 (1978), 182 n. 6, from H. J. Gurland, *Ginze Israel* (St. Petersburg, 1865), p. 34. For the author Moses Yerushalmi (meaning: who has made the pilgrimage to Jerusalem) b. Elijah ha-Levi, a prolific author, see Mann, *Texts*, II, 1427–1428.

[51]Maqrīzī, *Khiṭaṭ*, II, 464, bottom, often quoted.

[52]TS 20.117*v*, ed. Assaf, *Texts*, pp. 160–162. (The Arabic text was established and translated into Hebrew by D. H. Baneth.) In fact this is the recto. On the reverse side (catalogued as recto) the same hand wrote a court record repeatedly referring to Solomon Gaon, whether Solomon b. Judah or his predecessor Solomon ha-Kohen is not evident. The script is that of Samuel ha-Kohen b. Avṭalyōn, who signed a document in Fustat, 1016, and ten years later was head of the Palestinian congregation of Fustat (see *Med. Soc.*, II, 511, sec. 5, and Mann, I, 95). It stands to reason that this document was written before al-Ḥākim's anti-Christian drive turned against the Jews too, approximately around 1010.

In *Med. Soc.*, II, 553, n. 11, I ascribed TS 20.117 to Samuel's contemporary Japheth b. David (see *Med. Soc.*, II, 227). Although the matter is irrelevant for connecting this document with al-Ḥākim's reforms, a new examination of the manuscript convinced me that it was written by Samuel b. Avṭalyōn. Contemporaries often had similar handwritings, probably because they had studied calligraphy with the same teacher.

[53]Spelled *Dmwy*. The text has this: "The sanctuary called [about five words missing], which is situated in the town named D." I assume that the official title was "The Great Synagogue of the Rabbanite Jews" for, according to the famous report of R. Obadyah Bertinoro (visited Egypt in 1488), the Karaites, too, had a synagogue there (see Assaf, *Texts*, p. 156, n. 12; see *Med. Soc.*, II, 6, for naming a synagogue in this way). Had the official name of the sanctuary been "The Synagogue of Our Teacher Moses," it would certainly always have been referred to thus in daily use—but, as far as we know, it never was in the classical Geniza period.

[54]Ar. *khayāl*, flat figures manipulated behind a lit white screen, now known as "shadow play" (a translation of German *Schattenspiel*, which has not yet gained a proper foothold in English), see Dozy, *Supplément*, I, 418*a–b*, and *EI*², IV, 601–603 s.v. "Karagöz," where, however, the medieval Arabic shadow play is referred to only by bibliographical hints. The latter is treated, albeit briefly, in "Khayāl al-ẓill," *ibid.*, pp. 1136–1137.

[55]Text: *wa-lā yuʿmal fi ʾl-mawḍiʿ mizr*. See *Med. Soc.*, IV, 261 and n. 54. Since the

white Egyptian beer was made from wheat, which was probably grown around Dammūh, the quantities needed for the pilgrims were produced locally.

[56]Apostate: *pōshēʿa* (Heb.). The prohibition means that at Dammūh people were gathered for prayer, not for a party to which one could bring guests, whoever they were.

[57]A renewed emphasis that the synagogue building proper was like any other synagogue: a place of worship, not one for merely getting together, as had obviously happened to Dammūh because one did not regularly pray there.

[58]Keeping the laws of the Sabbath (on which, for instance, cooking is prohibited) at home was alleviated by special arrangements, which were missing in the camp at Dammūh. Cf. n. 22, above.

[59]Since chess was played for money, it was like gambling and, consequently, prohibited or, at least, disapproved.

[60]Drawing water from a well for purposes other than drinking was regarded as work prohibited on a Sabbath.

[61]It is evident from the Geniza that in Fustat segregation of sexes in the synagogue was complete, with women confined to the gallery upstairs, cf. *Med. Soc.*, II, 144. That here it was necessary to invoke an ancient *sunna* seems to show that during the visit to the Dammūh synagogue considerable laxity had prevailed.

[62]The editor read *(al-)yṣyʿh* *(al-madhkūra)* obviously taking it as Heb. *yaṣīʿa*, a gallery, which makes no sense and is grammatically impossible (the masculine term cannot be followed by a feminine attribute). Read *ḍayʿah*, farm, village (see *Med. Soc.*, I, 117), a proper designation for Dammūh, a place comprising fields, gardens, and date palm plantations, all mentioned in our sources.

[63]TS 13 J 26, f. 6, cf. *Med. Soc.*, II, 333 n. 29.

[64]TS 10 J 20, f. 5*v*, *Med. Soc.*, II, 422, sec. 103, ed. Goitein, *Tarbiz*, 32 (1963), 184–188, re-ed. Gil, *Foundations*, pp. 321–322: a letter by Moses Maimonides to Abraham b. Yaḥyā al-Najīb al-Wāthīq (Heb.), the administrator of Dammūh, shows him taking care of the smallest details related to its upkeep. In DK XXI, *Med. Soc.*, II, 419–420, sec. 41, ed. Gil, *Foundations*, pp. 322–324, this man receives help for the payment of his poll tax in the court (not: yeshiva) of Maimonides. In TS 10 J 4, f. 11*v*, *Med. Soc.*, II, 422, sec. 100, ed. Gil, *Foundations*, 319–321, the same person leases from the community a piece of land near the sanctuary for the token price of 8 dirhems a year for the duration of thirty years in order to revive the plot and to constantly supervise the synagogue. For a note of Maimonides sent to al-Wāthīq see n. 80, below. The circular TS 10 J 32, f. 12, in which the community is exhorted to donate for Dammūh, after it had been neglected for some time, is in the hand of Mevōrākh b. Nathan, who was Maimonides' confidant and secretary. (Partly ed. by me in "New Documents from the Cairo Geniza," in *Homenaje a Millás-Vallicrosa* (Barcelona, 1954), I, 718, where "f. 12" is omitted, and *tusammā* is erroneously read for *tasmaḥ*; correct *ibid.*, p. 711, n. 13, accordingly.) For Abraham Maimonides see *Med. Soc.*, II, 485, sec. 36. In TS Arabic Box 54, f. 66, ll. 3–4, a letter from Alexandria to chief justice Hananel b. Samuel, the writer remembers with pride the days he was privileged to spend with him in Dammūh and, at the end of the letter, sends 50 dirhems for its repair (May 1235). About this Hananel see Goitein, *Letters*, p. 57, and *idem*, "Chief Justice Hananel b. Samuel," *Tarbiz*, 50 (1981/2), 371–395.

[65]The sources on the visits to Dammūh, its legendary history, and the donations pledged and fines imposed for the benefit of its upkeep are conveniently summarized in Gil, *Foundations*, pp. 100–102. See also Strauss, *Mamluks*, I, 245–246, and *passim*; see *ibid.*, III, 189, Index. For the *mawlid* (Muhammad's birthday) see *EI*, III, 419–422, and P. Shinar, "Traditional and Reformist Mawlid Celebrations in the Maghrib," *Studies in Memory of Gaston Wiet*, ed. Myriam Rosen-Ayalon (Jerusalem, 1977), pp. 373–376.

[66]See the end of the preceding note.

[67]TS 13 J 4, f. 16, ed. Strauss-Ashtor, *Mamluks*, III, 112–115. See *Med. Soc.*, III, 211 and 471 n. 224.

[68]TS Arabic Box 52, f. 247*d* (1182/3), see *Med. Soc.*, II, 427 n. 137, ed. Gil,

Foundations, pp. 324–325. Instead of *khafīr*, Gil read *kufayr*, "the little infidel, a Christian of European extraction." As far as I remember, nowhere in the classical Geniza is a Christian or Muslim described as a *kāfir*, or a person denying the existence of God. The name of the watchman, Abū Kallabūṣ, means wearing a cap called *kallabūṣ*; no "Clovis" is hidden there (see Dozy, *Supplément*, II, 482, where the word ends in *sh*, not *ṣ*).

[69]TS 8 J 15, f. 5 (early thirteenth century). From the contents of the letter it is evident that it was written either on the day the company assembled in Dammūh or the day after. Since a Jewish holiday, outside Palestine, is always celebrated for two days, and activities like writing or undertaking a journey are prohibited, the Pentecost visit cannot be meant here. The seventh of Adar (see n. 65 above) could. In this case the good wishes at the beginning of the letter would refer to Purim (14 Adar), for which it was indeed customary to send congratulations, see p. 352, below).

[70]See Richler, "New Inscriptions" (see n. 50, above), p. 183.

[71]Details about Taṭay and the Torah scrolls, mostly from the Geniza, in Golb, "Topography of the Jews of Medieval Egypt" (see n. 48, above), *JNES*, 33 (1974), 142–143, who spells Tatai. Another minor shrine in the Nile Delta, the synagogue of Jawjar (Goger), was named after the Prophet Elijah (see *ibid.*, p. 131) and was visited by a traveler on the Purim day (which was celebrated in Geniza times as a memorial of salvation rather than an opportunity for merrymaking): TS 13 J 26, f. 7, ed. Strauss-Ashtor, *Mamluks*, III, 123–125, where l. 18, for *r'yt*, translated "I saw" (which makes no sense) the MS has *r'yḥ*, "I am going, traveling" (see Goitein, *Education*, p. 97).

[72]For al-Maḥalla see Israel Ben-Ze'eb's important article "The Hebrew Documents from the Cairo Community Archives," *Sefunot*, 9 (1964), esp. 266–270. On p. 268 he reports that Muslims and local Christians took part in the processions with the Torah, the dancing, the lighting of the oil candles on the night of the pilgrimage and that the meat of the animals donated was distributed indiscriminately among the poor of the three religions. Among the many miracles ascribed to that Torah scroll was this: anyone giving a false oath in its name would die within a year.

The name Abū *ʿwy* on the inscription of the case (*ibid.*, p. 267) was probably Abū ʿAwn. The enigmatic letters *'bm* at the end were no doubt *'ns*, an acrostic meaning "Amen, for ever and eternity" (*'mn, nṣḥ, slh*).

[73]See pp. 350–351, and 401–402, and *passim* under Jerusalem.

[74]Women's rights: TS 8 J 29, f. 13, where the four terms are mentioned together: *iftiqād*, a short call, lit., "inquiring," namely about the host's well-being; *ziyāra*, a more prolonged visit; *hanā'* and *ʿazā*, congratulations and condolences. See *Med. Soc.*, III, 216–217, and 191. "Talk and spindle": Kafih, *Jewish Life in Sanʿa*, p. 58.

[75]BT Taʿanit 23*a*; *Med. Soc.*, III, 172.

[76]TS 13 J 26, f. 18*v*, l. 10, ed. Goitein, *Palestinian Jewry*, p. 155.

[77]TS 10 J 19, f. 7, l. 3: *waḥda, ghurba, tashattut*, lit., "dispersion, separation from family and friends," said here and elsewhere of an individual and not only of a group. Written by a man who had traveled from Fustat to Alexandria, where he hoped his mother would join him. The most common word for this notion is "desolation," *wuḥsha*, lit., "living in the wilderness," e.g., Bodl. MS Heb. c 28 (Cat. 2876), f. 58, l. 6, see *Med. Soc.*, III, 229, n. 34, a letter reporting that the writer was put up by a local VIP, who did not let him stay alone for a single night!

[78]For the social aspects of illness see nn. 348 ff., below.

[79]Mosseri L-31, *recto* and *verso*. For *maqṭaʿ* see *Med. Soc.*, IV, 454, n. 82.

[80]Mosseri L-19; see S. D. Goitein, "Moses Maimonides, Man of Action: A Revision of the Master's Biography in Light of the Geniza Documents," in *Hommage à Georges Vajda*, ed. G. Nahon and C. Touati (Louvain, 1980), p. 166 n. 47. For al-Wāthīq and Dammūh see n. 64, above. Another such message on an evenly cut slip (3½ × 3½ inches): Mosseri L-129.1: Mukarram and Abū Manṣūr are requested to send to "the illustrious sheikh at Makīn Abu 'l-ʿIzz al-Levi" 1 dinar they had pledged for the first installment of the poll tax (to be used for the payment of a cantor's tax).

[81]Cf., e.g., TS 24.56*v*, ll. 3–19, ed. Goitein, *Palestinian Jewry*, p. 167: unworthiness

as an excuse for not appearing; Dropsie 394, ll. 23–32: ten lines of excuses (sore eyes which the Nagid would not like) for not coming to Cairo from Alexandria to congratulate Mevōrākh b. Saadya on his new titles; Mosseri L-209.1: excuse for being unable to convey in person congratulations on Sar Shalom ha-Levi's reinstatement in office, ca. 1176; TS Arabic Box 54, f. 66, ll. 5–6: "I had no opportunity to congratulate you on entering the new property," *mā kān li furja nubārik dukhūl al-mulk.*

Morocco: cf. I. Ben-Ami, "Le mariage traditionnel chez les Juifs marocains," *Studies in Marriage Customs*, ed. I. Ben-Ami and Dov Noy (Jerusalem, 1974), pp. 9–103; Yemen: Brauer, *Ethnologie der Jemenitischen Juden*, pp. 124–173.

[82]See *Med. Soc.*, III, 230–233, especially 233, nn. 61 and 62. The horoscope (TS 12.512, mentioned *ibid.*, 476 n. 62), dated 18 May 1113, has been edited by B. R. Goldstein and David Pingree, "Horoscope from the Cairo Geniza," *JNES*, 36 (1977), 113–144, esp. 121–125. The anniversary horoscope made on the sixteenth birthday of the person concerned (17 June 1066–17 June 1082) (*Med. Soc.*, III, 113 and 115–121) was probably made before a betrothal in order to to find out whether the proposed union was favored by the stars or whether the date chosen for the wedding was propitious. It could also have been requested by a physician. At certain periods birthday celebrations were held for the Fatimid caliphs (cf. Paula Sanders, "The Court Ceremonial of the Fatimid Caliphate in Egypt" [Ph.D. diss., Princeton University, 1984], *passim*). But in the Geniza I have not come across such festivities honoring private persons.

[83]Cf. Brauer, *Ethnologie der Jemenitischen Juden*, pp. 298–299. Bar-mitzvah as term for a family event was used by Brauer's informants when *answering questions of the ethnologists*, not among themselves. I believe I have not found the term or a reference to such a ceremony in Kafih's detailed *Jewish Life in Sanʿa.* Long ago it was observed that the term "bar-mitzvah" for a ceremony appeared only in the Late Middle Ages in Central Europe. A kind of ceremony seems to have been older (see *EJ*, IV, 344). A recent study by Arnaldo Momigliano, "A Medieval Jewish Autobiography" (about *Opusculum de conversione sua* of Hermannus quondam Judaeus), *H. Trevor-Roper Jubilee Volume* (London, 1981), pp. 26–32, makes it likely that some such ceremony was in vogue in Germany around 1100, that is, in Geniza times.

[84]Subsection A, 3, below.

[85]P. Randel, "Huxley in America," *Proceedings of the American Philosophical Society*, 114 (1970), 83.

[86]Qurʾān, Sura 90:6.

[87]BT Sabbath 127*a*, which also contains this saying of Rav, the founder of one of the Babylonian schools: "Putting up a wayfarer is like receiving the divine Presence." From the time of the early Church, hospitality was one of the most emphasized traits of Christian charity.

[88]TS 16.128. Whether this letter was really written by the Nāsī Daniel b. Azarya, as Mann, II, 260, believed, is doubtful (see Goitein, *Palestinian Jewry*, p. 133). The famine of 1025: see Lane-Poole, *History of Egypt*, pp. 135–136, and *Med. Soc.*, II, 130. For letters of introduction in general see *ibid.*, I, 347.

[89]The writer, Judah b. Aaron Ibn al-ʿAmmānī, as cantor and court clerk, kept the lists of the *ṣaʿlūk*, the poor, who were in receipt of the weekly distribution of bread, and knew therefore their approximate number.

[90]TS 12.299, ed. in Goitein, *Palestinian Jewry*, pp. 338–343.

[91]Alexandria 1235: see *Med. Soc.*, I, 67 and n. 38, and Robert Chazan, *Medieval Jewry in Northern France* (Baltimore and London, 1973), pp. 109–116. Tinnīs: TS 10 J 6, f. 2, margin, l. 2 (*Nahray* 219).

[92]See n. 40, above.

[93]"Not remiss [in the duties of hospitality]," *mā qaṣṣarū*, is the standing phrase in this connection.

[94]TS 8 J 40, f. 8, esp., ll. 13–23, and *verso*, l. 4, ed. S. D. Goitein, "On the Way to the Tomb of Ezekiel," *Studies in the History of the Jews of Iraq* (Heb.), ed. Samuel

Moreh (Jerusalem, 1981), pp. 12–18. "Pay no attention," *lā yaltafitūn ʿalā* (not: *ilā*) *gharīb.*

[95]Westminster College, Frag. Cairens. 35, ed. with Engl. trans. in S. D. Goitein, "Tyre, Tripoli-ʿArqa: Geniza Documents from the Beginnings of the Crusader Period," *JQR*, 66 (1975), 69–88; re-edited in Goitein, *Palestinian Jewry*, pp. 278–282, where the *JQR* article's concept of the interesting letter is changed with the following explanation (among others): Since the refugees from Jerusalem brought with them a crate of books, they could not have done so in Crusader times, even if they had left the city long before the siege.

[96]Messenger sent with mount: *Med. Soc.*, IV, 265 and n. 22. An *allūf*, or distinguished member of the Baghdad yeshiva, while arriving in Alexandria, "did not inconvenience the community by compelling them to meet him outside the town": TS 16.149, ll. 4–5. See p. 75 at n. 111, below. The Great Rav, Isaac b. Samuel, the Sefaradi, of Fustat was greeted by a letter of invitation by Baruch b. Isaac, the Great Rav of Aleppo, Syria, when he was still in Maʿarrat al-Nuʿmān, a town quite a distance from Aleppo (see Mann, *Texts*, I, 392 n. 16). List of notables meeting the guest outside the town: see n. 103.

[97]"An apartment becoming his honored rank": BT Bava Meṣiʿa 83*b*.

[98]"We" can always mean "I," but it stands to reason that the dignitary writing this letter was accompanied by a servant. Describing his state of exhaustion he writes expressly *wṣltw*, "I arrived." But he does not mention a travel companion.

[99]"The judge," the local rabbi.

[100]A person coming from, or named after, the town of Ashmūn (probably Ashmūn Ṭanāḥ).

[101]A man bearing the title "Scholar" and probably reading courses for adults.

[102]Al-Makīn, "The Solid," a title borne by a physician, ENA 2727, f. 9A (approached by his disciple for prescription for a disease of the eye); a banker, TS K 15, f. 107 (making a pledge for a charity); proprietor of a sugar mill, TS 13 J 37, f. 6 [1238]; and even a glassmaker, ULC Or 1080 J 2, col. II, l. 11 (paying arrears of pledge).

[103]ENA 2592, f. 3, ll. 7–14. A personal letter addressed to the Nāsī Solomon (b. Yishay-Jesse) (see *Med. Soc.*, II, 19, n. 49) containing greetings to the Nagid David (b. Abraham b. Moses) Maimonides and members of his family. Thus the writer must have belonged to the higher echelons of Jewish society in Egypt.

[104]TS NS Box 321, f. 1, l. 4. About this voyage on the Nile see *Med. Soc.*, I, 298, n. 27. "A place which could be locked," with separate entrance: *ṭabaqa bi-mughallaqihā* or *bi-mughlaqihā*. For similar expressions see *Med. Soc.*, IV, 363 n. 45 and 368 n. 136.

[105]ENA 2730, f. 1. Although much effaced, the name of (Samuel) Ibn Ṭalyūn (early eleventh century) is mentioned.

[106]ULC Or 1080, Box 6, f. 25 + TS 13 J 17, f. 16*v*, ed. Goitein, *Palestinian Jewry*, pp. 64–68. Because of the strict dietary laws to be observed during Passover week, it was difficult for the new arrival to manage alone. Moreover, during holidays he would have an opportunity to meet numerous members of the community in his host's house.

[107]This Aaron b. Yeshūʿa Ibn al-ʿAmmānī is frequently mentioned in *Med. Soc.*, II, 619, Index s.v.

[108]S. D. Goitein, "The Biography of Rabbi Judah Ha-Levi in the Light of the Cairo Geniza Documents," *PAAJR*, 28 (1959), 41–46.

[109]About this man and his correspondence with Nahray and others see Goitein, *Letters*, pp. 119–133.

[110]ENA 2805, f. 12, margin, ed. Goitein, *Palestinian Jewry*, pp. 186–187. Daniel b. Azarya was Gaon or head of the Jerusalem yeshiva 1051–1063. Such titles were by no means merely honorary. The Palestinian (or main) congregation in Alexandria was "under the authority" of the Gaon of Jerusalem. Without a certificate from the Gaon the itinerant preacher would not have been permitted to deliver a sermon.

[111]See n. 96, above.

[112]TS 16.149, ll. 3 and 5–14. To the story as told in *Med. Soc.*, II, 217–218, is to be added that this most successful speaker was unable to produce a certificate that he was indeed a member of the Baghdad yeshiva (see n. 110, above).

[113]A letter of safe conduct which any traveler from a non-Muslim country needed in Muslim territory. It seems that the document was indeed attached to the recipient's clothing for his protection.

[114]Dropsie 393, ll. 11–16. About the traveler and his benefactor see Mann, I, 218, II, 271 ff. The reference to the pantry seems to indicate that Isaac took most of his meals at his lodgings. In a contemporary source both Isaac and his father, Benveniste, are described as the Rav, or highest religious authority of the Jews of Narbonne (see Mann, I, 218, n. 1). He was only passing through Egypt, for in another letter to Joshua he asks for safe conduct through the ports of the eastern Mediterranean, then under Fatimid domination.

[115]BM Or 5566 D, f. 24, l. 10, said about travelers from Egypt, who claimed to be important people in their homeland, but did not conduct themselves accordingly, while sojourning in Aden, South Arabia. Ed. in Goitein, *The Yemenites*, pp. 67–68.

[116]See *Med. Soc.*, IV, 228 and n. 6, and *ibid.*, II, 162 and n. 26. A visitor from faraway Ṣaʿda in northern Yemen is invited to lead the community in prayer in Aden: TS 20.37, ll. 6–12, ed. Goitein, *The Yemenites*, p. 58.

[117]Such a poem—and not a bad one—was recited when the Spanish Great Rav Isaac b. Samuel left the capital of Egypt for Aleppo in northern Syria: TS Loan 32, ed. I. Davidson, *Genizah Studies*, Vol. III (New York, 1928), pp. 284 and 301–302, cf. Mann, *Texts*, I, 391, n. 13*a*. This journey must have been undertaken some years before the Crusaders made their appearance in northern Syria (early 1098), at a time when Isaac was a visitor and not yet a member of the rabbinical court in Fustat (see *Med. Soc.*, II, 512, sec. 13). He signed documents there as of 1098 (five in my *India Book* and one in *Med. Soc.*, I, illus. 5, after p. 20).

[118]According to the Talmud, a scholar should behave according to accepted standards and not regard them as beneath his dignity (see n. 120, below).

[119]Ar. *bākir*, lit., "early."

[120]Heb. *tēʿārēv daʿtekhā ʿim ha-beriōth*: BT Ketubbot 17*a*.

[121]TS 8 J 26, f. 1. The third postscript means that a person permits doing to friends what he would not do to others. As Goethe's Torquato Tasso said: "By Freunden laesst man leicht sich gehen" (with friends one takes leave of one's manners).

[122]The three *ʾ-sh-l* planted by Abraham (Gen. 21:33) is taken as a symbol for hospitality, namely, as initials of the Hebrew words denoting food, drink, and company after leaving. This acrostic is widely quoted in rabbinic literature (see *Berēshīth Rabba*, ed. J. Theodor [Berlin, 1912], p. 583, the commentary). (It is characteristic of the change of times and customs, that in modern Hebrew the last letter *l* is understood as the initial of *līnā*, lodging, so that today, *ʾēshel*, the symbol of hospitality, means "full board.")

[123]TS 8 J 18, f. 22, margin, *sālim ghānim*. In ll. 4–5, the same idea is expressed in Heb. *shalōm el shelōmīm* (for *shālēm el shelēmīm*), *ibid.*, ll. 4–5.

[124]TS 28.22, l. 10, *India Book* 14: *shayyaʿtanī*.

[125]Woman: see *Med. Soc.*, II, 136, n. 55. Scholarly person: *fīh rēʾaḥ Torah*, TS 8 J 17, f. 13.

[126]TS 20.28, l. 46: "the termination of 'my' hospitality," that is, the hospitality granted to me: *ākhir ḍiyāfatī*; "you will bid me farewell": *tuwaddiʿnī*. Several members of the al-Jāzifīnī family appear in the Geniza during the eleventh and twelfth centuries. Cf. n. 145, below.

[127]TS 8 J 18, f. 28. The letter was dictated.

[128]*India Book* 41–44, 331*b* (the last number contains drafts of three poems). For Ḥasan b. Bundār see p. 84, above.

[129]Typical examples of such poems: TS 13 J 26, f. 1 (see, in particular, ll. 20–21) and n. 126, above. "Wayfarer," *ʿōvēr wa-shāv*, common in the Talmud. Frequently used also in letters. See n. 140, below, asking for help, e.g., TS 8 J 16, f. 29*v*, l. 13,

where a complaint is made that no one else had paid attention to the writer or given him a morsel of bread. He was "from a faraway place, al-Raḥba" (in Iraq) and confident that the recipient, famous for his hospitality, would look after him. See p. 90.

[130]At public service: see *Med. Soc.*, II, 162. In warehouses and social gatherings: "Thanking your high excellency and invoking blessings upon you *fī kull makhzan wa-kull maḥḍar jamāʿa*": TS 10 J 19, f. 7, ll. 10–11.

[131]TS AS 146, f. 9, in Hebrew, of course, since destined to be read out at services.

[132]Bodl. MS Heb. b13, f. 52 (Cat. 2834, no. 33), ll. 12–15. In ll. 22–25, thanks, praise, and promise to spread the addressee's care for him are expressed by another man who had just arrived in the sender's house while the letter was written. As the script and the very specific style prove, the writer was Nathan b. Judah of Alexandria (see n. 287, below).

[133]The spiritual leader of the Jewish community of al-Maḥalla.

[134]Bodl. MS Heb. c 50 (no Cat.), f. 24. Although the name (al-)Sitt (al-)Ghazāl is common, there can be little doubt that this one was the wife of the judge Elijah b. Zechariah; the sender was her elder son Abū Zikrī, and the brother referred to was her younger son Solomon. See Goitein, *Palestinian Jewry*, pp. 321–332. The letter is not in Abū Zikrī's hand. It was dictated, and, I suspect, to the prospective guest himself. Abū Zikrī was a whimsical person; for the strange procedure that a recommendation is dictated to the recommended because he had a good handwriting, see *ibid.*, p. 49, n. 21.

[135]BT Bava Meṣiʿa 87*a*: *Ishshā ṣārā ʿēnēhā be-ōreḥīm yōtēr min hā-īsh.*

[136]ENA 4100, f. 8A, ll. 8–10. The letter is analyzed in Goitein, *Palestinian Jewry*, p. 204.

[137]TS 13 J 25, f. 2, l. 9. About Japheth b. David see *Med. Soc.*, II, 569, nn. 9, 19, and 22, and the Index, s.v.

[138]TS 13 J 21, f. 27. The addressee was Abu ʾl-Majd (b. Yākhīn b. Meir), the cantor, court clerk, and secretary of Abraham Maimonides. Greetings are extended to Rebekah, probably the recipient's wife and to Sitt Masʿūd, his mother-in-law. Combs and even spindles were sometimes made of costly materials (see *Med. Soc.*, IV, 224 and nn. 546–547). This was probably not the case here. But since the combs are sent here from Alexandria to Fustat, it is probable that they were made of European boxwood (see *ibid.*).

[139]ULC Or 1080 J 50. See *Med. Soc.*, IV, 123 and 382 n. 100. Richard Ettinghausen actually assigned the placard to the fifteenth century, cf. my note in *Genizah Fragments* (Newsletter of Cambridge University's Taylor Schechter Genizah Research Unit), 6 (Oct. 1983), 4, with reference to a note by Dr. Paul Fenton on the same subject in the April 1983 issue.

[140]Similarly, the Talmudic term for "wayfarer," so commonly found in Geniza letters (see n. 129, above) means "one who passes by and comes back."

[141]When Joseph contrived to placate his suspicious brothers, he arranged that they "drank and got drunk with him" (Genesis 43:34). In Yemen they used to say: "God plagues the Jews with brandy and the Muslims with *qāt*" (a stimulating plant, which is chewed by everyone who can afford it but which has harmful side effects) (Goitein, *Jemenica*, p. 116, no. 840). My remark about the Sabbath meal is based on observation.

[142]See *Med. Soc.*, IV, 253–261 (the subsection on wine).

[143]In his *Guide of the Perplexed*, III:8 (trans. S. Pines [Chicago, 1963], p. 434), Maimonides compares participants in a drinking bout to naked persons defecating in daylight while sitting together. I surmise that this is not an expansion of Isa. 28:7–8, which is strong enough (for otherwise he would have quoted the verses) but goes back to a Greek source.

[144]Westminster College, Frag. Cairens. 104 (formerly 42), ed. Dan Pagis with an important commentary in "Wine Songs Preceding the Spanish Period," *Dov Sadan Jubilee Volume* (Tel Aviv, 1977), pp. 245–255 (Heb.). Mixing wine with water before consuming it was common practice in antiquity. As I learned from the eminent

archaeologist Ernst Herzfeld, who excavated in Iraq in the first decade of this century, even then the local wine offered to him was, as he said, "such a thick soup that it was palatable only with a strong admixture of water." "Water into Wine" has significant symbolic connotations in various religions, cf. the book with this title by Lady Ethel Stefana Drower (London, 1956).

[145]"Crown of the revelers": ENA 2738, f. 22, an invitation sent by "the son of the cantor al-Jāzifīnī," cf. n. 126, above. "Kingdom": see *Med. Soc.*, IV, 255 n. 8.

[146]Maimonides, *Responsa*, I, 167, bottom.

[147]Oath: Goitein, *Letters*, p. 256. Bequest: TS 10 J 17, f. 4, l. 13, ed. in Goitein, "Chief Justice Hananel b. Samuel" (see n. 64, above), 377–378, *India Book* 37.

[148]TS 16.305*v*, ll. 5–7: "He drank to my health," *sharib sirrī*. Dozy, *Supplément*, I, 644 and 740, has only *shariba surūran bihi*, or *lahu*. Thus the Geniza letter of 1217 is perhaps the oldest testimony for modern *bi-sirrkum*, "skoal"! The uncle addicted to wine: TS 10 J 25, f. 3*v*, ll. 16–17.

[149]Maimonides, *Responsa*, II, 340 and 516. There were types of Egyptian *nabīdh* which were definitely intoxicating, see *Med. Soc.*, IV, 254 and n. 5.

[150]Aden: Bodl. MS Heb. d 66 (Cat. 2878), f. 21, *India Book* 177, ed. in Goitein, *The Yemenites*, pp. 47–52 (early thirteenth century). Town in Egypt: TS 12.312, l. 21. Toviahu ha-Kohen b. Eli writes to (his cousin) Nathan ha-Kohen b. Solomon (second quarter of twelfth century). One gets the impression that the temporary prohibition of wine was ordered by the Jewish authorities in the capital, and the local judge reported that he had carried out the orders.

[151]TS Misc. Box 8, f. 99, see *Med. Soc.*, II, 492, sec. 55, end of first paragraph (a list of contributors from the beginning of the thirteenth century). The proprietor, named al-Shaykh Abū Naṣr al-saʿīd (The Blessed One), was a respectable person. Meat to be consumed together with wine: in the poem described in n. 144, above.

[152]Son: TS 24.78, see B, 2, pp. 249–254, below. Fiancé: see *Med. Soc.*, III, 157 and n. 75.

[153]Text *yifshaʿ* (Heb.), usually meaning in the Geniza renouncing the Jewish religion. Here, where the boy remained with his grandmother, the meaning can only be that he did not keep the religious rituals and injunctions.

[154]TS 13 J 28, f. 12*v*, ll. 7–11. The term "fate" translates the Arabic *zamān*, literally, "time," see C, 1, below. Text: *taḥtamilī al-madaḍ minhu min al-zamān ḥattā yataʿammal ṣanʿa*.

[155]TS NS J 24, ll. 8–14. Another part of this letter is trans. in *Med. Soc.*, II, 63. Since the brawl took place at the gate of the cantor's house and one of those beaten up fell down as if killed, the affair reflected unfavorably on the community.

[156]ULC Or 1080 J 86, ll. 11–23, and top. Cf. *Med. Soc.*, II, 368–369 n. 32.

[157]Maimonides, *Responsa*, II, 398–400. See Boaz Cohen, "The Responsum of Maimonides concerning Music," in *Law and Tradition in Judaism* (New York, 1959), pp. 167–181, where the literature on the subject is assembled and discussed. The very extended article on Music in *EJ*, XII, 554–678, as far as I can see, does not treat the legal aspect in concentrated form.

[158]See *EI*, III, 809–816, s.v. "*Mūsīkī*," which deals with the Islamic science of music, not music life. The latter is concisely and beautifully described by A. Shiloah, "The Dimensions of Sound," in *The World of Islam*, ed. Bernard Lewis (London, 1976), pp. 161–180. Illustrations opposite p. 172 show a female dancer, a lute player, and a musician with a double flute, as depicted on ivory plaques from the Fatimid period, that is, the time and place of the Geniza documents.

[159]Music, *laʿb*, at funerals (in al-Mahdiyya, Tunisia): Bodl. MS Heb. c 28 (Cat. 2876), f. 52, l. 11, probably meaning flutes, as in Antiquity, see Krauss, *Talmudische Archäologie*, II, 64–65, and III, 88.

[160]TS 16.179, l. 5: The judge Labraṭ I b. Moses I Ibn Sighmār writes to his brother Judah, cf. *Med. Soc.*, III, 17.

[161]TS 18 J 2, f. 10, ll. 23–24, ed. Goitein, *Palestinian Jewry*, pp. 260 and 266. The word *wa-laʿb-hum*, "and their 'play'" is added above the line—as a special attraction. The Egyptians' pleasant company: *mukhālaṭat al-Miṣriyyīn*.

[162]TS 24.78, l. 31: "Drums and flutes in my house, as well as *laᶜb*." *Ibid.*, ll. 59 and 60 (twice): *jiwār al-laᶜb*, "the company of the musicians," could also be read *jawāri*, [singing or dancing] girls.

[163]The visitor to the capital: Daniel b. Azarya, condemned *all* instrumental music, ENA 3765, f. 10*v*, ll. 23–24, ed. Goitein, *Palestinian Jewry*, p. 134, see Mark R. Cohen, "New Light on the Conflict over the Palestinian Gaonate, 1038–1042, and on Daniel b. ᶜAzariah: A Pair of Letters to the Nagid of Qayrawan," *AJSreview*, 1 (1976), 12–13, and 25. Provincial town: ENA 2727, f. 31, l. 6, "they drink while listening to musical instruments," *mīnē zemer* (Heb.); the text is in Arabic.

[164]Player of flutes: *zāmir*, ENA 2556, f. 1*v* (dated 997). Maker of flutes: *mazāmīrī* (a banker or money changer), TS Arabic Box 40, f. 53, cf. *Med. Soc.*, II, 508, sec. 137. Lute-player: *ᶜawwād*, TS K 15, f. 6 (1178), TS NS J 76, all contributors to charity. Player of a *miᶜzaf*, a stringed instrument: *ᶜāzif*, TS Arabic Box 39, f. 79, *Med. Soc.*, II, 506, sec. 131 (several persons, contributors). Musician: *ālatī*, TS K 15, f. 14, and TS K 15, f. 93 (beneficiary of handouts). Buffoon, *zaffān*, seems to have been the name of a ramified and respected family: TS 20.160 (1047), summarized in *Med. Soc.*, III, 157, see also 460 n. 75, ed. M. A. Friedman, *Dine Israel*, 6 (1975), 107–114.

[165]"The son of the woman abstaining from wine": TS 24.76, l. 15 (receives bread at a handout). See *Med. Soc.*, III, 352–353.

[166]The inconsolable divorcée who could not accept the betrayal of her former husband "did not enter the bathhouse except on New moon's day, nor attend a wedding nor pass a night at a feasting party," DK XIII, ll. 8–9, *Med. Soc.*, III, 275 and n. 150. My translation there "once a month" is inexact. Right to go out for visiting the bath, *ibid.*, 217. Price of admission, *ibid.*, 186. Edward W. Lane, *An Account of the Manners and Customs of the Modern Egyptians* (London, 1836), p. 349. About the bathhouse visit in general, see pp. 96 ff. and n. 255, below.

[167]*Thousand and One Nights*: see *Med. Soc.*, III, 507 n. 217. *Kalīla wa-Dimna*: TS Arabic Box 40, f. 9. Cf. Sofie Walzer, "An Illustrated Leaf from a Lost Mamluk Kalila wa-Dimna Manuscript," *Ars Orientalis*, 2 (1957), 503–505, publication of an unmarked leaf from the Cairo Geniza depicting a lion and its mother given to the author by the late S. M. Stern.

[168]See n. 54, above.

[169]Play with dice: n. 16. Chess: n. 59, above, and nn. 172–174, below.

[170]*Med. Soc.*, II, 47, bottom.

[171]TS 12.56, top, and *verso*, ll. 1–10. Seller of beer: *fuqqāᶜī*. See EI^2, V, 108–110, s.v. "Ḳimār"; Franz Rosenthal, *Gambling in Islam* (Leiden, 1975).

[172]TS Arabic Box 40, f. 48. Breakup of friendship: *qaṭᶜ*, rhyming with *naṭᶜ*, the hide that served as chessboard.

[173]TS Arabic Box 54, f. 48. The chessboard is called here *ruqᶜat al-shaṭranj*, a piece of paper serving as such. The word "checkmate" is voweled *shēh mēt* (which is not Hebrew, but Arabic, pronounced with *imāla*). For the wicked Jewish woman who was such an excellent chess player that she was able to rob her Christian lover of all his possessions, see *Med. Soc.*, III, 344 and n. 151.

[174]The poem is conveniently available in Schirmann's *Hebrew Poetry in Spain and Provence*, I, 585–587. For its authorship, see *EJ*, V, 402.

[175]Pigeon race from the roof of a synagogue: *Med. Soc.*, II, 85 and n. 88. Pigeon house: *ibid.*, IV, 339 and 464, n. 251. Carriers: *Med. Soc.*, I, 291. Talmud: Krauss, *Talmudische Archäologie*, II, 238–239. Baghdad: M. C. Lyons, "The Sīrat Baybars," in *F. M. Pareja Jubilee Volume* (Leiden, 1974), I, 495. Bukhara: Ephraim Hay Zirkiyoff told me (in Jerusalem) that his grandfather banished the Jewish devotees of pigeon races from that Central-Asian city "for the benefit of the community and their own safety." For Islam in general, see EI^2, III, 108–110, s.v. "Ḥamām." Cf. the recent *A Fancy for Pigeons* by Joseph Kligerman (New York, 1978).

[176]The relevant passage from a commentary by Isaac b. Samuel the Spaniard is quoted in a later Yemenite compilation, see Mann, II, 464–465, Cohen, Mark R., *Self-government*, p. 120 n. 72.

2. Challenges

[1]"May He avert the bad things from you and turn them upon others," *ṣaraf al-aswāʾ ʿannak wa-aḥall-hā dūnak*: ULC Or 1080 J 154 (Aug. 1008), ed. Goitein, *Tarbiz*, 37 (1968), 158. "May God guard you from what is dreaded and let you meet what is enjoyable," *waqāk allāh al-maḥdhūr // wa-laqāk al-masrūr //*: TS 12.175, l. 2, ed. Goitein, *Tarbiz*, 34 (1965), 170. As the rhyme shows, these and similar phrases were stereotyped. They were in use throughout the classical period.

[2]Then the main port of Tunisia. The meaning of this laconic sentence is that Qayrawān had to be given up, and that the writer was unable to return to his hometown.

[3]Another port city of Tunisia. The most illustrious Jewish refugee from Qayrawān, R. Nissīm b. Jacob, also settled in Sūsa after the disaster of 1057 (see Goitein, *Letters*, pp. 163–165).

[4]ENA NS 18, f. 24, ll. 2–4.

[5]TS 12.227, ed. Goitein, *Tarbiz*, 37 (1968), 52, trans. Norman Stillman, "A Case of Labor Problems in Medieval Egypt," *IJMES*, 5 (1974), 197–200.

[6]*Wal-ḥāl salāma wa-naʿma bi-baqā mawlāy*: ENA NS 22, f. 1, l. 3. The sender: Ibrāhīm b. Faraḥ, who acted not only as mail agency but also as representative of merchants in Alexandria. Many missives of his have been identified since *Med. Soc.*, I, 304 and n. 20. In this important letter "the man with the outrageous script" is at his best.

[7]TS 13 J 24, f. 3, l. 4. Ḥalfōn b. Manasse, the court clerk, writes to his brother-in-law, Eli b. Hillel.

[8]"Things have stabilized," *aḥwāl mustawiya*: TS 13 J 23, f. 14, ll. 2–3. See pp. 16 ff. and nn. 33 and 37, above. Besides the paper mentioned in *Med. Soc.*, I, 81, there were several other orders.

[9]TS NS J 270, ed. Goitein, *Palestinian Jewry*, p. 308. The Arabic version *ʿāfiya* is here translated by "prosperity," since the writer's financial situation is intended. Compare above, p. 46.

[10]ENA NS 22, f. 20*v*, ll. 3–10. "Comfort," *naʿma*, as common as *ʿāfiya*, and actually used as its synonym. Written at least a century later than the letter cited in n. 6, above.

[11]ULC Or 1080 J 21, ed. Goitein, *Palestinian Jewry*, p. 276.

[12]Mishna, Berakhot 9:5. Actually "*all* that God does is good": TS 16.286, l. 30. See p. 595, n. 8, below.

[13]TS 13 J 14, f. 2, *Nahray* 17. Written probably around 1065 (see Lane-Poole, *History of Egypt*, pp. 146–150) although anxious watching for the rising of the Nile was not confined to those catastrophic years, as numerous Geniza letters show.

[14]TS 16.13, l. 3. The sixteen or so references to this letter in these volumes testify to the seriousness of the troubles recorded in it. Similarly in ENA NS 18, f. 31, l. 3, words of a much worried Isaac b. Barhūn.

[15]TS 8.32, *India Book* 349.

[16]TS 10 J 15, f. 33, ll. 2–3, Yaḥyā b. Mūsā al-Majjānī, Tunisia, writing to Barhūn b. Maṣlīaḥ (usually called Ṣāliḥ) temporarily in Egypt. His complaint refers to the troubles he was having in Tunisia. Later in the letter, he describes his lawsuits with one of the customers of his late father in Egypt, because he wished that Barhūn should act in that matter. About other troubles of our Yaḥyā see Goitein, *Letters*, pp. 95–101.

[17]The word is in Hebrew (*galgal*) because the concept of fate as "a wheel revolving in the world" is Talmudic (BT Shabbat 151*b*) (probably taken over from the Greek). The corresponding Arabic word *dāʾira* simply means misfortune. The Hebrew metaphor is taken from the water-wheel: the bucket is full when it comes up—a simile for the rich; it goes down empty—the rich have become poor; it comes up again full—the poor have become rich (Wayyiqra Rabba 34:9, ed. Mordecai (*thus*) Margulies, *Midrash Wayyikra Rabbah* [Jerusalem, 1953–61], pp. 792–793).

[18]TS 12.433*v*.

[19]Ar. *iḥan al-zamān wa-taqallubātih.*

[20]Proofs for the writer's integrity and worthiness.

[21]A reminiscence of the nineteenth and last benediction of the main Jewish daily prayer. In the seventeenth benediction, which speaks about God's miracles that surround us day in day out, a somewhat different phrase is used. A conflation of phrases, the like of which is natural.

[22]TS 13 J 25, f. 12, margin. Abūn b. Ṣadaqa al-Maghrebi (from Tunisia), living in Jerusalem, writes to Ḥayyīm b. ʿAmmār of Palermo, Sicily, staying in Fustat.

[23]*Ibid.*, ll. 5–6, 27–29, 10–11 (in this order). "In this time, after the death of the head of the community," l. 15, refers to Daniel b. Azarya (1063), while "in the Court of the Rayyis," l. 32, alludes to the session of a lawsuit presided over by him before his death.

[24]TS 16.196, ll. 25–28, see *Med. Soc.*, II, 72 n. 17, and 193 n. 2; ed. Mark R. Cohen, "Geniza Documents concerning a Conflict in a Provincial Egyptian Jewish Community during the Nagidate of Mevorakh b. Saadya," *Studies in Judaism and Islam, 1981*, pp. 123–154, esp. pp. 130–131, where the conflict is described, and p. 148, where the passage cited here is translated (somewhat differently). The Hebrew words for *enmity and strife* are used because they often occur in connection with communal discord, but are repeated in Arabic (see Cohen's translation), probably because the clerk assumed that not everyone in al-Maḥalla was familiar with them. Partisanship in worldly affairs is mentioned because one faction seems to have accused the *dayyān* of "currying favor with some people at the expense of others."

Disregard of the lesson to be learned from suffering: *kol ha-mvaʿēṭ be-yissurīn yissurīn neḥezāqīn ʿalāw* (Heb.), in a letter of Evyatar b. Elijah, the future Gaon, when he was still a "Fourth," ed. Goitein, *Palestinian Jewry*, pp. 128–129.

[25]See Mez, *Renaissance*, VI, p. 70: *ṣāḥib al-akhbār*; and see *Med. Soc.*, I, 271–272.

[26]TS AS 148, f. 9, *India Book* 363: Khalaf b. Isaac writing to Abraham Ben Yijū, both frequently corresponding with one another. Family names preserved: ʿAkkāwī, from Akko, Palestine; Maghrebi; ʿAfṣī, dealer in gall apples, a common export from northern Syria.

[27]TS NS J 180, *India Book* 293. A fragment.

[28]TS NS J 285, *India Book* 297. Maḍmūn to Ben Yijū.

[29]ENA NS 2, f. 13. The New Series of the Elkan Nathan Adler Collection of the Jewish Theological Seminary of America, New York, was established long after the publication of *Med. Soc.*, I, therefore this important letter with its valuable price lists and other information has not been treated there. The beginning of the letter is lost and with it the address, which was written, as usual, on the corresponding part of the reverse side. The writer mentions himself by his first name, Nissīm, a very common name among North African Jews. The time of the letter can be ascertained approximately by various persons mentioned in it: Abū Zikrī Judah b. Mūsā Ibn Sighmār, *verso*, l. 8, known from dated documents between 1055 (TS 18 J 1, f. 8) and 1098 (ULC Add 3416*c*, *India Book* 17, and see the Index); Abu ʾl-Faḍl he-Ḥāvēr, ENA NS 2, f. 13, l. 15, who was addressed thus in the 1060s and slightly later, before he became known as the Nagid Mevōrākh b. Saadya (see Cohen, Mark R., *Self-government*, p. 139); and Mūsa Majjānī, Jr., l. 17, also known to have lived in the 1060s (TS 8 J 7, f. 15), not to be confused with his namesake and grandfather who was dead in 1040 (Goitein, *Letters*, pp. 96–101, 354). The siege of Alexandria dominating the scene of our letter might have been that by the viceroy Badr al-Jamālī (1074) or some similar event happening in these turbulent times (see Lane-Poole, *History of Egypt*, p. 151), but hardly that of 1084/5, when Badr again had to besiege the city (see J. al-Shayyāl, *Tārīkh Madīnat al-Iskandariyya* [Alexandria, 1967], p. 53).

[30]TS 16.286, l. 30, quoting this Talmudic saying (BT Berakhot 60*b*) in the original Aramaic (but without the final *ʿāved*). The letter is summarized below (see n. 46). In *Med. Soc.*, I, 98–99, one of his afflictions is described.

[31]Ar. *al-ʿāqiba lil-khayr*, and the like, as in the passage translated above (n. 4);

although Qayrawān was devastated and mostly destroyed, God was expected "to turn the end to the good." In Palestine they would conclude the most harrowing reports with the phrase *biṣīr khēr*, "it will be good."

[32]See n. 29, above.

[33]See p. 516 n. 152. A facsimile of the original of the letter, reduced in size, is attached to the article cited there.

[34]See n. 22, above. Isaiah 33:24. Cf. BT Ketubbot 111*a*.

[35]Genesis chapters 32 and 33. The teachings to be derived from Jacob's preparations for the dreaded meeting with his brother were largely expanded by the Talmudic preachers.

[36]The verbs commonly used for expressing this idea are *khlf* and *ʿwḍ*; hence the frequent names Khalaf and Makhlūf and ʿIwāḍ, also ʿIwaḍ, meaning sons substituting for children who had died.

[37]Before making an important decision, one must ask God for guidance as to how to make the choice (see *Med. Soc.*, I, 346).

[38]TS 20.130, *India Book* 28. Mangalore is the name of a port city on the west coast of India.

[39]William M. Brinner, trans., *An Elegant Composition concerning Relief after Adversity* by Nissīm ben Jacob Ibn Shāhīn (New Haven and London, 1977). For the *Faraj baʿd al-Shidda* works in Arabic literature as compared with R. Nissīm's book, see *ibid.*, pp. xxiv–xxix.

[40]Goitein, *Jemenica*, p. 122, no. 879 end. The examples cited there could be increased easily.

[41]BT Berakhot 13*a*. TS 13 J 19, f. 20, ll. 13–14, *Nahray* 88, Goitein, *Letters*, p. 170.

[42]R. Nissīm b. Jacob had been given jurisdiction over the entire Maghreb by Hay Gaon, the head of the leading Baghdad yeshiva, *aṭlaq loh al-naẓar ʿalā sāʾir al-maghrib*: Mosseri L-135, margin, Mann, *Texts*, I, 246.

[43]See nn. 32–38, above.

[44]TS 20.113, trans., see pp. 374–379, below.

[45]TS 16.9, ed. Goitein, *Palestinian Jewry*, pp. 312–320; trans. by *idem* in "Moses Maimonides, Man of Action: A Revision of the Master's Biography in Light of the Geniza Documents," in *Hommage à Georges Vajda*, ed. G. Nahon and C. Touati (Louvain, 1980), pp. 158–159.

[46]TS 16.286. Four loaves cost 1⅛ dirhems, a high price indeed for "inedible bread," ll. 14–15, cf. *Med. Soc.*, IV, 238 nn. 87–90. The "voluntary contribution" amounted to 5,000 dinars, plus 1,000 for *ʾajʿāl* (sing. *juʿl*), "payments," probably to the officials collecting the imposition, *verso* ll. 3–5. "I am powerless," *mā fī yadī ḥīla*, ll. 29 and 33. See n. 30, above.

[47]TS 8 J 20, f. 26. The ditch was probably intended to protect the city at the seaside. The bazaars were closed so that everyone would be free to participate in the digging. The city gates were locked up probably to impede the infiltration of spies or troublemakers. Alexandria was famous for its textile industry, and *malḥafas* were ordered there.

[48]In addition to the letter from 1074 or so, n. 29, above, and the one just cited.

[49]Probably because the events in the city had taken a particularly dangerous turn. The New Year's holiday was celebrated in that year on Thursday and Friday, so that Sunday was the first day when disembarking was possible for an observant Jew.

[50]At a standstill: *al-balad qad qām ʿalā sāq*.

[51]A leader of the Arab tribe Lakhm was in temporary control of the capital itself in 1163 (see Lane-Poole, *History of Egypt*, p. 176). Gh. is spelled *ghrbyʾ*, but probably stands for *Ghurābiyya*, the "Raven," that is, black troops (suggested by Bernard Lewis).

[52]The governor: *al-wālī*. Throughout the Geniza the governor of Alexandria (and other large cities) is called *amīr*, whereas wālī usually designates the head of the police. But wālī is a good general term for governor, and the writer who clearly had been out of the country for a long time could use it in this sense.

[53]Run-down, *muhajjan*, clearly written so, but not seen by me elsewhere to describe a town.

[54]The Dockyard: [dār] *al-ṣināʿa*, lit., "workshop," in Alexandria as in Cairo, served also as customhouse and was situated outside the city. See *Med. Soc.*, I, 340.

[55]TS 10 J 31, f. 6. In the original manuscript, I believe, one more line can be deciphered. I read: *idh . . . . . . baʿd dhālika wa-kānat khayran*, "when . . . . . . afterward and will be good. . . ."

[56]The latest date given for R. Ḥiyyā, son of Isaac the Spaniard, in *Med. Soc.*, II, 513, sec. 19, is 1160.

[57]ENA 4020, f. 42, ed. Mann, II, 180–182. (In Mann's time, the manuscript did not yet have a mark.) Tortures: that the male genitals may be used as an object for torture seems to have been known prior to the discovery of electricity (see l. 5). Virgins (l. 33): unmarried women were recognized by their different hairdress and headcover. I believe, however, that the writer used the term "virgins" only because in the preceding sentence the word "women" was mentioned. In the report on the conquest of Jerusalem in 1099 it is said expressly that the Crusaders, unlike Muslims (see p. 375, below), did not rape women, and there married women were meant.

[58]See Goitein, *Palestinian Jewry*, pp. 191–192, where the erroneous assumption that the elegy was written in the time of the caliph al-Ḥākim is disproved.

[59]This arabicized Hebrew term, *ʾafshaʿū*, is said of a Jew who renounces his faith. I do not believe that the writer also thought about orthodox Muslims accepting the Almohad creed.

[60]The Jews were on firm legal ground since Islamic law clearly prohibits forced conversions. But sectarians, including the Shiʿites, both in Iran and Yemen, often found pretexts to interpret the law in their own way.

[61]The Hebrew phrase *yiḥūd ha-shēm* is used.

[62]Not a biblical quotation, but a benediction to be pronounced when hearing bad tidings, such as the death of a relative, friend, spiritual leader, or a martyr. See p. 595 n. 8, below.

[63]If here *ʿumūmatī* has the usual meaning "the brothers of my father" (and not merely "relatives on my father's side"), we have a problem: etiquette requires mention of a person as related to the addressee not to the writer. Solomon should have said: "Your brothers." Since something ominous is reported about them here, he might have preferred to describe them as his own uncles. The names of respectable persons are preceded by *Mār*, Sir, Lord, Master, which is more than English Mr.

[64]Ar. *khawārij*; a sect by this name is represented in North Africa, but it cannot be meant here, for Meknes was the last stronghold of the Almoravids, which withstood the siege by the Almohads for seven years until 1150, that is, over two years after the writing of our letter. See *EI*, III, 527, s.v. "Meknes."

[65]The MS has *bādū*, not the senseless *biʾidhn*, as read and translated in Hirschberg's edition (see n. 71, below).

[66]Only *jabal* is legible and that only with difficulty. Gibraltar is the European form of the name Jabal Ṭāriq. What the writer wishes to say is that from Bijāya, a port town in Algeria, to the Atlantic Ocean no one in North Africa could openly practice the Jewish religion.

[67]MS: *ukhidhat waʾashyāʾ*, "that B. has been taken and other things." This news was premature. B. did not fall to the Almohads until 1152 (see *EI*², I, 1205, s.v. "Bidjāya"). On the rest of the margin, which is much damaged, it is reported that the people of Spain had also submitted to ʿAbd al-Muʾmin.

[68]The name of this city from which the European name of the country is derived (because Marrākesh served also as a residence for its rulers) is here clearly spelled *mrwkwsh*, as if it was then pronounced *Ma*[or: *o*]*rrōkosh*. The Hebrew letter *w* designates long or short *o* or *u*; any short vowel is mostly not written.

[69]These phrases, lit., "I am informing you of this," customarily conclude, as here, one item of a letter, before the writer goes on to another; they are not intended to stress a point. The phrase is repeated here because the last sentence is a kind of postscript to the report about the Almohad persecutions, added as an afterthought.

[70]See *Med. Soc.*, III, 241 n. 25.

[71]Sassoon 713, ed. J. M. Toledano, "Documents from Manuscripts" (Heb.) *HUCA*, 4 (1927), 449–458; re-ed. H. Z. Hirschberg, "The Almohade Persecutions and the

India Trade," *I. Baer Jubilee Volume*, ed. Samuel Ettinger (Jerusalem, 1960), pp. 134–153 (*India Book* 263).

[72]Goitein, *Letters*, pp. 212–220.

[73]See the important study of Abraham S. Halkin, "On the History of the Almohad Forced Conversions," *Joshua Starr Memorial Volume* (New York, 1953), pp. 101–110 (Heb.). For Judah b. Farḥūn see Toledano, "Documents from Manuscripts," p. 456, and Hirschberg, "Almohade Persecutions," p. 138 n. 16 (see n. 71, above).

[74]Ismāʿīlīs, different from the Shiʿites of Yemen and Iran, and totally different from the Almohads. But all of them were infected by missionary zeal. See *EI*^{2}, IV, 198–206 (W. Madelung).

[75]The unhappy father of a profligate son (see p. 254 and n. 187), after having told all his misfortunes unashamedly, quotes BT Yoma 75a, "Sorrow in a man's heart bows him down [Proverbs 12:25, and] makes him talkative."

[76]See p. 58 and n. 57, above.

[77]Not found in the Bible in this form. Approximate quotations are introduced in subsequent notes.

[78]A conflation of Amos 9:5 and Hosea 4:3.

[79]The southern part of Palestine was called Filasṭīn, which is Latin Palaestina, ultimately meaning "Land of the Philistines," whose Hebrew equivalent is used here.

[80]The Hebrew name of the city presently known as Nablus, halfway between Jerusalem and Tiberias.

[81]The poetical name of the Holy Land in the Book of Daniel, perhaps used here as a designation for the northern province of the country (see n. 79, above).

[82]The slash indicates rhymed prose.

[83]TS 18 J 3, f. 9, ed. Mann, II, 176–178, trans. *ibid.*, I, 156–158. Occasionally the translation provided above differs not only in style but also in substance.

[84]See *Med. Soc.*, II, 19 and n. 49, and *ibid.*, pp. 492 and 493.

[85]TS 8 J 14, f. 18, ed. Paul Fenton, "A Meeting with Maimonides," *BSOAS*, 45 (1982), 1–4 (with facsimile). Maimonides not only asked the young man to sit down and talked with him but ordered the "curtain-keeper" to bring in the little boy, who was left outside with a friend, and played and laughed with him.

[86]Bodl. MS Heb. a 3 (Cat. 2873), f. 24, ed. (in its totality) Goitein, *Braslavi Volume*, pp. 486–501, with facsimile (plate 9 at the very end of the book). The passage translated here was edited before in *Levi Della Vida Jubilee Volume* (Rome, 1956), pp. 398–401, 405–408. In view of the great expansion of Geniza studies since, a number of comments made in connection with the letter in that paper must now be qualified. As is evident from p. 339 there, the date 1136 on p. 405 is a misprint for 1236.

[87]TS 20.128, ed. in Goitein, *Braslavi Volume*. This document, although written a few months later than Bodl. a 3, f. 24 (preceding note), is treated there first because it contains more material about housing, which was the main topic of that article, cf. *Med. Soc.*, IV, 66 and n. 103, 76 and n. 164.

[88]Yāqūt, III, 723, ll. 9–11. In Yāqūt, II, 388, ll. 14–15, it is stated that the Khāzer river (famous in Islamic history because of a decisive battle fought there), flows between al-ʿImrāniyya and the Khilibtā mountain. But I doubt whether this mountain could be meant in our letter, for nothing is said in it about the necessity of crossing a river. It could be, however, that the synagogue was situated on the other side of the river and near the Khilibtā.

[89]A Muslim term denoting a nobleman, especially one belonging to the family of the Prophet Muhammad (see *EI*, IV, 349–354, s.v. "Sharīf").

[90]The word omitted in Goitein, *Braslavi Volume*, p. 496, l. 7, n. 29 is Heb. *ōnes*, acts of God, accidents not under one's control. Dots over a word may mean either "omission," as wrongly assumed there, or "Hebrew, not Arabic." Thus diacritical signs were necessary; for instance the letters marked here with dots *ʾwns*, if read as Arabic (*uns*) would mean "meeting friends" and the like.

[91]No doubt the Tatars had been mentioned in a previous letter to Solomon b. Jesse.

[92]The word omitted in *ibid.*, l. 9, is *al-jumʿa*, Friday. The writer and his company probably intended to pass the Sabbath at the holy shrine. The reading tried in the *Levi Della Vida Volume* (see n. 86, above), "Day of Fasting," is wrong.

[93]Ar. *khubz nukhāla*, lit., "bread consisting of bran."

[94]See n. 86, above.

[95]Four fragments of three copies of this letter have been identified thus far. (Because of the risks of sea travel they sent copies of the same letter in different boats.) In this case the recipient kept all the copies and, after many years of sojourn in India and Yemen, took them with him back to Egypt, where they finally found their way into the Geniza.

The passage translated is found in TS 20.137, ll. 9–22, *India Book* 29, ed. in S. D. Goitein, "Two Eyewitness Reports on an Expedition of the King of Kīsh (Qais) against Aden," *BSOAS*, 16 (1954), 247–257, where the date and other technical details are discussed. These matters are taken up again in my *India Book.*

[96]Kīsh was pronounced also, as spelled here, Kīs, see *EI*, II, 695–697, s.v. "Ḳais."

[97]This flotilla, similar to naval expeditions on the Mediterranean (see *Med. Soc.*, I, 306–307 and 476–477) was composed of three types of boats: (*a*) heavy sailing ships with a wide, roundish hull, capable of carrying troops, war materials, and provisions, *burma*, I read *burmatayn*, although the first letter is closer to an *n* (*b* and *n* are similar in Hebrew), for the Muslim historian Ibn al-Mujāwir (d. 1291) (*Descriptio Arabiae Meridionalis*, ed. O. Löfgren [Leiden, 1951], pp. 124–126) uses this word in his account of the event ("cooking-pot" in Arabic, a suitable name for a roundship); (*b*) oar-propelled galleys, *shaffāra*, "cutting the waves," like a *shafra*, a large, sharp knife; and (*c*) launches, *jāshujiyyāt*, which is derived from Persian *jāshū*, "sailor," according to O. Löfgren, *Arabische Texte zur Kenntnis der Stadt Aden im Mittelalter* (Uppsala, 1936), I, 44, still used in the Persian gulf.

[98]The eastern, natural harbor of Aden, called *makallaʾ*, an Arabic term, meaning "protected" (from the waves), was situated between the town and the island of Ṣīra (see the following passage); details in *EI*^{2}, I, 180–181, s.v. "ʿAdan." See also n. 101, below.

[99]About him see S. M. Stern, "Rāmisht of Sīrāf: A Merchant Millionaire of the Twelfth Century," *JRAS*, n.v. (April, 1967), 10–14.

[100]The large merchant ships also carried a number of soldiers, as noted in *Med. Soc.*, I, 307, and see now Richard W. Unger, *The Ship in the Medieval Economy, 600–1600* (London and Montreal, 1980), p. 123.

[101]The western, larger, and partly artificial harbor of Aden, separated from the eastern one by a volcanic mountain, was designated by the Persian term *bandar*.

[102]Ar. *dīwān*, lit., "[registered in the government] payroll." In the parallel report the word *ʿaskar*, "troops," is used.

[103]TS 18 J 5, f. 5, *India Book* 149.

[104]See *Med. Soc.*, IV, 146 and n. 51, 166 and n. 119.

[105]TS AS 149, f. 3, *India Book* 370, damaged. Greetings to ʿArūs the purple maker put the letter into the end of the eleventh and beginning of the twelfth century. It seems to be addressed to "the illustrious elder Abu ʾl-Ḥusayn, the brother-in-law [sihr = ṣihr] of Abu [Yaḥyā], that is, Nahray b. Nissīm, which makes it likely that the letter was written in the last third of the eleventh century. Professor Jean-Claude Garcin, the expert on medieval history of Upper Egypt, informed me in his detailed letter of 15 September 1975, that no Muslim account of this event was known to him. "The Bulyanī" was the way in which the merchants designated the chieftain, probably after his birthplace Bulyanā, a town on the Nile in Upper Egypt (Yāqūt, I, 735); it was not his official designation.

Ibn Zubayr, *Dhakhāʾir* (The Book of Treasures and Presents), contains endless stories about princely presents, mostly in a vein similar to our letter. The "amber chain with jewels" is to be understood as a wall decoration and the like. In *ʿanbariyya mukallala bi-jawhar* the first word should not be taken as a variant of *anbār* (with *alif*), "storage room" (cf. Dozy, *Supplément*, II, 179*b*, top). The phrase means "a chain of pieces of amber intersected by jewels."

[106]Goitein, *Letters*, p. 265, nn. 11–12. "Usurper" there translates *khārijī*, pl. *khawārij*, anyone fighting the dominant authority. Here, in n. 64, I translated "dissenters," because the Almoravids, who are intended there, could not be described as usurpers, since they ruled the country for about a hundred years. For the civil population both Almoravid and Almohad conquerors were the same. Whatever their religious tenets and tribal allegiances, they were bloodstained troublemakers.

[107]*Ibid.*, p. 169, esp. n. 2, for which see Lane-Poole, *History of Egypt*, pp. 145–150. The details provided there refer mostly to the subsequent years (p. 149).

[108]TS AS 147, f. 2, written around 1055. In *Med. Soc.*, III, 91, the year 1085 is a misprint.

[109]Cf. *Med. Soc.*, II, 348–349.

[110]E.g., *nahb al-Fayyūm*, see *Med. Soc.*, III, 208. "We [in Alexandria] learned about the pillage of al-Maḥalla. I hope So-and-So has been saved; please find out" (TS 8 J 22, f. 6, ll. 16–17). The writer himself was held up during a business trip and robbed of everything, including his clothing, so that he had to traverse the Buḥayra district "naked," that is, without proper cover. (He mentions later that he had nothing to wear except an Aleppo robe, probably made of cotton.) A man who suffered during both a pillage and a holdup appears in a lawsuit in September 1075 claiming that his house was emptied during the pillage of Malīj, when the entire population was affected by the *nahb*, while he was waylaid by the Lawāta (Berber contingents), who robbed him of his clothing (Bodl. MS Heb. d 66 [Cat. 2878], f. 10). The pillage had certainly occurred during the period of lawlessness and famine, 1062–1074. In the second quarter of the twelfth century we read about *nahb*, famine, and the persecution of Jews it entailed, with reference to the towns of Sunbāṭ and Bilbays; because of famine and the robberies travel was rendered impossible (TS 13 J 25, f. 15).

A papyrus in Hebrew script and Arabic language (Ann Arbor pap. 6710) concerning the wholesale flight of the inhabitants of a village, including its Jews, reflects conditions in early Islamic times. Then, as in Late Antiquity, the rural population, unable to bear the burden of taxation, sought salvation in exodus to the towns, creating there an additional proletariat. Conversely, reports about the late Ayyubid period refer to the pillaging of districts in Fustat. In a letter to Solomon b. Yishay, the doyen of the Mosul Davidites (see n. 84, above), the writer describes how, at his arrival in the capital after a dangerous journey, he found the population in a state of terror because it was menaced with pillage: the bazaar of the wool merchants and the stores of the clothiers were plundered; one acquaintance lost 100 dinars worth of textiles belonging to him and others; but, thanks to God, "the end turned out to be good," that is, there was no general *nahb* (TS 13 J 21, f. 24, ll. 9–14). A grandmother, informing her son that his children were seriously ill, inserts into the letter, which is written in calligraphic Arabic script (of course, by a scribe), seven lines in equally calligraphic Hebrew script. In these, she reports that *mamlūks*, "slave soldiers," had plundered the Dār al-Fāʾizī quarter (see Ibn Duqmāq, IV, 35), leaving not a single mill, oil press, or house untouched; in the house of the Ibn Muzaghlil family ("Dazzler," occurring in several letters of the period), nothing remained in the room overlooking the Nile (certainly the reception hall of the house). All this had now been going on for a week. Why is this told in Hebrew script? Because troops running wild are a disgrace for the government, and any offense to the authorities had to be avoided.

(This is also a characteristically human document. Throughout the letter the mother speaks to her son: there is no money for the prescribed medical potions, not even for bread. At the end we read: "She [the wife] would not have dared to trouble you, had it not been for the seriousness of the children's illness" [TS 8 J 23, f. 7].)

In a third letter from this period the writer says, "We were plundered and came out of it 'naked' and hungry" (TS Arabic Box 38, f. 88, l. 7). Thus we see that even under the Ayyubids, who kept stricter discipline than most of the Fatimids were able to do, the people of the Egyptian capital were not always safe from their protectors. Needless to say, the great pillage of Fustat in 1168, *nahb miṣr* (referred to also as the affliction, *nawba*, or burning), the last notorious demonstration of Fatimid impotence, is reflected in the Geniza. The districts preferred by Jews for their homes seem to have been less affected. But a loss of deposits worth about 10,000 dinars, a sum unheard of in the Geniza, shows that the community was by no means spared during that infamous sack (TS NS J 174; see *Med. Soc.*, II, 81).

When "the two Sultans"—as they were called in the Geniza, the cousins who held the two forts of Aden, South Arabia—fought each other (see p. 68 and nn. 103, 104, above), there was robbery and plunder, *nahb*, in the town and the population was in great danger (TS Misc. Box 28, f. 256, l. 11, *India Book* 207).

For travel overland, river traffic, and piracy on the high seas see *Med. Soc.*, I, 279–280, 299, 327–332.

[111]ENA NS 2, f. 37, l. 21: *wa-qalbī mashghūl bil-mā*, "I ım worried about the water," in a letter from Palestine in the hand of Eli I b. Ezekiel.

[112]"May God bring us out of this hard year," *yukhalliṣnā min hādhihi ʾl-sana al-ṣaʿba* (ENA NS 2, f. 17, l. 10), echoed in the same letter (*verso*, l. 1), by *yōṣīʾēnū be-shālōm min* (Heb.!) *hādhihi ʾl-sana*. Also, TS 8 J 22, f. 6, l. 2, where the writer's extreme personal misfortune is connected with the disaster befalling the community. Same phrase in the text quoted in the next note.

[113]TS 13 J 26, f. 8*v*, ll. 6–8. See preceding note.

[114]See *Med. Soc.*, IV, 239 and nn. 100–102.

[115]See *ibid.*, pp. 234–244.

[116]*Ibid.*, p. 238 n. 91.

[117]Goitein, *Letters*, p. 222.

[118]See pp. 94–116, below.

[119] Ar. *itmām al-maʿrūf khayr min ibtidāh*, which is the writer's Arabic version of the Talmudic "He who begins a good work is advised: finish it!" (PT Megilla, chap. 2, end, and parallels).

[120]An allusion to Ecclesiastes 10:5, as used in the Talmud in many places, namely, that even a learned and pious man may err and thus bring upon himself sin and disaster.

[121]TS 8.33, ll. 3–9. Only a few lines are missing at the beginning.

[122]Heb. *gezērōt qāshōt*, used throughout the Talmud and the synagogal liturgy.

[123]Cf. Goitein, *Letters*, p. 222.

[124]The most common word for slump, *kasād*, e.g., TS NS J 380, l. 10, *al-balad kharib bil-kasād*, "the city is in ruins because of the slump," or ENA 1822, f. 47, ll. 6–7, *wāqif*, "at a standstill."

[125]"Out of work," *baṭṭāl*, common, said of merchants, craftsmen, and intellectuals alike. This term should not be translated as "unemployed," for people were mostly not *hired* for work, but entered it through partnerships or other forms of mutual agreement, cf. *Med. Soc.*, I, 82–85, 164–183. Without livelihood, *bilā maʿīsha*, as in TS 8 J 22, f. 6, ll. 6–7.

[126]Merchant: ENA NS 2, f. 17*v*, ll. 14, 17–18, see n. 112, above. Craftsman: *Med. Soc.*, II, 8. Intellectuals, see pp. 76 ff., below.

[127]Both expressions at the end of TS 16.286, see n. 46, above.

[128]In ENA NS 22, f. 20, ll. 8–16, an ordinary family letter (see n. 10, above). The writer, addressing his first cousin, a woman, who probably was also his in-law, expresses the wish that the extended family, *al-bayta*, may be reunited in one place, "for just as he has dispersed us [meaning Israel, the extended family in the wider sense of the word] among the nations, thus he will gather us in a place he will choose, as he has promised in his Book given to me through his Prophet [Moses]—Peace be upon him: *Even if your dispersed are at the end of the world, from there the Lord your God will gather you* [Deuteronomy 30:4]. May he ease our heart and yours from the tidings which are not good, and may he act for you and us *for his great name's sake*, for we are *between lions' teeth* [Joel 1:6]. *May he rescue us from them, as it is said: Even then, when they are in the land of their enemies, I shall not spurn them, etc.* [Leviticus 26:44]."

[129]Michel Mollat, *Les pauvres au Moyen Âge, étude sociale* (Paris, 1978) (deals with the subject historically as divided into four periods between the fifth and the beginning of the sixteenth centuries); Evelyne Patlagean, *Pauvreté économique et pauvreté sociale à Byzance, 4e–7e siècle* (Paris and La Haye, 1977) (eye-opening arrangement according to subject matter); Demetrius J. Constantelos, *Byzantine Philanthropy and Social Welfare* (New Brunswick, 1968); Brian Tierney, *Medieval Poor Law: A Sketch of Canonical Theory and Its Application in England* (Berkeley and Los Angeles, 1959). For literature on the social services in the Jewish community, see *Med. Soc.*, II, 542, n. 1, and *EJ*, V, 338–354, s.v. "Charity."

[130]The recurrent famines due to the failing of the Nile or other natural causes affected all layers of the society, not only the poor. The same was true of wars and states of anarchy, which impeded the sowing of the fields on time. The problem of agricultural supply is not treated in this book: the Geniza provides plenty of information for the side of the consumers, but only little for that of the producers.

[131]*Med. Soc.*, II, 91–145, 411–510, 542–550; Gil, *Foundations*.

[132]*Med. Soc.*, III, 363–422, esp. 418–419. Since the printing of that volume, additional documents have been identified, so that the distribution of the population in the light of marriage contracts is now as follows:

		Documents	
I.	Destitute	62	Totally underprivileged
II*a*.	Poor	51	
II*b*.	Very modest	71	
II*c*.	Modest	54	
III*a*.	Lower middle class	78	
III*b*.	Upper middle class	64	
IV.	Wealthy	16	
	Total	396	

Attention is drawn to the document analyzed in *Med. Soc.*, II, 468, sec. 110, where the Fustat community submits to the government a statement specifying that it harbored 150 residents entirely and permanently destitute and another 150 whose condition was unknown, but from whom not more than the usual minimum of 2 dinars could be taken and this only in installments. *Takers* and *givers* (Hebrew in an Arabic text): TS 13 J 27, f. 5 + 13 J 13, f. 13*v*, l. 23, ed. M. Gil, in *Studies in* [*the*] *Geniza and Sepharadi Heritage 1981*, p. 72.

[133]*Med. Soc.*, II, 139–142; Kenneth L. Brown, "Mellah and Madina: A Moroccan City and its Jewish Quarter" [Salé, ca. 1880–1930], in *Studies in Judaism and Islam, 1981*, p. 261.

[134]Baron, *History of the Jews*, 17 (1980), 164.

[135]*Med. Soc.*, III, 250–312, 189–205, 171–189.

[136]Mothers dictating letters to their boys: n. 175, below, and *Med. Soc.*, III, 193–194. Court clerks: *ibid.*, I, 90. Attitudes toward poverty: *ibid.*, II, 138–143.

[137]"Uncovering one's face," *kashaf wajhoh*. In times of general want both the *mastūr* and the *ṣaʿlūk* perish, TS 20.133, l. 23. In the jargon of the businessmen a merchant with little cash was called a ṣaʿlūk, TS 12.434, l. 11 (ca. 1100), TS 12.793, l. 11, *Nahray* 148: "These are not coins handled by ṣaʿlūks and craftsmen, but by landed proprietors, *muzāriʿ*, and the like."

[138]See n. 145, below.

[139]*EI*, I, 872, s.v. "Ceuta."

[140]At the beginning of this century, when Paul Eudel described the art of sil-

versmiths in North Africa, he stated in detail that this craft was almost entirely in Jewish hands (see his *L'orfèvrerie algérienne et tunisienne* [Paris, 1902], pp. 69–72). In Yemen, silversmithing was the livelihood preferred by scholarly persons, although learned men were found also among weavers and blacksmiths.

[141]Only about thirty words have been preserved of the introduction. The upper part of the sheet was neatly cut off.

[142]The name of the father is found in l. 2, that of the recipient in l. 27. The Bible verses: ". . . you will give loans to many peoples, but you will not take any" (Deuteronomy 28:12); ". . . you will lend to many peoples, but you shall not borrow" (*ibid.*, 15:6). Unlike the Jews of medieval western and central Europe, those of the Geniza were not significantly engaged in lending money to gentiles (see *Med. Soc.*, I, 254–258).

[143]TS 12.3, ll. 16–28. Later, our Ephraim b. Isaac, more successful elsewhere, became disappointed with R. Moses (see TS 8 J 20, f. 24).

[144]Ar. Siqilliyya (spelled here, as the Maghrebis did, with *s* instead of *ṣ*) denotes both the island of Sicily and its capital, Palermo. As l. 26 shows, here Palermo is intended.

[145]"There, too," meaning in Palermo, as when leaving Ceuta. While speaking about his flight from his native city, the writer did not mention what happened to him then. The Maghrebis knew that those who escaped from the sword were prone to fall into the hands of robbers. Cf. the lot of the persons fleeing from Sijilmāsa, n. 63, above.

[146]Boys were taught to read also upside down and from both sides, so that four boys could use one book. Our Ephraim probably possessed only one redundant copy of the Pentateuch which he was prepared to expose to the wear and tear of teaching (see *Med. Soc.*, II, 181).

[147]A trained scribe, like our Ephraim, is able to write even after losing half of his eyesight, but silversmithing with its filigree and other delicate techniques required full ocular capacity.

[148]The last letter is clearly a *t*, not an *m*, as required in *ḥayyīm*, life. Since "Land of Life" is a synonym for the Holy Land, the writer changed the word to *ḥiyyūt*, a land where one can live; he tampered with the second *y*, trying to convert it into a *w*.

[149]Flour might have been requested as usual for Passover (for the preparation of the unleavened bread). In this case, good wishes for the holiday would have been imperative. They might have been found in the part of the introductory passage which was cut away (see n. 141, above).

[150]TS 20.148. The name Joel, so common today even in the United States, is next to absent from the Geniza. The social—not economic!—position of the *melammed*, the schoolmaster, was higher in the Geniza world than later in European Jewry (see *Med. Soc.*, II, 188, 190).

[151]For Abraham the Pious and the pietist movement, see p. 481, below.

[152]Heb.: *mi-mēvīkh maḥashāvōt. The Guide of the Perplexed* was completed "sometime between 1185 and 1190" (see I. Twersky, *Maimonides' Reader* [New York, 1972], p. 19). Our letter was almost certainly written before 1201 (see n. 156, below).

[153]Heb. *ḥōser yād* seems to be a translation of Ar. *qalīl dhāt al-yad*, a man with little or no means. "Poverty" refers to his state as teacher, his income, which was insufficient and did not permit him to make savings. Cf. Mosseri L-227, l. 3, "a large family and no means."

[154]A Hebrew pun: when I remember the tax, *mas*, my heart melts, *yimmas*.

[155]See *Med. Soc.*, IV, 161 and n. 81.

[156]*Ibid.*, II, 141. The wish expressed that Abraham be blessed with children presupposes a time when he was still middle-aged. He died in 1223.

[157]See *Med. Soc.*, II, 138–143; III, 350, top (Wuḥsha's will); in more detail in *JQR Anniversary Volume*, 75 (1967), pp. 234–235; Maimonides: see n. 242, below.

[158]See Mann, II, 338 (3); *Med. Soc.*, II, 355–356, 604–605, nn. 2, 4, 5. The name of the recipient is alluded to when he is addressed, *verso*, l. 19, as "the Thiqa . . . excellency," referring to one of his Arabic titles, Thiqat al-Mulk, "The Trusted [ser-

vant] of the State." Only the elder of his two sons (see TS 13 J 33, f. 3, ll. 14–15, a letter addressed to him by Abu ʾl-Ḥasan Ibrahīm [with short *a* in Arabic script] al-Zayyāt), is mentioned, probably because the other had not yet been born, or because Elazar, also a government official, was regarded as a kind of successor to his father's eminence. Moreover, it was customary to single out the firstborn for special mention. For a probable identification of the writer, see n. 167, below.

[159]BT Ketubbot 67*b*, top. Cf. Nahum N. Glatzer, *Hillel the Elder: The Emergence of Classical Judaism* (New York, 1957), p. 44.

[160]Since we have a court record from December 1175, in which Judah b. Elazar was a party (*Med. Soc.*, II, 605 n. 4), and another from May 1178, where his son Elazar signs a document mentioning his father as being alive, we are here probably in the difficult years after the pillage and conflagration of Fustat, 1168, and the termination of the Fatimid caliphate in 1171.

[161]An allusion to wine, obligatory on Passover. For "adornments" by clothing, *tajammul*, see *Med. Soc.*, IV, 397 n. 44.

[162]Celebrated four weeks before Passover, when presents should be sent to friends and gifts to the poor according to the Book of Esther 9:22. The writer reminds the Trusted that he has saved him something.

[163]A hint that a fine piece of clothing from the wardrobe of the women in the Trusted's house would be a welcome gift for the writer's new wife.

[164]Ar. *barr*, the dedication one owes to close relatives, such as parents ("piety"), and intimate friends.

[165]TS 24.27*v*, ll. 23–37. The word *Selah*, which concludes so many psalms (e.g., 3, 9, 24), is used occasionally for ending a letter, but (almost) always in connection with Amen or similar expressions, as in TS 13 J 33, f. 7*v*, l. 31 (see nn. 169 and 173, below).

[166]BT Sanhedrin 105*a*.

[167]He signs as "Manasse the schoolmaster" in TS 12.425, the reminder for a Hanukkah bonus, and calls himself the "Alexandrian schoolmaster" when sending congratulations to a man from Yemen in the epistle concerning the competition to his school in TS 13 J 33, f. 8, both trans. into Heb. in Goitein, *Education*, pp. 49–50 and 92–95, respectively. The script in the two later letters is more calligraphic, especially in TS 12.425, which is written with a fine pen.

[168]See A. L. Udovitch, "A Tale of Two Cities . . . ," in *The Medieval City*, ed. H. A. Miskimin et al. (New Haven and London, 1977), pp. 143–162.

[169]The poet Judah ha-Levi was also known by the name "the Castilian," so that there was complete identity between the names of the addressee and the sender. But the man from Badajoz did not rub that point in (cf. Schirmann, *Studies*, II, 232, Heb.).

[170]This verse is usually quoted in requests for material things.

[171]Ecclesiastes 8:1. Again a case, as with Zechariah 4:13–15, quoted by the Maghrebi from Ceuta, above, in which the relevant part of the biblical passage is omitted, leaving it to the knowledgeable reader to complement it.

[172]The problem of modesty and meekness, so often ascribed to a Geniza personality, is studied on pp. 196–199, below.

[173]TS 13 J 33, f. 7, ed. with facsimile and Hebrew trans. by S. D. Goitein in *Tarbiz*, 30 (1961), 379–384. Judah ha-Levi, known to posterity as a great poet and man of thought, was a well-to-do physician, generously devoting of his time to public welfare and personal charity (cf. *Med. Soc.*, II, 260).

[174]Goitein, *Jemenica*, p. 173, no. 1348.

[175]Westminster College, Frag. Cairens. 35, ed. S. D. Goitein, "Tyre, Tripoli-ʿArqa: Geniza Documents from the Beginnings of the Crusader Period," *JQR*, 66 (1975), 79–83, re-edited, with important corrections in Goitein, *Palestinian Jewry*, pp. 278–282, see p. 30 and n. 95, above.

[176]Cf. n. 181, below.

[177]It seems strange that a person addressed in the preceding line as "illustrious"

is called "boy" here. This means only that he belonged to a younger age group, for instance, that he was the writer's husband's nephew.

[178]The words in brackets were supplemented on the basis of the following paragraph. The way in which al-Muntaṣir, a Muslim commander or official, is introduced here shows that he was known to the addressee. Most probably he had had his seat before in Jerusalem, where Abu ʾl-Khayr had lived, and the relations between the two men had been mentioned before to the receiver of the letter or he had witnessed them when visiting Jerusalem.

[179]Namely, God. Before thanking a benefactor one thanks God who has created him and made him a good human being. Ar. *yurīd* is used here, as in spoken Arabic today, in the sense of "he requires."

[180]She mentions this in the midst of the passage on the books probably in order to explain why she did not learn about the contents of the crate before.

[181]An allusion to communal troubles which the Nagid might have experienced a few years before. Ar. *ḥaraṣ* for *ḥaras.*

[182]The crate with the books of Abu ʾl-Khayr and the addressee had been pawned with a Muslim. The dinars lent to the family had been used up. Retrieving the books was like ransoming a human being. It was a deed of charity; but the Nagid is promised the books.

[183]Abu ʾl-Wafāʾ, Abu ʾl-Khayr's brother, was, like him, connected with Muslim authorities; perhaps he was a *kātib al-ʿArab*, paymaster in a Bedouin auxiliary regiment, as we know of other Jews (see *Med. Soc.*, II, 379).

[184]Who was captured or killed. Ar. *shanāʿa*, in the usage of the Geniza letters, may also have the meaning of mere rumors, not certain bad news.

[185]The Jewish and Christian communities in whose neighborhood the captives are held, who would take care of their coreligionists.

[186]Her husband.

[187]The brother's family.

[188]An approximate translation of a partly effaced text.

[189]Called here *al-maqdis*, abbreviated from *bayt al-maqdis*, a common form, echoed in Hebrew by *miqdāsh* as a name for the Holy City.

[190]Ar. *ḥaḍḍ*, to be understood as *ḥaẓẓ*, share of a donation. Everyone donated for Jerusalem. Since Abu ʾl-Khayr was probably a communal official, a donation could be sent directly to his family.

[191]Ar. *kamā ḥaṣalat*, "as it occurs." Perhaps the mother of the addressee, *recto*, l. 20, was the woman's sister.

[192]Ar. *wal-aʿyān*, misheard, or otherwise an error, for *wal-ān.*

[193]Opening a letter with greetings from God was not uncommon, especially in a missive to a congregation. But I have never read this as personal greetings, at the end of a Geniza letter. The writer doubted whether it was proper that she, as a woman, should send regards directly to the Nagid. Therefore she left it to God to convey her greetings. See pp. 602–603 nn. 87 and 88, below.

The combination "my lord, the Nagid and my lord, the Ḥāvēr" is found as referring to Judah b. Saadya and his brother Mevōrākh, the later Nagid (see Mann (1970), II, 250, bottom). The history of these two brothers is now dealt with in detail in Cohen, Mark R., *Self-government.*

[194]Meaning: God will reward you for safely delivering this letter. It was given to one of the merchants who traveled from Tripoli (via Damietta or Tinnīs) to Cairo.

[195]See *Med. Soc.*, III, 171–172.

[196]ʿAfīf's activities in Safed are described in Gottheil-Worrell, pp. 252–255, ll. 71–94. His letter, TS 20.149, is edited in Strauss-Ashtor, *Mamluks*, III, 127–133. Despite the late date, I include him here because his script and style are very similar to those of the "classical" Geniza period, which means that he was a local Arabic-speaking Jew, not an immigrant from Europe. He is called "the Egyptian" in the Gottheil-Worrell document.

[197]Amshāṭī: see *Med. Soc.*, II, 498, sec. 81 (dated 1161). The same Amshāṭī is

mentioned in several letters in the *India Book*, *Med. Soc.*, IV, 224–225, Strauss-Ashtor, *Mamluks*, III, 162, Index, s.v. Numerous other documents.

[198]ʿAfīf is mentioned in the Gottheil-Worrell document as being in Safed in the company of a highly revered man named Peres. In our letter it is said that this man died while trying to return there. Thus the letter must have been written when ʿAfīf was on his way back to the town where he practiced.

[199]TS 20.149, l. 35. Read: *al-mara baqat*, and translate accordingly.

[200]*Ibid.*, ll. 24, 30, 34, 37, *verso*, 17, 22, 24. In l. 42 he addresses God, using I Samuel 2:7, *mōrīsh mashpīl u-maʿashīr* (so the MS). "He makes poor and makes rich," a warning that we are all exposed to the vicissitudes of life.

[201]"By his own fault," *ʿamil* (not *ʿāl*) *bi-nafso*, l. 38.

[202]His extreme poverty is evident from his request to sell a share of his in a family house, which share would bring two *anṣāfs*, half-dirhems, per month (*verso*, l. 8, MS *btaʾkhudh*).

[203]Not all physicians were well off. See *Med. Soc.*, II, 257 and n. 88. An example of glaring want is TS 13 J 6, f. 16, about a physician who formerly used to treat a noble Muslim family.

[204]Ar. *naʿt*, the totality of honorary titles possessed by a person (see next note).

[205]TS 8 J 16, f. 7, ll. 5 and 15–16. This Abū Sahl b. Moses *hā-āhūv* is the person so highly recommended for the post of a cantor in TS 10 J 26, f. 7 (see Mann, II, 374, and *Med. Soc.*, II, 222, and 569 n. 16). For singling out the firstborn by name, see, e.g., n. 158, above.

[206]Family sacrifice with distributions to the poor: *dhabīḥa lil-tafriqa*, TS 8 J 16, f. 7*v*, ll. 13–15.

[207]See *Med. Soc.*, II, 128.

[208]They swore by anything that came to mind in connection with the topic of their letters. The writer of TS 8 J 16, f. 7, in n. 206, above, who wished to stress the literal truth of his assertions, swears by "the religion of the Unity of God" (the first article of the Jewish faith) *verso*, l. 9, or "the faith of the children of Israel, *ibid.*, l. 1. The oath "by the truth of your generosity" sounds like a slight joke; that truth remains to be revealed: live up to your reputation. See also n. 223, below.

[209]TS 8 J 24, f. 17. The *verso*, the original letter, was addressed to the writer of the *recto*, the letter analyzed here, cf. *bēt ʿammak*, "your uncle's wife," *verso*, l. 12, with *bēt ʿammā*, "my uncle's wife."

[210]The reader is reminded that a letter usually is concluded with "*And Peace.*" Any postscript must again have this expression of taking leave.

[211]Abraham Maimuni, *Responsa*, p. 206 (ca. 1220).

[212]TS 13 J 1, f. 22, ll. 11–12 (1091), when the Jewish High Court of Jerusalem had its seat in Tyre. For women working with silk, see *Med. Soc.*, I, 128 and n. 11.

[213]Maimonides, *Responsa*, I, 50, no. 34.

[214]*Mā ʿindō ḥaqq al-zayt*: J. L. Burckhardt, *Arabische Sprüchwörter oder die Sitten und Gebräuche der neueren Aegyptier* (Arab Proverbs, or the Manners and Customs of the Modern Egyptians) (Weimar, 1834), p. 25 n. 61.

[215]"Utmost humiliation through poverty," *wa-hī fī dhull ʿaẓīm min al-qilla*: Maimonides, *Responsa*, I, 50, no. 34. The woman's story: *Med. Soc.*, III, 344–346.

[216]TS 10 J 15, f. 27; see *Med. Soc.*, II, 107 and n. 18; III, 305 and n. 134.

[217]TS 8.200. A person could not *sign* as "the Scholar" *ha-talmīd* unless he had received this title from a religious authority. The Hebrew letter is addressed to Japheth b. Nathan Tinnīsi (with *sh* for *s*, the writer probably knew no Arabic) who is promised that for reviving a starving soul he would acquire a merit as if he had brought "a whole offering" to the altar of the Temple. "Not even a pound of bread": also in TS 13 J 21, f. 3, l. 16; about the writer see *Med. Soc.*, II, 188 and n. 18.

[218]Bodl. MS Heb. e 94 (no Cat.), f. 27.

[219]TS 13 J 25, f. 2, see *Med. Soc.*, IV, 243 and n. 129.

[220]ENA NS 22, f. 7. In the Karaite sect, a "presbyterian" denomination, one applied to "the elders," as here, not to "a judge," as with the main Jewish community (see, e.g., n. 218, above). A list of contributors on the reverse side shows that a collection was made in response to the widow's appeal.

[221]TS Arabic Box 40, f. 187.

[222]ENA 2727, f. 7B.

[223]TS NS J 323. "In private," *sitran,*" lit., "secretly," same root as *mastūr* (see n. 137, above). "By the truth of your generosity": see n. 208, above. In TS NS J 98, Yedūthūn, heading the list of receivers of bread from the community, gets five loaves, probably showing that his family was small. In the margin of our letter Yedūthūn signs with his Arabic name "Abu ʾl-Ḥasan b. Abu ʾl-Faraj, the cantor of the Synagogue of the Palestinians." Thus he suffered hunger while in office. His script and style reflect a good education; the fact that he used the reverse side of a letter in Arabic characters betrays his poverty (cf. n. 209, above).

[224]Quoted, for instance, in the letter covered in the preceding note.

[225]TS Arabic Box 30, f. 67, col. III, ll. 13–17, cf. *Med. Soc.*, II, 457, sec. 65.

[226]TS 8 J 21, f. 30.

[227]TS 8 J 37, f. 11, ll. 4–6, 15–16; much damaged, signed by Jacob b. Aaron when his father was still alive. In the margin he offers to write down for the recipient the "Prayer for Rain," a long and extremely difficult liturgy (recited on the concluding holiday of the Feast of the Tabernacles). Jacob obviously knew it by heart.

[228]TS 8 J 16, f. 29*v*. The original user of the paper wrote on *recto*. "Standing in this posture" may be meant literally: waiting outside the gate of the house for a reply. The letter of the blind man was dictated to an "Ashkenazi," a fellow Jew from Europe, who spelled Alexandria *ʾqsdryʾh*. For Eli, the parnās, see *Med. Soc.*, II, 78. Scheiber, *Geniza Studies*, pp. 78–79, edited the letter of the blind man.

[229]"No cover, no couch" is an attempt to translate the Arabic rhyme *lā ghaṭā wa-lā waṭā*. The second term denotes anything spread out on which one sleeps.

[230]TS AS 150, f. 13. "Rich food" translates *zafar*, cf. *Tāj al-ʿArūs*, III, 239, l. 3. Dozy, *Supplément*, I, 595*a*–*b*, Wahrmund, *Handwörterbuch* I, 836a.

[231]TS 13 J 6, f. 15, l. 16, *India Book* 302. BT Bava Qamma 92*a*, bottom, where the accepted text has *ʿanyā*, the poor in the singular, whereas the writer of the Geniza letter spells *ʿnyy* in the plural.

[232]"No affliction in the world is as grave as poverty, for anyone crushed (or ground) by poverty feels as if hit by all the curses enumerated in the Book of Deuteronomy (28:15–68), which is indeed a gruesome catalog. Shemot Rabba 31:14, "Crushed," *meduqdaq*; "ground," *medukhdakh*. The differentiation between poverty from childhood, for instance by blindness, and other types in Wayyiqrā Rabba 34:13, ed. Margulies (see n. 17, above), p. 800.

[233]As noted above in n. 131, a perusal of the sources analyzed in *Med. Soc.*, II, App. B, comparable with that done by Gil, *Foundations*, for App. A., could result in a detailed picture of the world of the underprivileged referred to here. The deserted wives, widows, and female orphans who addressed a congregation or communal leader, as in *Med. Soc.*, II, 170, 324; III, 197, 215, 217–218, were all comparatively young women and should be compared with the writers of the letters analyzed in this subsection. They were not resigned to their fate, but spoke up.

[234]Jews described as rich in a polemical poem: *Med. Soc.*, II, 374.

[235]For statistics about poverty see n. 132, above.

[236]A man who reports that his wife and children had died *qad mātū*, of hunger (probably meaning: were starving?), because he had to go into hiding for evading the poll tax and that he had to leave for Alexandria immediately, where he was promised work, adds this postscript: "Your servant stands here seeking the mercy of his master; with the help of Heaven I shall no longer be here the coming Saturday."

[237]Heb. *baʿal ha-bayit*, "master of the house," as opposed to the poor, corresponds to Ar. *mastūr* (see n. 137, above).

[238]Wayyiqra Rabba 34:8, ed. Margulies (see n. 17, above), p. 791, with a reference to the Book of Ruth 2:19, where Ruth's benefactor Boaz is described as the man *for* (text: *with*) whom she had worked.

[239]The word *ṣedāqā*, lit., "righteousness," was understood as "charity" in rabbinic Judaism.

[240]Wayyiqra Rabba 34:9, ed. Margulies (see n. 17, above), pp. 791–792.

[241]*Med. Soc.*, II, 142–143.

[242]Maimonides, *Commentary on the Mishna*, Introduction to Sanhedrin, ch. 10:1, ed. J. Qāfiḥ (Jerusalem, 1964), IV, 197 and 207.

[243]Midrash Tanḥuma Yelamdenu, Mishpaṭim 9; a pun on Psalms 61:8. In the mid-1930s when the religious kibbutz (communal settlements) movement came into being in Israel, I was told by one of its founders, Moses Unna, that his father, Dr. Isaac Unna, formerly rabbi in Karlsruhe, Germany, had some misgivings: how can the individual obligation of charity be fulfilled when everything is in common and the members do not possess private property with which to help others?

Illness

[244]Maimonides, *Code*, Book of Knowledge 2:4.

[245]See *Med. Soc.*, IV, 226–253. For sexual mores see pp. 307 ff., below.

[246]See *Med. Soc.*, IV, 229–230. In my youth, when I read Maimonides' chapter I was confident that he but copied Greek science, for I could not imagine Maimonides doing Swedish gymnastics before breakfast like myself. Here, as so often, the Geniza provides the actual background for the writings of medieval authors. By the way, in the Israeli kibbutzim, breakfast is served after an hour and a half or so of hard work.

[247]See pp. 12–13 and nn. 13–15.

[248]In TS 10 J 30, f. 9, the recipient is admonished to come out to the countryside, *ukhruj*, for a full month to find relief, *faraj*, from his stress, *ḍīqa*, and to bring also his boys with him who would have it better in the country than in the Bible school (cf. *Med. Soc.*, II, 182, n. 29). Physician: TS 10 J 16, f. 16, margin: *ukhruj itfarraj* (early thirteenth century).

[249]DK 75, ed. Schirmann, *New Hebrew Poems from the Genizah*, pp. 381–382, trans. here with omissions. For Qalyūb see *EI*^{2}, IV, 514, and our Index.

[250]In his famous *Guide to Good Health*, written in 1198 for an Ayyubid prince, who suffered from depression, Maimonides recommends walks in pleasant surroundings as conducive to recuperations (cf. *EJ*, IX, 779). Our poem here was written about twenty years earlier, but that "scientific" medical advice was commonplace.

[251]This should not be taken as a list of fruit trees found in the orchards of Qalyūb around 1180. The writer was constrained by meter and rhyme as well as by his endeavor to use in poetry as far as possible only Hebrew words occurring in the Bible.

[252]For example, cows or sheep, but not wild animals, which the Bible regards as impure.

[253]The wine is mentioned here because one drank wine at outings to groves and gardens.

[254]I should not be surprised if it will be found out that this Hebrew poem is an adaptation of an encomium in Arabic in praise of Qalyūb.

[255]Cf. the story of the Alexandrian merchant who apologizes for the extreme shortness of his urgent letter by saying: "It is Friday and I have already had my bath," Bodl. MS Heb. d 66 (Cat. 2878), f. 52*v*, ll. 2–3; Goitein, *Letters*, p. 51.

[256]Smoke from bathhouses: noted by the physician Ibn Riḍwān (998–1061), a native of Fustat (see Wiet, *Cairo*, p. 37), who complains about the excessive amount of smoke emanating from the bathhouses. When we call a steam bath a Turkish bath, we must remember that it, like many other achievements, was a creation of antiquity which has come to the West through the mediation of the medieval civilization of the Near East.

[257]*Ḥammām al-Kaʿkī*: TS 13 J 19, f. 30, address; Kaʿkī is to be understood here as a family name. Casanova, *Reconstruction*, pp. 303–304. Bath of the Cock: TS 12.298, top. (The judge Nathan ha-Kohen b. Solomon, *Med. Soc.*, II, 513, sec. 17, is asked to hand over a small sum to a person described as "the one who had served the notable Ben Dōsā and who had lived in the Bath of the Cock.") The Bath of

the Mice, repeatedly mentioned in the Geniza (see *ibid.*, I, 293 n. 74; II, 227 n. 45) and also by the Muslim antiquarians, derived its unsavory name probably from some unpleasant experience. See also n. 269, below. For Cairo see A. Raymond, "La localisation des bains publics au Caire au quinzième siècle d'après les Khiṭaṭ de Maqrīzī," *BEOIF Damas*, 30 (1978), 347–360 (with maps on pp. 359 and 360).

[258]See Krauss, *Talmudische Archäologie*, I, 217–233, 674–686.

[259]*Ibid.*, pp. 227–228. As a boy of twelve or so I studied Talmud with a lonely young man who was a chain smoker. Once I asked him whether he could not stop it while we were studying. "No, this is absolutely impossible." "So, what do you do on Sabbath" [when smoking is forbidden]? "Yes, this is a great tribulation. When I cannot stand it any longer, I go out into the street and walk behind a person with a cigar or a cigarette in his mouth. Thus I can at least inhale the smoke."

[260]I remember having seen somewhere *ḥammām al-yahūdī*, but this could simply designate a bathhouse owned by a Jew. The Muslim legal texts seem to assume that Muslims and members of the minority religions used the same facilities, wherefore the latter bore distinguishing marks showing them as such even while in the water.

[261]ENA 2805, f. 16B, l. 10. "Swooned": Ar. *subita.*

[262]TS 12.373, ll. 4–5. The sender is Mardūk b. Mūsā, but the letter was written by Mūsā b. Abi ʾl-Ḥayy. Mardūk was probably still too weak to write the long letter himself (end of eleventh century).

[263]E.g., TS 13 J 23, f. 3, *Nahray* 71 (expressing the hope that the recovery should be enduring; eleventh century). TS 12.654*v*, l. 16 (after lengthy description of illness, diarrhea, and sore eyes, and many other matters, a postscript written four days after the original letter: "Do not worry, I shall presently enter the bathhouse"; thirteenth century), TS 8 J 21, f. 33, ll.12–13 (Heb., fourteenth century or later).

[264]Intercession: TS 10 J 14, f. 20. A husband abroad promising his wife that he is not forgetful of her: *Med. Soc.*, III, 193 n. 157. A dejected divorcée: DK XIII, l. 10, see *ibid.*, p. 275 n. 150.

[265]Excommunicated person: ENA 4009, f. 11, l. 8, ed. S. D. Goitein, "The Communal Activities of Elḥanan b. Shemarya" (Heb.), in *Joshua Finkel Volume* (New York, 1974), p. 135, sec. 14; see *Med. Soc.*, II, 571, and Cohen, Mark R., *Self-government*, p. 198 n. 67, bottom.

[266]Bathrobe: *minshafa.* Utensil with compartments: *majmaʿ*. The boxes put one into the other: *ḥuqqa.* Shallow drinking bowl: *ṭāsa* (e.g., TS 10 J 12, f. 10*v*, l. 15: *ṭāsa nuḥās lil-ḥammām*). Entrance fee: a dirhem, *Med. Soc.*, III, 186.

[267]New Moon day: DK XIII, l. 10, see n. 264, above. For the celebration of the New Moon by women see *EJ*, XII, 1039.

[268]See, esp., *Ḥammām* in EI^2, III, 139–146, and H. Grotzfeld, *Das Bad im arabisch-islamischen Mittelalter* (Wiesbaden, 1970).

[269]Ar. *ḥammām al-māliḥa*, namely, *al-amyāh*, "the waters." The antiquarian Ibn Duqmāq, IV, 23, l. 19, calls it *al-māliḥ*, certainly a later abbreviation. Casanova, *Reconstruction*, seems not to note it.

[270]The list, or rather a draft of it, is written on the back of two letters, DK 18 and TS 12.374, sent from Jerusalem to Fustat, ed. Goitein, *Palestinian Jewry*, pp. 205–218. The passage translated is found on p. 218, ll. 5–8. The list is enigmatic because most of the sums, millions of dinars, are entirely fantastic, but realistic sums and other details are also mentioned.

[271]For the burying of coins in general see *Med. Soc.*, I, 265.

[272]Ar. *furnāq*, derived from Latin *fornax*, like English furnace; Dozy, *Supplément*, II, 262*b*, has *furnaj* (with short *a*, Spain, sixteenth century).

[273]Bodl. MS Heb. b 3, f. 32 (Cat. 2806, no. 30), ll. 8–21. "The middle room": *bayt al-wasaṭ*; stucco work: *tajṣīṣ*. Toilet: *mustaḥamm*; although this word, as its literal English translation, means "bathroom," it has, as in English, the meaning of "toilet"; see TS NS J 4, l. 11, where a prisoner asks to be admitted to the mustaḥamm, since he feels an urge to move his bowels (cf. *Med. Soc.*, IV, 69 and n. 116). "To conduct the heat": *lindifāq al-sukhn fī ḥawḍih.*

[274]Gottheil-Worrell XXVII, p. 121, l. 30. The recipient of the letter is assured that his relative had found a comfortable dwelling "in the vicinity of the bathhouse" (in Jerusalem).

[275]See nn. 264–267, above.

[276]Tosefta, Berakhot 2:23; cf. Saul Lieberman, *Tosefta Kifshutah* (New York, 1955), I, 26.

[277]BT Shabbat 129*b*. TS 8 J 20, f. 1, ed. Mann, II, 160–170. The manuscript has *hqznw*, "I had bloodletting" (as Dr. Davidson 'suggested,' see *ibid.*, p. 170 and n. 4). "Modern ills": *The New York Times*, Science Times, April 27, 1982, front page.

[278]*Med. Soc.*, IV, 255 and nn. 8–9.

[279]Food products: "The cheese [sent from Hebron to Jerusalem as a present] was prepared in my house with utmost attention to [ritual] purity and [physical] cleanliness, *fī ghāyat al-ṭahāra wal-naẓāfa*, TS 10 J 11, f. 12, ll. 13–14. Living quarters: *Med. Soc.*, IV, 91 n. 42. Housewife: *ibid.*, III, 166 and n. 36.

[280]*Med. Soc.*, IV, 139 and n. 1.

[281]*Ibid.*, pp. 225–226 and nn. 550–554. Day of Atonement: Mishna Yōmā 8:1.

[282]Tooth powder: Bodl. MS Heb. e 98 (no Cat.), f. 63, l. 9 (1139). (In my youth one still used powder, not paste.)

[283]TS 12.428. This Sicilian, writing one hundred and forty years after the conquest of the island by the Normans, has full command of (Middle) Arabic.

[284]Ibn Riḍwān: see Wiet, *Cairo*, p. 39, and above, n. 256.

[285]Wind catcher: see *Med. Soc.*, IV, 65 and 365 and n. 97. No complaints about colds caught there (see *ibid.*) have been found by me in the Geniza. Ibn Jumayᶜ: *Med. Soc.*, II, 577 n. 36. See David A. King, "Architecture and Astronomy: The Ventilators of Medieval Cairo and Their Secrets," *JAOS*, 104 (1984), 97–133, illustrated. Deals with the relationship of the direction of the "wind catcher" and the direction of prayer to the Kaᶜba of Mecca.

[286]ENA 2805, f. 6, ll. 8–12: "After my arrival [in Alexandria] I remained with the flax in the Khalīj canal for three days, unable to transport it to town because of the heavy rain, the slipperiness, and the mud. The pack animals could not move until the fourth day. I then transported the flax on sliding planks, *jurar*, and stored it somewhere along the road, but, because of the slipperiness, was not able to get it to the warehouses of the merchants." (This interesting letter, with others from ENA 2805, is in preparation for publication by A. L. Udovitch.)

[287]TS 8 J 27, f. 9.

[288]TS 13 J 20, f. 3, l. 14, ed. Mann, II, 303, ll. 13–14.

[289]TS Arabic Box 54, f. 48.

[290]TS 10 J 10 f. 3.

[291]TS 13 J 36, f. 11*v*, ll. 7 and 14. Frost: *saqīᶜ* (s = ṣ).

[292]Bodl. MS Heb. b 3 (Cat. 2806, no. 16), f. 17, *Nahray* 87.

[293]See n. 225, above.

[294]ENA 4100, f. 12, l. 24. Verse: Ezra 10:13 (the quotation is not literal).

[295]TS 13 J 21, f. 3, l. 20. See *Med. Soc.*, II, 188 n. 18, and n. 217, above.

[296]TS 8 J 21, f. 20.

[297]TS 12.57. Beautifully written by Ḥalfōn b. Manasse.

[298]From Egypt to Jerusalem: ENA 2805, f. 9, l. 5 (a man from Libya), and often; Tyre, Lebanon, to Jerusalem: Mosseri L-39 (writing on Passover: for four months connection interrupted); from Damascus to Baalbek, Syria: TS Box J 2, f. 74, ed. Mann, II, 323. (Despite the snow that impeded the writer, another traveler succeeded in making the trip.)

[299]TS 8 J 18, f. 20, ed. Joseph Eliash, *Sefunot*, 2 (1958), 22. The faultily read and partly omitted words at the end of l. 2 are: *fa-rassam ᶜalayy rajul.* The writer carried with him goods belonging to Abū Naṣr, probably the famous Tustari, of Cairo, for which he had no sufficient authority. A delegate of the qadi was to accompany him so that he might not sell part of the goods on his way, for instance in Ascalon. Fifteen days were plenty of time for a letter going to Cairo and coming back with Abū Naṣr's instructions to the qadi. The writer mentions also that he did not feel

well on that day. For the legal term *rassam*, see *Med. Soc.*, II, 372 (*tarsīm*) and 609 n. 46.

[300]TS 12.654*v*, ll. 2–3, see nn. 304–307, below.

[301]Heard from travelers: e.g., TS 10 J 17, f. 17. Assumption that addressee was ill: TS 13 J 18, f. 4, l. 3.

[302]"When I parted from you on Sunday I was gravely ill to a degree only God knows but I set out for Qūṣ [Upper Egypt] and arrived there after fourteen days in good health and safety," TS AS 149, f. 3, *India Book* 370. Another India trader was not as lucky. His illness in Qūṣ forced him to give up his voyage and to return to Fustat, TS 20.37, ll. 34–37, *India Book* 91. Ḥalfōn b. Nethanel complains that during two years of travel in Spain and North Africa he was constantly ill, ENA NS 18, f. 30, *India Book* 359, and other letters of his.

[303]TS 10 J 24, f. 4, ll. 7–16, *India Book* 121, ed. Goitein, *Tarbiz*, 24 (1955), 44, a letter addressed to Ḥalfōn b. Nethanel.

[304]Accompanied by nn. 84–93, esp. n. 86, above.

[305]Doctor, Ar. *ḥakīm*, both meaning "learned."

[306]The Sabbath on which the lection beginning with the word "Judges" (Deuteronomy 16:18) is read.

[307]TS 12.654, l. 12–*verso*, l. 4, much torn and effaced, beginning and end missing. The letter was sent from Fustat to the nāsī Solomon b. Yishay (Jesse), sojourning temporarily in Bilbays.

[308]Lane-Poole, *History of Egypt*, pp. 161–162.

[309]They seem to have believed that a sick person needed more nourishment, especially bread, than a healthy one, see *Med. Soc.*, IV, 233 n. 55. For *wayba* see p. 543 n. 58, below and *Med. Soc.*, I, 361, sec. 10.

[310]TS 12.693, ll. 6–16. There follow twenty-eight lines dealing with business and legal affairs. The forced contribution is called here *muṣādara*, lit., "confiscation." In 1219, when the Crusaders laid siege to Damietta, a similar war imposition in Alexandria bore the more oblique name *tabarruᶜ*, voluntary donation (TS 16.286*v*, l. 4). For this letter see the text accompanied by n. 46, above.

[311]TS NS J 260. "I did not work," Ar. *mā taṣarraft.*

[312]TS 13 J 18, f. 27, ll. 19–20. Although fairly prosperous the writer also complains about the losses incurred.

[313]*Med. Soc.*, II, 384, top.

[314]TS 13 J 15, f. 20, ll. 6–7, and TS 13 J 19, f. 23, l. 12, see Goitein, *Tarbiz*, 24 (1955), 28 n. 23.

[315]TS 18 J 4, f. 10.

[316]Bread crumbs, Ar. *labāba* (or *lubāba*), Dozy, *Supplément* II, 509*b*.

[317]I hiccupped, Ar. *tafāhaqt*; a hiccup, *fihāq*: not yet seen by me elsewhere with this precise meaning. The assumption, already known to ancient Greek medicine, that hiccups might be an indication of approaching death ("he who hiccups dies") is found in Bodl. MS Heb. b 11 (Cat. 2874), f. 7, a letter on the capture of Jerusalem by the Crusaders, written in 1100, see S. D. Goitein, "Contemporary Letters on the Capture of Jerusalem by the Crusaders," *JJS*, 3 (1952), 170 n. 2; for the letter itself (where this detail is omitted) see pp. 374–379.

[318]"Greek cheeses, such as Halumi [Ar. *ḥālūm*, see *Med. Soc.*, I, 429 n. 66] . . . which are hard and salty, are delicious when cut into cubes, grilled or fried, and served with a squeeze of lemon juice," Roden, *Middle Eastern Food*, p. 38.

[319]Call of nature: *mā jā'anī ṭabᶜ*, a common expression.

[320]Enema: *fatīla mā aqdir ataḥaqqanhā.*

[321]TS AS 152, f. 4.

[322]The later letter: TS 13 J 25, f. 15*v*, ll. 1–2.

[323]Active in Fustat 1125 through 1150 (*Med. Soc.*, II, 513, sec. 17).

[324]In this world and in the World to Come, cf. Mishna Peah 1:1. Commonly used in a request for a legal opinion, not in regular correspondence.

[325]Attack: Ar. *fawra.*

[326]At the same time: Ar. *fi 'l-ghuḍūn*, for: *fī ghuḍūn dhālika.*

[327]Bodl. MS Heb. d 66 (Cat. 2878), f. 141. Palpitation: *min kathrat al-takarrub yalḥaq-hā ʿalā fuʾād-hā raghīf yasīr*. Meaning mild, but unusual.

[328]Pp. 60 ff.

[329]Bloated: Ar. *tarahhal.*

[330]Blisters: *ḥabb.*

[331]Permanent: *wa-yanqalib ḥabb baqiyyatī.*

[332]Pockmarks: *wa-ṣār ʿalayy ruʾa ʾl-buʾaq wa-mā nafaʿat rūḥī baʿd bi-nafʿa.*

[333]TS 13 J 20, f. 16.

[334]Perhaps caused by the terrible tidings from the Maghreb, reported in the same letter.

[335]Tertiary fever: *bil-muthallatha.*

[336]"Made up my mind": *fa-lawlā mā alḥaq* (or *ulḥiq*) *rūḥī wa-aqūm min al-dukkān.*

[337]Sassoon 713, ll. 19–25 (*India Book* 263). This passage is found near the beginning of this long letter.

[338]DK 278 d, see *Med. Soc.*, I, 299 and n. 37. At the time of the writing of the article cited the manuscript did not yet have a mark.

[339]TS 8 J 15, f. 3, ll. 9 ff. The cantor, who describes himself as "expert" (see *Med. Soc.*, II, 223) and his father as *shōfēṭ* (*ibid.*, p. 315) addressed the Nagid Mevōrākh also in ENA 2736, f. 20, probably written at an earlier period.

[340]TS 10 J 14, f. 11, addressed to Abraham (Barhūn) b. Yaḥyā Fāsī, also an India trader.

[341]See n. 307, above.

[342]TS 13 J 17, f. 8, l. 7. In the preceding line he says: "You know how sick I am after having been a man [strong] as a lion."

[343]Cf. *The Treatise of the Pool*, trans. Paul Fenton (London, 1981), pp. 84, 100–101.

[344]TS 10 J 17, f. 16, l. 6.

[345]TS Misc. Box 25, f. 130, ll. 19–22, *Nahray* 142. The letter was sent from the Mediterranean port city of Tinnīs. The good wishes for Nahray's health do not mean that he was ill. But "to avert the evil," one distances the recipient of the letter from the writer's own misery by sending him good wishes.

[346]TS 8.11, l. 19, and *verso*, l. 8. The *muqaddam* of the provincial town, Malīj, sends good wishes for recovery to Japheth, the son of the notable Abu ʾl-Ḥasan Aaron, who himself had just escaped a dangerous intrigue undertaken against him. The long calligraphic letter, which is replete with biblical quotations about healing (also of the water by Moses [Exodus 15:25] and by Elisha [II Kings 2:19–22]), ends with one line reminding the recipient that, in addition to prayer, works of charity (for instance, done to the poor muqaddam) are conducive to recovery from illness.

[347]Westminster College, Glass 40, ed. Scheiber, *Geniza Studies*, pp. 256–259.

[348]TS 10 J 17, f. 17, a note especially written for that purpose.

[349]Complete recovery: TS 13 J 22, f. 23, ll. 11–12, *tammam allāh ʿafiyatoh.* Relapse: *al-naksa ashadd min al-maraḍ.*

[350]TS 8 J 18, f. 23, l. 5.

[351]Bodl. MS Heb. d 65 (Cat. 2877), f. 17*v*, l. 8. Beginning and address are cut away, but the identity of the sender, ʿAllūsh b. Yeshūʿā, and recipient, Ismaʿīl b. Abraham al-Andalūsī, is established by comparison with *JNUL* 12, where, in ll. 3–17,the same subject matter, as here in ll. 25–26, is treated (eleventh century). See *Med. Soc.*, III, 481 n. 170.

[352]TS 8 J 41, f. 13.

[353]TS Box G 1, f. 52, l. 1, ed. Gershon Weiss, "A Testimony from the Cairo Geniza Documents," *JQR*, 68 (1977), 101. Similar hoaxes led to a question of religious law; hence we learn about the funny story. The document, which is a declaration in Hebrew by the husband, ends in a vow made in Spanish to refrain from wine and a promise, that, it seems, he would not leave his wife alone on Sabbath (meaning that he would fulfill his conjugal obligations, cf. *Med. Soc.*, III, 168). He signs Shem Tov ("Good Name") *al-ḥāmī*, watchman of a quarter, cf. *Med. Soc.*, II, 608 n. 41. I have not seen the manuscript of this document; therefore, I cannot say anything

about its time. But Spanish-speaking Jews might have come to Egypt as early as the twelfth century. The purpose of the declaration was, of course, that the impulsive watchman thirsted for wine and wished to be absolved from his overhasty vow.

[354]ULC 1080 J 27, prayers for Moses, a man connected with the government. (He is wished to gain, or retain, favor with "this sultan [the new one, probably Saladin] and his entourage," ll. 18–19.) The writer led the prayer in the synagogue and inquired, *iftiqād*, about Moses' health "every morning and evening," ll. 13–14. ENA NS 22, f. 9, ll. 17 ff., the cantor, Abu ʾl-Majd, known to us through many documents because he served as secretary to the Nagid Abraham Maimonides for a considerable time, complains to his brother, Abu ʾl-Najm, that he was unable to go down to the synagogue to lead the congregation in the prayer for their sick sister because he himself was not well, *takhallaft ʿan al-nuzūl ila ʾl-duʿāʾ li-ukhtī*. The *duʿāʾ*, or special prayer service, was held without him.

[355]TS 12.92, Israel b. Joseph writes to Abū Sahl Manasse b. David.

[356]TS 10 J 17, f. 16. An allusion to the Talmudic: "He who asks for God's mercy for someone else, while he is in need of the same thing, is answered first," BT Bava Qamma 92*a*. The letter contains mainly official business, see *Med. Soc.*, II, 591 n. 9; *ibid.*, III, 81 and 443 n. 45.

[357]The main part is preserved in ULC Add 3342; the shorter fragment is in TS 8 J 19, f. 8.

[358]TS NS 108, f. 50, ed. Schirmann, *New Hebrew Poems from the Genizah*, pp. 128–129. The poet was Gamliel b. Moses, who is known also otherwise.

[359]TS 13 J 17, f. 2, end, *Nahray* 76. The sender: (Abū Yaʿqūb) Joseph b. Eli Kohen al-Fāsī.

[360]INA 55-D, f. 13, ed. Goitein, *Tarbiz*, 36 (1966), 59–72, see *ibid.*, pp. 64–65. The spiritual leader: R. Nissīm b. Jacob. Written ca. 1061, when Nahray was comparatively young, a man in his forties.

[361]I have some doubts on this point, at least as far as the higher middle class is concerned. Since the Muslims were far richer than the Jews, they had the means to buy more expensive, and hence, more sophisticated medication, and, consequently, possessed the opportunity for a more variegated knowledge of the *materia medica*.

[362]See Michael W. Dols, *The Black Death in the Middle East* (Princeton, 1977), which is far more comprehensive in content than indicated by the title, and later publications by the same specialist in the subject. See also L. Conrad, "Arabic Plague Chronologies and Treatises: Social and Historical Factors in the Formation of a Literary Genre," *Studia Islamica*, 54 (1981), 51–93.

[363]"When those *illnesses* happened in Egypt [in the year 1099/1100], that plague, *wabāʾ*, that pest, *fanāʾ*, that disaster, *balāʾ*," TS 20.113, l. 6, ed. Goitein, "New Sources on the Fate of the Jews during the Crusaders' Conquest of Jerusalem" (Heb.) *Zion*, 17 (1952), 136, Goitein, *Palestinian Jewry*, pp. 241–242. But later, in l. 32, the writer is precise: "[The refugees] arrived at the height of that plague, *wabāʾ*, and quite a number of them died." For the use of *wabāʾ* as the technical term, see TS 13 J 17, f. 6, l. 6, a letter from Damascus, where a merchant from Fustat anxiously inquires about his relatives, *fī ʿām al-wabāʾ*, "in the year of the plague" (ca. 1066), or TS NS J 285, ll. 10–11, *India Book* 291, where it is reported that no travelers from Egypt had arrived in Aden, South Arabia, for two years because of the *wabāʾ* prevailing in that country (ca. 1145).

[364]Great and small plagues: *dever gādōl-qāṭān* (Heb.), Westminster College, Frag. Cairens, 16, col. III, 2–3, a magical text. Perhaps a translation of Arabic *wabāʾ ʿaẓīm*, see p. 114, below.

[365]TS 18 J 2, f. 11, summarized in *Med. Soc.*, II, 44–45.

[366]See n. 283, above.

[367]In the theophany granted to Moses after the catastrophe of the golden calf, God introduced himself as "the merciful and gracious" (Exodus 34:6), hence God is called in the Talmud simply *raḥmānā*, the Merciful.

[368]ULC Or 1081 J 24, ll. 17–20. A letter from Mūsā b. Isaac b. Nissīm al-ʿĀbid ("Devout," a family name) to Ismaʿīl b. Barhūn (middle third of the eleventh century).

[369]Bodl. MS Heb. b 13, (Cat. 2834, no. 33), f. 52. The time and place of the writer are evident from his letter, TS 10 J 6, f. 5, to the judge, Sāsōn b. Meshullām, *Med. Soc.*, II, 514, sec. 24.

[370]TS Arabic Box 54, f. 91, esp. ll. 11–13. The chief justice, R. Hananel (early thirteenth century), is mentioned.

[371]Business sluggish because of "illnesses in town": DK 15*v*, l. 3, a Maghrebi writes from Fustat to Jerusalem. See also Goitein, *Letters*, pp. 240–241. Shamṭūniyya: TS 8 J 40, f. 8, ll. 13–23, see p. 512 n. 94, above.

[372]The date for Mevōrākh's death given in *Med. Soc.*, II, 30 and 527 n. 37, is to be corrected in light of Cohen, Mark R., *Self-government*, p. 147 n. 148.

[373]Designating here the Raʾīs al-Yahūd, the official head of the Jewish community.

[374]Although this idea goes back to a biblical notion (cf. Psalms 49:8: "No one can be ransomed by his brother" before God's judgment), it is likely that the Arabic expression used here is based on the qurʾānic descriptions of the Last Judgment.

[375]The *nāsī* (see nn. 85–87 and 304, above) writes TS NS Box 321, f. 93, ll. 8–14, and *verso*, ll. 3–6. The fragment, TS Arabic Box 54, l. 91, referring to the (a) great plague is dated Kislev 128 of the Era of the Documents (omitting the initial ʾ*t* = 1400 = 1528, less 312 = 1216). The month of Kislev began on November 13, 1216. The other letter from the years 1216/7 is discussed in the next note.

[376]TS 16.305*v*, ll. 23–31. This letter is repeatedly quoted in *Med. Soc.*, e.g., II, 529 n. 61.

[377]TS 8 J 22, f. 6, l. 15. Surūr b. Ḥayyim Ben Sabra, or Sabrī, is addressed by his son-in-law Mubārak b. Isaac. See n. 110, above. The pillage of al-Maḥalla is also mentioned in ULC Or 1080 J 264, sent by the same Mubārak.

[378]Dols, *Black Death* (see n. 362, above), pp. 22–25, and *passim* (see his Index, p. 380).

[379]ULC Or 1080 J 161, ll. 15–17.

[380]Heb. *negef, qeṣef, mashḥīth*, all common biblical phrases.

[381]That is, may the children be spared to replace and represent their parents in the family after the latter's death.

[382]The nightly sky, where, with the exception of the planets, all the stars appear continuously in the same order, aroused the thought and admiration of early man. Up there, God is really the landlord who assigns everyone his proper place. Down here, we can only hope and pray for similar order and peace.

[383]TS Box K 15, f. 105. Attention is drawn to the list of the persons who died during an epidemic in 1126, TS NS Box 320, f. 7, in *Med. Soc.*, II, 140.

[384]See the publications noted in n. 362, and for the great epidemics of the years 1100, 1111/2, 1126, ca. 1145, nn. 363, 372, and 383, above.

[385]Maimonides: see Goitein, *Letters*, p. 207. See also n. 420, below.

[386]BT Sota 49*a*. Cf. the Hebrew version in Bava Bathra 139*a* (top).

[387]This point was made to me by Professor Carmel Schrire-Steiger with regard to tribes outside the monotheistic world.

[388]Even so prominent a court clerk as Japheth b. David did not add the eulogy after his father's name in 1040, since the latter had already been dead for fifteen years, ENA NS 17, f. 21. Marriage: see the lists in *Med. Soc.*, III, 394–416 s.v. "Status." Brothers: *ibid.*, pp. 21 ff.

[389]TS 20.103. The name of the town is not preserved. But the judge, Joseph b. Elazar, is known as stationed in Tinnīs, TS 12.657, Goitein, *Letters*, pp. 173–174 (second half of eleventh century).

[390]TS 13 J 1, f. 14, ed. S. Assaf, *Tarbiz*, 9 (1938), 199.

[391]TS 16.186, see *Med. Soc.*, II, 62 and n. 128.

[392]Richardson, *Old Age among the Ancient Greeks*, pp. 231–236, 277–360, esp. pp. 231–232.

393Schirmann, *Hebrew Poetry in Spain and Provence*, I, 494. Trans. Nina Salaman, *Selected Poems by Jehudah Halevi* (Philadelphia, 1924), p. 10.

394Schirmann, *Hebrew Poetry in Spain and Provence*, I, 589.

395Quoted by Leopold Löw, *Die Lebensalter in der jüdischen Literatur* (Szegedin, 1875), p. 38. Y. Ratzaby ("The Motif of Old Age in the Hebrew Poetry of Spain," *Bar-Ilan University Yearbook*, 16–17 [Ramat Gan, 1979], 193–220, Hebrew and Arabic with English summary) studies twenty poetical devices depicting (mostly the misery of) old age. Many of these devices are also found in Arabic poetry.

396Bodl. MS Heb. c 28 (Cat. 2876), f. 52. See *Med. Soc.*, II, 185 and n. 1.

397ULC Or 1080 J 24, *India Book* 124, quoted concerning other matters in *Tarbiz*, 24 (1955), 147–148. Other letters of Amram b. Isaac are partly treated in *ibid.*, pp. 25, 34, 43, and *Med. Soc.*, III, 61–62.

398TS 13 J 23, f. 15*v*, l. 4. A letter from al-Mahdiyya, Tunisia. In a postscript, the writer explains that, in addition to small children, he had to take care of a very old person.

399TS 12.780, ll. 33–36 (addressed to Nahray b. Nissīm).

400ULC Or 1081 J 8: An old woman says, "As long as I was healthy and my eyesight not impaired, I was not in need of support." Westminster College, Frag. Cairens, 113, ll. 17–18: "With little strength for work," *ḍaʿīfat al-qudra.*

401Heb. *ben gīlī*, "of the same age as myself," but meaning also "of similar rank."

402TS 12.217, ll. 19–25, ed. Mann, II, 146. The letter is addressed to Sahlān, the son of Solomon's "peer."

403ENA 2804, f. 4, postscript l. 4, ed. Mann, II, 165.

404See *Med. Soc.*, I, 264–265; III, 348–349; III, 151 and n. 37. Cf. n. 422, below.

405TS 16.171, ed. Mann, *Texts*, II, 196–198.

406Abraham Maimuni, *Responsa*, pp. 162–164. See pp. 138–139.

407*Med. Soc.*, I, 175–176 and n. 25.

408*Med. Soc.*, IV, 88 and nn. 27–29.

409TS 24.14, written by Ḥalfōn b. Manasse; ed. Gershon Weiss, *Azriel Shochat Jubilee Volume* (Haifa, 1978), pp. 161–173.

410JNUL 4° 577, no. 83, ed. S. D. Goitein, "Court Records from the Cairo Geniza in JNUL" (Heb.) *Kirjath Sepher*, 41 (1966), 272–275.

411TS 13 J 3, f. 2, dated 1142, ed. S. D. Goitein, *Sefunot*, 8 (1964), 113–115.

412*Med. Soc.*, IV, 232–233 and nn. 49–54.

413BM Or 5566 C 10, col. II, l. 2. See facsimile in Braslavsky, *Our Country*, opp. p. 97: "For the one in R. Nathan's house: 4 [dirhems]." Nathan's solicitation in TS NS J 354.

414Mosseri L-224, item 3. The mother's name: Naẓar b. Dā'ūd.

415Mosseri A 16, see *Med. Soc.*, III, 174 and n. 73.

416PT Nedarim 9:1. TS AS 151, f. 2, ll. 9–14. Here "blessed" does not mean "cursed." It means "may he be blessed despite his bad behavior."

417ULC Add 3417 (b). In many cases, the community paid the poll tax for the indigent.

418See *Med. Soc.*, III, 227 and n. 23; 250–260, esp. 259–260.

419Eight years: see *ibid.*, I, 130 and n. 22. Seven years: ENA 2748. Maimonides' sister: *Med. Soc.*, I, 351 and n. 35. Disinheriting: TS 12.466. An elder daughter got all the old man possessed. Written by Ḥalfōn b. Manasse.

420TS 8 J 15, f. 18. Since the death of the boy, the old man had been confined to his bed, cf. n. 385, above.

421TS 10 J 12, f. 14.

422E.g., TS 13 J 3, f. 3, ed. Goitein, *Sefunot*, 8 (1964), 122–125. *Med. Soc.*, III, 151 and n. 37, cf. n. 404, above.

423TS Arabic Box 42, f. 165. The recipient: Sābiq al-Kohen b. Maḥfūẓ. The copyist: "al-ḥāvēr Yaʿqūb, your paternal cousin." The sender: Barakāt al-Jiblī (letters not provided with dots). It is not excluded that this letter was sent from Yemen to Fustat.

[424]Bodl. MS Heb. d 74 (no Cat.), f. 37. The concluding paragraph means that one must always keep a distance between misfortune, such as the infirmity of old age, blindness, and need, reported in the letter, and the person addressed.

[425]John Rylands Library, Manchester, Gaster Collection L 213, ed. S. D. Goitein, with a facsimile, a transcript in Hebrew characters, and a detailed commentary, containing the biographical data for the writer, Ṣedāqā ha-Levi b. Solomon-Salāma b. Saʿīd Ibn Nufayʿ, *Bulletin of the John Rylands Library,* 54 (1971), 94–102. The ends of the lines are eaten away, but can be safely supplemented in view of the traditional style used by Ṣedāqā.

[426]That is, may all misfortunes destined for the father be diverted from him to the son. A common phrase, see p. 518 n. 1, above.

[427]All are common phrases.

[428]One coming from the north "went up" to Cairo because one traveled by boat upstream.

[429]He wishes to have his father's blessings, although he felt that he was not entirely blameless in his filial conduct. See *Med. Soc.*, III, 244–245.

[430]Normally, Jews did not date according to Muslim months. But Ramadan, the Muslim month of fasting, so disrupted their economic and social life that it is often referred to in the Geniza.

[431]TS NS J 134*v*, l. 10: the physician Abū Zikrī addressing his father, judge Elijah.

[432]TS 13 J 23, f. 10, and Bodl. MS Heb. d 75 (no Cat.), f. 19. In both letters, Nahray b. Nissīm is addressed by Amram b. Joseph, a Tunisian living in Alexandria.

[433]Ar. *aḥsan Allāh khātimat-hā.* TS 16.250, margin, ll. 17–19. A letter sent from Palestine to Egypt at the beginning of the Crusader period, ed. in Goitein, *Palestinian Jewry,* p. 293.

[434]Each point in the imaginary description of a satisfactory old age in Geniza times made in the text can be illustrated by Nahray b. Nissīm's correspondence of nearly three hundred items: his business, his material position, the transition from hired premises to real estate acquired; his son Nissīm, born comparatively late but fulfilling his warmest hopes. In 1050, he attended the wedding of his friend and Tunisian compatriot Abraham b. Isaac, the scholar; in 1093, he still corresponded with him; he remained in close contact with other Tunisian emigrants to Egypt, such as Judah b. Moses Ibn Sighmār (*Med. Soc.*, I, 158–159), Mūsā b. Abi ʾl-Ḥayy Khalīla (*ibid.*, II, 445, sec. 27; letters addressed to Nahray: *Nahray* 94–99, 115), or Yeshūʿā b. Ismaʿīl, with whom he had also studied together (Goitein, *Letters*, pp. 168 ff.), and several others. From "Member" of the Jerusalem yeshiva, itself a high honor, he advanced to "Most prominent member," and finally to Rav, designating him as an independent jurisprudent.

[435]See the story of Nahray b. ʿAllān, Goitein, *Letters*, pp. 197–201, esp. n. 23.

[436]TS AS 147, f. 4. Because of the shortness of the fragment, I am reluctant to try to identify its writer.

[437]See n. 392, above.

[438]Mann, *Texts,* I, 118–119.

[439]*Med. Soc.*, II, 14, 522 and n. 32.

[440]Mann, I, 185–187.

[441]The problem of longevity in spiritually creative minds is discussed by Richardson, *Old Age among the Ancient Greeks*, pp. 215–224 (see n. 392, above).

3. Death

[1]Referring to BT Shabbat 152*b*: "Return to God your spirit as you have received it from him; he gave it to you in purity; return it to him in the same state."

[2]An ancient prayer, already formulated in the Talmud, BT Berakhot 60*b* (originally destined for private devotion), and found in official prayer books, including the very first one, of R. Amram (ninth century), also Maimonides, *Code*, Book Two ("Love [of God]"), chap. II. "Prayer," 7:3.

Note: "Who gives back souls to dead bodies" (not: the souls to the dead bodies"), leaving it to God to choose which souls should be "returned." See Messianic Expectations and the World to Come" (pp. 391–415), below.

Although the sages of the Talmud had taught that in the world to come there is no food, drink, or sex (BT Berakhot 17*a*), Moses Maimonides found it difficult to defend the philosophical concept of the incorporeity of the soul; see Joshua Finkel, *Maimonides' Treatise on Resurrection* (New York, 1939), pp. 66–69.

[3]Before bringing up the repellent image of death, the writer assures the recipient three times that he is destined for life.

[4]This is a play on words. Heb. *Joseph* means "may He [God] add."

[5]If I have read and understood the phrase correctly, it may mean: you and I would prefer life to the most beautiful funeral.

[6]TS 16.279, ll. 1–15, Ṣāliḥ b. Bahlūl, Tunisia, writes to Nahray b. Nissīm, Egypt, *Nahray* 196.

[7]"Perfect saint": *ṣaddīq gāmūr* (Heb.), an approximative translation.

[8]"It is a good sign for a man, when he dies on the eve of the Sabbath," BT Ketubbot 103*b*.

[9]The popular view: "May my death be an atonement for all my sins" (Mishna Sanhedrin 6:2). With theological precision: Death expiates in conjunction with the Day of Atonement, repentance (and confession) (Mishna Yoma 8:8). The obligatory character of confession is emphasized in Sanhedrin 6:2. Our writer confesses, so to speak, for the community.

"I was afraid of the punishment of the Creator" simply means "I was afraid I might die," ULC Or 1080 J 22, Goitein, *Letters*, p. 319 and n. 18.

[10]Also *al-amr al-maḥtūm*, PER H 21, l. 2; TS 16.57, ll. 7–8, ed. G. Weiss, "Financial Arrangements for a Widow in a Cairo Geniza Document," *Gratz College Anniversary Volume*, ed. I. D. Passow and S. T. Lachs (Philadelphia, 1971), p. 279; or simply *al-maḥtūm*, TS 10 J 6, f. 4*v*, and often.

[11]Proverbs 9:11 quoted as a wish in TS 24.27*v*, l. 16, cf. p. 528 n. 165, above. "*May life be added for you,*" a common wish at the end of letters. A man from northern Syria writes to his brother: "I learned about the death of my father—[may he] r[est in] E[den]—only from your letter. May God add the years taken from his lifespan to yours," TS 13 J 15, f. 18, ll. 4–5, cf. *Med. Soc.*, IV, 398 n. 61. (From the same letter of his brother he had learned about the latter's marriage and the birth of a son to him.)

[12]BT Sanhedrin 29*a*, quoted as a popular saying.

[13]Especially the common wish, "may the fixed term of your death be forgotten," e.g., TS 12.270*v*, ll. 18–19, and even "may God forget his [your] ajal," TS 16.262 (*India Book* 308). See EI^2, I, 204, s.v. "*Adjal,*" TS 16.339, *Nahray* 17*a*.

[14]With this I qualify what I said in "Dispositions in Contemplation of Death," *PAAJR Jubilee Volume*, 46–47 (New York, 1979–1980), p. 157. I still believe that *ʿindanā* means "I, Maimonides," not "we Jews," for Maimonides goes on to give scientific reasons for the impossibility of a predestined lifespan, reasons that have nothing to do with Judaism; but the gist of his essay is certainly to prove that the idea contradicts the basic teachings of the Torah. See Gotthold Weil, *Maimonides über die Lebensdauer* (Basel and New York, 1953), widely expanded in a valuable Hebrew version by Michael Schwartz, *Teshūvōt ha-Rambam bish'ēlat ha-qēṣ ha-qāṣūv la-ḥayyīm* (Tel Aviv, 1979).

[15]Goitein, *Jemenica*, p. 153, no. 1144. In Sura 2:96, the Christians seem to be included, for 2:111 states: "They say, only Jews and Christians enter Paradise," to which Muhammad retorts: "Then, why are they so eager to remain on this earth?"

[16]See Yaron, *Gifts in Contemplation of Death*, and *EI*, IV, 1225–1226, s.v. "*Waṣīya*" (Joseph Schacht), abbreviated in Schacht, *Islamic Law*, pp. 173–174.

[17]See *Med. Soc.*, I, 204–205, and cf. the Talmudic saying: "God's blessing does not rest on anything weighed, measured, or counted, but only on what is concealed from the eye," BT Taʿanit, 8*b*.

[18]Aaron Skaist ("Inheritance Laws and Their Social Background," *JAOS*, 95 [1975], 242–247), in a review article on a volume of essays on Oriental laws of succession (Ancient Mesopotamian, Egyptian, Islamic, Modern Chinese), emphasizes that the statutory laws of succession in a certain people often do not conform with its social structure and notions.

[19]"Testator." I should have used "legator," since, as explained, there are no "testaments" in Islamic and Jewish laws. But I prefer to use more familiar terms and crave the indulgence of the legalistically minded reader for loose terminology. (A friend reading this section had taken "legator" as meaning "legislator.")

[20]See Yaron, *Gifts in Contemplation of Death,* and *EI*, III, 585–586, s.v. "Mīrāth" (Joseph Schacht).

[21]"Complete will," *ʿan waṣiyya kāmila tāmma*, TS 16.279, l. 7, see n. 6, above, *Nahray* 196. No will: TS 18 J 2, f. 16 (Spring 1026), ed. Assaf, *Yerushalayim* (Jerusalem, 1953), p. 113. Complications: TS 18 J 4, f. 13 (Jan. 1254). Recovered: TS 13 J 36, f. 6, l. 13, a letter from Ramle by Eli I b. Ezekiel I ha-Kohen (ca. 1060).

[22]For the Arabic, Aramaic, and Hebrew terms used in such documents see the six texts edited by me in *Sefunot*, 8 (1964), 111–119, 122–126.

[23]A typical and complete example: TS Misc. Box 24, f. 137, p. 4*v*, in the hand of Mevōrākh b. Nathan (about him see *Med. Soc.*, II, 514, sec. 22).

[24]TS 13 J 3, f. 2, ed. *Sefunot*, 8 (1964), 113–114 (1142).

[25]TS 13 J 2, f. 6*v*. It was a time of *ḥāmās*, oppression (Heb.). Hand of the cantor and court clerk Hillel b. Eli. Cf. Gershon Weiss, "Documents Written by Hillel Ben Eli: A Study in the Diplomatics of the Cairo Geniza Documents" (M.A. thesis, University of Pennsylvania, 1967).

[26]TS 12.631, Yāʾīr (Heb., also called Zuhayr) b. Abraham, Jan. 1113. As explicitly stated (ll. 6–7), this is only that part of the will which dealt with the funeral arrangements and which the person charged with them had asked to be set down in a separate document. TS 12.613 [not a misprint], l. 26, and TS 16.44, l. 35, an old aunt making her declaration—a long one—on Thursday night, April 29, 1126, and dying the following Saturday. See Weiss, "Halfon b. Manasse," II, 100, 103, 123.

[27]ULC Add. 3339 (b). This is a court record reproducing a report of Salmān al-Levi b. Solomon on the deathbed declaration of his brother Barakāt, who had died on the New Moon day of Shevat, January 11, 1217. In the date of the record itself the clerk erroneously omitted a *q* (= 100); it was, of course, Kislev *ʾt⟨q⟩l*, 1530, corresponding to 1218. For stipulations with regard to the remarrying of a widow see *Med. Soc.*, III, 271–277.

[28]Westminster College, Frag. Cairens. 113 and 115.

[29]Mosseri A 11 (Spring 1215), ed. Assaf, *Texts*, p. 172.

[30]TS 16.262, *India Book* 307, a letter addressed to "the Prince of Princes," that is, the Nagid Mevōrākh.

[31]TS 13 J 14, f. 4, *India Book* 259, see *Med. Soc.*, I, 264 and n. 209, and *ibid.*, 263 and n. 205.

[32]ULC Or 1080 J 62 (middle piece of incomplete 13 lines).

[33]TS 18 J 1, f. 15 (Nov. 1104). In *Sefunot*, 8 (1964), 107 n. 3, TS 18 J 1, f. 17, is a misprint for f. 15.

[34]See *Med. Soc.*, III, 232 and n. 54.

[35]TS 16.196*v*, written by Hillel b. Eli immediately beneath the draft (or copy) of a letter of the Nagid Mevōrākh to the community of al-Maḥalla, also written by him (entry in a record book). Eli ha-Kohen b. Yaḥyā: see *Med. Soc.*, II, 78; Isaac b. Samuel: see *ibid.*, II, 512, sec. 13. "Withdraw," *istajarr* (l. 25).

[36]ENA NS 16, f. 11, right upper corner of a document in the hand of Ḥalfōn b. Manasse. The maidservant: Nashū. The niece: Nājiya.

[37]E.g., Bodl. MS Heb. a 2 (Cat. 2805), f. 9, discussed in *Med. Soc.*, II, 399, in connection with the interplay of Islamic and Jewish laws.

[38]ENA 4011, f. 51 (June 1166, under the authority of the "Lion in Scholarship" *arī ha-tōrā*, Nethanel ha-Levi [b. Moses], "the Head of the yeshiva of the Diaspora").

The testator might have made other declarations on that occasion. But the document we have is concerned solely with the matter reported, cf. n. 26, above.

[39]TS 18 J 1, f. 24 (May 1156. The last digit is *z*, not ʾ.) Line 19: *in quḍiya ʿalā wālidih bil-maḥtūm.*

[40]TS 13 J 3, f. 18 (November 1203). *Al-Lebdī* is spelled with one *l*, wherefore in *Med. Soc.*, I, 427 n. 31, I rendered the name as *al-Baddī.* But since then Abu ʾl-Barakāt al-Lebdī was identified by me in several documents as a sugar merchant and producer, which makes the reading *Lebdī* preferable. The elliptic spelling of *ll* as *l* is common.

[41]TS 10 J 6, f. 7. Since this is a draft, the month and the last digit of the year were omitted; 155 corresponds to 1238–1248. The testator: Amram ha-Kohen b. Abu ʾl-Majd Ibn al-Ṣanānīrī, see *Med. Soc.*, I, 421 n. 62.

[42]"Six equal shares," *suds dāʾir*, lit., "the sixth of the [all comprising] circle." A comparison with TS Misc. Box 24, f. 137, p. 4*v*, l. 10, *thulth dāʾir*, taught me the right meaning, see Goitein, *Tarbiz*, 42 (1973), 501, English summary: *ibid.*, pp. xiv–xv, where *sadas* is to be corrected to *suds*.

[43]TS 8.143 (Aug. 3, 1250), ed. Strauss-Ashtor, *Mamluks*, III, 4.

[44]TS AS 146, f. 2, comprising twenty-five lines (June 1244). Elazar ha-Levi Abū Naṣr b. Abu ʾl-Ḥasan appoints Barakāt b. Yeshūʿā, the son of a late government purveyor, *al-mūrid.*

[45]TS 18 J 1, f. 21 (Jan. 1127). Ṣedāqā *ha-meshōrēr* (see *Med. Soc.*, II, 224), "the esteemed young man," son of the late ṣemaḥ, is agent of Abu ʾl-Maʿālī al-Dhahabī Solomon b. Yākhīn in a *qirāḍ biḍāʿa*, see *Med. Soc.*, I, 183, and 446 n. 3. The pharmaceuticals: *ʿanzarūt*, Sarcocolla, used as an eye-powder, a purgative, and also for other purposes (Maimonides-Meyerhof, p. 6, no. 4), and an important article in overseas trade, cf. TS 8 J 8, f. 9, devoted in its entirety to this commodity; *ʿunnāb*, jujube (Maimonides-Meyerhof, no. 291). These products were mostly imported from Syria, see *Med. Soc.*, I, 213, and for *ʿanzarūt*, DK XV, ll. 16–21. The carefully executed document is without signatures; it was a copy given to a party for information, not for use in a court action.

[46]TS 8 J 21, f. 4, and TS 8 J 8, f. 12 (in this sequence), copy in the hand of Hillel b. Eli, of a last will, made in June 1085. Something (one or a few lines) is lost between the two fragments, and the end is not preserved.

[47]TS 18 J 1, f. 10 (July 1072), ed. N. Golb, "Legal Documents from the Cairo Genizah," *JSS*, 20 (1958), 41–44. For the scarcity of cash see *Med. Soc.*, I, 200.

[48]See *Med. Soc.*, III, 259 and n. 56.

[49]Cf. *ibid.*, p. 42.

[50]This passage is translated and discussed in *Med. Soc.*, I, 180, where "the cows" is to be inserted before "the sheep."

[51]"Abū Naṣr is my firstborn son, my brother has taken responsibility for him," that is, he will make the proper arrangements that Abū Naṣr will get his additional share.

[52]The signed, final document: Bodl. MS Heb. b 13 (Cat. 2834, no. 27) f. 46; the note on the firstborn: *ibid.*, ll. 44–45; draft or copy: TS 20.99, both by Hillel b. Eli (1066–1108).

[53]TS NS J 347 (1219/20), written, it seems, by Solomon b. Elijah. For counting and accountbooks see *Med. Soc.*, I, 204–209.

[54]Cash and kind: *ʿayn wa-ʿarḍ.* When I translated Abraham Maimuni, *Responsa*, p. 165 n. 17, I was not yet familiar with this phrase. I have already corrected that mistake in *Med. Soc.*, I, 458 n. 2.

[55]Minors are not obliged to pay the poll tax according to Muslim law. But the tax collectors took a different view, see *Med. Soc.*, II, 383.

[56]Abraham Maimuni, *Responsa*, pp. 161–167.

[57]See *Med. Soc.*, I, 263–266.

[58]An *irdabb* measured about 24 gallons, see *Med. Soc.*, I, 361. In another will, TS NS Box 320, f. 23, irdabbs of wheat were assigned to charity and another purpose.

Saadya Gaon, according to Yemenite tradition, translated biblical *ēfā* with *wayba* (which is 1/6 of an irdabb), cf. *Tāj* (the Yemenite Pentateuch), reprint (Jerusalem, 1968), II, 5*a*, on Leviticus 5:11, and J. Qāfiḥ, *The Five Scrolls* (Jerusalem, 1962), p. 145, on Ruth 2:17. The wayba referred to there might have been different in size from the Egyptian measure, cf. Hinz, *Masse*, pp. 52–53.

59ENA NS 17, f. 21, Moses b. ʿAdāyā and his wife Laylā b. David.

60TS 8 J 6, f. 14. Abu ʾl-Fakhr ("Famous") al-Jabbān b. Saadya (d.); his partner: Abu ʾl-Faḍl ("Generous") al-Ṣabbāgh (dyer) b. Abu ʾl-Izz al-Jabbān. The house was in the "Sun Lane," seemingly not known otherwise, near the *zarība*, or cattle pen. The daughter: Karam ("Nobility of character"); the wife: Ḥasab ("Noble descent"); the granddaughter: Rashīda ("Following God's ways"). Cattle pens were found also near the houses of the rich.

61TS 10 J 7, f. 10 c, copy of the will of Khulla ("Beloved") b. Shābāt (spelled thus), who had shares in three different houses, but owed small sums to different persons, among them her own slave. Her two sisters and other heirs would take care of these debts. For Nathan b. Samuel see *Med. Soc.*, II, 513; for the restoration of a Bible codex, *ibid.*, p. 239 and n. 52. The reverse of TS 10 J 7, f. 10 c (page d), is dated 1135.

62TS 8 J 34, f. 10 *r* and *v*; ENA 1822, f. 17. Abu ʾl-Ḥusayn Moses, son of the late *ʿaṭṭār* Solomon. The wife Sitt al-Kull ("Mistress over everyone"), daughter of the late elder Amram. A judge present asking questions: TS NS J 94.

63For the "symbolic purchase" see *Med. Soc.*, II, 329–330. Whether the *qinyān*, as this formality is called, was required at a deathbed declaration seems to have been a moot point. TS 8 J 6, f. 14, l. 13 (see n. 60, above), says expressly that the testator was able to make legally valid transaction "at the time of the qinyān." TS 13 J 22, f. 2, ll. 12–13, ed. *Sefunot*, 8 (1964), 111–113, says that because of the Sabbath no qinyān was taken from the testator's husband. It was taken for granted that the testator himself was exempted. See on the entire question Yaron, *Gifts in Contemplation of Death*, pp. 90 ff.

64"I and those who were with me said *the confession of sins*, for we were sure we would be killed," Bodl. MS Heb. a 3 (Cat. 2873), f. 24, l. 18 (Dec., 1236), see pp. 66 ff., above. The full text of this long letter is edited in *Joseph Braslavi Jubilee Volume*, ed. L. Benzion (Jerusalem, 1970), pp. 495–501. For death as atonement see n. 9, above.

65Government (poll tax): Bodl. MS Heb. f. 56 (Cat. 2821, no. 16) f. 45, cf. *Med. Soc.*, I, 253 and n. 138 (1182); TS 13 J 3, f. 2, l. 12 ("the balance of the poll tax, 2 dinars").

66ENA 3795, f. 8 (early twelfth century).

67Cf. TS 16.115, dispositions of a woman with regard to a house, some parts of which she had formerly sold to relatives (1006); see n. 97, below.

68ENA 3795, f. 8*v*, cf. n. 66, and pp. 355 ff.

69See *Med. Soc.*, III, 104 and n. 29.

70*Ibid.*, II, 120. See Gil, *Foundations*, *passim.*

71In the will made in Alexandria, March 1201 (nn. 54–56, above) the two daughters receive 50 dinars each, while the estate left to the infant boy amounted to about 2,500 dinars. The girls were no doubt married; otherwise, funds for a dowry would have been left to them. Cf. the cheesemaker's will of May 1241 (p. 139 and n. 60, above), who left his two thirds share in a house, probably the only substantial property he possessed, to his virgin daughter who had come of age. The son would simply carry on with the father's workshop.

72See, e.g., n. 31, above, and *Med. Soc.*, II, 395–397.

73ENA Laminated 159 (2558), l. 10, *India Book* 288*a*, a will made by Abu ʾl-Barakāt II b. Joseph III al-Lebdī in August 1222. The remark was made when the dying man was reminded that the law assigned a double share to the firstborn.

74See preceding note and nn. 51–52, above, and *Med. Soc.*, II, 398–399.

75I so interpreted it in *Sefunot*, 8 (1964), 108, when I was still unaware of Geniza documents showing that persons from other Mediterranean countries were as much concerned with funeral pomp as those living in Egypt.

Exceptions: TS NS Box 320, f. 23, where a man who makes a number of dispositions for the community (*heqdēsh*) and relatives, says this: "I possess two *talthīmas* [covers]; one should be given to the younger son of my sister, while the other should be sold by auction, and the proceeds be used for what is needed in a case of death. I possess also ten *irdabbs* of wheat; one should be used for charity (distribution to the poor) and one for the consolation ceremonies. The rest should be given to my wife and to the orphan children of my sister [who probably lived in the testator's house]." Ten irdabbs (ca. 150 liters) of wheat amounted to a considerable stock, found only in a well-ordered household.

The *talthīma*, originally a cover for the face, denoted a long shawl; white ones were worn even by qadis (see Dozy, *Supplément*, II, 516*a*). As the term *talthīma fuwaṭ*, a sari-like *t*., shows, it could even reach to the lower parts of the body (ENA 3030, f. 7*v*, ll. 1–2; TS 8 J 4, f. 23 d, l. 7). Sulayman b. Abū Zikrī Kohen sent three talthīmas from Cairo to Aden as a gift to the sons of Maḍmūn b. Ḥasan, representative of merchants in that town (TS 28.20, l. 37, *India Book* 280). This piece of clothing could not have cost more than a few dinars. The testator gave no special thought to how his body would be disposed of.

76BT Bava Bathra 10*a*. In his article, "Sedākā, Charity," *HUCA*, 23 (1950–1951), 411–430, Franz Rosenthal inquires how the biblical term for *justice* assumed in postbiblical Hebrew the meaning *charity*.

77Such as the will of Yeshūʿā b. Samuel (= Ismaʿīl), Alexandria, 1090, see pp. 144 ff., below.

78See p. 138, above. Silver case: In *Eretz-Israel* 7 (1964), 91, l. 5, I supplemented: *tāj fiḍḍa*, "a silver crown," but the right half of the manuscript, found in TS Misc. Box 28, f. 5, has *tīq* (Heb.), "case," see *Tarbiz*, 38 (1969), 397.

79About this extraordinary woman, see *Med. Soc.*, III, 346–352.

80Despite Leviticus 25:46 ("You may keep them in bondage forever"), rabbinical law was by no means unequivocal on this point, cf. *EJ*, 14, 1658–1660, and the bibliography noted there.

81Since the manumission of slaves was regarded as a highly meritorious deed in both Christianity and Islam, the Jews followed suit, although in the Geniza society slavery (mostly the legal status of maidservants and business factotums) did not have the harsh character it had in the surrounding world.

82See Israel Abrahams, *Hebrew Ethical Wills* (Philadelphia, 1926).

83Goitein, *Letters*, pp. 168–176. More about Yeshūʿā: *ibid.*, pp. 119–135.

84About him, see *ibid.*, p. 173, and the Index of that book, p. 355, s.v. "the Rav."

85BT Taʿanit 21*a*, Giṭṭin 14*b*, and parallels.

86Lichen or moss, Ar. *ushna* (not to be confused with *ushnān*), used as leaven and for other purposes, see Maimonides-Meyerhof, p. 10, no. 11.

87Wicker basket, Ar. *marjūna*, see Spiro, *Dictionary of Modern Arabic*, p. 422, cf. TS NS Box 320, f. 52: *marjūna fīhā ḥavāʾij al-safar*, a *m.* containing travel utensils. This translation fits better than *Kürbisflasche* (pumpkin bottle), Wahrmund, *Handwörterbuch*, II, 765, although *marjūn* is the name of a plant, Maimonides-Meyherhof, p. 24 n. 44. Score: *kūraja*, common in Yemen and in the Geniza letters of the India trade, see E. V. Stace, *English-Arabic Vocabulary for the Use of Students of the Colloquial* [of Aden, South Arabia] (London, 1893), p. 149.

88This is Mūsā b. Abi ʾl-Ḥayy, "the Treasure" (of the yeshiva), *segullat* (*ha-yeshiva*), also a Tunisian who had emigrated to Egypt, see p. 540 n. 434, above. His title in Dropsie 394*v*: TS 10 J 16, f. 2, *Nahray* 123; Bodl. MS Heb. d 75 (no Cat.), f. 19—all to be included in the final version of the *India Book.*

89Spelled here without final *h*.

90Several persons prominent in the Geniza correspondence are called Samuel b. Judah. The person probably intended here was Samuel b. Judah, "Pride of the Enlightened," "Support of the Yeshiva," to whom the huge fragment TS 20.171 is addressed, a letter from the head of the Jerusalem yeshiva, which, in 1090, had its seat in Tyre, Lebanon. As far as I am able to judge, the exceptionally beautiful hand in the official missive TS 20.171 is identical with that in the University

Museum, Philadelphia, E 16516, trans. S. D. Goitein, in "Parents and Children: A Geniza Study on the Medieval Jewish Family," *Gratz College Annual*, 4 (1975), 50–55, a letter by a copyist and clerk from Tyre, who happened to be in Damascus and wrote home to his family in the Lebanese port. I have no doubt that he wrote 20.171 in Tyre, a letter showing that our Samuel b. Judah was held in high esteem by the yeshiva.

[91]The *maqṭaʿ* robes were manufactured in Alexandria (see *Med. Soc.*, IV, 180 and n. 222) and sent to Fustat for sale.

[92]If he had recovered, the declaration would have needed additional legal formalities to become valid.

[93]Aug. 29–Sept. 27, 1090.

[94]TS 13 J 34, f. 5*v*.

[95]See *Med. Soc.*, IV, App. A, Group V.

[96]See nn. 101 and 104, below.

[97]TS 16.115, in Hebrew, ed. S. Assaf, *Tarbiz*, 9 (1938), 19–20, 206–208. I translated it in a collection of Geniza papers submitted to the University of California Press in December 1958. I planned to enlarge the collection into a separate volume with the title *Mediterranean People*, see *Med. Soc.*, I, ix and the Preface of this volume. Gil, *Foundations*, re-edited TS 16.115 with a new English translation and a detailed and valuable commentary. (On p. 127, he refers to *Mediterranean People*, which was put at his disposal.) The differences in our translations are mostly matters of style; *natattī* means "I hereby give," not "I gave."

[98]Ar. *al-Masākīn*, stretching between the two synagogues. Various parts of buildings in this lane were converted into pious foundations. Originally, probably a prestigious neighborhood, it deteriorated owing to the exodus from the Fortress of the Candles to the newly founded city of Fustat.

[99]See *Med. Soc.*, IV, 37 and n. 183.

[100]About five words are missing here, which is a pity. See next note.

[101]See n. 85, above. By quoting here this general principle, the woman intended perhaps to emphasize the special purpose (lost to us) for which she donated so large a share of her property to the synagogues.

[102]Positive condition preceding a negative one: a principle of Jewish law, based on Numbers 32:20 ff.

[103]For burial in Jerusalem and the Holy Land in general, see Gil, *Foundations*, pp. 126–127 n. 14, and below.

[104]The complete maxim says: "The sons of sons are sons, the sons of daughters are not" (see *Med. Soc.*, III, 227 and n. 22), which, of course, does not apply here. I suspect that the person from whom our woman learned that saying politely omitted the second part. She took it to mean; my brother's daughter is in her father's place and therefore gets the same share as her uncle.

[105]For Sitt al-Ḥusn b. Saʿāda see *Med. Soc.*, III, 269 and n. 122; p. 274 and n. 146. For the significance of the husband's marriage gift of 50 dinars see *ibid.*, p. 419. Nathan's hospice: see pp. 122, ff., above. Nathan was a poet (*Med. Soc.*, II, 574 n. 36), and Judah ha-Levi praised him in a long poetical epistle (*Diwan*, ed. H. Brody [Berlin, 1894], I, 214–216).

[106]TS 13 J 22, f. 2, ed. Goitein, *Sefunot*, 8 (1964), 111–113.

[107]Members of the family of the Head of the Diaspora, who derived their origin from King David, see *Med. Soc.*, II, 19.

[108]From Ramle, Palestine. In this time of the Crusades, Egypt was flooded with immigrants from Palestine or their descendants.

[109]Heb. *asher yifrosh* or *yifros*, spreading out one's hands for the priestly blessings (Numbers 6:23–27). Every Kohen present in the synagogue may participate in blessing the congregation. This one might have led the Kohens or have been selected to do it daily. If the dot on the right end of the letter *sh* is correct (reading *yifrosh*), the meaning would be "who practices continence." A Jewish husband is permitted to practice continence if his wife agrees. But this reading cannot be accepted until it is confirmed by another case.

[110]The Nagid, or Head of the Egyptian Jews, Samuel b. Hananyah (1140–1159).

[111]*Dhahab*, "Gold," is most probably identical with the three-year-old "maidservant" of this name, who was given by a Jewish widow to her brother in 1145, probably only a few years prior to our document; see *Med. Soc.*, I, 433 n. 28. The deed of gift was written and signed by our Nathan b. Samuel. *Sitt al-Sumr*, the Queen of the brown-skinned. This color was liked in both men and women.

[112]More commonly called Mamṣūṣa, see *Med. Soc.*, IV, 17–19.

[113]Text, *qōdesh*, holy, originally the treasure preserved in the sanctuary.

[114]This declaration was made to emphasize that the other half did not belong to him, when he inherited her estate.

[115]The two Kohens noted last in item A. There was no point in mentioning the deferred installment of the marriage gift, since nothing was to be paid when she died. The matter was mentioned, however, and the conscientious clerk noted it.

[116]Probably the mosque in the street in which the two synagogues were situated, see Gil *Foundations*, p. 123 n. 6.

[117]Shares in houses could pass into the hands of the government by confiscation, inheritance, and even gift.

[118]A Jewish husband is obliged to bear the burial expenses for his wife. Taking care of this herself was another act of piety or considerateness on the part of Sitt al-Ḥusn.

[119]Since the husband is responsible for his wife's property entrusted to him, he must confirm her legal actions. But on Saturday, even a symbolic transaction is not permitted. For the symbolic purchase, see *Med. Soc.*, II, 329.

[120]TS 8 J 12, f. 2. For the general problem of manumission, see *Med. Soc.*, I, 144–147. A list of bills of manumission: *ibid.*, I, 436 n. 97. Add TS NS J 484 (1096), and the formulary TS Box J 3, f. 16, where the slave's children receive the right to attend the Bible school (found also in the bill for the remarkable slavegirl Nujūm, *Med. Soc.*, I, 144).

[121]Bodl. MS Heb. a 2 (Cat. 2805), f. 9, ed. Goitein, *Sefunot*, 8 (1964), 125–126.

[122]Sar Shalom ha-Levi was head of the Egyptian Jews approximately 1176–1195 (between the first and second tenures of Moses Maimonides in this office).

[123]Written above the line, see n. 128, below.

[124]For this populous and mixed district, see *Med. Soc.*, IV, 17–19.

[125]That means that the heirs could not sue her for repayment of these 3 dinars.

[126]Even in regular transactions, it was customary for a merchant charged with selling the goods of an absent business friend to be assisted by another person. The often mentioned (Abu ʾl-) Ṭāhir was the confidant of the rich and the poor.

[127]The copper vessels are not included in the possessions to be sold according to item C, above.

[128]See n. 123, above.

[129]PER H 22, ed. Goitein, *Sefunot*, 8 (1964), 115–119.

[130]TS 13 J 3, f. 3, ed. *ibid.*, pp. 122–125. Some misprints in the edited text are silently corrected here in the translation.

[131]See n. 110, above.

[132]A neighborhood in the vicinity of the Fortress of the Greeks, originally a part of the prestigious Rāya quarter, see *Med. Soc.*, IV, 34 and nn. 166 and 167. "Large house" is a technical term, see *ibid.*, p. 56 and n. 37.

[133]One sees that the judge noted the woman's words, although they were redundant. At the end of the document it is stated that these words were added above the lines.

[134]Since a husband inherits the estate of his wife, the house would belong to him.

[135]*Fūq*, exceedingly (unpleasantly) tall. Women advanced in years would bring up young slavegirls who would serve them later in life, cf. pp. 148 ff., above.

[136]This quantity of wheat for a year was standard for a family. But the husband wanted Sitt al-Ahl to get enough in order to have her parents at her table, see *Med. Soc.*, IV, 235–236 and nn. 71–79.

[137]This word is in Hebrew to indicate that this agreement was made before a Jewish court.

[138]The half-and-half *niṣāfī* usually designated silk and cotton woven together, see

Dozy, *Supplément* II, 680*b*. Even men had first quality silk, *khazz*, in their burial attire. TS Box J 1, f. 31, see *Med. Soc.*, IV, 160 and n. 72. Bier, *farāsh*. The braid, *ḥuzza*, held the corpse in proper position. The 35 or so dinars listed here represented only a fraction of the burial expenses, although they are far above the sums usually spent for this purpose by the middle class. The husband, who was obliged to pay for his wife's burial, would contribute the balance when the time came.

[139]Hārūn is the Arabic form of the name Aaron.

[140]For the seven days of mourning, see p. 174.

[141]Black like ink: TS Arabic Box 51, f. 111, ll. 28–30, after two other, normal cases of death are mentioned. Holiday: INA D–55, f. 4*v*, ll. 4–8. The person concerned was the brother of the cantor and clerk Abu ʾl-Majd, a secretary of Abraham Maimonides for many years.

[142]Bankruptcy: *Med. Soc.*, I, 248 and n. 107.

[143]Scheiber, *Geniza Studies*, Heb. sec., p. 69.

[144]See n. 8, above.

[145]Cf. Brandon, *Judgment of the Dead*, p. 113.

[146]See p. 66 and n. 94, above.

[147]See p. 110 nn. 351–354, above.

[148]TS NS J 419, l. 2: *bukā wa-laṭm*. See n. 263, below.

[149]BT Moʿed Qaṭan 27*b*.

[150]BT Sanhedrin 46*b*.

[151]TS AS 150, f. 6, middle part of a letter. Burial: *madfan*, not common.

[152]TS NS J 419. Poems: *aqāwīl*. Pall: *basāṭ*, cf. Spiro, *Dictionary of Modern Arabic*, II, 56*a*: *basāṭ* (*al-raḥma*). Childless widow: see *Med. Soc.*, III, 310–311. The handwriting is identical with that of TS 13 J 22, f. 29 (see *Med. Soc.*, II, 430 n. 15), where Japheth b. Manasse Ibn al-Qaṭāʾif of Alexandria addresses his brothers Peraḥya (in address) and Ḥalfōn (l. 7, the famous clerk, *ibid.*, p. 231). In TS NS J 419, only the words "Son of Manasse ha-Levi" in the name of the writer are preserved. The family were Levis. Probably here, too, the same brothers were addressed.

[153]Mishna Ketubbot 4:4.

[154]"Bringing flutes for a bride or a dead," Mishna Bava Meṣiʿa 6:1. In addition to arousing attention, music had, of course, many other purposes. "My heart moans like flutes," Jeremiah 48:36. The magical effect of keeping bad spirits away might also have been intended.

[155]Funeral expenses for a poor man amounting to 92½ dirhems or about 2½ dinars: Bodl. MS Heb. f. 103 (no Cat.), f. 40, see p. 162. An approximate total of 2½ + 1½ = 4 dinars also in TS 12.284*v*, where the total was 165 dirhems. This document is a request for a legal opinion, and will be treated by M. A. Friedman together with other such material found in the Geniza. For expenses on *ʿazā* and *thawāb*, condolences and charities, see n. 75, above.

[156]During the seven days of mourning, one sits on the floor and is not supposed to be distracted from the pious duty of mourning by letter writing and similar pastimes. The dead son was a firstborn and, as usual, is named after his grandfather.

[157]Mourning begins after the burial. The previous letter was written immediately after the death, but before the funeral.

[158]The ransoming of captives was one of the most stringent and most heeded injunctions, see *Med. Soc.*, II, 137. The man could be regarded as "captive" because he was a refugee.

[159]Heb. *mēt miṣwā*, a forsaken corpse. Anyone finding him and able to do so was obliged to bury him.

[160]The poor man was buried in whatever clothing he possessed, but fresh underpants, *ṣarāwīl*, were supplied. This detail is rarely mentioned, probably because its price was insignificant. Its actual provision might have been common. The purpose of this custom is self-evident.

[161]What I expressed here with twelve English words is said in Arabic in one: *wa-sābaʿahū* (from *sabʿ*, "seven"), lit., "he sevened him." The cost of the condolence

ceremonies was such an important fact of life that one had to form a special verb for it.

[162]Bodl. MS Heb. c 28 (Cat. 2876), f. 52. The first meal after the burial to be consumed by mourners, must be furnished by others. Here *yuʿazziyūnī* clearly means that the visitors brought food throughout the week.

[163]TS 8 J 5, f. 1, sec. 1. See below, n. 233.

[164]Al-Malik al-Afḍal: *Med. Soc.*, II, 394 and n. 57. Payments to Muslim authorities on the day of the burial: nn. 196–200, below.

[165]TS 12.530, written by Ḥalfōn b. Manasse, see n. 172, below.

[166]A native, or son of a native, of Bône, medieval Būna, an ancient city east of Algiers, Algeria, called today al-ʿAnnāba, under which name it is listed in *EI*^{2}, I, 511. An Ibn al-Būnī, a silk merchant, is mentioned in Egypt a generation later, TS 20.80, ll. 18 and 38, *India Book* 273.

[167]All expressions of grief, including announcements of death, are discouraged on Sabbath.

[168]Meaning, I, the judge.

[169]*Sukkarī*, sugar-maker or merchant, a very common family name, cf. *Med. Soc.*, III, 14.

[170]Abū ʿAlī is the *kunya*, or by-name, of Ḥasan or Ḥusayn. It is most likely that this man was the grandson of Japheth (Hebrew equivalent of Ḥasan or Ḥusayn) b. David b. Shekhanya, a family of cantors, see *Med. Soc.*, II, 94, top; 227 and n. 45.

[171]Flax merchant, Ar. *al-katt⟨ā⟩nāni*, the second *a* being short as in DK XXVIII throughout.

[172]Ibn al-Qaṭāʾif was the family name of the ubiquitous court clerk, Ḥalfōn b. Manasse, see *Med. Soc.*, II, 231 and n. 16. He did not mention himself by his proper name, as then he would have had to write R(abbī) Ḥalfōn, which would have been awkward and presumptuous, since he was the writer (Rabbī means my master).

[173]Simḥā was a gravedigger, see *ibid.*, p. 456, sec. 63. This Hebrew word means Joy, a word befitting his occupation.

[174]Masarra means Joy in Arabic.

[175]Ar. *ithbāt-hum*, which could also mean: to identify them.

[176]Ar. *al-bayt.* For "house," *dār* would have been used at that time.

[177]Courtyard of the place: *ṣaḥn al-makān.* Disrobed, *ʿuryān*, meaning: without outer garment.

[178]The list of objects found sounds more like that of a trousseau than that of the possessions of a man. They were distributed (it seems, before the death of the foreigner) in containers of different descriptions: one filled with copper vessels; one with jewelry, mostly in silver, and female toilet vessels and implements; a third, with tableware; a fourth—the largest, but the words mostly lost—with clothing and bedding; and still another with small carpets, runners, and mattresses. Outside the containers, small quantities of raw flax (seven and two pounds) and spun flax, used clothing, and the like, were found. The whole gives the impression that the man had come from Alexandria not long before he died.

[179]The same sum of 6 dinars for the coffin, trestles (see n. 182, below), and general expenses of the burial in TS 12.636 (frgt. of a will by a woman with limited means, written by Ḥalfōn b. Manasse). Muslim funeral expenses: when the caliph al-Ḥākim succeeded his father, he ordered the bodies of persons crucified at the time of disturbances to be returned to their families and paid for each 10 dinars for shrouds and burial, Maqrīzī, *Khiṭaṭ*, II, 196, ll. 25–26.

[180]Tunic, Ar. *ghilāla*, worn directly on the body.

[181]Scarf, Ar. *radda*, worn around the neck, one of the most frequently mentioned pieces of clothing in the Geniza, but seemingly not noted in the glossaries of classical Arabic. *Med. Soc.*, IV, 197, and *passim.*

[182]Trestles, Ar. *dawāmīs*, mentioned in the same connection below, item C, and in TS 12.636 (see n. 179, above), a word that goes back to Greek *demos*, people. It designated a public bath, a vaulted building, finally a vault, see Dozy, *Supplément*,

I, 460*b*. On the way to the cemetery and in the cemetery itself, the coffin or bier was put on trestles during the prayers and eulogies.

183From here to the end, all sums refer to dirhems; this is self-evident, and confirmed by the first number in item C, 24. Had these been qirāṭs, the scribe would have written 1 dinar, since a dinar was worth 24 qirāṭs.

184Watchman: *man yanṭur*. A watchman is still called *nāṭūr* in Palestine.

185TS Box J 1, f. 31. The total spent on the burial amounted to 6½ dinars, 3½ qirāṭs, and 134½ dirhems, which were worth ca. 3½ dinars, depending on the fluctuations of the exchange rate of dinar:dirhem. This makes approximately 10 dinars; but since a balance of 2½ dirhems is noted, it stands to reason that the amount earmarked for the burial was precisely 10 dinars.

186See *Med. Soc.*, IV, 160 and nn. 71 and 72, and 188–189 and nn. 286–296.

187Goitein, *Jews and Arabs*, pp. 171–172.

188Saadia Gaon (Rosenblatt), chap. VII, secs. 1 and 4.

189BT Ketubbot 111*b*. Mordechai Friedman draws my attention to *Bereshith Rabba*, ed. J. Theodor-Ch. Albeck, p. 1186, where numerous sources expressing the same belief are quoted. Friedman deals with this matter in his book, *Jewish Polygyny in the Middle Ages: New Documents from the Caīro Geniza* (Jerusalem and Tel Aviv, 1986) (Heb.), chap. 9, n. 3.

190See *EI*^{2}, V, 236*b*, s.v. "Ḳiyāmah" (L. Gardet), and Abraham Geiger, *Was hat Mohammed aus dem Judenthume aufgenommen* (Leipzig, 1902), p. 78. (Needless to say such beliefs were not specifically Jewish but were widely accepted in Late Antiquity.)

191Maimonides, *Commentary on the Mishna*, ed. J. Qāfiḥ (Jerusalem, 1964), IV, 197 (Sanhedrin chap. X, Introduction). "Please tailor for me . . .": TS 13 J 3, f. 2. Maimonides, *Treatise on Resurrection*, ed. J. Finkel (New York, 1939), Heb. sec., pp. 7–8; see Robert S. Kirschner, "Maimonides' Fiction of Resurrection," *HUCA*, 52 (1981), 163–193, particularly p. 187, bottom.

192For Jewish burial customs, see Krauss, *Talmudische Archäologie*, II, 60–82, 478–491 (nn. 442–563), a real gold mine for anthropologists and ethnologists, and Lamm, *Death and Mourning*, *passim*. Lieberman, *After Life*, must always be consulted. For Islam, see *EI*^{2}, II, 441–442, s.v. "Djanāza" (A. S. Tritton).

193New coffin: TS 13 J 3, f. 3, called, as usual, *tābūt*; TS 13 J 3, f. 2, called *durj*, lit., "box"; new and not to be reused: TS NS J 284. When Maimonides, *Code*, Book 14, sec. Mourning, 4:4, says: "they may bury him in a coffin made of wood," he is quoting the Talmud, the law, not describing a contemporary custom.

194See n. 182, above.

195See *Med. Soc.*, II, 163 and n. 32. The Palestinian custom of instrumental music during a funeral has also been found only in Alexandria, see p. 289 and nn. 153 and 154, above. In a letter from Alexandria, written in 1200, we read: "No news, except that the vault they intended to erect for funerals behind the synagogue has been built," ENA NS 19, f. 10, ll. 23–24. This vault was obviously built after Maimonides had ruled that a coffin could not be brought into the synagogue itself.

196The sum mentioned here was probably 3½ dirhems as in TS 10 J 7, f. 6. The second numeral here is not clearly visible.

197Cf. Lane-Poole, *History of Egypt*, pp. 173–176. The document translated, TS 10 J 7, f. 6*c*, ll. 6–13, forms part of a bunch of notes made by Mevōrākh b. Nathan and other court clerks.

With this account for funeral expenses for a foreigner may be compared a similar document referring to a man who had lived in a pious foundation belonging to the community, Bodl. MS Heb. f. 103 (no Cat.), f. 40.

	[Dirhems]
Found as belonging to R . . . may God have mercy upon him,	166
Deduct from this, as due to the [rent] collector Hiba	18

	[Dirhems]
To the collectors of the poll tax	10
To the bearers of the bier, the gravediggers, and the building of the tomb	30
A washer	5
Cantors	5
Release	4
To the guards	6 + 1 = 7
For trestles, an ʿAbbadānī *ʿataba* (longish mat), and a runner, and their transport	25
The price of the casket, *durj*	19
	[18 + 105]
[Grand Total	123]
Balance 166 – 123	43.

The man had owed rent in the amount of 18 dirhems. Hiba, the rent collector, is probably identical with Hiba the parnēs in TS Misc. Box 28, f. 184, col. I, l. 26, where he receives two waybas of wheat, see *Med. Soc.*, II, 457, sec. 66. Whether the 10 dirhems "to the collectors of the *jāliya*" were considerations given to officials, or, at least, partial payments of installments due, is difficult to say. The release, *iṭlāq*, from an inheritance tax, where next to nothing was to be inherited, was a formality. Together with payments for a guard accompanying the cortege the total paid to Muslim authorities was 21 out of 105 dirhems, considerably less than the sums noted in the document from 1159 translated in the text.

The ʿAbbadānī mat (see *Med. Soc.*, IV, 126 and 383 n. 123; 128 and nn. 140, 142–148) appears here for the first time as used at a funeral. The runner probably served as the pall.

198 Release, *iṭlāq*. The term occurs again four lines later in connection with the poll tax. Thus here only the inheritance tax could have been meant. In later documents the office of the *mawārīth*, estates, is expressly mentioned. "Release" does not mean, here and later, that the deceased was freed from the inheritance tax, but that the little that was to be paid had been paid.

199 The deceased had receipts for poll tax paid either in Damascus or in Cairo, or both. Poll tax, especially of the poor, was mostly paid in installments. Here, only a small installment was due. See Maimonides, *Responsa*, I, 103, l. 12, where *iṭlāqih ʿan jāliya* means not that death freed from the payment of a poll tax due but, as our text here and the Geniza throughout shows, that a release was granted after the tax due was paid, and for the release itself, in later times, a fee was charged. The messenger of the office received an additional consideration.

200 The policeman or soldier (for *ḥāmī*, see *Med. Soc.*, II, 370, and 608, n. 41) who had to protect the cortege sent instead a *ghulām*, a slave, or a young man employed by him. This "young man" received 5 dirhems, as much as the cantor (the "funeral director," see n. 202, below), and the washer combined. In TS 12.581, an account from Minyat Ziftā contains only two items, "coffin and *rufqa*, the guard accompanying the cortege," if my explanation of the term, not found by me elsewhere in connection with a funeral, is correct.

201 About the role of the *ḥazzān*, see *Med. Soc.*, II, 219–224.

202 TS 12.631, l. 12: *al-ḥazzanīn alladhī yuṭliʿū* (*yukhrijū*, see Dozy, *Supplément*, II, 54) *al-mīṭṭā* (the last word is Hebrew). The Hebrew term: *hōṣāʾat ha-mēt.*

203 Several cantors; see preceding note; TS Box J 1, f. 31, see n. 185, above, and

next note; Bodl. MS Heb. f. 103 (no Cat.), f. 40, where two or more cantors receive 5 dirhems, the same as one washer of the dead.

[204]TS Arabic Box 4, f. 5, p. 4, l. 5. "Rank and renown": *mawḍiʿih wa-jalālatih*, see S. D. Goitein, "A Jewish Business Woman of the Eleventh Century," *JQR, Anniversary Volume,* 75 (1967), p. 232, text, p. 241.

[205]For the separation of genders at funerals in Jewish and Islamic tradition, see the sources noted in n. 192, above. When Muqaddasi, p. 440, l. 19, reports that in Fārs (southwest Iran) the woman walked behind the coffin, he seems to have noted this as exceptional.

[206]The son of the wailing woman, *nāʾiḥa*, receives (for herself and her family) two waybas at a distribution of wheat, TS Misc. Box 28, f. 184*v*, col. I, l. 19, cf. *Med. Soc.*, II, 457, sec. 66. A nāʾiḥa proprietor of a house: *ibid.*, p. 433, sec. 164. The Aramaic word for wailing woman was also used: TS Box K 15, f. 14*v*, col. II, Ibn *al-allāyā.*

[207]See p. 154, above, item I.

[208]ENA 4011, f. 73, l. 16 (Feb. 1100). E. N. Adler, *Catalogue of Hebrew Manuscripts* (London, 1921), facsimile 14.

[209]*Med. Soc.*, IV, 160 and n. 70.

[210]They appear rarely in the relevant documents, cf. p. 157 and n. 152, above: "All Alexandria had come; the spiritual leader—called there *ḥāvēr*, or member of the Jerusalem academy—sent the chief cantor. . . ." Had he himself visited the house of mourning, it certainly would have been mentioned. For the appellations of the rabbis in the Geniza period, see *Med. Soc.*, II, 215–218.

[211]Cf. *Med. Soc.*, I, 48, and III, 171–172.

[212]Ed. H. Schirmann, *Studies of the Research Institute for Hebrew Poetry in Jerusalem,* 6 (1945), 291–296, it seems, one dirge for each of the seven days of mourning. Cf. *Med. Soc.*, II, 574 n. 36, where another, long, dirge of Nathan b. Samuel, found in the Geniza, is referred to.

[213]Ar. *tuʾallif lī fī ẓahr hādhihi ʾl-ruqʿa alfiyya.* It is difficult to see how an alphabetical poem of twenty-two verses could be written on a small piece of paper. They did not, however, always begin a verse on a new line.

[214]Ar. *al-nawba qad akhadhat khādimak.*

[215]TS NS J 236, a piece of paper measuring about 15.5 × 8.5 cm., disfigured by stains and holes.

[216]See n. 212, above, and Krauss, *Talmudische Archäologie*, II, 68.

[217]Heb. *Ibn al-meqōnēn*, a contributor, Gottheil-Worrell XIII, p. 68, l. 26, see *Med. Soc.*, II, 473, sec. 7. The *safdānīm u-meqōnenīm*, eulogizers and lamenters, mentioned in a letter of Eli b. Amram to Joseph b. Samuel ha-Nagid of Spain shortly after his father's demise (ENA 3765, f. 8, Mann, II, 461 = *HUCA*, 3, 286–287) were not professionals but cantors and scholars who fulfilled those tasks.

[218]As shown in the lists translated or discussed here.

[219]As in INA D-55, f. 8 (Jan. 1061), trans. and with commentary by me for a publication on partnerships.

[220]For the holy brotherhoods of the washers of the dead, see the article "Ḥevra Kaddisha," *EJ*, XV, 442–446.

[221]ENA 4010, f. 41, written and signed by Ḥusayn (= Japheth) b. David b. Shekhanyah when his father was still alive. Unfortunately, only the left third or so of the document is preserved, yet the word *ḥizb* occurs in the fragment six times. The leader of one ḥizb of gravediggers was called Wusayd b. ʿUqayb, Little Lion, son of Young Eagle, an appropriate name for a troublemaker (*lammā kathura ʾl-khiṭāb*, ll. 2 and 7).

[222]TS 13 J 4, f. 10, ll. 7–8, ed. Strauss-Ashtor, *Mamluks*, III, 13. Owing to a slip in reading, the document was misunderstood. Instead of *bi-[th]aman nabīdh*, "for the price of wine," *bi[d]afn nabīr* was read, which makes no sense.

[223]For the watchman, see n. 184, above.

[224]TS NS J 284, l. 5. See *Med. Soc.*, IV, 160 and n. 70.

[225]Āmul: see *Med. Soc.*, I, 61 and n. 12, also 63 and nn. 25 and 26. "The city of the tombs of your forefathers": *ibid.*, IV, 41 and n. 204. Cf. also Nehemiah 2:3.

[226]See p. 160, item C, above.

[227]P. 170, item N, below.

[228]Pp. 158 ff. and nn. 163–179.

[229]Cf. Cohen, Mark R., *Self-government*, p. 241, where the Alexandrian branch of the family is noted. Our Abū Yaʿqūb and his grandfather lived in Fustat, and his father Samuel was solicited there for a public appeal, *Med. Soc.*, II, 504, sec. 124. Abū Yaʿqūb's sister, Munā, was married to Jekuthiel b. Moses, representative of merchants in Fustat, and was repudiated by him, under circumstances described, *ibid.*, III, 261 and 266. At least a dozen other Ben Nahums who left us their writings, are addressed or are mentioned in the Geniza, among them one Abu ʾl-Faraj Hiba, whom Abraham b. Sahlān, the leader of the Fustat Iraqi community around 1040, praised in a *qaṣīda* poem (TS 16.6*v*), and one Abū Thābit b. al-Rayyis, who was *muqaddam* of the Jewish community in Damīra, Lower Egypt (TS Arabic Box 41, f. 109). The writer of the letter addressed to Abū Thābit was Abu ʾl-Khayr Ben Nahum, one of the notables listed in TS NS J 403, *Med. Soc.*, II, 477, sec. 18.

[230]TS Misc. Box 28, f. 199, addressed to the grandfather, is translated in Goitein, *Letters*, pp. 108–110 (with omissions). One detail omitted is mentioned in *Med. Soc.*, II, 548 n. 46.

[231]University Museum Philadelphia E 16 510, see S. D. Goitein, "The Geniza Collection of the University Museum of the University of Pennsylvania," *JQR*, 49 (1958), 36–38. Her name: Qurrat al-ʿAyn Sitt al-Milāḥ.

[232]"Fashioned for himself," *ḥaly maṣāgh . . . ṣāghahu lahu*, item J. This could hardly mean "ordered for himself," in which case *istaʿmal* or *ʿamil* would have been used.

[233]TS 8 J 5, f. 1 (four pages). For the convenience of the reader, the text, where appropriate, is arranged in table form. The document was written by Ḥalfōn b. Manasse, who signed last.

[234]Although Fustat was the main seat of the Jewish judiciary, Cairo is mentioned first because Abraham b. Nathan, the first signatory, who had his seat there, had been a member of the Jewish High Court of Palestine and, as such, had precedence, see *Med. Soc.*, II, 512, sec. 14. Abraham b. Shemaʿya, *ibid.*, sec. 12, the second signatory, also belonged to the Palestinian nobility. The outsider, Isaac b. Samuel, the Andalusian, *ibid.*, sec. 13, without a doubt the most important scholar of the three, signed last.

[235]This and the three dates that follow are according to Muslim months.

[236]Shallow bowl, *qihf.*

[237]Text *sarsīm sabāʾik*, which I take as Persian *sar*, high quality; *sīm*, silver. As a term, however, the word is not found in Arabic or Persian dictionaries (as confirmed to me by Professor J. Clinton). The first letter is corrected and might be different. According to Grohmann, *Einführung*, p. 213, *sabīka* (sg. of sabāʾik) itself might designate pure silver.

[238]Molded pieces of silver with gold luster, *fiḍḍat dhahab sabāʾik*, which I take as an abbreviated form of *fiḍḍa* (*jamīʿuhā*) *mujrā bil-dhahab*, Ibn al-Zubayr, *Dhakhāʾir*, p. 256, sec. 389. For *mujrā*, see *Med. Soc.*, IV, 453 n. 70.

[239]Gold for gilding, *dhahab ṭalī*, see Dozy, *Supplément*, II, 58*b*.

[240]Silver dust *d[u,i,a]qq fiḍḍa*.

[241]Heb. *ṣorkhē ha-mēt*, lit., "the needs of the deceased," expressed in the following line in Arabic *nawāʾib al-mutawaffā*.

[242]The exact nature of this transaction escapes me, also to whom the fee, *wājib*, had to be paid (to the government? the banker?). *Jāʾiz*(*a*) usually means consideration, reward, and the like. If the banker got the wājib, it looks as if Abu ʾl-Ḥasan owed 65 dinars, but received only 61¾ dinars. This would be veiled interest, unlikely in the early years of the twelfth century.

[243]The silk weaver, Mūsā b. Musallam, was Jewish; therefore, it had to be said that his note—*wathīqa*—was certified by a non-Jewish notary; of the two following debtors one was a Christian and one a Muslim, probably known as such to the merchant community. The rare name Naḥrīr (meaning skilled) was borne also by Jews, cf. TS 6 J 3, f. 5, where a *tājir*, respectable merchant, Naḥrīr b. Mawhūb, appeared in the rabbinical court of Fustat in the fall of 1127. He might have been

identical with the Naḥrīr mentioned as well known to the addressee in the fragmentary end of a letter, TS NS J 209, l. 3, where persons known from that period are mentioned.

[244]See n. 234, above, and next note.

[245]For *mbsl* read *mghsl*. The name of this signatory, Mevassēr b. Yeshūʿā ("Herald" [of Salvation], son of "Salvation"), has not yet been found by me elsewhere in the Geniza.

[246]*Med. Soc.*, II, 266.

[247]All items enumerated here are listed in items C and E, above. Silver covers of vessels of earthenware or other nonmetallic materials are common in the trousseau lists. Two silver covers are mentioned in the last line of item E.

[248]A house owned by her in common with her sister formed the object of the lawsuit of 1120, mentioned p. 167 and n. 231, above.

[249]The manuscript clearly has *lahu*, "for himself," not *lahā*, "for her." But the meaning is not in doubt: in addition to the ornaments brought in at the marriage, the wife had received from her husband jewelry he had crafted himself.

[250]Sitt al-Ahl: pp. 152 ff., above. Wuḥsha: Goitein, "Jewish Business Woman" (see n. 204, above), 229–230. Wife of Nathan b. Samuel, p. 147, above.

[251]For such cases, see *Med. Soc.*, III, 253, and *passim*.

[252]Almost all notes were from one bank, Abū Sahl and Son. This was a deviation from the main business principle apparent in the Geniza: spreading the risk. In *Med. Soc.*, I, 264 and nn. 212 and 213, I ascribed this to old age, when the supervision of one debtor would be less laborious. Meanwhile, I found that even an Abū Zikrī Kohen, a renowned India trader and representative of merchants in Fustat, did, during one period, all his brisk monetary business with one banker. About the place of gold specie in the Geniza world, see *ibid.*, I, 391 and nn. 25–28.

The small sums listed in item K, a kind of appendix, were not investments or hoardings, but owed from loans or respites granted. One amounted to a quarter dinar!

[253]See *ibid.*, pp. 264–265, where the example of the great of Islamic society is adduced as a possible additional factor.

[254]See *ibid.*, III, 285 and nn. 41–45.

[255]Coppersmith: ENA 1822, f. 46, see *Med. Soc.*, IV, 338–339, App. D, doc. VIII; *sharābī*: TS NS J 27, see *ibid.*, II, 264 and n. 22; physician: ULC 1080 J 142 and TS Misc. Box 25, f. 53, see *ibid.*, IV, 335–338, App. D, doc. VII; tax farmer: TS Box K 15, f. 91, see *ibid.*, II, 362 and n. 47. For the sources cited here, consult the Index of Geniza texts.

[256]Closing accounts: *Med. Soc.*, I, 208 and n. 81.

[257]See Goitein, *Letters*, p. 207.

[258]BT Moʿed Qaṭan 27*b*, quoted in the Geniza letter, translated here, see n. 280, below.

[259]BT, *ibid.*, alluded to in the same letter.

[260]TS 13 J 22, f. 24, ed. Goitein, *Palestinian Jewry*, pp. 321–326, written by him in 1196, when he sojourned in Jerusalem at the time the sultan al-Malik al-ʿAzīz, whom he served, laid siege to Damascus. His father's letter: Bodl. MS Heb. d 66 (Cat. 2878), f. 57, ed. *ibid.*, pp. 327–332. We have other letters in Abū Zikrī's hand, which are, however, mostly from a later period and not connected with the relations of the family with the court of al-Malik al-ʿAzīz. Cf. A. L. Motzkin, "A Thirteenth-Century Jewish Physician in Jerusalem," *Muslim World*, 60 (1970), 344–349. The article was written when only a part of the relevant correspondence had been identified; consequently, some statements there need qualification.

[261]See *Med. Soc.*, II, 254 and n. 64.

[262]TS 24.72, ed., trans. (Heb.), and discussed in Goitein, *Palestinian Jewry*, pp. 260–263, 268–275.

[263]Loincloth, lit., "[waist]band." Ar. *ḥuzza*, *Med. Soc.*, IV, 340 and n. 253. The turban consists of a thin and precious cloth wound around a cap and fastened tightly. One could remove the fastened cloth and leave the cap on the head. Abū Zikrī untied the cloth so that part of it fell on the ground. In TS 8.213*v*, a fragment

of a calligraphic letter in which the receipt of bad tidings was confirmed, described the immediate reaction to them thus: "We wept bitterly, struck hand against hand, took the turbans down, and sat on the earth, groaning and full of grief." The turban is a person's status symbol and pride (comparable to the crown of a ruler). Disaster (a visitation by God) must be accepted with humility. Abū Zikrī's behavior was intended to express the degree of his commotion.

[264]This Mufaḍḍal is possibly identical with the supporter of the Nagid Abraham Maimonides during the reign of al-Malik al-ʿĀdil (1198–1218), the uncle and successor of al-ʿAzīz, see Goitein, "New Documents from the Cairo Geniza," in *Homenjae a Millās-Vallicrosa* (Barcelona, 1954), p. 710.

[265]The father knew all the persons mentioned, of course. That even Muslim women came to extend their sympathies demonstrates what impression Abū Zikrī's mourning for his brother had made on the circle around the court (Shams al-Dīn, "The sun of the religion," is a Muslim name), but Alkyn if to be read as Alcuin, might indicate that he was a Christian converted to Islam (tentative suggestion by D. H. Baneth).

[266]Fakhr al-Dīn Taṭar (spelled *ṭaṭṭar*), alias Iyāz (or Ayāz) Jahārkes, the commander of the Ṣalāḥiyya division and Sultan ʿAzīz's right hand, see Ibn al-Athīr, *Taʾrīkh*, ed. C. J. Tornberg (Leiden, 1851 ff.), XII, 92, l. 3. I assume he was once treated by Abū Zikrī (or, rather, by his father).

[267]In *Palestinian Jewry*, p. 268, l. 11, I took *kbr* as *kabbar*, "said Allah is Great," meaning "how terrible." I prefer now to read *khabbar*, "spread the news," but am not sure that this is a change for the better.

[268]A Mamluk officer, who was formerly the Sultan's slave, hence bynamed al-ʿAzīzī, and who now served as his personal attendant.

[269]As a court physician, Abū Zikrī lived in a Muslim neighborhood, wherefore the tidings of his misfortune had not yet reached the Jewish community, with the exception of Mufaḍḍal, who, if my identification is correct (see n. 264, above), was himself connected with the court. Later, Jews sat with him day and night and also intended to bring him food, as customary. The week of mourning begins the moment one receives the information about the death of a close relative, who had passed away sometime before.

[270]D. H. Baneth suggested that the relapse of the ophthalmia (Ar. *ramad*) was perhaps attributed to the ashes (ramād) smeared on the face. But Abū Zikrī speaks of a second relapse when another case of death occurred, see n. 278, below.

[271]*Muʿallim* means here probably a young physician who had not received government permission to practice independently, see *Med. Soc.*, II, 246.

[272]See n. 265, above.

[273]Abū Zikrī explains that he wished to stay the entire week of mourning at home, as required by Jewish law, but official duties interfered. The Yemenite mentioned here was the son of a learned Yemenite whose acquaintance Abū Zikrī had made while in Jerusalem, accompanying the Sultan in 1196, see *Palestinian Jewry*, p. 325 and here, n. 260, above.

[274]In this paragraph, Abū Zikrī thanks his father for having prepared him for the terrible news by repeated allusions in previous letters. Without these he would have been unable to write a reply.

[275]He seems to have in mind Isaiah 66:13: "As a mother comforts her child, so I shall comfort you." In the next sentence the quotation from Job 1:21 is also in Arabic.

[276]Akko, where the brother died, was regarded as not belonging to the Holy Land, wherefore he willed to be buried in Haifa, which is only a few hours' walk away and was believed to be part of the Promised Land. Abū Zikrī regrets that he was not buried in Jerusalem.

[277]A person separated from his family feels like an orphan. For this phrase, see *Med. Soc.*, III, 302 and n. 115.

[278]This seems to imply that he wept again much, which led to a relapse of his sore eyes. For another explanation, see n. 270, above.

[279]At the time of the writing of the letter (1196) sent by Abū Zikrī's father to him,

see n. 260, above, the family lived in Jerusalem. The Holy City, we remember, had been conquered by Saladin in 1187. The Crusaders left, and Muslims and Jews repopulated the city. Abū Zikrī's family was among them, but, for reasons unknown to us, was forced to leave. Since life in Jerusalem was difficult, holding out there was regarded as religiously meritorious. But the end of this paragraph is characteristic: the sanctity of Jerusalem is paramount, but being united with one's family, wherever that might be, takes precedence.

[280]Another version of the sayings quoted above, nn. 258 and 259.

[281]Labored breath, *ḍīq al-nafas*, also in the report about the Almohad massacres in Morocco, cf. p. 107, above. In *Palestinian Jewry*, p. 274, l. 42, I wrongly read *nafs* instead of *nafas*, and translated accordingly.

[282]Four months and twelve days had passed since the death of the brother.

[283]Another brother of Abū Zikrī was at the time of the writing of this letter still a boy in the early years of his schooling, see *ibid.*, p. 331.

[284]I do not find the name al-Amjad among the eighteen sons of Saladin listed in E. de Zambour, *Manuel de généalogie et de chronologie pour l'histoire de l'Islam* (Hanover, 1927), p. 100. But the name is found in the Ayyubid family. This Amjad probably died as a youth before he could reach historical significance, and therefore was not listed by the Muslim historians.

[285]For the father's letter, see nn. 260 and 279, above.

[286]*Diwan of Shemuel Hannaghid*, ed. David Solomon Sassoon (Oxford and London, 1934), pp. 28–34, poems nos. 33–50. Medieval Arabic poetry was of a similar type; cf. what R. Blachère (*Analecta* [Damascus, 1975], p. 417) says about how the prince of Arabic lyrics, al-Mutanabbī, confronted the death of his grandmother whom he loved so much. Letter from Alexandria: TS 10 J 6, f. 5, *margin*, l. 12 to *verso*, l. 3, p. 31, no. 40, ll. 3–5 (=*Diwan*, cf. preceding note), Nathan b. Judah, Alexandria, writing to Sāsōn b. Meshullām, Cairo. The general content of this long letter is discussed in Cohen, Mark R., *Self-government*, pp. 215/6 and 241/2. This judge Sāsōn b. Meshullām was probably not identical with the one described in *Med. Soc.*, II, 514, sec. 24, but probably belonged to the same family. Nathan b. Judah authored also the lovely family letter quoted above, p. 36 n. 132.

[287]For the visit at midnight see *Med. Soc.*, IV, 256–266 and n. 24. Thirty dirges: TS 12.299, ll. 10–14, ed. Goitein, *Palestinian Jewry*, p. 399 (early thirteenth century). Zadok (also a cantor): TS 16.287, ed. Strauss-Ashtor, *Mamluks*, III, 101. For the correct translation of that passage see Goitein, *Tarbiz*, 41 (1971), 70, bottom, but since, at that time, I was not yet aware of the passage in TS 12.299, I believed erroneously that Heb. *qīnōt* referred, as usual, to lamentations recited (like the biblical Book of Lamentations) on the Fast of the Ninth of Av. In TS 12.299 it is expressly said: lamentations for the dead.

Professor Ezra Fleischer of the Hebrew University, Jerusalem, informs me that the Geniza contains uncounted numbers of dirges; most of them are found in only one copy, which indicates that they were not literary creations of renowned poets but local products (combining lamentations with justifications of God's judgment).

[288]*Med. Soc.*, III, 242 and n. 133.

[289]TS 10 J 9, f. 1, cf. *ibid.*, p. 431 n. 39.

[290]Isaiah 66:13. God is speaking. The verse, like other biblical quotations in the letter, is equipped with vowel-signs, perhaps to make the reading easier for the addressee.

[291]Lit., "the mistress over the chiefs [an allusion to her name Rayyisa, chief], the noble (pl.), the understanding, the prudent and the learned; the leader of the people with common sense, *sayyidat al-ʿuqalā*."

[292]The name of the mother was probably Jawhara or the like. See n. 294, and p. 305 and n. 163, below.

[293]Good deeds, Ar. *thawāb*, lit., "something for which one is rewarded" (mostly: in the World to Come).

[294]BT Megilla 15*a*, bottom.

[295]The writer wishes to stress that despite his great despair, Ecclesiastes (12:13) comes to the conclusion: "Fear God and observe his commandments."

[296]There exist a number of books in Arabic with this title (*Al-faraj baʿd al-shidda*), but here no doubt that written by Rabbenu Nissīm b. Jacob of Qayrawān is intended; now available in an English translation with a good commentary by William M. Brinner (New Haven and London, 1977).

[297]An Arabic adaptation of the Aramaic phrase: "He who has gone away, but left behind someone like himself, has not gone away," used, for instance, by Samuel ha-Nagid, Granada, in his letter of condolence to R. Hananel of Qayrawān on the death of his father Hushiel, cf. J. Mann, "Remarks," *Tarbiz*, 6 (1935), 239.

[298]Jeremiah 22:10, where "goes away" refers to a king who went into exile. The Hebrew word for "going away," *hlkh*, means in Arabic "perishing"; the writer uses the verse as meaning: weep for him who destroys himself by excessive mourning.

[299]Ar. *yuʿāwiḍ ghabīnatahā*, see Dozy, *Supplément*, II, 201*a*.

[300]Ar. *wa-lā yuwaḥḥidik min wāḥidik* (spelled *ywḥdyh min wʾḥidyk*).

[301]We should never ask God to correct the ways of sinners without remembering that we, too, need atonement. A common way of speaking.

[302]Text: *fa-hādhih saʿīda*, may be translated as: and this is fortunate.

[303]It was common for elderly women to marry again. Many Geniza texts reflect this situation. The writer wished this in particular so that she should overcome her loneliness. The brothers referred to, but not greeted, did not live at Rayyisa's home; they had come there only to be at their mother's bedside during her last days.

[304]The two books: TS 8 J 15, f. 20, ll. 13–14, end of a letter of congratulation for the New Year and the Day of Atonement: "May you be inscribed in the *Book of Life and in the Book of Record for life in the World to Come.*" Omitting the blessing for a deceased person in the presence of a relative as an offense: *Med. Soc.*, III, 191 and n. 45. Omitting the blessing for a living person: *ibid.*, p. 215.

[305]The blessing *yizke le-ḥayyē ʿad* is found, e.g., in: TS 16.124, Abraham b. Amram (dated 1017), signed by four other prominent persons, each blessing his father in a different way; TS 10 J 2, f. 1, David b. Shekhanya (1024); Bodl. MS Heb. a 3 (Cat. 2873), f. 38 (1067), Hillel b. Eli, who probably had arrived from Baghdad only a short time before: *yeḥī l-ʿad yizke le-ḥ*[ayyē haʿōlām habā?]; TS 16.138, Shiloh b. R. Mevassēr, Alexandria (1077); TS Box K 27, Mann, II, 225, l. 1: *yiḥyē we-yizke le-ḥayyē ʿad*, said about a nāsī who was a liturgical poet (eleventh century).

[306]TS 13 J 6, f. 9*v*, Moses b. Peraḥya, *zlhh*, an acronym of *zikhrō le-ḥayyē ha-ʿōlām ha-bā*; TS 8 J 33, f. 4 (1 for 4 is a misprint), Mann, II, 304, Yehiel b. Isaac (1200 and later), a common blessing. Another signatory blesses his father with *yḥbyʿm*, an acronym of the initials of the verse Psalm 149:5 (rarely used: see below). For the document itself, see *Med. Soc.*, III, 124–125 and nn. 34 and 37, also *ibid.*, p. 422, sec. 379.

[307]See nn. 1–2, 76, 187–192, 224–225, above, and "Messianism and the World to Come," pp. 391 ff., below.

[308]Leopold Zunz, the "father of the science of Judaism" (1794–1886), dedicated a special study to the blessings for the dead ("The Memory of the Righteous" in *Zur Geschichte und Literatur* [Berlin, 1845], pp. 304–317). The Geniza would provide some additions to his list. The most common Muslim formula used in the Geniza, "may God have mercy upon him," is a replica of the Jewish prayer for the dead; the less common *raḍiya ʾl-lāhu ʿanhu*, "may God be pleased with him," said by Muslims only for some of Muhammad's "Companions" and other saints, was easily taken up by Jews because it is the translation or equivalent of the Hebrew religious term *rāṣā bō*. "May God brighten his face," TS 10 J 30, f. 8, l. 14, recalls, of course, the often quoted verse from Daniel 12:3: "the righteous will shine like the bright sky," but the phrase itself is derived from the Qurʾān, Sura 75:22.

[309]It is this form of the saying, not that in I Kings 8:46, which is usually quoted in the Geniza.

[310]TS 10 J 10, f. 20, l. 10, and margin. Joseph b. Jacob of Hebron, Palestine, "The

servant of the Fathers of the World" (i.e., keeper of the tombs of the biblical patriarchs), whose brother David died on a voyage, inquires where he was temporarily interred. "I shall travel there, build his tomb, *wa-uraḥḥim ʿalayh*, and invoke for him mercy." See next note.

[311]Such a prayer in a memorial service is called *tarḥīm*, see *Med. Soc.*, II, 162–163, and 554 nn. 28 and 31, because it opened with the words "may our God have mercy with," cf. Mann, *Texts*, II, 259–280 (from a Karaite source), or *dukhrān tāv*, "may the record of the deceased be beautiful," cf. *Med. Soc.*, II, 163. TS NS Box 135, a leaf from an ancient Palestinian (Rabbanite) prayer book, contains the end of a prayer for the dead, in which each of the three passages preserved opens with: "[May] the Merciful," see Margalioth, *Hilkhot* (cf. *Med. Soc.*, III, p. xx, bottom), p. 129.

[312]A custom prevailing for the centuries, e.g., TS 28.7 (April 1060); about the nature of this contract, see *Med. Soc.*, I, 183 and n. 15; TS 13 J 4, f. 7 (June 1244, see *ibid.*, III, 218 and n. 243). For release, see *ibid.*, I, 11, top.

[313]TS 16.11 (late eleventh century), see "Note on the Sources," n. 4, above.

[314]A Geniza manuscript from the library of the Jewish community in Berlin, which has been lost, but a photograph of which is preserved in the Schocken Library, Jerusalem; ed. Schirmann, *New Hebrew Poems from the Genizah*, pp. 97–102. I do not believe that this poem was composed by the Nagid Moses b. Mevōrākh himself, for it betrays a considerable degree of artistry. Had the Nagid been a poet, we would certainly have more of his creations, as we do of the communal leader Sahlān b. Abraham, many of whose poems have been preserved in the Geniza. Lamentations recited on the anniversary of the death of a relative: e.g., in TS 12.594*v*.

[315]Bodl. MS Heb. d 68 (Cat. 2836, no. 10), f. 28*v*, ll. 5–8, ed. Mann, II, 261, poem III. Heb. *ṣiyyūn* designates a tombstone with an inscription. The tombstones in Fustat might have looked then as later: a hollow sandstone cylinder lying on the ground, see I. Ben-Zeʾev, "Documents Pertaining to the Ancient Jewish Cemetery in Cairo," *Sefunot*, 1 (1956), 7–24, a tombstone above the graves of the two brothers Isaac and Jacob, sons of Meshullam, the former getting four and the latter three long lines of inscriptions dated 1746/7 (photograph opposite p. 23; in the offprint given to me by the author in 1957, opposite p. 15). Many, if not most, of the graves were probably marked in some primitive way that did not require much expense.

[316]Heb. *lishka* in the poem cited corresponds to Ar. *ḥujra*, a small room, a sepulcher, see TS Box K 6, f. 118 b, ll. 8–11, where a mother gives to a son and a daughter a quarter of a house each on condition that if they should die without producing an heir a ḥujra be erected over both with whatever remained of these gifts, see *Med. Soc.*, III, 244 and n. 146. The same Hebrew term corresponds to *maghāra*, cave, vault, see p. 144, above. A family burial ground was later called *ḥōsh* (Ar.), which I have not found in this sense in the Geniza. Our poem has *ṭīrā* (Heb.), designating in the Bible an enclosed camp of nomads.

[317]A document concerning the litigation of August 1227 was produced by the head of the community in 1482 when the ownership of the cemetery was again contested, see I. Ben-Zeʾev's article cited in n. 315, above, p. 22, ll. 26–27 of the document. The document of 1482 was preserved in the archives of the Jewish community of Cairo, not in the Geniza.

[318]As at the earthquake in Ramle, see p. 64, above. The supplication of Muslim, Christian, and Jewish schoolboys in the cemeteries of their communities for the recovery of the mighty sultan Aḥmad Ibn Ṭalūn (which was of no avail; he died in May 884 at the age of fifty), was clearly supposed to invoke the merits of the ancestors together with the innocence of the children, Ibn al Jawzi, *Al-Muntaẓam fī Taʾrīkh al-Mulūk wa ʾl-Umam* (Hyderabad, 1938), V b, 73, Tritton, *Muslim Education*, p. 14. Years ago, I learned that in Yemen, even in this century, such prayers of schoolboys in cemeteries were arranged.

[319]TS 20.102, ed. Schechter, *Saadyana*, p. 112, ll. 27–34, esp. l. 28. The writer of this letter was the Palestinian Gaon Solomon b. Judah, who uses here the ancient term for cemetery, *meʿārā*, lit., "cave," whereas in his report on the earthquake, see

preceding note, he writes *bēt ha-qevārōt,* lit., "the house of tombs," see Mann, II, 128, l. 28. See A. Yaari, "Excommunication on a Cemetery," *Tarbiz,* 21 (1950), 207–208; TS Arabic Box, 4, f. 5, trans. by Goitein in "Jewish Business Woman" (see n. 204, above), 230 n. 18; Goitein, *Palestinian Jewry,* p. 233 n. 9. Moshe Gil's surmise that meʿārā means synagogue, in "The Jewish Quarters of Jerusalem . . . ," *JNES,* 41 (1982), 278, cannot be sustained.

[320]On the mass vigil in the cemetery during the night preceding the eve of the Day of Atonement, see I. Ben-Ze'ev's article mentioned in n. 315, above. For Capusi, see *EJ,* V, 156.

[321]For holy shrines, see pp. 18 ff., above.

[322]On "memorial lists" or, rather, combined prayers for the dead and the living, see *Med. Soc.,* II, 162–163, and 554, nn. 28–31; *ibid.,* III, 2–6.

[323]Isaiah 25:8 is the concluding quotation of BT Moʿed Qaṭan, which deals in its last chapter with the rules for mourning, and contains much of the Talmudic lore about death. The reverse side of the long letter ULC Or 1080, Box 6, f. 25 + TS 13 J 17, f. 16*v,* ed. in Goitein, *Palestinian Jewry,* pp. 60–69, reproduces much of this material, probably to be used for sermons or study in houses of mourning. Paul's use of Isaiah 25:8 (together with Hosea 13:14) in I Corinthians 15:55, seems to show that his audience was not unfamiliar with these verses.

B. AWARENESS OF PERSONALITY

1. The Ideal Person

[1]TS 18 J 1, f. 5, l. 9: *al-akhlāq kamā yuʿraf.*

[2]TS 24.78*v,* l. 23: *mā yakhfā ʿannak khuluqī.* Trans. pp. 249–254, below.

[3]Bodl. MS Heb. d 66 (Cat. 2878), f. 57*v,* l. 8: *khuluqoh mā yaḥtamil.*

[4]DK 22, *Nahray* 194, l. 20: *qaḍā' ḥawā'ij al-nās min akhlāqak bil-ṭabʿ.*

[5]For *akhlāq* in the meaning of ethics see EI^2, I, 325–329.

[6]ENA NS 18, f. 7. In the address of a letter to Ṣadaqa b. Ḥakmūn, his "brother from father and mother" (that is, friend, not related), Joseph b. Samuel says of himself: *shākir awṣāfoh,* lit., "grateful for his [friend's] descriptions." For the singular *waṣf* see n. 11, below.

[7]Bodl. MS Heb. d 65 (Cat. 2877), f. 9, l. 29, ed. S. Assaf, *J. N. Epstein Jubilee Volume* (= *Tarbiz* 20) (Jerusalem, 1950), p. 180, French trans. N. Stillman, "Un témoignage contemporain de l'histoire de la Tunisie ziride," *Hespéris talmuda,* 13 (1972), 51–59. Mind: *ʿaql,* cf. W. Madelung, review of J.R.T.M. Peters, *God's Created Speech* (Leiden, 1976), in *Der Islam,* 55 (1978), 103.

[8]Cf. *Med. Soc.,* III, 17 and n. 8.

[9]TS 8 J 20, f. 26*v,* l. 8: *nafsoh nafs zawjtak.*

[10]TS 16.286*v,* ll. 8–9, an often cited letter from Alexandria. Resembling one's maternal uncle: *Med. Soc.,* III, 25–26. A son's actions are like those of his father: TS 10 J 18, f. 10, *ibid.,* p. 35.

[11]TS 13 J 20, f. 8*v,* ll. 1–2: *waṣfī bi'annī nāhiḍ wa-ghayrī muhmil.* See n. 6, above.

[12]TS 20.127: *mithlī lā yuʿtaraḍ ʿalayh.* Cf. *Med. Soc.,* I, 168 and n. 13.

[13]TS 16.294, the muqaddam of Minyat Ghamr referring to that of Minyat Ziftā. See *ibid.,* II, 49 and n. 55.

[14]Bodl. MS Heb. a 3 (2873), f. 13*v,* l. 4: *ant ṣaḥīfat rūḥak,* Goitein, *Letters,* p. 125 and n. 23.

[15]TS 16.303, l. 12, Manṣūr Kohen writing to judge Elijah: kān al-mawlā *takhallaq* min *akhlāq* al-shaykh Abū Saʿd. . . . Cf. TS 10 J 15, f. 9, l. 6: *takhālaq,* simulate a good character which one does not possess.

[16]Bodl. MS Heb. a 2 (Cat. 2805), f. 21*v,* l. 19: *ḍāqat akhlāqī.* See nn. 26, 27, below.

[17]Unable to describe: TS 10 J 14, f. 12, ll. 27–28. "Obstinacy and difficulty of character": TS 10 J 13, f. 10*v.* Mind (cf. n. 7): *irjaʿ ila llāh wa-rudd ʿaqlak ʿalayk,* TS Arabic Box 18 (1), f. 137, l. 16. Another important letter on the same affair is TS 12.415, to be added to *Med. Soc.,* II, 610 n. 27.

[18]Bodl. MS Heb. d 66 (2878), f. 57, l. 17: *taʿawwaḍ khuluqak.*

[19]Husband complaining: TS 12.69*v*, ll. 14–18, ed. A. L. Motzkin, "A Young Couple in Thirteenth-Century Cairo" (Heb.), in *Zvi Avneri Memorial Volume* (Haifa, 1970), p. 122. Wife: TS 8 J 22, f. 27, trans. *Med. Soc.*, III, 186. The original does not have "bad" (as I translated there), and is more forceful.

[20]TS 13 J 26, f. 22, ll. 23–24: *mā yaqdir yakhruj ʿan ṭabʿ ahl al-gharb.*

[21]TS 10 J 30, f. 7: *fa-kun ʿind al-ẓann fīk*; TS 16.27, l. 23: *fal-takun ʿalā mā ʿulimt bih.* Beautiful habit: TS NS J 120, and very common.

[22]TS 16.42, l. 16 (and see l. 9): *fī maknūn ṭawiyyatak al-khayr*, ed. Goitein, *Tarbiz*, 38 (1969), 20; said in a letter by the Berachiah brothers to the powerful Joseph Ibn ʿAwkal; *ṭawiyya*: what is folded up inside a man. A similar term for character is *sajiyya*, what is covered (as with a garment): TS 10 J 31, f. 9, l. 15.

[23]In the preceding notes about a dozen synonyms for character were cited: *khuluq, akhlāq, khalīqa, ṭabʿ, ʿaql, rūḥ, nafs, waṣf, awṣāf, qālab, ṭawiyya, sajiyya.* To these may be added *ʿarīka*, n. 68, below, and *shariyya*: *kull insān yalfiẓ bi-qadr shariyyatoh*, "everyone speaks in accordance with his nature [as he pleases]," TS 13 J 25, f. 12, l. 14 (Jerusalem, eleventh century). Here also belong words that always occur in the plural and are always accompanied by an attribute: *hū min al-faḍl wal-ʿilm wal-dīn wal-khilal al-jalīla ʿalā mā hū mash-hūr*, he is famous by his nobility, learnedness, and piety, and his lofty dispositions, TS 20.113*v*, ll. 12–13, Goitein, *Palestinian Jewry*, p. 247; *alladhī kammal allāhū fīh jamīʿ al-khiṣal al-fāḍila*, TS 13 J 23, f. 3, *Nahray* 71. For *dimāgh*, "brain," see nn. 30 and 31, below; for *khāṭir*, TS 10 J 17, f. 7*v*, l. 10; for *wasm*, p. 569 n. 30, below.

[24]I believe I found up to seventy synonyms. Compare this with Hebrew. Biblical Hebrew seems not to possess a word for character. The postbiblical *dēʿā*, "mind," comes close to the notion of character, but does not cover it completely; *midda*, "measurement," "quality," is regularly used in the plural; cf. TS 10 J 16, f. 11, l. 5: "I praised in the assemblies of elders the beauty of his character, the strength of his intelligence, and his perfect honesty," *yōfī* [for *yefī*] *daʿtō we-ḥōsen sikhlō we-rōv mūsārō*; TS AS 148, f. 17: *mā ʿahidnā min middōt al-mawlā*, "as we are accustomed with regard to our lord's character," where the writer, addressing judge Elijah b. Zachariah, uses the Hebrew word *middōt* as corresponding to Arabic *akhlāq* in a letter written in Arabic. This passing from one language to another was done perhaps under the subconscious assumption that the judge's helpfulness was due to his religious learning. The expression *middōt ṭōvōt*, "good qualities," said of a person or a community, is common in Hebrew letters, for instance, TS 16.196, l. 38, and *verso*, l. 7, trans. in Mark R. Cohen's article in *Studies in Judaism and Islam, 1981*, pp. 327 and 328. Nor do the Hebrew terms *ṭīv* (originally *ṭibb*) and *ṭevaʿ* cover the meaning of character completely, while *ōfī*, used today in this sense, was not a common word, and, as far as I know, never occurs in the Geniza.

[25]Cf. the opening of a famous poem by Samawʾal: *shabābun tasāmā lil-ʿulā wa-kuhūla*, A. J. Arberry, *Arabic Poetry* (Cambridge, 1965), pp. 30–31, "young and old vying for the highest." See Franz Rosenthal's important discussion of the place of competitiveness in Islamic society in his *Study of Muslim Intellectual and Social History*, pp. 8–11.

[26]TS 12.224, ll. 13–15: *bi-ʿilmī bi-ḍīq khuluqak* (eleventh century). Westminster College, Frag. Cairens. 100, l. 16: *khuluqoh ḍīq al-ṣadr* (same time). Worry about the illness of a relative: TS 13 J 23, f. 3, l. 3, *Nahray* 71.

[27]TS 10 J 13, f. 15, ll. 11–12: *fa-bi-ḥaqq mā baynanā fi ʾllāh ubsuṭ nafsī bi-kitāb tunfidhōh lī min kull bidd; innanī kullamā kunt an aktub lak mā ajid ṭībat nafsī walā inshirāḥī. mā khallayt katb kitāb surʿa illā ḍīq ṣadrī. wa-aqūl mā aktub loh illā wa-anā fī ṭīb al-nafs.* More about this in subsection "Moods," p. 241, below. "Wideness": *saʿat ṣadr*, TS 13 J 20, f. 6 m.

[28]TS 20.69, ll. 48–49. Light: *khiff.* See *Med. Soc.*, I, 372, sec. 14. "Mr. Heavy," *Mūsā al-thaqīl*: Bodl. MS Heb. c 28 (Cat. 2876), f. 24, l. 10.

[29]TS 12.337, *margin, India Book* 73: *qāṣī* (ṣ = s) *al-qalb.* Hence the common phrase:

mā nuqāsī minhū or *min khuluqoh*, TS 13 J 21, f. 14, "the difficulties we have with him."

[30]ULC Or 1080 J 78, *Nahray* 46, ll. 11–12: *bārid al-dimāgh*; neglecting family: *bārid al-qalb wal-niyya*, TS 18 J 2, f. 10, ll. 13–14, ed. Goitein, *Palestinian Jewry*, p. 265. Warmth: *ḥamiyya*, and derivatives from the root *ḥrq*, see n. 53, below.

[31]TS 12.405*v*, ll. 5–6: *jayyid al-qaʿīda raṭb al-dimāgh*, "pleasant to talk to, possessed of a fresh brain."

[32]TS 8 J 21, f. 12*v*, l. 1: *wa-badhalat nafs-hā muruwwatan minhā*. See *Med. Soc.*, II, 160 and 553 n. 21.

[33]TS NS J 134, l. 3: *muruwwatī jassaratni ʿala ʾl-maqām al-sharīf bi-katb hādhihi ʾl-waraqa ilayh*. The handwriting in this fragment is that of the oculist Abū Zikrī (son of the judge Elijah b. Zachariah) in TS 10 J 16, f. 16.

[34]For instance, TS 8 J 11, f. 14, l. 12, see *Med. Soc.*, I, 173 and 442 n. 14.

[35]TS 16.294, l. 15, and *verso*, ll. 2–3. Cf. *ibid.*, II, 49 and 533 n. 55; and here, n. 13, above.

[36]TS 13 J 8, f. 23, ll. 17–21, cf. *Med. Soc.*, III, 164 and 462 n. 24. Sense of honor: *nakhwa* (see nn. 43–51, below). Learnedness: *qirāʾa*. The writer probably had in mind a famous passage in BT Giṭṭin 6*b*–7*a*, where the husband is warned not to become angry when his wife commits some oversight in the exact observance of the religious ritual, such as kindling the Sabbath lights a full hour before sunset. (This was only a precautionary injunction; kindling immediately before sunset is no desecration of the Sabbath.)

[37]TS NS J 23, *India Book* 214: *wa-lays hū balad an yadfaʿ fīha insān ḥaqq illā bil-muruwwa*.

[38]TS 8 J 9, f. 15, l. 13. It seems that the letter emanated from the office of the Nagid Joshuah (d. 1355), a descendant of Moses Maimonides.

[39]TS 13 J 28, f. 17, ll. 32–34, a father addressing his son. Cf. *Med. Soc.*, I, 477 n. 14.

[40]TS 8 Ja 1, f. 4: *itrajjal fī hādha ʾl-amr ghāyat al-tarajjul*.

[41]TS 13 J 17, f. 15, ll. 2–7.

[42]TS 8 J 23, f. 20*v*, *India Book* 267. Humaneness: *insāniyya*. My well-read mother used to teach us: "A man does his duty when he does more than his duty." This oxymoron was probably a quotation, but I have not come upon it elsewhere. The praise of benefactors who have done with the needy "more than was their obligation" is found in the Geniza more than once, for instance, in the long letter of a formerly well-to-do foreigner who had lost everything but had been kept by the Fustat-Jewish community, famed for its charity (see *Med. Soc.*, II, 168), for a year and a half, ULC Add. 3345, l. 41.

It is worthy of note that muruwwa is not counted among the ten cardinal virtues enumerated by ʿĀʾisha, the Prophet's favorite wife, which Ibn Abī d-Dunyā (spelled so by the editor) took as the framework for his book *The Noble Qualities of Character*, ed. James A. Bellamy (Wiesbaden, 1973), text, p. 8, para. 36, Introduction, p. 2. Because of its composite character muruwwa did not easily lend itself to being pigeonholed together with the other, mostly very specific qualities mentioned by ʿĀʾisha.

[43]*Nakhwat al-jāhiliyya*, see Ibn ʿAbd Rabbihi, *Al-ʿIqd al-farīd* (Cairo, 1962), III, 403.

[44]TS 13 J 23, f. 8, l. 5: *fa-tantakhi maʿoh wa-tuʿīnoh*, "be generous to him and help him"; but *intakhā ʿalayh*, "he treated him superciliously" (not from the Geniza).

[45]BM Or 5542, f. 23, ll. 4–5, summarized in *Med. Soc.*, II, 465, sec. 98. A notable with the title Rāṣūy is addressed.

[46]ULC Add. 3345, ll. 11–23 (Heb.), l. 55 (Ar.).

[47]TS 13 J 23, f. 17, l. 16: *hādha waqt al-ṣanīʿa wal-nakhwa*. For the writer see *Med. Soc.*, II, 481, sec. 29.

[48]See n. 36, above.

[49]TS 13 J 30, f. 6, bottom. See *Med. Soc.*, II, 293 and n. 12.

[50]TS 12.652, bottom, said of the foreigner described in *Med. Soc.*, II, 136 and n. 56. One sees how untranslatable terms like *nakhwa* and *muruwwa* are when they are said with respect to entirely different objects.

[51]Job 23:28 is one of the Bible verses opening the fragment TS 8 J 20, f. 4, margin (not in *India Book*), written by Peraḥyā b. Joseph, the learned nephew of the India trader Abraham Ben Yijū: *wa-anā aʿrif nakhwatak wa-ʿazamātak.*

[52]TS 20.28, ll. 44–45. The circumstances provoking this praise are summarized above, p. 35 and n. 126.

[53]PER H 21, l. 8, *India Book* 167: *wa-taḥarruqoh ʿala ʾl-aytām wa-shahāmatoh wa-jasāratoh.* A rare term with a similar meaning is *buzūla*, efficiency, resoluteness, cf. classical *bazala ʾl-umūra qaṭaʿahā.* A newcomer from Yemen in Fustat adjures his brother in Alexandria: *bi-ḥaqq al-bazūla,* "by the virtue of resoluteness, do not neglect me," TS 12.13, l. 6. An efficient housewife is described as *bāzila, Med. Soc.*, III, 462 n. 36.

[54]Christ College, Cambridge, Abrahams Collection no. IX, l. 8: *tataʿaṣṣab maʿī—le-shem shāmayīm.* TS NS J 120, l. 11: *yirʾat shāmayīm u-z(e)rīzūt.* TS 8 J 15, f. 9, l. 14: *yataʿaṣṣab maʿoh.*

[55]TS NS J 16, ll. 16–20. The request is different from that mentioned in *Med. Soc.*, I, 135 and n. 24. Religious merit: *lā sabīl ilā thawāb illā bi-mashaqqa,* TS 13 J 28, f. 10, l. 20.

[56]DK 13, ll. 18–19: *li-miqdārak ʿindī wa-jalālatak wa-manzilatak fi ʾl-faḍl wal-diyāna,* ed. Goitein, *Tarbiz,* 37 (1968), 65. Cf. *ibid., verso,* ll. 1–2: *wa-anā wāthiq bi-jamīlak* (your kindness) *wa-diyānatak*; but *ibid.*, l. 19: *ka-mā yalzam fi ʾl-dīn wal-muruwwa.*

[57]TS 13 J 15, f. 14, l. 27. Cf. Mann, II, 83–84, who copied only the Hebrew proemium (ll. 1–25). For Abraham b. Isaac Ibn al-Furāt see *Med. Soc.*, II, 243–244. In the very short, Arabic part of the letter cited, the word *faḍl*, nobility, kindness, occurs three times.

[58]TS 13 J 23, f. 3, l. 9, *Nahray* 71, Benayah b. Mūsā writing to Nahray. Mevōrākh b. Saadya is the central figure in Cohen, Mark R., *Self-government.*

[59]Mosseri L-288, l. 4, *India Book* 292: *fa-ʾabā llāh an yajʿal al-faḍl illā li-ahlōh, wa-hū fa-qad jaʿaloh allāh fīmā yakhtaṣṣ boh.* At the beginning of this letter Joseph b. Abraham refers gratefully to the large order that he had placed with Ḥalfōn, Westminster College, Cambridge, Frag. Cairens. 9, *India Book* 50, often cited in *Med. Soc.*, IV. In both letters the address is lost. But ENA 3793, f. 2, l. 11, *India Book* 93, a letter addressed to Ḥalfōn refers to the same matter as the main topic of Mosseri L-288, which establishes that this letter was sent to Ḥalfōn.

[60]ULC Add. 3340, trans. S. D. Goitein, "Judaeo-Arabic Letters from Spain," *Orientalia Hispanica, F. M. Pareja Jubilee Volume,* Vol. I (Leiden, 1974), p. 343; text (transcribed into Arabic characters), p. 341, ll. 22–24.

[61]See the Arabic and Hebrew terms together in M. Maimonides, *Commentary on the Mishna*, ed. J. Qāfiḥ (Jerusalem, 1964), IV, 206–207.

[62]The Muslim formula "[Only] God is great" is known today even to attentive readers of newspapers. But it occurs frequently in the Old Testament and is the first epithet of God in the Jewish daily prayers (following Deuteronomy 10:17).

[63]TS 13 J 9, f. 3, l. 30.

[64]TS 16.255, *India Book* 350. The writer, Jacob ha-Kohen b. Isaiah, was probably the leader of the Jewish community of Dhū Jibla, which then (around 1094) was the capital of inner Yemen. About him see Goitein, *The Yemenites*, p. 87.

[65]TS 16.291, see *Med. Soc.*, II, 248 and n. 37.

[66]TS 13 J 19, f. 21. Isaac b. Nissīm Fārisī (the Persian, or dealer in the textile of that name, see *Med. Soc.*, I, 400 n. 2) writes to Abū Zikrī Yiḥye b. Mevōrākh. Both were young. Yiḥye had sent to Fārisī a poem by the illustrious Spanish Hebrew poet Solomon Ibn Gabirol.

[67]Bodl. MS Heb. d 75, f. 13, ll. 17–18 (Spring 1112). The writer, Tovia, the son of Eli, "the distinguished member of the Academy," is perhaps not identical with his namesake (the cousin of judge Nathan ha-Kohen b. Solomon), see *Med. Soc.*, III, 30, sec. 8), from whose hand we have numerous letters, for the style and spelling of our Tovia is defective. For instance, *bōrē*, the Creator, is spelled *byry*, which seems to show that he pronounced ō similarly to ē (as is found in some other medieval texts and was common in some parts of Yemen and in Lithuania).

[68]TS 13 J 9, f. 1: *luṭf akhlāqak wa-līn ʿarīkatak*, ed. S. Assaf, *The Gaonic Period and its Literature* (Jerusalem, 1955), pp. 286–287 (Heb.). For Hezekiah b. David see Mann, *Texts*, I, 179–184.

[69]*Mose Ben Maimon, Epistulae*, ed. D. H. Baneth (Jerusalem, 1946), pp. 95–96 (Heb.). The reader is advised to read Baneth's introduction, translation into modern Hebrew, comments, and notes.

[70]Ed. and trans. by Samuel Rosenblatt under title *High Ways to Perfection of Abraham Maimonides*, Vol. II (Baltimore, 1938), pp. 10–89. The chapter is superscribed with Arabic *tawāḍuʿ*, humility; the quotations are all in Hebrew.

[71]The scale of values: BT ʿAvoda Zara 20*b*. The opinion that humility is the highest value was expressed by R. Joshua b. Levi, the same who sang the praise of that virtue elsewhere; see p. 197 and n. 68, above.

[72]The poet Ibn Maṭrūḥ (1196–1251), born in Upper Egypt. See Jawdat Rikabi, *La poésie profane sous les Ayyūbides et ses principaux représentants* (Paris, 1949), p. 210 and n. 4; p. 315, App. I, no. 142 (Arabic text). For Ibn Maṭrūḥ see *ibid.*, pp. 105–120.

[73]*Iḥyāʾ* (Cairo, 1939), III, 330–334. Ghazālī's sections on pride and haughtiness also belong here. Abraham Maimonides includes these topics in his chapter on humility.

[74]E.g., the refugee from Spain, mentioned in n. 21, above, is described as "modest and of blocked tongue," *ʿafīf munqaṭiʿ al-lisān*, TS NS J 120, l. 10; of a respectable person, who fell on bad days, it is said that he was *bashful* (Heb.) and unable to speak for himself, TS 10 J 13, f. 13, ll. 9–14.

[75]TS 13 J 15, f. 15, l. 16: *muḥtashim kathīr al-ḥayāʾ*.

[76]TS 13 J 22, f. 12, margin.

[77]ULC Add. 3341, ll. 9–10. Inexperienced in troublemaking: *lays loh maʿrifa bil-sharr*. The opposite in ll. 13–14. See *Med. Soc.*, II, 44 and n. 17.

[78]Ibn Abī d-Dunyā, *The Noble Qualities*, p. 2 (Introduction); Ar. text: secs. 36, 38, 72–114.

[79]At Mount Sinai: BT Nedarim 20*a*. "This community is marked by three traits; they are compassionate, bashful, and charitable": BT Yevamot 79*a*.

[80]Ibn Abī d-Dunya, *The Noble Qualities*, secs. 98–99. When Ibn Kaʿb, a Jewish convert to Islam, adduced (apocryphal) quotations from the Bible praising shame, his Arab interlocutor chided him: "I tell you what Muhammad has said, and you quote your Scriptures."

[81]Cf. *Honour and Shame: The Values of Mediterranean Society*, ed. J. G. Peristiany (London, 1966). Harold W. Glidden ("The Arab World," *American Journal of Psychiatry*, 128 [1972], 984–988) describes shame as the driving force in Arab social life.

[82]It is noteworthy that Bellamy, the editor of *Ibn Abī d-Dunya*, translates *ḥayaʾ* mostly as modesty (e.g., p. 58, sec. 105), and only occasionally as shame (p. 59, sec. 107). I believe, however, that these variations were attributable to the exigencies of English style rather than to considerations similar to those suggested here with reference to the Geniza.

[83]The minuscules of Isaac b. Samuel: TS 16.57 (dated 1120), ed. Gershon Weiss, "Financial Arrangements for a Widow in a Cairo Geniza Document," *Gratz College Anniversary Volume*, ed. I. D. Passow and S. T. Lachs (Philadelphia, 1971), pp. 275–283, esp. p. 283 n. 30; Bodl. MS Heb. c 13 (Cat. 2807), f. 1 (1124), where he adds the acronym *zikh(rō) le-ḥay(yē) hā-ʿō(lām) ha-b(ā)*, "may he be remembered as one worthy of life in the World to Come"; Bodl. MS Heb. c 28 (Cat. 2876), f. 68 (1125; same addition) and others. For the grace see BT Berakhot 46*a*, "world" and "eternity" both translate the Hebrew word *ʿōlām*.

[84]Mosseri A-28. The signatory, Aaron b. Peraḥyā, has not been found by me elsewhere. The document seems to have originated in the thirteenth century.

[85]Farès also wrote the article "ʿIrḍ" in *EI*^{2}, IV, 77–78. The term is not mentioned in the Koran and has a somewhat checkered history in Islamic literature. In modern usage, according to Farès, it is more confined to the honor of women.

[86]*Arabian Nights*, the 989th night: the story of Maʿrūf, the cobbler of old shoes, "a man of gentle disposition, who cared for his good repute," and was justified in

invoking his honor, cf. Mia I. Gerhardt, *The Art of Story-telling* (Leiden, 1963), pp. 334 ff. In the original, *ʿirḍ* is used.

[87]The article, "Honor (in the Talmud)," *EJ*, VIII, 966–967, a useful collection of sayings, gives some idea, but not a full feeling, of the place the subject occupies in Talmudic literature. M. Lazarus (*Die Ethik des Judenthums* [Frankfurt a. Main, 1901], p. 313) reminds the reader that the motive of honor is in itself by no means an expression of moral virtue.

[88]All concerns of life, but not the "field of honor," war, a field not frequented by the Geniza people and the sedentary population in general, cf. *Med. Soc.*, II, 379.

[89]A Jewish husband who suspects his wife of infidelity is not permitted to stay with her under one roof for even a single night. After the young woman had told her story to "the judges," it is difficult to understand that they took no action, if the husband had accused her of adultery.

[90]A similar appeal was made to Maṣlīʾaḥ Gaon, translated in *Med. Soc.*, II, 186, where his name is mentioned. Another guess would be Sar Shalom ha-Levi (second term ca. 1177–1195), see *Med. Soc.*, II, 32–33, who was often approached in family matters, *ibid.*, III, 81, 252, 336, including, as here, a question concerning a wife's earnings, *ibid.*, p. 133.

[91]TS NS J 68, cf. *Med. Soc.*, III, 307 and n. 149. Colloquialisms: *fī sana*, "it is now a year"; *arbaḥ ʿirḍī*, "to save [lit., "to win"] my honor"; *qad* [perhaps *ʿalima* omitted] *allāh ʿirḍī bi-shay ilā ʿindī*, "God knows [or: by God], my honor is worth something to me." Clearing of honor: cf. BM Or 5542, f. 24, ll. 7 and 10, where the expression *abrī* (for *ubriʾ*) *ʿirḍī*, "I wish to clear my honor," is used twice. See n. 95, below.

[92]INA D-55, f. 3*v*, l. 12, see *Med. Soc.*, III, 194 and n. 164. The phrase used here: *yunqiṣū bi-miqdārī*, "who detract from my worthiness."

[93]TS 8 J 5, f. 24 (1172). The quarrelsome communal official was Abraham al-Najīb I (see Gil, *Foundations*, Index, pp. 526 and 575), who in summer 1150 had a serious encounter with the cantor Sayyid al-kull b. Abū Yaʿqūb, and a third one with the author of the beautiful letter TS NS J 87, see p. 307 and n. 175.

[94]Ar. *aʿrif ma bitqūl.*

[95]BM Or 5542, f. 24, see Goitein, *Education*, pp. 60–61. At that time (1962) the manuscript mark was f. 13, not 24.

[96]In informal notes and petitions it was customary to put the sender's name at the top of the page on the right side. Not mentioning the writer's name and only alluding to his identity emphasizes his close relationship to the recipient.

[97]Ar. *fa-mahmā kān ʿlyh* [= *ʿalayy*] *wa-lazimani* [*mā*] *rught minhū*. In the concluding part of the letter (not completely preserved) the unhappy writer notes that he had not accepted the post in that little place so that people should report about him what he said or did, and asks, of course, God not to pardon the spreader of false rumors.

[98]Goitein, *Letters*, p. 32.

[99]TS 12.362, l. 8 and margin, *Nahray* 238. The insinuation was that a person who transported a turban to someone let another get it.

[100]TS 13 J 24, f. 4, l. 26, see Goitein, *Tarbiz*, 54 (1985), 88.

[101]ENA 1822, f. 44, ll. 17–18, Ar. *wa-law ahdānī Allāh awwal wuṣūlī, la-fīhim kān al-dīn wal-ʿirḍ sālimīn*: A letter by Abraham b. Nathan to Nahray b. Nissīm, when the latter was already "the eminent member" of the Jerusalem yeshiva. See *Med. Soc.*, II, 512, sec. 14 and here p. 327 and n. 19, below.

[102]TS 18 J 3, f. 1, ll. 22–23. The strange thing is that the dayyān is mentioned in a row with other charitable people who supported the writer. The remark about the worth of the dinar is meant factually, not in a perjorative sense.

[103]TS 10 J 7, f. 27, ll. 15–16: *mashhūr baynanā bil-dīn wal-amāna* . . . (see next note). See *Med. Soc.*, III, 295–296 and n. 86.

[104]TS 10 J 5, f. 9, l. 6 (1102). Trustworthiness: *amāna* (from the Semitic root from which *Amen* is derived). Equity: *iʿtidāl*, the making of a just decision after weighing the two aspects of a matter, an echo of the Aristotelian "sound middle." Circumspection: *iḥtiyāṭ*, lit., "caution."

[105]Westminster College, Frag. Cairens. 113, l. 8 (Alexandria, 1097). In the will in

which a person appoints his mother-in-law (and not his young wife) as executrix of his will and sole guardian of his three children, he mentions her circumspection, called here *iḥtirāz*, before her religiosity: PER H 22, l. 10, ed. Goitein, *Sefunot*, 8 (1964), 115.

[106]ULC Add. 3340, l. 7, see p. 288 and n. 71, where this pair of human excellences is rhymed: diyāna (for dīn)-amāna.

[107]Business practices: *Med. Soc.*, I, esp. pp. 198, 202, 205; customs evasions: *ibid.*, p. 344; court procedures: *ibid.*, II, 338–339, and 601 nn. 29 and 30.

[108]TS AS 147, f. 4, upper part of a large letter. For carob seed see *ibid.*, I, 360, sec. 10.

[109]"Closing of the account:" *ibid.*, I, 208 and n. 81. Maghreb: TS 8 J 19, f. 24, l. 15, *Nahray* 151.

[110]TS 13 J 19, f. 9, l. 29, an important business letter, from Faraḥ b. Ismaʿīl b. Faraḥ to his father. About this family, originally from Gabes, Tunisia, but based in Alexandria, see Goitein, *Letters*, pp. 153–158. For grain see *Med. Soc.*, I, 359, sec. 7.

[111]*Med. Soc.*, II, 358 and n. 16, and elsewhere. See Franz Rosenthal, "Gifts and Bribes: The Muslim View," *Proceedings of the American Philosophical Society*, 108 (1964), 135–144.

[112]Normal procedures: *Med. Soc.*, I, 341–343. Overweight: TS 8 J 16, f. 31, l. 14.

[113]Goitein, *Letters*, pp. 95–101. For other references to Ibn ʿAllān see *ibid.*, pp. 106 and 118 (where a ship of his is mentioned). For Yaḥyā (Ar. = Yiḥye, Heb., both meaning "May he live!") Ibn al-Majjānī see also *ibid.*, p. 32 and n. 24, where his father Moses is referred to many years before as the Tunisian representative of "the merchant prince" Joseph Ibn ʿAwkal of Fustat.

[114]See *ibid.*, pp. 101–107.

[115]Fustat, 1040: Mosseri A 101, ll. 16 and 26, ed. Mann, *Texts*, I, 343–345 (Mann noted erroneously L–101. The two main parts of the Mosseri Collection are documents labeled L, Lettres, and A, Actes). Zawīlat al-Mahdiyya, 1047: TS 13 J 9, f. 5, l. 6. His son Moses (b. Yiḥye) Majjānī, who was named, as usual, after his grandfather, signed TS 8 J 7, f. 15 in the 1060s and is repeatedly referred to in the accounts of Nahray b. Nissīm, TS NS J 111 (1059) and 127. For the office of the representative of merchants see *Med. Soc.*, I, 186–192.

[116]See Goitein, *Letters*, p. 105.

[117]Ibn ʿAllān threatened also to appeal to the Jewish High Court in Jerusalem and "the meetings of the Muslims and their judges," *ibid.*, p. 97. (The word "gentiles" printed there means "Muslims," see *Med. Soc.*, II, 278.)

[118]Goitein, *Letters*, pp. 128 and 161, sec. D.

[119]Taking advantage: *ibid.*, pp. 126 and 127. For Yeshūʿā's correspondence see *ibid.*, p. 119 n. 2. See also the devastating letter addressed to him by a senior partner, *ibid.*, pp. 119–125. For "constrained chest" see nn. 26 and 27, above.

[120]The enclosure: Mosseri L-162. I mention script last, because the handwriting is that of a professional scribe, who could have served others, too. The letter of Joseph b. Berechiah: TS 16.64, ed. Goitein, *Tarbiz*, 38 (1968), 22–26. This letter, like other letters by him, was sent in both his own name and that of his brother Nissīm, see *ibid.*, 34 (1965), 174 and 178; *ibid.*, 38 (1968), 18–22; S. Assaf (see n. 7, above), pp. 181 and 185; he speaks in them always in the first person, and only he is addressed in the highly laudatory letters of the presidents of the Baghdad yeshivas, Hay Gaon, see Mann, *Texts*, I, 121, ll. 25–28, and Samuel b. Ḥofnī, see *ibid.*, p. 159, ll. 2–7.

[121]Abridged from TS 16.64, ll. 13–22 ed. Goitein, *Tarbiz*, 38 (1968), 25. Although the Jews of Qayrawān were inveterate town dwellers, they had many dealings with the peasants (called here, as by Ibn Khaldūn, *badū*, not to be translated as "Bedouins," but as "those living outside towns"). This refers mainly to growers of olive trees, oil then being the main agricultural export of Tunisia. The text that follows: Mosseri L-162.

[122]In order to save his money, Joseph b. Berechiah had to swear a false oath. But this was out of the question for both religious and other considerations.

[123]Large sums were quoted conveniently in dinars (as is done here twice), but in

Tunisia actual payments were often made in silver pieces, called here, as usual, *waraq*.

[124]Abū Yaʿqūb ʿUqbān, a Qayrawanese VIP, probably a banker, mentioned also in ENA 2556, f. 1, l. 20, ed. Goitein, "The Qayrawān United Appeal," *Zion*, 27 (1962), 162, and Bodl. MS Heb. d 65 (Cat. 2877), f. 9, top, see Assaf (see n. 7, above), p. 181, where for *Naḥshon*(?) the manuscript has *ʿqbʾn* = ʿUqbān.

[125]Abū Ibrahīm Isḥāq Ibn al-Sahl ("The Obliging," a family name) carried the body of the father of the Nagid Abraham b. ʿAṭāʾ (or Nathan, both meaning "gift [of God]") from Qayrawān to Fustat and from there to Jerusalem, but suffered wounds and loss of money when he was attacked on the second leg of his journey, TS 10 J 9, f. 26, ll. 15 and 22, ed. Goitein, *Tarbiz*, 34 (1965), 166 and 167. He seems to have been a Maghrebi settled in Jerusalem, cf. Assaf (see n. 7, above), p. 179, l. 4, where Joseph b. Berechiah, as here, requests Ibn ʿAwkal to forward to him a letter, and TS 16.64, ll. 24–25 (see n. 120), where Joseph reports having received a letter from the Head of the Jerusalem yeshiva through him. A person by the name of al-Sahl was a brother of the President of the High Court in Jerusalem: TS NS Box 320, f. 16, l. 4. This name seems to have been used only in the Maghreb. One Sulaymān b. Samḥūn Ibn al-Sahl sent a letter from Tlemçen, Algeria, to Egypt: TS 8 J 22, f. 23.

[126]Several families named al-Fāsī are known from Tunisia during the eleventh century. Had this Isaiah been a compatriot, Joseph Berechiah probably would have known better than to stand surety for him.

[127]Bodl. MS Heb. d 65 (Cat. 2877), f. 4; see Mann, I, 94 and n. 1; 123 and n. 1; and 124, where both the text and a complete translation are supplied.

[128]TS 16.64, see n. 120, above.

[129]For the "ban in general terms" see *Med. Soc.*, II, 340. A good example of the replacement of an oath by a settlement is provided, *ibid.*, III, 266 and n. 107. Settlements had to be arranged by the elders, not by the presiding judge, whose interference could be taken as partiality.

[130]TS 8 J 4, f. 14a.

[131]For Abu ʾl-Munajjā's story see *Med. Soc.*, II, 356–357. Damietta is the eastern seaport of Egypt, from which one sailed to "Palestine and Syria," called Shām (originally *shaʾm*), a geographical, not political term, comprising the lands between Egypt and Mesopotamia.

[132]Written above the line.

[133]"The proceeds" translates *thaman*, the last word in l. 12, which is only partly visible. Shelah had brought, probably from a trip to the Maghreb, highly valued Murābiṭī dinars and asked Tiqwā to "sell" them and with the proceeds "buy" currencies in vogue in Palestine and Syria.

[134]The initial deposition of the plaintiff was probably longer, wherefore it is summarized by the clerk in the third person. The reply of the defendant, which refutes the allegations made point for point, is given in his own words.

[135]The handwriting of Nissīm b. Nahray is so similar to that of the text of the document that I was first inclined to believe that he had written it. A prolonged examination convinced me that the copyist was Hillel b. Eli, and that very likely Nissīm, who was a child or not yet born when Hillel started to serve as court clerk in Fustat (at latest 1066), later learned the art of calligraphy from Hillel, who was clearly trained in one of the yeshivas of Baghdad, cf. *Med. Soc.*, II, 231 and n. 17, 234 and n. 35.

[136]TS 16.196*v*, the story told above, p. 134 and n. 35, without mentioning the name of the partner. The last document signed by Eli was TS 8 J 4, f. 14d, November 1098. In *Med. Soc.*, II, 444, sec. 24, I assumed that an undated document signed by him belonged together with others from 1107, and assigned therefore his latest signature to that year, see *ibid.*, p. 78. But in summer 1100, he was already dead, as is evident from TS 28.4; see next note.

[137]TS 28.4 (1100), missing the beginning but still comprising sixty-two long lines.

Written also by Hillel b. Eli and signed by the same two chief judges as our TS 8 J 4, f. 14a.

[138]Mosseri A-74. Tiqwā b. Amram had given the letter in private (possibly in Fustat) to Ezekiel ha-Kohen he-Ḥavēr b. Eli, who was the third signatory on TS 28.4; see preceding note.

[139]Westminster College, Frag. Cairens. 45.

[140]TS 12.683. For 1100 see TS 28.4, l. 56, where the blessing for his father Amram is *s(āfēh) ṭ(āv)*, "may his end be blessed," a good wish for the living. The blessing in 1105: "may he rest in Eden." The name of Tiqwā's wife, Sitt al-Nasab, "the Noble Lady," sounds special, but was common in the twelfth century.

[141]A good example of a court session with a long list of contradictory depositions is contained in TS 13 J 7, f. 17, a record written in Damsīs, Lower Egypt, in spring 1150. A younger brother, probably when coming of age, sued his elder sibling for many diverse pieces of jewelry, for 400 dinars, also for silver, clothing, silk, and one hundred and fifty measures, *damāwiya* (for *ṭamāwiya*, see *Med. Soc.*, IV, 256) of wine, demands mostly denied by the latter. In the course of the session, a smaller item had to be conceded by him in the face of witnesses who appeared in court. In general, it seems, however, that the claims made by the younger man were exaggerated. He probably had obtained possession of a copy of the marriage contract of his late mother (whose estate was inherited by his late father) and simply demanded a share in all the items forming part of her trousseau. Baseless claims made by orphans attaining majority are not absent from the Geniza.

2. *"Your Noble Self." Considerateness*

[1]"Individualism and Conformity in Medieval Western Europe," in *Individualism and Conformity in Classical Islam*, 5th Giorgio Levi Della Vida Conference, ed. Amin Banani and Speros Vryonis, Jr. (Wiesbaden, 1977).

[2]The dissertation, completed in 1923, was not printed because of the catastrophic inflation then rampant in Germany.

[3]Benton in the volume cited in n. 1, pp. 145–158. See also Colin Morris, *The Discovery of the Individual 1050–1200* (New York and London, 1972). Walter Ullmann, *The Individual and Society in the Middle Ages* (Baltimore, 1966). See also Robert S. Lopez, "Still another Renaissance?" *American Historical Review*, 57 (1951), 1–21 (referring to the tenth century).

[4]*Med. Soc.*, III, 221–223.

[5]*Ibid.*, pp. 218–220.

[6]*Ibid.*, pp. 220–221. Her father was a cantor in the capital, who probably had no son, wherefore he taught his daughter Hebrew and the Bible in order to fulfill the commandment, "teach your children," and married her to a young man of his profession. About a similar case, see *ibid.*, p. 235 and n. 77.

[7]His name, Solomon b. Japheth (ENA 2739, f. 16, l. 5, *India Book* 176, added by him above the line), appears in other documents, but not from the same period. Thus, for the time being, our letter is the only source for the knowledge of his status and personality.

[8]Cf. Goitein, *Letters*, p. 319, a husband writing from Sicily to Egypt: "I wrote her the bill of divorce not because I do not love her, but because I was afraid of the punishment of the Creator," meaning that he might die in an accident and be declared missing, whereupon his wife would never be able to marry again.

[9]TS 10 J 15, f. 23. "Not less than 20 dinars exactly, *sawā*," seems to be a modest minimum, but that sum was regarded as sufficient for starting a small business.

[10]Mosseri L-197, ed. S. D. Goitein, "A Maghrebi Living in Cairo Implores His Karaite Wife to Return to Him," *JQR*, n.s. 73 (1982–83), 138–143. The letter was written by him, as is proved by the way the pages, including the four margins of page two (almost never found elsewhere) and the two free ones on page one are filled with writing.

[11]She was a Karaite woman. The Karaite house of prayer is not called synagogue here, for theoretically (and often in practice), new synagogues were not permitted to be erected in Muslim countries, and Karaism originated after the advent of Islam. I believe that the husband was of the same persuasion, for he alludes to phrases used in Karaite (not Rabbinic) marriage contracts.

[12]For the restriction of the freedom of movement of wives, see *Med. Soc.*, III, 153–155 and *passim.* Sitt al-Sāda was from Tripoli, Libya, that is, she was a Maghrebi like her husband. But she might have been interested in learning new embroidery techniques and models, for her husband emphasizes twice that he will permit her to take with her embroidery frames (*mansaj*, pronounced *menseg*; see the illustration in Edward W. Lane, *An Account of the Manners and Customs of the Modern Egyptians* [London, 1836], p. 195). Some were in the house of a *qawwās*, "bow maker, archer, policeman," possibly a Muslim, where the women met. About the importance of embroidery, see *Med. Soc.*, III, 342.

[13]See, eg., BT Eruvin 100*b*. As might be expected, there existed a deviating opinion on this delicate subject.

[14]In the very extensive letter, nothing is said about a child, which would have been incredible had one existed.

[15]ULC Or 1080 J 71. The name of the boy was Salāma, as on the address, not Sālma, as in the text. The first two words in the second line of the address are *aḥmāhā ʾllāh* (for *ḥamāhā*, a common mistake), "may God protect her," namely, the city of Alexandria, which is mentioned later in the line. The boy copied the address (and the phrases in the first three lines) from other letters and was not quite sure where to put the word.

[16]ʿAllān b. Ḥassūn's letter to his sons: TS 8 J 17, f. 15, *India Book* 380. His letter to ʿArūs b. Joseph: TS AS 156, fs. 237 and 238, *ibid.*, 384. When in *Med. Soc.*, III, 468 n. 163, I noted the sources identifying ʿAllān as an India trader, I was not yet aware of the new ones cited here. The TS AS manuscript was communicated to me by Dr. Paul Fenton, formerly at the University Library, Cambridge. Zayn al-Dār, who wrote the letter to his father translated in *Med. Soc.*, III, 193–194, was certainly the eldest of the brothers. When his father inquired about him in his letter from ʿAydhāb, Zayn al-Dār was probably himself an overseas trader away from home.

[17]TS 13 J 24, f. 22, *India Book* 360. On 23 May 1492, a Jew from Granada, called Isaac Perdonel, receives from King Ferdinand and Queen Isabella special permission to leave Spain with his wife, children, and extended family and all his possessions in cash and kind. This was done at the special request of the former Muslim King of Granada. The relevant document is printed in F. Baer, *Die Juden im Christlichen Spanien* (Berlin, 1936), p. 413. From a communication by Professor M. Benayahu, I learned that the family was also active in Palestine, not only, as here, in Egypt.

[18]I first assumed that the mother referred to the wives of the young men. But had they existed, greetings had to be mentioned either to, or from, them. She means that they gave more of their time to their friends (some of whom are mentioned) than to her.

[19]Bodl. MS Heb. d 66 (Cat. 2878), f. 21, *India Book* 177, ed. Goitein, *The Yemenites*, pp. 48–52. The letter must have been written between 1226 and 1228, for only in those years did the Muslim feast of the breaking of the fast coincide with the Jewish New Year after ca. 1218, when the Nagid Maḍmūn b. David, whose death is reported in this letter, was still alive, cf. the relevant tables in Eugen Mahler and Wüstenfeld-Mahler, noted in *Med. Soc.*, I, 355 (with one day difference in each case, which often happened).

[20]For the Dōsā family, in which the names Joshua and Dōsā alternate for generations, see Mann, II, 270 (TS Box K 15, f. 7; at Mann's time the folios did not yet have a mark). The references to Jerusalem show that our letter was written before ca. 1070. The script points to ca. 1050. In his article, "Jews in Latakia [= al-Lādhiqiyya] during the Crusader Period," *Joseph Braslavi Jubilee Volume*, ed. L. Ben-zion (Jerusalem, 1970), pp. 475–485, E. Ashtor had no reason to include our letter,

which is addressed to Dōsā b. Joshua al-Ḥāvēr al-Lādhiqī as it clearly precedes the Crusader period.

[21]See *Med. Soc.*, III, 227 and n. 23.

[22]See *ibid.*, n. 24.

[23]TS 13 J 23, f. 5. The sender, her son-in-law, was Sahl b. Ḥātim. Excellent hand. The preceding letters were sent on the ninth of Av, a day of fasting in memory of the destruction of the Temple of Jerusalem. She emphasizes this to show in what mood she had written them.

[24]Cf., e.g., pp. 146–147 and nn. 101, 104, above.

[25]She knew the customary openings of a letter by heart. But instead of *al-raḥmān al-raḥīm*, she dictated the first word twice, and the clerk faithfully noted what he heard.

[26]It should have been, of course, "in all *my* affairs"; but since she had her son in mind, she dictated "yours"; or this was simply a slip of the tongue, which the clerk set down in writing with gusto.

[27]A mother does not address her son in this way; but since she knew that polite parlance required occasional use of the words "my lord," she did so anyhow. In order not to overload this modest missive with notes, I remark on such matters later only for the sake of clarity.

[28]To address a person with his by-name was a greater honor than to call him by his given name.

[29]Ar. *fa'an shakar* ("the fact that he was grateful") *tḥj lillāh*. How she pronounced *tḥj*, I cannot know. The verb is derived from *ḥujja*, "a proof that a person is on the right way or represents a right cause." (The same word as the title, *hojjat el-Islam*, "personifying [the truth of] Islam," so commonly found now in news from Iran.)

[30]Ar. *wasm*, lit., "a stamp branded on cattle," another word for character, see p. 190 and n. 23, above. The triad of piety, reason, and character was a commonplace in Islamic literature.

[31]Ṣiraqūṣī, a native, or son of a native, of Syracuse in Sicily. The word *aghzal* is the elative of *ghazil*, "courting women." The Ṣiraqūṣī had apparently tried to enlighten Abū Sulaymān on these matters, whereupon the latter indignantly retorted that he was more versed in them than a notorious philanderer of their circle, of whose name, or nickname, only the first two letters, *Ss*, are visible.

[32]Ar. *khuṣṣ nafsak al-sharīfa 'l-salām*. Abbreviated, since the writer had reached the bottom of the sheet. The addition in the narrow margin is also somewhat misformed. Khalaf was the given name of Abū Ṭayyib. The habit of mentioning a person by a name different from that used repeatedly before was indulged by the finest scribes, see *Med. Soc.*, II, 236–237. It was clearly regarded as a stylistic refinement, cf. Exodus 1:1: "These are the names of the sons of Israel who came to Egypt with Jacob." Jacob is, of course, Israel.

[33]TS 8.9. Barqa was the main city of the ancient country known as Cyrenaica, today the eastern province of Libya.

[34]The schoolmistress: *Med. Soc.*, III, 344–346. Wuḥsha: *ibid.*, pp. 346–352.

[35]P. 201 and n. 91, above. Translated.

[36]The unhappy wife: *ibid.*, III, 217–218. The orphan girl driven from her house: *ibid.*, II, 324 and nn. 58–62. Both translated.

[37]The fugitive husband: trans. *ibid.*, III, 197. "I am a captive": trans. *ibid.*, p. 186.

[38]Escaped from Crusaders: *ibid.*, II, 170; trans., see p. 555 n. 60. (The mark ENA Uncatalogued 98 is now ENA NS I, f. 62a.) Son killed: *ibid.*, p. 501, sec. 95. Daughter treated: *ibid.*, sec. 96. No fees asked by a court clerk: *ibid.*, p. 230 and n. 10.

[39]Pp. 145–147, above. The phrases containing mere legal technicalities were, of course, added by the court clerk, as usual.

[40]Pp. 152–155, above.

[41]The trauma of marriage: *ibid.*, III, 171–172. Marital strife: *ibid.*, pp. 212–218. Divorce: *ibid.*, pp. 260–272. In his recent study, "Polygyny in Jewish Tradition and Practice: New Sources from the Cairo Geniza," *PAAJR*, 49 (1982), 60, Mordechai A. Friedman tells about a man who repudiated his wife, took a divorcée who

stipulated "that he undertake not to return to his divorcée." He did, however, take her back, whereupon his second wife sued for a divorce, "but afterwards relented and remarried him."

[42]See *Med. Soc.*, III, 4 and 5. Depravity: *ibid.*, p. 176.

[43]TS 16.278, l. 8, *kitābī maqām ḥuḍūrī*, trans. *Med. Soc.*, III, 221, bottom. This is the letter discussed pp. 216–217, above. Cf. ULC Or 1080 J 25, l. 24: *Kutubkum ḥūḍūrkum*, "Your letters are like your presence." I.e., you need not come in person, your written word is influential enough.

[44]TS 18 J 3, f. 19, ll. 4–5 Acknowledgment of the receipt of the letter of a brother after long separation: *hī* (*kitāb* is often treated as fem.) *ʿindī mithl rūyat wajhak al-sharīfa.* (This is a mistake; the writer of this long letter was a boy who wished to show his uncle in faraway Egypt what an excellent scribe he was [Libya, Aug. 1089].) Najmiyya, writing about five hundred years later, uses the same expression for acknowledging a letter on business in Yemen from her father, see n. 17, above. Used as a request in TS 13 J 23, f. 5, l. 7, by the unhappy mother of Dōsā, cf. nn. 21–23, above. Bodl. MS Heb. b 11 (Cat. 2874), f. 15*v*, l. 11, *India Book* 79: long letter sent from Sicily at a time of naval warfare to two brothers who had emigrated to Egypt (July 1156).

[45]TS 13 J 9, f. 4, see *Med. Soc.*, III, 19 and n. 21.

[46]An exuberant example is a long letter of thanks addressed by Hay Gaon, Baghdad, to Judah Alluf and Rosh ha-Seder b. Joseph of Qayrawān, Tunisia, ed. Mann, *Texts*, I, 126–134, see *ibid.*, pp. 115–117. Although written entirely in Hebrew—and a very rich and original one—it reflects the Arab ambiance that inspired it.

[47]Dropsie 389 and 414, which form one letter, cited more than thirty times in this book.

[48]Goitein, *Letters*, p. 203.

[49]*Ibid.*, p. 209.

[50]E.g., ULC Or 1080 J 55, l. 1: *amtaʿanā baqāk*, Mūsā b. Abi ʾl-Ḥayy, Alexandria, writing to his nephew.

[51]*Letters*, p. 53.

[52]*Ibid.*, p. 187, a good example of a short, unassuming introduction to a letter exchanged between educated people. Khalaf b. Isaac b. Bundār of Aden, South Arabia, addressing Abraham b. Yijū in India (1139).

[53]For *shawqiyya* see Wahrmund, *Handwörterbuch*, I, 1021*a*, not found by me in the Geniza.

[54]Reynold A. Nicholson, *Selected Poems from the Dīvāni Shamsi Tabrīz* (Cambridge, 1898), pp. 152–153: *Īn ʿejebter ke men ō tū bi-yekī kunj īnjā Hem der īn dem be-ʿirāqīm ō khorāsān men ō tū.* Nicholson politely translates "Thou and I." But in the original it is "I and you," and for good reasons; the I, the person speaking, expresses his feelings.

[55]Goitein, *Letters*, p. 192. See n. 52, above.

[56]*Ibid.*, p. 75.

[57]"An instrument of God," *ʿuddat allāh*, Dropsie 394, l. 12, *India Book* 217*a*, addressed to Mūsā b. Abi ʾl-Ḥayy.

[58]TS 12.64, Rudeness, insensitivity, *jafā*, the usual term. The mark TS 12.64 in *Med. Soc.*, III, 452 n. 14, last item, is a mistake for TS 20.64, as printed correctly *ibid.*, p. 395, no. 16 (1241).

[59]TS 8 J 16, f. 3, ll. 9–10, ed. Goitein, *Palestinian Jewry*, pp. 129–130: *yuʿaffir al-khabb.* This should not be understood as a translation of Heb. *mithʾabbēq be-ʿafar* (Mishna Avot 1:4) "cover yourself with the dust of the feet of the scholars," that is, study with them constantly. The Arabic is classical, and both phrases are certainly derived from ancient Near Eastern wisdom.

[60]TS 13 J 34, f. 12, ll. 1–7, and end of letter. The reference was certainly to inner-Jewish affairs.

[61]P. Heid. 913, l. 16. A communal official who could not live on his meager emoluments in the Rīf asks a friend to rent a temporary domicile for him in the

capital. The writer must have been in a somewhat disturbed mood, for he changes continually from Arabic to Hebrew script and vice versa, and writes Hebrew words with Arabic letters.

[62]Nothing is mentioned about enemies in this correspondence. But rendering enemies harmless is always welcome. The wish is repeated five times! (Ll. 7, 13/14, margin, *verso*, l. 12).

[63]TS 10 J 5, f. 12, ll. 11–15, *Nahray* 157. Isma'īl b. Isḥāq al-Andalusī from Baṭalyaws, today Badajoz, Spain, writing to Nahray b. Nissīm from Tyre, Lebanon. Other letters from the same to the same are preserved in TS 8 J 25, f. 6, *Nahray* 160 (from Aleppo, the first we have) and TS 13 J 28, f. 11, *Nahray* 159 (from Jerusalem, the last). A letter from him to his *ṣihr*, "in-law," Yeshū'ā b. Isma'īl, in which Nahray is mentioned, from Tyre, TS 13 J 23, f. 22, was designated by me as *Nahray* 223.

[64]TS 13 J 7, f. 10*v*, ll. 3–4.

[65]Bodl. MS Heb. d 66 (Cat. 2878) f. 21, ed. Goitein, *The Yemenites*, p. 49, ll. 15–16.

[66]*Med. Soc.*, III, 117.

[67]TS AS 147, f. 2, ll. 22–24. See *Med. Soc.*, III, 91 and n. 79, where 1085 is a misprint for 1055, and *ibid.*, p. 5 and n. 17.

[68]More about this in subsection 4, below.

[69]TS Arabic Box 5, f. 1, ll. 5–7, ed. Goitein, *Tarbiz*, 37 (1968), 168. Instead of Ar. *baraka*, "blessing," Heb. *zekhūth*, "religious merit," is probably more common in such connections. "Get near to one perfumed etc.," a popular Near Eastern maxim, quoted in BT Shevu'ot 47*b*.

[70]TS 12.305*v*, margin; a passage from this letter is translated in *Med. Soc.*, IV, 238 and n. 91. Son to father: TS 12.21, l. 7. The wife might have been a stepmother. In this case, *'ammatī*, "my aunt," would have been the expression related to the writer. "My cherished ones, your sons": Bodl. MS Heb. c 28 (Cat. 2876) f. 16*v*, l. 16, Mann, II, 280 n. 2.

[71]TS 12.303, ll. 3–6.

[72]TS 24.43, ll. 34–35, ed. Goitein, *Palestinian Jewry*, p. 74. A Gaon of Jerusalem asks a notable to obtain for him a caliphal rescript of installation, which was overdue.

[73]TS 13 J 27, f. 15, cf. ll. 18, 25, 26. A man from Alexandria complains not to have heard from his relatives in the capital for four months, although he was worried about their well-being in the face of the epidemics ravaging there (thirteenth century). TS 13 J 36, f. 1, l. 24, Joseph b. Berechiah of Qayrawān, castigating Joseph Ibn 'Awkal for neglecting to forward letters from the Gaons of Baghdad, ed. Goitein, *Tarbiz* 34 (1965), 177. See also p. 269 and n. 69, below.

[74]Persons of high standing were addressed by the title, see sec. B, 3, "Rank and Renown," below.

[75]TS AS 148, f. 3, and TS 8 J 19, f. 15, both ed. Goitein, *Palestinian Jewry*, pp. 179–180. I assumed there that the sender of the first item was Daniel b. Azarya and that of the second Eli b. Amram, see the Index.

[76]TS 12.21, ll. 8–12.

[77]One invokes the name of God as self-protection before saying something ominous or, at least, uncommon. The same, p. 232, above.

[78]TS AS 150, f. 2*v*.

[79]TS Misc. Box 28, f. 225, ll. 4–6, *Nahray* 161.

[80]DK 18, ll. 10–11, ed. Goitein, *Palestinian Jewry*, p. 209. The mother, p. 225 and n. 30, above. Brother to brother: n. 58, above.

[81]Ar. *wa-ra'yōh al-'a'lā*, or *al-muwaffaq*: TS 13 J 20, f. 2*v*, l. 14.

[82]Urge: *ēn mezārezīm ellā li-mzōrāz*, BT Makkot 23*a*; e.g., TS 16.293*v*, ll. 25–26, ed. Goitein, *Tarbiz*, 50 (1981), 390. The omission of *ellā* in TS 8 J 17, f. 17, ll. 19–20, is not another version of that maxim but is due to the carelessness of the copyist in moving from one line to the other, as is proved by Deuteronomy 3:28, quoted there and in Bamidbar Rabba 7:7. This letter is discussed in *Med. Soc.*, III, 258 and n. 52.

[83]Bodl. MS Heb. d 66 (Cat. 2878), f. 57, top, said by a father to his son after long admonitions, fortified by Bible quotations, ed. Goitein, *Palestinian Jewry*, p. 329.

[84]Slave girl: TS 10 J 17 f. 22, l. 23, see *Med. Soc.*, III, 24 and n. 54. Pitfalls: *āfāt al-kutub*, TS 10 J 11, f. 13*v*, l. 13.

[85]TS 13 J 22, f. 10, l. 31, reporting to a communal leader suspicions cast upon him: *ramzā le-ḥakīmā* (Aramaic). "A hint is sufficient for a wise man": *remez le-ḥākhām dāy* (*d'y* for *dy*), TS 16.293*v*, l. 5, see n. 82, above. Even more common is the abbreviation *wdl* = *we-day le-ḥākhām*," this is sufficient for a wise man." The quotation of II Samuel 14:20, e.g., TS 10 J 5, f. 12, *Nahray* 157, top, last words, is rather common.

[86]Bodl. MS Heb. a 3 (Cat. 2873), f. 15, ll. 17–18, the Nagid Abraham Maimonides after reprimanding a *muqaddam* for his unkindness toward a worthy colleague (1234), see *Med. Soc.*, II, 49 and n. 54. "Had I said less etc." is a common phrase in conclusions of letters, as here, or of an argument, as in TS 16.339*v*, ll. 8–9, *Nahray* 179.

[87]TS 12.383, Isaac b. Janūn writing to "Abī [sic!] Bishr Jacob Ibn Joseph and to Abī Jacob Joseph Ibn Jacob," ed. Goitein, *Tarbiz*, 37 (1968), 171–172.

[88]TS 8 J 36, f. 2, Judah b. Joseph of Qayrawān addressing the three Tustarīs, ed. Gil, *The Tustaris*, pp. 67–68 (with facs.). Tāhertīs-Tustarīs: TS 12.133, ed. *ibid.*, pp. 69–75, trans. Goitein, *Letters*, pp. 73–79. In a letter from Iran to the three Tustarīs, however, they are always addressed together in the plural, TS 13 J 25, f. 18, ed. Gil, *The Tustaris*, pp. 76–79, trans. Goitein, *Letters*, p. 34–39. Thus the custom that only the senior member of a family firm speaks or is addressed was perhaps a Mediterranean tradition.

[89]Loss of friendship: TS 12.175, ed. Goitein, *Tarbiz*, 34 (1965), 169–172, trans. pp. 281–283, below. Confidential: TS 12.171, ed. *ibid.*, 37 (1968), 160–162.

[90]TS 16.339, *Nahray* 179, l. 31, and *verso*, ll. 4 and 5.

[91]About family partnerships see *Med. Soc.*, I, 180–183, esp. pp. 443–444 n. 5. To the examples cited there may be added TS Arabic Box 38, f. 41 (written on vellum), where Isma'īl b. Ezra and his son Ezra appear in the address but the writer turns exclusively to the father.

[92]For the technical aspects of writing see *Med. Soc.*, II, 231–237. It seems that the custom of regularly discarding letters in the Geniza was first observed by merchants from Tunisia and other places excelling in Jewish learning and was imitated by the general public only later. During the Fatimid period, and especially the eleventh century, the Geniza was filled by the long letters of overseas traders; later the carelessly written and styled shorter messages of smaller fry dominated the scene. To be sure, many traders had a quick, cramped hand, but it had personality and style; it was regular, not erratic. The learned merchants, like Nahray b. Nissīm or Abraham Ben Yijū, were calligraphers, whatever they wrote.

[93]Paper: e.g., TS 18 J 4, f. 3*v*, ll. 3–4, ed. Goitein, *The Yemenites*, p. 128, exemplary also in script and style. A similar case: TS 13 J 20, f. 18*v*, ll. 1–2, ed. Mann, II, 301, where the writer craves indulgence also with respect to his script because of sore eyes and intestinal troubles, forcing him to write while lying down. In fact, his paper seems to be all right and his writing is clear, but certainly not as perfect as he would have desired to see in a letter addressed to the Gaon Sar Shalom.

[94]Dropsie 410, Goitein, *Education*, p. 108. It seems strange that the writer, Solomon, son of the judge Elijah, who was both a schoolteacher and a court clerk, could plead *jahl*, "ignorance," to excuse himself. But his script and style, poor in general, were particularly unpleasant here. As often, he was recovering from an illness.

[95]TS 10 J 17, f. 8. The word in brackets was omitted by the writer, probably because he had not found the right term.

[96]TS 13 J 24, f. 8, l. 30, ed. Goitein, *Tarbiz*, 28 (1959), 354: a letter from Alexandria to the Spanish Hebrew poet Judah ha-Levi sojourning in Cairo. Written in Hebrew characters, it has this addition in Arabic script: "To be read and destroyed immediately." TS 12.279, *Nahray* 154, l. 5: Abūn b. Ṣadaqa of Jerusalem thanks Nahray for having destroyed his letter of best wishes for the Passover holiday—it certainly had also contained more sensitive matters. In TS 13 J 16, f. 7, l. 15, *Nahray*

47, a letter was torn up by a friend before it was sent because it dealt with "great secrets," the discovery of which could be dangerous.

Similar requests are found in Arabic papyri. Grohmann, *World of Arabic Papyri*, p. 179, ll. 9–10, reads *yuḥraq*, "should be burned." Unpunctuated Arabic script does not distinguish between *ḥ* and *kh*, but Hebrew does, wherefore the word should be read *yukhraq*, "to be destroyed." In the Near East, during most of the year, there was no permanent fire available in the house.

[97] ʿAllān b. Ḥassūn: see pp. 221–222 and n. 16, above. Maḥrūz: Goitein, *Letters*, pp. 62–65, esp. p. 65 and n. 5.

[98] Ibn ʿAwkal: TS 12.291*v*, l. 13, ed. Goitein, *Tarbiz*, 37 (1968), 75. Daniel Ibn al-Shāma for Abraham b. Joseph. Nahray: e.g., *Nahray* 76, 78, 103, 108, 110, 114, 183. India: see preceding note. Elsewhere: see next note.

[99] The writer extends greetings, but does not mention his name: TS 13 J 21, f. 28, margin, Samuel b. Aaron, Alexandria, to Abraham, the scholar, son of Moses, the teacher, Fustat, both young merchants dealing in pharmaceuticals, spices, copper, and silk (and probably other items). When Samuel says, "I dyed the better silk with gold," one should not assume that his main occupation was dyeing, for he refers also to his travels; the sentence probably means "I had it dyed." Since his friend was a scholar, he preferred to address him in a dignified way. (Abraham was from Alexandria and was expected there; the two were not accustomed to correspond with one another.)

DK XVII: A father writes to his family in Dimyāṭ (Damietta), the Mediterranean port, from the capital, where he had traveled in matters of a mysterious lawsuit connected somehow with the forthcoming delivery of his wife. The *rayyis*, that is, the Nagid, as well as a Jewish judge, and the head of the police had been approached. The son is instructed not to budge from his mother until she had given birth. A common friend with a beautiful hand, but, unfortunately, not a very clear mind, put the confidential and complicated story into writing.

The scribe of TS 18 J 2, f. 3, top, see Cohen, Mark R., *Self-government*, p. 113 n. 58, was a relative of the recipient, and other letters of his to the same are known, but still he says only *wa-kātibōh yakhuṣṣōh*, "he who has written this sends you a special."

[100] TS 12.287, ll. 1–10, *India Book* 120*a*, see Goitein, *Tarbiz*, 24 (1955), 31; the major part of ll. 1–5 is lost. Abū Naṣr, who was a prominent merchant like Ḥalfōn, and, like him, cherished poetry, asks him to elicit from Judah ha-Levi the end of a poem of which he had heard and memorized the preceding verses (while the poet sojourned in Alexandria). As we know from other letters, he had visited the poet there, but in writing a stricter adherence to classical Arabic was expected than in talking. He complains indeed of lacking *lafẓ ṣāʾib wa-maʿnā*, correct use of language and style.

[101] See Franz Rosenthal, "Abū Ḥayyān al-Tawḥīdī on Penmanship," *Ars Islamica*, 13–14 (1948), 19–20, Arabic text on p. 27.

[102] Quoted in a letter from Jerusalem, DK 18, ed. Goitein, *Palestinian Jewry*, p. 209 (middle of eleventh century).

[103] The fact that the relevant Talmudic saying, "New troubles let one forget old ones," BT Berakhot 13*a* (and parallels), appears here in the form *ṣārōt meshakkeḥōt zō eth zō* proves that it was in common use. Goitein, *Letters*, p. 170.

[104] TS 10 J 17, f. 7*v*, ll. 8–19. "I would be again as is proper": *wa-akūn kamā yajib*. "Turned my mind upside down": *wa-aʿkasat khāṭirī*. Expressing regret that one's own character has changed: p. 189 and n. 16, above. No sender or addressee.

[105] TS 8 J 27, f. 22, l. 3: *ʿan salāma fi ʾl-jism wa-maraḍ* [no: *fī*] *qalb*, Daʾūd b. Nahum addressing Ismaʿīl b. Faraḥ al-Qābisī. ULC Or 1080 J 55, l. 3: *wa-shughl fi ʾl-sirr*, Mūsā b. Abi ʾl-Khayr addressing the son of his widowed sister. TS 10 J 12, f. 20, l. 4, *Nahray* 144: *min kull al-wujūh*, Mubashshir b. Daʾūd b. Mubashshir writing to Nahray b. Nissīm.

[106] TS 12.34*v*, l. 12, Nathan b. Samuel (ca. 1240): *ēn ādām nitpas ʿal* (in BT Bava Bathra 16*b*: *bi-shʿath*) *ṣaʿrō*.

[107]TS 8 J 25, f. 16, l. 2. A fragment.

[108]Bodl. MS Heb. a 3 (Cat. 2873) f. 17*v*, ll. 1–2, ed. Goitein, *Palestinian Jewry*, p. 160: *taʿib naṣib wa-ghull al-qalb bi-lā hudūʾ wa-lā qarār.*

[109]TS 16.13*v*, l. 2: *laʿalla yahtadī qalbī.* The identity of the writer of this long letter is established by *verso*, l. 11, where he mentions himself and his brother Ḥayyīm.

[110]ENA 2727, f. 6*b*, top, in a report of various disasters at sea.

[111]DK 3*v*, l. 2, trans. Goitein, *Letters*, p. 242, sec. F, second paragraph (twelfth century): *wa-mā itmakkan lī rūḥiyya.* I had doubts concerning the letter *ḥ*, but saw that in l. 11, the *ḥ* in *ḥāja* is written in the same way. The word is self-explanatory, derived from *rūḥ*, spirit, but I have not seen it elsewhere, either in literature or in a dictionary. Lack of initiative, *lam ajid min rūḥī nahḍa*, is given by Hilāl b. Abraham as the reason why he had not yet opened a store in Alexandria. A few lines later he eloquently demands from his brother "to take heavy loads upon his back," see p. 194 and n. 55, above, and TS NS J 16, ll. 11–12.

[112]TS 13 J 20, f. 6, margin. The name of the brother: Yehōsef. For details about the VIP, see Mann, II, 338.

[113]TS 13 J 20, f. 22. The daughter of Hillel (called here "Hilāl, the Cantor from Baghdad") b. Eli, writing to her brother Eli.

[114]TS 13 J 36, f. 3, margin. About Saʿdān see Goitein, *Letters*, p. 255.

[115]See pp. 94 ff., above.

[116]TS 8 J 22, f. 18. Clearly written, but fragmentary.

[117]TS 12.435, ll. 20–23. Trans. Goitein, *Letters*, p. 53.

[118]TS 16.286*v*, top, the very end of a long letter, repeatedly cited in this book. Dry tumor: *ḥabba yābisa.*

[119]ENA NS 2, f. 5, esp. l. 24, and *verso*, ll. 17–18.

[120]E.g., Gottheil-Worrell, p. 55, *India Book* 174.

[121]TS 8 J 15, f. 18, ll. 6–7. Maimonides: Goitein, *Letters*, p. 207. See also p. 578 n. 27, below, describing the "cup of sorrow" over the death of a father as poison pervading and weakening the body of the mourner.

[122]Bodl. MS Heb. c 28 (Cat. 2876), f. 31, *India Book* 99.

[123]*Letters*, p. 104.

[124]TS 13 J 18, f. 27, l. 18. The letter is analyzed in detail in *Med. Soc.*, III, 34 and n. 2. The same writer, Abū ʿAlī Ḥasan b. ʿImrān of Alexandria, writes to the same person in Fustat, Abū Mūsā Hārūn, son of the late teacher Yaʿqūb (c/o the store of the scholar Abū Naṣr), a nephew of his, in TS 8 J 17, f. 22. In this letter he scolds him for neglecting his mother (the writer's sister). In the letter cited here, she was already dead.

[125]Gottheil-Worrell, p. 119, ll. 10–11, and p. 123, l. 39. Abūn b. Ṣadaqa (or Ṣedāqā) writing to Nahray b. Nissīm.

[126]See Franz Rosenthal, "On Suicide in Islam," *JAOS*, 66 (1946), 239–259, and more recently (1971) EI^2, III, 1246–1248, "Intiḥār" (suicide); for Jewish attitudes, see *EJ*, XV, 489–491.

[127]TS Arabic Box 40, f. 56, l. 21, *India Book* 314. Abū ʿAlī in Ceylon: *India Book* 240.

[128]TS 8 J 17, f. 33, ll. 12–13.

[129]TS 10 J 12, f. 20*v*, l. 8, *Nahray* 144. He still found strength to write about a hundred lines, mostly on current business.

[130]TS 16.281. "I would commit suicide," *afʿal bi-rūḥī.*

[131]ULC Or 1080 J 39.

[132]Bodl. MS Heb. b 13 (Cat. 2834, no. 36) f. 55, l. 20. The list (fourteenth century) is discussed in *Med. Soc.*, II, 496, sec. 68. For nicknames as family names see S. D. Goitein, "Nicknames as Family Names," *JAOS*, 90 (1970), 517–524.

[133]See pp. 174–178 and nn. 260–285, above. He is called there Abū Zikrī, son of Abu ʾl-Faraj b. al-Rayyis, the Arabic name of Elijah b. Zechariah, as his father was later referred to, when he became judge. Condolences to father, mother, and sister are sporadically expressed in items G, H, L, and O, while the main part of the letter, from beginning to end, A-F, M-N, P, are outpourings about the writer's own state.

[134]See pp. 207–208 and nn. 113–117, above and Goitein, *Letters*, pp. 95–101 and 105.

[135]See above, pp. 208–209 and nn. 118–119, and *ibid.*, pp. 119–127, 134, 168–171.

[136]House in Alexandria: see the letter translated below. In Barqa: see n. 144, below. Makhlūf was by-named *Ibn ʿayn (ayn) sārra*, the son of the man with the gladdening eye(s), if my translation of *srh* or *shrh* (they pronounced *sh* = *s*) is correct, TS NS J 241, l. 1, *India Book* 296; TS 12.392, l. 7, *India Book* 173.

[137]Second source mentioned in the preceding note.

[138]See *Med. Soc.*, I, 320 and nn. 47 and 48.

[139]TS 16.54, ll. 30–32, ed. Assaf, *Texts*, p. 133.

[140]ENA 4020, f. 8, l. 9, *India Book* 153: Makārim b. Mūsā b. Nufayʿ writes that he, Nahray (b. ʿAllān), see Goitein, *Letters*, p. 198, and Ibn al-Yatīm (Makhlūf) booked one cabin together for the passage from ʿAydhāb to Aden. At the same time Maḍmūn refers to Makhlūf as *al-yatīm*, see n. 142, below.

[141]ULC Or 1081 J 3 margin, *India Book* 61.

[142]TS NS J 1, l. 1, *India Book* 199, Maḍmūn b. Ḥasan writes to Abraham Ben Yijū: see *ibid.*, ll. 12–19.

[143]TS 8 J 40, f. 1, Makhlūf writing to Abū ʿAlī Ezekiel Dimyāṭī, the brother of the India trader Ḥalfōn b. Nethanel. The other man accused: Abū Naṣr b. Elisha.

[144]Bodl. MS Heb. d 66 (Cat. 2878), f. 137. He had let his house in Barqa for two years because he set out for Aden to settle his affairs with Ben Yijū. See n. 185, below.

[145]TS 8 J 17, f. 16, ll. 9–15, margin and top. The money was sent in Sicilian *ṭarī*, or quarter dinars. Makhlūf probably had returned to Alexandria from a trip to Sicily.

[146]TS 10 J 14, f. 11, addressed to Abraham b. Yaḥyā Fāsī, not known to me otherwise. Toothache: see p. 108 and n. 340, above.

[147]Some of Makhlūf's letters summarized above were certainly written after 1131; the others, too, might have been from that period.

[148]Ar. *mushrif ʿalā-marākib al-sulṭān*, see item G.

[149]A special chapter by Claude Cahen is devoted to "The Monk" Abū Najāḥ in the *Histoires Coptes*, in *BIFAO*, 59 (1960), 141–142, where the other sources dealing with him are also cited.

[150]TS 24.78, ed. and trans. S. D. Goitein with facsimile of the Hebrew original and transcription into Arabic characters in "The Tribulations of an Overseer of the Sultan's Ships: *A Letter from the Geniza*," *Arabic and Islamic Studies in Honor of Hamilton A. R. Gibb*, ed. George Makdisi (Leiden, 1965), pp. 270–284.

[151]"A locality in the district of Barqa, between Alexandria and Tripoli," Yāqūt, 4, 364. Occurring also in other Geniza documents.

[152]Text: *kān yakūn lī sawiyat*, cf. Dozy, *Supplément*, I, 709*a*: valoir *plus*.

[153]After this sentence the text has a *q* with a dot. This could be the number one hundred and mean "a hundred times," or, more likely, the dot indicates that the letter is to be deleted.

[154]The Jewish Day of Atonement.

[155]The capital of *al-wāḥ al-thālitha*, the "third oasis," in the westernmost part of Egypt, "between the Fayyūm and Fazzān," Yāqūt, 3, 157, Ibn Duqmāq, 5, 14. The assertion that the place was not visited by Jews is an exaggeration. In ENA 154(2558), l. 21, business worth 100 dinars is done there. To be sure, that letter is dated 1158, but the transaction is mentioned as an ordinary affair. See *EI*, IV, 1173, s.v. "al-Wāḥ."

[156]Since Jews were not allowed to travel on Saturday for religious reasons, the Jewish traveler had to stay behind and catch up with his caravan after the Sabbath, a procedure both dangerous and expensive, since special guides and guards had to be hired.

[157]The Egyptian *wāḥ*, see n. 155, above.

[158]That is, since he left Lukk in the Barqa district of Eastern Libya.

[159]The traveler spent all his money on his arrangements for his Sabbath rest, see n. 156, while he begged for his food.

[160]Except the hypothetical phrase "I would have been content with bread made of barley," no other reference to the use of this foodstuff for human consumption has been traced thus far in the Geniza papers, see *Med. Soc.*, IV, 243 and n. 132.

[161]The verb *dakhal*, even without the qualification "from the Rīf," means traveling to the city (Cairo or Alexandria) from the countryside, cf. line 59 of the manuscript and its translation.

[162]A tentative rendering of "Eri and Arodi," two names mentioned in Genesis 46:16. The origin of this usage has not yet been traced.

[163]That is, a low-class district, serving as a hiding place.

[164]Closed by the court, in order to protect the rights of orphans.

[165]Most likely a scribal error for Māshiṭī, a well-known family.

[166]Selling on the market means getting a low price. Normally one sold to, or through, business friends.

[167]Stripped: Ar. *mubaṣṣal.* Our translation is tentative.

[168]TS NS J 60, which was written around 1130, contains the lower part of a contract in which a man receives one buhār of lacquer for doing business with it in *diyār al-gharb*, or the Muslim West. The contract might refer to our writer. If and when the upper part of the manuscript is found, we shall learn his name and other details about him.

[169]"Musicians" could also be translated as "girls" (playing instruments or dancing), see p. 517 n. 162, above.

[170]The reference is to Maṣlīʾaḥ, the Head of the Jewish Academy of Jerusalem, which at that time, because of the Crusaders, had its seat in Cairo. Maṣlīʾaḥ was the highest juridical authority for the Jews of the Fatimid Empire and it was certainly in this capacity that he summoned the young man to appear before him.

[171]A common Jewish name at that time, being regarded as having the same meaning as Hebrew Solomon ("The Perfect").

[172]Abū Zikrī Kohen, representative of merchants in Fustat.

[173]In those days, one traveled from Cairo to Alexandria on the western (Rosetta) branch of the Nile down to Fuwwa, whence one continued on the Khalīj, the canal connecting Alexandria with the Nile.

[174]Perhaps another judge, or a general expression, namely, "he who brought me to court," is intended.

[175]That is, he pawned cloths worth ten dinars for sixty dirhems, which is less than two dinars.

[176]The quotations are from Jeremiah 23:9, 31:19, and 6:24.

[177]Ḥayyīm was the Hebrew name of the unworthy son. See n. 188, below.

[178]"The lead workers," an important Jewish family in that period.

[179]Literally, "the son of the candidate." The Jerusalem academy conferred honorary titles on donors. As a first step, they were appointed as "candidates" for a certain title, which in itself was regarded as an honor. When a "candidate" died before obtaining the title, the epithet "son of the candidate" remained as a family name.

[180]A quotation from I Samuel 26:10. The Arabic words following the quotation seem to mean: His being far away from us is preferable to mourning him (*taʿdīd*).

[181]Most probably, Nahrāy b. ʿAllān, an Alexandrian merchant prominent at that time, is intended. Cf. Goitein, *Letters*, pp. 197–201.

[182]"Pocketed" is a tentative translation of *mṣrm* (*muṣrim* or *muṣarrim*).

[183]An India trader, known from other Geniza papers.

[184]Numbers 32:14.

[185]It is possible that Makhlūf made good this threat, sold his house in Alexandria and bought another one in Barqa, Libya, see n. 144, above.

[186]Beggars, Ar. *saʿālīq* (*s* = *ṣ*), "small shopkeepers."

[187]Proverbs 12:25, as interpreted in BT Yoma 75*a*.

[188]The *kunya* of his son Ḥayyīm.

[189]Job 32:20.

3. Rank and Renown

[1]Ibn Ḥamdūn, *Tadhkira*, BM Or 3179, I, f. 82*a*: *al-rutba nasab tajmaʿ ahlahā*, quoted by M. J. Kister (and M. Plessner) in "Notes on Caskel's Ǧamharat An-Nasab," *Oriens*, 25–26 (1976), 50 n. 1.

[2]*Ibid.*, n. 2.

[3]On the specific question of whether government service or large-scale commerce was the preferable nonmilitary occupation cf. Goitein, *Studies*, pp. 239–241.

[4]For small shopkeepers called *ṣaʿālik* see *Med. Soc.*, I, 79, and here, above, p. 232 and n. 58.

[5]*Ibid.*, I, 75–80.

[6]Ar. *maqām, makān, manzil, maḥall*; Heb. *māqōm.*

[7]Bodl. MS Heb. b 3 (Cat. 2806, no. 15), f. 16, margin and top. For Judah Ibn Sighmār see *Med. Soc.*, I, 158–159 and *passim.*

[8]TS 13 J 23, f. 15, ll. 8–9. About this letter see Cohen, Mark R., *Self-government*, pp. 144–145 and n. 142.

[9]Goitein, *Letters*, p. 32, section F. "High position": *jāh.*

[10]TS 28.17. A translation in full of this interesting document is provided in a special study on partnership prepared by me for publication. The Fustat merchant finally agreed to join the partnership, which led, however, to some friction.

[11]ENA 4020, f. 43, margin, l. 1: *wa-lays gharaḍī bidhālika tijāra bal iqāmat jāh.* Faraḥ b. Ismaʿīl is the writer.

[12]The *Actes* of the 1961 Colloque were published in Brussels, n.d. Sir Hamilton Gibb's remarks are on pp. 262–263. My address is reprinted (with some changes) in Goitein, *Studies*, pp. 242–254. Ibn Khaldūn, *Muqaddima*, book V, sec. 5 (Cairo ed., n.d.), p. 389: "jāh is profitable for gaining wealth." Professor A. L. Udovitch drew my attention to Abdessalam Cheddadi, "Le système du pouvoir en Islam d'après Ibn Khaldûn," *Annales: Économies, Sociétés, Civilisations*, 35 (1980), 534–550.

[13]TS 8 J 22, f. 9, l. 13 (the concluding words of a letter): may God *yaḥbis ʿalayh waladō wa-jāhō*, "preserve for him his children and his honored position."

[14]Physician: *Med. Soc.*, II, 257 and n. 89. Bible school: *ibid.*, III, 345, last para. (the schoolmistress and her two assistants, her sons).

[15]TS 13 J 24, f. 18, ll. 11–12, 15–18. The writer does not mention himself by name; but, the name of the addressee, Sitt Rayḥān, wife of the physician Joseph, and the reference to his father identify him as Solomon b. Elijah.

[16]TS 13 J 8, f. 27, ll. 27–28: *lī᾿ anna ᾿l-insān bi-jāhō*, adding "and it is no shame for a man of low standing to aspire to the highest goals," which shows the ambivalence of such notions as rank. The story is told in *Med. Soc.*, III, 59–60.

[17]For details about the use of the phrase (from BT Pesaḥim 49*a*) in the Geniza see *Tarbiz*, 50 (1980–1981), 391 n. 77.

[18]Bodl. MS Heb. a 3 (Cat. 2873), f. 17, ll. 18–19, ed. Goitein, *Palestinian Jewry*, p. 159. The young Ibn al-Furāt had received not only a robe of honor from the vizier but also a substantial monetary gift, *ibid.*, p. 160.

[19]Mosseri L-197, end, edited by S. D. Goitein, *JSQR*, 73 (1982), 138–145. See p. 567 n. 10, above.

[20]TS 13 J 27, f. 20, l. 6 and ll. 16–24. Ar. *mā ḥaṣal lak min qiyām al-jāh.*

[21]TS 12.303, ll. 7–8. The Gaon Maṣlī᾿aḥ is addressed. Proverbs 3:4 is one of the most quoted Bible verses in the Geniza. For the system of succession and the prerogatives of the Gaonate see *Med. Soc.*, II, 14–17.

[22]ULC Or 1080 J 28, ll. 8–9. "Secure in his honored position" *qayyim al-jāh.* The title *hadrath ha-nesī᾿ūth* (Heb.), "The Pride of the nāsīs," that is, of "the princes of the House of David" (see *Med. Soc.*, II, 19), could be acquired by a generous present to the nāsī living in Alexandria at that time. A certain measure of religious conduct, education, and standing in the community, however, was required for any such title. The writer of this letter identifies himself in the first line as Solomon, son of the judge Elijah, but calls himself in the Hebrew address simply "Ben al-Rayyis," and in the Arabic address: "Abu ᾿l-Barakāt, son of the judge Abu ᾿l-Faraj Ibn

al-Rayyis." For this predilection for variety, so strange to us, see *ibid.*, II, 236–237. The family name Ibn al-Rayyis could either mean that his grandfather was a physician, see *ibid.*, II, 246, or could refer to his title "Head of the Congregation," mentioned elsewhere.

[23]See Goitein, *Letters*, pp. 173–174.

[24]About Mevōrākh's stay in Alexandria see Cohen, Mark, R., *Self-government*, pp. 214–217. About David b. Daniel see *ibid.*, pp. 178–212.

[25]About the most recent discussion of Daniel b. Azarya's progeny see *ibid.*, p. 185 n. 16. Since the beginning and end of the letter are lost, the names of the sender and the recipient are not preserved. The recipient is referred to as *maskīl* (a teacher, master, in Karaite usage), and both his son and grandson are addressed.

[26]Samuel b. Daniel b. Azarya later became "Third" (after the Head of the Yeshiva and the President of the High Court) and in this capacity wrote and signed a legal document in Damascus in October 1074, see Mann, II, 221, and the preceding note. Given the difference between a solemn communication and a legal document of little importance the script in both manuscripts must be regarded as identical. The misspelling *ṣanṭerōth* (ṭ for t) in l. 4, a reference to Zechariah 12:4, is to be explained phonetically (ṭ influenced by ṣ). As the calligraphically executed document DK 120, ed. Goitein, *Palestinian Jewry*, p. 169, proves, Samuel's father Daniel himself seems not always to have been fussy about spelling.

[27]TS 13 J 17, f. 21. Samuel describes his illness as caused by the bitter cup (his father's death), which was like poison pervading his entire body, an impressive figure of speech symbolizing the influence of emotions on physical health, see pp. 243–244 and nn. 115–122, above.

[28]Mosseri L-290, B-C, ll. 31–43, ed. Goitein, *Palestinian Jewry*, pp. 94–95. Slight deviations here from the Hebrew translation: in the (Heb.) translation on p. 95, l. 38, the word *lō* is erroneously omitted.

[29]I am using here Jacob's given name for easier identification. As good manners required, the writer mentions him with the honorific title by which he was known in Fustat before he received the title *ḥāvēr*.

[30]Mishna, The Sayings of the Fathers 6:6.

[31]See pp. 196 ff., above.

[32]Title, *Laḳab*, *EI*^{2}, V, 618–631. For the controversy about "the place in life," the sociological importance of titles, between M. van Berchem and J. H. Kramers see *ibid.*, p. 629*a*, referring to p. 621*b*.

[33]See Bosworth in *EI*^{2}, V, 624*b*.

[34]*Ibid.*, p. 625*a*.

[35]See *Med. Soc.*, II, 18–19; Mann, I, 252, 272 n. 1; II, 101, top, l. 14; Cohen, Mark R., *Self-government*, p. 282 and n. 35; above, p. 546 n. 107.

[36]When the synagogue of the Palestinians in Fustat was partly demolished during al-Ḥākim's persecution of non-Muslims, and needed repairs, its head repeatedly admonished his superior, the Gaon of the Jerusalem yeshiva, to follow the example of the Iraqi yeshivas and to grant attractive titles to the well-off Maghrebi merchants to induce them to join his synagogue.

[37]The exact meaning and weight of titles of the Baghdad yeshivas, such as *rōsh ha-seder* or *rōsh ha-shūrā*, "head of the row," or *allūf*, "distinguished member" (cf. *Med. Soc.*, II, 198–199), and others are still under scrutiny, cf. Abramson, *Bamerkazim*, pp. 43–46. For the entire system of attendance at the yeshiva and the titles awarded and offices assigned by it see *Med. Soc.*, II, 211–217, esp. p. 214.

[38]Mann's lists (I, 272–280) may easily be expanded. His table of "benefactors and well-wishers" contains titles given only to the top-ranking scholars, e.g., *gedōl ha-yeshīvā*, "the great, the most prominent member of the yeshiva," was borne by Nahray b. Nissīm, sometime "great Rav," a kind of mufti for Egyptian Jews, and before him by Elhanan b. Shemarya. Both were closely connected with the yeshivas of both Baghdad and Jerusalem. In the 1140s the title was held by Ḥalfōn ha-Levi b. Joseph, who was so well known as "great" that in a list of persons with titles from

that period he appears only as "The Great" without his proper name. See TS NS Box 246, f. 22, l. 19, ed. N. Allony, *Sefunot*, 8 (1964), 131. See *ibid.*, p. 130 n. 4. This Ḥalfōn already bore the title *meʿulle*, "prominent member of the yeshiva," at his wedding in November 1116, TS 24.75, and, thirty years later, in autumn 1147, also the title "The Greatest," TS 13 J 18, f. 15. His father had borne these titles, while Ḥalfōn, a physician, had them as an aspirant, almost as a family name, TS K 15, f. 47, ll. 1–2. Sahlān b. Abraham, the head of the Iraqian congregation in Fustat, a learned creator of liturgical poetry, was titled *segan* (not "adjutant"—this is later usage—but "leader"). Mann himself sends the reader to the proper references. His list, however, may confuse the uninitiated reader.

[39]Abramson, *Bamerkazim*, p. 44, top.

[40]See *Med. Soc.*, II, 525 n. 6, where "Yeshiva" in "Splendor of the Yeshiva" is to be replaced by "the Elders." For Ibn Faḍlān II see *ibid.*, p. 18, bottom. He survived Daniel, and could not have been meant here. For the Būyid title Bahāʾ al-dawla see E. de Zambaur, *Manuel de généalogie et chronologie pour l'histoire de l'Islam* (Hanover, 1927), pp. 212–213, for the ruler, and p. 214 for the viziers. Also C. E. Bosworth, *The Islamic Dynasties* (Edinburgh, 1967), pp. 94–95.

[41]The title *hōd ha-malkhūth* "heading a family tree," in TS 8 J 11, f. 2*v*, ll. 1–2, is a translation of Bahāʾ al-dawla. The manuscript is in a hand from the thirteenth century. But see n. 80 below, where a title borne by a very high Muslim dignitary is given also to a Jewish contemporary.

[42]BM Or 5544, f. 8. The main, mostly Hebrew, part ed. in Mann, II, 86, the Arabic ed. in Goitein, *Palestinian Jewry*, p. 185, where, in n. 13, last line, *Levi* has to be replaced by *lō*.

[43]The word omitted by Mann (see preceding note) is *hākadhā*. "Text": *nasaq*, lit., "arrangement."

[44]These three high-sounding ancient appellatives were widely used, which, to a certain extent, should be regarded as an indication of the general esteem for the individual.

[45]"*My* master and *our* lord," *mārī wa-rabbānā*, clearly written so in the manuscript (not *mār* with a dot or *r*, as in Mann), also twice in Mosseri L-21, Mann, *Texts*, I, 164, in a letter sent by the Gaon Israel b. Samuel b. Ḥofnī in summer 1008. This strange form of address was obviously common in the Babylonian yeshivas, whence Daniel hailed.

[46]For *lā* (*yusamma*) read *lam*, as in the manuscript.

[47]His first title was given to Ibn al-Furāt by Daniel's predecessor, the Head of the Yeshiva Solomon b. Judah, Bodl. MS Heb. c 28 (Cat. 2876), f. 67, ll. 1–2, ed. Goitein, *Palestinian Jewry*, p. 123. Bodl. MS Heb. a 3 (Cat. 2873), f. 17, ll. 2–3, ed. *ibid.*, p. 159, a letter sent by Daniel to him from Damascus, shows that Ibn al-Furāt had been honored by a fourth, also secular title, the "Mighty of the people of God." (At least the name of God is there.)

[48]See Allony's list cited in n. 38, above. In *Med. Soc.*, II, 480, sec. 26, 1142 is noted as its approximate date. It must have been written between 1140, when Samuel b. Hananyah assumed the leadership of Egyptian Jews, for he heads the list with many high-sounding titles, and 1146, when Abu ʾl-Faḍl Ben al-Baṣrī, mentioned in the list, ll. 36–37, was already dead, see *Med. Soc.*, IV, 325.

[49]For the (fourteen) titles of Mevōrākh b. Saadya see Cohen, Mark R., *Self-government*, pp. 220–221 and 383, Index, s.v. "*sar ha-sārīm*." For the Nagid Samuel b. Hananyah see preceding note and Mann, Index, s.v. The translation of the biblical word *sar* as "prince" (to which I, too, have often adhered following the accepted usage) is not appropriate for the Geniza period. "Chief," "master," "notable," "noble" might be used according to the circumstances. A person would occasionally be described as one who is called "the esteemed notable, *ha-sar he-nikhbād*, by order of our lord, *adōnēnū*," where the latter term could refer to the official head of the community, but those cases are ambiguous and rare.

[50]See Mann, I, 260. The persons mentioned there as benefactors to both Rabbanite

and Karaite congregations were all Karaites. The term *pēʾā* (Heb.), used for group, may seem strange to anyone familiar with Hebrew. But the Geniza people spoke Arabic, and Heb. *pēʾā* is only a phonetic variant of Ar. *fiʾa*, which does mean group.

[51]*Med. Soc.*, II, 75–77.

[52]About the role of the elders see *ibid.*, pp. 58–60.

[53]For *zāqēn* as distinguished scholar see Marcus Jastrow, *A Dictionary of the Targumim, the Talmud* . . . (Repr.; New York, 1950), I, 409, s.v. "zāqēn," II, no. 2.

[54]Heb. *muflā, mumḥe*, see Mann, I, 266, top. As the signatures under court records show, the practices concerning the presidency at court sessions changed with the times and circumstances, cf. *Med. Soc.*, II, 313, and *passim*. See also next note.

[55]Heb. *māhīr*, in Allony's list (see n. 38 above), twice, ll. 8–16; *addīr*, *ibid.*, l. 10. A judge described as *muflā*, chief judge, bore the title "Diadem, *nēzer*, of the Judges," ENA 4020, f. 49. Note that judge Nathan b. Samuel (*Med. Soc.*, II, 513, sec. 18) often referred to as "The Diadem" (without his name) had the title *nēzer ha-ḥavērīm*, "Diadem of the Members [of the Academy]."

[56]For the special ranks of cantors see *ibid.*, p. 223, and *passim*.

[57]For the honorific titles of cantors see Mann, II, 416, 421, 423, Index, s.v. "hōd," "nēzer," and "peʾēr," respectively. For the chorister, *meshōrēr*, called *hōd*, see Allony's list (n. 38, above), last item, where "*pʾr* ?" is probably Ar. Fakhr, his personal name. (I have no facsimile of this manuscript.)

[58]Ibn Jamāhir (spelled *jmyyhr*, pronounced Jamēhir, with Imāla) in Allony (see n. 38, above), l. 50: *hadar benē Levi, ʿaṭṭeret ha-nedīvīm.* The texts telling his story trans. Goitein, *Letters*, pp. 335–338. "Splendor of the Kohens," twice in Allony, ll. 40–41 and 55. In both cases the Kohen was also a "Friend" or "Delight" of the yeshiva. For messianic expectations see subsection "Messianic Expectations and the World to Come," pp. 391 ff., below.

[59]Abraham, son of Isaac the Scholar, is described as "Son of the Scholar" (without the name of his father) in JNUL 2*v*, l. 6, *Nahray* 19, which shows the rarity of this title in the first half of the eleventh century. At the time of Abraham's wedding in 1050, his father was already dead: TS 20.7, l. 2.

[60]A title such as *mumḥe*, "expert," for a *ḥazzān*, "cantor," testifying that he possessed sufficient knowledge in Hebrew language and literature to compose liturgical poetry as expected from a man in his position (see *Med. Soc.*, II, 220–221); or "the accomplished scribe" (cf. Ezra 7:6) for a court clerk, bearing witness to his expertise in the law and in legal parlance.

[61]TS 20.94, ll. 24–25, 28–29, ed. Mann, II, 205–206.

[62]TS 16.291, ll. 39 and 45, see *Med. Soc.*, II, 248 and n. 37. The term *zakī* (for *dhakī*) is Arabic and might refer to attainments in the field of medical knowledge. In Bodl. MS Heb. a 3 (Cat. 2873), f. 16, l. 9, "the sheikh al-Zakī Peraḥya, the esteemed talmīd, son of the teacher Nissīm," however, zakī referred probably to religious study. The two Lebdi brothers appearing in this document of 1240 also bore the title talmīd.

[63]E.g., Bodl. MS Heb. d 66 (Cat. 2878), f. 92, ll. 5–6: Abu ʾl-Baqāʾ Elazar, *ha-talmīd ha-mēvīn*, son of Evyatar, the chief speaker (autumn 1229). For the Talmudic origin of the title ha-mēvīn cf. Jastrow, *Dictionary* (see n. 53, above), I, 162*b*.

[64]The shorter branch of the family: TS 8 K 22, f. 1, ed. Mann, II, 320. The longer branch: TS Box K 15, f. 69. As Mann rightly observes (I checked the manuscript), the caption was added in another hand and is abbreviated. The full name of the family is given in TS Box K 15, f. 69: "The House of the Daughter of Nafīs *al-sharābī*." The story behind the strange name was probably this: Nafīs had no son, and, as was done elsewhere in such a case, gave his daughter a thorough religious education. When he married her to the ḥāvēr Ḥalfōn, the founder of the new family, he stipulated that it should be named after her, which meant, in reality, after himself.

[65]In a letter addressed to a cantor Samuel, "the esteemed notable," greetings are extended to a number of distinguished persons, among them a talmīd, "and to the

talmīds [probably meaning fledgling scholars], who gather in your midrāsh," TS 10 J 17, f. 25*v*, ll. 2–6. The writer, the newly appointed spiritual leader of the important Jewish community of al-Maḥalla, invites Samuel to honor Maḥalla with his visit, probably for a *derāsh*, a public exposition of the Scriptures.

[66]"Chief speaker and Master of the midrāsh": Munā the physician (in Ar.) *rōsh ha-medabberīm, sār ha-midrāsh*, Allony's list (see n. 38, above), ll. 40–41. For the 13th century see n. 63 above. For the original bearer of the title "Chief speaker," Rabbi Judah bar Ilai, see *EJ*, X, 337–339, and bibliography, and Mordecai Margalioth, *Encyclopedia of Talmudic and Geonic Literature* (Tel Aviv, 1950), I, 395–403.

[67]TS 16.293, ll. 4–24, ed. Goitein, *Tarbiz*, 50 (1980–1981), 389. The term *mushtaghil maʿa*, "studying with" was also used in Muslim education, see George Makdisi, *The Rise of Colleges* (Edinburgh, 1981), pp. 164, 208; in both cases "working" means studying. The phrase is an abbreviation of *mushtaghil bil-ʿilm*, TS 18 J 3, f. 15, l. 10.

[68]For the dates see *Med. Soc.*, III, 427–428 nn. 39–42 and 492 n. 90. I do not possess manuscripts of all the documents in which Samuel Ben Asad is mentioned. About him see *ibid.*, pp. 9 and 296–297. "Master of the Discerning" is an attempt to translate *gevīr ha-mevīnīm.*

[69]For the use of this verse see p. 236 and nn. 72 and 73, above.

[70]TS Arabic Box 30, f. 156. Prince of Wisdom: *sār ha-bīnā*. The saying of the sages quoted is not known to me in this form; cf. BT Bava Meṣiʿa 49*a*.

[71]TS 16.298, *India Book* 190: *tifʾereth ha-zeqēnīm, ʿaṭṭereth ha-nevōnīm.* For rhymes in late lists of titles see, e.g., the texts edited in Strauss-Ashtor, *Mamluks*, III, 88 and 89, both dated 1378. An earlier example is Mann, II, 329 (4), dated 1292.

[72]Smart: *dihqān*, see Dozy, *Supplément*, I, 467*a*; TS Box K 15, f. 106, l. 10 and Bodl. MS Heb. e 94 (no Cat.), f. 21. Abu ʾl-Ḥasan *al-dihqān*, contributor to appeals: cf. *Med. Soc.*, II, 477, sec. 16 (early eleventh century). Maʿālī *Ibn al-dihqān*, recipient of handouts: BM Or 5566 C, f. 9, l. 20, *ibid.*, pp. 447–448, sec. 32; 454, sec. 55. There I still assumed that this Persian word had retained its original meaning of "squire, nobleman of the low gentry," but further findings convinced me that it had acquired the meaning noted by Dozy. *Al-duhayqīn* ("The little *d.*," diminutive as expression of endearment), contributor: TS Misc. Box 8, f. 102, *ibid.*, p. 478, sec. 19. *Dihqān al-adhiqā*, "Smartest of the smart": TS NS J 292*v*, l. 15, dated 1120; his wife (i.e., widow) owed the community for rent 20¾ dinars, more than ten times as much as any one else in the list; she must have inherited some of her husband's smartness. Gil, *Foundations*, p. 241, who edited the text, left the two words out, probably because *adhiqā* is indeed an irregular form of the plural of *dihqān*, not seen by me elsewhere. There are more references to the by-name dihqān in the Geniza.

[73]Gaons, or heads of yeshivas, existed in al-Najīb's lifetime both in Cairo (in the 1180s, when this contract was written; Sar Shalom ha-Levi, the Head of the Jews, who was preceded by his brother) and in Damascus. The quarrelsome al-Najīb (see pp. 202 ff. and nn. 93–94, above) must at one time have behaved impudently toward the Egyptian Gaon, for a curious entry in the record book of the court of 1183 has this: "Our Gaon, the Head [of the Jews], will not shake hands [*yusāqif* for *yusāfiq* as in TS 13 J 24, f. 4, l. 19] with al-Najīb Abraham, the Levi, for the duration of a month," Bodl. MS Heb. f 56 (Cat. 2821, no. 16), f. 52*v*.

[74]The lease: TS 10 J 4, f. 11*v*, ll. 11–13, ed. Assaf, *Texts*, p. 159; re-edited with useful notes in Gil, *Foundations*, pp. 319–321. For Niẓām al-Mulk see n. 34, above.

[75]Blessings for the bearers of titles, *neqūvē ha-shēm* (cf. Numbers 1:16–17): TS NS Box 110, f. 26, ll. 38–39, ed. Goitein, "Prayers from the Geniza for Fatimid Caliphs . . . ," *Studies in Judaica, Karaitica and Islamica, Presented to Leon Nemoy* (Ramat Gan, 1982), pp. 47–57 (Engl.). This document was written between 1127 and 1131, see *ibid.*, p. 50.

[76]Mez, *Renaissance*, p. 78 n. 3, is almost shocked that a Christian vizier in Cairo should be addressed as "our illustrious lord," and takes it for granted that a great Jewish banker in Baghdad, *ibid.*, p. 450, should be blessed with "May God keep

you," according to Mez, the lowest wish accorded a person. On the bestowing of titles on non-Muslims by the government see also *EI*², II, 178*b* (F. Rosenthal).

In Mosseri L-246 a Jewish notable *al-shaykh al-thiqa al-amīn*, "the reliable elder, trusted [by the government]" is asked to act in matters of the delayed marriage gift of a divorcée or widow, who had embraced Islam. One or more of the five brothers-in-law of Moses Maimonides might have borne one of these titles or both, like their father, but since a number of Jews possessed them, the identification is doubtful. Correct *Hommage à Georges Vajda*, ed. G. Nahon and C. Touati (Louvain, 1980), p. 166 n. 47, accordingly. "The Levite" there is a misreading for *waliyyī*, "my friend." Mosseri L-246 is not in the handwriting of Maimonides.

77 The Sound: *Med. Soc.*, II, 246–247. In TS 20.128*v*, the nāsī Solomon b. Jesse is addressed thus in 1237. At approximately the same time a physician living in Damascus and bearing that title is mentioned in TS 12.413*v*, l. 3, a fragmentary letter sent to the same.

78 Sadīd al-Dawla Abū Saʿd: TS Arabic Box 38, f. 117, l. 10; TS Arabic Box 30, f. 40, bottom. For Saʿd al-Dīn, see D. H. Baneth, "The Library of a Physician in Egypt in Maimonides' Time," *Tarbiz*, 30 (1961), 171 n. 3.

79 Maimonides: TS 16.291, l. 20, and *Med. Soc.*, II, 248 and n. 37.

80 *Abu ʾl-Barakāt al-Kohen al-kātib al-sadīd*; Bodl. MS Heb. a 3 (Cat. 2873), f. 6, l. 15 (1169), see *ibid.*, III, 299 and n. 99. *Al-qāḍī al-sadīd* carried a considerable sum belonging to Jewish orphans on his way back from Aden, South Arabia, to Egypt, TS NS J 242, *India Book* 311.

81 Al-Asʿad the physician: *Med. Soc.*, III, 81–82 and nn. 46 and 47 (dated 1217), esp. p. 465 n. 120 (where Ibn Abī Uṣaybiʿa II, 218, is a misprint for II, 118).

82 The banker, *ṣayrafī*: *ibid.*, II, 428, secs. 141 and 142, and 502, sec. 113; as contributor in ULC Or 1080 J 2, col. I, l. 15; Gil, *Foundations*, pp. 453–456, 464 n. 8, 467.

83 Clerk in the army: *Med. Soc.*, II, 435, sec. 173, dated 1302. For *kātib al-ʿArab* see *ibid.*, p. 379 and n. 38. Representative of merchants: TS 16.298, *India Book* 190. Customs director: TS NS Box 321, f. 23, ll. 3 and 6, *India Book* 320. The writer of the Arabic letter was a Muslim; whether al-Asʿad himself was a Muslim, Jew, or Christian is not evident.

84 Cf. *EI*², II, 178*b* (Franz Rosenthal) on titles composed with dawla borne by non-Muslims.

85 TS 8 J 16, f. 18. Only the first seventeen lines of the letter are preserved, which show, however, that Obadiah, the bearer of these titles, possessed also a certain familiarity with Hebrew literature. For "favor, good luck," *ḥazz*, needed in contact with rulers, see *Med. Soc.*, II, 604 n. 32.

86 We have no Geniza from Iraq from the High Middle Ages. But the divan of the gifted poet Eleazar b. Jacob ha-Bavli (d. ca. 1250), ed. H. Brody (Jerusalem, 1935) is replete with creations extolling persons bearing titles composed with *dawla* and *mulk*. See about him *EJ*, VI, 590 (W. J. Fischel). *Gharas al-dawla*: Divan, p. 104, no. 222; his father was a *muʿīd*, "repetitor" (not *muʿīr*), see Makdisi, *The Rise of Colleges* (see n. 67, above), p. 127, bottom and *passim*.

4. *Friendship and Enmity*

1 Saʿīd ʿAbbūd, *5000 arabische Sprichwörter aus Palästina* (Berlin, 1933), p. 19, no. 426. The Yemenite version of the saying is milder: "Try to have few enemies and many friends," Goitein, *Jemenica*, p. 123, no. 883. In both cases the word for friend is *ṣāḥib*.

2 Goitein, *Jemenica*, p. 181, no. 1425. A weaker parallel in ʿAbbūd, p. 106, no. 2406.

3 Mishna Avot (Sayings of the Fathers) 5:16. Referred to in TS 16.294, ll. 9–11, see n. 57, below.

4 Attention is drawn to Wolfram von den Steinen, *Der Kosmos des Mittelalters* (Bern and Munich, 1959), p. 220: "It was not courtly love, which, around 1100, represented the moving moral power, but the comradeship in battle which bound man to man" (trans.).

[5]David's friend: I Chronicles 27:33, in a list of officials and dignitaries. In II Samuel 15:37 and 16:16–17, conceived as a friend owing special allegiance. Solomon's friend: I Kings 4:5. This "friend" was a son of the prophet Nathan to whom Solomon owed his throne.

[6]Amnon, the firstborn of David: II Samuel 13:3. Rehoboam, son of Solomon: I Kings 12:8. His friends became his servants who "stood before him."

[7]I Samuel 18:3. Professor Moshe Greenberg drew my attention to the ancient Mesopotamian phrase *ka napashtum*, "like his own self," corresponding exactly to Heb. *ke-nafshō*, here, and in Deuteronomy 13:17. (The Mesopotamian vassal promises to love his overlord like himself.) TS 8 J 20, f. 11, l. 2: "You are dearer to me than my own soul," letter by Zechariah b. Ḥayyīm of Palermo, Sicily, written in autumn 1172. As his name indicates, he belonged to the distinguished family of the brothers Zakkār-Zechariah and Ḥayyīm b. ʿAmmār from the same city, active a hundred years before him. The recipient, not a relative, is addressed with eight lines of superlative expressions of yearning.

[8]Malachi 2:14, "she is your companion and wife by convenant."

[9]I Samuel 10:5–6, and 19:20–24.

[10]I Kings 19:19–21.

[11]Genesis 2:24. See Ruth 3:9.

[12]I found this pair of verses rather impressive:

Make friends with noble men,
  If you can find a way to their friendship.
And drink out of their cup,
  Even if it is poison right down to the dregs.

T. Nöldeke (*Beiträge zur Kenntnis der Poesie der alten Araber* [Hanover, 1864], p. 79) calls this a marvelous pair of verses. The poet happened to be Jewish, but there was no substantial difference between Jewish and pagan pre-Islamic poets. The term for concluding a friendship, used here twice, is *ikhāʾ*, lit., "taking as brother," see n. 14, below.

[13]*Ḥamāsa of Abū Tammām*, ed. G. Freytag (Bonn, 1828–1847), p. 327. See also R. A. Nicholson, *A Literary History of the Arabs* (New York, 1907), p. 84.

[14]"The true-believers are brothers," Koran 49:10. Also 9:12. In order to emphasize that the new brotherhood of religion cut through the bonds of tribal allegiance, the prophet Muhammad concluded formal brotherhood between each Muslim member of his own tribe and one of the Muslims of Medina, to which he emigrated. This was called *ikhāʾ*, see n. 12, above, and n. 19 below.

[15]Goitein, *Studies*, pp. 149–167.

[16]*Tahdhīb al-akhlāq*, ed. C. K. Zurayk (Beirut, 1967), who provided an English translation (Beirut, 1968); French trans., Mohammed Arkoun, *Miskawayh, Traité d'Éthique* (Damascus, 1969). See also: M. Arkoun, *Contribution à l'étude de l'humanisme arabe au iv/xe siècle: Miskawayh, philosophe et historien* (Paris, 1970). A contemporary of Miskawayh, at-Tawḥīdī, wrote a treatise on friendship, which is deeply influenced by Greek thinking. An excellent study of it is found in Marc Bergé, "Une Anthologie sur l'amitié d'Abū Ḥayyān at-Tawḥīdī," *BEOIF Damas*, 16 (1961), 15–58.

[17]Details in *Med. Soc.*, I, 164–169.

[18]*Ibid.*, pp. 347 and 489 nn. 9–13. However, *Mawhūb ha-mitḥabbēr le-Ben Yeshaʿyā* (Heb.) in Bodl. MS Heb. d 65 (Cat. 2877), f. 4, l. 9, a letter sent from Qayrawān, Tunisia, to Fustat in 1035, should not be translated "Mawhūb, who traveled with Ben Yeshaʿyā," but ". . . who is befriended by . . ." or ". . . who is the *ṣaḥib* of . . . "; see the usage in Pirqē Avot 1:7.

[19]TS 13 J 21, f. 5, ll. 15–18, ed. Goitein, *The Yemenites*, pp. 131–132. This Arabian Jew does not use the term "rafīq," but writes *kunt muʾākhī*, "I concluded a brotherhood"; see n. 14, above.

[20]*Friends and Lovers* (New York, 1976).

[21]*Ibid.*, pp. 12–13, 32–33, 38, 222. David's dirge: II Samuel 1:17–27.

[22]*Ibid.*, pp. 42–43.

[23]Text: *ṭalāq [not ṭalāqat] al-wajh li[ʾl]-ṣadīq wal-thānī al-taraddud lahu.*

[24]TS 16.274, ll. 26–30, a very long letter, beginning and end missing. Preserved: 40 complete and 33 defective lines, the latter containing often only a few words or letters. The writer, I am convinced, was none other than Makhlūf b. Mūsā al-Nafūsī Ibn al-Yatīm, whose extremely moody letter is translated above, pp. 249–254. The handwriting and the style, including numerous quotations, are his. His original home was Barqa, Libya. He tells the recipient, *verso*, l. 4, that he would give "to my lady, your mother" 10 dinars and a sum for maintenance (obviously as requested). "My lady" in such a context probably means "my elder sister." The letter must have been written when Makhlūf was comparatively young, for he complains about separation from his small children, l. 15, and asks the addressee to buy a beautiful pair of earrings for "the baby girl," i.e., his wife, *verso*, l. 26. It is remarkable that most of the products ordered had come from India. I copied this letter in August 1953, but refrained from publishing it because I hoped that some of the missing parts would be found.

[25]See n. 16, above. See also Marc Bergé, *Pour un humanisme vécu: Abū Ḥayyān al-*[*l*, not *t*, as above] *Tawḥīdī* (Damascus, 1979), p. 430, s.v. "amitié," where the reader is sent to the Arabic terms. Miskawayh, *Traité d'Éthique*, trans. Arkoun (see n. 16, above), pp. 211–231, esp. p. 214.

[26]Westminster College, Frag. Cairens, f. 43, ll. 9–14. The writer Isaac the Jerusalemite had probably become acquainted with Elijah when both still lived in Jerusalem. The style and content of the letter show that both were intimately acquainted with each other.

[27]TS 8 J 27, f. 1, l. 4. In l. 5 he quotes Proverbs 17:17, which expresses the idea that only enduring friendship is genuine; *bi-ḥaqq al-ahavā*, "in the name of our friendship" (lit., "love," Heb.), TS 8 J 28, f. 5, l. 22, an old letter on vellum.

[28]TS 13 J 25, f. 8, ll. 27–28, *Nahray* 183. Jacob b. Nahum b. Ḥakmūn travels to Alexandria *li-natamattaʿ bi-ruʾyatak, li-nujaddid bihā ʿahda*[*n*]*ā*, "for the pleasure of seeing you and the renewal of our covenant." The same in TS 8 J 25, f. 15, l. 8. TS 24.65, ll. 26–27, ed. Goitein, *Palestinian Jewry*, p. 286, and elsewhere. However, the signature *berīth shalōm*, "covenant of peace," added to one's name, refers to Malachi 2:5, characterizing the writer as a Kohen. TS 8 J 28, f. 5, address, see preceding note.

[29]Dropsie 389, ll. 7–8. Bodl. MS Heb. d 66 (Cat. 2878), f. 5, ll. 12–13: "Friendship, *ṣadāqa*, and *ṣuḥba* were between us." See also *Med. Soc.*, I, 169.

[30]ENA 1822, f. 47: Simḥā, the son of Isaac b. Simḥā Nīsabūrī, Alexandria, greets Abū Saʿd (Nissīm), the son of Nahray b. Nissīm. TS 10 J 10, f. 27 and TS 10 J 17, f. 21, *Nahray* 114 and 115: the son of ʿIwāḍ b. Hananel greets Abū Saʿd.

[31]TS 13 J 29, f. 3, l. 11. The recipient is asked to grant a delay in the payment of a debt because the writer got stuck with his money since sums owed him had not been paid. The date mentioned, Tuesday, first of Nisan (47)89 = March 18, 1029, designates the arrival of the letter, as it was customary to note this in letters of the early years of the eleventh century. The date cannot refer to Muslim Rabīʿ al-awwal, (4)89 = 1096, for in that year the Jewish and Muslim months mentioned did not coincide. Differences of one or two days between the Jewish and Muslim dates are common in the Geniza.

[32]TS 12.92, ll. 5–6: Israel b. Joseph, Qayrawān, writing to Abū Sahl Manasse b. David, Fustat. Wife: *ahl al-dār.*

[33]ULC Or 1080 J 36, margin, end, *Nahray* 178: *mā naghīb mawḍiʿ taḥḍur*. The writer was Barhūn b. Moses, about whose personality see pp. 129–130 and nn. 3–9, above.

[34]Cf. Goitein, *Letters*, pp. 168–173, and n. 53, below.

[35]Bodl. MS Heb. c 28 (Cat. 2876), f. 22, top, ll. 5–6, *India Book* 83. Abū Naṣr means victorious (our Victor).

[36]ENA NS 21, f. 14, a loose sheet, originally attached to a letter, which has not yet been found. It is identified by script, style, and subject matter. In the final version of the *India Book*, which includes items found of late, this manuscript is numbered chap. IV, 72.

[37]TS 13 J 19, f. 17, margin, ed. Goitein, *Tarbiz*, 28 (1959), 355. Cf. Bodl. MS Heb. a 2 (Cat. 2805), f. 21*v*, ll. 4–5: "Every son of Israel owes his *ṣāḥib* affection and love in times of distress and happiness," said of two brothers-in-law (in a letter addressed to their father). Relatives by definition should be friends.

[38]About Jacob b. Nissīm and Joseph b. Berechiah, see Mann, *Texts*, I, 112 ff.

[39]This is Moses (Mūsā) Ibn al-Majjānī, the representative of Ibn ʿAwkal in Qayrawān, see Goitein, *Letters*, p. 32, and above, pp. 564–565 nn. 98 and 113.

[40]Mishna, Berakhot 9:5.

[41]David, the presumed author of the Book of Psalms.

[42]By the rearrangement of the verses the writer makes the point brought home by the Mishna text alluded to earlier.

[43]Ar. *karārīs*. The learned *responsa*, or answers from the academies, which often extended over several pages, were written not on single leaves but on quires. Many of them, or their copies, written in the same way, have been preserved in the Geniza.

[44]Reference to the Head of the Academy Sherira Gaon (d. 1006) and his son Hay, who served as vice-president from 985.

[45]The three senior Tustarīs of Fustat.

[46]Time (here *waqt*) means fortune. The word translated two lines later as fortune, *dahr*, also means time. Time-fortune as destroyer of friendship was a constant theme in Arabic poetry; see p. 294 at n. 108.

[47]TS 12.175, ed. Goitein, *Tarbiz*, 34 (1965), 169–174.

[48]Religion is compared with a tent.

[49]Song of Songs 1:8, as explained in BT Shabbat 33*b* (especially there in Rashi; the great commentator was born around 1040, but his comments are based on ancient traditions).

[50]The biblical text refers to the upkeep of the Temple service. Our writer had in mind the efforts made to reform the loose mores for which Egypt was notorious. In a letter written in or around 1039 the nāsī Daniel b. Azariah is praised for cleansing the Jewish community of Fustat of its abuses: "He removed the slave girls [meaning: concubines] from the houses, made a partition between pure and impure, and banned music and those listening to it": ENA 3765, f. 10*v*, ll. 22–24, see Mark R. Cohen, "New Light on the Conflict over the Palestinian Gaonate, 1038–1042," *AJSreview*, 1 (1976), 25.

[51]As the verse is explained in BT Berakhot 8*a*.

[52]See the comment on Proverbs 27:19 in BT Yevamot 117*a*, bottom.

[53]TS 16.269, a long letter, beautiful in script and style, but much damaged by water and tears. The names of the sender and the recipient are not preserved. The part translated is in ll. 12–25, the details about the Torah scroll on the margin of page one. The very badly defaced and shorter reverse side contains postscripts. The greetings to Rabbēnū are found on the two uppermost lines of the margin on *verso*, continued on the top.

For the topics treated in this subsection see also S. D. Goitein, "Formal Friendship in the Medieval Near East," *Proceedings of the American Philosophical Society*, 115 (1971), 484–489, a paper read at the Society on April 23, 1971.

[54]Abū Ḥayyān al-Tawḥīdī, *Kitāb al-imtāʿ wal-muʾānasa*, ed. A. Amīn and A. al-Zayn (3d ed.; Beirut, 1966).

[55]Product of culture: Brain, *Friends and Lovers* (see n. 20, above), p. 223. Primitive societies: *ibid.*, p. 35.

[56]Ar. *muḥāḍara*, which in modern Arabic means lecture, but at the time of the writing of this letter: "exchange of ideas between people present." The book of Moses Ibn Ezra, which has the form of questions and answers, uses the same word in its title.

[57]TS 16.294, ll. 5 ff. The writer alludes here to Mishna Avot 5:16, see n. 3, above. About the circumstances of the writing of this letter see *Med. Soc.*, II, 49 and n. 55. The Nagid referred to (of whom he says that he was liked by him) seems to have been Abraham Maimonides (d. 1237).

[58]TS 13 J 15, f. 14, ed. Mann, II, 83–84, who omits, however, the addition in

Arabic. The term *muḥāwara* is still used.

[59]Bodl. MS Heb. a 3 (Cat. 2873), f. 17, ed. Goitein, *Palestinian Jewry*, p. 159, ll. 5–20, are all dedicated to this topic. "Blaze," Ar. *ghurra*, the white fleck on the head of a horse, is a typically Arabic expression for splendor. Jews did not ride horses.

[60]TS 24.56*v*., ll. 31–33, ed. *ibid*., p. 168.

[61]TS 24.49, ll. 13–30, ed. *ibid*., p. 127. For Eli see *Med. Soc*., II, 78. He was a prominent member of the community; documents emanating from him and letters addressed to him might fill a monograph. Documents signed by him range from 1057 to 1098. (In II, 78, I wrote the date 1107, based on II, 444, top, sec. 24, where Eli signed a list of handouts to the poor from that time, but the sheet on which he signed had been incorrectly inserted there, by whom we cannot know. In TS 28.4, ll. 39–40, dated summer 1100, Eli is mentioned as dead.) Our letter was written in 1067 (or 1070), see Goitein, *Palestinian Jewry*, p. 126, top.

[62]TS 8 J 13, f. 1. As often, the introductory lines are cut away. The reverse side was used for a carefully written list of household expenses, ranging from a wide variety of products bought to payments to a laborer and for a visit to the bathhouse. The list is in Arabic script and notes numbers with Coptic, not Hebrew, numerals. It might well have been written by the friend. We are here in an environment well acquainted with Arabic. For other lists of this type see *Med. Soc*., IV, 230–234.

[63]TS 13 J 24, f. 14, esp. ll. 12–18, *verso*, ll. 11–15, 21–25. The fact that the cantor makes inquiries of travelers from both Cairo and Alexandria, *verso*, l. 9, shows that he served in a provincial town; he sends his letters with "Alexandrians," *recto*, l. 14.

[64]Like the cantor Etan (cf. Psalms 89:1, heading) in *Med. Soc*., III, 221, top.

[65]A person kisses a *newly arrived* letter from a friend, and puts it on his eyes and head *before* reading it.

[66]TS 13 J 19, f. 21. Vernacular forms like *ẓannayt* for *ẓanant*, *verso*, l. 3, are found even in the writings of Maimonides; see J. Blau, *A Grammar of Mediaeval Judaeo-Arabic* (Jerusalem, 1980), p. 80, para. 88.

[67]For Solomon Ibn Gabirol (d. ca. 1057), see *EJ*, VII, 235–246. His divan and that of Judah ha-Levi were eagerly studied in the countries of the eastern Mediterranean, see *Med. Soc*., II, 221 and n. 10, 238 and n. 48 (Egypt, Damascus, Byzantium). The poem, or rather piece of one, written by Ibn Gabirol at sixteen: *Solomon Ibn Gabirol: Secular Poems*, ed. H. Brody and J. Schirmann (Jerusalem, 1974), p. 77, no. 129, and often printed; I searched for a model in *ibid*., pp. 17–19, where poems with the same rhyme and meter as Parsī's are edited, but in vain. I wish to thank Professor Ezra Fleischer for his helpful comments on this poem.

[68]These verses might well have been inspired by a poem of Ibn Gabirol.

[69]See pp. 15–16 and n. 32, above.

[70]"The Life of Judah ha-Levi," ed. Goitein, *Tarbiz*, 9 (1938), 35–54, 219–240, 284–305; reprinted in Schirmann, *Studies*, I, 250–318, followed by an Appendix, pp. 319–341, examining the Geniza letters on the subject, edited or discussed by me.

[71]ULC Add. 3340, ed. Goitein, *Tarbiz*, 24 (1955), 138–146; Eng. trans. S. D. Goitein, "Judaeo-Arabic Letters from Spain," in *Orientalia Hispanica*, ed. J. M. Barral (Leiden, 1974), pp. 339–345, with the text transcribed into Arabic letters. See pp. 448 ff., below.

Al-Ukhtūsh: spelled by the writer himself *ʾlkhtūsh*. About fifty years before this letter, Nahray b. Nissīm was informed by his cousin Nathan b. Nahray: "The son of Ben Lukhtūj has arrived in Alexandria from Denia, Spain," TS 10 J 16, f. 17, l. 20, *Nahray* 37. We see that this family, which bore a Berber name (probably of a chieftain, under whose protection they had been while still living in Morocco) had long-standing commercial connections with Egypt. This explains why the mother of our Ibn al-Ukhtūsh was a sister of Ḥalfōn's father, an Egyptian, an example of a "diplomatic" overseas marriage, see *Med. Soc*., I, 48.

[72]It was a year of messianic expectations, as is evident from a poem by Judah ha-Levi, see *Tarbiz*, 9 (1938), 140. But there is no allusion to it here. Letters were dated when it was not certain when they would be received by the addressee. Ḥalfōn's arrival in Spain was expected—this is a letter of welcome—and Judah

ha-Levi traveled to meet him, but it was not sure if and when he would arrive.

[73]The paper on which this letter is written is the best ever seen by me in the Geniza. It is still almost entirely white, strong, and pleasantly smooth.

[74]Ar. *rayyis* (*raʾīs*) has many meanings. Here it should be taken as "dignitary" and the like, since Ḥalfōn came from a family of divines and scholars.

[75]Ḥalfōn had been in Spain before, and Joseph Ibn al-Ukhtūsh most probably had visited Egypt. Therefore he was eager to know everything happening among the intellectuals there.

[76]"Quintessence and embodiment," Ar. *jumlat bilādnā wa-maʿnāhā*, l. 23. Ha-Levi's uniqueness was fully recognized during his lifetime, although the preeminent poet Moses Ibn Ezra was still alive, albeit very old, and the younger Abraham Ibn Ezra still lived in Spain at the writing of this letter.

[77]Merchants usually traveled in the company of others. Joseph assumed that Ḥalfōn's traveling companions were people whom he had met in Egypt.

[78]Abu ʾl-Barakāt b. Ḥārith was a Levi like Ḥalfōn and appears in at least four other letters in his company; he might have been a relative of his and of Ibn al-Ukhtūsh.

[79]The writer's mother. It was good manners to mention common relatives by their relationship to the recipient.

[80]Humorous allusion to friends belonging to the circle to which both Ḥalfōn and Ibn al-Ukhtūsh belonged. Potter: (Samuel b. Isaac) Ibn al-Fakhkhār (meaning potter), who wrote TS 12.66 and TS 12.816, to Ḥalfōn. Philosopher: Joseph b. Barzel, who is called *ḥakīm*, man of secular erudition, also in the letter of Judah ha-Levi translated p. 465, below. Bragger, *fashshāṭ* (this is the correct reading), name of an important family in Fustat (members mentioned between 965 and 1016, at least) and later in Tudela, Spain, 1305, see I. F. Baer, *A History of the Jews in Christian Spain* (Tel Aviv, 1959), p. 131 (Heb.); perhaps only the name was common to these Egyptian and Spanish families. Cantors is an incomplete translation; *ḥazzānīn* means here composers of *ḥazzanūth*, synagogue liturgy, often concocted by cantors with few poetical gifts, here said humorously of verse makers belonging to the circle in general.

[81]Text and trans. of this will in Israel Abrahams, *Hebrew Ethical Wills* (Philadelphia, 1926), II, 186–187, and see p. 163, mentioned in Mann, *Texts*, who used an older edition. The story that everyone present testified that the face of the dead man lit up is not as strange as it sounds on first reading. My father died, when I, not yet fourteen, was away. When I came home for the funeral, the attending physician opened the coffin for me, and I was astounded to see how relaxed, almost happy, my father's face looked. For a moment I had the feeling that he was aware of my presence.

[82]The text of this pact is conveniently available in B. Dinur, *Israel in the Diaspora*, Vol. II, Book 1 (Tel Aviv, 1965), pp. 532–533. It did not work out as planned. In the years that followed, Portuguese pirates made seafaring almost impossible for Jews and Muslims. One of the partners lost four children during the subsequent years and regarded it as a punishment for not carrying out his vows. See Alfred Freimann, "Asher ben Jechiel," *Jahrbuch der Jüdisch–Literarischen Gesellschaft*, 12 (1918), 281 (repr., p. 45) and n. 4.

[83]The reader might form an inkling of the rules of behavior drawn up for the members of brotherhoods from Solomon Schechter, *Studies in Judaism*, Vol. II (Philadelphia, 1945), pp. 238–239. For the contracts themselves see M. Benayahu, *Azulay*, Vol. I (Jerusalem, 1959), pp. 16–18, where further literature.

[84]Firkovitch II, 236, no. 5, f. 2*v*., ed. Mann, *Texts*, I, 472–474, esp. pp. 453–454. I do not possess a copy of the manuscript, but the text is clear.

[85]*We-shalōm* is to be added; the phrase is taken from the last of the seven benedictions at a wedding ceremony.

[86]Heb. *she-nisṭarkhū* for *nisṭarēkh*, a Maghrebi Arabic dialect form of the first person plural transferred to Hebrew—an interesting case of bilingualism.

[87]A synagogue reputed to be of particular holiness and miracular faculties,

founded by a refugee from Spain, a cabalist, see Sambari, *Chronicle*, ed. Ad. Neubauer (Oxford, 1887), *passim*, esp. p. 159.

[88]The word is not completely preserved. Probably *le-halwōtō* was intended.

[89]Such as a wedding or a funeral, both expensive affairs.

[90]Not the usual simile of one soul in two bodies, but two persons being like one body, meaning that each should feel the other's pains or well-being as if they had been his own. Found also in contemporary contracts of group friendship.

[91]The most prominent religious leaders of the time, the first three living in Palestine, R. Meir b. Isaac Katzenellenbogen in Padua, Italy, and the last, Ibn Sīd (of the same family as the second signatory but probably not his father), in Cairo.

[92]I.e., Yōm Tōv's father was still alive.

[93]See *Med. Soc.*, II, 180, and III, 236–237, and above, p. 289, where two boys conclude a pact of friendship at the age of ten.

[94]See p. 279 and nn. 23, 24, above. That a man should meet another member of a religious brotherhood at least once a day was stipulated in the rules summarized by Schechter, *Studies* (see n. 83, above), p. 239.

[95]See *ibid.*, pp. 238 and 292–294 (Hebrew Appendix). Also Benayahu, *Azulay*, I, 16–18 (see n. 83, above).

[96]In the Arab world the sixteenth century certainly must be regarded as belonging to the Late Middle Ages.

[97]See pp. 282–283 and nn. 48 and 53, and p. 284 and n. 57, above.

[98]For Hillel b. Eli see *Med. Soc.*, II, 231. First document signed by him: 1066. He retired around 1108. Out of wedlock: *Med. Soc.*, III, 350. I plan to deal with this and similar booklets of divination preserved in the Geniza separately.

[99]TS Arabic Box 44, f. 54, f. 3*a*, no. 4. A dubious friendship is a disgrace for the friends, like an unsuccessful marriage for the spouses, and provides joy to their enemies.

[100]*Ibid.*, f. 5*a*, no. 5.

[101]*Ibid.*, f. 8*a*, no. 5.

[102]Dropsie 389*v*, ll. 4–5, 29–30, and Dropsie 414 (the continuation of 389). Communicate: *wa-qulūb-nā ʿalā baʿḍ-hā baʿḍ illā ʾl-wasāʾiṭ*. Your loving: *min wādd-hi.*

[103]After the pillage of Qayrawān in 1057, R. Nissīm b. Jacob lived in Sūsa, Tunisia, see Goitein, *Letters*, p. 168, but at his death there in 1062, was buried in al-Mahdiyya, see *ibid.*, p. 170. Our letter, TS 10 J 31, f. 3, speaks twice about the transport of his body, *verso*, ll. 1 and 7–8.

[104]Brother: meaning here [distant] relative, for in ll. 11–13 he is described as "head, *sayyid*, of our house and family," while Ibn Qayyōmā is only "our dear friend and brother."

[105]TS 10 J 31, f. 3*v*, ll. 3–7.

[106]Joseph b. Berechiah: see pp. 281–282 and nn. 38–47, above.

[107]Forgotten: see pp. 285 ff., above.

[108]See Rosenthal, *Complaint and Hope in Medieval Islam*, esp. pp. 4–18.

[109]Mann, I, 226–228; II, 279–280. The letter is in Hebrew. The translated lines are mostly in rhyme; often every second word is rhymed. See also p. 48 and n. 18 and p. 53 and n. 38, above.

[110]See n. 106 above.

[111]"Twenty" meant "many" in the Middle Ages, it seems, from India to Western Europe. As we would say: "I wrote you ten letters."

[112]TS 8 J 26, f. 20, much damaged. See also p. 247 and n. 142.

[113]TS 13 J 17, f. 10, ll. 3 and 14. Same complaint in TS 12.348.

[114]TS AS 148, f. 2. Separation is called here both *firqa* and *mufāraqa*(*tak*).

[115]TS 13 J 24, f. 20*v*. The *recto* is damaged to such an extent that the dispute referred to cannot be completely understood.

[116]PER H 129*v*, ll. 4–5: *al-ṣabr ʿala ʾl-ḥabīb walā faqdō*, see ʿAbbūd, *Sprichwörter*, p. 113, no. 2544. The term *ḥabīb* is normally not used in the classical Geniza, but is, of course, classical Arabic, cf. n. 121, below. The text of the letter and a full translation (into Hebrew) is provided in my article "The Twilight of the House of Maimonides," *Tarbiz*, 54 (1985), 67–104.

[117]Text *al-mṣh*, in the postscript, l. 2, for *maṣāṣa*, sugarcane that had gone through the sugar mill once, see Dozy, *Supplément*, II, 597*a*. Since sugar was widely used in medicine, physicians often kept sugar workshops, see *Med. Soc.*, II, 258 and n. 92, IV, 441–442 and nn. 157–159.

[118]The identity of the writer is established by "our lord" in the postscript, l. 7, the date 1334, and the superscription "Here is the God of my salvation" (Isaiah 12:2), which is regularly used in the missives emanating from Joshua's office. The word *al-ḥaqq*, "The Truth," in *verso*, l. 7, simply means God, a common usage in the Late Middle Ages.

[119]TS 12.405, ll. 6–7.

[120]Pp. 237–238 and n. 78, above.

[121]Cf. Proverbs 27:10; "Alphabet of Ben Sira," *Ozar Midrashim*, ed. J. D. Eisenstein (New York, 1915), I, 42: "You never disown an old friend." Abū Nuʿaym al-Iṣfahānī, *Ḥilyat al-Awliyā* (Hyderabad, 1932), III, 71, last but one line: *ʿalayka bil-ḥabībi ʾl-awwali*, "keep your first friend." Goitein, *Jemenica*, p. 94, no. 640. *Med. Soc.*, I, 169.

[122]Allusion to Genesis 15:16. The writer means to say that part of the accusations made by him in a previous letter had already been substantiated, but the full guilt of the recipient had become evident in the latest events which gave rise to the break.

[123]Sarcastic reference to the bad behavior of his friend.

[124]An imitation of a Muslim blessing for Muhammad, which itself is an echo of Psalms 72:15, "May he [God] always pray for him" [the messianic king].

[125]TS Arabic Box 41, f. 53.

[126]For this cf. pp. 233 ff. and nn. 61–65, above.

[127]ENA 2560, f. 32, l. 11, ed. Goitein, *Palestinian Jewry*, p. 300. The son of a notable in Bilbays, Lower Egypt, writes to a friend who had carried donations made by the local congregation to a synagogue and to a group of scholars in Jerusalem. He asks him now to send an official confirmation that "the gold" had been safely delivered to its destinations. "For as long as such a confirmation has not been received, there might be [bad] talk about my father [the local VIP] and you." The sentence translated here corrects my Hebrew translation accompanying the edited text.

[128]See pp. 230, 234, 235, and 249, above, and *passim*.

[129]ULC Or 1080 J 70, ll. 2–5.

[130]Letter: TS 6 J 4, f. 14, *India Book* 23–25: three fragments of two copies of one complete letter. Maḍmūn, representative of merchants in Aden, writes to Abraham Ben Yijū in India. Note: TS NS Box 320, f. 58, *India Book* 328, addressed to Abū Saʿīd (Ḥalfōn b. Nethanel).

[131]Mann, I, 152.

[132]Salo W. Baron's brilliant essay "Saadia's Communal Activities" in *Saadia Anniversary Volume* (New York, 1943), pp. 9–74, is a good introduction to the world of Babylonian-Iraqian Jewry of the tenth century. The supplication in Saadya Gaon, *Siddur*, p. 356, ll. 10–12, is in Aramaic, then still partly spoken by the Jews of Babylonia-Iraq.

[133]DK 120, ed. Goitein, *Palestinian Jewry*, p. 169, and before by Alexander Scheiber in "Drei Briefe von Osten," *Acta Orientalia Hungarica*, 17 (1964), 217–219, who kindly put the manuscript at my disposal. Now in Scheiber, *Geniza Studies*, p. 219. The house of the Head of the Diaspora derived its origin from King David.

[134]See S. D. Goitein, "Prayers from the Geniza for Fatimid Caliphs, the Head of the Jerusalem Yeshiva, the Jewish Community, and the Local Congregation," *Studies in Judaica, Karaitica, and Islamica, Presented to Leon Nemoy on his Eightieth Birthday* (Ramat-Gan, 1982), pp. 47–57 (in English).

[135]See p. 263 n. 42, above.

[136]TS 12.654*v*, ll. 2–3, a letter to the nāsī Solomon b. Jesse. The writer, after having been afflicted with a protracted case of *ishāl*, "diarrhea," was suffering from ophthalmia, which was particularly painful.

[137]ULC Add. 3345, l. 44. A learned foreigner, after praising the charitable people of Fustat for what they had done for him during a year and a half, complains of failing to find work.

[138]Rosenthal, *Study of Muslim Intellectual and Social History*, p. 8.

[139]Qur'ān, Sura 113:5; cf. 15:17, 81:35.

[140]*Ibid.*, 15:30–33, and *EI*^{2}, III, 668, s.v. "Iblīs," and, preferably, I, 177, s.v. "Ādam," where the Satan story and its sources are explained in more detail.

[141]Cf. Goitein, *Letters*, p. 75. Here the father and the two uncles of Abu Saʿd are addressed.

[142]TS 10 J 24, f. 2, ll. 14–15, *India Book* 92: *ʿalā asarr surūd wa-rajm kull ḥasūd.* In the introduction to the letters, the enviers are listed before the enemies. For the poem and other quotations, see Rosenthal, *Study of Muslim Intellectual and Social History*, p. 10.

[143]TS 13 J 23, f. 3*v*, l. 6, said in connection with the troubles incurred by the Maghrebi merchants sojourning in Alexandria, see *Med. Soc.*, II, 67 and n. 148; *ʿumila ʿalā damī*, and similar phrases meaning spilling blood denote extreme harm inflicted on a man's possessions or reputation.

[144]ULC Add. 3336, ll. 6–7, addressed to Abū ʿAlī Ezekiel, the brother of Ḥalfōn b. Nethanel.

[145]Competition between physicians: *Med. Soc.*, II, 257; teachers: *ibid.*, pp. 186–187. Tribulations of public servants: *ibid.*, pp. 88–89 and n. 116: "I am most miserable. Some envy me [again: first item], others despise me; others, again, are hostile."

[146]Gloating of enemies: above, p. 177, item N. Letter of Abū Zikrī's brother (Solomon): TS 13 J 27, f. 20, ll. 14–19. Shedding blood (see n. 143, above, and n. 152, below): *baʿalē dāmīm* is a misquotation, see Psalms 26:9. Position: *jāh.*

[147]TS 18 J 3, f. 5, l. 35, ed., Goitein, *Palestinian Jewry*, p. 304. The Alexandrians paid the Crusaders a tax for permitting them to do work in Acre at an occupation that they had probably inherited from their forefathers.

[148]TS 13 J 15, f. 24, ll. 11 and 15–21. The addressee: Abraham, son of Nathan the "Seventh," a confidant of the Nagid Mevōrākh b. Saadya, see Cohen, Mark R., *Self-government*, pp. 130–131. The income of a community official consisted of (writing and) issuing legal documents, teaching, occasionally also ritual killing of animals, but mainly of sums pledged (and mostly paid weekly) by individual members. Had the person about whom the writer complained been sufficiently learned, he would have taken the post of spiritual leader himself.

[149]TS 10 J 20, f. 2, ll. 6–15; *verso*, ll. 13–16. The Ibn al-Naʿja ("female sheep, ewe") were a well-known family. A Musallam Ibn al-Naʿja, probably the father of the physician mentioned here, signed a promissory note of 100 dinars in TS Box K 15, f. 91, Col. I, bottom, around 1145, see *Med. Soc.*, I, 263–264 and nn. 206 and 207, and II, 479, sec. 23. Thus the Nagid intended here was probably Samuel b. Hananyah. The physician may also have claimed religious scholarship, as the one mentioned above, p. 268 and n. 66.

[150]PER H 21, *India Book* 167, see p. 194 and n. 53, above.

[151]BT Qiddushin 70*a*.

[152]TS 10 J 18, f. 2, ll. 2–4, 11–15, 23–24. In l. 24, the manuscript clearly has *hdh*, but this is a slip for *hdr* (*hadar damī*, "he shed my blood"; for this usage see nn. 143 and 146, above).

[153]*Ibid.*, ll. 19–20. The word used for denunciation to the government: *yimsor, masrūth* (Heb.).

[154]BT Shabbat 97*a*, top. Said by Rēsh Laqīsh. An allusion to the story of Miriam, sister of Moses (Numbers 12:10–15).

[155]*Ibid.*, 118*b*.

[156]TS 13 J 25, f. 12, ll. 11–12, 19–23. I have prepared a fully annotated English translation of this remarkable letter. Text in Gil, *Palestine during the First Muslim Period (634–1099)*, III, 218–224.

[157]TS 13 J 25, f. 12, l. 17, *ʿāmil wa-ṣāḥib mawārīth.*

[158]TS 24.49, margin, ed. Goitein, *Palestinian Jewry*, pp. 128–129. The meaning of the first quotation (from BT ʿAvoda Zara 18*b*): When a man incurs misfortune, he must ascribe this to his sins and mend his ways.

[159]See pp. 298–299 and nn. 132, 133, and 135, above.

[160]TS 12.415, ll. 17–20.

[161]TS 8.32, *India Book* 349.

[162]TS 16.286, l. 23. The story is told on pp. 55–56 and n. 46, above.

[163]TS 13 J 15, f. 16, ll. 16–17, continued in TS 13 J 15, f. 20, ll. 1–2, *India Book* 122, the letter in which Amram b. Isaac, Ḥalfōn's brother-in-law, informed him about the arrival in Alexandria of the Spanish Hebrew poet Judah ha-Levi, partly edited in Goitein, *Tarbiz*, 24 (1955), 25–28. The passage translated here is not included there. *Ibid.*, p. 28 n. 23, and p. 148, sec. 4, I still understood Ar. *karīma*, according to modern usage, as daughter; but in the Geniza, as in Fatimid inscriptions, it means sister; see *Med. Soc.*, III, 22 and n. 37. The fatherly tone of the letters addressed by Amram to Ḥalfōn proves that his wife was an elder sister of Ḥalfōn. For the meaning of "Pearl" as a designation for a deceased dear relative, see p. 180 and n. 294.

[164]Bodl. MS Heb. d 66 (Cat. 2878), f. 57, ed. Goitein, *Palestinian Jewry*, pp. 329–330, where (Cat. 2787) is a misprint for (Cat. 2878), but is correct on the preceding pages there.

[165]Maimonides, *Commentary on the Mishna*, ed. J. Qāfiḥ (Jerusalem, 1964), IV (Neziqin), 204.

[166]Bodl. MS Heb. e 101 (no Cat.), f. 15, referred to in *Med. Soc.*, III, 47 and n. 64. The date of the year is missing here, but found on e 101, f. 14, with the same month. The father of the two brothers was a *muzanjir*, a specialist dyer working with *zinjār*, a copper sulfate exposed to the air, which provided a light green color (not mentioned among the colors in *Med. Soc.*, IV, 172–177, because it did not appear in connection with clothing). That a Jew should physically attack his brother is an offense to Jewish religion. I have not found the name Shamūn elsewhere; but since it appears here three times, it cannot be a mistake. "And Peace" means that this is a draft to be made, perhaps by another clerk, into a full-fledged document.

[167]ENA 1822, f. 51, ll. 7–13. Much damaged.

[168]*Med. Soc.*, III, 175 and n. 15.

[169]*Ibid.*, IV, 162 and 399 n. 88.

[170]*Ibid.*, II, 168.

[171]*Ibid.*, III, 259 and n. 60.

[172]*Ibid.*, II, 111–112 and n. 41.

[173]In a letter written many years after the demise of (Abraham b. Jacob) al-Darʿī, Alexandria, Nathan b. Judah reports that al-Darʿī accused him on his deathbed of having exchanged a medication sent to him with another causing his death. The fact is mentioned only to illustrate the degree of al-Darʿī's hatred of Nathan because Mevōrākh b. Saadya, the Nagid, had entrusted him with some of the public functions formerly handled by al-Darʿī. For the general background of this strange letter see Cohen, Mark R., *Self-government*, pp. 215 and 241–242.

[174]The same idea in the letter referred to in p. 301 and n. 148, above. Both writers certainly had in mind Maimonides' rulings about the humane treatment of slaves; see *Med. Soc.*, I, 142, third paragraph.

[175]TS NS J 87, beginning and end torn away.

[176]BT Shabbat 88*b*. Sufferings are regarded by pious men with joy because they reveal God as a loving father castigating his son; cf. Proverbs 13:24.

5. Sex

[1]*Islam et sexualité,* thèse présentée devant l'Université de Paris V le 3 Juin 1972, Service de reproduction des thèses, Université de Lille III (Lille, 1973) (hereafter Bouhdiba, *Sexualité*). (Bouhdiba's book on the subject came to my knowledge after the completion of this volume.)

[2]Hayyim J. Cohen, "The Economic Background and the Secular Occupations of Muslim Jurisprudents and Traditionists in the Classical Period of Islam (until the Middle of the Eleventh Century)," *JESHO*, 13 (1970), 16–61.

[3]In ULC Or 1080 J 15*v*, l. 7, *Nahray* 45, a first cousin of Nahray, an old man, extends greetings "to those that are with you." Since no children are mentioned,

the phrase should mean "members of your household." The name of the wife who survived him is known to us from a legal document, by which the widow purchased a maidservant about thirteen years after her husband's death (*Med. Soc.*, I, 137 and n. 39).

[4]TS 16.277, trans. in S. D. Goitein, "Parents and Children: A Geniza Study on the Medieval Jewish Family," *Gratz College Annual*, 4 (1975), 61–64.

[5]Muqaddasi, p. 200, l. 5, and p. 166, l. 3 (on the chastity of the people of Jerusalem).

[6]Maqrīzī, *Khiṭaṭ*, I, 39, ll. 6–10.

[7]*Med. Soc.*, II, 292–293.

[8]See, e.g., *ibid.*, III, 329 and nn. 69–71, which is complemented by *ibid.*, IV, 372 n. 24, end.

[9]*Ibid.*, II, 144–145. Attention is drawn to al-Bukhārī, *Al-Jāmiʿ al-Ṣaḥiḥ*, Adhān, para. 163, where ʿĀʾisha, the Prophet's favorite wife, is cited as prohibiting women from entering the mosque, saying, "had the Messenger of God known what the women do in public gatherings, he would have prohibited them from attending, as the Children of Israel have done with their women." I see in this legend an allusion to the separation of sexes in medieval synagogues and Oriental churches (Children of Israel means both Christians and Jews). Quoted by Moshe Perlmann, "A Seventeenth Century Exhortation Concerning al-Aqṣā," *Israel Oriental Studies*, 3 (1973), 263.

[10]Details in *Med. Soc.*, III, 147–148.

[11]Leviticus 20:13.

[12]In both Palestinian and Babylonian sources, see Saul Lieberman, *Tosefta Kifshutah* (New York, 1955), Part VIII, p. 980.

[13]Rachid Boujedra, *La Répudiation* (Paris, 1970), pp. 106–107, quoted in Bouhdiba, *Sexualité*, pp. 468–469. For homosexuality in Islam, see the (1983) article "Liwāṭ" in *EI*², V, 776–779, which, however, cannot be regarded as an entirely satisfactory treatment of the complex phenomenon.

[14]Mosseri A 68, based on a Talmudic source.

[15]Geniza data about this in *Med. Soc.*, III, 53.

[16]*Ibid.*, p. 263 and n. 85.

[17]Details, *ibid.*, pp. 147–150, 205–210, and *passim.*

[18]Such observations have been made regarding other polygamous societies. For the interesting reports of travelers in Yemen about Jewish polygyny see Brauer, *Ethnologie der Jemenitischen Juden*, pp. 74–76, who emphasizes the sexual aspects. As far as I know, the marriage of a young woman to an old man—joining May to December, as they say now—although not uncommon in the past, was disapproved in principle by the Yemenites, as it was in the Talmud, BT Yevamot 44*a*, top. The story of the "reverse Job" (seven daughters and three sons) is told in my *The Yemenites*, p. 313.

[19]Gottheil-Worrell IX, pp. 44–57, *India Book* 174. Text and translation need revision. For instance, p. 53, where the text clearly says that the child was born after fourteen months, we read "on the fourteenth of the month," which is grammatically impossible and nonsensical in the context of the report. Also TS Box G 1, f. 61*v*, ll. 2–3, *India Book* 371 (dated April–May 1176).

[20]*Med. Soc.*, III, 176.

[21]TS 12.242, ll. 3–13.

[22]The story is told in more detail in the article noted in n. 51, below, pp. 55–56, where source is not given. It is Firkovitch II, 1701.

[23]ULC Or 1080 J 93. See the Comments following the translation.

[24]TS 20.38, ll. 55–56. His full name was Nethanel ha-Levi b. Amram, known as Abu ʾl-Faraj Ibn Maʿmar al-Sharābī. Another Nethanel b. Amram—not ha-Levi—lived seventy years later.

[25]ENA 3765, f. 10, ll. 19–24. See Mark R. Cohen, "New Light on the Conflict over the Palestinian Gaonate, 1038–1042," *AJSreview*, 1 (1976), 12–13 and 21–22, also Goitein, *Palestinian Jewry*, p. 134.

[26]For the role of the *māshiṭa*, see *Med. Soc.*, I, 127 and n. 5.

[27]See *ibid.*, II, 246 and nn. 25 and 26.

[28]Ar. *qalānisiyyīn*, makers of *qalansuwas*, a tall headgear worn mostly by qadis and other high dignitaries.

[29]See n. 25, above. Unless Sayyid Nāṣir is a nickname (like that of Abu ʾl-Dīk, "the man with the cock"), the name claims descent from the Arab prophet, and he might have felt himself particularly responsible for the morality of his contemporaries. Today several million Muslims make such a claim. For the translation of *rājil* (the singular of *rajjāla*, *Med. Soc.*, II, 608 n. 38) as police, namely a policeman on foot, as opposed to mounted police, see *ibid.*, p. 370, second paragraph.

[30]See "The World of Women—outside men's purview," *ibid.*, III, 312 ff.

[31]See Shraga Abramson, *R. Nissīm Gaon* (Jerusalem, 1965), p. 273 (Heb.). The responsum is mentioned in a list of the entries in R. Nissīm's notebook called *Megillat Setārīm* (Private) as no. 215, with the remark: "He discussed women *mesōlelōt* [the Hebrew word has the same double meaning as Latin *salire*] extensively." The responsum itself, as far as I know, is not extant. The ancient law was concerned with this problem, because it was questionable whether a *mesōlelet*, "lesbian," was to be regarded as a prostitute and therefore unfit for marrying a priest (Kohen), cf. BT Yevamot 76*a*, middle, PT 8:10, f. 49*c*, bottom. Maimonides, *Code*, Book "Holiness," sec. "Forbidden Relations," chap. 21:8.

[32]For a short survey see *EI*^{2}, IV, 118–119, s.v. "ʿIshq" (M. Arkoun).

[33]Saadya Gaon, *Kitāb al-Amānāt wal-iʿtiqādāt*, chap. x, sec. 4, ed. J. Qāfiḥ (Jerusalem, 1970), pp. 300–303. Samuel Landauer's edition (Leiden, 1880) is not available to me at the moment.

[34]The splitting of an originally androgynous being into two halves, who henceforth would be seeking out one another, is familiar to everyone from Plato's *Symposium.* It is less well known that Aristophanes, the reputed inventor of this philosophical myth, also created (to satisfy the gays of both sexes) two "double-faced" prototypes of the human race, two males and two females, respectively, in one body. The spheres (our word, *ukar*, pl. of *ukra*, designates small balls with which children play) have their origin in the round form that Aristophanes gave to the creations of his fantasy.

Saadya Gaon knew, of course, that both aspects of this myth are repeatedly referred to in Talmudic literature, even with the Greek terms *androgynous* and *dy-prosopos*, double-faced, the former as explained by Genesis 5:2 (understood as "Adam was created male and female") and the latter by Psalms 139:5 (taken as "you formed me being the same behind and before"). Saadya had no reason to argue with those quotations. All the ancient sages wanted to show was that those esoteric terms of the Greeks were foreshadowed in the Bible. That male and female were originally one body and therefore always yearn to be reunited was sufficiently brought home by the story of the rib (Genesis 2:21–24). The double-faced Adam was only another version of the same idea, not an explanation of homosexuality. See *Bereschit Rabba*, 8:1, ed. J. Theodor (Berlin, 1912), p. 55 (with numerous parallels), and Krauss, *Griechische und lateinische Lehnwörter*, p. 202*a*.

[35]The word used, *ilfa*, means social, not physical contact.

[36]TS 20.117, ed. Assaf, *Texts*, p. 161. See p. 21, above.

[37]TS 8 J 22, f. 25, ed. Goitein, *Palestinian Jewry*, pp. 170–171. For a former edition, see *Med. Soc.*, II, 555 n. 54, and 168, where, however, the cause of the fistfight is omitted.

[38]Cantors, like singers of any type, were suspected of somewhat light mores, see *Med. Soc.*, II, 222–223.

[39]TS Loan 170, ed. Israel Davidson, *Genizah Studies*, Vol. III (New York, 1928), 218–223. Corrections by S. M. Stern, *Tarbiz*, 19 (1948), 62–63.

[40]See Schirmann, *New Hebrew Poems from the Genizah*, pp. 157–158 and 281, a strong and outspoken example from the very beginnings of Hebrew poetry in Spain. On pp. 392–394 Schirmann discusses Davidson's text (see preceding note).

[41]"The Ephebe in Medieval Hebrew Poetry," *Sefarad*, 15 (1955), 55–68.

[42]TS NS Box 200, f. 55, ed. Zvi Malachi, *Israel Oriental Studies*, 2 (1972), 288–289.

[43]I have not seen in the Geniza any notice about a slave girl with musical training, as is so common in Arabic literature. But since instrumental music and the keeping of concubines are constantly mentioned together as the main corrupters of morality, I believe that when one talked, and talked much, about music, one had in mind also the musician. About prices of slave girls, see *Med. Soc.*, I, 137–140.

[44]This estimate is a combination of the data derived from *ibid.*, IV, 449 n. 3, and III, 418–422.

[45]See *ibid.*, I, 134.

[46]TS 24.56*v*, ll. 34–37, ed. Goitein, *Palestinian Jewry*, p. 168.

[47]ENA 3765, f. 10, ll. 15–28, see *ibid.*, p. 134, and here, n. 25, above.

[48]See Goitein, *Letters*, pp. 335–358: "The Abandoned Concubine."

[49]TS Arabic Box 54, f. 93, *India Book* 375. Loosening of communal discipline was noticeable also by the fact that the case of Ibn Sighmār was seemingly brought to the notice of the Muslim authorities by some Jews. The letter, which includes a detailed list of the prices of Oriental and Indian goods, is addressed to Elazar b. Ismaʿīl-Samuel, who signed TS 13 J 1, f. 8 in 1033/4.

[50]This idea is expressed in many places, one of the most elaborate being *Midrash Wayyikra Rabbah*, chap. 24:6, ed. Mordecai (*thus*) Margulies (Jerusalem, 1953–61), pp. 559–560.

[51]Some parts of this subsection are treated in more detail in S. D. Goitein, "The Sexual Mores of the Common People," *Society and the Sexes in Medieval Islam*, Sixth Giorgio Levi Della Vida Conference (in honor of Franz Rosenthal), ed. Afaf Lutfi al-Sayyid-Marsot (Malibu, Calif., 1979), pp. 43–61. See n. 22, above.

C. THE TRUE BELIEVER

1. *Trust in the Merciful*

[1]Attention is drawn to M. Piamenta, *Islam in Everyday Arabic Speech* (Leiden, 1979), where, on 220 tightly packed printed pages, phrases using the name of God are judiciously discussed. Although, as his bibliography shows (pp. 223–230), he utilizes material from many countries throughout Islamic history, he distinguishes carefully between the usages in different places and communities. We learn, for instance, what a Jew in Basra, Iraq, or one in Yemen must wish a Muslim, when the latter sneezes (p. 13). As a young man, Piamenta served the mandatory British government of Palestine in a capacity that gave him opportunity to listen to speakers of Arabic from every imaginable provenance.

[2]This Arabic aphorism (Goitein, *Jemenica*, p. 81, no. 543 and parallels) echoes an Aramaic popular saying, cited in the Talmud. BT Berakhot 63*a*, ʿĒn Yaʿqov version. Both are ultimately derived from an ancient Babylonian hymn on the Sun-god, in which it is said: "Even the burglar, albeit an enemy of the Sun, beseeches you," see J. B. Pritchard, ed., *Ancient Near Eastern Texts Relating to the Old Testament* (Princeton, 1955), p. 389, sec. III. ll. 31–32, and B. Meissner, *Babylonien und Assyrien* (Heidelberg, 1925), II, 168.

[3]BT Soṭa 49*b*, top, and parallels. Matthew 9:6; see H. L. Strack and P. Billerbeck, *Das Evangelium nach Matthäus, erläutert aus Talmud und Midrasch* (Munich, 1922), pp. 392–396, 410–411.

[4]The opening of Exodus 34:5 should not be translated "The Lord, the Lord," because the second word is to be understood as an adjective along with the other attributes. The word translated in the English Bible as "the Lord," YHWH (Jehova), means "the passionate," in the double meaning of compassionate and jealous; see S. D. Goitein, "YHWH the Passionate: The Monotheistic Meaning and Origin of the name YHWH," *Vetus Testamentum*, 6 (1956), 1–9.

[5]BT Rosh ha-Shana 17*b*: "A covenant has been made with the thirteen attributes (*middōt*) that [their recitation] will not come back empty-handed [from God]."

[6]The basmalah is somehow connected with the opening of the "thirteen attributes": *Allāh al-raḥmān al-raḥīm* corresponds exactly to *ēl raḥūm we-ḥannūn*, with the difference that Ar. *ḥanīn* has the meaning of "yearning" and is therefore replaced by the repetitive *raḥīm*.

[7]Psalm 145, which contains other verses with the same content, was said in both the morning and afternoon prayers on workdays and Sabbaths, wherefore everyone knew it by heart.

[8]Saadya Gaon, *Siddur*, pp. 92–93. For use of the first benediction, TS 12.245, ll. 7–10, is a typical case. A man with a Spanish hand had received letters from two friends telling him "what God, the exalted, had wrought for you and for me through you [God's mercy with the friend is a bounty for the writer]; blessed be the Good One who dispenses goodness; may he follow up his boons." After a visit in Jerusalem at the time of its second occupation by Crusaders, a traveler reports that a Jewish dyer was permitted to live there, "blessed be the Good One . . ." (Muslims and Jews were not permitted to live in Jerusalem after it was delivered to the emperor Frederic II). ENA 2559, f. 178, postscript, l. 6, ed. Goitein, *Palestinian Jewry*, p. 301.

Even more extreme is this report in TS 12.258, ll. 14–20: Edom (the Crusaders) had taken everything the writer possessed, his wife and son were captured, the latter sold as slave. "But God wrought miracles and wonders with me; my wife and boy were rescued from Edom; now, we need only bread and clothing; blessed be the Good One. . . ."

As the readers of the New Testament know, letters were occasionally introduced by greetings from God. This custom and the use of Aramaic is still recognizable in early Geniza letters: "Good greetings of Peace from the good Lord who in his bounty dispenses goodness to his world." TS 12.179, l. 3, ed. *ibid.*, p. 277.

[9]BT Berakhot 60*b*. This Aramaic saying is quoted in the original in the Geniza only by more educated persons, see p. 51 and n. 30, above, but is present in various Arabic forms in practically every other letter. The Hebrew "this [misfortune], too, is to the good," BT Taʿanit 21*a* and parallels, is also occasionally quoted.

[10]Mosseri L-290, l. 13, ed. Goitein, *Palestinian Jewry*, p. 92.

[11]TS 8.60, margin, *India Book* 275, Ḥalfōn b. Nethanel writing to his brother Ezekiel.

[12]Cf. the extract from a letter translated, above, p. 46.

[13]TS NS Box 264, f. 1, *India Book* 264*b*, *bi-shmākh raḥmānā roḥṣanenā* (rwḥṣnnʾ), "in your name, O Merciful, we trust" (Aram.), a letter sent from Aden, South Arabia, to Egypt by Saʿīd b. Marḥab, a clerk of the rabbinic court of that city. The Jews of Yemen have often preserved old and original formulations. Professor M. A. Friedman of Tel Aviv University drew my attention to S. Lieberman's *Texts and Studies* (New York, 1974), pp. 21 ff. (quoted in Friedman, *Marriage*, I, 92, n. 17), where he supposes that the ancient superscription "In your name, O Merciful (or Creator)" was originally followed by the word "I [or we] trust."

[14]Maybe Isaiah conceived here the term "Hosts" in the sense of Genesis 2:1 ("The heaven and the earth and all their host were completed"), namely, as the totality of nature. (Heard so from my mentor R. Nehemiah Nobel, although I could not accept this interpretation of his for Psalms 24:10.) H. Gunkel (*Die Psalmen* [Göttingen, 1926], pp. 103–104) has rightly explained that the gates of the Temple opened themselves only after the real name of the warrior "God of Hosts" was pronounced. The *Sanctus* in the Eucharist preserves the Hebrew *Sebaot* (Lord of Hosts).

[15]Saadya Gaon, *Siddur*, pp. 18, l. 1, and 90–91.

[16]"Because of our sins"; p. 60, above. "The sin has caused this": ENA 2805, f. 12, l. 2, see n. 18, below. Earthquake: p. 64, above.

[17]Nīsabūrī: DK XI, ll. 10–30, esp. l. 21. For Time (Fortune) as the inveterate ıater of mankind, see p. 48 and n. 19, above.

[18]ENA 2805, f. 12, ll. 6–7 and 9. This letter is not included in Dr. M. Michael's dissertation on the Nahray correspondence.

[19]ENA 1822, f. 45, ll. 5–7, f. 44, ll. 17–19. This is one letter (although f. 45 is not the direct continuation of f. 44) addressed by Abraham b. Nathan Āv to Nahray b. Nissīm (not in Michael's dissertation). See Gil, "Megillat Evyatar," p. 64, and Cohen, Mark R., *Self-government*, pp. 123–125. What Cohen, p. 125, read (in TS 10 J 13, f. 11, l. 4, also addressed by Abraham to Nahray) as *bmnf* is actually *be-minnuy*: "I am head of my congregation by appointment" (from the nāsī David b. Daniel). What is said about religious slaughtering of animals and of one congregation in this letter fits only a major city like Alexandria. Abraham b. Nathan's connection with Alexandria is confirmed also by Gil, "Megillat Evyatar," p. 89, ll. 29–30. In *Med. Soc.*, II, 512, sec. 14, following Mann, I noted that Abraham signed a document in Ramle, Palestine in 1096. This is now to be corrected to 1076. About the combination of "religion and honor" see p. 564 n. 101, above. Abraham b. Nathan was very much concerned that his involvement in communal strife might be damaging to his *dīn*, "correct service of God," see TS 10 J 13, f. 11, l. 14 (read *dīnī*, but, in l. 15, *al-dayn*, cf. l. 24).

[20]Dropsie 389, l. 11. See p. 348 and n. 1.

[21]Goitein, *Letters*, p. 213, B.

[22]*Ibid.*, p. 328, first paragraph of letter. TS 13 J 15, f. 22, ll. 23–32 (both in Hebrew). TS 13 J 25, f. 12, margin, Abūn b. Ṣadaqa, see pp. 48–49 and nn. 22–23, above.

[23]*Med. Soc.*, I, 352.

[24]Goitein, *Letters*, p. 90, top.

[25]*Ibid.*, p. 211 and n. 20.

[26]TS 13 J 29, f. 10, ll. 15–16. The Day of Atonement falls on the 10th of Tishri, the opening and closing holidays of the Feast of Tabernacles on the 15th and 22d, respectively. The writer had to leave when the caravan set out for its long journey.

[27]*Med. Soc.*, IV, 230 and 433 n. 32.

[28]TS 12.270, l. 14: *Allāh taʿālā wa-hū* (meaning you) *alladhī nastanid ilayh, allāh yuḥyīh wa-yūqīnī.*

[29]TS 12.357, ll. 3–4.

[30]TS 10 J 19, f. 26, l. 20, Ar. *mā li-aḥad fī nafsō ḥukm.*

[31]TS 13 J 23, f. 10, ll. 23–28, *India Book* 45, *Nahray* 120.

[32]See the passage translated on p. 48 and n. 17, above.

[33]BT Shabbat 156*a* and *b*, and parallels.

[34]The Italian poet (Yehiel b. Abraham, the father of the renowned Nathan b. Yehiel): see Schirmann, *Studies*, II, 30–43. Maimonides: see Alexander Marx, "The Correspondence between the Rabbis of Southern France and Maimonides about Astrology," *HUCA*, 3 (1926), 311–358, which also contains a general discussion of the subject.

[35]ULC Add. 3345, ll. 35–37.

[36]TS 13 J 36, f. 2, ll. 12–15, cf. p. 93 and n. 236, above.

[37]DK 22, ll. 19–20, *Nahray* 194, a long letter with changing moods.

[38]ENA 2738, f. 20, *India Book* 353. "Rabbēnū Judah" is addressed. On the reverse side an account in the hand of Abū Zikrī Judah b. Joseph ha-Kohen.

[39]The net of Time: TS 13 J 20, f. 28, ll. 10–11, *ulkhadāhu ha-zemān ba-ḥavalāw* (Heb.). Time as betrayer: TS 13 J 20, f. 20, ll. 10–13. The lovely invitation described above, p. 15 and n. 28, is a postscript to this letter of recommendation for an esteemed and bashful person, who had fallen on bad times.

[40]The Aramaic *we-gavrōhī le-mazzālēh* was the original and common form. The Hebrew forms were derived from it and therefore varied. Daniel b. Azariah uses twice in a letter the phrase *yaʿalē ṣūr mazzālō*, "may the Rock [God] heighten your Star," Bodl. MS Heb. a 3 (Cat. 2873), f. 17, l. 33, and *verso*, l. 16, ed. Goitein, *Palestinian Jewry*, pp. 160–161. "May he [God] heighten your star and your lot," TS 13 J 15, f. 12, ll. 11–12, shows that the astrological connotation of mazzāl, was almost forgotten, although perhaps not as completely as in present-day *mazel tov*, "congratulations," *American Heritage Dictionary*, 1973, p. 809*b*. When in the family letter TS

13 J 20, f. 20, l. 4 (see preceding note) "high mazzāl" is wished together with all the blessings said in the Bible, the "innocent" character of mazzāl is evident.

[41]See *Med. Soc.*, III, 107–108, and 448 nn. 38–42. Auspicious hour made by God: ENA NS 18, f. 35, l. 32.

[42]BT Moʿed Qaṭan 28*a*. Rava adduces as a proof for the validity of the saying the fate of two equally learned and pious sages, one of whom lived ninety-two years, the other forty.

[43]TS 20.80, top, *India Book* 273.

[44]TS 10 J 10, f. 14, l. 14, Abi(!) ʾl-Ḥay b. Ṣalḥūn writes to Barhūn b. Mūsā b. Barhūn Tāhertī, quoting himself as the man with the weak star.

[45]Pp. 130–131 and nn. 10–14, above.

[46]BT Berakhot 29*b*. ENA 2808, f. 17*v*, ll. 25–26, in a Hebrew letter by Solomon, the son of judge Elijah.

[47]See *Med. Soc.*, I, 346. For the Islamic *istikhāra*, see s.v. in *EI²*, IV, 259–260 (by T. Fahd, the author of a work on divination), and *EI*, II, 600–601 (by I. Goldziher, "the father of Islamology").

[48]TS 12.250, ll. 8–9: Joseph b. Berechiah (see Index), writing from Qayrawān, informs Barhūn b. Ṣāliḥ Tāhertī that he had asked for God's guidance and commissioned Barhūn's cousin Abū Sahl ʿAṭāʾ to take delivery of a costly shipment (early eleventh century).

DK I, ll. 17–24, *Nahray* 167: about the sending of three bales of sumac from Ascalon to Egypt (probably in the 1050s).

TS 12.464: Ṣedāqā ha-Levi b. Moses admits his son Moses as a partner in his perfumer's store (1092). A much damaged, but interesting document. Father and son each contribute 6 dinars, l. 7; the son receives a daily allowance of 1½ dirhems, the father 3, because he brought into the partnership the shop and its inventory. In l. 4 the parties declare, as is necessary in a contract, that the partnership was their own choice, *bi-khtiyarinā*, but in l. 6, *istakharnā*, "we asked for God's choice."

TS 16.170: A partnership, also in a perfumer's store, of 300 + 300 = 600 dinars, an unheard-of sum for such an enterprise, is formed between two in 1095, see *Med. Soc.*, I, 173–174 and n. 19.

[49] See *Med. Soc.*, III, 135–136 and n. 92. Another example for "looking into the Scriptures": *ibid.*, I, 349. I can make a personal contribution to this topic. I did not have to "look" into the Scriptures; I was in them. It happened on September 11, 1923, when Erich Fromm (to become renowned for his psychoanalytical writings) and I officiated as cantors at the Jewish New Year's service in the house of the philosopher Franz Rosenzweig in Frankfurt, am Main; cf. Franz Rosenzweig, *Briefe* (Berlin, 1935), p. 446, which refers to 1922. When I recited Genesis 21:12, "God hears the voice of the boy wherever he might be," I suddenly paused; for it occurred to me that "the boy" could very well be me; I was to leave the next day for Palestine, then a voyage of eight days (not today's flight of four hours), and the country was very, very much underdeveloped. That the boy in the biblical story was Ishmael seemed to be altogether appropriate for a fledgling Arabist.

[50]For divination without use of the horoscope see p. 292, above.

[51]See my remarks on this topic on p. 297, above (general), *Med. Soc.*, II, 352–353 (government and court), 317 (Muslim judiciary), and *passim.*

[52]BT Berakhot 58*a*.

2. Close to God

[1]TS 8 J 5, f. 8, see *Med. Soc.*, III, 196 and n. 171.

[2]Bodl. MS Heb. c 28 (Cat. 2876), f. 67, ll. 20–21, ed. Goitein, *Palestinian Jewry*, p. 124, the Gaon Solomon b. Judah writing to Abraham Ibn al-Furāt. TS 8 J 15, f. 24, request sent from Aden to secure the rights of the orphans of an India trader, *India Book* 22.

[3]In a famous passage of his book *Die Religion der Vernunft aus den Quellen des*

Judentums (The Religion of Reason based on the Sources of Judaism) (Leipzig, 1919), p. 190, para. 34, Hermann Cohen, referring to these verses of Psalm 73, defines nearness to God as the absolute good. The Geniza people were not theologians, but, as far as they were thinking at all, their basic attitude was consonant with Cohen's concept.

[4]TS 8 J 24, f. 1, ll. 7–10. *ʿAlā aḥsan qaḍiyya* (Ar.) *ʿim elōhīm we-ʿim anāshīm* (Heb.), *wa-dhālika kulloh min faḍl allāh.* A note from a father to his son about a *ṣulḥ*, "peaceful agreement," with "the man whom you know." The brother mentioned was obviously involved in the case.

[5]TS NS J 242, l. 13, *India Book* 311. The Nagid is called Shemaryā (Protected by God), which is the Hebrew equivalent of his Arabic name Maḍmūn (II), about whom see Goitein, *Letters*, p. 213 and n. 4.

[6]Aram. *mehemnūthā di-shmāyā*, "reliability and fidelity" in cases where no human control is possible.

[7]TS 12.830 and TS 8 J 5, f. 13, which form one document, *India Book* 115, Ḥalfōn b. Nethanel, the India trader contracting a partnership (a bilateral commenda) with Yūsuf b. Shuʿayb Ibn al-Naghira of Fez. This contract between two learned observant persons is superscribed: "*with a good and propitious augury*" (Aram.). The meaning: may this propitious contract be a good augury for similar successful joint undertakings. One avoided superscribing documents with the name of God, see Friedman, *Marriage*, I, 92.

[8]Bodl. MS Heb. a 3 (Cat. 2873), f. 8, see *Med. Soc.*, I, 363, sec. 9.

[9]TS 6 J 1, f. 5, l. 10, *India Book* 306: *mā yukhalliṣak min Allāh*, Judah b. Joseph ha-Kohen al-Sijilmāsī is addressed in matters of the India trader Nissīm b. Jacob. TS 16.339, margin, *Nahray* 179, concerning a shipment destined to be spent for the poor.

[10]Common, e.g., TS 28.6 A, ll. 33 and 35, June 1079, a release after the dissolution of a partnership in precious stones, in which women were also involved, see *Med. Soc.*, III, 45–46 and n. 55; IV, 206 and n. 396.

[11]Despite what is said in *EI*[2], II, 293, s.v. "Dīn" (L. Gardet), I prefer Theodor Nöldeke's derivation of this word in the meaning religion from Pehlevi (Middle Persian) *dēn*, which is essentially different from the Heb.-Aram. *dīn*, "judgment."

[12]Westminster College, Frag. Cairens. 113, l. 8.

[13]TS Box K 6, f. 189, l. 18, see *Med. Soc.*, I, 451 n. 69, and, Gil, *The Tustaris*, p. 56.

[14]ULC Or 1080 J 42, margin, trans. Goitein, *Letters*, p. 93.

[15]TS 10 J 15, f. 33, l. 16, *fat-bayyan lil-nās khissat dīnoh*, written by Yaḥyā Ibn al-Majjānī (see Index).

[16]TS NS J 272, l. 9, see *Med. Soc.*, II, 281 and 588 n. 34.

[17]He does not fear God; e.g., TS 12.18, l. 11; TS 12.568, l. 9, both written by Ḥalfōn b. Manasse, who was also a master of Hebrew style. In postbiblical Hebrew one preferred to say "fear of Heaven" to "fear of God" (the biblical). "Write for him [a letter of recommendation] to a person who possesses fear of Heaven and readiness to exert himself for others," *yirʾat shāmayim u-zrīzūth*, TS NS J 120, l. 11.

[18]TS 12.65, l. 10. Depraved: *fāsid.* The writer must have been very serious about this matter, for he threatens to cut off all relations with his sister and her family if the marriage goes through.

[19]TS 8 J 17, f. 22, ll. 7–10, (Abū ʿAlī) Ḥasan b. ʿImrān, Alexandria, writing to the son of his sister Abū Mūsā Hārūn, son of R. Jacob, the teacher (who was still alive). The Muslim scholars dealing scientifically with the history of religions were better informed about the nature of Zoroastrianism than the scholars of Islamic law, see *EI*, III, 104–108, s.v. "Madjūs" (V. F. Büchner).

[20]Walter B. Denny in his review of Oleg Grabar, *The Alhambra* (Cambridge, Mass., 1978), in *Speculum*, 55 (1980), 793.

[21]In Jewish law "taking the Lord's name in vain" meant pronouncing a false oath while using it.

[22]Cf. p. 323 and n. 1, above.

[23]Abode, *ha-māqōm barūkh hū.* This ancient postbiblical term is very common in

the Geniza. The translation "Abode" is based on such biblical passages as "The Lord is coming out from his abode" (Isaiah 26:21), and "I shall return to my abode" (Hosea 5:15).

As of the second half of the twelfth century it became customary in Geniza letters sent to a high-standing person to address not him but his *majlis*, "reception hall." Although this usage could be compared semantically to that of Heb. *māqōm* (abode, place, seat) for God, it has nothing to do with it historically, since the Hebrew term appears about 1,200 years earlier. For its origin and original meaning see Urbach, *The Sages*, pp. 53–64.

[24]Mosseri L-268. As the script betrays, the Aramaic and Arabic names Nahray b. Abū Najm of the sender are a playful version of his Hebrew and real name Meir b. Hillel b. Zadok Āv. He addresses three young cousins, all of them with the title *rayyis*, "chief," designating even a fledgling physician. Cf. *Med. Soc.*, II, 193 and n. 7, and 421, sec. 97. Further details about the writer in Goitein, *Tarbiz*, 34 (1965), 232–233.

[25]Predilection for variety: *Med. Soc.*, II, 236–237.

[26]Mosseri L-133. For Yeshūʿā b. Ismaʿīl see the Index.

[27]TS NS J 473, l. 1: *rabbī sallim bi-raḥmatik yā arḥam al-rāḥimīn*, "Lord, grant safety in your mercifulness, you most merciful of those who have mercy." The shipment, described in one and a half lines, belonged to the brothers Barhūn and Nissīm Tāhertī. The signature of Barhūn is followed by another supplication: "May God keep it safe in his mercy." Another short bill of lading in Goitein, *Letters*, pp. 333–334. More elaborate: TS AS 149, f. 7, ll. 1, 12–13, 16. An unusually long bill, listing the goods of at least eight merchants, is superscribed: "God's blessing makes rich" (Proverbs 10:22) and opens with the words: "I trust in the might of the most merciful of those who have mercy." The conclusion is provided in the text, above. TS 12.378 (mid-eleventh century). See *Med. Soc.*, I, 336 and n. 25.

[28]INA D-55, f. 8 (1061); TS 10 J 27, f. 3c (1107); Bodl. MS Heb. a 3, f. 8 (1134), all partnerships.

[29]See Lopez-Raymond, *Medieval Trade*, pp. 176–204. When we find about 200 merchants from Amalfi, Italy, in Cairo in 996, and commerce between that city and the Muslims of Spain and Sicily already underway a century earlier, Muslim ways of doing business must have been well known to Italian traders before the eleventh century, see Cl. Cahen, "Le commerce d'Amalfi dans le Proche-Orient Musulman" in *Comptes Rendus, Académie des Inscriptions et Belles-Lettres* (Paris, 1977), pp. 291–292.

[30]TS 12.464, l. 8: *ayy* (Ar.) *she-meraḥamīm min shāmayim* (Heb.), "whatever Heaven may give us." Cf. p. 331 and n. 48, above.

[31]PT Berakhot 9:1, f. 13*a*, bottom. The entire section is dedicated to a comparison of the directness of approach to God with the difficulty of getting help from a Roman emperor. It is noteworthy that al-Qūmisī, one of the early Karaite authors, denied the existence of angels. The biblical word (which literally means "messenger") was a metaphoric term for any of God's agents. See Nemoy, *Karaite Anthology*, pp. 30–31.

[32]For angels in the Talmud see Urbach, *The Sages*, pp. 115–160, and, succinctly, *EJ*, II, 968–972. The name Gabriel was unpopular with Jews under Islam probably because he was the bearer of Allāh's message to Muhammad, see *EI*[2], II, 362–364 s.v. "Djabra'īl" (usually pronounced *Jibrīl* and even *Jibrīn*) (J. Pedersen). The tax collector Jibrīn in INA D-55, f. 3, l. 14 (see *Med. Soc.*, III, 194 and n. 164) was certainly a Christian. (Among Christians the name was already common in early classical Islamic times and has remained so until today).

[33]TS 12.41. The strange name of the heavenly court clerk Zeganzāl (Zgnzāl) occurs in two different forms in late Midrashim, see Urbach, *The Sages*, p. 152 and n. 50, both different from the one clearly written here. This formulary belongs to the world of magic rather than of religion.

[34]This is the more surprising, as Psalm 91, "the prayer against accidents," *shīr shel pegāʿīm*, was recited by a Talmudic sage before retiring at night, see BT Shevuʿoth 15*b*, and as such was incorporated in the Jewish book of prayers (but not in Saadya

Gaon's *Siddur*, p. 87). The "Order of Prayers" by R. Amram Gaon (d. ca. 875) contains the text of a nightly adjuration invoking three angels with uncommon names (ed. Warsaw, 1863, p. 54), but the book contains many later additions, see *EJ*, II, 891–893, s.v. "Amram b. Sheshna." A similar adjuration, containing the names of the four archangels and admitted to the Jewish prayer book is based on late Midrashim, see Baer, *Prayer-Book*, p. 576, commentary.

[35]G. G. Coulton, *Medieval Panorama: The English Scene from Conquest to Reformation* (Cambridge, 1938; Meridian Books, 1958), p. 109.

[36]John M. Steadman, "The Idea of Satan as the Hero of *Paradise Lost*," *Proceedings of the American Philosophical Society*, 120 (1976), 253–294. Jeffrey Burton Russell dedicated three volumes to the study of Satan, of which the latest, *Lucifer: The Devil in the Middle Ages* (Ithaca, 1984), is the most comprehensive.

[37]See *Med. Soc.*, III, 54 and n. 25.

[38]Cf. *EJ*, XIV, 903–905, which, however, does not do full justice to the subject.

[39]Saadya Gaon, *Siddur*, p. 107, based on BT Berakhot 46*a* and parallel sources.

[40]BT Berakhot 16*b*, bottom. In the Warsaw edition of Amram Gaon's Order of Prayers (see n. 34), p. 1*b*, the reference to Satan is omitted. See Baer, *Prayer-Book*, pp. 43–44.

[41]Cf. pp. 329–331.

[42]See pp. 17–25, above. For prayer at the tombs of the Sages in Galilee, see p. 18 and n. 39.

[43]TS 12.247, ed. Mann, II, 118. Mann's deviations from the text of the manuscript are indicated only where they change the meaning.

[44]For *mḥlh* in the printed edition the manuscript has *tḥlt* (*teḥillat*).

[45]For *ʿmdtk* read *ʿtyrtk* (*ʿathīrātkhā*), cf. *we-neʿethar* in l. 10.

[46]The countenance of God, a postbiblical version of the corresponding biblical phrase, cf. BT Hagiga 5*b*.

[47]The manuscript has the correct reading, not the one attributed to it by the editor.

[48]The word *bimhērā* is omitted in the printed edition.

[49]For *wyshmrk* the manuscript has the correct *wi-sammēḥakhā*. "Joy" refers to weddings; none of the three sons of the Gaon (cf. Mann, II, 133, l. 35) was married at that time.

[50]The ending of this sentence is correctly supplied by the editor. Cf. *Med. Soc.*, II, 285.

[51]See p. 247 and n. 137, above. The family, however, was not entirely strange to the India trade. In Dahlak our writer met a paternal cousin, who carried corals belonging to the recipient of our letter.

[52]I am not sure which of the two is meant: "God will save me anyhow, because of his mercy, even if you do not pray for me" or "God will accept your supplication and save me."

[53]Ar. *tuḥālilnī*, cf. Dozy, *Supplément*, I, 312*a*: *déclarer quelqu'un innocent.*

[54]By asking God to exculpate his in-laws the writer indicates that he has already forgiven them.

[55]This refers to the writer's married sister and an orphan sister who lived with her in her husband's house, where the latter's mother was in command, the connecting link between the world of men and that of women. Our novice in the India trade asked the recipient to destroy the letter and let no one know about its arrival (*verso*, ll. 1–2 and 12).

[56]This Qurʾānic phrase "God is sufficient for me: I trust in him" (9:129) appears often in letters of Jewish persons, especially from the Muslim West, even when they were not in a dangerous situation.

[57]"My brother from father and mother," meaning in the phraseology of that time a friend *not* related to me.

[58]TS 12.392, l. 24, margin, ll. 1–14, *verso*, ll. 2–6, *India Book* 173. He writes "my sister" to avoid writing "your wife," cf. p. 309, above.

[59]Cf. TS 12.34*v*, ll. 12–13, where a man in a provincial town excuses himself for

something done to his brother in the capital, but adds: "Learn from the ways of the Holy one, may he be blessed, 'who pardons iniquity and passes over transgression'" (Micah 7:18). Both the writer and the recipient were educated persons, no doubt, and understood the biblical quotation in the sense given to it in BT Rosh ha-Shana 17*a*, bottom: "When a person pardons the iniquities of others, God passes over his own transgressions." Our novice in the India trade was also learned, as his excellent command of both Arabic and Hebrew shows. Moreover, he writes that he had forgotten his Mishna volume *Moʿed* (Holidays) in the synagogue and asks his brother-in-law in deferential terms to take the trouble to bring it home.

[60]A merchant sending his wife a bill of divorce (which she was at liberty to use or not), because he was afraid he might perish on the high sea during a naval war, expresses this with these words: "I was afraid of the punishment of the Creator," Goitein, *Letters*, p. 319 and n. 18. In the Talmud this idea is expressed thus: "In an hour of danger Satan accuses," i.e., reminds God of the sins committed by the person in jeopardy. I have not found this often-quoted saying about Satan's absence (PT Shabbat 2:3, fol. 5*b*, top and parallels) in the Geniza, cf. p. 337, above.

[61]Cf. p. 323 and n. 1.

[62]See *EJ*, V, 760–783, where all 613 commandments are described; 365 is, of course, the number of days in a "sun-year," and 248, according to the Talmud, is the number of "members" in the human body. The symbolic meaning: serve God with your entire being every day in the year. Many of these commandments had become obsolete by Geniza times, for example, those connected with the Temple service, capital punishment, and most of the laws concerning the agriculture of Palestine.

[63]Mishna Makkot 3:16, recited at the conclusion of a meeting of study.

[64]*Med. Soc.*, III, 224–225.

[65]Saadya Gaon, *Siddur*, pp. 87–89.

[66]Another prayer at awakening is translated on p. 129 and n. 2, above. Both are found in BT Berakhot 60*b*, and both are quoted in Maimonides' *Code*, which follows the Talmud more exactly than Saadya Gaon's *Siddur*. The deviations are minor. I quoted Saadya because his was the prevailing authority prior to the appearance of Maimonides.

[67]Maimonides, *Code*, Book Two ("Love [of God]"), chap. II, "Prayer," 7:9. His argument, as usual, was logical: if you do not make the relevant movement, do not pronounce the benediction prescribed for it. More about this in Saadya Gaon, *Siddur*, pp. 24–25, Introduction.

[68]In those days people did not as a rule read prayers from a book; they knew them by heart. They were said aloud in the synagogue, partly in unison, and were learned by practice (not in school). The parts selected as suitable for recitation during work are not prayers in the strict sense, but sections from the Torah (Deuteronomy 11:13–22, and Numbers 15:39–41), recited after the "Hear Israel" (Deuteronomy 6:4–10).

[69]For the service on the Sabbath see *Med. Soc.*, II, 158–163, for its social aspects, see pp. 11–14, above, for its general significance, *Med. Soc.*, IV, 155. The Sabbath as a foretaste of the World to Come: BT Berakhot 57*b* ("The Sabbath is 1/60 of the World to Come"); another saying on the same page, mentioning the Sabbath together with the sun and sex, is of dubious reading.

[70]Saadya Gaon, *Siddur*, p. 113, ll. 11–15 and the commentary referring to the Geniza texts.

[71]The poet: Abu ʾl-ʿAlāʾ al-Maʿarrī (973–1057), see Reynold A. Nicholson, *Studies in Islamic Poetry* (Cambridge, 1921), p. 188, Ar. text, p. 280, no. 293, l. 2. On Jewish participation in caravan travel see *Med. Soc.*, I, 280–281, and II, 274 and 586 n. 1, where the dayyān of Barqa, eastern Libya, praises his Muslim compatriots for their helpfulness concerning the Sabbath rest and other matters. In TS 8 J 26, f. 4*v*, l. 5, however, when the writer learns that a business friend had decided to travel from Barqa to Alexandria by land, he is very worried "because of the dangers connected

with the Sabbath," *khawf ʿalayh fi ʾl-sabt.* (The fragmentary, but important, letter is addressed to Nahray b. Nissīm, as is evident from the almost illegible greetings to the latter's brothers-in-law scribbled upside down on the top of p. 1.)

[72]Elbogen, *Gottesdienst* (p. 118, bottom) rightly observes that the words about the jubilant patriarchs clearly lead up to the climax represented by Moses.

[73]An allusion to BT Yoma 75*a*, middle, where Israel gets this title because of its chastity.

[74]Based on BT Shabbat 119*a*, top, where it is reported of a Palestinian sage of the third century that after donning his festive attire on the eve of Sabbath, he would say: "Come, O bride, come O bride!" (In this context, "bride" means beautiful, not chaste). Nothing is said there about holidays. The preacher added it here, because, as the conclusion shows, he gave this sermon on a holiday.

[75]Love, Heb. *ʿōnā*, lit., "a fixed time," meaning sex. See *Med. Soc.*, III, 168, and above pp. 312 and 323.

[76]Ar. *sawāqī*, places irrigated with the *sakieh*, the Egyptian waterwheel. Dozy, *Supplément*, I, 665*a*, near bottom: *jardin.*

[77]TS 13 J 19, f. 7. *Verso* blank. See next note.

[78]As his script and style indicate, the writer was an educated man and interested in preaching. In the very wide margin he wrote a sermon with many quotations on the harmfulness of anger. On preachers in general see *Med. Soc.*, II, 216–219.

[79]One of the complaints of Samawʾal al-Maghribī, a convert to Islam, about the difficulty of life under Judaism was this: "When a rabbi learned that some young Jew sat alongside the road on a Sabbath, he would rebuke and curse the fellow at a gathering of the town's Jews and would disparage him," Moshe Perlmann, ed., *Ifḥām al-Yahūd* (New York, 1964), p. 70. One has the impression that the author himself had had such an experience.

[80]ULC Or 1080 J 181*v*, a longish, narrow piece of paper (25½ × 9½ cm), folded longitudinally into two columns, like an account or songbook, which could be tucked up one's sleeve. The *recto* is a letter in Arabic script.

[81]Shavuoth, the Jewish Pentecost, is celebrated on the sixth (or seventh) of the month of Sivan.

[82]Ar. *kharajnā ilā barrā natanazzah* (text: *sh* = *s* = *z*) *fi ʾl-raṣad.* About the history of this observatory see Ibn Duqmāq, IV, 58; Maqrīzī, *Khiṭaṭ*, I, 125–128. A meeting of astronomers, among them the renowned Ibn al-Haytham, is reported from April 1119 in connection with the newly erected observatory. Since a few years later the observatory was transferred to a more remote place, our story must have taken place around 1120.

[83]Abraham, "the Father of the Monotheistic Faith," was also regarded as possessed of esoteric knowledge and as author of "the earliest Jewish text on speculative thought," the *Sefer Yeṣīrā* (Book of the Creation), see *EJ*, XVI, 782–787. About this attribution see Louis Ginzberg, *The Legends of the Jews* (Philadelphia, 1925), V, 210 nn. 13 and 15. The real mountain: not the physical Mount Sinai but its spiritual meaning.

[84]Solomon Buber, ed., *Midrāsh Tehillīm* (Vilna, 1891), pp. 206–207, where many parallel sources are quoted.

[85]Three biblical stories and their legendary embellishments in rabbinic sources are here intertwined. The elders appointed by Moses prior to the revelation on Mount Sinai were professionally qualified, but not God-fearing, cf. Exodus 18:21, where Moses is recommended to choose only God-fearing men with 18:24, where "God-fearing" is missing. The elders again showed this deficiency in Exodus 24:10–11, where the punishment was postponed to Numbers 11:1, where "the top of the camp," which was destroyed, refers to them. But our mentor opens his comments with Numbers 11:16, a wrong quotation.

[86]The words *esfāh lī*, "assemble for me," Numbers 11:16, he spells as one word *esfalī.*

[87]The Talmudic "under no circumstances should one [i.e., a man] greet a woman"

(BT Qiddushin 70*a* bottom, and *b*, ll. 1–3) was meant to apply to oral address, but, as the Geniza shows, was soon extended to correspondence.

[88]See p. 85 and n. 193, where further details.

3. Member of God's community

[1]For the problem of merits see pp. 327–328 and nn. 20–23, and p. 341 and nn. 63–64, above.

[2]My translation follows Saadya Gaon, *Siddur*, p. 359, l. 18: *hayyē ʿōlām* (not: *we-ḥayyē*). "Eternal life": in the World to Come, after the resurrection of the dead (see Daniel 12:2).

[3]The special benediction for all holidays, including the Day of Atonement, concludes thus: "Blessed be . . . who hallows Israel and the Day of Atonement. . . ." The benediction for the Sabbath omits "Israel."

[4]See *Med. Soc.*, I, 124.

[5]BT Shabbat 119*b*, top (Rav Hamnūnā).

[6]According to a well-known ancient interpretation of Genesis 2:2 ("God completed on the seventh day all his work"): "What did he create on the Sabbath? What the world was missing—rest."

[7]See *Med. Soc.*, IV, 397 n. 41.

[8]And not on the New Year holiday, see *ibid.*, IV, 156 and nn. 36–40. I. Goldziher, "Usages juifs d'après la littérature religieuse des Musulmans," *REJ*, 28 (1894), 83, quotes an Arabic account in which the Muslims express their astonishment that the Jewish women of Khaybar put on their most beautiful jewelry on the Day of Atonement.

[9]The social aspects of the holidays are discussed pp. 14–17 and nn. 26–38, above.

[10]TS 10 J 9, f. 3, sent from Tunisia to Egypt five days before the New Year, which means, that the letter would arrive after all the holidays had passed; see p. 17, above.

[11]TS 13 J 15, f. 3, ll. 4–8. The writer excuses himself after fifty lines that the letter was written in a hurry.

[12]TS 12.81, ll. 19–20, a calligraphic Hebrew letter to Āraḥ b. Nathan, "the Seventh."

[13]TS 18 J 4, f. 19, ll. 12–15.

[14]TS 24.27*v*, ll. 13–23 (these are ll. 67–77 of the letter; see pp. 80 ff. and nn. 158–168, above). TS 13 J 18, f. 11, ll. 9–13, the writer begins in Arabic: "This festive time, in which God freed our prisoners from the servitude to Pharaoh. . . ." TS 13 J 16, f. 9, ll. 22–24; TS 10 J 20, f. 19, ll. 9–13.

[15]TS 10 J 17, f. 25, ll. 8–10, written by Ṭōviyā (spelled thus) ha-Kohen b. Judah b. Ṭōviyāhū, dayyān in al-Maḥalla and Sammanūd.

[16]TS 8 J 23, f. 27, ll. 1–3. I copied this from the original many years ago, but have no photo of the manuscript. There may be a mistake in the MS mark.

[17]TS 8 J 24, f. 17, ll. 3–7: ". . . and visit in his Temple; and may you witness the joy of the water plays, while you are happy, alive and fit, well-to-do and healthy, as willed by the Rock." The paper of this letter was reused for the letter discussed on pp. 87–88 and nn. 208–210, above. For the water libations in the Temple of Jerusalem see *EJ*, XV, 499, s.v. "Sukkot."

[18]Good wishes for Hanukka: ENA NS 2, f. 5*v*; *ibid.*, f. 16, l. 9 (ca. 1230); TS 8 J 22, f. 7 (ca. 1050); TS 10 J 14, f. 9. Consecration: TS 13 J 21, f. 3, ll. 8–9: *wī-zakkēhū la-ḥanukka hā-ʿatīdā le-hēʿasōth.* Consideration: TS 12.425. "Purim dinar": TS 13 J 20, f. 26, l. 5, *Nahray* 34. (The father sent it, although he himself had not more than 1 dinar in his purse, l. 18.) Good wishes for *al-mōʿēd al-Purim al-sharīf* (the dayyān Abraham b. Shabbetay): TS 12.56, ll. 13–15; TS 13 J 21, f. 1, *India Book* 260 (dated 1110), where, after mōʿēd of Purim is mentioned *al-ḥag*, referring to Passover; TS NS J 84, *India Book* 250; and often. The liturgical poem for Hanukka, TS AS 145, f. 14*b*, published by Simon Hopkins, *A Miscellany of Literary Pieces from the Cambridge Genizah Collections* (Cambridge, 1978), pp. 46–48, seems to be in the

hand of the India trader Abraham Ben Yijū. In TS 10 J 13, f. 23, ll. 22–23, an old teacher expects to receive a gift from a former student on the great holidays of the fall and the spring, as well as on Hanukka and Purim.

[19]Very common. Cf. Zechariah 8:19. Discreet gifts on the Ninth of Āv: TS 24.46, l. 47, see *Med. Soc.*, II, 123 and n. 9 (*qirṭās darāhim*).

[20]Saadya Gaon, *Siddur*, p. 93. See also *Med. Soc.*, IV, 137–138 and 228.

[21]For meat see *Med. Soc.*, II, 224–228; IV, 248–250; wine: I, 123–124, IV, 254–255, 258; cheese: IV, 251–252. The numerous references to cheese in this book (see Index) concern mostly certificates issued by religious authorities that cheeses imported or offered by merchants were fit for consumption by (Rabbanite) Jews. Bread: II, 307–308.

[22]See *Med. Soc.*, II, 137–138. To the examples given there add the efforts to ransom the Jewish captives from Bilbays, Lower Egypt, who were taken in November 1168, when the troops of the Frankish king Amalric of Jerusalem conquered that town, massacred many of its inhabitants, and carried others away to Palestine, cf. S. D. Goitein, "Moses Maimonides, Man of Action: A Revision of the Master's Biography in Light of the Geniza Documents," *Hommage à Georges Vajda*, ed. G. Nahon and C. Touati (Louvain, 1980), pp. 155–162; *idem*, *Palestinian Jewry*, pp. 312–320.

[23]See pp. 73–76 and nn. 129–136, above. The sections on widows in *Med. Soc.*, III, 254–260, 324–325, and orphans, 302–312, should also be consulted.

[24]Numerous Geniza letters with requests for help presuppose such a situation.

[25]Besides this most common reference to the reward in the World to Come (see p. 93 and n. 239, above) there were others, e.g., TS NS J 337, ll. 1, 4, 8, where Deuteronomy 22:6, "You may have it good," is explained, following the rabbinic interpretation in BT Ḥullin 142, as "in the World that is entirely good," fragment of a calligraphic begging letter with wide space between the lines, as in caliphal chancelleries.

[26]Routine and sincerity are not always mutually exclusive. ULC Or 1080 J 35, a very much down-to-earth, factual business letter (often cited in this book), combines profuse quotes of religious phraseology with substantial and convincing expressions of gratitude. In one place, ll. 27–28, the writer, Judah b. Joseph b. Simḥā (not known to me otherwise), addressing the brothers Ismaʿīl and Sāliḥ Tāhertī, says of himself: "Even small kindnesses remain firmly implanted in my heart forever, let alone the good you have done for me, which was all-comprising and rendered me respectable [or: protected me], *wa-kayf jamīl-kum alladhī ashmal-nī wa-satar-nī.*

During my first year in Jerusalem, when, still unmarried, I had to go for lunch to a certain place (there was almost no other one at that time), I used to meet, at a street crossing, a wonderful old beggar. He invariably stretched out to me his big open hand, saying with a radiant face, *zekhē ʿimmī*, "acquire religious merit through me" (see n. 59, below), and I, of course, never failed to put something into his hand. He certainly had no doubt that he did a bigger favor to the young man than I did to him. I do not remember on what grounds Chaucer said of his Friar that he was the best beggar in his "house." Probably for a similar reason.

[27]ENA 3795, f. 8, beginning and right margin torn away. Handwriting of Ḥalfōn b. Manasse (1100–1138), extremely fleeting here; he certainly took no payment for the writing; this was his charitable contribution. The identity of R. Isaac is established by Ḥalfōn's period of service as court clerk; see *Med. Soc.*, II, 512, sec. 13. In general, deathbed declarations did not require the "symbolic purchase" enacted here (see *ibid.*, p. 329), but under specific circumstances one preferred to apply it. On the reverse side Ḥalfōn wrote a somewhat similar declaration by an extremely poor woman who left a son, two daughters, and an old mother; the ending "I do not owe a thing to anyone, nor does anyone owe me a thing" is common.

[28]Day and month not preserved.

[29]"Little Turk" (in the masculine!), a name of particular endearment for a girl with a fair complexion, see S. D. Goitein, "Nicknames as Family Names," *JAOS*, 90 (1970), 522.

[30]*Qurdūs* is known to me only in its diminutive form *quraydis*, which means shrimps, see Dozy, *Supplément*, II, 326*a*, Barthélemy, *Dictionnaire arabe-français*, p. 646, Yāqūt, I, 886, l. 9, where it is enumerated among the seventy-nine types of "fishes" found on the coast of Tinnīs, Egypt. Shrimps are not eaten by Jews: a forefather of Turayk might have been a fishmonger (many Jews were), and one day a few shrimps might have been among his fish; he was nicknamed "shrimp monger," and the nickname stuck as family name; see Goitein,"Nicknames as Family Names" (preceding note).

[31]His uncle had been representative of the merchants, see Mann, II, 78 n. 7, and he had served as his helper or partner. Now, despite the fact that he was a father of six and a prominent citizen (see TS 24.43, ll. 13–34; TS 13 J 19, f. 16, l. 33), he still was called "Shimʿān's nephew." Muḥsin means "benefactor."

[32]This leopard-like animal was as faithful a companion to the oriental hunter as a dog or a falcon. It was customary to mention a wife, wherever feasible, after her children, so that she appears as a mother rather than a wife.

[33]Hailing from Athārib, a place near Aleppo, northern Syria.

[34]Five expressions to this effect.

[35]Five expressions.

[36]Sixty-two items of relationships or objects that might invite a claim.

[37]In the last but one line it is even stated that his father-in-law was a Kohen. So honorific a statement is normally made when a person is first introduced.

[38]The three fragments: BM Or 5542, f. 6; TS 20.169; TS 10 J 8, f. 9.

[39]JNUL 5, ed. S. D. Goitein, "Court Records from the Cairo Geniza in *JNUL*" (Heb.) *Kirjath Sepher*, 41 (1966), 267–271.

[40]TS 13 J 3, f. 12. Samuel b. Judah b. Asad had rented a house of his in Alexandria, see the Index under his name.

[41]*Med. Soc.*, II, 514, sec. 22. His father Nathan, *ibid.*, p. 513, sec. 18.

[42]Bodl. MS Heb. d 66 (Cat. 2878), f. 78 (summer 1161).

[43]TS 20.80, *India Book* 273 (ca. 1141).

[44]I wish to thank Mr. Friedenberg for the permission to publish the translation of his *unicum*.

[45]They would be put into prison, and, if no one cared, even sold into slavery.

[46]Genesis 41:39, said of Joseph in Egypt.

[47]This strange Hebrew title (*gevīr ha-mevīnīm*), found thus far only in connection with this Samuel, lauds his farsighted judgment.

[48]About four words are effaced here.

[49]Abbreviated from Sitt al-Sumr, "the Queen of the Tawny," see below. Although a fair complexion was highly appreciated, a healthy tan was regarded as a mark of beauty in both men and women.

[50]This form of invoking God against oneself has not yet been found by me in other documents of release.

[51]The sons, not the widow, are heirs according to Jewish law. There follow four lines containing a release for the elder Samuel from any other obligations connected with previous transactions with his protégés and also from any oath.

[52]In large, monumental characters, probably in order to set the signature apart from the text, also written by Mevōrākh. The blessing attached to the name of the father shows that he was still alive.

[53]Psalms 25:13.

[54]About him see *Med. Soc.*, II, 513, sec. 19.

[55]*Ibid.*, sec. 20.

[56]MS Friedenberg, private, see n. 44, above. Since the manuscript is in private hands, I preferred to provide a complete translation.

[57]PT Qiddushin 4:1, f. 65*a*; BT Yevamot 79*a*.

[58]BT Bava Bathra 9*a*.

[59]TS 13 J 17, f. 8, ll. 8, 9, 11, 15, 17, 22. "You have been making rounds, *timshī*, in acquiring religious merits [both Heb. *zekhūth* and Ar. *thawāb* are used] from your early youth to your old age." The letter is in a good hand and superscribed, as begging letters often were, with Proverbs 21:14 ("A gift in secret averts wrath,"

referring in the original to bribe, but understood here as charity [cf. BT Soṭa 5*a*, l. 1 and parallels]) and Proverbs 11:4 ("Riches are of no avail on the day of wrath, but charity delivers from death"). In both cases wrath is taken as referring to God. Two fund raisers are more effective than one, and this was also the law or, at least, custom, see *Med. Soc.*, II, 79 and n. 51.

The writer addresses his relative Abu ʾl-Khayr Ṣedāqā, son of the late Ṣamōʾaḥ b. Sāsōn (name not found by me elsewhere) and despite his own plight asks for help also for another person. "Make the rounds for him at his friends, this is the most meritorious you can do" (ll. 17–18). Friends might be more discreet.

60 To be sure, one would not withhold a loaf of bread from a needy Muslim, even during a communal handout (which was Jewish law, "the poor of the gentiles must be maintained together with those of the Jews," BT Giṭṭin 61*a*), and members of the same profession belonging to different religions would assist one another under certain circumstances, cf. *Med. Soc.*, II, 128, 293–299, and *passim.*

4. Schism and Counter reformation

1 See Leon Nemoy, "Elijah Ben Abraham and His Tract against the Rabbanites," *HUCA*, 51 (1980), 64–65. "Religion," Heb. *dāth*, probably corresponding to Ar. *milla.*

2 Cf. S. D. Goitein, "The Rise of Middle-Eastern Bourgeoisie in Early Islamic Times," *Journal of World History*, 3 (1957), 583–604, revised in Goitein, *Studies*, pp. 217–241, and *idem, Jews and Arabs* (1974), pp. 89–124, on the socioeconomic transformation of the Jewish people in Islamic times, where the pre-Islamic elements of Jewish social life surviving in Islam are also considered.

3 Formerly it was taught that Islam was spread "by fire and sword." This was not true, or, at least, it was true only indirectly. Today, one is inclined to exaggerate in the other direction, as if the Muslim conquest was but a transition from one administration to another. The deadly silence that affected Iranian and Jewish literatures for untold years is an eloquent testimony to what really happened during those dark centuries. One should keep in mind that the devastation of the Middle East started long before the Muslim conquest.

4 The best introduction to the world of Karaism is Nemoy's comprehensive *Karaite Anthology*, selected texts translated with introductions and notes. He also wrote a summary of Karaite history, literature, theology, and practice for EI^2, IV, 603–609 (1978), and a somewhat older, but more extensive version in *EJ*, X, 761–785, both with valuable bibliographies. Note also Nemoy's "Ibn Kammūnah's Treatise on the Differences between the Rabbanites and the Karaites," *JQR*, 63 (1973), 222–246, and "Mourad Farag and His Work *The Karaites and Rabbanites*," *REJ*, 135 (1976), 87–112, where the very useful study of an Arabic-writing modern Karaite (Cairo, 1918) is summarized. See also n. 1, above. EI^2, I, 481, s.v. "ʿĀnāniyya," contains another, short, article on Karaism by Georges Vajda, in which the Muslim sources about the sect are briefly surveyed. During the last decade of his life Vajda has given us a comprehensive study of the theology of Yūsuf al-Baṣīr, one of the most influential Karaite thinkers, published in continuations in *Journal Asiatique* (1974), 305–367, (1975), 7–48, and *REJ*, 134, fasc. 3–4 (1975), 31–74, and 137, fasc. 3–4 (1978), 279–365, where he demonstrates the dependence, "thought through and controlled," of al-Baṣīr upon his contemporary, the Muslim theologian ʿAbd al-Jabbār. (For al-Baṣīr see *EJ*, IV, 301–302, s.v.) See also H. Ben-Shammai, "A Note on some Karaite Copies of Muʿtazilite Writings," *BSOAS*, 37 (1974), 295–304, fourteenth century (perhaps earlier?), copies in Hebrew script of parts of ʿAbd al-Jabbār's work. Jacob Mann's *Texts and Studies*, II (1935) is entirely dedicated to Karaism and will remain the standard work on the topic. Zvi Ankori's *Karaites in Byzantium* (New York, 1959) (546 closely printed pages), despite its title, contains much material for the "Geniza" countries. Simon Szyszman's *Le Karaisme, ses doctrines et son histoire* (Lausanne, 1980), is characterized by a reviewer as "Karaism, as a modern Karaite wishes to see it" (Guy D. Sixdenier, *Journal Asiatique*, 169 [1981], 494–497).

5 Nemoy, *Karaite Anthology*, p. 111 n. 7.

[6]Al-Qūmisī in *ibid.*, pp. 36–38 and p. 329, sec. II. It was Muslim custom that a person unable to make the pilgrimage to Mecca himself sent a substitute, paying him part or all of his expenses. Since the country from which al-Qūmisī hailed is very remote from the holy cities of Islam, it might well have been that the inhabitants of a town put their resources together to send a group of five substitutes. Five is a holy number in Zoroastrianism and in Islamic popular religion. One is also reminded of Nehemiah 11:1–2. When Nehemiah rebuilt the walls of Jerusalem and had to fill the city with people, every village had to designate one out of ten men to live there. The selection was in part by lot and in part by volunteering.

[7]See Mann, I, 274–277, and Mann, *Texts*, II, 58–61, where further literature on the subject.

[8]Nemoy, *Karaite Anthology*, pp. 113–114 a tract of Sahl b. Maṣlīʾaḥ, translated in full.

[9]A technical term, Heb. *āvēl*, an ascetic, who renounces the pleasures of this world, mourning the symbolic absence of God after the destruction of his Temple, see Mann, II, 413.

[10]From Sahl b. Maṣlīʾaḥ's *Book of Precepts*, quoted by Solomon L. Skoss, *The Hebrew-Arabic Dictionary of the Bible of David b. Abraham al-Fāsī* (New Haven, 1936), I, xlix n. 59. Skoss adduces this passage in order to explain why al-Fāsī, who, as his name indicates, hailed from Fez, Morocco, on the other end of the Muslim world, uses so many Persian words. To be true, with one exception all the Persian words listed by Skoss, pp. xliv-xlviii, have also been encountered in the Arabic Geniza correspondence. It shows only that because of the many immigrants from Iran in Palestine and Egypt, the Arabic spoken there was filled with Persian elements; see *Med. Soc.*, IV, 78, and the Index, s.v. "Persian(s)."

[11]Al-Qūmisī in Nemoy, *Karaite Anthology*, pp. 36–37.

[12]Sahl b. Maṣlīʾaḥ, in *ibid.*, p. 114, top. See n. 8, above.

[13]See Goitein, *Studies*, pp. 146–148. Al-Qūmisī (*Karaite Anthology*, p. 37, sec. 8) emphatically extols "nations" from the four corners of the world who come to Jerusalem for prayer, and requests his fellow Jews to imitate their praiseworthy ways.

[14]Saadya Gaon, *Book of Beliefs and Opinions*, chap. X, pp. 364–367, the first of the thirteen types of behavior discussed (in Joseph Qāfiḥ's edition [Jerusalem, 1970], pp. 293–294). That Saadya chose withdrawal from the world as the first item in his chapter on ethics seems to indicate that serious differences existed between Karaites and Rabbanites on this point. As I understand the context, Saadya speaks here about a religious anchorite, not about a recluse seeking solitude for the purpose of philosophical meditation.

[15]The Rabbanite yeshiva and, with it, most of the members of the community had left Jerusalem in the 1070s. It was the Karaites who suffered most at the time of the Crusaders' conquest in 1099. See p. 54 n. 44, above, and pp. 372 ff., below.

[16]A good example: Japheth b. Eli's commentary on the Book of Ruth, partly translated in *Karaite Anthology*, pp. 84–107, with his characterization of Naomi, Orpah, Ruth, and other biblical women. Japheth b. Eli (not ʿAlī) is the Hebrew form of his name. In Arabic he called himself Abū ʿAlī Ḥasan b. ʿAlī al-Baṣrī (from Basra in southern Iraq), which he also used as an acrostic in a Hebrew poem of his, ed. Mann, *Texts* II, 31–32. About the time Japheth wrote his commentaries in Jerusalem, see Haggai Ben-Shammai, "Versions of Japheth b. Eli's Commentaries on the Bible," in *ʿAlē Sefer* (Ramat-Gan), 2 (1976), 29–31 (of the offprint, Heb.).

[17]See n. 10, above. The value of this dictionary consists for us in the information about how Arabic-speaking Jews understood the Bible a thousand years ago.

[18]The literature on this subject is well discussed in a colloquium organized by Moshe Gil, "Immigration and Pilgrimage to Palestine during the Years 634–1099," *Cathedra* (Jerusalem) 8 (1978), 124–144, esp. p. 125 n. 7 (Heb.). *Idem, Palestine during the First Muslim Period (634–1099)*, I, 499–519.

[19]See L. Nemoy's detailed article on Kirkisani (*K* for *Q*) in *EJ*, X, 1047–1048. He edited *The Book of Lights* in five volumes (New Haven, 1939–1943), patching it

together from numerous manuscripts, none complete. Students of Islamic letters should pay attention to the book (ed. in Arabic script, with quotations from the Bible and postbiblical Hebrew literature in Hebrew script). Dr. Larry B. Miller, in his Princeton University 1984 dissertation "Islamic Disputation Theory" makes considerable use of this work.

[20]See *EI*, IV, 1329–1330 s.v. "Zindīḳ" (Louis Massignon).

[21]These verses are quoted in Sahl b. Maṣlīʾaḥ's missionary epistle as the biblical affirmation of independent reasoning, *Karaite Anthology*, p. 118.

[22]See for instance, n. 33, below.

[23]Qirqisānī, *Book of Lights*, ed. Nemoy, p. 645. See n. 19, above, discussed by H. Ben-Shammai, "Hebrew in Arabic Script," in Sheldon R. Brunswick, ed., *Studies in Judaica, Karaitica, and Islamica, Presented to Leon Nemoy* (Ramat Gan, 1982), pp. 115–126, esp. p. 126 n. 49.

[24]See *Karaite Anthology*, pp. 61–64. It is noteworthy that ʿAbd al-Jabbār, the eminent Muslim theologian (and contemporary of Qirqisānī), wished to prove the inauthenticity of Christianity by the fact that the Gospels are written in a language other than Hebrew, the language in which God revealed himself to the (pre-Islamic) "prophets" including Jesus, see S. M. Stern, "ʿAbd al-Jabbār's Account of How Christ's Religion Was Falsified by the Adoption of Roman Customs," *Journal of Theological Studies*, n.s. 19, Part I (1968), 135–136.

[25]See Nemoy, *Karaite Anthology*, pp. 250–257, where Elijah Bashyatchi's interesting discourse on the learning of Hebrew, the sixth principle of Karaite faith, is translated. The discourse is taken from Bashyatchi's Code, entitled after his death *Addereth Eliyahu*, "The Mantle of Elijah" (cf. I Kings 19:19, and II Kings 2:14). The Israeli edition of 1966, brought out by the Karaite community there (no place-name mentioned), is a photographic reproduction of the Odessa, Russia, print of 1870, enriched by a detailed introduction from the pen of Z. Ankori, see n. 4, above.

[26]Cf. *Karaite Anthology*, p. 117, bottom, where Sahl b. Maṣlīʾaḥ (see pp. 361–362 and nn. 8–10, above) asserts that "the Disciples of the Rabbanites" in Jerusalem and Ramle are stricter in the observance of the Law "because they walk the path of the Karaite students, from whom they have learned it." A kernel of truth must be contained in this statement, since the epistle in which it is found is addressed to a Rabbanite scholar who had complained that Sahl was out to procure converts from the Rabbanite ranks (p. 109).

[27]BT Giṭṭin 62*a*, bottom.

[28]ʿĀnān, the reputed founder of Karaism, was credited with the saying: "Forsake the words of the Mishnah and the Talmud; I will compose for you a Talmud of my own." (Reported by the Gaon Naṭrōnay, who lived about a century after ʿĀnān, *Karaite Anthology*, p. 3, bottom.)

[29]TS 8 J 26, f. 2, a fragment; script: late twelfth century. Qirqisānī (*Book of Lights*, I, 63–64), after discussing such discrepancies, "which are increasing every day," stresses that they are a title of honor for the Karaites, since their law is based on free reasoning. Cf. the Islamic saying attributed to Muhammad: "Dissension in my community is a gift of mercy [by God]."

[30]See *Med. Soc.*, I, 356, fourth and fifth paragraphs, on these matters.

[31]In 1973, the Karaite Day of Atonement was a day later than the generally accepted one. Thus for them the war that began on that day was not a "Yōm Kippūr war."

[32]Sahl b. Maṣlīʾaḥ goes so far as to say to his Rabbanite brethren: "You have used the Sabbath lamp . . . so as to prevent the Karaites from coming to you and revealing to everyone that which is hidden from your eyes," *Karaite Anthology*, p. 120, sec. 21, end.

[33]They came to this conclusion by taking literally, "man and his wife becoming one flesh" (Genesis 2:24).

[34]In Judaism wine possessed a strongly sacramental character, see *Med. Soc.*, I, 123, IV, 258–259, and *passim*. Abraham Maimuni, *Responsa*, pp. 104–105, confirmed, of course, the ruling of his father, but in TS 6 J 2, f. 17, ll. 5, 6, 9 (frag.),

another scholar categorically prohibits the consumption of Karaite wine. The statement in *Med. Soc.*, I, 136 and n. 32, that a freedman was more trustworthy than a Karaite refers to meat, concerning which the Rabbanite law differed considerably from that of the other dispensation (ULC Or 1080 J 110, sec. 4). A merchant from Cairo could lose face even in faraway Aden, South Arabia, when it was said of him that he would *eat* (not, to drink wine) in Karaite houses, cf. *Med. Soc.*, I, 424 n. 99.

[35]Maimonides, *Responsa,* II, 729–732 (selected passages). The first question of the newcomer, who was perhaps a physician, was whether a Rabbanite was permitted to circumcise a Karaite boy on a Sabbath (when born on the preceding Sabbath, cf. Genesis 21:4). Unless there was danger of life, no operation was permitted on Sabbath except the circumcision of a Jewish newborn. By answering this question in the affirmative, Maimonides made it clear that Karaites had to be regarded as Jews in the religious (and not only the ethnic) sense.

[36]*Umma*: Goitein, *Letters,* p. 74 and nn. 3 and 4, p. 75 and n. 9. For the general meaning of the word see *Med. Soc.*, II, 274.

[37]See now Gil, *The Tustaris,* an excellent study with rich documentation and original texts illuminated by facsimiles. The Tustarīs mentioned "according to ancient customs" in the public prayer of the Karaite congregations between ʿĀnān, the founder of the sect, and "the scholars" (p. 59 and n. 86) were probably not the Tustarīs of Fustat-Cairo but the tenth-century teachers in Tustar, Iran, about whom Qirqisānī reports (pp. 61–62).

[38]E.g., Dropsie 393, ll. 53–59. Isaac b. Benveniste of Narbonne, France, in another letter written by him to Joshua b. Dōsā (see p. 33 n. 114, above) extols Abū Riḍā (spelled by him Rādā), "one of our Karaite brethren," who brought him in safety to Tinnīs, provided him with supplies and other needs, and, when taking leave of him, pressed into his hand a purse containing 10 dinars. Isaac now asks the addressee to request his brother to induce Abū Riḍā to intervene with the governor of Damietta that he not put obstacles in the way of the French traveler's passage to Palestine. It was the time of the first Crusade. Abū Riḍā and Joshua's brother obviously lived in that Mediterranean port city.

[39]About David b. Isaac ha-Levi, see S. M. Stern, "A Petition to the Fāṭimid Caliph al-Mustanṣir Concerning a Conflict within the Jewish Community," *REJ*, 128 (1969), 209–210, published posthumously. "Pride of the Two Denominations," *peʾēr shetē ha-pēʾōth* (Heb.); *pēʾā* in the meaning of group, denomination, is a Hebraization of Ar. *fiʾa.*

[40]TS 13 J 14, f. 14, see *Med. Soc.*, I, 85, and 411 n. 17. The *ṣāḥib diwān* of Minya might have had his office in Cairo. His name Ben al-Bērūtī probably indicates that in the late eleventh century the Jewish community of Beirut, Lebanon, included some Karaite families; cf. Goitein, *Palestinian Jewry,* pp. 294–296. Mevōrākh b. Saadya is addressed.

[41]See Mann, I, 88–93, referring to 1028–1030; cf. *Med. Soc.*, II, 137.

[42]See *Med. Soc.*, II, 472, sec. 4.

[43]TS 16.347, in the beautiful hand of Yeshūʿā ha-Kohen b. Joseph ha-dayyān, the same person who wrote other such missives from the congregations of Alexandria to those of Fustat in and around 1028, see Mann, I, 88 and 92. Although the fragment is about 33 cm. (13 in.) long and 17 cm. (7 in.) wide, it contains only a part of the eloquent introduction. About *shetē ha-pēʾōth,* in l. 24, and in the address, l. 2, see n. 39, above. The "Scribes of the Government," *sōferē ha-melūkhā,* are mentioned in l. 2. At the end of the proem three groups of leaders are addressed: the students of the Mishna and Gemara (Talmud), "the skilled scribes" (in the double meaning of students of the Torah, see Ezra 7:6, and government officials), and the experienced representatives of the merchants, that is, the great merchants.

[44]TS AS 147, f. 2, ll. 16–18. Eli ha-Kohen I b. Ezekiel I, Jerusalem (written in Arabic script as ʿĀlī b. Ḥazqīl) addressing Eli ha-Kohen b. Yaḥyā in Fustat. The letter has been repeatedly referred to before e.g., *Med. Soc.*, III, 91, third paragraph, where 1085 is a misprint for 1055, and p. 70 n. 108, above. See also Cohen, Mark R., *Self-government,* p. 112 n. 55, and *Med. Soc.*, II, 53 and nn. 83–84.

A freedman (a gentile who had embraced Judaism), however, willed one-fourth of his estate to "the poor of the Holy City of the Rabbanite persuasion with the exclusion of the Karaites," see *ibid.*, I, 146–147 and n. 110 (early eleventh century).

[45]PER H 92 and TS 16.334, which together form a long document, in which the partnership is dissolved. The proprietor of the store Ezekiel b. Nethanel ha-Levi al-Dimyāṭī gives his former partner, the Karaite Banīn b. Jacob, a loan of 20 dirhems for a down payment to rent a store from a Muslim (December 1125).

[46]TS 13 J 19, f. 16, ll. 24–25: "If they think so low of us, why do they strive to multiply through us [by taking our daughters, *yatakaththarū binā*] or to marry into our families [*yataẓāharūnā*]?" The late D. H. Baneth intended to publish this highly interesting, but incomplete, letter in the 1960s (see *Med. Soc.*, I, 521 n. 13); perfectionist that he was, he never gave his imprimatur to his version. Moshe Gil edited it with a very useful Introduction in *D. H. Baneth Memorial Volume* (Jerusalem, 1979), pp. 1–16.

[47]See the Index, s.v. "Karaites," and Friedman, *Marriage*, pp. 290–291, who is going to take up this phenomenon in a larger context.

[48]TS 13 J 6, f. 33, "The conditions imposed on . . . Abū Saʿīd, son of the illustrious sheikh Abū Naṣr b. Isaiah, marrying the daughter [not named!] of . . . R. Amram. The girl will stay with her mother and not be permitted to leave her." This strange first condition finds its explanation in a number of others near the end: "If he marries another wife, or takes a concubine, *yatasarrā*, he must pay 100 dinars [an exceptionally large fine, see *Med. Soc.*, II, 110] for the poor of the Rabbanites and Karaites and cannot compel her to stay with him overnight. Her dowry will be deposited and protected, with no one having access to it." The reputation of this young man from the prominent Isaiah-Shaʿya family (see *Med. Soc.*, III, 9–10, 290, 331) seems to have been rather shaky, but the girl might have been attracted to him. It is possible that stipulations of a religious nature were included in the marriage contract itself and were perhaps entered by the clerk of the court issuing the document as a matter of routine.

[49]See Mann, *Texts*, II, 61–66, "The Gaon Solomon b. Yehudah and his relations with the Karaites," a summary with additional sources. More Geniza texts on the topic were identified after Mann's death. See the following note.

[50]TS 13 J 7, f. 29, ed., S. D. Goitein, "A Caliph's Decree in Favour of the Rabbanite Jews of Palestine," *JJS*, 5 (1954), 118–125. S. M. Stern (*Fāṭimid Decrees* [London, 1964], pp. 31–34) transcribed the document into Arabic letters and discussed it within the frame of his searching study on Fatimid decrees. On p. 31 n. 2, Stern held that the chronological relationship of the two documents cannot be established. But since the banishment of the Rabbanite leaders is so outstanding a topic in Solomon b. Judah's letters, the caliph's action in favor of the Rabbanites, which alludes to it, must be later than the year 1026, when Solomon assumed office.

[51]See Mann, *Texts*, II, 63, top. In a letter to his son, Solomon alludes delicately to misunderstandings between them, TS NS J 14, l. 14, ed. Goitein, *Palestinian Jewry*, p. 105 n. 59.

[52]ENA 4010, f. 32, Eli I b. Ezekiel I. Jerusalem, signing only in Arabic script as ʿĀlī b. Ḥazqīl, writing to Ephraim b. Shemarya in Fustat.

[53]TS 13 J 19, f. 16, ll. 30 ff.; see n. 46, above.

[54]*Ibid.*, ll. 21–23.

[55]TS 8.106. Beginning and end and some words within the preserved text are missing. But the main content of the letter can be fully restored. See S. D. Goitein, "Petitions to Fatimid Caliphs from the Cairo Geniza," *JQR*, 45 (1954), 30–38, cf. *Med. Soc.*, I, 82 and n. 3. S. M. Stern ("Three Petitions of the Fatimid Period," *Oriens*, 15 [1962], 188–189) discussed the formal aspects of petitions addressed to the government. The text was printed by Joseph Eliash, *Sefunot*, 2 (1958), 20–22, who, for comments, sent the reader to my *JQR* article. Various readings can be improved; e.g., in *verso*, l. 10, read: *fī ākhir kull ṣalāt*, "at the end of each obligatory prayer." In the mutilated l. 2 *thiyāb baladī*, "clothes in the local fashion," are men-

tioned. Whether our artisan was a weaver, tailor, or embroiderer, and which work he was required to do for the government, cannot be made out. Perhaps they worked for the army, not for the caliphal wardrobe.

[56]The instructions for the manager of the workshop obviously envisaged that he could force inhabitants of Damascus to work for the government but could not prevent people from leaving the city.

[57]It seems that the preceding letters were written in Hebrew script only, which takes much time to read for persons like Abū Naṣr, who mostly wrote and read Arabic in Arabic script. On the other hand, the letter(s) sent now had to be written also in Hebrew script since some or most of the signatories, craftsmen, as I surmised, were not familiar with Arabic script (and one was not permitted to sign what one could not read).

[58]ENA NS 2, f. 21. As usual in Karaite correspondence, the congregation or its elders, not its spiritual leader (*rabbi* means lord), is addressed. Only at the end, l. 17, a blessing is said upon him, the *maskīl* (meaning teacher as in Daniel 9:33), as well as upon the nāsīs, the pretended scions of the house of King David. Ca. 1100.

[59]ENA 3787, f. 10, a "wanted" circular sent from Damascus, ed. M. A. Friedman in *Leshonenu* (in press); see *Med. Soc.*, III, 199 and n. 184. "The name [of the fugitive husband] is Joseph. He is accompanied by a young man with reddish hair, also called Joseph. His distinguishing mark [of the fugitive] is that he was a Karaite, a man not accepting the words of our Sages, and now has become a *rabbān*." Strange that the writer of the circular finds it necessary to define the term "Karaite." For the reputation of Fustat, see *ibid.*, II, 138.

[60]TS 13 J 34, f. 8, cf. *ibid.*, II, 390 and n. 41; III, 473, n. 8. About Maimonides' attitude toward Karaites, see p. 366, above, and Baron, *History of the Jews*, V, 280–281.

[61]See *Med. Soc.*, III, App., Part II, 395–422, nos. 1–379. The distribution of means at Karaite marriages (according to item number) compared with the general stratification of society summarized in *ibid.*, pp. 418–419 (slightly qualified here, p. 526 n. 132, above) was this: poor and very modest, 206, 211, 252; modest, 95 (translated in full, *ibid.*, IV, App. D, 314–317), 371 (I did not note that this was a Karaite marriage, nor that the betrothal contract of the same couple is preserved in TS 16.109); lower middle class, 154; upper middle class, 159, 173 (also TS 12.644); wealthy, 189, 191, 192, 194, 196, 237, 319 (frag. in Heb.), 366.

[62]Literary sources, too, seem not to contribute anything substantial in this respect, see "The Literary Defenders of Rabbinism in Palestine" in Mann, *Texts*, II, 57–61.

[63]Baron, *History of the Jews*, V, 275 ff., "Rabbanite Reactions."

[64]In Skoss, *Hebrew-Arabic Dictionary of the Bible of David b. Abraham al-Fāsī*, see n. 10, above.

[65]On Judah Ibn Qoraysh see *EJ*, VIII, 1192–1193, and Baron, *History of the Jews*, VII, 17–18.

[66]See Solomon S. Skoss's Introduction to David al-Fāsī's *Dictionary*, p. xxxvii and n. 33, and pp. cxxix-cxxx, and a reproduction of the beautifully written and moving colophon by Abraham b. Shabbetay on p. xv. Because of the anarchic state of the Near East a few years before the advent of the Crusaders he concludes his postscript with the prayer that God may protect him on his travels and save him from villains and highwaymen. His prayer was granted. He and his copy arrived safely in Egypt, see *Med. Soc.*, II, 47. His copy landed finally in the Geniza; a fragment of it with the colophon is preserved in the State Library in Leningrad.

[67]See Assaf, *Texts*, p. 106, n. 37.

[68]See the substantial articles on Ben Asher, Aaron (by Z. Ben-Hayyim), and Ben Asher, Moses (by A. Dotan) in *EJ*, IV, 463–469. The article "Masorah" in *EJ*, XVI, 1401–1479 (by A. Dotan) is not intended for the general reader. The length of the article reflects the complexities of medieval Bible research.

[69]TS AS 146, f. 3, ed. Goitein, *Palestinian Jewry*, pp. 254–256, trans. Goitein, "Geniza Sources for the Crusader Period," *Outremer*, 1982, pp. 308–311.

[70]*Ibid.*, pp. 313–315. On p. 313 n. 34, I must correct a mistake of mine. The correct translation of the sentence referred to is as follows: "How can I, a Kohen, become a Christian?" Gil, *The Tustaris*, p. 65, has the correct translation.

[71]TS 20.113, ed. Goitein, "New Sources on the Fate of the Jews during the Crusaders' Conquest of Jerusalem," *Zion*, 17 (1952), 129–147, trans. by *idem*, "Contemporary Letters on the Capture of Jerusalem by the Crusaders," *JJS*, 3 (1952), 162–177.

[72]TS 10 J 5, f. 6, ed. Goitein, *Palestinian Jewry*, pp. 231–250. A detailed commentary is provided there for this historic document.

[73]See n. 80 and sec. D, below.

[74]In Ar. *al-wabā wal-aʿlāl wal-amrāḍ*, ed. Goitein, *Palestinian Jewry*, p. 253, ll. 39–40; see n. 79, below.

[75]Bodl. MS Heb. b 11 (Cat. 2874), f. 7, ed. *ibid.* The Egyptian army: K. M. Setton, *A History of the Crusades*, Vol. I (Berkeley, 1909), pp. 332–333.

[76]Sections A and B are from TS 10 J 5, f. 6; secs. C–M (until n. 90, below) are from TS 20.113. For the continuation see that note.

[77]The terms "captives" and "refugees" are usually expressed in Hebrew to emphasize the religious character of the duty to help them.

[78]In accordance with the space available on the effaced part I read *q*[*ad fukka*].

[79]Ar. *wabā, fanā, balā*, cf. n. 74, above. In Geniza usage *wabā* means plague and *mubtalī* is a person afflicted with leprosy. But here the writers obviously were left in the dark about these "evil diseases of Egypt" (Deuteronomy 7:15, quoted in the letter of the Maghrebi).

[80]They had intended to send a messenger from Ascalon. But because of the epidemics they did not find one. Now "here," in Egypt, they had found one.

[81]This scion of the noble banking family of Shaʿyā (Isaiah) had good reason to be present in Ascalon during the winter of 1099/1100; he married there on 23 January 1100, see Bodl. MS Heb. e 98, f. 60, where he is called "Shēlā, the prince of the House of Israel." For the fragmentary copy of the marriage contract, see Friedman, *Marriage*, II, 388–396.

[82]Possibly identical with the boy from a noble family, reported as still being held by the Crusaders in Antioch in TS 24.65, l. 15, ed. Goitein, *Palestinian Jewry*, p. 286.

[83]The man was a Kohen and a stepson of a renowned Karaite from the Tustarī family (who were not Kohens). Gil (*The Tustaris*, pp. 65–66) quotes a Muslim traveler from Spain who visited Jerusalem in the 1090s and attended a religious disputation in which the Jewish side was represented by "the Tustarī," most likely the one referred to here.

[84]The Ashkenaz, the European Christians, did not violate women at the fall of Jerusalem as "the others," the Muslims, did at the conquest of a city. For details see Goitein, "Geniza Sources for the Crusader Period" (see n. 69, above), p. 312 and nn. 29–30.

[85]For references to caravan travel on a Sabbath or holiday, see p. 344 and n. 71, above.

[86]Taken from houses of worship or study, not from private homes.

[87]The ransom for any free person, Christian, Jew, or Muslim, was 33⅓ dinars, see *Med. Soc.*, I, 329. In 1099 the Crusaders acted differently, certainly not out of ignorance of this international rule but because they wanted to get rid of their prisoners as quickly as possible in view of the precarious military situation.

[88]Four Arabic and four Hebrew terms.

[89]Psalms 44:12–13. Followed by Isaiah 1:9.

[90]"This winter" seems to refer not to the harshness of the weather but to contributions levied by the government for the war effort. The last few lines (Goitein, *Palestinian Jewry*, p. 245, ll. 59–246, l. 65) are written partly in the margin of TS 20.113 and mainly in the margin of TS 10 J 5, f. 6; not everything can be read accurately. (Also: *shḥwh*, l. 59, is a misprint for *shtwh*, and *qnaʿ* is a misprint for *qṭʿ*, l. 61).

The rest of sec. M, and secs. N, O, P, Q are on TS 20.113.

[91]The first donation (see sec. B, above) had been transferred by a letter of credit charged to a banker or merchant, who had paid the equivalent to the elders of Ascalon (in Alexandria), a procedure that was obviously more expedient than waiting for the collection of the pledges and safer than sending cash.

[92]On TS 10 J 5, f. 6*v*.

[93]The first three signatures and greetings are below the text on TS 10 J 5, f. 6*v*; the other three are in the margin, partly on TS 20.113 and partly on TS 10 J 5, f. 6*v*. With the exception of no. 3, all the greetings are in the Arabic language, but only nos. 2 and 4 use Arabic script.

[94]The *physician* in Hebrew, see *Med. Soc.*, II, 246. Physicians were often selected as community leaders, because they had contacts with the non-Jewish environment and because their profession was surrounded with a halo of learning and spirituality.

[95]Musallam—arabicized Heb. Meshullam, a messianic name, cf. Isaiah 42:19. On messianic names in general see pp. 396–397, below.

[96]Indulgent—for imperfect script and style; in fact, both are excellent. As often done, the scribe uses cursive script for the text and writes his signature and additional personal remarks in rectangular (Torah) script.

[97]The writer obviously had been held up, robbed, and wounded, and was still suffering.

[98]He enumerates five generations in order to get to one ancestor of distinction.

[99]See, e.g., *The Fihrist of al-Nadīm* (commonly called *Ibn al-Nadīm*, cf. *EI*^{2}, III, 895–896), trans. Bayard Dodge (New York, 1970), Vol. I, on the works of al-Jāḥiẓ (d. 869), pp. 402–409, and al-Shāfiʿī (d. 819/20), pp. 517–519.

[100]Malter, *Saadia Gaon*. Jacob Mann's review of the book, *REJ*, 73 (1922), 105–112, brings home the tragic fact that Malter's studious work was written prior to the publication of Mann's voluminous contributions (some of which are repeatedly quoted here). See also *EJ*, XIV, 543–555.

The memorial volumes:

Saadia Anniversary Volume, American Academy for Jewish Research, ed. Boaz Cohen [not on the title page] (New York, 1943).

Saadia Studies (Philadelphia, 1943). Actually a special edition of *JQR*, 32 (1943), 109–401.

Saadya Studies, ed. Erwin I. J. Rosenthal (Manchester, 1943).

Rab Saadia Gaon, ed. Louis Finkelstein (New York, 1944).

Rav Saadya Gaon, ed. J. L. Fishman (Jerusalem, 1943) (in Heb.), twenty-six contributions, among which are such massive studies as S. Assaf, "The Book of Legal Documents by Saadya" (mostly from the Geniza), pp. 65–97 and 674–677; B. M. Lewin, *Essā meshālī* (a book of rhymed polemics, all from the Geniza, not even known to Malter), pp. 481–536; and I. Heineman's penetrating inquiry "Saadya's Rationalism," pp. 191–240.

[101]See Malter, *Saadia Gaon*, pp. 272–295, "Saadia's Influence on Later Generations."

[102]*Ibid.*, p. 295. The Arabic original is printed in Hebrew characters on the page immediately following the title page. It is taken from Malter's edition of *Sēfer ha-Gālūy* (see n. 115, below). H. Malter, "Saadia Studies," *JQR*, n.s., 3 (1912), 497, ll. 15–18, trans. p. 492. The continuation: ". . . I have witnessed God's bounty toward me and toward them through me."

[103]The parts of the two versions of the *Egron* preserved were edited by N. Allony with facsimiles in a magnificent publication of 600 pages (Jerusalem, 1969). The form Agron used by Malter and others is not essentially different, since the vowel signs for short *e* and *a* were pronounced as the same sound in certain communities (as the Yemenites still do). Saadya voweled the Introduction to his Hebrew version and supplied it with cantillation signs (see Allony, *Egron*, pp. 156–161), as was done with the Bible and (exceptionally) other sacred texts. The young man had a high opinion of his mission. In his old age he did the same; see n. 115, below. Fayyūmi as acrostic: Saadya Gaon, *Siddur*, p. 418.

[104]Allony, *Egron*, pp. 156–160. That mankind, at the end, will return to paradisiacal conditions is part of the ancient Near Eastern concept of the circular movement of world history.

[105]See *Med. Soc.*, II, 159–161.

[106]According to Jewish law, a slave was a member of the household, who had, for instance, to observe the Sabbath rest. BT Ketubbot 104*a* presents the maidservant in the house of R. Yehuda ha-Nasi as an accomplished Hebraist.

[107]Allony, *Egron*, p. 159, ll. 45–46, 55–57. See also A. S. Halkin, "The Medieval Jewish Attitude toward Hebrew," in A. Altmann, ed., *Biblical and Other Studies* (Cambridge, Mass., 1963), pp. 233–248.

[108]Solomon L. Skoss, *Saadia Gaon: The Earliest Hebrew Grammarian* (Philadelphia, 1955). The Arabic title of Saadya's book: *Kitāb faṣīḥ lughat al-ʿibrāniyīn*, or, simply, *Kitāb al-lugha*, see *ibid.*, pp. 1–2.

[109]"Explanation of Seventy Difficult Words," known simply as *Kitāb al-sabʿīn lafẓa*. A shortened, flawed version has been repeatedly printed, see Malter, *Saadia Gaon*, pp. 140–141, 307–308. Large parts of the original version are contained in at least ten Geniza fragments, which, together with the shorter version, make the text almost complete. It was edited by N. Allony in *Ignace Goldziher Memorial Volume*, Vol. II, ed. S. Löwinger (Jerusalem, 1958), Heb. sec., pp. 1–48. Allony's edition contains 96, not 70, words requiring explanation (see p. 45).

[110]For the use of the piyyūṭ in the synagogue service, see *Med. Soc.*, II, 159–161.

[111]That Saadya must have spent some time in Palestine before he wrote his *Egron* at the age of twenty seems to be warranted by the books quoted in it: all books of the Bible, about sixty treatises of the Mishna, twenty-nine of the Babylonian Talmud, and twelve of the Palestinian; see Allony, *Egron*, pp. 477–508. Being aware of the difficulties incurred in obtaining volumes of the Babylonian Talmud in the capital of Egypt even in the middle of the eleventh century, I assume that around 900, Saadya could have had constant use of the books quoted only in Jerusalem or Tiberias, cf. Goitein, "Books: Migrant and Stationary," in *A. Scheiber Memorial Volume* (Budapest, 1987), pp. 127–146.

[112]Abraham Ibn Ezra, *Commentary on Ecclesiastes* 5:1. These words of praise for Saadya are the continuation of his renowned diatribe against the piyyūṭ and its most prominent representative Eleazar Kallir.

[113]Maimonides, *Responsa*, II, 366–370. The question was sent to him from Aleppo, northern Syria.

[114]M. Zulay (d. 1954), *The Liturgical Poetry of Saʿadya Gaon and His School* (Jerusalem, 1964) (Heb., publ. posthumously). Must be studied together with the extensive review of Ezra Y. Golè in *Tarbiz*, 34 (1965), 382–397. Golè ("The Exiled," namely to Siberia for his love of Zion) was the nom de plume adopted by Professor Ezra Fleischer shortly after his arrival in Israel, but was later abandoned by him. The Tōkhēḥā was edited in the *Siddur* on the basis of 17 Geniza fragments (the Leningrad manuscript also came from the Geniza). Zulay had 34 fragments at his disposal, preserved in ten different places (pp. 63–77). Another grand composition of Saadya for the Day of Atonement, based on the first ten half verses of Psalm 104 was pieced together by Zulay from 39 Geniza fragments (pp. 99–141). The style of its ten poems is mixed and shows Saadya in midstream. He did not include them in his *Siddur*. Much can be learned from Benjamin Klar's review of the edition of the *Siddur* in *Kirjath Sepher*, 18 (1941/42), 342–348.

[115]I am referring to his *Sēfer ha-Gālūy*, best translated as "Open Letter," in which he defended himself in his conflict with the Exilarch David b. Zakkay claiming that he (Saadya) was the true spiritual leader of his people. Soon he found it necessary to publish another version, each Hebrew verse followed by an Arabic translation and still another version with comments in Arabic. One of the purposes of writing the book was to teach refined Hebrew style. See Schechter, *Saadyana*, pp. 1–7, for the Hebrew text, and Malter, "Saadia Studies" (see n. 102, above), 487–499, for the highly interesting Arabic translation (rendered also into English). See Yosef Tobi, "Saʿadia's Theory of Poetry and Language as Reflected in His Linguistic Writings,"

Sefunot, n.s., 2 (17) (1983), 309–337, and *idem*, "Saʿadia's Piyyūṭs" (Ph.D. diss., Jerusalem, 1980) (both Heb.).

[116]See Malter, *Saadia Gaon*, pp. 69–88, esp. pp. 409–419. The medieval scholar: Jacob Tam (twelfth century), see *ibid.*, p. 87 n. 186. The Geniza texts were collected, arranged, and critically evaluated by H. J. Bornstein "The Controversy between R. Saadia Gaon and Ben Meir in Fixing the Years 4622–4624 A.M.: A Chapter in the History of the Calculation of Intercalculations among the Jews" (Heb.) in the *N. Sokolow Jubilee Volume* (Warsaw, 1904), pp. 45–102. Bornstein was a man with a good grasp of anatomy.

[117]See *Med. Soc.*, II, 148. I am inclined to believe that Saadya's own family were immigrants from Iraq.

[118]Cf. Malter, *Saadia Gaon*, pp. 263–267. Solomon Gandz in *Saadia Anniversary Volume*, ed. Boaz Cohen (see n. 100, above), pp. 141–195, esp. p. 142, where Gandz seems to say that Saadya was (in his youth) a professional arithmetician and calculator. His treatise entitled *Law of Inheritance* (preserved), in which he could give vent to his passion for calculation, is regarded by Louis Ginzberg and others as an earlier work, an opinion that Gandz upheld (against Malter, *Saadia Gaon*, p. 165 n. 376).

[119]Cf. Malter, *Saadia Gaon*, pp. 157–167, esp. p. 164: "No Jewish author before Saadya had written an Introduction to his work."

[120]For the monograph on *The Law of Inheritance*, see n. 118, above.

[121]N. Allony, "The Writings of Saadya Gaon, Samuel b. Ḥofnī, and Hay Gaon in a Booklist of the 11th Century," in *ʿAlē Sēfer*, 6–7 (1979), 28–49. On pp. 31–32, he supplements the list of Samuel b. Ḥofnī's monographs, found in TS NS J 125, edited by him, with BM Or 5552 B, edited by G. Margoliouth, "Some British Museum Genizah Texts," *JQR*, 14 (1902), 311. For *ʾsfʾt*, p. 32, n. 17 (also p. 31, l. 11) in Allony's paper read *asfātij*, "letters of credit," with Margoliouth, cf. *Med. Soc.*, II, 328 and n. 5, where I still used the translation, formerly in vogue, "bills of exchange."

[122]TS 6 J 9, f. 1, ed. J. Mann, "A Fihrist of Saʿadya's Works," *JQR*, 11 (1921), 423–428, and since then much discussed. *The Book of Flowers* is also mentioned in the booklist in the preceding note, see Allony, "Writings . . . in a Booklist . . . ," p. 44, n. 99. Saadya also wrote introductions to the Pentateuch, Proverbs, and Job, see Malter, *Saadia Gaon*, p. 146.

[123]Mann, "Fihrist," 426 n. 10. The date 1111 given there must be a misprint for 1211.

[124]For Aaron b. Joseph ha-Kohen b. Sarjādo see *EJ*, I, 13–14. Some details there need qualification. The vehemence of Saadya's attacks against him is best understood, if, before the communal strife, Aaron had been a dedicated disciple.

[125]See Boaz Cohen, "Quotations from Saadia's Arabic Commentary from Two Manuscripts of Abraham b. Solomon," in *Saadia Anniversary Volume* (see n. 100, above), pp. 75–139, esp. p. 76. Cohen does not deal with this problem.

[126]See Allony, "Writings of Saadya Gaon," pp. 6–7, 34–35 (see n. 121, above).

[127]Dozy, *Supplément*, II, 720.

[128]He even used Arabic *script* in his translations and commentaries, see Malter, *Saadia Gaon*, p. 142 n. 305. These were later all copied into Hebrew characters, because the wider Jewish public (with the exception of clerks, physicians, wholesale merchants, government officials, and the like) was no longer fluent in Arabic script.

[129]For instance, nothing seems to have been published from Saadya's commentaries on the books of the earlier prophets (Joshua-Kings) prior to Malter, *Saadia Gaon*, p. 316, although such eminent commentators as Abraham Ibn Ezra and David Kimḥī refer to them. The Yemenite Abraham b. Moses provides us with twenty-eight quotations from them, some very extended. See Cohen, "Quotations from Saadia's Arabic Commentary . . ." (n. 125, above), pp. 76–77.

[130]The details of this process of integration are very controversial. This is evident from M. Zucker's monumental *Rav Saadya Gaon's Translation of the Torah* (New York, 1959) (Heb. with Engl. summary), to be followed by a volume containing fragments

of the originals of the commentary. Since Malter's characterization of Saadya's Bible exegesis, as he himself concedes, is very restricted, *Saadia Gaon*, pp. 141–146, the English reader will find a welcome supplement in Cohen, "Quotations from Saadia's Arabic Commentary . . ." (n. 125, above), pp. 78–87.

[131]G. Vajda's essay on the teachings of Ecclesiastes as seen by Saadia Gaon forms the opening section of his book *Deux commentaires Karaites sur l'Ecclésiaste* (Leiden, 1971). Saadya's philosophical chef d'oeuvre, *Emūnōth we-dē'ōth*, is available in a full, well-organized, and pleasant English rendering by Samuel Rosenblatt, *Saadia Gaon: The Book of Beliefs and Opinions* (New Haven, 1948). Alexander Altmann's selective and abridged translation, first published under the title *Book of Doctrines and Beliefs* in 1946, is available as a paperback in *Three Jewish Philosophers* (New York, 1982). It omits, however, the tenth treatise. Saadya's discussion of Ecclesiastes is found in Saadia Gaon (Rosenblatt), pp. 239–243, 275, 361–366, in the concluding section, pp. 404–408, and *passim*; see the list on pp. 490–491, and Vajda, *Deux commentaires Karaites sur l'Ecclésiaste*, p. 2.

[132]Ar. *wa-hādhā ghazwī*. S. Landauer, ed., *Kitāb al-Amānāt wal-iʿtiqādāt* (Leiden, 1880), p. 320, ll. 3–4. The manuscript from which this edition was made is written in Hebrew characters. Landauer transcribed them into Arabic letters, since they were used by Saadya in writing this book.

[133]Two literary devices underline Saadya's awareness of the unity of his spiritual world: the frequent cross-references to other books of his or to other chapters of the same work, and the autobiographic story form of his disquisitions: I wondered; I asked myself; I met; I found; it became clear to me, and the like.

[134]See Herbert Davidson, "Saadia's List of Theories of the Soul," in A. Altmann, ed., *Jewish Medieval and Renaissance Studies* (Cambridge, Mass., 1967), pp. 75–94, where cf. "I have met people who imagine the soul consists of air" with "I found people who argued thus" in Altmann, ed., *Three Jewish Philosophers* (see n. 131), p. 143, secs. 2 and 3; p. 148, sec. 3.

For the problem of the transmission of knowledge in Arabic literature through attendance at learned assemblies, see the bibliography of recent research on the subject in *Studia Islamica*, 59 (1984), 195, n. 1 (in a review by Cl. Gilliot of W. Werkmeister's comprehensive [German] study of the sources of the Spanish Arabic author Ibn ʿAbd Rabbih [860–940, a contemporary of Saadya]).

[135]The complete translation in Saadia Gaon (Rosenblatt), pp. 50–83. For Saadya's sources see Altmann's translation in *Three Jewish Philosophers*, pp. 62–73. Research, naturally, has progressed since 1946; see, e.g., A. Altmann and S. M. Stern, *Isaac Israeli* (Oxford, 1958), p. 217.

[136]As against about 1,300 quotations from the Bible there are less than 70 from postbiblical literature, see Saadia Gaon (Rosenblatt), pp. xxvi, and 478–494.

[137]See Malter, *Saadia Gaon*, pp. 386–387.

[138]*Ibid.*, pp. 384–386. Ḥiwwī is a biblical name. The proper pronunciation of this Arabic-Persian word is Ḥayaway(hi).

[139]E. Fleischer, *Tarbiz*, 51 (1981/82), 49–57, where the main literature about the subject (after Malter) is also listed.

[140]Malter, *Saadia Gaon*, pp. 194–260, provides a well-written and richly commentated survey of the entire content of Saadya's philosophical chef d'oeuvre. The participation of the gentile pious in the spiritual World to Come is a well-known Talmudic dictum, Tosefta 13:2, and accepted, of course, also by Maimonides, *Code*, "Book of Knowledge," "Return to God," 3:5, end.

[141]For Saadya's chronistic writings, see Malter, *Saadia Gaon*, pp. 171–173, 353–355; for Sherira, see *EJ*, XIV, 1381–1382. The continuity of the school of Pumbeditha, over which Sherira presided, was better preserved than that of Sura, and probably more records had been available there. Jacob b. Nissīm b. Shāhīn, as the name of his grandfather indicates, was of Iranian-Iraqian origin, and, as the representative of the Baghdadian yeshivas, served as the head of the North African diocese with its seat in Qayrawān. He was the father of Nissīm b. Jacob, often mentioned in this book.

[142]For the multifaced aspects of Hay Gaon's role, see, e.g., *Med. Soc.*, I, 52,

paragraphs two and four, and II, 24, 25, 177, 337, 338, 344.

[143]The quotations from Samuel ha-Nagid's corpus have been collected by Mordecai Margalioth, *Hilkhot Hannagid* (Jerusalem, 1962) (Heb.), a lifetime's work. The opinion of Samuel about his book, cited in the text, is taken from a postscript in verse, following a poem of a hundred lines, in which he described his rescue and vow, David Solomon Sassoon, ed., *Diwan of Shemuel Han-naghid* (Oxford, 1934), p. 84 n. 108, ll. 1 and 4.

5. Messianic Expectations and the World to Come

[1]Saadya (*Siddur*, p. 25) substantiates his decision with the rather weak explanation that the prayer refers to the light of every morning, not to the light brought by the advent of the Messiah.

[2]Al-Qūmisī: see p. 607 n. 11, above. Arrival in Jerusalem after a snowstorm: Goitein, *Letters*, p. 159 (TS Misc. Box 25, f. 124, *Nahray* 185).

[3]Judah ha-Levi, *Diwan*, ed. H. Brody (Berlin, 1896–1897), II, 157, l. 31. Carmi, *Hebrew Verse*, p. 348, bottom.

[4]Goitein, *Letters*, pp. 34–39: *as'al allāh al-ijtimāʿ be-vinyan qudsih*. I translated *qudsih* as "his sanctuary," but prefer now "holy city." On Karaism in southwestern Iran, see Sha'ul Shaked, "An Early Karaite Document in Judaeo-Persian," *Tarbiz*, 41 (1971), 51, n. 13 (Heb.).

[5]TS Misc. Box 28, f. 37, see *Med. Soc.*, I, 521. Similar wishes are found in letters written about two hundred years later, such as TS 28.10, l. 6 ("in Jerusalem, the seat of God's mercy"), TS 32.10, l. 23, both addressed to a Nagid.

[6]Other letters of Labrāṭ to his brother Judah are analyzed in *Med. Soc.*, III, 17, 20, 161, 226.

[7]ENA NS 18, f. 35.

[8]TS 20.69*v*, l. 27, where he is referred to with his Arabic designation Abū Zikrī Ibn Sighmār.

[9]ULC Or 1080 J 255, ll. 13–14, *India Book* 246. The writer, Jacob b. Salīm, had exiled himself from Aden to al-Juwwa, a three-day ride from there, because of strife in the Adenese Jewish community. He was very active in collecting donations for the Jerusalem yeshiva, which then had its seat in Cairo; see Goitein, *Tarbiz*, 31 (1962), 368–369. The other letter, TS 20.173, was partly edited by Mann, II, 366–367. The understanding of the Bible verse is based on BT Ketubbot 111*a*; see *ibid.*

[10]ULC Or 1080 J 28, ll. 17–21. Details about Solomon's family in Goitein, *Palestinian Jewry*, pp. 97–105.

[11]E.g., TS 13 J 14, f. 11 (to Mevōrākh b. Saadya, d. 1111, see next note); TS 13 J 15, f. 3, ll. 6–8 (written around 1110).

[12]TS 10 J 11, f. 15: *wa-jamaʿanā wa-iyyākum we-khol Yisrā'ēl le-vēt miqdāshō be-qibbūṣ qehālō uv-shikhlūl hēkhālō.* Another Hebrew rhyme, TS 12.386, ll. 5–6: *tizke le-vīat gō'ēl u-vinyan ariēl we-qibbūṣ kol Yisrā'ēl*, "May you witness the coming of the Redeemer, the erection of the Temple, and the ingathering of Israel."

[13]Passover: TS 13 J 16, f. 9, end; TS 13 J 18, f. 11, ll. 9–13. Sukkot: TS 8 J 24, f. 17. For the water libation see *EJ*, XV, 499–500.

[14]Fragment: TS 8 J 23, f. 27. Complete letter: TS 10 J 17, f. 25. Both were written around 1200. The fragment also contained the wish: "May God make your sons Elazar and Solomon great in knowledge ['Torah']." No doubt, the notable Meshullām b. Elazar ha-Kohen Kelīl ha-Yōfī (Perfect Beauty, an honorific title) is addressed. In another letter of congratulation for a holiday, TS 20.78, Meshullām is wished (by a dayyān, son of a "great rav") success, welfare, and a prominent position. The dayyān probably knew the addressee better than did the pious well-wisher cited above.

[15]ENA NS 2, I, f. 16, l. 9: *ʿīd al-ḥanukka.* TS 12.56, ll. 13–15: *al-mōʿēd al-pūrīm al-sharīf.* ENA NS 2, I, f. 5: *hādhihi 'l-ayyām al-sharīfa* (Hanukka).

[16]TS 8 J 22, f. 7; TS 10 J 14, f. 9; and the letters cited in the preceding note.

[17]TS 13 J 26, f. 15 (letter of 25 ll., Purim wishes addressed to Joseph b. Jacob Ibn ʿAwkal). TS NS J 84, *India Book* 250: "The Galut does not let man reach his goals. May this Purim be a good sign for the coming redemption, *yeshūʿā*," see p. 395 at n. 18, below. TS 13 J 11, f. 7, ed. Mann, II, 40–41: "May you witness the new heaven . . ." (Purim). The writer: Elhanan b. Shemarya Rosh ha-Seder.

[18]Travel for celebrating Hanukka: Westminster College, Cambridge, Geniza, Liturgy, II, f. 140, Jawjar (pronounced today Goger): TS 13 J 26, f. 7, l. 17, see N. Golb, "The Topography of the Jews of Medieval Egypt," *JNES*, 33 (1974), 131.

[19]Wedding: *Med. Soc.*, III, 108 and 118. Circumcision feast: TS 20.66; TS 20.111. Expressed in rhymed prose or verses.

[20]TS 13 J 26, f. 24, ll. 33–34: *wa-yuwaṣṣil ayyāmō bi-ayyām al-yeshūʿā* (to the Gaon Solomon b. Judah in the 1030s); ULC Or 1080 J 40 (*gōʾēl*, written by Ḥalfōn b. Manasse, 1100–1138); Mosseri A 67.2 (*mōre ṣedeq*, Damascus, eleventh century).

[21]See Mann, I, 179. Daniel b. Azarya's sons: *ibid.*, II, 85, ll. 24–25. For Hay Gaon: Mann, *Texts*, I, 122–123. For Solomon b. Judah's predecessor: TS 24.43, ed. S. D. Goitein, "New Sources on the Palestinian Gaonate," *S. W. Baron Jubilee Volume* (Jerusalem, 1974), II, pp. 517–523, 531–533. His son: ULC Or 1080 J 265. References to "the new covenant": TS 13 J 16, f. 1 (a head cantor), ULC Or 1080 J 132 (an itinerant preacher), TS 13 J 15, f. 8, l. 11 (in begging letter of a French[?] scholar).

[22]Palermo: TS 24.6, ed. J. Mann, "The Responsa of the Babylonian Geonim as a Source of Jewish History," *JQR*, n.s., 9 (1918/19), 176, ll. 10–11. Tyre: Bodl. MS Heb. a 3 (Cat. 2873), f. 37, see Shaked, *Bibliography*, p. 205.

[23]See p. 394 and n. 10, above.

[24]TS 18 J 1, f. 6, l. 13: *yeḥayyēhū ēl ʿad yāvō gōʾēl.* For those who go to decipher the manuscript, I must note that before these minuscules is written: *hū Ḥalfōn nīn Ephraim*, "identical with H. son of E." The name of the parnas was Aaron b. Ephraim, but on some occasion his name had been changed to Ḥalfōn, "Substitute," perhaps when his father was seriously ill, and his mother preferred to lose him rather than her husband (for, as a Yemenite woman once said to me, "children I can bear"). Aaron had long been known by his adopted name but had returned to the original one. In Geniza letters a son regularly addresses his father with the words "May I be your ransom," meaning, may all the evil destined for you come upon me.

[25]TS 12.719: *yeshaʿ rāv be-ḥayyāw.* The name of the man was Job, rare in Geniza documents.

[26]TS 12.459. As common in the Geniza, only the last word of the verse has been preserved. The script (square) is about 6 cm. high and put between borders above and below, consisting of a broader stripe in red on the outside and a narrower one in black on the inside. The inscription, as it stands, would be copied by embroidery or some other technique on a band of textile, to appear on one of the many hangings embellishing the walls of a house.

[27]Unlike our own times, where the meaning of a name is mostly unknown to the parents. Cf. *Med. Soc.*, III, 314–319, "The Message of Women's Names."

[28]Mordecai Margalioth, *Encyclopedia of Talmudic and Geonic Literature* (Jerusalem, n.d.), pp. 630, 747–750, 874. This should not be regarded as an imitation of the regnal titles of the first Abbasid caliphs, cf. Bernard Lewis, "The Regnal Titles of the First Abbasid Caliphs," *Dr. Zakir Husain Presentation Volume* (Delhi, 1969), pp. 13–30, for the names of the Gaons were given at birth, not at installation. But there was a connection: the messianic stirrings at the time of the advent of the Abbasids.

[29]I do not believe that the very common name *shylh*, mostly spelled *shlh*, should be read Shiloh (Genesis 49:10), but its frequency might have been caused by the messianic meaning given to the name Shela in BT Sanhedrin 98*b*, see E. E. Urbach, *The Sages* (Jerusalem, 1969), p. 617 n. 32 (Heb.).

[30]See Mann, II, 99 (1029).

[31]TS 8 J 9, f. 6 (spring 1100).

[32]TS 16.34 (1079).

[33]M. Steinschneider, "An Introduction to the Arabic Literature of the Jews," *JQR*,

10 (1898), 127. I do not believe that the name implies thanks to God for the mother's safe delivery. At the birth of a girl the family was congratulated that everything went well, at the birth of a boy—that it was a boy, see *Med. Soc.*, III, 226–227. Because of its frequency the name was abbreviated to Shūʿa from which the form of endearment Shuwayʿ was derived. Its Arabic equivalent was Furqān (Karaite and Rabbanite, but not common).

34 TS 13 J 14, f. 4, l. 3, *India Book* 259.

35 See Saadia Gaon (Rosenblatt), chap. 8 (superscribed Furqān, the Arabic equivalent of Heb. Yeshūʿā; see n. 33 above). Cf. also the reasoning of the first Jewish theologian whose Arabic writings have come down to us, albeit in fragmentary state, the Karaite David Ibn al-Muqammiṣ: Miracles (as performed by Moses) are decisive proof of the truth of his sending; military success (as achieved by the Muslims) cannot serve as a proof; many pagans, who do not know God, have vanquished their enemies. See G. Vajda, "La prophétologie de Dāwūd ibn Marwān al-Muqammiṣ, théologien juif arabophone du IXᵉ siècle," *Journal Asiatique*, 265 (1977), 227–233 and the Ph.D. diss. of Sarah Stroumsa, "Ibn al-Muqammiṣ and his ʿIshrūn Maqāla" (Hebrew University, Jerusalem, 1983).

36 Josef van Ess, *Chiliastische Erwartungen und die Versuchung der Göttlichkeit* (Millennial Expectations and the Temptation of Being God): *Der Kalif al-Ḥākim* (386–411 H.) (Heidelberg, 1977).

37 One of the less obnoxious, but still troublesome, edicts was the prohibition of eating *mulūkhiya*, a mallow plant made into a dish that was as popular in Geniza times as in modern Egypt (see *Med. Soc.*, IV, 475, s.v. "Garden mallow"), or that of eating eels and other fish without scales (which is, of course, biblical, Deuteronomy 14:10). When a man said a supererogatory prayer not approved by the Shiʿa, however, he was executed.

38 Mann, II, 432–436, formerly in *HUCA*, 3 (1926), 258–262. An additional fragment in ENA 4096*a* contains some better readings. E.g., Mann, II, 434, l. 3 from bottom, for the second *be-sahadūtām*, read with ENA *be-ʿēdūtām.*

39 Paul Kraus, "Hebräische und Syrische Zitate in ismaelitischen Schriften," *Der Islam*, 19 (1931), 241–263.

40 The use of the numerical value of letters in homiletic or mystical interpretation, see *EJ*, VII, 370 and 374, and S. Sambursky, *Tarbiz*, 45 (1976), 268–271. For instance, the Prophet has said that the Mahdi would come when the sun (*shams* in Arabic) would rise in the West (Egypt): *sh-m-s* (only the consonants count) = 300 + 40 + 60 = 400.

41 TS 13 J 22, f. 19, written on a piece of paper 24.5 cm. long and 8 cm. broad, as used in letters. The Shiʿite book: Ibn Shuʿba, *Tuḥaf al-ʿuqūl min āl al-rasūl* (Precious Gifts to the Minds from the Family of the Messenger) (Beirut, 1969), pp. 64–67. I am indebted to Professor M. J. Kister for the identification.

42 The letter of the chief missionary is discussed and fully translated in S. M. Stern, *Studies in Early Ismāʿīlism* (Jerusalem and Leiden, 1983), pp. 243–245; photos of the originals and transcripts on pp. 254–256. See also n. 35 on p. 253 of the editors of this posthumous publication.

Stern, "Fatimid Propaganda among Jews," in *ibid.*, pp. 84–95. The study is based on the Commentary on the Book of Daniel by Japheth b. Eli al-Baṣrī, who was active in Jerusalem during the second half of the tenth century, see p. 363 and n. 16, above. The prophecies contained in Daniel (which referred, of course, to the events and expectations of the times of the author of the book) were understood by Japheth as revealing the problems of his own environment, e.g., the annihilation of the Abbasid caliphate by the Fatimids, as anticipated by "the learned" of his time.

43 S. D. Goitein, "A Report on Messianic Troubles in Baghdad in 1120–21," *JQR*, 43 (1952), 57–76. On p. 75, the end of the line on the single leaf is to be read: *wa-lak ʿuluww al-ray*, "yours is the final decision" (lit., "the highest opinion").

44 Although the article is written in English, I provided the translation in Hebrew (opposite the Arabic text written in Hebrew characters) to make the American typesetter's task easier.

45 Something noble women did not do in those days.

[46]It was now exactly five hundred years after Muhammad's death. See p. 397, above.

[47]Goitein, "Messianic Troubles" (see n. 43 above), p. 76, f. 17*b*, l. 12 *nṣrh* is to be read as *naẓarahū.*

[48]*Ibid.*, p. 61, and in greater detail, *Med. Soc.*, II, 286–287.

[49]See pp. 392–394, above.

[50]TS Box K 21, f. 29, ed. Joseph Eliash, *Sefunot*, 2 (1958), 24.

[51]See *EJ*, XI, 1407–1427, esp. pp. 1416–1417 and 1427. Z. W. Werblowsky's short, but penetrating paper "Messianism in Jewish History," in *Jewish Society through the Ages*, ed. H. H. Ben-Sasson and Shmuel Ettinger (New York, 1971), pp. 30–45, is recommended as an introduction to the subject.

[52]Cf. Norman Cohn, *The Pursuit of the Millennium* (rev. ed.; New York, 1970), and C. Morris, *The Discovery of the Individual*, pp. 148–152, "The Jerusalem Literature." For Islam see *EI*, III, 120–124, s.v. "al-Mahdī," *EI*[2], IV, 198–206, s.v. "Ismāʿīliyya"; Goitein, *Studies*, pp. 135–148, "The Sanctity of Jerusalem and Palestine in Early Islam"; Hava Lazarus-Yafeh, *Some Religious Aspects of Islam* (Leiden, 1981), pp. 58–71, "The Sanctity of Jerusalem in Islam."

[53]See p. 362 and n. 13, above.

[54]The Kohens, that is, persons recognized as descendants of priests who officiated in the Temple of Jerusalem, possessed, of course, in Geniza times the same privileges that they still enjoy in orthodox Jewish congregations: they "spread their hands out" to bless the community, TS 20.94, l. 17, see Mann, II, 206, TS 13 J 22, f. 2, see p. 148 n. 109, above; at public service they were called up as first to read the Torah; anyone pronouncing grace after a banquet had first to ask the scholars and Kohens present for permission, and so on. In addition, it was common usage in the Geniza to invite the Kohens present to sign legal documents or official letters first. Karaites: ULC Add. 3430, see *Med. Soc.*, IV, 316, four Kohens, followed by two Levis (1028); ENA NS 18, f. 37; TS 12.644. Rabbanites: ENA NS 17, f. 21 (1040); ENA 2804, f. 20 (the mark was changed; in Mann, II, 115, it was f. 1), two Kohens, eight others; according to the custom of the Jerusalem yeshiva the Gaon Solomon b. Judah, preceded by his young son Abraham, signed last. In TS 16.177 the Kohens (3 out of 22 signatories) with an untrained hand signed after the scholars (City of Tunis, early eleventh century).

More important was the custom of wishing a Kohen to be granted to officiate in the Temple after its restoration: Mann, II, 151, ll. 9–10; (the manuscript now has the mark ENA 4020, f. 32); TS 24.49*v*, ll. 5–6, ed. Goitein, *Palestinian Jewry*, p. 130. Still more significant is the fact that from a Kohen more was expected than from the common Jew: "How can I, a Kohen, become a Christian?!" see p. 375, above. "The bearer of this letter is a Kohen, an excellent person, charitable, intelligent," TS 8 J 27, f. 8*v*.

During the period of the Second Temple, the service in it was divided among twenty-four "watches," or sections, each serving a week. The Kohens lived all over the country. During the week the "watch" had its turn, its members moved to Jerusalem. When Jacob Saphir visited Yemen in 1858 (see *Med. Soc.*, I, 395, n. 4), he still met Kohens claiming to belong to one of these "watches." In 1970 W. W. Müller, and again in 1971 P. A. Graznievitch came upon a large fragment of a stone tablet containing the names of the "watches" in a mosque of a small town east of Sanʿa, the capital of Yemen. Fragments of similar lists had been identified before in Palestine. Geniza finds show that it was customary each Sabbath to study one of the twenty-four chapters of the Mishnaic treatise "Sabbath" and to dedicate it in turn to one of the "watches." A document dated 1034 describes the custom of asking the congregation each Sabbath, "Whose Sabbath is it today?" With the answer given in unison, numerous liturgical poems dedicated to this subject have been preserved in the Geniza. See E. Fleischer, "News about the 'Watches' in Piyyūṭim," *Dov Sadan Jubilee Volume* (Jerusalem, 1977), pp. 256–284. All this proves that expectations of an early renewal of the Temple service were widespread. Moses Maimonides took the trouble to collect, arrange, and discuss in his Code of Jewish law the enormous mass of injunctions connected with the Temple service.

For the Yemenite tablet discovered in 1970 see R. Degen, "An Inscription of the Twenty-four Priestly Courses from the Yemen," *Tarbiz*, 42 (1973), 300–303, with photograph, and esp. E. E. Urbach, in *ibid.*, pp. 304–327, esp. p. 309. For the topic in general see *EJ*, XII, 89–93.

55See M. Gil, "The Sixty Years' War (969–1029)," *Shalem*, 3 (1981), 1–55 (Heb. with Engl. summary). Also Gil, *Palestine during the First Muslim Period (634–1099)*, I, 278–346.

56See Ezra Fleischer, "Studies in the Poetry of R. Hay Gaon," in *Habermann Memorial Volume* (Jerusalem, 1977), pp. 257–258 (Heb.). For the penitentiary poem see Carmi, *Hebrew Verse*, pp. 101 and 303–304. For Hay see pp. 127–128 and n. 438, above.

57Schirmann, *Hebrew Poetry in Spain and Provence*, I, 472–474, ll. 1–6, 9–10, 17–19, 38–39. This *geʾulla* is still recited in Yemenite synagogues. A stanza (ll. 20–28) referring to noble girls who were captured (in the border warfare between Christians and Muslims in northern Spain) but refused to convert (to a religion "with icons") is perhaps connected with Judah ha-Levi's endeavor to ransom a captured woman, see pp. 456 ff. and nn. 185, 186.

58Schirmann, *Hebrew Poetry in Spain and Provence*, I, 247–249. About the poet, see *EJ*, VII, 235–246, s.v., "Gabirol."

59Schirmann, p. 617, l. 7. About this poet, see *EJ*, VIII, 1163–1170, s.v. "Ibn Ezra Abraham." Abraham Ibn Ezra lived in the period of the terrible Almohad slaughters (not only of Jews), which he lamented in a famous elegy. His son Isaac converted to Islam in Baghdad, but returned later to his father's faith, see *Med. Soc.*, II, 302–303 and 592 n. 17. See now *Isaac Ben Abraham Ibn Ezra: Poems*, ed. Menahem H. Schmelzer (New York, 1980).

60Maimonides, *Commentary on the Mishna*, ed. J. Qāfiḥ (Jerusalem, 1964), IV, 197, "Nezīqīn" (Ar. and Heb.).

61For the originally private prayer see p. 129 and n. 2, above; for the obligatory prayer: Saadya Gaon, *Siddur*, p. 18, l. 6; for Maimonides, p. 407 and n. 71, below.

62Read Altmann, *Saadya Gaon*, pp. 155–162.

63Revelation to John, especially from 20:5 ("This is the first resurrection") through 20:11 (disappearance of sky and earth, see Isaiah 51:6, and Altmann, *Saadya Gaon*, pp. 155–162); 20:12 (the judgment of the newly resurrected, the book of life for the saved ones) to 21:3–4 (God dwelling with men, for "death will not be more," Isaiah 25:8).

64See above, p. 161 and nn. 188–190.

65BT Berakhot 17*a*. My rendering of Exodus 24:11 is not a translation, but expresses Rav's audacious interpretation of the verse. Wreaths were worn by the ancients at banquets and symposiums.

66Altmann, *Saadya Gaon*, p. 189. See also Malter, *Saadia Gaon*, p. 246 n. 528*a*, who refers the reader to BT Nedarim 8*b*, where the exposure to the miraculously intensified sunlight has the same opposite effect on the pious and the wicked as "the light of the Presence," see preceding note. Saadya does not refer to these Talmudic sources expressly, probably because their colorful wording might arouse additional questions.

67Cf. Saadia Gaon (Rosenblatt), p. 133, and 355, where he again emphasizes that the precise nature of the heavenly reward can be envisaged only at the time of the final redemption itself.

68As far as I can make out, the latest comprehensive and authoritative exposition of Maimonides' thought, Isadore Twersky's *Introduction to the Code of Maimonides* (New Haven, 1980), does not deal with the problem of resurrection. For what he has to say about Maimonides' famous *Treatise on Resurrection of the Dead*, ed. J. Finkel (New York, 1939), is its characterization as "a poignant spiritual-intellectual autobiography" (see pp. 503 and 43–45), but does not treat the subject itself.

69Harold Blumberg, "The Problem of Immortality . . . ," *Harry Austryn Wolfson*

Jubilee Volume (Jerusalem, 1965), I, 165–185, available also in *Essays in Medieval Jewish and Islamic Philosophy* (New York, 1977), pp. 95–115. Repeated again in Jacob I. Dienstag, *Eschatology in Maimonidean Thought* (New York, 1983), pp. 76–96.

[70]If Blumberg is right, Avicenna (see *EI*, III, s.v. "Ibn Sīnā"), born into an Ismāʿīlī environment, applied *taqiyya*, "concealing thoughts" about controversial topics, as is accepted in Shiʿism. Avicenna left over a hundred writings, however, many of them voluminous and still unpublished. Therefore any *argumentum ex silentio* with regard to him is hazardous.

[71]The nature of the "acquired intellect" is briefly explained by Maimonides, *Code*, Book One, "Knowledge," Sec. I, chap. 4:9, but he emphasizes that this is only "a drop in the bucket." I mention this detail only to show that Maimonides did not refrain from incorporating it in his Code.

[72]As taught by Saadya Gaon, see p. 387 and n. 132, above.

[73]Maimonides, *Code*, Book One, "Knowledge," Sec. V, chap. 8. The numbers in parentheses refer to the paragraphs of the chapter.

[74]Explained thus in BT Ḥullin 142*a*, the last page of that long treatise.

[75]See n. 71, above.

[76]In the biblical text the final clause is also omitted.

[77]BT Berakhot 34*b*, a saying by R. Yohanan, one of the most prominent sages of Palestine (third century).

[78]Robert S. Kirschner, "Maimonides' Fiction of Resurrection," *HUCA*, 52 (1982), 163–193. Similarly, Maimonides explains the place of animal sacrifices in Jewish religion historically: because all nations of antiquity brought such offerings to their gods, the Jews would have felt they were irreverent if they did not do the same. But despite this relativistic attitude toward sacrifices Maimonides dedicated a large part of his Code to the Temple Service (Book Eight). All laws of the Torah (Scriptures and rulings of the Sages) stand forever and must therefore find their place in the Code.

[79]Ezra Fleischer, "Second Thoughts about the Character of the Hebrew Poetry in Spain," *Peʿamim*, 2 (1979), 15–20, esp. p. 19 (Heb.). Solomon Ibn Gabirol, *The Kingly Crown*, trans. Bernard Lewis (London, 1961), esp. pp. 34–52.

[80]The scope of the creations of Islamic philosophers might be guessed from Charles E. Butterworth, "The Study of Arabic Philosophy Today," *MESA Bulletin*, 17 (1983), 8–24.

[81]See p. 130 and n. 8, above.

[82]TS Box K 25, f. 244, l. 7, ed. Goitein, *Palestinian Jewry*, p. 144. Rachel, although the younger, precedes Leah, as in the Book of Ruth 4:11. In this order the four matriarchs appear on the tombstone of a woman buried in Buda, Hungary, in September 1350, and another in a small town in Italy in 1572. Of the woman of Buda it is also said: "She departed for life in the Garden of Eden," and the names of the matriarchs are given only by their initials, which shows that by 1350 such an inscription must have been very common. See A. Scheiber, *Jewish Inscriptions in Hungary* (Budapest and Leiden, 1983), pp. 117–119.

[83]These formulas are usually translated as "*may* he rest in Paradise," which is acceptable, since everything depends on God's mercy, but as the wording on p. 129 proves, the speaker relies on the piety of the deceased that his soul finds rest immediately after his demise.

[84]BT Berakhot 18*b*, based on Job 14:22, "he feels the pain of his flesh." Cf. p. 185, where a mother complains to her children visiting her tomb about the worms tormenting her.

[85]Cf. Goitein, *Jews and Arabs*, p. 188.

[86]See p. 129 and n. 3, and, in particular, p. 183 and n. 312.

[87]See p. 130 and n. 5.

[88]See Mann, II, 259 n. 7, and *ibid.*, p. xxxiv, Reader's Guide. The copyist was Abraham b. Shabbetay, about whom see *Med. Soc.*, II, 47. Even in his old age the Gaon Solomon b. Judah used to sign: "S. b. J., the contrite, may he be granted to

witness God's Salvation." Heb. *nidke* must be understood here as in Psalms 51:19, as "crushed and contrite" by the weight of sin: "May I be deemed to be worthy to witness the miracle despite my sins." E.g., in Goitein, *Palestinian Jewry*, p. 108, l. 31.

[89]As it was in Talmudic times: "There is no difference between this world and the days of the Messiah except [the liberation from] the oppressive kingdoms." BT Berakhot 34*b* and parallels.

[90]The identification of the days of the Messiah with the general resurrection of the dead, criticized by Maimonides, see n. 60 above, was a popular simplification.

[91]See Scheiber, *Geniza Studies*, p. 571, ll. 10–11, who adduces another example for the phrase (n. 9).

[92]Letters might fall into other people's hands and be misused.

[93]TS 10 J 11, f. 13*v*, ll. 11–16, forming, together with TS 10 J 5, f. 10, a very long letter in the hand of Abūn b. Ṣadaqa, cf. Goitein, *Palestinian Jewry*, p. 176. The "young" [meant as a pejorative] preacher speaking about "the mysteries of the Torah," which he himself did not understand, probably also spoke about the things to come; *Med. Soc.*, II, 219 and n. 43.

[94]Cf. nn. 14 and 21, above.

[95]Cf. pp. 404 ff., above.

[96]See n. 11, above.

[97]*Med. Soc.*, III, 275 and n. 150, where the responsibility of the husband for certain sins of his wife is explained. DK XIII, ll. 12–13. Immediately after this sentence, the writer, the father of the woman, adds, "[when I try to quiet her] and say, 'remember how badly he treated you,' she answers: 'I wished I had remained with that bad treatment.'"

[98]Goitein, *Palestinian Jewry*, p. 95, ll. 43–44; p. 101, l. 1.

[99]See p. 332 and n. 1, above.

[100]See subsections 2 and 3 of section X, C, "Close to God" and "Member of God's Community."

[101]See pp. 404 ff., above.

[102]The poem beginning with the words *shūvī nafshī*, "Return my soul," ed. Schirmann, *Hebrew Poetry in Spain and Provence*, I, 514–515, often printed. As Professor Ezra Fleischer informs me (letter of March 8, 1984), the poem is found on five different Geniza fragments in the University Library, Cambridge.

[103]BT Sabbath 152*b* and Ḥagiga 12*b*, both quoting I Samuel 25:29.

[104]Cf. Malter, *Saadia Gaon*, pp. 190–191.

[105]An allusion to Micah 2:10, "Arise and go, for *this* is no place to rest; it is defiled."

[106]Refers to the Talmudic story of Mar ʿUqbā, who asked on his deathbed to be shown his account book for charity; when he found that he had given only 7,000 gold pieces (an enormous sum in those days), he said: "These are scanty supplies for a long journey," BT Ketubbot 67*b*.

[107]Cf. Ecclesiastes 3:1, and, in particular, verse 17.

[108]When, if not now? the well-known saying of Hillel, Mishna Avot 1:14.

[109]A reference to Mishna, Eduyot 5:7, where Aqavya b. Mahalalel (*EJ*, II, 478), asked by his son to commend him to his colleagues, answers: "Your own deeds will bring you near to them or will estrange you from them."

[110]A letter from Granada, May 1130, describes ha-Levi as *jumlat bilādnā wa-maʿnāhā*, "quintessence and embodiment of our country," see p. 449 and n. 168, below. His sojourn of eight months in Egypt on his way to Palestine in 1140/1 was a communal event of the first order.

[111]BT Berakhot 17*a*: "May you see your world during your life, and your end shall be for life in the World to Come"; this was the blessing said by the students to their masters when taking leave of them.

[112]"The day is short and much is to be done," Mishna Avot 2:17. But the poet says: "*your* day"; he was not young any more.

[113]See n. 96 and n. 11, above.

[114]BT Pesaḥim 78*a*. The question discussed: whether the newlywed should partake

of the first Passover meal after her wedding in the house of her father or her husband. Answer (or rather, one of the answers): the choice is left to her, especially if she is a *shulamit*, a "perfect" woman accepted favorably in both houses.

D. THE PRESTIGE OF SCHOLARSHIP

[1]Mishna Avot 1:2. Maimonides, *Commentary on the Mishna*, ed. J. Qāfiḥ (Jerusalem, 1964), IV, 408. See Cohen, Gerson D., *Soteriology*, p. 97 n. 74.

[2]Other works of charity are enumerated here: putting up wayfarers, visiting the ill, fitting out (poor) brides, and (honoring the dead by) joining the funeral procession.

[3]Baer, *Prayer-Book*, pp. 38–39, where the different versions are discussed.

[4]BT Qiddushin 40*b*, bottom. The sages assembled in Lydda to discuss whether doing or studying was more meritorious. The great Rabbi Aqiba decided for the latter "because study engenders action," which opinion was generally accepted. See what follows (cited in next note).

[5]BT Qiddushin 31*b*, bottom.

[6]See also *Med. Soc.*, III, 224–225.

[7]See *ibid.*, II, 192–195, "Adult Education."

[8]See *EJ*, XI, 1507–1523, s.v. "Midrash." For the relationship between these homilies and the biblical lections, see, e.g., Jacob Mann, *The Bible as Read and Preached in the Old Synagogue*, first published in 1940 and reprinted with a useful "Prolegomenon" by Ben Zion Wacholder (New York, 1971). See also *Med. Soc.*, II, 158 and nn. 14 and 15.

[9]*Ibid.*, pp. 159–162.

[10]See p. 342 and n. 66, above. In the congregational prayer of Saturday afternoon, the same request is made for the community at large, see p. 343 and n. 70, above.

[11]On her deathbed, the rich businesswoman Wuḥsha laid aside a sum for the education of her young son, hiring a teacher who would live in the house with him and "teach him the Bible and the prayers to the extent proper for him to know," *wa-yuqri'h al-miqrā* (Heb.) *wal-ṣalāt mā yaṣluḥ an yaʿlamoh*, ed. Goitein, "A Jewish Business Woman of the Eleventh Century," *JQR Anniversary Volume*, 75 (1967), p. 241, ll. 9–10, and p. 232, sec. H.

[12]Abbreviation of Beth-ha-Midrāsh, House of Study, see *Med. Soc.*, II, 199 and 202–205. For Ramle see Goitein, *Palestinian Jewry*, p. 69.

[13]ENA 1822, f. 45, last line, letter by Abraham b. Nathan Āv.

[14]TS 16.293, ll. 20–21, ed. Goitein, *Tarbiz*, 50 (1980–1981), p. 389.

[15]*Ibid.*, p. 381, from a now lost manuscript in Frankfurt, ed. J. Horovitz, "Ein arabischer Brief an R. Chananel," *ZfHB*, 4 (1900), 155–158.

[16]ENA 2727, f. 11 E. The "illustrious judge" was Isaac b. Ḥalfōn, mentioned in a court record from Alexandria dated 1235, see Abraham Maimuni, *Responsa*, p. 182 and n. 33.

[17]See pp. 432–438, below.

[18]See *Med. Soc.*, I, 51–54, for but a few examples which may easily be augmented with other examples from the Geniza.

[19]See p. 382 and n. 111.

[20]*Med. Soc.*, II, 195–217.

[21]About the economic activities of Christian Patriarchs and Muslim qadis, see *Med. Soc.*, I, 311, top, and n. 14, II, 366–367 and *passim*. For Hananel b. Samuel see Goitein, *Tarbiz*, 50 (1980–1981), 377–382.

[22]As on p. 339, above.

[23]*Med. Soc.*, II, 39 and nn. 76–77, where donations to Christian Patriarchs are also noted. Jacob Neusner's remarks on "the Glory of the Sage on Earth . . ." (*A History of the Jews in Babylonia* [Leiden, 1970], V 168 ff.) are also applicable to the Geniza period.

[24]See *Med. Soc.*, II, 240–261, "Medical Profession."

[25]This would not impede a physician from buying books of a renowned physician who was his own elder contemporary. See *ibid.*, p. 249. In a letter from Aden, South Arabia, written in July 1202, that is, in Maimonides' lifetime, to Cairo, Maḍmūn II b. David ordered all the medical writings of the master to be copied for him, see Goitein, *Letters*, p. 219, sec. G.

[26]The unique manuscript of Isḥāq al-Ruhāwī's *Adab al-ṭabīb* (The Education of a Physician) was discovered by the renowned bibliographer Fu'ad Sezgin in the 1960s. On the title page of the manuscript the name of the author was accompanied by the appellation *al-yahūdī*, "the Jew." This line was crossed out and the name was repeated without the word "the Jew." Whether the author was really a Jew (probably true) is irrelevant. He wrote in the spirit of the Greek authors so copiously referred to by him. The translation by Martin Levey, under the title *Medical Ethics of Medieval Islam, with Special Reference to al-Ruhāwī* . . . (Philadelphia, 1967) is not reliable; see the detailed review by J. Christoph Bürgel, *Göttingische Gelehrte Anzeigen*, 220 (1968), 215–227. Bürgel's summary "Die Bildung des Arztes" in *Sudhoffs Archiv . . . für Geschichte der Medizin*, 50 (Wiesbaden, 1966), 337–360, is a good introduction to a moving book about the high standards expected of a physician.

[27]There were exceptions. The court physician Abraham b. Isaac b. Furāt, the great benefactor and protector of the community, was flattered in a letter by Eli b. Amram, the head of the Palestinian congregation in Fustat, as "outstanding in [the knowledge of] the Torah, a champion of *miqrā* [the parts of the Bible outside the five books of Moses], great in Gemara [the Talmud]," but he was not. His intimate friend, Daniel b. Azarya, the head of the Jerusalem yeshiva, decorated him with an exceptionally rare title given only once before by a Babylonian yeshiva to an outstanding public figure, but stopped short of making him an (honorary) "member." See Goitein, *Palestinian Jewry*, pp. 185–186.

[28]Lynn White, Jr., "Medical Astrologers and Late Medieval Astrology," *Viator, Medieval and Renaissance Studies*, 6 (1975), 296. Bernard R. Goldstein and David Pingree, "Horoscopes from the Cairo Geniza," *JNES*, 36 (1977), 113–144: five Geniza documents with calculated dates 1082–1149. The Hebrew scribe was not Hillel b. Eli (as assumed by me, cf. *ibid.*, p. 124, and *Med. Soc.*, III, 233), but his son-in-law Ḥalfōn b. Manasse, who had certainly learned the scriptorial art from his father-in-law, so that it is sometimes difficult to discern between them. Since the person to whom the horoscope refers was born in 1113, the scribe must have been Ḥalfōn (documents: 1100–1138). B. R. Goldstein and D. Pingree, "More Horoscopes from the Cairo Geniza," *Proceedings of the American Philosophical Society*, 125 (1981), 155–189: two for determining events befalling all mankind, the rest for individuals; three of the ten horoscopes are later than 1200. *Idem*, "Astrological Almanacs from the Cairo Geniza," *JNES*, 38 (1979), 153–175, 231–256: ten documents predicting astronomical phenomena and the corresponding judgments (about this term see n. 32 below). Since all can be dated between 1132 and 1158, one individual may have been responsible for all of them (*ibid.*, p. 154). *Idem*, "Additional Astrological Almanacs from the Cairo Geniza," *JAOS*, 103 (1983), 673–690: four documents, also all originating in the years 1132–1158, which confirms that assumption. The authors of the article suppose that the tables were produced by the members of the new observatory founded in the capital of Egypt in 1120, and were copied into Hebrew script. The copyist, as far as I am able to judge, was Nathan, "the Scribe of the Yeshiva," son of Samuel, member of the academy; documents signed by him: 1128–1153, see *Med. Soc.*, II, 513, sec. 18; he died between October 1163 and 5 January 1164, see *ibid.*, III, 501–502 n. 96. He probably used the ten years of retirement to copy material other than court records. For another example of his copying an important text, see *ibid.*, II, 513. For Jews taking Sabbath afternoon walks to the observatory, see p. 346, above.

[29]*Med. Soc.*, II, 444, sec. 25: two male and the son of a female *munajjim* each receive a *jūkāniyya* robe (col. I, l. 2; col. II, l. 10; col. I, l. 12). *Ibid.*, p. 447, sec. 32, and 455, sec. 61: distribution of bread. See also p. 464, secs. 95–96, about a cantor

described as son of a munajjim. All these documents are from the first half of the twelfth century.

[30]Mosseri A 30, dated 1148, Ṭāhōr ha-Levi al-munajjim b. Nāmēr promised his divorced wife not to marry another wife before paying her 3 dinars, the balance of her delayed marriage gift of 15 dinars. This man was not destitute.

[31]TS 16.307, l. 17. The writer had suffered from a "burnt gall" and had to refrain from drinking wine. He was certainly under medical treatment. For *qaṭʿ* see Dozy, *Supplément*, II, 370b, bottom, *conjonction d'astres qui est dangereuse.*

[32]TS 16.71, see Friedman, *Marriage*, II, 219. "Judgment," *ḥukm*, is the practical conclusion derived by the astrologer from the astral phenomena observed.

[33]See p. 329 and n. 33, above.

[34]*Ibid.*, p. 330 and n. 42, above.

[35]*Med. Soc.*, III, 448 nn. 39–42. I experienced this myself. In the early 1950s I was invited as guest of honor to a wedding in a community of immigrants who had recently arrived from Yemen. I took the trouble to get to that place, and everything was ready for the ceremony. But the wedding was postponed, for the person expert in these matters (not their *mōrī*, "spiritual leader") had just found out that the hour was not propitious. That person had already left, so I could not find out how he arrived at his lamentable decision. The Geniza has preserved fragments of books of divination which their authors assert were not based on horoscopes, see p. 292 and nn. 99–101, above.

[36]Israel Zangwill, *Selected Religious Poems of Solomon Ibn Gabirol, Translated into English Verse* from a *Critical Text* "The Royal Crown," ed. Israel Davidson (Philadelphia, 1923), pp. 91–99, Secs. XIII–XXII. An English translation freed from the shackles of rhyme and therefore more exact by Bernard Lewis, *The Kingly Crown* (London, 1961), pp. 17–44. For Maimonides, see p. 329 and n. 34, above.

[37]Shortcomings in epistolary art: *wa-yasʾalō basṭ ʿudhrō fiʾl-mukātaba, fa-hū muqaṣṣir ʿalā kull ḥāl*, "I am asking you to forgive my shortcomings in writing." TS 16.250*v*, 1.7, ed. Goitein, *Palestinian Jewry*, p. 294, after fifty-eight lines containing all the habitual ornaments of speech. A letter from Palestine requesting the relations in peaceful Egypt to renew family and commercial connections since under the Crusaders life had become normal again. For its content see S. D. Goitein, "Geniza Sources for the Crusader Period," in *Outremer*, 1982, p. 314.

[38]TS 10 J 17, f. 8, margin: *daʿīf* (*d* for *ḍ*) [. . .] *wal-ʿibāra*. Abu ʾl-Faḍl b. Sahl writes to his relative Ibrahīm b. Ṣalḥūn. His spelling and diction reveal a man with little education.

[39]TS 8 J 11, f. 10, ll. 9–11: *badīʿ lafẓak . . . fahmak, ḥusn mantiqak, kathrat tajammulak.* The left side of the letter is lost. But the fragment, as well as other letters from Japheth ha-Levi b. Manasse's hand, e.g., TS 13 J 22, f. 29, referred to in *Med. Soc.*, III, 19, n. 15, and p. 157 and n. 152, above, show that he was in full command of the style accepted in family and business letters. His brother Ḥalfōn was not only the most prolific author of legal documents in the Geniza known to us (see Weiss, "Halfon b. Manasse"), but, as his exuberant letter of thanks to Khalaf b. Isaac of Aden proves, a master of Hebrew epistolography, Bodl. MS Heb. a 2 (Cat. 2805), f. 16, *India Book* 150.

[40]*Med. Soc.*, II, 41 and n. 5.

[41]TS 24.29, ed. Mann, *Texts*, I, 367–368.

[42]Bodl. MS Heb. a 3 (Cat. 2873), f. 28, ed. Arthur Cowley, "Bodleian Geniza Fragments," *JQR*, 19 (1906/7), 253–254, see Shaked, *Bibliography*, p. 205, where *Joshua* should be replaced by *Yeshūʿā*.

[43]TS 20.111, ll. 14–17, 21–23. The wording is interesting: *we-khol millā mehuddarā gevīrā āsaftah keʾesōf* . . . (Heb.). Cf. Cohen, Mark R., *Self-government*, p. 151 n. 159.

[44]TS AS 146, f. 3, l. 14, trans. in *Outremer*, 1982, p. 310; see Goitein, *Palestinian Jewry*, pp. 255–256, for Arabic original and Hebrew translation.

[45]TS 12.252, letter of Misgavyā b. Moses, see *Med. Soc.*, III, 29, bottom, sec. 1, and *ibid*, p. 434 n. 79 (1). The reader is reminded that Heb. *payṭān*, derived from

Greek *poiētēs* (like Eng. *poet*), designated in the early Middle Ages a writer of liturgical poetry.

[46]For Samuel "the Third" see *EJ*, XIV, 818–819, s.v. "Samuel ha-shelishi ben Hoshana"; for Ibn Abitur, see *ibid.*, VIII, 1152–1153, s.v. "Ibn Abitur, Joseph b. Isaac." More data about Jacob he-Ḥāvēr b. Joseph Āv in n. 91, below. The space accorded to Ibn Abitur and Samuel the Third in Ezra Fleischer, *The Yoẓer* [a branch of liturgical poetry] (Jerusalem, 1984), is larger than that given to any other payṭān—with the exception of Saadya Gaon, of course. See *ibid.*, pp. 765 and 773.

[47]TS NS Box 320, f. 44. The left half, which also contained the name of the poet, is torn away. But his identity is not in doubt, since the poem, *Mī zōth kemō shaḥar*, is well known, see Schirmann, *Hebrew Poetry in Spain and Provence*, I, 205, no. 72. "Metrical deviation in one foot," Ar. *al-izḥāf* (spelled here *ʾl-zḥf*), see Dozy, *Supplément*, I, 582*a*. "Onyxed and jaspered," *meshōhemeth meyushshāfā*, in l. 10 of the poem.

[48]The Arabs themselves did not remain untouched by the Near Eastern literary atmosphere of the early Middle Ages. For instance, the rhyme was known there long before the rise of pre-Islamic Arabic poetry. Cf. for these problems J. Schirmann, "Hebrew Liturgical Poetry and Christian Hymnology," *JQR*, 44 (1953), 123–161. The Arabs, taking advantage of the structure of Arabic words and endings, overdid the use of rhyme, in which they were imitated by others with gusto.

[49]For Saadya see pp. 380–383, above. For cooperation between Karaites and Rabbanites, p. 372.

[50]See p. 39 and n. 144, above, and the article by Dan Pagis cited there.

[51]TS Misc. Box 24, f. 28. Famous poets of the pre-Islamic, early Islamic, and Umayyad periods are, of course, also noted: "*min shiʿr Ṭarafa*;" and ʿAntar (*so*, not ʿAntara), and al-Shammākh; dīwān al-Quṭāmī; of the ʿAbbasid period, Abū Nuwās. The poet Ṭahir al-ḥaddād, "the blacksmith," was perhaps a contemporary of the proprietor. The bearer of this name could have been a Muslim, Christian, or Jew.

[52]ENA NS 7, f. 76.

[53]TS NS J 173, ed. D. H. Baneth, *Tarbiz*, 30 (1961), 174, l. 5. See *Med. Soc.*, II, 249 and n. 41. About Abu ʾl-Faraj al-Iṣfahānī see *EI*², I, 118.

[54]*Med. Soc.*, IV, 338–339. The coppersmith presided, perhaps, over a small congregation (in the Street of the Coppersmiths?), for which he needed the holy texts when entertaining his friends with his Arabic book of poems.

[55]Cf. J. Schirmann, "The Function of the Hebrew Poet in Medieval Spain," *JSS*, 16 (1954), 235–252; Raymond P. Scheindlin, "Rabbi Moshe Ibn Ezra on the Legitimacy of Poetry," *Medievalia et Humanistica*, 7 (1976), 101–115. Scheindlin's article refers to Moshe (Moses b. Jacob) Ibn Ezra's book on Hebrew poetry (written in Arabic). He was a kind of arbiter of the rules to be observed and a chronicler of their application.

[56]Samuel ha-Nagid, the statesman, in addition to his massive and distinguished contributions to poetry, was a leading expert in Halakha (Jewish religious law). It is noteworthy that a work of his youth on this subject, written in Arabic, is partly preserved in Geniza fragments, whereas his classic, the *Hilkhāthā Gavrāthā* (The Well-Established Laws), written in the Talmudic mixture of Aramaic and Hebrew, was widely used in Europe, but, as far as is known to me, is not represented by Geniza fragments. See Mordecai Margoliouth, *Hilkhoth Hannagid: A Collection of Extant Halakhic Writings of R. Shmuel Hannagid* (Jerusalem, 1962), esp. pp. 193–217 (with numerous facsimiles from the Geniza), compared with pp. 77–189 (quotations in medieval literature).

Abraham (b. Meir) Ibn Ezra (d. 1167), who was the last great representative of twelfth-century Hebrew literature in Spain, was also its most versatile author. Besides his poetry, his commentaries on the Bible were perhaps the best known of his manifold creations.

[57]Cf. Westminister College, Heb. Frag. in Glass, no. 1: "Abū Hārūn [that is Moses] Ibn Ezra, of blessed memory, composed in honor of M. Judah ha-Levi, may his Rock [God] preserve him, the following." Thus, this poem was copied during

ha-Levi's lifetime. Facsimile in Schirmann, *Hebrew Poetry in Spain and Provence*, I, opposite p. 512. A Hebrew poem copied above the one dedicated to ha-Levi concludes with verses in Arabic. *Ibid.*, *verso*, contains facsimiles from two other manuscripts reproducing creations of minor Spanish Hebrew poets, one a love song and another written for a wedding, also copied during each author's lifetime.

[58]TS Arabic Box 30, f. 250*v*, l. 7. See *Med. Soc.*, II, 221 and n. 10. As I understand the concluding remark, the cantor sang the stanzas improvised by him in a melody different from that used for the Spanish poem. It is still customary in Oriental synagogues that of longer liturgical creations each stanza is recited by a different member of the congregation after the cantor, or the audience in unison, has introduced the piece.

[59]See pp. 448 ff.

[60]Calligraphic note: TS Misc. Box K 25, f. 64. For Nethanel ha-Levi b. Moses, "the Sixth" (i.e., member no. six of the seven leaders of the Jerusalem Academy), see Mann, II, 292–294 and *passim*; Mann, *Texts*, I, 256–262, where his father Moses is also spoken of; *Med. Soc.*, II, *passim*, esp. pp. 244 and 576 n. 16.

[61]Ar. *wa'ant tadhkur fīh mā dhakart*, obviously a hint as to how to meet his friends in secret.

[62]Ar. *Abū Murra*, "Bringer of bitterness," the devil, see Wahrmund, *Handwörterbuch*, II, 774*b*.

[63]"No one's eye"; he writes *ʿayn yahūdī*, "a Jew's eye." This manner of speaking is also found elsewhere in the Geniza.

[64]The following is arranged in five sentences of rhymed prose, which gives the text a humorous, bittersweet flair.

[65]Intertwining the signature with letters forming the acrostic of a biblical phrase, as here, or of another motto expressing a prayer was customary among scholars in Geniza times. Such mottos would be transmitted from father to son, and since our very young Nethanel adds it to both of the missives discussed here, it was probably so with him too.

The Islamist is reminded of the *ʿalāma*, the motto used in Abbasid and Fatimid chanceries *instead* of the signature by name; see Stern, *Fatimid Decrees*, pp. 123–165. The Jewish custom of *combining* the religious motto with the name, and in the form of an acrostic, was probably older. It corresponds to the ancient practice of ascribing to a sage a particular ethical teaching, as in the Sayings of the Fathers or in the Talmudic *margelā be-fūmēh*, "he was accustomed to say" (e.g., BT Berakhot 17*a*).

In the family of Abraham Maimonides, when the motto *took the place of the name* and was put, as in Muslim documents, at the *head* of the paper, I am inclined to see it as a direct imitation of the Muslim practice. Cf. S. D. Goitein, "The Twilight of the House of Maimonides," *Tarbiz*, 54 (1985), 67–104.

The use of the vernacular forms, such as *baṣaddiq* for *uṣaddiq* (l. 9), in an intimate letter to a friend was not exceptional in Middle Arabic written around the middle of the twelfth century.

[66]BM Or 5566B, f. 30. See n. 70.

[67]This should not be taken to mean that the friend was the father of a son borne out of wedlock, but as an apt witticism uttered on a certain occasion, which then stuck as a nickname. The code was an *at-Bash*, that is the last letter *t* stands for the first (*'a*), the last but one *sh* stands for *b*, and so on. This code, used in the Bible (Jeremiah 25:26, *Sheshakh* for *Babel*) is well known.

[68]A lower middle class family could live for a year on 25 dinars.

[69]I.e., the book was entrusted to the recipient of the letter and not to be handled by strangers.

[70]See n. 66, above. In the address the recipient is called Joseph ha-Kohen b. Ḥalfōn (a name found elsewhere in the Geniza, but not fitting the time and circumstances of our letter); in the text he is repeatedly addressed as Hiba ("Gift" [of God]), a common Arabic equivalent of Heb. Nathan, but here a name of endearment. At its first occurrence (l. 10), it is accompanied by the epithet *al-muhayya'ī* (spelled *mhyy'ȳ*) "one who prepares"; see Steingass, *Persian-English Dictionary*, p.

1357*b*, who gives the pronunciation *muhaiyi*. He was probably honored with this title for providing liberally for his friends, ll. 12–13.

[71]Ibn Abī Uṣaybiʿa, II, 116. The author extols the medical knowledge, art, and success of Nethanel, but does not mention any medical writing from his pen.

[72]Mann, I, 234 n. 3, and Mann, *Texts*, I, 256–257. Mann's (tentatively made) conjecture that the Moses concerned was Maimonides and the poet Joseph Ibn ʿAqnīn is untenable in view of the express superscription in ha-Levi's diwan and the realization made by later research that there was little contact between Ibn ʿAqnīn and Maimonides. The phrase in the superscription "ha-Levi *wrote* to [Moses b. Nethanel]" may be explained by assuming that while he was still in Alexandria, Moses had written a letter of welcome to him after his arrival from Spain, whereupon ha-Levi answered with the laudatory poem.

[73]Bodl. MS Heb. a 3 (Cat. 2873), f. 6, ll. 16–17 and 30–31. Saladin's appointment: Andrew S. Ehrenkreutz, *Saladin* (Albany, N.Y., 1972), p. 65.

[74]When a busy merchant like Judah b. Moses Ibn Sighmār is congratulated by his elder brother on the birth of his firstborn and even more on completing the reading of the Bible a second time and knowing it, the reference is certainly to the completion of a round of daily readings; see *Med. Soc.*, II, 193 and n. 6. In old communities like al-Ḥugariyya in southwest Yemen and neighboring places, it was customary to read a chapter from the second and third parts of the Bible every morning after the service. (Communication from Ephraim Jacob, B.A., from Nahariyya, Israel, where a group of immigrants from al-Ḥugariyya have their own synagogue and still observe the old rites.)

[75]See pp. 443 ff., below, "Interconfessional learned contacts."

[76]For al-Muḥāsibī see Brockelmann, *GAL*, First Supplement Volume, 352, no. 10. For his influence on Baḥyā see A. S. Yahuda, *Al-Hidāja ilā Farāʾiḍ al-Qulūb* (Leiden, 1912), p. 72. Since 1912, a complete revolution in our knowledge of al-Muḥāsibī has occurred. He is now one of the best-known authors of ancient Islamic ascetism.

[77]TS 13 J 6, f. 27, ll. 2–3; the document is translated in Goitein, "Side Lights on Jewish Education," pp. 94–95. The internal conflicts alluded to by Mann, I, 234–236, and Mann, *Texts*, I, 395–396, were not those immediately following the death of Nethanel's predecessor, Samuel ha-Nagid in 1159, as here, but occurred about a decade later.

[78]Small town: Minyat al-sharīf; *rōsh ha-yeshūʿā* (Heb.), ENA 4011, f. 26, l. 4 (not noted by Mann, II, 293[a]).

[79]Antonin Collection, Leningrad no. 1154, ed. Mann, *Texts*, I, 261–262, l. 4. Mann had to rely on a transcript by the famous Orientalist Abraham Harkavy. Professor A. E. Katsh secured for me a photograph, which showed that Mann's assumption that the letter was written by Mevōrākh b. Nathan (*Med. Soc.*, II, 514, sec. 22) was right. For *wa-akhūh*, "and his brother," read *li-abūh*, "to his father," and correct on p. 260 Mann's note about Mevōrākh's brother accordingly. The corrections by Mann on p. 262 are actually in the original manuscript.

[80]See the two preceding notes. Latest dated court record while Nethanel was Head of the Jews: TS 13 J 3, f. 12, l. 3, Mann, II, 293 (d). The document from 1169 (see n. 73, above) was written when he had already renounced that post. The beginning of that document, where the persons in charge are usually mentioned with their full titles, is lost. The expression *arī ha-tōrāh*, "a lion of knowledge," is Talmudic. For Samuel b. Saadya see *Med. Soc.*, II, 514, sec. 23.

[81]TS Misc. Box 24, f. 137, p. 4 (mid-January 1160).

[82]See esp. pp. 265–266, above.

[83]Mann, II, 294, top.

[84]*The Itinerary of Benjamin of Tudela*, ed. and trans. Marcus N. Adler (London, 1907; repr. New York, n.d.), trans. pp. 70–71. Prince of Princes, *sār ha-sārīm*, was the title of Nethanel's predecessor Samuel ha-Nagid b. Hananya. Since this title does not occur in the document from November 1165, nor, as far as I can see, in any of the previous Geniza records referring to Nethanel, he must have received or adopted it only during the last years of his incumbency.

[85]For ʿĀna see Le Strange, *Eastern Caliphate*, p. 106 and *passim*. For the caliph's exile there, by which ʿĀna became proverbial ("So, the caliph is still in ʿĀna," meaning: the world is still leaderless, in anarchy), see Yāqūt, III, 595, ll. 10–12, and *EI*², I, 1074*b*, s.v. "al-Basāsīrī," the mutinous general.

Professor Robert McC. Adams of the University of Chicago and, in particular, Professor McGuire Gibson of the University of Arizona, Tucson, were most helpful with regard to the identification of the place, which was complicated, since at the beginning I had to rely on S. Schechter's edition, who read *h* (5) instead of *ḥ* (8), as in the manuscript, which I received later. Gibson's detailed letter of 26 November 1971, stating that all the literature assembled showed that six and a half days were the minimum for a boat ride from ʿĀna to Baghdad, settled the matter.

[86]See "Responsa by R. Yom-tov Ṣahlūn to the Community of ʿĀna," *Kobez ʿal Yad*, ed. Meir Benayahu (Jerusalem, 1950), pp. 139–193, no. 1 and *passim*, and Abraham Ben-Yaʿaqov, *The Jews of Babylonia from the End of the Gaonic Period to Our Time* (Jerusalem, 1965), pp. 84–85 and 320–323. A Karaite congregation in ʿĀna is noted in Mann, *Texts*, II, 338 n. 24.

[87]In 1612, about 600 years after the writing of our letter, this occurred in ʿĀna: the two synagogues had chosen a rabbi and made a contract with him for three years. Only a few days after the rabbi's arrival the members of one synagogue declared that they really had no need for a rabbi; all that was required were schoolmasters and a cantor. Ben-Yaʿaqov, *The Jews of Babylonia* (see preceding note), pp. 320–321.

[88]Mosseri L-290, ed. Goitein, *Palestinian Jewry*, pp. 91–96, esp. p. 95, l. 32.

[89]On the Palestinian quadrangular script see *Med. Soc.*, II, 234–235.

[90]See pp. 358 ff., above.

[91]The material about him is collected in Mann, I, 36–37. The letter of invitation to him from Buzāʿa, a small town in northern Syria, probably was extended to him when he was a refugee during the persecution of non-Muslims under al-Ḥākim, ca. 1013, Mosseri L-183, ed. J. Mann, *HUCA*, 3, 263–264, included in Mann, II, 437–438. TS 12.252 is a letter addressed to him while in Aleppo; the writer asks him for certain liturgical texts and sends him two and a half pounds of truffles as a present. For the remarks about him by Solomon b. Judah see n. 88, above.

[92]Ed. S. Schechter, "Genizah Manuscripts," in *Festschrift zum siebzigsten Geburtstag Abraham Berliners* (Frankfurt a. Main, 1903), pp. 108–112. See Shaked, *Bibliography*, p. 49, no. *9. Now preserved in the library of the Jewish Theological Seminary of America, New York, in the new special collection "Schechter Geniza," as no. 4.

[93]Referring to a king of Israel, an allusion to the appointment of the recipient as the Jewish chief judge of Aleppo; see below, n. 95.

[94]A judge was normally seated, not standing, but the writer is alluding to biblical verses such as Psalms 82:1: "God stands up in the heavenly assembly when he judges in the midst of the heavenly crowd."

[95]The office of the judge is compared to that of the king (see n. 93, above), one of whose prerequisites was beauty, Psalms 45:3.

[96]Expressed in twelve beautifully ascending phrases.

[97]Karmī is a biblical name, appearing in the Geniza mostly in the thirteenth century (but then for Oriental Jews). Lectures: *shemāʿūthēnū*.

[98]Meaning the judge's wife (see n. 10), sister, or another female relative.

[99]One of the very rare occurrences in the Geniza, where mention is made of good food.

[100]The judge's first wife had died and he had married into an important family in the community over which he now presided. He had a son, to whom greetings are extended; see below.

[101]The written and the oral law, that is, the five books of Moses (or the Hebrew Bible in general) and the Mishna and the Talmud; see above.

[102]The name is spelled here, as in Hezekiah's own letters, *Yḥzqyhw*. He was already in office in 1021 and survived Hay, who died in 1038; see Mann, *Texts*, I, 183.

[103]Saʿdel. Like the more common Saadya, the Hebrew name is not found in the

Bible, but was created in Islamic times. In Hebrew the meaning is "God helps," but "Saʿd" might have been felt more in the Arabic connotation of "good fortune," "propitious star."

[104]Ḥayyān. I have never encountered this Mesopotamian derivative of the root "life" in Egypt or the Maghreb.

[105]Mevōrākh b. Sahl was a Karaite who contributed to a joint appeal of Karaites and Rabbanites in Fustat around 1030; see *Med. Soc.*, II, 472, sec. 4.

[106]Probably identical with the representative of merchants Caleb b. Aaron, Fustat, who, according to a document from Tyre, dated 1011, had received bales of glass sent from that Lebanese port, see *Med. Soc.*, I, 421 n. 65, and who is mentioned also in a letter to Joseph Ibn ʿAwkal, ed. Goitein, *Tarbiz*, 37 (1968), 176, top. He might have left Fustat for Aleppo during the al-Ḥākim persecutions. He was probably a native of Syria, for the name Caleb was used by Palestino-Syrian and Byzantine Jews, but rarely elsewhere.

[107]Meaning: may your welfare be permanent. I believe that this is the correct translation, and not "may the reward be peace," Mann, II, 128 n. 2, for this Heb. phrase: *weʿēqev shālōm* is an adaptation of Ar. *al-ʿāqiba ilā ʾl-khayr.*

[108]My clumsy translation renders the meaning of the blessing for the dead father, consisting of an acrostic *nbtḥm*, which is a combination of Psalms 25:13 and Deuteronomy 33:25. Mann put a question mark after *ḥm*; it is an abbreviation of *ḥelqat meḥōqeqī*, which, according to the ancient translator Onkelos and a passage in the BT Sōṭā 13*b* and parallels, refers to the burial place of Moses. The meaning is that the dead father should be in the company of Moses in the World to Come and study with him. In modern Hebrew meḥōqēq means lawgiver; but Moses was not a legislator, he was "my scribe" (God is speaking). The Gaon Solomon b. Judah, signing a letter *ḥelqī* (not *ḥelqat*), purposely changes the text; the resulting meaning is: "Moses [i.e., the Torah] is my lot." Goitein, *Palestinian Jewry*, p. 81.

[109]The Head of the Diaspora, called here nāsī.

[110]The yeshivas of Babylonia-Iraq.

[111]Instead of the printed text the manuscript has: *kī gam hēm nihyū birshūthēnū.*

[112]"To tutor." The writer uses the felicitous verb *padgēg* (derived from Greek *paidagogos*, cf. English *pedagogue*), not listed in the standard Hebrew dictionaries.

[113]For Monday and Thursday as days for the sessions of courts and audiences of rulers see *Med. Soc.*, II, 342–343. For *wywm(?)* the manuscript has *wḥmyshy.*

[114]A euphemism for "cursed you."

[115]The usual preparations for a confiscation.

[116]The blessing is followed by the addition "with 7 and 8," *ʿim z we-ḥ*, meaning "together with numerous groups of pious men." The blessing to be united in Paradise with seven groups of pious men, based on an ancient Midrash (Midrash Tehillim to Psalms 11:7) occurs occasionally in the Geniza. The phrase "seven and [even] eight" (Ecclesiastes 11:2) is used in wishes for many sons.

[117]A form of greeting used by Kohens (originally, priests), see Numbers 6:23–26; 25:12; Malachi 2:5–6.

[118]The large, orderly, vertical Arabic characters seem to be related to Elijah's Hebrew script. Despite the absolute diversity between Arabic and Hebrew, I have often observed such kinship between the two scripts emanating from the same person.

[119]Looks like *imām*, the Muslim dignitary who leads the community in prayer. I have not seen this Islamic term applied to a Jewish divine in a Geniza letter, but this might have been common practice among the Muslim mail carriers in northern Syria, and therefore used also by Elijah ha-Kohen.

[120]For the Islamic commercial mail service, see *Med. Soc.*, I, 281–295.

[121]TS Arabic Box 53, f. 37, ed., with a facsimile and a commentary, by S. D. Goitein, *Sefunot*, 11 (1972), 11–22, and summarized in *Med. Soc.*, I, 57–58.

[122]Referring to the daughter who accompanied him, see sec. C, below.

[123]The writer's room was in the synagogue compound. When the service was conducted by a professional cantor, the voice carried to him. On weekdays, mostly

laymen officiated, who could not be heard so well. Saturday night is expressed in Hebrew, as usual, by the phrase "night of Sunday." It is interesting to see that the night after the Sabbath, which is actually the beginning of the work week, was celebrated here, as in ancient times, by a prolonged special service, cf. Elbogen, *Gottesdienst*, pp. 120–122. In the magnificent, hyperorthodox synagogue of Frankfurt am Main (now destroyed, of course) that service did not take more than twenty minutes at most, but endless rows of cars waited outside to take busy executives to their offices.

[124]The eldest daughter from the second wife. "Your mother" is the writer's first, repudiated wife.

[125]This name, whose Hebrew equivalent was invariably Samuel, not Ishmael (because this was then a term designating Arabs or Muslims), was extremely common.

[126]Only the year 4848 of the Creation, corresponding to 1087/88, can be meant. Miss (now Professor) Paula Sanders drew my attention to Ibn Taghribirdī, *al-Najūm al-Zāhira* (Cairo), V, 128: "In the year 481 [corresponding to 1088] the Nile rose 18 cubits and 4 fingers above its former level; everything sown and grown and in the storehouses perished because of the inundations."

[127]The members of the Jerusalem yeshiva, or high council, normally were promoted (from "Seventh," the lowest rank, to "Sixth," and so on) when a more senior colleague died. The writer assumes that his in-law, during the years in which there was no contact between him and the family, had risen in rank. The reference here might have been to honorary membership.

[128]The Nahum family was prominent in Alexandria through several generations. ʿImrān, the Arabic equivalent of Amram, the father of Moses, was not a common Jewish name.

[129]"By-named": *mṭʾqlʾ*, *metakala* (late Greek, as I learned from Professor Moshe Gil). The writer emphasizes that his son should not forget the title of the man (as he did with the titles of his own father), see n. 131, below. We see that the visiting scholar lived in the house of the leader of the community or in a building nearby in the immediate vicinity of the synagogue.

[130]Ismaʿīl-Samuel knew how to write, of course, but was ignorant of the calligraphic style in which a scholar (like his father) had to be addressed. About this problem, see *Med. Soc.*, II, 178–179, 236. "Only once" refers to a preceding letter.

[131]A large part of the last five lines on page 1 is blotted out or totally lost. In ll. 38–39 I read now *wa-nisīt* (l. 39) *al . . . alladhī nuʿittoh fī Dimashq*. The verb and noun *nʿt* is commonly used for honorific titles, cf., e.g., above, p. 87 and n. 204. Damascus also had a yeshiva, from which our writer had received an additional laudatory epithet while sojourning there. His son had omitted both the title(s) given by the Gaon of Jerusalem and that received in Damascus.

[132]I.e., not to be buried with them. A son, just as he should serve his father during his lifetime, should strive to be buried next to him, see p. 166 and n. 225, above.

[133]Read *ḥālat yadī min*.

[134]The second daughter of his second wife.

[135]Probably: the means for a dowry for the girl.

[136]From here to the end of the letter the writer combines two warnings: against certain heretics who had traveled from Salonika to Cairo (probably on a pilgrimage to Jerusalem) and whose teachings perhaps on the immediate and miraculous fulfillment of messianic expectations had made an impression on his son; and against the suspicion that he refused to join the family in Cairo, because he had accumulated riches on his travels and did not want to share them with others.

[137]The heretical teachings probably had something to do with the theory of retribution and God's justice. The writer seems to remind his children that owing to his efforts they and their possessions were spared during the terrible years of famine, plague, and anarchy that harassed Egypt in the late 1060s and early 1070s; see Lane-Poole, *History of Egypt*, pp. 145–150. Owing to lack of room (see next note), the text is ambiguous.

[138]The abrupt ending can be explained only by assuming that the copyist informed

the old man that he had arrived at the bottom of the page, and the latter did not wish to fill a third sheet (or had none).

[139]The answer of the Talmud: "So that people should not think that 'Torah,' knowledge, has come to scholars as an heirloom," BT Nedarim 81*a*, top. Another answer, provided on the same page: "So that scholars should not become haughty and supercilious."

[140]The words "blind" (secs. A and C) and "naked" are not always to be taken literally in the Geniza. I pondered a long time whether this letter was written by the sender or dictated. Finally, I decided for the latter because (*a*) the style of the handwriting is not the one that was usual in Egypt at that time; (*b*) the lively tone of the letter resembles speech; (*c*) the conclusion is so abrupt (see n. 138, above).

[141]See pp. 430 ff. and n. 75, above.

[142]See *EI*², III, 929, where further literature is indicated.

[143]The latest translation known to me is found and discussed in Franz Rosenthal's article cited in n. 145, below. In the printed version these verses are omitted. Abū ʿImrān is Moses Maimonides.

[144]See also *The Guide of the Perplexed*, trans. Shlomo Pines (Chicago, 1963), pp. cxxiv-cxxxv, the translator's remarks on the Kalām.

[145]Franz Rosenthal, "Maimonides and a Discussion on Muslim Speculative Theology," in *Jewish Tradition in the Diaspora: Studies in Memory of Professor Walter J. Fischel*, ed. Mishael [an uncommon name, see, e.g., Daniel 1:6] Maswari Caspi (Berkeley, Los Angeles and London, 1981), pp. 109–112. Unfortunately, as the reader easily recognizes, and as was confirmed to me by the author, the article is marred by omissions and other mishaps. Rosenthal most kindly put at my disposal a copy of his original text.

[146]Cf. *Med. Soc.*, I, 253 (and 463 n. 138, where the publication of the document is promised); *ibid.*, II, 298.

[147]The original text of Bodl. MS Heb. f 56 (Cat. 2821), f. 45, *recto*, is contained in my article "The Moses Maimonides–Ibn Sanāʾ al-Mulk Circle," in *Studies in Islamic History and Civilization in Honour of Professor David Ayalon*, ed. M. Sharon (Jerusalem and Leiden, 1986), pp. 399–405.

[148]Corresponding to 24 March 1182. The Muslim year was 577. Some readers might notice that the document was written on one of "the middle days" between the first and last holidays of Passover, during which some people refrained from conducting business and writing documents. But death does not wait; therefore we see that here and also in another case in which Maimonides was directly involved (*Med. Soc.*, IV, 335–336, App. D, doc. VII) the rabbinic court acted.

[149]This phrase, taken from the biblical story of Joseph (Genesis 44:39), is frequently attached to the name of a respectable person.

[150]The dying man had not mentioned her name, and since his declaration was to be rendered verbatim, the name was provisionally omitted. Later she would be invited to the court (or visited by a judge) and her identity established by proper witnesses.

[151]Firkovitch, II, 1700, f. 15, see *Med. Soc.*, III, 130, 365 n. 9, and 454 n. 67.

[152]TS NS J 422, see *Med. Soc.*, II, 479, sec. 24, and 579 n. 73. Ibn al-Kallām in TS NS J 296*v* (another list of contributors) might also refer to him.

[153]Four dinars were the maximum poll tax. The additional ⅙ dinar was for the *ḥāshir*, "tax collector," or a fine, *tarsīm*, for late payment (i.e., the policeman guarding the door of the taxpayer until payment was made).

[154]Cf. *Med. Soc.*, I, 200 ff., "Business principles and policies."

[155]See my latest summary, "Moses Maimonides, Man of Action: A Revision of the Master's Biography in Light of the Geniza Documents," *Hommage à Georges Vajda*, ed. Gerard Nahon and Charles Touati (Louvain, 1980), pp. 155–167. Attention is also drawn to a charming description of "A Meeting with Maimonides," published by Paul Fenton, "A Meeting with Maimonides," *BSOAS*, 45 (1982), 1–4, which betrays the master as a very sociable being.

[156]See E. Ashtor-Strauss, "Saladin and the Jews," *HUCA*, 37 (1956), 310–311.

Another Jewish physician attending Saladin, Ibn Shūʿa (*ibid.*, p. 310), also bore the title al-Muwaffaq, but since he died in 1183/4, he was probably an old man at the time of Abu ʾl-Faraj's voyage and would hardly have been chosen by him to take care of such vital matters as the purchase of wheat, a toilsome affair.

[157]A famous example is the India trader Ḥalfōn b. Nethanel, the dedicated friend of the poet Judah ha-Levi and of other Spanish intellectuals; see below, pp. 453 ff., and his correspondence edited by me in *Tarbiz*, 24 (1955), 21–47, 134–149, and *passim*.

[158]*Kallām*, derived from *kalm*, wound, cut, slash; designated perhaps not a physician proper, but a male nurse bandaging wounds; cf. *Med. Soc.*, II, 255 n. 73.

[159]To whom we owe valuable information about the lives of Moses Maimonides and his son Abraham, which we do not get from Jewish sources.

[160]Cf. Maimonides' frequent remarks in his *Responsa* about Muslim judges.

[161]Some minor questions raised by this document are answered here.

a. Why does a man who pays the top poll tax assign to his wife as the delayed portion of the marriage gift (the one to be paid at his death) only 10 dinars? At the very least 50 dinars would have been more appropriate. The answer is found in the document itself: she was his maternal cousin. It was a family arrangement. Both were probably widowed; she did not bring in a dowry because her future husband's house was replete with everything she needed; consequently, on his side, only a token marriage gift was required.

b. The first signatory, Samuel ha-Levi b. R. Saadya, was a prominent member of Moses Maimonides' rabbinic court, see *Med Soc.*, II, 514, sec. 23. He attended the deathbed declaration in person. The other witness, Elazar b. Michael, is known to me as a signatory of documents from the years 1182 (TS 12.487; a few months before our document) and 1181 (TS 12.451*v*); a scholarly person, as his good hand shows.

[162]The term "the Jew" (in the passage from Ibn Sanāʾ al-Mulk's book translated above) following the name of Moses Maimonides should by no means be understood as demeaning. In each biography in which a Jew or Christian appears, Ibn Abī Uṣaybiʿa, the most liberal of Muslim biographers, notes this, because this detail fixed the place of a person in society. But Ibn Sanāʾ al-Mulk describes Maimonides as "chief physician" and gives him the kunya Abū ʿImrān (Father of Amram, which pertains to the name Moses), as he would bestow an honorary epithet on any respectable Muslim.

[163]See p. 289 and n. 76, above. Also p. 288 and n. 71.

[164]See *EJ*, X, 355–366; for the bibliography of ha-Levi's poetry: *ibid.*, pp. 361–362. Schirmann, *Studies*, I, 250–318 (originally published in *Tarbiz*, 9 [1938], in three continuations) contains a complete biography, based mainly on ha-Levi's poetry, followed by Supplements, pp. 319–341, a critical, mostly positive review of ten Geniza publications of mine on the life of the poet, listed, on p. 341, as Goitein 1–10. For the English reader my paper "The Biography of Rabbi Judah Ha-Levi in the Light of the Cairo Genizah Documents," in *PAAJR*, 18 (1959), 41–56, presents a survey on the Geniza finds on the subject. Nina Salaman's *Selected Poems by Jehudah Halevi* (Philadelphia, 1924, still in print) is perhaps the best choice for the English reader, although one misses there some of the favorite pieces. See also n. 168, below.

[165]See *EJ*, X, 366, for a bibliography of editions, translations, and treatments of the *Kuzari*. The final edition of the Arabic original by David H. Baneth, prepared for posthumous publication by Haggai Ben-Shammai, appeared in Jerusalem in 1977. Isaac Heineman's abridged translation with introduction and commentary in *Three Jewish Philosophers* (1946, repr. New York, 1982) intends to present ha-Levi's teachings "from the modern [i.e., 1946] view-point," perhaps not always acceptable to the present-day reader. The translation, too, could be improved here and there.

[166]The *Kuzari* is divided into five chapters and, within each, the utterings of the participants bear running numbers. Thus the book can be referred to by chapter and number of uttering, irrespective of the edition.

[167]Leon Roth, *Judaism: A Portrait* (New York, 1961), pp. 104–110. Leon Roth, a

former professor of philosophy and rector of the Hebrew University, and I often took walks in England between Cambridge and Grantchester, a village nearby, and Judah ha-Levi was frequently discussed. While we were inclined to agree on many topics, Judah ha-Levi was not among them. Philosopher and historian do not always see eye to eye.

[168]Trans. Salaman, *Selected Poems* (see n. 164, above), p. 127. German poetic translation in Franz Rosenzweig, *Jehuda Halevi, Zweiund-neunzig Hymnen und Gedichte* (Ninety-two Hymns and Poems) (Berlin: Lambert Schneider, n.d.), p. 87. This controversial but highly artistic work, with its epilogue and notes full of ideas, is recommended to everyone interested in the subject and in full command of the German language.

[169]Ha-Levi was not the only poet using the vocabulary of love poetry for depicting the relation between Israel and its God; see p. 404, above.

[170]Cf., for instance, what ha-Levi had to say about the physical nature of the human heart in the famous passage where Israel is described by him as the heart in the body of humanity, *Kuzari*: II, 36–42.

[171]The hymn *yeḥaw lāshōn* has often been printed, e.g., Schirmann, *Hebrew Poetry in Spain and Provence*, I, 528–531; Germ. trans., Rosenzweig, *Jehuda Halevi* (see n. 168), pp. 39–42, with his remarkable comments on pp. 185–188.

[172]"Devārēkhā be-mōr ʿōvēr": Schirmann, *Hebrew Poetry in Spain and Provence*, I, 492–494; Salaman, *Selected Poems* (see n. 164, above), pp. 14–17, esp. pp. 16–17; Rosenzweig, *Jehuda Halevi* (see n. 168, above), pp. 130–132, nn. 244–245. The straight road: lit., "the mother of roads."

[173]On the meaning of the Kaddish in Geniza times see *Med. Soc.*, III, 245 and n. 154. See also *EJ*, X, 660–663.

[174]"Yāh shimkhā": Salaman, *Selected Poems* (see n. 164, above), pp. 127–129. Rosenzweig, *Jehuda Halevi* (see n. 168, above), pp. 13–17 (the very first poem translated in that book).

[175]Alexander Altmann, "The Delphic Maxim in Medieval Islam and Judaism," in *Biblical and Other Studies*, ed. A. Altmann (Cambridge, Mass., 1963), pp. 196–232. The reference to ha-Levi's poem *im nafshekhā yeqārā be-ʿēnēkhā*: *ibid.*, p. 199 n. 21.

[176]ULC Or 1080 J 94, l. 2, *India Book* 101.

[177]Or *Khatūsh*; written also *Lakhtuj* (not *ū*). TS 10 J 16, f. 17.

[178]See J. Schirmann, *Tarbiz*, 9 (1938), 295; *idem*, *Studies* (see n. 164), I, 307–308.

[179]Cf. Goitein, *Tarbiz*, 24 (1955), 141–143. In Arabic *nasīb*, which, in the language of that age, could designate almost any form of relationship; see Dozy, *Supplément*, II, 665*a*; Ḥalfōn's letter, *India Book* 99. It seems that Nethanel's family was related to the Ibn Ezras.

[180]It is not always easy to distinguish between a literary and a documentary paper from the Geniza. The rule is that a poetical composition, even if it is found on a single sheet or on scattered papers, is to be regarded as literary and not as documentary. Therefore, the fragments of Judah ha-Levi's epistle to Samuel the Nagid, or Head of the Jews of Egypt, published by S. Abramson "R. Judah ha-Levi's Letter on his Emigration to the Land of Israel" (Heb.) *Kirjath Sepher*, 29 (1953/4), 133 ff., or his epistle to Ḥabīb of al-Mahdiyya, published by Madame Starkova (cf. J. Schirmann, "Studies in Hebrew Poetry, 1948–1949" (Heb.) *Kirjath Sepher*, 26 [1950], 198–199) cannot be described as "documentary," as they obviously originally formed parts of a collection of the poet's works.

[181]The fragment of a letter by Judah ha-Levi addressed to the Nagid Samuel b. Hananyah, published by A. Scheiber in *Tarbiz*, 36 (1967), 156–157 with facsimile (= Scheiber, *Geniza Studies*, pp. 72–74) is no doubt identical with the letter referred to in Abū Naṣr b. Abraham's note. But it was not the original (which was, of course, forwarded to the Nagid immediately after it had been copied). What we have is a copy made after ha-Levi's death. Its beginning, mostly lost, is to be restored thus: "[This is what Rabbenū Judah ha-Levi, may he be remembered with blessings] and for resurrection, wrote to our lord and Nagid Samuel—may he rule forever—while on board ship [in the port of Alexan]dria." See my remarks in *Tarbiz*, 36 (1967), 299.

[182]See pp. 462–468, below.

[183]Cf. the well-known passage "how they did congratulate him on being in the service of kings" in Judah ha-Levi's *Diwan*, ed. H. Brody (Berlin, 1896/7), II, 185, l. 25. See also Salaman, *Selected Poems* (see n. 164, above), p. 10, l. 4, ("service of men," as opposed to God) in the poem *ha-tirdof naʿarūth*, and *ibid.*, p. 27, l. 21, "I ceased to walk on my hand and my nose" in *heṣiqathnī teshūqāthī*.

[184]The letter is translated in full, pp. 464–465.

[185]Translated pp. 463–464, below.

[186]Ha-Levi was in close contact with Ibn Migash. He wrote poems in his honor for his wedding and other occasions, sent a rhymed letter in Ibn Migash's name to a scholar in al-Mahdiyya, Tunisia (see n. 180, above), who inquired whether the Rav had dealt with the juridical questions he had submitted to him, and another poetic missive to scholars in Narbonne, France; see n. 178, above.

[187]Cf. my "The Oldest Documentary Evidence for the Title *1001 Nights*," *JAOS*, 78 (1958), 301, and "Communal Officials and Physicians Dealing in Books," *Kirjath Sepher*, 44 (1969), 125–128.

[188]Goitein, *Tarbiz*, 24 (1955), 136–138.

[189]TS 16.54; Assaf, *Texts*, p. 133. See also *Med. Soc.*, II, 256 and n. 82.

[190]See J. Schirmann, *Tarbiz*, 9 (1938), 230, esp. n. 52.

[191]Bodl c 28, f. 31, ll. 13–20, *India Book* 99.

[192]TS 10 J 11, f. 1, ll. 14–15, *India Book* 128.

[193]Pp. 288 and 454 ff.

[194]See my provisional list in *Tarbiz*, 25 (1956), 395.

[195]Most likely, this ship is referred to in a letter sent in Nisan 1137 from Spain to Egypt as being constructed at that time. See my "Glimpses from the Cairo Geniza on Naval Warfare in the Mediterranean . . . , " in *Studi Orientalistici in onore di Giorgio Levi Della Vida* (Rome, 1956), I, p. 405, *verso*, ll. 13–14.

[196]When Badr al-Jamālī, the great Armenian soldier, sailed in December 1073 from Acre to Egypt, it was regarded as an exceptional feat, see Lane-Poole, *History of Egypt*, pp. 150–151.

[197]See above p. 454, and, in particular, no. 6. The poem, *Diwan*, ed. Brody (see n. 183, above) p. 172, no. 13, Salaman, *Selected Poems* (see n. 164, above), p. 26, where the poet takes leave of Isaac and others, probably was composed while he was still in Spain; on the other hand, in no. 11, Brody, II, 170, Salaman, p. 23, which gives the impression of being written at sea, only his daughter and grandson are greeted as being far away.

[198]*Diwan*, ed. Brody (see n. 183, above), I, 13, no. 11. *Diwan*, I, 67–68, no. 50. Ibn Gabbay was an India trader whom we find in Aden in the fall of 1149, TS 10 J 10 f. 15, l. 12, *India Book* 68, l. 12.

[199]TS 13 J 24, f. 8, l. 8 ff., Goitein, *Tarbiz*, 28 (1959), 352–354.

[200]This family name may be derived from the Banū Maṭrūḥ, who ruled Tripoli in Libya around 1140, see Amari, *Musulmani di Sicilia*, III, 414–416.

[201]In Arabic *wālī*, to be distinguished from *amīr*, the governor of the town (occurring in other letters of Abū Naṣr). Concerning this use of the term *wālī* see Marius Canard, *Vie de l'Ustadh Jaudhar* (Algiers, 1958), n. 336 (for Mamluk times).

[202]See, e.g., his verses "Oh those girls on the banks of the Nile," *Med. Soc.*, IV, 200.

[203]Reference is made here to ULC Or 1080 J 258.

[204]The first poem in *Diwan*, ed. Brody (see n. 183, above), II, 171, the second in *ibid.*, p. 168, Salaman, *Selected Poems* (see n. 164, above), pp. 24 and 22, respectively.

[205]F. I. Baer might be right in his assumption ("The Political Situation of the Spanish Jews in the Times of Judah ha-Levi," *Zion*, 1 [1936], 23) that the poet did not believe in the prospect of the Jews persecuted in Muslim countries finding a refuge in Christian Spain; but leaving Alexandria, which, at exactly that time, was particularly oppressive, he might have found relief in the idea of leaving the realm of Muslim domination. One is reminded of ha-Levi's younger compatriot, the Spanish Muslim Ibn Jubayr, who was full of praise for the Crusaders' state when he crossed it in 1184.

[206]From the letter published by me in *Tarbiz*, 24 (1955), 33, taken together with ULC Or 1080 J 258, which shows that the death occurred in the month of Av. See also my "Did Judah ha-Levi Arrive in the Holy Land?" *Tarbiz*, 46 (1977), 245–250, where the answer is affirmative.

[207]The autographs are numbered in the sequence in which I identified them.

[208]D. Antonio Ballesteros y Beretta, *Historia d'España* (Barcelona, 1920), II, 254–258. J. Schirmann (*Tarbiz*, 25 [1956], 412) thought that "the wicked woman" might perhaps refer to an oppressive government. But D. H. Baneth (*Tarbiz*, 26 [1957], 301) points out that the Hebrew term *mirsha'ath*, found here in the midst of an Arabic text, is used in the Bible referring to the wicked queen Athaliah (II Chronicles 24:7) and the references here are to a person rather than to an institution.

[209]TS 10 J 15, f. 3, margin, l. 2, *India Book* 103. On the ransoming of captives, see *Med. Soc.*, I, 328–329, and II, 96 and 137.

[210]This and the two following letters are edited by me with facsimilies, *Tarbiz*, 25 (1956), 393–408.

[211]The poet Judah b. Ghiyāth (often spelled Ghayyāth) lived in Granada and was a personal friend of Ḥalfōn b. Nethanel.

[212]Ghuzz are the Turkish people that we loosely call Seljuks. I assume that these Ghuzz had taken (paid) responsibility for the travelers in their caravan.

[213]Lucena, halfway between Granada and Cordova, was the Jewish "capital" of Muslim Spain. Therefore, it was expected that a sum equal to that collected in Toledo, the main Jewish center of Christian Spain, would be brought together there.

[214]This translation follows Baneth, *Tarbiz*, 26 (1957), 301. In Yemen it was common practice to send imprisoned Jews home on their Sabbaths.

[215]The month of the Jewish autumn holidays. After the lapse of the term, the girl could be sold as a slave. If she was beautiful, a price far higher than 33⅓ dinars could be obtained for her.

[216]The text has *ṣihrak*, "relative," but since the word precedes "your paternal aunt," Ḥalfōn's prominent uncle, Samuel Ibn Al-Ukhtūsh, is no doubt intended.

[217]"Head of the Police," *ṣāḥib ash-shurṭa*, was a title rather than an office in those days. Abū Ibrāhīm Ibn Barōn once sent to Judah ha-Levi almonds, figs, grapes, and other fruits from Malaga, to which gift the poet alluded in a poem dedicated to him, see Schirmann, *Tarbiz*, 9 (1938), 225. As I learned from S. M. Stern, Barōn is simply Spanish *varón*, "man."

[218]I.e., a man from the city of Jaén.

[219]Again Hebrew, but a different word.

[220]Read, with Baneth, *Tarbiz*, 26 (1957), 302, *sababan*.

[221]Joseph Ibn Migash, then the spiritual leader of the Jews of Spain, was referred to in this way. The poet had submitted to him a question (in legal or religious matters) for his compatriots and asks now his friend Halfōn, who either happened to be in Lucena or was expected to travel there, to expedite the matter.

[222]Before setting out on a voyage or before sending something, one made an *istikhāra*, lit., "asking God for guidance," trying to find out whether the time and other circumstances were propitious for the undertaking. See *Med. Soc.*, I, 346, II, 581 n. 111.

[223]The dinar donated by Ḥalfōn.

[224]Ḥalfōn was an avid collector of books. The son of Obadiah: Isaac, known from other Geniza letters.

[225]Excuse, please: the shortness and informality of the note.

[226]This shows that at the writing of this note the poet was already in Muslim territory. Although vizier was an office of low rank in Spain of those days, the greetings show that the India trader from Egypt must have been quite at home in Spain by that time. The phrase "scented and most fragrant greetings" might have had its origin in the custom of refined people to perfume the paper of letters sent to distinguished or beloved persons.

[227]Obviously, [*ghayr*] *al-khāsira min al-shawq* is to be read.

[228]Ar. *sakhāfa*. It seems that it was common for authors to speak in this way about

their creations. In TS 12.280, the poet Isaac b. Abraham Ibn Ezra uses this word three times in referring to his own writings. Joseph b. Barzel was a physician and also wrote poetry, see Schirmann, *Studies*, II, 175–178.

[229]Certainly a poem ordered by Ḥalfōn. In TS 10 J 11, f. 1, a common friend of the two sends Ḥalfōn a *muwashshaḥ*, "strophic poem," by Judah ha-Levi, ordered by him.

[230]A verse from a hitherto unidentified poem alluding to the dictum: man's feet "guarantee" that he goes where Fate has destined him to go (BT, Sukka 53*a*). Elegantly changing the ancient saying, the poet emphasizes that his heart's desire is the best guarantee that he will ultimately meet his friend.

[231]The end of the line is torn away. Very likely nothing followed here, as in the three preceding letters by the poet, where the name of the sender is also omitted.

[232]The letter has been edited by me with an introduction and Hebrew translation in *Tesoro de los Judíos Sefardiés* (Jerusalem, 1965), pp. 7–10. The left half of the superscription, consisting of one blank line and two other lines, has been carefully cut away. It probably contained the signature of the sender. Here, where ha-Levi was not yet on intimate terms with the recipient, he certainly signed his name in full.

[233]TS Arabic Box 48 f. 270, *India Book* 86, and ULC 18 J f. 5, *India Book* 149.

[234]I take this as Ar. *ḥabr*, Jewish scholar, not as Heb. *ḥāvēr*, member of the Academy. There is not a single Hebrew word in the entire letter. In an almost official letter to a learned patient, doctors were advised to keep to one, unmixed language. Arabic Spain, a border country, was jealous of its classic language. Later, when ha-Levi became familiar with Ḥalfōn b. Nethanel, he slightly softened this strictness.

[235]Ẓumyāṭī (for Dimyāṭī, of Damietta). Ha-Levi obviously had heard the name pronounced in this way by the Maghrebi merchants mentioned below.

[236]Ar. *min kamāl dhātih wa-adawātih*. The word *kamāl* is missing in the printed text.

[237]This does not mean that ha-Levi, too, had been ill, but that his patient's recovery increased his own health.

[238]Certainly referring to a trip from Spain to North Africa in the company of the two Maghrebi merchants mentioned in the following. "Benefactions to your friends" means permanent success for Ḥalfōn, which makes his friends happy.

[239]Ezrah, spelled thus, and not Ezrā, as usual. There were Ezrah families, which probably preferred that spelling in order to differentiate themselves from the famous Ibn Ezrās.

[240]Ar. *al-adab ghayroh*, which I have not seen elsewhere. But such excuses at the end of letters are very common: "My scriptorial performance is not up to standard; please condone." In effect, the letter is a calligraphic masterpiece.

[241]These personal references, when intimate friends or eminent persons are mentioned, seem to be characteristic of ha-Levi's style at that early time. In item 1 ha-Levi transmits a letter of Judah Ibn Ghiyāth to ha-Levi. In item 9 a sum of 150 dinars is sent to Ḥalfōn b. Nethanel through the same. In item 1 ha-Levi introduces the fellow poet as "lord of mine and admirer of you, may God let me enjoy your company." In item 5 ha-Levi extends "greetings commensurate with my love, corresponding to my yearnings and expressing my admiration and partisanship for you." "Finally greetings, repeated, reiterated, and renewed" emphasizes the intensity of feelings for a dear patient, whose treatment had not yet been completed. In no. 4, when the friendship with Ḥalfōn was well established, more sophisticated combinations were used.

[242]Salaman, *Selected Poems* (see n. 164, above), p. 10, ll. 3–6, *ha-tirdōf naʿarūth*.

[243]*Ibid.*, pp. 87–88; Carmi, *Hebrew Verse*, pp. 336–337, *adōnāy, negdekhā kol taʾavāthī*.

[244]Salaman, *Selected Poems* (see n. 164, above), pp. 90–92, 121, 127, and *passim*, in particular, p. 108, *yeqārā shākhenā*, where the longing of the soul to separate from the body is extolled: on the day of separation the soul will enjoy the fruit of her faith.

[245]For the education of women in Geniza times see *Med. Soc.*, II, 183–185, III, 321–322, and *passim*.

[246]Ḥisday (also Ḥasday) Ibn Shaprūṭ: *Med. Soc.*, I, 191 and n. 23.

[247]TS NS Box 143, f. 46. Ezra Fleischer has published this fragment in *Jerusalem Studies in Hebrew Literature*, 5 (1984), 189–202.

[248]The wording of the concluding verse is illogical; what she wishes to say seems to be: even if he had left her as much as he took, or more, nothing could substitute for his presence. First, I translated: "In the entire land of Spain shall nothing remain of its lord [meaning Ḥisday], even if he takes one half of the kingdom with him," meaning, let Ḥisday go into exile instead of Dunash. The version put in the text is a more likely conclusion of the train of thought recognizable in the poem.

[249]Ring and bracelets on upper arm: *Med. Soc.*, IV, 219–220, esp. p. 220 and n. 518.

[250]A man wearing his wife's cloak: *ibid.*, pp. 153–155.

[251]Chains: *ibid.*, pp. 216–218, esp. pp. 217–218 and nn. 489–497.

[252]The entourage of Samuel ha-Nagid b. Hananyah: Salaman *Selected Poems* (see n. 164, above), p. 75, l. 6, and 77, l. 31; poem *mivḥar nezārīm.*

[253]Mosseri Collection (where the copy is torn across the middle into two pieces): see Taylor-Schechter *Newsletter*, and Fleischer, *Jerusalem Studies* (see n. 247, above), facsimile opposite p. 192.

[254]The answer of the husband (far inferior to her little piece) begins with the words: "You [pl.] killed me by what you have written," meaning by her implication that he might be able to forget her. Referring to one's wife in the plural masculine was a common way of speaking, see *Med. Soc.*, III, 160, and here it was required by the meter. It should not be deduced from this use that someone else wrote the piece.

[255]Jalāl al-Dīn al-Suyūṭī, *Nuzhat al-julasāʾ fī ashʿār al-nisāʾ* (Entertaining the Company with Poems by Women), ed. S. Munajjid (Beirut, 1958), pp. 86–87.

[256]James A. Bellamy, "Qasmūna the Poetess: Who Was She?" *JAOS*, 103 (1983), 423–424. (For the reader not acquainted with medieval Arabic writing: in unpunctuated texts *b* and *n* have the same form. A long ā was often pronounced as ē.)

[257]*Diwan of Shemuel Hannaghid*, ed. David Solomon Sassoon (London, 1934), pp. xxxiv-xxxv, Introduction.

[258]*Diwan* (see preceding note), pp. 58–60, ll. 22–23, in poem no. 87. For Qasmūna's verses see J. M. Nichols, "The Arabic Verses of Qasmūna . . . ," *IJMES*, 13 (1981), 155–158, and Bellamy, "Qasmūna" (see n. 256, above).

[259]Samuel al-Maghrebi's mother and her two sisters knew how to read and to write both Arabic and Hebrew, see *Med. Soc.*, III, 355. See also *ibid.*, p. 359.

[260]Subkī, *Ṭabaqāt al-Shāfiʿiyya*, IV, 251, quoted by I. Goldziher, *ZDMG*, 62 (1908), 10.

[261]Zekī Mubārak, *Al-Taṣawwuf al-Islāmī* (Cairo, 1938), II, 300. On the catastrophic extent of conversion to Islam in the late Middle Ages see Strauss-Ashtor, *Mamluks*, I, 281–291.

[262]Al-Kūrānī is a *nisba* (by-name) borne by many Muslim scholars and writers of Kurdish descent, see Brockelmann, *GAL*, Supplement Volume III, 638. No one, however, fits the situation described in our letter except Yūsuf al-ʿAjamī.

[263]Brockelmann, *GAL*, II, 282, has 1366. The Muslim year 768, in which al-Kūrānī died, began on 7 September 1366. The exact date of his death was the 15th of the fifth Muslim month, which coincides with January 1367.

[264]Strauss, *Mamluks*, I, 300–302, 355, II, 26–30.

[265]Ibn Taghribirdī, *al-Nujūm al-zāhira*, ed. W. Popper (Berkeley, 1909 ff.), V, 247, and al-Shaʿrānī, *Al-Tabaqāt al-Kubrā al-Musammāh bi-Lawāqih al-Anwār fī Tabaqāt al-Akhyār* (Cairo, 1954), II, 72–73.

[266]Like many other stories in the *Ṭabaqāt*, this one reads like a parody written by an opponent of the Sufis to ridicule their beliefs and practices. But it is not. Al-Shaʿrānī concludes his report with the words: "Look, when al-Kūrānī's eye was able to perform such a miracle with a dog, you can imagine what happened when his eye fell on a man."

[267]Baṣīr, "clear-sighted," is often used as a euphemism for a blind man; but here, no doubt, it is a proper name. *Jalājil* are the small bells suspended from the necks

of beasts of burden; they were mandatory, see Ibn al-Ukhuwwa, *Maʿālim al-Qurba fī aḥkām al-ḥisba*, ed. R. Levy (London, 1938), p. 97 of the English summary. A number of persons with this occupation are mentioned in the Geniza, see, e.g., *Med. Soc.*, II, 488, sec. 44, where one of them contributes to a charity.

[268]Life in these convents is vividly described in Shaʿrānī's mystical autobiography *Laṭāʾif al-Minān wa ʾl-Akhlāq* (Cairo, 1938), II, 112–123. To be sure, Shaʿrānī was very far from adhering to the ideal of poverty as propagated by al-Kūrānī.

[269]*Taṭawwuʿ* in late Arabic (e.g., in the usage of *The Arabian Nights*) means plainly "leading the life of a Sufi," cf. Dozy, *Supplément*, II, 68*b*, s.v., where *lābisa lubs muṭṭawiʿa* in one edition corresponds to *ʿmutahayyiʾa bihayʾat al-ṣūfiyya* in another, both meaning "she was dressed like a Sufi."

[270]The sender calls herself "the [and not even: your] maidservant" and "kisses the ground," an introductory formula obligatory when addressing a Jewish or a Muslim religious authority, such as a judge. She does not address the Nagid himself, but only his "court," *mōshāv* = Ar. *majlis*, cf. D. H. Baneth, *J. N. Epstein Jubilee Volume* (= *Tarbiz* 20) (Jerusalem, 1950), p. 207.

[271]Since the house, or a part of it, was certainly mortgaged to the sum promised in her marriage contract, it could not be sold without her permission.

[272]*Widne* for *udhn* is a dialect form found in various present-day Arabic vernaculars.

[273]The Hebrew original is printed in my "A Jewish Addict to Sufism in the Time of the Nagid David II Maimonides," *JQR*, 44 (1953), 37–49, esp. pp. 46–47. Simon Hopkins (now professor of Arabic at the Hebrew University, Jerusalem) kindly compared the manuscript for me in 1978.

[274]For basic studies about Abraham Maimonides see: S. Eppenstein, "Abraham Maimuni, sein Leben und seine Schriften," *Jahresbericht des Rabbinerseminars* (Berlin, 1912–1913); Abraham Maimonides, *High Ways*, I, 1–128. Introduction; Abraham Maimuni, *Responsa*, pp. ix–xxii; Reuben Margaliot (Margulies), *R. Abraham b. Moses Maimonides* (Jerusalem, 1953) (Heb.), see the review of G. Vajda, *REJ*, 113 (1954), 25 ff.; N. Wieder, *Islamic Influences on the Jewish Worship*, East and West Library (Oxford, 1957) (Heb.), see pp. 95–96, index; E. Wiesenberg in *Pērūsh Rabbēnū Avrāhām* . . . ed. S. D. Sassoon (London, 1959), pp. 11–63. Earlier literature is listed in the last cited, p. 12. Cohen, Gerson D., "Soteriology."

[275]Abraham Maimonides, *High Ways*, I, 43–46. The title *The High Ways to Perfection* was chosen by the editor Samuel Rosenblatt. I refer to the book mostly as *Kifāya*, the title given to the book by its author and thus quoted by him.

[276]TS 8 J 20, f. 20, l. 3: *shekhīnā sherūyā bēnēnū*. While it was not uncommon in the Talmud to *compare* a scholar (or one's own mother, Qiddushim 31*b*) to the Presence of God (see BT Berakhot 64*a* and Sanhedrin 110*a*), I do not remember having seen in the Geniza another instance of a person *addressed* thus. ULC Or 1080 J 244 seems to be another version of this letter; both are superscribed with the outcry "Is there no balm in Gilead!?" (Jeremiah 8:22), and both deal with the so-called laws of purity incumbent on a wife (see *Med. Soc.*, III, 107 and *passim*), which, despite Maimonides' reforms, were not meticulously observed in Egypt. ULC Or 1080 J 244 contains more titles and laudatory epithets for Abraham Maimonides than TS 8 J 20, f. 20, but not the one quoted in the latter noted above.

[277]*Mose Ben Maimon, Epistulae*, ed. D. H. Baneth (Jerusalem, 1946), pp. 95–96.

[278]See p. 490 and n. 326, and p. 490 and n. 329, below.

[279]See Wieder, *Islamic Influences* (see n. 274, above), *passim*.

[280]Abraham Maimonides, *High Ways*, I, 54 ff.

[281]*Ibid.*, pp. 124–126.

[282]Quoted *ibid.*, pp. 123–124. Ibn Abī Uṣaybiʿa, p. 118.

[283]Raʾīs means here not "Head of the Jews" but "Head of a department of a hospital," often given as an honorific title to a physician.

[284]*Abu ʾl-Munā*, "object of my wishes," namely, a son. Maimonides married his Egyptian wife not long after his arrival in Fustat around 1168; see Goitein, *Letters*, p. 211 nn. 17–18. Abraham was born in 1186. That late arrival was preceded by many years of waiting.

[285]The author did not remember the unit digit. The years 630–639 of the Muslim era correspond to 1232–1241. Abraham Maimonides died in 1237.

[286]*Responsa*, ed. Freimann, p. 18 (see n. 274, above).

[287]See Brockelmann, *GAL*, I, 367, Supplement Volume I, 627.

[288]Rosenblatt, in Abraham Maimonides, *High Ways*, I, 50.

[289]*Kirjath Sepher*, 15 (1938/9), 442–444.

[290]*Responsa*, ed. Freimann (see n. 274, above), pp. 19 and 62. In his *Pērūsh* Abraham always calls his book *al-Kifāya*, see, e.g., Wiesenberg, *Pērūsh* (see n. 274, above), p. 539.

[291]*Responsa*, ed. Freimann (see n. 274, above), pp. 123, 131, 133, 146, and elsewhere. Until recently the *Mishneh Torah* was referred to by Oriental Jews as *al-ḥibbūr*.

[292]See Wieder, *Islamic Influences* (n. 274, above), *passim*.

[293]Ed. M. J. Kister (Jerusalem, 1954).

[294]See, e.g., *High Ways*, II, 276–277.

[295]I have not examined Bodl. MS Heb. d 23 (Cat. 2752), which contains eleven much damaged and obliterated leaves from the *Kifāya*.

[296]See n. 281, above.

[297]*Responsa*, ed. Freimann (see n. 274, above), pp. 124, 126, 133: *al-maqāla al-ṣalawiyya*.

[298]Bodl. MS Heb. c 28 (Cat. 2876), ff. 45 and 46, ed. by me with an Engl. trans. in "A Treatise in Defense of the Pietists by Abraham Maimonides" in *JSS*, 16 (1966), 105–114.

[299]*High Ways*, I, 146–147. See also Wieder, *Islamic Influences* (see n. 274, above), pp. 39–40.

[300]The *kunya* Abu ʾl-Rabīʿ is invariably connected with the name Solomon. The manuscript quoting Abraham Ibn Abu ʾl-Rabīʿ he-ḥāsīd (Bodl. MS Heb. e 74 [Cat. 2862], f. 7) (see Wieder, *Islamic Influences* [see n. 274, above], p. 34) was perhaps written during his lifetime, since the eulogy for the dead is attached only to the name of his father. According to the catalog, the manuscript bears the date "14 Tammuz . . . 93 Sel.," which corresponds to 1182, i.e., four years before Abraham Maimonides was born. Abraham he-ḥāsīd died at the beginning of 1223, or at least his library was auctioned after his death in February and March of that year (TS 20.44, *JQR*, 20 [1929/30], 460–463), approximately fourteen years before Abraham Maimuni's death. About Abraham the Pious and his brother Joseph see pp. 79–80, above.

[301]He is already referred to as *Raʾīs* in the month of Nisan 1205; TS 16.187, ed. by me in *Ignace Goldziher Memorial Volume*, Vol. II, ed. S. Löwinger, A. Scheiber, and J. Somogyi (Jerusalem, 1958), pp. 52–53. He assumed the title Nagid a number of years later, apparently in 1213.

[302]TS Box K 15, f. 68, ed. by me in *Tarbiz*, 33 (1963/64), 181–197.

[303]Mann, II, 319 (TS 8 K 22). In Mann's text the name of the fifth brother of Abraham's mother was omitted. It was (Abu ʾl-) Makārim Jekuthiel. The kunya of the fourth brother was Abu ʾl-Ṭāhir, not Abu ʾl-Ṭār.

[304]ULC Or 1080 J 281. See *Med. Soc.*, I, 135 and n. 20. The full text in Mordechai A. Friedman, *Jewish Polygyny in the Middle Ages: New Documents from the Cairo Geniza* (Jerusalem and Tel Aviv, 1986) (Heb.).

[305]TS 10 J 13, f. 14, ed. in *Tarbiz* (see n. 302, above), pp. 184–186.

[306]This phrase must be of Islamic origin since in Arabic it rhymes: *ṣiyām al-ayyām qiyām al-layālī*. It is common in Sufic writings, but it was used in Hebrew long before the time of Abraham Maimonides. Judah ha-Levi quotes it in a vigil prayer, *yāshēn al tērādam*, Schirmann, *Hebrew Poetry in Spain and Provence*, I, 518, l. 12.

[307]TS 10 J 13, f. 8, ed. in *Tarbiz* (see n. 302, above), pp. 186–189.

[308]TS 12.289, ed. *ibid.*, pp. 189–192.

[309]ULC Or 1080 J 281; cf. *Med. Soc.*, I, 135 and n. 20.

[310]TS 10 J 14, f. 5, ed. in *Tarbiz*, 33 (see n. 302, above), pp. 192–195.

[311]TS 10 J 30, f. 11, ed. *ibid.*, pp. 195–196.

[312]Bodl. MS Heb. d 66 (Cat. 2878, no. 84), f. 85. When I discovered this item, I was not aware that it was included in the published responsa and that I had

translated it into Hebrew twenty-seven years before. Therefore, I translated it again, but was disappointed when I found that I had already translated it once and that my Hebrew style of 1936 was definitely superior to that of 1963. This reminds me of an answer given to me by an old teacher of Arabic in Safed, Israel, whom I asked why he did not speak a single sentence of Arabic in his lesson: "Does your honor, the inspector [I was then senior education officer to the mandatory government of Palestine] not know that speaking a language means spoiling it?"

[313]ULC Or 1080 J 110.

[314]TS 8 J 16, f. 4. See *Med. Soc.*, I, 146 and n. 105.

[315]BM Or 10652; DK XXV; ULC Or 1080 J 281. See *Med. Soc.*, I, 134–135 and nn. 20 and 21.

[316]TS 13 J 9, f. 10, *Med. Soc.*, I, 124.

[317]Goitein, *Letters*, pp. 228–229, autograph of Abraham Maimonides; reproductions after p. 156, nos. 2*a* and 2*b*.

[318]MS David Kaufmann (no shelf mark provided), published by A. Scheiber, "A Legal Question Sent to Abraham Maimonides" (Heb.) *Sinai*, 46 (1960), 268–270; reprinted in Scheiber, *Geniza Studies*, Heb. section, pp. 58–60.

[319]TS 13 J 3, f. 21*v*, *Med. Soc.*, I, 384, sec. 67.

[320]TS 10 J 4, f. 4.

[321]TS 8 J 10, f. 19. The person was called Evyatar ha-Kohen al-Āmidī (from Āmid; i.e., Diyārbakr, now in southeastern Turkey).

[322]TS 13 J 3, f. 27*v*.

[323]ULC Or 1080 J 287, published by Israel Abrahams, "A Formula and a Responsum," *Jews' College Jubilee Volume* (London, 1906), pp. 101–108. At the time of publication the document did not have a shelf mark.

[324]See my "The Title and Office of the Nagid: A Re-examination," *JQR*, 53 (1962), 93–119, *Med. Soc.*, II, 23–40, and Cohen, Mark R., *Self-government*, pp. 3–49.

[325]Bodl. MS Heb. a 3 (Cat. 2873), f. 15. The Nagid explains a principle of ethics ("for the sake of peace") by the ritual law of the *ʿērūv*; for the latter see *EJ*, VI, 849–850.

[326]TS 13 J 21, f. 11*v*, ll. 6–12.

[327]TS 18 J 3, f. 12, the main document, written by Abu ʾl-Barakāt Solomon, son of the judge Elijah. At least sixty items have come down to us in the unpleasant hand of this scribe, who served also as schoolteacher, bookseller, and wine merchant. TS 8 J 22, f. 22, contains the eloquent complaint of the divorced woman, who, by the way, was eager to give her younger son a good education, but she was afraid that her former husband would take him away from her and then neglect him. ULC Or 1080 J 285 is a ruling in this matter by Abraham Maimonides. The story is told in *Med. Soc.*, III, 268–269. See Friedman, *Jewish Polygyny* (see n. 304, above), pp. 230–240.

[328]TS Box K 25, f. 240; see *Med. Soc.*, II, 420–421, and Gil, *Foundations*, p. 526, Index, top, s.v. "Abraham b. Moses Maimuni."

[329]TS 16.305*v*, ll. 20–23.

[330]TS 18 J 3, f. 11.

[331]Bodl. MS Heb. f. 56 (Cat. 2821, no. 38), f. 126, l. 4. See *Med. Soc.*, II, 254 and n. 67.

[332]TS 10 J 12, f. 27.

[333]E.g., TS 8 J 9, f. 16.

[334]TS 16.187, in *Goldziher Volume* (see n. 301, above), II, 52–53.

[335]See Mann, II, 327 (b).

[336]S. D. Goitein, "New Documents from the Cairo Geniza," *Homenaje a Millás-Vallicrosa*, Vol. I (Barcelona, 1954), pp. 707–719. (The manuscript published there, p. 717, should now be cited as TS Arabic Box 51, f. 111.) The manuscript published by Richard Gottheil, "Some Genizah Gleanings," in *Mélanges Hartwig Derenbourg* (Paris, 1909), p. 98, refers to the same affair.

[337]See my "Yemenites in Jerusalem and Egypt at the Time of Maimonides and His Son Abraham," *Harel, Refāʾēl al-Shaykh Memorial Volume* (Tel Aviv, 1962), p. 142 (Heb.). Reprinted in my *The Yemenites*, pp. 125–129.

[338]That Abraham Maimonides lived in Fustat and not in Cairo is proved by Bodl., MS Heb. b 3 (Cat. 2806), f. 6, dated 1213/4, which deals with his domicile there, and by TS NS J 59, where he is asked when he could come to Cairo and spend a weekend there. It is possible, perhaps, even likely, that later in life he moved to Cairo.

[339]Proverbs 6:27–28 (said about adultery); Abraham Maimonides, *High Ways*, II, 263.

[340]*Ibid.*, I, 124–126.

[341]Cf. Mann, II, 294, and my "Moses Maimonides, Man of Action" (see n. 155, above), esp. pp. 165–167.

[342]Abraham Maimonides, *High Ways*, II, 263. Here, Abraham takes great pains to explain how the pious King David and other meritorious heads of the community were spared the evils caused by the distractions of leadership.

[343]No other author of distinction on Jewish subjects is known from Egypt or Syria-Palestine in this period.

[344]See David R. Blumenthal, *The Commentary of R. Ḥōṭer Ben Shelōmō to the Thirteen Principles of Maimonides* (Leiden, 1974), p. 65 and pp. 204–205.

[345]Reynold A. Nicholson, *Selected Poems from the Dīvāni Shamsi Tabrīz* (Cambridge, 1898), pp. 250–251.

[346]See the Introduction to ʿObadyāh Maimonides, *The Treatise of the Pool*, trans. Paul Fenton (London, 1981).

[347]*JAOS*, 104 (1984), 135–164.

[348]Goitein, *Studies*, pp. 54–70. The book was translated into Arabic and edited by ʿAṭiyya al-Qawmī (Kuwait, 1980), but I understand that this chapter was not included.

Index

Compositor: Prestige Typography
Text: 10/12 Baskerville
Display: Baskerville
Printer: BookCrafters
Binder: BookCrafters